Collins
English
Dictionary

HarperCollins Publishers
Westerhill Road
Bishopbriggs
Glasgow
G64 2QT
Great Britain

www.collins.co.uk

Third Edition 2005

Reprint 10 9 8 7 6 5 4 3 2 1

© HarperCollins Publishers 1990,
2002, 2005

Collins Gem® is a registered
trademark of HarperCollins
Publishers Limited

Collins Gem and HarperResource
are imprints of HarperCollins
Publishers

HarperCollins Publishers,
10 East 53rd Street,
New York, NY 10022

ISBN-13 978-0-06-082571-3
ISBN-10 0-06-082571-5

HarperCollins books may be
purchased for educational,
business or sales promotional use.
For information, please write to:
Special Markets Department,
HarperCollins Publishers,
10 East 53rd Street,
New York, NY 10022

www.harpercollins.com

Designed by Mark Thomson

Typeset by Wordcraft, Glasgow

Printed in Italy by
Legoprint S.p.A.

Acknowledgements
We would like to thank those
authors and publishers who kindly
gave permission for copyright
material to be used in the Collins
Word Web. We would also like to
thank Times Newspapers Ltd for
providing valuable data.

EDITORIAL STAFF

EDITORS
Frank Abate
Jennifer Sagala
Susan Gillespie
Elspeth Summers
Paige Weber

FOR THE PUBLISHERS
Morven Dooner
Elaine Higgleton
Lorna Knight

CONTENTS

USING THIS DICTIONARY

Main Entry Words printed in large bold type, eg

ab·bey

All main entry words,
including abbreviations and
combining forms, in one
alphabetical sequence, eg

al·ge·bra
ALGOL
al·go·rithm

Variant spellings shown in full, eg

an·eu·rysm, an·eu·rism

Pronunciations given in square brackets; the
word is respelt as it is
pronounced, with the stressed
syllable in capital letters, eg

ca·chet [ka-SHAY]

Note: the symbol schwa (ə) is
used to represent the neutral
vowel sound typically
occurring in unstressed
syllables

In some entries, the
pronunciation is adequately
shown by placing a mark (ˇ)
immediately after the syllable
that carries the main stress, as
in **mon·soon'**.

	Center dots, as in **ab·sinthe** and **mol·lusk**, are used to indicate divisions between syllables
Parts of Speech	shown in italics as an abbreviation, eg
	a·blaze [ə-BLAYZ] *adj*
	When a word can be used as more than one part of speech, the change of part of speech is shown after an empty arrow, eg
	mock [mok] *vt* make fun of, ridicule; mimic ▷ *vi* scoff ▷ *n* act of mocking; laughingstock...
	Parts of speech may be combined for some words, eg
	an·y [EN-ee] *adj, pron* one indefinitely; some; every
Cross References	shown in small capitals and bold type, eg
	lawyer see LAW
Irregular Parts	or confusing forms of verb, nouns, adjectives, and adverbs shown in bold type, eg
	be·gin [bi-GIN] *v* **be·gan, be·gun, be·gin·ning** **col·o·ny** [KOL-ə-nee] *n, pl* **–nies** **hap·py** *adj* **–pi·er, -pi·est**

Meanings	separated by semicolons, eg
	cas·u·al [KAZH-oo-ə-l] *adj* accidental; unforeseen; occasional; unconcerned; informal
Phrases and Idioms	included immediately after the meanings of the main entry word, eg
	salt [sawlt] *n ... vt ...* **with a pinch of salt** allowing for exaggeration **worth one's salt** efficient
Related Words	shown in smaller bold type in the same paragraph as the main entry word, eg
	ab·surd′ *adj* contrary to reason **ab·surd′i·ty** *n*
	Note: where the meaning of a related word is not given, it may be understood from the main entry word, or from another related word.
Compounds	shown in alphabetical order at the end of the paragraph, eg
	hand *n ...* **hand′stand** *n* act of supporting body in upside-down position by hands alone **hand′writ·ing** *n* way person writes

ABBREVIATIONS USED IN THIS DICTIONARY

abbrev	abbreviation	*fem*	feminine
AD	anno Domini	*foll*	followed
adj	adjective	*geom*	geometry
adv	adverb	*Ger*	German
Afr	Africa(n)	*Gr*	Greek
Amer	America(n)	*hist*	history
approx	approximately	*ie*	that is
Aust	Australia(n)	*impers*	impersonal
BC	before Christ	*ind*	indicative
Brit	British	*inf*	infomal
Can	Canada, Canadian	*interj*	interjection
chem	chemistry	*intr*	intransitive
comb	combining	*It*	Italian
comp	comparative	*k*	kilogram(s)
conj	conjunction	*km*	kilometer(s)
cu	cubic	*l*	liter(s)
dial	dialect	*Lat*	Latin
dim	diminutive	*lb*	pound(s)
E	East	*lit*	literally
eg	for example	*m*	meter(s)
esp	especially	*etc*	et cetera

masc	masculine	*pron*	pronoun
math	mathematics	*pr p*	present participle
med	medicine	*pt*	past tense
mil	military	®	trademark
mm	millimeter(s)	*refl*	reflexive
mus	music	*Russ*	Russian
n	noun	*S*	South
N	North	*sing*	singular
NZ	New Zealand	*sl*	slang
obs	obsolete	*Sp*	Spanish
offens	offensive	*sq*	square
oft	often	*sup*	superlative
orig	originally	*tr*	transitive
pers	person	*usu*	usually
pert	pertaining	*v*	verb
pl	plural	*v aux*	auxiliary verb
poss	possessive	*vi*	intransitive verb
pp	past participle	*vt*	transitive verb
prep	preposition	*vulg*	vulgar
pres t	present tense	*W*	West

a *adj* indefinite article, used before a noun being mentioned for the first time

aard•vark [AHRD-vahrk] *n* S African mammal feeding on ants and termites

a•back [ə-BAK] *adv* **taken aback** startled

ab•a•cus [AB-ə-kəs] *n* counting device of beads on wire frame; flat tablet at top of architectural column

ab•a•lo•ne [ab-ə-LOH-nee] *n* edible shellfish, yielding mother-of-pearl

a•ban•don [ə-BAN-dən] *vt* desert; give up altogether ▷ *n* freedom from inhibitions, etc **a•ban'doned** *adj* deserted, forsaken; uninhibited; wicked

a•base [ə-BAYS] *vt* **-based, -bas•ing** humiliate, degrade **a•base'ment** *n*

a•bash [ə-BASH] *vt* (usu passive) confuse, make ashamed **a•bash'ment** *n*

a•bate [ə-BAYT] *v* **-bat•ed, -bat•ing** make or become less, diminish **a•bate'ment** *n*

ab•at•toir [AB-ə-twahr] *n* slaughterhouse

ab•bey [AB-ee] *n, pl* **-beys** dwelling place of community of monks or nuns; church of an abbey

ab•bot [AB-ət] *n* (*fem* **ab'bess**) head of abbey or monastery

ab•bre•vi•ate [ə-BREE-vee-ayt] *vt* **-at•ed, -at•ing** shorten, abridge **ab•bre•vi•a'tion** *n* shortened form of word or phrase

ab•di•cate [AB-di-kayt] *v* **-cat•ed, -cat•ing** formally give up (throne, etc) **ab•di•ca'tion** *n*

ab•do•men [AB-də-mən] *n* belly **ab•dom'i•nal** *adj*

ab•duct [ab-DUKT] *vt* carry off, kidnap **ab•duc'tion** *n*

ab•er•ra•tion [ab-ə-RAY-shən] *n* deviation from what is normal; flaw; lapse **ab•er'rant** [ə-BER-ənt] *adj*

a•bet [ə-BET] *vt* **-bet•ted, -bet•ting** assist, encourage, esp in doing wrong **a•bet'tor, -ter** *n*

a•bey•ance [ə-BAY-əns] *n* condition of not being in use or action

ab•hor [ab-HOR] *vt* **-horred, -hor•ring** dislike strongly, loathe **ab•hor'rent** *adj* hateful

a•bide [ə-BĪD] *v* **a•bode'** or **a•bid'ed, a•bid'ing** ▷ *vt* endure, put up with ▷ *vi obs* stay, reside **abide by** ▷ *vi*

a•bil•i•ty [ə-BIL-i-tee] *n, pl* **-ties** competence, power; talent

ab•ject [AB-jekt] *adj* humiliated, wretched; despicable **ab•ject'ness** *n*

ab•jure [ab-JOOR] *vt* **-jured, -jur•ing** give up by oath, renounce **ab•ju•ra'tion** *n*

a•blaze [ə-BLAYZ] *adj* burning

a•ble [AY-bəl] *adj* capable, competent **a'bled** *adj* having a range of physical powers as specified: *differently abled* **a'bly** *adv* **a'ble-bod'ied** *adj*

ab•lu•tion [ə-BLOO-shən] *n* (usu

pl) act of washing (oneself)

ab·ne·gate [AB-ni-gayt] *vt* **-gat·ed, -gat·ing** give up, renounce **ab·ne·ga'tion** *n*

ab·nor·mal [ab-NOR-məl] *adj* irregular; not usual or typical; freakish, odd **ab·nor·mal'i·ty** *n, pl* **-ties ab·nor'mal·ly** *adv*

a·board [ə-BORD] *adv* on board, on ship, train, or aircraft

a·bode [ə-BOHD] *n* home; dwelling; *pt/pp* of **ABIDE**

a·bol·ish [ə-BOL-ish] *vt* do away with **ab·o·li'tion** *n* **ab·o·li'tion·ist** *n* one who wishes to do away with something, esp slavery

a·bom·i·nate [ə-BOM-ə-nayt] *vt* **-nat·ed, -nat·ing** detest **a·bom'i·na·ble** *adj* **a·bom·i·na'tion** *n* loathing; the object loathed **abominable snowman** large legendary apelike creature said to inhabit the Himalayas

ab·o·rig·i·nal [ab-ə-RIJ-ə-nl] *adj* (of people, etc) original or earliest known in an area; of, relating to aborigines **ab·o·rig·i·ne** [-ə-nee] *n* one of race of people inhabiting an area when European settlers arrived; original inhabitant of country, etc; **(A-)** one of a race of people originally inhabiting Australia

a·bort [ə-BORT] *v* (cause to) end prematurely (esp pregnancy) ▷ *vi* give birth to dead fetus; fail **a·bor'tion** *n* operation to terminate pregnancy; something deformed **a·bor'tion·ist** *n* one who performs abortion, esp illegally **a·bor'tive** *adj* unsuccessful

a·bound [ə-BOWND] *vi* be plentiful; overflow **a·bound'ing** *adj*

a·bout [ə-BOWT] *adv* on all sides; nearly; up and down; out, on the move ▷ *prep* around; near;

concerning; ready to **about turn** reversal, complete change

a·bove [ə-BUV] *adv* higher up ▷ *prep* over; higher than, more than; beyond

a·brade [ə-BRAYD] *vt* **-brad·ed, -brad·ing** rub off, scrape away

a·bra·sion [ə-BRAY-zhən] *n* place scraped or worn by rubbing (on skin); scraping, rubbing **a·bra'sive** [-siv] *n* substance for grinding, polishing, etc ▷ *adj* causing abrasion; grating **a·bra'sive·ness** *n* tendency to annoy

a·breast [ə-BREST] *adv* side by side; keeping up with

a·bridge [ə-BRIJ] *vt* cut short, abbreviate **a·bridg'ment** *n*

a·broad [ə-BRAWD] *adv* to or in a foreign country; at large

ab·ro·gate [AB-rə-gayt] *vt* cancel, repeal **ab·ro·ga'tion** *n*

ab·rupt [ə-BRUPT] *adj* sudden; blunt; hasty; steep

abs [ABZ] *pl n inf* abdominal muscles

ab·scess [AB-ses] *n* gathering of pus in any part of the body

ab·scis·sa [ab-SIS-ə] *n, pl* **-sae** [-see] *mathematics* distance of point from the axis of coordinates

ab·scond [ab-SKOND] *vi* leave secretly, esp having stolen something

ab·sent [AB-sənt] *adj* away; not attentive ▷ *vt* [ab-SENT] keep away **ab'sence** *n* **ab·sen·tee'** *n* one who stays away esp habitually **ab·sen·tee'ism** *n* persistent absence from work, etc

ab·sinthe [AB-sinth] *n* potent aniseed-flavored liqueur

ab·so·lute [AB-sə-loot] *adj* complete; not limited, unconditional; pure: *absolute alcohol* ▷ *n* **ab'so·lute·ly** *adv* completely

▷ *interj* [-LOOT-lee] certainly

ab•solve [ab-ZOLV] *vt* **-solved,
-solv•ing** free from; pardon; acquit

ab•so•lu•tion [-sà-LOO-shàn] *n*

ab•sorb' *vt* suck up, drink in;
engage, occupy (attention, etc);
receive impact **ab•sorb'ent** *adj*

ab•sorp'tion *n*

ab•stain [ab-STAYN] *vi* keep from,
refrain from drinking alcohol, voting,
etc **ab•sten'tion** *n* **ab'sti•nence** *n*

ab•ste•mi•ous [ab-STEE-mee-
ès] *adj* sparing in food or esp drink,
temperate **ab•ste'mi•ous•ness** *n*

ab•stract [ab-STRAKT] *adj* existing
only in the mind; not concrete; (of
art) not representational ▷ *n* [AB-
strakt] summary, abridgment ▷ *vt*
[ab-STRAKT] draw from, remove;
steal **ab•stract'ed** *adj* preoccupied

ab•strac'tion *n*

ab•struse [ab-STROOS] *adj*
obscure, difficult to understand,
profound

ab•surd' *adj* contrary to reason

ab•surd'i•ty *n*

a•bun•dance [à-BUN-dàns] *n*
great amount **a•bun'dant** *adj*
plentiful

a•buse [à-BYOOZ] *vt* **-bused,
-bus•ing** misuse; address rudely
▷ *n* [à-BYOOS] **a•bu'sive** [-siv] *adj*

a•bu'sive•ness *n*

a•but [à-BUT] *vi* **-but•ted,
-but•ting** adjoin, border on

a•but'ment *n* support, esp of bridge
or arch

a•bys•mal [à-BIZ-màl] *adj*
immeasurable, very great; *inf*
extremely bad **a•bys'mal•ly** *adv*

a•byss [à-BIS] *n* very deep gulf
or pit

Ac *chemistry* actinium

a•cad•e•my [à-KAD-à-mee] *n,
pl* **-mies** society to advance arts or
sciences; institution for specialized

training; secondary school

ac•a•dem•ic [ak-à-DEM-ik] *adj* of
academy, university, etc; theoretical

ac•cede [ak-SEED] *vi* **-ced•ed,
-ced•ing** agree, consent; attain
(office, right, etc)

ac•cel•er•ate [ak-SEL-à-rayt] *v*
-at•ed, -at•ing (cause to) increase
speed, hasten **ac•cel•er•a'tion** *n*

ac•cel'er•a•tor *n* mechanism to
increase speed, esp in automobile

ac•cent [AK-sent] *n* stress or
pitch in speaking; mark to show
such stress; local or national style of
pronunciation; particular attention
or emphasis ▷ *vt*

ac•cen•tu•ate [ak-SEN-choo-ayt]
vt **-at•ed, -at•ing** stress, emphasize

ac•cept [ak-SEPT] *vt* take,
receive; admit, believe; agree to

ac•cept'a•ble *adj* **ac•cept'ance** *n*

ac•cess [AK-ses] *n* act, right, or
means of entry **ac•ces'si•ble** *adj*
easy to approach

ac•ces•sion [ak-SESH-àn] *n*
attaining of office, right, etc;
increase, addition

ac•ces•so•ry [ak-SES-à-ree] *n, pl*
-ries additional or supplementary
part of automobile, woman's dress,
etc; person inciting or assisting in
crime ▷ *adj* contributory, assisting

ac•ci•dent [AK-si-dànt] *n* event
happening by chance; misfortune
or mishap, esp causing injury;
nonessential quality **ac•ci•den'tal**
adj

ac•claim [à-KLAYM] *vt*
applaud, praise ▷ *n* applause

ac•cla•ma'tion *n*

ac•cli•mate [AK-klà-mayt] *v*
-mat•ed, -mat•ing acclimatize

ac•cli•ma•tize [à-KLÏ-mà-tiz]
v **-tized, -tiz•ing** accustom to
new climate or environment

ac•cli•ma•ti•za'tion *n*

ac·co·lade [AK-ə-layd] *n* praise, public approval; award, honor; token of award of knighthood, etc

ac·com·mo·date [ə-KOM-ə-dayt] *vt* **-dat·ed, -dat·ing** supply, esp with board and lodging; oblige; harmonize, adapt **ac·com·mo·dat·ing** *adj* obliging **ac·com·mo·da·tion** *pl n* lodgings

ac·com·pa·ny [ə-KUM-pə-nee] *vt* **-nied, -ny·ing** go with; supplement; occur with; provide a musical accompaniment **ac·com'pa·ni·ment** *n* that which accompanies, esp in music, part that goes with solos, etc **ac·com'pa·nist** *n*

ac·com·plice [ə-KOM-plis] *n* one assisting another in criminal deed

ac·com·plish [ə-KOM-plish] *vt* carry out; finish **ac·com'plished** *adj* complete, perfect; proficient **ac·com'plish·ment** *n* completion; personal ability

ac·cord [ə-KORD] *n* agreement, harmony ▷ *v* (cause to) be in accord with ▷ *vt* grant **ac·cord'ing·ly** *adv* as the circumstances suggest; therefore

ac·cor·di·on [ə-KOR-dee-ən] *n* portable musical instrument with keys, metal reeds and a bellows

ac·cost [ə-KAWST] *vi* approach and speak to, often aggressively

ac·count [ə-KOWNT] *n* report, description; importance, value; statement of moneys received, paid, or owed; person's money held in bank; credit available to person at store, etc ▷ *vt* reckon; judge ▷ *vi* give reason, answer (for) **ac·count'a·ble** *adj* responsible **ac·count'an·cy** *n* keeping, preparation of business accounts, financial records, etc **ac·count'ant** *n* one practicing accountancy

ac·count'ing *n* skill or practice of keeping and preparing business accounts ▷ *adj*

ac·cred·it·ed [ə-KRED-i-tid] *adj* authorized, officially recognized

ac·cre·tion [ə-KREE-shən] *n* growth; something added on

ac·crue [ə-KROO] *vi* **-crued, -cru·ing** be added to; result

ac·cu·mu·late [ə-KYOO-myə-layt] *v* **-lat·ed, -lat·ing** gather, become gathered in increasing quantity; collect **ac·cu·mu·la·tion** *n*

ac·cu·rate [AK-yər-it] *adj* exact, correct, without errors **ac'cu·ra·cy** *n*

ac·curs·ed [ə-KUR-sid] *adj* under a curse; hateful, detestable

ac·cuse [ə-KYOOZ] *vt* **-cused, -cus·ing** charge with wrongdoing; blame **ac·cu·sa·tion** [ak-yə-ZAY-shən] *n* **ac·cu'sa·tive** *n* grammatical case indicating the direct object **ac·cu'sa·to·ry** *adj*

ac·cus·tom [ə-KUS-təm] *vt* make used to, familiarize **ac·cus'tomed** *adj* usual; used (to); in the habit (of)

ace *n* the one at dice, cards, dominoes; *tennis* winning serve untouched by opponent; very successful fighter pilot ▷ *vt* **aced, ac·ing** score an ace; *golf* make hole in one; *inf* make grade of A

ac·er·bi·ty [ə-SUR-bi-tee] *n* severity, sharpness; sour tasting **ac·erb'** *adj*

ac·e·tate [AS-i-tayt] *n* salt or ester of acetic acid; synthetic textile fiber

ac·e·tic [ə-SEE-tik] *adj* derived from or having the nature of vinegar

ac·e·tone [AS-i-tohn] *n* colorless liquid used as a solvent

ac·et·y·lene [ə-SET-l-een] *n* colorless, flammable gas used esp in welding metals

ache [ayk] *n* continuous pain ▷ *vi*

ached, ach•ing to be in pain

a•chieve [ə-CHEEV] vt **-chieved, -chiev•ing** accomplish, perform successfully; gain **a•chieve'ment** n something accomplished

ac•id [AS-id] adj sharp, sour ▷ n sour substance; *chemistry* one of a class of compounds that combine with bases (alkalis, oxides, etc) to form salts **a•cid'ic** adj **a•cid'i•fy** vt **-fied, -fy•ing a•cid'i•ty** n **a•cid'u•lous** adj caustic **acid rain** rain acidified by atmospheric pollution **acid test** conclusive test of value

ac•knowl•edge [ak-NOL-ij] vt **-edged, -edg•ing** admit, own to knowing, recognize; say one has received **ac•knowl'edg•ment** n

ac•me [AK-mee] n highest point

ac•ne [AK-nee] n pimply skin disease

ac•o•lyte [AK-ə-līt] n follower or attendant, esp of priest

a•cous•tic [ə-KOO-stik] adj pert to sound and to hearing **a•cous'tics** n science of sounds ▷ pl features of room or building as regards sounds heard within it

ac•quaint [ə-KWAYNT] vt make familiar with others **ac•quaint'ance** n person known; personal knowledge

ac•qui•esce [ak-wee-ES] vi **-esced, -esc•ing** agree, consent without complaint **ac•qui•es'cence** n

ac•quire [ə-KWĪR] vt **-quired, -quir•ing** gain, get **ac•qui•si•tion** [ak-wə-ZISH-ən] n act of getting; material gain **ac•quis'i•tive** adj desirous of gaining

ac•quit [ə-KWIT] vt **-quit•ted, -quit•ting** declare innocent; settle, discharge, as a debt; behave (oneself) **ac•quit'tal** n declaration of innocence in court

a•cre [AY-kər] n measure of land, 43,560 square feet ▷ pl **lands, estates;** *inf* large area or plenty of **a•cre•age** n the extent of land in acres

ac•rid [AK-rid] adj pungent, sharp; irritating

ac•ri•mo•ny [AK-rə-moh-nee] n bitterness of feeling or language **ac•ri•mo'ni•ous** adj

ac•ro•bat [AK-rə-bat] n one skilled in gymnastic feats, esp as entertainer in circus, etc **ac•ro•bat'ic** adj **ac•ro•bat'ics** pl n activities requiring agility

ac•ro•nym [AK-rə-nim] n word formed from initial letters of other words, such as NATO

a•crop•o•lis [ə-KROP-ə-lis] n citadel, esp in ancient Greece

a•cross [ə-KRAWS] adv, prep crosswise; from side to side; on or to the other side; **get, put it across** explain, make (something) understood

a•cros•tic [ə-KRAW-stik] n word puzzle (or verse) in which the first, middle, or last letters of each line spell a word or words

a•cryl•ic [ə-KRIL-ik] n variety of synthetic materials, esp paint and textiles

act [akt] n thing done, deed; doing; law or decree; section of a play ▷ v perform, as in a play ▷ vi exert force, work, as mechanism; behave **act'ing** n performance of a part ▷ adj temporarily performing the duties of **action** n operation; deed; gesture; expenditure of energy; battle; lawsuit **ac'tion•a•ble** adj subject to lawsuit **ac'ti•vate** vt **-vat•ed, -vat•ing** make active; make radioactive; make chemically active **ac•ti•va'tion** n **ac'tive** adj moving, working; brisk, energetic

ac·ti·vist n one who takes (direct) action to achieve political or social ends **ac·tiv·i·ty** n **ac·tor, ac·tress** n one who acts in a play, film, etc

ac·tin·i·um [ak-TIN-ee-əm] n radioactive element occurring as decay product of uranium

ac·tu·al [AK-choo-əl] adj existing in the present; real **ac·tu·al·i·ty** n **ac·tu·al·ly** adv really, indeed

ac·tu·ar·y [AK-choo-ar-ee] n, pl **-ar·ies** statistician who calculates insurance risks, premiums, etc **ac·tu·ar·i·al** adj

ac·tu·ate [AK-choo-ayt] vt **-at·ed, -at·ing** activate; motivate **ac·tu·a·tor** n mechanism for controlling or moving something indirectly

a·cu·i·ty [ə-KYOO-i-tee] n keenness, esp in vision or thought

a·cu·men [ə-KYOO-mən] n sharpness of wit, perception, penetration

ac·u·punc·ture [AK-yə-pungk-chər] n medical treatment involving insertion of needles at various points on the body

a·cute [ə-KYOOT] adj keen, shrewd; sharp; severe; of angle, less than 90° ▷ n accent (′) over a letter to indicate the quality or length of its sound, as in café **a·cute'ness** n

ad·age [AD-ij] n much wise saying, proverb

a·da·gio [ə-DAH-joh] adv, n, pl **-gios** music leisurely, slow (passage)

ad·a·mant [AD-ə-mənt] adj very hard, unyielding **ad·a·man'tine** [-MAN-teen] adj

Adam's apple [AD-əmz] projecting part at front of the throat, the thyroid cartilage

a·dapt [ə-DAPT] vt alter for new use; fit, modify; change **a·dapt'a·ble** adj **ad·ap·ta'tion** n

a·dapt'er, -tor n device for connecting several electrical appliances to single socket

add v join; increase by; say further **ad·di·tion** [ə-DISH-ən] n **ad·di·tion·al** adj **ad'di·tive** n something added, esp to food

ad·den·dum [ə-DEN-dəm] n, pl **-da** [-də] thing to be added

ad·der [AD-ər] n small poisonous snake

ad·dict [AD-ikt] n one who has become dependent on something, esp drugs **ad·dict'ed** adj **ad·dic'tion** n **ad·dic'tive** adj causing addiction

ad·dle [AD-l] v **-dled, -dling** make or become rotten, muddled

ad·dress [ə-DRES, AD-res] n direction on letter; place where one lives; computing number giving the location of a piece of stored information; speech ▷ vt mark destination, as on envelope; speak to; direct; dispatch **address ball** golf adjust club before striking ball **ad·dress·ee'** n person addressed

ad·duce [ə-DOOS] vt **-duced, -duc·ing** offer as proof; cite **ad·duc'i·ble** adj

ad·e·noids [AD-n-oidz] pl n tissue at back of nose and throat, sometimes obstructing breathing

a·dept [ə-DEPT] adj skilled ▷ n [AD-ept] expert

ad·e·quate [AD-i-kwit] adj sufficient, enough, suitable; not outstanding **ad'e·qua·cy** n

ad·here [ad-HEER] vi **-hered, -her·ing** stick to; be firm in opinion, etc **ad·her'ent** n, adj **ad·he'sion** [-HEE-zhən] n **ad·he'sive** [-siv] adj, n

ad hoc [ad-HOK] adj, adv for a particular occasion only; improvised

a·dieu [ə-DYOO] interj farewell ▷ n,

pl **a·dieus, a·dieux** [ə-DYOOZ] act of taking leave

ad in·fi·ni·tum [in-fə-Nī-təm] *Lat* endlessly

ad·i·pose [AD-ə-pohs] *adj* of fat, fatty

ad·ja·cent [ə-JAY-sənt] *adj* lying near, next (to)

ad·jec·tive [AJ-ik-tiv] *n* word that modifies or limits a noun **ad·jec·ti·val** [-Tī-vəl] *adj* of adjective

ad·join [ə-JOIN] *v* be next to; join **ad·join'ing** *adj* next to, near

ad·journ [ə-JURN] *v* postpone temporarily, as meeting; *inf* move elsewhere

ad·judge [ə-JUJ] *vt* **-judged, -judg·ing** declare; decide; award

ad·ju·di·cate [ə-JOO-di-kayt] *v* **-cat·ed, -cat·ing** try, judge; sit in judgment **ad·ju·di·ca·tion** *n*

ad·junct [AJ-ungkt] *adj* joined, added ▷*n* person or thing added or subordinate

ad·jure [ə-JOOR] *vt* **-jured, -jur·ing** beg, earnestly entreat **ad·ju·ra·tion** [aj-ə-RAY-shən] *n*

ad·just [ə-JUST] *vt* make suitable, adapt; alter slightly, regulate ▷*vi* adapt or conform to new conditions, etc **ad·just·a·ble** *adj*

ad·ju·tant [AJ-ə-tənt] *n* military officer who assists superiors **ad·ju·tan·cy** *n* office, rank of adjutant

ad-lib *v* **-libbed, -lib·bing** improvise and speak spontaneously **ad lib** *n* such speech, etc

ad·min·is·ter [ad-MIN-ə-stər] *vt* manage, look after; dispense, as justice, etc; apply **ad·min·is·tra·tion** *n* **ad·min·is·tra·tive** *adj*

ad·mi·ral [AD-mər-əl] *n* naval officer of highest sea rank

ad·mi·ral·ty *n law* court having jurisdiction over maritime matters

ad·mire [ad-MĪR] *vt* **-mired, -mir·ing** look on with wonder and pleasure; respect highly **ad·mi·ra·ble** *adj* **ad·mi·ra·bly** *adv* **ad·mi·ra·tion** *n* **ad·mir·er** *n* **ad·mir·ing·ly** *adv*

ad·mit [ad-MIT] *vt* **-mit·ted, -mit·ting** confess; accept as true; allow; let in **ad·mis·si·ble** *adj* **ad·mis·sion** *n* permission to enter; entrance fee; confession **ad·mit·tance** *n* permission to enter **ad·mit·ted·ly** *adv*

ad·mix·ture [ad-MIKS-chər] *n* mixture; ingredient

ad·mon·ish [ad-MON-ish] *vt* reprove; advise; warn; exhort **ad·mo·ni·tion** [-mə-NISH-ən] *n* **ad·mon·i·to·ry** *adj*

ad nau·se·am [NAW-zee-əm] *Lat* to a boring or disgusting extent

a·do [ə-DOO] *n* fuss

a·do·be [ə-DOH-bee] *n* sun-dried brick

ad·o·les·cence [ad-l-ES-əns] *n* period of life just before maturity **ad·o·les·cent** *n* a youth ▷*adj*

a·dopt [ə-DOPT] *vt* take into relationship, esp as one's child; take up, as principle, resolution **a·dop'tion** *n* **a·dop'tive** *adj* that which adopts or is adopted

a·dore [ə-DOR] *v* **-dored, -dor·ing** love intensely; worship **a·dor'a·ble** *adj* **ad·o·ra·tion** *n*

a·dorn [ə-DORN] *vt* beautify, embellish, deck **a·dorn'ment** *n* ornament, decoration

ad·re·nal [ə-DREEN-l] *adj* near the kidney **adrenal glands** glands covering the top of the kidneys **a·dren·a·line** [ə-DREN-l-in] *n* hormone secreted by adrenal glands; this substance used as drug

a·drift [ə-DRIFT] *adj, adv* drifting free; *inf* detached; *inf* off course

a·droit [ə-DROIT] *adj* skillful, expert; clever **a·droit·ness** *n* dexterity

ad·sorb [ad-SORB] *v* (of gas, vapor) condense and form thin film on surface **ad·sorb·ent** *adj, n* **ad·sorp·tion** *n*

ad·u·la·tion [aj-ə-LAY-shən] *n* flattery **ad·u·late** *vt* **-lat·ed, -lat·ing** flatter **ad·u·la·to·ry** *adj*

a·dult [ə-DULT] *adj* grown-up, mature ▷ *n* grown-up person; full-grown animal or plant

a·dul·ter·ate [ə-DUL-tə-rayt] *vt* **-at·ed, -at·ing** make impure by addition **a·dul·ter·ant** *n*

a·dul·ter·y [ə-DUL-tə-ree] *n* sexual unfaithfulness of a husband or wife **a·dul·ter·er, a·dul·ter·ess** *n* **a·dul·ter·ous** *adj*

ad·vance [ad-VANS] *v* **-vanced, -vanc·ing** ▷ *vt* bring forward; suggest; encourage; pay beforehand; *auto* to time spark earlier in engine cycle ▷ *vi* go forward; improve in position or value ▷ *n* movement forward; improvement; a loan ▷ *pl* personal approach(es) to gain favor, etc ▷ *adj* ahead in time or position **ad·vanced** *adj* at a late stage; not elementary; ahead of the times **ad·vance·ment** *n* promotion

ad·van·tage [ad-VAN-tij] *n* superiority; more favorable position or state; benefit **ad·van·ta·geous** [-vən-TAY-jəs] *adj*

ad·vent [AD-vent] *n* a coming, arrival; **(A-)** the four weeks before Christmas **the Advent** the coming of Christ **Ad·vent·ist** *n* one of number of Christian sects believing in imminent return of Christ

ad·ven·ti·tious [ad-vən-TISH-əs] *adj* added; accidental, casual

ad·ven·ture [ad-VEN-chər] *n* risk; bold exploit; remarkable happening; enterprise; commercial speculation **ad·ven·tur·er, ad·ven·tur·ess** *n* one who seeks adventures; one who lives on his wits **ad·ven·tur·ous** *adj*

ad·verb [AD-vurb] *n* word used with verb, adjective, or other adverb to modify meaning **ad·ver·bi·al** *adj*

ad·verse [ad-VURS] *adj* opposed to; hostile; unfavorable, bringing harm **ad·ver·sar·y** *n, pl* **-sar·ies** enemy **ad·verse·ly** *adv* **ad·ver·si·ty** *n* distress, misfortune

ad·ver·tise [AD-vər-tīz] *v* **-tised, -tis·ing** ▷ *vt* publicize; make known; give notice of in newspapers, etc ▷ *vi* make public request (for) **ad·ver·tise·ment** *n* **ad·ver·tis·ing** *adj, n*

ad·vice [ad-VĪS] *n* opinion given; counsel; information; (formal) notification

ad·vise [ad-VĪZ] *vt* **-vised, -vis·ing** offer advice; recommend a line of conduct; give notice (of) **ad·vis·a·ble** *adj* expedient **ad·vised** *adj* considered, deliberate; *well-advised* **ad·vis·ed·ly** [-zid-lee] *adv* **ad·vis·er** *n* **ad·vi·so·ry** *adj*

ad·vo·cate [AD-və-kit] *n* one who pleads the cause of another, esp in court of law; attorney ▷ *vt* [-kayt] uphold, recommend **ad·vo·ca·cy** [-kə-see] *n*

ad·ware [AD-wair] *n* computer software that collects information about a user's interests in order to display relevant advertisements to that user; computer software that is given to a user with advertisements already embedded

ae·gis [EE-jis] *n* sponsorship, protection (orig shield of Zeus)

aer·ate [AIR-ayt] *vt* **-at·ed, -at·ing** charge liquid with gas, as

effervescent drink; expose to air
aer·a·tion n **aer·a·tor** n apparatus for charging liquid with gas

aer·i·al [AIR-ee-əl] adj of the air; operating in the air; pertaining to aircraft ▷ n part of radio, etc receiving or sending radio waves

aer·ie, aer·y n see EYRIE

aero- comb form air or aircraft: aerodynamics

aer·o·bat·ics [air-ə-BAT-iks] pl n stunt flying

aer·o·bics [air-OH-biks] n exercise system designed to increase the amount of oxygen in the blood

aer·o·dy·nam·ics [air-oh-di-NAM-iks] n study of air flow, esp around moving solid bodies

aer·o·naut [AIR-ə-nawt] n pilot or navigator of lighter-than-air craft **aer·o·nau·tics** n science of air navigation and flying in general **aer·o·nau·ti·cal** adj

aer·o·sol [AIR-ə-sawl] n (substance dispensed as fine spray from) pressurized can

aer·o·space [AIR-oh-spays] n Earth's atmosphere and space beyond ▷ adj

aes·thet·ic [es-THET-ik] adj relating to principles of beauty, taste and art **aes·thet·ics** n study of art, taste, etc **aes·thete** [ES-theet] n one who affects extravagant love of art

a·far [ə-FAHR] adv from, at, or to, a great distance

af·fa·ble [AF-ə-bəl] adj easy to speak to, polite and friendly **af·fa·bil·i·ty** n

af·fair [ə-FAIR] n thing done or attended to; business; happening; sexual liaison ▷ pl personal or business interests; matters of public interest

af·fect [ə-FEKT] vt act on,

influence; move feelings; make show of, make pretense; assume; have liking for **affect** [AF-ekt] n psychology emotion, feeling, desire **af·fec·ta·tion** n show, pretense

af·fect·ed adj making a pretense; moved; acted upon **af·fect·ing** adj moving the feelings **af·fec·tion** n fondness, love **af·fec·tion·ate** adj

af·fi·da·vit [af-i-DAY-vit] n written statement under oath

af·fil·i·ate [ə-FIL-ee-ayt] vt **-at·ed, -at·ing** connect, attach, as society to federation, etc; adopt ▷ n [-ee-it] affiliated organization

af·fin·i·ty [ə-FIN-i-tee] n, pl **-ties** natural liking; resemblance; relationship by marriage; chemical attraction

af·firm [ə-FURM] v assert positively, declare; maintain statement; make solemn declaration **af·fir·ma·tion** n **af·firm·a·tive** adj asserting ▷ n word of assent

af·fix [ə-FIKS] vt fasten (to); attach, append ▷ n [AF-fiks] addition, esp to word, as suffix, prefix

af·flict [ə-FLIKT] vt give pain or grief to, distress; trouble, vex **af·flic·tion** n

af·flu·ent [AF-loo-ənt] adj wealthy; abundant ▷ n tributary stream **af'flu·ence** n wealth, abundance

af·ford [ə-FORD] vt be able to buy; be able to spare the time, etc; produce, yield, furnish

af·front [ə-FRUNT] vt insult openly ▷ n insult; offense

a·field [ə-FEELD] adv away from home; in or on the field

a·fire [ə-FIR] adv on fire

a·flame [ə-FLAYM] adv burning

a·float [ə-FLOHT] adv floating; at sea; in circulation

a·foot [ə-FUUT] adv astir; on foot

a·fore [ə-FOR] *prep, adv* before, usually in compounds: *aforesaid; aforethought*

a·foul [ə-FOWL] *adj, adv* into difficulty with

a·fraid [ə-FRAYD] *adj* frightened; regretful

a·fresh [ə-FRESH] *adv* again, anew

Af·ri·can [AF-ri-kən] *adj* belonging to Africa ▷ *n* native of Africa **African-American** *n* American of African descent ▷ *adj* of African-Americans

Af·ri·kaans [af-ri-KAHNS] *n* language used in S Africa, derived from 17th cent Dutch **Af·ri·ka·ner** *n* white native of S Afr with Afrikaans as mother tongue

aft *adv* toward stern of ship or tail of aircraft

af·ter [AF-tər] *adv* later; behind ▷ *prep* behind; later than; on the model of; pursuing ▷ *conj* at a later time than ▷ *adj* behind; later; nearer stern of ship or tail of aircraft

af·ter·birth [-burth] *n* membrane expelled after a birth

af·ter·care [-kair] *n* care, esp medical, bestowed on person after period of treatment

af·ter·ef·fect [-ə-fekt] *n* subsequent effect of deed, event, etc

af·ter·glow [-gloh] *n* light after sunset; reflection of past emotion

af·ter·math [-math] *n* result, consequence

af·ter·noon *n* time from noon to evening

af·ter·taste [-tayst] *n* taste remaining or recurring after eating or drinking something

af·ter·thought [-thawt] *n* idea occurring later

af·ter·ward(s) [-wərd, -wərdz] *adv* later

Ag *chemistry* silver

a·gain [ə-GEN] *adv* once more; in addition; back, in return; besides

a·gainst [ə-GENST] *prep* in opposition to; in contact with; opposite; in readiness for

a·gape [ə-GAYP] *adj, adv* open-mouthed as in wonder, etc

ag·ate [AG-it] *n* colored, semiprecious, decorative form of quartz

age [ayj] *n* length of time person or thing has existed; time of life; period of history; maturity; long time ▷ *v* **aged, ag·ing** make or grow old **aged** [AY-jid, ayjd] *adj* old ▷ *pl n* [AY-jid] old people **aging** *n, adj* **age·less** *adj* not growing old, not showing signs of age **age-old** *adj* ancient

a·gen·da [ə-JEN-də] *n* things to be done; program of business meeting

a·gent [AY-jənt] *n* one authorized to carry on business or affairs for another; person or thing producing effect; cause; natural force **a'gen·cy** *n* instrumentality; business, place of business, of agent

agent pro·vo·ca·teur [prə-vok-ə-TUR] *n, pl* **agents pro·vo·ca·teur** *Fr* police or secret service spy

ag·glu·ti·nate [ə-GLOOT-n-ayt] *vt* **-nat·ed, -nat·ing** unite with glue, etc; form words into compounds ▷ *adj* [-n-it] united, as by glue **ag·glu·ti·na'tion** *n*

ag·gran·dize [ə-GRAN-dīz] *vt* **-dized, -diz·ing** make greater in size, power, or rank **ag·gran'dize·ment** [-diz-mənt] *n*

ag·gra·vate [AG-rə-vayt] *vt* **-vat·ed, -vat·ing** make worse or more severe; *inf* annoy **ag·gra·va'tion** *n*

ag·gre·gate [AG-ri-gayt] *vt* **-gat·ed, -gat·ing** gather into mass ▷ *adj* [-git] gathered thus ▷ *n* [-git] mass, sum total; rock consisting of mixture of minerals; mixture of gravel, etc for concrete **ag·gre·ga'tion** n

ag·gres·sion [ə-GRESH-ən] n unprovoked attack; hostile activity **ag·gres'sive** adj **ag·gres'sive·ness** n **ag·gres'sor** n

ag·grieve [ə-GREEV] vt **-grieved, -griev·ing** pain, injure

a·ghast [ə-GAST] adj struck, stupefied with horror or terror

ag·ile [AJ-əl] adj nimble; active; quick **a·gil'i·ty** n

ag·i·tate [AJ-i-tayt] v **-tat·ed, -tat·ing** ▷ vt disturb, excite; keep in motion, stir, shake up; trouble ▷ vi stir up public opinion (for or against) **ag·i·ta·tor** n

a·glow [ə-GLOH] adj glowing

ag·nos·tic [ag-NOS-tik] n person who believes that it is impossible to know whether God exists ▷ adj of this theory **ag·nos'ti·cism** n

a·go [ə-goh] adv in the past

a·gog [ə-GOG] adj, adv eager, astir

ag·o·ny [AG-ə-nee] n, pl **-nies** extreme suffering of mind or body, violent struggle **ag·o·nize** vi **-nized, -niz·ing** suffer agony; worry greatly **agony column** newspaper or magazine feature column containing advertisements relating to personal problems, esp to missing friends or relatives

ag·o·ra·pho·bi·a [ag-ər-ə-FOH-bee-ə] n abnormal fear of open spaces

a·grar·i·an [ə-GRAIR-ee-ən] adj of agriculture, land or its management

a·gree [ə-GREE] v **-greed, -gree·ing** be of same opinion; consent; harmonize; settle suit **a·gree'a·ble** adj willing; pleasant **a·gree'ment** n concord; contract

ag·ri·cul·ture [AG-ri-kul-chər]

n art, practice of cultivating land **ag·ri·cul'tur·al** adj

a·gron·o·my [ə-GRON-ə-mee] n the study of the management of the land and the scientific cultivation of crops **a·gron'o·mist** n

a·ground [ə-GROWND] adv (of boat) touching bottom

a·head [ə-HED] adv in front; forward; in advance

a·hoy [ə-HOI] interj shout used at sea for hailing

aid [ayd] vt to help ▷ n help, support, assistance

aide [ayd] n person acting as an assistant

aide-de-camp [AYD-də-KAMP], pl **aides-de-camp** [AYD-də-KAMP] military officer personally assisting superior

AIDS acquired immune deficiency syndrome

ail [ayl] vt trouble, afflict, disturb ▷ vi be ill **ail'ing** adj sickly **ail'ment** n illness

ai·ler·on [AY-lə-ron] n movable section of wing of aircraft that gives lateral control

aim [aym] v give direction to weapon, etc; direct effort toward, try to ▷ n direction; object, purpose **aim'less** adj without purpose

ain't [aynt] nonstandard am not; is not; are not; has not; have not

air n mixture of gases we breathe, the atmosphere; breeze; tune; manner ▷ pl affected manners ▷ vt expose to air to dry or ventilate **air'i·ly** adv **air'i·ness** n **air'ing** v time spent in the open air; exposure to public view; radio or TV broadcast **air'less** adj stuffy **air'y** adj **air'i·er, air·i·est air'borne** adj flying, in the air **air bag** n safety device in car which inflates automatically in an accident to protect the driver or passenger **air brake** brake worked by compressed air; method of slowing down an aircraft **air'brush** n atomizer spraying paint by compressed air **air·con·di·tion** vt maintain constant stream of clean fresh air in building at correct temperature **air conditioner** n **air'craft** n collective name for flying machines; airplane **aircraft carrier** warship with a long flat deck for the launching and landing of aircraft **air cushion** pocket of air supporting hovercraft **air'field** n landing and takeoff area for aircraft **air force** military organization of country for air warfare **air gun** gun discharged by force of compressed air **air'lift** n transport of goods, etc by aircraft **air'line** n company operating aircraft **air'lock** n air bubble obstructing flow of liquid in pipe; airtight chamber **air pocket** less dense air that causes airplane to drop suddenly **air'port** n station for civilian aircraft **air pump** machine to extract or supply air **air raid** attack by aircraft **air shaft** passage for air into a mine, etc **air'ship** n lighter-than-air flying machine with means of propulsion and steering **air'sick·ness** n nausea caused by motion of aircraft in flight **air'speed** n speed of aircraft relative to air **air'strip** n small airfield with only one runway **air'tight** adj not allowing passage of air **air'way** n regular aircraft route **air'wor·thy** adj fit for service in air **air'wor·thi·ness** n **air·plane** [-playn] n heavier-than-air flying machine **aisle** [il] n passageway separating seating areas in church, theater, etc **a·jar** [ə-JAHR] adv partly open **a·kim·bo** [ə-KIM-boh] adv with

hands on hips and elbows outward **a·kin** [ə-KIN] adj related by blood; alike, having like qualities **Al** chemistry aluminum **al·a·bas·ter** [AL-ə-bas-tər] n soft, white, semitransparent stone **al·a·bas'trine** [-BAS-trin] adj of, like this **à la carte** [ah lä KAHRT] selected freely from the menu **a·lac·ri·ty** [ə-LAK-ri-tee] n quickness, briskness, readiness **à la mode** [ä lä MOHD] in fashion; topped with ice cream **a·larm** [ə-LAHRM] n sudden fright; apprehension; notice of danger; bell, buzzer; call to arms ▷ vt frighten; warn of danger **a·larm'ist** n one given to prophesying danger or exciting alarm esp needlessly **a·las** [ə-LAS] interj cry of grief, pity, or concern **al·ba·tross** [AL-bə-traws] n large oceanic bird, of petrel family; someone or something thought to make accomplishment difficult **al·be·it** [awl-BEE-it] conj although **al·bi·no** [al-Bī-noh] n, pl -nos person or animal with white skin and hair, and pink eyes, due to lack of pigment **al·bi·nism** [AL-bə-niz-əm] n **al·bum** [AL-bəm] n book of blank leaves, for photographs, stamps, autographs, etc; one or more long-playing phonograph records or tape recordings **al·bu·men** [al-BYOO-mən] n egg white **al·bu·min** [al-BYOO-mən] n constituent of animal and vegetable matter, found nearly pure in white of egg **al·che·my** [AL-kə-mee] n medieval chemistry, esp attempts to turn base metals into gold and find elixir of life **al·che·mist** n

al·co·hol [AL-kə-hawl] n intoxicating fermented liquor; class of organic chemical substances **al·co·hol·ic** adj of alcohol ▷ n one addicted to alcoholic drink **al·co·hol·ism** n disease, alcohol poisoning

al·cove [AL-kohv] n recessed section of a room

ale [ayl] n fermented malt liquor, type of beer, orig without hops

a·lert [ə-LURT] adj watchful; brisk, active ▷ n warning of sudden attack or surprise ▷ vt warn, esp of danger; draw attention to **a·lert'ness** n **on the alert** watchful

al·fal·fa [al-FAL-fə] n plant widely used as fodder

al·fres·co [al-FRES-koh] adv, adj in the open air

al·gae [AL-jee] pl n, sing **-ga** [-gə] various water plants, including seaweed

al·ge·bra [AL-jə-brə] n method of calculating, using symbols to represent quantities and to show relations between them, making a kind of abstract arithmetic **al·ge·bra'ic** [-BRAY-ik] adj

ALGOL, Algol [AL-gol] computing algorithmic oriented language

al·go·rithm [AL-gə-rith-əm] n procedural model for complicated calculations

a·li·as [AY-lee-əs] adv otherwise known as ▷ n, pl **-as·es** assumed name

al·i·bi [AL-ə-bi] n plea of being somewhere else when crime was committed; inf excuse

a·li·en [AY-lee-ən] adj foreign; different in nature; repugnant (to) ▷ n foreigner **a'li·en·a·ble** adj able to be transferred to another owner **a'li·en·ate** [-nayt] vt

-at·ed, -at·ing estrange; transfer **a·li·en·a'tion** n

a·light [ə-LIT] vi get down; land, settle

a·light[2] adj lit up

a·lign [ə-LIN] vt bring into line or agreement

a·like [ə-LIK] adj like, similar ▷ adv in the same way

al·i·men·ta·ry [al-ə-MEN-tə-ree] adj of food **alimentary canal** food passage in body

al·i·mo·ny [AL-ə-moh-nee] n allowance paid under court order to separated or divorced spouse

a·live [ə-LIV] adj living; active; aware; swarming

al·ka·li [AL-kə-li] n, pl **-lis** substance that combines with and neutralizes acid, forming a salt **al'ka·line** adj **al·ka·lin'i·ty** n

all [awl] adj the whole of, every one of ▷ adv wholly, entirely ▷ n the whole; everything, everyone ▷ pron everything, everyone **all fours** hands and feet **all in** exhausted **all'-a·round'** adj showing ability in many fields **all right** satisfactory; well, safe; pleasing; very well; beyond doubt

Al·lah [AH-lə] n Muslim name for the Supreme Being

al·lay [ə-LAY] vt lighten, relieve, calm, soothe

al·lege [ə-LEJ] vt **-leged, -leg·ing** state without or before proof; produce as argument **al·le·ga·tion** [al-i-GAY-shən] n **al·leged'** adj **al·leg·ed·ly** adv

al·le·giance [ə-LEE-jəns] n duty of a subject or citizen to sovereign or government; loyalty (to person or cause)

al·le·go·ry [AL-i-gor-ee] n, pl **-ries** story with a meaning other than literal one; description of

one thing under image of another
al·le·gor·i·cal *adj*
al·le·gret·to [al-i-GRET-oh] *adv, adj, n music* lively (passage) but not so quick as allegro
al·le·gro [ə-LEG-roh] *adv, adj, n music* fast (passage)
al·ler·gy [AL-ər-jee] *n, pl* **-gies** abnormal sensitivity to some food or substance harmless to most people **al'ler·gen** *n* substance capable of inducing an allergy **al·ler·gic** [ə-LUR-jik] *adj* having or caused by an allergy; *inf* having an aversion (to)
al·le·vi·ate [ə-LEE-vee-ayt] *vt* **-at·ed, -at·ing** ease, lessen, mitigate; make light **al·le·vi·a·tion** *n*
al·ley [AL-ee] *n, pl* **-leys** narrow street esp through the middle of a block; walk, path; hardwood lane for bowling; building housing bowling lanes
al·li·ance [ə-Lï-əns] *n* state of being allied; union between families by marriage, and states by treaty; confederation
al·li·ga·tor [AL-i-gay-tər] *n* animal of crocodile family; leather made from its hide
al·lit·er·a·tion [ə-lit-ə-RAY-shən] *n* beginning of two or more words in close succession with same sound, e.g *Sing a Song of Sixpence* **al·lit·er·a·tive** *adj*
al·lo·cate [AL-ə-kayt] *vt* **-cat·ed, -cat·ing** assign as a share; designate **al·lo·ca·tion** *n*
al·lo·mor·phism [al-ə-MOR-fiz-əm] *n* variation of form without change in essential nature; variation of crystalline form of chemical compound **al·lo·morph** *n* **al·lo·mor·phic** *adj*
al·lop·a·thy [ə-LOP-ə-thee] *n* orthodox treatment of medicine;

opposite of homeopathy
al·lot [ə-LOT] *vt* **-lot·ted, -lot·ting** distribute as shares; give out **al·lot'ment** *n* distribution; portion of land rented for cultivation; portion of land, pay, etc allotted
al·low [ə-LOW] *vt* let happen; permit; acknowledge; set aside ▷ *vi* (usu with *for*) take into account **al·low'a·ble** *adj* **al·low'ance** *n* portion or amount allowed, esp at regular times
all right SEE ALL
all·spice [AWL-spis] *n* berry of West Indian tree; the tree; aromatic spice prepared from its berries
al·lude [ə-LOOD] *vi* **-lud·ed, -lud·ing** mention lightly, hint at, make indirect reference to; refer to **al·lu·sion** [-LOO-zhən] *n* **al·lu·sive** [-siv] *adj*
al·lure [ə-LOOR] *vt* **-lured, -lur·ing** entice, win over, fascinate ▷ *n* attractiveness **al·lur'ing** *adj* charming, seductive
al·lu·vi·al [ə-LOO-vee-əl] *adj* deposited by rivers **al·lu'vi·on** [-vee-ən] *n* land formed by washed-up deposit **al·lu'vi·um** [-vee-əm] *n, pl* **-vi·a** [-vee-ə] water-borne matter deposited by rivers, floods, etc
al·ly [ə-LĪ] *vt* **-lied, -ly·ing** join in relationship by treaty, marriage, or friendship, etc ▷ *n* [AL-ī], *pl* **-lies** country or ruler bound to another by treaty; confederate
al·ma ma·ter [AL-mə MAH-tər] *n* one's school, college, or university; its song or hymn
al·ma·nac [AWL-mə-nak] *n* yearly publication with detailed information on tides, events, etc
al·might·y [awl-Mī-tee] *adj*

having all power, omnipotent; *inf* very great **The Almighty** God

al•mond [AH-mànd] *n* kernel of the fruit of a tree related to the peach; tree that bears it

al•most [AWL-mohst] *adv* very nearly, all but

alms [ahmz] *pl n* gifts to the poor

al•oe [AL-oh] *n* genus of plants of medicinal value ▷ *pl* bitter drug made from plant

a•loft [à-LAWFT] *adv* on high; overhead; in ship's rigging

a•lone [à-LOHN] *adj* single, solitary ▷ *adv* separately, only

a•long [à-LAWNG] *adv* lengthwise; forward (with); forward ▷ *prep* over the length of **a•long'side'** *adv*, *prep* beside

a•loof [à-LOOF] *adv* withdrawn; at a distance; apart ▷ *adj* uninvolved **a•loof'ness** *n*

al•o•pe•ci•a [al-à-PEESH-à] *n* baldness

a•loud [à-LOWD] *adj* in a voice loud enough to be heard ▷ *adv* loudly; audibly

alp *n* high mountain **Alps** *pl* esp mountains of Switzerland **al•pine** [AL-pīn] *adj* of, growing on, high mountains; (**A-**) of the Alps ▷ *n* mountain plant **al•pin•ist** [AL-pà-nist] *n* mountain climber

al'pen•stock [-pàn-stok] *n* iron-tipped staff used by climbers

al•pac•a [al-PAK-à] *n* Peruvian llama; its wool; cloth made from this

al•pha•bet [AL-fà-bet] *n* the set of letters used in writing a language **al•pha•bet'i•cal** *adj* in the standard order of the letters

al•pha male *n* dominant animal or person in a group

al-Qae•da [al-KAY-dà, al-Kī-dà] *n* militant Islamic organization believed to be behind various

operations against Western interests

al•read•y [awl-RED-ee] *adv* before, previously; sooner than expected

al•so [AWL-soh] *adv* as well, too; besides; moreover

al•tar [AWL-tàr] *n* raised place, stone, etc, on which sacrifices are offered; in Christian church, table on which priest consecrates the eucharist elements **al'tar•cloth** *n* **al'tar•piece** *n* **al'tar rails** *n*

altar boy *n* acolyte

al•ter [AWL-tàr] *v* change, make or become different; castrate, spay (animal) **al'ter•a•ble** *adj* **al•ter•a•bly** *adv* **al•ter•a'tion** *n*

al•ter•ca•tion [awl-tàr-KAY-shàn] *n* dispute, wrangling, noisy controversy

al•ter•e•go [AWL-tàr EE-goh] second self; close friend

al•ter•nate [AWL-tàr-nayt] *v* **-nat•ed, -nat•ing** occur or cause to occur by turns **al'ter•nate** [-nit] *adj, n* (one) after the other, by turns **al•ter•na•tive** [awl-TUR-nà-tiv] *n* one of two choices ▷ *adj* offering or expressing a choice **al•ter•na•tor** *n* electric generator for producing alternating current **alternative medicine** treatment of disease by non-traditional methods such as homeopathy and acupuncture

al•though [awl-THOH] *conj* despite the fact that

al•tim•e•ter [al-TIM-i-tàr] *n* instrument for measuring height

al•ti•tude [AL-ti-tood] *n* height, eminence, loftiness

al•to [AL-toh] *n, pl* **-tos** *music* male singing voice or instrument above tenor; contralto

al•to•geth•er [awl-tà-GETH-àr] *adv* entirely; on the whole; in total **in the altogether** nude

al•tru•ism [AL-troo-iz-àm] *n*

principle of living and acting for good of others **al'tru•ist** n **al•tru•is'tic** adj

a•lu•mi•num [ə-LOO-mə-nəm] n light nonrusting metal resembling silver **a•lu'mi•na** n oxide of aluminum

a•lum•na [ə-LUM-nə] n, pl **-nae** [-nee] girl or woman graduate of a particular school, college, or university

a•lum•nus [ə-LUM-nəs] n, pl **-ni** [-nī] graduate of a particular school, college, or university

al•ways [AWL-wayz] adv at all times; forever

am first person sing pres ind of BE

Am chemistry americium

am, am ante meridiem: before noon

a•mal•gam [ə-MAL-gəm] n compound of mercury and another metal; soft, plastic mixture; combination of elements

a•mal•ga•mate [ə-MAL-gə-mayt] v **-mat•ed, -mat•ing** mix, combine or cause to combine **a•mal•ga•ma'tion** n

a•man•u•en•sis [ə-man-yoo-EN-sis] n, pl **-ses** [-seez] one who writes from dictation; copyist, secretary

a•mass [ə-MAS] v collect in quantity

am•a•teur [AM-ə-chuur] n one who carries on an art, study, game, etc for the love of it, not for money; unskilled practitioner **am•a•teur'ish** adj imperfect, untrained

am•a•to•ry [AM-ə-tor-ee] adj relating to love

a•maze [ə-MAYZ] vt **-mazed, -maz•ing** surprise greatly, astound **a•maze'ment** n **amazing** adj

Am•a•zon [AM-ə-zon] n female warrior of legend; tall, strong woman **Am•a•zo'ni•an** [-ZOH-nee-ən] adj

am•bas•sa•dor [am-BAS-ə-dər] n senior diplomatic representative sent by one government to another **am•bas•sa•do'ri•al** adj

am•ber [AM-bər] n yellowish, translucent fossil resin ▷ adj made of, colored like amber

am•ber•gris [AM-bər-grees] n waxy substance secreted by the sperm whale, used in making perfumes

am•bi•dex•trous [am-bi-DEK-strəs] adj able to use both hands with equal ease **am•bi•dex•ter'i•ty** n

am•bi•ence, -ance [AM-bee-əns] n atmosphere of a place

am•bi•ent [AM-bee-ənt] adj surrounding

am•big•u•ous [am-BIG-yoo-əs] adj having more than one meaning; obscure **am•bi•gu'i•ty** n

am•bi•tion [am-BISH-ən] n desire for power, fame, honor; the object of that desire **am•bi'tious** adj

am•biv•a•lence [am-BIV-ə-ləns] n simultaneous existence of two conflicting desires, opinions, etc **am•biv'a•lent** adj

am•ble [AM-bəl] vi **-bled, -bling** move along easily and gently; move at an easy pace ▷ n this movement or pace

am•bro•sia [am-BROH-zhə] n mythology food of the gods; anything smelling, tasting particularly good

am•bu•lance [AM-byə-ləns] n conveyance for sick or injured

am•bush [AM-buush] n a lying in wait (for) ▷ vt waylay, attack from hiding, lie in wait for

a•mel•io•rate [ə-MEEL-yə-rayt] v **-rat•ed, -rat•ing** make better, improve **a•mel•io•ra'tion** n

a•men [AY-MEN] interj surely; so let it be

a•me•na•ble [ə-MEE-nə-bəl] adj

easy to be led or controlled; subject to, liable **a•me'na•bly** adv

a•mend [ə-MEND] vi grow better ▷ vt correct; improve; alter in detail, as bill in legislature, etc **a•mend'ment** n **a•mends'** pl n reparation

a•men•i•ty [ə-MEN-i-tee] n, pl -**ties** useful or pleasant facility or service

A•mer•i•can [ə-MER-i-kən] adj of, relating to, the North American continent or the United States of America

am•e•thyst [AM-ə-thist] n bluish-violet precious stone; its color

a•mi•a•ble [AY-mee-ə-bəl] adj friendly, kindly **a•mi•a•bil'i•ty** n

am•i•ca•ble [AM-i-kə-bəl] adj friendly **am•i•ca•bil'i•ty** n

a•mid [ə-MID], **a•midst** [ə-MIDST] prep in the middle of; among; during

a•mid•ships [ə-MID-ships] adv near, toward, middle of ship

a•mi•no acid [ə-MEE-noh] organic compound found in protein

a•miss [ə-MIS] adj wrong ▷ adv faultily, badly **take amiss** to be offended (by)

am•i•ty [AM-i-tee] n friendship

am•me•ter [AM-mee-tər] n instrument for measuring electric current

am•mo•nia [ə-MOHN-yə] n pungent alkaline gas containing hydrogen and nitrogen

am•mo•nite [AM-ə-nīt] n whorled fossil shell like ram's horn

am•mu•ni•tion [am-yə-NISH-ən] n any projectiles (bullets, rockets, etc) that can be discharged from a weapon; facts that can be used in an argument

am•ne•sia [am-NEE-zhə] n loss of memory

am•nes•ty [AM-nə-stee] n, pl -**ties**

general pardon ▷ vt -**tied, -ty•ing** grant this

am•ni•ot•ic fluid [am-nee-OT-ik] fluid surrounding fetus in womb

a•moe•ba [ə-MEE-bə] n, pl -**bas** microscopic single-celled animal found in ponds, etc and able to change its shape

a•mok, a•muck [ə-MUK] adv **run amok** rush about in violent frenzy

a•mong [ə-MUNG], **a•mongst** [ə-MUNGST] prep mixed with, in the midst of, of the number of, between

a•mor•al [ay-MOR-əl] adj nonmoral, having no moral qualities **a•mo•ral•i•ty** [ay-mə-RAL-i-tee] n

am•o•rous [AM-ər-əs] adj inclined to love; in love **am'o•rous•ness** n

a•mor•phous [ə-MOR-fəs] adj without distinct shape

am•or•tize [AM-ər-tīz] vt pay off a debt by a sinking fund **am'or•tiz•a•ble** adj

a•mount [ə-MOWNT] vi come, be equal (to) ▷ n quantity; sum total

a•mour [ə-MOOR] n (illicit) love affair

am•pere [AM-peer] n unit of electric current **am•per•age** [AM-pə-rij] n strength of current in amperes

am•per•sand [AM-pər-sand] n the character (&), meaning and

am•phet•a•mine [am-FET-ə-meen] n synthetic liquid used medicinally as stimulant, a dangerous drug if misused

am•phib•i•ous [am-FIB-ee-əs] adj living or operating both on land and in water **am•phib'i•an** n animal that lives first in water then on land; vehicle able to travel on land or water; aircraft that can alight on land or water

am•phi•the•a•ter [AM-fə-thee-ə-tàr] n building with tiers of seats rising around an arena; room with gallery above from which one can observe surgical operations, etc

am·pho·ra [AM-fər-ə] n, pl **-rae** [-ree] two-handled vessel of ancient Greece and Rome

am·ple [AM-pəl] adj big enough; large, spacious **am'ply** adv

am·pli·fy [AM-plə-fī] vt **-fied, -fy·ing** increase; make bigger, louder, etc **am·pli·fi·ca'tion** n **am'pli·fi·er** n

am·pli·tude [AM-pli-tood] n spaciousness, width; maximum departure from average of alternating current, etc **amplitude modulation** modulation of amplitude of radio carrier wave; broadcasting system using this

am·pule [AM-pyool] n container for hypodermic dose

am·pu·tate [AM-pyə-tayt] vi **-tat·ed, -tat·ing** cut off (limb, etc) **am·pu·ta'tion** n

amuck see AMOK

am·u·let [AM-yə-lit] n something carried or worn as a charm

a·muse [ə-MYOOZ] vt **-mused, -mus·ing** divert; occupy pleasantly; cause to laugh or smile **a·muse'ment** n entertainment, pastime

an adj form of a used before vowels, and sometimes before h: an hour

an·a·bol·ic ster·oid [an-ə-BOL-ik STEER-oid] any of various hormones used by athletes to encourage muscle growth

a·nach·ro·nism [ə-NAK-rə-niz-əm] n mistake of time, by which something is put in wrong historical period; something out-of-date

an·a·con·da [an-ə-KON-də] n large semi-aquatic snake that kills by constriction

an·a·gram [AN-ə-gram] n word or sentence made by reordering the letters of another word or sentence, such as ant from tan

anal see ANUS

an·al·ge·si·a [an-lJEE-zee-ə] n absence of pain **an·al·ge'sic** adj, n (drug) relieving pain

a·na·log [A-nə-log] n physical object or quantity used to measure or represent another quantity; something that is analogous to something else ▷ adj displaying information by means of a dial

a·nal·o·gy [ə-NAL-ə-jee] n, pl **-gies** agreement or likeness in certain respects; correspondence **a·nal'o·gize** v **-gized, -giz·ing** explain by analogy **a·nal'o·gous** [-ə-gəs] adj similar; parallel

a·nal·y·sis [ə-NAL-ə-sis] n, pl **-ses** [-seez] separation into elements or components **an·a·lyze** [AN-l-īz] vt **-lyzed, -lyz·ing** examine critically; determine the constituent parts **an·a·lyst** [AN-l-ist] n one skilled in analysis, esp chemical analysis; psychoanalyst **an·a·lyt·i·cal** [an-l-IT-i-kəl] **an·a·lyt·ic** [an-l-IT-ik] adj

an·ar·chy [AN-ər-kee] n lawlessness; lack of government in a country; confusion **an·ar·chic** [an-AHR-kik] adj **an'ar·chism** n **an'ar·chist** n one who opposes all government

a·nath·e·ma [ə-NATH-ə-mə] n, pl **-mas** anything detested, hateful; ban of the church; curse **a·nath'e·ma·tize** vt **-tized, -tiz·ing**

a·nat·o·my [ə-NAT-ə-mee] n science of structure of the body; detailed analysis; the body **an·a·tom'i·cal** adj

an·ces·tor [AN-ses-tər] n person from whom another is descended;

early type of later form or product **an·ces·tral** adj **an·ces·try** n

an·chor [ANG-kər] n heavy (usu hooked) implement dropped on cable, chain, etc to bottom of sea, etc to secure vessel; radio and TV principal announcer in program of news, sports, etc ▷ vt fasten by or as with anchor; perform as anchor **an'chor·age** n act of, place of anchoring

an·cho·rite [ANG-kə-rīt] n hermit, recluse

an·cho·vy [AN-choh-vee] n, pl (**-vies**) small fish of herring family

an·cient [AYN-shənt] adj belonging to former age; old; timeworn ▷ n one who lived in an earlier age **ancient history** history of ancient times; common knowledge

an·cil·lar·y [AN-sə-ler-ee] adj, n, pl **-ies** subordinate, subservient, auxiliary

and conj joins words, phrases, clauses, and sentences to introduce a consequence, etc

an·dan·te [ahn-DAHN-tay] adv, n music moderately slow (passage)

and·i·ron [AND-ī-ərn] n steel bar or bracket for supporting logs in a fireplace

an·drog·y·nous [an-DROJ-ə-nəs] adj having characteristics of both male and female

an·ec·dote [AN-ik-doht] n very short story dealing with single incident. **an'ec·do·tal** adj **an·ec·do'tal·ist** n one given to recounting anecdotes

a·ne·mi·a [ə-NEE-mee-ə] n deficiency in number of red blood cells **a·ne'mic** adj suffering from anemia; pale, sickly

an·e·mom·e·ter [an-ə-MOM-ə-tər] n wind gauge

a·nem·o·ne [ə-NEM-ə-nee] n flower related to buttercup **sea anemone** plantlike sea animal

an·er·oid [AN-ə-roid] adj denoting a barometer that measures atmospheric pressure without use of mercury or other liquid

an·es·the·si·ol·o·gy [an-is-thee-zi-OL-ə-jee] n branch of medicine dealing with anesthetics

an·es·thet·ic [an-əs-THET-ik] n, adj (drug) causing loss of sensation **an·es·the·sia** [-THEE-zhə] n loss of sensation **an·es·the·tist** [ə-NES-thi-tist] n expert in use of anesthetics **an·es·the·tize** vt **-tized, -tiz·ing**

an·eu·rysm, an·eu·rism [AN-yə-riz-əm] n swelling out of a part of an artery

a·new [ə-NOO] adv afresh, again

an·gel [AYN-jəl] n divine messenger; ministering or attendant spirit; person with the qualities of such a spirit, as gentleness, purity, etc **an·gel'ic** adj

An·ge·lus [AN-jə-ləs] n devotional service in R C Church in memory of the Incarnation, said at morning, noon and sunset; bell announcing the time for this service

an·ger [ANG-gər] n strong emotion excited by a real or supposed injury; wrath; rage ▷ vt excite to wrath; enrage **an'gri·ly** adv **an'gry** adj full of anger; inflamed

an·gi·na (pec·to·ris) [an-jī-nə PEK-tər-is] n severe pain accompanying some heart diseases

an·gle¹ [ANG-gəl] vi **-gled, -gling** fish with hook and line **an'gler** n

angle² n meeting of two lines or surfaces; corner; point of view; inf devious motive ▷ vt bend at an angle

An·gli·can [ANG-gli-kən] adj, n

(member) of the Church of England **An'gli·can·ism** n

An·gli·cize [ANG-glə-siz] vt **-cized, -ciz·ing** express in English; turn into English form **An'gli·cism** n English idiom or peculiarity

Anglo- comb form English: Anglo-Scottish; British: Anglo-American

an·glo·phil·ia [ang-glə-FIL-ee-ə] n excessive admiration for English **an'glo·phile** [-fil] n

An·glo·pho·bi·a [ang-glə-FOH-bee-ə] n dislike of England, etc **an'glo·phobe** n

an·go·ra [ang-GOR-ə] n variety of goat, cat, or rabbit with long silky hair; hair of the angora goat or rabbit; cloth made from this hair

an·gos·tu·ra bark [ang-gə-STOOR-ə] n bitter bark of certain S American trees, used as flavoring in alcoholic drinks

angst [ankst] n feeling of anxiety

ang·strom [ANG-strəm] n unit of length for measuring wavelengths of electromagnetic radiation

an·guish [ANG-gwish] n great mental or bodily pain ▷ v suffer this pain; cause to suffer it

an·gu·lar [ANG-gyə-lər] adj (of people) bony, awkward; having angles; measured by an angle **an·gu·lar'i·ty** n

an·hy·drous [an-HĪ-drəs] adj (of chemical substances) free from water

an·i·line [AN-l-in] n product of coal tar or indigo that yields dyes

an·i·mal [AN-ə-məl] n living creature, having sensation and power of voluntary motion; beast ▷ adj of, pert to animals; sensual **an·i·mal·cule** [an-ə-MAL-kyool] n very small animal, esp one that cannot be seen by naked eye **animal husbandry** branch of agriculture concerned with raising domestic animals

an·i·mate [AN-ə-mayt] vt **-mat·ed, -mat·ing** give life to; enliven; inspire; actuate; make cartoon film of **an'i·mat·ed** adj lively; in form of cartoons **an·i·ma'tion** n life, vigor; cartoon film

an·i·mism [AN-ə-miz-əm] n primitive religion, belief that natural effects are due to spirits, that inanimate things have spirits **an'i·mist** n

an·i·mos·i·ty [an-ə-MOS-i-tee] n, pl **-ties** hostility, enmity

an·i·mus [AN-ə-məs] n hatred; animosity

an·i·on [AN-ī-ən] n ion with negative charge

an·ise [AN-is] n plant with aromatic seeds, which are used for flavoring

an·i·seed [AN-ə-seed] n the licorice-flavored seed of anise

an·kle [ANG-kəl] n joint between foot and leg **an·klet** [ANG-klit] n ankle-ornament; short sock reaching just above the ankle

an·nals [AN-lz] pl n historical records of events **an'nal·ist** n

an·neal [ə-NEEL] vt toughen (metal or glass) by heating and slow cooling; temper

an·ne·lid [AN-l-id] n one of class of invertebrate animals, including the earthworm, etc

an·nex [a-NEKS] vt add, append, attach; take possession of (esp territory) **an·nex·a·tion** [an-ik-SAY-shən] n annex n [AN-eks] supplementary building; something added

an·ni·hi·late [ə-Nī-ə-layt] vt **-lat·ed, -lat·ing** reduce to nothing, destroy utterly **an·ni·hi·la'tion** n

an·ni·ver·sa·ry [an-ə-VUR-sə-ree] *n* yearly return of a date; celebration of this

an·no Dom·i·ni [AN-oh DOM-ə-nee] *Lat* in the year of our Lord

an·no·tate [AN-ə-tayt] *vt* **-tat·ed, -tat·ing** make notes upon, comment **an·no·ta·tion** *n*

an·nounce [ə-NOWNS] *vt* **-nounced, -nounc·ing** make known, proclaim **an·nounce·ment** *n* **an·nounc·er** *n* broadcaster who announces items in program, introduces speakers, etc

an·noy [ə-NOI] *vt* vex; make slightly angry; tease **an·noy'ance** *n*

an·nu·al [AN-yoo-əl] *adj* yearly; of, for a year ⊳ *n* plant that completes its life cycle in a year; book published each year **an·nu·al·ly** *adv*

an·nu·i·ty [ə-NOO-i-tee] *n, pl* **-ties** sum or grant paid every year **an·nu'i·tant** [-tnt] *n* holder of annuity

an·nul [ə-NUL] *vt* **-nulled, -nul·ling** make void, cancel, abolish **an·nul·ling** *n*

an·nu·lar [AN-yə-lər] *adj* ring-shaped **an'nu·lat·ed** [-lay-tid] *adj* formed in rings **an'nu·let** [-lit] *n* small ring or molding in shape of ring

An·nun·ci·a·tion [ə-nun-see-AY-shən] *n* angel's announcement of Incarnation to the Virgin Mary (a-) announcing; announcement **an·nun'ci·ate** *vt* **-at·ed, -at·ing** proclaim, announce

an·ode [AN-ohd] *n* electricity the positive electrode or terminal **an·o·dize** [AN-ə-diz] *vt* cover (metal object) with protective film by using it as an anode in electrolysis **an·o·dyne** [AN-ə-din] *adj* relieving pain, soothing ⊳ *n* pain-relieving drug; something that soothes

a·noint [ə-NOINT] *vt* smear with oil or ointment; consecrate with oil **a·noint·ment** *n* the Anointed; the Messiah

a·nom·a·lous [ə-NOM-ə-ləs] *adj* irregular, abnormal **a·nom'a·ly** *n, pl* **-lies** irregularity; deviation from rule

a·non [ə-NON] *adv* obs in a short time, soon; now and then

a·non·y·mous [ə-NON-ə-məs] *adj* nameless, esp without an author's name **an·o·nym·i·ty** [an-ə-NIM-i-tee] *n*

an·o·rak [AN-ə-rak] *n* lightweight, warm, waterproof, usu hooded jacket; parka

an·o·rex·i·a ner·vo·sa [an-ə-REK-see-ə nur-VOH-sə] *n* psychological disorder characterized by fear of becoming fat and refusal to eat

an·oth·er [ə-NUTH-ər] *pron, adj* one other; a different one; one more

an·ser·ine [AN-sə-rin] *adj* of or like a goose; silly

an·swer [AN-sər] *v* reply (to); solve; reply correctly; pay; meet; be accountable (for, to); match; satisfy, suit ⊳ *n* reply; solution **an'swer·a·ble** *adj* accountable **answering machine** apparatus for answering a telephone automatically and recording messages

ant *n* small social insect, proverbial for industry **ant'eat·er** *n* animal that feeds on ants by means of a long, sticky tongue **ant'hill** the mound raised by ants

an·tag·o·nist [an-TAG-ə-nist] *n* opponent, adversary **an·tag·o·nism** *n* **an·tag·o·nis·tic** *adj* **an·tag'o·nize** *vt* **-nized, -niz·ing** arouse hostility in

Ant·arc·tic [ant-AHRK-tik] *adj* south polar ⊳ *n* these regions

an·te [AN-tee] *n* player's stake in poker ⊳ *vt* **-ted, -te·ing** (often with up) stake

ante- *prefix* before in time or position: *antedate; antechamber*

an·te·ced·ent [an-tə-SEED-nt] *adj, n* (thing) going before

an·te·di·lu·vi·an [an-tee-di-LOO-vee-ən] *adj* before the flood; ancient

an·te·lope [AN-tl-ohp] *n* deer-like ruminant animal, remarkable for grace and speed

ante me·rid·i·em [AN-tee mə-RID-ee-əm] before noon

an·ten·na [an-TEN-ə] *n, pl* **-nae** [-nee] insect's feeler; aerial

an·te·pe·nult [an-tee-PEE-nult] *n* last syllable but two in a word **an·te·pe·nul·ti·mate** *adj, n*

an·te·ri·or [an-TEER-ee-ər] *adj* to the front; before

an·them [AN-thəm] *n* song of loyalty, esp to a country; Scripture passage set to music; piece of sacred music, originally sung in alternate parts by two choirs

an·ther [AN-thər] *n* in flower, part at top of stamen containing pollen

an·thol·o·gy [an-THOL-ə-jee] *n, pl* **-gies** collection of poems, literary extracts, etc **an·thol·o·gist** *n* maker of such **an·thol·o·gize** *vt* **-gized, -giz·ing** compile or publish in an anthology

an·thra·cite [AN-thrə-sīt] *n* hard coal burning slowly almost without flame or smoke

an·thrax [AN-thraks] *n* malignant disease in cattle, communicable to people; sore caused by this

an·thro·poid [AN-thrə-poid] *adj* like man ▷ *n* ape resembling human being

an·thro·pol·o·gy [an-thrə-POL-ə-jee] *n* scientific study of origins, development of human race **an·thro·po·log·i·cal** [-pə-LOJ-i-kəl]

adj **an·thro·pol·o·gist** *n*

an·thro·po·mor·phize [an-thrə-pə-MOR-fīz] *vt* **-pized, -piz·ing** ascribe human attributes to God or an animal **an·thro·po·mor·phic** *adj*

anti- *prefix* against, opposed to: *anti-war*; opposite to: *anticlimax*; counteracting: *antifreeze*

an·ti·bi·ot·ic [an-ti-bi-OT-ik] *n* any of various chemical, fungal or synthetic substances, esp penicillin, used against bacterial infection ▷ *adj*

an·ti·bod·y [AN-ti-bod-ee] *n* substance in, or introduced into, blood serum that counteracts the growth and harmful action of bacteria

an·tic·i·pate [an-TIS-ə-payt] *vt* **-pat·ed, -pat·ing** expect; take or consider beforehand; foresee; enjoy in advance **an·tic·i·pa·tion** *n* **an·tic·i·pa·to·ry** [-pə-tor-ee] *adj*

an·ti·cli·max [an-ti-KLI-maks] *n* sudden descent to the trivial or ludicrous set **an·ti·cli·mac·tic** *adj*

an·tics [AN-tiks] *pl n* absurd or grotesque movements or acts

an·ti·cy·clone [an-tee-SI-klohn] *n* system of winds moving around center of high barometric pressure

an·ti·dote [AN-ti-doht] *n* counteracting remedy

an·ti·freeze [AN-ti-freez] *n* liquid added to water to lower its freezing point, as in automobile radiators

an·ti·gen [AN-ti-jən] *n* substance stimulating production of antibodies in the blood

an·ti·his·ta·mine [an-ti-HIS-tə-meen] *n* drug used esp to treat allergies

an·ti·mo·ny [AN-tə-moh-nee] *n* brittle, bluish-white metal

an·tip·a·thy [an-TIP-ə-thee] *n, pl* **-thies** dislike, aversion

an·ti·per·spi·rant [an-ti-PUR-spər-ənt] n substance used to reduce sweating

an·ti·phon [AN-tə-fon] n composition in which verses, lines are sung alternately by two choirs; anthem **an·tiph·o·nal** [an-TIF-ə-nl] adj

an·tip·o·des [an-TIP-ə-deez] pl n countries, peoples on opposite side of the globe (often refers to Aust and N Zealand) **an·tip·o·de'an** adj

an·ti·pope [AN-ti-pohp] n pope elected in opposition to the one regularly chosen

an·tique [an-TEEK] n relic of former times, usu a piece of furniture, etc that is collected ▷ adj ancient; old-fashioned **an·ti·quar·i·an** n student or collector of old things **an·ti·quat·ed** adj out-of-date **an·tiq·ui·ty** [an-TIK-wi-tee] n great age; former times

an·ti-Se·mit·ic [an-tee-sə-MIT-ik] adj hostile or discriminating against Jews **an·ti-Sem'i·tism** n **an·ti-Sem'ite** n

an·ti·sep·tic [an-tə-SEPT-ik] n, adj (substance) preventing infection ▷ adj free from infection

an·tith·e·sis [an-TITH-ə-sis] n, pl **-ses** [-seez] direct opposite; contrast; opposition of ideas **an·ti·thet'i·cal** adj

an·ti·tox·in [an-ti-TOK-sin] n serum used to neutralize disease poisons

an·ti·trust [an-ti-TRUST] adj (of laws) opposing business monopolies

an·ti·tus·sive [an-ti-TUS-iv] n, adj (substance) controlling or preventing coughing

an·ti·ven·in [an-tee-VEN-in] n antitoxin to counteract specific venom, esp of snake or spider

an·ti·vi·rus [an-tee-VĪ-rus] adj relating to software designed to protect computer files from viruses

ant·ler [ANT-lər] n branching horn of certain deer

an·to·nym [AN-tə-nim] n word of opposite meaning to another, eg cold is an antonym of hot

a·nus [AY-nəs] n the lower opening of the bowels **a'nal** adj

an'vil n heavy iron block with steel face on which a blacksmith hammers metal into shape

anx·ious [ANGK-shəs] adj troubled, uneasy; concerned **anx·i·e·ty** [ang-ZĪ-ə-tee] n

an·y [EN-ee] adj, pron one indefinitely; some; every **an'y·bod·y** n **an'y·how** adv **an'y·one** n **an'y·thing** n **an'y·way** adv **an'y·where** adv

a·part [ə-PAHRT] adv separately, aside; in pieces

a·part·heid [ə-PAHRT-hayt] n former official government policy of racial segregation in S Africa

a·part·ment [ə-PAHRT-mənt] n room or suite of rooms in larger building used for dwelling

ap·a·thy [AP-ə-thee] n, pl **-thies** indifference; lack of emotion **ap·a·thet'ic** adj

ape [ayp] n tailless monkey such as the chimpanzee or gorilla; coarse, clumsy person; imitator ▷ vt **aped**, **ap·ing** imitate

a·pe·ri·od·ic [ay-peer-ee-OD-ik] adj electricity having no natural period or frequency

a·pe·ri·tif [ə-per-i-TEEF] n alcoholic appetizer

ap·er·ture [AP-ər-chər] n opening, hole

a·pex [AY-peks] *n, pl* **a·pex·es** top, peak; vertex

a·pha·sia [ə-FAY-zhə] *n* dumbness, or loss of speech control, due to disease of the brain

a·phe·li·on [ə-FEE-lee-ən] *n* point of planet's orbit farthest from the sun

a·phid [AY-fid] *n* any of various sap-sucking insects

a·phis [AY-fis] *n, pl* **a·phi·des** [AY-fi-deez] an aphid

aph·o·rism [AF-ə-riz-əm] *n* maxim, pithy saying **aph·o·ris'tic** [-RIS-tik] *adj*

aph·ro·dis·i·ac [af-rə-DEE-zee-ak] *adj* exciting sexual desire ▷ *n* substance that so excites

a·pi·ar·y [AY-pee-er-ee] *n, pl* **-ar·ies** place where bees are kept **a'pi·a·rist** *n* beekeeper **a'pi·cul·ture** *n*

a·piece [ə-PEES] *adv* for each

a·plomb [ə-PLOM] *n* self-possession, coolness, assurance

a·poc·a·lypse [ə-POK-ə-lips] *n* prophetic revelation esp of future of the world; (**A-**) revelation to St John, recounted in last book of the New Testament **a·poc·a·lyp'tic** *adj*

a·poc·ry·pha [ə-POK-rə-fə] *pl n* religious writing of doubtful authenticity; (**A-**) collective name for 14 books originally in the Old Testament **a·poc'ry·phal** *adj* spurious

ap·o·gee [AP-ə-jee] *n* point farthest from Earth in orbit of moon or satellite; climax; highest point

a·pol·o·gy [ə-POL-ə-jee] *n, pl* **-gies** acknowledgment of offense and expression of regret; written or spoken defense; justification (*with* **for**) poor substitute **a·pol·o·get'ic** *adj* **a·pol·o·get'ics** *n* branch of theology charged with defense

of Christianity **a·pol'o·gist** *n* **a·pol'o·gize** *vi* **-gized, -giz·ing**

ap·o·plex·y [AP-ə-plek-see] *n* loss of sense and often paralysis caused by broken or blocked blood vessel in the brain; a stroke **ap·o·plec'tic** *adj*

a·pos·ta·sy [ə-POS-tə-see] *n, pl* **-sies** abandonment of one's religious or other faith **a·pos'tate** [-tayt] *n, adj*

a·pos·te·ri·o·ri [ay po-steer-ee-OR-ī] *adj* denoting form of inductive reasoning that arrives at causes from effects; empirical

a·pos·tle [ə-POS-əl] *n* ardent supporter; leader of reform (**A-**) one sent to preach the Gospel, esp one of the first disciples of Jesus; founder of Christian church in a country **ap·os·tol'ic** *adj*

a·pos·tro·phe [ə-POS-trə-fee] *n* a mark (') showing the omission of a letter or letters in a word; digression to appeal to someone dead or absent

ap·o·thegm [AP-ə-them] *n* terse saying, maxim

a·poth·e·o·sis [ə-poth-ee-OH-sis] *n, pl* **-ses** [-seez] deification, act of raising any person or thing into a god

ap·pall [ə-PAWL] *vt* dismay, terrify **ap·pall'ing** *adj* inf dreadful, terrible

ap·pa·ra·tus [ap-ə-RAT-əs] *n* equipment, tools, instruments, for performing any experiment, operation, etc; means by which something operates

ap·par·el [ə-PAR-əl] *n* clothing ▷ *vt* **-eled, -el·ing** clothe

ap·par·ent [ə-PAR-ənt] *adj* seeming; obvious; acknowledged: *heir apparent*

ap·pa·ri·tion [ap-ə-RISH-ən] *n* appearance, esp of ghost

ap·peal [ə-PEEL] *vi* (*with* **to**) call upon, make earnest request; be

attractive; refer to, have recourse to; apply to higher court ▷ *n* request, reference, supplication **ap·peal'ing** *adj* making appeal; pleasant, attractive **ap·pel'ant** [-PEL-ənt] *n* one who appeals to higher court **ap·pel'late** [-it] *adj* of appeals

ap·pear [ə-PEER] *vi* become visible or present; seem, be plain; be seen in public **ap·pear'ance** *n* an appearing; aspect; pretense

ap·pease [ə-PEEZ] *vt* **-peased, -peas·ing** pacify, quiet, allay, satisfy **ap·pease'ment** *n*

appellant SEE APPEAL

ap·pel·la·tion [ap-ə-LAY-shən] *n* name

ap·pend [ə-PEND] *vt* join on, add **ap·pend'age** *n*

ap·pen·di·ci·tis [ə-pen-də-SĪ-tis] *n* inflammation of vermiform appendix

ap·pen·dix [ə-PEN-diks] *n*, *pl* **-di·ces** [-də-seez] subsidiary addition to book, etc; *anatomy* projection, esp the small worm-shaped part of the intestine

ap·per·cep·tion [ap-ər-SEP-shən] *n* perception; apprehension; the mind's perception of itself as a conscious agent

ap·per·tain [ap-ər-TAYN] *vi* belong, relate to, be appropriate

ap·pe·tite [AP-i-tīt] *n* desire, inclination, esp desire for food **ap·pe·tiz·er** *n* something stimulating to appetite **ap·pe·tiz·ing** *adj*

ap·plaud [ə-PLAWD] *vt* praise by handclapping; praise loudly **ap·plause'** [-PLAWZ] *n* loud approval

ap·ple [AP-əl] *n* round, firm, fleshy fruit; tree bearing it

ap·plet [AP-lət] *n* computing computing program that runs within

a page on the World Wide Web

ap·pli·ance [ə-PLĪ-əns] *n* piece of equipment esp electrical

ap·pli·qué [ap-li-KAY] *n* ornaments, embroidery, etc, secured to surface of material ▷ *vt* **-quéd, -qué·ing** ornament thus

ap·ply [ə-PLĪ] *v* **-plied, -ply·ing** ▷ *vt* utilize, employ; lay or place on; administer, devote ▷ *vi* have reference (to); make request (to) **ap·pli·ca·ble** *adj* relevant **ap'pli·cant** *n* **ap·pli·ca'tion** *n* applying something for a particular use; relevance; request for a job, etc; concentration, diligence **applied** *adj* (of skill, science, etc) put to practical use

ap·point [ə-POINT] *vt* name, assign to a job or position; fix, settle; equip **ap·point'ment** *n* engagement to meet; (selection for a) position ▷ *pl* equipment, furnishings

ap·por·tion [ə-POR-shən] *vt* divide out in shares **ap·por'tion·ment** *n*

ap·po·site [AP-ə-zit] *adj* suitable, apt **ap'po·site·ness** *n* **ap·po·si'tion** [-ZISH-ən] *n* proximity; the placing of one word beside another that it describes

ap·praise [ə-PRAYZ] *vt* **-praised, -prais·ing** set price on, estimate value of **ap·prais'al** *n* **ap·prais'er** *n*

ap·pre·ci·ate [ə-PREE-shee-ayt] *v* **-at·ed, -at·ing** ▷ *vt* value at true worth; be grateful for; understand; enjoy ▷ *vi* rise in value **ap·pre'ci·a·ble** [-shə-bəl] *adj* estimable; substantial **ap·pre'ci·a·bly** *adv* **ap·pre·ci·a'tion** *n* **ap·pre'ci·a·tive** [-shə-tiv] *adj* capable of expressing pleasurable recognition

ap·pre·hend [ap-ri-HEND] *vt*

arrest, seize by authority; take hold of; recognize, understand; dread **ap·pre·hen·si·ble** [-HEN-sə-bəl] adj **ap·pre·hen·sion** [-shən] n dread, anxiety; arrest; conception; ability to understand **ap·pre·hen·sive** [-siv] adj **ap·pre·hen·sive·ly** adv

ap·pren·tice [ə-PREN-tis] n person learning a trade under specified conditions; novice ▷ vt **-ticed, -tic·ing** bind, set to work as, apprentice **ap·pren·tice·ship** n

ap·prise [ə-PRĪZ] vt **-prised, -pris·ing** inform

ap·proach [ə-PROHCH] v draw near (to); set about; address request to; approximate to; make advances to ▷ n a drawing near; means of reaching or doing; approximation; (oft pl) friendly or amatory overture(s) **ap·proach·a·ble** adj

ap·pro·ba·tion [ap-rə-BAY-shən] n approval

ap·pro·pri·ate [ə-PROH-pree-ayt] vt **-at·ed, -at·ing** take for oneself; put aside for particular purpose ▷ adj [-it] suitable, fitting **ap·pro·pri·ate·ness** [-nis] n **ap·pro·pri·a·tion** n act of setting apart for purpose; legislative vote of money

ap·prove [ə-PROOV] vt **-proved, -prov·ing** think well of, commend; authorize, agree to **ap·prov·al** n **ap·prov·ing·ly** adv

ap·prox·i·mate [ə-PROK-sə-mit] adj very near, nearly correct; inexact, imprecise ▷ v [-mayt] **-mat·ed, -mat·ing** ▷ vt bring close ▷ vi come near; be almost the same as **ap·prox·i·mate·ly** adv

ap·pur·te·nance [ə-PUR-tn-əns] n thing that appertains to; accessory

après-ski [ah-pray-SKEE] n social activities after day's skiing

ap·ri·cot [AP-ri-kot] n orange-colored fruit related to the plum ▷ adj of the color of the fruit

A·pril fool [AY-prəl] n butt of a joke or trick played on April Fools' Day, April 1

a pri·o·ri [ay-prī-OR-ī] adj denoting deductive reasoning from general principle to expected facts or effects; denoting knowledge gained independently of experience

a·pron [AY-prən] n cloth, piece of leather, etc, worn in front to protect clothes, etc, as part of costume; in theater, strip of stage before curtain; on airfield, paved area where aircraft stand, are refueled, etc; pl any of a variety of things resembling these

ap·ro·pos [ap-rə-POH] adv to the purpose; with reference to ▷ adj apt, appropriate **apropos of** concerning

apse [aps] n arched recess, esp in a church

apt adj suitable; likely; prompt, quick-witted; dexterous **ap·ti·tude** [AP-ti-tood] n capacity, fitness **apt·ly** adv **apt·ness** n

aq·ua·ma·rine [ak-wə-mə-REEN] n precious stone, a transparent beryl ▷ adj greenish-blue, sea-colored

aq·ua·plane [AK-wə-playn] n plank or boat towed by fast motorboat and ridden by person standing on it ▷ vi **-planed, -plan·ing** ride on aquaplane; (of automobile) be in contact with water on road, not with road surface **aquaplaning** n

a·quar·i·um [ə-KWAIR-ee-əm] n, pl **-i·ums** tank or pond for keeping water animals or plants

a·quat·ic [ə-KWAT-ik] adj living, growing, done in or on water **a·quat·ics** pl n water sports

aq·ua·vit [AH-kwə-veet] n Scandinavian liquor usu flavored with caraway seeds

aq•ue•duct [AK-wi-dukt] *n* artificial channel for water, esp one like a bridge; conduit

a•que•ous [AY-kwee-əs] *adj* of, like, containing water

aq•ui•fer [AK-wə-fər] *n* geological formation containing or conveying ground water

aq•ui•line [AK-wə-lin] *adj* relating to eagle; hooked like an eagle's beak

Ar *chemistry* argon

Ar•ab [AR-əb] *n* general term for inhabitants of Middle Eastern countries; Arabian horse **Ar'a•bic** *n* language of Arabs ▷ *adj* **Ar'ab•ist** *n* specialist in Arabic language or in Arabic culture

ar•a•besque [ar-ə-BESK] *n* classical ballet position; fanciful painted or carved ornament of Arabian origin ▷ *adj*

ar•a•ble [AR-ə-bəl] *adj* suitable for plowing or planting crops

a•rach•nid [ə-RAK-nid] *n* one of the Arachnida (spiders, scorpions, and mites) **a•rach'noid** *adj*

ar•bi•ter [AHR-bi-tər] *n* judge, umpire **ar•bi•trar'i•ly** [-TRER-ə-lee] *adv* **ar'bi•trar•y** *adj* not bound by rules, despotic; random **ar'bi•trate** [-trayt] *v* decide dispute; submit to, settle by arbitration; act as an umpire **ar•bi•tra'tion** *n* hearing, settling of disputes, esp industrial and legal, by impartial referee **ar'bi•tra•tor** *n*

ar•bor [AHR-bər] *n* leafy glade, etc, sheltered by trees

ar•bo•re•al [ahr-BOR-ee-əl] *adj* relating to trees **ar•bo•re'tum** [-bə-REE-təm] *n*, *pl* **-tums** place for cultivating specimens of trees

ar•bor•i•cul•ture [AHR-bər-i-kul-chər] *n* forestry, cultivation of trees **ar'bor•ist** *n*

ar•bor vi•tae [ahr-bər-Vi-tee] a kind of evergreen conifer

arc [ahrk] *n* part of circumference of circle or similar curve; luminous electric discharge between two conductors **arc lamp, light** light source in which an arc between two electrodes produces intense white illumination

ar•cade [ahr-KAYD] *n* row of arches on pillars; covered walk or avenue, esp lined by shops

ar•cane [ahr-KAYN] *adj* mysterious; esoteric

arch¹ [ahrch] *n* curved structure in building, supporting itself over open space by pressure of stones one against the other; any similar structure; a curved shape; curved part of sole of the foot ▷ *v* form, make into, an arch **arched** *adj* **arch'way** *n*

arch² [ahrch] *adj* chief; experienced; expert; superior, knowing, coyly playful **arch'ly** *adv* **arch'ness** *n*

arch- *comb form* chief, principal; archenemy

ar•cha•ic [ahr-KAY-ik] *adj* old, primitive **ar•cha•ism** [AHR-kee-iz-əm] *n* obsolete word or phrase

ar•che•ol•o•gy [ahr-kee-OL-ə-jee] *n* study of ancient times from remains of art, implements, etc **ar•che•o•log'i•cal** *adj*

ar•cher [AHR-chər] *n* one who shoots with bow and arrow **arch'er•y** [AHR-chə-ree] *n* skill, sport of shooting with bow and arrow **arch'er** *n*

ar•che•type [AHR-ki-tip] *n* prototype; perfect specimen **ar'che•ty'pal** [-Ti-pəl] *adj*

ar•chi•pel•a•go [ahr-kə-PEL-ə-goh] *n*, *pl* **-goes, -gos** group of islands; sea with many small islands, esp Aegean

ar·chi·tect [AHR-ki-tekt] n one qualified to design and supervise construction of buildings; contriver **ar·chi·tec·tur·al** [-TEK-chər-əl] adj **ar'chi·tec·ture** n

ar·chive [AHR-kiv] n (oft pl) collection of records, documents, etc about an institution, family, etc; place where these are kept; computing data on tape or disk for long-term storage ▷ vt store in an archive **ar·chi'val** adj **ar'chi·vist** [-kə-vist] n

Arc·tic [AHRK-tik] adj of northern polar regions; (a-) very cold ▷ n region around north pole

ar·dent [AHR-dnt] adj fiery; passionate **ar'dent·ly** adv **ar'dor** [-dər] n enthusiasm; zeal

ar·du·ous [AHR-joo-əs] adj laborious, hard to accomplish, difficult, strenuous

are¹ [ahr] pres ind pl of BE

are² [air] n unit of measure, 100 square meters

ar·e·a [AIR-ee-ə] n extent, expanse of any surface; two-dimensional expanse enclosed by boundary (area of square, circle, etc); region; part, section; subject, field of activity

a·re·na [ə-REE-nə] n enclosure for sports events, etc; space in middle of amphitheater or stadium; sphere, scene of conflict

ar·gon [AHR-gon] n a gas, inert constituent of air

ar·go·sy [AHR-gə-see] n, pl -sies poetry large richly-laden merchant ship

ar·got [AHR-goh] n slang

ar·gue [AHR-gyoo] v -gued, -gu·ing ▷ vi quarrel, dispute; prove; offer reasons ▷ vt prove by reasoning; discuss **ar'gu·a·ble** adj **ar'gu·ment** n

quarrel; reasoning; discussion; theme **ar·gu·men·ta·tion** n **ar·gu·men·ta·tive** adj

a·ri·a [AHR-ee-ə] n air or rhythmical song in cantata, opera, etc

ar'id adj parched with heat, dry; dull **a·rid·i·ty** [ə-RID-i-tee] n

a·right [ə-RĪT] adv rightly

a·rise [ə-RĪZ] vi a·rose, a·ris·en [ə-RIZ-ən], a·ris·ing come about; get up; rise (up); ascend

ar·is·toc·ra·cy [ar-ə-STOK-rə-see] n, pl -cies government by the best in birth or fortune; nobility; upper classes **a·ris·to·crat** [ə-RIS-tə-krat] n **a·ris·to·crat·ic** adj noble; elegant

a·rith·me·tic [ə-RITH-mə-tik] n science of numbers; art of reckoning by figures **ar·ith·met'ic** adj **ar·ith·met'i·cal·ly** adv

ark [ahrk] n Noah's vessel; (A-) coffer containing scrolls of the Torah

arm¹ [ahrm] n limb extending from shoulder to wrist; anything projecting from main body; as branch of sea, supporting rail of chair, etc **arm'chair** n **arm'ful** n, pl -fuls **arm'hole** n **arm'pit** n hollow under arm at shoulder **arm-twisting** n use of personal pressure to achieve a desired result

arm² vt supply with weapons, furnish; prepare bomb, etc for use ▷ vi take up arms ▷ n weapon; branch of army ▷ pl weapons; war, military exploits; official heraldic symbols **arm'a·ment** n

ar·ma·da [ahr-MAH-də] n large number of ships or aircraft

ar·ma·dil·lo [ahr-mə-DIL-oh] n, pl -los small Amer animal protected by bands of bony plates

ar·ma·ture [AHR-mə-chər] n revolving structure in electric

mo·tor, generator; framework used by a sculptor to support modeling clay, etc

ar·mi·stice [AHR-mə-stis] *n* truce, suspension of fighting

ar·mor [AHR-mər] *n* defensive covering or dress; plating of tanks, warships, etc; armored fighting vehicles, as tanks **ar·mor·y** *n*, *pl* **-mor·ies**

ar·my [AHR-mee] *n*, *pl* **-mies** large body of soldiers armed for warfare and under military command; host; great number

a·ro·ma [ə-ROH-mə] *n* sweet smell; fragrance; peculiar charm **ar·o·mat·ic** [ar-ə-MAT-ik] *adj*

a·rose pt of ARISE

a·round [ə-ROWND] *prep* on all sides of; somewhere in or near; approximately (of time) ▷ *adv* on every side; in a circle; here and there, nowhere in particular; *inf* present in or at some place

a·rouse [ə-ROWZ] *vt* **-roused, -rous·ing** awaken, stimulate

ar·peg·gio [ahr-PEJ-ee-oh] *n*, *pl* **-gios** *music* notes sounded in quick succession, not together; chord so played

ar·raign [ə-RAYN] *vt* accuse, indict, put on trial **ar·raign·ment** *n*

ar·range [ə-RAYNJ] *v* **-ranged, -rang·ing** set in order; make agreement; adjust; plan; adapt, as music; settle, as dispute **ar·range·ment** *n*

ar·rant [AR-ənt] *adj* downright, notorious

ar·ras [AR-əs] *n* tapestry

ar·ray [ə-RAY] *n* order, esp military order; dress; imposing show, splendor ▷ *vt* set in order; dress, equip, adorn

ar·rears [ə-REERZ] *pl n* amount unpaid or undone

ar·rest [ə-REST] *vt* detain by legal authority; stop; catch attention ▷ *n* seizure by warrant; making prisoner **ar·rest·ing** *adj* attracting attention, striking **ar·rest·er** *n* person who arrests; mechanism to stop or slow moving object

ar·rive [ə-RIV] *vi* **-rived, -riv·ing** reach destination; (with *at*) reach, attain; *inf* succeed **ar·riv·al** *n*

ar·ro·gance [AR-ə-gəns] *n* aggressive conceit **ar·ro·gant** *adj* proud; overbearing

ar·ro·gate [AR-ə-gayt] *vt* **-gat·ed, -gat·ing** seize or claim without right

ar·row [AR-oh] *n* pointed shaft shot from bow **ar·row·head** *n* head of arrow; any triangular shape

ar·row·root [AR-oh-root] *n* nutritious starch from W Indian plant, used as a food

ar·se·nal [AHR-sə-nl] *n* place for manufacture, storage weapons and ammunition; *fig* repertoire (of skills, skilled personnel, etc)

ar·se·nic [AHR-sə-nik] *n* soft, gray, metallic element; its oxide, a powerful poison **ar·se·nate** [-nayt] *n* **ar·sen·i·cal** *adj*

ar·son [AHR-sən] *n* crime of intentionally setting property on fire

art [ahrt] *n* skill; human skill as opposed to nature; creative skill in painting, poetry, music, etc; any of the works produced thus; profession, craft; knack; contrivance, cunning, trick; system of rules ▷ *pl* certain branches of learning, languages, history, etc, as distinct from natural science; wiles **art·ful** *adj* wily **art·ful·ly** *adv* artist *n* one who practices fine art, esp painting; one who makes a fine art of a craft **ar·tiste** [-TEEST] *n* professional entertainer, singer, dancer, etc

ar·tis'tic adj **art'ist·ry** n **art'less** adj natural, frank **art'less·ness** n **art'y** adj **art·i·er, art·i·est** ostentatiously artistic

ar·te·ri·o·scle·ro·sis [ahr-teer-ee-oh-sklə-ROH-sis] n hardening of the arteries **ar·te·ri·o·scle·rot'ic** adj

ar·ter·y [AHR-tə-ree] n, pl **-ter·ies** one of the vessels carrying blood from heart; any main channel of communications **ar·te'ri·al** [-TEER-ee-əl] adj pert to an artery; (of a route) major

ar·te·sian [ahr-TEE-zhən] adj describes deep well in which water rises by internal pressure

ar·thri·tis [ahr-THRI-tis] n painful inflammation of joint(s) **ar·thrit'ic** [-THRIT-ik] adj, n

ar·thro·pod [AHR-thrə-pod] n invertebrate with jointed limbs and segmented body eg; insect, spider

ar·ti·choke [AHR-ti-chohk] n thistle-like perennial, edible flower

ar·ti·cle [AHR-ti-kəl] n item, object; short written piece; paragraph, section; grammar any of the words the, a, or an; clause in a contract; rule, condition

ar·tic·u·late [ahr-TIK-yə-lit] adj able to express oneself fluently; jointed; of speech, clear, distinct ▷ v [-layt] **-lat·ed, -lat·ing** ▷ vt joint; utter distinctly ▷ vi speak **ar·tic·u·late·ly** adv **ar·tic·u·la'tion** n

ar·ti·fact [AHR-tə-fakt] n something made by a person, esp by hand

ar·ti·fice [AHR-tə-fis] n contrivance, trick, cunning, skill **ar·tif'i·cer** [-TIF-ə-sər] n craftsperson **ar·ti·fi'cial** [-FISH-əl] adj manufactured, synthetic; insincere **ar·ti·fi'cial·ly** adv

artificial intelligence ability of machines, esp computers, to imitate intelligent human behavior

artificial respiration method of restarting person's breathing after it has stopped

ar·til·ler·y [ahr-TIL-ə-ree] n large guns on wheels; the troops that use them

ar·ti·san [AHR-tə-zən] n craftsperson, skilled mechanic, manual worker

ar·tiste see ART

Ar·y·an [AIR-ee-ən] adj relating to Indo-European family of nations and languages

As chemistry arsenic

as [az] adv, conj denoting: comparison; similarity; equality; identity; concurrence; reason

as·bes·tos [as-BES-təs] n fibrous mineral that does not burn **as·bes·to·sis** [as-be-STOH-sis] n lung disease caused by inhalation of asbestos dust

as·cend [ə-SEND] vi climb, rise ▷ vt walk up, climb, mount **as·cend'an·cy** n control, dominance **as·cend'ant** adj rising **as·cen·sion** [-shən] n **as·cent'** n rise

as·cer·tain [as-ər-TAYN] v get to know, find out, determine **as·cer·tain'a·ble** adj

as·cet·ic [ə-SET-ik] n one who practices severe self-denial ▷ adj rigidly abstinent, austere **as·cet'i·cism** [-ə-siz-əm] n

ASCII [ASS-kee] n a code for transmitting data between computers

a·scor·bic acid [ə-SKOR-bik] vitamin C, present in green vegetables, citrus fruits, etc

as·cribe [ə-SKRIB] vt **-cribed, -crib·ing** attribute, impute, assign

a·scrib·a·ble adj

a·sep·tic [ə-SEP-tik] adj germ-free

a·sep·sis n

a·sex·u·al [ay-SEK-shoo-əl] adj without sex

ash¹ n dust or remains of anything burned ▷ pl ruins; remains after burning, esp of a human body after cremation **ash·en** adj like ashes; pale

ash² n deciduous timber tree; its wood **ash·en** adj

a·shamed [ə-SHAYMD] adj affected with shame, abashed

a·shore [ə-SHOR] adv on shore

Ash Wednesday first day of Lent

A·sian [AY-zhən] adj pert to continent of Asia ▷ n native of Asia or descendant of one **A·si·at·ic** [-zhee-AT-ik] adj

a·side [ə-SĪD] adv to or on one side; privately ▷ n words spoken in an undertone meant to be heard by some person present

as·i·nine [AS-ə-nin] adj of or like an ass, silly **as·i·nin·i·ty** [-NIN-i-tee] n

ask vt request, require, question, invite ▷ vi make inquiry or request

a·skance [ə-SKANS] adv sideways, awry; with a sidelong look or meaning **look askance** view with suspicion

a·skew [ə-SKYOO] adv aside, awry

a·sleep [ə-SLEEP] adj, adv sleeping, at rest

asp n small venomous snake

as·par·a·gus [ə-SPA-rə-gəs] n plant whose young shoots are a table delicacy

as·pect [AS-pekt] n look, view, appearance, expression

as·pen [AS-pən] n type of poplar tree

as·per·i·ty [ə-SPER-i-tee] n, pl **-ties** roughness; harshness; coldness

as·per·sion [ə-SPUR-zhən] n cast

aspersions on make derogatory remarks about

as·phalt [AS-fawlt] n black, hard bituminous substance used for road surfaces, etc

as·phyx·i·a [as-FIK-see-ə] n suffocation **as·phyx·i·ate** [-ayt] v **-at·ed, -at·ing as·phyx·i·a·tion** n

as·pic [AS-pik] n jelly used to coat or make a mold of meat, eggs, fish, etc

as·pire [ə-SPĪR] vi **-pired, -pir·ing** desire eagerly; aim at high things; rise to great height **as·pi·rant** [AS-pər-ənt] n one who aspires; candidate **as·pi·rate** [-pə-rayt] vt pronounce with full breathing, as h **as·pir·ing** adj

as·pi·rin [AS-pər-in] n (a tablet of) drug used to allay pain and fever

ass n quadruped of horse family; stupid person

as·sail [ə-SAYL] vt attack, assault **as·sail·a·ble** adj **as·sail·ant** n

as·sas·sin [ə-SAS-in] n one who kills, esp prominent person, by treacherous violence; murderer **as·sas·si·nate** vt **-nat·ed, -nat·ing as·sas·si·na·tion** n

as·sault [ə-SAWLT] n attack, esp sudden ▷ vt attack

as·say [ə-SAY] vt test, esp proportions of metals in alloy or ore ▷ n [AS-ay] analysis, esp of metals; trial, test

as·sem·ble [ə-SEM-bəl] v **-bled, -bling** meet, bring together; collect; put together (of machinery, etc) **as·sem·blage** [-blij] n **as·sem·bly** n, pl **-blies** gathering, meeting; assembling **assembly line** sequence of machines, workers in factory assembling product

as·sent [ə-SENT] vi concur, agree ▷ n acquiescence, agreement, compliance

as·sert [ə-SURT] vt declare strongly, insist upon **as·ser·tion** n **as·ser·tive** adj **as·ser·tive·ly** adv

as·sess [ə-SES] vt fix value, evaluate, estimate, esp for taxation; fix amount (of tax or fine); tax or fine **as·sess·ment** n **as·ses·sor** n

as·set [AS-et] n valuable or useful person, thing ▷ pl property available to pay debts, esp of insolvent debtor

as·sid·u·ous [ə-SIJ-oo-əs] adj persevering, attentive, diligent **as·si·du·i·ty** [as-i-DOO-i-tee] n

as·sign [ə-SIN] vt appoint to job, etc; allot, apportion; fix, ascribe; transfer **as·sign·a·ble** adj **as·sig·na·tion** [as-ig-NAY-shən] n secret meeting; appointment to meet **as·sign·ment** n act of assigning; allotted duty

as·sim·i·late [ə-SIM-ə-layt] vt -lat·ed, -lat·ing learn and understand; make similar; absorb into the system **as·sim·i·la·tion** n

as·sist [ə-SIST] v give help; aid **as·sis·tance** n **as·sis·tant** n helper

as·so·ci·ate [ə-SOH-shee-ayt] v -at·ed, -at·ing ▷ vt link, connect, esp as ideas in mind; join ▷ vi formerly, keep company with; combine, unite ▷ n [-it] companion, partner; friend, ally; subordinate member of association ▷ adj affiliated **as·so·ci·a·tion** n society, club

as·sort [ə-SORT] vt classify, arrange ▷ vi match, agree with, harmonize **as·sort·ed** adj mixed **as·sort·ment** n

as·suage [ə-SWAYJ] vt -suaged, -suag·ing soften, pacify; soothe

as·sume [ə-SOOM] vt -sumed, -sum·ing take for granted; pretend; take upon oneself; claim **as·sump·tion** [-SUMP-shən] n

as·sure [ə-SHOOR] vt -sured, -sur·ing tell positively, promise; make sure; insure against loss, esp of life; affirm **as·sured** adj sure **as·sur·ed·ly** [-id-lee] adv

as·ter·isk [AS-tə-risk] n star (*) used in printing ▷ vt mark thus

a·stern [ə-STURN] adv in, behind the stern; backward in direction

as·ter·oid [AS-tə-roid] n small planet ▷ adj star-shaped

asth·ma [AZ-mə] n illness in which one has difficulty in breathing **asth·mat·ic** adj

a·stig·ma·tism [ə-STIG-mə-tiz-əm] n inability of lens (esp of eye) to focus properly **as·tig·mat·ic** [as-tig-MAT-ik] adj

a·stir [ə-STUR] adv on the move; out of bed; in excitement

as·ton·ish [ə-STON-ish] vt amaze, surprise **as·ton·ish·ing** adj **as·ton·ish·ment** n

as·tound [ə-STOWND] vt astonish greatly; stun with amazement **as·tound·ing** adj startling

as·tra·khan [AS-trə-kən] n lambskin with curled wool

as·tral [AS-trəl] adj of the stars or spirit world

a·stray [ə-STRAY] adv off the right path, wanderingly

a·stride [ə-STRID] adv with the legs apart, straddling

as·trin·gent [ə-STRIN-jənt] adj severe, harsh; sharp; constricting (body tissues, blood vessels, etc) ▷ n astringent substance

as·trol·o·gy [ə-STROL-ə-jee] n foretelling of events by stars; medieval astronomy **as·trol·o·ger** n **as·tro·log·i·cal** adj

as·tro·naut [AS-trə-nawt] n one trained for travel in space

as·tron·o·my [ə-STRON-ə-mee] n scientific study of heavenly bodies **as·tron·o·mer** n **as·tro·nom·i·cal**

[-trə-NOM-i-kəl] adj very large; of astronomy **astronomical unit** unit of distance used in astronomy equal to the mean distance between Earth and the sun

as·tro·phys·ics [as-troh-FIZ-iks] n the science of the chemical and physical characteristics of heavenly bodies **as·tro·phys·i·cist** n

as·tute [ə-STOOT] adj perceptive, shrewd **as·tute·ly** adv **as·tute·ness** n

a·sun·der [ə-SUN-dər] adv apart; in pieces

a·sy·lum [ə-Sī-ləm] n refuge, sanctuary, place of safety; old name for hospital for mentally ill

a·sym·me·try [ay-SIM-i-tree] n lack of symmetry **a·sym·met·ric** [-sə-MET-rik] adj

as·ymp·tote [AS-im-toht] n straight line that continually approaches a curve, but never meets it

at prep, adv denoting: location in space or time; rate; condition or state; amount; direction; cause

At chemistry astatine

at·a·vism [AT-ə-viz-əm] n appearance of ancestral, not parental, characteristics in human beings, animals or plants **at·a·vis·tic** adj

a·tax·i·a [ə-TAK-see-ə] n lack of muscular coordination

ate [ayt] pt of **EAT**

at·el·ier [at-l-YAY] n workshop, artist's studio

a·the·ism [AY-thee-iz-əm] n belief that there is no God **a·the·ist** n **a·the·is·tic** adj

ath·lete [ATH-leet] n one trained for physical exercises, feats or contests of strength; one good at sports **ath·let·ic** adj **ath·let·ics** pl n sports such as running, jumping,

throwing, etc **ath·let·i·cal·ly** adv

a·thwart [ə-THWORT] prep across ▷ adv across, esp obliquely

at·las [AT-ləs] n volume of maps

at·mos·phere [AT-məs-feer] n mass of gas surrounding heavenly body, esp Earth; prevailing tone or mood (of place, etc); unit of pressure in cgs system **at·mos·pher·ic** [-FER-ik] adj **at·mos·pher·ics** pl n noises in radio reception due to electrical disturbance in the atmosphere; politics mood or atmosphere

at·oll [AT-awl] n ring-shaped coral island enclosing lagoon

at·om [AT-əm] n smallest unit of matter that can enter into chemical combination; any very small particle **a·tom·ic** [ə-TOM-ik] adj of, arising from atoms **at·om·ic·i·ty** [at-ə-MIS-i-tee] n number of atoms in molecule of an element **at·om·ize** vt -ized, -iz·ing reduce to atoms or small particles **at·om·iz·er** n instrument for discharging liquids in a fine spray **atom(ic) bomb** one whose immense power derives from nuclear fission or fusion, nuclear bomb **atomic energy** nuclear energy **atomic number** the number of protons in the nucleus of an atom **atomic reactor** see also **REACTOR** **atomic weight** the weight of an atom of an element relative to that of carbon 12

a·tone [ə-TOHN] vi -toned, -ton·ing make reparation, amends (for); expiate; give satisfaction **a·tone·ment** n

a·ton·ic [ay-TON-ik] adj unaccented

a·top [ə-TOP] adv at or on the top; above

a·tro·cious [ə-TROH-shəs] adj extremely cruel or wicked; horrifying;

very bad **a·troc·i·ty** [-TROS-i-tee] n, pl **-ties** wickedness

at·ro·phy [A-trà-fee] n wasting away, emaciation ▷ vi **-phied, -phy·ing** waste away, become useless **atrophied** adj

at·tach [ə-TACH] vt (mainly tr) join, fasten; unite; be connected with; attribute; appoint; seize by law **at·tached** adj (with to) fond of **at·tach'ment** n

at·ta·ché [a-ta-SHAY] n, pl **-chés** specialist attached to diplomatic mission **attaché case** small suitcase for papers

at·tack [ə-TAK] vt take action against (in war, etc); criticize; set about with vigor; affect adversely ▷ n attacking action; bout of sickness

at·tain [ə-TAYN] vt arrive at; reach, gain by effort, accomplish **at·tain'a·ble** adj **at·tain'ment** n esp personal accomplishment

at·tain·der [ə-TAYN-dàr] n history loss of civil rights usu through conviction of treason

at·tar [AT-àr] n a fragrant oil made esp from rose petals

at·tempt [ə-TEMPT] vt try, endeavor ▷ n trial, effort

at·tend [ə-TEND] vt be present at; accompany ▷ vi (with to) take care of; give the mind (to), pay attention to **at·tend'ance** n an attending; presence; persons attending **at·tend·ee** [ə-ten-DEE] n **at·tend'ant** n, adj **at·ten'tion** n notice; heed; act of attending; care; courtesy **at·ten'tive** adj **at·ten'tive·ness** n

at·ten·u·ate [ə-TEN-yoo-ayt] v **-at·ed, -at·ing** weaken or become weak; make or become thin **at·ten'u·at·ed** adj **at·ten·u·a'tion** n reduction of

intensity **at·ten'u·a·tor** n device for attenuating, esp for reducing the amplitude of an electrical signal

at·test [ə-TEST] vt bear witness to, certify **at·tes·ta·tion** [a-tes-TAY-shàn] n formal confirmation by oath, etc

at·tic [AT-ik] n space within roof where ceiling follows line of roof **Attic** adj of Attica, Athens; (of literary or artistic style) pure, refined, elegant

at·tire [ə-TĪR] vt **-tired, -tir·ing** dress, array ▷ n dress, clothing

at·ti·tude [AT-i-tood] n mental view, opinion; posture, pose; disposition, behavior **at·ti·tu·di·nize** vi **-nized, -niz·ing** assume affected attitudes

at·tor·ney [ə-TUR-nee] n, pl **-neys** one legally appointed to act for another, esp a lawyer **attorney-at-law** n, pl **-neys-at-law** a lawyer

at·tract [ə-TRAKT] v draw (attention, etc); arouse interest of; cause to come closer (as magnet, etc) **at·trac'tion** n power to attract; something offered so as to interest, please **at·trac'tive** adj **at·trac'tive·ness** n

at·trib·ute [ə-TRIB-yoot] vt **-ut·ed, -ut·ing** regard as belonging to or produced by ▷ n [A-trà-byoot] quality, property or characteristic of anything **at·trib'ut·a·ble** adj **at·tri·bu'tion** n

at·tri·tion [ə-TRISH-àn] n wearing away of strength, etc; rubbing away, friction

at·tune [ə-TOON] vt **-tuned, -tun·ing** tune, harmonize; make accordant

Au chemistry gold

au·burn [AW-bàrn] adj reddish brown ▷ n this color

au cou·rant [oh koo-RAHN] up-to-date; acquainted with

auc·tion [AWK-shən] n public sale in which bidder offers increase of price over another and what is sold goes to one who bids highest ▷ b

auc·tion·eer' n auction bridge card game **Dutch auction** one in which price starts high and is reduced until purchaser is found

au·da·cious [aw-DAY-shəs] adj bold; daring, impudent **au·dac'i·ty** [-DAS-i-tee] n

au·di·ble [AW-də-bəl] adj able to be heard **au'di·bly** adv

au·di·ence [AW-dee-əns] n assembly of spectators or listeners; act of hearing; judicial hearing; formal interview

audio- comb form relating to sound or hearing

au·di·o·phile [AW-dee-ə-fil] n one who is enthusiastic about sound reproduction, esp of music

au·di·o·vis·u·al [aw-dee-oh-VIZH-oo-əl] adj (esp of teaching aids) involving both sight and hearing

au·dit [AW-dit] n formal examination or settlement of financial accounts ▷ vt examine such accounts **au'di·tor** n

au·di·tion [aw-DISH-ən] n screen or other test of prospective performer; hearing ▷ vt conduct such a test **au·di·to'ri·um** n, pl **-ri·ums** hall; place where audience sits **au'di·to·ry** adj pert to sense of hearing

aufWie·der·seh·en [owfVEE-dər-zay-ən] Ger goodbye

au·ger [AW-gər] n carpenter's tool for boring holes, large gimlet

aught [awt] pron obs anything whatever

aug·ment [awg-MENT] v increase, enlarge **aug·men·ta'tion**

n **aug'ment'a·ble** adj able to increase in force or size

au grat·in [oh GRAHT-n] cooked or baked to form light crust

au·gur [AW-gər] n among the Romans, soothsayer ▷ v be a sign of future events, foretell **au'gu·ry** [-gə-ree] n divination from omens, etc; omen

au·gust [aw-GUST] adj majestic, dignified **au·gust'ly** adv

auk [awk] n northern web-footed seabird with short wings used only as paddles

aunt [ant] n father's or mother's sister, uncle's wife

au pair [oh PAIR] n young foreign person, usu a girl, who receives free board and lodging and usu an allowance in return for housework, etc

au·ra [OR-ə] n, pl **-ras** quality, air, atmosphere considered distinctive of person or thing; medical symptom warning of impending epileptic seizure, etc

au·ral [OR-əl] adj of, by ear **au'ral·ly** adv

au·re·ole [OR-ee-ohl] n gold disk around head in sacred pictures; halo

au re·voir [oh rə-VWAHR] Fr goodbye

au·ri·cle [OR-i-kəl] n outside ear; an upper cavity of heart **au·ric·u·lar** [aw-RIK-yə-lər] adj of the auricle; aural

au·rif·er·ous [aw-RIF-ər-əs] adj gold-bearing

au·ro·ra [aw-ROR-ə] n, pl **-ras** dawn; lights in the atmosphere seen radiating from regions of the poles **aurora bo·re·al·is** [bor-ee-AL-is] the northern lights **aurora aus·tra·lis** [aw-STRAY-lis] the southern lights

aus·cul·ta·tion [aw-skəl-TAY-shàn] *n* listening to sounds of heart and lungs with stethoscope

aus·pice [AW-spiss-siz] *pl n* **under the auspices of** with the support and approval of

aus·pi·cious [aw-SPISH-əs] *adj* of good omen, favorable

aus·tere [aw-STEER] *adj* harsh, strict, severe; without luxury **aus·tere·ly** *adv* **aus·ter·i·ty** [aw-STER-i-tee] *n*

aus·tral [AW-strǝl] *adj* southern **Austral** *adj* Australian

Aus·tral·a·sian [aw-strǝ-LAY-zhǝn] *adj, n* (native or inhabitant) of Australasia (Australia, N Zealand and adjacent islands)

Aus·tral·ian [aw-STRAYL-yǝn] *n, adj* (native or inhabitant) of Australia

au·tar·chy [AW-tahr-kee] *n, pl* **-chies** despotism, absolute power, dictatorship

au·then·tic [aw-THEN-tik] *adj* real, genuine, true; trustworthy **au·then·ti·cal·ly** *adv* **au·then·ti·cate** [-ti-kayt] *vt* make valid, confirm; establish truth, authorship, etc of **au·then·tic·i·ty** *n*

au·thor [AW-thǝr] *n* writer of book; originator, constructor

au·thor·i·ty [ǝ-THOR-i-tee] *n, pl* **-ties** legal power or right; delegated power; influence; permission; expert; body or board in control, esp in pl **au·thor·i·ta·tive** [-tay-tiv] *adj* **au·thor·i·ta·tive·ly** *adv* **au·thor·i·za·tion** *n* **au·thor·ize** *vt* **-ized, -iz·ing** empower; permit, sanction

au·tis·tic [aw-TIS-tik] *adj* withdrawn and divorced from reality **au'tism** *n* this condition

auto- *comb form* self-: *autobiography*

au·to [AW-toh] *n* automobile

au·to·bi·og·ra·phy [aw-tǝ-bi-OG-rǝ-fee] *n, pl* **-phies** life of person written by that person **au·to·bi·o·graph'i·cal** *adj*

au·toch·thon [aw-TOK-thǝn] *n* primitive or original inhabitant; native plant or animal **au·toch'tho·nous** *adj* indigenous, native

au·to·crat [AW-tǝ-krat] *n* absolute ruler; despotic person **au·toc'ra·cy** [-TOK-rǝ-see] *n, pl* **-cies** **au·to·crat'ic** *adj*

au·to·er·o·tism [aw-toh-ER-ǝ-tiz-ǝm] *n* self-produced sexual arousal

au·to·gi·ro [aw-tǝ-JÍ-roh] *n, pl* **-ros** aircraft like helicopter using horizontal airscrew for vertical ascent and descent

au·to·graph [AW-tǝ-graf] *n* a signature; one's own handwriting ▷ *vt* sign

au·to·in·tox·i·ca·tion [aw-toh-in-tok-si-KAY-shǝn] *n* poisoning of tissues of the body as a result of the absorption of bodily waste

au·to·mate [AW-tǝ-mayt] *vt* **-mat·ed, -mat·ing** make manufacturing process, etc; automatic **au·to·ma'tion** *n* use of automatic devices in industrial production

au·to·mat·ic [aw-tǝ-MAT-ik] *adj* operated or controlled mechanically; done without conscious thought ▷ *adj, n* self-loading (weapon) **au·to·mat'i·cal·ly** *adv* **au·tom'a·ton** *n, pl* **-ta** [-tǝ] self-acting machine, esp simulating a human being

au·to·mo·bile [AW-tǝ-mǝ-BEEL] *n* motor car

au·ton·o·my [aw-TON-ǝ-mee] *n, pl* **-mies** self-government **au·ton'o·mous** *adj*

au·top·sy [AW-top-see] *n, pl*

-sies postmortem examination to determine cause of death

au·to·sug·ges·tion [aw-toh-sàg-JES-chàn] *n* process of influencing the mind (toward health, etc, conducted by oneself)

au·tumn [AW-tàm] *n, adj* (typical of) the season after summer

au·tum·nal [aw-TUM-nl] *adj* typical of the onset of winter

aux·il·ia·ry [awg-ZIL-yà-ree] *adj* helping, subsidiary ▷ *n, pl* **-ries** helper; something subsidiary, as troops; verb used to form tenses of others

a·vail [à-VAYL] *v* be of use, advantage, value (to) ▷ *n* use or advantage: *to no avail*

a·vail·a·bil·i·ty *n* **a·vail·a·ble** *adj* obtainable; accessible **avail oneself of** make use of

av·a·lanche [AV-à-lanch] *n* mass of snow, ice, sliding down mountain; a sudden overwhelming quantity of anything

a·vant-garde [ah-vahnt-GAHRD] *adj* markedly experimental or in advance

av·a·rice [AV-àr-is] *n* greed for wealth **av·a·ri·cious** [-RISH-às] *adj*

a·vast [à-VAST] *interj* nautical stop

av·a·tar [AV-à-tahr] *n* Hinduism descent of god to Earth in bodily form

a·venge [à-VENJ] *vt* **-venged, -veng·ing** take vengeance on behalf of (person) or on account of (thing) **a·veng·er** *n*

av·e·nue [AV-à-nyoo] *n* route; a way of approach, a channel

a·ver [à-VUR] *vt* **-verred, -ver·ring** affirm, assert

av·er·age [AV-rij] *n* the mean value or quantity of a number of values or quantities ▷ *adj* calculated as an average; medium, ordinary ▷ *v* **-aged, -ag·ing** ▷ *vt* fix or calculate a

mean ▷ *vi* exist in or form a mean

a·verse [à-VURS] *adj* disinclined, unwilling **a·ver·sion** [-zhàn] *n* dislike; person or thing disliked

a·vert [à-VURT] *vt* turn away; ward off

a·vi·ar·y [AY-vee-er-ee] *n, pl* **-ar·ies** enclosure for birds **a·vi·a·rist** *n*

a·vi·a·tion [ay-vee-AY-shàn] *n* art of flying aircraft; transport by aircraft **a·vi·a·tor** *n*

av·id [AV-id] *adj* keen, enthusiastic; greedy (for) **a·vid·i·ty** *n* **av·id·ly** *adv*

av·o·ca·do [av-à-KAH-doh] *n* tropical tree; its green-skinned edible fruit, alligator pear

av·o·ca·tion [av-à-KAY-shàn] *n* vocation; employment, business

a·void [à-VOID] *vt* keep away from; refrain from; not allow to happen **a·void·a·ble** *adj* **a·void·ance** *n*

av·oir·du·pois [av-àr-dà-POIZ] *n* system of weights used in many English-speaking countries based on pounds and ounces

a·vow [à-VOW] *vt* declare; admit **a·vow·al** *adj* **a·vow·al** *n* **a·vowed'** *adj* **a·vow·ed·ly** *adv*

a·vun·cu·lar [à-VUNG-kyà-làr] *adj* like or of an uncle esp in manner

a·wait [à-WAYT] *vt* wait or stay for; be in store for

a·wake [à-WAYK] *v* **a·wak·ing, a·woke, a·wok·en** emerge or rouse from sleep; become or cause to become alert **a·wak·en·ing** *n*

a·wak·en [à-WAY-kàn] *vt* arouse (feelings, etc) or cause to remember (memories, etc)

a·ward [à-WORD] *vt* to give formally (esp a prize or punishment) ▷ *n* prize; judicial decision, amount awarded

a·ware [à-WAIR] *adj* informed,

conscious **a·ware·ness** n

a·wash [ə-WOSH] adv level
with the surface of water; filled or
overflowing with water **awash in**
marked by an abundance of

a·way [ə-WAY] adv absent, apart,
at a distance, out of the way ▷ adj
sport played on opponent's
grounds

awe [aw] n dread mingled with
reverence **awe·some** [-səm] adj
awe·some·ly adv **awe·some·ness**
n **awe·struck** adj filled with awe

aw·ful [AW-fəl] adj very bad,
unpleasant; inspiring awe; inf
very great **aw·ful·ly** adv in an
unpleasant way; inf very much

a·while [ə-HWĪL] adv for a time

awk·ward [AWK-wərd] adj clumsy,
ungainly; difficult; inconvenient;
embarrassed **awk·ward·ly** adv
awk·ward·ness n

awl n pointed tool for marking or
boring wood, leather, etc

awn·ing n (canvas, etc) roof or
shelter, to protect from weather

awoke pt/pp of AWAKE

a·wry [ə-Rī] adv crookedly; amiss;
at a slant ▷ adj crooked, distorted;
wrong

ax, axe [aks] n tool with handle
and heavy, sharp blade for chopping;
inf dismissal from employment,
etc ▷ vt **axed, ax·ing** inf dismiss,
dispense with

ax·iom [AK-see-əm] n received or
accepted principle; self-evident truth
ax·i·o·mat·ic adj

ax·is [AK-sis] n, pl **ax·es** [AK-seez]
(imaginary) line around which a
body spins; line or column about
which parts are arranged **ax'i·al**
adj **ax'i·al·ly** adv

Ax·is n coalition of Germany, Italy
and Japan, 1936–45

ax·le [AK-səl] n shaft on which
wheel turns

a·ya·tol·lah [ah-yə-TOH-lə] adj
one of a class of Islamic religious
leaders

aye [ī] adv yes ▷ n affirmative
answer or vote ▷ pl those voting
for motion

a·zal·ea [ə-ZAYL-yə] n any of
group of shrubby plants of the
rhododendron genus

az·i·muth [AZ-ə-məth] n vertical
arc from zenith to horizon; angular
distance of this from meridian

Az·tec [AZ-tek] adj, n (member) of
people ruling Mexico before Spanish
conquest

az·ure [AZH-ər] n sky-blue color;
clear sky ▷ adj sky-blue

b

B chemistry boron

Ba chemistry barium

bab·ble [BAB-əl] v **-bled, -bling** speak foolishly, incoherently, or childishly ▷ n foolish, confused talk **bab'bler** n

babe [bayb] n baby; guileless person

ba·bel [BAY-bəl] n confused noise or scene, uproar

ba·boon [ba-BOON] n large monkey of Africa and Asia

ba·by [BAY-bee] n, pl **-bies** very young child, infant **ba'by·ish** adj **ba'by·sit** v **-sat, -sit·ting ba'by·sit·ter** n one who cares for children when parents are out

bac·ca·lau·re·ate [bak-ə-LOR-ee-it] n degree of bachelor; service held at college or university awarding degree; sermon delivered at this service

bac·ca·rat [BACH-kà-rah] n gambling card game

bach·e·lor [BACH-lər] n unmarried man; holder of lowest four-year college or university degree

ba·cil·lus [bə-SIL-əs] n, pl **-cil·li** [-SIL-ī] minute organism sometimes causing disease

back [bak] n hinder part of anything, eg human body; part opposite front; part or side of something farther away or less used; (position of) player in football and other games behind other (forward) players ▷ adj situated behind; earlier ▷ adv at, to the back; in, into the past; in return ▷ vi move backward ▷ vt support; put wager on; provide with back or backing **back'er** n one supporting another, esp in contest or election campaign; one betting on horse, etc in race **back'ing** n support; material to protect the back of something **back'ward, back'wards** adv to the rear; to the past; to worse state **back'ward** adj directed toward the rear; (of a country, region or people) retarded in economic development; behind in education; reluctant, bashful **back'ward·ness** n **back'bite** vt **-bit, -bit·ten, -bit·ing** slander absent person **back'bit·er** n **back'bit·ing** n **back'bone** n spinal column **back'date** vt **-dat·ed, -dat·ing** make effective from earlier date **back'drop** n painted cloth at back of stage **back'fire** vi **-fired, -fir·ing** ignite at wrong time, as fuel in cylinder of internal-combustion engine; (of plan, scheme, etc) fail to work, esp to the detriment of the instigator; ignite wrongly, as gas burner, etc **back'gam·mon** [-gam-ən] n game played with counters and dice **back'ground** n space behind chief figures of picture; past history of person **back'hand** n stroke with hand turned backward **back'hand·ed** adj (of compliment, etc) with second, uncomplimentary meaning **back'lash** n sudden and adverse reaction **back'log** n accumulation of work, etc to be dealt with

back`pack** n type of knapsack ▷vi **-packed, -pack`ing hike with this **back`side** n buttocks **back`slash** n backward-sloping diagonal mark (\) **back`slide** vi **-slid, -slid** or **-slid`den, -slid`ing** fall back in faith or morals **back`stab`bing** n actions or remarks that betray trust and are likely to cause harm to a person **back`stroke** n swimming stroke performed on the back **back`talk** n impudent or insolent answer **back`up** n a support or reinforcement; a reserve or substitute **back up** v support; *computing* make a copy of (a data file), esp as a security copy **back`wash** n water thrown back by ship's propellers, etc; a backward current; a reaction **back`wa`ter** n still water fed by back flow of stream; backward or isolated place or condition **back`woods`** pl n remote forest areas; remote or backward area

ba·con [BAY-kən] n cured and smoked meat from side of pig

bac·te·ri·a [bak-TEER-ee-ə] pl n, sing **-ri·um** microscopic organisms, some causing disease **bac·te·ri·al** adj **bac·te·ri·cide** [-TEER-ə-sid] n substance that destroys bacteria **bac·te·ri·ol·o·gist** [-OL-ə-jist] n **bac·te·ri·ol·o·gy** n study of bacteria

bad adj **worse, worst** of poor quality; faulty; evil; immoral; offensive; severe; rotten, decayed **bad`ly** adv **bad`ness** n **bad-mouth** vt sl speak unfavourably about

bade [bad] pt of **BID**

badge [baj] n distinguishing emblem or sign

badg·er [BAJ-ər] n burrowing night animal, about the size of fox; its pelt or fur ▷vt pester, worry

bad·i·nage [bad-n-AHZH] n playful talk, banter

bad·min·ton [BAD-min-tn] n game like tennis, played with rackets and shuttlecocks over high net

baf·fle [BAF-əl] vt **-fled, -fling** check, frustrate, bewilder **baffling** adj **baffle** n device to regulate or divert flow of liquid, gas, sound waves, etc

bag n sack, pouch; measure of quantity; woman's handbag; *offens* unattractive woman ▷v **bagged, bag·ging** vi swell out; bulge; sag ▷vt put in bag; kill as game, etc **bag`gy** adj **-gi·er, -gi·est** loose, drooping **bag lady** homeless woman who carries her possessions in shopping bags, etc **bag`man** n, pl **-men** person who collects and distributes illicitly obtained money for another

bag·a·telle [bag-ə-TEL] n trifle; game like billiards

bag·gage [BAG-ij] n suitcases, etc, packed for journey; *offens* woman

bag·pipe [BAG-pip] n (oft pl) musical wind instrument, of windbag and pipes **bag`pip`er** n

bail[1] [bayl] n law security given for person's reappearance in court; one giving such security ▷vt release, or obtain release of, on security; inf help a person, firm, etc out of trouble

bail[2] vt empty out water from boat **bail out** leave aircraft by parachute; give up on or abandon something

bail·iff [BAY-lif] n minor court officer

bail·i·wick [BAY-li-wik] n a person's domain or special area of competence

bait [bayt] n food to entice fish; any lure or enticement ▷vt set a lure; annoy, persecute

baize [bayz] n smooth woolen cloth

bake [bayk] v **baked, bak•ing** ▷ vt cook or harden by dry heat ▷ vi make bread, cakes, etc; be scorched or tanned **bak•er** n **bak•er•y** n **baking powder** leavening agent containing sodium bicarbonate, etc used in making baked goods

bal•a•cla•va [bal-ə-KLAH-və] n close-fitting woolen helmet, covering head and neck

bal•a•lai•ka [bal-ə-LĪ-kə] n Russian musical instrument, like guitar

bal•ance [BAL-əns] n pair of scales; equilibrium; surplus; sum due on an account; difference between two sums ▷ vt **-anced, -anc•ing** weigh; bring to equilibrium **balance sheet** tabular statement of assets and liabilities **balance wheel** regulating wheel of watch

bal•co•ny [BAL-kə-nee] n, pl **-nies** railed platform outside window; upper seats in theater

bald [bawld] adj hairless; plain; bare **bald'ing** adj becoming bald **bald'ness** n

bale [bayl] n bundle or package ▷ vt **baled, bal•ing** make into bundles or pack into cartons **bal'er** n machine that does this

ba•leen [bə-LEEN] n whalebone

bale•ful [BAYL-fəl] adj menacing **bale'ful•ly** adv

balk [bawk] vi swerve, pull up; baseball commit a balk ▷ vt thwart, hinder; shirk ▷ n hindrance; rafter, beam; baseball illegal motion of pitcher before releasing ball to batter **balk at** recoil; stop short

ball[1] [bawl] n anything round; globe, sphere, esp as used in games; a ball as pitched; bullet ▷ v clog, gather into a mass **ball bearings** hardened steel balls used to lessen friction on bearings **ball'park** n

stadium used for baseball games; inf approximate range ▷ adj inf approximate **ball'point, ball'point pen** pen with tiny ball bearing as nib

ball[2] n formal social gathering for dancing; inf a very good time **ball'room** n

bal•lad [BAL-əd] n narrative poem; simple song

bal•lade [bə-LAHD] n short poem with refrain and envoi; piece of music

bal•last [BAL-əst] n heavy material put in ship to give steadiness; that which renders anything steady ▷ vt hold with ballast, steady

bal•let [ba-LAY] n theatrical presentation of dancing and miming to musical accompaniment **bal•le•ri•na** [bal-ə-REE-nə] n

bal•lis•tic [bə-LIS-tik] adj moving as, or pertaining to motion of, a projectile **bal•lis'tics** n scientific study of ballistic motion

bal•loon [bə-LOON] n large bag filled with air or gas to make it rise in the air ▷ vi puff out; increase rapidly **bal•loon'ing** n **bal•loon'ist** n

bal•lot [BAL-ət] n method of voting secretly, usually by marking ballot paper and putting it into box ▷ vi vote or decide by ballot **ballot box** box into which voting papers are dropped on completion

bal•ly•hoo [BAL-ee-hoo] n noisy confusion or uproar; flamboyant, exaggerated publicity or advertising

balm [bahm] n aromatic substance, healing or soothing ointment; anything soothing **balm'y** adj **balm•i•er, balm•i•est** soothing; (of climate) mild; (of a person) foolish **balm'i•ness** n

ba•lo•ney [bə-LOW-nee] n inf nonsense

bal•sa [BAWL-sə] n Amer tree with light but strong wood

bal·sam [BAWL-səm] *n* resinous aromatic substance obtained from various trees and shrubs; soothing ointment **bal·sam'ic** *adj*

Baltimore oriole oriole of eastern N Amer

bal·us·ter [BAL-ə-stər] *n* short pillar used as support to rail of staircase, etc **bal'us·trade** [-strayd] *n* row of short pillars topped by rail

bam·boo' *n, pl* **-boos** large tropical treelike reed

bam·boo·zle [bam-BOO-zəl] *vt* **-zled, -zling** mystify, hoodwink

ban *vt* **banned, ban·ning** prohibit, forbid, outlaw ▷ *n* prohibition; proclamation **banns** *pl n* proclamation of marriage

ba·nal [bə-NAL] *adj* commonplace, trivial, trite **ba·nal'i·ty** *n*

ba·nan·a [bə-NAN-ə] *n* tropical treelike plant; its fruit

band¹ *n* strip used to bind; range of values, frequencies, etc, between two limits **band·age** [BAN-dij] *n* strip of cloth for binding wound

band² *n* company, group; company of musicians ▷ *v* bind together **band'mas·ter** *n* **band'stand** *n*

ban·dan·na [ban-DAN-ə] *n* large decorated handkerchief

band·box [BAND-boks] *n* light box of cardboard for hats, etc; theater or other public structure of small interior dimensions

ban·deau [ban-DOH] *n, pl* **-deaux** [-DOHZ] band, ribbon for the hair; narrow bra or top

ban'dit *n* outlaw; robber; brigand

ban·do·leer [ban-də-LEER] *n* shoulder belt for cartridges

band·wag·on [BAND-wag-ən] *n* **climb, jump, get on the bandwagon** join something that seems sure of success

ban·dy [BAN-dee] *vt* **-died,** **-dy·ing** beat to and fro, toss from one to another **ban·dy-leg·ged** [-leg-id] *adj* bowlegged, having legs curving outward

bane [bayn] *n* poison; person or thing causing misery or distress **bane'ful** *adj*

bang¹ *n* sudden loud noise, explosion; heavy blow ▷ *vt* make loud noise; beat; strike violently, slam

bang² *n* (usu pl) fringe of hair cut straight across forehead

ban·gle [BANG-gəl] *n* ring worn on arm or leg

ban'ish *vt* condemn to exile; drive away; dismiss **ban'ish·ment** *n* exile

ban·is·ter [BAN-ə-stər] *n* handrail held up by balusters

ban·jo [BAN-joh] *n, pl* **-jos** musical instrument like guitar, with circular body **ban'jo·ist** *n*

bank¹ [bangk] *n* mound or ridge of earth; edge of river, lake, etc; rising ground in sea ▷ *v* enclose with ridge; pile up; (of aircraft) tilt inward in turning

bank² *n* establishment for keeping, lending, exchanging, etc money; any supply or store for future use, as **a blood bank** ▷ *vt* put in bank ▷ *vi* keep with bank **bank'er** *n* **bank'ing** *n* **bank teller** bank cashier **bank'note** *n* written promise of payment acceptable as money **bank on** rely on

bank³ *n* arrangement of switches, keys, oars, etc in a row or in tiers

bank·rupt [BANGK-rupt] *n* one who fails in business, insolvent debtor ▷ *adj* financially ruined; broken; destitute ▷ *vt* make, cause to be, bankrupt **bank'rupt·cy** *n*

ban·ner [BAN-ər] *n* long strip with slogan, etc; placard; flag used as ensign

banns n see BAN

ban·quet [BANG-kwit] n feast ▷ vi feast ▷ vt treat with feast

ban·quette [bang-KET] n upholstered bench usu along a wall; raised firing step behind parapet

ban·shee n (in Irish folklore) female spirit with a wail portending death

ban·tam [BAN-tàm] n dwarf variety of domestic fowl; person of diminutive stature **ban'tam·weight** n boxer weighing no more than 118 pounds

ban·ter [BAN-tàr] vt make fun of ▷ n light, teasing language

Ban·tu [BAN-too] n collective name for large group of related tribes in Africa; family of languages spoken by Bantu peoples

ban·yan [BAN-yàn] n Indian fig tree with spreading branches that take root

ba·o·bab [BAY-oh-bab] n Afr tree with thick trunk and angular branches

Bap'tist n member of Protestant Christian denomination believing in necessity of baptism by immersion, esp of adults **baptist** n one who baptizes

bap·tize [BAP-tiz] vt **-tized, -tiz·ing** immerse in, sprinkle with water ceremonially; christen **bap'tism** [-tiz-àm] n **bap·tis'mal** [-TIZ-màl] adj **bap'tist·ry** n, pl **-ries** place where baptism is performed

bar¹ [bahr] n rod or block of any substance; obstacle; bank of sand at mouth of river; rail in law court; body of lawyers; room or counter where drinks are served, esp in hotel, etc; unit of music ▷ vt **barred, bar·ring** fasten; obstruct; exclude ▷ prep except **barring** prep excepting **bar code** arrangement of numbers and parallel lines on package, electronically scanned at checkout to give price, etc **bar'maid** n **bar'ten·der** n

bar² n unit of pressure

barb [bahrb] n sharp point curving backward behind main point of spear, fishhook, etc; cutting remark **barbed** adj **barbed wire** fencing wire with barbs at close intervals

bar·ba·rous [BAHR-bàr-às] adj savage, brutal, uncivilized **bar·bar'ian** [-BAIR-ee-àn] n **bar·bar·ic** adj **bar'ba·rism** n **bar·bar'i·ty** n

bar·be·cue [BAHR-bi-kyoo] n food cooked outdoors over hot charcoal; fireplace, grill used for this ▷ vt **-cued, cu·ing** cook meat, etc in this manner

bar·ber [BAHR-bàr] n one whose job is to cut hair and shave beards ▷ v **-bered, -ber·ing** perform this service

bar·bi·tu·rate [bahr-BICH-àr-it] n derivative of barbituric acid used as sedative drug

bar·ca·role [BAHR-kà-rohl] n gondolier's song; music imitative of this

bard [bahrd] n Celtic poet; wandering minstrel; poet **the Bard of Avon** Shakespeare

bare [bair] adj **bar·er, bar·est** uncovered; naked; plain; scanty ▷ vt **bared, bar·ing** make bare **bare'ly** adv only just, scarcely **bare'back, -backed** adj on unsaddled horse **bare'faced** adj shameless

barf v sl vomit

bar·gain [BAHR-gàn] n something bought at price favorable to purchaser; contract, agreement ▷ vi haggle, negotiate; make bargain

barge [bahrj] n flat-bottomed freight boat propelled by towing; roomy pleasure boat ▷ vi inf

bar·i·tone [BAR-i-tohn] n (singer with) second lowest adult male voice ▷ adj written for or possessing this vocal range

bar·i·um [BA-ree-əm] n white metallic element

bark¹ [bahrk] n sharp loud cry of dog, etc ▷ v make, utter with such sound **bark'er** n one who stands outside entrance to a circus, etc calling out its attractions **bark up the wrong tree** misdirect one's efforts; pursue a wrong course

bark² n outer layer of trunk, branches of tree ▷ vt strip bark from; rub off (skin), graze (shins, etc)

bark³ n sailing ship, esp large, three-masted one

bar·ley [BAHR-lee] n grain used for food and making malt **bar'ley·corn** n a grain of barley **John Barleycorn** personification of intoxicating liquor

bar mitz·vah [bahr MITS-və] n Jewish boy at age 13 who participates in religious ceremony signifying entry into adulthood; the ceremony

barn [bahrn] n building to store grain, hay, etc **barn dance** (party with) country music and dancing **barn'yard** n area adjoining barn **barnyard humor** earthy or smutty humor

bar·na·cle [BAHR-nə-kəl] n shellfish that adheres to rocks, logs, ships' bottoms, etc

ba·rom·e·ter [bə-ROM-i-tər] n instrument to measure pressure of atmosphere **bar·o·met·ric** [bar-ə-ME-trik] adj **bar·o·graph** [BA-rə-graf] n recording barometer

bar·on [BA-rən] n member of lowest rank of peerage in Great Britain; powerful businessman **bar'on·ess** n **bar'o·ny** n

ba·ro·ni·al [-ROH-nee-əl] adj

bar·on·et [BA-rə-nit] n lowest British hereditary title, below baron but above knight **bar'o·net·cy** n

ba·roque [bə-ROHK] adj extravagantly ornamented, esp in architecture and music **baroque pearl** one irregularly shaped

bar·rack [BA-rək] n (usu in pl) building for housing soldiers; bare, barnlike building ▷ vt house in barracks

bar·ra·cu·da [ba-rə-KOO-də] n type of large, elongated, predatory fish, mostly tropical

bar·rage [bə-RAHZH] n heavy artillery fire; continuous and heavy delivery, esp of questions, etc

bar·rel [BA-rəl] n round wooden vessel, made of curved staves bound with hoops; its capacity; great amount or number; anything long and hollow, as tube of gun, etc ▷ v **-reled, -rel·ing** put in barrel; move at high speed **bar'rel·ful** n, pl **-fuls** as much, as many, as a barrel can hold; large amount or number **over a barrel** helpless

bar·ren [BA-rən] adj unfruitful, sterile; unprofitable; dull **bar'ren·ness** n

bar·ri·cade [BA-ri-kayd] n improvised fortification, barrier ▷ vt **-cad·ed, -cad·ing** to protect by building barrier; block

bar·ri·er [BAR-ee-ər] n fence, obstruction, obstacle, boundary **barrier reef** coral reef lying parallel to shore

bar·row¹ [BA-roh] n small wheeled handcart; wheelbarrow

barrow² n castrated male swine

barrow³ n burial mound of earth or stones

bar·ter [BAHR-tər] v trade by exchange of goods ▷ n trade by exchange of goods

bar·y·on [BA-ree-on] n physics elementary particle of matter

ba·salt [bə-SAWLT] n dark-colored, hard, compact, igneous rock **ba·sal·tic** adj

base¹ [bays] n bottom, foundation; starting point; center of operations; fixed point; chemistry compound that combines with an acid to form a salt; medium into which other substances are mixed ▷ vt **based, bas·ing** found, establish **base·less** adj **base·ment** n lowest floor of building, partly or entirely below ground

base² adj **-er, -est** low, mean; despicable **base·ly** adv **base·ness** n

base·ball [BAYS-bawl] n game played with bat and ball between teams of 9 (sometimes 10) players; the ball they use

ba·sen·ji [bə-SEN-jee] n small African hunting dog that seldom barks

bash v inf strike violently ▷ n blow; attempt; festive party

bash·ful [BASH-fəl] adj shy, modest **bash·ful·ly** adv

BASIC [BAY-sik] n computer programing language that uses common English words

ba·sic [BAY-sik] adj relating to, serving as base; fundamental; necessary **ba·si·cal·ly** adv

ba·sil·i·ca [bə-SIL-i-kə] n type of church with long hall and pillars

bas·i·lisk [BAS-ə-lisk] n legendary small fire-breathing dragon; type of tropical lizard related to iguanas

ba·sin [BAY-sən] n deep circular dish; harbor; land drained by river

ba·sis [BAY-sis] n, pl **-ses** [-seez] foundation; principal constituent

bask vi lie in warmth and sunshine

bas·ket [BAS-kit] n vessel made of woven cane, straw, etc **bas·ket·ry** [-ki-tree] n **bas·ket·ball** n ball game played by two teams of 5 players who score points by throwing ball through baskets suspended above ends of playing area; the ball they use

Basque [bask] n one of a people from W Pyrenees; their language

bas·re·lief [bah-ri-LEEF] n sculpture with figures standing out slightly from background

bass¹ [bays] n lowest part in music; bass singer or voice ▷ adj

bass² [bas] n any of large variety of freshwater or seawater fishes

bas·set hound [BAS-it] n type of smooth-haired short-legged dog

bas·soon [bə-SOON] n woodwind instrument of low tone **bas·soon·ist** n

bas·tard [BAS-tərd] n child born of unmarried parents; sl person, esp a man: a lucky bastard ▷ adj illegitimate; spurious

baste¹ [bayst] vt **bast·ed, bast·ing** moisten (meat) during cooking with hot fat; beat severely **bast·er** n

baste² vt **bast·ed, bast·ing** sew loosely, tack

bas·ti·na·do [bas-tə-NAY-doh] n, pl **-does** beating with stick, etc esp on soles of feet ▷ vt **-doed, -do·ing**

bas·tion [BAS-chən] n projecting part of fortification, tower; strong defense or bulwark

bat¹ n any of various types of clubs used to hit ball in certain sports, eg baseball ▷ vt **bat·ted, bat·ting** strike with bat or use bat in sport **batting** n performance with bat

bat² n nocturnal mouselike flying animal

bat³ vt **bat·ted, bat·ting** flutter (one's eyelids)

batch [bach] n group or set of similar objects, esp cakes, etc baked

together
bat·ed [BAY-tid] *adj* **with bated breath** anxiously
bath *n* vessel or place to bathe in; water for bathing; act of bathing
bath·house *n* building with dressing and washing facilities for bathers
bath·room *n* room with toilet and washing facilities **take a bath** *sl* experience serious, esp financial, losses in a venture
bathe [bayth] *v* **bathed, bath·ing** apply liquid; wash; immerse in water ▷ *n* **bath·er** *n*
ba·thos [BAY-thos] *n* ludicrous descent from the elevated to the ordinary in writing or speech
ba·tik [bà-TEEK] *n* dyeing process using wax
ba·ton [bà-TON] *n* stick, esp of conductor, marshal, member of relay team
ba·tra·chi·an [bà-TRAY-kee-àn] *n, adj* (of) any amphibian, esp frog or toad
bat·tal·ion [bà-TAL-yàn] *n* military unit consisting of three or more companies; *fig* a large group
bat·ten¹ [BAT-n] *n* narrow piece of board, strip of wood ▷ *vt* (esp with *down*) fasten, make secure
batten² *vi* (usu with *on*) thrive, esp at someone else's expense
bat·ter [BAT-àr] *v* strike continuously ▷ *n* mixture of flour, eggs, liquid, used in cooking
bat·ter·y [BAT-à-ree] *n, pl* **-ter·ies** connected group of electrical cells; any electrical cell; number of similar things occurring together; *law* assault by beating; number of guns; place where they are mounted; unit of artillery; *baseball* pitcher and catcher as a unit
bat·ting [BAT-ing] *n* cotton or wool fiber as stuffing or lining

bat·tle [BAT-l] *n* fight between armies, combat ▷ *vi* **-tled, -tling** fight, struggle **battle-ax** *n sl* sharp-tempered, domineering woman
bat·tle·ment [BAT-l-mànt] *n* wall, parapet on fortification with openings for cannon
bat·tle·ship [BAT-l-ship] *n* heavily armed and armored fighting ship of the largest and heaviest class
bat·ty [BAT-ee] *adj inf* **-ti·er, -ti·est** crazy, silly
bau·ble [BAW-bàl] *n* showy trinket
baud [bawd] *n* unit of data transmission speed
baux·ite [BAWK-sit] *n* mineral yielding aluminum
bawd *n* prostitute; brothel keeper **bawd·y** *adj* **bawd·i·er, bawd·i·est** obscene, lewd
bawl *vi* cry; shout ▷ *n* loud shout or cry **bawl out** *vt inf* reprimand severely
bay¹ *n* wide inlet of sea; space between two columns; recess **bay window** window projecting from a wall
bay² *n* bark; cry of hounds in pursuit ▷ *v* bark (at) **at bay** cornered
bay³ *n* laurel tree
bay⁴ *adj* reddish-brown ▷ *n* horse with body of this color and black mane
bay·o·net [BAY-à-nit] *n* stabbing weapon fixed to rifle ▷ *vt* **-net·ed, -net·ing** stab with this
bay·ou [BI-oo] *n, pl* **-ous** marshy inlet or outlet of lake, river, etc, usu sluggish
ba·zaar [bà-ZAHR] *n* market (esp in Orient); sale of goods for charity
ba·zoo·ka [bà-ZOO-kà] *n* antitank rocket launcher
be *v, present sing 1st person* **am**, *2nd person* **are**, *3rd person is* **is**; *pl present* **are**, *past sing, 1st person was*, *2nd person*

were, 3rd person was, past pl were, present participle being, past participle been exist or live; pay a visit: *have you been to Spain?*; take place: *my birthday was last Monday*; used as a linking between the subject of a sentence and its complement: *John is a musician*; forms the progressive present tense: *the man is running*; forms the passive voice of all transitive verbs: *a good movie is being shown on television tonight*

Be chemistry beryllium

beach [beech] *n* shore of sea ▷ *vt* run boat on shore **beach'comb·er** [-koh-màr] *n* one who habitually searches shore debris for items of value; loafer spending days aimlessly on beach **beach'head** *n* area on beach captured from enemy; base for operations; foothold

bea·con [BEE-kòn] *n* signal fire; lighthouse, buoy; (radio) signal used for navigation

bead [beed] *n* little ball pierced for threading on thread of necklace, rosary, etc; drop of liquid; narrow molding ▷ *vt* string together or furnish with beads **bead'ing** *n* **bead'y** *adj* **bead·i·er, bead·i·est** small and bright

bea·gle [BEE-gàl] *n* small hound

beak [beek] *n* projecting horny jaws of bird; anything pointed or projecting; *sl* nose

beak·er [BEE-kàr] *n* large drinking cup; glass vessel used by chemists

beam [beem] *n* long squared piece of wood; ship's cross timber, side, or width; ray of light, etc; broad smile; bar of a balance ▷ *vt* aim light, radio waves, etc (to) ▷ *vi* shine; smile benignly

bean [been] *n* any of various leguminous plants or their seeds; head **full of beans** *inf* lively bean

sprout edible sprout of newly germinated bean, esp mung bean

bear¹ [bair] *vt* **bore, borne** or **born, bear·ing** carry; support; produce; endure; press (upon) **bear'er** *n*

bear² *n* heavy carnivorous quadruped; other bearlike animals, such as the koala **bear'skin** *n* tall fur helmet

beard [beerd] *n* hair on chin ▷ *vt* oppose boldly

bear·ing [BAIR-ing] *n* support or guide for mechanical part, esp one reducing friction; relevance; behavior; direction; relative position

beast [beest] *n* animal; four-footed animal; brutal man **beast'li·ness** *n* **beast'ly** *adj*

beat [beet] *v* **beat, beat·en, beat·ing** *vt* strike repeatedly; overcome; surpass; stir vigorously with striking action; flap (wings); make, wear (path) ▷ *vi* throb; pulsation; appointed course; basic rhythmic unit in piece of music ▷ *adj sl* exhausted **beat'er** *n* instrument for beating; one who rouses game for shooters

be·at·i·fy [bee-AT-à-fī] *vt* **-fied, -fy·ing** make happy; *R C Church* pronounce in eternal happiness (first step in canonization) **be·a·tif·ic** [bee-à-TIF-ik] *adj* **be·at·i·fi·ca'tion** *n* **be·at'i·tude** *n* blessedness

beau [boh] *n, pl* **beaux** [bohz] suitor

Beau·fort scale [BOH-fàrt] system of indicating wind strength (from 0, calm, to 17, hurricane)

beau·ty [BYOO-tee] *n, pl* **-ties** loveliness, grace; beautiful person or thing **beau·ti·cian** [byoo-TISH-àn] *n* one who gives treatment in beauty parlor **beau'ti·ful** *adj* **beau'ti·fy** [-tà-fī] *vt* **-fied, -fy·ing** beauty

parlor establishment offering hairdressing, manicure, etc

bea·ver [BEE-vər] *n* amphibious rodent; its fur; exceptionally hard-working person

be·calmed [bi-KAHMD] *adj* (of ship) motionless through lack of wind

became pt of BECOME

be·cause [bi-KAWZ] *adv, conj* by reason of, since

beck [bek] *n* **at someone's beck and call** subject to someone's slightest whim

beck·on [BEK-ən] *v* summon or lure by silent signal

be·come [bi-KUM] *v* **be·came, be·come, be·com·ing** ▷ *vi* come to be ▷ *vt* suit **becoming** *adj* suitable to; proper

bed *n* piece of furniture for sleeping on; garden plot; supporting structure; bottom of river; layer, stratum ▷ *vt* **bed·ded, bed·ding** lay in a bed; plant **bedding** *n* **bed'bug** *n* wingless bug infesting beds and sucking blood **bed'pan** *n* container used as toilet by bedridden person **bed'rid·den** *adj* confined to bed by age or sickness **bed'rock** *n* solid rock beneath the surface soil; basic facts or principles **bed'room** *n* **bed'spread** [-spred] *n* cover for bed when not in use **bed'stead** [-sted] *n* framework of a bed

be·dev·il [bi-DEV-əl] *vt* **-iled, -il·ing** confuse; torment **be·dev·il·ment** *n*

bed·lam [BED-ləm] *n* noisy confused scene

Bed·ou·in [BED-oo-in] *n* nomadic Arab of the desert; nomad

be·drag·gle [bi-DRAG-əl] *vt* **-gled, -gling** dirty by trailing in wet or mud

bee *n* insect that makes honey

bee'hive *n* **bee'line** *n* shortest route **bees'wax** *n* wax secreted by bees **bee in one's bonnet** an obsession

beech *n* tree with smooth grayish bark and small nuts; its wood

beef *n* flesh of cattle raised and killed for eating; *inf* complaint ▷ *vi inf* complain **beef'y** *adj* **beef·i·er, beef·i·est** fleshy, stolid **beef'burg·er** *n* hamburger

been pp of BE

beep *n* short, loud sound of automobile horn, etc ▷ *v* make this sound **beep'er** *n* small portable electronic signaling device

beer *n* fermented alcoholic drink made from hops and malt **beer'y** *adj* **beer·i·er, beer·i·est** affected by, smelling of, beer

beet *n* any of various plants with root used for food or extraction of sugar

bee·tle [BEET-l] *n* class of insect with hard upper-wing cases closed over the back for protection **bee·tle-browed** [browd] *adj* with prominent brows

be·fall [bi-FAWL] *v* **be·feil, be·fall·en, be·fall·ing** happen (to)

be·fit [bi-FIT] *vt* **be·fit·ted, be·fit·ting** be suitable to

be·fog [bi-FOG] *vt* **-fogged, -fog·ging** perplex, confuse

be·fore [bi-FOR] *prep* in front of; in presence of; in preference to; earlier than ▷ *adv* earlier; in front ▷ *conj* sooner than **be·fore'hand** *adv* previously

be·foul [bi-FOWL] *vt* make filthy **be·friend** [bi-FREND] *vt* make friend of

beg *v* **begged, beg·ging** ▷ *vt* ask earnestly, beseech ▷ *vi* ask for or live on charity **beg·gar** [BEG-ər] *n*

began pt of BEGIN

be·get [bi-GET] vt **be·got** or **be·gat**, **be·got·ten** or **be·got**, **be·get·ting** obs produce, generate

be·gin [bi-GIN] v **be·gan**, **be·gun**, **be·gin·ning** (cause to) start; initiate; originate **be·gin·ner** n novice

be·go·nia [bi-GOHN-yə] n genus of tropical plant

be·got pt/pp of **BEGET**

be·grudge [bi-GRUJ] vt **-grudged**, **-grudg·ing** grudge, envy anyone the possession of

be·guile [bi-GĪL] vt **-guiled**, **-guil·ing** charm, fascinate; amuse; deceive **beguiling** adj

be·gun pp of **BEGIN**

be·half [bi-HAF] n **on behalf of** in the interest of or for the benefit of

be·have [bi-HAYV] vi **-haved**, **-hav·ing** act, function in particular way **be·hav·ior** [bi-HAYV-yər] n conduct **behave oneself** conduct oneself well

be·head [bi-HED] vt cut off head

be·held pt/pp of **BEHOLD**

be·hest [bi-HEST] n charge, command

be·hind [bi-HĪND] prep farther back or earlier than; in support of ▷ adv in the rear **behind-the-scenes** kept or made in secret

be·hold [bi-HOHLD] vt **-held**, **-hold·ing** watch, see **be·hold·er** n

be·hol·den [bi-HOHL-dən] adj bound in gratitude

be·hoove [bi-HOOV] vi **-hooved**, **-hoov·ing** be necessary or fitting for

beige [bayzh] n color of undyed woolen cloth

be·ing [BEE-ing] n existence; that which exists; creature; prp of **BE**

bel n unit for comparing two power levels

be·la·bor [bi-LAY-bər] vt beat soundly; discuss (a subject) endlessly

be·lat·ed [bi-LAY-tid] adj late; too late

be·lay [bi-LAY] vt fasten rope to peg, pin, etc

belch vi void gas by mouth ▷ vt eject violently; cast up ▷ n emission of gas, etc

be·lea·guer [bi-LEE-gər] vt besiege

bel·fry [BEL-free] n, pl **-fries** bell tower

be·lie [bi-LĪ] vt **-lied**, **-ly·ing** contradict; misrepresent

be·lieve [bi-LEEV] v **-lieved**, **-liev·ing** ▷ vt regard as true or real ▷ vi have faith **be·lief** n **be·liev·a·ble** adj credible **be·liev·er** n esp one of same religious faith

be·lit·tle [bi-LIT-l] vt **-tled**, **-tling** regard, speak of, as having little worth or value **be·lit·tler** n

bell n hollow metal instrument giving ringing sound when struck; electrical device emitting ring or buzz as signal **bell·hop** n hotel employee who carries luggage, conducts guests to rooms, etc

bel·la·don·na [bel-ə-DON-ə] n deadly nightshade

belle [bel] n beautiful woman, reigning beauty

bel·li·cose [BEL-i-kohs] adj warlike

bel·lig·er·ent [bə-LIJ-ər-ənt] adj hostile, aggressive; making war ▷ n warring person or nation

bel·low [BEL-oh] vi roar like bull; shout ▷ n roar of bull; any deep cry or shout

bel·lows [BEL-ohz] pl n instrument for creating stream of air

bel·ly [BEL-ee] n, pl **-lies** part of body that contains intestines; stomach ▷ vt **-lied**, **-ly·ing** swell out

belly laugh n hearty laugh

be·long [bi-LAWNG] vi be the property or attribute of; be a member or inhabitant of; have an allotted place; pertain to **be·long·ings** pl n personal possessions

be·lov·ed [bi-LUV-id or bi-LUVD] adj much loved ▷ n dear one

be·low [bi-LOH] adv beneath ▷ prep lower than

belt n band; girdle; zone or district ▷ vt surround, fasten with belt; mark with band; inf thrash

be·moan [bi-MOHN] vt grieve over (loss, etc)

be·muse [bi-MYOOZ] v -mused, -mus·ing confuse, bewilder

bench n long seat; seat or body of judges, etc ▷ vt provide with benches **bench**mark n fixed point, criterion

bend v bent, bend·ing (cause to) form a curve ▷ n curve **the bends** pl n decompression sickness **bend over backward** exert oneself to the utmost

be·neath [bi-NEETH] prep under, lower than ▷ adv below than

ben·e·dic·tion [ben-i-DIK-shàn] n invocation of divine blessing

ben·e·fit [BEN-à-fit] n advantage, favor, profit, good; money paid by a government or business, etc to unemployed, etc ▷ v -fit·ed, -fit·ing do good to; receive good **ben'e·fac·tor** n one who helps or does good to others; patron **ben'e·fice** [-à-fis] n an ecclesiastical livelihood **be·nef'i·cence** n **be·nef'i·cent** adj doing good; kind **ben·e·fi'cial** [-FISH-àl] adj advantageous, helpful **ben·e·fi'ci·ar·y** n, pl -ar·ies **benefit society** organization providing life insurance, sickness benefit, etc, to its members, and often also social activities

be·nev·o·lent [bà-NEV-à-lànt] adj kindly, charitable **be·nev'o·lence** n

be·night·ed [bi-NĪ-tid] adj ignorant, uncultured

be·nign [bi-NĪN] adj kindly, mild, favorable **be·nign'ly** adv

bent pt/pp of **BEND** adj curved; resolved (on); determined ▷ n inclination, personal propensity

be·numb [bi-NUM] vt make numb, deaden

ben·zene [BEN-zeen] n one of group of related flammable liquids used in chemistry and as solvents, cleaning agents, etc

be·queath [bi-KWEETH] vt leave property, etc by will **be·quest** [bi-KWEST] n bequeathing; legacy

be·rate [bi-RAYT] vt -rat·ed, -rat·ing scold harshly

be·reave [bi-REEV] vt -reaved, -reft, -reav·ing deprive of, esp by death **be·reave'ment** n loss, esp by death

be·ret [bà-RAY] n round, close-fitting hat

ber·i·ber·i [ber-ee-BER-ee] n tropical disease caused by vitamin B deficiency

ber·ke·li·um [bàr-KEE-lee-àm] n artificial radioactive metallic element

ber·ry [BER-ee] n, pl -ries small juicy stoneless fruit ▷ v -ried, -ry·ing look for, pick, berries

ber·serk [bàr-SURK] adj frenzied

berth [burth] n ship's mooring place; place to sleep on ship or train ▷ vt to moor

ber·yl [BER-àl] n variety of crystalline mineral including aquamarine and emerald

be·ryl·li·um [bà-RIL-ee-àm] n strong brittle metallic element

be·seech [bi-SEECH] vt -sought

or **-seeched, -seech·ing** entreat, implore

be·set [bi-SET] *vt* **-set, -set·ting** assail, surround with danger, problems

be·side [bi-SĪD] *adv, prep* by the side of, near; distinct from **be·sides'** *adv, prep* in addition (to)

be·siege [bi-SEEJ] *vt* **-sieged, -sieg·ing** surround (with armed forces, etc)

be·sot·ted [bi-SOT-id] *adj* drunk; foolish; infatuated

besought pt/pp of **BESEECH**

be·speak [bi-SPEEK] *vt* **-spoke, -spok·en, -speak·ing** engage beforehand

best *adj, adv* sup of **GOOD** or **WELL** ▷ *vt* defeat **best seller** book or other product sold in great numbers; author of one or more of these books

bes·tial [BES-chǎl] *adj* like a beast, brutish **bes·ti·al·i·ty** [-chee-AL-i-tee] *n*

be·stir [bi-STUR] *vt* **-stirred, -stir·ring** rouse (oneself) to activity

be·stow [bi-STOH] *vt* give, confer **be·stow'al** *n*

be·stride [bi-STRĪD] *vt* **-strode** or **-strid, -strid·den** or **-strid, -strid·ing** sit or stand over with legs apart, mount horse

bet *v* **bet** or **bet·ted, bet·ting** agree to pay money, etc if wrong (or win if right) in guessing result of contest, etc ▷ *n* money risked in this way

be·tel [BEET-l] *n* species of pepper **betel nut** the nut of the betel palm

bête noire [bet NWAHR] *n, pl* **bêtes noires** *Fr* pet aversion

be·tide [bi-TĪD] *v* **-tid·ed, -tid·ing** happen (to)

be·to·ken [bi-TOH-kǎn] *vt* be a sign of

be·tray [bi-TRAY] *vt* be disloyal to, esp by assisting an enemy; reveal,

divulge; show signs of **be·tray'al** *n* **be·tray'er** *n*

be·troth [bi-TROHTH] *vt* promise to marry **be·troth'al** *n* **be·trothed'** *n, adj*

bet·ter [BET-ər] *adj, adv* comp of **GOOD** or **WELL** ▷ *v* improve **bet'ter·ment** *n*

be·tween [bi-TWEEN] *prep, adv* in the intermediate part in space or time; indicating reciprocal relation or comparison

be·twixt [bi-TWIKST] *prep, adv obs* between

bev·el [BEV-əl] *n* surface not at right angle to another; slant ▷ *v* **-eled, -el·ing** slope, slant; cut on slant **bev'eled** *adj* slanted

bev·er·age [BEV-rij] *n* drink

bev·y [BEV-ee] *n, pl* **bev·ies** flock or group

be·wail [bi-WAYL] *vt* lament

be·ware [bi-WAIR] *vi* be on one's guard, take care

be·wil·der [bi-WIL-dər] *vt* puzzle, confuse **be·wil'der·ing** *adj* **be·wil'der·ment** *n*

be·witch [bi-WICH] *vt* cast spell over; charm, fascinate **be·witch'ing** *adj*

be·yond [bee-OND] *adv* farther away; besides ▷ *prep* on the farther side of; later than; surpassing, out of reach of

Bh *chemistry* bohrium

Bi *chemistry* bismuth

bi·as [BĪ-əs] *n, pl* **-as·es** personal slant; inclination or preference; onesided inclination ▷ *vt* **-ased, -as·ing** influence, affect **bi'ased** *adj* prejudiced

bib *n* cloth put under child's chin to protect clothes when eating; part of apron or overalls above waist

Bi·ble [BĪ-bəl] *n* the sacred writings of Christianity and Judaism **bible**

n fig book or journal considered unchallengeably authoritative

Bib·li·cal [BIB-li-kəl] *adj*

bib·li·og·ra·phy [bib-lee-OG-rə-fee] *n, pl* **-phies** list of books on a subject; history and description of books **bib·li·og'ra·pher** *n*

bib·li·o·phile [BIB-lee-ə-fil] *n* lover, collector of books

bib·u·lous [BIB-yə-ləs] *adj* given to drinking

bi·cam·er·al [bi-KAM-ər-əl] *adj* (of a legislature) having two chambers

bi·car·bo·nate [bi-KAHR-bə-nit] *n* chemical compound releasing carbon dioxide when mixed with acid

bi·cen·ten·ni·al [bi-sen-TEN-ee-əl] *n* two hundredth anniversary; its celebration ▷ *adj* relating to this

bi·ceps [Bi-seps] *n* two-headed muscle, esp muscle of upper arm

bick·er [BIK-ər] *vi, n* quarrel over petty things **bick'er·ing** *n*

bi·cy·cle [Bi-si-kəl] *n* vehicle with two wheels, one in front of other, pedaled by rider **bi'cy·clist** *n*

bid *vt* **bade**, **bid** or **bid·den**, **bid·ding** offer; say; command; invite ▷ *n* offer, esp of price; try **bid'der** *n*

bide [bid] *v* **bid·ed**, **bid·ing** ▷ *vi* remain; dwell ▷ *vt* await **bid'ing** *n*

bi·det [bi-DAY] *n* low basin for washing genital area

bi·en·ni·al [bi-EN-ee-əl] *adj* happening every two years; lasting two years ▷ *n* plant living two years **bi·en'ni·um** [-əm] *n* period of two years

bier [beer] *n* frame for bearing dead to grave; stand for holding dead; coffin and its stand

bi·fo·cal [bi-FOH-kəl] *adj* having two different focal lengths **bi·fo'cals** *pl n* eyeglasses having bifocal lenses

for near and distant vision

big *adj* **big·ger**, **big·gest** of great or considerable size, height, number, power, etc **big cheese** *inf* important person **big'head** *n inf* conceit **big'head·ed** *adj* **big shot** *inf* important or influential person **big'-time** *adv inf* very much, to a great extent

big·a·my [BIG-ə-mee] *n, pl* **-mies** crime of marrying a person while one is still legally married to someone else **big'a·mist** *n*

bight [bit] *n* curve or loop in rope; long curved shoreline or water bounded by it

big·ot [BIG-ət] *n* person intolerant or not receptive to ideas of others (esp on religion, race, etc) **big'ot·ed** *adj* **big'ot·ry** *n*

bike [bik] *n* short for bicycle or motor bike

bi·ki·ni [bi-KEE-nee] *n, pl* **-nis** woman's brief two-piece swimming costume

bi·lat·er·al [bi-LAT-ər-əl] *adj* two-sided

bile [bil] *n* fluid secreted by the liver; anger, ill temper **bil·ious** [BIL-yəs] *adj* nauseous, nauseating **bil'ious·ness** *n*

bilge [bilj] *n* bottom of ship's hull; dirty water collecting there; *inf* nonsense

bi·lin·gual [bi-LING-gwəl] *adj* speaking, or written in, two languages **bi·lin'gual·ism** *n*

bill *n* written account of charges; draft of legislative act; poster; commercial document; paper money ▷ *vt* present account of charges; announce by advertisement **bill'able** *adj* referring to time worked on behalf of a client and for which that client is to pay **bill'ing** *n* degree of importance (esp in theater, etc)

bill·board n large panel for outdoor advertising

bill[2] n bird's beak ▷ vi touch bills, as doves; caress affectionately

bil·let [BIL-it] n civilian quarters for troops; resting place ▷ vt quarter, as troops

bil·let-doux [bil-ee-DOO] n, pl **billets-doux** [bil-ee-DOOZ] love letter

bil·liards [BIL-yårdz] n game played on table with balls and cues

bil·lion [BIL-yån] n thousand millions

bil·low [BIL-oh] n great swelling wave ▷ vi surge; swell out

bi·month·ly [bi-MUNTH-lee] adv, adj every two months; oft twice a month

bin n box, etc used for storage

bi·na·ry [Bī-nå-ree] adj composed of, characterized by, two; dual

bind [bind] v **bound, bind·ing** ▷ vt tie fast; tie around, gird; tie together; oblige; seal; constrain; bandage; cohere; unite; put (book) into cover **bind·er** n one who, or that which binds **bind·er·y** n, pl **-er·ies** **bind·ing** n cover of book; tape for hem, etc

binge [binj] n inf excessive indulgence in eating or drinking; spree

bin·go [BING-goh] n game of chance in which numbers drawn are matched with those on a card

bin·na·cle [BIN-å-kål] n box holding ship's compass

bin·oc·u·lar [bå-NOK-yå-lår] adj seeing with, made for, both eyes **bin·oc·u·lars** pl n telescope made for both eyes

bi·no·mi·al [bi-NOH-mee-ål] adj, n (denoting) algebraic expression consisting of two terms

bio- comb form life or living

organisms: biology

bi·o·de·fense [bi-oh-di-FENS, bi-oh-DEE-fens] n procedures used to defend against attacks involving biological weapons

bi·o·de·grad·a·ble [bi-oh-di-GRAY-då-bål] adj capable of decomposition by natural means

bi·o·di·ver·si·ty [bi-oh-di-VURZ-å-tee] n existence of a wide variety of species in their natural environment

bi·og·ra·phy [bi-OG-rå-fee] n, pl **-phies** story of one person's life **bi·og·ra·pher** n **bi·o·graph·i·cal** adj

bi·ol·o·gy [bi-OL-å-jee] n study of living organisms **bi·o·log·i·cal** adj **bi·ol·o·gist** n

bi·o·met·ric [bi-oh-MET-rik] adj relating to digital scanning of physiological or behavioral traits of individuals for identification

bi·on·ics [bi-ON-iks] n study of relation of biological and electronic processes **bionic** adj having physical functions controlled, augmented by electronic equipment

bi·op·sy [Bi-op-see] n, pl **-sies** examination of tissue removed surgically from a living body

bi·o·rhythm [Bi-oh-rith-åm] n cyclically recurring pattern of physiological states

bi·o·se·cu·ri·ty [bi-oh-si-KYOOR-i-tee] n precautions taken to protect against the spread of harmful organisms and diseases

bi·o·ter·ror·ism [bi-oh-TER-år-iz-åm] n use of viruses, bacteria, etc by terrorists **bi·o·ter·ror·ist** n

bi·par·ti·san [bi-PAHR-tå-zån] adj consisting of or supported by two political parties

bi·par·tite [bi-PAHR-tit] adj consisting of two parts, parties

bi·ped [BI-ped] n two-footed animal

bi·plane [BI-playn] n airplane with two pairs of wings

birch [burch] n tree with silvery bark; rod for punishment, made of birch twigs ▷ vt flog **birch'en** adj

bird [burd] n feathered animal ▷ v observe or identify wild birds as a hobby **bird'brain** n stupid person

bird·ie [BUR-dee] n, v golf (make) score of one under par for a hole

bi·ret·ta [bə-RET-ə] n square cap with three or four ridges worn usu by Catholic clergy

birth [burth] n bearing, or the being born, of offspring; parentage, origin **birth control** limitation of childbearing usu by artificial means **birth'mark** n blemish, usu dark, formed on skin before birth **birth'right** n right one has by birth

bis·cuit [BIS-kit] n quick bread made from spoonful of rolled dough

bi·sect [bī-SEKT] vt divide into two equal parts

bi·sex·ual [bī-SEK-shoo-əl] adj sexually attracted to both men and women; of both sexes

bish·op [BISH-əp] n clergyman typically governing diocese; chess piece **bish'op·ric** n diocese or office of a bishop

bis·muth [BIZ-məth] n reddish-white metal used in medicine, etc

bi·son [BĪ-sən] n large wild ox; N Amer buffalo

bis·tro [BIS-troh] n, pl -tros small restaurant

bit¹ n fragment, piece; biting, cutting part of tool; mouthpiece of horse's bridle

bit² pt/pp of BITE

bit³ n computing smallest unit of information

bitch [bich] n female dog, fox or wolf; offens spiteful woman; inf complaint ▷ vi inf complain **bitch'y** adj **bitch·i·er, bitch·i·est bitch'i·ness** n

bite [bīt] vt **bit, bit·ten, bit·ing** cut into esp with teeth; grip; rise to bait; etch with acid ▷ n act of biting; wound so made; mouthful **biting** adj having power to bite

bit·ter [BIT-ər] adj **-er, -est** sharp, sour tasting; unpleasant; (of person) angry, resentful; sarcastic **bit'ter·ly** adv **bit'ter·ness** n **bit'ters** pl n essence of bitter usu aromatic herbs **bitter end** final extremity

bi·tu·men [bi-TOO-mən] n viscous substance occurring in asphalt, tar, etc **bi·tu'mi·nous coal** coal yielding much bitumen on burning

bi·valve [BI-valv] adj having a double shell ▷ n mollusk with such shell

biv·ou·ac [BIV-oo-ak] n temporary encampment of soldiers, hikers, etc ▷ vi **-acked, -ack·ing** pass the night in temporary camp

bi·zarre [bi-ZAHR] adj unusual, weird

Bk chemistry berkelium

blab v blabbed, blab'bing reveal secrets; chatter idly ▷ n chatter **blab·ber** v -bered, -ber·ing blab

black [blak] adj of the darkest color; without light; dark; evil; somber; dishonorable ▷ n darkest color; black dye, clothing, etc; (B-) person of dark-skinned race; African-American **black'en** v **black'ing** n substance used for blacking and cleaning leather, etc **black'ball** vt vote against, exclude **black'bird** n common American black bird **black'board** n dark-colored surface for writing on with chalk **black box** inf name for FLIGHT RECORDER

black economy illegally undeclared income **black·head** n dark, fatty plug blocking pore in skin **black·list** n list of people, organizations considered suspicious, untrustworthy, etc ▷ vt put on blacklist **Black Ma·ri·a** [mə-Rī-ə] police van for transporting prisoners **black market** illegal buying and selling of goods **black widow** highly poisonous N Amer spider

black·guard [BLAG-ahrd] n scoundrel

black·mail [BLAK-mayl] vt extort money from (a person) by threats ▷ n act of blackmailing; money extorted thus **black'mail·er** n

black·out [BLAK-owt] n complete failure of electricity supply; sudden turning off of all stagelights; state of temporary unconsciousness; obscuring of all lights as precaution against night air attack **black out** vi lose consciousness, memory, or vision temporarily

black·smith [BLAK-smith] n smith who works in iron

blad·der [BLAD-ər] n membranous bag to contain liquid, esp urinary bladder

blade [blayd] n edge, cutting part of knife or tool; leaf of grass, etc; sword; obs dashing fellow; flat of oar

blame [blaym] n censure; culpability ▷ vt **blamed, blam·ing** find fault with; censure **blame'less** adj **blame'wor·thy** [-wur-thee] adj

blanch v whiten, bleach, take color out of; (of foodstuffs) briefly boil or fry; turn pale

bland adj **-er, -est** devoid of distinctive characteristics; smooth in manner

blan·dish vt coax; flatter **bland'ish·ment** n

blank adj without marks or writing; empty; vacant, confused; (of verse) without rhyme ▷ n empty space; void; cartridge containing no bullet

blan·ket [BLANG-kit] n thick woven covering for bed, horse, etc; concealing cover ▷ vt cover with blanket; cover, stifle

blare [blair] v **blared, blar·ing** sound loudly and harshly ▷ n such sound

blar·ney [BLAHR-nee] n flattering talk

bla·sé [blah-ZAY] adj indifferent through familiarity; bored

blas·pheme [blas-FEEM] v show contempt for God or sacred things, esp in speech **blas·phem'er** n **blas·phe·mous** [-fə-məs] adj **blas'phe·my** n

blast n explosion; high-pressure wave of air coming from an explosion; current of air; gust of wind or air; loud sound; reprimand; sl riotous party ▷ vt blow up; remove, open, etc by explosion; blight; ruin **blast furnace** furnace for smelting ore, using blast of heated air

bla·tant [BLAYT-nt] adj obvious **bla'tan·cy** n

blaze¹ [blayz] n strong fire or flame; brightness; outburst ▷ vi **blazed, blaz·ing** burn strongly; be very angry

blaze² v **blazed, blaz·ing** (mark trees to) establish trail ▷ n mark on tree; white mark on horse's face

blaze³ vt **blazed, blaz·ing** proclaim

blaz·er [BLAY-zər] n type of sports jacket

bla·zon [BLAY-zən] vt make public, proclaim

bleach [bleech] v make or become white ▷ n bleaching substance

bleak [bleek] adj **-er, -est** cold and cheerless; exposed **bleak'ly** adv **bleak'ness** n

blear•y [BLEER-ee] adj **blear•i•er, blear•i•est** (of the eyes) dimmed, as with tears, sleep

bleat [bleet] v cry, as sheep; say, speak, plaintively ▷ n sheep's cry

bleed v **bled, bleed•ing** lose blood; draw blood or liquid from; extort money from

bleep n short high-pitched sound eg from electronic device ▷ vt obscure sound eg of TV program by making bleep **bleep•er** n small portable radio receiver that makes a bleeping signal

blem'ish n defect; stain ▷ vt make (something) defective, dirty, etc **blem'ished** adj

blend vt mix ▷ n mixture **blend'er** n one who, that which blends, esp electrical kitchen appliance for mixing food

bless vt **blessed** or **blest, bless•ing** consecrate; give thanks to; ask God's favor for; (usu passive) endow (with); glorify; make happy **bless'ed** [-id] adj **bless'ing** n (ceremony asking for) God's protection, aid; short prayer; approval; welcome event, benefit

blew pt of BLOW

blight [blit] n plant disease; harmful influence ▷ vt injure as with blight

blimp n small, nonrigid airship used for observing

blind [blind] adj unable to see; heedless; random; dim; closed at one end; sl very drunk ▷ n something cutting off light; window screen; pretext; place of concealment for hunters **blind'ly** adv **blind'ness** n **blind flying** navigation of aircraft by use of instruments alone **blind'fold** vt cover the eyes of so as to prevent vision ▷ n, adj **blind•man's buff** game in which one player is blindfolded

blink [blingk] vi wink; twinkle; shine intermittently ▷ n gleam **blink'ers** pl n leather flaps to prevent horse from seeing to the side **blink at** see, know about, but ignore **on the blink** inf not working (properly)

blip n repetitive sound or visible pulse, eg on radar screen ▷ vt **blipped, blip•ping** bleep

bliss n perfect happiness **bliss'ful** adj **bliss'ful•ly** adv

blis•ter [BLIS-tər] n bubble on skin; surface swelling, eg on paint ▷ v form blisters (on) **blis'ter•ing** adj (of verbal attack) bitter **blister pack** package for goods with hard, raised, transparent cover

blithe [blith] adj happy, gay; heedless **blithe'ly** adv **blithe'ness** n

blitz [blits] n sudden, concentrated attack **blitz'krieg** [-kreeg] n sudden concentrated military attack; war conducted in this way

bliz•zard [BLIZ-ərd] n a blinding storm of wind and snow

bloat [bloht] v puff or swell out ▷ n distention of stomach of cow, etc by gas **bloat'ed** adj swollen

blob n soft mass, esp drop of liquid; shapeless form

bloc [blok] n (political) grouping of people or countries

block [blok] n solid piece of wood, stone, etc; history rectangular piece of wood on which people were beheaded; obstacle; stoppage; pulley with frame; group of buildings; urban area enclosed by intersecting streets ▷ vt obstruct, stop up; shape on block; sketch (in) **block'age** n obstruction **block'head** n fool, simpleton **block letters** written capital letters

block•ade [blo-KAYD] n physical prevention of access, esp to port, etc

▷ vt **-ad•ed, -ad•ing**

blog [blawg] n person's online journal; (also **weblog**) **blog'ger** n

blonde (*masc*), **blond** adj, n fair-haired (person)

blood [blud] n red fluid in veins; race; kindred; good parentage; temperament; passion ▷ vt initiate (into hunting, war, etc) **blood'less** adj **blood'y** adj slaughterous ▷ adj, adv sl a common intensifier ▷ v make bloody **blood bank** (institution managing) store of human blood preserved for transfusion **blood'cur•dling** adj horrifying **blood'hound** n breed of large hound noted for keen powers of scent **blood'shed** n slaughter, killing **blood'shot** adj inflamed (said of eyes) **blood sport** sport in which animals are killed, eg fox hunting **blood'suck•er** n parasite (eg mosquito) living on host's blood; parasitic person **blood test** examination of sample of blood **blood'thirst•y** adj murderous, cruel **blood transfusion** transfer of blood from one person into another

bloom n flower of plant; blossoming; prime, perfection; glow; powdery deposit on fruit ▷ vi be in flower; flourish

bloom•er [BLOO-mǝr] n inf plant in bloom; person reaching full competence; person reaching puberty; ludicrous mistake

bloo•mers [BLOO-mǝrz] pl n girls' or women's wide, baggy underpants

blos•som [BLOS-ǝm] n flower; flower bud ▷ vi flower; develop

blot n spot, stain; disgrace ▷ vt **-ted, -ting** spot, stain; obliterate; detract from; soak up ink, etc from **blot'ter** n **blotting paper** soft absorbent paper for soaking up ink

blotch [bloch] n dark spot on skin ▷ vt make spotted **blotch'y** adj **blotch•i•er, blotch•i•est**

blouse [blows] n light, loose upper garment

blow¹ [bloh] v **blew, blown, blow•ing** ▷ vi make a current of air; pant; emit sound ▷ vt drive air upon or into; drive by current of air; sound; spout (of whales); fan; sl squander ▷ n blast; gale **blow-dry** vt **-dried, -dry•ing** style hair after washing using stream of hot air **blow fly** fly that infects food, etc **blow'pipe** n dart tube **blow'out** n sudden puncture in tire; uncontrolled escape of oil, gas, from well; sl festive party **blow up** explode; inflate; enlarge (photograph); inf lose one's temper

blow² n stroke, knock; sudden misfortune, loss

blown pp of **BLOW¹**

blows•y [BLOW-zee] adj **blows•i•er, blows•i•est** slovenly, sluttish; red-faced

blub•ber [BLUB-ǝr] vi weep ▷ n fat of whales; weeping

bludg•eon [BLUJ-ǝn] n short thick club ▷ vt strike with one; coerce (someone else)

blue [bloo] adj **blu•er, blu•est** of the color of sky or shades of that color; livid; depressed; indecent ▷ n the color; dye or pigment ▷ vt **blued, blu•ing** make blue; dip in blue liquid **blues** pl n inf depression; song in slow tempo originating with Amer Blacks, employed in jazz music **blu'ish** adj **blue baby** baby born with bluish skin caused by heart defect **blue blood** (person of) royal or aristocratic descent **blue-col•lar** adj denoting factory workers **blue jeans** pants made usu of blue denim **blue-pen•cil** vt **-ciled, -cil•ing** alter, delete parts of, esp to censor **blue·print** n copy of drawing; original plan **blue state** n US state with a majority of Democrat voters **blue·stock·ing** n scholarly, intellectual woman

bluff¹ n cliff, steep bank ▷ adj **-er, -est** hearty; blunt; steep; abrupt

bluff² vt deceive by pretense of strength ▷ n pretense

blu·ing [BLOO-ing] n indigo powder used in laundering

blun·der [BLUN-dər] n clumsy mistake ▷ vi make stupid mistake; act clumsily

blun·der·buss [BLUN-dər-bus] n obsolete short gun with wide bore

blunt adj **-er, -est** not sharp; (of speech) abrupt ▷ vt make blunt **blunt'ly** adv **blunt'ness** n

blur v blurred, blur·ring make, become less distinct ▷ n something vague, indistinct **blur'ry** adj **-ri·er, -ri·est**

blurb n statement advertising, recommending book, etc

blurt vt (usu with out) utter suddenly or unadvisedly

blush vi become red in face; be ashamed; redden ▷ n this effect

blus·ter [BLUS-tər] vi, n (indulge in) noisy, aggressive behavior **blus'ter·ing, -ter·y** adj (of wind, etc) noisy and gusty

bo·a [BOH-ə] n, pl **bo·as** large, nonvenomous snake, esp boa constrictor; long scarf of fur or feathers

boar [bor] n male pig; wild pig

board [bord] n broad, flat piece of wood; sheet of rigid material for specific purpose; table; meals; group of people who administer company; governing body; thick, stiff paper ▷ pl stage ▷ vt cover with planks; supply food daily; enter ship, etc ▷ vi take daily meals **board'er**

n **board·ing house** lodging house where meals may be had **boarding school** school providing living accommodation for pupils **board'room** n room where board of company or governing body meets **above board** beyond suspicion **on board** aboard

boast [bohst] vi speak too much in praise of oneself, one's possessions ▷ vt brag of; have to show ▷ n something boasted (of) **boast'er** n **boast'ful** adj

boat [boht] n small open vessel; ship ▷ vi sail about in boat **boat'ing** n **boat'swain** [BOH-sən] n ship's petty officer in charge of maintenance

bob v bobbed, bob·bing ▷ vi move up and down ▷ vt move jerkily; cut (women's) hair short ▷ n short, jerking motion; short hair style; weight on pendulum, etc **bobbed** adj

bob·bin [BOB-in] n cylinder on which thread is wound

bob·ble [BOB-əl] v, n baseball **-bled, -bling** fumble ▷ n fumbled ball

bob·cat [BOB-kat] n N Amer lynx

bob·o·link [BOB-ə-lingk] n Amer songbird

bode [bohd] vt **bod·ed, bod·ing** be an omen of

bod·ice [BOD-is] n upper part of woman's dress

bod·y [BOD-ee] n, pl **bod·ies** entire frame of person or animal; main part of such frame; corpse; main part of anything; substance; mass; person; number of persons united or organized; matter, opposed to spirit **bod'i·ly** adj, adv bodyward **bod'y·guard** n escort to protect important person **body stocking** undergarment covering body, oft including arms and legs **bod'y·work** n body of motor vehicle; repair of this

Boer [bor] *n* a S Afr of Dutch or Huguenot descent

bof•fo [BOF-oh] *adj sl* excellent; highly successful

bog *n* wet, soft ground **bog'gy** *adj* **-gi•er, -gi•est** marshy **bog down** stick as in a bog

bo•gey [BOH-gee] *n* evil or mischievous spirit; source of fear; *golf* one stroke over par on a hole **bo'gey•man** *n*

bog•gle [BOG-əl] *v* **-gled, -gling** ▷ *vi* be surprised; be baffled ▷ *vt* overwhelm with wonder; bewilder

bo•gus [BOH-gəs] *adj* sham, false

bo•he•mi•an [boh-HEE-mee-ən] *adj* unconventional ▷ *n* one who leads an unsettled life **bo•he'mi•a** *n* district, social circles of bohemians

boil[1] *vi* change from liquid to gas, esp by heating; become cooked by boiling; bubble; be agitated; seethe; *inf* be hot; *inf* be angry ▷ *vt* cause to boil; cook by boiling ▷ *n* boiling state **boil'er** *n* vessel for boiling **boil'er•mak•er** *n* repairman, worker on boilers; whiskey with beer chaser **boil'ing point** temperature at which boiling occurs; point at which anger becomes uncontrollable

boil[2] *n* inflamed suppurating swelling on skin

bois•ter•ous [BOI-stər-əs] *adj* wild; noisy; turbulent **bois'ter•ous•ness** *n*

bold [bohld] *adj* **-er, -est** daring, fearless; presumptuous; striking, prominent **bold'ly** *adv* **bold'ness** *n* **bold'face** *n printing* heavy-faced type

bole [bohl] *n* trunk of a tree

bo•le•ro [bə-LAIR-oh] *n, pl* **-ros** Spanish dance; loose jacket

boll [bohl] *n* seed capsule of cotton, flax, etc **boll weevil** beetle infesting

the cotton plant

Bol•she•vik [BOHL-shə-vik] *n* violent revolutionary, esp member of Russian group active in overthrow of czarist regime

bol•ster [BOHL-stər] *vt* support, uphold ▷ *n* long pillow; pad, support

bolt [bohlt] *n* bar or pin (esp with thread for nut); rush; discharge of lightning; roll of cloth ▷ *vt* fasten with bolt; swallow hastily ▷ *vi* rush away; break from control

bomb [bom] *n* explosive projectile; any explosive device; a failure ▷ *vt* attack with bombs **the bomb** nuclear bomb **bom•bard'** *vt* shell; attack (verbally) **bom•bar•dier'** [-bər-DEER] *n* person in military aircraft who aims and releases bombs **bom•bard'ment** *n* **bomb'er** *n* aircraft capable of carrying bombs; person using bombs illegally **bomb'shell** *n* shell of bomb; surprise; *inf* very attractive woman

bom'bast *n* pompous language; pomposity **bom•bas'tic** *adj*

bo•na fide [BOH-nə fid] *Lat* genuine(ly); sincere(ly) **bona fi•des** [Fi-deez] good faith, sincerity

bo•nan•za [bə-NAN-zə] *n* sudden good luck or wealth

bond *n* that which binds; link, union; written promise to pay money or carry out contract ▷ *vt* bind; store goods until duty is paid on them **bond'ed** *adj* placed in bond; mortgaged **bonds'man** [-mən] *n law* one whose work is to enter into bonds as surety

bond•age [BON-dij] *n* slavery

bone [bohn] *n* hard substance forming animal's skeleton; piece of this ▷ *v* **boned, bon•ing** ▷ *vt* take out bone ▷ *vi* (foll with *up*) study hard **bone'less** *adj* **bon'y** *adj* **bon•i•er, bon•i•est** **bone'head** *n*

inf stupid person
bon·fire [BON-fīr] *n* large outdoor fire
bon·go [BONG-goh] *n, pl* **-gos, -goes** small drum, usu one of a pair, played with the fingers
bon·net [BON-it] *n* hat (usu with strings)
bon·sai [BON-sī] *n* (art of growing) dwarf trees, shrubs
bo·nus [BOH-nəs] *n, pl* **-nus·es** extra (oft unexpected) payment or gift
boob *n* fool; *sl* female breast
boo·by [BOO-bee] *n, pl* **-bies** fool; tropical marine bird **booby hatch** *inf* insane asylum **booby prize** mock prize for poor performance **booby trap** harmless-looking object that explodes when disturbed; form of practical joke
boog·ie-woog·ie [BUUG-ee-WUUG-ee] *n* kind of jazz piano playing, emphasizing a rolling bass in syncopated eighth notes
book [buuk] *n* collection of sheets of paper bound together; literary work; main division of this ▷ *vt* reserve (table, ticket, etc); charge with legal offense; enter name in book; schedule engagements for **book'ing** *n* performance for entertainer, etc; reservation **book·ie** *n inf* bookmaker **book'ish** *adj* studious, fond of reading **book'keep·ing** *n* systematic recording of business transactions **book'keep·er** *n* **book'let** *n* **book'mak·er** *n* one whose work is taking bets; (also **book'ie**) **book'mark** *n* strip of some material put between the pages of a book to mark a place; *computing* identifier put on a website that enables the user to return to it quickly and easily ▷ *vt computing* identify and store

a website so that one can return to it quickly and easily **book'worm** *n* great reader
boom [1] *n* sudden commercial activity; prosperity ▷ *vi* become active, prosperous
boom [2] *vi, n* (make) loud, deep sound
boom [3] *n* long spar, as for stretching the bottom of a sail; barrier across harbor, river, etc; pole carrying overhead microphone, etc
boo·mer·ang [BOO-mə-rang] *n* curved wooden missile of Aust Aborigines that returns to the thrower ▷ *vi* recoil; return unexpectedly; backfire
boon *n* something helpful, favor
boon·docks [BOON-doks] *pl n* rural, backward area
boon·dog·gle [BOON-dog-əl] *n, vi* **-gled, -gling** (do) work of no practical value performed merely to appear busy
boor *n* rude person **boor'ish** *adj* **boor'ish·ness** *n*
boost *n* encouragement, help; upward push; increase ▷ *vt* **boost'er** *n* person or thing that supports, increases power, etc
boot *n* covering for the foot and ankle; *inf* kick ▷ *vt inf* kick; start up (a computer) **boot'ed** *adj*
booth *n* stall; cubicle
boot'leg *v* **-legged, -leg·ging** make, carry, sell illicit goods, esp alcohol ▷ *adj* **boot'leg·ger** *n*
boo·ty [BOO-tee] *n, pl* **-ties** plunder, spoil
booze [booz] *n, vi inf* **boozed, booz·ing** (consume) alcoholic drink; drinking spree **booz'er** *n* inf person fond of drinking
bo·rax [BOR-aks] *n* white soluble substance, compound of boron **bo·rac·ic** [bə-RAS-ik] *adj*
bor·der [BOR-dər] *n* margin;

bore¹ [bor] vt **bored, bor·ing** pierce, making a hole ▷ n hole; caliber of gun **bor'er** n instrument for making holes; insect that bores holes

bore² vt **bored, bor·ing** make weary by repetition, etc ▷ n tiresome person or thing **bore'dom** [-dəm] n

bore³ pt of BEAR

borne, born pp of BEAR

bo·ron [BOR-on] n chemical element used in hardening steel, etc

bor·ough [BUR-oh] n political subdivision in some states

bor·row [BOR-oh] vt obtain on loan or trust; appropriate

bor'zoi n breed of tall hound with long, silky coat

bos·om [BUUZ-əm] n human breast; seat of passions and feelings **boss¹** [baws] n person in charge of or employing others ▷ vt be in charge of; be domineering over **boss'y** adj **boss·i·er, boss·i·est** overbearing

boss² n knob or stud; raised ornament ▷ vt emboss

bo·sun [BOH-sən] n boatswain

bot·a·ny [BOT-n-ee] n study of plants **bo·tan·i·cal** [bə-TAN-ik-əl] adj **bot'a·nist** n **botanical garden** garden for exhibition and study of plants

botch [boch] vt spoil by clumsiness

both [bohth] adj, pron the two ▷ adv, conj as well

both·er [BOTH-ər] vt pester; perplex ▷ vi, n fuss, trouble

bot·tle [BOT-l] n vessel for holding liquid; its contents ▷ vt **-tled, -tling** put into bottle; restrain **bot'tler** n **bot'tle·neck** n narrow outlet that impedes smooth flow of traffic or

production of goods; person who hampers flow of work, information, etc

bot·tom [BOT-əm] n lowest part of anything; bed of sea, river, etc; buttocks ▷ vt put bottom to; base (upon); get to bottom of **bot'tom·less** adj **bottom line** last line of financial statement; crucial or deciding factor

bot·u·lism [BOCH-ə-liz-əm] n kind of food poisoning

bou·clé [boo-KLAY] n looped yarn giving knobbly effect

bou·doir [BOO-dwahr] n woman's bedroom, private sitting room

bough [rhymes with **cow**] n branch of tree

bought pt/pp of BUY

boul·der [BOHL-dər] n large weather-worn rounded stone

boul·e·vard [BUUL-ə-vahrd] n broad street or promenade

bounce [bowns] v **bounced, bounc·ing** (cause to) rebound (repeatedly) on impact, as a ball ▷ n rebounding; quality in object causing this; inf vitality, vigor **bounc'er** n esp one employed to evict undesirables (forcibly) **bounc'ing** adj vigorous, robust **bounc'y** adj **bounc·i·er, bounc·i·est** lively

bound¹ [bownd] n, vt limit **bound'a·ry** n, pl **-ries bound'ed** adj **bound'less** adj

bound² vi, n spring, leap

bound³ adj on a specified course: homeward bound

bound⁴ pt/pp of BIND adj committed; certain; tied

boun·ty [BOWN-tee] n, pl **-ties** liberality; gift; premium **boun'te·ous** [-tee-əs] **boun'ti·ful** adj liberal, generous

bou·quet [boo-KAY] n bunch

of flowers; perfume of wine; compliment

bour·bon [BUR-bàn] n whiskey made from corn, malt and rye

bour·geois [buur-ZHWAH] n, adj disparaging middle class; smugly conventional (person) **bourgeoisie** [buur-zhwah-ZEE] n middle classes

bout [bowt] n contest, fight; period of time spent doing something

bou·tique [boo-TEEK] n small shop, esp one selling clothes

bo·vine [BOH-vin] adj of cattle; oxlike; stolid, dull

bow¹ [boh] n weapon for shooting arrows; implement for playing violin, etc; ornamental knot of ribbon, etc; bend, bent line ▷ v bend **bow'leg·ged** [-leg-id] adj having legs curved outward **bow window** one with outward curve

bow² [rhymes with cow] vi bend body in respect, assent, etc; submit ▷ vt bend downward; cause to stoop; crush ▷ n

bow³ [rhymes with cow] n fore end of ship; prow; rower nearest bow

bowd·ler·ize [BOHD-là-rīz] vt -ized, -iz·ing expurgate, censor

bow·el [BOW-àl] n (oft pl) part of intestine (esp with reference to defecation); inside of anything

bow·er [BOW-àr] n shady retreat, arbor

bowl¹ [bohl] n round vessel, deep basin; drinking cup; hollow

bowl² n wooden ball ▷ pl outdoor game played with such balls ▷ v roll or throw ball in various ways **bowl'ing** n indoor game, played usu with large, heavy balls **bowling green** place where bowls is played **bowling alley** place where bowling is played

box¹ [boks] n (wooden) container, usu rectangular with lid; its contents; small enclosure; any boxlike cubicle, shelter or receptacle ▷ vt put in box; confine

box² v fight with fists, esp with padded gloves on ▷ vt strike ▷ n blow **box'er** n one who boxes; breed of pug-faced large dog

boy [boi] n male child; young man **boy'hood** [-huud] n

boy·cott [BOI-kot] vt refuse to deal with or participate in ▷ n

Br chemistry bromine

bra [brah] n brassiere

brace [brays] n tool for boring; clasp, clamp; pair, couple; strut, support ▷ pl dental appliance worn to help straighten teeth ▷ vt **braced, brac·ing** steady (oneself) as before a blow; support, make firm **bracing** adj invigorating **brace'let** n ornament for the arm ▷ pl sl handcuffs

brack·et [BRAK-it] n support for shelf, etc; group ▷ pl marks [ ], used to enclose words, etc ▷ vt enclose in brackets; connect

brack·ish [BRAK-ish] adj (of water) slightly salty

bract [brakt] n small scalelike leaf

brad n small nail

brag vi **bragged, brag·ging** boast ▷ n boastful talk **brag'gart** [-àrt] n

Brah·man [BRAY-màn] n breed of beef cattle

Brah·min [BRAH-min] n member of priestly Hindu caste; socially or intellectually aloof person

braid [brayd] vt interweave (hair, thread, etc); trim with braid ▷ n length of anything interwoven or plaited; ornamental tape

Braille [brayl] n system of printing for blind, with raised dots instead of letters

brain [brayn] n mass of nerve tissue in head; intellect ▷ vt kill by hitting

on head **brain'less** adj **brain'y** adj
brain·i·er, brain·i·est brain'child
n invention **brain'storm** n sudden
mental aberration; sudden clever
idea ▷ v practice, subject to,
brainstorming **brain'storm·ing**
n technique for coming upon
innovative ideas **brain trust** group
of experts without official status
who advise government officials
brain'wash vt change, distort a
person's ideas or beliefs **brain wave**
electrical impulse in brain

braise [brayz] vt **braised, brais·ing**
cook slowly in covered pan

brake [brayk] n instrument for
retarding motion of wheel on vehicle
▷ vt **braked, brak·ing** apply
brake to

bram·ble [BRAM-bəl] n prickly
shrub **bram'bly** adj **-bli·er, -bli·est**

bran n sifted husks of cereal grain

branch n limb of tree; offshoot or
subsidiary part of something larger
or primary ▷ vi bear branches;
diverge; spread **branched** adj
branch'less adj

brand n trademark; class of goods;
particular kind, sort; mark made
by hot iron; burning piece of wood;
sword; mark of disgrace ▷ vt burn
with iron; mark; stigmatize **brand-
new** adj absolutely new

bran'dish vt flourish, wave
(weapon, etc)

bran·dy [BRAN-dee] n, pl **-dies**
alcoholic liquor distilled from wine
or fruit juice ▷ vt **-died, -dy·ing**
flavor or preserve with brandy

brash adj **-er, -est** bold, impudent

brass n alloy of copper and zinc;
group of brass wind instruments
forming part of orchestra or band;
inf (military) officers ▷ adj **brass'y**
adj **brass·i·er, brass·i·est** showy;
harsh **brass'i·ness** n

bras·siere [brə-ZEER] n woman's
undergarment, supporting breasts,
bra

brat n contemptuous term for
a child

bra·va·do [brə-VAH-doh] n showy
display of boldness

brave [brayv] adj **brav·er, brav·est**
bold, courageous; splendid, fine
▷ n NAmer Indian warrior ▷ vt
braved, brav·ing defy, meet boldly
brav'er·y n, pl **-er·ies**

bra·vo [BRAH-voh] interj well done!

brawl vi fight noisily ▷ n **brawl'er**
n

brawn n muscle; strength **brawn'y**
adj **brawn·i·er, brawn·i·est**
muscular

bray n donkey's cry ▷ vi utter this;
give out harsh or loud sounds

braze [brayz] vt **brazed, braz·ing**
solder with alloy of brass or zinc

bra·zen [BRAY-zən] adj of,
like brass; impudent, shameless
▷ vt (usu with out, through) face,
carry through with impudence
bra'zen·ness n effrontery

bra·zier [BRAY-zhər] n pan
for burning charcoal or coals;
brassworker

breach [breech] n break, opening;
breaking of rule, duty, etc; quarrel
▷ vt make a gap in; break (rule, etc)

bread [bred] n food made of flour
or meal baked; food; sl money
bread'fruit n breadlike fruit found
in Pacific islands **bread'win·ner** n
person who works to support family

breadth [bredth] n extent across,
width; largeness of view, mind

break [brayk] v **broke, bro·ken,
break·ing** ▷ vt part by force;
shatter; burst; destroy; fail to
observe; disclose; interrupt;
surpass; make bankrupt; relax;
mitigate; accustom (horse) to

being ridden; decipher (code) ▷ *vi* become broken, shattered, divided; open, appear; come suddenly; crack, give way; part, fall out; (of voice) change in tone, pitch ▷ *n* fracture; gap; opening; separation; interruption; respite; interval; *inf* opportunity; dawn; *pool* opening shot in a game; *boxing* separation after a clinch **break·a·ble** *adj* **break·age** *n* **break·er** *n* person or device that breaks, for example an electrical circuit; wave beating on rocks or shore **break dance** *n* acrobatic dance style associated with hip-hop ▷ *vi* **break'down** *n* collapse, as nervous breakdown; failure to function effectively; analysis **break·fast** [BREK-fəst] *n* first meal of the day **break'-in** *n* illegal entering of building, esp by thieves **break'neck** *adj* dangerous **break'through** *n* important advance **break'wa·ter** *n* barrier to break force of waves

breast [brest] *n* human chest; milk-secreting gland on chest of human female; seat of the affections; any protuberance ▷ *vt* face, oppose; reach summit of **breast'stroke** *n* stroke in swimming

breath [breth] *n* air used by lungs; life; respiration; slight breeze **breathe** [breeth] *v* **breathed, breath·ing** ▷ *vi* inhale and exhale air from lungs; live; pause, rest ▷ *vt* inhale and exhale; utter softly, whisper **breath'er** [-thər] *n* short rest **breath·less** [BRETH-lis] *adj* **breath'tak·ing** *adj* causing awe or excitement

Breath·a·lyz·er [BRETH-ə-li-zər] *n* ⑧ device that estimates amount of alcohol in breath

bred *pt/pp of* **BREED**

breech *n* buttocks; hinder part of

anything, esp gun **breech'load·er** *n*

breed *v* **bred, breed·ing** ▷ *vt* generate, bring forth, give rise to; rear ▷ *vi* be produced; be with young ▷ *n* offspring produced; race, kind **breeding** *n* producing; manners; ancestry **breeder reactor** *n* nuclear reactor producing more fissionable material than it consumes

breeze [breez] *n* gentle wind **breez'i·ly** *adv* **breez'y** *adj* **breez·i·er, breez·i·est** *adj;* jovial, lively; casual **in a breeze** easily

breth·ren [BRETH-ràn] *obs* pl of **BROTHER**

breve [breev] *n* long musical note

bre·vi·ar·y [BREE-vee-er-ee] *n, pl* **-ar·ies** book of daily prayers, hymns, etc

brev·i·ty [BREV-i-tee] *n* conciseness of expression; short duration

brew [broo] *vt* prepare liquor, as beer from malt, etc; make drink, as tea, by infusion; plot, contrive ▷ *vi* be in preparation ▷ *n* beverage produced by brewing **brew'er** *n* **brew'er·y** *n*

bri·ar¹, bri·er [BRĪ-ər] *n* prickly shrub, esp the wild rose

briar², brier *n* European shrub **briar pipe** pipe made from its root

bribe [brīb] *n* anything offered or given to someone to gain favor, influence ▷ *vt* **bribed, brib·ing** influence by bribe **brib'er·y** *n, pl* **-er·ies**

bric-a-brac [BRIK-ə-brak] *n* miscellaneous small objects, used for ornament

brick [brik] *n* oblong mass of hardened clay used in building; good-hearted person ▷ *vt* build, block, etc with bricks

bride [brīd] *n* woman about to be, or

just, married **brid'al** adj of, relating to, a bride or wedding **bride'groom** n man about to be, or just, married **brides'maid** n

bridge¹ [brij] n structure for crossing river, etc; something joining or supporting other parts; raised narrow platform on ship; upper part of nose; part of violin supporting strings ▷vt **bridged, bridg·ing** make bridge over, span

bridge² n card game

bri·dle [BRĪD-l] n headgear of horse harness; curb ▷v **-dled, -dling** ▷vt put on bridle; restrain ▷vi show resentment **bridle path** path suitable for riding horses

brief [breef] adj **-er, -est** short in duration; concise; scanty ▷n summary of case for judge or lawyer's use; papal letter; instructions ▷pl underpants; panties ▷vt give instructions, information **brief'ly** adv **brief'case** n hand case for carrying papers **briefing book** one prepared to provide (participant) information on meeting, etc

brier SEE BRIAR

brig n two-masted, square-rigged ship; inf ship's jail, guardhouse

bri·gade [bri-GAYD] n subdivision of army; organized band **brig·a·dier gen·er·al** [-ə-DEER] one-star general

brig·an·tine [BRIG-ən-teen] n two-masted vessel, with square-rigged foremast and fore-and-aft mainmast

bright [brīt] adj **-er, -est** shining; full of light; cheerful; clever **bright'en** v

bril·liant [BRIL-yənt] adj shining; sparkling; splendid; very intelligent or clever; distinguished **bril'liance** n

brim n margin, edge, esp of river, cup, hat **brim·ful** adj **brim'less** adj

brim'ming adj to the brim; until it can hold no more

brim·stone [BRIM-stohn] n sulfur

brin·dled [BRIN-dld] adj brownish with streaks of other color **brin'dle** n this color; a brindled animal

brine [brīn] n salt water **brin'y** adj

brin·i·er, brin·i·est very salty ▷n inf the sea

bring vt **brought, bring·ing** fetch; carry with one; cause to come

brink [bringk] n edge of steep place; verge, margin **brink'man·ship** n technique of attempting to gain advantage through maneuvering dangerous situation to limit of tolerance

bri·quette [bri-KET] n block of compressed coal dust

brisk adj **-er, -est** active, vigorous **brisk'ly** adv **brisk'ness** n

bris·ket [BRIS-kit] n cut of meat from breast of animal

bris·tle [BRIS-əl] n short stiff hair ▷vi **-tled, -tling** stand erect; show temper **bris'tly** adj **-tli·er, -tli·est**

brit·tle [BRIT-l] adj easily broken, fragile; curt, irritable **brit'tle·ness** n

broach [brohch] vt pierce (cask); open; begin

broad [brawd] adj **-er, -est** wide, spacious, open; plain, obvious; coarse; general; tolerant; (of pronunciation) dialectal **broad'en** vt **broad'ly** adv **broad'ness** n **broad·cast** vt **-cast** or **-cast·ed, -cast·ing** transmit by radio or television; make widely known; scatter, as seed ▷n radio or TV program **broad'cast·er** n **broad'loom**, n adj (carpet) woven on wide loom **broad·mind·ed** [-MĪN-did] adj tolerant; generous **broad'side** n discharge of all guns on one side; strong (verbal) attack

bro·cade [broh-KAYD] n rich

woven fabric with raised design

broc·co·li [BROK-ə-lee] n type of cabbage

bro·chette [broh-SHET] n small spit; skewer

bro·chure [broh-SHUUR] n pamphlet, booklet

brogue [brohg] n stout shoe; dialect, esp Irish accent

broil vt cook over hot coals; grill ▷ vi be heated

broke see **BREAK** adj inf penniless

bro·ker [BROH-kər] n one employed to buy and sell for others; dealer **bro'ker·age** n business of broker; payment to broker

bro·mide [BROH-mīd] n chemical compound used in medicine and photography; hackneyed, commonplace statement

bro·mid·ic [-MID-ik] adj lacking in originality

bro·mine [BROH-meen] n liquid element used in production of chemicals

bron·chus [BRONG-kəs] n, pl **-chi** [-kee] branch of windpipe **bron'chi·al** adj **bron·chi·tis** [-Kī-tis] n inflammation of bronchi

bron·co [BRONG-koh] n, pl **-cos** Amer half-tamed horse

bron·to·sau·rus [bron-tə-SOR-əs] n very large herbivorous dinosaur

bronze [bronz] n alloy of copper and tin ▷ adj made of, or colored like, bronze ▷ vt **bronzed, bronz·ing** give appearance of bronze to

brooch [brohch] n ornamental pin or fastening

brood n family of young, esp of birds; tribe, race ▷ vi sit, as hen on eggs; meditate, fret over **brood'y** adj **brood·i·er, brood·i·est** moody, sullen

brook[1] [bruuk] n small stream

brook[2] vt put up with, endure, tolerate

broom n brush for sweeping; yellow-flowered shrub **broom'stick** n handle of broom

broth [brawth] n thick soup; stock

broth·el [BROTH-əl] n house of prostitution

broth·er [BRUTH-ər] n son of same parents; one closely united with another **broth'er·hood** [-huud] n relationship; fraternity, company **broth'er·ly** adj **broth'er-in-law** n brother of husband or wife; husband of sister

brought pt/pp of **BRING**

brow n ridge over eyes; forehead; eyebrow; edge of hill **brow'beat** vt **-beat, -beat·en, -beat·ing** bully

brown adj **-er, -est** of dark color inclining to red or yellow ▷ n the color ▷ v make, become brown **browned off** sl angry; fed up

Brown·ie [BROW-nee] n Girl Scout 7 to 10 years old; (**b-**) small, nutted square of chocolate cake **Brownie point** notional mark to one's credit for being seen to do the right thing

browse [browz] vi **browsed, brows·ing** look through (book, articles for sale, etc) in a casual manner; feed on shoots and leaves; computing read hypertext, esp on the Internet **brows'er** n computing software package that enables a user to read hypertext, esp on the Internet

bruise [brooz] vt **bruised, bruis·ing** injure without breaking skin ▷ n contusion, discoloration caused by blow **bruis'er** n inf strong, tough person

brunch n inf breakfast and lunch combined

bru·nette [broo-NET] n person of dark complexion and hair ▷ adj dark brown

brunt *n* shock of attack, chief stress; first blow

brush *n* device with bristles, hairs, wires, etc used for cleaning, painting, etc; act, instance of brushing; brief contact; skirmish; fight; bushy tail; bushy haircut; dense growth of bushes, shrubs, etc; (carbon) device taking electric current from moving to stationary parts of generator, etc ▷ *v* apply, remove, clean, with brush; touch, discuss lightly **brush'off** *n* *inf* dismissal; refusal; snub; rebuff **brush'fire** *n* fire in area of bushes, shrubs, etc **brush'wood** *n* broken-off branches; land covered with scrub

brusque [brusk] *adj* rough in manner, curt, blunt

brute [broot] *n* any animal except man; crude, vicious person ▷ *adj* animal; sensual, stupid; physical **bru'tal** *adj* **bru•tal'i•ty** *n* **bru'tal•ize** vt **-ized, -iz•ing** **brut'ish** *adj* bestial, gross

Btu British thermal unit

bub•ble [BUB-əl] *n* hollow globe of liquid, blown out with air; something insubstantial, not serious; transparent dome ▷ *vi* **-bled, -bling** rise in bubbles; make gurgling sound

bu•bon•ic plague [byoo-BON-ik playg] *n* acute infectious disease characterized by swellings and fever

buc•ca•neer [buk-ə-NEER] *n* pirate; unscrupulous adventurer **buc•ca•neer'ing** *n*

buck [buk] *n* male deer, or other male animal; act of bucking; *sl* dollar ▷ *v* of horse, attempt to throw rider by jumping upward, etc; resist, oppose (something) **buck'shot** *n* lead shot in shotgun shell **buck•teeth** *pl n* projecting upper teeth **pass the buck** shift blame or responsibility to another person

buck•et [BUK-it] *n* vessel, round with arched handle, for water, etc; anything resembling this **buck'et•ful** *n*, *pl* **-fuls** **bucket seat** seat with back shaped to occupier's figure

buck•le [BUK-əl] *n* metal clasp for fastening belt, strap, etc ▷ *v* **-led, -ling** ▷ *vt* fasten with buckle ▷ *vi* warp, bend **buckle down** start work

bu•col•ic [byoo-KOL-ik] *adj* rustic

bud *n* shoot or sprout on plant containing unopened leaf, flower, etc ▷ *v* **bud•ded, bud•ding** ▷ *vi* begin to grow ▷ *vt* to graft

Bud•dhism [BOO-diz-əm] *n* religion founded in India by Buddha **Bud'dhist** *adj*, *n*

bud•dy [BUD-ee] *n* *inf*, *pl* **-dies** pal, chum

budge [buj] *vi* budged, budg•ing move, stir

budg•et [BUJ-it] *n* annual financial statement; plan of systematic spending ▷ *v* prepare financial statement; plan financially

buff¹ *n* light yellow color; bare skin; polishing pad ▷ *vt* polish

buff² *n* *inf* expert on some subject

buf•fa•lo [BUF-ə-loh] *n*, *pl* **-los, -loes** of several species of large oxen

buff•er [BUF-ər] *n* contrivance to lessen shock of concussion; person, country that shields another against annoyance, etc

buf•fet¹ [BUF-it] *n* blow, slap; misfortune ▷ *vt* strike with blows; contend against **buf'fet•ing** *n*

buf•fet² [bə-FAY] *n* refreshment bar; meal at which guests serve themselves; sideboard

buf•foon [bə-FOON] *n* clown; fool **buf•foon'er•y** *n* clowning

bug *n* any small insect; *inf* disease, infection; concealed listening device

▷ vt **bugged, bug·ging** install secret microphone, etc; *inf* annoy

bug·a·boo [BUG-ə-boo] *n, pl* **-boos** something that causes fear or worry

bug·bear [BUG-bair] *n* object of needless terror; nuisance

bug·ger [BUG-ər] *n vulg* sodomite; *inf* worthless person; *inf* lad

bu·gle [BYOO-gəl] *n* instrument like trumpet **bu'gler** *n*

build [bild] *v* **built, build·ing** make, construct, by putting together parts or materials ▷ *n* make, form; physique **build'ing** *n*

bulb *n* modified leaf bud emitting roots from base, eg onion; anything resembling this; globe surrounding filament of electric light ▷ *vi* form bulbs **bul'bous** *adj*

bulge [bulj] *n* swelling, protuberance; temporary increase ▷ *vi* **bulged, bulg·ing** swell out **bulg'i·ness** *n*

bu·li·mi·a [byoo-LEE-mee-ə] *n* disorder characterized by compulsive overeating followed by self-induced vomiting **bu·lim'ic** [byoo-LEE-mik] *adj, n*

bulk *n* size; volume; greater part; cargo ▷ *vi* be of weight or importance **bulk'i·ness** *n* **bulk'y** *adj* **bulk·i·er, bulk·i·est**

bulk·head [BULK-hed] *n* partition in interior of ship

bull[1] [buul] *n* male of cattle; male of various other animals **bull'dog** *n* thickset breed of dog **bull'doze** [-dohz] *v* **-dozed, -doz·ing** **bull'doz·er** *n* powerful tractor with blade for excavating, etc **bull'lock** [-lək] *n* castrated bull **bull's-eye** *n, pl* **-eyes** middle part of target

bull[2] *n* papal edict

bull[3] *n sl* nonsense ▷ *v* talk nonsense (to)

bul·let [BUUL-it] *n* projectile discharged from rifle, pistol, etc

bul·le·tin [BUUL-i-tn] *n* official report

bul·lion [BUUL-yən] *n* gold or silver in mass

bul·ly [BUUL-ee] *n, pl* **-lies** one who hurts, persecutes, or intimidates weaker people ▷ *vt* **-lied, -ly·ing** intimidate, overawe; ill-treat ▷ *adj, interj* first-rate

bul·rush [BUUL-rush] *n* tall reedlike marsh plant with brown velvety spike

bul·wark [BUUL-wərk] *n* rampart; any defense or means of security; raised side of ship; breakwater

bum *n* loafer, scrounger ▷ *v inf* **bummed, bum·ming** get by scrounging ▷ *adj sl* worthless; inferior; disabled

bum·ble [BUM-bəl] *v* **-bled, -bling** perform clumsily **bum'bler** *n*

bum·ble·bee [BUM-bəl-bee] *n* large bee

bump *n* heavy blow, dull in sound; swelling caused by blow; protuberance; sudden movement ▷ *vt* strike or push against **bump'er** *n* horizontal bar at front and rear of automobile to protect against damage; full glass ▷ *adj* full, abundant **bump off** *sl* murder

bump·kin [BUMP-kin] *n* rustic

bump·tious [BUMP-shəs] *adj* offensively self-assertive

bun *n* small, round bread or cake; round knot of hair; *sl* enough liquor to make one drunk

bunch *n* number of things tied or growing together; cluster; tuft, knot; group, party ▷ *vt* put together in bunch ▷ *vi* gather together

bun·dle [BUN-dl] *n* package; number of things tied together; *sl* lot of money ▷ *vt* **-dled, -dling** tie in bundle; send (off) without ceremony

bung n stopper for cask; large cork ▷vt stop up, seal, close **bung'hole** n

bun·ga·low [BUNG-gə-loh] n one-storied house

bun·gle [BUNG-gəl] v **-gled, -gling** ▷vt do badly from lack of skill, botch ▷vi act clumsily, awkwardly ▷n blunder, muddle **bun'gler** n

bun·ion [BUN-yən] n inflamed swelling on foot or toe

bunk[1] [bungk] n narrow, shelflike bed ▷vi stay the night (with) **bunk bed** one of pair of beds constructed one above the other

bunk[2] n bunkum

bun·ker [BUNG-kər] n large storage container for oil, coal, etc; sandy hollow on golf course; (military) underground defensive position

bun·ko [BUNG-koh] n, pl **-kos** swindling scheme or game

bun·kum [BUNG-kəm] n nonsense

bun·ny [BUN-ee] n inf, pl **-nies** rabbit

Bun·sen burner [BUN-sən] gas burner, producing great heat, used for chemical experiments

bunt·ing[1] n material for flags

bunt·ing[2] n bird with short, stout bill

bu·oy [BOO-ee] n floating marker anchored in sea; lifebuoy ▷vt mark with buoy; keep from sinking; support **bu·oy·an·cy** [BOI-ən-see] n **buoy'ant** adj

bur·ble [BUR-bəl] vi **-bled, -bling** gurgle, as stream or baby; talk idly

bur·den [BUR-dn] n load; weight, cargo; anything difficult to bear ▷vt load, encumber **burd'en·some** [-səm] adj

bu·reau [BYUUR-oh] n, pl **-reaus, -reaux** [-rohz] office; government department **bu·reauc·ra·cy** [byuu-ROK-rə-see] n, pl **-cies**

government by officials; body of officials; body **bu·reau·crat** [BYUUR-ə-krat] n

bur·geon [BUR-jən] vi bud; develop rapidly

burg·er [BUR-gər] n hamburger

bur·gess [BUR-jis] n member of colonial Maryland or Virginia legislature

bur·glar [BUR-glər] n one who enters building to commit theft **bur'gla·ry** [-glə-ree] n **bur'gle** [-gəl] vt **-gled, -gling**

Bur·gun·dy [BUR-gən-dee] n, pl **-dies** red or white wine produced in Burgundy, France; (**b-**) similar wine made elsewhere **bur·gun·dy** adj dark-purplish red

bur·lap n coarse canvas

bur·lesque [bər-LESK] n (artistic) caricature; ludicrous imitation; provocative and humorous stage show ▷vt **-lesqued, -lesqu·ing** caricature

bur·ly [BUR-lee] adj **-li·er, -li·est** sturdy, stout, robust

burn v **burned** or **burnt, burn·ing** ▷vt destroy or injure by fire; record data on (a CD) ▷vi be or feel hot; be consumed by fire ▷n injury, mark caused by fire

bur·nish vt make bright by rubbing; polish ▷n gloss, luster

burp v inf belch (esp of baby) ▷n

burr[1] n soft trilling sound given to letter r in some dialects

burr[2] n rough edge left after cutting, drilling, etc

burr[3] n head of plant with prickles or hooks

bur·ro [BUR-oh] n, pl **-ros** small donkey

bur·row [BUR-oh] n hole dug by rabbit, etc ▷vt make holes in ground; bore; conceal oneself

bur·sar [BUR-sər] n official

managing finances of college, monastery, etc

burst v burst, burst•ing ▷ vi fly asunder; break into pieces; rend; break suddenly into some expression of feeling or wish ▷ vt shatter, break violently ▷ n bursting; explosion; outbreak; spurt

bur•y [BER-ee] vt **bur•ied, bur•y•ing** put underground; inter; conceal **bur'i•al** n, adj

bus n large motor vehicle for passengers ▷ vt travel or transport by bus; work as busboy **bus'man's holiday** vacation spent in an activity closely resembling one's work

bus•boy [BUS-boi] n waiter's helper in public dining room

bush [buush] n shrub; woodland, thicket; uncleared country, backwoods, interior **bushed** adj inf tired out **bush'y** adj **bush•i•er, bush•i•est** shaggy **bush jacket** shirtlike jacket with patch pockets

bush•el [BUUSH-əl] n dry measure of eight gallons

busi•ness [BIZ-nis] n profession, occupation; commercial or industrial establishment; commerce, trade; responsibility, affair, matter; work **business** style of casual clothing worn by businesspeople at work

bust¹ n sculpture of head and shoulders of human body; woman's breasts

bust² v inf burst; make, become bankrupt ▷ vt sl raid; arrest ▷ adj inf broken; bankrupt ▷ n sl police raid or arrest; inf punch

bus•tle¹ [BUS-əl] vi **-tled, -tling** be noisily busy, active ▷ n fuss, commotion

bustle² n history pad worn by ladies to support back of the skirt

bus•y [BIZ-ee] adj **bus•i•er,**

bus•i•est actively employed; full of activity ▷ vt **bus•ied, bus•y•ing** occupy **bus'y•bod•y** n, pl **-bod•ies** meddler

but prep, conj without; except; only; yet; still; besides

bu•tane [BYOO-tayn] n gas used for fuel

butch [buuch] adj, n sl markedly or aggressively masculine (person)

butch•er [BUUCH-ər] n one who kills, dresses animals for food, or sells meat; bloody, savage man ▷ vt slaughter, murder; spoil work **butch'er•y** n

but•ler [BUT-lər] n chief male servant

butt¹ n the thick end; target; object of ridicule; bottom or unused end of anything ▷ v lie, be placed end on to

butt² v strike with head; push ▷ n blow with head, as of sheep **butt in** interfere, meddle **butt•in'sky** n, pl **-skies** sl meddler

but•ter [BUT-ər] n fatty substance got from cream by churning ▷ vt spread with or as if with butter; flatter

but•ter•fly [BUT-ər-flī] n, pl **-flies** insect with large wings; inconstant person; stroke in swimming ▷ vt **-flied, -fly•ing** split (foodstuff) into shape resembling butterfly

but•ter•milk [BUT-ər-milk] n milk that remains after churning

but•tock [BUT-ək] n (usu pl) rump, protruding hinder part

but•ton [BUT-n] n knob, stud for fastening dress; knob that operates doorbell, machine, etc ▷ vt fasten with buttons **but'ton•hole** n slit in garment to pass button through as fastening ▷ vt **-holed, -hol•ing** detain (unwilling) person in conversation

but•tress [BU-tris] n structure to

support wall; prop ▷ *vt*

bux•om [BUK-səm] *adj* full of health, plump, gay; large-breasted

buy [bī] *vt* **bought, buy•ing** get by payment, purchase; bribe **buy'er** *n*

buzz *vi* make humming sound ▷ *n* humming sound of bees; *inf* telephone call **buzz'er** *n* any apparatus that makes buzzing sound **buzz word** *inf* word, oft orig jargon, that becomes fashionable

buz•zard [BUZ-ərd] *n* bird of prey of hawk family

by [bī] *prep* near; along; across; past; during; not later than; through use or agency of; in units of ▷ *adv* near; away, aside; past **by and by** soon, in the future **by and large** on the whole; speaking generally **come by** obtain

bye [bī] *n sport* in early round of a tournament, a situation in which player, team not paired with opponent advances to next round without playing

by•gone [Bī-gawn] *adj* past, former ▷ *n* (oft pl) past occurrence

by•law [Bī-law] *n* law, regulation made by an organization

by•line [Bī-līn] *n* printed line identifying author of news story, article, etc

by•pass [Bī-pas] *n* road for diversion of traffic from crowded centers; secondary channel carrying fluid around a part and back to the main stream ▷ *vt*

by•play [Bī-play] *n* diversion, action apart from main action of play

byte [bīt] *n computing* sequence of bits processed as single unit of information

by•word [Bī-wurd] *n* a well-known name, saying

C

C *chemistry* Carbon; Celsius

Ca *chemistry* calcium

cab *n* taxi; driver's enclosed compartment on locomotive, truck, etc **cab'driv·er** *n* **cab'stand** *n* place where taxis may wait to be hired

ca·bal [kə-BAL] *n* small group of intriguers; secret plot

cab·a·ret [kab-ə-RAY] *n* night club

cab·bage [KAB-ij] *n* green vegetable with usu round head of leaves

ca·ber [KAY-bər] *n* pole tossed as trial of strength at Scottish games

cab·in [KAB-in] *n* hut, shed; small room esp in ship **cabin cruiser** power boat with cabin, bunks, etc

cab·i·net [KAB-ə-nit] *n* piece of furniture with drawers or shelves; outer case of television, radio, etc; body of advisers to head of state **cab'i·net·mak·er** *n* artisan who makes fine furniture

ca·ble [KAY-bəl] *n* strong rope; wire or bundle of wires conveying electric power, telegraph signals, etc; message sent by this; cable TV ▷ *v* **-bled, -bling** telegraph by cable **ca'ble·gram** *n* cabled message **cable TV** TV service conveyed by cable to subscribers

ca·boo·dle [kə-BOOD-l] *n inf* **the whole caboodle** the whole lot

ca·boose [kə-BOOS] *n* (usu last) car of freight train, for use by train crew

ca·ca·o [kə-KAH-oh] *n* tropical tree from the seeds of which chocolate and cocoa are made

cache [kash] *n* secret hiding place; store of food, arms, etc

ca·chet [ka-SHAY] *n* mark, stamp; mark of authenticity; prestige, distinction

cack·le [KAK-əl] *vi* **-led, -ling** make chattering noise, as hen ▷ *n* cackling noise or laughter; empty chatter

ca·coph·o·ny [kə-KOF-ə-nee] *n*, *pl* **-nies** disagreeable sound; discord of sounds **ca·coph·o·nous** *adj*

cac·tus [KAK-təs] *n*, *pl* **-ti** [-tī] spiny succulent plant

cad *n* dishonorable, ungentlemanly person

ca·dav·er [kə-DAV-ər] *n* corpse **ca·dav'er·ous** *adj* corpselike; sickly-looking; gaunt

cad·die [KAD-ee] *n* person hired to carry golfer's clubs, find the ball, etc

ca·dence [KAYD-ns] *n* fall or modulation of voice in music, speech, or verse

ca·den·za [kə-DEN-zə] *n* *music* elaborate passage for solo instrument or singer

ca·det [kə-DET] *n* youth in training, esp for officer status in armed forces

cadge [kaj] *v* **cadged, cadg·ing** get (food, money, etc) by begging **cadg'er** *n* sponger

cad·mi·um [KAD-mee-əm] *n* metallic element

ca·dre [KAD-ree] *n* nucleus or framework, esp skeleton of military unit

Cae·sar·e·an section [si-ZAIR-ee-ən] *n* surgical incision through abdominal wall to deliver a baby

café [ka-FAY] *n* small or inexpensive restaurant serving light refreshments; bar **caf·e·te·ri·a** [kaf-ə-TEE-ree-ə] *n* restaurant designed for self-service

caf·feine [ka-FEEN] *n* stimulating alkaloid found in tea and coffee plants

caf·tan [KAF-tan] *n* long coatlike Eastern garment; imitation of it, esp as woman's long, loose dress with sleeves

cage [kayj] *n* enclosure, box with bars or wires, esp for keeping animals or birds; place of confinement; enclosed platform of elevator, esp in mine ▷ *vt* **caged, cag·ing** put in cage, confine **cag'ey** *adj* **cag·i·er, cag·i·est** wary, shrewd

ca·hoots [kə-HOOTS] *pl n sl* partnership, as **in cahoots with**

cairn [kairn] *n* heap of stones, esp as monument or landmark

cais·son [KAY-son] *n* chamber for working under water; apparatus for lifting vessel out of the water; ammunition wagon **caisson disease** the bends

ca·jole [kə-JOHL] *vt* **-joled, -jol·ing** persuade by flattery, wheedle **ca·jol'er** *n*

cake [kayk] *n* baked, sweetened, bread-like food; compact mass ▷ *v* **caked, cak·ing** make into a cake; harden (as of mud)

cal·a·boose [KAL-ə-boos] *n inf* jail

cal·a·mine [KAL-ə-mīn] *n* pink powder used medicinally in soothing ointment

ca·lam·i·ty [kə-LAM-i-tee] *n*, *pl* **-ties** great misfortune; deep distress, disaster **ca·lam'i·tous** *adj*

cal·ci·um [KAL-see-əm] *n* metallic element, the basis of lime **cal·car·e·ous** [-KAIR-ee-əs] *adj* containing lime **cal'ci·fy** *v* **-fied, -fy·ing** convert, be converted, to lime

cal·cu·late [KAL-kyə-layt] *v* **-lat·ed, -lat·ing** ▷ *vt* estimate; compute ▷ *vi* make reckonings **cal'cu·lat·ing** *adj* able to perform calculations; shrewd, designing, scheming **cal'cu·la·tor** *n* electronic or mechanical device for making calculations **cal'cu·lus** *n*, *pl* **-li** [-lī] branch of mathematics; stone in body

cal·en·dar [KAL-ən-dər] *n* table of months and days in the year; list of events, documents; register

calf [kaf] *n*, *pl* **calves** [kavz] young of cow and other animals; leather made of calf's skin **calve** [kav] *vi* **calved, calv·ing** birth to calf

calf[2] *n*, *pl* **calves** fleshy back part of leg below knee

cal·i·ber [KAL-ə-bər] *n* size of bore of gun; capacity, character **cal'i·brate** [-brayt] *vt* **-brat·ed, -brat·ing** mark scale of measuring instrument, etc **cal·i·bra'tion** *n*

cal·i·co [KAL-i-koh] *n*, *pl* **-coes, -cos** printed cotton fabric

cal·i·per [KAL-ə-pər] *n* instrument for measuring diameters; thickness, esp of tree, paper

cal·is·then·ics [kal-əs-THEN-iks] *pl n* light gymnastic exercises

call [kawl] *vt* speak loudly to attract attention; summon; (often with *up*) telephone; name ▷ *vi* shout; pay visit ▷ *n* shout; animal's cry; visit; inner urge, summons, as to be minister, etc; need, demand **call'ing** *n* vocation, profession **call box** outdoor telephone for calling police or fire department

call girl prostitute who accepts appointments by telephone **call up** summon to reserve in army; imagine

cal·lig·ra·phy [kə-LIG-rə-fee] n handwriting, penmanship **cal·li·graph·ic** adj

cal·lous [KAL-əs] adj hardened, unfeeling **cal'lous·ness** n

cal·low [KAL-oh] adj inexperienced; immature

cal·lus [KAL-əs] n, pl **-lus·es** area of thick, hardened skin

calm [kahm] adj **-er, -est** still, quiet, tranquil ▷ n stillness; tranquility; absence of wind ▷ v become, make, still or quiet **calm'ly** adv

cal·o·rie [KAL-ə-ree] n unit of heat; unit of energy obtained from foods **cal·o·rif'ic** adj heat-making **cal·o·rim'e·ter** n

cal·u·met [KAL-yə-met] n tobacco pipe of N Amer Indians; peace pipe

cal·um·ny [KAL-əm-nee] n, pl **-nies** slander, false accusation **ca·lum'ni·ate** vt **-at·ed, -at·ing** **ca·lum·ni·a'tion** n

ca·lyp·so [kə-LIP-soh] n, pl **-sos** (West Indies) improvised song on topical subject

ca·lyx [KAY-liks] n, pl **-lyx·es** covering of bud

cam [kam] n device to change rotary to reciprocating motion **cam'shaft** n in motor vehicles, rotating shaft to which cams are fixed to lift valves

ca·ma·ra·de·rie [kah-mə-RAH-də-ree] n spirit of comradeship, trust

cam·ber [KAM-bər] n convexity on upper surface of road, bridge, etc; curvature of aircraft wing; setting of motor vehicle wheels closer together at bottom than at top

cam·bric [KAYM-brik] n fine white linen or cotton cloth

cam·cord·er [KAM-kor-dər] n combined portable video camera and recorder

came pt of COME

cam·el [KAM-əl] n animal of Asia and Africa, with humped back, used as beast of burden

cam·e·o [KAM-ee-oh] n, pl **-e·os** medallion, brooch, etc with profile head or design carved in relief; single brief scene or appearance in film, etc by well-known performer

cam·er·a [KAM-ər-ə] n apparatus used to make photographs **cam'er·a·man** n photographer, esp for TV or film **camera ob·scu·ra** [ob-SKYUUR-ə] darkened chamber in which views of external objects are shown on sheet by means of lenses **camera phone** cell phone that includes a camera **in camera** (of legal proceedings, etc) conducted in private

cam·i·sole [KAM-ə-sohl] n woman's short sleeveless undergarment

cam·ou·flage [KAM-ə-flahzh] n disguise, means of deceiving enemy observation, eg paint, screen ▷ vt **-flaged, -flag·ing** disguise

camp [kamp] n (place for) tents of hikers, army, etc; cabins, etc for temporary accommodation; group supporting political party, etc ▷ adj inf consciously artificial ▷ vi form or lodge in a camp

cam·paign [kam-PAYN] n series of coordinated activities for some purpose, eg political or military campaign ▷ vi serve in campaign **cam·paign'er** n

cam·pa·nol·o·gy [kam-pə-NOL-ə-jee] n art of ringing bells musically

cam·phor [KAM-fər] n solid

essential oil with aromatic taste and smell **cam'phor·at·ed** *adj*

cam·pus [KAM-pəs] *n, pl* **-pus·es** grounds of college or university

can¹ [kan] *vi* **could** *pt* be able; have the power; be allowed

can² *n* container, usu metal, for liquids, foods ▷ *v* **canned, can·ning** put in can; prepare (food) for canning **canned** *adj* preserved in jar or can; (of music, TV or radio programs, etc) previously recorded **can·ner·y** *n, pl* **-ner·ies** factory where food is canned

Can·a·da Day [KAN-ə-də] July 1st, anniversary of establishment of Confederation in 1867

Canada goose large grayish-brown N Amer goose

Ca·na·di·an [kə-NAY-dee-ən] *n, adj* (native) of Canada

ca·nal [kə-NAL] *n* artificial watercourse; duct in body

can·al·ize [KAN-l-īz] *vt* **-ized, -iz·ing** convert into canal; direct (thoughts, energies, etc) into one channel

can·a·pé [KAN-ə-pay] *n* small piece of toast, etc with cheese, etc topping

ca·nar·y [kə-NAIR-ee] *n, pl* **-nar·ies** yellow singing bird

ca·nas·ta [kə-NAS-tə] *n* card game played with two packs

can·can [KAN-kan] *n* high-kicking (orig French music-hall) dance

can·cel [KAN-səl] *vt* **-celed, -cel·ing** cross out; annul; invalidate; call off later **can·cel·la·tion** *n*

can·cer [KAN-sər] *n* malignant growth or tumor **can'cer·ous** *adj*

can·de·la [kan-DEE-lə] *n* basic unit of luminous intensity

can·did [KAN-did] *adj* frank, open, impartial **can'did·ly** *adv* **can'dor** [-dər] *n* frankness

can·di·date [KAN-di-dayt] *n* one who seeks office, employment, etc; person taking examination or test **can'di·da·cy** [-də-see] *n, pl* **-cies**

can·dle [KAN-dl] *n* stick of wax with wick; light **can·de·la'brum** [-AH-brəm], *pl* **-bra** [-brə] *n* large, branched candle holder **can'dle·pow·er** *n* unit for measuring light **can't hold a candle to** compare unfavorably with

can·dy [KAN-dee] *n, pl* **-dies** crystallized sugar; confectionery in general ▷ *v* **-died, -dy·ing** preserve with sugar; become encrusted with sugar

cane [kayn] *n* stem of small palm or large grass; walking stick ▷ *vt* **caned, can·ing** beat with cane

ca·nine [KAY-nīn] *adj* like, pert to, dog **canine tooth** one of four sharp, pointed teeth, two in each jaw

can·is·ter [KAN-ə-stər] *n* container, oft of metal, for storing dry food

can·ker [KANG-kər] *n* spreading sore; thing that eats away, destroys, corrupts **canker sore** painful ulcer esp in mouth

can·na·bis [KAN-ə-bis] *n* hemp plant; drug derived from this; marijuana; hashish

can·nel·lo·ni [kan-l-OH-nee] *n* tubular pieces of pasta filled with meat, etc

can·ni·bal [KAN-ə-bəl] *n* one who eats human flesh ▷ *adj* relating to this practice **can'ni·bal·ism** *n* **can'ni·bal·ize** *vt* **-ized, -iz·ing** use parts from one machine, etc to repair another

can·non [KAN-ən] *n, pl* **-nons** or **-non** large gun **can'non·ball** *n*

can·not [KAN-ot] negative form of CAN¹

can·ny [KAN-ee] *adj* **-ni·er,**

-ni•est shrewd; cautious; crafty **can'ni•ly** adv

ca•noe [kà-NOO] n, pl **-noes** very light boat propelled with paddle or paddles **ca•noe'ist** n

can•on¹ [KAN-ən] n law or rule, esp of church; standard; body of books accepted as genuine; list of saints **can•on•i•za'tion** n **can'on•ize** vt **-ized, -iz•ing** enroll in list of saints

canon² n church dignitary, member of cathedral or collegiate chapter or staff **ca•non'i•cal** adj **ca•non'i•cals** pl n canonical vestments

can•o•py [KAN-à-pee] n, pl **-pies** covering over throne, bed, etc; any overhanging shelter ▷ vt **-pied, -py•ing** cover with canopy

cant¹ [kant] n hypocritical speech; whining; language of a sect; technical jargon; slang; argot of thieves

cant² v **cant•ed, cant•ing** tilt, slope; bevel

can•ta•loupe [KAN-tà-lohp] n variety of muskmelon

can•tan•ker•ous [kan-TANG-kàr-às] adj ill-natured, quarrelsome

can•ta•ta [kàn-TAH-tà] n choral work like, but shorter than, oratorio

can•teen [kan-TEEN] n flask for carrying water; place in factory, school, etc where light meals are provided; post exchange

can•ter [KAN-tàr] n easy gallop ▷ v move at, make to canter

can•ti•le•ver n beam, girder, etc fixed at one end only ▷ vi project like a cantilever ▷ vt build to project in this manner

can•to [KAN-toh] n, pl **-tos** division of a poem

can•ton [KAN-tn] n division of country, esp Swiss federal state

can•ton•ment [kan-TON-mànt] n quarters for troops

can•tor [KAN-tàr] n chief singer of liturgy in synagogue

can•vas [KAN-vàs] n coarse cloth used for sails, painting on, etc; sails of ship; picture

can•vass [KAN-vàs] vt solicit votes, contributions, etc; discuss, examine ▷ n solicitation

can•yon [KAN-yàn] n deep gorge

cap [kap] n covering for head; lid, top, or other covering ▷ vt **capped, cap•ping** put a limit on; outdo; excel (a well)

ca•pa•ble [KAY-pà-bàl] adj able, gifted; competent; having the capacity, power **ca•pa•bil'i•ty** n

ca•pac•i•ty [kà-PAS-i-tee] n, pl **-ties** power of holding or grasping; room; volume; character; ability, power of mind **ca•pa'cious** [-PAY-shàs] adj roomy **ca•pac'i•tance** n (measure of) ability of system to store electric charge **ca•pac'i•tor** n

cape¹ [kayp] n covering for shoulders

cape² n point of land running into sea, headland **Cape Cod** common type of cottage in Mass. and elsewhere in Northeast

ca•per¹ [KAY-pàr] n skip; frolic; escapade ▷ vi skip, dance

caper² n pickled flower bud of Sicilian shrub

cap•il•lar•y [KAP-à-ler-ee] adj hairlike ▷ n, pl **-lar•ies** tube with very small bore, esp small blood vessel

cap•i•tal [KAP-i-tl] n chief town; money, stock, funds; large-sized letter; headpiece of column ▷ adj involving or punishable by death; serious; chief; leading; excellent **cap'i•tal•ism** n economic system based on private ownership of industry **cap'i•tal•ist** n owner of capital; supporter of capitalism ▷ adj run by, possessing, capital, as capitalist state **cap•i•tal•ize** v **-ized, -iz•ing** convert into capital; (with on) turn to advantage

Cap•i•tol [KAP-i-tl] n building in which US Congress meets; **(c-)** a state legislature building

ca•pit•u•late [kə-PICH-ə-layt] vi **-lat•ed, -lat•ing** surrender on terms, give in **ca•pit•u•la•tion** n

ca•pon [KAY-pon] n castrated male fowl fattened for eating **ca•pon•ize** vt **-ized, -iz•ing**

cap•puc•ci•no [kap-ə-CHEE-noh] n espresso coffee with steamed milk

ca•price [kə-PREES] n whim, freak **ca•pri•cious** [-PRISH-əs] adj

cap•size [KAP-siz] v **-sized, -siz•ing** ▷ vt (of boat) upset ▷ vi be overturned

cap•stan [KAP-stən] n machine to wind cable, esp to hoist anchor

cap•sule [KAP-səl] n gelatin case for dose of medicine or drug; any small enclosed area or container; seed vessel of plant **cap•sul•ize** vt **-ized, -iz•ing** enclose in a capsule; put (news or information) in concise form

cap•tain [KAP-tən] n commander of ship or company of soldiers; leader, chief ▷ vt be captain of

cap•tion [KAP-shən] n heading, title of article, picture, etc

cap•tious [KAP-shəs] adj ready to find fault; critical; peevish **cap•tious•ness** n

cap•tive [KAP-tiv] n prisoner ▷ adj taken, imprisoned **cap•ti•vate** vt **-vat•ed, -vat•ing** fascinate **cap•ti•vat•ing** adj delightful **cap•tiv•i•ty** n

cap•ture [KAP-chər] vt **-tured, -tur•ing** seize, make prisoner ▷ n seizure, taking **cap•tor** n

car [kahr] n automobile; passenger compartment, as in cable car; vehicle

running on rails **car park** area, building where vehicles may be left for a time

ca•rafe [kə-RAF] n glass water bottle for the table, decanter

car•a•mel [KAR-ə-məl] n burned sugar or syrup for cooking; type of confectionery **car•a•mel•ize** v **-ized, -iz•ing** change (sugar, etc) into caramel; become caramel

car•at [KAR-ət] n small weight used for gold, diamonds, etc; proportional measure of twenty-fourths used to state fineness of gold

car•a•van [KAR-ə-van] n company of merchants traveling together for safety in the East

car•a•way [KAR-ə-way] n plant whose seeds are used as a spice in bread, etc

carb [kahrb] n short for **CARBOHYDRATE**

car•bide [KAHR-bid] n compound of carbon with an element, esp calcium carbide

car•bine [KAHR-been] n light rifle

car•bo•hy•drate [kahr-boh-Hi-drayt] n any of large group of compounds containing carbon, hydrogen and oxygen, esp sugars and starches as constituents of food

car•bol•ic ac•id [kahr-BOL-ik] n disinfectant derived from coal tar

car•bon [KAHR-bən] n nonmetallic element, substance of pure charcoal, found in all organic matter **car'bon•ate** n salt of carbonic acid **car•bon'ic** adj **car'bon•ize** vt **-ized, -iz•ing** **car•bon'ic ac•id** carbon dioxide; compound formed by carbon dioxide and water **carbon dioxide** colorless gas exhaled in respiration of animals **carbon paper** paper coated with a dark, waxy pigment, used for duplicating written or typed matter, producing **carbon copy**

car·bo·run·dum [kahr-bə-RUN-dəm] n artificial silicate of carbon

car·bun·cle [KAHR-bung-kəl] n inflamed ulcer, boil or tumor

car·bu·re·tor [KAHR-bə-ray-tər] n device for vaporizing and mixing gasoline with air in internal combustion engine

car·cass [KAHR-kəs] n dead animal body; orig skeleton

car·cin·o·gen [kahr-SIN-ə-jən] n substance producing cancer

car·ci·no·ma [kahr-sə-NOH-mə] n, pl -mas a cancer

card¹ [kahrd] n thick, stiff paper; piece of this giving identification, etc; greeting card; one of the 48 or 52 playing cards making up a pack; inf a character, eccentric ▷ pl n any card game **card'board** n thin, stiff board made of paper pulp **card'hold·er** n person who owns a credit or debit card

card² n instrument for combing wool, etc ▷ vt comb

car·di·ac [KAHR-dee-ak] adj pert to the heart ▷ n person with heart disease **car'di·o·graph** [-ə-graf] n instrument that records movements of the heart **car'di·o·gram** n graph of such

car·di·gan [KAHR-di-gən] n knitted sweater opening in front

car·di·nal [KAHR-dn-l] adj chief, principal ▷ n highest rank, next to the Pope in Cath church; N Amer finch, male of which is bright red in summer **cardinal numbers** 1, 2, 3, etc **cardinal points** N, S, E, W

care [kair] vi cared, car·ing be anxious; have regard or liking (for); look after; be disposed to ▷ n attention; pains, heed; charge, protection; anxiety; caution **care'free** adj **care'ful** adj **care'less** adj **care'tak·er** n person in charge

of premises ▷ adj temporary, interim

ca·reen [kə-REEN] vt cause ship to list; lay ship over on its side for cleaning and repair ▷ vi keel over; sway dangerously

ca·reer [kə-REER] n course through life; profession; rapid motion ▷ vi run or move at full speed

ca·ress [kə-RES] vt fondle, embrace, treat with affection ▷ n act or expression of affection

car·et [KAR-it] n mark (∧) showing where to insert something omitted

car·go [KAHR-goh] n, pl -goes load, freight, carried by ship, plane, etc

car·i·bou [KAR-ə-boo] n N Amer reindeer

car·i·ca·ture [KAR-i-kə-chər] n likeness exaggerated or distorted to appear ridiculous ▷ vt -tured, -tur·ing portray in this way **car'i·ca·tur·ist** n

car·ies [KAIR-eez] n tooth decay

car·il·lon [KAR-ə-lon] n set of bells usu hung in tower and played by set of keys, pedals, etc; tune so played

car·min·a·tive [kahr-MIN-ə-tiv] n medicine to remedy flatulence ▷ adj acting as this

car·mine [KAHR-min] n brilliant red color (prepared from cochineal) ▷ adj of this color

car·nage [KAHR-nij] n slaughter

car·nal [KAHR-nl] adj fleshly, sensual; worldly

car·na·tion [kahr-NAY-shən] n cultivated flower; flesh color

car·ni·val [KAHR-nə-vəl] n festive occasion; traveling fair; show or display for amusement

car·niv·o·rous [kahr-NIV-ər-əs] adj flesh-eating **car'ni·vore** [-nə-vor] n

car·ob [KAR-əb] n Mediterranean tree with edible pods

car·ol [KAR-əl] *n* song or hymn of joy or praise (esp Christmas carol) ▷ *vi* **-oled, -ol·ing** sing (carols)

car·om [KAR-əm] *n* billiard stroke, hitting both object balls with one's own ▷ *vi* make this stroke; rebound, collide

ca·rouse [kə-ROWZ] *vi* **-roused, -rous·ing** have merry drinking spree ▷ *n* **ca·rous·er** *n*

car·ou·sel [kar-ə-SEL] *n* merry-go-round

carp[1] [kahrp] *n* freshwater fish

carp[2] *vi* complain about small faults or errors **carp'ing** *adj*

car·pen·ter [KAHR-pən-tər] *n* worker in timber as in building, etc **car'pen·try** [-tree] *n* this art

car·pet [KAHR-pit] *n* heavy fabric for covering floor ▷ *vt* cover floor **car'pet·bag** *n* traveling bag **car'pet·bag·ger** *n* political adventurer **on the carpet** called up for censure

car·riage [KA-rij] *n* bearing, conduct; horse-drawn vehicle; act, cost, of carrying

car·ri·on [KA-ree-ən] *n* rotting dead flesh

car·rot [KA-rət] *n* plant with orange-red edible root; inducement **car'rot-top** *n* person with red hair

car·ry [KA-ree] *v* **-ried, -ry·ing** ▷ *vt* convey, transport; capture; win; effect; behave ▷ *vi* (of projectile, sound) reach ▷ *n* range **car'ri·er** *n* one that carries goods; immune person who communicates a disease to others; aircraft carrier; kind of pigeon **carry on** continue; *inf* fuss unnecessarily

cart [kahrt] *n* open (two-wheeled) vehicle, esp pulled by horse ▷ *vt* convey in cart; carry with effort **cart'er** *n* **cart'horse** *n* **cart'wheel** *n* large, spoked wheel; sideways somersault **cart'wright** *n* maker of carts

carte blanche [kahrt blanch] *n*, *pl* **cartes blanches** [kahrts blanch] complete discretion or authority

car·tel [kahr-TEL] *n* commercial combination for the purpose of fixing prices, output, etc; alliance of political parties, etc to further common aims

Car·te·sian [kahr-TEE-zhən] *adj* pert to the French philosopher René Descartes (1596–1650) or his system of coordinates ▷ *n* an adherent of his philosophy

car·ti·lage [KAHR-tl-ij] *n* firm elastic tissue in the body; gristle **car·ti·lag'i·nous** *adj*

car·tog·ra·phy [kahr-TOG-rə-fee] *n* map making **car·tog'ra·pher** *n*

car·ton [KAHR-tn] *n* cardboard or plastic container

car·toon [kahr-TOON] *n* drawing, esp humorous or satirical; sequence of drawings telling story; animated cartoon

car·tridge [KAHR-trij] *n* case containing charge for gun; container for film, magnetic tape, etc; unit in head of phonograph pickup

carve [kahrv] *vt* **carved, carv·ing** cut; hew; sculpture; engrave; cut in pieces or slices (meat) **carv'er** *n*

car·y·at·id [kar-ee-AT-id] *n* supporting column in shape of female figure

cas·cade [kas-KAYD] *n* waterfall; anything resembling this ▷ *vi* **-cad·ed, -cad·ing** fall in cascades

case[1] [kays] *n* instance; event, circumstance; question at issue; state of affairs, condition; arguments supporting particular action, etc; *medicine* patient under treatment; law suit; grounds for suit; grammatical relation of words in sentence

case² n box, sheath, covering; receptacle; box and contents ▷vt **cased, cas·ing** put in a case **case'hard·en** vt harden by carbonizing the surface of (esp iron) by converting into steel; make hard, callous

case·ment [KAYS-mənt] n window opening on hinges

cash [kash] n money, bills and coin ▷vt turn into or exchange for money **cash·ier** [ka-SHEER] n one in charge of receiving and paying of money **cash dispenser** computerized device outside a bank for supplying cash **cash register** till that records amount of money put in

cash·ier [ka-SHEER] vt dismiss from office or service

cash·mere [KAZH-meer] n fine soft fabric; yarn made from goat's wool

ca·si·no [kə-SEE-noh] n, pl **-nos** building, institution for gambling; type of card game

cask [kask] n barrel; container for wine

cas·ket [KAS-kit] n small case for jewels, etc; coffin

Cas·san·dra [kə-SAN-drə] n prophet of misfortune or disaster

cas·se·role [KAS-ə-rohl] n fireproof cooking and serving dish; food cooked in this

cas·sette [kə-SET] n plastic container for film, magnetic tape, etc

cas·sock [KAS-ək] n long tunic worn by clergymen

cast [kast] v throw or fling; shed; throw down; deposit (a vote); allot, as parts in play; mold, as metal ▷n throw; distance thrown; squint; mold; that which is shed or ejected; set of actors; type or quality **cast'ing** n **cast'a·way** n shipwrecked

person **cast-iron** adj made of a hard but brittle type of iron; definite, unchallengeable

cas·ta·nets [kas-tə-NETS] pl n (in Spanish dancing) two small curved pieces of wood, etc clicked together in hand

caste [kast] n section of society in India; social rank

cast·er [KAS-tər] n container for salt, etc with perforated top; small swiveled wheel on table leg, etc

cas·ti·gate [KAS-ti-gayt] vt **-gat·ed, -gat·ing** punish, rebuke severely, correct; chastise **cas'ti·ga·tor** n

cas·tle [KAS-əl] n fortress; mansion; chess piece **castle in the air** pipe dream

cas·tor oil [KAS-tər] vegetable medicinal oil

cas·trate [KAS-trayt] vt **-trat·ed, -trat·ing** remove testicles, deprive of power of generation; deprive of vigor **cas·tra'tion** n

cas·tra·to [ka-STRAH-toh] n, pl **-ti** [-tee] singer castrated in boyhood to preserve soprano or alto voice

cas·u·al [KAZH-oo-əl] adj accidental; unforeseen; occasional; unconcerned; informal **cas'u·al·ty** n, pl **-ties** person killed or injured in accident, war, etc; thing lost, destroyed, in accident, etc

cas·u·ist [KAZH-oo-ist] n one who studies and solves moral problems; quibbler **cas'u·ist·ry** n

cat [kat] n any of various feline animals, including, eg small domesticated furred animal, and lions, tigers, etc **cat'ty** adj **-ti·er, -ti·est** spiteful **cat'call** n derisive cry **cat'fish** n mainly freshwater fish with catlike whiskers **cat'kin** n drooping flower spike **cat'nap** vi, n doze **cat's-eye** n, pl **-eyes**

glass reflector set in road to reflect beams from automobile headlights

cat'walk n narrow, raised path or plank

ca·tab·o·lism [kə-TAB-ə-liz-əm] n breaking down of complex molecules, destructive metabolism

cat·a·clysm [KAT-ə-kliz-əm] n (disastrous) upheaval; deluge **cat·a·clys'mic** adj

cat·a·comb [KAT-ə-kohm] n underground gallery for burial ▷pl series of underground tunnels and caves

cat·a·lep·sy [KAT-l-ep-see] n condition of unconsciousness with rigidity of muscles **cat·a·lep'tic** adj

cat·a·log [KAT-l-awg] n descriptive list ▷vt make such list of; enter in catalog

cat·a·lyst [KAT-l-ist] n substance causing or assisting a chemical reaction without taking part in it; person or thing that precipitates event or change **cat'a·lyze** [-līz] vt -lyzed, -lyz·ing **ca·tal'y·sis** n **cat·a·lyt'ic** adj **catalytic converter** type of antipollution device for automotive exhaust system

cat·a·ma·ran [kat-ə-mə-RAN] n type of sailing boat with twin hulls; raft of logs

cat·a·pult [KAT-ə-pult] n small forked stick with elastic sling used for throwing stones; history engine of war for hurling arrows, stones, etc; launching device ▷vt

cat·a·ract [KAT-ə-rakt] n waterfall; downpour; disease of eye

ca·tas·tro·phe [kə-TAS-trə-fee] n great disaster, calamity; culmination of a tragedy **cat·a·stroph'ic** adj

catch [kach] v caught, catch·ing ▷vt take hold of, seize, understand; hear; contract (disease); be in time for; surprise, detect ▷vi be contagious; get entangled; begin to burn ▷n seizure; thing that holds, stops, etc; what is caught; inf snag, disadvantage; form of musical composition; thing, person worth catching, esp as spouse

catch'er catching adj **catch'y** adj **catch·i·er, catch·i·est** pleasant, memorable; tricky **catch'word** n popular phrase or idea **catch 22** inescapable dilemma **catch'ment area** drainage basin, area in which rainfall collects to form the supply of river, etc; area from which water is allocated to a particular social service agency, hospital, etc **catch-as-catch-can** adj using any method that can be applied

cat·e·chize [KAT-i-kīz] vt -chized, -chiz·ing instruct by question and answer; question **cat'e·chism** n such instruction **cat'e·chist** n

cat·e·go·ry [KAT-i-gohr-ee] n, pl -ries class, order, division **cat·e·gor'i·cal** adj positive; of category **cat·e·gor'i·cal·ly** adv **cat'e·go·rize** vt -ized, -iz·ing

ca·ter [KAY-tər] v provide what is required or desired, esp food, etc **ca'ter·er** n

cat·er·pil·lar [KAT-ə-pil-ər] n hairy grub of moth or butterfly

cat·er·waul [KAT-ər-wawl] vi wail, howl; argue noisily

ca·the·dral [kə-THEE-drəl] n principal church of diocese ▷adj pert to, containing cathedral

cath·ode [KATH-ohd] n negative electrode **cathode rays** stream of electrons

cath·o·lic [KATH-lik] adj universal; including whole body of Christians; **(C-)** relating to Catholic Church ▷n **C-** adherent of Catholic Church **Ca·thol·i·cism** [kə-THOL-ə-siz-əm] *n* **cath·o·lic·i·ty** [kath-ə-LIS-i-tee] *n*

CAT scan [kat skan] computerized axial tomography; (also **CT scan**)

cat·tle [KAT-l] *pl n* beasts of pasture, esp steers, cows **cat'tle·man** *n* cattle guard heavy grid over ditch in road to prevent passage of livestock

Cau·ca·sian [kaw-KAY-zhən] *adj, n* (of, pert to) light-complexioned racial group of mankind **Cau'ca·soid** [-kə-soid] *adj, n*

cau·cus [KAW-kəs] *n* group, meeting, esp of members of political party, with power to decide policy, etc

caught *pt/pp of* **CATCH**

caul·dron [KAWL-drən] *n* large pot used for boiling

cau·li·flow·er [KAW-li-flow-ər] *n* variety of cabbage with edible white flowering head

caulk [kawk] *vt* stop up cracks (orig of ship) with waterproof filler **caulk'er** *n* **caulk'ing** *n* **caulking compound** filler used in caulking

cause [kawz] *n* that which produces an effect; reason, origin; motive, purpose; charity, movement; lawsuit ▷ *vt* **caused, caus'ing** bring about, make happen **caus'al** *adj* **cau·sal'i·ty** *n* **cau·sa'tion** *n* **cause'less** *adj* groundless

cause cé·lè·bre [kawz sə-LEB-rə] *n, pl* **causes cé·lè·bres** [kawz sə-LEB-rəz] great controversy eg famous legal case

cause·way [KAWZ-way] *n* raised way over marsh, etc; highway

caus·tic [KAW-stik] *adj* burning; bitter, severe ▷ *n* corrosive substance **caus'ti·cal·ly** *adv*

cau·ter·ize [KAW-tə-rīz] *vt* **-ized, -iz·ing** burn with caustic or hot iron **cau·ter·i·za'tion** *n*

cau·tion [KAW-shən] *n* heedfulness, care; warning ▷ *vt* warn **cau'tion·ary** *adj* containing warning or precept **cau'tious** *adj*

cav·al·cade [KAV-əl-kayd] *n* column or procession of riders; series

cav·a·lier [kav-ə-LEER] *adj* careless, disdainful ▷ *n* courtly gentleman; *obs* horseman

cav·al·ry [KAV-əl-ree] *n, pl* **-ries** mounted troops

cave [kayv] *n* hollow place in the earth; den **cav·ern** [KAV-ərn] *n* deep cave **cav'ern·ous** *adj* **cav'i·ty** *n, pl* **-ties** hollow **cave'man** *n* prehistoric cave dweller **cave in** fall inward; submit; give in

cav·i·ar [KAV-ee-ahr] *n* salted sturgeon roe

cav·il [KAV-əl] *vi* **-iled, -il·ing** find fault without sufficient reason, make trifling objections **cav'il·ing** *n* **cav'il·er** *n*

cav·i·ta·tion [kav-i-TAY-shən] *n* rapid formation of cavities or bubbles **cav'i·tate** *vi* **-tat·ed, -tat·ing** undergo cavitation

ca·vort [kə-VORT] *vi* prance, frisk

caw [kaw] *n* crow's cry ▷ *vi* cry so

cay·enne pepper [ki-EN] *n* pungent red pepper

Cd *chemistry* cadmium

CD compact disk; certificate of deposit **CD-R** compact disk recordable **CD-ROM** compact disk storing digitized read-only data **CD-RW** compact disk read-write

cease [sees] *v* **ceased, ceas·ing** bring or come to an end **cease'less** *adj*

ce·dar [SEE-dər] *n* large evergreen tree; its wood

cede [seed] *vt* **ced·ed, ced·ing** yield, give up, transfer, esp of territory

ce·dil·la [si-DIL-ə] *n* hooklike mark

placed under a letter c to show the sound of s

ceil·ing [SEE-ling] n inner, upper surface of a room; maximum price, wage, etc; *aviation* lower level of clouds; limit of height to which aircraft can climb

cel·e·brate [SEL-ə-brayt] v **-brat·ed, -brat·ing** rejoice or have festivities to mark (happy day, event, etc) ▷ vt observe (birthday, etc); perform (religious ceremony, etc); praise publicly **cel'e·brant** n celebrated *adj* famous **cel·e·bra'tion** n **ce·leb'ri·ty** n, pl **-ties** famous person; fame

ce·ler·i·ty [sə-LER-i-tee] n swiftness

cel·er·y [SEL-ə-ree] n vegetable with long juicy edible stalks

ce·les·tial [sə-LES-chəl] *adj* heavenly, divine; of the sky

cel·i·ba·cy [SEL-ə-bə-see] n sexual abstinence **cel'i·bate** [-bit] n, *adj*

cell [sel] n small room, esp in prison; small cavity; minute, basic unit of living matter; device converting chemical energy into electrical energy; small local group operating as nucleus of larger political or religious organization; short for CELL PHONE **cel·lu·lar** [SEL-yə-lər] *adj* **cell phone, cellular phone** portable telephone operating by radio communication via a network of transmitters each serving a small area

cel·lar [SEL-ər] n underground room or story; stock of wine; wine cellar

cel·lo [CHEL-oh] n, pl **-los** stringed instrument of violin family **cel·lo·phane** [SEL-ə-fayn] n transparent wrapping **cel·lu·loid** [SEL-yə-loid] n

synthetic plastic substance with wide range of uses; motion-picture film

cel·lu·lose [SEL-yə-lohs] n substance of vegetable cell wall; group of carbohydrates

Cel·si·us [SEL-see-əs] *adj*, n (of) scale of temperature from 0° (melting point of ice) to 100° (boiling point of water)

Celt·ic [KEL-tik, SEL-] n branch of language including Gaelic and Welsh ▷ *adj* of, or relating to the Celtic peoples or languages

ce·ment [si-MENT] n fine mortar; adhesive, glue ▷ vt unite with cement; join firmly

cem·e·ter·y [SEM-i-ter-ee] n, pl **-ter·ies** burial ground

cen·o·taph [SEN-ə-taf] n monument to one buried elsewhere

cen·ser [SEN-sər] n pan in which incense is burned

cen·sor [SEN-sər] n one authorized to examine films, books, etc and suppress all or part if considered morally or otherwise unacceptable ▷ vt **cen·so·ri·al** [sen-SOHR-ee-əl] *adj* of censor **cen·so'ri·ous** *adj* faultfinding **cen'sor·ship** n

cen·sure [SEN-shər] n blame; harsh criticism ▷ vt **-sured, -sur·ing** blame; criticize harshly

cen·sus [SEN-səs] n, pl **-sus·es** official counting of people, things, etc

cent [sent] n hundredth part of dollar, etc

cen·taur [SEN-tor] n mythical creature, half man, half horse

cen·ten·a·ry [sen-TEN-ə-ree] n, *adj* centennial **cen·te·nar·i·an** [sen-tn-AIR-ee-ən] n person a hundred years old

cen·ten·ni·al [sen-TEN-ee-əl] *adj* lasting, happening every hundred years ▷ *n* 100 years; celebration of hundredth anniversary

cen·ter [SEN-tər] *n* midpoint; pivot, axis; point to or from which things move or are drawn; place for specific organization or activity **cen·tral** [-trəl] *adj* **cen·tral·i·ty** *n* **cen·tral·ize** *vt* -ized, -iz·ing bring to a center; concentrate under one control **cen·tral·ly** *adv* **cen·trif·**u·gal [-TRIF-yə-gəl] *adj* tending away from center **cen·trip·e·tal** [-TRIP-i-tl] *adj* tending toward center **central heating** method of heating building from one central source **central processing unit** *computing* part of a computer that performs logical and arithmetical operations

cen·ti·grade [SEN-ti-grayd] *adj* another name for Celsius; having one hundred degrees

cen·ti·me·ter [SEN-tə-mee-tər] *n* hundredth part of meter

cen·ti·pede [SEN-tə-peed] *n* small segmented animal with many legs

cen·tu·ry [SEN-chə-ree] *n, pl* -ries 100 years; any set of 100

CEO chief executive officer

ce·ram·ic [sə-RAM-ik] *n* hard brittle material of baked clay; object made of this ▷ *adj* **ce·ram·ic** *n* hard brittle material made by heating clay to a very high temperature; object made of this ▷ *pl* art of producing ceramic objects ▷ *adj* made of ceramic

ce·re·al [SEER-ee-əl] *n* any edible grain, such as wheat, rice, etc; (breakfast) food made from grain ▷ *adj*

ce·re·bral [sə-REE-brəl] *adj* pert to brain or intellect

cer·e·mo·ny [SER-ə-moh-nee] *n, pl* -nies formal observance; sacred rite; courteous act **cer·e·mo·ni·al** *adj, n* **cer·e·mo·ni·ous** *adj*

ce·rise [sə-REES] *n, adj* clear, pinkish red

cer·tain [SUR-tn] *adj* sure; settled, inevitable; some, one; of moderate (quantity, degree, etc) **cer·tain·ly** *adv* **cer·tain·ty** *n, pl* -ties **cer·ti·tude** *n* confidence

cer·ti·fy [SUR-tə-fī] *vt* -fied, -fy·ing declare formally; endorse, guarantee; declare legally insane **cer·tif·i·cate** [-kit] *n* written declaration [-kayt] *-cat·ed, -cat·ing give written declaration **cer·ti·fi·ca·tion** *n*

ce·ru·le·an [sə-ROO-lee-ən] *adj* sky blue; deep blue

cer·vix [SUR-viks] *n, pl* -**vix·es** neck, esp of womb **cer·vi·cal** *adj*

ces·sa·tion [se-SAY-shən] *n* ceasing or stopping, pause

ces·sion [SESH-ən] *n* yielding up

cess·pit [SES-pit] *n* pit for receiving sewage or other refuse **cess·pool** [SES-pool] *n* catch basin in which sewage collects; filthy place; place of moral filth

Cf *chemistry* californium

cf. compare

CFC chlorofluorocarbon

cgs units metric system of units based on *centimeter, gram, second*

chad *n* small pieces removed during the punching of holes in punch cards, printer paper, etc

chafe [chayf] *vt* **chafed, chaf·ing** make sore or worn by rubbing; make warm by rubbing; vex, irritate

chaff *n* husks of corn; worthless matter; banter ▷ *v* tease good-naturedly

cha·grin [shə-GRIN] *n* vexation, disappointment ▷ *vt* embarrass; annoy; disappoint

chain [chayn] *n* series of connected

links or rings; thing that binds; connected series of things or events; surveyor's measure ▷ *vt* fasten with a chain; confine; restrain

chair *n* movable seat, with back, for one person; seat of authority; professorship ▷ *vt* preside over; carry in triumph **chair'lift** *n* series of chairs fixed to cable for conveying people (esp skiers) up mountain **chair'per·son, -wom·an, -man** *n* one who presides over meeting **chair'man·ship** *n*

chaise [shayz] *n* light horse-drawn carriage **chaise longue** [lawng] *n* sofa

chal·ced·o·ny [kal-SED-n-ee] *n* whitish, bluish-white variety of quartz

cha·let [sha-LAY] *n* Swiss wooden house; house in this style

chal·ice [CHAL-is] *n* cup or bowl; communion cup

chalk [chawk] *n* white substance, carbonate of lime; crayon ▷ *v* rub, draw, mark with chalk **chalk'y** *adj* **chalk·i·er, chalk·i·est**

chal·lenge [CHAL-inj] *vt* **-lenged, -leng·ing** call to fight to account; dispute; stimulate; object to; claim ▷ *n* **chal'lenged** *adj* disabled as specified: *physically challenged; mentally challenged* **chal'leng·er** *n* **chal'leng·ing** *adj* difficult but stimulating

cham·ber [CHAYM-bər] *n* room for assembly; body of legislators; compartment; cavity; *obs* room; chamber pot ▷ *pl* office of lawyer or judge; lodgings **cham'ber·lain** [-lin] *n* official at court of a monarch having charge of domestic and ceremonial affairs **cham'ber·maid** *n* female servant with care of bedrooms **chamber music** music for performance by

a few instruments **chamber pot** vessel for urine

cha·me·le·on [kə-MEEL-yən] *n* small lizard famous for its power of changing color

cham·fer [CHAM-fər] *vt* groove; bevel; flute ▷ *n* groove

cham·ois [SHAM-ee] *n* goatlike mountain antelope; a soft pliable leather

champ[1] *v* munch (food) noisily, as horse; be nervous, impatient

champ[2] *n* short for **CHAMPION**

cham·pagne [sham-PAYN] *n* light, sparkling white wine from Champagne region of France; similar wine made elsewhere

cham·pi·on [CHAM-pee-ən] *n* one that excels all others; defender of a cause; one who fights for another; hero ▷ *vt* fight for, maintain **cham'pi·on·ship** *n*

chance [chans] *n* unpredictable course of events; fortune, luck; opportunity; possibility; risk; probability ▷ *v* **chanced, chanc·ing** ▷ *vt* risk ▷ *vi* happen ▷ *adj* casual, unexpected **chanc'y** *adj* **chanc·i·er, chanc·i·est** risky

chan·cel [CHAN-səl] *n* part of a church where altar is

chan·cel·lor [CHAN-sə-lər] *n* high officer of state; head of university, state educational system

chan·cer·y [CHAN-sə-ree] *n, pl* **-ies** court of equity

chan·de·lier [shan-dl-EER] *n* hanging frame with branches for holding lights

change [chaynj] *v* **changed, chang·ing** alter, make or become different; put on (different clothes, fresh coverings) ▷ *vt* put or give for another; exchange, interchange ▷ *n* alteration, variation; variety; conversion of money; small money,

coins; balance received on payment
change·a·ble *adj* **change·less** *adj*
change·ling *n* child exchanged
for another
chan·nel [CHAN-l] *n* bed of stream;
strait; deeper part of strait, bay,
harbor; groove; means of passing or
conveying; band of radio frequencies;
TV broadcasting station ▷ *vt* groove,
furrow; guide, convey
chant *n* simple song or melody;
rhythmic or repetitious slogan
▷ *v* sing or utter chant; speak
monotonously or repetitiously
chan·tey [SHAN-tee] *n* sailor's
song with chorus
chan·ti·cleer [CHAN-tə-kleer]
n rooster
cha·os [KAY-os] *n* disorder,
confusion; state of universe
before Creation **cha·ot·ic** *adj*
cha·ot·i·cal·ly *adv*
chap¹ *v* **chapped, chap·ping** of
skin, become dry, raw and cracked,
esp by exposure to cold and wind
chapped *adj*
chap² *n* inf fellow, man
chap·el [CHAP-əl] *n* private
church; subordinate place of
worship; division of church with its
own altar; place of worship used by
a nonconforming Christian group;
print shop
chap·er·on, chaperone
[SHAP-ə-rohn] *n* one who attends
young unmarried woman in public
as protector ▷ *vt* **-oned, -on·ing**
attend in this way
chap·lain [CHAP-lin] *n*
clergyman attached to chapel,
regiment, warship, institution,
etc **chap·lain·cy** *n* office or term
of chaplain
chaps *pl n* cowboy's leggings of
thick leather
chap·ter [CHAP-tər] *n* division of

book; section, heading; assembly
of clergy, bishop's council, etc;
organized branch of society,
fraternity
char [chahr] *vt* **charred, char·ring**
scorch, burn to charcoal **charred** *adj*
char·ac·ter [KAR-ik-tər] *n*
nature; total of qualities making
up individuality; moral qualities;
reputation of possessing them;
statement of qualities of person;
an eccentric; personality in
play or novel; letter, sign, or
any distinctive mark; essential
feature **char·ac·ter·is·tic** *adj,
n* **char·ac·ter·is·ti·cal·ly** *adv*
char·ac·ter·ize *vt* **-ized, -iz·ing**
mark out, distinguish; describe by
peculiar qualities
cha·rade [shə-RAYD] *n* absurd act;
travesty ▷ *pl* word-guessing parlor
game with syllables of word acted
char·coal [CHAHR-kohl] *n*
black residue of wood, bones, etc,
produced by smothered burning;
charred wood
charge [chahrj] *v* **charged,
charg·ing** ▷ *vt* ask as price;
bring accusation against; lay task
on; command; attack; deliver
injunction; fill with electricity;
fill, load ▷ *vi* make onrush, attack
▷ *n* cost, price; accusation; attack,
onrush; command; exhortation;
accumulation of electricity ▷ *pl*
expenses **charge·a·ble** *adj* **charg'er**
n strong, fast battle horse; that
which charges, esp electrically
char·i·ot [CHAR-ee-ət] *n* two-
wheeled vehicle used in ancient
fighting **char·i·ot·eer'** *n*
cha·ris·ma [kə-RIZ-mə] *n*
special power of person to
inspire fascination, loyalty, etc
char·is·mat·ic [kar-iz-MAT-ik] *adj*
char·i·ty [CHAR-i-tee] *n, pl* **-ties**

the giving of help, money, etc to those in need; organization for doing this; the money, etc given; love, kindness; disposition to think kindly of others **char·i·ta·ble** adj

char·la·tan [SHAHR-lə-tn] n quack, impostor

charm [chahrm] n attractiveness; anything that fascinates; amulet; magic spell ▷ vt bewitch; delight, attract **charmed** adj **charm·ing** adj

char·nel house [CHAHR-nl] n vault for bones of the dead

chart [chahrt] n map of sea; diagram or tabulated statement ▷ vt map; represent on chart

char·ter [CHAHR-tər] n document granting privileges, etc ▷ vt let or hire; establish by charter

char·wom·an [CHAHR-wuum-ən] n woman paid to clean office, house, etc

char·y [CHAIR-ee] adj **char·i·er, char·i·est** cautious, sparing **char·i·ly** adv **char·i·ness** n caution

chase¹ [chays] vt **chased, chas·ing** hunt, pursue; drive from, away, into, etc ▷ n pursuit, hunting; the hunted; hunting ground **chas·er** n drink of beer, soda, etc, taken after straight whiskey

chase² vt **chased, chas·ing** ornament, engrave (metal) **chas·er** n **chas·ing** n

chasm [KAZ-əm] n deep cleft, fissure; abyss

chas·sis [CHAS-ee] n, pl **chassis** [-eez] frame, wheels and machinery of motor vehicle on which body is supported

chaste [chayst] adj virginal; pure; modest; virtuous **chaste·ly** adv **chas·ti·ty** [CHAS-ti-tee] n

chas·ten [CHAY-sən] vt correct by punishment; restrain, subdue **chas'tened** adj **chas·tise** [chas-

TĪZ] vt **-tised, -tis·ing** inflict punishment on

chas·u·ble [CHAZ-yə-bəl] n priest's long sleeveless outer vestment

chat vi **chat·ted, chat·ting** talk idly, or familiarly ▷ n familiar idle talk **chat'bot** n computer program in the form of a virtual e-mail correspondent **chat'room** n site on the Internet where users have group discussions by e-mail

châ·teau [shat-TOH] n, pl **-teaus** or **-teaux** [-TOHZ] (esp in France) castle, country house

chat·tel [CHAT-l] n any movable property

chat·ter [CHAT-ər] vi talk idly or rapidly; rattle teeth ▷ n idle talk **chat'ter·er** n **chat'terbox** n one who chatters incessantly

chauf·feur [SHOH-fər] n paid driver of automobile ▷ vt perform this work

chau·vin·ism [SHOH-və-niz-əm] n aggressive patriotism **male chauvinism** smug sense of male superiority over women **chau'vin·ist** n

cheap [cheep] adj **-er, -est** low in price; inexpensive; easily obtained; of little value or estimation; mean, inferior **cheap'en** vt

cheat [cheet] vt deceive, defraud, swindle; impose upon ▷ vi practice deceit to gain advantage; (oft followed by on) be sexually unfaithful **cheat, cheat'er** n one who cheats **cheat'ers** pl n sl eyeglasses

check [chek] vt stop; restrain; hinder; repress; control; examine for accuracy, quality, etc ▷ n repulse; stoppage; restraint; brief examination for correctness or accuracy; pattern of squares on fabric; threat to king at chess;

written order to banker to pay money from one's account; printed slip of paper used for this **check'book** n book of checks **check'mate** n chess final winning move; any overthrow, defeat ▷ vt **-mat·ed, -mat·ing** chess make game-ending move; defeat **check'out** n counter in supermarket where customers pay **check'up** n examination (esp medical) to see if all is in order

checked [chekt] adj having pattern of small squares

check·er [CHEK-ər] n marking as on checkerboard; piece in game of checkers ▷ vt mark in squares; variegate **check'ered** adj marked in squares; uneven, varied **check'ers** n game played on checkered board of 64 squares with flat round playing pieces **check'er·board** n

Ched·dar [CHED-ər] n smooth hard cheese

cheek n side of face below eye; impudence; buttock ▷ vt inf address impudently **cheek by jowl** in close intimacy

cheep vi, n (utter) high-pitched cry, as of young bird

cheer vt comfort; gladden; encourage by shouts ▷ vi shout applause ▷ n shout of approval; happiness, good spirits; mood **cheer'ful** adj **cheer'i·ly** adv **cheer'less** adj

cheese [cheez] n curd of milk coagulated, separated from the whey and pressed **chees'y** adj **chees·i·er, chees·i·est** suggesting cheese in aroma, etc; sl cheap, shabby **cheese'cake** n cake made with cottage or cream cheese and oft with fruit mixture; inf photograph of shapely, scantily clad woman **cheese'cloth** n loosely woven cotton cloth

chee·tah [CHEE-tə] n large, swift, spotted feline animal

chef [shef] n head cook, esp in restaurant

chef-d'oeu·vre [shay-DUR-vr] Fr masterpiece

chem·is·try [KEM-ə-stree] n science concerned with properties of substances and their combinations and reactions; interaction of one personality with another **chem'i·cal** n, adj **chem'ist** n one trained in chemistry **chemical peeling** cosmetic process in which a chemical substance is applied to the face and peeled away to remove dead skin cells

che·mo·ther·a·py [kee-moh-THER-ə-pee] n treatment of disease by chemical means

che·nille [shə-NEEL] n soft yarn, fabric of silk, wool, etc

cher'ish vt treat with affection; protect; foster

che·root [shə-ROOT] n cigar with both ends open

cher·ry [CHER-ee] n small red fruit with stone; tree bearing it ▷ adj ruddy, bright red

cher·ub [CHER-əb] n, pl **cher·u·bim, cher·ubs** winged creature with human face; angel **che·ru·bic** [chə-ROO-bik] adj

cher·vil [CHUR-vil] n an herb

chess n game of skill played by two with 32 pieces on checkered board of 64 squares **chess'board** n **chess'man** n, pl **-men** piece used in chess

chest n upper part of trunk of body; large, strong box **chest of drawers** piece of furniture containing drawers

chest·nut [CHES-nut] n large reddish-brown nut growing in prickly husk; tree bearing it; horse of chestnut color; old joke ▷ *adj* reddish-brown

chev·ron [SHEV-rən] *n* military V-shaped band of braid worn on sleeve to designate rank

chew [choo] *v* grind with teeth ▷ *n* **chew'y** *adj* **chew·i·er, chew·i·est** firm, sticky when chewed

chi·an·ti [kee-AHN-tee] *n* dry red Italian wine

chic [sheek] *adj* **-er, -est** stylish, elegant ▷ *n*

chi·can·er·y [shi-KAY-nə-ree] *n, pl* **-er·ies** quibbling; trick, artifice

chick [chik], **chick·en** [CHIK-ən] *n* young of birds, esp of hen; *sl soft offens* girl, young woman **chicken feed** trifling amount of money **chick'en·heart·ed** *adj* cowardly **chick'en·pox** *n* infectious disease, esp of children **chick'pea** *n* legume bearing pods containing pealike seeds; seed of this plant

chic·o·ry [CHIK-ə-ree] *n* salad plant; ground root of the plant used with, or instead of, coffee

chide [chid] *vt* **chid·ed** or **chid, chid·ed** or **chid** or **chid·den, chid·ing** scold, reprove, censure

chief [cheef] *n* head or principal person ▷ *adj* principal, foremost, leading **chief'ly** *adv* **chief'tain** [-tən] *n* leader, chief of clan or tribe

chif·fon [shi-FON] *n* thin gauzy material

chi·gnon [SHEEN-yon] *n* roll, knot, of hair worn at back of head

chi·hua·hua [chi-WAH-wah] *n* breed of tiny dog, orig from Mexico

chil·blain [CHIL-blayn] *n* inflamed sore on hands, legs, etc, due to cold

child [chīld] *n, pl* **chil·dren** [CHIL-drən] *n* young human being; offspring **child'ish** *adj* of or like a child; silly; trifling **child'ish·ly** *adv* **child'less** *adj* **child'like** *adj* of or like a child;

innocent; frank; docile **child'birth** *n* **child'hood** *n* period between birth and puberty **child's play** very easy task

chil·i [CHIL-ee] *n, pl* **chil·ies** small red hot-tasting seed pod; plant producing it; chili con carne **chili con carne** [kon KAHR-nee] *n* Mexican-style dish of chilies or chili powder, ground beef, onions, etc

chill *n* coldness; cold with shivering; anything that damps, discourages ▷ *v* make, become cold (esp food, drink) **chill'i·ness** *n* **chill'y** *adj* **chill·i·er, chill·i·est** chill out *sl* relax, calm down; spend time in trivial occupations; keep company (with) **chill pill** imaginary medicinal pill with a calming effect

chime [chīm] *n* sound of bell; harmonious, ringing sound ▷ *v* **chimed, chim·ing** ▷ *vi.* ring harmoniously; agree ▷ *vt* strike (bells) **chime in** break into a conversation to express an opinion

chi·me·ra [ki-MEER-ə] *n* fabled monster, made up of parts of various animals; wild fancy **chi·mer·i·cal** [-MER-i-kəl] *adj* fanciful

chim·ney [CHIM-nee] *n, pl* **-neys** a passage for smoke; narrow vertical cleft in rock

chim·pan·zee [chim-pan-ZEE] *n* gregarious, intelligent ape of Africa

chin *n* part of face below mouth

chi·na [CHĪ-nə] *n* fine earthenware, porcelain; cups, saucers, etc collectively

chin·chil·la [chin-CHIL-ə] *n S Amer* rodent with soft, gray fur; its fur

chine [chīn] *n* backbone; cut of meat including backbone; ridge or crest of land; intersection of bottom and side of boat

chink[1] [chingk] *n* cleft, crack

chink² n light metallic sound ▷ v (cause to) make this sound

chintz [chints] n cotton cloth printed in colored designs

chip n splinter; place where piece has been broken off; tiny wafer of silicon forming integrated circuit in computer, etc ▷ v **chipped, chip·ping** ▷ vt chop into small pieces; break small pieces from; shape by cutting off pieces ▷ vi break off **chip** in contribute; butt in **chip'set** n circuit in a computer that controls many of its data transfer functions; the main processing circuitry on many video cards

chip·munk [CHIP-mungk] n small, striped N Amer squirrel

chi·rop·o·dist [ki-ROP-ə-dist] n one who treats disorders of feet **chi·rop'o·dy** n

chi·ro·prac·tor [KÏ-rə-prak-tər] n one skilled in treating bodily disorders by manipulation, massage, etc **chi·ro·prac'tic** n

chirp [churp] n short, sharp cry of bird ▷ vi make this sound **chirp'y** adj inf **chirp·i·er, chirp·i·est** happy

chis·el [CHIZ-əl] n cutting tool, usu bar of steel with edge across main axis ▷ vt **-eled, -el·ing** cut, carve with chisel; sl cheat

chit¹ n signed note for money owed; informal receipt

chit² n child, esp young girl

chiv·al·ry [SHIV-əl-ree] n bravery and courtesy; medieval system of knighthood **chiv'al·rous** adj

chive [chÏv] n herb with mild onion flavor

chlo·rine [KLOR-een] n nonmetallic element, yellowish-green poison gas, used as disinfectant **chlo'rate** [-ayt] n salt of chloric acid **chlo'ric** adj **chlo'ride** n compound of chlorine; bleaching agent **chlo·ri·nate** [KLOR-ə-nayt] vt **-nat·ed, -nat·ing** disinfect; purify with chlorine

chlo·ro·fluo·ro·car·bon [klor-ə-fluur-ə-KAHR-bən] n (also **CFC**) any of various gaseous compounds of carbon, hydrogen, chlorine, and fluorine, used in refrigerants and aerosol propellants, some of which break down the ozone in the atmosphere

chlo·ro·form [KLOR-ə-form] n volatile liquid formerly used as anesthetic ▷ vt render insensible with it

chlo·ro·phyll [KLOR-ə-fil] n green coloring matter in plants

chock [chok] n block or wedge to prevent heavy object from rolling or sliding **chock'-full** adj packed thick

choc·o·late [CHAWK-lit] n paste from ground cacao seeds; candy, drink made from this ▷ adj dark brown

choice [chois] n act or power of choosing; alternative; thing or person chosen ▷ adj select, fine, worthy of being chosen

choir [kwÏr] n company of singers, esp in church; part of church set aside for them

choke [chohk] v **choked, chok·ing** ▷ vt hinder, stop the breathing of; smother, stifle; obstruct ▷ vi suffer choking ▷ n act, noise of choking; device in carburetor to increase richness of fuel-air mixture

chol·er [KOL-ər] n bile, anger **chol'er·ic** adj irritable

chol·er·a [KOL-ə-rə] n deadly infectious disease marked by vomiting and diarrhea

cho·les·ter·ol [kə-LES-tə-rawl] n substance found in animal tissue and fat

chomp v chew noisily

choose [chooz] v **chose, cho·sen, choos·ing** ▷vt pick out, select; take by preference ▷vi decide, think fit **choos'y** adj **choos·i·er, choos·i·est** fussy

chop vt **chopped, chop·ping** cut with blow; hack ▷n hewing blow; slice of meat containing rib or other bone **chop'per** n short axe; inf helicopter **chop'py** adj **-pi·er, -pi·est** (of sea) having short, broken waves

chops pl n jaw, mouth

chop·sticks [CHOP-stiks] pl n implements used by Chinese and others for eating food

cho·ral [KOR-əl] adj of, for, sung by, a choir

cho·rale [kə-RAL] n slow, stately hymn tune

chord [kord] n emotional response, esp of sympathy; simultaneous sounding of musical notes; straight line joining ends of arc

chore [chor] n (unpleasant) task; odd job

cho·re·og·ra·phy [kor-ee-OG-rə-fee] n art of arranging dances, esp ballet; art, notation of ballet dancing **cho·re·og'ra·pher** n **cho·re·o·graph'ic** adj

chor·tle [CHOR-tl] vi **-tled, -tling** chuckle happily ▷n

cho·rus [KOR-əs] n group of singers; combination of voices singing together; refrain ▷vt **-rused, -rus·ing** sing or say together **cho'ris·ter** n

chose pt of CHOOSE **cho'sen** pp of CHOOSE

chow¹ inf n food ▷vi (oft with down) eat heartily **chow'hound** n sl glutton

chow² n thick-coated dog with curled tail, orig from China

chow·der [CHOW-dər] n thick soup of seafood, vegetables, etc; soup resembling it, such as corn chowder

Christ [krist] n Jesus of Nazareth, regarded by Christians as the Messiah

Chris·tian [KRIS-chən] n follower of Christ ▷adj following Christ; relating to Christ or his religion **chris'ten** [-ən] vt baptize, give name to **Chris'ten·dom** [-ən-dəm] n all the Christian world **Chris·ti·an'i·ty** [-chee-AN-i-tee] n religion of Christ **Christian name** name given at baptism **Christian Science** religious system founded by Mary Baker Eddy

Christ·mas [KRIS-məs] n festival of birth of Christ

chro·mat·ic [kroh-MAT-ik] adj of color; music of scale proceeding by semitones

chro·ma·tin [KROH-mə-tin] n part of protoplasmic substance in nucleus of cells that takes color in staining tests

chrome [krohm], **chro'mi·um** [-mee-əm] n metal used in alloys and for plating

chro·mo·some [KROH-mə-sohm] n microscopic gene-carrying body in the tissue of a cell

Chron. Chronicles

chron·ic [KRON-ik] adj lasting a long time; habitual

chron·i·cle [KRON-i-kəl] n record of events in order of time; account ▷vt **-cled, -cling** record **chron'i·cler** n

chro·nol·o·gy [krə-NOL-ə-jee] n, pl **-gies** determination of sequence of past events; arrangement in order of occurrence; account of events, reference work arranged in order of time **chron·o·log'i·cal** [kron-l-OJ-i-kəl] adj arranged in order of time

chro·nom·e·ter [krə-NOM-i-tər] *n* instrument for measuring time exactly; watch

chrys·a·lis [KRIS-ə-lis] *n, pl* **chry·sal·i·des** [kri-SAL-i-deez] resting state of insect between grub and butterfly, etc; case enclosing it

chry·san·the·mum [kri-SAN-thə-məm] *n* garden flower of various colors

chub·by [CHUB-ee] *adj* **-bi·er, -bi·est** plump

chuck[1] [chuk] *vt inf* throw; pat affectionately (under chin); give up, reject

chuck[2] *n* cut of beef; device for gripping, adjusting bit in power drill, etc

chuck·le [CHUK-əl] *vi* **-led, -ling** laugh softly ▷ *n* such laugh

chuk·ker [CHUK-ər] *n* period of play in game of polo

chum *n inf* close friend **chum'my** *adj* **-mi·er, -mi·est**

chunk [chungk] *n* thick, solid piece **chunk'y** *adj* **chunk·i·er, chunk·i·est**

church *n* building for Christian worship; (**C-**) whole body or sect of Christians; clergy **church'ward·en** *n* officer who represents interests of Anglican parish; long clay pipe **church'yard** *n*

churl *n* rustic; rude, boorish person **churl'ish** *adj* **churl'ish·ness** *n*

churn *n* vessel for making butter ▷ *v* shake up, stir (liquid) violently; make (butter) in churn; (of a stockbroker) trade (stocks) excessively to increase commissions

chute [shoot] *n* slide for sending down parcels, coal, etc; channel; narrow passageway, eg for spraying, counting cattle, sheep, etc; *inf* short for **PARACHUTE**

chut·ney [CHUT-nee] *n* condiment

of fruit, spices, etc

chutz·pah [HUUT-spə] *n* shameless audacity; gall

ci·ca·da [si-KAY-də] *n* cricketlike insect

cic·a·trix [SIK-ə-triks] *n* scar of healed wound

cic·e·ro·ne [sis-ə-ROH-nee] *n* guide for sightseers

ci·der [SĪ-dər] *n* drink made from apples **hard cider** cider after fermentation **soft cider** cider before fermentation

ci·gar [si-GAHR] *n* roll of tobacco leaves for smoking **cig·a·rette** [sig-ə-RET] *n* finely cut tobacco rolled in paper for smoking

ci·lan·tro [si-LAN-troh, -LAHN-] *n* coriander

cinch [sinch] *n inf* easy task, certainty; strong girth used on saddle

cin·der [SIN-dər] *n* remains of burned coal

cin·e·ma [SIN-ə-mə] *n* building used for showing of motion pictures; these generally or collectively

cin·na·mon [SIN-ə-mən] *n* spice got from bark of Asian tree; the tree ▷ *adj* light-brown color

ci·pher [SĪ-fər] *n* secret writing; arithmetical symbol; person of no importance; monogram ▷ *vt* write in cipher

cir·ca [SUR-kə] *Lat* about, approximately

cir·cle [SUR-kəl] *n* perfectly round figure; ring; *theater* balcony or tier of seats above main level of auditorium; group, society with common interest; class of society ▷ *v* **-cled, -cling** move in circle **cir'cu·lar** [-kyə-lər] *adj* round; in a circle ▷ *n* letter, etc intended for wide distribution **cir'cu·late** [-kyə-layt] *v* **-lat·ed,**

-lat·ing ▷ *vi* move around; pass from hand to hand or place to place ▷ *vt* send around **cir·cu·la·tion** *n* flow of blood from, and back to, heart; act of moving around; extent of sale of newspaper, etc **cir·cu·la·to·ry** *adj*

cir·cuit [SUR-kit] *n* complete round or course; area; path of electric current; round of visitation, esp of judges; series of sporting events; district **cir·cu·i·tous** [sər-KYOO-i-təs] *adj* roundabout, indirect **cir·cuit·ry** *n* electrical circuit(s)

cir·cum·cise [SUR-kəm-siz] *vt* **-cised, -cis·ing** cut off foreskin of (penis) **cir·cum·ci·sion** [-SIZH-ən] *n*

cir·cum·fer·ence [sər-KUM-fər-əns] *n* boundary line, esp of circle

cir·cum·flex [SUR-kəm-fleks] *n* accent (^) over vowel to indicate length of its sound

cir·cum·lo·cu·tion [sur-kəm-loh-KYOO-shən] *n* roundabout speech

cir·cum·nav·i·gate [sur-kəm-NAV-i-gayt] *vt* **-gat·ed, -gat·ing** sail or fly right around

cir·cum·scribe [SUR-kəm-skrīb] *vt* **-scribed, -scrib·ing** confine, bound, limit, hamper

cir·cum·spect [SUR-kəm-spekt] *adj* watchful, cautious, prudent **cir·cum·spec·tion** *n*

cir·cum·stance [SUR-kəm-stans] *n* detail; event; matter of fact ▷ *pl* state of affairs; condition in life, esp financial; surroundings or things accompanying an action **cir·cum·stan·tial** *adj* depending on detail or circumstances; detailed; minute; incidental

cir·cum·vent [sur-kəm-VENT] *vt* outwit, evade, get round **cir·cum·ven·tion** *n*

cir·cus [SUR-kəs] *n, pl* **-cus·es** (performance of) traveling group of acrobats, clowns, performing animals, etc; circular place for public shows

cir·rho·sis [si-ROH-sis] *n* any of various chronic progressive diseases of liver **cir·rhot·ic** [-ROT-ik] *adj*

cir·rus [SIR-əs] *n, pl* **cirrus** high wispy cloud

cis·tern [SIS-tərn] *n* water tank, esp for rain water

cit·a·del [SIT-ə-dl] *n* fortress in, near, or commanding a city

cite [sīt] *vt* **cit·ed, cit·ing** quote; bring forward as proof **ci·ta·tion** [sī-TAY-shən] *n* quoting; commendation for bravery, etc

cit·i·zen [SIT-ə-zən] *n* native, naturalized member of state, nation, etc; inhabitant of city **cit·i·zen·ship** *n*

cit·ron [SI-trən] *n* fruit like a lemon; the tree **cit·ric** *adj* of the acid of lemon or citron **cit·rus fruit** citrons, lemons, limes, oranges, etc

cit·y [SIT-ee] *n, pl* **cit·ies** a large town

civ·et [SIV-it] *n* strong, musky perfume **civet cat** catlike animal producing it

civ·ic [SIV-ik] *adj* pert to city or citizen **civ·ics** *n* study of the responsibilities and rights of citizenship

civ·il [SIV-əl] *adj* relating to citizens of state; not military; refined, polite; *law* not criminal **ci·vil·ian** [si-VIL-yən] *n* nonmilitary person **ci·vil·i·ty** *n, pl* **-ties civ·il·ly** *adv* **civil service** service responsible for the public administration of the government of a city, state, or country

civ·i·lize [SIV-ə-līz] *vt* **-lized, -liz·ing** bring out of barbarism;

refine **civ·i·li·za'tion** n

Cl chemistry chlorine

clack [klak] n sound, as of two pieces of wood striking together ▷ v

clad pt/pp of CLOTHE

clad·ding [KLAD-ing] n metal bonded to inner core of another metal, as protection against corrosion

claim [klaym] vt demand as right; assert; call for ▷ n demand for thing supposed due; right; thing claimed; plot of mining land marked out by stakes as required by law **claim'ant** [-mənt] n

clair·voy·ance [klair-VOI-əns] n power of seeing things not present to senses, second sight **clair·voy'ant** n, adj

clam [klam] n edible mollusk

clam·ber [KLAM-bər] vi to climb with difficulty or awkwardly

clam·my [KLAM-ee] adj **-mi·er, -mi·est** moist and sticky **clam'mi·ness** n

clam·or [KLAM-ər] n loud shouting, outcry, noise ▷ vi shout, call noisily (for) **clam'or·ous** adj

clamp [klamp] n tool for holding or compressing ▷ vt fasten, strengthen with or as with clamp

clan [klan] n tribe or collection of families under chief and of common ancestry; faction, group **clan'nish** adj

clan·des·tine [klan-DES-tin] adj secret; sly

clang [klang] v (cause to) make loud ringing sound ▷ n loud ringing sound

clank [klangk] n short sound as of pieces of metal struck together ▷ v cause, move with such sound

clap¹ [klap] v **clapped, clap·ping** (cause to) strike with noise; strike (hands) together; applaud ▷ vt

pat; place or put quickly ▷ n hard, explosive sound; slap **clap'per** n

clap'trap n empty words

clap² n sl gonorrhea

clar·et [KLAR-it] n a dry dark red wine of Bordeaux; similar wine made elsewhere

clar·i·fy [KLAR-ə-fī] v **-fied, -fy·ing** make or become clear, pure, or more easily understood **clar·i·fi·ca'tion** n **clar'i·ty** n clearness

clar·i·net [klar-ə-NET] n woodwind musical instrument

clar·i·on [KLAR-ee-ən] n clear-sounding trumpet; rousing sound

clash [klash] n loud noise, as of weapons striking; conflict, collision ▷ vi make clash; come into conflict; (of events) coincide; (of colors) look ugly together ▷ vt strike together to make clash

clasp [klasp] n hook or other means of fastening; embrace ▷ vt fasten; embrace, grasp

class [klas] n any division, order, kind, sort; rank; group of school pupils, etc taught together; division by merit; quality; inf excellence or elegance ▷ vt assign to proper division **clas'si·fy** [-ə-fī] vt **-fied, -fy·ing** arrange methodically in classes **clas·si·fi·ca'tion** n **clas·si·fied** adj arranged in classes; secret; (of advertisements) arranged under headings in newspapers, etc **class'room** n room in a school where lessons take place **class'y** adj **class·i·er, class·i·est** inf stylish, elegant

clas·sic [KLAS-ik] adj of first rank; of highest rank generally, but esp of art; refined; typical; famous ▷ n (literary) work of recognized excellence ▷ pl ancient Latin and Greek literature **clas'si·cal** adj of Greek and Roman literature, art, culture; of classic quality; *music* of established standards of form, complexity, etc **clas'si•cism** *n* **clas'si•cist** *n*

clat•ter [KLAT-ər] *n* rattling noise; noisy conversation ▷ *v* (cause to) make clatter

clause [klawz] *n* part of sentence, containing verb; article in formal document as treaty, contract, etc

claus•tro•pho•bia [klaw-strə-FOH-bee-ə] *n* abnormal fear of confined spaces

clav•i•chord [KLAV-i-kord] *n* musical instrument with keyboard, forerunner of piano

clav•i•cle [KLAV-i-kəl] *n* collarbone

claw [klaw] *n* sharp hooked nail of bird or beast; foot of bird of prey; clawlike article ▷ *vt* tear with claws; grip

clay [klay] *n* fine-grained earth, plastic when wet, hardening when baked; earth

clean [kleen] *adj* **-er, -est** free from dirt, stain, or defilement; pure; guiltless; trim, shapely ▷ *adv* **-er, -est** so as to leave no dirt; entirely ▷ *vt* free from dirt **clean•li•ness** [KLEN-lee-nis] *n* **clean•ly** [KLEEN-lee] *adv, adj* **-li•er, -li•est** clean **cleanse** [klenz] *vt* **cleansed, cleans•ing** make clean **come clean** *inf* confess

clear [kleer] *adj* **-er, -est** pure, undimmed, bright; free from cloud; transparent; plain, distinct; without defect or drawback; unimpeded ▷ *adv* **-er, -est** brightly; wholly, quite ▷ *vt* make clear; acquit; pass over or through; make as profit; free from obstruction, debt, difficulty ▷ *vi* become clear, bright, free, transparent **clear'ance** *n* making clear; removal of obstructions, surplus stock, etc; certificate that

ship has been cleared at custom house; space for moving part, vehicle, to pass within, through or past something **clear'ing** *n* land cleared of trees **clear'ly** *adv* **clear'head•ed** [-hed-id] *adj* discerning

cleat [kleet] *n* wedge; piece of wood or iron with two projecting ends round which ropes are made fast; (on shoes) projecting piece to furnish a grip ▷ *pl* shoes equipped with cleats

cleave¹ [kleev] *v* **cleft, cleaved** or **clove; cleft, cleaved** or **clo•ven; cleav•ing** ▷ *vt* split asunder ▷ *v* crack, part asunder **cleav'age** *n* space between a woman's breasts, as revealed by a low-cut dress, top, etc; division, split **cleav'er** *n* butcher's heavy knife with a square blade

cleave² *vi* **cleaved, cleav•ing** stick, adhere; be loyal

clef *n music* mark showing pitch of music on staff

cleft *n* crack, fissure, chasm; opening made by cleaving; pt/pp of **CLEAVE¹**

clem•ent [KLEM-ənt] *adj* merciful; gentle; mild **clem'en•cy** *n*

clench *vt* set firmly together; grasp, close (fist)

cler•gy [KLUR-jee] *n* body of ordained ministers in a religion **cler'gy•man** *n*

cler•ic [KLER-ik] *n* member of clergy

cler•i•cal [KLER-i-kəl] *adj* of clergy; of, connected with, office work

clerk [klurk] *n* employee who keeps files, etc in an office; officer in charge of records, correspondence, etc of court, government department, etc; sales or service employee

clev•er [KLEV-ər] *adj* quick to understand; able, skillful, adroit **clev'er•ly** *adv* **clev'er•ness** *n*

cli•ché [klee-SHAY] *n, pl* **-chés** stereotyped hackneyed phrase

click[1] [klik] *n* short, sharp sound, as of latch in door; catch ▷ *vi* make this sound ▷ *v* (usu foll by *on*) *computing* press and release (button on a mouse) **click'able** *adj* (of a website) having links that can be accessed by clicking a computer mouse **click through** navigate around (a website) using links provided to move onto different pages

click[2] *vi sl* be a success; *inf* become clear; *inf* strike up friendship

cli•ent [KLIY-ənt] *n* customer; one who employs professional person; *computing* program or work station that requests data from a server **cli•en•tele'** [-ən-TEL] *n* body of clients

cliff [klif] *n* steep rock face **cliff'hang•er** *n* tense situation

cli•mate [KLIY-mit] *n* condition of region with regard to weather; prevailing feeling, atmosphere **cli•mat'ic** *adj* of climate

cli•max [KLIY-maks] *n* highest point, culmination; point of greatest excitement, tension in story, etc **cli•mac'tic** *adj*

climb [klim] *v* go up or ascend; progress with difficulty; creep up, mount; slope upwards

clinch [klinch] *vt* clench; settle, conclude (an agreement) ▷ *vi* (in boxing) hold opponent close with arm or arms; *sl* embrace, esp passionately ▷ *n* clinching; *sl* embrace **clinch'er** *n inf* something decisive

cling *vi* clung, cling•ing adhere; be firmly attached to; be dependent

clin•ic [KLIN-ik] *n* hospital facility for examination, treatment of outpatients; medical training session with hospital patients as subjects **clin'i•cal** *adj* relating to clinic, care of sick, etc; unemotional; bare, plain **clinical thermometer** used for taking body temperature

clink[1] [klingk] *n* sharp metallic sound ▷ *v* (cause to) make this sound

clink[2] *n sl* prison

clink•er [KLING-kər] *n* fused coal residues from fire or furnace; hard brick

clip[1] *vt* **clipped, clip•ping** cut with scissors; cut short; *sl* cheat ▷ *n inf* sharp blow **clip'per** *n*

clip[2] *n* device for gripping or holding together, esp hair, clothing, etc **clip•per** [KLIP-ər] *n* fast commercial sailing ship

clique [kleek] *n* small exclusive set; faction, group of people **cli'quish** *adj* **cli'quish•ness** *n*

cli•to•ris [KLIT-ər-is] *n* small erectile part of female genitals

cloak [klohk] *n* loose outer garment; disguise, pretext ▷ *vt* cover with cloak; disguise, conceal

clob•ber [KLOB-ər] *vt inf* beat, batter; defeat utterly

clock [klok] *n* instrument for measuring time; device with dial for recording or measuring **clock'wise** *adv, adj* in the direction that the hands of a clock rotate **clock'work** *n* mechanism similar to that of a clock, as in a windup toy **clock in** or **on**, **out** or **off** record arrival, or departure, on automatic time recorder

clod [klod] *n* lump of earth; blockhead **clod'dish** *adj*

clog [klog] *vt* **clogged, clog•ging** hamper, impede, choke up ▷ *n* obstruction, impediment; wooden-soled shoe

cloi•son•né [kloi-zə-NAY] *n* enamel decoration in compartments formed by small strips of metal ▷ adj

clois·ter [KLOI-stər] n covered
pillared arcade; monastery or
convent **clois·tered** adj confined,
secluded, sheltered

clone [klohn] n group of organisms,
cells of same genetic constitution
as another, derived by asexual
reproduction, as graft of plant, etc;
person closely resembling another
in appearance, behavior, etc ▷ v
cloned, clon·ing

clop [klop] vi **clopped, clop·ping**
move, sound, as horse's hooves

close¹ [klohs] adj **clos·er, clos·est**
adjacent, near; compact; crowded;
affectionate, intimate; almost
equal; careful, searching; confined;
secret; unventilated, stifling;
reticent; niggardly; strict, restricted
▷ adv nearly; tightly **close·ly** adv
close·fist·ed adj mean; avaricious
close·up n close view, esp portion of
motion picture

close² [klohz] v **closed, clos·ing**
▷ vt shut; stop up; prevent access to;
finish ▷ vi come together; grapple
▷ n end **closed season** when it is
illegal to kill certain kinds of game
and fish **closed shop** place of work
in which all workers work belong
to a union

clos·et [KLOZ-it] n small room, etc
for storing clothing; small private
room ▷ v shut up in private room,
esp for conference **clos·et·ful** n,
pl **-fuls**

clo·sure [KLOH-zhər] n act of
closing; (sense of contentment
experienced after) resolution of a
significant event or relationship in a
person's life; cloture

clot [klot] n mass or lump; medicine
coagulated mass of blood ▷ v
clot·ted, clot·ting form into
lumps; coagulate

cloth [klawth] n woven fabric

clothes [klohthz] pl n dress; bed
coverings **clothe** [klohth] vt
clothed or **clad, cloth·ing** put
clothes on **clo·thier** [KLOHTH-yər]
n **cloth·ing** [KLOH-thing] n

clo·ture [KLOH-chər] n ending
of debate by majority vote or other
authority

cloud [klowd] n condensed water
vapor floating in air; state of gloom;
multitude ▷ vt overshadow,
dim, darken ▷ vi become cloudy
cloud'less adj **cloud'y** adj
cloud·i·er, cloud·i·est

clout [klowt] n inf blow; influence,
power ▷ vt strike

clove¹ [klohv] n dried flower bud
of tropical tree, used as spice; one of
small bulbs making up compound
bulb

clove² [klohv] pt of CLEAVE¹. **clo·ven** pp
of CLEAVE¹

clo·ver [KLOH-vər] n low-growing
forage plant **be in clover** be in
luxury

clown [klown] n comic entertainer
in circus; jester, fool

cloy [kloi] vt weary by sweetness,
sameness, etc

club [klub] n thick stick; bat, stick
used in some games; association
for pursuance of common interest;
building used by such association;
one of the suits at cards ▷ v
clubbed, club·bing strike with club;
combine for a common object **club
foot** deformed foot

cluck [kluk] vi, n (make) noise of hen

clue [kloo] n indication, esp
of solution of mystery or puzzle
not have a clue be ignorant or
incompetent

clump¹ [klump] n cluster of trees or
plants; compact mass

clump² vi walk, tread heavily ▷ n

clum·sy [KLUM-zee] adj **-si·er,
-si·est** awkward, unwieldy,
ungainly; badly made or arranged
clum'si·ly adv **clum'si·ness** n

clung pt/pp of CLING

clunk [klungk] n (sound of) blow or
something falling

clus·ter [KLUS-tər] n group, bunch
▷ v gather, grow in cluster

clutch[1] [kluch] v grasp eagerly;
snatch (at) ▷ n grasp, tight grip;
device enabling two rotating shafts
to be connected and disconnected
at will

clutch[2] n set of eggs hatched at one
time; brood of chickens

clut·ter [KLUT-ər] v strew; crowd
together in disorder ▷ n disordered,
obstructive mass of objects

Cm chemistry curium

Co chemistry cobalt

coach [kohch] n large four-wheeled
carriage; railway carriage; class of
airline travel; tutor, instructor ▷ vt
instruct **coach class** class of air
travel that is cheaper than first class

co·ag·u·late [koh-AG-yà-layt]
v **-lat·ed, -lat·ing** curdle, clot,
form into a mass; congeal, solidify
co·ag·u·la'tion n

coal [kohl] n mineral consisting of
carbonized vegetable matter, used as
fuel; glowing ember ▷ v supply with
or take in coal **coal'field** n area in
which coal is found

co·a·lesce [koh-à-LES] vi
-lesced, -lesc·ing unite, merge
co·a·les'cence n

co·a·li·tion [koh-à-LISH-àn] n
alliance, esp of political parties

coarse [kors] adj **coars·er,
coars·est** rough, harsh; unrefined;
indecent **coarse'ness** n

coast [kohst] n seashore ▷ v move
under momentum; proceed without
making much effort; sail by the coast

coast'er n small ship; that which,
one who, coasts; small table mat for
glasses, etc

coat [koht] n sleeved outer
garment; animal's fur or feathers;
covering layer ▷ vt cover with layer;
clothe **coat of arms** armorial
bearings

coax [kohks] vt wheedle, cajole,
persuade, force gently

co·ax·i·al [koh-AK-see-àl] adj
having the same axis **co·ax'i·al·ly**
adv

co·balt [KOH-bawlt] n metallic
element; blue pigment from it

cob·ble [KOB-àl] vt **-bled, -bling**
patch roughly; mend shoes ▷ n
round stone **cob'bler** n shoe mender

co·bra [KOH-brà] n venomous,
hooded snake of Asia and Africa

cob·web n spider's web

co·caine [koh-KAYN] n addictive
narcotic drug used medicinally as
anesthetic

coch·i·neal [koch-à-NEEL] n
scarlet dye from Mexican insect

cock [kok] n male bird, esp of
domestic fowl; tap for liquids;
hammer of gun; its position drawn
back ▷ vt draw back (gun hammer)
to firing position; raise, turn in alert
or jaunty manner **cock'eyed** [-id]
adj crosseyed; with a squint; askew
cock'fight n staged fight between
roosters

cock·a·trice [KOK-à-tris] n
fabulous animal similar to basilisk

cock·chaf·er [KOK-chay-fàr] n
large, flying beetle

cock·le [KOK-àl] n shellfish

Cock·ney [KOK-nee] n, pl **-neys**
native of East End of London; urban
dialect of London or its East End

cock·pit [KOK-pit] n pilot's seat,
compartment in small aircraft;
driver's seat in racing car; orig

enclosure for cockfighting

cock•roach [KOK-rohch] *n* kind of insect, household pest

cock•tail [KOK-tayl] *n* short drink of whiskey, gin, etc with flavorings, etc

cock•y [KOK-ee] *adj* **cock•i•er, cock•i•est** conceited, pert **cock'i•ness** *n*

co•coa [KOH-koh] *n* powder made from seed of cacao (tropical) tree; drink made from the powder

co•co•nut [KOH-kə-nut] *n* tropical palm; very large, hard nut from this palm

co•coon [kə-KOON] *n* sheath of insect in chrysalis stage; any protective covering

co•da [KOH-də] *n* *music* final part of musical composition

cod•dle [KOD-l] *vt* **-dled, -dling** overprotect, pamper; cook (eggs) lightly

code [kohd] *n* system of letters, symbols and rules for their association to transmit messages secretly or briefly; scheme of conduct; collection of laws **cod'i•fy** [KOD-] *vt* **-fied, -fy•ing cod•i•fi•ca'tion** *n*

co•deine [KOH-deen] *n* alkaline sedative, analgesic drug

co•de•pen•dent [koh-di-PEND-dənt] *adj* of a relationship involving an addict ▷ *n* **co•de•pen'den•cy** *n*

co•dex [KOH-deks] *n, pl* **-di•ces** [-də-seez] ancient manuscript volume, esp of Bible, etc

codg•er [KOJ-ər] *n inf* man, esp old

cod•i•cil [KOD-ə-səl] *n* addition to will

co•ed•u•ca•tion•al [koh-ej-ə-KAY-shə-nl] *adj* of education of boys and girls together in mixed classes **co•ed** [koh-ed] *n* (female student at) coeducational school ▷ *adj*

co•ef•fi•cient [koh-ə-FISH-ənt] *n* *mathematics* numerical or constant factor

co•erce [koh-URS] *vt* **-erced, -erc•ing** compel, force **co•er'cion** [-UR-shən] *n* forcible compulsion or restraint

co•ex•ist [koh-ig-ZIST] *vi* exist together **co•ex•ist'ence** *n*

cof•fee [KAW-fee] *n* seeds of tropical shrub; drink made from roasting and grinding these

cof•fer [KAW-fər] *n* chest for valuables; treasury, funds

cof•fer•dam [KAW-fər-dam] *n* watertight structure enabling construction work to be done underwater

cof•fin [KAW-fin] *n* box for corpse

cog [kog] *n* one of series of teeth on rim of wheel; person, thing forming small part of big process, organization, etc

co•gent [KOH-jənt] *adj* convincing, compelling, persuasive **co'gen•cy** *n*

cog•i•tate [KOJ-i-tayt] *vi* **-tat•ed, -tat•ing** think, reflect, ponder

co•gnac [KOHN-yak] *n* French brandy

cog•nate [KOG-nayt] *adj* of same stock, related, kindred

cog•ni•tion [kog-NISH-ən] *n* act or faculty of knowing **cog'ni•tive** *adj*

cog•ni•zance [KOG-nə-zəns] *n* knowledge, perception **cog'ni•zant** *adj*

co•gno•scen•ti [kon-yə-SHEN-tee] *pl n* people with knowledge in particular field, esp arts

co•hab•it [koh-HAB-it] *vi* live together as husband and wife

co•here [koh-HEER] *vi* **-hered, -her•ing** stick together, be consistent **co•her'ence** *n* **co•her'ent** *adj* capable of logical speech, thought; connected; making sense; sticking together

co·he·sion [-HEE-zhàn] n cohering **co·he·sive** adj

co·hort [KOH-hort] n troop; associate

coif·feur [kwah-FUUR] n hairdresser

coif·fure [kwah-FYUUR] n hairstyle

coil [koil] vt lay in rings; twist into winding shape ▷ vi twist, take up a winding shape or spiral ▷ n series of rings; device in vehicle, etc to transform low-voltage direct current to higher voltage for ignition purposes; contraceptive device inserted in womb

coin [koin] n piece of money; money ▷ vt make into money, stamp; invent **coin'age** n coining; coins collectively **coin money** inf make money rapidly

co·in·cide [koh-in-SĪD] vi **-cid·ed, -cid·ing** happen together; agree exactly **co·in'ci·dence** [-si-dàns] n **co·in'ci·dent** adj coinciding **co·in·ci·den'tal** adj

co·i·tus [KOH-i-tàs], **co·i'tion** [koh-ISH-àn] n sexual intercourse

coke¹ [kohk] n residue left from distillation of coal, used as fuel

coke² n sl cocaine

Col. Colossians

co·la [KOH-là] n tropical tree; its nut, used to flavor drink

col·an·der [KUL-àn-dàr] n culinary strainer perforated with small holes

cold [kohld] adj **-er, -est** lacking heat; indifferent, unmoved, apathetic; dispiriting; reserved or unfriendly; (of colors) giving an impression of coldness ▷ n lack of heat; illness, marked by runny nose, etc **cold'ly** adv **cold'-blood·ed**

adj lacking pity, mercy; having body temperature that varies with that of the surroundings **cold chisel** toughened steel chisel **cold feet** fear **cold storage** method of preserving perishable foods, etc by keeping them at artificially reduced temperature **cold turkey** sl abrupt halt in use of addictive drug, etc **cold war** economic, diplomatic stance of nonmilitary hostility

cole·slaw [KOHL-slaw] n salad dish based on shredded cabbage

col·ic [KOL-ik] n severe pains in the intestines **co·li·tis** [kà-LĪ-tis] n inflammation of the colon

col·lab·o·rate [kà-LAB-à-rayt] vi **-rat·ed, -rat·ing** work with another on a project **col·lab'o·ra·tor** n one who works with another, esp one who aids an enemy in occupation of his own country

col·lage [kà-LAHZH] n (artistic) composition of bits and pieces stuck together on background

col·lapse [kà-LAPS] vi **-lapsed, -laps·ing** fall; give way; lose strength, fail ▷ n act of collapsing; breakdown **col·laps'i·ble** adj

col·lar [KOL-àr] n band, part of garment, worn round neck; inf police arrest ▷ vt seize by collar; inf capture, seize **col'lar·bone** n bone from shoulder to breastbone

col·late [kà-LAYT] vt **-lat·ed, -lat·ing** compare carefully; place in order (as printed sheets for binding) **col·la'tion** n collating; light meal

col·lat·er·al [kà-LAT-àr-àl] n security pledged for repayment of loan ▷ adj accompanying; side by side; of same stock but different line; subordinate **collateral damage** unintentional civilian casualties or damage to civilian property caused by military action

col•league [KOL-eeg] *n* associate, companion in office or employment, fellow worker

col•lect [kə-LEKT] *vt* gather, bring together ▷ *vi* come together; *inf* receive money **col•lect'ed** *adj* calm; gathered **col•lec'tion** *n* **col•lec'tive** *n* factory, farm, etc, run on principles of collectivism ▷ *adj* **col•lec'tiv•ism** *n* theory that a government should own all means of production

col•lege [KOL-ij] *n* place of higher education; society of scholars; association **col•le•giate** [kə-LEE-jit] *adj* **col•le•gian** *n* student

col•lide [kə-LID] *vi* **-lid•ed, -lid•ing** strike or dash together; come into conflict **col•li'sion** [-LIZH-ən] *n* colliding

col•lo•di•on [kə-LOH-dee-ən] *n* chemical solution used in photography and medicine

col•loid [KOL-oid] *n* suspension of particles in a solution

col•lo•qui•al [kə-LOH-kwee-əl] *adj* pert to or used in informal conversation **col•lo'qui•al•ism** *n* **col•lo•quy** [KOL-ə-kwee] *n, pl* **-quies** conversation; dialogue

col•lu•sion [kə-LOO-zhən] *n* secret agreement for a fraudulent purpose, esp in legal proceedings **col•lu'sive** [-siv] *adj*

co•logne [kə-LOHN] *n* perfumed liquid

co•lon¹ [KOH-lən] *n* mark (:) indicating break in a sentence

colon² *n* part of large intestine from cecum to rectum

colo•nel [KUR-nl] *n* commander of regiment or battalion

col•on•nade [kol-ə-NAYD] *n* row of columns

col•o•ny [KOL-ə-nee] *n, pl* **-nies** body of people who settle in new country but remain subject to parent country; country so settled; distinctive group living together **co•lo•ni•al** [kə-LOH-nee-əl] *adj* of colony **co'lo•nist** *n* **col•o•ni•za'tion** *n* **col'o•nize** *vt* **-nized, -niz•ing**

col•or [KUL-ər] *n* hue, tint; complexion; paint; pigment; *fig* semblance, pretext; timbre, quality; mood ▷ *pl* flag; distinguishing symbol ▷ *vt* stain, dye, paint, give color to; disguise; influence or distort ▷ *vi* become colored; blush **col•or•a'tion** *n* **col'or•ful** *adj* with bright or varied colors; distinctive

co•los•sus [kə-LOS-əs] *n, pl* **-los•si** [-LOS-ī] huge statue; something, somebody very large **co•los'sal** *adj* huge, gigantic

colt [kohlt] *n* young male horse

col•umn [KOL-əm] *n* long vertical cylinder; pillar; support; division of page; body of troops **co•lum•nar** [kə-LUM-nər] *adj* **col'um•nist** *n* journalist writing regular feature for newspaper

com-, con- *prefix* together, jointly: commingle

co•ma [KOH-mə] *n* state of unconsciousness **co'ma•tose** [-tohs] *adj*

comb [kohm] *n* toothed instrument for tidying, arranging, decorating hair; rooster's crest; mass of honey cells ▷ *vt* use comb on; search with great care **comb'-o•ver** *n* hairstyle in which long hairs from the side of the head are swept over the scalp to cover a bald patch

com•bat [KOM-bat] *n* fight or struggle ▷ *vt* [kəm-BAT] fight, contest **com•bat•ant** [kəm-BAT-nt] *n* **combat boot** heavy army boot **com•bat'ive** *adj*

com•bine [kəm-BIN] *v* join together; ally ▷ *n* [KOM-bin] trust, syndicate, esp of businesses, trade organizations, etc **com·bi·na·tion** [kom-bə-NAY-shən] n **com'bine** n machine to harvest and thresh grain in one operation

com·bus·tion [kəm-BUS-chən] n process of burning **com·bus'ti·ble** adj

come [kum] vi **came, come, com·ing** approach, arrive, move toward; reach; happen to; occur; be available; originate (from); become; turn out to be **come'back** n inf return to active life after retirement; retort **come'down** n setback; descent in social status

com·e·dy [KOM-i-dee] n, pl **-dies** dramatic or other work of light, amusing character; humor **co·me·di·an** [kə-MEE-dee-ən] n entertainer who tells jokes, etc; actor in comedy

come·ly [KUM-lee] adj fair, pretty, good-looking **come'li·ness** n

co·mes·ti·bles [kə-MES-tə-bəlz] n food

com·et [KOM-it] n luminous heavenly body consisting of diffuse head, nucleus and long tail

com·fort [KUM-fərt] n well-being; ease; consolation; means of consolation or satisfaction ▷ vt soothe; cheer, gladden, console **com·fort·a·ble** [KUMF-tə-bəl] adj free from pain, etc; inf financially secure **com'fort·a·bly** adv **com'fort·er** n one who comforts; woolen scarf; quilt **comfort food** food that makes the eater feel better emotionally

com·ic [KOM-ik] adj relating to comedy; funny, laughable ▷ n comedian; magazine consisting of strip cartoons **com'i·cal** adj

com·ma [KOM-ə] n punctuation mark (,) separating parts of sentence

com·mand [kə-MAND] vt order; rule; compel; have in one's power; overlook, dominate ▷ vi exercise rule ▷ n order; power of controlling, ruling, dominating, overlooking, knowledge, mastery; post of one commanding; district commanded, jurisdiction **com'man·dant** [KOM-ən-dant] n **com·man·deer'** vt seize for military use, appropriate **com·mand'er** n **com·mand'ing** adj in command; with air of authority **com·mand'ment** n

com·man·do [kə-MAN-doh] n, pl **-dos** (member of) special military unit trained for airborne, amphibious attack

com·mem·o·rate [kə-MEM-ə-rayt] vt **-rat·ed, -rat·ing** celebrate, keep in memory by ceremony; be a memorial of **com·mem·o·ra'tion** n **com·mem'o·ra·tive** adj

com·mence [kə-MENS] v **-menced, -menc·ing** begin **com·mence'ment** n beginning; graduation of students

com·mend [kə-MEND] vt praise; commit, entrust **com·mend'a·ble** adj **com·men·da'tion** n

com·men·su·rate [kə-MEN-sər-it] adj equal in size or length of time; in proportion, adequate

com·ment [KOM-ent] n remark, criticism; gossip; note, explanation ▷ vi remark; note; annotate, criticize **com'men·tar·y** n pl **-tar·ies** explanatory notes or comments; spoken accompaniment to film, etc **com'men·ta·tor** n author, speaker of commentary

com·merce [KOM-ərs] n buying and selling; dealings; trade **com·mer·cial** [kə-MUR-shəl] adj of, concerning, business, trade, profit, etc ▷ n advertisement on radio or TV

com·mis·er·ate [kə-MIZ-ə-rayt]
vt **-at·ed, -at·ing** pity, condole,
sympathize with

com·mis·sion [kə-MISH-ən] *n*
something entrusted to be done;
delegated authority; body entrusted
with some special duty; payment
by percentage for doing something;
warrant, esp presidential warrant,
giving authority; document
appointing person to officer's rank;
doing, committing ▷ *vt* charge with
duty or task; *military* confer a rank;
give order for **com·mis·sion·er**
n one empowered to act by
commission or warrant; member of
commission or government board;
administrative head of professional
sport

com·mit [kə-MIT] *vt* **-mit·ted,
-mit·ting** entrust, give in charge;
perpetrate, be guilty of; pledge,
promise; compromise, entangle;
place in prison or mental institution
com·mit'ment *n*

com·mit·tee [kə-MIT-ee] *n*
body appointed, elected for special
business usu from larger body

com·mode [kə-MOHD] *n* chest of
drawers; toilet

com·mo·di·ous [kə-MOH-dee-
əs] *adj* roomy

com·mod·i·ty [kə-MOD-i-tee] *n*,
pl **-ties** article of trade; anything
useful

com·mon [KOM-ən] *adj* shared
by or belonging to all, or to several;
public, general; ordinary, usual,
frequent; inferior; vulgar ▷ *n* land
belonging to community ▷ *pl*
ordinary people; **(C-)** lower house of
British parliament **com'mon·ly**
adv **Common Market** former name for
EUROPEAN UNION com'mon·place
adj ordinary, everyday ▷ *n* trite
remark; anything occurring

frequently **common sense**
sound, practical understanding
com'mon·wealth *n* republic;
state of the US; federation of self-
governing countries

com·mo·tion [kə-MOH-shən] *n*
stir, disturbance, tumult

com·mune¹ [kə-MYOON] *vi*
-muned, -mun·ing converse
together intimately **com·mun'ion**
n sharing of thoughts, feelings, etc;
fellowship; body with common faith;
(C-) participation in sacrament of the
Lord's Supper; **(C-)** that sacrament,
Eucharist

com·mune² [KOM-yoon] *n*
group of families, individuals living
together and sharing property,
responsibility, etc **com·mu·nal**
[kə-MYOON-l] *adj* for common use

com·mu·ni·cate [kə-MYOO-
ni-kayt] *v* **-cat·ed, -cat·ing** ▷ *vt*
impart, convey; reveal ▷ *vi* give
or exchange information; have
connecting passage, door; receive
Communion **com·mu·ni·ca·ble**
adj **com·mu'ni·cant** *n* one
who receives Communion
com·mu·ni·ca'tion *n* act of giving,
esp information; information,
message; (usu *pl*) passage (road,
railway, etc), or means of exchanging
messages (radio, mail, etc)
between places ▷ *pl* connections
between military base and front
com·mu'ni·ca·tive *adj* free with
information

com·mu·ni·qué [kə-myoo-ni-
KAY] *n* official announcement

com·mu·nism [KOM-yə-niz-əm]
n doctrine that all goods, means of
production, etc, should be property
of community **com'mu·nist** *n, adj*

com·mu·ni·ty [kə-MYOO-ni-
tee] *n, pl* **-ties** body of people
with something in common,

eg neighborhood, religion, etc; society, the policy; joint ownership; similarity, agreement

com·mute [kə-MYOOT] v **-mut·ed, -mut·ing** ▷ vi travel daily some distance to work ▷ vt exchange; change (punishment, etc) into something less severe; change (payment, etc) into another form ▷ n journey made by commuting **com·mu·ta·tion** [kom-yə-TAY-shən] n **com'mu·ta·tor** n device to change alternating electric current into direct current **com·mut'er** n one who daily travels some distance to work

com·pact¹ [kəm-PAKT] adj neatly arranged or packed; solid, concentrated; terse ▷ v make, become compact; compress **com·pact'ness** n **com·pact disk** [KOM-pakt] small disk on which sound is recorded as series of metallic pits enclosed in polyvinyl chloride and played back by optical scanning by laser

com·pact² [KOM-pakt] n small case to hold face powder, powder puff and mirror

com·pact³ [KOM-pakt] n agreement, covenant, treaty, contract

com·pan·ion¹ [kəm-PAN-yən] n chum, fellow, comrade, associate; person employed to live with another **com·pan'ion·a·ble** adj

companion² n raised cover over staircase from deck to cabin of ship; deck skylight **com·pan'ion·way** n staircase from deck to cabin

com·pa·ny [KUM-pə-nee] n, pl **-nies** gathering of persons; companionship, fellowship; guests; business firm; division of regiment under captain; crew of ship; actors in play

com·pare [kəm-PAIR] vt **-pared, -par·ing** notice or point out likenesses and differences of things; liken; make comparative and superlative of adjective or adverb ▷ vi be like; compete with **com·pa·ra·bil·i·ty** [kom-pər-ə-BIL-i-tee] n **com'pa·ra·ble** adj **com·par'a·tive** adj that may be compared; not absolute; relative, partial; grammar denoting form of adjective, adverb, expressing "more" ▷ n **com·par'a·tive·ly** adv **com·par'i·son** n act of comparing

com·part·ment [kəm-PAHRT-mənt] n division or part divided off; section

com·pass [KUM-pəs] n instrument for showing the north; instrument for drawing circles; circumference, measurement around; space, area; scope, reach ▷ vt surround; comprehend; attain, accomplish

com·pas·sion [kəm-PASH-ən] n pity, sympathy **com·pas'sion·ate** [-it] adj

com·pat·i·ble [kəm-PAT-ə-bəl] adj capable of harmonious existence; consistent, agreeing with **com·pat·i·bil'i·ty** adv

com·pa·tri·ot [kəm-PAY-tree-ət] n fellow countryman ▷ adj

com·pel [kəm-PEL] vt **-pelled, -pel·ling** force, oblige; bring about by force

com·pen·di·um [kəm-PEN-dee-əm] n, pl **-di·ums** abridgment, summary **com·pen'di·ous** adj brief but inclusive

com·pen·sate [KOM-pən-sayt] vt **-sat·ed, -sat·ing** make up for; recompense suitably; reward **com·pen·sa'tion** n

com·pete [kəm-PEET] vi **-pet·ed, -pet·ing** (oft with with) strive

in rivalry, contend for, vie with
com·pe·ti·tion [kom-pi-TISH-ən] *n* **com·pet'i·tive** [kəm-] *adj* **com·pet'i·tor** *n*

com·pe·tent [KOM-pi-tənt] *adj* able, skillful; properly qualified; proper, due, legitimate; suitable, sufficient **com'pe·tence** *n* efficiency

com·pile [kəm-PĪL] *vt* **-piled, -pil·ing** make up (eg book) from various sources or materials; gather, put together **com·pi·la·tion** [kom-pə-LAY-shən] *n* **com·pil'er** *n*

com·pla·cent [kəm-PLAY-sənt] *adj* self-satisfied; pleased or gratified **com·pla'cen·cy** *n*

com·plain [kəm-PLAYN] *vi* grumble; bring charge, make known a grievance; (with *of*) make known that one is suffering from **com·plaint'** *n* statement of a wrong, grievance; ailment, illness **com·plain'ant** *n*

com·ple·ment [KOM-plə-mənt] *n* something making up a whole; full allowance, equipment, etc ▷ *vt* add to, make complete **com·ple·men'ta·ry** *adj*

com·plete [kəm-PLEET] *adj* full, perfect; finished, ended; entire; thorough ▷ *vt* **-plet·ed, -plet·ing** make whole, perfect; finish **com·plete'ly** *adv* **com·ple'tion** *n*

com·plex [kəm-PLEKS] *adj* intricate, compound, involved ▷ *n* [KOM-pleks] complicated whole; group of related buildings; psychological abnormality, obsession **com·plex'i·ty** *n*

com·plex·ion [kəm-PLEK-shən] *n* look, color, of skin, esp of face, appearance; aspect, character; disposition

compliant see **COMPLY**

com·pli·cate [KOM-pli-kayt]

vt **-cat·ed, -cat·ing** make intricate, involved, difficult; mix up **com·pli·ca'tion** *n*

com·plic·i·ty [kəm-PLIS-i-tee] *n*, *pl* **-ties** partnership in wrongdoing

com·pli·ment [KOM-plə-mənt] *n* expression of regard, praise; flattering speech ▷ *pl* expression of courtesy, formal greetings ▷ *vt* praise, congratulate **com·pli·men'ta·ry** *adj* expressing praise; free of charge

com·ply [kəm-PLĪ] *vi* **-plied, -ply·ing** consent, yield, do as asked **com·pli'ance** *n* **com·pli'ant** *adj*

com·po·nent [kəm-POH-nənt] *n* part, element, constituent of whole ▷ *adj* composing, making up

com·port [kəm-PORT] *v* agree; behave

com·pose [kəm-POHZ] *vt* **-posed, -pos·ing** arrange, put in order; write, invent; make up; calm; settle, adjust **com·posed'** *adj* calm **com·pos'er** *n* one who composes, esp music **com·pos·ite** [kəm-POZ-it] *adj* made up of distinct parts **com·po·si·tion** [kom-pə-ZISH-ən] *n* **com·pos·i·tor** [kəm-POZ-i-tər] *n* typesetter, one who arranges type for printing **com·po·sure** [kəm-POH-zhər] *n* calmness

com·pos men·tis [KOM-pəs MEN-tis] *Lat* of sound mind

com·post [KOM-pohst] *n* fertilizing mixture of decayed vegetable matter for soil

com·pote [KOM-poht] *n* fruit stewed or preserved in syrup

com·pound¹ [KOM-pownd] *n* mixture, joining; substance, word, made up of parts ▷ *adj* not simple; composite, mixed ▷ *vt* [kəm-POWND] mix, make up, put together; intensify, make worse; compromise, settle debt by partial payment

com·pound² [KOM-pownd]
n (fenced or walled) enclosure
containing houses, etc

com·pre·hend [kom-pri-HEND]
vt understand, take in; include,
comprise **com·pre·hen·si·ble**
adj **com·pre·hen·sion** n
com·pre·hen·sive adj wide, full;
taking in much

com·press [kəm-PRES] vt squeeze
together; make smaller in size,
bulk ▷ n [KOM-pres] pad of cloth
applied to wound, inflamed part, etc
com·press·i·ble adj **com·pres·sion**
[kəm-PRESH-ən] n in internal
combustion engine, squeezing of
explosive charge before ignition, to
give additional force **com·pres·sor**
n esp machine to compress air, gas

com·prise [kəm-PRIZ] vt -prised,
-pris·ing include, contain

com·pro·mise [KOM-prə-miz] n
meeting halfway, coming to terms
by giving up part of claim; middle
course ▷ v -mised, -mis·ing settle
(dispute) by making concessions
▷ vt expose to risk or suspicion

comp·trol·ler [kən-TROH-lər] n
controller (in some titles)

com·pul·sion [kəm-PUL-shən]
n act of compelling; irresistible
impulse **com·pul·sive** adj
com·pul·sive·ly [-sə-rə-lee] adv
com·pul·so·ry adj not optional

com·punc·tion [kəm-PUNGK-
shən] n regret for wrongdoing

com·pute [kəm-PYOOT] v
-put·ed, -put·ing reckon,
calculate, esp using computer
com·pu·ta·tion [kom-pyə-TAY-
shən] n reckoning, estimate
com·put'er n electronic device
for storing, retrieving information
and performing calculations
com·put'er·ize v -ized, -iz·ing

equip with, perform by computer

com·rade [KOM-rad] n chum,
companion, friend **com'radeship** n
com'rade·ly adj

con¹ [kon] v inf **conned**, **con·ning**
swindle, defraud; cajole

con² [kon] **conned**, **con·ning** direct
steering (of ship)

con- prefix see com-

con·cat·e·nate [kon-KAT-n-ayt]
vt -nat·ed, -nat·ing link together
con·cat·e·na'tion n connected
chain (as of circumstances)

con·cave [kon-KAYV] adj hollow,
rounded inward **con·cav'i·ty** n

con·ceal [kən-SEEL] vt hide, keep
secret

con·cede [kən-SEED] vt -ced·ed,
-ced·ing admit, admit truth of;
grant, allow, yield

con·ceit [kən-SEET] n vanity,
overweening opinion of oneself; far-
fetched comparison **con·ceit'ed** adj

con·ceive [kən-SEEV] v -ceived,
-ceiv·ing think of, imagine; believe;
form in the mind; become pregnant
con·ceiv'a·ble adj

con·cen·trate [KON-sən-trayt] v
-trat·ed, -trat·ing ▷ vt focus (one's
efforts, etc); increase in strength;
reduce to small space ▷ vi devote
all attention; come together ▷ n
concentrated material or solution
con·cen·tra'tion n **concentration
camp** prison camp, esp one in Nazi
Germany

con·cen·tric [kən-SEN-trik] adj
having the same center

con·cept [KON-sept] n
abstract idea; mental expression
con·cep·tu·al [kən-SEP-choo-
əl] adj

con·cep·tion [kən-SEP-shən] n
idea, notion; act of conceiving

con·cern [kən-SURN] vt relate,
apply to; interest, affect, trouble;

(with *in*, *with*) involve (oneself) ▷ *n* affair; regard; worry; importance; business, enterprise **con·cerned'** *adj* connected with; interested; worried; involved **con·cern'ing** *prep* respecting, about

con·cert [KON-surt] *n* musical entertainment; harmony; agreement ▷ *vt* [kän-SURT] arrange, plan together **con·cert'ed** [-əns] mutually arranged, planned; determined **con·cer·ti·na** [kon-sər-TEE-nə] *n* musical instrument with bellows and keys **con·cer·to** [kən-CHER-toh] *n*, *pl*-**tos** musical composition for solo instrument and orchestra

con·ces·sion [kən-SESH-ən] *n* act of conceding; thing conceded; grant; special privilege

conch [kongk] *n* seashell

con·chol·o·gy [kong-KOL-ə-jee] *n* study, collection of shells and shellfish

con·cierge [kon-see-AIRZH] *n* in France esp, caretaker, doorkeeper

con·cil·i·ate [kän-SIL-ee-ayt] *vt* -**at·ed**, -**at·ing** pacify, win over from hostility **con·cil'i·a·tor** *n* **con·cil'i·a·to·ry** *adj*

con·cise [kän-SĪS] *adj* brief, terse **con·cise'ly** *adv* **con·cise'ness** *n*

con·clave [KON-klayv] *n* private meeting; assembly for election of a pope

con·clude [kän-KLOOD] *v* -**clud·ed**, -**clud·ing** ▷ *vt* end, finish; deduce; settle ▷ *vi* come to end; decide **con·clu·sion** [-KLOO-zhän] *n* **con·clu'sive** *adj* decisive, convincing

con·coct [kän-KOKT] *vt* make mixture, prepare with various ingredients; make up; contrive, plan **con·coc'tion** *n*

con·com·i·tant [kän-KOM-i-tənt] *adj* accompanying

con·cord [KON-kord] *n* agreement; harmony ▷ *vi* [kän-KORD] agree **con·cord'ance** [-əns] *n* agreement; index to words of book (esp Bible)

con·course [KON-kors] *n* crowd; large, open place in public area; boulevard

con·crete [KON-kreet] *n* mixture of sand, cement, etc, used in building ▷ *adj* made of concrete; particular, specific; perceptible, actual; solid **con·crete'ly** *adv*

con·cu·bine [KONG-kyə-bīn] *n* woman living with man as his wife, but not married to him; mistress **con·cu·bi·nage** [kon-KYOO-bə-nij] *n*

con·cu·pis·cence [kon-KYOO-pi-səns] *n* lust

con·cur [kän-KUR] *vi* -**curred**, -**cur·ring** agree, express agreement; happen together; coincide **con·cur'rence** *n* **con·cur'rent** *adj* **con·cur'rent·ly** *adv* at the same time

con·cus·sion [kän-KUSH-ən] *n* brain injury; physical shock

con·demn [kän-DEM] *vt* blame; find guilty; doom; find, declare unfit for use **con·dem·na·tion** [kon-dem-NAY-shän] *n* **con·dem'na·to·ry** *adj*

con·dense [kän-DENS] *v* -**densed**, -**dens·ing** ▷ *vt* concentrate, make more solid; turn from gas into liquid; pack into few words ▷ *vi* turn from gas to liquid **con·den·sa·tion** [kon-den-SAY-shän] *n* **con·dens'er** *n* electricity apparatus for storing electrical energy, a capacitor; apparatus for reducing gas to liquid form; a lens or mirror for focusing light

con·de·scend [kon-də-SEND] *vi* treat graciously one regarded as inferior; do something below one's dignity **con·de·scend'ing** adj **con·de·scen'sion** n

con·di·ment [KON-də-mənt] n sauce, seasoning for food

con·di·tion [kən-DISH-ən] n state or circumstances of anything; thing on which statement or happening or existing depends; stipulation, prerequisite; health, physical fitness; rank ▷ vt accustom; regulate; make fit, healthy; be essential to happening or existence of; stipulate **con·di'tion·al** adj dependent on circumstances or events ▷ n grammar form of verbs

con·do [KON-doh] n, pl -dos condominium (building)

con·dole [kən-DOHL] vi -doled, -dol·ing grieve with, offer sympathy; commiserate with **con·do'lence** n

con·dom [KON-dəm] n sheathlike usu rubber contraceptive device worn by man

con·do·min·i·um [kon-də-MIN-ee-əm] n joint rule by two or more countries; building with apartments, offices, etc; individually owned

con·done [kən-DOHN] vt -doned, don·ing overlook, forgive, treat as not existing

con·duce [kən-DOOS] vi -duced, -duc·ing help, promote; tend toward **con·du'cive** adj

con·duct [KON-dukt] n behavior; management ▷ vt [kən-DUKT] escort, guide; lead, direct; manage; transmit (heat, electricity) **con·duc'tion** n **con·duc'tive** adj **con·duc·tiv'i·ty** n **con·duc'tor** n employee on bus, train, etc who collects fares; director of orchestra; one who leads, guides; substance capable of transmitting heat, electricity, etc

con·du·it [KON-doo-it] n channel or pipe for conveying water, electric cables, etc

cone [kohn] n solid figure with circular base, tapering to a point; fruit of pine, fir, etc **con·ic** [KON-ik] **con'i·cal** adj

con·fab·u·late [kən-FAB-yə-layt] vi -lat·ed, -lat·ing chat **con·fab** [KON-fab] n inf shortened form of confabulation **con·fab·u·la'tion** n confidential conversation

con·fec·tion [kən-FEK-shən] n prepared delicacy, esp something sweet; candy **con·fec'tion·er** n dealer in candies, fancy cakes, etc **con·fec'tion·er·y** n confectioner's shop; things confectioner sells

con·fed·er·ate [kən-FED-ər-it] n ally; accomplice ▷ v [-ə-rayt] -at·ed, -at·ing unite **con·fed'er·a·cy** n **con·fed·er·a'tion** n alliance of political units

con·fer [kən-FUR] v -ferred, -fer·ring ▷ vt grant, give; bestow; award ▷ vi talk with, take advice **con·fer·ence** [KON-fər-əns] n meeting for consultation or deliberation

con·fess [kən-FES] vt admit, own; (of priest) hear sins of ▷ vi acknowledge; declare one's sins orally to priest **con·fes'sion** [-FESH-ən] n **con·fes'sion·al** n confessor's stall **con·fes'sor** n priest who hears confessions

con·fet·ti [kən-FET-ee] n small bits of colored paper for throwing at weddings

con·fide [kən-FID] v -fid·ed, -fid·ing ▷ vi (with in) tell secrets, trust ▷ vt entrust **con·fi·dant** [KON-fi-dant] n (fem **con·fi·dante**) one entrusted with secrets **con'fi·dence** n trust; boldness,

assurance; intimacy; something confided, secret **con'fi·dent** adj
con·fi·den·tial [-shəl] adj private; secret; entrusted with another's confidences **con'fi·dent·ly** adv
confidence game con game, swindle in which victim entrusts money, etc to thief, believed honest

con·fig·u·ra·tion [kən-fig-yə-RAY-shən] n shape, aspect, conformation, arrangement

con·fine [kən-FĪN] vt **-fined, fin·ing** keep within bounds; keep in house, bed, etc; shut up, imprison **con·fines** [KON-fīnz] pl n boundaries, limits **confine'ment** n esp childbirth; imprisonment

con·firm [kən-FURM] vt make sure, verify; strengthen, settle; make valid, ratify; administer confirmation to **con·fir·ma·tion** [kon-fər-MAY-shən] n making strong, certain; Christian rite administered to confirm vows made at baptism; Jewish ceremony to admit boys, girls to adult status **con·firm'a·to·ry** adj tending to confirm or establish; corroborative **con·firmed'** adj (of habit, etc) long-established

con·fis·cate [KON-fə-skayt] vt **-cat·ed, -cat·ing** seize by authority **con·fis·ca'tion** n **con·fis·ca·to·ry** [kən-FIS-kə-tor-ee] adj

con·fla·gra·tion [kon-flə-GRAY-shən] n great destructive fire

con·flict [KON-flikt] n struggle, trial of strength; disagreement ▷ vi [kən-FLIKT] be at odds with, be inconsistent with; clash

con·flu·ence [KON-floo-əns] n union of streams; meeting place **con'flu·ent** adj

con·form [kən-FORM] v comply with accepted standards, conventions, etc; adapt to rule, pattern, custom, etc

con·for·ma·tion [kon-for-MAY-shən] n structure, adaptation

con·form'ist n one who conforms, esp excessively **con·form'i·ty** n compliance

con·found [kon-FOWND] vt baffle, perplex; confuse; defeat **con·found'ed** adj old-fashioned damned

con·front [kən-FRUNT] vt face; bring face to face with **con·fron·ta·tion** [kon-frən-TAY-shən] n

con·fuse [kən-FYOOZ] vt **-fused, -fus·ing** bewilder; jumble; make unclear; mistake (one thing) for another; disconcert **con·fu'sion** n

con·geal [kən-JEEL] v solidify by cooling or freezing

con·gen·ial [kən-JEEN-yəl] adj pleasant, to one's liking; of similar disposition, tastes, etc **con·ge·ni·al'i·ty** n

con·gen·i·tal [kən-JEN-i-tl] adj existing at birth; dating from birth

con·ge·ries [KON-jə-reez] n sing and pl collection or mass of small bodies, conglomeration

con·gest [kən-JEST] v overcrowd or clog **con·ges'tion** n abnormal accumulation, overcrowding **con·gest'ed** adj

con·glom·er·ate [kən-GLOM-ər-it] n thing, substance (esp rock) composed of mixture of other, smaller elements or pieces; business organization comprising many companies ▷ v [-ə-rayt] **-at·ed, -at·ing** gather together ▷ adj **con·glom·er·a'tion** n

con·grat·u·late [kən-GRACH-ə-layt] vt **-lat·ed, -lat·ing** express pleasure at good fortune, success, etc **con·grat·u·la'tion** n **con·grat·u·la·to·ry** adj

con·gre·gate [KONG-gri-

gayt] v **-gat·ed, -gat·ing**
assemble; collect, flock together
con·gre·ga·tion n assembly, esp
for worship **con·gre·ga'tion·al** adj
con·gre·ga·tion·al·ism n form
of Protestant church organization
in which local churches are self-
governing
con·gress [KONG-gris] n meeting;
sexual intercourse; formal assembly
for discussion; legislative body
con·gres·sion·al [kən-GRESH-ə-nl]
adj **con'gress·man** n member of US
House of Representatives
con·gru·ent [KONG-groo-ənt] adj
suitable, accordant; fitting together,
esp triangles **con·gru'ence** n
con·gru'i·ty n **con·gru·ous** adj
conic see **CONE**
con·i·fer [KON-ə-fər] n cone-
bearing tree, as fir, pine, etc
co·nif·er·ous [koh-NIF-ər-əs] adj
con·jec·ture [kən-JEK-chər] n
guess, guesswork ▷ v **-tured,
-tur·ing** guess, surmise
con·jec'tur·al adj
con·join·ed twins [kən-JOIND
twinz] pl n the technical name for
SIAMESE TWINS
con·ju·gal [KON-jə-gəl] adj
relating to marriage; between
married persons **con·ju·gal'i·ty** n
con·ju·gate [KON-jə-gayt] v
-gat·ed, -gat·ing inflect verb in its
various forms (past, present, etc)
con·ju·ga'tion n
con·junc·tion [kən-JUNGK-shən]
n union; simultaneous happening;
part of speech joining words,
phrases, etc **con·junc'tive** adj
con·junc·ti·va [kon-jungk-TĪ-və]
n mucous membrane lining eyelid
con·junc·ti·vi·tis [kən-jungk-tə-
VĪ-tis] n inflammation of this
con·jure [KON-jər] v **-jured,
-jur·ing** produce magic effects;

perform tricks by sleight of hand, etc;
invoke devils; [kən-JUUR] implore
earnestly **con·ju·ra'tion** [kon-jə-
RAY-shən] n **con'jur·er** n
conk [kongk] vt inf strike (esp on
head) **conk out** vi inf break down,
stall; faint; fall asleep
con·nect [kə-NEKT] v join
together, unite; associate in the
mind **con·nec'tion** n association;
train, etc timed to enable passengers
to transfer from another; family
relation; social, commercial, etc
relationship **con·nec'tive** adj
con·nec·ti·vi·ty n state of being
or being able to be connected;
state of being connected to the
Internet; capacity of a machine to
be connected to other machines
connecting rod part of engine that
transfers motion from piston to
crankshaft
con·ning tower [KON-ing] n raised
observation tower containing the
periscope on a submarine
con·nive [kə-NĪV] vi **-nived,
-niv·ing** plot, conspire; assent,
refrain from preventing or forbidding
con·niv'ance n
con·nois·seur [kon-ə-SUR] n
critical expert in matters of taste, esp
fine arts; competent judge
con·note [kə-NOHT] vt **-not·ed,
-not·ing** imply, mean in addition to
primary meaning **con·no·ta·tion**
[kon-ə-TAY-shən] n
con·nu·bi·al [kə-NOO-bee-əl] adj
of marriage
con·quer [KONG-kər] vt win by
force of arms, overcome; defeat
▷ vi be victorious **con'quer·or** n
con·quest [KON-kwest] n
con·san·guin·i·ty [kon-
sang-GWIN-i-tee] n kinship
con·san·guine·ous adj
con·science [KON-shəns] n sense

of right or wrong governing person's words and actions **con·sci·en·tious** [-shee-EN-shàs] adj scrupulous; obedient to the dictates of conscience **con·sci·en·tious·ly** adv **conscientious objector** one who refuses military service on moral or religious grounds

con·scious [KON-shàs] adj aware; awake to one's surroundings and identity; deliberate, intentional **con·scious·ly** adv **con·scious·ness** n being conscious

con·script [KON-skript] n one compulsorily enlisted for military service ▷ vt [kàn-SKRIPT] enrol (someone) for compulsory military service **con·scrip·tion** n

con·se·crate [KON-si-krayt] vt **-crat·ed, -crat·ing** make sacred **con·se·cra·tion** n

con·sec·u·tive [kàn-SEK-yà-tiv] adj in unbroken succession

con·sen·sus [kàn-SEN-sàs] n widespread agreement, unanimity

con·sent [kàn-SENT] vi agree to, comply ▷ n acquiescence; permission; agreement

con·se·quence [KON-si-kwens] n result, effect, outcome; that which naturally follows; significance, importance **con·se·quent** adj **con·se·quen·tial** adj important **con·se·quent·ly** adv therefore, as a result

con·serv·a·to·ry [kàn-SUR-và-tor-ee] n, pl **-ries** school for teaching music or painting, etc; greenhouse

con·serve [kàn-SURV] vt **-served, -serv·ing** keep from change or decay; preserve; maintain ▷ n [KON-surv] jam, preserved fruit, etc **con·ser·va·tion** [kon-sàr-VAY-shàn] n protection, careful management of natural resources and environment

con·ser·va·tion·ist n, adj

con·serv·a·tive adj tending or wishing to conserve; moderate ▷ n politics one who desires to preserve institutions of country against change and innovation; one opposed to hasty changes or innovations **con·serv·a·tism** n

con·sid·er [kàn-SID-àr] vt think over; examine; make allowance for; be of opinion that; discuss **con·sid·er·a·ble** adj important; somewhat large **con·sid·er·ate** [-it] adj thoughtful for others' feelings, careful **con·sid·er·ate·ly** adv **con·sid·er·a·tion** n deliberation; point of importance; thoughtfulness; bribe, recompense

con·sign [kàn-SĪN] vt commit, hand over; entrust to carrier **con·sign·ee** [kon-sī-NEE] n **con·sign·or** n **con·sign·ment** n goods consigned

con·sist [kàn-SIST] vi be composed of; (with in) have as basis; agree with, be compatible **con·sist·en·cy** n agreement; harmony; degree of firmness **con·sist·ent** adj unchanging, constant; agreeing (with)

con·sis·to·ry [kàn-SIS-tà-ree] n, pl **-ries** ecclesiastical court or council, esp of pope and cardinals

con·sole¹ [kàn-SOHL] vt **-soled, -sol·ing** comfort, cheer in distress **con·so·la·tion** [kon-sà-LAY-shàn] n

con·sole² [KON-sohl] n bracket supporting shelf; keyboard, stops, etc, of organ; cabinet for TV, radio, etc

con·sol·i·date [kàn-SOL-i-dayt] vt **-dat·ed, -dat·ing** combine into connected whole; make firm, secure **con·sol·i·da·tion** n

con·som·mé [kon-sà-MAY] n clear meat soup

con·so·nant [KON-sə-nənt] *n* sound making a syllable only with vowel; non-vowel ▷ *adj* agreeing with, in accord **con'so·nance** *n*

con·sort [kən-SORT] *vi* associate, keep company with ▷ *n* [KON-sort] husband, wife, esp of ruler; ship sailing with another **con·sor'ti·um** [-SOR-shee-əm] *n, pl* **-ti·a** [-shee-ə] ▷ *n* association of banks, companies, etc

con·spic·u·ous [kən-SPIK-yoo-əs] *adj* striking, noticeable, outstanding; prominent; eminent

con·spire [kən-SPĪR] *vi* **-spired, -spir·ing** combine for evil purpose; plot, devise **con·spir'a·cy** [-SPIR-ə-see] *n, pl* **-cies con·spir'a·tor** *n* **con·spir·a·to'ri·al** *adj*

con·stant [KON-stənt] *adj* fixed, unchanging; steadfast; always duly happening or continuing ▷ *n* quantity that does not vary **con'stan·cy** *n* steadfastness; loyalty

con·stel·la·tion [kon-stə-LAY-shən] *n* group of stars

con·ster·na·tion [kon-stər-NAY-shən] *n* alarm, dismay, panic **con'ster·nate** *v* **-nat·ed, -nat·ing**

con·sti·pa·tion [kon-stə-PAY-shən] *n* difficulty in emptying bowels **con'sti·pate** *vt* **-pat·ed, -pat·ing** affect with this disorder

con·stit·u·ent [kən-STICH-oo-ənt] *adj* going toward making up whole; having power to make, alter constitution of a government ▷ *n* component part; element; voter **con·stit'u·en·cy** *n* body of constituents, supporters

con·sti·tute [KON-sti-toot] *vt* **-tut·ed, -tut·ing** compose, set up, establish, form; make into, found, give form to **con·sti·tu'tion** *n* structure, composition; health; character, disposition; principles

on which country, state is governed **con·sti·tu'tion·al** *adj* pert to constitution; in harmony with political constitution ▷ *n* walk taken for health's sake

con·strain [kən-STRAYN] *vt* force, compel **con·straint'** *n* compulsion; restraint; embarrassment, tension

con·stric·tion [kən-STRIK-shən] *n* compression, squeezing together **con·strict'** *vt* **con·stric'tive** *adj* **con·stric'tor** *n* that which constricts; see also **BOA**

con·struct [kən-STRUKT] *vt* make, build, form; put together; compose **con·struct** [KON-strukt] *n* **con·struc'tion** *n* **con·struc'tive** *adj* serving to improve; positive

con·strue [kən-STROO] *vt* **-strued, -stru·ing** interpret; deduce; analyze grammatically

con·sul [KON-səl] *n* official appointed by a government to represent it in a foreign country; in ancient Rome, one of the chief magistrates **con'su·lar** *adj* **con'su·late** [-lit] *n*

con·sult [kən-SULT] *v* seek counsel, advice, information from **con·sult'ant** *n* specialist, expert **con·sul·ta·tion** [kon-səl-TAY-shən] *n* consulting; appointment to seek professional advice, esp of doctor, lawyer **con·sult'a·tive** [kən-SUL-tə-tiv] *adj* having privilege of consulting, but not of voting; advisory

con·sume [kən-SOOM] *vt* **-sumed, -sum·ing** eat or drink; engross, possess; use up; destroy **con·sum'er** *n* buyer or user of commodity; one who consumes **con·sump·tion** [-SUMP-shən] *n* using up; destruction; *old-fashioned* pulmonary tuberculosis **con·sump'tive** *adj, n*

con·sum·mate [KON-sə-mayt] *vt* **-mat·ed, -mat·ing** perfect; fulfill; complete (esp marriage by sexual intercourse) ▷ *adj* [kən-SUM-it] of greatest perfection or completeness **con·sum'mate·ly** *adv* **con·sum·ma'tion** *n*

con·tact [KON-takt] *n* touching; being in touch; junction of two or more electrical conductors; useful acquaintance ▷ *vt* **contact lens** lens fitting over eyeball to correct defect of vision

con·ta·gion [kən-TAY-jən] *n* passing on of disease by touch, contact; contagious disease; harmful physical or moral influence **con·ta'gious** *adj* communicable by contact, catching

con·tain [kən-TAYN] *vt* hold; have room for; include, comprise; restrain (oneself) **con·tain'er** *n* box, etc for holding; large cargo-carrying standard-sized receptacle for various modes of transport

con·tam·i·nate [kən-TAM-ə-nayt] *vt* **-nat·ed, -nat·ing** stain, pollute, infect; make radioactive **con·tam·i·na'tion** *n* pollution

con·tem·plate [KON-təm-playt] *vt* **-plat·ed, -plat·ing** reflect, meditate on; gaze upon; intend **con·tem·pla'tion** *n* thoughtful consideration; spiritual meditation **con·tem·pla·tive** [kən-TEM-plə-tiv] *adj, n*

con·tem·po·rar·y [kən-TEM-pə-rer-ee] *adj* existing or lasting at same time; of same age; modern ▷ *n, pl* **-rar·ies** one existing at same time as another **con·tem·po·ra'ne·ous** [-RAY-nee-əs] *adj*

con·tempt [kən-TEMPT] *n* feeling that something is worthless, despicable, etc; expression of this feeling; state of being despised, disregarded; willful disrespect of authority

con·tend [kən-TEND] *vi* strive, fight; dispute ▷ *vt* maintain (that) **con·ten'tion** *n* strife; debate; subject matter of dispute **con·ten'tious** *adj* quarrelsome; causing dispute

con·tent[1] [KON-tent] *n* that contained; holding capacity ▷ *pl* that contained; index of topics in book

con·tent[2] [kən-TENT] *adj* satisfied; willing (to) ▷ *vt* satisfy ▷ *n* satisfaction **con·tent'ed** *adj*

con·ter·mi·nous [kən-TUR-mə-nəs] *adj* of the same extent (in time, etc); meeting along a common boundary; meeting end to end **co·ter'mi·nous** *adj*

con·test [KON-test] *n* competition; conflict ▷ *vt* [kən-TEST] dispute, debate; fight or compete for **con·test'a·ble** *adj* **con·test'ant** *n*

con·text [KON-tekst] *n* words coming before, after a word or passage; conditions and circumstances of event, fact, etc **con·tex·tu·al** [kən-TEKS-choo-əl] *adj*

con·tig·u·ous [kən-TIG-yoo-əs] *adj* touching, near **con·ti·gu'i·ty** *n*

con·ti·nent[1] [KON-tə-nənt] *n* large continuous mass of land **con·ti·nen'tal** *adj*

continent[2] *adj* able to control one's urination and defecation; sexually chaste **con'ti·nence** *n*

con·tin·gent [kən-TIN-jənt] *adj* depending (on); possible; accidental ▷ *n* group (of troops, supporters, etc); part of or representative of a larger group **con·tin'gen·cy** *n*

con·tin·ue [kən-TIN-yoo] *v* **-ued, -u·ing** remain, keep in existence;

carry on, last, go on; resume; prolong
con·tin·u·al *adj* **con·tin·u·a·tion**
n extension, extra part; resumption;
constant succession, prolongation
con·ti·nu·i·ty *n* logical sequence;
state of being continuous
con·tin·u·ous *adj*

con·tort [kən-TORT] *vt* twist
out of normal shape **con·tor·tion**
n **con·tor·tion·ist** *n* one who
contorts own body to entertain

con·tour [KON-tuur] *n* outline,
shape, esp of mountains, coast,
etc; (also **contour line**) line on map
drawn through places of same height

contra- *prefix* against or
contrasting: *contradistinction;
contrapuntal*

con·tra·band [KON-trə-band]
n smuggled goods; illegal traffic in
such goods ▷ *adj* prohibited by law

con·tra·cep·tion [kon-trə-SEP-
shən] *n* prevention of conception
usu by artificial means, birth control
con·tra·cep'tive *adj, n*

con·tract [kən-TRAKT] *v* make or
become smaller, shorter; enter into
agreement; agree upon ▷ *vt* incur,
become affected by ▷ *n* [KON-
trakt] bargain, agreement; formal
document recording agreement;
agreement enforceable by law
con·tract'ed *adj* drawn together
con·trac·tile [kən-TRAK-tl] *adj*
tending to contract **con·trac'tion**
n **con'trac·tor** *n* one making
contract, esp builder **con·trac·tu·al**
[-choo-əl] *adj*

con·tra·dict [kon-trə-DIKT] *vt*
deny; be at variance or inconsistent
with **con·tra·dic'tion** *n*
con·tra·dic'to·ry *adj*

con·tral·to [kən-TRAL-toh] *n, pl*
-tos lowest of female voices

con·trap·tion [kən-TRAP-shən] *n*
gadget; device; construction, device

often overelaborate or eccentric

con·tra·pun·tal [kon-trə-PUN-tl]
adj music pert to counterpoint

con·tra·ry [KON-trer-ee] *adj*
opposed; opposite, other; [kən-
TRAIR-ee] perverse, obstinate
▷ *n* something the exact opposite
of another ▷ *adv* in opposition
con'trar·i·ness *n*

con·trast [kən-TRAST] *vt* bring
out differences; set in opposition
for comparison ▷ *vi* show great
difference ▷ *n* [KON-trast] striking
difference; TV sharpness of image

con·tra·vene [kon-trə-VEEN]
vt **-vened, -ven·ing** transgress,
infringe; conflict with; contradict
con·tra·ven'tion *n*

con·tre·temps [KON-trə-tahn] *n*
unexpected and embarrassing event
or mishap

con·trib·ute [kən-TRIB-yoot]
v **-ut·ed, -ut·ing** give, pay to
common fund; help to occur; write
for the press **con·tri·bu·tion** [kon-
trə-BYOO-shən] *n* **con·trib'u·tive**
adj **con·trib'u·tor** *n* one who
writes articles for newspapers, etc;
one who donates **con·trib'u·to·ry**
adj partly responsible; giving to
pension fund, etc

con·trite [kən-TRĪT] *adj* remorseful
for wrongdoing, penitent
con·trite'ly *adv* **con·tri'tion**
[-TRISH-ən] *n*

con·trive [kən-TRĪV] *vt* **-trived,
-triv·ing** manage; devise, invent,
design **con·triv'ance** *n* artifice or
device **con·trived'** *adj* obviously
planned, artificial

con·trol [kən-TROHL] *vt* **-trolled,
-trol·ling** command, dominate;
regulate; check, test ▷ *n*
power to direct or determine; curb,
check; standard of comparison
in experiment ▷ *pl* system of

instruments to control automobile, aircraft, etc **con·trol'la·ble** adj
con·trol'ler n one who controls; official controlling expenditure
control tower tower in airport from which takeoffs and landings are directed

con·tro·ver·sy [KON-trə-vur-see] n, pl **-sies** dispute, debate, esp over public issues **con·tro·ver'sial** adj **con'tro·vert** vt deny; argue **con·tro·vert'i·ble** adj

con·tu·ma·cy [KON-tuu-mə-see] n, pl **-cies** stubborn disobedience **con·tu·ma'cious** [-MAY-shəs] adj

con·tu·me·ly [kon-TUU-mə-lee] n, pl **-lies** insulting language or treatment **con·tu·me'li·ous** [-MEE-lee-əs] adj abusive, insolent

con·tu·sion [kən-TOO-zhən] n bruise

co·nun·drum [kə-NUN-drəm] n riddle, esp with punning answer

con·ur·ba·tion [kon-ər-BAY-shən] n densely populated urban sprawl formed by spreading of towns

con·va·lesce [kon-və-LES] vi **-lesced, -lesc·ing** recover health after illness, operation, etc **con·va·les'cence** n **con·va·les'cent** adj, n

con·vec·tion [kən-VEK-shən] n transmission, esp of heat, by currents in liquids or gases **con·vec'tor** n **con·vec'tive** adj

con·vene [kən-VEEN] vt **-vened, -ven·ing** call together, assemble, convoke **con·ven'tion** n assembly; treaty, agreement; rule; practice based on agreement; accepted usage **con·ven'tion·al** adj (slavishly) observing customs of society; customary; (of weapons, war, etc) not nuclear

con·ven·ient [kən-VEEN-yənt] adj handy; favorable to needs, comfort;

well adapted to one's purpose **con·ven'ience** n ease, comfort, suitability ▷ adj (of food) quick to prepare

con·vent [KON-vent] n religious community, esp of nuns; their building

con·verge [kən-VURJ] vi **-verged, -verg·ing** approach, tend to meet **con·ver'gence, -gen·cy** n **con·ver'gent** adj

con·ver·sant [kən-VUR-sənt] adj acquainted, familiar (with), versed in **conversation** see **CONVERSE**[1]

con·verse[1] [kən-VURS] vi **-versed, -vers·ing** talk (with) **con·ver·sa'tion** n **con·ver·sa'tion·al** adj

con·verse[2] [KON-vurs] adj opposite, turned around, reversed ▷ n the opposite, contrary

con·vert [kən-VURT] vt apply to another purpose; change; transform; cause to adopt (another) religion; opinion; football make a conversion ▷ n [KON-vurt] converted person **con·ver'sion** [-zhən] n change of state; unauthorized appropriation; change of opinion, religion, or party; football extra point scored after a touchdown **con·vert'er** n one who, that which converts; electrical device for changing alternating current into direct current; vessel in which molten metal is refined **con·vert'i·ble** n car with folding roof ▷ adj

con·vex [kon-VEKS] adj curved outward; of a rounded form **con·vex'i·ty** n

con·vey [kən-VAY] vt carry, transport; impart, communicate; law make over, transfer **con·vey'ance** n carrying; vehicle; act by which title to property is transferred **con·vey'or** belt continuous moving belt for transporting things, esp in factory

con·vict [kən-VIKT] vt prove or declare guilty ▷ n [KON-vikt] person found guilty of crime; criminal serving prison sentence

con·vic·tion n verdict of guilty; being convinced, firm belief, state of being sure

con·vince [kən-VINS] vt **-vinced, -vinc·ing** firmly persuade, satisfy by evidence or argument **con·vinc·ing** adj capable of compelling belief, effective

con·viv·i·al [kən-VIV-ee-əl] adj sociable, festive, jovial **con·viv·i·al·i·ty** n

con·voke [kən-VOHK] vt **-voked, -vok·ing** call together **con·vo·ca·tion** [kon-və-KAY-shən] n calling together, assembly, esp of clergy, college faculty, etc

con·vo·lute [KON-və-loot] vt **-lut·ed, -lut·ing** twist, coil, tangle **con·vo·lut·ed** adj **con·vo·lu·tion** n

con·voy [KON-voi] n party (of ships, troops, trucks, etc) traveling together for protection ▷ vt escort for protection

con·vulse [kən-VULS] vt **-vulsed, -vuls·ing** shake violently; affect with violent involuntary contractions of muscles **con·vul·sion** n violent upheaval ▷ pl spasms; fits of laughter or hysteria **con·vul·sive** adj

coo [koo] n cry of doves ▷ vi **cooed, coo·ing** make such cry

cook [kuuk] vt prepare (food) for table, esp by heat; inf falsify (accounts, etc) ▷ vi undergo cooking; act as cook ▷ n one who prepares food for table **cook'er** n cooking apparatus **cook'ie** n small cake made from sweet dough **cook'out** n (party featuring) meal

cooked and served outdoors **cook up** inf invent, plan; prepare (meal)

cool [kool] adj moderately cold; unexcited, calm; lacking friendliness or interest; inf calmly insolent; inf sophisticated, elegant ▷ v make, become cool ▷ n cool time, place, etc; inf calmness, composure **cool'ant** n fluid used for cooling tool, machinery, etc **cool'er** n vessel in which liquids are cooled; iced drink usu with wine or whiskey base; sl jail **cool one's heels** be kept waiting, esp because of deliberate discourtesy

coon [koon] n raccoon

coop [koop] n cage or pen for pigeons, etc ▷ vt shut up in a coop; confine

co-op [KOH-op] n cooperative enterprise; apartment or business run by one

coop·er [KOO-pər] n one who makes casks

co·op·er·ate [koh-OP-ə-rayt] vi **-at·ed, -at·ing** work together **co·op·er·a·tion** n **co·op·er·a·tive** adj willing to cooperate; (of an enterprise) owned collectively and managed for joint economic benefit ▷ n cooperative organization

co·opt [koh-OPT] vt preempt, appropriate as one's own; elect by votes of existing members

co·or·di·nate [koh-OR-dn-ayt] vt **-nat·ed, -nat·ing** bring into order as parts of whole; place in same rank; put into harmony ▷ n [-it] mathematics any of set of numbers defining location of point ▷ adj equal in degree, status, etc **co·or·di·na·tion** n

coot [koot] n small black water fowl; inf silly (old) person

cop [kop] vt sl **copped, cop·ping** catch ▷ n inf policeman **cop a plea**

sl plead guilty in return for light sentence

cope [kohp] *vi* **coped, cop•ing** deal successfully (with)

Co•per•ni•can [koh-PUR-ni-kən] *adj* pert to Copernicus, Polish astronomer (1473–1543), or to his system

cop•ing [KOH-ping] *n* top course of wall, usu sloping to throw off rain

co•pi•ous [KOH-pee-əs] *adj* abundant; plentiful; full, ample

cop•per[1] [KOP-ər] *n* reddish-brown malleable ductile metal; bronze money, coin ▷ *vt* cover with copper **copper beech** tree with reddish leaves **cop'per•plate** [-playt] *n* plate of copper for engraving, etching; print from this; copybook writing; first-class handwriting

copper[2] *n sl* policeman

co•pra [KOH-prə] *n* dried coconut kernels

copse [kops] *n* a wood of small trees

cop•u•la [KOP-yə-lə] *n, pl* **-las** word, esp verb acting as connecting link in sentence; connection, tie **cop•u•late** [KOP-yə-layt] *vi* **-lat•ed, -lat•ing** unite sexually **cop•u•la'tion** *n*

cop•y [KOP-ee] *n, pl* **cop•ies** imitation; single specimen of book; matter for printing ▷ *vt* **cop•ied, cop•y•ing** make copy of; imitate; transcribe; follow an example **cop'y•right** *n* legal exclusive right to print and publish book, article, work of art, etc ▷ *vt* protect by copyright **cop'y•writ•er** *n* one who writes advertisements

co•quette [koh-KET] *n* woman who flirts ▷ *vi* **co•quet'ry** [KOH-ki-tree] *n* **co•quet'tish** *adj*

Cor. Corinthians

cor•al [KOR-əl] *n* hard substance made by sea polyps and forming growths, islands, reefs; ornament of coral ▷ *adj* made of coral; of deep pink color

cord [kord] *n* thin rope or thick string; rib on cloth; ribbed fabric ▷ *vt* fasten with cord **cord'age** *n*

cor•date [KOR-dayt] *adj* heart-shaped

cor•dial [KOR-jəl] *adj* hearty, sincere, warm ▷ *n* sweet, fruit-flavored alcoholic drink; liqueur **cor•di•al•i•ty** [kor-jee-AL-i-tee] *n* warmth

cord•ite [KOR-dit] *n* explosive compound

cor•don [KOR-dn] *n* chain of troops or police; fruit tree grown as single stem ▷ *vt* form cordon around **cor•don bleu** [kor-DAWN BLUU] *adj* (esp of food preparation) of highest standard

cor•du•roy [KOR-də-roi] *n* cotton fabric with velvety, ribbed surface

core [kor] *n* horny seed case of apple and other fruits; central or innermost part of anything ▷ *vt* **cored, cor•ing** take out the core

co•re•spond•ent [koh-ri-SPON-dənt] *n* one cited in divorce case, alleged to have committed adultery with the respondent

cor•gi [KOR-gee] *n* short-legged sturdy dog

co•ri•an•der [KOR-ee-an-dər] *n* plant grown for its aromatic seeds and leaves

Co•rin•thi•an [kə-RIN-thee-ən] *adj* of Corinth; of Corinthian order of architecture, ornate Greek ▷ *pl* books in New Testament

cork [kork] *n* bark of an evergreen Mediterranean oak tree; piece of it or other material, esp used as stopper for bottle, etc ▷ *vt* stop up with cork **cork'age** *n* charge for opening wine bottles in restaurant

cork'er n sl something, someone outstanding **cork'screw** n tool for pulling out corks

corn¹ [korn] n (kernels of) sweet corn, corn on the cob; inf oversentimental, trite quality in play, film, etc ▷ vt preserve (meat) with salt or brine **corn'y** adj **corn·i·er, corn·i·est** inf trite, oversentimental, hackneyed **corn'cob** n ear of sweet corn **corn'flour** n finely ground corn **corn'flow·er** n blue flower, oft growing in grainfields

corn² n painful horny growth on foot or toe

cor·ne·a [KOR-nee-ə] n transparent membrane covering front of eye

cor·ner [KOR-nər] n part of room where two sides meet; remote or humble place; point where two walls, streets, etc meet; angle; projection; business buying up of whole existing stock of commodity, shares ▷ vt drive into position of difficulty, or leaving no escape; establish monopoly ▷ vi turn around corner **cor'ner·stone** n indispensable part, basis **corner kick** soccer free kick from corner of field

cor·net [kor-NET] n trumpet with valves

cor·nice [KOR-nis] n projection near top of wall; ornamental, carved molding below ceiling

cor·nu·co·pia [kor-nə-KOH-pee-ə] n symbol of plenty, consisting of goat's horn, overflowing with fruit and flowers

co·rol·la [kə-ROL-ə] n flower's inner envelope of petals

cor·ol·lar·y [KOR-ə-ler-ee] n, pl **-lar·ies** inference from a preceding statement; deduction; result

co·ro·na [kə-ROH-nə] n, pl **-nas** halo around heavenly body; flat projecting part of cornice; top or crown

cor·o·nar·y [KOR-ə-ner-ee] adj of blood vessels surrounding heart ▷ n, pl **-nar·ies** coronary thrombosis **coronary thrombosis** disease of the heart

cor·o·na·tion [kor-ə-NAY-shən] n ceremony of crowning a sovereign

cor·o·ner [KOR-ə-nər] n officer who holds inquests on bodies of persons supposed killed by violence, accident, etc

cor·o·net [KOR-ə-net] n small crown

cor·po·ral¹ [KOR-pər-əl] adj of the body; material, not spiritual **corporal punishment** (flogging, etc) of physical nature

corporal² n noncommissioned officer below sergeant

cor·po·ra·tion [kor-pə-RAY-shən] n association, body of persons legally authorized to act as an individual; authorities of town or city **cor'po·rate** [-rit] adj

cor·po·re·al [kor-POR-ee-əl] adj of the body, material; tangible

corps [kor] n, pl **corps** [korz] military force, body of troops; any organized body of persons

corpse [korps] n dead body

cor·pu·lent [KOR-pyə-lənt] adj fat **cor'pu·lence** n

cor·pus [KOR-pəs] n collection or body of works, esp by single author; main part or body of something

cor·pus·cle [KOR-pə-səl] n minute organism or particle, esp red and white corpuscles of blood

cor·ral [kə-RAL] n enclosure for cattle, or for defense ▷ vt **-raled, -ral·ing**

cor·rect [kə-REKT] vt set right; indicate errors in; rebuke, punish;

counteract, rectify ▷ *adj* right, exact, accurate; in accordance with facts or standards **cor·rec·tion** *n*, *adj* **cor·rec·tive** *n*, *adj*

cor·re·late [KOR-ĕ-layt] *vt* **-lat·ed, -lat·ing** bring into reciprocal relation ▷ *n* [-lit] either of two things or words necessarily implying the other **cor·re·la·tion** *n* **cor·rel·a·tive** [kŏ-REL-ă-tiv] *adj, n*

cor·re·spond [kor-ĕ-SPOND] *vi* be in agreement, be consistent with; be similar (to); exchange letters **cor·re·spond·ence** *n* agreement, corresponding; similarity; exchange of letters; letters received **cor·re·spond·ent** *n* writer of letters; one employed by newspaper, etc to report on particular topic, country, etc

cor·ri·dor [KOR-i-dăr] *n* passage in building, etc; strip of territory (or air route) not under control of country through which it passes; densely populated area incl. two or more major cities

cor·ri·gen·dum [kor-i-JEN-dăm] *n, pl* **-da** [-dă] thing to be corrected

cor·rob·o·rate [kă-ROB-ă-rayt] *vt* **-rat·ed, -rat·ing** confirm, support (statement, etc) **cor·rob·o·ra·tion** *n* **cor·rob·o·ra·tive** *adj*

cor·rode [kă-ROHD] *vt* **-rod·ed, -rod·ing** eat, wear away, eat into (by chemical action, disease, etc) **cor·ro·sion** [-ROH-zhŏn] *n* **cor·ro·sive** *adj*

cor·ru·gate [KOR-ă-gayt] *v* **-gat·ed, -gat·ing** wrinkle, bend into wavy ridges

cor·rupt [kă-RUPT] *adj* lacking integrity; open to, or involving, bribery; wicked; spoiled by mistakes, altered for the worse (of words, literary passages, etc) ▷ *vt* make evil, pervert; bribe; make rotten **cor·rupt·i·ble** *adj* **cor·rup·tion** *n*

cor·sage [kor-SAHZH] *n* (flower, spray, worn on) bodice of woman's dress

cor·sair [KOR-sair] *n* pirate (ship)

cor·set [KOR-sit] *n* close-fitting undergarment stiffened to give support or shape to the body

cor·tege [kor-TEZH] *n* formal (funeral) procession

cor·tex [KOR-teks] *n, pl* **-ti·ces** [-tă-seez] *anatomy* outer layer; bark; sheath **cor·ti·cal** *adj*

cor·ti·sone [KOR-tă-zohn] *n* synthetic hormone used in the treatment of a variety of diseases

cor·vette [kor-VET] *n* lightly armed warship for escort and antisubmarine duties

co·sine [KOH-sin] *n* in a right triangle, the ratio of a side adjacent to a given angle and the hypotenuse

cos·met·ic [koz-MET-ik] *n* preparation to beautify or improve skin, hair, etc ▷ *adj* designed to improve appearance only

cos·mic [KOZ-mik] *adj* relating to the universe; of the vastness of the universe **cos·mog·ra·pher** *n* **cos·mog·ra·phy** *n* description or mapping of the universe **cos·mo·log·i·cal** [koz-mă-LOJ-i-kăl] *adj* **cos·mol·o·gy** *n* the science or study of the universe

cosmic rays high-energy electromagnetic rays from space

cos·mo·naut [KOZ-mă-nawt] *n* the Russian name for an astronaut

cos·mo·pol·i·tan [koz-mă-POL-i-tn] *n* person who has lived and traveled in many countries ▷ *adj* familiar with many countries; sophisticated; free from national prejudice

cos·mos¹ [KOZ-măs] *n* the world or universe considered as an ordered system

cosmos² n, pl **-mos** plant cultivated for brightly colored flowers

cos•sack [KOS-ak] n member of tribe in SE Russia

cost [kawst] n price; cost price; expenditure of time, labor, etc ▷ pl expenses of lawsuit ▷ vt **cost, cost•ing** have as price; entail payment, or loss, as price; sacrifice of **costing** n system of calculating cost of production, sale **cost'li•ness** n **cost'ly** adj **-li•er, -li•est** valuable; expensive **cost price** price at which article is bought by one intending to resell it

cos•tal [KOS-tl] adj pert to side of body or ribs

cos•tume [KOS-toom] n style of dress of particular place or time, or for particular activity; theatrical clothes **cos'tum•er** n dealer in costumes **costume jewelry** inexpensive jewelry

cot [kot] n narrow, usu collapsible bed

cote [koht] n shelter, shed for animals or birds: dovecote

co•te•rie [KOH-tà-ree] n exclusive group of people with common interests; social clique

coterminous see **CONTERMINOUS**

cot•tage [KOT-ij] n small house **cottage cheese** mild, soft cheese **cottage industry** industry in which workers work in their own homes

cot•ter [KOT-àr] n pin, wedge, etc to prevent relative motion of two parts of machine, etc

cot•ton [KOT-n] n plant; white downy fibrous covering of its seeds; thread or cloth made of this **cotton (on) to** begin to like, understand (idea, person, etc)

cot•y•le•don [kot-I-EED-n] n primary leaf of plant embryos

couch [kowch] n piece of furniture for sitting or reclining on by day, sofa ▷ vt put into (words), phrase; cause to lie down **couch potato** inf lazy person whose only hobby is watching television **on the couch** under psychiatric treatment

cou•gar [KOO-gàr] n mountain lion

cough [kawf] vi expel air from lungs with sudden effort and noise, often to remove obstruction ▷ n act of coughing

could pt of **CAN¹**

cou•lomb [KOO-lom] n unit of quantity of electricity

coun•cil [KOWN-sàl] n deliberative or administrative body; one of its meetings; local governing authority of town, etc **coun'ci•lor** n member of council

coun•sel [KOWN-sàl] n advice, deliberation or debate; lawyer or lawyers; plan, policy ▷ vt advise, recommend **coun'se•lor** n adviser; lawyer **keep one's counsel** keep a secret

count¹ [kownt] vt reckon, calculate, number; include; consider to be ▷ vi be reckoned in; depend (on); be of importance ▷ n reckoning; total number reached by counting; item in list of charges or indictment; act of counting **count'less** adj too many to be counted

count² n European nobleman of rank corresponding to that of British earl

coun•te•nance [KOWN-tn-àns] n face, its expression; support, approval ▷ vt **-nanced, -nanc•ing** give support, approve

count•er¹ [KOWN-tàr] n horizontal surface in bank, store, etc, on which business is transacted; work surface in kitchen; disk, token used for counting or scoring, esp in board games **coun·ter·top** flat upper surface of counter, display case, etc

coun·ter² *adv* in opposite direction; contrary ▷ *vi* oppose, contradict; *fencing* parry ▷ *n* parry

counter- *prefix* opposite, against: *counterattack*; complementary, corresponding: *counterpart*

coun·ter·act [kown-tər-AKT] *vt* neutralize or hinder

coun·ter·at·tack [KOWN-tər-ə-tak] *v, n* attack after enemy's advance

coun·ter·bal·ance [KOWN-tər-bal-əns] *n* weight balancing or neutralizing another ▷ *vt* **-anced, anc·ing**

coun·ter·feit [KOWN-tər-fit] *adj* sham, forged ▷ *n* imitation, forgery ▷ *vt* imitate with intent to deceive; forge

coun·ter·mand [kown-tər-MAND] *vt* cancel (previous order)

coun·ter·part [KOWN-tər-pahrt] *n* thing so like another as to be mistaken for it; something complementary to or correlative of another

coun·ter·point [KOWN-tər-point] *n* melody added as accompaniment to given melody; art of so adding melodies

coun·ter·sign [KOWN-tər-sin] *vt* sign document already signed by another; ratify ▷ *n* military secret sign

coun·ter·sink [KOWN-tər-singk] *v* **-sunk, -sink·ing** enlarge upper part of hole (drilled in wood, etc) to take head of screw, bolt, etc below surface

count'ess *n* wife or widow of count or earl

coun·try [KUN-tree] *n, pl* **-tries** region, district; territory of

nation; land of birth, residence, etc; rural districts as opposed to city; nation **coun'tri·fied** [-fid] *adj* rural in manner or appearance **coun·try·man** *n* rustic; compatriot **country music** popular music based on Amer folk music **coun'try·side** *n* rural district; its inhabitants

coun·ty [KOWN-tee] *n, pl* **-ties** division of a state

coup [koo] *n, pl* **coups** [kooz] successful stroke, move or gamble; coup d'état **coup d'é·tat** [koo-day-TAH] sudden, violent seizure of government

cou·ple [KUP-əl] *n* two, pair; husband and wife; any two persons ▷ *v* **-pled, -pling** *vt* connect, fasten together; associate, connect in the mind ▷ *vi* join, associate **cou'plet** *n* two lines of verse, esp rhyming and of equal length **cou'pling** *n* connection

cou·pon [KOO-pon] *n* ticket or voucher entitling holder to discount, gift, etc; detachable slip used as order form

cour·age [KUR-ij] *n* bravery, boldness **cou·ra·geous** [kə-RAY-jəs] *adj*

cour·i·er [KUUR-ee-ər] *n* express messenger

course [kors] *n* movement in space or time; direction of movement; successive development, sequence; line of conduct or action; series of lessons, exercises, etc; any of successive parts of meal; continuous line of masonry at particular level in building; area where golf is played; track or ground on which a race is run ▷ *v* **coursed, cours·ing** ▷ *vt* hunt ▷ *vi* run swiftly, gallop about; (of blood) circulate

court [kort] *n* space enclosed by buildings, yard; area marked off or enclosed for playing various games; retinue and establishment of sovereign; body with judicial powers, place where it meets, one of its sittings; attention, homage, flattery ▷ vt woo, try to win or attract; seek, invite **cour·ti·er** [KOR-tee-ər] n one who frequents royal court **court'li·ness** n **court'ly** adj **-li·er, -li·est** ceremoniously polite; characteristic of a court

court martial n, pl **courts martial** court of naval or military officers for trying naval or military offenses **court'yard** n paved space enclosed by buildings or walls

cour·te·san [KOR-tà-zàn] n court mistress; high-class prostitute

cour·te·sy [KUR-tà-see] n, pl **-sies** politeness, good manners; act of civility **cour'te·ous** adj polite

court·ship [KORT-ship] n wooing

cous·in [KUZ-ən] n son or daughter of uncle or aunt

cove [kohv] n small inlet of coast, sheltered bay

cov·en [KUV-ən] n gathering of witches

cov·e·nant [KUV-ə-nənt] n contract, mutual agreement; compact ▷ v agree to a covenant

cov·er [KUV-ər] vt place or spread over; extend, spread; bring upon (oneself); screen, protect; travel over; include; be sufficient; point a gun at ▷ n lid, wrapper, envelope, binding, screen, anything that covers **cov'er·age** n amount, extent covered **cov'er·let** n bedspread **cover girl** attractive model whose picture appears on magazine cover

co·vert [KOH-vàrt] adj secret, veiled, concealed, sly ▷ n [KUV-àrt] thicket, place sheltering game

cov·et [KUV-it] vt long to possess, esp what belongs to another

cov·et·ous adj greedy

cov·ey [KUV-ee] n, pl **-eys** brood of partridges or quail

cow¹ [kow] n mature female of cattle and of certain other mammals, such as the elephant or seal **cow'boy** n ranch hand in charge of cattle on western plains of US; inf reckless driver, etc

cow² vt frighten into submission, overawe, subdue

cow·ard [KOW-àrd] n one who lacks courage, shrinks from danger **cow'ard·ice** [-dis] n **cow'ard·ly** adj

cow·er [KOW-àr] vi crouch, shrink in fear

cowl [kowl] n monk's hooded cloak; its hood; cowling

cowl·ing [KOW-ling] n covering for aircraft engine

cow·rie [KOW-ree] n brightly colored sea shell

cox·swain [KOK-sàn] n steersman of boat **cox** v inf act as coxswain

coy [koi] adj **-er, -est** (pretending to be) shy, modest **coy'ness** n

coy·o·te [ki-OH-tee] n NAmer prairie wolf

co·zy [KOH-zee] adj **-zi·er, -zi·est** snug, comfortable, sheltered; suggesting conspiratorial intimacy **co'zi·ly** adv **co'zi·ness** n

CPU computing central processing unit

Cr chemistry chromium

crab [krab] n edible crustacean with ten legs, noted for sidelong and backward walk; type of louse ▷ vi **crabbed, crab'bing** catch crabs; move sideways **crab·bed** [KRAB-id] adj of handwriting, hard to read **crab'by** adj **-bi·er, -bi·est** irritable

crack [krak] v break, split partially; break with sharp noise; cause to make sharp noise, as of whip, rifle, etc; break down, yield; *inf* tell (joke); solve, decipher ▷ *vi* make sharp noise; split, fissure; of the voice, lose clearness when changing from boy's to man's ▷ *n* sharp explosive noise; split, fissure; flaw; *inf* joke, esp sarcastic; chat; *sl* pure, highly addictive form of cocaine ▷ *adj inf* special, smart, of great reputation for skill or fashion **crack'er** *n* thin dry biscuit; (C-) *sl offens* native or inhabitant of Georgia **crack'le** [-əl] *n* sound of repeated small cracks ▷ *vi* **-led, -ling** make this sound **crack'ling** *n* crackle; crisp skin of roast pork, etc

cra·dle [KRAYD-l] *n* infant's bed (on rockers); *fig* earliest resting place or home; supporting framework ▷ *vt* **-dled, -dling** hold or rock as in a cradle; cherish

craft[1] [kraft] *n* skill, ability, esp manual ability; cunning; skilled trade; members of a trade **craft'i·ly** *adv* **craft'y** *adj* **craft·i·er, craft·i·est** cunning, shrewd **crafts'man** *n* **crafts'man·ship** *n*

craft[2] *n* vessel; ship

crag [krag] *n* steep rugged rock **crag'gy** *adj* **-gi·er, -gi·est** rugged

cram [kram] *vt* **crammed, cram·ming** fill quite full; stuff, force; pack tightly ▷ *vi* feed to excess; prepare quickly for examination

cramp [kramp] *n* painful muscular contraction; clamp for holding masonry, woodwork, etc together ▷ *vt* restrict or hamper; hem in, keep within too narrow limits

cram·pon [KRAM-pon] *n* spike in shoe for mountain climbing esp on ice

crane [krayn] *n* wading bird with long legs, neck, and bill; machine for moving heavy weights ▷ *vi* **craned, cran·ing** stretch neck to see

cra·ni·um [KRAY-nee-əm] *n* skull **cra·ni·al** *adj*

crank [krangk] *n* arm at right angles to axis, for turning main shaft, changing reciprocal into rotary motion, etc; *inf* eccentric person, faddist ▷ *v* start (engine) by turning crank **crank'y** *adj* **crank·i·er, crank·i·est** bad-tempered; eccentric **crank'shaft** *n* principal shaft of engine

cran·ny [KRAN-ee] *n, pl* **-nies** small opening, chink **cran'nied** *adj*

crap [krap] *n* gambling game played with two dice; (also **craps**)

crape [krayp] *n* crepe, esp when used for mourning clothes

crash [krash] *v* (cause to) make loud noise; (cause to) fall with crash ▷ *vi* break, smash; collapse, fail, esp financially; (cause (aircraft) to hit land or water; collide with (another car, etc); move noisily or violently ▷ *vi* of computer system or program) fail suddenly because of malfunction ▷ *n* loud, violent fall or impact; collision, esp between vehicles; sudden, uncontrolled descent of aircraft to land; sudden collapse or downfall, esp of economy; bankruptcy ▷ *adj* requiring, using, great effort to achieve results quickly **crash helmet** worn by motorcyclists, etc to protect head

crass [kras] *adj* **-er, -est** grossly stupid; insensitive **crass'ness** *n*

crate [krayt] *n* large (usu wooden) container for packing goods

cra·ter [KRAY-tər] *n* mouth of volcano; bowl-shaped cavity, esp one made by explosion of large shell, bomb, mine, etc

cra·vat [krə-VAT] *n* man's neckband or scarf

crave [krayv] *v* **craved, crav·ing** have very strong desire for, long for

▷ vt ask humbly; beg **craving** n

cra•ven [KRAY-vən] adj cowardly, abject, spineless ▷ n coward **cra'ven•ness** n

craw [kraw] n bird's or animal's stomach; bird's crop

crawl [krawl] vi move on belly or on hands and knees; move very slowly; ingratiate oneself, cringe; swim with crawl stroke; be overrun (with) ▷ n crawling motion; very slow walk; racing stroke at swimming

cray•fish [KRAY-fish] n edible freshwater crustacean like lobster; (also **craw'fish**)

cray•on [KRAY-on] n stick or pencil of colored chalk, wax, etc

craze [krayz] n short-lived current fashion; strong desire or passion, mania; madness **crazed** adj demented; (of porcelain) having fine cracks **cra'zy** adj **-zi•er, -zi•est** insane; very foolish; madly eager (for) **crazy quilt** patchwork quilt of irregular patches; jumble

creak [kreek] n harsh grating noise ▷ vi make creaking sound

cream [kreem] n fatty part of milk; various foods, dishes, resembling cream; cosmetic, etc with creamlike consistency; yellowish-white color; best part of anything ▷ vt take cream from; take best part from; beat to creamy consistency **cream'y** adj **cream•i•er, cream•i•est**

crease [krees] n line made by folding; wrinkle; ice hockey rectangular area in front of goal cage; superficial bullet wound ▷ v **creased, creas•ing** make, develop creases

cre•ate [kree-AYT] v **-at•ed, -at•ing** ▷ vt bring into being; give rise to; make ▷ vi inf make a fuss **cre•a'tion** n **cre•a'tive** adj **cre•a'tor** n

crea•ture [KREE-chər] n living being; thing created; dependent, tool (of another) **creature comforts** bodily comforts

crèche [kresh] n representation of the Nativity scene

cre•dence [KREED-ns] n belief, credit; small table for bread and wine of the Eucharist

cre•den•tials [kri-DEN-shəlz] pl n testimonials; letters of introduction, esp those given to ambassador

cred•i•ble [KRED-ə-bəl] adj worthy of belief; trustworthy **cred•i•bil'i•ty** n

cred•it [KRED-it] n commendation, approval; source, cause, of honor; belief, trust; good name; influence, honor or power based on trust of others; system of allowing customers to take goods for later payment; money at one's disposal in bank, etc; side of ledger on which such sums are entered; reputation for financial reliability ▷ pl list of those responsible for production of film, etc ▷ vt attribute, believe that person has; believe; put on credit side of account **cred'it•a•ble** adj bringing honor **cred'i•tor** n one to whom debt is due

cred•u•lous [KREJ-ə-ləs] adj too easy of belief, easily deceived or imposed on, gullible **cre•du•li•ty** [krə-DOO-li-tee] n

creed [kreed] n formal statement of religious beliefs; statement, system of beliefs or principles

creek [kreek] n narrow inlet on seacoast

creel [kreel] n angler's fishing basket

creep [kreep] vi **crept, creep•ing** make way along ground, as snake; move with stealthy, slow movements; crawl; act in servile way; of skin or flesh, feel shrinking, shivering sensation, due to fear or repugnance ▷ *n* creeping; *sl* repulsive person ▷ *pl* feeling of fear or repugnance **creep·er** *n* creeping or climbing plant, such as ivy **creep·y** *adj* **creep·i·er, creep·i·est** *inf* uncanny, unpleasant; causing flesh to creep

cre·ma·tion [kri-MAY-shən] *n* burning as means of disposing of corpses **cre·mate** [KREE-mayt] *vt* **-mat·ed, -mat·ing** **cre·ma·to·ri·um** [kree-mə-TOR-ee-əm] *n* place for cremation

cre·ole [KREE-ohl] *n* hybrid language; **(C-)** native born W Indian, Latin American, of European descent

cre·o·sote [KREE-ə-soht] *n* oily antiseptic liquid distilled from coal or wood tar, used for preserving wood ▷ *vt* **-sot·ed, -sot·ing** coat or impregnate with creosote

crepe [krayp] *n* fabric with crimped surface; crape; thin, light pancake **crepe rubber** rough-surfaced rubber used for soles of shoes

crept *pt/pp of* **CREEP**

cre·scen·do [kri-SHEN-doh] *n* gradual increase of loudness, esp in music ▷ *adj, adv*

cres·cent [KRES-ənt] *n* (shape of) moon as seen in first or last quarter; any figure of this shape; curved portion of a street

crest [krest] *n* comb or tuft on bird's or animal's head; plume on top of helmet; top of mountain, ridge, wave, etc; badge above shield of coat of arms, also used separately on seal, plate, etc ▷ *vi* crown ▷ *vt* reach top of **crest'fall·en** *adj* cast down by failure, dejected

cre·ta·ceous [kri-TAY-shəs] *adj* chalky

cre·tin [KREET-n] *n offens* stupid

or mentally defective person; *obs* person afflicted with deficiency in thyroid gland causing physical and mental retardation

cre·vasse [kri-VAS] *n* deep open chasm, esp in glacier

crev·ice [KREV-is] *n* cleft, fissure, chink

crew [kroo] *n* ship's, boat's or aircraft's company, excluding passengers; *inf* gang or set ▷ *v* serve as crew **crew cut** closely cropped haircut

crew·el [KROO-əl] *n* fine worsted yarn, used in needlework and embroidery

crib [krib] *n* child's cot; barred rack used for fodder; plagiarism; translation used by students, sometimes illicitly ▷ *vt* **cribbed, crib·bing** confine in small space; copy unfairly

crib·bage [KRIB-ij] *n* card game for two, three, or four players

crick [krik] *n* spasm or cramp in muscles, esp in neck

crick·et[1] [KRIK-it] *n* chirping insect

crick·et[2] *n* outdoor game played with bats, ball and wickets by teams of eleven a side **crick·et·er** *n*

crime [krīm] *n* violation of law (usu a serious offense); wicked or forbidden act; *inf* something to be regretted **crim·i·nal** [KRIM-ə-nl] *adj, n* **crim·i·nal·i·ty** *n* **crim·i·nol'o·gy** *n* study of crime and criminals

crimp [krimp] *vt* pinch into tiny parallel pleats; wrinkle

crim·son [KRIM-zən] *adj, n* (of) rich deep red

cringe [krinj] *vi* **cringed, cring·ing** shrink, cower; behave obsequiously

crin·kle [KRING-kəl] *v, n* **-kled, -kling** wrinkle

crin·o·line [KRIN-l-in] *n* hooped

petticoat or skirt of stiff material

crip•ple [KRIP-əl] n offens one not having normal use of limbs, disabled or deformed person ▷ vt **-pled, -pling** maim, disable, impair; weaken, lessen efficiency of

cri•sis [KRĪ-sis] n, pl **-ses** [-seez] turning point or decisive moment, esp in illness; time of acute danger or difficulty

crisp [krisp] adj **-er, -est** brittle but firm; brisk, decided; clear-cut; fresh, invigorating; crackling; of hair, curly ▷ n dessert of fruit baked with a crunchy mixture **crisp'er** n refrigerator compartment for storing salads, etc

cri•te•ri•on [kri-TEER-ee-ən] n, pl **-ri•a** [-ree-ə] standard of judgment

crit•i•cal [KRIT-i-kəl] adj faultfinding; discerning; skilled in or given to judging; of great importance, crucial, decisive **crit'ic** n one who passes judgment; writer expert in judging works of literature, art, etc **crit'i•cism** n **crit'i•cize** vt **-cized, ciz•ing cri•tique** [kri-TEEK] n critical essay, carefully written criticism

croak [krohk] v utter deep hoarse cry, as raven, frog; talk dismally ▷ vi sl die ▷ n deep hoarse cry

cro•chet [kroh-SHAY] n kind of handicraft like knitting, done with small hooked needle ▷ v do, make such work

crock [krok] n earthenware jar or pot; broken piece of earthenware **crock'er•y** n earthenware dishes, utensils, etc

croc•o•dile [KROK-ə-dīl] n large amphibious reptile **crocodile tears** insincere grief

crois•sant [krwah-SAHN] n buttery, crescent-shaped roll of leavened dough or puff pastry

crone [krohn] n witchlike old woman

cro•ny [KROH-nee] n, pl **-nies** intimate friend

crook [kruuk] n hooked staff; any hook, bend, sharp turn; inf swindler, criminal **crook'ed** adj bent, twisted; deformed; dishonest

croon [kroon] v hum, sing in soft, low tone **croon'er** n

crop [krop] n produce of cultivation of any plant or plants; harvest; pouch in bird's gullet; stock of whip; hunting whip; short haircut ▷ v **cropped, crop'ping** cut short; raise, produce or occupy land with crop; (of animals) bite, eat down; poll or clip **crop'-dust•ing** n spreading fungicide, etc on crops from aircraft **crop-top** n short T-shirt or vest that reveals the wearer's midriff **crop up** inf happen unexpectedly

cro•quet [kroh-KAY] n lawn game played with balls, wooden mallets and hoops

cro•quette [kroh-KET] n breaded, fried ball of minced meat, fish, etc

cro•sier [KROH-zhər] n bishop's or abbot's staff

cross [kraws] n structure or symbol of two intersecting lines or pieces (at right angles); such a structure of wood as means of execution by tying or nailing victim to it; symbol of Christian faith; any thing or mark in the shape of cross; misfortune, annoyance, affliction; intermixture of breeds, hybrid ▷ v move or go across (something); intersect; meet and pass ▷ vt mark with lines across; (with out) delete; place or put in form of cross; make sign of cross on or over; modify breed of animals or plants by intermixture; thwart, oppose ▷ adj out of temper, angry; peevish, perverse;

transverse; intersecting; contrary; adverse **cross'ing** n intersection of roads, rails, etc; part of street where pedestrians are expected to cross **cross'ly** adv **cross'wise** adv, adj **cross'bow** [-boh] n bow fixed across wooden shoulder stock

cross'breed n breed produced from parents of different breeds **cross-country** adj, n (long race) held over open ground **cross'-ex·am'ine** vt examine witness already examined by other side **cross'-eyed** adj having eye(s) turning inward **cross'-fer·ti·li·za'tion** n fertilization of one plant by pollen of another **cross'-grained'** adj having fibers running diagonally, etc; perverse **cross'-ref'er·ence** n reference within text to another part of text **cross section** transverse section; group of people fully representative of a nation, community, etc **cross'word puzzle** puzzle built up of intersecting words, of which some letters are common, the words being indicated by clues

crotch [kroch] n angle between legs, genital area; fork **crotch·et** [KROCH-it] n musical note, equal to half the length of a minim **crotch·et·y** [KROCH-i-tee] adj peevish; irritable

crouch [krowch] vi bend low; huddle down close to ground; stoop servilely, cringe ▷ n

croup [kroop] n throat disease of children, with cough

crou·pi·er [KROO-pee-ər] n person dealing cards, collecting money, etc at gambling table

crow' [kroh] n large black scavenging bird **crow's'-foot** n wrinkle at corner of eye **crow's'-nest** n lookout platform high on ship's mast

crow' vi utter rooster's cry; boast one's happiness or superiority ▷ n rooster's cry

crow·bar [KROH-bahr] n iron or steel bar, usu wedge-shaped, for levering

crowd [krowd] n throng, mass ▷ vi flock together ▷ vt cram, force, thrust, pack; fill with people **crowd out** exclude by excess already in

crown [krown] n monarch's headdress; wreath for head; monarch; monarchy; royal power; various foreign coins; top of head; summit, top; completion or perfection of thing ▷ vt put crown on; confer title; occur as culmination of series of events; inf hit on head **crown prince** heir to throne

cru·cial [KROO-shəl] adj decisive, critical; inf very important

cru·ci·ble [KROO-sə-bəl] n small melting pot

cru·ci·fy [KROO-sə-fī] vt **-fied, -fy·ing** put to death on cross; treat cruelly; inf ridicule **cru·ci·fix** [-fiks] n cross; image of (Christ on the) Cross **cru·ci·fix'ion** n

crude [krood] adj **crud·er, crud·est** lacking taste, vulgar; in natural or raw state, unrefined; rough, unfinished **crud'i·ty** n, pl **-ties**

cru·el [KROO-əl] adj **-er, -est** delighting in others' pain; causing pain or suffering **cru'el·ly** adv **cru'el·ty** n, pl **-ties**

cru·et [KROO-it] n small container for salt, pepper, vinegar, oil, etc; stand holding such containers

cruise [krooz] vi **cruised, cruis·ing** travel about in a ship for pleasure, etc; (of vehicle, aircraft) travel at safe, average speed ▷ n cruising voyage **cruis'er** n ship that cruises; warship lighter and faster than battleship

cruise missile subsonic missile guided throughout its flight

crumb [krum] *n* small particle, fragment, esp of bread ▷ *vt* reduce to, break into, cover with crumbs

crum·ble [KRUM-bəl] *v* **-bled, -bling** break into small fragments, disintegrate, crush; perish, decay ▷ *vi* fall apart or away **crum'bly** *adj* **-bli·er, -bli·est**

crum·my [KRUM-ee] *adj* sl **-mi·er, -mi·est** inferior, contemptible

crum·ple [KRUM-pəl] *v* **-pled, -pling** (cause to) collapse; make or become crushed, wrinkled, creased

crunch [krunch] *n* sound made by chewing crisp food, treading on gravel, hard snow, etc; *inf* critical moment or situation ▷ *v* make crunching sound

cru·sade [kroo-SAYD] *n* medieval Christian war to recover Holy Land; campaign against something believed to be evil; concerted action to further a cause ▷ *vi* **-sad·ed, -sad·ing crusad'er** *n*

crush[1] [krush] *vt* compress so as to break, bruise, crumple; break to small pieces; defeat utterly, overthrow ▷ *n* act of crushing; crowd of people, etc

crush[2] *n inf* infatuation

crust [krust] *n* hard outer part of bread; similar hard outer casing on anything ▷ *v* cover with, form, crust **crust'i·ly** *adv* **crust'y** *adj* **crust·i·er, crust·i·est** having, or like, crust; harsh, surly; rude

crus·ta·cean [kru-STAY-shən] *n* hard-shelled animal, eg crab, lobster ▷ *adj*

crutch [kruch] *n* staff with crosspiece to go under armpit of lame person, device resembling this; support; groin, crotch

crux [kruks] *n, pl* **-es** that on which a decision turns; anything that puzzles very much

cry [kri] *v* **cried, cry·ing** ▷ *vi* weep; wail; utter call; shout; clamor or beg (for) ▷ *vt* utter loudly, proclaim ▷ *n* loud utterance; scream, wail, shout; call of animal; fit of weeping; watchword

cry·o·gen·ics [kri-ə-JEN-iks] *n* branch of physics concerned with phenomena at very low temperatures **cry·o·gen'ic** *adj*

crypt [kript] *n* vault, esp under church **cryp'tic** *adj* secret, mysterious **cryp'ti·cal·ly** *adv* **cryp'to·gram** *n* piece of writing in code **cryp·tog'ra·phy** *n* art of writing, decoding ciphers

crys·tal [KRIS-tl] *n* clear transparent mineral; very clear glass; cut-glass ware; characteristic form assumed by many substances, with definite internal structure and external shape of symmetrically arranged plane surfaces **crys'tal·line** [-tl-in] *adj* **crys·tal·li·za'tion** *n* **crys'tal·lize** *v* **-lized, -liz·ing** form into crystals; become definite

Cs *chemistry* cesium

Cu *chemistry* copper

cub [kub] *n* young of fox and other animals; cub scout ▷ *v* **cubbed, cub·bing** bring forth cubs **cub scout** member of junior division of the Boy Scouts

cub·by·hole [KUB-ee-hohl] *n* small, enclosed space or room; pigeonhole

cube [kyoob] *n* regular solid figure contained by six equal square sides; cube-shaped block; product obtained by multiplying number by itself twice ▷ *vt* **cubed, cub·ing** multiply thus **cu'bic** *adj* **cub'ism** *n* style of art in which objects are presented as assemblage of geometrical shapes

cub'ist n, adj

cu·bi·cle [KYOO-bi-kəl] n partially or totally enclosed section of room, as in study hall

cu·bit [KYOO-bit] n old measure of length, about 18 inches

cuck·old [KUK-əld] n man whose wife has committed adultery ▷ vt

cuck·oo [KOO-koo] n, pl -oos migratory bird that deposits its eggs in the nests of other birds; its call ▷ adj sl crazy ▷ vi -ooed, -oo·ing

cu·cum·ber [KYOO-kum-bər] n plant with long fleshy green fruit; the fruit, used in salad

cud [kud] n food that ruminant animal brings back into mouth to chew again **chew the cud** reflect, meditate

cud·dle [KUD-l] v -dled, -dling ▷ vt hug ▷ vi lie close and snug, nestle ▷ n

cudg·el [KUJ-əl] n short thick stick ▷ vt -eled, -el·ing beat with cudgel

cue¹ [kyoo] n last words of actor's speech, etc as signal to another to act or speak; signal, hint, example for action

cue² n long tapering rod used in pool, billiards, etc

cuff¹ [kuf] n ending of sleeve; wristband **off the cuff** inf without preparation

cuff² vt strike with open hand ▷ n blow with hand

cui·sine [kwi-ZEEN] n style of cooking; menu, food offered by restaurant, etc

cul-de-sac [KUL-də-SAK] n, pl **culs-** [kulz-] street, lane open only at one end; blind alley

cu·li·nar·y [KYOO-lə-ner-ee] adj of, for, suitable for, cooking or kitchen

cull [kul] vt gather, select; take out selected animals from herd ▷ n

something culled

cul·mi·nate [KUL-mə-nayt] vi -nat·ed, -nat·ing reach highest point; come to climax, to a head **cul·mi·na·tion** n

cul·pa·ble [KUL-pə-bəl] adj blameworthy **cul·pa·bil·i·ty** n

cul·prit [KUL-prit] n one guilty of usu minor offense

cult [kult] n system of religious worship; pursuit of, devotion to, some person, thing, or idea **cult'ism** n practices of a religious cult **cult'ist** n

cul·ti·vate [KUL-tə-vayt] vt -vat·ed, -vat·ing till and prepare (soil) to raise crops; develop, improve, refine; devote attention to, cherish; foster **cul·ti·va·tion** n

cul·ture [KUL-chər] n state of manners, taste, and intellectual development at a time or place; cultivating; artificial rearing; set of bacteria so reared **cul'tur·al** adj **cul'tured** adj refined, showing culture **cultured pearl** pearl artificially induced to grow in oyster shell

cul·vert [KUL-vərt] n tunneled drain for passage of water under road, railroad, etc

cum·ber·some [KUM-bər-səm] adj awkward, unwieldy

cu·mu·la·tive [KYOO-myə-lə-tiv] adj becoming greater by successive additions; representing the sum of many items

cu·mu·lus [KYOO-myə-ləs] n, pl -li [-lī] cloud shaped in rounded white woolly masses

cu·ne·i·form [kyoo-NEE-ə-form] adj wedge-shaped, esp of ancient Babylonian writing

cun·ning [KUN-ing] adj crafty, sly; ingenious; cute ▷ n skill in deceit or evasion; skill, ingenuity

cup [kup] *n* small drinking vessel with handle at one side; any small drinking vessel; contents of cup; various cup-shaped formations, cavities, sockets, etc; cup-shaped trophy as prize; portion or lot; iced drink of wine and other ingredients ▷ *vt* **cupped, cup·ping** shape as cup (hands, etc) **cup·ful** *n, pl* **-fuls**

cup·board [KUB-ərd] *n* piece of furniture, recess in room, with door, for storage

Cu·pid [KYOO-pid] *n* god of love

cu·pid·i·ty [kyoo-PID-i-tee] *n* greed for possessions; covetousness

cu·po·la [KYOO-pə-lə] *n* dome

cu·pre·ous [KYOO-pree-əs] *adj* of, containing, copper

cur [kur] *n* dog of mixed breed; surly, contemptible, or mean person

cu·ra·re [kyuu-RAHR-ee] *n* poisonous resin of S Amer tree, now used as muscle relaxant in medicine

cu·rate [KYUUR-it] *n* parish priest **cu'ra·cy** *n* office or term of office of curate

cur·a·tive [KYUUR-ə-tiv] *adj* tending to cure disease ▷ *n*

cu·ra·tor [kyuur-AY-tər] *n* person in charge, esp of museum, library, etc

curb [kurb] *n* check, restraint; chain or strap passing under horse's lower jaw and giving powerful control with reins; edging, esp of stone or concrete, along street, path, etc ▷ *vt* restrain; apply curb to

curd [kurd] *n* coagulated milk **cur·dle** [KUR-dl] *v* **-dled, -dling** turn into curd, coagulate

cure [kyuur] *vt* **cured, cur·ing** heal, restore to health; remedy; preserve (fish, skins, etc) ▷ *n* remedy; course of medical treatment; successful treatment, restoration to health **cur·a·ble** *adj*

cu·rette [kyuu-RET] *n* surgical instrument for removing dead tissue, etc from some body cavities **cu·ret·tage** [kyuur-i-TAHZH] *n*

cur·few [KUR-fyoo] *n* official regulation restricting or prohibiting movement of people, esp at night; time set as deadline by such regulation

cu·rie [KYUUR-ee] *n* standard unit of radium emanation

cu·ri·o [KYUUR-ee-oh] *n, pl* **-ri·os** rare or curious thing of the kind sought for collections

cu·ri·ous [KYUUR-ee-əs] *adj* eager to know, inquisitive; prying; puzzling, strange, odd **cu·ri·os'i·ty** *n, pl* **-ties** eagerness to know; inquisitiveness; strange or rare thing

cu·ri·um [KYUUR-ee-əm] *n* element produced from plutonium

curl [kurl] *vi* take spiral or curved shape or path ▷ *vt* bend into spiral or curved shape ▷ *n* spiral lock of hair; spiral, curved state, form or motion **curl'ing** *n* target game played with large rounded stones on ice **curl'y** *adj* **curl·i·er, curl·i·est**

cur·mudg·eon [kər-MUJ-ən] *n* surly or miserly person

cur·rent [KUR-ənt] *adj* of immediate present, going on; up-to-date, not yet superseded; in circulation or general use ▷ *n* body of water or air in motion; tendency, drift; transmission of electricity through conductor **cur'ren·cy** *n* money in use; state of being in use; time during which thing is current

cur·ric·u·lum [kə-RIK-yə-ləm] *n, pl* **-la** [-lə] specified course of study

cur·ry¹ [KUR-ee] *n, pl* **-ries** highly-flavored, pungent condiment; meat, etc dish flavored with curry ▷ *vt* **-ried, -ry·ing** prepare, flavor dish with curry

curry² *vt* **-ried, -ry•ing** groom (horse) with comb; dress (leather) **curry favor** try to win favor unworthily, ingratiate oneself

curse [kurs] *n* profane or obscene expression of anger, etc; utterance expressing extreme ill will toward some person or thing; affliction, misfortune, scourge ▷ *v* **cursed, curs•ing** utter curse, swear (at); afflict **curs•ed** [KUR-sid] *adj* hateful; wicked; deserving of, or under, a curse

cur•sive [KUR-siv] *adj, n* (written in) running script, with letters joined

cur•so•ry [KUR-sə-ree] *adj* rapid, hasty, not detailed, superficial **cur'so•ri•ly** *adv*

curt [kurt] *adj* **-er, -est** short, rudely brief, abrupt **curt'ness** *n*

cur•tail [kər-TAYL] *vt* cut short, diminish

cur•tain [KUR-tn] *n* hanging drapery at window, etc; cloth hung as screen; screen separating audience and stage in theater; end to act or scene, etc ▷ *pl sl* death ▷ *vt* provide, cover with curtain **curtain call** return to stage by performers to acknowledge applause

curt•sy [KURT-see] *n, pl* **-sies** woman's bow or respectful gesture made by bending knees and lowering body ▷ *vi* **-sied, sy•ing**

curve [kurv] *n* line of which no part is straight; bent line or part ▷ *v* bend into curve **cur•va'ceous** [-VAY-shəs] *adj* shapely **cur'va•ture** [-və-chər] *n* a bending; bent shape

cush•ion [KUUSH-ən] *n* bag filled with soft stuffing or air, to support or ease body; any soft pad or support; resilient rim of pool table ▷ *vt* provide, protect with cushion; lessen effects of

cush•y *adj* **cush•i•er, cush•i•est**

inf easy

cusp [kusp] *n* pointed end, esp of tooth; *astrology* point marking the beginning of a house or sign **cus'pid** *n* pointed tooth

cus•pi•dor [KUS-pi-dor] *n* spittoon

cus•tard [KUS-tərd] *n* dessert made of eggs, sugar and milk

cus•to•dy [KUS-tə-dee] *n, pl* **-dies** safekeeping, guardianship, imprisonment **cus•to'di•an** *n* keeper, caretaker

cus•tom [KUS-təm] *n* habit; practice; fashion, usage; business patronage; tax ▷ *pl* duties levied on imports; government department that collects these; area in airport, etc where customs officials examine baggage for dutiable goods **cus•tom•ar'i•ly** *adv* **cus'tom•ar•y** *adj* usual, habitual **cus'tom•er** *n* one who enters store to buy, esp regularly; purchaser

cut [kut] *vt* **cut, cut•ting** sever, penetrate, wound, divide, or separate with pressure of edge or edged instrument; pare, detach, trim, or shape by cutting; divide; intersect; reduce, decrease; abridge; *inf* ignore (person); strike (with whip, etc); *inf* deliberately stay away from ▷ *n* act of cutting; stroke; blow, wound (of knife, whip, etc); reduction, decrease; fashion, shape; incision; engraving; piece cut off; division; excavation (for road, canal, etc) through high ground; *inf* share, esp of profits **cut'ter** *n* one who, that which, cuts; ship's boat for carrying stores, etc; small armed government boat **cut'ting** *n* act of cutting, thing cut off or out; shoot, twig of plant ▷ *adj* sarcastic, unkind **cutting edge** *n* the leading position in any field ▷ *adj* leading **cut'throat**

adj merciless ▷ *n* murderer **cut dead** refuse to recognize an acquaintance

cu•ta•ne•ous [kyoo-TAY-nee-əs] *adj* of skin

cute [kyoot] *adj* **cut•er, cut•est** appealing, attractive, pretty

cu•ti•cle [KYOO-ti-kəl] *n* dead skin, esp at base of fingernail

cut•lass [KUT-ləs] *n* short broad-bladed sword

cut•ler•y [KUT-lə-ree] *n* knives, forks, spoons, etc

cut•let [KUT-lit] *n* small piece of meat broiled or fried

cy•a•nide [SĪ-ə-nīd] *n* extremely poisonous chemical compound

cy•a•no•sis [sī-ə-NOH-sis] *n* blueness of the skin **cy•a•not'ic** *adj*

cyber- [SĪ-bər] *comb form* indicating computers: *cyberspace*

cy•ber•net•ics [sī-bər-NET-iks] *n* comparative study of control mechanisms of electronic and biological systems

cy•ber•space [SĪ-bər-spays] *n* hypothetical environment containing all the data stored in computers

cy•ber•squat•ting [SĪ-bər-skwot-ing] *n* registering an Internet domain name belonging to another person in the hope of selling it to them for a profit **cy•ber•squat•ter** *n*

cy•cle [SĪ-kəl] *n* recurrent series or period; rotation of events; complete series or period; development following course of stages; series of poems, etc; bicycle ▷ *vi* **-cled, -cling** move in cycles; ride bicycle **cy'clist** *n* bicycle rider

cy•clone [SĪ-klohn] *n* system of winds moving around center of low pressure; circular storm **cy•clon'ic** [-KLON-ik] *adj*

cy•clo•tron [SĪ-klə-tron] *n* powerful apparatus that accelerates the circular movement of subatomic particles in a magnetic field, used for work in nuclear disintegration

cyg•net [SIG-nit] *n* young swan

cyl•in•der [SIL-in-dər] *n* roller-shaped solid or hollow body, of uniform diameter; piston chamber of engine **cy•lin'dri•cal** *adj*

cym•bal [SIM-bəl] *n* one of pair of two brass plates struck together to produce ringing or clashing sound in music

cyn•ic [SIN-ik] *n* one who expects, believes, the worst about people, their motives, or outcome of events **cyn'i•cal cyn'i•cism** *n* being cynical

cy•no•sure [SĪN-nə-shuur] *n* center of attraction

cyst [sist] *n* sac containing liquid secretion or pus **cys'tic** *adj* of cysts; of the bladder **cys•ti'tis** *n* inflammation of bladder

Czar [zahr] *n* history emperor of Russia **Cza•ri•na** [zah-REE-nə] *n* wife of Czar

d

D *chemistry* deuterium

dab *vt* **dabbed, dab·bing** apply with momentary pressure, esp anything wet and soft; strike feebly ▷ *n* smear; slight blow or tap; small mass

dab·ble [DAB-əl] *vi* **-bled, -bling** splash about; be desultory student or amateur (in) **dab'bler** *n*

dac·tyl [DAK-til] *n* metrical foot of one long followed by two short syllables

dad·dy [DAD-ee] *n inf, pl* **-dies** father

da·do [DAY-doh] *n, pl* **-dos** lower part of room wall when lined or painted separately

dag·ger [DAG-ər] *n* short, edged stabbing weapon

da·guerre·o·type [də-GAIR-ə-tip] *n* early photographic process; photograph by it

dahl·ia [DAL-yə] *n* garden plant of various colors

dai·ly [DAY-lee] *adj* done, occurring, published every day ▷ *adv* every day ▷ *n, pl* **-lies** daily newspaper

dain·ty [DAYN-tee] *adj* **daint·i·er, daint·i·est** delicate; elegant, choice; pretty and neat; fastidious ▷ *n, pl* **-ties** delicacy **dain'ti·ly** *adv* **dain'ti·ness** *n*

dair·y [DAIR-ee] *n, pl* **-ries** place for processing milk and its products **dair'y·ing** *n*

da·is [DAY-is] *n* raised platform, usually at end of hall

dai·sy [DAY-zee] *n, pl* **-sies** flower with yellow center and white petals

Da·lai La·ma [DAH-lī-LAH-mə] *n* head of Buddhist hierarchy in Tibet

dale [dayl] *n* valley

dal·ly [DAL-ee] *vi* **-lied, -ly·ing** trifle, spend time in idleness or amusement; loiter **dal'li·ance** *n*

Dal·ma·tian [dal-MAY-shən] *n* large dog, white with black spots

dam[1] *n* barrier to hold back flow of waters; water so collected ▷ *vt* **dammed, dam'ming** hold with or as with dam

dam[2] *n* female parent (used of animals)

dam·age [DAM-ij] *n* injury, harm, loss ▷ *pl* sum claimed or adjudged in compensation for injury ▷ *vt* **-maged, -mag·ing** harm

dam·ask [DAM-əsk] *n* figured woven material of silk or linen, esp white table linen with design shown up by light; color of damask rose, velvety red

dame [daym] *n obs* lady; *sl* woman

damn [dam] *v* **damned, damn·ing** ▷ *vt* condemn to hell; be the ruin of; give hostile reception to ▷ *vi* curse ▷ *interj* expression of annoyance, impatience, etc **dam'na·ble** *adj* deserving damnation; hateful, annoying **dam·na'tion** *n*

damp *adj* moist; slightly moist ▷ *n* diffused moisture; in coal mines, dangerous gas ▷ *vt* make damp; (often with *down*) deaden, discourage **damp'en** *v* make,

become damp ▷ vt stifle,
deaden **damp'er** n anything that
discourages or depresses; plate in a
flue to control draft

Dan. Daniel

dance [dans] v **danced, danc·ing**
▷ vi move with measured rhythmic
steps, usu to music; be in lively
movement; bob up and down ▷ vt
perform (dance); cause to dance
▷ n lively, rhythmical movement;
arrangement of such movements;
tune for them; social gathering for
the purpose of dancing **danc'er** n
dan·seuse [dahn-SUUZ] n female
battle dancer

dan·de·li·on [DAN-dl-i-ən] n
yellow-flowered wild plant

dan·der [DAN-dər] n inf temper,
fighting spirit

dan·druff [DAN-drəf] n dead skin
in small scales on the scalp, in hair

dan·dy [DAN-dee] n, pl -**dies**
man excessively concerned with
smartness of dress ▷ adj inf
excellent

dan·ger [DAYN-jər] n liability
or exposure to harm; risk, peril
dan'ger·ous adj

dan·gle [DANG-gəl] v -**gled, -gling**
hang loosely and swaying; hold
suspended; tempt with

dank [dangk] adj -**er, -est**
unpleasantly damp and chilly
dank'ness n

dap·per [DAP-ər] adj neat and
precise, esp in dress, spruce

dap·ple [DAP-əl] v -**pled, -pling**
mark with spots **dappled** adj
spotted; mottled; variegated
dapple-gray adj (of horse) gray
marked with darker spots

dare [dair] vt **dared, dar·ing**,
venture, have courage (to); challenge
▷ n challenge **daring** adj bold ▷ n
adventurous courage **dare'dev·il**

adj, n reckless (person)

dark [dahrk] adj -**er, -est** without
light; gloomy; deep in tint; dim,
secret; unenlightened; wicked
▷ n absence of light or color or
knowledge **dark'en** v **dark'ness** n
dark horse somebody, something,
esp competitor in race, about
whom little is known **dark'room** n
darkened room for processing film

dar·ling [DAHR-ling] adj, n much
loved or very lovable (person)

darn[1] [dahrn] vt mend by filling
(hole) with yarn ▷ n place so
mended **darn'ing** n

darn[2] interj mild expletive

dart [dahrt] n small light pointed
missile; darting motion; small seam
or intake in garment ▷ pl indoor
game played with numbered target
and miniature darts ▷ vt cast, throw
rapidly (dart glance, etc) ▷ vi go
rapidly or abruptly

dash vt smash, throw, thrust, send
with violence; cast down; tinge,
flavor, mix ▷ vi move, go with great
speed or violence ▷ n rush; vigor;
smartness; small quantity; tinge;
stroke (–) between words **dash'ing**
adj spirited, showy **dash'board** n
in car, etc, instrument panel in front
of driver

da·shi·ki [də-SHEE-kee] n, pl -**kis**
loose pullover garment, orig African

das·tard [DAS-tərd] n does
contemptible, sneaking coward
das'tard·ly adj

da·ta [DAY-tə] n information
consisting of observations,
measurements, or facts; numbers,
digits, etc, stored by a computer
database systematized collection
of data that can be manipulated by
data-processing system for specific
purpose **data processing** handling
of data by computer

date[1] [dayt] n day of the month;
statement on document of its time
of writing; time of occurrence; period
of work of art, etc; engagement,
appointment ▷ v **dat•ed, dat•ing**
▷ vt mark with date; refer to date;
reveal age of; inf accompany on
social outing ▷ vi exist (from);
betray time or period of origin,
become old-fashioned **date'less** adj
without date; immemorial

date[2] n sweet, single-stone fruit of
palm; the palm

da•tive [DAY-tiv] n case indicating
indirect object, etc

da•tum n, pl **da•ta** single piece
of information in the form of a fact
or statistic

daub [dawb] vt coat, plaster,
paint coarsely or roughly ▷ n crude
picture; smear **daub'er** n

daugh•ter [DAW-tər] n one's
female child **daugh'ter-in-law** n, pl
daugh'ters-in-law son's wife

daunt [dawnt] vt frighten, esp into
giving up purpose **daunt'less** adj
intrepid, fearless

dav•en•port [DAV-ən-port] n
small writing table with drawers;
large couch or settee

Da•vy Jones's locker [DAY-vee
JOHN-ziz] bottom of sea, considered
as sailors' grave

daw•dle [DAWD-l] vi **-dled, -dling**
idle, waste time, loiter **daw'dler** n

dawn n first light, daybreak; first
gleam or beginning of anything ▷ vi
begin to grow light; appear, begin;
(begin to) be understood

day n period of 24 hours; time
when sun is above horizon; point
or unit of time; daylight; part of day
occupied by certain activity, time
period; special or designated day
day'break n dawn **day'-care center**
place providing daytime care,

meals, etc for preschool children,
etc **day'dream** n idle fancy ▷ vi
day'light n natural light; dawn
▷ pl consciousness, wits **daylight
saving** in summer, time set one hour
ahead of local standard time, giving
extra daylight in evenings **day'time**
n time between sunrise and sunset

daze [dayz] vt **dazed, daz•ing**
stupefy, stun, bewilder ▷ n
stupefied or bewildered state

daz•zle [DAZ-əl] vt **-zled, -zling**
blind, confuse or overpower with
brightness, light, brilliant display
or prospects ▷ n brightness that
dazzles the vision

Db chemistry dubnium

D-day [DEE-day] n day selected for
start of something, orig the Allied
invasion of Europe on June 6th 1944

de- prefix indicating: removal:
dethrone; reversal: declassify;
departure: decamp

dea•con [DEE-kən] n in
hierarchical churches, member of
the clergy next below priest; in other
churches, one who superintends
secular affairs **dea'con•ess** n fem

dead [ded] adj **-er, -est** no longer
alive; obsolete; numb, without
sensation; no longer functioning,
extinguished; lacking luster or
movement or vigor; sure, complete
▷ adv utterly **the dead** dead person
or persons **dead'en** vt **dead'ly** adj
-li•er, -li•est fatal; deathlike ▷ adv
as if dead **dead'beat** n inf one who
avoids payment of debts; lazy, useless
person **dead'head** n log sticking out
of water as hindrance to navigation;
boring person; train, aircraft, etc
operating empty, as when returning
to terminal **dead heat** race in
which competitors finish exactly
even **dead letter** rule no longer
observed; letter that post office

cannot deliver **dead·line** n limit of time allowed **dead·lock** n standstill **dead·pan** adj expressionless **dead reckoning** calculation of ship's position from log and compass, when observations cannot be taken **dead set** absolutely; resolute attack **dead of night** time of greatest stillness and darkness

deaf [def] adj **-er, -est** wholly or partly without hearing; unwilling to listen **deaf·en** vt make deaf

deal [deel] v **dealt, deal·ing** ▷ vt distribute, give out; inflict (on) ▷ vi act; treat; do business (with, in) ▷ n agreement; treatment; share; business transaction **deal·er** n one who deals (esp cards); trader **deal·ings** pl n transactions or relations with others **deal with** handle, act toward (someone)

dean [deen] n university or college official; head of cathedral chapter

dear [deer] adj beloved; precious; costly, expensive ▷ n beloved one ▷ adv at a high price **dear·ly** adv

dearth [durth] n scarcity

death [deth] n dying; end of life; end, extinction; annihilation; (D-) personification of death, as skeleton **death·less** adj immortal **death·ly** adj, adv like death **death mask** cast of person's face taken after death **death·watch** n vigil at dying person's bedside

de·ba·cle [day-BAH-kəl] n utter collapse, rout, disaster

de·bar [di-BAHR] vt **-barred, -bar·ring** shut out from; stop; prohibit; preclude

de·bark [di-BAHRK] v disembark

de·base [di-BASE] vt **-based, -bas·ing** lower in value, quality or character; adulterate coinage **de·base·ment** n

de·bate [di-BAYT] v **-bat·ed,**

-bat·ing argue, discuss, esp in a formal assembly; consider ▷ n discussion; controversy **de·bat·a·ble** adj

de·bauch [di-BAWCH] vt lead into a life of depraved self-indulgence ▷ n bout of sensual indulgence **de·bauch·ee** [deb-aw-CHEE] n dissipated person **de·bauch·er·y** n

de·ben·ture [di-BEN-chər] n bond of company or corporation

de·bil·i·ty [di-BIL-i-tee] n, pl **-ties** feebleness, esp of health; languor **de·bil'i·tate** vt weaken, enervate

deb·it n accounting entry in account of sum owed; side of ledger in which such sums are entered ▷ vt charge, enter as due

deb·o·nair [deb-ə-NAIR] adj suave, genial, affable

de·brief [dee-BREEF] v of soldier, etc, report to superior on result of mission

de·bris [də-BREE] n fragments, rubbish

debt [det] n what is owed; state of owing **debt'or** n

de·bug [dee-BUG] vt inf find and remove defects in (computer program); remove concealed microphones from (room or telephone)

de·bunk [di-BUNGK] vt expose falseness, pretentiousness of, esp by ridicule

de·but [day-BYOO] n first appearance in public **deb·u·tante** [DEB-yuu-tahnt] n young woman making official debut into society

deca- comb form tech: decagon

dec·ade [DEK-ayd] n period of ten years; set of ten

dec·a·dent [DEK-ə-dənt] adj declining, deteriorating; morally corrupt **dec'a·dence** n

de·caf·fein·at·ed [dee-KAF-ə-nay-tid] adj (of coffee) with the caffeine removed

dec·a·gon [DEK-ə-gon] n figure of 10 angles

dec·a·he·dron [dek-ə-HEE-drən] n solid of 10 faces

de·cal·ci·fy [dee-KAL-si-fī] vt **-fied, -fy·ing** deprive of lime, as bones or teeth

Dec·a·logue [DEK-ə-lawg] n the Ten Commandments

de·camp [di-KAMP] vi make off, break camp, abscond

de·cant [di-KANT] vt pour off (liquid, as wine) to leave sediment **de·cant'er** n stoppered bottle for wine or whiskey

de·cap·i·tate [di-KAP-i-tayt] vt behead **de·cap·i·ta'tion** n

de·cath·lon [di-KATH-lon] n athletic contest with ten events

de·cay [di-KAY] v rot, decompose; fall short, decline ▷ n rotting; a falling away, break up

de·cease [di-SEES] n death ▷ vi **-ceased, -ceas·ing** die **deceased** adj dead ▷ n person lately dead

de·ceive [di-SEEV] vt **-ceived, -ceiv·ing** mislead, delude, cheat **de·ceit'** n fraud; duplicity **de·ceit'ful** adj

de·cel·er·ate [dee-SEL-ə-rayt] vi **-at·ed, -at·ing** slow down

de·cen·ni·al [di-SEN-ee-əl] adj of period of ten years

de·cent [DEE-sənt] adj respectable; fitting, seemly; not obscene; adequate; inf kind **de'cen·cy** n

de·cen·tral·ize [dee-SEN-trə-līz] vt **-ized, -iz·ing** divide (government, organization) among local centers

de·cep·tion [di-SEP-shən] n deceiving; illusion; fraud; trick **de·cep'tive** adj misleading; apt to mislead

deci- comb form one tenth: *decimetre*

dec·i·bel [DES-ə-bəl] n unit for measuring intensity of a sound

de·cide [di-SĪD] v **-cid·ed, -cid·ing** ▷ vt settle, determine, bring to resolution; give judgment ▷ vi come to a decision, conclusion **de·cid'ed** adj unmistakable; settled; resolute **de·cid'ed·ly** adv certainly, undoubtedly **de·ci'sion** [-SIZH-ən] n **de·ci'sive** adj **de·ci'sive·ness** n

de·cid·u·ous [di-SIJ-oo-əs] adj of trees, losing leaves annually; of antlers, teeth, etc being shed at the end of a period of growth

dec·i·mal [DES-ə-məl] adj relating to tenths; proceeding by tens ▷ n decimal fraction **decimal system** system of weights and measures, or coinage, in which value of each denomination is ten times the one below it

dec·i·mate [DES-ə-mayt] vt **-mat·ed, -mat·ing** destroy or kill a tenth of, large proportion of **dec·i·ma'tion** n

de·ci·pher [di-SĪ-fər] vt make out meaning of; decode **de·ci'pher·a·ble** adj

deck [dek] n platform or floor, esp one covering whole or part of ship's hull; cassette deck; pack of playing cards; sl small packet of a narcotic ▷ vt array, decorate **deck chair** folding chair made of canvas suspended in wooden frame

de·claim [di-KLAYM] v speak dramatically, rhetorically or passionately; protest loudly **dec·la·ma'tion** [dek-lə-MAY-shən] n **de·clam'a·to·ry** adj

de·clare [di-KLAIR] v **-clared, -clar·ing** ▷ vt announce formally; state emphatically; show; name (as liable to customs duty) ▷ vi take sides (for); bridge bid (a suit or no trump) **dec·la·ra·tion** [dek-lə-RAY-shən] n **de·clar'a·tive** adj **de·clar'er** n bridge person who plays the contract

de·cline [di-KLIN] v **-clined, -clin·ing** refuse; slope, bend or sink downward; deteriorate gradually; grow smaller, diminish; list the case endings of nouns, pronouns, adjectives ▷n gradual deterioration; movement downward; diminution; downward slope **de·clen'sion** n in grammar, set of nouns, pronouns, etc; falling off; declining **de·clin'a·ble** adj **dec·li·na'tion** n sloping away, deviation; angle

de·cliv·i·ty [di-KLIV-i-tee] n downward slope

de·code [dee-KOHD] vt **-cod·ed, -cod·ing** put in intelligible terms a message in code or secret alphabet

dé·colle·té [day-kol-TAY] adj (of women's garment) having a low-cut neckline **dé·colle'tage'** [-TAHZH] n low-cut neckline

de·com·mis·sion [dee-kə-MISH-ən] vt dismantle (nuclear reactor, industrial plant) sufficiently to abandon safely; remove (ship) from service

de·com·pose [dee-kəm-POHZ] v **-posed, -pos·ing** separate into elements; rot **de·com·po·si·tion** [dee-kom-pə-ZISH-ən] n decay

de·com·press [dee-kəm-PRES] vt free from pressure; return to condition of normal atmospheric pressure **de·com·pres'sion** n

de·con·ges·tant [dee-kən-JES-tənt] adj, n (drug) relieving (esp nasal) congestion

de·con·struct·ed [dee-kən-STRUKT-əd] adj having no formal structure

de·con·tam·i·nate [dee-kən-TAM-ə-nayt] vt **-nat·ed, -nat·ing** free from contamination eg from poisons, radioactive substances

de·con·trol [dee-kən-TROHL] vt **-trolled, -trol·ling** release from government control

dé·cor [day-KOR] n decorative scheme of a room, etc; stage decoration; scenery

dec·o·rate [DEK-ə-rayt] vt **-rat·ed, -rat·ing** beautify by additions; select paint, furniture, etc for room, apartment, etc; award (medal, etc) **dec·o·ra'tion** n **dec'o·ra·tive** [-rə-tiv] adj

de·co·rum [di-KOR-əm] n seemly behavior, propriety, decency **dec·o·rous** [DEK-ə-rəs] adj

de·coy [DEE-koi] n something used to entrap others or to distract their attention; bait, lure ▷v [di-KOI] lure, be lured as with decoy

de·crease [di-KREES] v **-creased, -creas·ing** diminish, lessen ▷n [DEE-krees] lessening

de·cree [di-KREE] n order having the force of law; edict ▷v **-creed, -cree·ing** determine judicially; order

dec·re·ment [DEK-rə-mənt] n act or state of decreasing; quantity lost by decrease

de·crep·it [di-KREP-it] adj old and feeble; broken down, worn out **de·crep'i·tude** n

de·cry [di-KRI] vt **-cried, -cry·ing** disparage

ded·i·cate [DED-i-kayt] vt **-cat·ed, -cat·ing** commit wholly to special purpose or cause; inscribe or address (book, etc); devote to God's service **ded·i·ca'tion** n **ded'i·ca·to·ry** [-kə-tor-ee] adj

de·duce [di-DOOS] vt **-duced, -duc·ing** draw as conclusion from facts **de·duct** [di-DUKT] vt take

away, subtract **de·duct'i·ble** adj
de·duc'tion n deducting; amount
subtracted; conclusion deduced;
inference from general to particular
de·duc'tive adj

deed n action or fact; exploit; legal
document

deem vt judge, consider, regard

deep adj **-er, -est** extending far
down, in or back; at, of given depth;
profound; heartfelt; hard to fathom;
cunning; engrossed; intense, of
color, dark and rich; of sound, low
and full ▷ n deep place; the sea ▷ adv
far down, etc **deep'en** vt **deep'ly**
adv **deep freeze** condition or period
of suspended activity

deer n, pl **deer** family of ruminant
animals typically with antlers in
male **deer'stalk·er** n one who
stalks deer; kind of cloth hat with
visor in front and behind

de·face [di-FAYS] vt **-faced,
-fac·ing** spoil or mar surface;
disfigure **de·face'ment** n

de fac·to [day FAK-toh] Lat existing
in fact, whether legally recognized
or not

de·fal·ca·tion [dee-fal-KAY-
shăn] n misappropriation of money
held by trustee, etc; the money
taken **de·fal·cate** [di-FAL-kayt] vi
-cat·ed, -cat·ing

de·fame [di-FAYM] vt
-famed, -fam·ing speak ill of,
dishonor by slander or rumor
def·a·ma·tion [def-ă-MAY-shăn] n
de·fam'a·to·ry adj

de·fault [di-FAWLT] n failure,
neglect to act, appear or pay;
computing instruction to a computer
to select a particular option unless
the user specifies otherwise ▷ v
fail (to pay) **de·fault'er** n one who
defaults

de·feat [di-FEET] vt overcome,

vanquish; thwart ▷ n overthrow;
lose battle or encounter; frustration
de·feat'ism n attitude tending to
accept defeat **de·feat'ist** n, adj

def·e·cate [DEF-i-kayt] vt
-cat·ed, -cat·ing empty the bowels;
clear of impurities **def·e·ca'tion** n

de·fect [DEE-fekt] n lack, blemish,
failing ▷ vi [di-FEKT] desert
one's country, cause, etc, esp to
join opponents **de·fec'tion** n
abandonment of duty or allegiance
de·fec'tive adj incomplete; faulty

de·fend [di-FEND] vt protect, ward
off attack; support by argument,
evidence; (try to) maintain (title,
etc) against challenger **de·fense'**
n **de·fend'ant** n person accused in
court **de·fend·er** n **de·fen'si·ble**
adj **de·fen'sive** adj serving for
defense ▷ n position or attitude
of defense

de·fer¹ [di-FUR] vt **-ferred,
-fer·ring** put off, postpone
de·fer'ment, de·fer'ral n

de·fer² vi **-ferred, -fer·ring**
submit to opinion or judgment of
another **def'er·ence** n respectful
submission to views, etc of another
def·er·en'tial [-shăl] adj

defiance, defiant see **DEFY**

de·fi·cient [di-FISH-ănt] adj
lacking or falling short in something,
insufficient **de·fi'cien·cy** n

def·i·cit [DEF-ă-sit] n amount by
which sum of money is too small;
lack, shortage

de·file¹ [di-FIL] vt **-filed, -fil·ing**
make dirty, pollute, soil; sully;
desecrate

de·file² n narrow pass or valley ▷ vi
-filed, -fil·ing march in file

de·fine [di-FIN] vt **-fined, -fin·ing**
state contents or meaning of;
show clearly the form; lay down
clearly, fix; mark out **de·fin'a·ble**

adj **def·i·ni·tion** [-NISH-ən] *n* **def'i·nite** [-nit] *adj* exact, defined; clear, specific; certain, sure **de·fin'i·tive** *adj* conclusive, to be looked on as final

de·flate [di-FLAYT] *v* **-flat·ed, -flat·ing** (cause to) collapse by release of gas from; take away (person's) self-esteem; *economics* cause deflation **de·fla'tion** *n* deflating; *economics* reduction of economic and industrial activity **de·fla'tion·ar·y** *adj*

de·flect [di-FLEKT] *v* (cause to) turn from straight course **de·flec'tion** *n*

de·flow·er [di-FLOW-ər] *vt* deprive of virginity, innocence, etc **de·flo·ra'tion** *n*

de·fo·li·ate [dee-FOH-lee-ayt] *v* **-at·ed, -at·ing** (cause to) lose leaves, esp by action of chemicals **defo'li·ant** *n* **de·fo·li·a'tion** *n*

de·form [di-FORM] *vt* spoil shape of; make ugly; disfigure **de·formed'** *adj* **de·form'i·ty** *n, pl* **-ties**

de·fraud [di-FRAWD] *vt* cheat, swindle

de·fray [di-FRAY] *vt* provide money for (expenses, etc)

de·frock [di-FROK] *vt* deprive (priest, minister) of ecclesiastical status

de·frost [di-FRAWST] *v* make, become free of frost, ice; thaw

deft *adj* **-er, -est** skillful, adroit **deft'ly** *adv* **deft'ness** *n*

de·funct [di-FUNGKT] *adj* dead, obsolete

de·fuse [dee-FYOOZ] *vt* **-fused, -fus·ing** remove fuse of bomb, etc; remove tension (from situation, etc)

de·fy [di-FI] *vt* **-fied, -fy·ing** challenge, resist successfully; disregard **de·fi'ance** *n* resistance **de·fi'ant** *adj* openly and aggressively hostile; insolent

de·gauss [dee-GOWS] *vt* neutralize magnetic field (of ship's hull, electronic apparatus, etc)

de·gen·er·ate [di-JEN-ə-rayt] *vi* **-rat·ed, -rat·ing** deteriorate to lower mental, moral, or physical level ▷ *adj* [-rit] fallen away in quality ▷ *n* [-rit] degenerate person **de·gen'er·a·cy** *n*

de·grade [di-GRAYD] *v* **-grad·ed, -grad·ing** dishonor; debase; reduce to lower rank ▷ *vi* decompose chemically **de·grad'a·ble** *adj* capable of chemical, biological decomposition **de·grad'ed** *adj* shamed, humiliated **deg·ra·da'tion** *n*

de·gree [di-GREE] *n* step, stage in process, scale, relative rank, order, condition, manner, way; academic title conferred by university or college; unit of measurement of temperature or angle **third degree** severe, lengthy examination, esp of accused person by police, to extract information, confession

de·hu·mid·i·fy [dee-hyoo-MID-ə-fī] *vt* **-fied, -fy·ing** extract moisture from

de·hy·drate [dee-Hī-drayt] *vt* **-drat·ed, -drat·ing** remove moisture from **de·hy·dra'tion** *n*

de-ice [dee-IS] *vt* **-iced, -ic·ing** to dislodge ice from (eg windshield) or prevent its forming

de·i·fy [DEE-ə-fī] *vt* **-fied, -fy·ing** make god of; treat, worship as god **de·i·fi·ca'tion** *n*

deign [dayn] *vt* condescend, stoop; think fit

de·ism [DEE-iz-əm] *n* belief in god but not in revelation **de'ist** *n*

de·i·ty [DEE-i-tee] *n, pl* **-ties** divine status or attributes; a god

dé·jà vu [DAY-zhah VOO] *Fr*

experience of perceiving new situation as if it had occurred before

de·ject [di-JEKT] vt dishearten, cast down, depress **de·ject'ed** adj **de·jec'tion** n

de·jure [di·JUUR-ee] Lat in law, by right

de·lay [di-LAY] vt postpone, hold back ▷ vi be tardy, linger ▷ n act or instance of delaying; interval of time between events

de·lec·ta·ble [di-LEK-tə-bəl] adj delightful delicious **de·lec·ta·tion** [dee-lek-TAY-shən] n pleasure

del·e·gate [DEL-i-git] n person chosen to represent another ▷ vt [-gayt] **-gat·ed, -gat·ing** send as deputy; commit (authority, business, etc) to a deputy **del·e·ga'tion** n

de·lete [di-LEET] vt **-let·ed, -let·ing** remove, cancel, erase **de·le'tion** n

del·e·te·ri·ous [del-i-TEER-ee-əs] adj harmful, injurious

de·lib·er·ate [di-LIB-ər-it] adj intentional; well considered; without haste, slow ▷ v [-rayt] **-rat·ed, -rat·ing** consider, debate **de·lib·er·a'tion** n

del·i·cate [DELi-kit] adj exquisite; not robust, fragile; sensitive; requiring tact; deft **del'i·ca·cy** n

del·i·ca·tes·sen [del-i-kə-TES-ən] n store selling ready-to-eat foods; the food sold

de·li·cious [di-LISH-əs] adj delightful, pleasing to senses, esp taste

de·light [di-LĪT] vt please greatly ▷ vi take great pleasure (in) ▷ n great pleasure **de·light'ful** adj charming

de·lin·e·ate [di-LIN-ee-ayt] vt **-at·ed, -at·ing** portray by drawing or description; represent accurately **de·lin·e·a'tion** n

de·lin·quent [di-LING-kwənt] n someone, esp young person, guilty of delinquency ▷ adj **de·lin'quen·cy** n, pl **-cies** (minor) offense or misdeed

del·i·quesce [del-i-KWES] vi **-quesced, -quesc·ing** become liquid **del·i·ques'cence** n **del·i·ques'cent** adj

de·lir·i·um [di-LEER-ee-əm] n disorder of the mind, esp in feverish illness; violent excitement **de·lir'i·ous** adj raving; light-headed, wildly excited

de·liv·er [di-LIV-ər] vt carry (goods, etc) to destination; hand over; release; give birth or assist in birth (of); utter or present (speech, etc) **de·liv'er·ance** n rescue **de·liv'er·y** n

Del·phic [DEL-fik] adj pert to Delphi or to the oracle of Apollo

del·ta [DEL-tə] n alluvial tract where river at mouth breaks into several streams; fourth letter in the Greek alphabet; shape of this letter

de·lude [di-LOOD] vt **-lud·ed, -lud·ing** deceive; mislead **de·lu'sion** [-zhən] n

del·uge [DEL-yooj] n flood, great flow, rush, downpour, cloudburst ▷ vt **-uged, -ug·ing** flood, overwhelm

de·luxe [də-LUKS] adj rich, sumptuous; superior in quality

delve [delv] v **delved, delv·ing** (with into) search intensively; dig

de·mag·net·ize [dee-MAG-nə-tiz] vt **-tized, -tiz·ing** deprive of magnetic polarity

dem·a·gogue [DEM-ə-gog] n mob leader or agitator **dem·a·gog'ic** [-GOJ-ik] adj **dem'a·go·gy** [-goh-jee] n

de·mand [di-MAND] vt ask as giving an order; ask as by right; call for as due, right or necessary ▷ n urgent request, claim, requirement; call for (specific commodity) **de·mand·ing** adj requiring great skill, patience, etc

de·mar·cate [di-MAHR-kayt] vt **-cat·ed, -cat·ing** mark boundaries or limits of **de·mar·ca·tion** n

de·mean [di-MEEN] vt degrade, lower, humiliate

de·mean·or [di-MEEN-ər] n conduct, bearing, behavior

de·ment·ed [di-MEN-tid] adj mad, crazy; beside oneself

de·men·tia [-shə] n form of insanity

de·mer·it [di-MER-it] n bad mark; undesirable quality

demi- comb form half: demigod

de·mil·i·ta·rize [dee-MIL-i-tə-rīz] vt **-rized, -riz·ing** prohibit military presence or function in (an area)

dem·i·monde [DEM-ee-mond] n class of women of doubtful reputation; group behaving with doubtful legality, etc

de·mise [di-MĪZ] n death; conveyance by will or bequest; transfer of sovereignty on death or abdication

dem·i·urge [DEM-ee-urj] n name given in some philosophies (esp Platonic) to the creator of the world and man

dem·o [DEM-oh] n inf short for **DEMONSTRATION**

de·mo·bi·lize [dee-MOH-bə-līz] vt **-lized, -liz·ing** disband (troops); discharge (soldier)

de·moc·ra·cy [di-MOK-rə-see] n, pl **-cies** government by the people or their elected representatives; country so governed **dem·o·crat** [DEM-ə-krat] n advocate of democracy **dem·o·crat·ic** adj connected with democracy; favoring popular rights **de·moc·ra·tize** vt

-tized, -tiz·ing

de·mog·ra·phy [di-MOG-rə-fee] n study of population statistics, as births, deaths, diseases **dem·o·graph·ic** [dem-ə-GRAF-ik] adj

de·mol·ish [di-MOL-ish] vt knock to pieces; destroy utterly, raze **dem·o·li·tion** [dem-ə-LISH-ən] n

de·mon [DEE-mən] n devil, evil spirit; very cruel or malignant person; person very good at or devoted to a given activity **de·mo·ni·ac** [di-MOH-nee-ak] n one possessed with a devil **de·mo·ni·a·cal** [dee-mə-NĪ-ə-kəl] adj **de·mon·ic** [di-MON-ik] adj of the nature of a devil **de·mon·ol·o·gy** [dee-] n study of demons

dem·on·strate [DEM-ən-strayt] v **-strat·ed, -strat·ing** ▷ vt show by reasoning, prove; describe, explain by specimens or experiments ▷ vi make exhibition of support, protest, etc by public parade, demonstration; make show of armed force **de·mon·stra·ble** [di-MON-strə-bəl] adj **dem·on·stra·tion** n making clear, proving by evidence; exhibition and description; organized public expression of opinion; display of armed force **de·mon·stra·tive** adj expressing feelings, emotions easily and unreservedly; pointing out; conclusive **dem·on·stra·tor** n one who demonstrates equipment, products, etc; one who takes part in a public demonstration

de·mor·al·ize [di-MOR-ə-līz] vt **-ized, -iz·ing** deprive of courage and discipline; undermine morally **de·mor·al·i·za·tion** n

de·mote [di-MOHT] vt **-mot·ed, -mot·ing** reduce in status or rank **de·mo·tion** n

de·mur [di-MUR] vi **-murred,
-mur·ring** make difficulties, object
de·mur·ral n raising of objection;
objection raised **de·mur·rer** n

de·mure [di-MYUUR] adj
-mur·er, -mur·est reserved, quiet
de·mure·ly adv

den n cave or hole of wild beast; lair;
small room, esp study; site, haunt

de·na·tion·a·lize [dee-NASH-
ə-nl-iz] vt **-lized, -liz·ing** return
(an industry) from public to private
ownership

de·na·ture [dee-NAY-chər] vt
-tured, -tur·ing deprive of essential
qualities, adulterate **denatured
alcohol** alcohol made undrinkable

den·gue [DENG-gee] n an
infectious tropical fever

denial see **DENY**

de·nier [DEN-yər] n unit of weight
of silk and synthetic yarn

den·i·grate [DEN-i-grayt] vt
-grat·ed, -grat·ing belittle or
disparage character of

den·im [DEN-əm] n strong twilled
cotton fabric for trousers, overalls,
etc > pl garment made of this

den·i·zen [DEN-ə-zən] n
inhabitant

de·nom·i·nate [di-NOM-ə-nayt]
vt **-nat·ed, -nat·ing** give name
to **de·nom·i·na·tion** n distinctly
named church or sect; name, esp of
class or group **de·nom·i·na·tion·al**
adj **de·nom·i·na·tor** n arithmetic
divisor in fraction

de·note [di-NOHT] vt **-not·ed,
-not·ing** stand for, be the
name of; mark, indicate, show
de·no·ta·tion [dee-noh-TAY-shən]
n esp explicit meaning of word or
phrase

de·noue·ment [day-noo-MAHN]
n unraveling of dramatic plot; final
solution of mystery

de·nounce [di-NOWNS] vt
-nounced, -nounc·ing speak
violently against; accuse; terminate
(treaty) **de·nun·ci·a·tion** n
denouncing

dense [dens] adj **dens·er, dens·est**
thick, compact; stupid **den·si·ty** n,
pl **-ties** mass per unit of volume

dent n hollow or mark left by blow
or pressure > vt make dent in; mark
with dent

den·tal [DEN-tl] adj of, pert to
teeth or dentistry; pronounced
by applying tongue to teeth
den·ti·frice [-fris] n powder,
paste, or wash for cleaning teeth
den·tist n one skilled in care,
repair of teeth **den·tis·try** n art
of dentist **den·ti·tion** n teething;
arrangement of teeth **den·ture**
[-chər] n (usu pl) set of false teeth
dental floss soft thread, often waxed,
for cleaning between teeth
den·tine [DEN-teen] n the hard
bonelike part of a tooth

de·nude [di-NOOD] vt **-nud·ed,
-nud·ing** strip, make bare; expose
(rock) by erosion of plants, soil, etc

denunciation see **DENOUNCE**

de·ny [di-Nī] vt **-nied, -ny·ing**
declare untrue; contradict; reject,
disown; refuse to give; refuse;
(reflex.) abstain from **de·ni·a·ble**
adj **de·ni·al** n

de·o·dor·ize [dee-OH-də-rīz]
vt **-ized, -iz·ing** rid of smell or
mask smell of **de·o·dor·ant** n
de·o·dor·iz·er n

de·ox·i·dize [dee-OK-si-dīz]
vt **-dized, -diz·ing** deprive of oxygen

de·part [di-PAHRT] vi go away;
start out, set forth; deviate, vary; die
de·par·ture [-chər] n

de·part·ment [di-PAHRT-mənt]
n division; branch; province
de·part·men·tal adj

de·pend [di-PEND] vi (usu with *on*) rely entirely; live; be contingent; await settlement or decision **de·pend'a·ble** adj reliable **de·pend'ent** n one for whose maintenance another is responsible ▷ adj depending on **de·pend'ence** n **de·pend'en·cy** n dependence; subject territory

de·pict [di-PIKT] vt give picture of; describe in words **de·pic'tion** n

de·pil·a·to·ry [di-PIL-à-tor-ee] n, pl **-ries** substance that removes unwanted hair ▷ adj

de·plete [di-PLEET] vt **-plet·ed, -plet·ing** empty; reduce; exhaust **de·ple'tion** n

de·plore [di-PLOR] vt **-plored, -plor·ing** lament, regret; deprecate, complain of **de·plor'a·ble** adj lamentable; disgraceful

de·ploy [di-PLOI] v of troops, ships, aircraft (cause to) adopt battle formation; arrange **de·ploy'ment** n

de·po·nent [di-POH-nànt] adj of verb, having passive form but active meaning ▷ n deponent verb; one who makes statement under oath

de·pop·u·late [di-POP-yà-layt] v **-lat·ed, -lat·ing** (cause to) be reduced in population **de·pop·u·la'tion** n

de·port [di-PORT] vt expel from foreign country, banish **de·por·ta'tion** [dee-] n

de·port·ment [di-PORT-mànt] n behavior, conduct, bearing **de·port'** v behave, carry (oneself)

de·pose [di-POHZ] v **-posed, -pos·ing** ▷ vt remove from office, esp of ruler ▷ vi make statement under oath, give evidence **de·pos'al** n removal from office

de·pos·it [di-POZ-it] vt set down, esp carefully; give into safekeeping, esp in bank; let fall (as sediment) ▷ n

thing deposited; money given in part payment or as security; sediment

dep·o·si·tion [dep-à-ZISH-àn] n statement written and attested; act of deposing or depositing

de·pos·i·tor n **de·pos'i·to·ry** n, pl **-ries** place for safekeeping

de·pot [DEE-poh] n storehouse; building for storage and servicing of buses, trains, etc; railroad, bus station

de·prave [di-PRAYV] vt **-praved, -prav·ing** make bad, corrupt, pervert **de·prav'i·ty** n, pl **-ties** wickedness, viciousness

dep·re·cate [DEP-ri-kayt] vt **-cat·ed, -cat·ing** express disapproval of; advise against **dep·re·ca'tion** n **dep're·ca·to·ry** adj

de·pre·ci·ate [di-PREE-shee-ayt] v **-at·ed, -at·ing** ▷ vt lower price, value or purchasing power of; belittle ▷ vi fall in value **de·pre·ci·a'tion** n

dep·re·da·tion [dep-ri-DAY-shàn] n plundering, pillage **dep're·date** v **-dat·ed, -dat·ing** plunder, despoil

de·press [di-PRES] vt affect with low spirits; lower, in level or activity **de·pres'sion** [-PRESH-àn] n hollow; low spirits, dejection, despondency; poor condition of business, slump **de·pres'sant** adj, n

de·prive [di-PRĪV] vt **-prived, -priv·ing** strip, dispossess **dep·ri·va·tion** [dep-rà-VAY-shàn] n **deprived** adj lacking adequate food, care, amenities, etc

depth n (degree of) deepness; deep place, abyss; intensity (of color, feeling); profundity (of mind) **depth charge** bomb for use against submarines

de·pute [di-PYOOT] vt **-put·ed, -put·ing** vt allot; appoint as an agent or substitute **dep·u·ta'tion**

[dep-yə-TAY-shən] *n* persons sent to speak for others **dep'u·tate** *vi* **-tized, -tiz·ing** act for another ▷*vt* **depute dep'u·ty** *n, pl* **-ties** assistant; substitute, delegate

de·rail [dee-RAYL] *v* (cause to) go off the rails, as train, etc **de·rail'ment** *n*

de·rail·leur [di-RAY-lər] *n* gear-changing mechanism for bicycles

de·range [di-RAYNJ] *vt* **-ranged, -rang·ing** put out of place, out of order; upset; make insane **de·range'ment** *n*

der·by [DUR-bee] *n* horserace, esp Kentucky Derby, held at Churchill Downs, Kentucky; contest between teams of skaters, etc; man's low-crowned stiff felt hat

de·reg·u·late [dee-REG-yə-layt] *vt* **-lat·ed, -lat·ing** remove regulations or controls from

der·e·lict [DER-ə-likt] *adj* abandoned, forsaken; falling into ruins, dilapidated ▷*n* social outcast, vagrant; abandoned property, ship, etc **der·e·lic'tion** *n* neglect (of duty); abandoning

de·ride [di-RĪD] *vt* **-rid·ed, -rid·ing** speak of or treat with contempt, ridicule **de·ri'sion** [-RIZH-ən] *n* ridicule **de·ri'sive** [-RĪ-siv] *adj*

de ri·gueur [də ri-GUR] Fr required by etiquette, fashion or custom

de·rive [di-RĪV] *vt* **-rived, -riv·ing** deduce, get from; show origin of ▷*vi* issue, be descended (from) **der·i·va·tion** [der-ə-VAY-shən] *n* **de·riv·a·tive** [di-RIV-ə-tiv] *adj, n*

der·ma·ti·tis [dur-mə-TĪ-tis] *n* inflammation of skin

der·ma·tol·o·gy [dur-mə-TOL-ə-jee] *n* science of skin **der·ma·tol'o·gist** *n* physician specializing in skin diseases

der·o·ga·to·ry [di-ROG-ə-tor-ee] *adj* disparaging, belittling, intentionally offensive **der·o·gate** [DER-ə-gayt] *v* **-gat·ed, -gat·ing** ▷*vt* disparage ▷*vi* detract

der·rick [DER-ik] *n* hoisting machine; framework over oil well, etc

der·ring-do [DER-ing DOO] *n* (act of) spirited bravery, boldness

der·rin·ger [DER-in-jər] *n* short-barreled pocket pistol

der·vish [DUR-vish] *n* member of Muslim ascetic order, noted for frenzied, whirling dance

des·cant [DES-kant] *n music* decorative variation sung as accompaniment to basic melody ▷*vi* [des-KANT] *music* sing or play a descant; talk about in detail; dwell (on) at length

de·scend [di-SEND] *vi* come or go down; slope down; stoop, condescend; spring from (ancestor, etc); pass to heir, be transmitted; swoop on or attack ▷*vt* go or come down **de·scen'dant** *n* person descended from an ancestor **de·scent'** *n*

de·scribe [di-SKRĪB] *vt* **-scribed, -scrib·ing** give detailed account of; pronounce or label; trace out (geometric figure, etc) **de·scrip'tion** [-SKRIP-shən] *n* detailed account; marking out; kind, sort, species **de·scrip'tive** *adj*

de·scry [di-SKRĪ] *vt* **-scried, -scry·ing** make out, catch sight of, esp at a distance espy

des·e·crate [DES-i-krayt] *vt* **-crat·ed, -crat·ing** violate sanctity of; profane; convert to evil use **des·e·cra'tion** *n*

des·ert¹ [DEZ-ərt] *n* uninhabited and barren region ▷*adj* barren, uninhabited, desolate

de·sert² [di-ZURT] *vt* abandon, forsake, leave ▷*vi* run away from

service, esp of soldiers, sailors, etc
de·sert·er n **de·ser·tion** n
de·sert³ [di-ZURT] n (usu pl) what
is due as reward or punishment;
merit, virtue
de·serve [di-ZURV] vt **-served,
-serv·ing** show oneself worthy
of; have by conduct a claim to
de·serv·ed·ly adv **de·serv·ing** adj
worthy (of reward, etc)
deshabille n see **DISHABILLE**
des·ic·cate [DES-i-kayt] v
-cat·ed, -cat·ing dry; dry up
de·sid·er·a·tum [di-sid-ə-RAH-
təm] n, pl **-ta** [-tə] something
lacked and wanted
de·sign [di-ZIN] vt make working
drawings for; sketch; plan out;
intend, select for ⊳ n outline
sketch; working plan; art of making
decorative patterns, etc; project,
purpose, mental plan **de·sign·ed·ly**
adv on purpose **de·sign·er** n
esp one who draws designs for
manufacturers or selects typefaces,
etc for books, etc **de·sign·ing** adj
crafty, scheming
des·ig·nate [DEZ-ig-nayt] vt
-nat·ed, -nat·ing name, pick
out, appoint to office ⊳ adj [-nit]
appointed but not yet installed
des·ig·na·tion n name, appellation
de·sire [di-ZIR] vt **-sired, -sir·ing**
wish, long for; ask for, entreat ⊳ n
longing, craving; expressed wish,
request; sexual appetite; something
wished for or requested **de·sir·a·ble**
adj worth desiring **de·sir·ous** adj
filled with desire
de·sist [di-ZIST] vi cease, stop
desk n table or other piece of
furniture designed for reading or
writing; counter; editorial section
of newspaper, etc covering specific
subject; section of State Department
having responsibility for particular

operations
des·o·late [DES-ə-lit] adj
uninhabited; neglected; barren,
ruinous; solitary; dreary, dismal,
forlorn ⊳ vt [-layt] depopulate, lay waste; overwhelm
with grief **des·o·la·tion** n
de·spair [di-SPAIR] vi lose hope
⊳ n loss of all hope; cause of this;
despondency
despatch see **DISPATCH**
des·pe·rate [DES-pər-it] adj
reckless from despair; difficult
or dangerous; frantic; hopelessly
bad; leaving no room for hope
des·per·a·do [-pə-RAH-doh] n,
pl **-dos** reckless, lawless person
des·per·ate·ly adv **des·per·a·tion**
n
de·spise [di-SPIZ] vt **-spised,
-spis·ing** look down on
as contemptible, inferior
des·pi·ca·ble [DES-pi-kə-bəl] adj
base, contemptible, vile
de·spite [di-SPIT] prep in spite of
de·spoil [di-SPOIL] vt plunder, rob,
strip of **de·spo·li·a·tion** [di-spoh-
lee-AY-shən] n
de·spond·ent [di-SPON-
dənt] adj dejected, depressed
de·spond·en·cy n
des·pot [DES-pət] n tyrant,
oppressor **des·pot·ic** [di-SPOT-ik]
adj **des·pot·ism** n autocratic
government, tyranny
des·sert [di-ZURT] n course of
pastry, fruit, etc served at end of meal
des·ti·na·tion [des-tə-NAY-shən]
n place a person or thing is bound
for; goal; purpose
des·tine [DES-tin] vt **-tined,
-tin·ing** ordain or fix beforehand;
set apart, devote
des·ti·ny [DES-tə-nee] n, pl **-nies**
course of events or person's fate; the
power that foreordains

des·ti·tute [DES-ti-toot] *adj* in absolute want; in great need, devoid (of); penniless **des·ti·tu·tion** *n*

de-stress [dee-STRES] *v* to become or cause to become less anxious

de·stroy [di-STROI] *v* ruin; pull to pieces; undo; put an end to; demolish; annihilate **de·stroy'er** *n* one who destroys; small, swift, heavily armed warship **de·struct** [di-STRUKT] *v* destroy (one's own missile, etc) for safety; be destroyed **de·struc'i·ble** *adj* **de·struc'tion** *n* ruin, overthrow; death **de·struc'tive** *adj* destroying; negative, not constructive

des·ue·tude [DES-wi-tood] *n* disuse, discontinuance

des·ul·to·ry [DES-əl-tor-ee] *adj* passing, changing fitfully from one thing to another; aimless; unmethodical

de·tach [di-TACH] *vt* unfasten, disconnect, separate **de·tach'a·ble** *adj* **de·tached'** *adj* standing apart, isolated; impersonal, disinterested **de·tach'ment** *n* aloofness; detaching; a body of troops detached for special duty

de·tail [di-TAYL, DEE-tayl] *n* particular; small or unimportant part; treatment of anything item by item; party or personnel assigned for duty in military unit ▷ *vt* relate in full; appoint for duty

de·tain [di-TAYN] *vt* keep under restraint; hinder; keep waiting **de·ten'tion** *n* confinement; arrest; detaining

de·tect [di-TEKT] *vt* find out or discover existence, presence, nature or identity of **de·tec'tion** *n* **de·tec'tive** *n* police officer or private agent employed in detecting crime ▷ *adj* employed in detection **de·tec'tor** *n* esp mechanical sensing device or device for detecting radio signals, etc

dé·tente [day-TAHNT] *n* lessening of tension in political or international affairs

detention *n* see **DETAIN**

de·ter [di-TUR] *vt* **-terred**, **-ter·ring** discourage, frighten; hinder, prevent **de·ter'rent** *adj*, *n*

de·ter·gent [di-TUR-jənt] *n* cleansing, purifying substance ▷ *adj* having cleansing power

de·te·ri·o·rate [di-TEER-ee-ə-rayt] *v* **-rat·ed**, **-rat·ing** become or make worse **de·te·ri·o·ra'tion** *n*

de·ter·mine [di-TUR-min] *v* **-mined**, **-min·ing** ▷ *vt* make up one's mind, decide; fix as known; bring to a decision; be deciding factor in; *law* end ▷ *vi* come to an end; come to a decision **de·ter'mi·nant** *adj*, *n* **de·ter'mi·nate** [-nit] *adj* fixed in scope or nature **de·ter·mi·na'tion** *n* determining; firm or resolute conduct or purpose; resolve **determined** *adj* resolute **de·ter'min·ism** *n* theory that human action is settled by forces independent of human will

de·test [di-TEST] *v* hate, loathe **de·test'a·ble** *adj* **de·tes·ta'tion** [dee-te-STAY-shən] *n*

de·throne [dee-THROHN] *vt* **-throned**, **-thron·ing** remove from throne, depose

det·o·nate [DET-n-ayt] *v* of bomb, mine, explosives, etc, (cause to) explode **det·o·na'tion** *n* **det'o·na·tor** *n* mechanical, electrical device, or small amount of explosive, used to set off main explosive charge

de·tour [DEE-toor] *n* course that leaves main route to rejoin it later; roundabout way ▷ *vi*

de·tox [DEE-toks] *inf n* treatment to rid the body of poisonous substances ▷ *v* [dee-TOKS] undergo or subject to such treatment

de·tract [di-TRAKT] *v* take away (a part) from, diminish **de·trac'tor** *n*

det·ri·ment [DE-trə-mənt] *n* harm done, loss, damage **det·ri·men'tal** *adj* damaging, injurious

de·tri·tus [di-TRĪ-təs] *n* worn-down matter such as gravel, or rock debris; debris

de trop [də TROH] *Fr* not wanted, superfluous

deuce [doos] *n* two; playing card with two spots; *tennis* forty all; in exclamatory phrases, the devil

Deut. Deuteronomy

deu·te·ri·um [doo-TEER-ee-əm] *n* isotope of hydrogen twice as heavy as the normal gas

de·val·ue [dee-VAL-yoo] -**ued**, -**u·ing** *v* (of currency) reduce or be reduced in value; reduce the value or worth of **de·val·u·a'tion** *n*

dev·as·tate [DEV-ə-stayt] *vt* -**tat·ed**, -**tat·ing** lay waste; ravage; *inf* overwhelm **dev·as·ta'tion** *n*

de·vel·op [di-VEL-əp] *vt* bring to maturity; elaborate; bring forth, bring out; evolve; treat photographic plate or film to bring out image; improve value or change use of (land) by building, etc ▷ *vi* grow to maturer state **de·vel'op·er** *n* one who develops land; chemical for developing film **de·vel'op·ment** *n*

de·vi·ate [DEE-vee-ayt] *vi* -**at·ed**, -**at·ing** leave the way, turn aside, diverge **de'vi·ant** *n*, *adj* (person) deviating from normal esp in sexual practices **de·vi·a'tion** *n* **de'vi·ous** *adj* deceitful, underhanded; roundabout; rambling; erring

de·vice [di-VĪS] *n* contrivance,

invention; apparatus; stratagem; scheme, plot; heraldic or emblematic figure or design

dev·il [DEV-əl] *n* personified spirit of evil; superhuman evil being; person of great wickedness, cruelty, etc; *inf* fellow; *inf* something difficult or annoying; energy, dash, unconquerable spirit; *inf* rogue, rascal ▷ *vt* -**iled**, -**il·ing** prepare (eggs, etc) with spicy seasoning **dev'il·ish** *adj* like, of the devil; evil ▷ *adv* very, extremely **dev'il·try** *n*, *pl* -**tries** wickedness; wild and reckless mischief, revelry, high spirits **dev'il-may-care'** *adj* happy-go-lucky **devil's advocate** one who advocates opposing, unpopular view, usu for sake of argument; *Catholic Church* one appointed to state disqualifications of person who has been proposed for sainthood

devious *adj* see **DEVIATE**

de·void [di-VOID] *adj* (usu *with of*) empty, lacking, free from

de·volve [di-VOLV] *vi* -**volved**, -**volv·ing** pass or fall (to, upon) ▷ *vt* throw (duty, etc) on to another **dev·o·lu·tion** [dev-ə-LOO-shən] *n* devolving, esp transfer of power from central to regional government

de·vote [di-VOHT] *vt* -**vot·ed**, -**vot·ing** set apart, give up exclusively (to person, purpose, etc) **devoted** *adj* loving, attached **dev·o·tee** [dev-ə-TEE] *n* ardent enthusiast; zealous worshiper **de·vo'tion** *n* deep affection, loyalty; dedication; religious earnestness ▷ *pl* prayers, religious exercises **de·vo'tion·al** *adj*

de·vour [di-VOWR] *vt* eat greedily; consume, destroy; read, gaze at eagerly

de·vout [di-VOWT] *adj* earnestly religious, pious; sincere, heartfelt

dew [doo] *n* moisture from air deposited as small drops on cool surface between nightfall and morning; any beaded moisture ▷ *vt* wet with or as with dew **dew'y** *adj* **dew·i·er, dew·i·est dew'claw** *n* partly developed inner toe of dogs **dew'lap** *n* fold of loose skin hanging from neck

dex·ter·i·ty [dek-STER-i-tee] *n* manual skill, neatness, deftness, adroitness **dex'ter·ous** *adj* showing dexterity, skillful

dex·trose [DEK-strohs] *n* white, soluble, sweet-tasting crystalline solid, occurring naturally in fruit, honey, animal tissue

di·a- *prefix* through

di·a·be·tes [dī-ə-BEE-tis] *n* various disorders characterized by excretion of abnormal amount of urine in which body fails to store and utilize glucose **di·a·bet'ic** *n, adj*

di·a·bol·ic [dī-ə-BOL-ik], **di·a·bol'i·cal** *adj* devilish; *inf* very bad **di·a·bol'i·cal·ly** *adv*

di·a·crit·ic [dī-ə-KRIT-ik] *n* sign above letter or character indicating special phonetic value, etc **di·a·crit'i·cal** *adj* of a diacritic; showing a distinction

di·a·dem [Dī-ə-dem] *n* a crown

di·ag·no·sis [dī-əg-NOH-sis] *n, pl* **-ses** [-seez] identification of disease from symptoms **di'ag·nose** [-nohz] *vt* **-nosed, -nos·ing di·ag·nos'tic** [-NOS-tik] *adj*

di·ag·o·nal [dī-AG-ə-nl] *adj* from corner to corner; oblique ▷ *n* line from corner to corner **di·ag·o·nal·ly** *adv*

di·a·gram [Dī-ə-gram] *n* drawing, figure in lines, to illustrate something being expounded **di·a·gram·mat'i·cal·ly** *adv*

di·al [Dī-əl] *n* face of clock, etc; plate marked with graduations on which a pointer moves (as on a meter, radio, scale, etc); numbered disk on front of telephone ▷ *vt* operate telephone; indicate on dial

di·a·lect [Dī-ə-lekt] *n* characteristic speech of region; local variety of a language **di·a·lec'tal** *adj*

di·a·lec·tic [dī-ə-LEK-tik] *n* art of arguing **di·a·lec'ti·cal** *adj* **di·a·lec·ti'cian** [-TISH-ən] *n* logician; reasoner

di·a·logue [Dī-ə-lawg] *n* conversation between two or more (persons); representation of such conversation in drama, novel, etc; discussion between representatives of two governments, etc

di·al·y·sis [dī-AL-ə-sis] *n, pl* **-ses** [-seez] *medicine* filtering of blood through membrane to remove waste products

di·am·e·ter [dī-AM-i-tər] *n* (length of) straight line from side to side of figure or body (esp circle) through center; thickness **di·a·met'ri·cal** *adj* opposite **di·a·met'ri·cal·ly** *adv*

di·a·mond [Dī-mənd] *n* very hard and brilliant precious stone, also used in industry; rhomboid figure; suit at cards; playing field in baseball **diamond jubilee** sixtieth anniversary of an event **diamond wedding** sixtieth anniversary of a wedding

di·a·pa·son [dī-ə-PAY-zən] *n* fundamental organ stop; compass of voice or instrument

dia·per [Dī-pər] *n* garment of absorbent material to absorb an infant's excrement ▷ *vt* put a diaper on

di·aph·a·nous [di-AF-ə-nəs] *adj* transparent

di·a·pho·ret·ic [di-ə-fə-RET-ik] *adj* drug promoting perspiration ▷ *adj*

di·a·phragm [Dĺ-ə-fram] *n* muscular partition dividing two cavities of body, midriff; plate or disk wholly or partly closing tube or opening; any thin dividing or covering membrane

di·ar·rhe·a [di-ə-REE-ə] *n* excessive looseness of the bowels

di·a·ry [Dĺ-ə-ree] *n, pl* **-ries** daily record of events or thoughts; book for this; book for noting appointments, memoranda, etc **di′a·rist** *n* writer of diary

di·as·to·le [di-AS-tl-ee] *n* dilatation of the chambers of the heart

di·a·ther·my [Dĺ-ə-thur-mee] *n* heating of body tissues with electric current for medical or surgical purposes

di·a·tom [Dĺ-ə-tom] *n* one of order of microscopic algae **di·a·tom′ic** *adj* of two atoms

di·a·ton·ic [di-ə-TON-ik] *adj music* pert to regular major and minor scales; (of melody) composed in such a scale

di·a·tribe [Dĺ-ə-trib] *n* violently bitter verbal attack, invective, denunciation

dice [dis] *n, pl* **dice** small cube each of whose sides has a different number of spots (1 to 6), used in games of chance ▷ *v* **diced, dic′ing** ▷ *vi* gamble with dice ▷ *vt cookery* cut vegetables into small cubes **dic′er** *n* **dic′ey** *adj* **dic·i·er, dic·i·est** *inf* dangerous, risky

di·chot·o·my [di-KOT-ə-mee] *n, pl* **-mies** division into two parts

dic·tate [DIK-tayt] *v* **-tat·ed, -tat·ing** say or read for another

to transcribe; prescribe, lay down; impose (as terms) ▷ *n* bidding **dic·ta′tion** **dic′ta·tor** *n* absolute ruler **dic·ta·to′ri·al** *adj* despotic; overbearing **dic·ta′tor·ship** *n*

dic·tion [DIK-shən] *n* choice and use of words; enunciation

dic·tion·ar·y [DIK-shə-ner-ee] *n, pl* **-ar·ies** book setting forth, alphabetically, words of language with meanings, etc; reference book with items in alphabetical order

dic·tum [DIK-təm] *n, pl* **-ta** [-tə] pronouncement, saying, maxim

did *pt* of **DO**

di·dac·tic [di-DAK-tik] *adj* designed to instruct; (of people) opinionated, dictatorial

die¹ [di] *vi* **died, dy·ing** cease to live; come to an end; stop functioning; *inf* be nearly overcome (with laughter, etc); *inf* look forward (to) **die′hard** *n* one who resists (reform, etc) to the end

die² see **DICE**

die³ *n* shaped block of hard material to form metal in forge, press, etc; tool for cutting thread on pipe, etc

di·e·lec·tric [di-i-LEK-trik] *n* substance through or across which electric induction takes place; nonconductor; insulator

di·er·e·sis [di-ER-ə-sis] *n, pl* **-ses** [-seez] mark (¨) placed over vowel to show that it is sounded separately from preceding one, for example in Noël

die·sel [DEE-zəl] *adj* pert to internal-combustion engine using oil as fuel ▷ *n* this engine; vehicle powered by it

di·et¹ [Dĺ-it] *n* restricted or regulated course of feeding; kind of food lived on; food ▷ *vi* follow a dietary regimen, as to lose weight **di′e·ta·ry** *adj* relating to diet

▷ n a regulated diet **di·e·tet'ic** adj **di·e·tet'ics** n science of diet **di·e·ti'tian** [-TISH-ən] n one skilled in dietetics **dietary fiber** fibrous substances in fruit and vegetables, consumption of which aids digestion

diet² n parliament of some countries; formal assembly

dif·fer [DIF-ər] vi be unlike; disagree **dif'fer·ence** n unlikeness; degree or point of unlikeness; disagreement; remainder left after subtraction **dif'fer·ent** adj unlike

dif·fer·en·tial [dif-ə-REN-shəl] adj varying with circumstances; special; mathematics pert to an infinitesimal change in variable quantity; physics relating to difference between sets of motions acting in the same direction or between pressures, etc ▷ n mathematics infinitesimal difference between two consecutive states of variable quantity; mechanism in automobile, etc permitting back wheels to revolve at different speeds when rounding corner; difference between rates of pay for different types of labor **dif·fer·en'ti·ate** [-shee-ayt] v **-at·ed, -at·ing** ▷ vt serve to distinguish between, make different ▷ vi discriminate **dif·fer·en·ti·a'tion** n **differential calculus** method of calculating relative rate of change for continuously varying quantities

dif·fi·cult [DIF-i-kult] adj requiring effort, skill, etc to do or understand, not easy; obscure **dif'fi·cul·ty** n, pl **-ties** being difficult; difficult task, problem; embarrassment; hindrance; obscurity; trouble

dif·fi·dent [DIF-i-dənt] adj lacking confidence, timid, shy **dif'fi·dence** n shyness

dif·fract [di-FRAKT] vi break up, esp of rays of light, sound waves **dif·frac'tion** [-FRAK-shən] n deflection of ray of light, electromagnetic wave caused by an obstacle

dif·fuse [di-FYOOZ] vt **-fused, -fus·ing** spread abroad ▷ adj [-FYOOS] widely spread; loose, verbose, wordy **dif·fuse'ly** adv loosely; wordily **dif·fu'sion** [-zhən] n **dif·fu'sive** adj

dig v **dug, dig·ging** ▷ vi work with spade; search, investigate ▷ vt turn up with spade; hollow out, make hole in; excavate; thrust into; discover by searching; sl understand ▷ n archaeological excavation; thrust; gibe, taunt **dig'ger** n

di·gest [di-JEST] vt prepare (food) in stomach, etc for assimilation; bring into handy form by sorting, tabulating, summarizing; reflect on; absorb ▷ vi of food, undergo digestion ▷ n [DI-jest] methodical summary, of laws, research, etc; magazine containing condensed version of articles, etc already published elsewhere **di·gest'i·ble** adj **di·ges'tion** n digesting

dig·it [DIJ-it] n finger or toe; any of the numbers 0 to 9 **dig'it·al** adj of, resembling digits; performed with fingers; displaying information (time, etc) by numbers rather than by pointer on dial; of, relating to device that can write, read, or store information represented in numerical form **digital recording** sound recording process that converts audio signals into pulses corresponding to voltage level **digital television** television in which the picture is transmitted in digital form and then decoded **dig'it·ized** adj recorded or stored in digital form

dig·i·tal·is [dij-i-TAL-is] *n* drug made from foxglove

dig·ni·ty [DIG-ni-tee] *n, pl* **-ties** stateliness, gravity; worthiness, excellence, repute; honorable office or title **dig'ni·fy** *vt* **-fied, -fy·ing** give dignity to **dig'ni·fied** *adj* stately, majestic **dig'ni·tar·y** [-ter-ee] *n, pl* **-tar·ies** holder of high office

di·gress [di-GRES] *vi* turn from main course, esp to deviate from subject in speaking or writing **di·gres'sion** *n*

di·he·dral [di-HEE-drəl] *adj* having two plane faces or sides

dike [dīk] *n* embankment to prevent flooding; ditch

di·lap·i·dat·ed [di-LAP-i-day-tid] *adj* in ruins; decayed

dil·a·ta·tion [dil-ə-TAY-shən] *n* widening of body aperture for medical treatment, for example for curettage

di·late [di-LAYT] *v* **-lat·ed, -lat·ing** ▷*vt* widen, expand ▷*vi* expand; talk or write at length (on) **di·la'tion** *n*

di·la·to·ry [DIL-ə-tor-ee] *adj* tardy, slow, belated ▷*vt* **di'la·to·ri·ness** *n* delay

di·lem·ma [di-LEM-ə] *n* position in fact or argument offering choice only between unwelcome alternatives; predicament

dil·et·tante [dil-i-TAHNT] *n* person with taste and knowledge of fine arts as pastime; dabbler ▷ *adj* amateur, desultory **dil'et·tant·ism** *n*

dil·i·gent [DIL-i-jənt] *adj* unremitting in effort, industrious, hardworking **dil'i·gence** *n*

di·lute [di-LOOT] *vt* **-lut·ed, -lut·ing** reduce (liquid) in strength, esp by adding water; thin; reduce in force, effect, etc ▷ *adj* weakened

thus **di·lu'tion** *n*

dim *adj* **dim·mer, dim·mest** indistinct, faint, not bright; mentally dull; unfavorable ▷*v* **dimmed, dim·ming** make, grow dim **dim'ly** *adv* **dim'mer** *n* device for dimming electric lights **dim'ness** *n*

dime [dīm] *n* 10-cent piece, coin of US and Canada

di·men·sion [di-MEN-shən] *n* measurement, size; aspect **fourth dimension** *physics* time; supernatural, fictional dimension additional to those of length, breadth, thickness

di·min·ish *v* lessen **dim·i·nu·tion** [dim-ə-NOO-shən] *n* **di·min·u·tive** [di-MIN-yə-tiv] *adj* very small ▷*n* derivative word, affix implying smallness

di·min·u·en·do [di-min-yoo-EN-doh] *adj, adv* music of sound, dying away

dim·ple [DIM-pəl] *n* small hollow in surface of skin, esp of cheek; any small hollow ▷*v* **-pled, -pling** mark with, show dimples

din *n* continuous roar of confused noises ▷*vt* **dinned, din·ning** repeat to weariness, ram (fact, opinion, etc) into

dine [dīn] *v* **dined, din·ing** ▷*vi* eat esp dinner ▷*vt* give dinner to **din'er** *n* one who dines; informal usu cheap restaurant **dining room** room where meals are eaten

din·ghy [DING-gee] *n, pl* **-ghies** small open boat; inflatable life raft

din·go [DING-goh] *n, pl* **-goes** Aust wild dog

din·gy [DIN-jee] *adj* **-gi·er, -gi·est** dirty-looking, shabby **din'gi·ness** *n*

din·ner [DIN-ər] *n* chief meal of the day; official banquet

di·no·saur [Dī-nə-sor] *n* extinct reptile, often of gigantic size

dint n force, power **by dint of** by means of

di·o·cese [DI-ə-sis] n ecclesiastical district under jurisdiction of bishop **di·oc·e·san** [di-OS-ə-sən] adj having jurisdiction over diocese

di·ode [DI-ohd] n electronics device for converting alternating current to direct current

di·op·ter [di-OP-tər] n unit for measuring refractive power of lens

di·o·ram·a [di-ə-RAM-ə] n miniature three-dimensional scene, esp as museum exhibit

di·ox·ide [di-OK-sid] n oxide with two parts of oxygen to one of the other constituents

di·ox·in [di-OK-sin] n extremely toxic byproduct of the manufacture of certain herbicides and bactericides

dip v **dipped, dip·ping** ▷vt put partly or for a moment into liquid; immerse, involve; lower and raise again; take up in ladle, bucket, etc ▷vi plunge partially or temporarily; go down, sink; slope downward ▷n act of dipping; brief swim; liquid chemical in which livestock are immersed to treat insect pests, etc; downward slope; hollow; creamy mixture in which cracker, etc is dipped before being eaten **dip into** glance at (book, etc)

diph·the·ri·a [dif-THEER-ee-ə] n infectious disease of throat with membranous growth

diph·thong [DIF-thawng] n union of two vowel sounds in single compound sound

di·plo·ma [di-PLOH-mə] n, pl **-mas** document vouching for person's proficiency; title to degree, honor, etc

di·plo·ma·cy [di-PLOH-mə-see] n management of international relations; skill in negotiation;

tactful, adroit dealing **dip·lo·mat** [DIP-lə-mat] n one engaged in official diplomacy **dip·lo·mat·ic** adj

di·plo·ma·tist n tactful person

di·plo·pi·a [di-PLOH-pee-ə] n double vision

di·po·lar [DI-POH-lər] adj having two poles

di·pole [DI-pohl] n type of radio and television antenna

dip·per [DIP-ər] n ladle, bucket, scoop

dip·so·ma·ni·a [dip-sə-MAY-nee-ə] n uncontrollable craving for alcohol **dip·so·ma·ni·ac** n victim of this

dip·tych [DIP-tik] n ancient tablet hinged in the middle, folding together like a book; painting, carving on two hinged panels

dire [dir] adj **dir·er, dir·est** terrible; urgent

di·rect [di-REKT] vt control, manage, order; point out the way; aim, point, turn; address (letter, etc); supervise actors, etc in play or film ▷adj frank, straightforward; straight; going straight to the point; immediate; lineal **di·rec·tion** n directing; aim, course of movement; address, instruction **di·rec·tive** adj, n **di·rec·tor** n one who directs, esp a film; member of board of directors of company **di·rec·to·rate** [-tər-it] n body of directors; office of director

di·rec·to·ry n, pl **-ries** book of names, addresses, streets, etc; computing area of a disk containing the names and locations of the files it currently holds **direction finder** radio receiver that determines the direction of incoming waves

dirge [durj] n song of mourning

dir·i·gi·ble [DIR-i-jə-bəl] adj steerable ▷n airship

dirt [durt] n filth; soil, earth;

obscene material; contamination

dirt'i•ness n **dirt'y** adj **-i•er, -i•est** unclean, filthy; obscene; unfair; dishonest

dis- prefix indicating: reversal: disconnect; negation or lack: dissimilar; disgrace; removal or release: disembowel

dis•a•ble [dis-AY-bl] vt **-bled, -bling** make ineffective, unfit, or incapable **dis'a'bled** adj lacking a physical power, such as the ability to walk **dis•a•bil'i•ty** n, pl **-ties** incapacity; drawback

dis•a•buse [dis-ə-BYOOZ] vt **-bused, -bus•ing** undeceive, disillusion; free from error

dis•ad•van•tage [dis-ad-VAN-tijj] n drawback; hindrance; detriment ▷ vt **-taged, -tag•ing** handicap **disadvantaged** adj deprived, discriminated against, underprivileged

dis•ad•van•ta•geous [-TAY-jəs] adj

dis•af•fect•ed [dis-ə-FEK-tid] adj ill-disposed, alienated, estranged **dis•af•fec'tion** n

dis•a•gree [dis-ə-GREE] vt **-greed, -gree•ing** be at variance; conflict; (of food, etc) have bad effect on **dis•a•gree'ment** n difference of opinion; discord; discrepancy **dis•a•gree'a•ble** adj unpleasant

dis•al•low [dis-ə-LOW] vt reject as untrue or invalid

dis•ap•pear [dis-ə-PEER] vi vanish; cease to exist; be lost **dis•ap•pear'ance** n

dis•ap•point [dis-ə-POINT] vt fail to fulfill (hope), frustrate **dis•ap•point'ment** n

dis•ap•prove vi (foll by of) consider wrong or bad **dis•ap•prov'al** n

dis•arm [dis-AHRM] v deprive of arms or weapons; reduce

country's war weapons; win over **dis•ar•ma•ment** n **dis•arm'ing** adj removing hostility, suspicion

dis•ar•range v throw into disorder

dis•ar•ray [dis-ə-RAY] vt throw into disorder, derange ▷ n disorderliness, esp of clothing

dis•as•ter [di-ZAS-tər] n calamity, sudden or great misfortune **dis•as'trous** adj calamitous

dis•band v (cause to) cease to function as a group

dis•bar [dis-BAHR] vt **-barred, -bar•ring** law expel from the bar

dis•be•lieve' vt reject as false ▷ vi (foll by in) have no faith (in) **dis•be•lief'** n

dis•burse [dis-BURS] vt **-bursed, -burs•ing** pay out (money) **dis•burse'ment** n

disc see **DISK** **disc jockey** person who introduces and plays pop records on a radio program or at a disco

dis•card [di-SKAHRD] v reject; give up; cast off, dismiss

dis•cern [di-SURN] vt make out; distinguish **dis•cern'i•ble** adj **dis•cern'ing** adj discriminating; penetrating **dis•cern'ment** n insight

dis•charge [dis-CHAHRJ] vt **-charged, -charg•ing** release; dismiss; emit; perform (duties), fulfill (obligations); let go; fire off; unload; pay ▷ n [DIS-chahrj] discharging; being discharged; release; matter emitted; document certifying release, payment, etc

dis•ci•ple [di-SĪ-pəl] n follower, one who takes another as teacher and model

dis•ci•pline [DIS-ə-plin] n training that produces orderliness, obedience, self-control; result of such training in order, conduct,

etc; system of rules, etc ▷ *vt*
-plined, -plin·ing train; punish
dis·ci·pli·nar·i·an *n* one
who enforces rigid discipline
dis·ci·pli·nar·y *adj*

dis·claim [dis-KLAYM] *vt*
deny, renounce **dis·claim'er** *n*
repudiation, denial

dis·close [dis-SKLOHZ] *vt* **-closed,
-clos·ing** allow to be seen; make
known **dis·clo'sure** [-zhǎr] *n*
revelation

dis·col·or [dis-KUL-ǎr] *vt* alter
color of, stain **dis·col·or·a'tion** *n*

dis·com·fit [dis-KUM-fit] *vt*
embarrass, disconcert, baffle
dis·com'fi·ture [-fi-chǎr] *n*

dis·com·pose *vt* disturb, upset
dis·com·po'sure *n*

dis·con·cert [dis-kǎn-SURT] *vt*
ruffle, confuse, upset, embarrass

dis·con·nect *vt* undo or break the
connection between (two things);
stop the supply of electricity or gas of
▷ *n* lack of a connection

dis·con·so·late [dis-KON-sǎ-lit]
adj unhappy, downcast, forlorn

dis·con·tent' *n* lack of
contentment **dis·con·tent'ed** *adj*
dis·con·tent'ment *n*

dis·con·tin·ue *v* come or bring
to an end **dis·con·tin'u·ous** *adj*
characterized by interruptions
dis·con·ti·nu'i·ty *n*

dis·cord [DIS-kord] *n* strife;
difference, dissension; disagreement
of sounds **dis·cord'ant** *adj*

dis·co·theque [DIS-kǎ-tek] *n*
club, etc for dancing to recorded
music

dis·count [dis-KOWNT] *vt*
consider as possibility but reject
as unsuitable, inappropriate, etc;
deduct (amount, percentage) from
usual price; sell at reduced price ▷ *n*
[DIS-kownt] amount deducted from

price, expressed as cash amount or
percentage

dis·coun·te·nance [dis-KOWN-
tn-ǎns] *vt* **-nanced, -nanc·ing**
abash; discourage; frown upon

dis·cour·age [di-SKUR-ij] *vt*
-aged, -ag·ing reduce confidence
of; deter; show disapproval of

dis·course [DIS-kors] *n*
conversation; speech, treatise,
sermon ▷ *vi* [dis-KORS] **-coursed,
-cours·ing** speak, converse, lecture

dis·cour·te·sy *n* showing bad
manners **dis·cour'teous·ly** *adv*

dis·cov·er [di-SKUV-ǎr] *vt* (be
the first to) find out, light upon;
make known **dis·cov'er·a·ble** *adj*
dis·cov'er·er *n*, *pl* **-er·ies**

dis·cred·it [dis-KRED-it] *vt*
damage reputation of; cast doubt on;
reject as untrue ▷ *n* disgrace; doubt
dis·cred'it·a·ble *adj*

dis·creet [di-SKREET] *adj* prudent,
circumspect **dis·creet'ness** *n*

dis·crep·an·cy [di-SKREP-ǎn-
see] *n*, *pl* **-cies** conflict, variation, as
between figures **dis·crep'ant** *adj*

dis·crete [di-SKREET] *adj* separate,
disunited, discontinuous

dis·cre·tion [di-SKRESH-ǎn] *n*
quality of being discreet; prudence;
freedom to act as one chooses
dis·cre'tion·ar·y *adj*

dis·crim·i·nate [di-SKRIM-ǎ-
nayt] *vi* **-nat·ed, -nat·ing** single
out for special favor or disfavor;
distinguish between; be discerning
dis·crim·i·na'tion *n*

dis·cur·sive [di-SKUR-siv] *adj*
passing from subject to subject,
rambling

dis·cus [DIS-kǎs] *n* disk-
shaped object thrown in athletic
competition

dis·cuss [di-SKUS] *vt* exchange

opinions about; debate **dis·cus·sion** n

dis·dain [dis-DAYN] n scorn, contempt ▷ vt scorn **dis·dain·ful** adj

dis·ease [di-ZEEZ] n illness; disorder of health

dis·em·bark v get off a ship, aircraft, or bus **dis·em·bar·ka·tion** n

dis·em·bod·ied [dis-em-BOD-eed] adj (of spirit) released from bodily form

dis·em·bow·el [dis-em-BOW-əl] vt take out entrails of

dis·en·chant·ed [dis-en-CHAN-tid] adj disillusioned

dis·en·gage v release from a connection **dis·en·gage·ment** n

dis·en·tan·gle v release from entanglement or confusion

dis·es·tab·lish vt remove state support from (a church etc) **dis·es·tab·lish·ment** n

dis·fa·vor n disapproval or dislike

dis·fig·ure [dis-FIG-yər] vt -ured, -ur·ing mar appearance of **dis·fig·ur·a·tion** n **dis·fig·ure·ment** n blemish, defect

dis·gorge [dis-GORJ] vt -gorged, -gorg·ing vomit; give up

dis·grace [dis-GRAYS] n shame, loss of reputation, dishonor ▷ vt -graced, -grac·ing bring shame or discredit upon **dis·grace·ful** adj shameful

dis·grun·tled [dis-GRUN-tld] adj vexed; put out

dis·guise [dis-GIZ] vt -guised, -guis·ing change appearance of, make unrecognizable; conceal, cloak; misrepresent ▷ n false appearance; device to conceal identity

dis·gust n violent distaste, loathing, repugnance ▷ vt affect with loathing

dish n shallow vessel for food; portion or variety of food; contents of dish; sl attractive person **dish out** inf put in dish; serve up; dispense (money, abuse, etc)

dis·ha·bille [dis-ə-BEEL] n state of being partly or carelessly dressed

dis·har·mo·ny n lack of agreement, discord

dis·heart·en vt weaken or destroy the hope, courage, or enthusiasm of

di·shev·eled [di-SHEV-əld] adj with disordered hair; ruffled, untidy, unkempt

dis·hon·est adj not honest or fair **dis·hon·est·ly** adv **dis·hon·es·ty** n

dis·hon·or vt treat with disrespect; refuse to cash (a check) ▷ n lack of respect; state of shame or disgrace; something that causes a loss of honor **dis·hon·or·a·ble** adj **dis·hon·or·a·bly** adv

dis·il·lu·sion [dis-i-LOO-zhən] vt destroy ideals, illusions, or false ideas of ▷ n

dis·in·fect·ant [dis-in-FEK-tənt] n substance that prevents or removes infection **dis·in·fect** vt

dis·in·for·ma·tion [dis-in-fər-MAY-shən] n false information intended to deceive or mislead

dis·in·gen·u·ous [dis-in-JEN-yoo-əs] adj not sincere or frank

dis·in·her·it [dis-in-HE-rit] vt to deprive of inheritance

dis·in·te·grate [dis-IN-tə-grayt] v -grat·ed, -grat·ing break up, fall to pieces **dis·in·te·gra·tion** n

dis·in·ter vt -ter·ring, -terred dig up; reveal, make known

dis·in·ter·est [dis-IN-trist] n freedom from bias or involvement **dis·in·ter·est·ed** adj

dis·joint vt put out of joint; break the natural order or logical arrangement of **dis·joint·ed** adj (of discourse) incoherent; disconnected

disk n thin, flat, circular object like a coin; *computing* storage device, consisting of a disk coated with a magnetic layer, used to record and retrieve data; a phonograph record **disk drive** *computing* controller and mechanism for reading and writing data on computer disks **disk harrow** harrow that cuts the soil with inclined disks **disk jockey, disc jockey** person who introduces and plays pop records on a radio program or at a disco

dis·lo·cate [DIS-loh-kayt] vt **-cat·ed, -cat·ing** put out of joint (eg dislocate shoulder); disrupt, displace **dis·lo·ca'tion** n

dis·lodge [dis-LOJ] vt **-lodged, -lodg·ing** drive out or remove from hiding place or previous position

dis·loy·al adj not loyal, deserting one's allegiance **dis·loy'al·ty** n

dis·mal [DIZ-məl] adj depressing; depressed; cheerless, dreary, gloomy **dis'mal·ly** adv

dis·man·tle [dis-MAN-tl] vt **-tled, -tling** take apart **dis·man'tle·ment** n

dis·may' vt dishearten, daunt ▷ n consternation, horrified amazement; apprehension

dis·mem·ber [dis-MEM-bər] vt tear or cut limb from limb; divide, partition **dis·mem'ber·ment** n

dis·miss' vt remove, discharge from employment; send away; reject **dis·miss'al** n

dis·mount' v get off a horse or bicycle

dis·o·bey [dis-ə-BAY] v refuse or fail to obey **dis·o·be'di·ence** [-BEE-dee-əns] n

dis·o·blige [dis-ə-BLIJ] vt **-bliged, -blig·ing** disregard the wishes, preferences of

dis·or·der [dis-OR-dər] n disarray, confusion, disturbance; upset of health, ailment ▷ vt upset order of; disturb health of **dis·or'der·ly** adj untidy; unruly

dis·or·gan·ize vt disrupt the arrangement or system of **dis·or·gan·i·za'tion** n

dis·o·ri·ent [dis-OR-ee-ənt] vt cause to lose one's bearings, confuse

dis·own [dis-OHN] vt refuse to acknowledge

dis·par·age [di-SPAR-ij] vt **-aged, -ag·ing** speak slightingly of; belittle **dis·par'age·ment** n

dis·pa·rate [DIS-pər-it] adj essentially different, unrelated **dis·par'i·ty** n, pl **-ties** inequality; incongruity

dis·pas·sion·ate [dis-PASH-ə-nit] adj unswayed by passion; calm, impartial

dis·patch [di-SPACH] vt send off to destination or on an errand; send off; finish off, get done with speed; *inf* eat up; kill ▷ n sending off; efficient speed; official message, report

dis·pel [di-SPEL] vt **-pelled, -pel·ling** clear, drive away, scatter

dis·pense [di-SPENS] vt **-pensed, -pens·ing** deal out; make up (medicine); administer (justice); grant exemption from **dis·pen'sa·ble** adj **dis·pen'sa·ry** n, pl **-ries** place where medical aid is given **dis·pen·sa'tion** n act of dispensing; license or exemption; provision of nature or providence **dis·pens·er** n **dispense with** do away with; manage without

dis·perse [di-SPURS] v **-persed, -pers·ing** scatter **dispersed** adj scattered; placed here and there **dis·per'sal, dis·per'sion** [-zhən] n

dis·pir·it·ed [di-SPIR-i-tid] adj dejected, disheartened

dis·pir·it·ing adj

dis·place [dis-PLAYS] vt **-placed,**
-plac·ing move from its place;
remove from office; take place
of **dis·place'ment** n displacing;
weight of liquid displaced by a
solid in it

dis·play [di-SPLAY] vt spread out
for show; show, expose to view ▷ n
displaying; parade; show, exhibition;
ostentation

dis·please [dis-PLEEZ] v
-pleased, pleas·ing offend; annoy
dis·pleas·ure [-PLEZH-ər] n anger,
vexation

dis·port [di-SPORT] v refl gambol,
amuse oneself, frolic

dis·pose [di-SPOHZ] v **-posed,**
-pos·ing ▷ vt arrange; distribute;
incline; adjust ▷ vi determine
dis·pos·a·ble adj designed to be
thrown away after use **dis·pos·al**
n **dis·po·si·tion** [dis-pə-ZISH-
ən] n inclination; temperament;
arrangement; plan **dispose of**
sell, get rid of; have authority over,
deal with

dis·pos·sess [dis-pə-ZES] vt cause
to give up possession (of)

dis·pro·por·tion n lack
of proportion or equality
dis·pro·por'tion·ate adj

dis·prove' vt show (an assertion or
claim) to be incorrect

dis·pute [di-SPYOOT] v **-put·ed,**
-put·ing ▷ vi debate, discuss ▷ vt
call in question; debate, argue;
oppose, contest **dis·put'a·ble** adj
dis·pu'tant n dis·pu·ta'tious adj
argumentative; quarrelsome

dis·qual·i·fy [dis-KWOL-ə-fī] vt
-fied, -fy·ing make ineligible, unfit
for some special purpose

dis·qui·et [dis-KWI-it] n anxiety,
uneasiness ▷ vt cause (someone)
to feel this

dis·qui·si·tion [dis-kwə-ZISH-
ən] n learned or elaborate treatise,
discourse or essay

dis·re·pute' n loss or lack of good
reputation **dis·rep'u·ta·ble** adj
having or causing a bad reputation

dis·re·spect' n lack of respect
dis·re·spect'ful adj

dis·rupt' vt interrupt; throw into
turmoil or disorder **dis·rup'tion** n
dis·rup'tive adj

dis·sat·is·fied vt not pleased or
contented **dis·sat·is·fac'tion** n

dis·sect [di-SEKT] vt cut up (body,
organism) for detailed examination;
examine or criticize in detail
dis·sec'tion n

dis·sem·ble [di-SEM-bəl] v
-bled, -bling conceal, disguise
(feelings, etc); act the hypocrite
dis·sem'bler n

dis·sem·i·nate [di-SEM-ə-nayt]
vt **-nat·ed, -nat·ing** spread abroad,
scatter **dis·sem·i·na'tion** n

dis·sent [di-SENT] vi differ in
opinion; express such difference;
disagree with doctrine, etc of
established church, etc ▷ n such
disagreement **dis·sent'er** n

dis·ser·ta·tion [dis-ər-TAY-shən]
n written thesis; formal discourse

dis·ser·vice [dis-SUR-vis] n ill
turn, wrong, injury

dis·si·dent [DIS-i-dənt] n, adj
(one) not in agreement, esp with
government **dis'si·dence** n dissent;
disagreement

dis·sim·i·lar adj not alike, different
dis·sim·i·lar'i·ty n

dis·sim·u·late [di-SIM-yə-
layt] v **-lat·ed, -lat·ing** pretend
not to have; practice deceit
dis·sim·u·la'tion n

dis·si·pate [DIS-ə-payt] vt
-pat·ed, -pat·ing scatter;
waste, squander **dis'si·pat·ed**

adj indulging in pleasure without restraint, dissolute; scattered, wasted **dis·si·pa·tion** *n* scattering; frivolous, dissolute way of life

dis·so·ci·ate [di-SOH-shee-ayt] *v* **-at·ed, -at·ing** separate, sever; disconnect

dis·so·lute [DIS-ə-loot] *adj* lacking restraint, esp lax in morals

dis·so·lu·tion [dis-ə-LOO-shən] *n* breakup; termination of legislature, meeting or legal relationship; destruction; death

dis·solve [di-ZOLV] *v* **-solved, -solv·ing** ▷ *vt* absorb or melt in fluid; break up, put an end to, annul ▷ *vi* melt in fluid; disappear, vanish; break up, scatter **dis·sol·u·ble** [di-SOL-yə-bəl] *adj* capable of being dissolved

dis·so·nant [DIS-ə-nənt] *adj* jarring, discordant **dis·so·nance** *n*

dis·suade [di-SWAYD] *vt* **-suad·ed, -suad·ing** advise to refrain, persuade not to **dis·sua·sion** [-zhən] *n* **dis·sua·sive** *adj*

dis·taff [DIS-taf] *n* cleft stick to hold wool, etc, for spinning **distaff side** maternal side; female line

dis·tance [DIS-təns] *n* amount of space between two things; remoteness; aloofness, reserve ▷ *vt* **-tanced, -tanc·ing** hold or place at distance **dis·tant** *adj* far off, remote; haughty, cold

dis·taste [dis-TAYST] *n* dislike of food or drink; aversion, disgust **dis·taste·ful** *adj* unpleasant, displeasing to feelings **dis·taste·ful·ness** *n*

dis·tem·per [dis-TEM-pər] *n* disease of dogs; method of painting on plaster without oil; paint used for this ▷ *vt* paint with distemper

by pressure from within, inflate **dis·ten·sion** *n*

dis·tich [DIS-tik] *n* couplet

dis·till [di-STIL] *vt* vaporize and recondense a liquid; purify, separate, concentrate liquids by this method; *fig* extract quality of ▷ *vi* trickle down **dis·til·late** [DIS-tə-lit] *n* distilled liquid, esp as fuel for some engines **dis·till·er** *n* one who distills, esp manufacturer of whiskey

dis·tinct [di-STINGKT] *adj* clear, easily seen; definite; separate, different **dis·tinc·tion** *n* point of difference; act of distinguishing; eminence, repute, high honor, high quality **dis·tinc·tive** *adj* characteristic **dis·tinct·ly** *adv*

dis·tin·guish [di-STING-gwish] *vt* make difference in; recognize, make out; honor; (usu refl) make prominent or honored; classify ▷ *vi* (usu with *between, among*) draw distinction, grasp difference **dis·tin·guish·a·ble** *adj* **dis·tin·guished** *adj* dignified; famous, eminent

dis·tort [di-STORT] *vt* put out of shape, deform; misrepresent; garble, falsify **dis·tor·tion** *n*

dis·tract [di-STRAKT] *vt* draw attention of (someone) away from work, etc; divert; perplex, bewilder, drive mad **dis·trac·tion** *n*

dis·traught [di-STRAWT] *adj* bewildered, crazed with grief; frantic, distracted

dis·tress [di-STRES] *n* severe trouble, mental pain; severe pressure of hunger, fatigue or want ▷ *vt* afflict, give mental pain **dis·tress·ful** *adj*

dis·trib·ute [di-STRIB-yoot] *vt* **-ut·ed, -ut·ing** deal out, dispense; spread, dispose at intervals; classify **dis·tri·bu·tion** *n* **dis·trib·u·tive**

adj **dis·trib'u·tor** *n* rotary switch distributing electricity in automotive engine

dis·trict [DIS-trikt] *n* region, locality; portion of territory

dis·trust' *v* regard as untrustworthy ▷ *n* feeling of suspicion or doubt **dis·trust'ful** *adj*

dis·turb' *vt* trouble, agitate, unsettle, derange **dis·turb'ance** *n*

dis·use [dis-YOOS] *n* state of being no longer used **dis·used'** [-YOOZD] *adj*

ditch [dich] *n* long narrow hollow dug in ground for drainage, etc ▷ *v* make, repair ditches; run car, etc into ditch ▷ *vt* sl abandon, discard

dith·er [DITH-ər] *vi* be uncertain or indecisive ▷ *n* this state

dith·y·ramb [DITH-ə-ram] *n* ancient Greek hymn sung in honor of Dionysus

dit·to [DIT-oh] *n, pl* **-tos** same, aforesaid (used to avoid repetition in lists, etc)

dit·ty [DIT-ee] *n, pl* **-ties** simple song

di·u·ret·ic [dī-ə-RET-ik] *adj* increasing the discharge of urine ▷ *n* substance with this property

di·ur·nal [dī-UR-nəl] *adj* daily; in or of daytime; taking a day

di·va·lent [dī-VAY-lənt] *adj* capable of combining with two atoms of hydrogen or their equivalent

di·van' *n* bed, couch without back or head

dive [dīv] *vi* **dived** or **dove, div·ing** plunge under surface of water; descend suddenly; disappear; go deep down into; reach quickly ▷ *n* act of diving; sl disreputable bar, club, etc **div·er** *n* one who descends into deep water **dive bomber** aircraft that attacks after diving steeply

di·verge [di-VURJ] *vi* **-verged, -verg·ing** get farther apart; separate **di·ver'gence** *n* **di·ver'gent** *adj*

di·vers [Dī-vərz] *adj obs* some, various

di·verse [di-VURS] *adj* different, varied **di·ver'si·ty** *n, pl* **-ties** quality of being different or varied; range of difference **di·ver·si·fy** *vt* **-fied, -fy·ing** make diverse or varied; give variety to **di·ver·si·fi·ca'tion** *n*

di·vert [di-VURT] *vt* turn aside, ward off; amuse, entertain **di·ver'sion** [-zhən] *n* a diverting; official detour for traffic when main route is closed; amusement

di·vest' *vt* unclothe, strip; dispossess, deprive; sell off

di·vide [di-VīD] *v* **-vid·ed, -vid·ing** ▷ *vt* make into two or more parts, split up, separate; distribute, share; diverge in opinion; classify ▷ *vi* become separated; part into two groups for voting, etc ▷ *n* division esp between adjacent drainage areas

div'i·dend *n* share of profits, of money divided among shareholders, etc; number to be divided by another **di·vid'ers** *pl n* pair of compasses

di·vine [di-VīN] *adj* **-vin·er, -vin·est** of, pert to, proceeding from, God; sacred; heavenly ▷ *n* theologian; clergyman ▷ *v* **-vined, -vin·ing** guess; predict, foresee, tell by inspiration or magic **div·i·na'tion** [div-ə-NAY-shən] *n* divining **di·vine'ly** *adv* **di·vin'er** *n* **di·vin'i·ty** *n* quality of being divine; god; theology **divining rod** [forked stick, etc said to move when held over ground where water is present]

di·vi·sion [di-VIZH-ən] *n* act of dividing; part of whole; barrier; section; difference in opinion, etc;

mathematics method of finding how many times one number is contained in another; army unit; separation, disunion **di·vis·i·ble** [di-VIZ-ə-bəl] *adj* capable of division **di·vi·sive** [-VI-siv] *adj* causing disagreement **di·vi·sor** [-VĪ-zər] *n mathematics* number that divides dividend

di·vorce [di-VORS] *n* legal dissolution of marriage; complete separation, disunion ▷ *vt* **-vorced, -vorc·ing** dissolve marriage; separate; sunder **di·vor·cee'** [-SAY]

div·ot [DIV-ət] *n* piece of turf

di·vulge [di-VULJ] *vt* **-vulged, -vulg·ing** reveal, let out (secret)

Dix·ie [DIK-see] *n* southern states of the US

diz·zy [DIZ-ee] *adj* **-zi·er, -zi·est** feeling dazed, unsteady, as if about to fall; causing or fit to cause dizziness, as speed, etc; *inf* silly ▷ *vt* **-zied, -zy·ing** make dizzy **diz·zi·ly** *adv* **diz·zi·ness** *n*

DJ *n* disc jockey ▷ *v* **DJ'd, DJ·ing** act as DJ

DNA *n* deoxyribonucleic acid, the main constituent of the chromosomes of all organisms

do¹ [doo] *v* **did, done, do·ing** ▷ *vt* perform, effect, transact, bring about, finish; work at; work out, solve; suit; cover (distance); provide; prepare; cheat, trick, frustrate; look after ▷ *vi* act; manage; work; fare; serve, suffice; happen ▷ *v aux* makes negative and interrogative sentences and expresses emphasis ▷ *n inf* celebration, festivity **do away with** destroy **do up** fasten; renovate **do with** need; make use of **do without** deny oneself

do² [doh] *n* first sol-fa note

doc·ile [DOS-əl] *adj* willing to obey, submissive

dock¹ [dok] *n* artificial enclosure near harbor for loading or repairing ships; platform for loading and unloading trucks ▷ *v* of vessel, put or go into dock; (of spacecraft) link or be linked together in space **dock'er** *n* longshoreman **dock'yard** *n* enclosure with docks, for building or repairing ships

dock² *n* solid part of animal's tail; cut end, stump ▷ *vt* cut short, esp tail; curtail, deduct (an amount) from

dock³ *n* enclosure in criminal court for prisoner

dock·et [DOK-it] *n* agenda; list of court cases to be heard ▷ *vt* place on docket

doc·tor [DOK-tər] *n* medical practitioner; one holding university's highest degree in any faculty ▷ *vt* treat medically; repair, mend; falsify (accounts, etc) **doc'tor·al** [-əl] *adj* **doc'tor·ate** [-it] *n*

doc·trine [DOK-trin] *n* what is taught; teaching of church, school, or person; belief, opinion, dogma **doc·tri·naire'** [-trə-NAIR] *adj* stubbornly insistent on applying theory without regard for circumstances ▷ *n* **doc·tri·nal** *adj*

doc·u·ment [DOK-yə-mənt] *n* piece of paper, etc providing information or evidence ▷ *vt* furnish with proofs, illustrations, certificates **doc·u·men·ta·ry** *adj, n, pl* **-ries** (of) type of film, TV program dealing with real life, not fiction **doc·u·men·ta'tion** *n*

dod·der [DOD-ər] *vi* totter or tremble, as with age

dodge [doj] *v* avoid or attempt to avoid (blow, discovery, etc) as by moving quickly; evade questions by cleverness ▷ *n* trick, artifice; ingenious method; act of dodging **dodg'er** *n* shifty person; evader

do·do [DOH-doh] *n, pl* **-dos** large extinct bird; person with old-fashioned ideas

doe [doh] *n* female of deer, hare, rabbit

Doe [doh] *n* **John** *or* **Jane Doe** unknown or unidentified person

does [duz] third pers sing, pres ind active of **do**

doff [dof] *vt* take off (hat, clothing); discard, lay aside

dog [dawg] *n* domesticated carnivorous four-legged mammal; person (in contempt, abuse or playfully); name given to various mechanical contrivances for gripping, holding; device with tooth that penetrates or grips object and detains it; andiron or firedog; *sl* ugly person; *sl* thing of extremely poor quality; *inf* a fellow ▷ *vt* **dogged, dog·ging** follow steadily or closely **dog'ged** [-gid] *adj* persistent, resolute, tenacious **dog'gy** *adj* **-gi·er, -gi·est dog days** hot season of the rising of Dog Star; period of inactivity **dog'-ear** *n* turned-down corner of page in book ▷ *vt* turn down corners of pages **dog'-eat-dog'** *n* action based on complete cynicism, ruthless competition **dog'fight** *n* skirmish between fighter planes; savage contest characterized by disregard of rules **doggy bag** bag in which diner may take leftovers (ostensibly for dog) **dog'house** *n* kennel **in the doghouse** *inf* in disfavor **dog'leg** *n* sharp bend or angle **dog's age** quite a long time **Dog Star** star Sirius **go to the dogs** degenerate

doge [dohj] *n* formerly, chief magistrate in Venice

dog·ger·el [DAW-gər-əl] *n* slipshod, unpoetic or trivial verse

do·gie [DOH-gee] *n* motherless calf

dog·ma [DAWG-mə] *n, pl* **-mas** article of belief, esp one laid down authoritatively by church; body of beliefs **dog·mat'ic** *adj* asserting opinions with arrogance; relating to dogma **dog·mat'i·cal·ly** *adv* **dog'ma·tism** *n* arrogant assertion of opinion

doi·ly [DOI-lee] *n, pl* **-lies** small cloth, paper, piece of lace to place under cake, dish, etc

Dol·by ® [DOHL-bee] *n* system used in tape recording to reduce unwanted noise

dol·ce [DOHL-chay] *adj* music sweet

dol·drums [DOHL-drəmz] *pl n* state of depression, dumps; region of light winds and calms near the equator

dole [dohl] *n* charitable allotment, gift ▷ *vt* **doled, dol·ing** (usu with **out**) deal out sparingly

dole·ful [DOHL-fəl] *adj* dreary, mournful **dole'ful·ly** *adv*

doll [dol] *n* child's toy image of human being; *sl* attractive person ▷ *v* dress (up) in latest fashion or smartly

dol·lar [DOL-ər] *n* standard monetary unit of many countries, esp US and Canada

dol·lop [DOL-əp] *n inf* semisolid lump; unmeasured amount, a dash

dol·ly [DOL-ee] *n, pl* **-lies** doll; wheeled support for film, TV camera; platform on wheels for moving heavy objects; various metal devices used as aids in hammering, riveting

dol·men [DOHL-mən] *n* prehistoric monument; stone table

do·lo·mite [DOH-lə-mīt] *n* a type of limestone

do·lor [DOH-lər] *n* grief, sadness, distress **dol'or·ous** [DOL-] *adj*

dol·phin [DOL-fin] *n* sea mammal

smaller than whale, with beaklike snout

dolt [dohlt] n stupid fellow **dolt·ish** adj

do·main [doh-MAYN] n lands held or ruled over; sphere, field of influence; province; *computing* group of computers with the same name on the Internet

dome [dohm] n a rounded vault forming a roof; something of this shape

Domes·day Book [DOOMZ-day] record of survey of England in 1086

do·mes·tic [də-MES-tik] adj of, in the home; homeloving; (of animals) tamed, kept by man; of, in one's own country, not foreign ▷ n household servant **do·mes·ti·cate** [-kayt] vt -cat·ed, -cat·ing tame (animals); accustom to home life; adapt to an environment **do·mes·tic·i·ty** [doh-me-STIS-i-tee] n

dom·i·cile [DOM-ə-sil] n person's regular place of abode **dom'i·ciled** adj living

dom·i·nate [DOM-ə-nayt] vt -nat·ed, -nat·ing rule, control, sway; of heights, overlook ▷ vi control, be the most powerful or influential member or part of something **dom'i·nant** adj **dom·i·na'tion** n **dom·i·neer'** v act imperiously, tyrannize

Do·min·i·can [də-MIN-i-kən] n priest or nun of the order of St Dominic ▷ adj pert to this order

do·min·ion [də-MIN-yən] n sovereignty, rule; territory of government

dom·i·noes [DOM-ə-nohz] n game played with 28 oblong flat pieces marked on one side with 0 to 6 spots on each half of the face **dom'i·no** n one of these pieces; cloak with eye mask for masquerading

don¹ [don] vt **donned, don·ning** put on (clothes)

don² n in English universities, fellow or tutor of college; Spanish title, Sir; in Mafia, head of a family or syndicate

do·nate [DOH-nayt] vt -nat·ed, -nat·ing give **do·na'tion** n gift to fund **do·nor** [DOH-nər] n **donor card** card specifying organs that may be used for transplant after cardholder's death

done pp of **DO**

don·key [DONG-kee] n, pl -keys ass; stupid or obstinate person **donkey engine** auxiliary engine **don'key·work** n drudgery

donned pt/pp of **DON**

doo·dle [DOOD-l] vi -dled, -dling scribble absentmindedly ▷ n

doom n fate, destiny; ruin; judicial sentence, condemnation; the Last Judgment ▷ vt sentence, condemn; destine to destruction or suffering **dooms'day** n the day of the Last Judgment

door [dor] n hinged or sliding barrier to close any entrance **door'way** n entrance with or without door

dope [dohp] n kind of varnish; sl drug, esp illegal, narcotic drug; inf information; inf stupid person ▷ vt **doped, dop·ing** drug (esp of racehorses) **dop·ey** [DOH-pee] adj **dop·i·er, dop·i·est** inf foolish; drugged; half-asleep

Dop·pler effect [DOP-lər] shift in frequency of sound, light, other waves when emitting source moves closer or farther from the observer

Dor·ic [DOR-ik] n dialect of Dorians; style of Greek architecture; rustic dialect ▷ adj **Do·ri·an** [DOR-ee-ən] adj, n (member) of early

Greek race

dork [dork] *n vulg sl* penis; *sl* stupid or clumsy person ▷ *adj* **dork·i·er, dork·i·est**

dor·mant [DOR-mənt] *adj* not active, in state of suspension; sleeping **dor'man·cy** *n*

dor·mer [DOR-mər] *n* upright window set in sloping roof; such a projecting structure

dor·mi·to·ry [DOR-mi-tor-ee] *n, pl -ries* sleeping room with many beds **dormitory suburb** suburb whose inhabitants commute to work

dor·mouse [DOR-mows] *n* small hibernating mouselike rodent

dor·sal [DOR-səl] *adj* of, on back

do·ry [DOR-ee] *n, pl -ries* flat-bottomed boat with high bow and flaring sides

dose [dohs] *n* amount (of drug, etc) administered at one time; *inf* instance or period of something unpleasant, esp disease ▷ *vt* **dosed, dos·ing** give doses to **dos'age** *n*

dos·si·er [DOS-ee-ay] *n* set of papers on some particular subject or event

dot *n* small spot, mark ▷ *vt* **dot·ted, dot·ting** mark with dot(s); sprinkle **dot'ty** *adj inf* **-ti·er, -ti·est** eccentric; crazy; (with *about*) *inf* extremely fond of **dot·com, dot·com** *n* company that conducts most of its business on the Internet

dote [doht] *vi* **dot·ed, dot·ing** (with *on, upon*) be passionately fond of; be silly or weak-minded **dot'age** [-ij] *n* senility **do'tard** [-tərd] *n* **dot'ing** *adj* blindly affectionate

dotty see **DOT**

dou·ble [DUB-əl] *adj* of two parts, layers, etc, folded; twice as much or many; of two kinds; designed for two users; ambiguous; deceitful ▷ *adv* twice; to twice the amount

or extent; in a pair ▷ *n* person or thing exactly like, or mistakable for, another; quantity twice as much as another; sharp turn; running pace ▷ *v* **-bled, -bling** make, become double; increase twofold; turn in two; turn sharply; get around, sail around **dou'bly** *adv* **double agent** spy employed simultaneously by two opposing sides **double bass** largest and lowest-toned instrument in violin form **dou'ble-cross'** *v* betray, swindle a colleague **dou'ble-cross'er** *n* **dou'ble-deal'ing** *n* artifice, duplicity **double Dutch** *sl* incomprehensible talk, gibberish **double dutch** form of the game of jump rope **double glazing** two panes of glass in a window to insulate against cold, sound, etc **dou'ble-head'er** *n sport* two games played consecutively on same day in same stadium **dou'ble-quick'** *adj, adv* very fast **dou'ble take** delayed reaction to a remark, situation, etc **dou'ble-talk** *n, vt* (engage in) intentionally garbled speech

dou·ble en·ten·dre [DUB-əl ahn-TAHN-drə] *n, pl -dres* [-drəz] word or phrase with two meanings, one usu indelicate

dou·blet [DUB-lit] *n* close-fitting body garment formerly worn by men

dou·bloon [du-BLOON] *n* ancient Spanish gold coin

doubt [dowt] *vt* hesitate to believe; call in question; suspect ▷ *vi* be wavering or uncertain in belief or opinion ▷ *n* uncertainty, wavering in belief; state of affairs giving cause for uncertainty **doubt'ful** *adj* **doubt'less** *adv*

douche [doosh] *n* jet or spray of water applied to (part of) body; device for douching ▷ *vt* **douched, douch·ing** give douche to

dough [doh] n flour or meal kneaded with water; sl money **dough·nut** n sweetened and fried, usu ring-shaped, piece of dough

dough·ty [DOW-tee] adj **-ti·er, -ti·est** valiant **dough·ti·ness** n boldness

dour [duur] adj grim, stubborn, severe

douse [dows] vt **doused, dous·ing** thrust into water; extinguish (light)

dove [duv] n bird of pigeon family; person opposed to war **dove·cote** [-koht] n house for doves **dove·tail** n joint made with fan-shaped tenon ▷ v fit closely, neatly, firmly together

dow·a·ger [DOW-ə-jər] n widow with title or property derived from deceased husband; dignified elderly woman, esp with wealth or social prominence

dow·dy [DOW-dee] adj **-di·er, -di·est** unattractively or shabbily dressed ▷ n woman so dressed

dow·el [DOW-əl] n wooden, metal peg, esp joining two adjacent parts

dow·er [DOW-ər] n widow's share for life of husband's estate ▷ vt endow **dow·ry** n property wife brings to husband at marriage; any endowment

down[1] adv to, in, or toward, lower position; below the horizon; (of payment) on the spot, immediate ▷ prep from higher to lower part of; at lower part of; along ▷ adj depressed, miserable ▷ vt knock, pull, push down; inf drink, esp quickly **down'ward** adj, adv **down·wards** adv **down·cast** adj dejected; looking down **down·er** n sl barbiturate, tranquillizer, or narcotic; state of depression **down·load** vt transfer (data) from the memory of one computer to that of another ▷ n data obtained in this way **down·pour** n heavy rainfall **down·right** adj plain, straightforward ▷ adv quite, thoroughly **down·stage** adj, adv at, to front of stage **down'-and-out**[1] finished, defeated **down in the mouth** dejected, discouraged **down East** New England, esp the state of Maine **down under** Australia and New Zealand

down[2] n soft underfeathers, hair or fiber; fluff **down'y** adj **down·i·er, down·i·est**

Down syndrome genetic disorder characterized by degree of mental and physical retardation

dowry SEE DOWER

dowse [dowz] v **dowsed, dows·ing** use divining rod **dows'er** n water diviner

dox·ol·o·gy [dok-SOL-ə-jee] n short hymn of praise to God

doy·en [doi-EN] n senior member of a body or profession **doyenne** n fem

doze [dohz] vi **dozed, doz·ing** sleep drowsily, be half-asleep ▷ n nap

doz·en [DUZ-ən] n (set of) twelve

drab adj dull, monotonous; of a dingy brown color ▷ n mud color; slut, prostitute

drach·ma [DRAK-mə] n, pl **-mas** former monetary unit of Greece

Dra·co·ni·an [dray-KOH-nee-ən] adj like the laws of Draco; (d-) very harsh, cruel

draft[1] n design, sketch; preliminary plan or layout for work to be executed; rough copy of document; order for money; current of air between apertures in room, etc; act or action of drawing; act or action of drinking; amount drunk at once; inhaling; depth of ship in water ▷ vt make sketch, plan, or rough design

draft | 166

of; make rough copy (of writing, etc) ▷ adj of beer, etc, for drawing; drawn **draft'y** adj **draft·i·er, draft·i·est** full of air currents **draft horse** horse for vehicles carrying heavy loads **drafts'man** n, pl **-men** one who makes drawings, plans, etc **drafts'man·ship** n

draft² vt select for compulsory military service; select (professional athlete) by draft; compel (person) to serve

drag v **dragged, drag·ging** ▷ vt pull along with difficulty or friction; trail, go heavily; sweep with net or grapnels; protract; *computing* move (an image) on screen by use of the mouse ▷ vi lag, trail; be tediously protracted ▷ n check on progress; checked motion; sledge, net, dragnet, rake; *sl* influence; *sl* tedious person or thing; *sl* women's clothes worn by (transvestite) man **drag'ster** n automobile designed, modified for drag racing; driver of such car **drag'net** n fishing net to be dragged along sea floor; comprehensive search, esp by police for criminal, etc **drag race** automobile race where cars are timed over measured distance

drag·on [DRAG-ən] n mythical fire-breathing monster, like winged crocodile; type of large lizard **drag'on·fly** n, pl **-flies** long-bodied insect with gauzy wings

dra·goon [drà-GOON] n formerly, cavalryman of certain regiments ▷ vt oppress; coerce

drain [drayn] vt draw off (liquid) by pipes, ditches, etc; dry; drink to dregs; empty, exhaust ▷ vi flow off or away; become rid of liquid ▷ n channel for removing liquid; sewer; depletion, strain **drain'age** [-ij] n

drake [drayk] n male duck

dram n small draft of strong drink; unit of weight, one eighth of fluid ounce, one sixteenth of avoirdupois ounce

dra·ma [DRAH-mà] n stage play; art or literature of plays; playlike series of events **dra·mat·ic** [drà-MAT-ik] adj pert to drama; suitable for stage representation; with force and vividness of drama; striking; tense; exciting **dram'a·tist** n writer of plays **dram·a·ti·za·tion** n **dram'a·tize** vt **-tized, -tiz·ing** adapt story, novel for acting

dram·a·tur·gy [DRAM-à-tur-jee] n the technique of writing and producing plays **dram'a·tur·gist** n playwright

drape [drayp] vt **draped, drap·ing** cover, adorn with cloth; arrange in graceful folds **dra·per·y** [DRAY-pà-ree] n, pl **-per·ies** covering, curtain, etc of cloth

dras·tic [DRAS-tik] adj extreme, forceful; severe

draw v **drew, drawn, draw·ing** ▷ vt pull, pull along, haul; inhale; entice; delineate, portray with pencil, etc; frame, compose, draft, write; attract; bring (upon, out, etc); get by lot; of ship, require (depth of water); take from (well, barrel, etc); receive (money); bend (bow) ▷ vi pull, shrink; attract; make, admit current of air; make pictures with pencil, etc; finish game in tie; write orders for money; come, approach (near) ▷ n act of drawing; casting of lots; unfinished game, tie **draw'er** n one who or that which draws; sliding box in table or chest ▷ pl undergarment for the lower body **draw'ing** n art of depicting in line; sketch so done; action of verb **draw'back** n anything that takes away from satisfaction; snag **draw'bridge** n hinged bridge to pull up **drawing room** living room, sitting room **draw near** approach **draw out** lengthen **draw up** arrange; come to a halt

drawl v speak slowly ▷ n such speech

drawn pp of DRAW

dread [dred] vt fear greatly ▷ n awe, terror ▷ adj feared, awful **dread'ful** adj disagreeable, shocking or bad **dread'locks** pl n Rastafarian hair style of long matted or tightly curled strands **dread'nought** n large battleship mounting heavy guns

dream [dreem] n vision during sleep; fancy, reverie, aspiration; very pleasant idea, person, thing ▷ v **dreamed** or **dreamt, dream·ing** ▷ vi have dreams ▷ vt see, imagine in dreams; think of as possible **dream'y** adj **dream·i·er, dream·i·est** given to daydreams, impractical, vague; inf wonderful

drear·y [DREER-ee] adj **drear·i·er, drear·i·est** dismal, dull **drear'i·ly** adv **drear'i·ness** n gloom

dredge[1] [drej] v **dredged, dredg·ing** bring up mud, etc, from sea bottom; deepen channel by dredge; search for, produce obscure, remote, unlikely material ▷ n form of scoop or grab **dredg'er** n ship for dredging

dredge[2] vt sprinkle with flour, etc **dredg'er** n

dregs [dregz] pl n sediment, grounds; worthless part

drench vt wet thoroughly, soak; make (an animal) take dose of medicine ▷ n soaking; dose for animal

dress vt clothe; array for show; trim, smooth, prepare surface of; prepare (food) for market or table;

put dressing on (wound); align (troops) ▷ vi put on one's clothes; form in proper line ▷ n one-piece garment for woman; clothing; clothing for ceremonial evening wear **dress'er** n one who dresses, esp actors or actresses; chest of drawers, oft with mirror **dress'ing** n something applied to something else, as sauce to food, ointment to wound, manure to land, etc **dress'y** adj **dress·i·er, dress·i·est** stylish; fond of dress **dress circle** usu first gallery in theater **dressing down** inf scolding **dressing gown** coat-shaped garment worn over pyjamas or nightdress **dressing room** room used for changing clothes, esp backstage in a theater **dressing table** piece of bedroom furniture with a mirror and drawers **dress'mak·er** n

dres·sage [drə-SAHZH] n method of training horse in special maneuvers to show obedience

drew pt of DRAW

drib·ble [DRIB-əl] v **-bled, -bling** flow in drops, trickle; run at the mouth; basketball work ball forward with short bounces; soccer work ball forward with short kicks ▷ n trickle, drop **drib'let** n small portion or installment

drift vi be carried as by current of air, water; move aimlessly or passively ▷ n process of being driven by current; slow current or course; deviation from course; tendency; speaker's, writer's meaning; wind-heaped mass of snow, sand, etc; material driven or carried by water **drift'er** n one who, that which drifts; inf aimless person with no fixed job, etc **drift'wood** [-wuud] n wood washed ashore by sea

drill[1] n boring tool or machine;

exercise of soldiers or others in handling of arms and maneuvers; repeated routine in teaching ▷ vt bore, pierce hole; exercise in military and other routine ▷ vi practice routine

drill² n machine for sowing seed; small furrow for seed; row of plants ▷ vt sow seed in drills or furrows

drill³ n coarsely woven twilled fabric

drink [dringk] v **drank, drunk, drink·ing** swallow liquid; absorb; take intoxicating liquor, esp to excess ▷ n liquid for drinking; portion of this; act of drinking; intoxicating liquor; excessive use of it **drink'a·ble** adj drink to, **drink the health of** express good wishes, etc by drinking a toast to

drip v **dripped, drip·ping** fall or let fall in drops ▷ n act of dripping; drop; medicine intravenous administration of solution; sl dull, insipid person **dripping** n melted fat that drips from roasting meat ▷ adj very wet **drip-dry** [-drī] adj (of fabric) drying free of creases if hung up while wet

drive [drīv] v **drove, driv·en, driv·ing** ▷ vt urge in some direction; make move and steer (vehicle, animal, etc); urge, impel; fix by blows, as nail; chase; convey in vehicle; hit a ball with force as in golf, baseball ▷ v keep machine, animal, going; steer it; be conveyed in vehicle; rush, dash, drift fast ▷ n act, action of driving; journey in vehicle; private road leading to house; capacity for getting things done; united effort, campaign; energy; forceful stroke in golf, baseball **driv'er** n one that drives; golf club **drive time** time in the morning or evening when people drive to and from work

driv·el [DRIV-əl] vi run at the mouth or nose; talk nonsense ▷ n silly nonsense

driz·zle [DRIZ-əl] vi **-zled, -zling** rain in fine drops ▷ n fine, light rain

drogue [drohg] n any funnel-like device, of canvas, used as sea anchor; small parachute; wind indicator; windsock towed behind target aircraft; funnel-shaped device on end of refueling hose of tanker aircraft to receive probe of aircraft being refueled

droll [drohl] **-er, -est** funny, odd, comical **droll'ness** n **drol'ly** adv

drone [drohn] n male of honey bee; lazy idler; deep humming; bass pipe of bagpipe; its note ▷ v **droned, dron·ing** hum; talk in monotonous tone

drool vi to slaver, drivel

droop vi hang down; wilt, flag ▷ vt let hang down ▷ n drooping condition **droop'y** adj **droop·i·er, droop·i·est**

drop n globule of liquid; very small quantity; fall, descent; distance through which thing falls; thing that falls, as gallows platform ▷ v **dropped, drop·ping** ▷ vt let fall; fall in drops; utter casually; set down, unload; discontinue ▷ vi fall; fall in drops; lapse; come or go casually **drop'let** n **drop'pings** pl n dung of birds, rabbits, etc **drop'out** n person who fails to complete course of study or one who rejects conventional society

dross [draws] n scum of molten metal; impurity, refuse; anything of little or no value

drought [drowt] n long spell of dry weather

drove¹ [drohv] pt of DRIVE

drove² n herd, flock, crowd, esp in motion **drov'er** n driver of cattle

drown v die or be killed by immersion in liquid; get rid of as by submerging in liquid; make sound inaudible by louder sound

drow·sy [DROW-zee] adj **-si·er, -si·est** half-asleep; lulling; dull **drowse** vi **drow·si·ly** adv **drow·si·ness** n

drub vt **drubbed, drub·bing** thrash, beat **drubbing** n beating

drudge [druj] vi work at menial or distasteful tasks, slave ▷ n one who drudges, hack **drudg·er·y** n, pl **-er·ies**

drug n medical substance; narcotic; merchandise that is unsalable because of overproduction ▷ vt **drugged, drug·ging** mix drugs with; administer drug to, esp one inducing unconsciousness **drug·store** n pharmacy where wide variety of goods is available **drug·gist** n

dru·id [DROO-id] n (**D-**) member of ancient order of Celtic priests

drum n percussion instrument of skin stretched over round hollow frame, played by beating with sticks; various things shaped like drum; part of ear ▷ v **drummed, drum·ming** play drum; tap, thump continuously **drum·mer** n one who plays drum; traveling salesman **drum·head** n part of drum that is struck **drumhead court-martial** summary one held at war front **drum major** leader of military band **drum·stick** n stick for beating drum; lower joint of cooked fowl's leg **drum out** expel from military service, etc

drunk [drungk] adj **-er, -est** overcome by strong drink; fig under influence of strong emotion **drunk·ard** [-ərd] n one given to excessive drinking **drunk·en** adj drunk; caused by, showing intoxication **drunk·en·ness** n

dry [drī] adj **dri·er, dri·est** without moisture; rainless; not yielding milk, or other liquid; cold, unfriendly; caustically witty; having prohibition of alcoholic drink; uninteresting; needing effort to study; lacking sweetness (as wines) ▷ v **dried, dry·ing** remove water, moisture; become dry; evaporate **dri'ly** adv **dry'ness** n **dry'er** n person or thing that dries; apparatus for removing moisture **dry battery** electric battery without liquid **dry'-clean** v clean clothes with solvent other than water **dry'-clean·er** n **dry ice** solid carbon dioxide **dry'point** needle for engraving without acid; engraving so made **dry rot** fungoid decay in wood **dry run** practice, rehearsal in simulated conditions

dry·ad [DRĪ-əd] n wood nymph

du·al [DOO-əl] adj twofold; of two, double, forming pair **du'al·ism** n recognition of two independent powers or principles, eg good and evil, mind and matter **du·al·i·ty** n

dub vt **dubbed, dub·bing** give title to; confer knighthood on; provide film with soundtrack not in original language; smear with grease, dubbin **dub'bin, dub'bing** n grease for making leather supple

du·bi·ous [DOO-bee-əs] adj causing doubt, not clear or decided; of suspect character **du·bi'e·ty** [-Bī-i-tee] n **-ties** uncertainty, doubt

du·cal [DOO-kəl] adj of, like a duke

duch·ess [DUCH-is] n duke's wife or widow

duch·y [DUCH-ee] n, pl **duch·ies** territory of duke, dukedom

duck¹ [duk] n common swimming bird ▷ v plunge (someone) under water; bob down **duck'ling** n **duck'billed platypus** see **PLATYPUS**

duck[2] n strong linen or cotton fabric ▷ pl trousers of it

duct [dukt] n channel, tube
duc•tile [DUK-til] adj capable of being drawn into wire; flexible and tough; easily led **duc•til′i•ty** n
duct•less adj (of glands) secreting directly certain substances essential to health

dud n futile, worthless person or thing; shell that fails to explode ▷ adj worthless

dude [dood] n city man, esp Easterner in the West; sl fellow **dude ranch** ranch operating as vacation resort

dudg•eon [DUJ-ən] n anger, indignation, resentment

duds [dudz] pl n inf clothes

due [doo] adj owing; proper to be given, inflicted, etc; adequate, fitting; under engagement to arrive, be present; timed for ▷ adv (with points of compass) exactly ▷ n person's right; (usu pl) charge, fee, etc **du′ly** adv properly; fitly; rightly; punctually **due** to attributable to; caused by

du•el [DOO-əl] n arranged fight with deadly weapons, between two persons; keen two-sided contest ▷ vi **-eled, -el•ing** fight in duel **du′el•ist** n

du•en•na [doo-EN-ə] n in Spain or Portugal, elderly governess, guardian, chaperone

du•et [doo-ET] n piece of music for two performers

duff n sl buttocks

duf•fel [DUF-əl] n coarse woolen cloth; coat of this

duff•er [DUF-ər] n inf stupid inefficient person; inept golfer

dug[1] pt/pp of **DIG**

dug[2] n udder, teat of animal

dug•out [DUG-owt] n covered excavation to provide shelter for troops, etc; canoe of hollowed-out tree; *baseball* roofed structure with bench for players when not on the field

duke [dook] n in Great Britain, peer of rank next below prince; ruler of duchy **duch′ess** n fem **duke′dom** [-dəm] n

dukes [dooks] pl n sl fists

dul•cet [DUL-sit] adj (of sounds) sweet, melodious

dul•ci•mer [DUL-sə-mər] n stringed instrument played with light hammers, ancestor of piano

dull adj **-er, -est** stupid; insensible; sluggish; tedious; lacking liveliness or variety; gloomy, overcast ▷ v make or become dull **dull′ard** [-ərd] n

duly see **DUE**

dumb [dum] adj **-er, -est** incapable of speech; silent; inf stupid **dumb′ly** adv **dumb′ness** n **dumb′bell** n weight for exercises; dolt **dumb′found** vt confound into silence

dumb down vt make less intellectually demanding or sophisticated **dumb show** gestures without speech

dum′dum n soft-nosed bullet that expands on impact

dum•my [DUM-ee] n, pl **-mies** tailor's, dressmaker's model; imitation object; *cards* hand exposed on table and played by partner ▷ adj sham, bogus **dummy up** inf to keep silent

dump vt throw down in mass; deposit; unload; send (low-priced goods) for sale abroad ▷ n place where garbage is dumped; inf dirty, unpleasant place; temporary depot of stores or munitions ▷ pl low spirits, dejection **dump′ling** n small round mass of boiled or steamed dough; dessert of fruit wrapped in dough and baked **dump truck** truck for hauling and dumping sand, stone, etc **dump·y** *adj* **dump·i·er, dump·i·est** short, stout

dun[1] *vt* **dunned, dun·ning** persistently demand payment of debts ▷ *n* one who duns; urgent request for payment

dun[2] *adj* of dull grayish brown ▷ *n* this color; dun horse

dunce [duns] *n* slow learner, stupid pupil

dune [doon] *n* sandhill on coast or desert

dung *n* excrement of animals; manure ▷ *vt* fertilize or spread with manure

dun·ga·ree [dung-gə-REE] *n* blue denim ▷ *pl* work clothes, etc of this material

dun·geon [DUN-jən] *n* underground cell or vault for prisoners; formerly, tower or keep of castle

dunk [dungk] *vt* dip bread, etc in liquid before eating it; submerge **dunk shot** *basketball* shot made by jumping high to thrust ball through basket

dun·nage [DUN-ij] *n* padding, loose material for packing cargo

du·o [DOO-oh] *n, pl* **du·os** pair of performers, etc

du·o·dec·i·mal [doo-ə-DES-ə-məl] *adj* computed by twelves; twelfth

du·o·dec·i·mo [doo-ə-DES-ə-moh] *n, pl* **-mos** size of book in which each sheet is folded into 12 leaves before cutting; book of this size ▷ *adj* of this size

du·o·de·num [doo-ə-DEE-nəm] *n* upper part of small intestine **du·o·de·nal** *adj*

dupe [doop] *n* victim of delusion or sharp practice ▷ *vt* **duped, dup·ing** deceive for advantage, impose upon

du·plex [DOO-pleks] *adj* twofold ▷ *n* apartment with rooms on two floors; two-family house

du·pli·cate [DOO-pli-kayt] *vt* **-cat·ed, -cat·ing** make exact copy of; double ▷ *adj* [-kit] double; exactly the same as something else ▷ *n* exact copy **du·pli·ca·tor** *n* machine for making copies (of typewritten matter, etc)

du·plic·i·ty [-PLIS-i-tee] *n, pl* **-ties** deceitfulness, double-dealing, bad faith

du·ra·ble [DUUR-ə-bəl] *adj* lasting, resisting wear **du·ra·bil·i·ty** *n*

du·ra·tion [duu-RAY-shən] *n* time thing lasts

du·ress [duu-RES] *n* compulsion by use of force or threats

dur·ing [DUUR-ing] *prep* throughout, in the time of, in the course of

dusk *n* darker stage of twilight; partial darkness **dusk·y** *adj* **dusk·i·er, dusk·i·est** dark; dark-colored

dust *n* fine particles, powder of earth or other matter, lying on surface or blown along by wind; ashes of the dead ▷ *vt* sprinkle with powder, fertilizer, etc; rid of dust **dust·er** *n* cloth for removing dust; housecoat **dust·y** *adj* **dust·i·er, dust·i·est** covered with dust **dust'bowl** *n* area in which dust storms have carried away the top soil

Dutch [duch] *adj* pert to the Netherlands, its inhabitants, its language **Dutch courage** drunken bravado **Dutch treat** one where each person pays own share

du·ty [DOO-tee] *n, pl* **-ties** moral or legal obligation; that which is due; tax on goods; military service; one's proper employment **du'te·ous** *adj* **du'ti·a·ble** *adj* liable to customs duty **du·ti·ful** *adj*

du·vet [doo-VAY] *n* quilt filled with down or artificial fiber

DVD Digital Versatile or Video Disk

dwarf [dworf] *n, pl* **dwarfs** or **dwarves** [dworvz] very undersized person; mythological, small, manlike creature ▷ *adj* unusually small, stunted ▷ *vt* make seem small by contrast; make stunted

dwell *vi* **dwelt** or **dwelled,** **dwell·ing** live, make one's abode (in); fix one's attention, write or speak at length (on) **dweller** *n* **dwell'ing** *n* house

dwin·dle [DWIN-dl] *vi* **-died,** **-dling** grow less, waste away, decline

Dy *chemistry* dysprosium

dye [dī] *vt* **dyed, dye·ing** impregnate (cloth, etc) with coloring matter; color thus ▷ *n* coloring matter in solution or that can be dissolved for dyeing; tinge, color **dy'er** *n*

dyke[1] [dīk] *n* wall built to prevent flooding

dyke[2] *n sl, oft offens* lesbian

dy·nam·ics [dī-NAM-iks] *n* branch of physics dealing with force as producing or affecting motion ▷ *pl* forces that produce change in a system **dy·nam'ic** *adj* of, relating to motive force, force in operation; energetic and forceful **dy·nam'i·cal·ly** *adv*

dy·na·mite [Dī-nə-mit] *n* high explosive mixture ▷ *vt* **-mit·ed,** **-mit·ing** blow up with this ▷ *adj* *inf* topnotch

dy·na·mo [Dī-nə-moh] *n, pl* **-mos** machine to convert mechanical into electrical energy, generator of electricity **dy·na·mom'e·ter** *n* instrument to measure energy expended

dy·nas·ty [Dī-nə-stee] *n, pl* **-ties** line, family, succession of hereditary rulers **dy'nast** *n* ruler **dy·nas'tic** *adj* of dynasty

dyne [din] *n* cgs unit of force

dys·en·ter·y [DIS-ən-ter-ee] *n* infection of intestine causing severe diarrhea

dys·func·tion [dis-FUNGK-shən] *n* abnormal, impaired functioning, esp of bodily organ

dys·lex·ia [dis-LEK-see-ə] *n* impaired ability to read, caused by condition of the brain **dys·lex'ic** *adj, n*

dys·pep·sia [dis-PEP-see-ə] *n* indigestion **dys·pep'tic** *adj, n*

dys·tro·phy [DIS-trə-fee] *n* wasting of body tissues, esp muscles

e

e- *prefix* electronic: *e-mail; e-tail*

each [eech] *adj, pron* every one taken separately

ea·ger [EE-gàr] *adj* having a strong wish (for something); keen, impatient **ea·ger·ness** *n*

ea·gle [EE-gàl] *n* large bird with keen sight that preys on small birds and animals; golf score of two strokes under par for a hole **ea·glet** [EE-glit] *n* young eagle

ear[1] [eer] *n* organ of hearing, esp external part of it; sense of hearing; sensitiveness to sounds; attention **ear·ache** *n* acute pain in ear **ear·mark** *vt* assign, reserve for definite purpose **ear·phone** *n* receiver for radio, etc held to or put in ear **ear·ring** *n* ornament for lobe of the ear **ear·shot** *n* hearing distance

ear[2] *n* spike, head of corn

earl [url] *n* British nobleman ranking next below marquis

ear·ly [UR-lee] *adj, adv* **-li·er, -li·est** before expected or usual time; in first part, near or nearer beginning of some portion of time

earn [urn] *vt* obtain by work or merit; gain **earn·ings** *pl n*

ear·nest[1] [UR-nist] *adj* serious, ardent, sincere **in earnest** serious, determined

earn·est[2] *n* money paid over in token to bind bargain, pledge; token, foretaste

earth [urth] *n* (E-) planet or world we live on; ground, dry land; mold, soil, mineral **earth·en** *adj* made of clay or earth **earth·ly** *adj* possible, feasible **earth·y** *adj* **earth·i·er, earth·i·est** of earth; uninhibited; vulgar **earth·en·ware** *n* (vessels of) baked clay **earth·quake** *n* convulsion of Earth's surface

ease [eez] *n* comfort; freedom from constraint, annoyance, awkwardness, pain or trouble; idleness ▷ *v* **eased, eas·ing** reduce burden; give bodily or mental ease to; slacken; (cause to) move carefully or gradually; relieve of pain **ease·ment** *n* right of way, etc, over another's land **eas·i·ly** *adv* **eas·y** *adj* **eas·i·er, eas·i·est** not difficult; free from pain, care, constraint or anxiety; compliant; characterized by low demand; fitting loosely; *inf* having no preference for any particular course of action **easy·going** *adj* not fussy; indolent

ea·sel [EE-zàl] *n* frame to support picture, etc

east [eest] *n* part of horizon where sun rises; (E-) eastern lands, Orient ▷ *adj* on, in, or nearer east; coming from east ▷ *adv* from, or to, east **east·er·ly** *adj, adv* from, or to, east **east·ern** *adj* of, dwelling in, east **east·ern·er** *n* **east·ward** *adj, adv, n* **east·ward, east·wards** *adv*

Eas·ter [EE-stàr] *n* annual festival of the resurrection of Christ

easy see EASE

eat [eet] *v* **ate, eat·en, eat·ing** chew and swallow; consume, destroy; gnaw; wear away

eaves [eevz] *pl n* overhanging edges of roof **eaves'drop** *v* **-dropped, -drop•ping** listen secretly **eaves'drop•per** *n*

ebb *vi* flow back; decay ▷ *n* flowing back of tide; decline, decay **at a low ebb** in a state of weakness

eb•on•y [EB-ə-nee] *n* **-on•ies** hard black wood ▷ *adj* made of, black as ebony

e-book [EE-buuk] *n* book in the form of a file that can be downloaded to a computer via the Internet ▷ *vt* book (tickets, etc) through the Internet

e•bul•lient [i-BUUL-yənt] *adj* exuberant; boiling **e•bul'lience** *n* **e•bul•li•tion** [eb-ə-LISH-ən] *n* boiling; effervescence; outburst

ec•cen•tric [ik-SEN-trik] *adj* odd, unconventional; irregular; not placed, or not having axis placed, centrally; not circular (in orbit) ▷ *n* odd, unconventional person; mechanical device to change circular into to-and-fro movement **ec•cen•tric'i•ty** *n*

Eccles. Ecclesiastes

ec•cle•si•as•tic [i-klee-zee-AS-tik] *n* clergyman ▷ *adj* of, relating to the Christian Church **ec•cle•si•as'ti•cal** *adj*

ech•e•lon [ESH-ə-lon] *n* level, grade, of responsibility or command; formation of troops, planes, etc in parallel divisions each slightly to left or right of the one in front

ech•o [EK-oh] *n, pl* **ech•oes** repetition of sounds by reflection; close imitation ▷ *v* **ech•oed, ech•o•ing** ▷ *vt* repeat as echo, send back the sound of; imitate closely ▷ *vi* resound; be repeated **echo sounding** system of ascertaining depth of water by measuring time required to receive an echo from sea bottom or submerged object

éclair [ee-KLAIR] *n* finger-shaped, chocolate-frosted cake filled with whipped cream or custard

éclat [ay-KLAH] *n* splendor, renown, acclamation

e•clec•tic [i-KLEK-tik] *adj* selecting; borrowing one's philosophy from various sources; catholic in views or taste ▷ *n* **e•clec'ti•cism** *n*

e•clipse [i-KLIPS] *n* blotting out of sun, moon, etc by another heavenly body; obscurity ▷ *vt* **-clipsed, -clips•ing** obscure, hide; surpass **e•clip'tic** *adj* of eclipse ▷ *n* apparent path of sun

e•col•o•gy [i-KOL-ə-jee] *n* science of plants and animals in relation to their environment **ec•o•log'i•cal** *adj* **e•col'o•gist** *n* specialist in or advocate of ecological studies

e-com•merce *n* business transactions conducted on the Internet

e•con•o•my [i-KON-ə-mee] *n, pl* **-mies** careful management of resources to avoid unnecessary expenditure or waste; sparing, restrained or efficient use; system of interrelationship of money, industry and employment in a country **ec•o•nom'ic** *adj* of economics; profitable; economical **ec•o•nom'i•cal** *adj* not wasteful of money, time, effort, etc; frugal **ec•o•nom'ics** *n* study of economies of nations; financial aspects **e•con'o•mist** *n* specialist in economics **e•con'o•mize** *v* **-mized, -miz•ing** limit or reduce expense, waste, etc

ec•ru [EK-roo] *n, adj* (of) color of unbleached linen

ec•sta•sy [EK-stə-see] *n, pl* **-sies** exalted state of feeling, mystic trance; frenzy; (**E-**) *sl* powerful drug that can produce hallucinations

ec·stat·ic [ik-STAT-ik] *adj*
ec·stat'i·cal·ly *adv*

ec·u·men·i·cal [ek-yuu-MEN-i-kəl] *adj* of the Christian Church throughout the world, esp with regard to its unity; interdenominational; universal
ec·u·men'i·cism *n*

ec·ze·ma [EK-sə-mə] *n* skin disease

ed·dy [ED-ee] *n, pl* **-dies** small whirl in water, smoke, etc ▷ *vi* **-died,** **-dy·ing** move in whirls

e·del·weiss [AY-dəl-vīs] *n* white-flowered alpine plant

e·de·ma [i-DEE-mə] *n* an abnormal excess of fluid in tissues, organs; swelling due to this

E·den [EE-dən] *n* garden in which Adam and Eve were placed at the Creation; any delightful, happy place or condition

edge [ej] *n* border, boundary; cutting side of blade; sharpness; advantage; acrimony, bitterness ▷ *vt* **edged, edg·ing** ▷ *vt* sharpen, give edge or border to; move gradually ▷ *vi* advance sideways or gradually
edge'ways, -wise *adv* **edg'i·er, edg·i·est** irritable, sharp or keen in temper **on edge** nervous, irritable; excited

ed·i·ble [ED-ə-bəl] *adj* eatable, fit for eating

e·dict [EE-dikt] *n* order proclaimed by authority, decree

ed·i·fice [ED-ə-fis] *n* building, esp big one

ed·i·fy [ED-ə-fī] *vt* **-fied,** **-fy·ing** improve morally, instruct
ed·i·fi·ca'tion *n* improvement of the mind or morals

ed'it *vt* prepare book, film, tape, etc for publication or broadcast

e·di·tion [i-DISH-ən] *n* form in which something is published; number of copies of new publication printed at one time **ed·i·to'ri·al** *adj* of editor ▷ *n* article stating opinion of newspaper, etc

ed·u·cate [EJ-uu-kayt] *vt* **-cat·ed,** **-cat·ing** provide schooling for; teach; train mentally and morally; train; improve, develop
ed·u·ca'tion *n* **ed·u·ca'tion·al** *adj* **ed'u·ca·tive** *adj* **ed'u·ca·tor** *n*

e·duce [i-DOOS] *vt* **-duced,** **-duc·ing** bring out, elicit, develop; infer, deduce

ee·rie [EER-ee] *adj* **-ri·er,** **-ri·est** weird, uncanny; causing superstitious fear

ef·face [i-FAYS] *vt* **-faced, -fac·ing** wipe or rub out **ef·face'a·ble** *adj*

ef·fect [i-FEKT] *n* result, consequence; efficacy; impression; condition of being operative ▷ *pl* movable property; lighting, sounds, etc to accompany film, broadcast, etc ▷ *vt* bring about, accomplish **ef·fec'tive** *adj* having power to produce effects; in effect, operative; serviceable; powerful; striking **ef·fec'tive·ly** *adv* **ef·fec'tu·al** [-choo-əl] *adj* successful in producing desired effect; satisfactory; efficacious **ef·fec'tu·ate** [-choo-ayt] *vt* **-at·ed, -at·ing** bring about, effect

ef·fem·i·nate [i-FEM-ə-nit] *adj* womanish, unmanly **ef·fem'i·na·cy** *n*

ef·fer·ent [EF-ər-ənt] *adj* conveying outward or away

ef·fer·vesce [ef-ər-VES] *vi* **-vesced, -vesc·ing** give off bubbles; be in high spirits **ef·fer·ves'cent** *adj*

ef·fete [i-FEET] *adj* worn out, feeble

ef·fi·ca·cious [ef-i-KAY-shəs] *adj* producing or sure to produce desired

effect; effective; powerful; adequate
ef·fi·ca·cy [-kə-see] *n* **-cies**
potency; force; efficiency
ef·fi·cient [i-FISH-ənt] *adj*
capable, competent, producing
effect **ef·fi·cien·cy** *n*, pl **-cies**
ef·fi·gy [EF-i-jee] *n*, pl **-gies** image,
likeness
ef·flo·resce [ef-lə-RES] *vi*
-resced, -resc·ing burst into flower
ef·flo·res·cence *n*
ef·flu·ent [EF-loo-ənt] *n* liquid
discharged as waste; stream flowing
from larger stream, lake, etc ▷ *adj*
flowing out **ef·flu·vi·um** [i-FLOO-
vee-əm] *n*, pl **-vi·a** something
flowing out invisibly, esp affecting
lungs or sense of smell
ef·fort [EF-ərt] *n* exertion,
endeavor, attempt or something
achieved **ef·fort·less** *adj*
ef·fron·ter·y [i-FRUN-tə-ree] *n*, pl
-ter·ies brazen impudence
ef·ful·gent [i-FUL-jənt]
adj radiant, shining brightly
ef·ful·gence *n*
ef·fu·sion [i-FYOO-zhən] *n*
(unrestrained) outpouring **ef·fuse**
[i-FYOOZ] *v* **-fused, -fus·ing** pour
out, shed; radiate **ef·fu·sive** [-siv]
adj gushing, demonstrative
eg for example
e·gal·i·tar·i·an [i-gal-i-TAIR-
ee-ən] *adj* believing that all people
should be equal; promoting this
ideal ▷ *n*
egg[1] *n* oval or round object produced
by female of bird, etc, from which
young emerge, esp egg of domestic
hen, used as food **egg'plant** *n*
egg-shaped dark purple fruit; plant
bearing it
egg[2] *vt* **egg on** encourage, urge;
incite
e·go [EE-goh] *n*, pl **e·gos** the self;
the conscious thinking subject; one's

image of oneself; morale **e'go·ism**
n systematic selfishness; theory
that bases morality on self-interest
e'go·tism selfishness; self-conceit
e'go·ist, ego'ist *n* **e·go·tis'tic,**
e·go·is'tic *adj* **e·go·cen'tric** *adj*
self-centered; egoistic; centered
in the ego
e·gre·gious [i-GREE-jəs] *adj*
outstandingly bad, blatant; absurdly
obvious, esp of mistake, etc
e·gress [EE-gres] *n* way out;
departure
e·gret [EE-grit] *n* one of several
white herons
ei·der [Ī-dər] *n* any of several
northern sea ducks; eiderdown
ei'der·down *n* its breast feathers;
quilt (stuffed with feathers)
eight [ayt] *n* cardinal number one
above seven; crew of eight-oared
shell ▷ *adj* **eight·een'** *adj, n* eight
more than ten **eight·eenth'** *adj, n*
eighth [ayth] *adj, n* ordinal number
eight'i·eth *adj, n* **eight'y** *adj, n, pl*
eight·ies ten times eight **figure**
eight a skating figure; any figure
shaped as 8
ei·ther [EE-thər] *adj, pron* one or the
other; one of two; each ▷ *adv, conj*
bringing in first of alternatives or
strengthening an added negation
e·jac·u·late [i-JAK-yə-layt]
v **-lat·ed, -lat·ing** eject
(semen); exclaim, utter suddenly
e·jac·u·la'tion *n*
e·ject [i-JEKT] *vt* throw out; expel,
drive out **e·jec'tion** *n*
eke out [eek] *vt* make (supply) last,
esp by frugal use; supply deficiencies
of; make with difficulty (a living, etc)
e·lab·o·rate [i-LAB-ər-it] *adj*
carefully worked out, detailed;
complicated ▷ *v* [-ayt] **-rat·ed,**
-rat·ing ▷ *vi* expand (upon) ▷ *vt*
work out in detail; take pains with

élan [ay-LAHN] n dash; ardor; impetuosity **élan vi·tal** [vee-TAL] esp in Bergsonian philosophy, the creative force within an organism that is responsible for growth, change, etc

e·lapse [i-LAPS] vi **-lapsed, -laps·ing** of time, pass

e·las·tic [i-LAS-tik] adj resuming normal shape after distortion, springy; flexible ▷n tape, fabric, containing interwoven strands of flexible rubber, etc **e·las·ti·cized** [-sīzd] adj **e·las·tic·i·ty** n

e·la·tion [i-LAY-shăn] n high spirits; pride **e·late** [i-LAYT] vt **-lat·ed, -lat·ing** (usu passive) be elated, etc; raise the spirits of; make happy; exhilarate

el·bow [EL-boh] n joint between fore and upper parts of arm (esp outer part of it); part of sleeve covering this; something resembling this, esp angular pipe fitting ▷vt shove, strike with elbow **elbow grease** hard work **elbow room** n sufficient room

eld·er¹ [EL-dăr] adj, senior; comp of OLD ▷n person of greater age; old person; official of certain churches **eld·er·ly** adj growing old **eld·est** adj oldest; sup of OLD

el·der² n white-flowered tree or shrub

El Do·ra·do [el dă-RAH-doh] n fictitious country rich in gold

e-learn·ing [EE-lurn-ing] n Internet-based teaching system

e·lect [i-LEKT] vt choose by vote; choose ▷adj appointed but not yet in office; chosen, select, choice **e·lec·tion** n choosing, esp by voting **e·lec·tion·eer** vi work in political campaign **e·lec·tive** adj appointed, filled, or chosen by election **e·lec·tor** n one who elects **e·lec·tor·al** adj

electoral college body of electors chosen by voters to elect President and Vice President **e·lec·tor·ate** n body of persons entitled to vote

e·lec·tric·i·ty [i-lek-TRIS-ĭ-tee] n form of energy associated with stationary or moving electrons or other charged particles; electric current or charge; science dealing with electricity **e·lec·tric** adj derived from, produced by, producing, transmitting or powered by electricity; excited, emotionally charged **e·lec·tri·cal** adj **e·lec·tri·cian** n one trained in installation, etc of electrical wiring and devices **e·lec·tri·fi·ca·tion** n **e·lec·tri·fy** vt **-fied, -fy·ing** **electric chair** chair in which criminals sentenced to death are electrocuted **electric organ** music organ in which sound is produced by electric devices instead of wind

electro- comb form operated by or caused by electricity: electrocute

e·lec·tro·car·di·o·graph [i-lek-troh-KAHR-dee-ă-graf] n instrument for recording electrical activity of heart **e·lec·tro·car·di·o·gram** n tracing produced by this

e·lec·tro·cute [i-LEK-tră-kyoot] vt **-cut·ed, -cut·ing** execute, kill by electricity **e·lec·tro·cu·tion** n

e·lec·trode [i-LEK-trohd] n conductor by which electric current enters or leaves battery, vacuum tube, etc

e·lec·tro·en·ceph·a·lo·graph [i-lek-troh-en-SEF-ă-lă-graf] n instrument for recording electrical activity of brain **e·lec·tro·en·ce·ph'a·lo·gram** n tracing produced by this

e·lec·tro·lyte [i-LEK-tră-līt] n solution, molten substance that conducts electricity **e·lec·tro·lyt·ic** [-LIT-ik] *adj*

e·lec·tro·lyze [i-LEK-trə-liz] *vt* **-lyzed, -lyz·ing** decompose by electricity **e·lec·trol·y·sis** [-TROL-ə-sis] *n*

e·lec·tro·mag·net [i-lek-troh-MAG-nit] *n* magnet containing coil of wire through which electric current is passed **e·lec·tro·mag·net·ic** *adj*

e·lec·tron [i-LEK-tron] *n* one of fundamental particles of matter identified with unit of charge of negative electricity and essential component of the atom **e·lec·tron·ic** *adj* of electrons or electronics; using devices, such as semiconductors, transistors, or vacuum tubes, dependent on action of electrons **electronic mail** see E-MAIL **e·lec·tron·ics** *n* technology concerned with development of electronic devices and circuits; science of behavior and control of electrons **electron volt** unit of energy used in nuclear physics

e·lec·tro·plate [i-LEK-trə-playt] *vt* **-plat·ed, -plat·ing** coat with silver, etc by electrolysis ▷ *n* articles electroplated

el·e·gant [EL-ə-gənt] *adj* graceful, tasteful; refined **el·e·gance** *n*

el·e·gy [EL-ə-jee] *n, pl* **-gies** lament for the dead in poem or song **el·e·gi·ac** [el-ə-JÏ-ak] *adj* suited to elegies; plaintive

el·e·ment [EL-ə-mənt] *n* substance that cannot be separated into other substances by ordinary chemical techniques; component part; small amount, trace; heating wire in electric kettle, stove, etc; proper abode or sphere ▷ *pl* powers of atmosphere; rudiments, first principles **el·e·men·tal** *adj*

fundamental; of powers of nature **el·e·men·ta·ry** *adj* rudimentary, simple

el·e·phant [EL-ə-fənt] *n* huge four-footed, thick-skinned animal with ivory tusks and long trunk **el·e·phan·ti·a·sis** *n* disease with hardening of skin and enlargement of legs, etc **el·e·phan·tine** [-FAN-teen] *adj* unwieldy, clumsy, heavily big

el·e·vate [EL-ə-vayt] *vt* **-vat·ed, -vat·ing** raise, lift up, exalt **el·e·va·tion** *n* raising; height, esp above sea level; angle above horizon, as of gun; drawing of one side of building, etc **el·e·va·tor** *n* cage raised and lowered in vertical shaft to transport people, etc

el·ev·en [i-LEV-ən] *n* number next above 10; team of 11 persons ▷ *adj* **el·ev·fold** *adj, adv* **el·ev·enth** *adj* the ordinal number **eleventh hour** latest possible time

elf *n, pl* **elves** fairy; woodland sprite **elf'in** *adj* roguish, mischievous

e·lic·it [i-LIS-it] *vt* draw out, evoke; bring to light

e·lide [i-LID] *vt* **e·lid·ed, e·lid·ing** omit in pronunciation a vowel or syllable **e·li·sion** [i-LIZH-ən] *n*

el·i·gi·ble [EL-ə-jə-bəl] *adj* fit or; qualified to be chosen; suitable, desirable **el·i·gi·bil'i·ty** *n*

e·lim·i·nate [i-LIM-ə-nayt] *vt* **-nat·ed, -nat·ing** remove, get rid of, set aside **e·lim·i·na·tion** *n*

elision see ELIDE

e·lite [i-LEET] *n* choice or select body; the pick or best part of society; typewriter type size (12 letters to inch) ▷ *adj* **e·lit'ism** *n* **e·lit'ist** *n*

e·lix·ir [i-LIK-sər] *n* preparation sought by alchemists to change base metals into gold, or to prolong life; panacea

elk n large deer

el·lipse [i-LIPS] n oval **el·lip·ti·cal** adj

el·lip·sis [i-LIP-sis] n, pl **-ses** [-seez] omission of parts of word or sentence; mark (...) indicating this

el·o·cu·tion [el-ə-KYOO-shən] n art of public speaking, voice management **el·o·cu·tion·ist** n teacher of this

e·lon·gate [i-LAWNG-gayt] v **-gat·ed, -gat·ing** lengthen, extend, prolong **e·lon·ga·tion** n

e·lope [i-LOHP] vi **-loped, -lop·ing** run away from home with lover; do this with intention of marrying **e·lope·ment** n

el·o·quence [EL-ə-kwəns] n fluent, powerful use of language **el·o·quent** adj

else [els] adv besides; instead; otherwise **else·where** adv in or to some other place

e·lu·ci·date [i-LOO-si-dayt] vt **-dat·ed, -dat·ing** throw light upon, explain **e·lu·ci·da·tion** n

e·lude [i-LOOD] vt **-lud·ed, -lud·ing** escape, slip away from, dodge; baffle **e·lu·sion** n act of eluding; evasion **e·lu·sive** adj difficult to catch hold of, deceptive **e·lu·sive·ness** n

elves, elvish see ELF

em n printing the square of any size of type

em- prefix see EN-

e·ma·ci·ate [i-MAY-see-ayt] v **-at·ed, -at·ing** make or become abnormally thin **e·ma·ci·a·tion** n

e-mail, email n (also **electronic mail**) sending of messages between computer terminals or other electronic devices ▷ v communicate in this way

em·a·nate [EM-ə-nayt] v **-nat·ed, -nat·ing** issue, proceed from, originate **em·a·na·tion** n

e·man·ci·pate [i-MAN-sə-payt] vt **-pat·ed, -pat·ing** set free **e·man·ci·pa·tion** n act of setting free, esp from social, legal restraint; state of being set free **e·man·ci·pa·tor** n

e·mas·cu·late [i-MAS--kyə-layt] vt **-lat·ed, -lat·ing** castrate; enfeeble, weaken **e·mas·cu·la·tion** n

em·balm [em-BAHM] vt preserve corpse from decay by use of chemicals, herbs, etc **em·balm'er** n

em·bank·ment [em-BANGK-mənt] n artificial mound carrying road, railway, or serving to dam water

em·bar·go [em-BAHR-goh] n, pl **-goes** order stopping movement of ships; suspension of commerce; ban ▷ vt **-goed, -go·ing** put under embargo

em·bark [em-BAHRK] v put, go, on board ship, aircraft, etc; (with on, upon) commence new project, venture, etc **em·bar·ka·tion** n

em·bar·rass [em-BAR-əs] vt perplex, disconcert; abash; confuse; encumber **em·bar·rass·ment** n

em·bas·sy [EM-bə-see] n, pl **-sies** office, work or official residence of ambassador; deputation

em·bed' vt **-bed·ded, -bed·ding** fix fast in something solid

em·bel·lish vt adorn, enrich **em·bel·lish·ment** n

em·ber [EM-bər] n glowing cinder ▷ pl red-hot ashes

em·bez·zle [em-BEZ-əl] vt **-zled, -zling** divert fraudulently, misappropriate (money in trust, etc) **em·bez·zle·ment** n **em·bez'zler** n

em·bit·ter [em-BIT-ər] vt make bitter **em·bit·ter·ment** n

em·bla·zon [em-BLAY-zən] vt

adorn richly, esp heraldically

em·blem [EM-blàm] n symbol; badge, device **em·ble·mat·ic** adj

em·bod·y [em-BOD-ee] vt **-bod·ied, -bod·y·ing** give body, concrete expression to; represent, include, be expression of **em·bod'i·ment** n

em·bo·lism [EM-bà-liz-àm] n medicine obstruction of artery by blood clot or air bubble

em·boss [em-BAWS] vt mold, stamp or carve in relief

em·brace [em-BRAYS] vt **-braced, -brac·ing** clasp in arms, hug; seize, avail oneself of, accept; comprise ▷ n

em·bra·sure [em-BRAY-zhàr] n opening in wall for cannon; widening of wall at sides of window

em·bro·ca·tion [em-brà-KAY-shàn] n lotion for rubbing limbs, etc to relieve pain **em'bro·cate** vt **-cat·ed, -cat·ing** apply lotion, etc

em·broi·der [em-BROI-dàr] vt ornament with needlework; embellish, exaggerate (story) **em·broi'der·y** n

em·broil vt bring into confusion; involve in hostility **em·broil'ment** n

em·bry·o [EM-bree-oh] n, pl **-os** unborn or undeveloped offspring, germ; undeveloped thing **em·bry·ol'o·gist** n **em·bry·ol'o·gy** n **em·bry·on'ic** adj

e·mend [i-MEND] vt remove errors from, correct **e·men·da'tion** n

em·er·ald [EM-àr-àld] n bright green precious stone ▷ adj the color of emerald

e·merge [i-MURJ] vi **-merged, -merg·ing** come up, out; rise to notice; issue into view; come out on inquiry **e·mer'gence** n **e·mer'gent** adj

e·mer·gen·cy [i-MUR-jàn-see] n,

pl **-cies** sudden unforeseen thing or event needing prompt action; difficult situation; exigency, crisis

e·mer·i·tus [i-MER-i-tàs] adj retired, honorably discharged but retaining one's title (eg professor) on honorary basis

em·er·y [EM-àr-ee] n hard mineral used for polishing **emery board** cardboard coated with powdered emery

e·met·ic [i-MET-ik] n, adj (medicine or agent) causing vomiting

em·i·grate [EM-i-grayt] vt **-grat·ed, -grat·ing** go and settle in another country **em'i·grant** [-gránt] n **em·i·gra'tion** n

é·mi·gré [EM-i-gray] n, pl -grés emigrant, esp one forced to leave native land for political reasons

em·i·nent [EM-à-nànt] adj distinguished, notable **em'i·nence** n distinction; height; rank; fame; rising ground; (E-) title of cardinal **em'i·nent·ly** adv **é·mi·nence grise** [ay-mee-nahns GREEZ] Fr person wielding unofficial power, oft surreptitiously

em·is·sar·y [EM-à-ser-ee] n, pl **-sar·ies** agent, representative (esp of government) sent on mission

e·mit [i-MIT] vt **-mit·ted, -mit·ting** give out, put forth **e·mis'sion** n **e·mit'ter** n

e·mol·lient [i-MOL-yànt] adj softening, soothing ▷ n ointment or other softening application

e·mol·u·ment [i-MOL-yà-mànt] n salary, pay, profit from work

e·mot·i·con [i-MOH-ti-kon] n series of keyed characters, used esp in e-mail, to indicate an emotion

e·mo·tion [i-MOH-shàn] n mental agitation, excited state of feeling, as joy, fear, etc **e·mo'tion·al**

given to emotion; appealing to the emotions **e·mo·tive** *adj* tending to arouse emotion

em·pa·thy [EM-pà-thee] *n* power of understanding, imaginatively entering into, another's feelings

em·per·or [EM-pàr-àr] *n* ruler of an empire **em·press** [-pris] *n fem*

em·pha·sis [EM-fà-sis] *n, pl* **-ses** [-seez] importance attached; stress on words; vigor of speech, expression **em·pha·size** *vt* **-sized, -siz·ing** **em·phat·ic** [-FAT-ik] *adj* forceful, decided; stressed

em·pire [EM-pīr] *n* large territory, esp aggregate of territories or peoples under supreme ruler, supreme control

em·pir·i·cal [em-PIR-i-kàl] *adj* relying on experiment or experience, not on theory **em·pir·i·cal·ly** *adv* **em·pir·i·cist** [-à-sist] *n* one who relies solely on experience and observation **em·pir·i·cism** *n*

em·place·ment [em-PLAYS-mànt] *n* putting in position; gun platform

em·ploy [em-PLOI] *vt* provide work for (a person) in return for money, hire; keep busy; use **em·ploy·ee** *n* **em·ploy·er** *n* **em·ploy·ment** *n* an employing, being employed; work, trade; occupation

em·po·ri·um [em-POHR-ee-àm] *n, pl* **-ri·ums** large store, esp one carrying general merchandise; center of commerce

em·pow·er [em-POW-àr] *vt* enable, authorize **em·pow·er·ment** *n*

empress see EMPEROR

emp·ty [EM-tee] *adj* **-ti·er, -ti·est** containing nothing; unoccupied; senseless; vain, foolish ▷ *v* **-tied, -ty·ing** make, become devoid of content; discharge (contents) into **emp·ties** *pl n* empty boxes, bottles,

etc **emp·ti·ness** *n*

EMT *n* emergency medical technician

e·mu [EE-myoo] *n* large Aust flightless bird like ostrich

em·u·late [EM-yà-layt] *vt* **-lat·ed, -lat·ing** strive to equal or excel; imitate **em·u·la·tion** *n* rivalry; competition **em·u·la·tive** *adj* **em·u·la·tor** *n*

e·mul·sion [i-MUL-shàn] *n* light-sensitive coating of film; milky liquid with oily or resinous particles in suspension; paint, etc in this form **e·mul·si·fi·er** *n* **e·mul·si·fy** *vt* **-fied, -fy·ing**

en *n* printing unit of measurement, half an em

en-, em- *prefix* put in, into, or on: *enrage*

en·a·ble [en-AY-bàl] *vt* **-bled, -bling** make able, authorize, empower, supply with means (to do something)

en·act [en-AKT] *vi* make law; act part **en·act·ment** *n*

e·nam·el [i-NAM-àl] *n* glasslike coating applied to metal, etc to preserve surface; coating of teeth; any hard outer coating ▷ *vt* **-eled, -el·ing**

e·nam·or [i-NAM-àr] *vt* inspire with love; charm; bewitch

en·camp [en-KAMP] *v* set up (in) camp **en·camp·ment** *n*

en·cap·su·late [en-KAP-sà-layt] *vt* **-lat·ed, -lat·ing** enclose in capsule; put in concise or abridged form **en·cap·su·la·tion** *n*

en·ceph·a·lo·gram [en-SEF-à-là-gram] *n* X-ray photograph of brain

en·chant *vt* bewitch, delight **en·chant·er** *n* **en·chant·ress** *n fem* **en·chant·ment** *n*

en·chi·la·da [en-chà-LAH-dà]

n rolled tortilla filled with sauce of meat, etc

en·cir·cle [en-SUR-kəl] *vt* **-cled, -cling** surround; enfold; go around so as to surround

en·clave [EN-klayv] *n* portion of territory entirely surrounded by foreign land; distinct area or group isolated within larger one

en·close [en-KLOHZ] *vt* **-closed, -clos·ing** shut in; surround; envelop; place in with something else (in letter, etc) **en·clo·sure** [-zhər] *n*

en·co·mi·um [en-KOH-mee-əm] *n* **-mi·ums** formal praise; eulogy **en·co·mi·ast** *n* one who composes encomiums

en·com·pass [en-KUM-pəs] *vt* surround, encircle, contain

en·core [ONG-kor] *interj* again, once more ▷ *n* call for repetition of song, etc; the repetition

en·coun·ter [en-KOWN-tər] *vt* meet unexpectedly; meet in conflict; be faced with (difficulty, etc) ▷ *n*

en·cour·age [en-KUR-ij] *vt* **-aged, -ag·ing** hearten, animate, inspire with hope; embolden **en·cour·age·ment** *n*

en·croach [en-KROHCH] *vi* intrude (on) as usurper; trespass **en·croach·ment** *n*

en·crust [en-KRUST] *vt* incrust **en·crus·ta·tion** *n*

en·cum·ber [en-KUM-bər] *vt* hamper; burden **en·cum·brance** *n* impediment, burden

en·cyc·li·cal [en-SIK-li-kəl] *adj* sent to many persons or places ▷ *n* circular letter, esp papal letter to all Catholic bishops

en·cy·clo·pe·dia [en-si-klə-PEE-dee-ə] *n* book, set of books of information on all subjects, or on every branch of subject, usu arranged alphabetically **en·cy·clo·pe·dic** *adj*

end *n* limit; extremity; conclusion, finishing; fragment; latter part; death; event, issue; purpose, aim; *football* one of two linemen stationed farthest from the center ▷ *v* put an end to; come to an end, finish **end·ing** *n* **end·less** *adj* **end·pa·pers** *pl n* blank pages at beginning and end of book

en·dear [en-DEER] *vt* to make dear or beloved **en·dear·ing** *adj* **en·dear·ment** *n* loving word; tender affection

en·deav·or [en-DEV-ər] *vi* try, strive after ▷ *n* attempt, effort

en·dem·ic [en-DEM-ik] *adj* found only among a particular people or in a particular place ▷ *n* endemic disease

en·dive [EN-div] *n* curly-leaved plant used in salad

endo- comb form within: endocrine

en·do·car·di·um [en-doh-KAHR-dee-əm] *n* lining membrane of the heart **en·do·car·di·tis** [-dī-tis] *n* inflammation of this

en·do·crine [EN-də-krin] *adj* of those glands (thyroid, pituitary, etc) that secrete hormones directly into bloodstream **en·do·cri·nol·o·gy** *n* science dealing with endocrine glands

en·dorse [en-DORS] *vt* **-dorsed, -dors·ing** sanction; confirm; write (esp sign name) on back of **en·dorse·ment** *n*

en·dow *vt* provide permanent income for; furnish (with) **en·dow·ment** *n*

en·dure [en-DUUR] *v* **-dured, -dur·ing** undergo; tolerate, bear; last **en·dur·a·ble** *adj* **en·dur·ance** *n* act or power of enduring

en·e·ma [EN-ə-mə] *n* medicine, liquid injected into rectum

en·e·my [EN-ə-mee] *n, pl* **-mies**

hostile person; opponent; armed foe; hostile force

en·er·gy [EN-ər-jee] *n, pl* **-gies** vigor, force, activity; source(s) of power, as oil, coal, etc; capacity of machine, battery, etc for work or output of power **en·er·get'ic** *adj* **en'er·gize** [-gized, -giz·ing] *vt* give vigor to

en·er·vate [EN-ər-vayt] *vt* **-vat·ed, -vat·ing** weaken, deprive of vigor enervate **en·er·va'tion** *n* lassitude, weakness

en·fee·ble [en-FEE-bəl] *vt* **-bled, -bling** weaken, debilitate

en·fi·lade [EN-fi-layd] *n* fire from artillery, sweeping line from end to end

en·force [en-FORS] *vt* compel obedience to; impose (action) upon; drive home **en·force'a·ble** *adj*

en·fran·chise [en-FRAN-chiz] *vt* **-chised, -chis·ing** give right of voting to; give legislative representation to; set free **en·fran'chise·ment** [-chiz-mənt] *n*

en·gage [en-GAYJ] *v* **-gaged, -gag·ing** *⊳ vt* employ; reserve, hire; bind by contract or promise; order; pledge oneself; betroth; undertake; attract; occupy; bring into conflict; interlock *⊳ vi* employ oneself (in); promise; begin to fight **en·gaged'** *adj* betrothed; in use; occupied, busy **en·gage'ment** *n* **engaging** *adj* charming

en·gen·der [en-JEN-dər] *vt* give rise to; beget; rouse

en·gine [EN-jin] *n* any machine to convert energy into mechanical work, as steam or gasoline engine; railroad locomotive; fire engine **en·gi·neer'** *n* one who is in charge of engines, machinery, etc or construction work (eg roads, bridges); one who originates,

organizes something; one trained and skilled in engineering *⊳ vt* construct as engineer; contrive **en·gi·neer'ing** *n*

Eng·lish [ING-glish] *n* the language of the US, Britain, most parts of the British Commonwealth and certain other countries; the people of England *⊳ adj* relating to England

engrain *vt* see **INGRAIN**

en·grave [en-GRAYV] *vt* **-graved, -grav·ing** cut in lines on metal for printing; carve, incise; impress deeply **en·grav'er** *n* **en·grav'ing** *n* copy of picture printed from engraved plate

en·gross [en-GROHS] *vt* absorb (attention); occupy wholly; write out in large letters or in legal form; monopolize

en·gulf' *vt* swallow up

en·hance [en-HANS] *vt* **-hanced, -hanc·ing** heighten, intensify, increase value or attractiveness **en·hance'ment** *n*

e·nig·ma [ə-NIG-mə] *n, pl* **-mas** puzzling thing or person; riddle **en·ig·mat'ic** *adj*

en·join [en-JOIN] *vt* command; impose, prescribe

en·joy [en-JOI] *vt* delight in; take pleasure in; have use or benefit of *⊳ v refl* be happy **en·joy'a·ble** *adj*

en·large [en-LAHRJ] *v* **-larged, -larg·ing** *⊳ vt* make bigger; reproduce on larger scale, as photograph *⊳ vi* grow bigger; talk, write about, in greater detail **en·large'a·ble** *adj* **en·large'ment** *n* **en·larg'er** *n* optical instrument for enlarging photographs

en·light·en [en-LI-tən] *vt* give information to; instruct, inform, shed light on **en·light'en·ment** *n*

en·list' *v* engage as soldier or helper

en·list·ment [en-Lĭ-vən] vt brighten,
make more lively, animate

en masse [ahn MAS] adv in a
group, body; all together

en·mesh vt entangle

en·mi·ty [EN-mi-tee] n, pl -ties ill
will, hostility

en·no·ble [en-NOH-bəl] vt
-**bled**, -**bling** make noble, elevate
en·no·ble·ment n

en·nui [ahn-WEE] n boredom

e·nor·mous [i-NOR-məs] adj
very big, vast **e·nor·mi·ty** n a
gross offense; great wickedness; inf
great size

e·nough [i-NUF] adj as much or
as many as need be; sufficient ▷ n
sufficient quantity ▷ adv (just)
sufficiently

enquire see INQUIRE

en·rap·ture [en-RAP-chər] vt
-**tured**, -**tur·ing** delight excessively;
charm

en·rich vt make rich; add to
en·rich·ment n

en·roll [en-ROHL] vt write name
of on roll or list; engage, enlist, take
in as member; enter, record ▷ vi
become member **en·roll·ment** n

en route [ahn ROOT] Fron the way

en·sconce [en-SKONS] vt
-**sconced**, -**sconc·ing** place snugly;
establish in safety

en·sem·ble [ahn-SAHM-bəl] n
whole; all parts taken together;
woman's complete outfit; company
of actors, dancers, etc; music group
of soloists performing together;
music concerted passage; general
effect

en·shrine [en-SHRĪN] vt -**shrined**,
-**shrin·ing** set in shrine, preserve
with great care and sacred affection

en·sign [EN-sin] n naval or military
flag; badge; navy, coast guard lowest
commissioned officer

ensilage see SILAGE

en·slave [en-SLAYV] vt -**slaved**,
-**slav·ing** make into slave
en·slave·ment n bondage

en·snare [en-SNAIR] vt -**snared**,
-**snar·ing** capture in snare or trap;
trick into false position; entangle

en·sue [en-SOO] vi -**sued**, -**su·ing**
follow, happen after

en·sure [en-SHUUR] vt -**sured**,
-**sur·ing** make safe or sure; make
certain to happen; secure

en·tail [en-TAYL] vt involve as
result, necessitate; law restrict
ownership of property to designated
line of heirs **en·tail'ment** n

en·tan·gle [en-TANG-gəl] vt
-**gled**, -**gling** ensnare, perplex
en·tan·gle·ment n

en·tente [ahn-TAHNT] n friendly
understanding between nations

en·ter [EN-tər] vt go, come into;
penetrate; join; write in, register ▷ vi
go, come in, join, begin **en'trance**
[-trăns] n going, coming in; door,
passage to enter; right to enter; fee
paid for this **en'trant** n one who
enters, esp contest **en'try** n, pl -**tries**
entrance; entering; item entered, eg
in account, list

en·ter·ic [en-TER-ik] adj of
or relating to the intestines
en·ter·i'tis n inflammation of
intestines

en·ter·prise [EN-tər-prīz] n bold
or difficult undertaking; bold spirit;
force of character in launching out;
business, company **en'ter·pris·ing**
adj

en·ter·tain [en-tər-TAYN] vt
amuse, divert; receive as guest;
maintain; consider favorable, take
into consideration **en·ter·tain'er** n

en·thrall [en-THRAWL] vt
captivate, thrill, hold spellbound

en·thu·si·asm [en-THOO-zee-az-əm] *n* ardent eagerness, zeal **en·thuse** *v* (cause to) show enthusiasm **en·thu·si·ast** *n* ardent supporter of **en·thu·si·as·tic** *adj*

en·tice [en-TĪS] *vt* **-ticed, -tic·ing** allure, attract; inveigle, tempt **en·tic·ing** *adj* alluring

en·tire [en-TĪR] *adj* whole, complete, unbroken **en·tire·ly** *adv* **en·tire·ty** *n, pl* **-ties**

en·ti·tle [en-TĪ-təl] *vt* **-tled, -tling** give claim to; qualify; give title to

en·ti·ty [EN-ti-tee] *n, pl* **-ties** thing's being or existence; reality; thing having real existence

en·to·mol·o·gy [en-tə-MOL-ə-jee] *n* study of insects **en·to·mol·o·gist** *n*

en·tou·rage [ahn-tuu-RAHZH] *n* associates, retinue; surroundings

en·trails [EN-traylz] *pl n* bowels, intestines; inner parts

en·trance¹ *n* see ENTER

en·trance² [en-TRANS] *vt* **-tranced, -tranc·ing** delight; throw into a trance

en·treat [en-TREET] *vt* ask earnestly; beg, implore **en·treat·y** *n, pl* **-treat·ies** earnest request

en·trée [AHN-tray] *n* main course of meal; right of access, admission

en·trench *vt* establish in fortified position with trenches; establish firmly

en·tre·pre·neur [ahn-trə-prə-NUR] *n* person who attempts to profit by risk and initiative

en·tro·py [EN-trə-pee] *n* unavailability of the heat energy of a system for mechanical work; measurement of

en·trust' *vt* commit, charge with; put into care or protection of

en·twine [en-TWĪN] *vt* **-twined, -twin·ing** interweave; wreathe with; embrace

e·nu·mer·ate [i-NOO-mə-rayt] *vt* **-at·ed, -at·ing** mention one by one; count **e·nu·mer·a·tion** *n* **e·nu·mer·a·tor** *n*

e·nun·ci·ate [i-NUN-see-ayt] *vt* **-at·ed, -at·ing** state clearly; proclaim; pronounce **e·nun·ci·a·tion** *n*

en·vel·op [en-VEL-əp] *vt* wrap up, enclose, surround; encircle **en·vel·op·ment** *n*

en·ve·lope [EN-və-lohp] *n* folded, gummed cover of letter; covering, wrapper

en·ven·om [en-VEN-əm] *vt* put poison, venom in; embitter

en·vi·ron [en-VĪ-rən] *vt* surround **en·vi·ron·ment** *n* surroundings; conditions of life or growth **en·vi·ron·men·tal** *adj* **en·vi·ron·men·tal·ist** *n* ecologist **en·vi·rons** *pl n* districts around (town, etc), outskirts

en·vis·age [en-VIZ-ij] *vt* **-aged, -ag·ing** conceive of as possibility; visualize

en·voy [EN-voi] *n* messenger, representative; diplomatic agent of rank below ambassador

en·vy [EN-vee] *n, pl* **-vies** bitter contemplation of another's good fortune; object of this feeling ▷ *vt* **-vied, -vy·ing** grudge another's good fortune, success or qualities; feel envy of **en·vi·a·ble** *adj* arousing envy **en·vi·ous** *adj* full of envy

en·zyme [EN-zim] *n* any of group of complex proteins produced by living cells and acting as catalysts in biochemical reactions

e·on [EE-ən] *n* age, very long period of time

ep·au·lette [EP-ə-let] *n* shoulder ornament on uniform

Eph. Ephesians

e·phem·er·al [i-FEM-ər-əl] *adj* short-lived, transient **e·phem'er·a** [i-FEM-ər-ə] *pl n* items designed to last only for a short time, such as programmes or posters

epi-, eph- (or before a vowel) **ep-** *prefix* upon, during: *epitaph; ephemeral; epoch*

ep·ic [EP-ik] *n* long poem or story telling of achievements of hero or heroes; film, etc about heroic deeds ▷ *adj* of, like, an epic; impressive, grand

ep·i·cene [EP-i-seen] *adj* common to both sexes; effeminate; weak ▷ *n* epicene person or thing

ep·i·cen·ter [EP-i-sen-tər] *n* focus of earthquake

ep·i·cure [EP-i-kyuur] *n* one delighting in eating and drinking **ep·i·cu·re'an** *adj* of Epicurus, who taught that pleasure, in the shape of practice of virtue, was highest good; given to refined sensuous enjoyment ▷ *n* such person or philosopher **ep·i·cu·re'an·ism** *n*

ep·i·dem·ic [ep-i-DEM-ik] *adj* (esp of disease) prevalent and spreading rapidly; widespread ▷ *n*

ep·i·der·mis [EP-i-DUR-mis] *n* outer skin

ep·i·du·ral [ep-i-DUUR-əl] *n, adj* (of) spinal anesthetic used esp for relief of pain during childbirth

ep·i·glot·tis [-pl·tis·es] cartilage that covers opening of larynx in swallowing **ep·i·glot'tal** [-GLOT-əl] *adj*

ep·i·gone [EP-i-gohn] *n* imitative follower

ep·i·gram *n* concise, witty poem or saying **ep·i·gram·mat'ic** [-grə-MAT-ik] *adj* **ep·i·gram'ma·tist** [-GRAM-ə-tist] *n*

ep·i·graph [EP-i-graf] *n* inscription

ep·i·lep·sy [EP-ə-lep-see] *n* disorder of nervous system causing convulsions **ep·i·lep'tic** *n* sufferer from this ▷ *adj* of, subject to, this

ep·i·logue [EP-ə-lawg] *n* short speech or poem at end, esp of play

E·piph·a·ny [i-PIF-ə-nee] *n, pl* **-nies** festival of the announcement of Christ to the Magi, celebrated January 6; **(e-)** sudden intuitive perception or insight

e·pis·co·pal [i-PIS-kə-pəl] *adj* of bishop; ruled by bishops **e·pis·co·pa·cy** [-pə-see] *n* government by body of bishops **E·pis·co·pa'li·an** [-PAYL-yən] *adj, n* (member, adherent) of Episcopalian church **e·pis'co·pate** [-kə-pit] *n* bishop's office, see, or duration of office; body of bishops

ep·i·sode [EP-ə-sohd] *n* incident; section of (serialized) book, TV program, etc **ep·i·sod'ic** [-SOD-ik] *adj*

e·pis·te·mol·o·gy [i-pis-tə-MOL-ə-jee] *n* study of source, nature and limitations of knowledge **e·pis·te·mo·log'i·cal** *adj*

e·pis·tle [i-PIS-əl] *n* letter, esp of apostle; poem in letter form **e·pis'to·lar·y** [-tə-ler-ee] *adj*

ep·i·taph [EP-i-taf] *n* memorial inscription on tomb

ep·i·thet [EP-ə-thet] *n* additional, descriptive word or name

e·pit·o·me [i-PIT-ə-mee] *n* embodiment, typical example; summary **e·pit'o·mize** [-ə-miz] *vt* **-mized, -miz·ing** typify

ep·och [EP-ək] *n* beginning of period; period, era, esp one of notable events **ep'o·chal** [-ə-kəl] *adj*

eq·ua·ble [EK-wə-bəl] *adj* even-tempered, placid; uniform, not easily disturbed **eq'ua·bly** *adv* **eq·ua·bil'i·ty** *n*

e·qual [EE-kwəl] *adj* the same in number, size, merit, etc; identical; fit or qualified; evenly balanced ▷ *n* one equal to another ▷ *vt* be equal to **e·qual·i·ty** [i-KWOL-i-tee] *n, pl* **-ties** state of being equal; uniformity

e·qual·ize *v* **-ized, -iz·ing** make, become, equal **e·qual·ly** *adv* **equal opportunity** nondiscrimination as to sex, race, etc in employment, pay, etc

e·qua·nim·i·ty [ee-kwə-NIM-i-tee] *n* calmness, composure, steadiness

e·quate [i-KWAYT] *vt* **-quat·ed, -quat·ing** make equal; bring to a common standard **e·qua·tion** [-zhən] *n* equating of two mathematical expressions; balancing

e·qua·tor [i-KWAY-tər] *n* imaginary circle around Earth equidistant from the poles **e·qua·to·ri·al** [ee-kwə-TOR-ee-əl] *adj*

e·ques·tri·an [i-KWES-tree-ən] *adj* of, skilled in, horseback riding; mounted on horse ▷ *n* rider

equi- *comb form* equal, at equal: equidistant

e·qui·an·gu·lar [ee-kwee-ANG-gyə-lər] *adj* having equal angles **e·qui·lat·er·al** [ee-kwə-LAT-ər-əl] *adj* having equal sides **e·qui·lib·ri·um** [ee-kwə-LIB-ree-əm] *n* state of steadiness, equipoise or stability

e·quine [EE-kwīn] *adj* of, like a horse

e·qui·nox [EE-kwə-noks] *n* time when sun crosses equator and day and night are equal; either point at which sun crosses equator

e·quip [i-KWIP] *vt* **-quipped, -quip·ping** supply, fit out, array **e·quip·ment** *n*

eq·ui·poise [EK-wə-poiz] *n* perfect balance; counterpoise; equanimity

eq·ui·ty [EK-wə-tee] *n, pl* **-ties** fairness; use of principles of justice to supplement law; system of law so made **eq·ui·ta·ble** *adj* fair, reasonable, just

e·quiv·a·lent [i-KWIV-ə-lənt] *adj* equal in value; having the same meaning or result; tantamount; corresponding **e·quiv·a·lence** *n* **e·quiv·a·len·cy** *n*

e·quiv·o·cal [i-KWIV-ə-kəl] *adj* of double or doubtful meaning; questionable; liable to suspicion **e·quiv·o·cate** *vi* **-cat·ed, -cat·ing** use equivocal words to mislead **e·quiv·o·ca·tion** *n*

Er *chemistry* erbium

e·ra [EER-ə] *n* system of time in which years are numbered from particular event; time of the event; memorable date, period

e·rad·i·cate [i-RAD-i-kayt] *vt* **-cat·ed, -cat·ing** wipe out, exterminate; root out **e·rad·i·ca·ble** *adj* **e·rad·i·ca·tion** *n*

e·rase [i-RAYS] *vt* **-rased, -ras·ing** rub out; remove, eg recording from magnetic tape **e·ra·ser** *n* **e·ra·sure** [-shər] *n*

ere [air] *prep, conj poetry* before; sooner than

e·rect [i-REKT] *adj* upright ▷ *vt* set up; build **e·rec·tile** [-tl] *adj* **e·rec·tion** *n* esp an erect penis **e·rec·tor** *n*

erg [urg] *n* cgs unit of work or energy

er·go·nom·ics [ur-gə-NOM-iks] *n* study of relationship between workers and their environment

er·got [UR-gət] *n* disease of grain; diseased seed used as drug

er·got·ism n disease caused by eating ergot-infested grain

er·mine [UR-min] n weasel in northern regions, esp in winter; its white winter fur

e·rode [i-ROHD] vt **-rod·ed, -rod·ing** wear away; eat into **e·ro·sion** [-zhən] n

e·rog·e·nous [i-ROJ-ə-nəs] adj sensitive to sexual stimulation

e·rot·ic [i-ROT-ik] adj relating to, or treating of, sexual pleasure **e·rot·i·ca** [-ə-kə] n sexual literature or art **e·rot·i·cism** [-ə-sizm] n

err [er] vi make mistakes; be wrong; sin **er·rat·ic** [i-RAT-ik] adj irregular in movement, conduct, etc **er·rat·i·cal·ly** adv **er·ra·tum** [i-RAH-təm] n, pl **-ta** [-tə] printing mistake noted for correction **er·ro·ne·ous** [i-ROH-nee-əs] adj mistaken, wrong **er·ror** n mistake; wrong opinion; sin

er·rand [ER-ənd] n short journey for simple business; the business, mission of messenger; purpose

er·rant [ER-ənt] adj wandering in search of adventure; erring **er·ran·cy** n, pl **-cies** erring state or conduct **er·rant·ry** n, pl **-ries** state or conduct of knight errant

erst·while [URST-hwil] adj of times past, former

er·u·dite [ER-yə-dīt] adj learned **er·u·di·tion** [-DISH-ən] n learning

e·rupt [i-RUPT] vi burst out **e·rup·tion** n bursting out, esp volcanic outbreak; rash on the skin **er·y·sip·e·las** [er-ə-SIP-ə-ləs] n acute skin infection

Es chemistry einsteinium

es·ca·late [ES-kə-layt] v **-lat·ed, -lat·ing** increase, be increased, in extent, intensity, etc

es·ca·la·tor [ES-kə-lay-tər] n moving staircase

es·cape [i-SKAYP] v **-caped, -cap·ing** ▷ vi get free; get off safely; go unpunished; find way out ▷ vt elude; be forgotten by ▷ n escaping

es·ca·pade n wild (mischievous) adventure **es·cap·ism** [-KAYP-izm] n taking refuge in fantasy to avoid facing disagreeable facts

es·carp·ment [i-SKAHRP-mənt] n steep hillside

es·cha·tol·o·gy [es-kə-TOL-ə-jee] n study of death, judgment and last things **es·cha·to·log·i·cal** adj

es·chew [es-CHOO] vt avoid, abstain from, shun

es·cort [ES-kort] n armed guard for traveler, etc; person or persons accompanying another **es·cort'** vt

es·cri·toire [es-kri-TWAHR] n type of writing desk

es·cut·cheon [i-SKUCH-ən] n shield with coat of arms; ornamental plate around keyhole, etc

Es·ki·mo [ES-kə-moh] n, pl **-mos** member of the aboriginal race inhabiting N Canada, Greenland, Alaska, and E Siberia; their language. Note that many of the peoples traditionally called **Eskimos** prefer to call themselves **Inuit**

e·soph·a·gus [i-SOF-ə-gəs] n, pl **-gi** [-ji] canal from mouth to stomach; gullet **e·soph·a·ge·al** [-JEE-əl] adj

es·o·ter·ic [es-ə-TER-ik] adj abstruse, obscure; secret; restricted to initiates

ESP extrasensory perception

es·pal·ier [i-SPAL-yər] n shrub, (fruit) tree trained to grow flat, as against wall, etc; trellis for this

es·pe·cial [i-SPESH-əl] adj preeminent, more than ordinary; particular **es·pe·cial·ly** adv

Es·pe·ran·to [es-pə-RAHN-toh]

n artificial language designed for universal use

es·pi·o·nage [ES-pee-ə-nahzh] *n* spying; use of secret agents

es·pla·nade [ES-plə-nahd] *n* level space, esp one used as public promenade

es·pouse [i-SPOWZ] *vt* -poused, -pous·ing support, embrace (cause, etc); marry **es·pous'al** *n*

es·pres·so [e-SPRES-oh] *n* strong coffee made by forcing steam through ground coffee beans; cup of espresso

es·prit [e-SPREE] *n* spirit; animation **esprit de corps** [də kor] attachment, loyalty to the society, etc, one belongs to

es·py [i-SPI] *vt* -pied, -py·ing catch sight of

es·quire [ES-kwir] *n* gentleman's courtesy title used on letters; formerly, a squire

es·say *n* prose composition; short treatise; attempt **es·say'** *vt* -sayed, -say·ing try, attempt; test **es'say·ist** *n*

es·sence [ES-əns] *n* all that makes thing what it is; existence, being; entity, reality; extract got by distillation **es·sen·tial** [ə-SEN-shəl] *adj* necessary, indispensable; inherent; of, constituting essence of thing ▷ *n* indispensable element; chief point

es·tab·lish [i-STAB-lish] *vt* make secure; set up; settle; prove **es·tab'lish·ment** *n* establishing; permanent organized body; place of business together with its employees, equipment, etc; household; public institution **established church** church officially recognized as national institution **the Establishment** *n* group, class of people holding authority within a profession, society, etc

es·tate [i-STAYT] *n* landed property; person's property; deceased person's property; class as part of nation; rank, state, condition of life

es·teem [i-STEEM] *vt* think highly of; consider ▷ *n* favorable opinion, regard, respect

es·ter [ES-tər] *n* chemistry organic compound produced by reaction between acid and alcohol

es·ti·mate [ES-tə-mayt] *vt* -mat·ed, -mat·ing form approximate idea of (amounts, measurements, etc); form opinion of; quote probable price for ▷ *n* [-mit] approximate judgment of amounts, etc; amount, etc, arrived at; opinion; price quoted by contractor **es'ti·ma·ble** *adj* worthy of regard **es·ti·ma'tion** *n* opinion, judgment, esteem

es·ti·vate [ES-tə-vayt] *vi* -vat·ed, -vat·ing spend the summer

es·trange [i-STRAYNJ] *vt* -tranged, -trang·ing lose affection of; alienate **es·trange'ment** *n*

es·tro·gen [ES-trə-jən] *n* hormone in females esp controlling changes, cycles, in reproductive organs **es·tro·gen·ic** *adj*

es·tu·ar·y [ES-choo-er-ee] *n, pl* -ar·ies tidal mouth of river, inlet

e-tail *n* selling of goods via the Internet

etc et cetera

et cet·er·a [et SET-ər-ə] and the rest, and others; or the like **etceteras** *pl n* miscellaneous extra things or people

etch [ech] *vt* make engraving by eating away surface of metal plate with acids, etc; imprint vividly **etch'er** *n* **etch'ing** *n*

e·ter·nal [i-TUR-nəl] *adj* without

beginning or end; everlasting; changeless **e·ter'ni·ty** n, pl **-ties**

e·ther [EE-thər] n colorless volatile liquid used as anesthetic; intangible fluid formerly supposed to fill all space; the clear sky, region above clouds **e·the·re·al** [i-THEER-ee-əl] adj light, airy; heavenly, spirit-like

eth·i·cal [ETH-i-kəl] adj relating to morals **eth'i·cal·ly** adv **eth'ics** n science of morals; moral principles, rules of conduct

eth·nic [ETH-nik] adj of race or relating to classification of humans into social, cultural, etc, groups **eth·nog'ra·phy** [-NOG-rə-fee] n description of human races **eth·nol'o·gy** n study of human races ethnic cleansing expulsion or extermination of other ethnic groups by the dominant ethnic group in an area

e·thos [EE-thos] n distinctive character, spirit, etc of people, culture, etc

eth·yl [ETH-əl] n of, consisting of, or containing the hydrocarbon group C_2H_5 **eth'y·lene** [-leen] n poisonous gas used as anesthetic and fuel

e·ti·ol·o·gy [ee-tee-OL-ə-jee] n, pl **-gies** study of causes, esp inquiry into origin of disease **e·ti·o·log'i·cal** adj

et·i·quette [ET-i-kit] n conventional code of conduct or behavior

é·tude [AY-tood] n short musical composition, study, intended often as technical exercise

et·y·mol·o·gy [et-ə-MOL-ə-jee] n tracing, account, of formation of word's origin, development; study of this **et'y·mo·log'i·cal** adj **et·y·mol'o·gist** n

eu-, ev- comb form well: eugenic;

euphony; evangelist

Eu chemistry europium

eu·ca·lyp·tus [yoo-kə-LIP-təs] n mostly Aust genus of tree, the gum tree, yielding timber and oil, used medicinally from leaves

Eu·cha·rist [YOO-kə-rist] n Christian sacrament of the Lord's Supper; the consecrated elements; **(e-)** thanksgiving

eu·gen·ic [yoo-JEN-ik] adj relating to, or tending toward, production of fine offspring **eu·gen'ics** n this science

eu·lo·gy [YOO-lə-jee] n, pl **-gies** speech or writing in praise of person esp dead person; praise **eu'lo·gist** n **eu'lo·gize** [-jiz] vt **-gized, -giz·ing**

eu·nuch [YOO-nək] n castrated man, esp formerly one employed in harem

eu·phe·mism [YOO-fə-miz-əm] n substitution of mild term for offensive or hurtful one; instance of this **eu·phe·mis'tic** adj **eu·phe·mis'ti·cal·ly** adv

eu·pho·ny [YOO-fə-nee] n, pl **-nies** pleasantness of sound **eu·phon'ic** [-FON-ik] adj **eu·pho'ni·ous** [-FOH-nee-əs] adj pleasing to ear

eu·pho·ri·a [yoo-FOR-ee-ə] n sense of well-being or elation **eu·phor'ic** adj

eu·phu·ism [YOO-fyoo-iz-əm] n affected high-flown manner of writing, esp in imitation of Lyly's Euphues (1580) **eu·phu·is'tic** adj

Eur·a·sian [yuu-RAY-zhən] adj of mixed European and Asiatic descent; of Europe and Asia ▷ n one of this people

eu·re·ka [yuu-REE-kə] interj exclamation of triumph at finding something

eu·ro n, pl **eu·ros** unit of the single currency of the European Union

Euro- *comb form* Europe or European: Euroland

Eu·ro·land *n* (also **Eurozone**) the countries within the European Union that have adopted the euro

Eu·ro·pe·an [yuur-ə-PEE-ən] *n, adj* (native) of Europe **European Union** (also **EU**) economic and political association of a number of European nations

Eu·sta·chian tube [yoo-STAY-shən] *n* passage leading from pharynx to middle ear

eu·tha·na·sia [yoo-thə-NAY-zhə] *n* gentle, painless death; putting to death in this way, esp to relieve suffering

e·vac·u·ate [i-VAK-yoo-ayt] *vt* **-at·ed, -at·ing** empty; withdraw from; discharge **e·vac·u·a'tion** *n* **e·vac·u·ee'** *n* person moved from dangerous area esp in time of war

e·vade [i-VAYD] *vt* **-vad·ed, -vad·ing** avoid, escape from; elude **e·va'sion** [-zhən] *n* subterfuge; excuse; equivocation **e·va'sive** *adj* elusive, not straightforward

e·val·u·ate [i-VAL-yoo-ayt] *vt* **-at·ed, -at·ing** find or judge value of **e·val·u·a'tion** *n*

ev·a·nesce [ev-ə-NES] *vi* **-nesced, -nesc·ing** fade away **ev·a·nes'cence** *n* **ev·a·nes'cent** *adj* fleeting, transient

e·van·gel·i·cal [ee-van-JEL-i-kəl] *adj* of, or according to, gospel teaching; of Protestant sect that stresses salvation by faith ▷ *n* member of evangelical sect **e·van'ge·lism** *n* **e·van'ge·list** *n* writer of one of the four gospels; ardent, zealous preacher of the gospel; revivalist **e·van'ge·lize** *vt* **-lized, -liz·ing** preach gospel to; convert

e·vap·o·rate [i-VAP-ə-rayt] *v*

-rat·ed, -rat·ing ▷ *vi* turn into, pass off in, vapor ▷ *vt* turn into vapor **e·vap·o·ra'tion** *n*

evasion see **EVADE**

eve [eev] *n* evening before (holiday, etc); time just before (event, etc)

e·ven [EE-vən] *adj* flat, smooth; uniform in quality, equal in amount, balanced; divisible by two; impartial ▷ *vt* make even; smooth; equalize ▷ *adv* equally; simply; notwithstanding; (used to express emphasis)

eve·ning [EEV-ning] *n* the close of day or early part of night; decline, end

e·vent [i-VENT] *n* happening; notable occurrence; issue, result; any one contest in series in sports program **e·vent'ful** *adj* full of exciting events **e·ven'tu·al** [-choo-əl] *adj* resulting in the end; ultimate; final **e·ven·tu·al'i·ty** [-AL-i-tee] *n* possible event **e·ven'tu·ate** *vi* **-at·ed, -at·ing** turn out; happen; end

ev·er [EV-ər] *adv* always; constantly; at any time **ev'er·green** *n, adj* (tree or shrub) bearing foliage throughout year **ev·er·more'** *adv* **ev'er·net** *n* hypothetical form of the Internet that is continuously accessible

eve·ry [EV-ree] *adj* each of all; all possible **ev'ery·body** *pron* **ev'ery·day** *adj* usual, ordinary **ev'ery·one** *pron* **ev'ery·thing** *pron*, *n* **ev'ery·where** *adv* in all places

e·vict [i-VIKT] *vt* expel by legal process, turn out **e·vic'tion** [-shən] *n*

ev·i·dent [EV-i-dənt] *adj* plain, obvious **ev'i·dence** *n* ground of belief; sign, indication; testimony ▷ *vt* **-denced, -denc·ing** indicate, prove **ev·i·den'tial** *adj* **ev'i·dent·ly** *adv* in evidence conspicuous

e·vil [EE-vəl] *adj* bad, harmful ▷ *n* what is bad or harmful; sin **e·vil·ly** *adv* **e·vil·do·er** *n* sinner

e·vince [i-VINS] *vt* -**vinced,** -**vinc·ing** show, indicate

e·voke [i-VOHK] *vt* -**voked,** -**vok·ing** draw forth; call to mind **ev·o·ca·tion** [ev-ə-KAY-shən] *n* **e·voc·a·tive** [i-VOK-ə-tiv] *adj*

e·volve [i-VOLV] *v* -**volved,** -**volv·ing** develop or cause to develop gradually ▷ *vi* undergo slow changes in process of growth **ev·o·lu·tion** [ev-ə-LOO-shən] *n* evolving; development of species from earlier forms **ev·o·lu·tion·ar·y** *adj* **ev·o·lu·tion·ist** *n* one who supports theory of evolution

ewe [yoo] *n* female sheep

ew·er [YOO-ər] *n* pitcher with wide spout

Ex. Exodus

ex-, e-, ef- *prefix* out from, from, out of, formerly: *exclaim; evade; effusive; exodus*

ex·ac·er·bate [ig-ZAS-ər-bayt] *vt* -**bat·ed,** -**bat·ing** aggravate, embitter, make worse **ex·ac·er·ba·tion** *n*

ex·act [ig-ZAKT] *adj* precise, accurate, strictly correct ▷ *vt* demand, extort; insist upon; enforce **ex·act·ing** *adj* making rigorous or excessive demands **ex·ac·tion** *n* act of exacting; that which is exacted, as excessive work, etc; oppressive demand **ex·act·ly** *adv* **ex·act·ness** *n* accuracy; precision

ex·ag·ger·ate [ig-ZAJ-ə-rayt] *vt* -**at·ed,** -**at·ing** magnify beyond truth, overstate; enlarge; overestimate **ex·ag·ger·a·tion** *n*

ex·alt [ig-ZAWLT] *vt* raise up; praise; make noble, dignify

ex·al·ta·tion [eg-zawl-TAY-shən] *n* an exalting; elevation in rank, dignity or position; rapture

ex·am·ine [ig-ZAM-in] *vt* -**ined,** -**in·ing** investigate; look at closely; ask questions of; test knowledge or proficiency of; inquire into **ex·am·i·na·tion** *n* **ex·am·in·er** *n*

ex·am·ple [ig-ZAM-pəl] *n* thing illustrating general rule; specimen; model; warning, precedent, instance

ex·as·per·ate [ig-ZAS-pə-rayt] *vt* -**at·ed,** -**at·ing** irritate, enrage; intensify, make worse **ex·as·per·a·tion** *n*

ex·ca·vate [EKS-kə-vayt] *vt* -**vat·ed,** -**vat·ing** hollow out; make hole by digging; unearth **ex·ca·va·tion** *n*

ex·ceed [ik-SEED] *vt* be greater than; do more than authorized; go beyond; surpass **ex·ceed·ing·ly** *adv* very; greatly

ex·cel [ik-SEL] *v* -**celled,** -**cel·ling** ▷ *vt* surpass, be better than ▷ *vi* be very good, preeminent **ex·cel·lence** *n* **ex·cel·len·cy** *n* title borne by certain high officials **ex·cel·lent** *adj* very good

ex·cept [ik-SEPT] *prep* not including; but ▷ *vt* leave or take out; exclude **ex·cept·ing** *prep* not including **ex·cep·tion** *n* thing excepted, not included in a rule; objection **ex·cep·tion·a·ble** *adj* open to objection **ex·cep·tion·al** *adj* not ordinary, esp much above average

ex·cerpt [EK-surpt] *n* quoted or extracted passage from book, etc **ex·cerpt** [*vt* extract, quote (passage from book, etc)

ex·cess [EK-ses] *n* an exceeding; amount by which things exceeds; too great amount; intemperance or immoderate conduct **ex·ces·sive**

[-siv] *adj*

ex·change [iks-CHAYNJ] *vt*
-changed, -chang·ing give
(something) in return for something
else; barter ▷ *n* giving one thing
and receiving another; giving or
receiving currency of one country
for that of another; thing given for
another; building where merchants,
dealers meet for business; central
telephone office **ex·change'a·ble**
adj

ex·cheq·uer [eks-CHEK-ər] *n*
treasury, eg of a government; *inf*
personal funds

ex·cise[1] [EK-siz] *n* tax levied on
domestic goods during manufacture
or before sale

ex·cise[2] [ik-SĪZ] *vt* **-cised, -cis·ing**
cut out, cut away **ex·ci·sion** [ek-
SIZH-ən] *n*

ex·cite [ik-SĪT] *vt* **-cit·ed, -cit·ing**
arouse to strong emotion, stimulate;
rouse up, set in motion; *electricity*
energize to produce electric activity
or a magnetic field **ex·cit·a·ble**
adj **ex·ci·ta·tion** [ek-si-TAY-shàn]
n **ex·cite'ment** *n* **ex·cit'ing** *adj*
thrilling; rousing to action

ex·claim [ik-SKLAYM] *v* speak
suddenly, cry out **ex·cla·ma·tion**
[ek-sklə-MAY-shàn] *n*
ex·clam·a·to·ry [ik-SKLAM-ə-
tor-ee] *adj*

ex·clude [ik-SKLOOD] *vt* **-clud·ed,**
-clud·ing shut out; debar from;
reject, not consider **ex·clu·sion**
[-zhàn] *n* **ex·clu·sive** *adj* excluding;
inclined to keep out (from society,
etc); sole, only; select ▷ *n* something
exclusive, esp story appearing only in
one newspaper **ex·clu'sive·ly** *adv*

ex·com·mu·ni·cate [eks-kə-
MYOO-ni-kayt] *vt* **-cat·ed, -cat·ing**
to cut off from the sacraments of the
Church **ex·com·mu·ni·ca'tion** *n*

ex·cre·ment [EKS-krə-mənt]
n waste matter from body, esp
from bowels; dung **ex·cre·ta** [ik-
SKREE-tə] *n* excrement **ex·crete'**
vi **-cret·ed, -cret·ing** discharge
from the system **ex·cre'tion** *n*
ex'cre·to·ry *adj*

ex·cres·cent [ik-SKRES-ənt]
adj growing out of; redundant
ex·cres'cence *n* unnatural
outgrowth

ex·cru·ci·ate [ik-SKROO-shee-
ayt] *vt* **-at·ed, -at·ing** torment
acutely, torture in body or mind

ex·cul·pate [EK-skul-payt]
vt **-pat·ed, -pat·ing** free from
blame, acquit **ex·cul·pa'tion** *n*
ex·cul'pa·to·ry *adj*

ex·cur·sion [ik-SKUR-zhàn] *n*
journey, ramble, trip for pleasure;
digression

ex·cuse [ik-SKYOOZ] *vt* **-cused,**
-cus·ing forgive, overlook; try to
clear from blame; gain exemption;
set free, remit ▷ *n* [-SKYOOS] that
which serves to excuse; apology
ex·cus·a·ble [ik-SKYOO-zə-bəl] *adj*

ex·e·cra·ble [EK-si-krə-bəl] *adj*
abominable, hatefully bad

ex·e·cute [EK-si-kyoot] *vt*
-cut·ed, -cut·ing inflict capital
punishment on, kill; carry out,
perform; make, produce; sign
(document) **ex·e·cu'tion** *n*
ex·e·cu'tion·er *n* one employed
to execute criminals **ex·ec·u·tive**
n person in administrative position;
executive body; executive branch
of government ▷ *adj* carrying into
effect, esp of branch of government
executing laws **ex·ec·u·tor** [ig-
ZEK-yə-tàr] *n* person appointed
to carry out provisions of a will
-u·trix *n fem*

ex·e·ge·sis [ek-si-JEE-sis] *n, pl*
-ses [-seez] explanation, esp of

Scripture **ex·e·gete** [-jeet] *n* one skilled in exegesis

ex·em·plar [ig-ZEM-plàr] *n* model type **ex·em·pla·ry** [-plà-ree] *adj* fit to be imitated; serving as example; commendable; typical

ex·em·pli·fy [ig-ZEM-plà-fī] *vt* **-fied, -fy·ing** serve as example of; illustrate; exhibit; make attested copy of **ex·em·pli·fi·ca'tion** *n*

ex·empt [ig-ZEMPT] *vt* free from; excuse ⊳ *adj* freed from, not liable for; not affected by **ex·emp'tion** *n*

ex·e·quies [EK-si-kweez] *pl n* funeral rites or procession

ex·er·cise [EK-sàr-sīz] *v* **-cised, -cis·ing** ⊳ *vt* use, employ; give exercise to; carry out, discharge; trouble, harass ⊳ *vi* take exercise ⊳ *n* use of limbs for health; practice for training; task for training; lesson; employment; use (of limbs, mind, etc)

ex·ert [ig-ZURT] *vt* apply (oneself) diligently, make effort; bring to bear **ex·er'tion** *n* effort, physical activity

ex·fo·li·ate [eks-FOH-lee-ayt] *v* wash (the body) with a granular cosmetic to remove dead cells from the skin's surface

ex·hale [eks-HAYL] *v* **-haled, -hal·ing** breathe out; give, pass off as vapor

ex·haust [ig-ZAWST] *vt* tire out; use up; empty; draw off; treat, discuss thoroughly ⊳ *n* used steam or fluid from engine; waste gases from internal combustion engine; passage for, or coming out of this **ex·haust'i·ble** *adj* **ex·haus'tion** [-chàn] *n* state of extreme fatigue; limit of endurance **ex·haus'tive** *adj* thorough; comprehensive

ex·hib·it [ig-ZIB-it] *vt* show, display; manifest; show publicly (often in competition) ⊳ *n* thing

shown, esp in competition or as evidence in court **ex·hi·bi·tion** [ek-sà-BISH-àn] *n* display, act of displaying; public show (of works of art, etc) **ex·hi·bi'tion·ist** *n* one with compulsive desire to draw attention to self or to expose genitals publicly **ex·hib'i·tor** *n* one who exhibits, esp in show

ex·hil·a·rate [ig-ZIL-à-rayt] *vt* **-rat·ed, -rat·ing** enliven, gladden **ex·hil·a·ra'tion** *n* high spirits, enlivenment

ex·hort [ig-ZORT] *vt* urge, admonish earnestly **ex·hor·ta·tion** [eg-zor-TAY-shàn] *n* **ex·hort'er** *n*

ex·hume [ig-ZOOM] *vt* **-humed, -hum·ing** unearth what has been buried, disinter **ex·hu·ma'tion** [eks-hyuu-MAY-shàn] *n*

ex·i·gent [EK-si-jànt] *adj* exacting; urgent, pressing **ex'i·gen·cy** *n*, *pl* **-cies** pressing need; emergency

ex·ig·u·ous [ig-ZIG-yoo-às] *adj* scanty, meager

ex·ile [EG-zīl] *n* banishment, expulsion from one's own country; long absence from abroad; one banished or permanently living away from own home or country ⊳ *vt* **-iled, -il·ing** banish, expel

ex·ist [ig-ZIST] *vi* be, have being, live **ex·ist'ence** *n* **ex·ist'ent** *adj*

ex·is·ten·tial·ism [eg-zi-STEN-shà-liz-àm] *n* philosophy stressing importance of personal responsibility and the free agency of the individual in a seemingly meaningless universe

ex·it [EG-zit] *n* way out; going out; death; actor's departure from stage ⊳ *vi* go out **exit strategy** *n* plan for freeing oneself from an undesirable situation

ex li·bris [eks LEE-bris] *Lat* from the library of

ex·o·crine [EK-sə-krin] *adj* of gland (eg salivary, sweat) secreting its products through ducts

ex·o·dus [EKS-ə-dəs] *n* departure, esp of crowd; (**E-**) second book of Old Testament **the Exodus** departure of Israelites from Egypt

ex of·fi·ci·o [eks-ə-FISH-ee-oh] *Lat* by right of position or office

ex·on·er·ate [ig-ZON-ə-rayt] *vt* **-at·ed, -at·ing** free, declare free, from blame; exculpate; acquit **ex·on·er·a·tion** *n*

ex·or·bi·tant [ig-ZOR-bi-tənt] *adj* very excessive, inordinate, immoderate **ex·or'bi·tance** *n*

ex·or·cise [EK-sor-siz] *vt* **-cised, -cis·ing** cast out (evil spirits) by invocation; free person of evil spirits **ex·or·cism** *n* **ex·or·cist** *n*

ex·ot·ic [ig-ZOT-ik] *adj* brought in from abroad, foreign; rare, unusual, having strange or bizarre allure ▷ *n* exotic plant, etc **ex·ot'i·ca** [-i-kə] *pl n* (collection of) exotic objects **ex·ot'i·cism** *n* **exotic dancer** stripper

ex·pand [ik-SPAND] *v* increase, spread out, dilate, develop **ex·pand'a·ble, -i·ble** *adj* **ex·panse'** *n* wide space; open stretch of land **ex·pan'si·ble** *adj* **ex·pan'sion** *n* **ex·pan'sive** *adj* wide; extensive; friendly, talkative

ex·pa·ti·ate [ik-SPAY-shee-ayt] *vi* **-at·ed, -at·ing** speak or write at great length (on); enlarge (upon) **ex·pa·ti·a'tion** *n*

ex·pa·tri·ate [eks-PAY-tree-ayt] *vt* **-at·ed, -at·ing** banish; exile; withdraw (oneself) from one's native land ▷ *adj, n* (-tree-it) **ex·pa·tri·a'tion** *n*

ex·pect [ik-SPEKT] *vt* regard as probable; look forward to; await; hope **ex·pect'an·cy** *n* state or act

of expecting; that which is expected; hope **ex·pect'ant** *adj* looking or waiting for, esp for birth of child **ex·pect'ant·ly** *adv* **ex·pec·ta·tion** [ek-spek-TAY-shən] *n* act or state of expecting; prospect of future good; what is expected; promise; value of something expected ▷ *pl* prospect of fortune or profit esp by inheritance

ex·pec·to·rate [ik-SPEK-tə-rayt] *v* **-rat·ed, -rat·ing** spit out (phlegm, etc) **ex·pec·to·ra'tion** *n*

ex·pe·di·ent [ik-SPEE-dee-ənt] *adj* fitting, advisable; politic; suitable; convenient ▷ *n* something suitable, useful, esp in emergency **ex·pe'di·en·cy** *n*

ex·pe·dite [EK-spi-dīt] *vt* help on, hasten; dispatch **ex·pe·di'tion** [-DISH-ən] *n* journey for definite purpose; people, equipment engaged in expedition; excursion; promptness **ex·pe·di'tion·ar·y** *adj* **ex·pe·di'tious** *adj* prompt, speedy

ex·pel [ik-SPEL] *vt* **-pelled, -pel·ling** drive, cast out; exclude; discharge **ex·pul'sion** *n*

ex·pend [ik-SPEND] *vt* spend, pay out; use up **ex·pend'a·ble** *adj* likely, or meant, to be used up or destroyed **ex·pend'i·ture** [-i-chər] *n* **ex·pense'** *n* cost; (cause of) spending ▷ *pl* charges, outlay incurred **ex·pen'sive** *adj*

ex·pe·ri·ence [ik-SPEER-ee-əns] *n* observation of facts as source of knowledge; being affected consciously by event; the event; knowledge, skill, gained from life, by contact with facts and events ▷ *vt* **-enced, -enc·ing** undergo, suffer, meet with **experienced** *adj* skilled, expert, capable **ex·pe·ri·en·tial** [ik-speer-ee-EN-shəl] *adj*

ex·per·i·ment [ik-SPER-ə-mənt]

n test, trial, something done in the hope that it may succeed, or to test hypothesis, principle, etc ▷ *vi* conduct experiment **ex·per·i·men·tal** *adj*

ex·pert [EK-spurt] *n* one skillful, knowledgeable, in something; authority ▷ *adj* practiced, skillful **ex·per·tise** [ek-spər-TEEZ] *n* expertness; know-how

ex·pi·ate [EK-spee-ayt] *vt* -**at·ed, -at·ing** pay penalty for; make amends for **ex·pi·a·tion** *n* **ex·pi·a·to·ry** [-ə-tor-ee] *adj*

ex·pire [ik-SPIR] *vi* -**pired, -pir·ing** come to an end; give out breath; die ▷ *vt* breathe out **ex·pi·ra·tion** *n*

ex·plain [ik-SPLAYN] *vt* make clear, intelligible; interpret; elucidate; give details of; account for **ex·pla·na·tion** [ek-splə-NAY-shən] *n* **ex·plan·a·to·ry** *adj*

ex·ple·tive [EK-spli-tiv] *n* exclamation; exclamatory oath ▷ *adj* serving only to fill out sentence, etc

ex·pli·ca·ble [ek-splik-2-bəl] *adj* explainable **ex·pli·cate** *vt* -**cat·ed, -cat·ing** develop, explain **ex·pli·ca·to·ry** *adj*

ex·plic·it [ik-SPLIS-it] *adj* stated in detail; stated, not merely implied; outspoken; clear, plain; unequivocal

ex·plode [ik-SPLOHD] *v* -**plod·ed, -plod·ing** *vi* go off with bang; burst violently; (of population) increase rapidly ▷ *vt* make explode; discredit, expose (a theory, etc) **ex·plo·sion** [-zhən] *n* **ex·plo·sive** *adj*, *n*

ex·ploit [EK-sploit] *n* brilliant feat, deed ▷ *vt* [ik-SPLOIT] turn to advantage; make use of for one's own ends **ex·ploi·ta·tion** [ek-] *n*

ex·plore [ik-SPLOHR] *vt* -**plored, -plor·ing** investigate; examine; scrutinize; examine

(country, etc) by going through it **ex·plo·ra·tion** [ek-splə-RAY-shən] *n* **ex·plor·a·to·ry** [ik-SPLOR-ə-tor-ee] *adj* **ex·plor·er** *n*

explosion SEE EXPLODE

exponent SEE EXPOUND

ex·port [ik-SPORT] *vt* send (goods) out of the country ▷ *n*, *adj* [EK-sport] **ex·por·ta·tion** [-TAY-shən] *n* **ex·port·er** *n*

ex·pose [ik-SPOHZ] *vt* -**posed, -pos·ing** exhibit; disclose, reveal; lay open (to); leave unprotected; expose photographic plate or film to light **ex·po·sure** [-zhər] *n*

ex·po·sé [ek-spoh-ZAY] *n* newspaper article, etc, disclosing scandal, crime, etc

exposition SEE EXPOUND

ex·pos·tu·late [ik-SPOS-chə-layt] *vi* -**lat·ed, -lat·ing** remonstrate; reason with (in a kindly manner) **ex·pos·tu·la·tion** *n*

ex·pound [ik-SPOWND] *vt* explain, interpret **ex·po·nent** [ik-SPOH-nənt] *n* one who expounds or promotes (idea, cause, etc); performer, executant; *mathematics* small, raised number showing the power of a factor **ex·po·nen·tial** [ek-spə-NEN-shəl] *adj* **ex·po·si·tion** [-ZISH-ən] *n* explanation, description; exhibition of goods, etc **ex·pos·i·tor** [ik-SPOZ-i-tər] *n* one who explains, interpreter **ex·pos·i·to·ry** *adj* explanatory

ex·press [ik-SPRES] *vt* put into words; make known or understood by words, behavior, etc; squeeze out ▷ *adj* definitely stated; specially designed; clear; positive; speedy; of train, fast and making few stops ▷ *adv* by express; with speed ▷ *n* express train; rapid parcel delivery service **ex·press·i·ble** [ik-] *adj* **ex·pres·sion** [-shən] *n* expressing;

word, phrase; look, aspect; feeling; utterance **ex·pres·sion·ism** n theory that art depends on expression of artist's creative self, not on mere reproduction **ex·pres·sive** adj **ex·press·ly** adv **ex·pres·sive·ness** n

ex·pro·pri·ate [eks-PROH-pree-ayt] vt **-at·ed, -at·ing** dispossess; take out of owner's hands **ex·pro·pri·a·tion** n

expulsion see EXPEL

ex·punge [ik-SPUNJ] vt **-punged, -pung·ing** strike out, erase

ex·pur·gate [EK-spǝr-gayt] vt **-gat·ed, -gat·ing** remove objectionable parts (from book, etc), purge **ex·pur·ga·tion** n

ex·qui·site [EK-skwiz-it] adj of extreme beauty or delicacy; keen, acute; keenly sensitive **ex·qui·site·ly** adv

ex·tant [EK-stǝnt] adj still existing

ex·tem·po·re [ik-STEM-pǝ-ree] adj, adv without previous thought or preparation **ex·tem·po·ra·ne·ous** adj **ex·tem·po·rize** vt **-rized, -riz·ing** speak without preparation; devise for the occasion

ex·tend [ik-STEND] vt stretch out, lengthen; prolong in duration; widen in area, scope; accord, grant ▷ vi reach; cover area; have range or scope; become larger or wider **ex·tend'i·ble** or **-a·ble** adj **ex·ten'si·ble** adj **ex·ten·sile** [ik-STEN-sǝl] adj that can be extended **ex·ten·sion** n stretching out, prolongation or enlargement; expansion; continuation, additional part, as of telephone, etc **ex·ten·sive** adj wide, large, comprehensive **ex·ten·sor** n straightening muscle **ex·tent** n space or degree to which thing is extended; size; compass; volume

ex·ten·u·ate [ik-STEN-yoo-ayt] vt **-at·ed, -at·ing** make less blameworthy, lessen; mitigate **ex·ten·u·a·tion** n

ex·te·ri·or [ik-STEER-ee-ǝr] n the outside; outward appearance ▷ adj outer, outward, external

ex·ter·mi·nate [ik-STUR-mǝ-nayt] vt **-nat·ed, -nat·ing** destroy utterly, annihilate, root out, eliminate **ex·ter·mi·na·tion** n **ex·ter·mi·na·tor** n destroyer

ex·ter·nal [ik-STUR-nǝl] adj outside, outward **ex·ter·nal·ly** adv

ex·tinct [ik-STINGKT] adj having died out or come to an end; no longer existing; quenched, no longer burning **ex·tinc·tion** n

ex·tin·guish [ik-STING-gwish] vt put out, quench; wipe out **ex·tin·guish·er** n device, esp spraying liquid or foam, used to put out fires

ex·tir·pate [EK-stǝr-payt] vt **-pat·ed, -pat·ing** root out, destroy utterly **ex·tir·pa·tion** n **ex·tir·pa·tor** n

ex·tol [ik-STOHL] vt **-tolled, -tol·ling** praise highly

ex·tort [ik-STORT] vt get by force or threats; wring out; exact **ex·tor·tion** n

ex·tra [EK-strǝ] adj additional; larger, better, than usual ▷ adv additionally; more than usually ▷ n extra thing; something charged as additional; films actor hired for crowd scenes

extra- prefix outside or beyond an area or scope: extradition; extramural; extraterritorial

ex·tract [ik-STRAKT] vt take out, esp by force; obtain against person's will; get by pressure, distillation, etc; deduce, derive; copy out, quote ▷ n [EK-strakt] passage from book, film, etc; matter got by distillation; concentrated solution **ex·trac·tion** n extracting, esp of tooth; ancestry

ex·tra·di·tion [ek-strə-DISH-ən] n delivery, under treaty, of foreign fugitive from justice to authorities concerned **ex·tra·dite** [-dīt] vt **-dit·ed, -dit·ing** give or obtain such delivery

ex·tra·mu·ral [ek-strə-MYUUR-əl] adj connected with but outside normal courses, etc of college or school; situated outside walls or boundaries of a place

ex·tra·ne·ous [ik-STRAY-nee-əs] adj not essential; irrelevant; added from without, not belonging

ex·tra·or·di·na·ry [ik-STROR-dn-er-ee] adj out of the usual course; additional; unusual, surprising, exceptional

ex·trap·o·late [ik-STRAP-ə-layt] vt **-lat·ed, -lat·ing** infer something not known from known facts; mathematics estimate a value beyond known values

ex·tra·sen·so·ry [ek-strə-SEN-sə-ree] adj of perception apparently gained without use of known senses

ex·tra·ter·res·tri·al [ek-strə-tə-RES-tree-əl] adj of, or from outside Earth's atmosphere

ex·trav·a·gant [ik-STRAV-ə-gənt] adj wasteful; exorbitant; wild, absurd **ex·trav·a·gance** n **ex·trav·a·gant·ly** adv **ex·trav·a·gan·za** [-GAN-zə] n elaborate, lavish, entertainment, display, etc

extravert SEE EXTROVERT

ex·treme [ik-STREEM] adj **-trem·er, -trem·est** of high or highest degree; severe; going beyond moderation; at the end; outermost ▷ n utmost degree; thing at one end or the other, first and last of series

ex·trem·ist n advocate of extreme measures **ex·trem·i·ty** [-TREM-i-tee] n, pl **-ties** farthest point ▷ pl hands and feet; utmost distress; extreme measures **extreme sport** any of various sports with a high risk of injury or death

ex·tri·cate [EK-stri-kayt] vt **-cat·ed, -cat·ing** disentangle, unravel, set free **ex·tri·ca·tion** n

ex·trin·sic [ik-STRIN-sik] adj accessory, not belonging, not intrinsic **ex·trin·si·cal·ly** adv

ex·tro·vert [EK-strə-vurt] n one who is interested in other people and things rather than own feelings **ex·tro·ver·sion** [-VUR-zhən] n

ex·trude [ik-STROOD] vt **-trud·ed, -trud·ing** squeeze, force out; (esp of molten metal or plastic, etc) shape by squeezing through suitable nozzle or die

ex·u·ber·ant [ig-ZOO-bər-ənt] adj high-spirited, vivacious; prolific, abundant, luxurious **ex·u·ber·ance** n

ex·ude [ig-ZOOD] v **-ud·ed, -ud·ing** ▷ vi ooze out ▷ vt give off (moisture)

ex·ult [ig-ZULT] vi rejoice, triumph **exult·an·cy** n **ex·ult·ant** adj triumphant **ex·ul·ta·tion** [eg-zul-TAY-shən] n

ex·urb [EKS-urb] n residential area outside the suburbs of a city

eye [ī] n organ of sight; look, glance; attention; aperture; view; judgment; watch, vigilance; thing, mark resembling eye; slit in needle for thread ▷ vt **eyed, ey·ing** look at; observe **eye'less** adj **eye'ball** n ball of eye **eye'brow** n fringe of hair above eye **eye'glass** n glass to assist sight; monocle **eye'lash** n hair fringing eyelid **eye'let**

n small hole for rope, etc to pass through **eye'lid** *n* lid or cover of eye **eye'o•pen•er** *n* surprising news; revealing statement **eye shadow** colored cosmetic put on around the eyes **eye'sore** *n* ugly object; thing that annoys one to see **eye'tooth** *n* canine tooth

eye'wash *n inf* deceptive talk, etc, nonsense **eye'wit•ness** *n* one who actually sees something and can give firsthand account of it

ey•rie [AIR-ee] *n* nest of bird of prey, esp eagle; high dwelling place

e-zine [EE-zeen] *n* magazine available only in electronic form

F *chemistry* fluorine

fa [fah] *n* fourth sol-fa note

fa·ble [FAY-bəl] *n* short story with moral, esp one with animals as characters; legend; fiction or lie ▷ *vt* invent, tell fables about **fab'u·list** *n* writer of fables **fab'u·lous** [-yə-ləs] *adj* amazing; *inf* extremely good; told of in fables; unhistorical

fab·ric [FAB-rik] *n* cloth; texture; frame, structure **fab'ri·cate** *vt* **-cat·ed, -cat·ing** build; frame; construct; invent (lie, etc); forge (document) **fab·ri·ca'tion** *n*

fa·cade [fə-SAHD] *n* front of building; *fig* outward appearance

face [fays] *n* front of head; distorted expression; outward appearance; front, upper surface, or chief side of anything; dial of a clock, etc; dignity ▷ *v* **faced, fac·ing** ▷ *vt* look or front toward; meet (boldly); give a covering surface ▷ *vi* turn **fac·et** [FAS-it] *n* one side of many-sided body, esp cut gem; one aspect **fa·cial** [FAY-shəl] *adj* pert to face ▷ *n* cosmetic treatment for face **fac'ings** *pl n* lining for decoration or reinforcement, sewn on collar, cuff, etc **face'less** *adj* without a face; anonymous **face'lift·ing** *n* operation to tighten skin of face to remove wrinkles **face recognition** ability of a computer to scan, store, and recognize human faces

fa·ce·tious [fə-SEE-shəs] *adj* (sarcastically) witty; humorous, given to jesting, esp at inappropriate time

facia *n* see **FASCIA**

fac·ile [FAS-il] *adj* easy; working easily; easygoing; superficial, silly **fa·cil'i·tate** *vt* make easy, help **fa·cil'i·ta·tor** *n* **fa·cil'i·ty** *n, pl* **-ties** easiness, dexterity ▷ *pl* good conditions; means, equipment for doing something

fac·sim·i·le [fak-SIM-ə-lee] *n* an exact copy

fact [fakt] *n* thing known to be true; deed; reality **fac'tu·al** [-choo-əl] *adj*

fac·tion [FAK-shən] *n* (dissenting) minority group within larger body; dissension **fac'tious** *adj* of or producing factions

fac·ti·tious [fak-TISH-əs] *adj* artificial; specially made up; unreal

fac·tor [FAK-tər] *n* something contributing to a result; one of numbers that multiplied together give a given number; agent, dealer; business that provides money to finance commerce **fac·to·tum** [-TOH-təm] *n* one performing all types of work

fac·to·ry [FAK-tə-ree] *n* building in which things are manufactured

fac·ul·ty [FAK-əl-tee] *n, pl* **-ties** inherent power; power of the mind; ability, aptitude; staff of school, college or university; department of university

fad *n* short-lived fashion; whim **fad'dish** *adj* **fad'dism** *n* **fad'dist** *n*

fade [fayd] *v* **fad·ed, fad·ing**

▷ *vi* lose color, strength; wither; grow dim; disappear gradually ▷ *vt* cause to fade **fad•in, -out** *n* radio variation in strength of signals; tv, film gradual appearance and disappearance of picture

fag *n sl offens* short for **FAGGOT**

fag•got [FAG-ət] *n* bundle of sticks for fuel, etc; *sl offens* male homosexual

Fahr•en•heit [FAR-ən-hīt] *adj* measured by thermometric scale with freezing point of water 32°, boiling point 212°

fa•ience [FAY-ahns] *n* glazed earthenware or china

fail [fayl] *vi* be unsuccessful; stop operating or working; be below the required standard; be insufficient; run short; be wanting in need; lose power; die away; become bankrupt ▷ *vt* disappoint, give no help to; neglect, forget to do; judge (student) to be below required standard **fail'ing** *n* deficiency; fault ▷ *prep* in default of **fail'ure** *n* **fail'safe** *adj* of device ensuring safety or remedy of malfunction in machine, weapon, etc **without fail** in spite of every difficulty; certainly

faint [faynt] *adj* -er, -est feeble, dim, pale; weak; dizzy, about to lose consciousness temporarily ▷ *vi* lose consciousness

fair[1] *adj* -er, -est just, impartial; according to rules, legitimate; blond; beautiful; ample; of moderate quality or amount; unblemished; plausible; middling; (of weather) favorable ▷ *adv* honestly **fair'ing** *n* aviation streamlined structure, or any part so shaped that it provides streamlined form **fair'ly** *adv* **fair'ness** *n* **fair'way** *n* golf trimmed turf between tee and green; navigable channel

fair[2] *n* traveling entertainment with sideshows, amusements, etc; large exhibition of farm, commercial or industrial products; periodical market often with amusements **fair'ground** *n*

fair•y [FAIR-ee] *n, pl* **fair•ies** imaginary small creature with powers of magic; *sl offens* male homosexual ▷ *adj* of fairies; like fairy, beautiful and delicate, imaginary **fair'y•land** *n* **fair'y•tale** *adj* of or like fairy tale **fairy tale** story of imaginary beings and happenings, esp as told to children

fait ac•com•pli [fay ta-kawn-PLEE] *n, pl* **faits accompli** [fe za-kawn-PLEE] *Fr* something already done that cannot be altered

faith [fayth] *n* trust; belief; belief without proof; religion; promise; loyalty, constancy **faith'ful** *adj* constant, true **faith'ful•ly** *adv* **faith'less** *adj*

fa•ji•tas [fa-HEE-taz] *pl n* Mexican dish of soft tortillas wrapped around fried strips meat or vegetables

fake [fayk] *vt* **faked, fak•ing** conceal defects of by artifice; touch up; counterfeit ▷ *n* fraudulent object, person, act ▷ *adj* **fak'er** *n* one who deals in fakes; swindler

fa•kir [fə-KEER] *n* member of Islamic religious order; Hindu ascetic

fa•la•fel [fə-LAH-fəl] *n* seasoned croquette of flour or ground chick peas

fal•con [FAL-kən] *n* small bird of prey, esp trained in hawking for sport **fal'con•er** *n* one who keeps, trains, or hunts with falcons **fal'con•ry** *n* hawking

fall [fawl] *vi* **fell, fall•en** drop, come down freely; become lower; decrease; hang down; come to the ground, cease to stand; perish; collapse; be captured; revert; lapse; be uttered; become; happen ▷ n falling; amount that falls; amount of descent; decrease; collapse, ruin; drop; (oft pl) cascade; cadence; yielding to temptation; autumn **fall'out** n radioactive particles spread as result of nuclear explosion; incidental effect or outcome **fall for** inf fall in love with; inf be taken in by

fal·la·cy [FAL-ə-see] n, pl -**cies** incorrect, misleading opinion or argument; flaw in logic; illusion **fal·la·cious** [fə-LAY-shəs] adj

fal·li·bil'i·ty n **fal'li·ble** adj liable to error

fallen pp of FALL

Fal·lo·pi·an tube [fə-LOH-pee-ən] either of a pair of tubes through which egg cells pass from ovary to womb

fal·low¹ [FAL-oh] adj plowed and harrowed but left without crop; uncultivated; neglected

fallow² adj brown or reddish yellow **fallow deer** deer of this color

false [fawls] adj **fals·er, fals·est** wrong, erroneous; deceptive; faithless; sham, artificial **false'ly** adv **false'ness** n faithlessness **fal·si·fi·ca'tion** n **fal'si·fy** vt -**fied, -fy·ing** alter fraudulently; misrepresent **fal'si·ty** n, pl -**ties** **false'hood** n lie

fal·set·to [fawl-SET-oh] n, pl -**tos** forced voice above natural range

Fal·staff·i·an [fawl-STAF-ee-ən] adj like Shakespeare's Falstaff; fat; convivial; boasting

fal·ter [FAWL-tər] vi hesitate; waver; stumble **fal'ter·ing·ly** adv

fame [faym] n reputation; renown **famed** adj **fa'mous** adj widely known; excellent

fa·mil·i·ar [fə-MIL-yər] adj well-known; frequent, customary; intimate; closely acquainted; unceremonious; impertinent, too friendly ▷ n familiar friend; familiar demon **fa·mil·i·ar'i·ty** n, pl -**ties** **fa·mil'iar·ize** vt -**ized, -iz·ing**

fam·i·ly [FAM-ə-lee] n, pl -**lies** group of parents and children, or near relatives; person's children; all descendants of common ancestor; household; group of allied objects **fa·mil·ial** [fə-MIL-yəl] adj **family leave** unpaid work leave for family reasons

fam·ine [FAM-in] n extreme scarcity of food; starvation **fam'ished** adj very hungry

famous see FAME

fan¹ n instrument for producing current of air, esp for ventilating or cooling; folding object of paper, etc, used, esp formerly, for cooling the face; outspread feathers of a bird's tail ▷ v **fanned, fan·ning** spread out like fan ▷ vt blow or cool with fan **fan'light** n (fan-shaped) window over door

fan² n inf devoted admirer; an enthusiast, particularly of a sport, etc

fa·nat·ic [fə-NAT-ik] adj filled with abnormal enthusiasm, esp in religion ▷ n fanatic person **fa·nat'ical** adj **fa·nat'i·cism** n

fan·cy [FAN-see] adj -**ci·er, -ci·est** ornamental, not plain; of whimsical or arbitrary kind ▷ n, pl -**cies** whim, caprice; liking, inclination; imagination; mental image ▷ vt -**cied, -cy·ing** imagine; be inclined to believe; inf have a liking for **fan'ci·er** n one with liking and expert knowledge (respecting some specific thing) **fan'ci·ful** adj **fan'ci·ful·ly** adv

fan·dan·go [fan-DANG-goh] n, pl -**goes** lively Spanish dance with castanets; music for this dance

fan·fare [FAN-fair] *n* a flourish of trumpets or bugles; ostentatious display

fang *n* snake's poison tooth; long, pointed tooth

fan·tail [FAN-tayl] *n* (kind of bird with) fan-shaped tail; projecting part of ship's stern

fan·ta·sy [FAN-tà-see] *n, pl* **-sies** power of imagination, esp extravagant; mental image; fanciful invention or design **fan·ta·sia** [-TAY-zhà] *n* fanciful musical composition **fan·ta·size** *v* **-sized, -siz·ing fan·tas·tic** *adj* quaint, grotesque, extremely fanciful, wild; *inf* very good; *inf* very large **fan·tas·ti·cal·ly** *adv*

FAQ *internet* frequently asked question or questions

far *adv* **far·ther** *or* **fur·ther, far·thest** *or* **fur·thest** at or to a great distance, or advanced point; at or to a remote time; by very much ▷ *adj* distant; more distant **far'-fetched'** *adj* incredible

far·ad [FA-ràd] *n* unit of electrical capacity

farce [fahrs] *n* comedy of boisterous humor; absurd and futile proceeding **far'ci·cal** *adj* ludicrous

fare [fair] *n* charge for passenger's transport; passenger; food ▷ *vi* **fared, far·ing** get on; happen; travel, progress **fare·well'** *interj* goodbye ▷ *n* leave-taking

far·i·na·ceous [far-à-NAY-shàs] *adj* mealy, starchy; made of flour or meal

farm [fahrm] *n* tract of land for cultivation or rearing livestock; unit of land, water, for growing or rearing a particular crop, animal, etc ▷ *v* cultivate (land); rear livestock (on farm) **farm'er** *n* **farm'house** *n*

farm'yard *n* **farm out** send (work) to be done by others; put into care of others

far·o [FAIR-oh] *n* card game

far·ra·go [fà-RAH-goh] *n, pl* **-gos** medley, hodgepodge

far·row [FA-roh] *n* litter of pigs ▷ *v* produce this

fart [fahrt] *n* *vulg* (audible) emission of gas from anus ▷ *vi*

far·ther [FAHR-thàr] *adv, adj* further; comp of **FAR far'thest** *adv, adj* furthest; sup of **FAR**

fas·ces [FAS-eez] *pl n* bundle of rods bound together around ax, forming Roman badge of authority; emblem of Italian fascists

fas·cia [FAY-shà] *n, pl* **-cias** *architecture* long flat surface between moldings under eaves; face of wood or stone in a building

fas·ci·nate [FAS-à-nayt] *vt* **-nat·ed, -nat·ing** attract and delight by arousing interest and curiosity; render motionless, as with a fixed stare **fas·ci·na·tion** *n*

fas·cism [FASH-iz-àm] *n* authoritarian political system opposed to democracy and liberalism; behavior (esp by those in authority) supposedly typical of this system **fas'cist** *adj, n* **fa·scis·tic** [fà-SHIS-tik] *adj*

fash·ion [FASH-àn] *n* (latest) style, esp of dress, etc; manner, mode; form, type ▷ *vt* shape, make **fash'ion·a·ble** *adj* **fash'ion·a·bly** *adv*

fast[1] *adj* **-er, -est** (capable of) moving quickly; permitting, providing, rapid progress; ahead of true time; firm, steady; permanent ▷ *adv* rapidly; tightly **fast'ness** *n* fast state; fortress, stronghold **fast'back** *n* car with back forming continuous slope from roof to rear **fast casual** style of fast food that is healthier and fresher than traditional fast food **fast food** food, esp hamburgers, etc, prepared and served very quickly

fast² *vi* **fast·ed, fast·ing** go without food, or some kinds of food ▷ *n* **fasting** *n*

fas·ten [FAS-ən] *vt* attach, fix, secure ▷ *vi* become joined; seize (upon)

fas·tid·i·ous [fa-STID-ee-əs] *adj* hard to please; discriminating; particular

fat *n* oily animal substance; fat part ▷ *adj* **fat·ter, fat·test** having too much fat; containing fat, greasy; profitable; fertile **fat'ten** *vt* feed (animals) for slaughter ▷ *vi* become **fat'ness** *n* **fat'ty** *adj* **-ti·er, -i·est** containing fat ▷ *n, pl* **-ties** *inf* fat person **fat'head** *n sl* dolt, fool **fat farm** resort for helping people lose weight

fate [fayt] *n* power supposed to predetermine events; goddess of destiny; destiny; person's appointed lot or condition; death or destruction ▷ *vt* **fat·ed, fat·ing** preordain **fa'tal** *adj* deadly, ending in death; destructive; disastrous; inevitable **fa'tal·ism** *n* belief that everything is predetermined; submission to fate **fa'tal·ist** *n* **fa·tal·is'tic** *adj* **fa·tal'i·ty** *n, pl* **-ties** accident resulting in death; person killed in war, accident **fa'tal·ly** *adv* **fate'ful** *adj* fraught with destiny; prophetic

fa·ther [FAH-*thər*] *n* male parent; forefather; originator; (**F-**) God; originator; early leader; priest; confessor; oldest member of a society ▷ *vt* beget; originate; pass as father or author of; act as father to **fa'ther·hood** *n* **fa'ther·less** *adj* **fa'ther·ly** *adj* **fa·ther-in-law** *n*

husband's or wife's father

fath·om [FATH-əm] *n* measure of six feet of water ▷ *vt* sound (water); get to bottom of, understand **fath'om·a·ble** *adj* **fath'om·less** *adj* too deep to fathom

fa·tigue [fə-TEEG] *n* weariness; toil; weakness of metals, etc, subjected to stress; soldier's nonmilitary duty ▷ *pl* clothing worn for such duty ▷ *vt* **-tigued, -tigu·ing** weary

fat·u·ous [FACH-oo-əs] *adj* very silly, idiotic **fat'u·ous·ness** *n*

fau·cet [FAW-sit] *n* device for controlling flow of liquid; tap

fault [fawlt] *n* defect; flaw; misdeed; blame, culpability; blunder; mistake; *tennis* ball wrongly served; *geology* break in strata ▷ *v* find fault in; (cause to) undergo or commit fault **fault'i·ly** *adv* **fault'less** *adj* **fault'y** *adj* **fault·i·er, fault·i·est**

faun [fawn] *n* mythological woodland being with tail and horns

fau·na [FAW-nə] *n, pl* **-nas** or **-nae** [-nee] animals of region or period collectively

faux pas [foh-PAH] *n, pl* **faux pas** [-PAHZ] social blunder or indiscretion

fa·vor [FAY-vər] *n* goodwill; approval; special kindness; partiality ▷ *pl* sexual intimacy granted by woman; small party gift for a guest ▷ *vt* regard or treat with favor; oblige; treat with partiality; aid; support; resemble **fa'vor·a·ble** *adj* **fa'vor·ite** [-it] *n* favored person or thing; horse, team, etc expected to win race (or game) ▷ *adj* chosen, preferred **fa'vor·it·ism** *n* practice of showing undue preference

fawn¹ *n* young deer ▷ *adj* light yellowish brown

fawn² *vi* of person, cringe, court

favor servilely; esp of dog, show affection by wagging tail and groveling

fax [faks] n facsimile ▷ vt transmit facsimile of (printed matter, etc) electronically

faze [fayz] vt **fazed, faz•ing** fluster; daunt

Fe chemistry iron

fear [feer] n dread, alarm, anxiety, unpleasant emotion caused by coming evil or danger ▷ vi have this feeling; be afraid ▷ vt regard with fear; hesitate, shrink from; revere **fear'ful** adj **fear'ful•ly** adv **fear'less** adj intrepid **fear'some** adj terrifying

fea•si•ble [FEE-zə-bəl] adj able to be done; likely **fea•si•bil'i•ty** n

feast [feest] n banquet, lavish meal; religious anniversary; something very pleasant, sumptuous ▷ vi partake of banquet, fare sumptuously ▷ vt regale with feast; provide delight for

feat [feet] n notable deed; surprising or striking trick

feath•er [FETH-ər] n one of the barbed shafts that form covering of birds; anything resembling this ▷ vt provide, line with feathers ▷ vi grow feathers ▷ v turn (oar, propeller) edgewise **feath'er•y** adj **feath'er•weight** n very light person (esp boxer) or thing; inf person of small consequence or ability **feather one's nest** enrich oneself **in fine feather** in good form

fea•ture [FEE-chər] n (usu pl) part of face; characteristic or notable part of anything; main or special item ▷ v -**tured, -tur•ing** ▷ vt portray; present in leading role in a film; give prominence to ▷ vi be prominent (in) **fea'ture•less** adj without striking features

fe•brile [FEE-brəl] adj of fever; feverish

fe•ces [FEE-seez] pl n excrement, waste matter **fe'cal** [-kəl] adj

feck•less [FEK-lis] adj spiritless, weak, irresponsible **feck'less•ness** n

fec•u•lent [FEK-yə-lənt] adj full of sediment, turbid, foul **fec'u•lence** n

fe•cund [FEE-kund] adj fertile, fruitful, fertilizing **fe'cun•date** vt -**dat•ed, -dat•ing** fertilize, impregnate **fe•cun•di•ty** [fi-KUN-di-tee] n

fed pt/pp of FEED **fed up** bored, dissatisfied

fed•er•al [FED-ər-əl] adj of, or like, the government of countries that are united but retain their internal independence of the separate states **fed'er•al•ism** n **fed'er•ate** [-ə-rayt] v -**at•ed, -at•ing** form into, become, a federation **fed•er•a'tion** n league; federal union

fee n payment for professional and other services

fee•ble [FEE-bəl] adj -**bler, -blest** weak; lacking strength or effectiveness, insipid **fee'bly** adv

feed v fed, feed•ing give food to; supply, support; take food ▷ n feeding; fodder, pasturage; allowance of fodder; material supplied to machine; part of machine taking in material **feed'er** n one who or that which feeds **feed'back** n return of part of output of electrical circuit or loudspeakers; information received in response to inquiry, etc **feed'lot** n area, building where cattle are fattened for market

feel v felt, feel•ing perceive, examine by touch; experience; proceed, find (one's way) cautiously; be sensitive to; show emotion (for); believe, consider ▷ n act or instance of feeling; quality or impression of something perceived by feeling; sense of touch **feel'er** n special organ of touch in some animals; proposal put forward to test others' opinions; that which feels **feel'ing** n sense of touch; ability to feel; physical sensation; emotion; sympathy, tenderness; conviction or opinion not solely based on reason ▷ adj susceptibilities ▷ pl sensitive, sympathetic, heartfelt **feel like** have an inclination for

feet see FOOT **feet of clay** hidden flaw in person's character

feign [fayn] v pretend, sham

feint [faynt] n sham attack or blow meant to deceive opponent; semblance, pretense ▷ vi make feint

feist•y [FI-stee] adj **feist•i•er, feist•i•est** spirited, spunky, plucky; ill-tempered **feist'i•ness** n

feld•spar [FELD-spahr] n crystalline mineral found in granite, etc

fe•lic•i•ty [fə-LIS-i-tee] n, pl **-ties** great happiness, bliss; appropriateness of wording **fe•lic'i•tate** vt **-tat•ed, -tat•ing** congratulate **fe•lic•i•ta'tion** pl n congratulations **fe•lic'i•tous** adj apt, well-chosen; happy

fe•line [FEE-lin] adj of cats; catlike

fell¹ pt of FALL

fell² vt knock down; cut down (tree)

fell³ adj fierce, terrible

fell⁴ n skin or hide with hair

fel•low [FEL-oh] n inf man, boy; person; comrade, associate; counterpart; like thing; member (of society); student granted university fellowship ▷ adj of the same class, associated **fel'low•ship** n fraternity; friendship; (in university, etc) research post or special scholarship

fel•on [FEL-ən] n one guilty of

felony **fe•lo•ni•ous** [fə-LOH-nee-əs] adj **fel'o•ny** n, pl **-nies** serious crime

felt¹ pt/pp of FEEL

felt² n soft, matted fabric made by bonding fibers chemically and by pressure; thing made of this ▷ vt make into, or cover with, felt ▷ vi become matted like felt **felt'-tip pen** n pen with writing point made of pressed fibers

fe•male [FEE-mayl] adj of sex that bears offspring; relating to this sex ▷ n one of this sex

fem•i•nine [FEM-ə-nin] adj of women; womanly; class or type of grammatical inflection in some languages **fem'i•nism** n advocacy of equal rights for women **fem'i•nist** n, adj **fem•i•nin'i•ty** n

femme fa•tale [FAHM fat-TAHL] n, pl **femmes fa•tales** Fr alluring woman who leads men into dangerous situations by her charm

fem•o•ral [FEM-ər-əl] adj of the thigh

fe•mur [FEE-mər] n thigh bone

fen n tract of marshy land, swamp

fence [fens] n structure of wire, wood, etc enclosing an area; (machinery) guard, guide; sl dealer in stolen property ▷ v **fenced, fenc•ing** erect fence; enclose; fight (as sport) with swords; avoid question, etc; sl deal in stolen property **fenc'ing** n art of swordplay

fend vt ward off, repel ▷ vi provide (for oneself, etc) **fend'er** n low metal frame in front of fireplace; name for various protective devices; frame; edge; buffer; mudguard of car **fender bender** inf collision between automobiles causing minor damage

fen•es•tra•tion [fen-ə-STRAY-shən] n arrangement of windows in a building; (in medicine) perforation in a structure; operation to create this

feng shui [FUNG SHWAY] *n* Chinese art of deciding the best design or position of a grave, building, furniture, etc, in order to bring good luck

fe·ral¹ [FER-əl] *adj* wild, uncultivated

feral² *adj* funereal, gloomy; causing death

fer·ment [FUR-ment] *n* leaven, substance causing thing to ferment; excitement, tumult ▷ *v* [fər-MENT] (cause to) undergo chemical change with effervescence, liberation of heat and alteration of properties, eg process set up in dough by yeast; (cause to) become excited **fer·men·ta·tion** [fur-] *n*

fern [furn] *n* plant with feathery fronds

fe·ro·cious [fə-ROH-shəs] *adj* fierce, savage, cruel **fe·roc·i·ty** [-ROS-i-tee] *n*

fer·ret [FER-it] *n* tamed animal like weasel, used to catch rabbits, rats, etc ▷ *vt* drive out with ferrets; search out ▷ *vi* search about, rummage

fer·ric [FER-ik], **fer·rous** [FER-əs] *adj* pert to, containing, iron **fer·ru·gi·nous** [fə-ROO-jə-nəs] *adj* containing iron; reddish-brown **fer·ro·con·crete** *n* reinforced concrete (strengthened by framework of metal)

Fer·ris wheel [FER-is] *n* amusement park, large, vertical wheel with seats for riding

fer·rule [FER-əl] *n* metal cap to strengthen end of stick, etc

fer·ry [FER-ee] *n, pl* **-ries** boat, etc for transporting people, vehicles, across body of water, esp as repeated or regular service ▷ *v* **-ried,**

-ry·ing carry, travel, by ferry; deliver (airplanes, etc) by air

fer·tile [FUR-tl] *adj* (capable of) producing offspring, bearing crops, etc; fruitful, producing abundantly; inventive **fer·til·i·ty** [fər-TIL-i-tee] *n* **fer·ti·li·za·tion** *n* **fer·ti·lize** *vt* **-lized, -liz·ing** make fertile **fer·ti·liz·er** *n*

fer·vent [FUR-vənt], **fer·vid** [-vid] *adj* ardent, vehement, intense **fer·ven·cy** *n* **fer·vent·ly** *adv* **fer·vor** [-vər] *n*

fes·cue [FES-kyoo] *n* grass for pasture or lawns, with stiff narrow leaves

fes·tal [FES-tl] *adj* of feast or holiday; merry

fes·ter [FES-tər] *v* (cause to) form pus ▷ *vi* rankle; become embittered

fes·ti·val [FES-tə-vəl] *n* day, period set aside for celebration, esp of religious feast; organized series of events, performances, etc usu in one place **fes·tive** [-tiv] *adj* joyous, merry; of feast **fes·tiv·i·ty** *n* gaiety, mirth; rejoicing ▷ *pl* celebrations

fe·stoon' *n* chain of flowers, ribbons, etc hung in curve between two points ▷ *vt* form, adorn with festoons

fetch [fech] *vt* go and bring; draw forth; be sold for; attract ▷ *n* act of fetching **fetch'ing** *adj* attractive

fete [fayt] *n, pl* **fetes** gala, bazaar, etc, esp one held out of doors; festival, holiday, celebration ▷ *vt*

fet·ed, fet·ing feast; honor with festive entertainment

fet'id *adj* stinking

fet'ish *n* (inanimate) object believed to have magical powers; excessive attention to something; object, activity, to which excessive devotion is paid; form of behaviour in which sexual pleasure is derived from looking at or handling an inanimate object **fet·ish·ism** n **fet·ish·ist** n

fet·lock [FET-lok] n projection behind and above horse's hoof, or tuft of hair on this

fet·ter [FET-ər] n chain or shackle for feet; check, restraint ▷ pl captivity ▷ vt chain up; restrain, hamper

fet·tle [FET-l] n condition, state of health

fe·tus [FEE-təs] n, pl **-tus·es** fully developed young in womb or egg **fe·tal** [FEE-tl] adj

feud [fyood] n bitter, lasting, mutual hostility, esp between two families or tribes; vendetta ▷ vi carry on feud

feu·dal [FYOOD-l] adj of, like, medieval social and economic system based on holding land from superior in return for service **feu·dal·ism** n

fe·ver [FEE-vər] n condition of illness with high body temperature; intense nervous excitement **fe·vered, fe·ver·ish** adj having fever; accompanied by, caused by, fever; in a state of restless excitement **fe·ver·ish·ly** adv **fever pitch** very fast pace; intense excitement

few [fyoo] adj **-er, -est** not many ▷ n small number **quite a few** several

fey [fay] adj supernatural, unreal; enchanted

fez n, pl **fez·zes** red, brimless, oriental Turkish tasseled cap

fi·an·cé [fee-ahn-SAY] n man engaged to be married **fi·an·cée** n fem

fi·as·co [fee-AS-koh] n, pl **-cos** breakdown, total failure

fi·at [FEE-aht] n decree; official permission

fib n trivial lie, falsehood ▷ vt

fibbed, **fib·bing** tell fib **fib·ber** n

fi·ber [FI-bər] n filament forming part of animal or plant tissue; substance that can be spun (eg wool, cotton) **fi·brous** adj made of fiber **fi·ber·board** n building material of compressed plant fibers **fi·ber·glass** n material made of fine glass fibers **fiber optics** use of bundles of long transparent glass fibers in transmitting light

fib·u·la [FIB-yə-lə] n slender outer bone of lower leg **fib·u·lar** adj

fick·le [FIK-əl] adj changeable, inconstant **fick·le·ness** n

fic·tion [FIK-shən] n prose, literary works of the imagination; invented statement or story **fic·tion·al** adj **fic·ti·tious** [-TISH-əs] adj not genuine, false; imaginary; assumed

fid·dle [FID-l] n violin ▷ v **-dled, -dling** ▷ vi play fiddle; make idle movements, fidget, trifle **fid·dle·sticks** interj nonsense

Fi·de·i De·fen·sor [FEE-de-ee de-FEN-sor] Lat defender of the faith

fi·del·i·ty [fi-DEL-i-tee] n, pl **-ties** (conjugal) faithfulness; quality of sound reproduction

fidg·et [FIJ-it] vi move restlessly; be uneasy ▷ n (oft pl) nervous restlessness, restless mood; one who fidgets **fidg·et·y** adj

fi·du·ci·ar·y [fi-DOO-shee-er-ee] adj held, given in trust; relating to trustee ▷ n trustee

fief [feef] n history land held of a superior in return for service **fief·dom** [-dəm] n estate of a feudal lord; inf organization, etc owned by controlled by one person

field [feeld] n area of (farming) land; enclosed piece of land; tract of land rich in specified product (eg gold field); players in a game or sport collectively; all competitors but the favorite; battlefield; area over which electric, gravitational, magnetic force can be exerted; sphere of knowledge; range, area of operation ▷v baseball stop and return ball; send player, team, on to field **field'er** n **field day** day of outdoor activities; important occasion **field events** throwing and jumping events in athletics **field glasses** binoculars **field hockey** hockey played on field, as distinct from ice hockey **field marshal** (in some countries) army officer of highest rank **field'work** n research, practical work, conducted away from the classroom, laboratory, etc **field of view** area covered in telescope, camera, etc

fiend [feend] n demon, devil; wicked person; person very fond of or addicted to something: *fresh-air fiend; drug fiend* **fiend'ish** adj wicked, difficult, unpleasant

fierce [feers] adj **fierc·er, fierc·est** savage, wild, violent; rough; severe; intense **fierce'ly** adv **fierce'ness** n

fier·y [Fí-ə-ree] adj **fier·i·er, fier·i·est** consisting of fire; blazing, glowing, flashing; irritable; spirited **fier'i·ness** n

fi·es·ta [fee-ES-tə] n (religious) celebration; carnival

fife [fíf] n high-pitched flute ▷v play on fife **fif'er** n

fifteen, fifth, fifty SEE FIVE

fig n soft, pear-shaped fruit; tree bearing it

fight [fit] v **fought, fight·ing** contend with in battle or in single combat; maintain against opponent; settle by combat ▷n a fight **fight'er** n one who fights; prizefighter; aircraft designed for destroying other aircraft

fig·ment [FIG-mənt] n invention, purely imaginary thing

fig·ure [FIG-yər] n numerical symbol; amount, number; form, shape; bodily shape; appearance, esp conspicuous appearance; space enclosed by lines, or surfaces; diagram, illustration; likeness; image; pattern, movement in dancing, skating, etc; abnormal form of expression for effect in speech, eg metaphor ▷v **-ured, -ur·ing** ▷vt calculate, estimate; represent by figure or diagram; ornament ▷vi (oft with in) show, appear, be conspicuous, be included **fig·ur·a·tive** adj metaphorical; full of figures of speech **fig·ur·a·tive·ly** adv **fig·ur·ine** [-REEN] n statuette **fig·ure·head** n nominal leader; ornamental figure under bowsprit of ship

fil·a·ment [FIL-ə-mənt] n fine wire in electric light bulb and vacuum tube that is heated by electric current; threadlike body

filch vt steal, pilfer

file[1] [fil] n box, folder, clip, etc holding papers for reference; papers so kept; information about specific person, subject; orderly line, as of soldiers, one behind the other; *computing* organized collection of related material ▷v **filed, fil·ing** ▷vt arrange (papers, etc) and put them away for reference; transmit (eg tax return); *law* place on records of a court; bring suit in law court ▷vi march in file **filing** n **single file** single line of people one behind the other

file[2] n roughened tool for smoothing or shaping ▷v **filed, fil·ing** apply file to, smooth, polish **filing** n action of using file; scrap of metal removed by file

filet SEE FILLET

fil·i·al [FIL-ee-əl] adj of, befitting,

son or daughter

fil·i·bus·ter [FIL-ə-bus-tər] n process of obstructing legislation by using delaying tactics ▷ vi

fil·i·gree [FIL-i-gree] n fine tracery or openwork of metal, usu gold or silver wire

fill vt make full; occupy completely; hold, discharge duties of; stop up; satisfy; fulfill ▷ vi become full ▷ n full supply; as much as desired; soil, etc, to bring area of ground up to required level **fill'ing** n **filling station** business selling oil, gasoline, etc **fill the bill** inf supply all that is wanted

fil·let [fi-LAY] n boneless slice of meat, fish; narrow strip ▷ vt cut into fillets, bone

fil·lip [FIL-əp] n stimulus; sudden release of finger bent against thumb; snap so produced

fil·ly [FIL-ee] n, pl **-lies** young female horse; inf girl, young woman

film n sequence of images projected on screen, creating illusion of movement; story, etc presented thus, and shown in movie theater or on TV; sensitized celluloid roll used in photography, cinematography; thin skin or layer; dimness on eyes; slight haze ▷ adj connected with movies ▷ vt photograph with movie camera; make movie of (scene, story, etc) ▷ v cover, become covered, with film **film'y** adj **film·i·er, film·i·est** membranous; gauzy **film star** popular movie actor or actress

fil·ter [FIL-tər] n cloth or other material, or a device, permitting fluid to pass but retaining solid particles; anything performing similar function ▷ vt act as filter, or as if passing through filter ▷ vi pass slowly (through) **fil·trate** [FIL-trayt] n filtered gas or liquid **fil·tra'tion** n

filth n disgusting dirt; pollution; obscenity **filth'i·ly** adv **filth'i·ness** n **filth'y** adj **filth·i·er, filth·i·est** unclean; foul

fin n propelling or steering organ of fish; vertical tailplane of an airplane; sl five-dollar bill

fi·nal [FIN-l] adj at the end; conclusive ▷ n game, heat, examination, etc, coming at end of series or school term **fi·na·le** [fi-NAL-ee] n closing part of musical composition, opera, etc; termination **fi·nal·i·ty** [fi-NAL-i-tee] n **fi·nal·ize** v **-lized, -liz·ing** **fi'nal·ly** adv

fi·nance [fi-NANS] n management of money ▷ pl money resources ▷ vt **-nanced, nanc·ing** find capital for **fi·nan'cial** [-shəl] adj of finance **fin·an·cier'** [-SEER] n

finch n one of family of small songbirds

find [fīnd] vt **found, find·ing** come across; light upon, obtain; recognize; experience, discover; discover by searching; ascertain; supply (as funds); law give a verdict ▷ n finding; (valuable) thing found **find'er** n **finding** n judicial verdict

fine¹ [fīn] adj **fin·er, fin·est** choice, of high quality; delicate, subtle; pure; in small particles; slender; excellent; handsome; showy; inf healthy, at ease, comfortable; free of rain ▷ vt **fined, fin·ing** make clear or pure; refine; thin **fine'ly** adv **fine'ness** n **fin'er·y** n, pl **-er·ies** showy dress **fi·nesse** [fi-NES] n elegant, skillful management **fine art** art produced for its aesthetic value **fine-tune** vt make fine adjustments to for optimum performance

fine² n sum fixed as penalty ▷ vt **fined, fin·ing** punish by fine **in fine** in conclusion; in brief

fin·ger [FING-gər] n one of the jointed branches of the hand; various things like this ▷ vt touch or handle with fingers; sl inform against (a criminal) **fin·ger·ing** n manner or act of touching; choice of fingers, as in playing musical instrument; indication of this **fin·ger·board** n part of violin, etc against which fingers are placed **fin·ger·print** n impression of tip of finger, esp as used for identifying criminals

fin·i·al [FIN-ee-əl] n ornament at apex of gable, spire, furniture, etc

fin·ick·y [FIN-i-kee] adj **-ick·i·er, -ick·i·est** fastidious, fussy; too fine

fin·is Lat end, esp of book

fin·ish v (mainly tr) bring, come to an end, conclude; complete; perfect; kill ▷ n end; way in which thing is finished of furniture: oak finish; final appearance

fi·nite [FI-nit] adj bounded, limited

fiord see **FJORD**

fir [fur] n kind of coniferous resinous tree; its wood

fire [fīr] n state of burning, combustion, flame, glow; mass of burning fuel; destructive burning, conflagration; burning fuel for heating a room, etc; ardor, keenness, spirit; shooting of firearms ▷ v **fired, fir·ing** ▷ vt discharge (firearm); propel from firearm; inf dismiss from employment; bake; make burn; supply with fuel; inspire; explode ▷ vi discharge firearm; begin to burn; become excited **fire·arm** n gun, rifle, pistol, etc **fire·brand** n burning piece of wood; energetic (troublesome) person **fire·break** [-brayk] n strip of cleared land to arrest progress of forest or grass fire **fire·bug** n inf person who practices arson **fire department** organized body of personnel and

equipment to put out fires and rescue those in danger **fire drill** rehearsal of procedures for escape from fire **fire engine** vehicle with apparatus for extinguishing fires **fire escape** means, esp metal stairs, for escaping from burning buildings **fire·fight·er** n member of fire department; person employed to fight forest fires **fire·fly** n, pl **-flies** insect giving off phosphorescent glow **fire·guard** n protective grating in front of fire **fire irons** tongs, poker and shovel **fire·man** n, pl **fire·men** firefighter; stoker; assistant to locomotive driver **fire·place** n recess in room for fire **fire·house** building housing fire department equipment and personnel **fire·work** n device to give spectacular effects by explosions and colored sparks ▷ pl show of fireworks; outburst of temper, anger **firing squad** group of soldiers ordered to execute an offender by shooting

fir·kin [FUR-kin] n small cask

firm [furm] adj **-er, -est** solid, fixed, stable; steadfast; resolute; settled ▷ v make, become firm ▷ n commercial enterprise; partnership

fir·ma·ment [FUR-mə-mənt] n expanse of sky, heavens

first [furst] adj earliest in time or order; foremost in rank or position; most excellent; highest, chief ▷ n beginning; first occurrence of something; baseball first base ▷ adv before others in time, order, etc **first'ly** adv **first aid** help given to injured person before arrival of doctor **first-hand** adj obtained directly from the first source **first mate, first officer** officer of merchant vessel immediately below captain **first-rate** adj of highest class or quality **first-strike** adj (of a nuclear missile) for use in an opening attack to destroy enemy nuclear weapons

fis·cal [FIS-kəl] *adj* of (government) finances

fish *n, pl* **fish** or **fish·es** vertebrate cold-blooded animal with gills, living in water; its flesh as food ▷ *v* (attempt to) catch fish; search (for); try to get information indirectly **fish'er** *n* **fish'er·y** *n, pl* **-er·ies** business of fishing; fishing ground **fish'y** *adj* **fish·i·er, fish·i·est** of, like, or full of fish; dubious, open to suspicion; unsafe **fish'er·man** *n* one who catches fish for a living or for pleasure **fish'plate** *n* piece of metal holding wooden beams, etc together **fish stick** small piece of fish covered in breadcrumbs

fis·sure [FISH-ər] *n* cleft, split, cleavage **fis'sile** [-əl] *adj* capable of splitting; tending to split **fis·sion** [FISH-ən] *n* splitting; reproduction by division of living cells into two parts, each of which becomes complete organism; splitting of atomic nucleus with release of large amount of energy **fis'sio·n·a·ble** *adj* capable of undergoing nuclear fission **fis·sip·a·rous** [fi-SIP-ər-əs] *adj* reproducing by fission

fist *n* clenched hand **fist'i·cuffs** *pl n* fighting

fis·tu·la [FIS-chuu-lə] *n, pl* **-las** pipelike ulcer

fit[1] *v* **fit·ted** or **fit, fit·ting** ▷ *vt* be suited to; be properly adjusted to; arrange, adjust, apply, insert; supply, furnish ▷ *vi* be correctly adjusted or adapted; be of right size ▷ *adj* suited to; be properly adjusted to; ready; in good condition or health ▷ *n* way anything fits, its style; adjustment **fit'ly** *adv* **fit'ment** *n* piece of equipment **fit'ness** *n* **fitter** *n* one who, that which, makes fit; one who supervises making and fitting of garments; mechanic skilled in fitting up metal work **fitting** *adj* appropriate, suitable; proper ▷ *n* fixture; apparatus; action of fitting

fit[2] *n* seizure with convulsions, spasms, loss of consciousness, etc, as of epilepsy, hysteria, etc; sudden passing attack of illness; passing state, mood **fit'ful** *adj* spasmodic, capricious **fit'ful·ly** *adv*

five [fiv] *adj, n* cardinal number after four **fifth** *adj, n* ordinal number **fifth'ly** *adv* **fif'teen** *adj, n* ten plus five **fif'teenth** *adj, n* **fif'ti·eth** *adj, n* **fif'ty** *adj, n, pl* **-ties** five tens **fifth column** organization spying for enemy within country at war

527 *n* non-profit US political organization that is exempt from taxes

fix [fiks] *vt* fasten, make firm or stable; set, establish; appoint, assign, determine; make fast; repair; *inf* influence the outcome of unfairly or by deception; bribe; *sl* treat someone vengefully ▷ *vi* become firm or solidified; determine ▷ *n* difficult situation; position of ship, aircraft ascertained by radar, observation, etc; *sl* dose of narcotic drug **fix·a'tion** *n* act of fixing; preoccupation, obsession; situation of being set in some way of acting or thinking **fix'a·tive** *adj* capable of, or tending to fix ▷ *n* **fix'ed·ly** [-sid-lee] *adv* intently **fix'ture** [-chər] *n* thing fixed in position; thing attached to house; sporting event that takes place regularly; person long-established in a place **fix up** arrange **fix (someone) up** attend to person's needs, esp arrange date

fizz *vi* hiss, splutter ▷ *n* hissing

noise; effervescent liquid such as champagne **fiz'zle** [-əl] vi **-zled, -zling** splutter weakly ▷ n fizzling noise; fiasco **fizzle out** inf come to nothing, fail

fjord [fyord] n (esp in Norway) long, narrow inlet of sea

flab·ber·gast [FLAB-ər-gast] vt overwhelm with astonishment

flab·by [FLAB-ee] adj **-bi·er, -bi·est** hanging loose, limp; out of condition, too fat; feeble; yielding **flab** n inf unsightly fat on the body **flab'bi·ness** n

flac·cid [FLAK-sid] adj flabby, lacking firmness **flac·cid'i·ty** n

flag¹ n banner, piece of bunting attached to staff or halyard as standard or signal ▷ vt **flagged, flag·ging** inform by flag signals **Flag Day** June 14 **flag'ship** n admiral's ship; most important ship of fleet **flag'staff** n pole for flag

flag² n flat slab of stone ▷ pl pavement of flags ▷ vt **flagged, flag·ging** pave with flags **flag'stone** n

flag³ vi **flagged, flag·ging** droop, fade; lose vigor

flag·el·late [FLAJ-ə-layt] vt **-lat·ed, -lat·ing** scourge, flog **flag'el·lant** [-lənt] n one who scourges self, esp in religious penance **flag·el·la'tion** n **flag'el·la·tor** n

flag·eo·let [flaj-ə-LET] n small flutelike instrument

flag·on [FLAG-ən] n large bottle of wine, etc

fla·grant [FLAY-grənt] adj glaring, scandalous, blatant **fla'gran·cy** n

flail [flayl] n instrument for threshing grain by hand ▷ v beat with, move as, flail

flair n natural ability; elegance

flak n antiaircraft fire; inf adverse criticism

flake [flayk] n small, thin piece, esp particle of snow; piece chipped off ▷ v **flaked, flak·ing** (cause to) peel off in flakes **flak'y** adj **flak·i·er, flak·i·est** of like flakes; sl eccentric **flake out** inf collapse, sleep from exhaustion

flam·boy·ant [flam-BOI-ənt] adj florid, gorgeous, showy; exuberant, ostentatious

flame [flaym] n burning gas, esp above fire; visible burning; passion, esp love; inf sweetheart; inf an abusive message sent by e-mail ▷ v **flamed, flam·ing** give out flames, blaze; shine; burst out; inf to send an abusive message by e-mail

fla·men·co [flə-MENG-koh] n Spanish dance to guitar; music for this

fla·min·go [flə-MING-goh] n, pl **-gos** or **-goes** large pink to scarlet bird with long neck and legs

flam·ma·ble [FLAM-ə-bəl] adj liable to catch fire, inflammable

flan n open sweet dessert with caramel topping; tartlike pastry

flange [flanj] n projecting flat rim, collar, or rib ▷ v **flanged, flang·ing** provide with or take form of flange

flank [flangk] n part of side between hips and ribs; side of anything, eg body of troops ▷ vt guard or strengthen on flank; attack or take in flank; be at, move along either side of

flan·nel [FLAN-l] n soft woolen fabric for clothing, esp trousers **flan'nel·mouth** n person of slow, thick speech or deceptively smooth speech

flap v **flapped, flap·ping** move (wings, arms, etc) as bird flying; (cause to) sway; strike with flat object; sl be agitated, flustered

▷ *n* act of flapping; broad piece of anything hanging from hinge or loosely from one side; movable part of aircraft wing; *inf* state of excitement or panic **flap'pa·ble** *adj inf* easily confused, esp under stress

flare [flair] *vi* **flared, flar·ing** blaze with unsteady flame; (*with up*) burst suddenly into anger; spread outward, as bottom of skirt ▷ *n* instance of flaring; signal light

flash *n* sudden burst of light or flame; sudden short blaze; very short time; brief news item; display ▷ *vi* break into sudden flame; gleam; burst into view; move very fast; appear suddenly; *sl* expose oneself indecently ▷ *vt* cause to gleam; emit (light, etc) suddenly **flash'er** *n* thing that flashes; *sl* one who indecently exposes self **flash'back** *n* break in continuity of book, play or film, to introduce what has taken place previously **flash'y** *adj* **flash·i·er, flash·i·est** showy, sham **flash point** temperature at which a vapor ignites; point at which violence or anger breaks out

flask *n* long-necked bottle for scientific use; metal or glass pocket bottle

flat[1] *adj* **flat·ter, flat·test** level; spread out; at full length; smooth; downright; dull, lifeless; *music* below true pitch; (of vehicle tire) deflated, punctured ▷ *n* what is flat; *music* note half tone below natural pitch **flat'ly** *adv* **flat'ness** *n* **flat'ten** *vt* **flat feet** feet with abnormally flattened arches **flat'foot** *n, pl* **-foots** *sl* police officer **flat race** horse race over level ground with no jumps **flat rate** the same price in all cases **flat out** at, with maximum speed or effort

flat[2] *n* apartment

flat·ter [FLAT-àr] *vt* fawn on; praise insincerely; inspire unfounded belief; gratify (senses); represent too favorably **flat'ter·er** *n* **flat'ter·y** *n, pl* **-ter·ies**

flat·u·lent [FLACH-à-lànt] *adj* suffering from, generating (excess) gases in intestines; pretentious **flat'u·lence** *n* flatulent condition; verbosity, emptiness

flaunt [flawnt] *v* show off; wave proudly

flautist *n* see **FLUTE**

fla·vor [FLAY-àr] *n* mixed sensation of smell and taste; distinctive taste, savor; undefinable characteristic, quality of anything ▷ *vt* give flavor to; season **fla'vor·ing** *n* **fla'vor·ful** *adj*

flaw *n* crack; defect, blemish ▷ *vt* make flaw in **flaw'less** *adj* perfect

flax [flaks] *n* plant grown for its textile fiber and seeds; its fibers, spun into linen thread **flax'en** *adj* of flax; light yellow or straw-colored

flay *vt* strip skin off; criticize severely

flea [flee] *n* small, wingless, jumping, blood-sucking insect **flea'bag** *n sl* worthless racehorse, unkempt dog, etc; shabby hotel, etc **flea'bite** *n* insect's bite; trifling injury; trifle **flea'-bit·ten** *adj* bitten by flea; mean, worthless; scruffy **flea market** market, us held outdoors, for used articles, cheap goods

fleck [flek] *n* small mark, streak, or particle ▷ *vt* mark with flecks

fled pt/pp of **FLEE**

fledged [flejd] *adj* (of birds) able to fly; experienced, trained **fledg'ling** *n* young bird; inexperienced person

flee *v* **fled, flee·ing** run away from

fleece [flees] *n* sheep's wool ▷ *vt* **fleeced, fleec·ing** rob **fleec'y** *adj* **fleec·i·er, fleec·i·est** resembling wool

fleet[1] n number of warships organized as unit; number of ships, automobiles, etc operating together

fleet[2] adj **-er, -est** swift, nimble **fleet'ing** adj passing, transient **fleet'ing·ly** adv

flesh n soft part, muscular substance, between skin and bone; in plants, pulp; fat; person's family **flesh'ly** adj **-li·er, -li·est** carnal, material **flesh'y** adj **flesh·i·er, flesh·i·est** plump, pulpy **flesh'pots** pl n (places catering to) self-indulgent living **in the flesh** in person, actually present

fleur-de-lis [flur-dl-EE] n, pl **fleurs-de-lis** [-dl-EEZ] heraldic lily with three petals

flew pt of FLY

flex [fleks] n act of flexing ▷ v bend, be bent **flex·i·bil'i·ty** n **flex'i·ble** adj easily bent; manageable; adaptable **flex'time** n system permitting variation in starting and finishing times of work, providing agreed total time is worked over a specified period

flib·ber·ti·gib·bet [FLIB-ər-tee-jib-it] n flighty, chattering person

flick [flik] vt strike lightly, jerk ▷ n light blow, jerk; sl motion picture

flick·er [FLIK-ər] vi burn, shine, unsteadily; waver, quiver ▷ n unsteady light or movement

flight [flīt] n act or manner of flying through air; number flying together, as birds; journey in aircraft; air force unit of command; power of flying; swift movement or passage; sally; distance flown; stairs between two landings; running away **flight recorder** electronic device in aircraft storing information about its flight **flight·y** [FLĪ-tee] adj **flight·i·er, flight·i·est** frivolous, erratic

flim·sy [FLIM-zee] adj **-si·er,**

-si·est frail, weak, thin; easily destroyed **flim'si·ness** n

flinch vi shrink, draw back, wince

fling v flung, **fling·ing** mainly tr throw, send, move, with force ▷ n throw; hasty attempt; spell of indulgence; vigorous dance

flint n hard steel-gray stone; piece of this; hard substance used (as flint) for striking fire **flint'y** adj **flint·i·er, flint·i·est** like or consisting of flint; hard, cruel

flip v flipped, **flip·ping** throw or flick lightly; turn over; sl react with astonishment, become irrational ▷ n instance, act, of flipping; drink with beaten egg **flip'pan·cy** n, pl **-cies flip'pant** adj treating serious things lightly **flip'per** n limb, fin for swimming ▷ pl sl fin-shaped rubber devices worn on feet to help in swimming

flirt [flurt] vi play with another's affections; trifle, toy (with) ▷ n person who flirts **flir·ta'tion** [-TAY-shən] n **flir·ta'tious** adj

flit vi flit·ted, flit·ting pass lightly and rapidly; dart; inf go away hastily, secretly

flitch [flich] n side of bacon

float [flōht] vi rest, drift on surface of liquid; be suspended freely; move aimlessly ▷ vt of liquid, support, bear alone; in commerce, get (company) started; obtain loan ▷ n light object used to help someone or something float; motor vehicle carrying tableau, etc, in parade; uncollected checks, etc in process of transfer between banks, etc **flo·ta'tion** n act of floating, esp floating of business venture

floc·cu·late [FLOK-yə-layt] vt **-lat·ed, -lat·ing** form into masses of particles **floc'cu·lant** [-lənt] n chemical for accomplishing this

floc·cu·lent [FLOK-yə-lənt] *adj* like tufts of wool

flock¹ [flok] *n* number of animals of one kind together; *fig* body of people; religious congregation ▷ *vi* gather in a crowd

flock² *n* lock, tuft of wool, etc; wool refuse for stuffing cushions, etc

floe [floh] *n* sheet of floating ice

flog *vt* **flogged, flog·ging** beat with whip, stick, etc; *sl* sell, esp vigorously

flood [flud] *n* inundation, overflow of water; rising of tide; outpouring; flowing water ▷ *vt* inundate; cover, fill with water; arrive, move, etc in great numbers **flood'gate** *n* gate, sluice for letting water in or out **flood'light** *n* broad, intense beam of artificial light **flood'lit** *adj* **flood tide** the rising tide

floor [flor] *n* lower surface of room; set of rooms on one level, story; flat space; (right to speak in) meeting or legislative chamber; lower limit ▷ *vt* supply with floor; knock down; confound **floor'ing** *n* material for floors **floor show** entertainment in nightclub, etc

flop *vi* **flopped, flop·ping** bend, fall, collapse loosely, carelessly; fall flat on floor, on water, etc; *inf* go to sleep; *inf* fail ▷ *n* flopping movement or sound; *inf* failure **flop'pi·ness** *n* **flop'py** *adj* **-pi·er, -pi·est** limp, unsteady **flop'house** *n* run-down rooming house **floppy disk** *computing* flexible magnetic disk that stores information

flo·ra [FLOR-ə] *n* plants of a region; list of them **flor'al** *adj* of flowers **flo·res·cence** [-əns] *n* state or time of flowering

flo·ret [FLOR-it] *n* small flower forming part of composite flower

flo·ri·cul·ture *n* cultivation of flowers **flo·ri·cul'tur·ist** *n* **flo'rist** *n* dealer in flowers

flor'id *adj* with red, flushed complexion; ornate

floss [flaws] *n* mass of fine, silky fibers; fluff **floss'y** *adj* **floss·i·er, floss·i·est** light and downy; excessively fancy

flotation SEE FLOAT

flo·til·la [floh-TIL-ə] *n* fleet of small vessels, esp naval vessels

flot·sam [FLOT-səm] *n* floating wreckage; discarded waste objects; penniless population of city, etc

flounce¹ [flowns] *vi* **flounced, flounc·ing** go, move abruptly and impatiently ▷ *n* fling, jerk of body or limb

flounce² *n* ornamental gathered strip on woman's garment

floun·der¹ [FLOWN-dər] *vi* plunge and struggle, esp in water or mud; proceed in bungling, hesitating manner ▷ *n* act of floundering

flounder² *n* type of flatfish

flour [FLOW-ər] *n* powder prepared by sifting and grinding wheat, etc; fine soft powder ▷ *vt* sprinkle with flour

flour·ish [FLUR-ish] *vi* thrive; be in the prime ▷ *vt* brandish, display; wave about ▷ *n* ornamental curve; showy gesture in speech, etc; waving of hand, weapon, etc; fanfare (of trumpets)

flout [flowt] *vt* show contempt for, mock; defy

flow [floh] *vi* glide along as stream; circulate, as the blood; move easily; move in waves; hang loose; be present in abundance ▷ *n* act, instance of flowing; quantity that flows; rise of tide; ample supply **flow chart** diagram showing sequence of operations in industrial, etc process

flow·er [FLOW-ər] *n* colored (not

green) part of plant from which fruit is developed; bloom, blossom; ornamentation; choicest part, pick ▷ vi produce flowers; bloom; come to prime condition ▷ vt ornament with flowers **flow·er·et** n small flower **flow·er·y** adj **-er·i·er, -er·i·est** abounding in flowers; full of fine words, ornamented with figures of speech **flower girl** girl selling flowers; young girl designated to attend bride at wedding ceremony

flown pp of **FLY**

flu n short for **INFLUENZA**

fluc·tu·ate [FLUK-choo-ayt] v **-at·ed, -at·ing** vary, rise and fall, undulate **fluc·tu·a'tion** n

flue [floo] n passage or pipe for smoke or hot air, chimney

flu·ent [FLOO-ənt] adj speaking, writing a given language easily and well; easy, graceful

fluff n soft, feathery stuff; down; inf mistake; inf anything insubstantial ▷ v make or become soft, light; inf make mistake **fluff'y** adj **fluff·i·er, fluff·i·est**

flu·id [FLOO-id] adj flowing easily, not solid ▷ n gas or liquid **flu·id'i·ty** n **fluid ounce** one sixteenth of a pint

fluke¹ [flook] n flat triangular point of anchor ▷ pl whale's tail

fluke² n stroke of luck, accident **fluk'y** adj **fluk·i·er, fluk·i·est** uncertain; got by luck

fluke³ n type of flatfish; parasitic worm

flume [floom] n narrow (artificial) channel for water

flum·mer·y [FLUM-ə-ree] n, pl **-mer·ies** nonsense, idle talk, humbug; dish of milk, flour, eggs, etc

flum·mox [FLUM-əks] vt inf bewilder, perplex

flung pt/pp of **FLING**

flun·ky [FLUNG-kee] n, pl **-kies** servant, esp liveried manservant; assistant doing menial work; servile person

fluo·res·cence [fluu-RES-əns] n emission of light or other radiation from substance when bombarded by particles (electrons, etc or other radiation, as in fluorescent lamp) **fluo·res'cent** adj

fluor·ide [FLUUR-id] n salt containing fluorine, esp as added to domestic water supply as protection against tooth decay **fluor'i·date** v **-dat·ed, -dat·ing** treat with fluoride **fluor·i·da'tion** n **fluor'ine** [-een] n nonmetallic element, yellowish gas

flur·ry [FLUR-ee] n, pl **-ries** squall, gust; bustle, commotion; fluttering (as of snowflakes) ▷ v **-ried, -ry·ing** agitate, bewilder, fluster

flush¹ vi blush; of skin, redden; flow suddenly or violently; be excited ▷ vt send water through (a toilet or pipe) so as to clean it; excite ▷ n reddening, blush; rush of water; excitement; elation; glow of color; freshness, vigor ▷ adj full, in flood; well supplied; level with surrounding surface

flush² v (cause to) leave cover and take flight

flush³ n set of cards all of one suit

flus·ter [FLUS-tər] v make or become nervous, agitated ▷ n

flute [floot] n wind instrument of tube with holes stopped by fingers or keys and blowhole in side; groove, channel ▷ v **flut·ed, flut·ing** ▷ vi play on flute ▷ vt make grooves in **flut'ist, flaut'ist** [FLOWT-] n flute player

flut·ter [FLUT-ər] v flap (as wings) rapidly without flight or in short flights; quiver; be or make excited, agitated ▷ n flapping movement;

nervous agitation

flu·vi·al [FLOO-vee-əl] adj of rivers

flux [fluks] n discharge; constant succession of changes; substance mixed with metal to clean, aid adhesion in soldering, etc; measure of strength in magnetic field

fly¹ [flī] v **flew, flown, fly·ing** move through air on wings or in aircraft; pass quickly (through air); float loosely; spring, rush; flee, run away ▷ vt operate aircraft; cause to fly; set flying ▷ vi run from ▷ n (zipper or buttons fastening) opening in trousers; flap in garment or tent; flying **flying** adj hurried, brief **fly'fish** v fish with artificial fly as lure **flying boat** airplane fitted with floats instead of landing wheels **flying buttress** architecture arched or slanting structure attached at only one point to a mass of masonry **flying colors** conspicuous success **flying fish** fish with winglike fins used for gliding above the sea **flying saucer** unidentified (disk-shaped) flying object, supposedly from outer space **flying squad** special detachment of police, etc, ready to act quickly **fly'leaf** n, pl **-leaves** blank leaf at beginning or end of book **fly'o·ver** n formation of aircraft in flight for observation from ground **fly'wheel** n heavy wheel regulating speed of machine

fly² n, pl **flies** two-winged insect, esp common housefly **fly'catch·er** n small insect-eating songbird

Fm chemistry fermium

foal [fohl] n young of horse, ass, etc ▷ v bear (foal)

foam [fohm] n collection of small bubbles on liquid; froth of saliva or sweat; light cellular solid used for insulation, packing, etc ▷ v (cause to) produce foam; be very angry

foam'y adj **foam·i·er, foam·i·est**

fob n short watch chain; small pocket in waistband of trousers or vest

fob off v **fobbed, fob·bing** ignore, dismiss someone or something in offhand (insulting) manner; dispose of

foci pl of **focus**

fo·cus [FOH-kəs] n, pl **-cus·es** or **-ci** [-sī] point at which rays meet after being reflected or refracted; state of optical image when it is clearly defined; state of instrument producing such image; point of convergence; point on which interest, activity is centered ▷ v **-cused, -cus·ing** ▷ vt bring to focus, adjust; concentrate ▷ vi come to focus; converge **fo'cal** [-kəl] adj of, at focus

fod·der [FOD-ər] n bulk food for livestock

foe [foh] n enemy

fog n thick mist; dense watery vapor in lower atmosphere; cloud of anything reducing visibility; stupor ▷ vt **fogged, fog·ging** cover in fog; puzzle **fog'gy** adj **-gi·er, -gi·est**
fog'horn n instrument to warn ships in fog

fo·gy [FOH-gee] n, pl **-gies** old-fashioned person

foi·ble [FOI-bəl] n minor weakness, idiosyncrasy

foil¹ vt baffle, defeat, frustrate ▷ n blunt sword, with button on point for fencing

foil² n metal in thin sheet; anything or person that sets off another to advantage

foist vt (usu with on, upon) sell, pass off inferior or unwanted thing as valuable

fold¹ [fohld] vt double up, bend part of; interlace (arms); wrap up;

clasp (in arms); *cookery* mix gently ▷ *vi* become folded; admit of being folded; *inf* fail ▷ *n* folding; coil; winding; line made by folding; crease; foldlike geological formation **fold'er** *n* binder, file for loose papers **fold²** *n* enclosure for sheep; body of believers, church

fo·li·age [FOH-lee-ij] *n* leaves collectively, leafage **fo·li·a·ceous** [-AY-shəs] *adj* of or like leaf **fo'li·ate** [-it] *adj* leaflike, having leaves

fo·li·o [FOH-lee-oh] *n, pl* **-li·os** sheet of paper folded in half to make two leaves of book; book of largest common size made up of such sheets; page numbered on one side only; page number

folk [fohk] *n* people in general; family, relatives; race of people **folk dance** traditional country dance **folk'lore** *n* tradition, customs, beliefs popularly held **folk song** music originating among a people

fol·li·cle [FOL-i-kəl] *n* small cavity, sac; seed vessel

fol·low [FOL-oh] *v* go or come after ▷ *vt* accompany, attend on; keep to (path, etc); take as guide, conform to; engage in; have a keen interest in; be consequent on; grasp meaning of ▷ *vi* come next; result **fol'low·er** *n* disciple, supporter **fol'low·ing** *adj* about to be mentioned ▷ *n* body of supporters **fol'low-through** *n* in ball games, continuation of stroke after impact with ball **fol'low-up** *n* something done to reinforce initial action

fol·ly [FOL-ee] *n, pl* **-lies** foolishness; foolish action, idea, etc; useless, extravagant structure

fo·ment [foh-MENT] *vt* foster, stir up; bathe with warm lotions

fond *adj* **-er, -est** tender, loving **fond'ly** *adv* **fond'ness** *n* fond of

having liking for

fon·dant [FON-dənt] *n* soft sugar mixture for candies; candy made of this

fon·dle [FON-dl] *vt* **-dled, -dling** caress

fon·due [fon-DOO] *n* Swiss dish of cheese and seasonings into which pieces of bread, etc are dipped

font *n* bowl for baptismal water usu on pedestal; productive source; assortment of printing type of one size

fon·ta·nel [fon-tn-EL] *n* soft, membranous gap between bones of baby's skull

food *n* solid nourishment; what one eats; mental or spiritual nourishment **food additive** natural or synthetic substance added to commercially processed food as preservative or to add color, flavor, etc **food group** any category into which a food may be placed according to its nutritional content **food processor** electric kitchen appliance for automatic chopping, blending, etc of foodstuffs **food'stuff** *n* food

fool *n* silly, empty-headed person; dupe; simpleton; *history* jester, clown ▷ *vt* delude; dupe ▷ *vi* act as fool **fool'er·y** *n, pl* **-er·ies** habitual folly; act of playing the fool; absurdity **fool'har·di·ness** *n* **fool'har·dy** *adj* **-di·er, -di·est** foolishly adventurous **fool'ish** *adj* ill-considered, silly, stupid **fool'proof** *adj* proof against failure **fool's cap** jester's or dunce's cap **fools'cap** *n* inexpensive paper, esp legal-size (formerly with fool's cap as watermark)

foot [fuut] *n, pl* **feet** lowest part of leg, from ankle down; lowest part of anything, base, stand; end of bed, etc; measure of twelve inches;

division of line of verse ▷ **v** (usu tr) dance **foot it** *inf* walk **foot the bill** pay the entire cost **foot'age** *n* length in feet; length, extent, of film used **foot'ing** *n* basis, foundation; firm standing, relations, conditions ▷ *pl* (concrete) foundations for walls of buildings **foot-and-mouth disease** infectious viral disease in sheep, cattle, etc **foot'ball** *n* game played with inflated oval ball; the ball **foot'ball pool** form of gambling on results of football games **foot brake** brake operated by pressure on foot pedal **foot fault** *tennis* fault of overstepping baseline while serving **foot'hold** *n* place affording secure grip for the foot; secure position from which progress may be made **foot'lights** *pl n* lights across front of stage **foot'loose** *adj* free of any ties **foot'note** *n* note of reference or explanation printed at foot of page **foot-pound** *n* unit of measurement of work in fps system **foot'print** *n* mark left by foot **playing foot'sie** flirting or sharing a surreptitious intimacy **foot'slog** *vi* **-slogged, slogging** walk, go on foot **foot'slog·ger** *n*

fop *n* man excessively concerned with fashion **fop'per·y** *n*, *pl* **-per·ies** **fop'pish** *adj*

for *prep* intended to reach, directed or belonging to; because of; instead of; toward; on account of; in favor of; respecting; during; in search of; in payment of; in the character of; in spite of ▷ *conj* because **in for it** *inf* liable for punishment or blame

for- *prefix* from, away, against: *forswear; forbid*

for·age [FOR-ijj] *n* food for cattle and horses ▷ *vi* **-aged, -ag·ing** collect forage; make roving search

for'ay *n* raid, inroad ▷ *vi* make one

for·bear [for-BAIR] *v* **-bore, -borne, -bear·ing** cease or refrain (from doing something) **for·bear'ance** *n* self-control, patience

for·bid [fər-BID] *vt* **-bade** or **-bad, -bid** or **-bid·den, -bid** or **-bid·ding** prohibit; refuse to allow **forbidding** *adj* uninviting, threatening

force [fors] *n* strength, power; compulsion; that which tends to produce a change in a physical system; mental or moral strength; body of troops, police, etc; group of people organized for particular task or duty; effectiveness, operative state; violence ▷ *vt* **forced, forc·ing** constrain, compel; produce by effort, strength; break open; urge, strain; drive; hasten maturity of **forced** *adj* accomplished by great effort; compulsory; unnatural; strained; excessive **force'ful** *adj* powerful, persuasive **for·ci·ble** *adj* done by force; efficacious, compelling, impressive; strong **for·ci·bly** *adv*

for·ceps [FOR-səps] *pl n* surgical pincers

ford *n* shallow place where river may be crossed ▷ *vt* **ford·a·ble** *adj*

fore¹ [for] *adj* in front ▷ *n* front part

fore² *interj* golfer's warning

fore- *prefix* before in time or rank: *forefather at the front: forecourt*

fore-and-aft [FOR-ənd-AFT] *adj* placed in line from bow to stern of ship

fore·arm [FOR-ahrm] *n* arm between wrist and elbow ▷ *vt* [for-AHRM] arm beforehand

fore·bear [FOR-bair] *n* ancestor

fore·bode [for-BOHD] *vt* **-bod·ed, -bod·ing** indicate in advance **foreboding** *n* anticipation of evil

fore·cast [FOR-kast] *vt* estimate beforehand (esp weather); prophesy

▷ *n* prediction

fore·castle [FOHK-səl] *n* forward raised part of ship; sailors' quarters

fore·close [for-KLOHZ] *vt* **-closed, -clos·ing** take away power of redeeming (mortgage); prevent, shut out, bar **fore·clo·sure** [-zhər] *n*

fore·court [FOR-kort] *n* courtyard, open space, in front of building; tennis part of court between service line and net

fore·fa·ther [FOR-fah-thər] *n* ancestor

fore·fin·ger [FOR-fing-gər] *n* finger next to thumb, index finger

foregather see FORGATHER

fore·go [for-GOH] *vt* **-went, -gone, -go·ing** precede in time, place **foregoing** *adj* going before, preceding **foregone** *adj* determined beforehand; preceding **foregone conclusion** result that might have been foreseen

fore·ground [FOR-grownd] *n* part of view, esp in picture, nearest observer

fore·hand [FOR-hand] *adj* of stroke in racquet games made with inner side of wrist leading

fore·head [FOR-id] *n* part of face above eyebrows and between temples

for·eign [FOR-in] *adj* not of, or in, one's own country; relating to, or connected with other countries; irrelevant; coming from outside; unfamiliar, strange **for'eign·er** *n*

fore·man [FOR-mən] *n, pl* **-men** one in charge of work; leader of jury

fore·mast [FOR-mast] *n* mast nearest bow

fore·most [FOR-mohst] *adj, adv* first in time, place, importance, etc

fore·noon [FOR-noon] *n* morning

fo·ren·sic [fə-REN-sik] *adj* of courts of law **forensic medicine** application of medical knowledge in legal matters

fore·play [FOR-play] *n* sexual stimulation before intercourse

fore·run·ner [FOR-run-ər] *n* one that goes before, precursor

fore·see [for-SEE] *vt* **-saw, -seen, -see·ing** see beforehand

fore·shad·ow [for-SHAD-oh] *vt* show, suggest beforehand, be a type of

fore·short·en [for-SHOR-tn] *vt* draw (object) so that it appears shortened; make shorter

fore·sight [FOR-sit] *n* foreseeing; care for future

fore·skin [FOR-skin] *n* skin that covers end of penis

for·est [FOR-ist] *n* area with heavy growth of trees and plants; these trees; *fig* something resembling forest ▷ *vt* plant, create forest (in an area) **for'est·er** *n* one skilled in forestry **for'est·ry** *n* study, management of forest planting and maintenance

fore·stall [for-STAWL] *vt* anticipate; prevent, guard against in advance

fore·taste [FOR-tayst] *n* anticipation; taste beforehand

fore·tell [for-TEL] *vt* **-told, -tel·ling** prophesy

fore·thought [FOR-thawt] *n* thoughtful consideration of future events

for·ev·er [for-EV-ər] *adv* always; eternally; *inf* for a long time

fore·warn [for-WORN] *vt* warn, caution in advance

forewent see FOREGO

fore·word [FOR-wurd] *n* preface

for·feit [FOR-fit] *n* thing lost by crime or fault; penalty, fine ▷ *adj* lost by crime or fault ▷ *vt* lose by penalty **for'fei·ture** [-fi-chər] *n*

for·gath·er [for-GATH-ər] *vi* meet together, assemble, associate

forge[1] [forj] *n* place where metal is worked, smithy; furnace, workshop for melting or refining metal ▷ *vt* **forged, forg·ing** shape (metal) by heating in fire and hammering; make, shape, invent; make a fraudulent imitation of thing; counterfeit **forg·er** *n* **for·ger·y** *n, pl* **-ger·ies** forged artwork, document, currency, etc; the making of it

forge[2] *vi* **forged, forg·ing** advance steadily

for·get [fər-GET] *vt* **-got, -got·ten** or **-got, -get·ting** lose memory of, neglect, overlook **for·get·ful** *adj* liable to forget

for·give [fər-GIV] *v* **-gave, -giv·en, -giv·ing** cease to blame or hold resentment against; pardon **for·give·ness** *n*

for·go [for-GOH] *vt* **-went, -gone, -go·ing** go without; give up **forgot, forgotten** SEE FORGET

fork *n* pronged instrument for eating food; pronged tool for digging or lifting; division into branches; point of this division; one of the branches ▷ *vi* branch ▷ *vt* dig, lift, throw, with fork; make fork-shaped **fork out** *inf* pay (reluctantly)

for·lorn[1] *adj* forsaken; desperate **forlorn hope** anything undertaken with little hope of success

form *n* shape, visible appearance; visible person or animal; structure; nature; species, kind; regularly drawn up document, esp printed one with blanks for particulars; condition, good condition; customary way of doing things; set order of words; *printing* frame for type ▷ *vt* shape, mold, arrange, organize; train, shape in the mind, conceive; to go to make up, make part of ▷ *vi* come into

existence or shape **for·ma·tion** *n* forming; thing formed; structure, shape, arrangement; military order **form·a·tive** *adj* of, relating to, development; serving or tending to form; used in forming **form·less** *adj*

for·mal [FOR-məl] *adj* ceremonial, according to rule; of outward form or routine; of, for, formal occasions; according to rule that does not matter; precise; stiff ▷ *n* formal dance **for·mal·ism** *n* quality of being formal; exclusive concern for form, structure, technique in an activity **for·mal·i·ty** *n, pl* **-ties** observance required by custom or etiquette; condition or quality of being formal; conformity to custom; conventionality, mere form; in art, precision, stiffness, as opposed to originality

for·mal·de·hyde [for-MAL-də-hīd] *n* colorless, poisonous, pungent gas, used in making antiseptics and in chemistry **for·ma·lin** [-mə-lin] *n* solution of formaldehyde in water, used as disinfectant, preservative, etc

for·mat *n* size and shape of book; organization of TV show, etc

for·mer [FOR-mər] *adj* earlier in time; of past times; first named ▷ *pron* first named thing or person or fact **for·mer·ly** *adv* previously

for·mi·da·ble [FOR-mi-də-bəl] *adj* to be feared; overwhelming, terrible, redoubtable; likely to be difficult, serious **for·mi·da·bly** *adv*

for·mu·la [FOR-myə-lə] *n, pl* **-las** or **-lae** [-lee] set form of words setting forth principle, method or rule for doing, producing something; substance so prepared; specific category of racing car; recipe; group of numbers, letters, or symbols expressing a scientific or mathematical rule **for•mu•late** [-layt] vt **-lat•ed, -lat•ing** reduce to, express in formula, or in definite form; devise **for•mu•la•tion** n

for•ni•ca•tion [for-ni-KAY-shən] n sexual intercourse outside marriage **for•ni•cate** vi **-cat•ed, -cat•ing**

for•sake [for-SAYK] vt **-sook, -sak•en, -sak•ing** abandon, desert; give up

for•sooth' adv obs in truth

for•swear [for-SWAIR] vt **-swore, -sworn, -swear•ing** renounce, deny; ▷ refl perjure

for•syth•i•a [for-SITH-ee-ə] n widely cultivated shrub with yellow flowers

fort n fortified place, stronghold

forte[1] [fort] n one's strong point, that in which one excels

forte[2] [FOR-tay] adv music loudly **for•tis•si•mo** adv music very loudly

forth adv onward, into view **forth•com•ing** adj about to come; ready when wanted; willing to talk, communicative **forth•with'** adv at once, immediately **forth•right** [FORTH-rīt] adj direct; outspoken

for•ti•eth see FOUR

for•ti•fy [FOR-tə-fī] vt **-fied, -fy•ing** strengthen; provide with defensive works **for•ti•fi•ca•tion** n

for•ti•tude [FOR-ti-tood] n courage in adversity or pain, endurance

fort•night [FORT-nīt] n two weeks **fort'night•ly** adv

FORTRAN [FOR-tran] computing a programming language for mathematical and scientific purposes

for•tress [FOR-tris] n large fort or fortified town

for•tu•i•tous [for-TOO-i-təs] adj accidental, by chance

for•tu•i•tous•ly adv **for•tune** [FOR-chən] n good luck, prosperity; wealth; stock of wealth; chance, luck **for'tu•nate** [-nit] adj **for'tu•nate•ly** adv **fortune hunter** person seeking fortune, esp by marriage **fortuneteller** n one who predicts a person's future

forty see FOUR

fo•rum [FOR-əm] n (place or medium for) meeting, assembly for open discussion or debate

for•ward [FOR-wərd] adj lying in front of; onward; presumptuous; impudent; advanced, progressive; relating to the future ▷ n player placed in forward position in various team games, eg basketball ▷ adv toward the future; toward the front, to the front, into view; as, in fore part of ship; onward, so as to make progress ▷ vt help forward; send, dispatch **for'ward•ly** adv pertly **for'ward•ness** n **for'wards** [-wərdz] adv **forward slash** forward-sloping diagonal mark (/)

forwent see FORGO

fos•sil [FOS-əl] n remnant or impression of animal or plant, esp prehistoric one, preserved in earth; inf person, idea, etc that is outdated and incapable of change **fos•sil•ize** v **-ized, -iz•ing** turn into fossil; petrify

fos•ter [FAW-stər] vt promote growth or development of; bring up child, esp not one's own ▷ adj of or involved in fostering a child: foster parents

fought pt/pp of FIGHT

foul [fowl] adj **-er, -est** loathsome, offensive; stinking; dirty; unfair; wet, rough; obscene, disgustingly abusive; charged with harmful matter, clogged, choked ▷ n act of unfair play; the breaking of a rule ▷ adv unfairly ▷ v (mainly tr) make, become foul; jam; collide with **foul·ly** adv

found[1] [fownd] pt/pp of **FIND**

found[2] vt establish, institute; lay base of; base, ground **foun·da·tion** n basis; base, lowest part of building; founding; endowed institution, etc **found·er** n **foundation stone** one of stones forming foundation of building, esp stone laid with public ceremony

found[3] vt melt and run into mold; cast **found·er** n **found·ry** n, pl **-ries** place for casting; art of this

found·er [FOWN-dər] vi collapse; sink; become stuck as in mud, etc

found·ling [FOWND-ling] n deserted infant

fount [fownt] n fountain

foun·tain [FOWN-tn] n jet of water, esp ornamental one; spring; source **foun·tain·head** [-hed] n source **fountain pen** pen with ink reservoir

four [for] n, adj cardinal number next after three **fourth** adj the ordinal number **fourth·ly** adv **for·ti·eth** adj **for·ty** adj, n, pl **-ties** four tens **four·teen'** n, adj four plus ten **four·teenth'** adj **four-stroke** adj describing an internal-combustion engine firing once every four strokes of piston **four·post·er** n bed with four posts for curtains, etc **four·some** n group of four people; game or dance for four people **four·square** adj firm, steady **on all fours** on hands and knees **401K** employer-run savings plan for retirement

fowl n domestic rooster or hen; bird, its flesh ▷vi hunt wild birds **fowling piece** gun for fowling

fox [foks] n red bushy-tailed animal; its fur; cunning person ▷vt perplex; discolor (paper) with brown spots;

mislead ▷vi act craftily; sham **fox·y** adj **fox·i·er, fox·i·est** foxlike; sl sexually appealing; attractive **fox·hole** n in war, small trench giving protection **fox·hound** n dog bred for hunting foxes **fox terrier** small dog now mainly kept as a pet **fox·trot** n (music for) ballroom dance ▷v

foy·er [FOI-ər] n entrance hall in theaters, hotels, etc; vestibule

Fr chemistry francium

fra·cas [FRAY-kəs] n noisy quarrel; uproar, brawl

frac·tion [FRAK-shən] n numerical quantity not an integer; fragment, piece **frac·tion·al** adj constituting a fraction; forming but a small part; insignificant

frac·tious [FRAK-shəs] adj unruly, irritable

frac·ture [FRAK-chər] n breakage, part broken; breaking of bone; breach, rupture ▷v **-tured, -tur·ing** break

frag·ile [FRAJ-əl] adj breakable; frail; delicate **fra·gil·i·ty** n

frag·ment [FRAG-mənt] n piece broken off; small portion, incomplete part ▷v (-ment) **frag·men·tar·y** [-te-ree] adj

fra·grant [FRAY-grənt] adj sweet-smelling **fra·grance** n scent

frail [frayl] adj **-er, -est** fragile, delicate; infirm; in weak health; morally weak **frail·ly** adv **frail·ty** n, pl **-ties**

frame [fraym] n that in which thing is set, as square of wood around picture, etc; structure; build of body; constitution; mood; individual exposure on strip of film ▷vt put together, make; adapt; put into words; put into frame; bring false charge against **frame-up** n plot, manufactured evidence **frame·work**

n structure into which completing parts can be fitted; supporting work

franc [frangk] *n* monetary unit of Switzerland and (formerly) France

fran·chise [FRAN-chiz] *n* right of voting; citizenship; privilege or right, esp right to sell certain goods ▷ *v* **-chised, -chis·ing**

fran·gi·pane [FRAN-jə-payn] *n* type of pastry cake; its filling

fran·gi·pan·i [fran-jə-PAN-ee] *n* tropical American shrub; perfume made of its flower

frank [frangk] *adj* **-er, -est** candid, outspoken; sincere ▷ *n* official mark on letter either canceling stamp or ensuring delivery without charge ▷ *vt* mark letter thus **frank'ly** *adv* candidly **frank'ness** *n*

frank·furt·er [FRANGK-fər-tər] *n* smoked sausage, hot dog

frank·in·cense [FRANG-kin-sens] *n* aromatic gum resin burned as incense

fran·tic [FRAN-tik] *adj* distracted with rage, grief, joy, etc; frenzied **fran'ti·cal·ly** *adv*

fra·ter·nal [frə-TUR-nl] *adj* of brother, brotherly **fra·ter'nal·ly** *adv* **fra·ter'ni·ty** *n, pl* **-ties** brotherliness; brotherhood; college society **frat·er·ni·za·tion** *n* **frat'er·nize** *vi* **-nized, -niz·ing** to associate, make friends **frat·ri·cid'al** [-SID-əl] *adj* **frat'ri·cide** *n* killing, killer of brother or sister

fraud [frawd] *n* criminal deception; swindle; imposture **fraud·u·lence** [FRAW-jə-ləns] *n* **fraud'u·lent** *adj*

fraught [frawt] *adj* filled (with), involving

fray[1] *n* fight; noisy quarrel

fray[2] *v* wear through by rubbing; make, become ragged at edge

fraz·zle [FRAZ-əl] *inf v* **-zled,**

-zling make or become exhausted; make or become irritated ▷ *n* exhausted state

freak [freek] *n* abnormal person, animal, thing ▷ *adj* **freak'ish** *adj* **freak'y** *adj* **freak·i·er, freak·i·est** **freak out** *sl* (cause to) hallucinate, be wildly excited, etc

freck·le [FREK-əl] *n* light brown spot on skin, esp caused by sun; any small spot ▷ *v* **-led, -ling** bring, come out in freckles

free *adj* **fre·er, fre·est** able to act at will, not under compulsion or restraint; not restricted or affected by; not subject to cost or tax; independent; not exact or literal; generous; not in use; (of person) not occupied, having no appointment; loose, not fixed ▷ *vt* **freed, free·ing** set at liberty; remove (obstacles, pain, etc); rid (of) **free'dom** *n* **free'ly** *adv* **free-for-all** *n* brawl **free'hand** *adj* drawn without guiding instruments **free'lance** [-lans] *adj, n* (of) self-employed, unattached person **Free·ma·son** [-may-sən] *n* member of secret fraternity for mutual help **freemasonry** *n* principles of Freemasons; fellowship, secret brotherhood **free'-range** *adj* (of livestock and poultry) kept, produced in natural, nonintensive conditions **free space** region that has no gravitational and electromagnetic fields **free speech** right to express opinions publicly **free-swinging** *adj* recklessly daring **free·think'er** *n* skeptic who forms own opinions, esp in religion **free trade** international trade free of protective tariffs **free'way** *n* express highway

freeze [freez] *v* **froze, fro·zen, freez·ing** change (by reduction of temperature) from liquid to solid,

freight | 226

as water to ice ▷ vt preserve (food, etc) by extreme cold, as in freezer; fix (prices, etc) ▷ vi feel very cold; become rigid as with fear; stop
freez'er n insulated cabinet for long-term storage of freezable foodstuffs
frozen adj of assets, etc, unrealizable
freezing point temperature at which liquid becomes solid
freight [frayt] n commercial transport (esp by rail, ship); cost of this; goods so carried ▷ vt send as or by freight **freight'er** n
French n language spoken by people of France ▷ adj of, or pertaining to France **French dressing** salad dressing **French fries** deep-fried strips of potato **French horn** musical wind instrument **French leave** unauthorized leave **French window** window extended to floor level and used as door
fre·net·ic [frə-NET-ik] adj frenzied
fren·zy [FREN-zee] n, pl -zies violent mental derangement; wild excitement **fren'zied** adj
fre·quent [FREE-kwənt] adj happening often; common; numerous ▷ vt [fri-KWENT] go often to **fre·quen·cy** n, pl -cies rate of occurrence; in radio, etc cycles per second of alternating current **fre·quen·ta·tive** [fri-KWEN-tə-tiv] adj expressing repetition
fres·co [FRES-koh] n, pl -coes method of painting in water color on plaster of wall before it dries; painting done thus
fresh adj -er, -est not stale; new; additional; different; recent; inexperienced; pure; not pickled, frozen, etc; not faded or dimmed; not tired; of wind, strong; inf unspoilt; forward **fresh'en** v **fresh'et** n rush of water at river mouth; flood of

river water **fresh'ly** adv **fresh'man** n first-year high school or college student
fret[1] v **fret·ted, fret·ting** be irritated, worry ▷ n irritation **fret'ful** adj irritable, (easily) upset
fret[2] n repetitive geometrical pattern; small bar on fingerboard of guitar, etc ▷ vt **fret·ted, fret·ting** ornament with carved pattern **fret saw** saw with narrow blade and fine teeth, used for fretwork **fret'work** n carved or open woodwork in ornamental patterns and devices
Freud·i·an [FROI-dee-ən] adj pert to Austrian psychologist Sigmund Freud, or his theories
fri·a·ble [FRI-ə-bəl] adj easily crumbled **fri·a·bil'i·ty,** n
fri·ar [FRI-ər] n member of mendicant religious order **fri'ar·y** n house of friars
fric·as·see [frik-ə-SEE] n dish of pieces of chicken or meat, fried or stewed and served with rich sauce ▷ vt **-seed, -see·ing** cook thus
fric·tion [FRIK-shən] n rubbing; resistance met with by body moving over another; clash of wills, etc, disagreement **fric·tion·al** adj
fried pt/pp of **FRY**
friend [frend] n one well known to another and regarded with affection and loyalty; intimate associate; supporter; (F-) Quaker **friend'less** adj **friend'li·ness** n **friend'ly** adj **-li·er, -li·est** having disposition of a friend, kind; favorable **friend'ship** n **friendly fire** military shooting or bombing that injures or kills comrades or allies
frieze [freez] n ornamental band, strip (on wall)
frig·ate [FRIG-it] n old (sailing) warship corresponding to modern cruiser; fast warship equipped for

escort and antisubmarine duties

fright [frīt] n sudden fear; shock; alarm; grotesque or ludicrous person or thing **fright'en** vt cause fear, fright in **fright'ful** adj terrible, calamitous; shocking; inf very great, very large **fright'ful•ly** adv inf terribly; very

frig•id [FRIJ-id] adj formal, dull; (sexually) unfeeling; cold **fri•gid'i•ty** n **frig'id•ly** n

frill n fluted strip of fabric gathered at one edge; ruff of hair, feathers around neck of dog, bird, etc; fringe; unnecessary words, politeness; superfluous thing; adornment ▷ vt make into, decorate with frill

fringe [frinj] n ornamental edge of hanging threads, tassels, etc; anything like this; edge, limit ▷ vt **fringed, fring•ing** adorn with, serve as, fringe **fringe benefit** benefit provided in addition to regular pay

frip•per•y [FRIP-ə-ree] n, pl **-per•ies** finery; trivia

fris•bee ® [FRIZ-bee] n disk-shaped object for throwing and catching as a sport or pastime

frisk vi move, leap, playfully ▷ vt wave briskly; search (person) for concealed weapons, etc ▷ n **frisk'y** adj **frisk•i•er, frisk•i•est**

frit•ter¹ [FRIT-ər] vt waste **fritter away** throw away, waste

fritter² n small deep-fried cake of batter often containing corn

friv•o•lous [FRI-ə-ləs] adj not serious, unimportant; flippant **fri•vol'i•ty** n

frizz vt curl into small crisp curls ▷ n frizzed hair **friz'zy** adj **-zi•er, -zi•est**

fro [froh] adv away: to and fro

frock [frok] n woman's dress; various garments ▷ vt dress with frock; invest with office of priest

frog¹ n tailless amphibious animal

developed from tadpole **frog'man** n swimmer equipped for swimming, working, underwater

frog² n ornamental coat fastening of button and loop; (military) attachment to belt to carry sword

frol•ic [FROL-ik] n merrymaking ▷ vi **-icked, -ick•ing** behave playfully **frol'ic•some** adj

from [frum] prep expressing point of departure, source, distance, cause, change of state, etc

frond n plant organ consisting of stem and foliage, usually with fruit forms, esp in ferns

front [frunt] n fore part; position directly before or ahead; battle line or area; meteorology dividing line between two air masses of different characteristics; outward aspect, bearing; inf something serving as a respectable cover for another, usu criminal, activity; field of activity; group with common goal ▷ v look, face; inf be a cover for ▷ adj of, at, the front **front'age** [-ij] n front of building; property line along street, lake, etc **fron'tal** [-əl] adj **fron'tier** [-TEER] n part of country that borders on another **fron'tis•piece** n illustration facing title page of book

frost [frawst] n frozen dew or mist; act or state of freezing; weather in which temperature falls below point at which water turns to ice ▷ v cover, be covered with frost or something similar in appearance; give slightly roughened surface **frost'i•ly** adv **frost'y** adj **frost•i•er, frost•i•est** accompanied by frost; chilly; cold; unfriendly **frost'bite** n destruction by cold of tissue, esp of fingers, ears, etc

froth [frawth] n collection of small bubbles, foam; scum; idle talk ▷ v (cause to) foam **froth'i•ly** adv

froth·y *adj* **froth·i·er, froth·i·est**

frown *vi* wrinkle brows ▷ *n*

frowz·y [FROW-zee] *adj*
frowz·i·er, frowz·i·est dirty,
unkempt

froze *pt of* **FREEZE frozen** *pp of*
FREEZE

fruc·ti·fy [FRUK-tə-fī] *v* **-fied,**
-fy·ing (cause to) bear fruit

fru·gal [FROO-gəl] *adj* sparing;
thrifty, economical; meager
fru·gal·i·ty *n*

fruit [froot] *n* seed and its envelope,
esp edible one; vegetable product;
(usu in pl) result, benefit ▷ *vi* bear
fruit **fruit'ful** [-fəl] *adj* **fru·i·tion**
[froo-ISH-ən] *n* enjoyment;
realization of hopes **fruit'less** *adj*
fruit'y *adj* **fruit·i·er, fruit·i·est**

frump *n* dowdy woman **frump'ish**
adj **frump'y** *adj* **frump·i·er,**
frump·i·est

frus·trate [FRUS-trayt] *vt*
-trat·ed, -trat·ing thwart; balk;
baffle; disappoint **frus·tra·tion** *n*

fry[1] [frī] *v* **fried, fry·ing** cook with
fat; be cooked thus; *sl* be executed
by electrocution

fry[2] *n*, *pl* **fry** young of fish **small fry**
young or insignificant beings

fuch·sia [FYOO-shə] *n* ornamental
shrub with purple-red flowers

fud·dle [FUD-l] *v* **-dled, -dling**
(cause to) be intoxicated, confused
▷ *n* this state

fudge[1] [fuj] *n* soft, variously
flavored candy

fudge[2] *vt* **fudged, fudg·ing** make,
do carelessly or dishonestly; fake

fuel [FYOO-əl] *n* material for
burning as source of heat or power;
something that nourishes ▷ *vt*
provide with fuel

fu·gi·tive [FYOO-ji-tiv] *n* one who
flees, esp from arrest or pursuit ▷ *adj*
fleeing; elusive

fugue [fyoog] *n* musical
composition in which themes are
repeated in different parts

F h·rer [FYUUR-ər] *n* Ger leader:
title used by Hitler as Nazi dictator

ful·crum [FUUL-krəm] *n*, *pl* **-crums**
point on which a lever is placed for
support

ful·fill [fuul-FIL] *vi* satisfy; carry
out; obey; satisfy (desire, etc)
ful·fill'ment *n*

full [fuul] *adj* **-er, -est** containing
as much as possible; abundant;
complete; ample; plump; (of
garment) of ample cut ▷ *adv* very;
quite; exactly **full'ness** *n*
ful·some [FUUL-səm] *adj* excessive
full·blown' [-BLOHN] *adj* fully
developed

ful·mi·nate [FUL-mə-nayt] *vi*
-nat·ed, -nat·ing criticize harshly
(with *against*) ▷ *n* chemical
compound exploding readily
ful·mi·na·tion *n*

fulsome *see* **FULL**

fum·ble [FUM-bəl] *v* **-bled, -bling**
grope about; handle awkwardly;
in football, etc, drop (ball) ▷ *n*
awkward attempt

fume [fyoom] *vi* be angry; emit
smoke or vapor ▷ *n* smoke; vapor
fu·mi·gate *vt* **-gat·ed, -gat·ing**
apply fumes or smoke to, esp for
disinfection **fu·mi·ga·tor** *n*

fun *n* anything enjoyable, amusing,
etc **fun'ni·ly** *adv* **fun'ny** *adj* **-ni·er,**
-ni·est comical; odd; difficult to
explain

func·tion [FUNGK-shən] *n* work
a thing is designed to do; (large)
social event; duty; profession;
mathematics quantity whose value
depends on varying value of another
▷ *vi* operate, work **func'tion·al** *adj*
having a special purpose; practical;
necessary; capable of operating

func·tion·ar·y n, pl **-ar·ies** official

fund n stock or sum of money; supply, store ▷ pl money resources ▷ vt (in financial, business dealings) provide or obtain funds in various ways

fun·da·men·tal [fun-də-MEN-tl] adj of, affecting, or serving as, the base; essential, primary ▷ n basic rule or fact **fun·da·ment** [-mənt] n buttocks; foundation **fun·da·men·tal·ism** n **fun·da·men·tal·ist** n one laying stress on belief in literal and verbal inspiration of Bible and other traditional creeds

fu·ner·al [FYOO-nər-əl] n (ceremony associated with) burial or cremation of dead **fu·ne·re·al** [-NEE-ree-əl] adj like a funeral; dark; gloomy

fun·gi·ble [FUN-jə-bəl] adj (of assets) freely exchangeable

fun·gus [FUNG-gəs] n, pl **-gi** [-jī] or **-gus·es** plant without leaves, flowers, or roots, as mushroom, mold **fun·gal** adj **fun·gous** adj **fun·gi·cide** [-jə-sīd] n fungus destroyer

fu·nic·u·lar [fyoo-NIK-yə-lər] n cable railway on mountainside with two counterbalanced cars

funk [fungk] n style of dance music with strong beat **funk·y** adj **funk·i·er, funk·i·est** (of music) having a strong beat; sl unconventional; sl fetid

fun·nel [FUN-l] n cone-shaped vessel or tube; chimney of locomotive or ship; ventilating shaft ▷ v **-neled, -nel·ing** (cause to) move as through funnel; concentrate, focus

funny see FUN

fur n soft hair of animal; garment, etc; of dressed skins with such hair;

furlike coating ▷ vt **furred, fur·ring** cover with fur **fur·ri·er** n dealer in furs; repairer, dresser of furs **fur·ry** adj **-ri·er, -ri·est** of, like fur

fur·bish vt clean up

fu·ri·ous [FYUUR-ee-əs] adj extremely angry; violent **fu·ri·ous·ly** adv

furl vt roll up and bind (sail, umbrella, etc)

fur·long [FUR-lawng] n eighth of mile

fur·lough [FUR-loh] n leave of absence, esp to soldier

fur·nace [FUR-nis] n apparatus for applying great heat to metals; closed fireplace for heating boiler, etc; hot place

fur·nish vt fit up house with furniture; equip; supply, yield **fur·ni·ture** [-chər] n movable contents of a house or room

fu·ror [FYUUR-or] n public outburst, esp of protest; sudden enthusiasm

fur·row [FUR-oh] n trench as made by plow; groove ▷ vt make furrows in

fur·ther [FUR-thər] adv more; in addition; at or to a greater distance or extent ▷ adj additional; more distant; comp of FAR ▷ vt help forward; promote **fur·ther·ance** n **fur·ther·more** adv besides **fur·thest** adj sup of FAR ▷ adv **fur·ther·most** adj

fur·tive [FUR-tiv] adj stealthy, sly, secret **fur·tive·ly** adv

fu·ry [FYUUR-ee] n, pl **-ries** wild rage, violent anger; violence of storm, etc; usu snake-haired avenging deity

fuse [fyooz] v **fused, fus·ing** blend by melting; melt with heat; amalgamate ▷ n (also **fuze**) soft wire, with low melting point, used as safety device in electrical systems; device (orig combustible cord) for igniting bomb, etc **fu'si·ble** [-zə-bəl] *adj* **fu·sion** [FYOO-zhən] *n* melting; state of being melted; union of things, as atomic nuclei, as if melted together

fu·se·lage [FYOO-sə-lahzh] *n* body of aircraft

fu·sil·lade [FYOO-sə-layd] *n* continuous discharge of firearms

fuss *n* needless bustle or concern; complaint; objection ▷ *vi* make fuss **fuss'i·ly** *adv* **fuss'i·ness** *n* **fuss'y** *adj* **fuss·i·er, fuss·i·est** particular; hard to please; overmeticulous; overelaborate

fus·tian [FUS-chən] *n* thick cotton cloth; inflated language

fus·ty [FUS-tee] *adj* **-ti·er, -ti·est** moldy; smelling of damp; old-fashioned **fus'ti·ness** *n*

fu·tile [FYOOT-l] *adj* useless, ineffectual, trifling **fu·til'i·ty** *n, pl* **-ties**

fu·ton [FOO-ton] *n* Japanese padded quilt, laid on floor as bed

fu·ture [FYOO-chər] *n* time to come; what will happen; tense of verb indicating this; likelihood of development ▷ *adj* that will be; of, relating to, time to come **fu'tur·ism** *n* movement in art marked by revolt against tradition **fu'tur·ist** *n, adj* **fu·tur·ist'ic** *adj* ultramodern **fu·tu'ri·ty** [-TUUR-i-tee] *n, pl* **-ties** future time

fuze see **FUSE**

fuzz *n* fluff; fluffy or frizzed hair; blur; *sl* police (officer) **fuzz'y** *adj* **fuzz·i·er, fuzz·i·est** fluffy, frizzy; blurred, indistinct

g

Ga chemistry gallium

gab·ar·dine, gab·er·dine [GAB-ər-deen] n fine twill cloth like serge; history loose outer garment worn by Orthodox Jews

gab·ble [GAB-əl] v **-bled, -bling** talk, utter inarticulately or too fast ▷ n such talk **gab** n, v **gabbed, gab·bing** inf talk, chatter **gab'by** adj **-bi·er, -bi·est** inf talkative **gift of gab** eloquence, loquacity

ga·ble [GAY-bəl] n triangular upper part of wall at end of ridged roof

gad vi **gad·ded, gad·ding gad about, around** go around in search of pleasure **gad'a·bout** n pleasure seeker

gad·fly [GAD-fli] n, pl **-flies** cattle-biting fly; worrying person

gadg·et [GAJ-it] n small mechanical device; object valued for its novelty or ingenuity **gadg'et·ry** n

Gael [gayl] n one who speaks Gaelic **Gael'ic** n language of Ireland and Scottish Highlands ▷ adj of Gaels, their language or customs

gaff n stick with iron hook for landing fish; spar for top of fore-and-aft sail ▷ vt seize (fish) with gaff

gaffe [gaf] n blunder; tactless remark

gaf·fer [GAF-ər] n inf old man; senior electrician on a TV or movie set

gag¹ v **gagged, gag·ging** stop up (person's mouth) with cloth, etc; retch, choke ▷ n cloth, etc put into, tied across mouth

gag² n joke, funny story

ga·ga [GAH-gah] adj inf foolishly enthusiastic; infatuated

gage¹ [gayj] n pledge, thing given as security; challenge, or something symbolizing one

gage² see GAUGE

gag·gle [GAG-əl] n flock of geese; inf disorderly crowd

gaiety see GAY

gain [gayn] vt obtain, secure; obtain as profit; win; earn; reach ▷ vi increase, improve; get nearer; (of watch, clock) operate too fast ▷ n profit; increase, improvement **gain'ful·ly** adv profitably; for a wage, salary

gain·say [GAYN-say] vt **-said, -say·ing** deny, contradict

gait [gayt] n manner of walking; pace

Gal. Galatians

ga·la [GAY-lə] n festive occasion; celebration; special entertainment ▷ adj festive; showy

gal·ax·y [GAL-ək-see] n, pl **-ax·ies** system of stars bound by gravitational forces; splendid gathering, esp of famous people **ga·lac·tic** [gə-LAK-tik] adj

gale [gayl] n strong wind; inf loud outburst, esp of laughter

gall¹ [gawl] n inf impudence; bitterness **gall'blad·der** n sac attached to liver, reservoir for bile **gall'stone** n hard secretion in gallbladder or ducts leading from it

gall² n painful swelling, esp on horse; sore caused by chafing ▷ vt make sore by rubbing; vex, irritate

gall³ n abnormal growth or excrescence on trees, etc

gal·lant [GAL-ənt] adj fine, stately, brave; [gə-LANT] chivalrous, very attentive to women ▷ n [gə-LANT] lover, suitor; dashing, fashionable young man **gall'ant·ly** adv **gall'ant·ry** n, pl -ries

gal·le·on [GAL-ee-ən] n large, high-built sailing ship of war

gal·ler·y [GAL-ə-ree] n, pl -ler·ies covered walk with side openings, colonnade; platform or projecting upper floor in theater, etc; group of spectators; long, narrow platform on outside of building; room or rooms for special purposes, eg showing works of art; passage in wall, open to interior of building

gal·ley [GAL-ee] n, pl -leys one-decked vessel with sails and oars, usu rowed by slaves or criminals; kitchen of ship or aircraft; printer's tray for composed type **galley proof** printer's proof before being made up into pages **galley slave** one condemned to row in galley; drudge

Gal·lic [GAL-ik] adj of ancient Gaul; French **Gal'li·cism** n French word or idiom

gal·li·um [GAL-ee-əm] n soft, gray metal of great fusibility

gal·li·vant [GAL-ə-vant] vi gad about

gal·lon [GAL-ən] n liquid measure of four quarts (3.7853 liters)

gal·lop [GAL-əp] v go, ride at gallop; move fast ▷ n horse's fastest pace with all four feet off ground together in each stride; ride at this pace **gal'lop·ing** adj at a gallop; speedy, swift

gal·lows [GAL-ohz] n structure, usu of two upright beams and crossbar, esp for hanging criminals

Gal·lup poll [GAL-əp] n method of finding out public opinion by questioning a cross section of the population

ga·loot [gə-LOOT] n inf silly, clumsy person

ga·lore [gə-LOR] adv in plenty

ga·losh·es [gə-LOSH-əz] pl n waterproof overshoes

gal·van·ic [gal-VAN-ik] adj of, producing, concerning electric current, esp when produced chemically; inf resembling effect of electric shock, startling **gal'va·nize** [-və-nīz] vt -nized, -niz·ing stimulate to action; excite, startle; cover (iron, etc) with protective zinc coating

gam'bit n chess opening involving sacrifice of a piece; any opening maneuver, comment, etc intended to secure an advantage

gam·ble [GAM-bəl] vi -bled, -bling play games of chance to win money; act on expectation of something ▷ n risky undertaking; bet, wager **gam'bler** n

gam·bol [GAM-bəl] vi -boled, -bol·ing skip, jump playfully ▷ n frolic

game¹ [gaym] n diversion, pastime; jest; contest for amusement; scheme, strategy; animals or birds hunted; their flesh ▷ adj **gam·er, gam·est** brave; willing **game'ster** n gambler **game'cock** n rooster bred for fighting **game'keep·er** n person employed to breed game, prevent poaching

game² adj lame, crippled (leg)

gam·ete [GAM-eet] n biology a sexual cell that unites with another for reproduction or the formation of a new individual

gam•ma [GAM-ə] *n* third letter of the Greek alphabet **gamma ray** a very penetrating electromagnetic ray

gam•mon [GAM-ən] *n* cured or smoked ham; lower end of side of bacon

gam•ut [GAM-ət] *n* whole range or scale (orig of musical notes)

gan•der [GAN-dər] *n* male goose; *sl* a quick look

gang *n* (criminal) group; organized group of persons working together ▷ *vi* (esp with *together*) form gang **gang up** *vi* form an alliance (against)

gang'ling *adj* lanky, awkward in movement

gan•gli•on [GANG-glee-ən] *n, pl* **-gli•a** [-glee-ə] nerve nucleus

gang•plank [GANG-plangk] *n* portable bridge for boarding or leaving vessel

gan•grene [GANG-green] *n* death or decay of body tissue as a result of disease or injury **gan'gre•nous** [-grə-nəs] *adj*

gang•sta rap [GANG-stə] *n* a style of rap music featuring lyrics that are anti-authority and often derogatory to women

gang•ster [GANG-stər] *n* member of criminal gang; notorious or hardened criminal

gang'way *n* bridge from ship to shore; anything similar ▷ *interj* make way!

gan•try [GAN-tree] *n, pl* **-tries** structure to support crane, railway signals, etc; framework beside rocket on launching pad

gap *n* breach, opening, interval; cleft; empty space

gape [gayp] *vi* **gaped, gap•ing** stare in wonder; open mouth wide, as in yawning; be, become wide open

ga•rage [gə-RAHZH] *n* (part of) building to house automobiles; refueling and repair center for them ▷ *vt* **-raged, -rag•ing** leave automobile in garage

garb [gahrb] *n* dress; fashion of dress ▷ *vt* dress, clothe

gar•bage [GAHR-bij] *n* rubbish; refuse **garbage can** large, usu cylindrical container for household rubbish

gar•ble [GAHR-bəl] *vt* **-bled, -bling** jumble or distort (story, account, etc)

gar•den [GAHR-dn] *n* ground for growing flowers, fruit, or vegetables ▷ *vi* cultivate garden **gar•den•er** [GAHRD-nər] *n* **gar•den•ing** [GAHRD-ning] *n*

gar•de•nia [gahr-DEE-nyə] *n* (sub)tropical shrub, with fragrant white or yellow flowers

gar•gan•tu•an [gahr-GAN-choo-ən] *adj* immense, enormous, huge

gar•gle [GAHR-gəl] *v* **-gled, -gling** ▷ *vi* wash throat with liquid kept moving by the breath ▷ *vt* wash (throat) thus ▷ *n* gargling; preparation for this purpose

gar•goyle [GAHR-goil] *n* carved (grotesque) face on waterspout, esp on Gothic church

gar•ish [GAIR-ish] *adj* showy; gaudy

gar•land [GAHR-lənd] *n* wreath of flowers worn or hung as decoration ▷ *vt* decorate with garlands

gar•lic [GAHR-lik] *n* (bulb of) plant with strong smell and taste, used in cooking and seasoning

gar•ment [GAHR-mənt] *n* article of clothing ▷ *pl* clothes

gar•ner [GAHR-nər] *vt* store up, collect, as if in granary

gar•net [GAHR-nit] *n* red semiprecious stone

gar•nish [GAHR-nish] *vt* adorn, decorate (esp food) ▷ *n* material for this

gar·ret [GAR-it] n small (usu wretched) room on top floor, attic

gar·ri·son [GAR-ə-sən] n troops stationed in town, fort, etc; fortified place ▷ vt furnish or occupy with garrison

gar·rote [gə-ROHT] n capital punishment by strangling; apparatus for this ▷ vt **-rot·ed, -rot·ing** execute, kill thus **gar·rot'er** n

gar·ru·lous [GAR-ə-ləs] adj (frivolously) talkative **gar·ru·li·ty** [gə-ROO-li-tee] n loquacity

gar·ter [GAHR-tər] n band worn around leg to hold up sock or stocking **garter snake** type of harmless snake

gas n, pl **-es** airlike substance, esp one that does not liquefy or solidify at ordinary temperatures; fossil fuel in form of gas, used for heating or lighting; gaseous anesthetic; poisonous or irritant substance dispersed through atmosphere in warfare, etc; gasoline; automobile accelerator; sl idle, boastful talk ▷ v **gassed, gas·sing** project gas over; poison with gas; fill with gas; sl talk idly, boastfully **gas·e·ous** [-ee-əs] adj of, like gas **gass'y** adj **-si·er, -si·est** filled with gas **gas'bag** n sl person who talks idly **gas mask** mask with chemical filter to guard against poisoning by gas

gash n gaping wound, slash ▷ vt cut deeply

gas·ket [GAS-kit] n rubber, neoprene, etc used as seal between metal faces, esp in engines

gas·o·hol [GAS-ə-hawl] n mixture of gasoline and ethyl alcohol used as fuel for automobiles

gas·o·line [gas-ə-LEEN] n refined petroleum used in automobiles, etc

gasp vi catch breath with open mouth, as in exhaustion or surprise

▷ n convulsive catching of breath

gas·tric [GAS-trik] adj of stomach **gas·tro·nom·i·cal** [-trə-NOM-ə-kəl] adj **gas·tron·o·my** [ga-STRON-ə-mee] n art of good eating

gas·tro·en·ter·i·tis [gas-troh-en-tə-Ri-tis] n inflammation of stomach and intestines

gas·tro·pod [GAS-trə-pod] n mollusk, eg snail, with disklike organ of locomotion on ventral surface

gate [gayt] n opening in wall, fence, etc; barrier for closing it; sluice; any entrance or way out; (entrance money paid by) those attending sports event **gate'-crash·er** n inf person who enters sports event, social function, etc uninvited

gath·er [GATH-ər] v (cause to) assemble; increase gradually; draw together ▷ vt collect; learn, understand; draw material into small tucks or folds **gath'er·ing** n assembly

gauche [gohsh] adj tactless, blundering **gau'che·rie** n awkwardness, clumsiness

gau·cho [GOW-choh] n, pl **-chos** cowboy of S Amer pampas

gaud [gawd] n showy ornament **gaud'i·ly** adv **gaud'i·ness** n **gaud'y** adj **gaud·i·er, gaud·i·est** showy in tasteless way

gauge, gage [gayj] n standard measure, as of diameter of wire, thickness of sheet metal, etc; distance between rails of railway; capacity; extent; instrument for measuring such things as wire, rainfall, height of water in boiler, etc ▷ vt **gauged, gaug·ing** measure; estimate

gaunt [gawnt] adj **-er, -est** extremely lean, haggard

gaunt·let [GAWNT-lit] n armored glove; glove covering part of arm; **run the gauntlet** formerly, run as punishment between two lines of men striking at runner with sticks, etc; be exposed to criticism or unpleasant treatment; undergo ordeal **throw down the gauntlet** offer challenge

gauss [gows] n unit of density of magnetic field

gauze [gawz] n thin transparent fabric of silk, wire, etc; this as surgical dressing

gave pt of **GIVE**

gav•el [GAV-əl] n mallet of presiding officer or auctioneer

ga•votte [gə-VOT] n lively dance; music for it

gawk vi stare stupidly **gawk'y** adj **gawk•i•er, gawk•i•est** clumsy, awkward

gay adj **-er, -est** homosexual; merry; lively; cheerful; bright; lighthearted; showy; given to pleasure ▷ n homosexual **gai'e•ty** n, pl **-ties** **gai'ly** adv

gaze [gayz] vi **gazed, gaz•ing** look fixedly ▷ n

ga•ze•bo [gə-ZEE-boh] n summerhouse, small roofed structure, with extensive view

ga•zelle [gə-ZEL] n small graceful antelope

ga•zette [gə-ZET] n name for newspaper **gaz•et•teer'** n geographical dictionary

ga•zil•lion [gə-ZIL-yən] n inf extremely large unspecified number

Gd chemistry gadolinium

Ge chemistry germanium

gear [geer] n set of wheels working together, esp by engaging cogs; connection by which engine, motor, etc is brought into work; arrangement by which movement of cycle, automobile, etc performs more or fewer revolutions relative to pedals, pistons, etc; equipment; clothing; goods, utensils; apparatus, tackle, tools; rigging; harness ▷ vt adapt (one thing) so as to conform with another; provide with gear; put in gear **gear'box** n case protecting gearing of bicycle, automobile, etc **in gear** connected up and ready for work **out of gear** disconnected

geek n inf boring, unattractive person

geese [gees] pl of **GOOSE**

gee•zer [GEE-zər] n sl (old, eccentric) man

ge•fil•te fish [gə-FIL-tə] in Jewish cookery, a dish of various freshwater fish chopped and blended with eggs, matzo meal, etc

Gei•ger count•er [GĪ-gər] n instrument for detecting radioactivity, cosmic radiation and charged atomic particles

gei•sha [GAY-shə] n in Japan, professional female entertainer and companion for men

gel [jel] n jelly-like substance ▷ vi **gelled, gel•ling** form a gel; jell

gel•a•tin [JEL-ə-tn] n substance prepared from animal bones, etc, producing edible jelly; anything resembling this **ge•lat•i•nous** [jə-LAT-n-əs] adj like gelatin or jelly

geld vt castrate **geld'ing** n castrated horse

gel•id [JEL-id] adj very cold

gem [jem] n precious stone, esp when cut and polished; treasure ▷ vt **gemmed, gem•ming** adorn with gems

Gen. Genesis

gen•darme [ZHAHN-dahrm] n policeman in France

gen•der [JEN-dər] n sex, male or female; grammatical classification of nouns, according to sex (actual or attributed)

gene [jeen] n biological factor determining inherited characteristics

ge·ne·al·o·gy [jee-nee-AL-ə-jee] n, pl -gies account of descent from ancestors; pedigree; study of pedigrees **ge·ne·a·log'i·cal** [-LOJ-ə-kəl] adj

genera pl of GENUS

gen·er·al [JEN-ər-əl] adj common, widespread; not particular or specific; applicable to all or most; usual, prevalent; miscellaneous; dealing with main element only; vague, indefinite ▷ n army officer of rank above colonel **gen·er·al'i·ty** n, pl -ties general principle; vague statement; indefiniteness **gen·er·al·i·za'tion** n general conclusion from particular instance; inference **gen'er·al·ize** v -ized, -iz·ing ▷ vt reduce to general laws ▷ vi draw general conclusions **general practitioner** physician with practice not restricted to particular branch of medicine

gen·er·ate [JEN-ə-rayt] vt -at·ed, -at·ing bring into being; produce **gen·er·a'tion** n bringing into being; all persons born about same time; average time between two such generations (about 30 years) **gen'er·a·tor** n apparatus for producing (steam, electricity, etc); begetter

ge·ner·ic [ji-NER-ik] adj belonging to, characteristic of class or genus **gen·er'i·cal·ly** adv **generic drug** one sold without brand name

gen·er·ous [JEN-ər-əs] adj liberal, free in giving; abundant **gen·er·os'i·ty** n, pl -ties

gen·e·sis [JEN-ə-sis] n, pl -ses [-seez] origin; mode of formation; (**G-**) first book of Bible

ge·net·ics [jə-NET-iks] n scientific study of heredity and variation in organisms **ge·net'ic** adj **ge·net'i·cist** n **genetic engineering** deliberate modification of heredity characteristics by treatment of DNA to transfer selected genes

gen·ial [JEEN-yəl] adj cheerful, warm in behavior; mild, conducive to growth **ge·ni·al'i·ty** n

ge·nie [JEE-nee] n in fairy tales, servant appearing by, and working, magic

gen·i·tal [JEN-i-tl] adj relating to sexual organs or reproduction **gen'i·tals** pl n the sexual organs **gen·i·tive** [JEN-i-tiv] adj, n possessive (case)

ge·nius [JEEN-yəs] n (person with) exceptional power or ability, esp of mind; distinctive spirit or nature (of nation, etc)

gen·o·cide [JEN-ə-sīd] n murder of a nationality or ethnic group

gen·re [ZHAHN-rə] n kind; sort; style; painting of homely scene

gen·teel [jen-TEEL] adj well-bred; stylish; affectedly proper

gen·tile [JEN-til] adj, n non-Jewish (person)

gen·tle [JEN-tl] adj -tler, -tlest mild, quiet, not rough or severe; soft and soothing; courteous; moderate; gradual; wellborn **gen·til'i·ty** n respectability, (pretentious) politeness **gen'tle·ness** n quality of being gentle; tenderness **gent'ly** adv **gen·tri·fi·ca'tion** n buying of properties in run-down urban neighborhoods by affluent people, thus increasing property values but displacing less affluent residents and owners of small businesses **gent'ry** n wellborn people **gen'tle·man** n well-bred man; man of good social position; man (used as a mark of politeness) **gen·tle·man·ly** adj **gentlemen's agreement** agreement binding by honor but not valid in law; unwritten law in private club, etc to discriminate against members of certain groups

gen·tri·fy v **-fied, -fy·ing** change by gentrification, undergo this change

gen·u·flect [JEN-yə-flekt] vi bend knee, esp in worship **gen·u·flec·tion** n

gen·u·ine [JEN-yoo-in] adj real, true, not sham, authentic; sincere; pure

ge·nus [JEE-nəs] n, pl **gen·e·ra** [JEN-ər-ə] class, order, group (esp of insects, animals, etc) with common characteristics usu comprising several species

ge·o·cen·tric [jee-oh-SEN-trik] adj astronomy measured, seen from Earth; having Earth as center

ge·ode [JEE-ohd] n cavity lined with crystals; stone containing this

ge·o·des·ic [jee-ə-DES-ik] adj of geometry of curved surfaces **geodesic dome** light but strong hemispherical construction formed from set of polygons

ge·og·ra·phy [jee-OG-rə-fee] n, pl **-phies** science of Earth's form, physical features, climate, population, etc **ge·og·ra·pher** n

ge·ol·o·gy [jee-OL-ə-jee] n science of Earth's crust, rocks, strata, etc **ge·o·log·i·cal** adj

ge·om·e·try [jee-OM-i-tree] n science of properties and relations of lines, surfaces, etc **ge·o·met·ric** adj

ge·o·phys·ics [jee-oh-FIZ-iks] n science dealing with physics of Earth **ge·o·phys·i·cal** adj

ge·o·sta·tion·ar·y [jee-oh-STAY-shə-ner-ee] adj (of satellite) in orbit around Earth so satellite remains over same point on surface

ger·bil [JUR-bəl] n burrowing, desert rodent of Asia and Africa

ger·i·at·rics [jer-ee-A-triks] n branch of medicine dealing with old age and its diseases **ger·i·at·ric** adj old ▷ n sl old person

germ [jurm] n microbe, esp causing disease; elementary thing; rudiment of new organism, of animal or plant **ger·mi·cide** [-mə-sid] n substance for destroying disease germs

Ger·man [JUR-mən] n, adj (language or native) of Germany **German measles** rubella, mild disease with symptoms like measles **german** adj of the same parents; closely akin: brother-german

ger·mane [jər-MAYN] adj relevant, pertinent

ger·mi·nate [JUR-mə-nayt] v **-nat·ed, -nat·ing** (cause to) sprout or begin to grow

ger·ry·man·der [JER-i-man-dər] vt manipulate election districts so as to favor one side

ger·und [JER-ənd] n noun formed from verb: living

ges·ta·tion [je-STAY-shən] n carrying of young in womb between conception and birth; this period

ges·tic·u·late [je-STIK-yə-layt] vi use expressive movements of hands and arms when speaking

ges·ture [JES-chər] n movement to convey meaning; indication of state of mind ▷ v **-tured, -tur·ing** make such a movement

get v got, got or got·ten, get·ting ▷ vt obtain, procure; contract; catch; earn; cause to go or come; bring into position or state; induce; engender; be in possession of, have (to do); inf understand ▷ vi succeed in coming or going; reach, attain; become **get'a·way** n escape **get across** vt understood **get at** gain access to; annoy; criticize; influence

gey·ser [GĪ-zàr] n hot spring throwing up spout of water from time to time

ghast·ly [GAST-lee] adj inf **-li·er, -li·est** unpleasant; deathlike; pallid; horrible ▷ adv horribly

gher·kin [GUR-kin] n small cucumber used in pickling

ghet·to [GET-oh] n, pl **-tos** densely populated (esp by one racial or ethnic group) slum area **ghet'to-blast·er** n inf large portable cassette or CD player and radio

ghost [gohst] n spirit, dead person appearing again; specter; semblance; faint trace; one who writes work to appear under another's name; ghostwriter ▷ v (also **ghost'write**) write another's work, speeches, etc **ghost'ly** adj

ghoul [gool] n malevolent spirit; person with morbid interests; fiend **ghoul'ish** adj of or like ghoul; horrible

gi·ant [JĪ-ənt] n mythical being of superhuman size; very tall person, plant, etc ▷ adj huge **gi·gan'tic** adj enormous, huge

gib·ber [JIB-àr] vi make meaningless sounds with mouth, jabber, chatter **gib'ber·ish** n meaningless speech or words

gib·bet [JIB-it] n gallows; post with arm on which executed criminal was hung; death by hanging ▷ vt hang on gibbet; hold up to scorn

gib·bon [GIB-àn] n type of ape

gibe [jīb] v **gibed, gib·ing** utter taunts; mock; jeer ▷ n insulting remark

gib·lets [JIB-lits] pl n internal edible parts of fowl, such as liver, gizzard, etc

gid·dy [GID-ee] adj **-di·er, -di·est** dizzy, feeling as if about to fall; liable to cause this feeling; flighty, frivolous **gid'di·ness** n

gift n thing given, present; faculty, power ▷ vt present (with); endow, bestow **gift'ed** adj talented

gig n light, two-wheeled carriage; inf single booking of musicians to play at club, etc

giga- prefix denoting 10^9: gigavolt; computing denoting 2^{30}: gigabyte

gigantic see GIANT

gig·gle [GIG-àl] vi **-gled, -gling** laugh nervously, foolishly ▷ n such a laugh

gig·o·lo [JIG-à-loh] n, pl **-los** man kept, paid, by (older) woman to be her escort, lover

gild vt gilded or **gilt, gild·ing** put thin layer of gold on; make falsely attractive **gilt** adj gilded ▷ n thin layer of gold put on

gill [jil] n liquid measure, quarter of pint

gills [gillz] pl n breathing organs in fish and other water creatures

gim·bals [JIM-bàlz] pl n pivoted rings, for keeping things, eg compass, horizontal at sea or in space

gim·let [GIM-lit] n boring tool, usu with screw point; drink of vodka or gin with lime juice

gim·mick [GIM-ik] n clever device, stratagem, etc, esp one designed to attract attention or publicity

gimp n narrow fabric or braid used as edging or trimming; sl a limp; sl person who limps

gin¹ [jin] n alcoholic liquor flavored with juniper berries

gin² n primitive engine in which vertical shaft is turned to drive horizontal beam in a circle; machine for separating cotton from seeds

gin·ger [JIN-jàr] n plant with

pungent spicy root used in cooking, etc; the root; *inf* spirit, mettle; light reddish-yellow color ▷ *vt* stimulate

gin·ger·y *adj* of, like ginger; spicy; high-spirited; reddish **ginger ale, beer** ginger-flavored soft drink
gin·ger·bread *n* cake, cookie flavored with ginger

gin·ger·ly [JIN-jər-lee] *adv* cautiously, warily, reluctantly

ging·ham [GING-əm] *n* cotton cloth, usu checked, woven from dyed yarn

gink·go [GING-koh] *n, pl* **-goes** large Chinese shade tree

gin·seng [JIN-seng] *n* (root of) plant believed to have tonic and energy-giving properties

gi·raffe [jə-RAF] *n* Afr ruminant animal, with spotted coat and very long neck and legs

gird [gurd] *vt* **gird·ed** or **girt, gird·ing** put belt around; fasten clothes thus; equip with, or belt on, a sword; prepare (oneself); encircle **gird·er** large beam, esp of steel

gir·dle [GURD-l] *n* corset; waistband; anything that surrounds, encircles ▷ *vt* **-dled, -dling** surround, encircle; remove bark (of tree) from a band around it

girl [gurl] *n* female child; young (formerly, an unmarried) woman **girl'hood** [-huud] *n*

girt *pt/pp of* **GIRD**

girth [gurth] *n* measurement around thing; leather or cloth band put around horse to hold saddle, etc ▷ *vt* surround, secure, with girth; girdle

gist [jist] *n* substance, main point (of remarks, etc)

give [giv] *v* **gave, giv·en, giv·ing** ▷ *vt* bestow, confer ownership of, make present of; deliver; impart; assign; yield, supply; utter; emit; be

host of (party, etc); make over; cause to have ▷ *vi* yield, give way, move ▷ *n* yielding, elasticity **give·a·way** *n* act of giving something away; what is given away; telltale sign **give up** acknowledge defeat; abandon

giz·zard [GIZ-ərd] *n* part of bird's stomach

gla·brous [GLAY-brəs] *adj* smooth; without hairs or any unevenness

gla·cier [GLAY-shər] *n* river of ice, slow-moving mass of ice formed by accumulated snow in mountain valleys **gla'cial** *adj* of ice, or of glaciers; very cold **gla·ci·a'tion** *n*

glad *adj* **-der, -dest** pleased; happy, joyous; giving joy **glad'den** *vt* make glad **glad'ly** *adv* **glad rags** *inf* dressy clothes for party, etc

glade [glayd] *n* clear, grassy space in wood or forest

glad·i·a·tor [GLAD-ee-ay-tər] *n* trained fighter in ancient Roman arena

glam·our [GLAM-ər] *n* alluring charm, fascination **glam'or·ize** *vt* **-ized, -iz·ing** make appear glamorous **glam'or·ous** *adj*

glance [glans] *vi* **glanced, glanc·ing** look rapidly or briefly; allude; touch; glide off something struck; pass quickly ▷ *n* brief look; flash; gleam; sudden (deflected) blow

gland *n* one of various small organs controlling different bodily functions by chemical means **glan·du·lar** [GLAN-jə-lər] *adj*

glare [glair] *vi* **glared, glar·ing** look fiercely; shine brightly, intensely; be conspicuous ▷ *n*

glass *n* hard transparent substance made by fusing sand, soda, potash, etc; things made of it; tumbler; its contents; lens; mirror; spyglass ▷ *pl* eyeglasses **glass'i·ness** *n* **glass'y** *adj* **glass·i·er, glass·i·est** like glass; expressionless **glass wool** insulating fabric of spun glass

glau·co·ma [glow-KOH-mə] *n* eye disease

glaze [glayz] *v* **glazed, glaz·ing** ▷*vt* furnish with glass; cover with glassy substance ▷*vi* become glossy ▷*n* transparent coating; substance used for this; glossy surface **gla·zier** [GLAY-zhər] *n* one who glazes windows

gleam [gleem] *n* slight or passing beam of light; faint or momentary show ▷*vi* give out gleams

glean [gleen] *v* pick up (facts, etc); gather, pick up, orig after reapers in grainfields **glean·er** *n*

glee *n* mirth, merriment; musical composition for three or more voices **glee'ful** *adj* **glee club** chorus organized for singing choral music

glen *n* narrow valley, usu wooded and with a stream

glib *adj* **-ber, -best** fluent but insincere or superficial; plausible **glib'ness** *n*

glide [glīd] *vi* **glid·ed, glid·ing** pass smoothly and continuously; of airplane, move without use of engines ▷*n* smooth, silent movement; *music* sounds made in passing from tone to tone **glid'er** *n* aircraft without engine that moves through the action of gravity and air currents; porch swing **glid'ing** *n* sport of flying gliders

glim·mer [GLIM-ər] *vi* shine faintly, flicker ▷*n* **glim'mer·ing** *n* faint gleam of light; faint idea, notion

glimpse [glimps] *n* brief or incomplete view ▷*vt* **glimpsed, glimps·ing** catch glimpse of

glint *v* flash, glance, glitter; reflect ▷*n*

glis·ten [GLIS-ən] *vi* gleam by reflecting light

glitch [glich] *n* small problem that stops something from working properly

glit·ter [GLIT-ər] *vi* shine with bright quivering light, sparkle; be showy ▷*n* luster; sparkle

gloam·ing [GLOH-ming] *n* evening twilight

gloat [gloht] *vi* regard, dwell on with smugness or malicious satisfaction

glob *n* soft lump or mass

globe [glohb] *n* sphere with map of Earth or stars; heavenly sphere, esp Earth; ball, sphere **glob'al** *adj* of globe; relating to whole world **glob·al·i·za'tion** [glohb-bəl-i-ZAY-shən] *n* broadening the scope, application, influence, or effect of something to the entire world **glob'u·lar** [-lər] *adj* globe-shaped **glob'ule** [-yool] *n* small round particle; drop **glob'u·lin** *n* kind of simple protein **global warming** increase in overall temperature worldwide believed to be caused by pollutants **globe'trot·ter** *n* (habitual) world traveler

glock·en·spiel [GLOK-ən-speel] *n* percussion instrument of metal bars struck with hammers

gloom *n* darkness; melancholy, depression **gloom'y** *adj* **gloom·i·er, gloom·i·est**

glo·ry [GLOR-ee] *n* renown, honorable fame; splendor; exalted or prosperous state; heavenly bliss ▷*vi* **-ried, -ry·ing** take pride (in) **glo'ri·fy** *vt* **-fied, -fy·ing** make glorious; invest with glory **glo'ri·ous** *adj* illustrious; splendid; excellent; delightful

gloss[1] *n* surface shine, luster ▷*vt* put gloss on; (esp with *over*) (try to) cover up, pass over (fault, error) **gloss·i·ness** n **gloss·y** adj **gloss·i·er, gloss·i·est** smooth, shiny ▷ n photograph printed on shiny paper

gloss² n marginal interpretation of word; comment, explanation ▷ vt interpret; comment; explain away **glos·sa·ry** n, pl **-ries** dictionary, vocabulary of special words

glot·tis n human vocal apparatus, larynx **glot'tal** [GLOT-l] adj

glove [gluv] n covering for the hand ▷ vt **gloved, glov·ing** cover with, or as with glove **glove compartment** storage area in dashboard of automobile **the gloves** boxing gloves

glow [gloh] vi give out light and heat without flames; shine; experience well-being or satisfaction; be or look hot; burn with emotion ▷ n shining heat; warmth of color; feeling of well-being; ardor **glow·worm** [GLOH-wurm] n female insect giving out green light

glow·er [GLOW-ər] vi scowl

glu·cose [GLOO-kohs] n type of sugar found in fruit, etc

glue [gloo] n any natural or synthetic adhesive; any sticky substance ▷ vt **glued, glu·ing** fasten (as if) with glue **glue sniffing** practice of inhaling fumes of glue for intoxicating or hallucinatory effects

glum adj **glum·mer, glum·mest** sullen, moody, gloomy

glut n surfeit, excessive amount ▷ vt **glut·ted, glut·ting** feed, gratify to the full or to excess; overstock

glu·ten [GLOOT-n] n protein present in cereal grain **glu'ti·nous** adj sticky, gluey

glut·ton [GLUT-n] n greedy person; one with great liking or capacity

for something, esp food and drink **glut'ton·ous** adj like gluttton, greedy **glut'ton·y** n

glyc·er·in [GLIS-ə-rin] n colorless sweet liquid with wide application in chemistry and industry

GM genetically modified

GMO genetically modified organism

gnarled [nahrld] adj knobbly, rugged, twisted

gnash [nash] v grind (teeth) together as in anger or pain

gnat [nat] n small, biting, two-winged fly

gnaw [naw] v bite or chew steadily; (esp with at) cause distress to

gneiss [nis] n coarse-grained metamorphic rock

gnome [nohm] n legendary creature like small old man; international financier **gnom'ish** adj

gno·mic [NOH-mik] adj of or like an aphorism

gnos·tic [NOS-tik] adj of, relating to knowledge, esp spiritual knowledge

gnu [noo] n S Afr antelope somewhat like ox

go [goh] vi **went, gone, go·ing** move along, make way; be moving; depart; function; make specified sound; fail, give way, break down; elapse; be kept, put; be able to be put; result; contribute to result; tend to; be accepted, have force; become ▷ n going; energy, vigor; attempt; turn **go-go dancer** dancer, usu scantily dressed, who performs rhythmic and oft erotic modern dance routines, esp in nightclub

goad [gohd] n spiked stick for driving cattle; anything that urges to action; incentive ▷ vt urge on; torment

goal [gohl] n end of race; object of effort; posts through which ball is to be driven in various games; the score so made

goat [goht] *n* four-footed animal with long hair, horns and beard **goat•ee'** *n* beard like goat's **get someone's goat** *inf* annoy (someone)

gob *n* lump; *sl* sailor **gob•ble** [GOB-əl] *vt* **-bled, -bling** eat hastily, noisily or greedily

gob•ble *n* throaty, gurgling cry of male turkey ▷ *vi* **-bled, -bling** make such a noise

gob•ble•dy•gook, -de•gook [GOB-əl-dee-guuk] *n* pretentious, usu incomprehensible language, esp as used by officials

gob•let [GOB-lit] *n* drinking cup

gob•lin *n* folklore small, usu malevolent being

god *n* superhuman being worshipped as having supernatural power; object of worship, idol; (**G-**) in monotheistic religions, the Supreme Being, creator and ruler of universe **god'dess** *n fem* **god'like** *adj* **god'li•ness** *n* **god'ly** *adj* **-li•er, -li•est** devout, pious **god'child** *n* child for whom a person stands as godparent **god'father** *n* **god'mother** *n* **god'parent** *n* sponsor at baptism **God-fearing** *adj* religious, good **god'for•sak•en** [-fər-say-kən] *adj* hopeless, dismal **God'head** *n* divine nature or deity **god'send** *n* something unexpected but welcome

gog•gle [GOG-əl] *vi* **-gled, -gling** (of eyes) bulge; stare ▷ *pl n* protective eyeglasses

goi•ter [GOI-tər] *n* neck swelling due to enlargement of thyroid gland

go-kart, go-cart SEE KART

gold [gohld] *n* very valuable precious metal; coins of this; wealth; beautiful or precious thing; color of gold ▷ *adj* of, like gold **gold'en** *adj* **gold digger** *inf* woman skillful in extracting money from men **golden mean** middle way between extremes **gold'en•rod** *n* tall plant with golden flower spikes **golden rule** important principle **golden wedding** fiftieth wedding anniversary **gold'field** *n* place where gold deposits are known to exist **gold'finch** *n* bird with yellow feathers **gold'fish** *n* any of various ornamental pond or aquarium fish **gold standard** financial arrangement whereby currencies of countries accepting it are expressed in fixed terms of gold

golf *n* outdoor game in which small hard ball is struck with clubs into a succession of holes ▷ *vi* play this game

go•nad [GOH-nad] *n* gland producing gametes

gon•do•la [GON-dl-ə] *n* Venetian canal boat **gon•do•lier'** *n* rower of gondola

gone [gawn] *pp* of **GO**

gong *n* metal plate with turned rim that resounds as bell when struck with soft mallet; anything used thus

gon•or•rhea [gon-ə-REE-ə] *n* a venereal disease

good [guud] *adj* **bet•ter, best** commendable; right; proper; excellent; beneficial; well-behaved; virtuous; kind; safe; adequate; sound; valid ▷ *n* benefit; well-being; profit ▷ *pl* property; wares **good'ly** *adj* large, considerable **good'ness** *n* **good will** kindly feeling, heartiness; value of a business in reputation, etc over and above its tangible assets

good-bye [guud-BĪ] *interj, n* form of address on parting

goof *n inf* mistake; stupid person ▷ *vi* make mistake **goof'y** *adj*

goof·i·er, goof·i·est silly

goo·gle [GOO-gәl] *vt* search for (something) on the Internet using a search engine; check (someone's) credentials) by entering that person's name into an Internet search engine

goon *n sl* stupid, awkward fellow; *inf* hired thug, hoodlum

goose [goos] *n, pl* **geese** web-footed bird; its flesh; simpleton **goose flesh** bristling of skin due to cold, fright **goose step** formal parade step

go·pher [GOH-fәr] *n* various species of Amer burrowing rodents **gopher ball** *baseball sl* pitched ball hit for home run

gore[1] [gor] *n* (dried) blood from wound **gor'y** *adj* **gor·i·er, gor·i·est**

gore[2] *vt* **gored, gor·ing** pierce with horns

gore[3] *n* triangular piece inserted to shape garment ▷ *vt* **gored, gor·ing** shape thus

gorge [gorj] *n* ravine; disgust, resentment ▷ *vi* **gorged, gorg·ing** feed greedily

gor·geous [GOR-jәs] *adj* splendid, showy, dazzling; *inf* extremely pleasing

gor·gon [GOR-gәn] *n* terrifying or repulsive woman; (**G-**) in Greek mythology, any of three sisters whose appearance turned any viewer to stone

go·ril·la [gә-RIL-ә] *n* largest anthropoid ape, found in Afr

gor·mand·ize [GOR-mәn-diz] *vt* **-ized, -iz·ing** eat hurriedly or like a glutton

gory see **GORE**[1]

gos'hawk *n* large hawk

gos·ling [GOZ-ling] *n* young goose

gos·pel [GOS-pәl] *n* unquestionable truth; (**G-**) any of first four books of New Testament

gos·sa·mer [GOS-ә-mәr] *n* filmy substance like spider's web; thin gauze or silk fabric

gos·sip [GOS-әp] *n* idle (malicious) talk about other persons, esp regardless of fact; one who talks thus ▷ *vi* **-siped, -sip·ing** engage in gossip; chatter

got see **GET**

Goth·ic [GOTH-ik] *adj architecture* of the pointed arch style common in Europe from twelfth to sixteenth century; of Goths; barbarous; gloomy; grotesque; (of type) German black letter

gouge [gowj] *vt* **gouged, goug·ing** scoop out; force out; extort from; overcharge ▷ *n* chisel with curved cutting edge

gou·lash [GOO-lahsh] *n* stew of meat and vegetables seasoned with paprika, etc

gourd [gord] *n* trailing or climbing plant; its large fleshy fruit; its rind as vessel

gour·mand [guur-MAHND] *n* glutton

gour·met [guur-MAY] *n* connoisseur of wine, food; epicure

gout [gowt] *n* disease with inflammation, esp of joints

gov [guv] *n* Internet domain name for a US governmental organization

gov·ern [GUV-әrn] *vt* rule, direct, guide, control; decide or determine; be followed by (grammatical case, etc) **gov'ern·a·ble** *adj* **gov'ern·ess** *n* woman teacher in private household **gov'ern·ment** *n* exercise of political authority in directing a people, country, etc; system by which community is ruled; body of people in charge of government of country; executive power; control; direction; exercise of authority **gov·ern·or** n one who governs, esp one invested with supreme authority in a state, etc; chief administrator of an institution; member of committee responsible for an organization or institution; regulator for speed of engine

gown n loose flowing outer garment; woman's (long) dress; official robe, as in university, etc

GPS Global Positioning System: a satellite-based navigation system

grab vt grabbed, grab·bing grasp suddenly; snatch ▷ n sudden clutch; quick attempt to seize; device or implement for clutching

grace [grays] n charm, elegance; accomplishment; goodwill, favor; sense of propriety; postponement granted; short thanksgiving before or after meal ▷ vt graced, grac·ing add grace to, honor **grace'ful** adj **grace'less** adj shameless, depraved **gra'cious** [-shəs] adj favorable; kind; pleasing; indulgent, beneficent, condescending **grace note** music melodic ornament

grade [grayd] n step, stage; degree of rank, etc; class; mark, rating; slope ▷ vt grad·ed, grad·ing arrange in classes; assign grade to; level ground, move earth with grader **gra·da'tion** n series of degrees or steps; each of them; arrangement in steps; in painting, gradual passing from one shade, etc to another **grad'er** n esp machine with wide blade used in road making **make the grade** succeed

gra·di·ent [GRAY-dee-ənt] n (degree of) slope

grad·u·al [GRAJ-oo-əl] adj taking place by degrees; slow and steady; not steep **grad'u·al·ly** adv

grad·u·ate [GRAJ-oo-ayt] v -at·ed, -at·ing ▷ vi receive diploma

or degree on completing course of study ▷ vt divide into degrees; mark, arrange according to scale ▷ n [-it] holder of diploma or degree **grad·u·a'tion** n

graf·fi·ti [grə-FEE-tee] pl n words or drawings scribbled or sprayed on walls etc

graft[1] n shoot of plant set in stalk of another; the process; surgical transplant of skin, tissue ▷ vt insert (shoot) in another stalk; transplant (living tissue in surgery)

graft[2] n inf self-advancement, profit by unfair means, esp through official or political privilege; bribe; swindle

grail [grayl] n cup or dish used by Christ at the Last Supper (also **Holy Grail**)

grain [grayn] n seed, fruit of cereal plant; wheat and allied plants; small hard particle; unit of weight, 0.0648 gram; texture; arrangement of fibers; any very small amount; natural temperament or disposition

gram n unit of weight (equivalent to 0.035 ounce) in metric system, one thousandth of a kilogram

gram·mar [GRAM-ər] n science of structure and usage of language; book on this; correct use of words **gram·mar·i·an** [grə-MAIR-ee-ən] n **gram·mat'i·cal** adj according to grammar **grammar school** elementary school

gra·na·ry [GRAY-nə-ree] n, pl -ries storehouse for grain; rich grain-growing region

grand adj -er, -est imposing; magnificent; majestic; noble; splendid; eminent; lofty; chief, of chief importance; final (total) **gran·deur** [GRAN-jər] n nobility; magnificence; dignity **gran·dil'o·quence** n

gran·dil·o·quent *adj* pompous in speech **gran'di·ose** [-dee-ohs] *adj* imposing; affectedly grand; striking **grand'child** *n* child of one's child **grand'daugh·ter** *n* female grandchild **grand'fa·ther** *n* male grandparent **grand'moth·er** *n* female grandparent **grand'par·ent** *n* parent of one's parent **grand piano** large harp-shaped piano with horizontal strings **grand'son** *n* male grandchild **grand'stand** *n* structure with tiered seats for spectators

grange [graynj] *n* farm with its farmhouse and farm buildings

gran·ite [GRAN-it] *n* hard crystalline igneous rock **gran'ite·like** *adj*

gran·ny [GRAN-ee] *n, pl* **-nies** *inf* grandmother

gra·no·la [grə-NOH-lə] *n* mixture of rolled oats, brown sugar, nuts, and fruit, eaten with milk

grant *vt* consent to fulfill (request); permit; bestow; admit ▷ *n* sum of money provided by government or other source for specific purpose, as education; gift; allowance, concession

gran·ule [GRAN-yool] *n* small grain; small particle **gran'u·lar** [-yə-lər] *adj* of or like grains

grape [grayp] *n* fruit of vine **grape'shot** *n* bullets scattering when fired **grape'vine** [-vīn] *n* grape-bearing vine; *inf* unofficial means of conveying information

grape·fruit [GRAYP-froot] *n* subtropical citrus fruit

graph [graf] *n* drawing depicting relation of different numbers, quantities, etc ▷ *vt* represent by graph

graph·ic [GRAF-ik] *adj* vividly descriptive; of, in, relating to,

writing, drawing, painting, etc **graphics** *pl n* diagrams, graphs, etc, esp as used in a TV programme or computer screen **graph'i·cal·ly** *adv* **graph'ite** [-īt] *n* form of carbon (used in pencils) **graph·ol'o·gy** *n* study of handwriting

grap·nel [GRAP-nel] *n* hooked iron instrument for seizing anything; small anchor with several flukes

grap·ple [GRAP-əl] *v* **-pled, -pling** come to grips with, wrestle; cope or contend ▷ *n* grappling; grapnel

grasp *v* (try, struggle to) seize hold; understand ▷ *n* act of grasping; grip; comprehension **grasp'ing** *adj* greedy, avaricious

grass *n* common type of plant with jointed stems and long narrow leaves (including cereals, bamboo, etc); such plants grown as lawn; pasture; *sl* marijuana ▷ *vt* cover with grass **grass'hop·per** *n* jumping, chirping insect **grass roots** ordinary people; fundamentals **grass-roots** *adj* coming from ordinary people, the rank and file

grate¹ [grayt] *n* framework of metal bars for holding fuel in fireplace **grat'ing** *n* framework of parallel or latticed bars covering opening

grate² *v* **grat·ed, grat·ing** ▷ *vt* rub into small bits on rough surface ▷ *vi* rub with harsh noise; have irritating effect **grat'er** *n* utensil with rough surface for reducing substance to small particles **grating** *adj* harsh; irritating

grate·ful [GRAYT-fəl] *adj* thankful; appreciative; pleasing **grat·i·tude** [GRAT-ə-tood] *n* sense of being thankful for favor

grat·i·fy [GRAT-ə-fī] *vt* **-fied, -fy·ing** satisfy; please; indulge **grat·i·fi·ca'tion** *n*

gratin see **AU GRATIN**

grat·is [adv, adj] free, for nothing

gra·tu·i·tous [grə-TOO-i-tàs] adj given free; uncalled for **gra·tu'i·tous·ly** adv **gra·tu'i·ty** n, pl **-ties** a tip

grave[1] [grayv] n hole dug to bury corpse; death **grave'stone** n monument on grave **grave'yard** n

grave[2] adj **grav·er, grav·est** serious, weighty; dignified, solemn; plain, dark in color; deep in note **grave'ly** adv

grave[3] n accent (`) over vowel to indicate special sound quality

grav·el [GRAV-əl] n small stones; coarse sand ▷ vt **-eled, -el·ing** cover with gravel **grav'el·ly** adj

grav·en [GRAY-vən] adj carved, engraved

grav·i·tate [GRAV-i-tayt] vi **-tat·ed, -tat·ing** move by gravity; tend (toward) center of attraction; sink, settle down **grav·i·ta'tion** n

grav·i·ty [GRAV-i-tee] n, pl **-ties** force of attraction of one body for another, esp of objects to Earth; heaviness; importance; seriousness; staidness

gra·vy [GRAY-vee] n, pl **-vies** juices from meat in cooking; sauce for food made from these; thing of value obtained unexpectedly

gray adj between black and white, as ashes or lead; clouded; dismal; turning white; aged; intermediate, indeterminate ▷ n gray color; gray or white horse

graze[1] [grayz] v **grazed, graz·ing** feed on grass, pasture

graze[2] vt **grazed, graz·ing** touch lightly in passing, scratch, scrape ▷ n grazing; abrasion

grease [grees] n soft melted fat of animals; thick oil as lubricant ▷ vt **greased, greas·ing** apply grease to **greas'i·ness** n **greas'y** adj

greas·i·er, greas·i·est grease gun appliance for injecting grease into machinery **grease monkey** inf mechanic **grease'paint** n theatrical makeup

great [grayt] adj **-er, -est** large, big; important; preeminent, distinguished; inf excellent **great-** prefix one generation older or younger than: great-grandfather **great'ly** adv **great'ness** n **Great Dane** breed of very large dog

Cre·cian [GREE-shòn] adj of (ancient) Greece

greed n excessive consumption of, desire for, food, wealth **greed'y** adj **greed·i·er, greed·i·est** gluttonous; eagerly desirous; voracious; covetous **greed'i·ly** adv

Greek n native language of Greece ▷ adj of Greece or Greek

green adj **-er, -est** of color between blue and yellow; grass-colored; emerald; unripe; inexperienced; gullible; envious ▷ n color; area of grass, esp in golf, for putting ▷ pl green vegetables **green'er·y** n, pl **-er·ies** vegetation **green belt** area of farms, open country around a community **green'horn** n inexperienced person; sl recent immigrant, newcomer **green'house** n, pl **-hous·es** [-how-ziz] (usu) glass house for rearing plants **greenhouse effect** rise in the temperature of the earth caused by heat absorbed from the sun being unable to leave the atmosphere **green'room** n room for actors, TV performers, when offstage **green thumb** talent for gardening

greet vt meet with expressions of welcome; accost, salute; receive **greet'ing** n

gre·gar·i·ous [gri-GAIR-ee-əs] adj fond of company, sociable; living in flocks **gre·gar·i·ous·ness** *n*

grem·lin *n* imaginary being blamed for mechanical and other troubles

gre·nade [gri-NAYD] *n* explosive shell or bomb, thrown by hand or shot from rifle

gren·a·dine [gren-ə-DEEN] *n* syrup made from pomegranate juice, for sweetening and coloring drinks

grew pt of **GROW**

grey·hound [GRAY-hownd] *n* swift slender dog used in racing

grid *n* network of horizontal and vertical lines, bars, etc; any interconnecting system of links; regional network of electricity supply

grid·dle [GRID-l] *n* frying pan, flat iron plate for cooking **grid·dle·cake** *n* pancake

grid·i·ron [GRID-i-ərn] *n* frame of metal bars for grilling; (field of play for) football

grid·lock [GRID-lok] *n* situation where traffic is not moving; point in a dispute at which no agreement can be reached **grid·locked** *adj*

grief [greef] *n* deep sorrow

griev·ance [GREE-vəns] *n* real or imaginary ground of complaint **grieve** *v* **grieved, griev·ing** ▷ *vi* feel grief ▷ *vt* cause grief to **griev·ous** *adj* painful, oppressive; very serious

grif·fin, grif·fon [GRIF-in] *n* fabulous monster with eagle's head and wings and lion's body

grill *n* grated utensil for broiling meat, etc; food cooked on grill; grillroom ▷ *v* cook (food) on grill; subject to severe questioning **grill'ing** *n* severe cross-examination **grill'room** *n* restaurant specializing in grilled food

grille [gril] *n* grating, crosswork of bars over opening

grim *adj* **grim·mer, grim·mest**
stern; of stern or forbidding aspect, relentless; joyless

grim·ace [GRIM-əs] *n* wry face ▷ *vi* **-aced, -ac·ing** make wry face

grime [grim] *n* ingrained dirt, soot ▷ *vt* **grimed, grim·ing** soil; dirty; blacken **grim'y** *adj* **grim·i·er, grim·i·est**

grin *vi* grinned, grin·ning show teeth, as in laughter ▷ *n* grinning smile

grind [grind] *v* **ground, grind·ing** ▷ *vt* crush to powder; oppress; make sharp, smooth; grate ▷ *vi* perform action of grinding; *inf* (with *away*) work (esp study) hard; grate ▷ *n* *inf* hard work, excessively diligent student; action of grinding

grin·go [GRING-goh] *n, pl* **-gos** in Mexico, contemptuous name for foreigner, esp American or Englishman

grip *n* firm hold, grasp; grasping power; mastery; handle; suitcase or traveling bag ▷ *vt* **gripped, grip·ping** grasp or hold tightly; hold interest or attention of

gripe [grip] *vi* **griped, grip·ing** complain (persistently) ▷ *n* *inf* complaint ▷ *vt* intestinal pain

gris·ly [GRIZ-lee] *adj* **-li·er, -li·est** grim, causing terror, ghastly

grist *n* grain to be ground **grist for one's mill** something that can be turned to advantage

gris·tle [GRIS-əl] *n* cartilage, tough flexible tissue

grit *n* rough particles of sand; coarse sandstone; courage ▷ *pl* hominy, etc coarsely ground and cooked as breakfast food ▷ *vt* **grit·ted, grit·ting** clench, grind (teeth) **grit'ty** *adj* **-ti·er, -ti·est**

griz·zle [GRIZ-əl] *v* **-zled, -zling** make, become gray **griz'zly** large Amer bear; (also **grizzly bear**)

groan [grohn] vi make low, deep sound of grief or pain; be in pain or overburdened ▷ n

groats [grohts] n hulled grain or kernels of oats, wheat, etc broken into fragments

gro·cer [GROH-sàr] n dealer in foodstuffs **gro'cer·ies** pl n commodities sold by a grocer **gro'cer·y** n, pl -**cer·ies** trade, premises of grocer

grog·gy [GROG-ee] adj unsteady, shaky, weak -**gi·er**, -**gi·est**

groin n fold where legs meet abdomen; euphemism for genitals

groom n person caring for horses; bridegroom ▷ vt tend or look after; brush or clean (esp horse); train (someone for something) **well-groomed** adj neat, smart

groove n narrow channel, hollow, esp cut by tool; rut, routine ▷ vt **grooved, groov·ing** cut groove in **groov'y** adj sl **groov·i·er, groov·i·est** attractive, exciting

grope [grohp] vi **groped, grop·ing** feel about, search blindly

gros·beak [GROHS-beek] n finch with large powerful bill

gross [grohs] adj -**er**, -**est** very fat; total, not net; coarse; flagrant; thick, rank ▷ n twelve dozen **gross out** sl disgust, sicken

gro·tesque [groh-TESK] adj (horribly) distorted; absurd ▷ n grotesque person, thing

grot·to [GROT-oh] n, pl -**toes** small picturesque cave

grouch [growch] n inf persistent grumbler; discontented mood ▷ vi grumble, be peevish

ground¹ [grownd] n surface of Earth; soil, earth; reason, motive; coating to work on with paint; background, main surface worked on in painting, embroidery, etc; special area; bottom of sea ▷ pl dregs; land around house and belonging to it ▷ vt establish; instruct (in elements); place on ground ▷ vi run ashore; strike ground **ground'ed** adj of aircraft or pilot, unable or not permitted to fly; inf of child, punished by restriction of activities **ground'ing** n basic general knowledge of a subject **ground'less** adj without reason **ground'speed** n aircraft's speed in relation to ground

ground² pt/pp of **GRIND**

group [groop] n number of persons or things near together, or placed or classified together; musical band of players or singers; class; two or more figures forming one artistic design ▷ v place, fall into group

grouse¹ [grows] n, pl **grouse** game bird; its flesh

grouse² vi **groused, grous·ing** grumble, complain ▷ n complain **grous'er** n grumbler

grout [growt] n thin fluid mortar ▷ vt fill up with grout

grove [grohv] n small group of trees

grov·el [GRUV-əl] vi -**eled**, -**el·ing** abase oneself; lie or crawl facedown

grow [groh] v grew, grown, **grow·ing** ▷ vi develop naturally; increase in size, height, etc; be produced; become by degrees ▷ vt produce by cultivation **growth** n growing; increase; what has grown or is growing **grown-up** adj **grownup** n adult

growl vi make low guttural sound of anger; rumble; murmur, complain ▷ n

grub v grubbed, grub·bing dig superficially; root up; dig, rummage; plod; drudge ▷ n larva of insect; sl food **grub'by** adj -**bi·er**, -**bi·est** dirty

grudge [gruj] vt grudged,

grudg·ing be unwilling to give, allow ▷ *n* ill will

gru·el [GROO-əl] *n* food of cereal boiled in milk or water

gru·el·ing *adj n* exhausting, severe (experience)

grue·some [GROO-səm] *adj* fearful, horrible, grisly **grue'some·ness** *n*

gruff *adj* **-er, -est** rough in manner or voice, surly **gruff'ness** *n*

grum·ble [GRUM-bəl] *vi* **-bled, -bling** complain; rumble, murmur; make growling sounds ▷ *n* complaint; low growl

grump·y [GRUM-pee] *adj* **grump·i·er, grump·i·est** ill-tempered, surly **grump'i·ness** *n*

grunge [grunj] *n* style of rock music with a fuzzy guitar sound; deliberately untidy and uncoordinated fashion style

grunt *vi* make sound characteristic of pig ▷ *n* pig's sound; gruff noise

G-string [JEE-string] *n* very small covering for genitals; *music* string tuned to G

gua·no [GWAH-noh] *n* manure of seabird

guar·an·tee [gar-ən-TEE] *n* formal assurance (esp in writing) that product, etc will meet certain standards, last for given time, etc ▷ *vt* **-teed, -tee'ing** give guarantee of, for something; secure (against risk, etc) **guar·an·tor** *n* one who guarantees **guar'an·ty** *n, pl* **-ties**

guard [gahrd] *vt* protect, defend ▷ *vi* be careful, take precautions (against) ▷ *n* person, group that protects, supervises, keeps watch; sentry; soldiers protecting anything; official in charge of train; protection; screen for enclosing anything dangerous; protector; posture of defense **guard'i·an**

[-ee-ən] *n* keeper, protector; person having custody of infant, etc **guard'i·an·ship** *n* care **guard'house** *n* place for stationing those on guard or for prisoners

gua·va [GWAH-və] *n* tropical tree with fruit used to make jelly

Guern·sey [GURN-zee] *n, pl* **-seys** breed of cattle

guer·ril·la [gə-RIL-ə] *n* member of irregular armed force, esp fighting established force, government, etc ▷ *adj*

guess [ges] *vt* estimate without calculation; conjecture, suppose; consider, think ▷ *vi* form conjectures ▷ *n*

guest [gest] *n* one entertained at another's house; one living in hotel **guest'house** *n* small house for guests, separate from main house

guff *n inf* silly talk; insolent talk

guf·faw [gə-FAW] *n* crude noisy laugh ▷ *vi* laugh in this way

guide [gid] *n* one who shows the way; adviser; book of instruction or information; contrivance for directing motion ▷ *vt* **guid·ed, guid·ing** lead, act as guide to; arrange **guid'ance** [-əns] *n* **guided missile** missile whose flight path is controlled by radio signals or programmed homing mechanism

guild [gild] *n* organization, club; society for mutual help, or with common object; *history* society of merchants or tradesmen

guile [gil] *n* cunning, deceit **guile'ful** *adj* **guile'less** *adj* sincere, straightforward

guil·lo·tine [GIL-ə-teen] *n* machine for beheading ▷ *vt* **-tined, -tin·ing** behead

guilt [gilt] *n* fact, state of having done wrong; responsibility for criminal or moral offense **guilt'less**

adj innocent **guilt'y** *adj* **guilt•i•er,**
guilt•i•est having committed an
offense

guin•ea pig [GIN-ee] *n* rodent
originating in S Amer; *inf* person
used in experiments

guise [giz] *n* external appearance,
esp one assumed

gui•tar [gi-TAHR] *n* usu six-
stringed instrument played by
plucking or strumming **gui•tar'ist** *n*

gulch *n* ravine; gully

gulf *n* large inlet of the sea; chasm;
large gap

gull[1] *n* long-winged web-footed
seabird

gull[2] *n* dupe, fool ▷ *vt* dupe, cheat
gul•li•bil'i•ty *n* **gul'li•ble** *adj* easily
imposed on, credulous

gul•let [GUL-it] *n* food passage
from mouth to stomach

gul•ly [GUL-ee] *n, pl* **-lies** channel or
ravine worn by water

gulp *vt* swallow eagerly ▷ *vi* gasp,
choke ▷ *n*

gum[1] *n* firm flesh in which teeth
are set ▷ *vt* **gummed, gum•ming**
chew with the gums

gum[2] *n* sticky substance issuing
from certain trees; an adhesive;
chewing gum; gum tree, eucalyptus
▷ *vt* **gummed, gum•ming** stick
with gum **gum'my** *adj* **-mi•er,**
-mi•est gum'shoe *n* shoe of rubber;
sl detective **gum tree** any species
of eucalyptus **gum up the works** *sl*
impede progress

gump•tion [GUM-shàn] *n*
resourcefulness; shrewdness; sense

gun *n* weapon with metal tube
from which missiles are discharged
by explosion; cannon, pistol, etc
▷ *v* **gunned, gun•ning** shoot;
pursue, as with gun; race engine (of
car) **gun'ner** *n* **gun'ner•y** *n* use
or science of large guns **gun'boat**

n small warship **gun dog** (breed
of) dog used to retrieve, etc game
gun'man *n* armed criminal
gun'met•al *n* alloy of copper and
tin or zinc, formerly used for guns
gun'pow•der *n* explosive mixture
of saltpeter, sulfur, charcoal
gun'shot *n* shot or range of gun
▷ *adj* caused by missile from gun
gun'wale, gun'nel [GUN-l] *n* upper
edge of ship's side

gunk [gungk] *n inf* any sticky, oily
matter

gun•ny [GUN-ee] *n, pl* **-nies** strong,
coarse sacking made from jute

gup•py [GUP-ee] *n, pl* **-pies** small
colorful aquarium fish

gur•gle [GUR-gàl] *n* bubbling
noise ▷ *vi* **-gled, -gling** utter, flow
with gurgle

gur•ney [GUR-nee] *n, pl* **-neys**
wheeled bed

gu•ru [GUUR-oo] *n* a spiritual
teacher, esp in India

gush *vi* flow out suddenly and
copiously, spurt ▷ *n* sudden and
copious flow; effusiveness **gush'er** *n*
gushing person; oil well

gus•set [GUS-it] *n* triangle or
diamond-shaped piece of material
let into garment **gus'set•ed** *adj*

gust *n* sudden blast of wind; burst of
rain, anger, passion, etc **gust'y** *adj*
gust•i•er, gust•i•est

gus•to [GUS-toh] *n* enjoyment,
zest

gut *n* (oft *pl*) entrails, intestines;
material made from guts of animals,
eg for violin strings, etc ▷ *pl inf*
essential, fundamental part; courage
▷ *vt* **gut•ted, gut•ting** remove
guts from (fish, etc); remove, destroy
contents of (house) **guts'y** *adj inf*
guts•i•er, guts•i•est courageous;
vigorous

gut•ter [GUT-àr] *n* shallow

trough for carrying off water from roof or side of street ▷ *vt* make channels in ▷ *vi* flow in streams; of candle, melt away by wax forming channels and running down **gutter press** journalism that relies on sensationalism **gut·ter·snipe** [-snip] *n* neglected slum child

gut·tur·al [GUT-ər-əl] *adj* of, relating to, or produced in, the throat ▷ *n* guttural sound or letter

guy¹ [gī] *n inf* person (usu male) ▷ *vt* **guyed, guy·ing** make fun of; ridicule **wise guy** *inf usu disparaging* clever person

guy² *n* rope, chain, etc to steady, secure something, eg tent ▷ *vt* **guyed, guy·ing** keep in position by guy

guz·zle [GUZ-əl] *v* **-zled, -zling** eat or drink greedily ▷ *n*

gym [jim] *n* short for **GYMNASIUM** or **GYMNASTICS**

gym·kha·na [jim-KAH-nə] *n* competition or display of horse riding or gymnastics; place for this

gym·na·si·um [jim-NAY-zee-əm] *n* place equipped for muscular exercises, athletic training **gym'nast** *n* expert in gymnastics **gym·nas'tics** *pl n* muscular exercises, with or without apparatus, eg parallel bars

gy·ne·col·o·gy [gī-ni-KOL-ə-jee] *n* branch of medicine dealing with functions and diseases of women **gy·ne·col'o·gist** *n*

gyp·sum [JIP-səm] *n* crystalline sulfate of lime, a source of plaster

Gyp·sy [JIP-see] *n, pl* **-sies** one of a wandering people originally from NW India, Romany

gy·rate [Jī-rayt] *vi* **-rat·ed, -rat·ing** move in circle, spirally, revolve **gy·ra'tion** *n*

gy·ro·com·pass [Jī-roh-kum-pəs] *n* compass using gyroscope

gy·ro·scope [Jī-rə-skohp] *n* disk or wheel so mounted as to be able to rotate about any axis, esp to keep disk (with compass, etc) level despite movement of ship, etc **gy·ro·scop'ic** [-SKOP-ik] *adj*

gy·ro·sta·bi·liz·er [jī-rə-STAY-bə-lī-zər] *n* gyroscopic device to prevent rolling of ship or airplane

h

H *chemistry* hydrogen

ha·be·as cor·pus [HAY-bee-əs KOR-pəs] *n* writ issued to produce prisoner in court

hab·er·dash·er [HAB-ər-dash-ər] *n* dealer in articles of dress, ribbons, pins, needles, etc **hab·er·dash·er·y** *n* **-er·ies**

hab·it *n* settled tendency or practice; constitution; customary apparel esp of nun or monk; woman's riding dress **ha·bit·u·al** [hə-BICH-oo-əl] *adj* formed or acquired by habit; usual, customary **ha·bit·u·ate** [-ayt] *vt* **-at·ed, -at·ing** accustom **ha·bit·u·a·tion** *n* **ha·bit·u·é** [-oo-ay] *n* constant visitor

hab·it·a·ble [HAB-i-tə-bəl] *adj* fit to live in **hab·i·tat** *n* natural home (of animal, etc) **hab·i·ta·tion** [-TAY-shən] *n* dwelling place

ha·ci·en·da [hah-see-EN-də] *n, pl* **-das** ranch or large estate in Sp Amer

hack¹ [hak] *vt* cut, chop (at) violently; *inf* utter harsh, dry cough; *sl* deal or cope with ▷ *n* **hack·er** *n sl* person who through personal computer breaks into computer system of company or government **hack around** *sl* pass time idly

hack² *n* drudge, esp writer of inferior literary works; cabdriver **hack·work** *n* dull, repetitive work

hack·le [HAK-əl] *n* neck feathers of rooster, etc ▷ *pl* hairs on back of neck of dog and other animals that are raised in anger

hack·ney [HAK-nee] *n, pl* **-neys** harness horse, carriage, coach kept for hire

hack·neyed [HAK-need] *adj* (of words, etc) stale, trite because of overuse

hack·saw [HAK-saw] *n* handsaw for cutting metal

had pt/pp of **HAVE**

Ha·des [HAY-deez] *n Greek myth* underworld home of the dead

haft *n* handle (of knife, etc) ▷ *vt* fit with one

hag *n* ugly old woman; witch

hag·gard [HAG-ərd] *adj* wild-looking; anxious, careworn

hag·gis *n* Scottish dish made from sheep's heart, lungs, liver, chopped with oatmeal, suet, onion, etc, and boiled in the stomach

hag·gle [HAG-əl] *vi* **-gled, -gling** bargain, wrangle over price ▷ *n*

hag·i·ol·o·gy [hag-ee-OL-ə-jee] *n, pl* **-gies** literature of the lives of saints **hag·i·og·ra·pher** [-rə-fər] *n* **hag·i·og·ra·phy** *n, pl* **-phies** writing of this

hail¹ [hayl] *n* (shower of) pellets of ice; intense shower, barrage ▷ *v* pour down as shower of hail **hail·stone** *n*

hail² *vt* greet (esp enthusiastically); acclaim, acknowledge; call ▷ *vi* come (from)

hair *n* filament growing from skin of animal, as covering of person's head; such filaments collectively **hair·i·ness** *n* **hair·y** *adj* **hair·i·er, hair·i·est hair·do** [-doo] *n, pl* **-dos**

way of styling hair **hair'dress·er** n one who attends to and cuts hair, esp women's hair **hair'line** adj, n very fine (line); lower edge of human hair eg on forehead **hair'pin** n pin for keeping hair in place **hairpin bend** U-shaped turn in road **hair'split·ting** n making of overly fine distinctions **hair'spring** n very fine, delicate spring in timepiece **hair trigger** trigger operated by light touch **hair-trigger** adj easily set off: a hair-trigger temper

hal·cy·on [HAL-see-ən] n bird fabled to calm the sea and to breed on floating nest **halcyon days** time of peace and happiness

hale [hayl] adj **hal·er, hal·est** robust, healthy: hale and hearty

half [haf] n, pl **halves** [havz] either of two equal parts of thing ▷ adj forming half ▷ adv to the extent of half **half'back** n football one of two players lining up on each side of fullback **half-baked** adj underdone; inf immature, silly **half'-breed** n offens person with parents of different races **half'-broth·er** n brother by one parent only **half-cocked** adj ill-prepared **half-heart·ed** adj unenthusiastic **half-life** n, pl **-lives** time taken for half the atoms in radioactive material to decay **half nel'son** hold in wrestling **half'-sis·ter** n sister by one parent only **half'time** n sport rest period between two halves of a game **half'tone** n illustration printed by photoengraving from plate, showing lights and shadows by means of minute dots **half vol'ley** sport striking of a ball the moment it bounces **half'wit** n feeble-minded person; stupid person

hal·i·but [HAL-ə-bət] n large edible flatfish

hal·i·to·sis [hal-i-TOH-sis] n bad-smelling breath

hall [hawl] n (entrance) passage; large room or building belonging to particular group or used for particular purpose esp public assembly

hal·le·lu·jah [hal-ə-LOO-yə] n, interj exclamation of praise to God

hall'mark [HAWL-mahrk] n mark used to indicate standard of tested gold and silver; mark of excellence; distinguishing feature

hal·low [HAL-oh] vt make, or honor as holy **Hal·low·een** [hal-ə-WEEN] n the evening of Oct 31st, the day before All Saints' Day

hal·lu·ci·nate [hə-LOO-sə-nayt] vi **-nat·ed, -nat·ing** suffer illusions **hal·lu·ci·na'tion** n illusion **hal·lu'ci·na·to·ry** adj **hal·lu'ci·no·gen** [-jən] n drug inducing hallucinations

ha·lo [HAY-loh] n, pl **-los, -loes** circle of light around moon, sun, etc; disk of light around saint's head in picture; ideal glory attaching to person ▷ vt **-loed, -lo·ing** surround with halo

halt¹ [hawlt] n interruption or end to progress, etc (esp as command to stop marching) ▷ v (cause to) stop

halt² vi falter, fail **halt'ing** adj hesitant, lame

hal·ter [HAWL-tər] n rope or strap with headgear to fasten horses or cattle; low-cut dress style with strap passing behind neck ▷ vt put halter on, fasten with one

halve [hav] vt **halved, halv·ing** cut in half; reduce to half; share

hal·yard [HAL-yərd] n rope for raising sail, signal flags, etc

ham [ham] n meat (esp salted or smoked) from thigh of pig; actor adopting exaggerated, unconvincing style;

amateur radio enthusiast; **ham it up** overact **ham'string** n tendon at back of knee ▷ vt **-strung, -string·ing** cripple by cutting thus; render useless; thwart

ham·burg·er [HAM-burg-gər] n broiled, fried patty of ground beef, esp served in bread roll

ham·let [HAM-lit] n small village

ham·mer [HAM-ər] n tool usu with heavy head at end of handle, for beating, driving nails, etc; machine for same purposes; contrivance for exploding charge of gun; auctioneer's mallet; heavy metal ball on wire thrown in sports ▷ v strike with, or as with, hammer **ham'mer·head** [-hed] n shark with wide, flattened head **ham'mer·toe** n deformed toe **hammer out** solve problem by painstaking work

ham·mock [HAM-ək] n bed of canvas, etc, hung on cords

ham·per[1] [HAM-pər] n large covered basket, such as for laundry; large parcel, box, etc of food, wines, etc, esp one sent as gift

ham·per[2] vt impede, obstruct movements of

ham·ster [HAM-stər] n type of rodent, sometimes kept as pet

ham·strung adj crippled, thwarted; see **HAM**

hand n extremity of arm beyond wrist; side, quarter, direction; style of writing; cards dealt to player; measure of four inches; manual worker; sailor; help, aid; pointer on dial; applause ▷ vt pass; deliver; hold out **hand'ful** n, pl **-fuls** small amount or number; inf person, thing causing problems **hand'i·ly** adv **hand'i·ness** n dexterity; state of being near, available **hand'y** adj **hand·i·er, hand·i·est** convenient; clever with the hands **hand'bag** n woman's bag for personal articles; bag for carrying in hand **hand'bill** n small printed notice **hand'book** n small reference or instruction book **hand'held** adj able to be held in the hand ▷ n computer that can be held in the hand **hand'cuff** n fetter for wrist, usu joined in pair ▷ vt secure thus **hand'i·craft** n manual occupation or skill **hand'i·work** n thing done by particular person **hand·ker·chief** [HANG-kər-chif] n small square of fabric carried in pocket for wiping nose, etc **hand'out** n inf money, food, etc given free; pamphlet giving news, information, etc **hands-on** adj involving practical experience of equipment **hand'stand** n act of supporting body in upside-down position by hands alone **hand'writ·ing** n way person writes **hand'y·man** n one employed to do various tasks; one skilled in odd jobs **hand in glove** very intimate

hand·i·cap [HAN-dee-kap] n something that hampers or hinders; race, contest in which chances are equalized by weights carried, golf strokes, etc; condition so imposed; any physical disability ▷ vt **-capped, -cap·ping** hamper; impose handicap on; attempt to predict winner of race, game **handicapped** dated physically or mentally disabled

han·dle [HAN-dl] n part of thing to hold it by ▷ v **-dled, -dling** touch, feel with hands; manage; deal with; trade **han'dle·bars** pl n curved metal bars used to steer bicycle, motorbike, etc **handlebar mustache** one resembling handlebar

hand·some [HAN-səm] adj of fine appearance; generous; ample

hang v hung or hanged, hang·ing

▷ *vt* suspend; kill by suspension by neck; attach, set up (wallpaper, doors, etc) ▷ *vi* be suspended, cling **hang'er** *n* frame on which clothes, etc can be hung **hang'dog** *adj* sullen, dejected **hang glider** glider like large kite, with pilot hanging in frame below **hang gliding** *n* **hang'man** *n* executioner **hang'o·ver** *n* aftereffects of too much drinking **hang out** *inf* reside, frequent **hang-up** *n sl* persistent emotional problem; preoccupation

hang·ar [HANG-ər] *n* large shed for aircraft

hank [hangk] *n* coil, skein, length, esp as measure of yarn

hank·er [HANG-kər] *vi* (oft with *after, for*) crave

han·ky-pan·ky [HANG-kee-PANG-kee] *n inf* trickery; illicit sexual relations

han·som [HAN-səm] *n* two-wheeled horse-drawn cab for two to ride inside with driver mounted up behind

hap·haz·ard [hap-HAZ-ərd] *adj* random, careless

hap·less [HAP-lis] *adj* unlucky

hap·pen [HAP-ən] *vi* come about, occur; chance to do **hap'pen·ing** *n* occurrence, event

hap·py *adj* **-pi·er, -pi·est** glad, content; lucky, fortunate; apt **hap'pi·ly** *adv* **hap'pi·ness** *n* **hap'py-go-luck'y** *adj* casual, lighthearted

ha·ra·ki·ri [HAHR-ə-KEER-ee] *n* in Japan, ritual suicide by disemboweling

ha·rangue [hə-RANG] *n* vehement speech; tirade ▷ *v* **-rangued, -rangu·ing**

ha·rass [hə-RAS] *vt* worry, trouble, torment **ha·rass'ment** *n*

har·bin·ger [HAHR-bin-jər] *n* one

who announces another's approach; forerunner, herald

har·bor [HAHR-bər] *n* shelter for ships; shelter ▷ *v* give shelter, protection to; maintain (secretly) esp grudge, etc

hard [hahrd] *adj* **-er, -est** firm, resisting pressure; solid; difficult to understand; harsh, unfeeling; difficult to bear; practical, shrewd; heavy, strenuous; of water, not making lather well with soap; of drugs, highly addictive ▷ *adv* vigorously; with difficulty; close **hard·en** *v* **hard'ly** *adv* unkindly, harshly; scarcely, not quite; only just **hard'ship** *n* bad luck; severe toil, suffering; instance of this **hard'ball** *n* baseball; *inf* forceful or ruthless methods of achieving a goal **hard-boiled** *adj* boiled so long as to be hard; *inf* of person, unemotional, unsentimental **hard copy** computer output printed on paper; original paper document **hard disk** *computing* rigid data-storage disk in a sealed container

hard drive mechanism on a computer that handles the reading, writing, and storage of data on a hard disk **hard-hat** *n* construction worker **hard'head·ed** *adj* shrewd **hard-pressed** *adj* heavily burdened **hard'ware** *n* tools, implements; necessary (parts of) machinery; *computing* mechanical and electronic parts **hard'wood** *n* wood from deciduous trees **hard of hearing** rather deaf **hard up** very short of money

har·dy [HAHR-dee] *adj* **-di·er, -di·est** robust, vigorous; bold; of plants, able to grow in the open all the year round **har'di·hood** [-huud] *n* extreme boldness, audacity **har'di·ly** *adv* **har'di·ness** *n*

hare [hair] *n* animal like large rabbit, with longer legs and ears, noted for speed **hare'brained** *adj* rash, wild **hare'lip** *n* fissure of upper lip

har•em [HAIR-əm] *n* women's part of Muslim dwelling; one man's wives and concubines

hark [hahrk] *vi* listen **hark back** return to previous subject of discussion

har•le•quin [HAHR-lə-kwin] *n* stock comic character, esp masked clown in diamond-patterned costume **har•le•quin•ade'** [-NAYD] *n* scene in pantomime; buffoonery

har•lot [HAHR-lət] *n* whore, prostitute **har'lot•ry** *n*

harm [hahrm] *n* damage, injury ▷ *vt* cause harm to **harm'ful** *adj* **harm'less** *adj* unable or unlikely to hurt

har•mo•ny [HAHR-mə-nee] *n*, *pl* **-nies** agreement; concord; peace; combination of notes to make chords; melodious sound **har•mon'ic** *adj* of harmony ▷ *n* tone or note whose frequency is a multiple of its pitch **har•mon'ics** *n* science of musical sounds **har•mon'i•ca** *n* various musical instruments, but esp mouth organ **har•mo'ni•ous** *adj* **har'mo•nize** [-mə-nīz] *v* **-nized, -niz•ing** ▷ *vt* bring into harmony; cause to agree; reconcile ▷ *vi* be in harmony

har•ness [HAHR-nis] *n* equipment for attaching horse to cart, plow, etc; any such equipment ▷ *vt* put on, in harness; utilize energy or power of (waterfall, etc)

harp [hahrp] *n* musical instrument of strings played by hand ▷ *vi* play on harp; dwell (on) persistently **harp'ist** *n* **harp'si•chord** [-si-kord] *n* stringed instrument like piano

har•poon [hahr-POON] *n* barbed spear with rope attached for catching whales ▷ *vt* catch, kill with this **har•poon'er** *n* **harpoon gun** gun for firing harpoon in whaling

Har•py [HAHR-pee] *n*, *pl* **-pies** monster with body of woman and wings and claws of bird; (**h-**) cruel, grasping person

har•ri•dan [HAHR-i-dn] *n* shrewish old woman, hag

har•row [HAR-oh] *n* implement for smoothing, leveling or stirring up soil ▷ *vt* draw harrow over; distress greatly **har'row•ing** *adj* heartrending; distressful

har•ry [HAR-ee] *vt* **-ried, -ry•ing** harass; ravage

harsh [hahrsh] *adj* **-er, -est** rough, discordant; severe; unfeeling **harsh'ness** *n*

har•um-scar•um [HAIR-əm-SKAIR-əm] *adj* reckless, wild; disorganized

har•vest [HAHR-vist] *n* (season for) gathering in grain; gathering; crop; product of action ▷ *vt* reap and gather in

has [haz] third person sing pres indicative of HAVE

hash *n* dish of chopped meat, etc; *inf* short for HASHISH mess, jumble ▷ *vt* cut up small, chop; mix up

hash•ish [hash-EESH] *n* resinous extract of Indian hemp, esp used as hallucinogen

hasp *n* clasp passing over a staple for fastening door, etc ▷ *vt* fasten, secure with hasp

has•sle [HAS-əl] *n* *inf* quarrel; a lot of bother, trouble ▷ *v* **-sled, -sling**

has•sock [HAS-ək] *n* cushion used as footstool, ottoman; tuft of grass

haste [hayst] *n* speed, quickness, hurry ▷ *v* **hast•ed, hast•ing** ▷ *vi* hasten **has•ten** [HAY-sən] *v* (cause to) hurry, increase speed **hast·i·ly** *adv* **hast·y** *adj* **hast·i·er, hast·i·est**

hat *n* head covering, usu with brim **hat·ter** *n* dealer in, maker of hats **hat trick** any three successive achievements, esp in sports

hatch¹ [hach] *v* of young, esp of birds, (cause to) emerge from egg; contrive, devise **hatch·er·y** *n*, *pl* **-er·ies**

hatch² *n* hatchway; trapdoor over it; lower half of divided door **hatch·back** *n* automobile with single lifting door in rear **hatch·way** *n* opening in deck of ship, etc

hatch³ *vt* engrave or draw lines on for shading; shade with parallel lines

hatch·et [HACH-it] *n* small ax **hatchet job** malicious verbal attack **hatchet man** person carrying out unpleasant assignments for another; professional assassin **bury the hatchet** make peace

hate [hayt] *vt* **hat·ed, hat·ing** dislike strongly; bear malice toward ▷ *n* this feeling; that which is hated **hate·ful** *adj* detestable **ha·tred** [HAY-trid] *n* extreme dislike, active ill will

haugh·ty [HAW-tee] *adj* **-ti·er, -ti·est** proud, arrogant **haugh·ti·ness** *n*

haul [hawl] *vt* pull, drag with effort ▷ *vi* move, shift in direction ▷ *n* hauling; what is hauled; catch of fish; acquisition; distance (to be) covered **haul·age** [HAW-lij] *n* carrying of loads; charge for this **haul·er** *n* firm, person that transports goods by road

haunch [hawnch] *n* human hip or fleshy hindquarter of animal; leg and loin of animal as food

haunt [hawnt] *vt* visit regularly; visit in form of ghost; recur to ▷ *n* esp place frequently visited

haunt·ed *adj* frequented by ghosts; worried

hau·teur [hoh-TUR] *n* haughty spirit; arrogance

have [hav] *vt* **had, hav·ing** hold, possess; be possessed, affected with; be obliged (to do); cheat, outwit; engage in, obtain; contain; allow; cause to be done; give birth to; used to form past tenses (with a past participle): *we have looked; she had done enough*

ha·ven [HAY-vən] *n* place of safety

hav·er·sack [HAV-ər-sak] *n* canvas bag for provisions, etc carried on back or shoulder when hiking, etc

hav·oc [HAV-ək] *n* devastation, ruin; *inf* confusion, chaos

hawk¹ *n* bird of prey smaller than eagle; supporter, advocate, of warlike policies ▷ *vi* hunt with hawks; attack like hawk

hawk² *vt* offer (goods) for sale, as in street **hawk·er** *n*

hawk³ *vi* clear throat noisily

haw·ser [HAW-zər] *n* large rope or cable

hay *n* grass mown and dried **hay·cock** *n* conical pile of hay for drying **hay fever** allergic reaction to pollen, dust, etc **hay·stack** *n* large pile of hay **hay·wire** *adj* crazy; disorganized

haz·ard [HAZ-ərd] *n* chance; risk, danger ▷ *vt* expose to risk; run risk of **haz·ard·ous** *adj* risky

haze [hayz] *n* mist, often due to heat; obscurity **ha·zy** *adj* **-zi·er, -zi·est** misty; obscured; vague

ha·zel [HAY-zəl] *n* bush or small tree bearing the nuts; yellowish-brown color of the nuts ▷ *adj* light brown

He chemistry helium

he [hee] *pron* third person masculine pronoun; person, animal already referred to ▷ *comb form* male: *he-goat*

head [hed] *n* upper part of person's or animal's body, containing mouth, sense organs and brain; upper part of anything; chief of organization, school, etc; chief part; aptitude, capacity; crisis; leader; title; headland; person, animal considered as unit; white froth on beer, etc; *inf* headache; *sl* addict, habitual user of drug ▷ *adj* chief, principal; of wind, contrary ▷ *vt* be at the top, head of; lead, direct; provide with head; hit (ball) with head ▷ *vi* make for; form a head **head'er** *n* headfirst plunge; brick laid with end in face of wall; action of striking ball with head **head'ing** *n* title **heads** *adv inf* with obverse side (of coin) uppermost **head'y** *adj* **head·i·er, head·i·est** apt to intoxicate or excite **head·ache** [-ayk] *n* continuous pain in head; worrying circumstance **head'board** *n* vertical board at head of bed **head'land** [-lànd] *n* promontory **head'light** *n* powerful lamp carried on front of locomotive, motor vehicle, etc **head'line** *n* news summary, in large type in newspaper **head'long** *adv* head foremost, in rush **head'quar·ters** *pl n* residence of commander-in-chief; center of operations **head'stone** *n* gravestone **head'strong** *adj* self-willed **head'way** *n* advance, progress

heal [heel] *v* make or become well **health** [helth] *n* soundness of body; condition of body; toast drunk in person's honor **health'i·ly** *adv* **health'y** *adj* **health·i·er, health·i·est** of strong constitution; of or producing good health, well-being, etc; vigorous **health food** vegetarian food, organically grown, eaten for dietary value

heap [heep] *n* pile of things lying one on another; great quantity ▷ *vt* pile, load with

hear [heer] *v* **heard** [hurd] **hear·ing** *n* perceive by ear; listen to; *law* try (case); heed; perceive sound; learn **hear'ing** *n* ability to hear; earshot; judicial examination **hear'say** *n* rumor ▷ *adj*

hark·en [HAHR-kàn] *vi* listen

hearse [hurs] *n* funeral carriage for coffin

heart [hahrt] *n* organ that makes blood circulate; seat of emotions and affections; mind, soul, courage; central part; playing card marked with figure of heart; one of these marks **heart'en** *v* make, become cheerful **heart'i·ly** *adv* **heart'less** [-lis] *adj* unfeeling **heart'y** *adj* **heart·i·er, heart·i·est** friendly, vigorous; in good health; satisfying the appetite **heart attack** sudden severe malfunction of heart **heart'burn** *n* pain in upper intestine **heart'rend·ing** *adj* overwhelming with grief; agonizing **heart'throb** *n* object of infatuation **heart'-to-heart** *adj* frank, sincere **by heart** by memory

hearth [hahrth] *n* floor of fireplace; part of room where fire is made; home

heat [heet] *n* hotness; sensation of this; hot weather or climate; warmth of feeling, anger, etc; sexual excitement caused by readiness to mate in female animals; one of many races, etc to decide persons to compete in finals ▷ *v* make, become hot **heat'ed** *adj* esp angry

heath [heeth] *n* tract of wasteland; low-growing evergreen shrub

hea·then [HEE-thàn] *adj* not adhering to a religious system; pagan; barbarous; unenlightened ▷ *n* heathen person **hea'then·ish**

adj of or like heathen; rough; barbarous

heath·er [HETH-ər] *n* shrub growing on heaths and mountains

heave [heev] *v* **heaved, heav·ing** ▷*vt* lift with effort; throw (something heavy); utter (sigh) ▷*vi* swell, rise; vomit ▷*n*

heav·en [HEV-ən] *n* abode of God; place of bliss; (also pl) sky **heav·en·ly** *adj* lovely, delightful; divine; beautiful; of or like heaven

heav·y [HEV-ee] *adj* **heav·i·er, heav·i·est** weighty, striking, falling with force; dense; sluggish; difficult, severe; sorrowful; serious; dull; *sl* serious, excellent **heav·i·ly** *adv* **heav·i·ness** *n* **heavy industry** basic, large-scale industry producing metal, machinery, etc **heavy metal** rock music with strong beat and amplified instrumental effects **heavy water** deuterium oxide, water in which normal hydrogen content has been replaced by deuterium

Heb. Hebrews

He·brew [HEE-broo] *n* member of an ancient Semitic people; their language; its modern form, used in Israel

heck·le [HEK-əl] *v* **-led, -ling** interrupt or try to annoy (speaker) by questions, taunts, etc

hect-, hecto- *comb form* one hundred: *hectoliter; hectometer*

hec·tare [HEK-tahr] *n* one hundred ares (10,000 square meters, 2.471 acres)

hec·tic [HEK-tik] *adj* rushed, busy

hec·tor [HEK-tər] *v* bully, bluster ▷*n* bully

hedge [hej] *n* fence of bushes ▷*v* **hedged, hedg·ing** ▷*vt* surround with hedge; obstruct; hem in; bet on both sides ▷*vi* make hedge;

be evasive; secure against loss **hedge'hog** *n* small animal covered with spines

he·don·ism [HEED-n-iz-əm] *n* doctrine that pleasure is the chief good **he'don·ist** *n*

heed *vt* take notice of, care for **heed'ful** *adj* **heed'less** *adj* careless

heel¹ *n* hinder part of foot; part of shoe supporting this; undesirable person ▷*vt* supply with heel; touch ground with heel ▷*vi* of dog, follow at one's heels

heel² *v* of ship, (cause to) lean to one side ▷*n* heeling, list

heft·y [HEF-tee] *adj* **heft·i·er, heft·i·est** bulky; weighty; strong

he·gem·o·ny [hi-JEM-ə-nee] *n, pl* **-nies** leadership, political domination

heif·er [HEF-ər] *n* young cow

height [hīt] *n* measure from base to top; quality of being high; elevation; highest degree; (oft pl) area of high ground; **heights** extremes: *dizzy heights of success* **height'en** *vt* make higher; intensify

hei·nous [HAY-nəs] *adj* atrocious, extremely wicked, detestable

heir [air] *n* person entitled to inherit property or rank **heir'ess** *n fem* **heir'loom** *n* thing that has been in family for generations

held *pt/pp of* HOLD

hel·i·cal [HEL-i-kəl] *adj* spiral

hel·i·cop·ter [HEL-i-kop-tər] *n* aircraft made to rise vertically by pull of rotating blades turning horizontally **hel'i·port** *n* airport for helicopters

helio- *comb form* sun: *heliograph*

he·li·o·graph [HEE-lee-ə-graf] *n* signaling apparatus employing a mirror to reflect sun's rays

he·li·o·ther·a·py [hee-lee-oh-THER-ə-pee] *n* therapeutic use of sunlight

he·li·o·trope [HEE-lee-ə-trohp] *n* plant with purple flowers; color of the flowers **he·li·o·trop·ic** [-TROP-ik] *adj* growing, turning toward source of light

he·li·um [HEE-lee-əm] *n* very light, nonflammable gaseous element

he·lix [HEE-liks] *n* spiral

hell *n* abode of the damned; abode of the dead generally; place or state of wickedness, or misery, or torture **hell'ish** *adj*

Hel·len·ic [he-LEN-ik] *adj* pert to inhabitants of Greece

hel·lo [he-LOH] *interj* expression of greeting or surprise

helm *n* tiller, wheel for turning ship's rudder

hel·met [HEL-mit] *n* defensive or protective covering for head

help *vt* aid, assist; support; succor; remedy, prevent ▷ *n* assistance or support **help'ful** *adj* **help'ing** *n* single portion of food taken at a meal **help'less** [-lis] *adj* useless, incompetent; unaided; unable to help **help'mate, -meet** *n* helpful companion; husband or wife

hel·ter-skel·ter [HEL-tər-SKEL-tər] *adv, adj, n* (in) hurry and confusion

hem *n* border of cloth, esp one made by turning over edge and sewing it down ▷ *vt* **hemmed, hem·ming** sew thus; confine, shut in **hem'stitch** *n* ornamental stitch ▷ *vt*

hemi- *comb form* half: *hemisphere*

hem·i·ple·gi·a [hem-i-PLEE-jə] *n* paralysis of one side of body **hem·i·ple·gic** *adj, n*

hem·i·sphere [HEM-i-sfeer] *n* half sphere; half of celestial sphere; half of Earth **hem·i·spher·i·cal**

[-sfe-rə-kəl] *adj*

hem·lock [HEM-lok] *n* poisonous plant; poison extracted from it; evergreen of pine family

hemo-, hema- *comb form* blood: *hemophilia*

he·mo·glo·bin [HEE-mə-gloh-bin] *n* coloring and oxygen-bearing matter of red blood corpuscles

he·mo·phil·i·a [hee-mə-FIL-ee-ə] *n* hereditary tendency to intensive bleeding as blood fails to clot **he·mo·phil'i·ac** *n*

hem·or·rhage [HEM-ər-ij] *n* profuse bleeding ▷ *vi* **-rhaged, -rhag·ing** bleed profusely; lose assets, esp in large amounts

hem·or·rhoids [HEM-ə-roidz] *pl n* swollen veins in rectum; (also **piles**)

hemp *n* Indian plant; its fiber used for rope, etc; any of several narcotic drugs made from varieties of hemp **hemp'en** [-pən] *adj* made of hemp or rope

hen *n* female of domestic fowl and others **hen'peck** *vt* (of a woman) harass (a man, esp husband) by nagging

hence [hens] *adv* from this point; for this reason **hence·for'ward, hence'forth** *adv* from now onward

hench·man [HENCH-mən] *n* trusty follower; unscrupulous supporter

hen·na [HEN-ə] *n* flowering shrub; reddish dye made from it

hen·o·the·ism [HEN-ə-thee-iz-əm] *n* belief in one god (of several) as special god of one's family, tribe, etc

hen·ry [HEN-ree] *n, pl* **-ries** SI unit of electrical inductance

he·pat·ic [hi-PAT-ik] *adj* pert to the liver **hep·a·ti·tis** [hep-ə-TI-tis] *n* inflammation of the liver

hepta- *comb form* seven: *heptagon*

hep·ta·gon [HEP-tə-gon] *n* figure

with seven angles **hep·tag'o·nal** adj

her [hur] adj objective and possessive case of **SHE hers** pron of her **her'self'** pron emphatic form of **SHE**

her·ald [HER-əld] n messenger, envoy; officer who makes royal proclamations, arranges ceremonies, etc ▷ vt announce; proclaim approach of **her·al·dic** [hi-RAL-dik] adj **her'ald·ry** n study of (right to have) heraldic bearings

herb [urb] n plant with soft stem that dies down after flowering; plant of which parts are used in cookery or medicine **her·ba·ceous** [hur-BAY-shəs] adj of, like herbs; perennially flowering **herb·al** [HUR-bəl] adj of herbs ▷ n book on herbs **herb'al·ist** n writer on herbs; collector, dealer in medicinal herbs **herb'i·cide** [-sid] n chemical that destroys plants **her·biv·o·rous** [-ə-rəs] adj feeding on plants

Her·cu·les [HUR-kyə-leez] n mythical hero noted for strength **her·cu·le·an** [-kyə-LEE-ən-ə] adj requiring great strength, courage; hard to perform

herd [hurd] n company of animals, usu of same species, feeding or traveling together ▷ v crowd together ▷ vt tend (herd) **herds·man** [HURDZ-mən] n

here [heer] adv in this place; at or to this point **here·af'ter** adv in time to come ▷ n future existence after death **here·to·fore'** [-tə-FOR] adv before

he·red·i·ty [hə-RED-i-tee] n tendency of organism to transmit its nature to its descendants **he·red'i·tar·y** [-ter-ee] adj descending by inheritance; holding office by inheritance; that can be transmitted from one generation to another

her·e·sy [HER-ə-see] n, pl -sies [-seez] opinion contrary to orthodox opinion or belief **her'e·tic** n one holding opinions contrary to orthodox faith **he·ret'i·cal** [-kəl] adj

her·it·age [HER-i-tij] n what may be or is inherited; anything from past, esp owned or handed down by tradition **her'it·a·ble** adj that can be inherited

her·maph·ro·dite [hur-MAF-rə-dit] n person, animal with characteristics or reproductive organs of both sexes

her·met·ic [hur-MET-ik] adj sealed so as to be airtight **her·met'i·cal·ly** adv

her·mit [HUR-mit] n one living in solitude, esp from religious motives **her'mit·age** [-tij] n this person's abode

her·ni·a [HUR-nee-ə] n projection of (part of) organ through lining encasing it

he·ro [HEER-oh] n, pl -roes one greatly regarded for achievements or qualities; principal character in poem, play, story; illustrious warrior; demigod **her·o·ine** [HER-oh-in] n fem **he·ro'ic** [hi-ROH-ik] adj, of, like hero; courageous, daring **he·ro'i·cal·ly** adv **he·ro'ics** pl n extravagant behavior **her'o·ism** n qualities of hero; courage, boldness **hero sandwich** large sandwich of meats, etc on loaf of Italian bread **hero worship** admiration of heroes of great men; excessive admiration of others

her·o·in [HER-oh-in] n white crystalline derivative of morphine, a highly addictive narcotic

her·on [HER-ən] n long-legged wading bird

her·pes [HUR-peez] *n* any of several diseases, including shingles and cold sores

her'ring *n* important food fish of northern hemisphere

hertz [hurts] *n, pl* **hertz** SI unit of frequency

hes·i·tate [HEZ-i-tayt] *vi* **-tat·ed, -tat·ing** hold back; feel, or show indecision; be reluctant **hes'i·tan·cy** [-tàn-see] *n* **hes·i·ta'tion** *n* wavering; doubt; stammering **hes'i·tant** *adj* undecided, pausing

hetero- *comb form* other or different: *heterosexual*

het·er·o·dox [HET-àr-à-doks] *adj* not orthodox **het'er·o·dox·y** *n, pl* **-dox·ies**

het·er·o·ge·ne·ous [het-àr-à-JEE-nee-às] *adj* composed of diverse elements **het·er·o·ge·ne'i·ty** [-jà-NEE-i-tee] *n*

het·er·o·sex·u·al [het-àr-à-SEK-shoo-àl] *n* person sexually attracted to members of the opposite sex

heu·ris·tic [hyuu-RIS-tik] *adj* serving to find out or to stimulate investigation

hew [hyoo] *v* **hewed, hewed** or **hewn, hew·ing** chop, cut with axe **hew'er** *n*

hex [heks] *n* magic spell ▷ *v* bewitch

hex-, hexa- *comb form* six: *hexagon*

hex·a·gon [HEK-sà-gon] *n* figure with six angles **hex·ag'o·nal** *adj*

hex·am·e·ter [hek-SAM-i-tàr] *n* line of verse of six feet

hey·day [HAY-day] *n* in bloom, prime

Hf *chemistry* hafnium

Hg *chemistry* mercury

hi·a·tus [hi-AY-tàs] *n, pl* **-tus·es** break or gap where something is missing

hi·ber·nate [Hì-bàr-nayt] *vi* **-nat·ed, -nat·ing** pass the winter, esp in a torpid state **hi·ber·na'tion** *n*

hi·bis·cus [hi-BIS-kàs] *n* flowering (sub)tropical shrub

hic·cup [HIK-up] *n* spasm of the breathing organs with an abrupt cough-like sound ▷ *vi* **-cupped, -cup·ping** have this

hick [hik] *adj inf* rustic; unsophisticated ▷ *n* person, place like this

hick·o·ry [HIK-à-ree] *n, pl* **-o·ries** N Amer nut-bearing tree; its tough wood

hide[1] [hid] *v* **hid, hid·den** or **hid, hid·ing** ▷ *vt* put, keep out of sight; conceal, keep secret ▷ *vi* conceal oneself **hide'out** *n* hiding place

hide[2] *n* skin of animal **hid'ing** *n* *sl* thrashing **hide'bound** *adj* restricted, esp by petty rules, etc; narrow-minded

hid·e·ous [HID-ee-às] *adj* repulsive, revolting

hi·er·ar·chy [Hì-à-rahr-kee] *n, pl* **-chies** system of persons or things arranged in graded order **hi·er·ar'chi·cal** *adj*

hi·er·o·glyph·ic [hi-àr-à-GLIF-ik] *adj* of a system of picture writing, as used in ancient Egypt ▷ *n* symbol representing object, concept or sound; symbol, picture, difficult to decipher **hi'er·o·glyph** *n*

hi-fi [Hì-Fì] *adj* short for **HIGH-FIDELITY** ▷ *n* high-fidelity equipment

high [hi] *adj* **-er, -est** tall, lofty; far up; of roads, main; of meat, tainted; of sound, acute in pitch; expensive; of great importance, quality, or rank; *inf* in state of euphoria, esp induced by alcohol or drugs ▷ *adv* far up; strongly, to a great extent; at, to a high pitch; at a high rate **high'ly**

adv **high'ness** *n* quality of being high; (**H-**) title of prince and princess **high'brow** *n* intellectual, esp intellectual snob ▷ *adj* intellectual; difficult; serious **high'-fi·del'i·ty** *adj* of high-quality sound-reproducing equipment **high-flown** *adj* extravagant, bombastic **high'-hand'ed** *adj* domineering, dogmatic **high'land** [-lənd] *n* relatively high ground **High'land** *adj* of, from the highlands of Scotland **high'light** *n* lightest or brightest area in painting, photograph, etc; outstanding feature ▷ *vt* bring into prominence **high·main'te·nance** *adj* (of equipment) requiring regular maintenance to keep it in working order; *inf* (of a person) requiring a high level of care and attention **high'-rise** *adj, n* (of) building that has many stories and elevators **high'-sound'ing** *adj* pompous, imposing **high-strung** *adj* excitable, nervous **high-tech** same as **HI-TECH high time** latest possible time **high'way** *n* main road **highway robbery** *inf* exorbitant fee or charge **high'way·man** [-mən] *n* (formerly) robber on road, esp mounted

hi·jack [HĪ-jak] *vt* divert or wrongfully take command of a vehicle (esp aircraft) or its contents or passengers; rob **hi'jack·er** *n*

hike [hīk] *v* **hiked, hik·ing** ▷ *vi* walk a long way (for pleasure) in country ▷ *vt* pull (up), hitch ▷ *n* **hik'er** *n*

hi·lar·i·ty [hi-LAR-i-tee] *n* cheerfulness, gaiety **hi·lar'i·ous** *adj*

hill *n* natural elevation, small mountain; mound **hill'ock** [-ək] *n* little hill **hill'y** *adj* **hill·i·er, hill·i·est hill'bil·ly** *n, pl* **-lies** *offens* unsophisticated country person

hilt *n* handle of sword, etc **up to the**

hilt completely

him *pron* objective case of pronoun **HE him·self'** *pron* emphatic form of **HE**

hind[1] [hīnd] *n* female of deer

hind[2] *adj* at the back, posterior; (also **hind·er**) [HĪN-dər]

hin·der [HIN-dər] *vt* obstruct, impede, delay **hin'drance** [-drəns] *n*

Hin·di [HIN-dee] *n* language of N central India **Hin'du** [-doo] *n* person who adheres to Hinduism **Hin'du·ism** the dominant religion of India

hinge [hinj] *n* movable joint, as that on which door hangs ▷ *v* **hinged, hing·ing** ▷ *vt* attach with, or as with, hinge ▷ *vi* turn, depend on

hint *n* slight indication or suggestion ▷ *v* give hint of

hin·ter·land [HIN-tər-land] *n* district lying behind coast, or near city, port, etc

hip *n* either side of body below waist and above thigh; angle formed where sloping sides of roof meet; fruit of rose, esp wild

hip-hop [HIP-hop] *n* pop-culture movement involving rap music, graffiti, and break dancing

hip·pie [HIP-ee] *n* (formerly) (young) person whose behavior, dress, etc implies rejection of conventional values

hip·po·pot·a·mus [hip-ə-POT-ə-məs] *n, pl* **-mus·es** or **-mi** [-mī] large Afr animal living in and near rivers

hire [hīr] *vt* **hired, hir·ing** obtain temporary use of by payment; engage for wage ▷ *n* hiring or being hired; payment for use of thing **hire'ling** *n* one who works for wages

hir·sute [HUR-soot] *adj* hairy

his [hiz] *pron, adj* belonging to him

His·pan·ic [hi-SPAN-ik] *adj*

relating to Spain or to Spanish-speaking Central and S America ▷ *n* Spanish-speaking person; U.S. resident of Hispanic descent

his·pid *adj* rough with bristles or minute spines; bristly, shaggy

hiss *vi* make sharp sound of letter S, esp in disapproval ▷ *vt* express disapproval, deride thus ▷ *n*

his·ta·mine [HIS-tə-meen] *n* substance released by body tissues, sometimes creating allergic reactions

his·tol·o·gy [hi-STOL-ə-jee] *n* science that treats of minute structure of organic tissues

his·to·ry [HIS-tə-ree] *n, pl* **-ries** record of past events; study of these; past events; train of events, public or private; course of life or existence; systematic account of phenomena **his·to·ri·an** *n* writer of history **his·tor·ic** *adj* noted in history **his·tor·i·cal** *adj* of, based on, history; belonging to past **his·tor·i·cal·i·ty** [-tə-RIS-i-tee] *n* historical authenticity **his·to·ri·og·ra·pher** *n* official historian; one who studies historical method **his·to·ri·og·ra·phy** *n* methods of historical research

his·tri·on·ic [his-tree-ON-ik] *adj* excessively theatrical, insincere, artificial in manner **his·tri·on·ics** *n* behavior like this

hit *v* **hit, hit·ting** ▷ *vt* strike with blow or missile; affect injuriously; find ▷ *vi* strike; light (upon) ▷ *n* blow; success; *computing* single visit to a website or single result of a search **hit·ter** *n* **hit man** *sl* hired assassin **hit it off** *inf* get along well (with person) **hit or miss** haphazard(ly) **hit the hay** *inf* go to bed **hit the road** *inf* proceed on journey; depart

hitch [hich] *vt* fasten with loop, etc;

raise, move with jerk ▷ *vi* be caught or fastened ▷ *n* difficulty; knot, fastening; jerk **hitch·hike** *vi* **-hiked, -hik·ing** travel by begging free rides

hi-tech *n* technology requiring sophisticated scientific equipment and engineering techniques; interior design using features of industrial equipment ▷ *adj*

hith·er [HITH-ər] *adv* to or toward this place **hith·er·to** *adv* up to now or to this time

hive [hiv] *n* structure in which bees live or are housed; *fig* place swarming with busy occupants ▷ *v* **hived, hiv·ing** gather, place bees, in hive

hives [hivz] *pl n* eruptive skin disease

HMO Health Maintenance Organization: an organization that provides health care to voluntarily enrolled clients in a particular US geographic area

Ho *chemistry* holmium

hoard [hord] *n* stock, store, esp hidden away ▷ *vt* amass and hide away; store

hoarse [hors] *adj* **hoars·er, hoars·est** rough, harsh sounding, husky

hoar·y [HOR-ee] *adj* **hoar·i·er, hoar·i·est** gray with age; grayish-white; of great antiquity; venerable **hoar'frost** *n* frozen dew

hoax [hohks] *n* practical joke; deceptive trick ▷ *vt* play trick on; deceive **hoax'er** *n*

hob *n* projection or shelf at side or back of fireplace, used for keeping food warm; tool for cutting gear teeth, etc **hob'nail** [-nayl] *n* large-headed nail for boot soles

hob·ble [HOB-əl] *v* **-bled, -bling** ▷ *vi* walk lamely ▷ *vt* tie legs together (of horse, etc); impede, hamper ▷ n straps or ropes put on an animal's legs to prevent it from straying; limping gait

hob·by [HOB-ee] n, pl **-bies** favorite occupation as pastime

hob'by·horse n toy horse; favorite topic, preoccupation

hob'gob·lin n mischievous fairy

hob'nob vi **-nobbed, -nob·bing** associate, be familiar (with)

ho·bo [HOH-boh] n, pl **-boes** shiftless, wandering person

hock [hok] n backward-pointing joint on leg of horse, etc, corresponding to human ankle ▷ vt disable by cutting tendons of hock, hamstring

hock·ey [HOK-ee] n team game played on a field with ball and curved sticks; ice hockey

ho·cus-po·cus [HOH-kàs-POH-kàs] n trickery; mystifying jargon

hod n small trough on a pole for carrying mortar, bricks, etc

hoe [hoh] n tool for weeding, breaking ground, etc ▷ vt **hoed, hoe·ing**

hog [hawg] n pig, esp castrated male for fattening; greedy, dirty person ▷ vt **hogged, hog·ging** inf eat, use (something) selfishly

hogs·head [HAWGZ-hed] n large cask; liquid measure of 63 to 140 gallons (238 to 530 liters) **hog'tie** vt **-tied, -ty·ing** hobble; hamper **hog'wash** n nonsense; pig food

ho·gan [HOH-gàn] n Navajo Indian dwelling of earth, branches, etc

hoi pol·loi [HOI pà-LOI] n the common mass of people; the masses

hoist vt raise aloft, raise with tackle, etc

ho·key·po·key [HO-kee-PO-kee] n kind of playful dance or its music

hold¹ [hohld] v **held, hold·ing** ▷ vt keep fast, grasp; support in or with hands, etc; maintain in position; have capacity for; own, occupy; carry on; detain; celebrate; keep back; believe ▷ vi cling; not to give away; abide (by); keep (to); last, proceed, be in force; occur ▷ n grasp; influence **hold'ing** n (oft pl) property, as land or stocks and bonds **hold'up** n armed robbery; delay

hold² n space in ship or aircraft for cargo

hole [hohl] n hollow place, cavity; perforation; opening; inf unattractive place; inf difficult situation ▷ v **holed, hol·ing** make holes in; go into a hole; drive into a hole

hol·i·day n day or other period of rest from work, etc, esp spent away from home

hol·low [HOL-oh] adj **-er, -est** having a cavity, not solid; empty; false; insincere; not full-toned ▷ n cavity, hole, valley ▷ vt make hollow, make hole in; excavate

hol·ly [HOL-ee] n, pl **-lies** [-leez] evergreen shrub usu with prickly leaves and red berries

hol·o·caust [HOL-à-kawst] n great destruction of life, esp by fire; (**H-**) mass slaughter of Jews in Nazi concentration camps during World War II

hol·o·gram [HOL-à-gram] n a three-dimensional photographic image

hol·o·graph [HOL-à-graf] n document wholly written by the signer

ho·log·ra·phy [hà-LOG-rà-fee] n science of using lasers to produce a photographic record that can reproduce a three-dimensional image

hol·ster [HOHL-stàr] n case for pistol, hung from belt, etc

ho·ly [HOH-lee] adj -li·er, -li·est belonging, devoted to God; free from sin; divine; consecrated **ho'li·ness** n sanctity; (**H-**) Pope's title **holy day** day of religious festival **Holy Communion** service of the Eucharist **Holy Week** that before Easter Sunday

hom·age [HOM-ij] n tribute, respect, reverence; formal acknowledgment of allegiance

home [hohm] n dwelling place; residence; native place; institution for the elderly, infirm, etc ▷ adj of, connected with, home; native ▷ adv to, at one's home; to the point ▷ v **homed, hom·ing** direct or be directed onto a point or target **home'boy** n sl close friend **home fries** boiled potatoes, sliced and fried in butter, etc **home'less** adj **home'ly** -li·er, -li·est unpretentious; warm and domesticated; plain **home'ward** [-wərd] adj, adv **home'wards** adv **home-brew** n alcoholic drink made at home, esp beer **bring home to** impress deeply upon **home free** sure of success **home'land** n country from which a person's ancestors came **homeland security** domestic governmental actions intended to protect against terrorist attacks **home page** internet introductory information about a website with links to the information or services provided **home'room** n classroom in a school used by a particular group of students as a base; group of students who use the same classroom as a base in school **home'sick** adj depressed by absence from home **home'spun** adj domestic; simple ▷ n cloth made of homespun yarn **home'stead** [-sted] n house

with outbuildings, esp on farm **home'stead·er** n **home'work** n school work done usu at home

ho·me·op·a·thy [hoh-mee-OP-ə-thee] n treatment of disease by small doses of what would produce symptoms in healthy person **ho·me·o·path'ic** adj

hom·i·cide [HOM-ə-sid] n killing of human being; killer **hom·i·cid'al** adj

hom·i·ly [HOM-ə-lee] n, pl -lies [-leez] sermon; religious discourse **hom·i·let'ic** adj of sermons **hom·i·let'ics** n art of preaching

Ho·mo [HOH-moh] n genus to which modern man belongs **homo-** comb form same, like: homophone; homosexual

ho·mo·ge·ne·ous [hoh-mə-JEE-nee-əs] adj formed of uniform parts; similar, uniform; of the same nature **ho·mo·ge·ne'i·ty** n **ho·mog·e·nize** [hə-MOJ-ə-niz] vt -nized, -niz·ing break up fat globules in milk and cream to distribute them evenly; make uniform or similar

ho·mol·o·gous [hə-MOL-ə-gəs] adj having the same relation, relative position, etc **ho·mo·logue** [HOH-mə-lawg] n homologous thing

hom·o·nym [HOM-ə-nim] n word of same form as another, but of different sense

ho·mo·sex·u·al [hoh-mə-SEK-shoo-əl] n person sexually attracted to members of the same sex ▷ adj **ho·mo·sex·u·al'i·ty** n **ho·mo·pho'bi·a** [-FOH-bee-ə] n hate or fear of homosexuals and homosexuality

hone [hohn] n whetstone for sharpening razors, etc ▷ vt **honed, hon·ing** sharpen on one

hon·est [ON-ist] adj not cheating,

lying, stealing, etc; genuine; without pretension **hon·est·y** n quality of being honest

hon·ey [HUN-ee] n, pl **-eys** sweet fluid made by bees **hon·ey·comb** [-kohm] n wax structure in hexagonal cells in which bees place honey, eggs, etc ▷ vt fill with cells or perforations **hon·ey·dew** [-doo] n sweet sticky substance found on plants; type of sweet melon **hon·ey·moon** n holiday taken by newly wedded couple; any new relationship with initial period of harmony ▷ vi spend one's honeymoon

honk [hongk] n call of goose; any sound like this, esp sound of automobile horn ▷ vi make this sound ▷ vt cause (automobile horn) to sound

hon·or [ON-ər] n personal integrity; renown; reputation; sense of what is right or due; chastity; high rank or position; source, cause of honor; pleasure, privilege ▷ pl mark of respect; distinction in examination ▷ vt respect highly; confer honor on; accept or pay (bill, etc) when due **hon'or·a·ble** adj **hon·o·rar·i·um** n, pl **-rar·i·a** a fee **hon'or·ar·y** adj conferred for the sake of honor only; holding position without pay or usual requirements; giving services without pay **hon·or·if·ic** adj conferring, indicating honor ▷ n in certain languages, form used to show respect, esp in direct address

hood¹ [huud] n covering for head and neck, often part of cloak or gown; hoodlike thing, as covering of engine compartment of automobile, etc **hood'ed** adj covered with or shaped like a hood **hood'wink** vt deceive

hood² n sl hoodlum

hood·lum [HUUD-ləm] n gangster; street ruffian

hoo'doo n cause of bad luck

hoof [huuf] n, pl **hoofs** or **hooves** horny casing of foot of horse, etc **on the hoof** (of livestock) alive

hoo-ha [HOO-hah] n uproar ▷ interj exclamation expressing excitement or surprise

hook [huuk] n bent piece of metal, etc, for catching hold, hanging up, etc; something resembling hook in shape or function; curved cutting tool; enticement; boxing blow delivered with elbow bent ▷ vt grasp, catch, hold, as with hook; fasten with hook; golf drive (ball) widely to the left (of right-handed golfer, and vice versa) **hooked** adj shaped like hook; caught; inf addicted to; sl married **hook'er** n sl prostitute **hook'up** n linking of radio, television stations **hook'worm** [-wurm] n parasitic worm infesting humans and animals **hook·ah** [HUUK-ə] n oriental pipe in which smoke is drawn through cooling water and long tube

hoo·li·gan [HOO-li-gən] n violent, irresponsible (young) person; ruffian **hoo'li·gan·ism** n

hoop n rigid circular band of metal, wood, etc such a band used for binding barrel, etc, for use as a toy, or for jumping through as in circus acts ▷ vt bind with hoops; encircle **put through the hoops** inf subject to ordeal or test

hoop·la [HOOP-lah] n inf excitement; hullabaloo

hoot n owl's cry or similar sound; cry of disapproval or derision; sl funny person or thing ▷ vi utter hoot (esp in derision) ▷ vt assail (someone) with derisive cries; drive (someone) away by hooting

hop¹ *vi* **hopped, hop·ping** spring on one foot; *inf* move quickly ▷ *n* leap, skip; one stage of journey **hop'scotch** [-skoch] *n* children's game of hopping in pattern drawn on ground

hop² *n* climbing plant with bitter cones used to flavor beer, etc ▷ *pl* the cones

hope [hohp] *n* expectation of something desired; thing that gives, or object of, this feeling ▷ *v* **hoped, hop·ing** feel hope (for) **hope'ful** *adj* **hope'less** *adj* young hopeful promising boy or girl

hop·per [HOP-ər] *n* one who hops; device for feeding material into mill or machine or grain into truck, etc **hopper car** railroad freight car, usu open at top and containing one or more hoppers, for transport and discharge of grain, etc

horde [hord] *n* large crowd (esp moving together)

ho·ri·zon [hə-RĪ-zən] *n* boundary of part of Earth seen from any given point; lines where Earth and sky seem to meet; boundary of mental outlook **hor·i·zon·tal** [hor-ə-ZON-tl] *adj* parallel with horizon, level

hor·mone [HOR-mohn] *n* substance secreted by certain glands that stimulates organs of the body; synthetic substance with same effect

horn *n* hard projection on heads of certain animals, eg cattle; substance of it; various things made of, or resembling it; *music* wind instrument orig made of a horn; device (esp in car) emitting sound as alarm, warning, etc **horned** *adj* having horns **horn'y** *adj* **horn·i·er, horn·i·est** hornlike; *sl* lustful **horn'pipe** *n* lively dance, esp associated with sailors

hor·net [HOR-nit] *n* large insect of wasp family **hornet's nest** much opposition, animosity

hor·o·scope [HOR-ə-skohp] *n* observation of, or scheme showing disposition of planets, etc at given moment, esp birth, by which character and abilities of individual are predicted; telling of person's fortune by this method

hor·ren·dous [haw-REN-dəs] *adj* horrific

hor·ror [HOR-ər] *n* terror; loathing, fear of; its cause **hor·ri·ble** *adj* exciting horror, hideous, shocking **hor·ri·bly** *adv* **hor·rid** *adj* unpleasant, repulsive; *inf* unkind **hor·ri·fy** *vt* **-fied, -fy·ing** move to horror **hor·rif·ic** *adj* particularly horrible

hors d'oeu·vre [or-DURV] *n, pl* **-vres** [-DURVZ] small appetizer served before main meal

horse [hors] *n* four-legged animal used for riding and work; cavalry; vaulting horse; frame for support; *sl* heroin ▷ *vt* **horsed, hors·ing** provide with horse or horses **hors'y** *adj* **hors·i·er, hors·i·est** having to do with horses; devoted to horses or horse racing **horse'fly** *n, pl* **-flies** large bloodsucking fly **horse laugh** harsh boisterous laugh usu expressing derision **horse'man** [-mən] **-wom·an** *n* rider on horse **horse'play** *n* rough, boisterous play **horse'pow·er** *n* unit of power of engine, etc, 550 foot-pounds per second **horse'shoe** [-shoo] *n* protective U-shaped piece of iron nailed to horse's hoof; thing so shaped **horse around** *sl* play roughly, boisterously

hor·ti·cul·ture [HOR-ti-kul-chər] *n* art or science of gardening **hor·ti·cul'tur·al** *adj*

Hos. Hosea

ho·san·na [hoh-ZAN-ə] *n, pl* **-nas** cry of praise, adoration

hose [hohz] *n* flexible tube for conveying liquid or gas; stockings ▷ *vt* **hosed, hos·ing** water with hose **ho·sier·y** *n* stockings or socks

hos·pice [HOS-pis] *n* traveler's house of rest kept by religious order; residence for care of terminally ill

hos·pi·tal [HOS-pi-tl] *n* institution for care of sick **hos·pi·tal·i·za'tion** *n* place for care in a hospital **hos'pi·tal·ize** *vt* **-ized, -iz·ing** to place for care in a hospital

hos·pi·tal·i·ty [hos-pi-TAL-i-tee] *n, pl* **-ties** friendly and liberal reception of strangers or guests **hos'pi·ta·ble** *adj* welcoming, kindly

host¹ [hohst] *n* one who entertains another; master of ceremonies of show; animal, plant on which parasite lives; *computing* computer that provides data or connectivity to others on a network ▷ *vt* act as a host **-ess** *n fem*

host² *n* large number

Host *n* consecrated bread of the Eucharist

hos·tage [HOS-tij] *n* person taken or given as pledge or security

hos·tel [HOS-tl] *n* building providing accommodation at low cost for particular category of people, as students, or the homeless

hos·tile [HOS-tl] *adj* opposed, antagonistic; warlike; of an enemy; unfriendly **hos·til'i·ty** *n* enmity **hos·til'i·ties** *pl n* acts of warfare

hot *adj* **hot·ter, hot·test** of high temperature, very warm, giving or feeling heat; angry; severe; recent, new; much favored; spicy; *sl* good, quick, smart, lucky, successful; *sl* stolen **hot'ly** *adv* **hot'ness** *n* **hot air** *inf* boastful, empty talk **hot'bed** *n* bed of earth heated by manure and grass for young plants; any place encouraging growth; center of activity **hot'-blood·ed** [-blud-id] *adj* passionate, excitable

hot dog frankfurter (in split bread roll) **hot'foot** [-fuut] *v, adv* (go) quickly **hot'head** [-hed] *n* hasty, intemperate person **hot'house** *n* forcing house for plants; heated building for cultivating tropical plants in cold or temperate climates **hot line** direct communication link between heads of governments, etc **hot pants** extremely brief and close-fitting pants for women; *sl* strong sexual desire **hot'plate** *n* heated plate on electric cooker; portable device for keeping food warm

ho·tel [hoh-TEL] *n* commercial establishment providing lodging

hound [hownd] *n* hunting dog ▷ *vt* chase, urge, pursue

hour [owr] *n* twenty-fourth part of day; sixty minutes; time of day; appointed time ▷ *pl* fixed periods for work, prayers, etc; book of prayers **hour'ly** *adv* every hour; frequently ▷ *adj* frequent; happening every hour **hour'glass** *n* instrument using dropping sand or mercury to indicate passage of an hour

hou·ri [HUUR-ee] *n, pl* **-ris** beautiful virgin provided in the Muslim paradise

house [hows] *n, pl* **hous·es** [HOW-ziz] building for human habitation; building for other specified purpose; legislative or other assembly; family; business firm; theater audience, performance ▷ *vt* [howz] **housed, hous·ing** give or receive shelter, lodging or storage; cover or contain **housing** *n* (providing of) houses; part or structure designed to cover, protect, contain **house'boat** *n* boat for living in on river, etc **house'break·er** [-brayk-ər] n burglar **house'coat** n woman's long loose garment for casual wear at home **house'hold** n inmates of house collectively **house'hold·er** n occupier of house as own dwelling; head of household **house'-hus·band** n man who runs a household **house'keep·er** n person managing affairs of household **house'keep·ing** n running household **house'warm·ing** n party to celebrate entry into new house **house'wife** n woman who runs a household

hov·el [HUV-əl] n mean dwelling

hov·er [HUV-ər] vi hang in the air (of bird, etc); loiter; be in state of indecision **hov'er·craft** n type of craft that can travel over land and sea on a cushion of air

how adv in what way; by what means; in what condition; to what degree; (in direct or dependent question) nevertheless ▷ adv in whatever way, degree; all the same

how·dah [HOW-də] n (canopied) seat on elephant's back

how·itz·er [HOW-it-sər] n short gun firing shells at high elevation

howl vi utter long loud cry ▷ n such cry **howl'er** n one that howls; embarrassing mistake

hoy·den [HOID-n] n wild, boisterous girl, tomboy

Hs chemistry hassium

HTML computing hypertext markup language: text description language that is used on the World Wide Web

hub n middle part of wheel, from which spokes radiate; central point of activity

hub'bub n confused noise of many voices; uproar

huck·ster [HUK-stər] n retailer, peddler; person using aggressive or questionable methods of selling ▷ vt sell goods thus

hud·dle [HUD-l] n crowded mass; inf impromptu conference, esp of offensive football team during game ▷ v **-dled, -dling** heap, crowd together; hunch; confer

hue [hyoo] n color, complexion

hue and cry public uproar, outcry; loud outcry usually in pursuit of wrongdoer

huff n passing mood of anger ▷ v make or become angry, resentful ▷ vi blow, puff heavily **huff'i·ly** adv **huff'y** adj **huff·i·er, huff·i·est**

hug vt hugged, hug·ging clasp tightly in the arms; cling; keep close to ▷ n fond embrace

huge [hyooj] adj very big **huge'ly** adv very much

hu·la [HOO-lə] n native dance of Hawaii

hulk n body of abandoned vessel; large, unwieldy thing **hulk'ing** adj unwieldy, bulky

hull n frame, body of ship; calyx of strawberry, raspberry, or similar fruit; shell, husk ▷ vt remove shell, hull

hul·la·ba·loo [HUL-ə-bə-loo] n, pl **-loos** uproar, clamor, row

hum v hummed, hum·ming ▷ vi make low continuous sound as bee; be very active ▷ vt sing with closed lips ▷ n humming sound; smell; great activity; in radio, disturbance affecting reception **hum'ming·bird** n very small bird whose wings make humming noise

hu·man [HYOO-mən] adj of people; relating to, characteristic of, people's nature **hu·mane'** [-MAYN] adj benevolent, kind; merciful **hu'man·ism** n belief in human effort rather than religion;

interest in human welfare and affairs; classical literary culture

hu·man·ist vt **hu·man·i·tar·i·an** n philanthropist ▷ adj **hu·man·i·ty** n, pl **-ties** [-teez] human nature; human race; kindliness ▷ pl study of literature, philosophy, the arts

hu·man·ize vt **-ized, -iz·ing** make human; civilize **hu·man·ly** adv

hu·man·kind [-kĭnd] n human race as a whole

hum·ble [HUM-bəl] adj **-bler, -blest** lowly, modest ▷ vt **-bled, -bling** bring low, abase, humiliate **hum·bly** adv

hum·bug n impostor; sham, nonsense, deception ▷ vt **-bugged, -bug·ging** deceive; defraud

hum·ding·er [HUM-DING-ər] n inf excellent person or thing

hum·drum adj commonplace, dull, monotonous

hu·mer·us [HYOO-mər-əs] n, pl **-mer·i** [-mə-rī] long bone of upper arm

hu·mid [HYOO-mĭd] adj moist, damp **hu·mid·i·fi·er** n device for increasing amount of water vapor in air in room, etc **hu·mid·i·fy** vt **-fied, -fy·ing hu·mid·i·ty** n

hu·mil·i·ate [hyoo-MIL-ee-ayt] vt **-at·ed, -at·ing** lower dignity of, abase, mortify

hu·mil·i·ty [hyoo-MIL-i-tee] n state of being humble; meekness

hum·mock [HUM-ək] n low knoll, hillock; ridge of ice

hum·mus [HEW-mus] n creamy dip of Middle East origin, made from puréed chickpeas

hu·mor [HYOO-mər] n faculty of saying or perceiving what excites amusement; state of mind, mood; temperament; obs one of four chief fluids of body ▷ vt gratify, indulge **hu·mor·ist** n person who

acts, speaks, writes humorously

hu·mor·ous adj funny; amusing

hump n normal or deforming lump, esp on back; hillock ▷ vt make hump-shaped; inf exert (oneself), hurry; sl carry or heave **hump'back** n person with hump **hump'backed** adj having a hump

hu·mus [HYOO-màs] n decayed vegetable and animal mold

hunch n inf intuition or premonition; hump ▷ vt thrust, bend into hump **hunch'back** n humpback

hun·dred [HUN-drĭd] n, adj cardinal number, ten times ten **hun'dredth** [-drĭdth] adj the ordinal number **hun'dred·fold** adj, adv **hun'dred·weight** n weight of 100 lbs (45.359 kg)

hung pt/pp of **HANG** adj (of jury, etc) unable to decide; not having majority **hung'o·ver** adj inf experiencing a hangover **hung up** inf delayed; stymied; baffled **hung up on** sl obsessed by

hun·ger [HUNG-gər] n discomfort, exhaustion from lack of food; strong desire ▷ vi **hun'gri·ly** adv **hun'gry** adj **-gri·er, -gri·est** having keen appetite **hunger strike** refusal of all food, as a protest

hunk [hungk] n thick piece; sl attractive man with excellent physique

hunt v seek out to kill or capture for sport or food; search (for) ▷ n chase, search; track of country hunted over; (party organized for) hunting; pack of hounds; hunting club **hunt'er** n one who hunts; horse, dog bred for hunting **-ress** n fem

hur·dle [HUR-dl] n portable frame of bars for temporary fences for jumping over; obstacle ▷ vi **-dled, -dling** race over hurdles **hurdles** n a

race over hurdles **hurd'ler** n
hurl vt throw violently **hurl·y-**
burl·y [HUR-lee-BUR-lee] n, pl
-burl·ies loud confusion
hur·rah [hə-RAH], **hur·ray**
[-RAY] interj exclamation of joy or
applause **last hurrah** final occasion
of achievement
hur·ri·cane [HUR-i-kayn] n very
strong, potentially destructive wind
or storm **hurricane lamp** lamp with
glass chimney around flame
hur·ry [HUR-ee] v **-ried, -ry·ing**
(cause to) move or act in great haste
▷ n, pl **-ries** undue haste; eagerness
hur'ried·ly adv
hurt v hurt, **hurt·ing** ▷ vt injure,
damage, give pain to, wound
feelings of; distress ▷ vi inf feel pain
▷ n wound, injury, harm **hurt'ful**
adj
hur·tle [HUR-tl] vi **-tled, -tling**
move rapidly; rush violently; whirl
hus·band [HUZ-bənd] n married
man ▷ vt economize; use to best
advantage **hus'ban·dry** [-dree] n
farming; economy
hush v make or be silent ▷ n
stillness; quietness **hush-hush** adj
inf secret **hush up** suppress rumors,
information; make secret
husk n dry covering of certain
seeds and fruits; worthless outside
part ▷ vt remove husk from **husk'y**
adj **husk·i·er, husk·i·est** rough
in tone; hoarse; dry as husk, dry
in the throat; of, full of, husks; big
and strong
husk·y [HUS-kee] n, pl **husk·ies**
Arctic sledge dog with thick hair and
curled tail
hus·sy [HUS-ee] n, pl **-sies** brazen
or immoral woman; impudent girl or
young woman
hus·tings [HUS-tingz] pl n any
place from which political campaign

speeches are made; political
campaigning
hus·tle [HUS-əl] v **-tled, -tling**
push about, jostle, hurry ▷ vi sl
solicit clients esp for prostitution
▷ n **hus·tler** [HUS-lər] industrious
person; sl prostitute
hut n any small house or shelter, usu
of wood or metal
hutch [huch] n boxlike pen for
rabbits, etc
hy·brid [HI-brid] n offspring of
two plants or animals of different
species; mongrel ▷ adj crossbred
hy'brid·ism n **hy'brid·ize** v **-ized,
-iz·ing** make hybrid; crossbreed
hy·dra [HI-drə] n, pl **-dras** [-drəz]
fabulous many-headed water
serpent; any persistent problem;
freshwater polyp **hy'dra·head·ed**
adj hard to understand, root out
hy·dran·gea [hi-DRAYN-jə] n
ornamental shrub with pink, blue, or
white flowers
hy·drant [HI-drənt] n water pipe
with nozzle for hose
hy·drau·lic [hi-DRAW-lik] adj
concerned with, operated by,
pressure transmitted through liquid
in pipe **hy·drau'lics** n science of
mechanical properties of liquid in
motion
hydro- comb form water:
hydroelectric; presence of hydrogen:
hydrocarbon
hy·dro·car·bon [hi-drə-KAHR-
bən] n compound of hydrogen and
carbon
hy·dro·chlor·ic ac·id [hi-drə-
KLOR-ik] strong colorless acid used
in many industrial and laboratory
processes
hy·dro·dy·nam·ics [hi-droh-di-
NAM-iks] n science of the motions
of system wholly or partly fluid
hy·dro·e·lec·tric [hi-droh-i-

LEK-trik] *adj* pert to generation of electricity by use of water

hy·dro·foil [Hĩ-drə-foil] *n* fast, light vessel with hull raised out of water at speed by action of vanes in water

hy·dro·gen [Hĩ-drə-jən] *n* colorless gas that combines with oxygen to form water **hydrogen bomb** atom bomb of enormous power in which hydrogen nuclei are converted into helium nuclei **hydrogen peroxide** colorless liquid used as antiseptic and bleach

hy·drog·ra·phy [hĩ-DROG-rə-fee] *n* description of waters of the earth **hy·dro·graph·ic** *adj*

hy·drol·y·sis [hĩ-DROL-ə-sis] *n* decomposition of chemical compound reacting with water

hy·drom·e·ter [hĩ-DROM-i-tər] *n* device for measuring relative density of liquid

hy·dro·pho·bi·a [hĩ-drə-FOH-bee-ə] *n* aversion to water, esp as symptom of rabies; rabies

hy·dro·plane [Hĩ-drə-playn] *n* light skimming motorboat; seaplane; vane controlling motion of submarine, etc

hy·dro·pon·ics [hĩ-drə-PON-iks] *n* science of cultivating plants in water without using soil

hy·dro·ther·a·py [hĩ-drə-THER-ə-pee] *n* medicine treatment of disease by external application of water

hy·drous [Hĩ-drəs] *adj* containing water

hy·e·na [hĩ-EE-nə] *n* wild animal related to dog

hy·giene [Hĩ-jeen] *n* principles and practice of health and cleanliness; study of these principles **hy·gi·en·ic** [hĩ-jee-EN-ik] *adj* **hy·gien'ist** [-JEE-nist] *n*

hy·grom·e·ter [hĩ-GROM-i-tər] *n* instrument for measuring humidity of air

hy·gro·scop·ic [hĩ-grə-SKOP-ik] *adj* readily absorbing moisture from the atmosphere

hy·men [Hĩ-mən] *n* membrane partly covering vagina of virgin; (**H-**) Greek god of marriage

hymn [him] *n* song of praise, esp to God ▷ *vt* praise in song **hym·nal** [HIM-nl] *adj* of hymns ▷ *n* book of hymns; (also **hymn book**)

hype[1] [hīp] *n* sl hypodermic syringe; drug addict

hype[2] *n* inf deception, racket; intensive publicity ▷ *v* **hyped, hyp·ing** inf promote (a product) using intensive publicity

hyper- *comb form* over, above, excessively: *hyperactive*

hy·per·bo·la [hĩ-PUR-bə-lə] *n* curve produced when cone is cut by plane making larger angle with the base than the side makes

hy·per·bo·le [hĩ-PUR-bə-lee] *n* rhetorical exaggeration **hy·per·bol'ic** *adj*

hy·per·bo·re·an [hĩ-pər-BOR-ee-ən] *adj, n* (inhabitant) of extreme north

hy·per·crit·i·cal [hĩ-pər-KRIT-i-kəl] *adj* too critical

hy·per·link [Hĩ-pər-lingk] *computing n* link from a hypertext file that gives users instant access to related material in another file ▷ *vt* link (files) in this way

hy·per·sen·si·tive [hĩ-pər-SEN-si-tiv] *adj* unduly vulnerable emotionally or physically

hy·per·ten·sion [hĩ-pər-TEN-shən] *n* abnormally high blood pressure

hy·per·text [Hĩ-pər-tekst] *n* computer software and hardware that allows users to store and view text and move between related items easily

hy·phen [HI-fən] n short line (-) indicating that two words or syllables are to be connected **hy·phen·ate** [-nayt] vt **-at·ed, -at·ing** join by a hyphen

hyp·no·sis [HIP-noh-sis] n, pl **-ses** [-seez] induced state like deep sleep in which subject acts on external suggestion **hyp·not·ic** adj of hypnosis or of the person or thing producing it; like something that induces hypnosis **hyp·no·tism** [HIP-nə-tiz-əm] n **hyp·no·tist** n **hyp·no·tize** vt **-tized, -tiz·ing** affect with hypnosis; affect in way resembling hypnotic state

hy·po [HI-poh] n short for hyposulfite (sodium thiosulfate), used as fixer in developing photographs

hypo-, hyph-, hyp- comb forms under, below, less: hypothermia **hy·po·al·ler·gen·ic** [hi-poh-al-ər-JEN-ik] adj (of cosmetics, etc) not likely to cause allergic reaction **hy·po·chon·dri·a** [hi-pə-KON-dree-ə] n morbid depression, without cause, about one's own health **hy·po·chon·dri·ac** adj, n **hy·po·cri·sy** [hi-POK-rə-see] n, pl **-sies** [-seez] assuming of false appearance of virtue; insincerity **hyp·o·crite** [HIP-ə-krit] n **hyp·o·crit·i·cal** adj **hy·po·der·mic** [hi-pə-DUR-mik] adj introduced, injected beneath the skin ▷n hypodermic syringe

or needle

hy·po·gas·tric [hi-pə-GAS-trik] adj relating to, situated in, lower part of abdomen

hy·pot·e·nuse [hi-POT-n-oos] n side of a right triangle opposite the right angle

hy·po·ther·mi·a [hi-pə-THUR-mee-ə] n condition of having body temperature reduced to dangerously low level

hy·poth·e·sis [hi-POTH-ə-sis] n, pl **-ses** [-seez] suggested explanation of something; assumption as basis of reasoning **hy·po·thet·i·cal** adj **hy·poth·e·size** [-POTH-ə-siz] v **-sized, -siz·ing**

hypso- comb form height: hypsometry **hyp·sog·ra·phy** [hip-SOG-rə-fee] n branch of geography dealing with altitudes **hyp·som·e·ter** [hip-SOM-i-tər] n instrument for measuring altitudes **hyp·som·e·try** [-tree] n science of measuring altitudes

hys·ter·ec·to·my [his-tə-REK-tə-mee] n, pl **-mies** surgical operation for removing the uterus **hys·ter·e·sis** [his-tə-REE-sis] n physics lag or delay in changes in variable property of a system **hys·te·ri·a** [hi-STER-ee-ə] n mental disorder with emotional outbursts; any frenzied emotional state; fit of crying or laughing **hys·ter·i·cal** adj **hys·ter·ics** pl n fits of hysteria; inf uncontrollable laughter

Hz hertz

I *chemistry* iodine

I *pron* the pronoun of the first person singular

i•amb [i-amb] *n* metrical foot of short and long syllable **i•am'bic** *adj*

i•bex [i-beks] *n, pl* **-bex•es** wild goat with large horns

ibid. [IB-id] (referring to a book, page, or passage already mentioned) in the same place

i•bis [i-bis] *n* storklike bird

ice [is] *n* frozen water; frozen dessert made of sweetened water and fruit flavoring ▷ *v* **iced, ic•ing** cover, become covered with ice; cool with ice; cover with icing **i'ci•cle** [-sǝ-kǝl] *n* tapering spike of ice hanging where water has dripped **i'ci•ly** *adv* in icy manner **i'ci•ness** *n* **i'cing** *n* mixture of sugar and water, etc used to decorate cakes **i'cy** *adj* **i•ci•er, i•ci•est** covered with ice; cold; chilling **ice'berg** [-burg] *n* large floating mass of ice **ice cream** sweetened frozen dessert made from cream, eggs, etc **ice floe** [-floh] sheet of floating ice **ice hockey** team game played on ice with puck **ich•thy•ol•o•gy** [ik-thee-OL-ǝ-jee] *n* scientific study of fish

icicle see **ICE**

i•con [i-kon] *n* image, representation, esp of religious figure; graphic representing a function, activated by clicking on **i•con•o•clast** *n* one who attacks established principles, etc; breaker of icons **i•con•o•clas'tic** *adj* **i•con•og'ra•phy** *n* icons collectively; study of icons

id *n psychoanalysis* the mind's instinctive energies

i•de•a [i-DEE-ǝ] *n* notion in the mind; conception; vague belief; plan, aim **i•de'al** *n* conception of something that is perfect; perfect person or thing ▷ *adj* perfect; visionary; existing only in idea **i•de'al•ism** *n* tendency to seek perfection in everything; philosophy that mind is the only reality **i•de'al•ist** *n* one who holds doctrine of idealism; one who strives after the ideal; impractical person **i•de•al•is'tic** *adj* **i•de'al•ize** *vt* **-ized, -iz•ing** portray as ideal

i•dem [i-dem] *Lat* the same

i•den•ti•ty [i-DEN-ti-tee] *n, pl* **-ties** individuality; being the same, exactly alike **i•den'ti•cal** *adj* very same **i•den'ti•fi•a•ble** *adj* **i•den'ti•fy** *v* **-fied, -fy•ing** establish identity of; associate (oneself) with; treat as identical **identity theft** crime of setting up and using bank accounts and credit facilities in another person's name without that person's knowledge

id•e•o•graph [ID-ee-ǝ-graf] *n* picture, symbol, figure, etc, suggesting an object without naming it; (also **id'e•o•gram**)

i•de•ol•o•gy [i-dee-OL-ǝ-jee] *n, pl* **-gies** body of ideas, beliefs of group, nation, etc **i•de•o•log'i•cal** *adj* **i'de•o•logue** [-lawg] *n* zealous advocate of an ideology

ides [īdz] *n* (in the Ancient Roman calendar) the 15th of March, May, July, or October, or the 13th of other months

idiocy see **IDIOT**

id·i·om [ID-ee-əm] *n* way of expression natural or peculiar to a language or group; characteristic style of expression **id·i·o·mat·ic** *adj* using idioms; colloquial

id·i·o·syn·cra·sy [id-ee-ò-SING-krà-see] *n* peculiarity of mind, temper or disposition in a person **id·i·o·syn·crat·ic** [-oh-sing-KRAT-ik] *adj*

id·i·ot [ID-ee-ət] *n* foolish, senseless person **id'i·o·cy** [-ə-see] *n* **id·i·ot'ic** *adj* utterly senseless or stupid

i·dle [ID-l] *adj* **-dler, -dlest** unemployed; lazy; useless, vain, groundless ▷ *vi* **-dled, -dling** be idle; (of engine) run slowly with gears disengaged ▷ *vt* (esp with *away*) waste **i'dle·ness** *n* **i'dler** *n* **i'dly** *adv*

i·dol [ID-l] *n* image of deity as object of worship; object of excessive devotion **i·dol'a·ter** *n* worshiper of idols **i·dol'a·trous** [-trəs] *adj* **i·dol'a·try** *n* **i'dol·ize** *vt* **-ized, -iz·ing** love or venerate to excess; make an idol of

i·dyll [ID-l] *n* short descriptive poem of picturesque or charming scene or episode, esp of rustic life **i·dyl'lic** [ī-DIL-ik] *adj* of, like, idyll; delightful

ie that is to say

if *conj* on condition or supposition that; whether; although ▷ *n* uncertainty or doubt: *no ifs, ands, or buts* **if'fy** [-ee] *adj* **-fi·er, -fi·est** dubious

ig·loo *n* dome-shaped Inuit house of snow and ice

ig·ne·ous [IG-nee-əs] *adj* esp of rocks, formed as molten rock cools and hardens

ig·nite [ig-NĪT] *v* **-nit·ed, -nit·ing** (cause to) burn **ig·ni'tion** [-NISH-ən] *n* act of kindling or setting on fire; in internal combustion engine, means of firing explosive mixture, usu electric spark

ig·no·ble [ig-NOH-bəl] *adj* mean, base; of low birth **ig·no'bly** *adv*

ig·no·min·y [IG-nə-min-ee] *n, pl* **-min·ies** dishonor, disgrace; shameful act **ig·no·min'i·ous** [-ee-əs] *adj*

ig·no·re [ig-NOR] *vt* **-nored, -nor·ing** disregard, leave out of account **ig·no·ra'mus** [-RA-məs] *n, pl* **-mus·es** ignorant person **ig'no·rance** [-rəns] *n* lack of knowledge **ig'no·rant** *adj* lacking knowledge; uneducated; unaware

i·gua·na [i-GWAH-nə] *n* large tropical American lizard

il- *prefix* same as **IN-¹** or **IN-²**

il·e·um [IL-ee-əm] *n* lower part of small intestine **il'e·ac** *adj*

ilk *adj* same of that ilk of the same type or class

ill *adj* not in good health; bad, evil; faulty; unfavorable ▷ *n* evil, harm; mild disease ▷ *adv* badly; hardly, with difficulty **ill'ness** *n* **ill-ad·vised'** *adj* imprudent; injudicious **ill'-fat'ed** [-FAY-tid] *adj* unfortunate **ill'-fa'vored** [-FAY-vərd] *adj* ugly, deformed; offensive **ill'-got·ten** *adj* obtained dishonestly **ill'-man'nered** *adj* boorish, uncivil **ill-timed** *adj* inopportune **ill-treat** *vt* treat cruelly **ill will** unkind feeling, hostility

il·le·gal *adj* against the law **il·le·gal·ly** *adv* **il·le·gal'i·ty** *n, pl* **-ties**

il·leg'i·ble *adj* unable to be read or

deciphered **il·leg·i·bil·i·ty** n

il·le·git·i·mate [il-i-JIT-ə-mit] adj born out of wedlock; unlawful; not regular ▷ n bastard

il·lic·it [i-LIS-it] adj illegal; prohibited, forbidden

il·lit·er·ate [i-LIT-ər-it] adj not literate; unable to read or write ▷ n illiterate person **il·lit·er·a·cy** n

il·log·i·cal adj unreasonable; not logical

il·lu·mi·nate [i-LOO-mə-nayt] vt **-nat·ed, -nat·ing** light up; clarify; decorate with lights; decorate with gold and colors **il·lu·mi·na·tion** n **il·lu·mine** vt **-mined, -min·ing** illuminate

il·lu·sion [i-LOO-zhən] n deceptive appearance or belief **il·lu·sion·ist** n conjurer **il·lu·so·ry** [-LOO-sə-ree] adj deceptive

il·lus·trate [IL-ə-strayt] vt **-trat·ed, -trat·ing** provide with pictures or examples; exemplify **il·lus·tra·tion** n picture, diagram; example; act of illustrating **il·lus·tra·tive** adj providing explanation

il·lus·tri·ous [i-LUS-tree-əs] adj famous; distinguished; exalted

IM see **INSTANT MESSAGING**

im- prefix same as **IN-¹** or **IN-²**

im·age [IM-ij] n representation or likeness of person or thing; optical counterpart, as in mirror; double, copy; general impression; mental picture created by words, esp in literature ▷ vt **-aged, -mag·ing** make image of; reflect **im·age·ry** n images collectively, esp in literature

im·ag·ine [i-MAJ-in] vt picture to oneself; think; conjecture **im·ag·i·na·ble** adj **im·ag·i·nar·y** adj existing only in fancy **im·ag·i·na·tion** n faculty of making mental images of things

not present; fancy; resourcefulness **im·ag·i·na·tive** adj

i·mam [i-MAHM] n Islamic minister or priest

im·bal·ance [im-BAL-əns] n lack of balance, proportion

im·be·cile [IM-bə-sil] n idiot ▷ adj idiotic **im·be·cil·i·ty** n

im·bibe [im-BĪB] v **-bibed, -bib·ing** ▷ vt drink in; absorb ▷ vi drink

im·bri·cate [IM-brə-kit] adj lying over each other in regular order, like tiles or shingles on roof **im·bri·ca·tion** n

im·bro·glio [im-BROHL-yoh] n, pl **-glios** disagreement; complicated situation, plot

im·bue [im-BYOO] vt **-bued, -bu·ing** inspire; saturate

im·i·tate [IM-i-tayt] vt **-tat·ed, -tat·ing** take as model; mimic, copy **im·i·ta·ble** adj **im·i·ta·tion** n act of imitating; copy of original; likeness; counterfeit **im·i·ta·tive** adj **im·i·ta·tor** n

im·mac·u·late [im-AK-yə-lit] adj spotless; pure; unsullied

im·ma·nent [IM-mə-nənt] adj abiding in, inherent **im·ma·nence** n

im·ma·te·ri·al [im-ə-TEER-ee-əl] adj unimportant, trifling; not consisting of matter; spiritual

im·ma·ture adj not fully developed; lacking wisdom or stability because of youth **im·ma·tu·ri·ty** n

im·me·di·ate [i-MEE-dee-it] adj occurring at once; direct, not separated by others **im·me·di·a·cy** n

im·me·mo·ri·al [im-ə-MOR-ee-əl] adj beyond memory

im·mense [i-MENS] adj huge, vast **im·men·si·ty** n vastness

im·merse [i-MURS] vt **-mersed, -mers·ing** dip, plunge, into liquid;

involve; engross **im·mer·sion** [-zhən] n immersing **immersion heater** n electric appliance for heating liquid in which it is immersed

im·mi·grate [IM-i-grayt] vi **-grat·ed, -grat·ing** come into country as settler **im·mi·grant** [-grənt] n, adj **im·mi·gra·tion** n

im·mi·nent [IM-ə-nənt] adj liable to happen soon; close at hand **im·mi·nence** n

im·mo·bile adj not moving; unable to move **im·mo·bil·i·ty** n **im·mo·bi·lize** vt make unable to move or work

im·mod·er·ate adj excessive or unreasonable

im·mod·est adj behaving in an indecent or improper manner; behaving in a boastful or conceited manner **im·mod·es·ty** n

im·mo·late [IM-ə-layt] vt **-lat·ed, -lat·ing** kill, sacrifice **im·mo·la·tion** n

im·mor·al [i-MOR-əl] adj corrupt; promiscuous; indecent; unethical **im·mo·ral·i·ty** n, pl **-ties**

im·mor·tal [i-MOR-tl] adj deathless; famed for all time ▷ n immortal being; god; one whose fame will last **im·mor·tal·i·ty** n **im·mor·tal·ize** vt **-ized, -iz·ing**

im·mov·a·ble adj unable to be moved; unwilling to change one's opinions or beliefs; not affected by feeling, emotionless

im·mune [i-MYOON] adj proof (against a disease, etc); secure, exempt **im·mu·ni·ty** n state of being immune; freedom from prosecution, etc **im·mu·ni·za·tion** n process of making immune to disease **im·mu·nize** vt **-nized, -niz·ing** make immune **im·mu·nol·o·gy** n branch of

biology concerned with study of immunity

im·mu·ta·ble [i-MYOO-tə-bəl] adj unchangeable

imp n little devil; mischievous child

im·pact [IM-pakt] n collision; profound effect **impact** [im-PAKT] vt drive, press

im·pair vt weaken, damage **im·pair·ment** n

im·pal·a [im-PAL-ə] n, pl **-pal·as** antelope of Africa

im·pale [im-PAYL] vt **-paled, -pal·ing** pierce with sharp instrument; make helpless as if pierced through

im·part [im-PAHRT] vt communicate (information, etc); give

im·par·tial [im-PAHR-shəl] adj not biased or prejudiced; fair **im·par·ti·al·i·ty** n

im·passe [IM-pas] n deadlock; place, situation, from which there is no outlet

im·pas·sioned [im-PASH-ənd] adj deeply moved, ardent

im·pas·sive [im-PAS-iv] adj showing no emotion; calm **im·pas·siv·i·ty** n

im·pa·tient adj irritable at any delay or difficulty; restless (to have or do something) **im·pa·tience** n

im·peach [im-PEECH] vt charge with crime; call to account; law challenge credibility of (a witness) **im·peach·a·ble** adj

im·pec·ca·ble [im-PEK-ə-bəl] adj without flaw or error

im·pe·cu·ni·ous [im-pi-KYOO-nee-əs] adj poor **im·pe·cu·ni·ous·ness** n **im·pe·cu·ni·os·i·ty** n

im·pede [im-PEED] vt **-ped·ed, -ped·ing** hinder **im·ped·ance** n electricity measure of opposition

offered to flow of alternating current
im·ped'i·ment [-PED-ə-mənt] n
obstruction; defect
im·pel' vt -**pelled**, -**pel'ling**
induce, incite; drive, force
im·pel'ler n
im·pend' vi threaten; be imminent;
hang over **im·pend'ing** adj
im·per·a·tive [im-PER-ə-tiv] adj
necessary; peremptory; expressing
command ▷ n imperative mood
im·per·cep'ti·ble adj too slight
or gradual to be noticed
im·per'fect adj having faults or
mistakes; not complete; grammar
denoting a tense of verbs describing
continuous, incomplete, or repeated
past actions ▷ n grammar imperfect
tense **im·per·fec'tion** n
im·pe·ri·al [im-PEER-ee-əl] adj
of empire, or emperor; majestic
im·pe'ri·al·ism n extension of
empire; belief in colonial empire
im·pe'ri·al·ist n
im·per·il [im-PER-əl] vt -**iled**,
-**il·ing** bring into peril; endanger
im·pe·ri·ous [im-PEER-ee-əs] adj
domineering; haughty; dictatorial
im·pe'ri·ous·ness n
im·per·son·al [im-PUR-sə-nl]
adj objective, having no personal
significance; devoid of human
warmth, personality, etc; (of
verb) without personal subject
im·per·son·al'i·ty n
im·per·son·ate [im-PUR-sə-nayt]
vt -**at·ed**, -**at·ing** pretend to be
(another person); play the part of
im·per·son·a'tion n
im·per·ti·nent [im-PUR-tn-ənt]
adj insolent, rude **im·per'ti·nence**
n
im·per·turb·a·ble [im-pər-TUR-
bə-bəl] adj calm, not excitable
im·per·vi·ous [im-PUR-vee-
əs] adj not affording passage;

impenetrable (to feeling, argument,
etc)
im·pe·ti·go [im-pi-TI-goh] n
contagious skin disease
im·pet·u·ous [im-PECH-
oo-əs] adj likely to act
without consideration, rash
im·pet·u·os'i·ty n
im·pe·tus [IM-pi-təs] n force with
which body moves; impulse
im·pinge [im-PINJ] vi **pinged**,
-**ping·ing** encroach (upon); collide
(with) **im·pinge'ment** n
im·pi·ous [IM-pee-əs] adj
irreverent, profane, wicked
im·pi'e·ty [-Pi-i-tee] n
im·plac·a·ble [im-PLAK-ə-bəl]
adj not to be appeased; unyielding
im·plac·a·bil'i·ty n
im·plant' vt insert, fix **im'plant** n
dentistry artificial tooth implanted
permanently in jaw; implanted
breast enhancement
im·ple·ment [IM-plə-mənt]
n tool, instrument, utensil ▷ vt
[-mənt] carry out (instructions, etc);
put into effect
im·pli·cate [IM-pli-kayt] vt
-**cat·ed**, -**cat·ing** involve, include;
entangle; imply **im·pli·ca'tion**
n something implied **im·plic'it**
[-PLIS-it] adj implied but not
expressed; absolute and unreserved
im·plore [im-PLOR] vt -**plored**,
-**plor·ing** entreat earnestly
im·ply [im-PLĪ] vt -**plied**, -**ply·ing**
indicate by hint, suggest; mean
im·po·lite' adj showing bad
manners
im·port' vt bring in, introduce (esp
goods from foreign country); imply
im'port n thing imported; meaning;
importance **im·port'er** n
im·por·tant [im-POR-tnt] adj of
great consequence; momentous;
pompous **im·por'tance** n

im·por·tune [im-por-TOON] vt **-tuned, -tun·ing** request, demand persistently **im·por·tu·nate** [-POR-chà-nit] adj persistent **im·por·tu·ni·ty** n

im·pose [im-POHZ] vt **-posed, -pos·ing** levy (tax, duty, etc, upon) ▷ vi take advantage (of), practice deceit on **im·pos'ing** adj impressive **im·po·si'tion** n that which is imposed; tax; burden; deception **im'post** n duty, tax on imports

im·pos·si·ble [im-POS-à-bàl] adj incapable of being done or experienced; absurd; unreasonable **im·pos·si·bil'i·ty** n, pl **-ties**

im·pos·tor [im-POS-tàr] n deceiver, one who assumes false identity

im·po·tent [IM-pà-tànt] adj powerless; (of males) incapable of sexual intercourse **im'po·tence** n

im·pound [im-POWND] vt take legal possession of and, often, place in a pound (automobile, animal, etc); confiscate

im·pov·er·ish [im-POV-àr-ish] vt make poor or weak **im·pov'er·ish·ment** n

im·prac·ti·ca·ble adj incapable of being put into practice

im·prac'ti·cal adj not sensible

im·pre·ca·tion [im-pri-KAY-shàn] n invoking of evil; curse **im'pre·cate** vt **-cat·ed, -cat·ing**

im·preg·na·ble [im-PREG-nà-bàl] adj proof against attack; unassailable; unable to be broken into **im·preg·na·bil'i·ty** n

im·preg·nate [im-PREG-nayt] vt **-nat·ed, -nat·ing** saturate, infuse; make pregnant **im·preg·na'tion** n

im·pre·sa·ri·o [im-prà-SAHR-ee-oh] n, pl **-ri·os** organizer of public entertainment; manager of opera, ballet, etc

im·press'¹ vt affect deeply, usu favorably; imprint; stamp; fix ▷ n [IM-pres] act of impressing; mark **impressed im·pres'sion** n effect produced, esp on mind; notion, belief; imprint; a printing; total of copies printed at once; printed copy **im·pres'sion·a·ble** adj susceptible to external influences **im·pres'sion·ism** n art style that renders general effect without detail **im·pres'sion·ist** n **im·pres'sive** adj making deep impression

im·press'² vt press into service

im·pri·ma·tur [im-pri-MAH-tàr] n license to print book, etc; sanction, approval

im'print n mark made by pressure; characteristic mark ▷ vt [im-PRINT] produce mark; stamp; fix in mind

im·pris·on [im-PRIZ-àn] n put in prison **im·pris'on·ment** n

im·prob·a·ble adj not likely to be true or to happen **im·prob·a·bil'i·ty** n, pl **-ties**

im·promp·tu [im-PROMP-too] adv, adj on the spur of the moment; unrehearsed

im·prop'er adj indecent; incorrect or irregular **improper fraction** fraction in which the numerator is larger than the denominator, as in 5/3

im·pro·pri'e·ty n, pl **-ties** unsuitable or slightly improper behaviour

im·prove [im-PROOV] v **-proved, -prov·ing** make or become better in quality, standard, value, etc **im·prove'ment** n

im·prov·i·dent [im-PROV-i-dànt] adj thriftless; negligent; imprudent **im·prov'i·dence** n

im·pro·vise [IM-prà-viz] v **-vised, -vis·ing** make use of materials at hand; compose, utter without

preparation **im·prov·i·sa'tion**
[-ZAY-shàn] n

im·pu·dent [IM-pyà-dànt]
adj disrespectful, impertinent
im'pu·dence n

im·pugn [im-PYOON] vt **-pugned,
-pugn·ing** call in question, challenge
as false

im·pulse [IM-puls] n sudden
inclination to act; sudden
application of force; motion caused
by it; stimulation of nerve moving
muscle **im·pul'sion** n impulse,
usu in its first sense **im·pul'sive** adj
given to acting without reflection,
rash

im·pu·ni·ty [im-PYOO-ni-tee] n
freedom, exemption from injurious
consequences or punishment

im·pure' adj having dirty or
unwanted substances mixed in;
immoral, obscene **im·pu'ri·ty** n,
pl **-ties**

im·pute [im-PYOOT] vt **-put·ed,
-put·ing** ascribe, attribute to
im·pu·ta'tion n that which
is imputed as a charge or fault;
reproach, censure

in prep expresses inclusion within
limits of space, time, circumstance,
sphere, etc ▷ adv in or into some
state, place, etc; inf in vogue, etc
▷ adj inf fashionable

In chemistry indium

in-[1], il-, im-, ir- prefix not, non:
incredible; lack of: inexperience

in-[2], il-, im-, ir- prefix in, into,
towards, within, on: infiltrate

in·a·bil·i·ty [in-à-BIL-i-tee] n
lack of means or skill
to do something

in·ac'cu·rate adj not correct
in·ac'cu·ra·cy n, pl **-cies**

in·ad'e·quate adj not enough;
not good enough **in·ad'e·qua·cy**
n, pl **-cies**

in·ad·vert·ent [in-àd-VUR-

tnt] adj not attentive; negligent;
unintentional **in·ad·vert'ence** n

in·ane [i-NAYN] adj foolish, silly,
vacant **in·a·ni'tion** [-NISH-àn] n
exhaustion; silliness **in·an'i·ty** n

in·an·i·mate [in-AN-à-mit] adj
lacking qualities of living beings;
appearing dead; lacking vitality

in·ap·pro'pri·ate adj not suitable

in·as·much as [in-àz-MUCH] conj
because or in so far as

in·au·gu·rate [in-AW-gyà-rayt]
vt **-rat·ed, -rat·ing** begin, initiate
the use of, esp with ceremony;
admit to office **in·au'gu·ral**
adj of or for the ceremony of
inaugurating; ceremony to celebrate
the initiation or admittance of
in·au·gu·ra'tion n act of
inaugurating; ceremony to celebrate
the initiation or admittance of

in·aus·pi·cious [in-aw-SPISH-
às] adj not auspicious; unlucky;
unfavorable **in·aus·pi'cious·ly** adv

in·board [IN-bord] adj inside hull
or bulwarks

in'born adj existing from birth;
inherent

in'breed vt **-bred, -breed·ing**
breed from union of closely related
individuals **in'bred** adj produced
as result of inbreeding; inborn,
ingrained

in·cal·cu·la·ble [in-KAL-kyà-
là-bàl] adj beyond calculation;
very great

in cam·er·a [KAM-à-rà] in secret
or private session

in·can·des·cent [in-kàn-DES-ànt]
adj glowing with heat, shining; of
artificial light, produced by glowing
filament **in·can·des'cence** n

in·can·ta·tion [in-kan-TAY-shàn]
n magic spell or formula, charm

in·ca·pa·ble adj (foll by of) unable
(to do something); incompetent

in·ca·pac·i·tate [in-kà-PAS-
i-tayt] vt **-tat·ed, -tat·ing**
disable; make unfit; disqualify

in·ca·pac·i·ty n

in·car·cer·ate [in-KAHR-sə-rayt] vt **-at·ed, -at·ing** imprison **in·car·cer·a·tion** n

in·car·nate [in-KAR-nayt] vt **-nat·ed, -nat·ing** embody in flesh, esp in human form ▷ adj [-nit] embodied in flesh, in human form; typified **in·car·na·tion** n

in·cen·di·ary [in-SEN-dee-er-ee] adj of malicious setting on fire of property; creating strife, violence, etc; designed to cause fires ▷ n arsonist; agitator; bomb, etc filled with inflammatory substance

in·cense¹ [in-SENS] vt **-censed, -cens·ing** enrage

in·cense² [IN-sens] n gum, spice giving perfume when burned; its smoke ▷ vt **-censed, -cens·ing** burn incense to; perfume with it

in·cen·tive [in-SEN-tiv] n something that arouses to effort or action; stimulus

in·cep·tion [in-SEP-shən] n beginning **in·cep·tive** [-tiv] adj

in·ces·sant [in-SES-ənt] adj unceasing

in·cest [IN-sest] n sexual intercourse between two people too closely related to marry **in·ces·tu·ous** [-SES-choo-əs] adj

inch n one twelfth of foot, or 2.54 centimeters ▷ v move very slowly

in·cho·ate [in-KOH-it] adj just begun; undeveloped

in·ci·dent [IN-si-dənt] n event, occurrence ▷ adj naturally attaching to; striking, falling (upon) **in·ci·dence** n degree, extent or frequency of occurrence; a falling on, or affecting **in·ci·den·tal** adj occurring as a minor part or an inevitable accompaniment or by chance **in·ci·den·tal·ly** adv by chance; by the way **in·ci·den·tals** pl

n accompanying items

in·cin·er·ate [in-SIN-ə-rayt] vt **-at·ed, -at·ing** burn up completely; reduce to ashes **in·cin·er·a·tor** n

in·cip·i·ent [in-SIP-ee-ənt] adj beginning

in·cise [in-SĪZ] vt **-cised, -cis·ing** cut into; engrave **in·ci·sion** [in-SIZH-ən] n **in·ci·sive** adj keen or biting (of remark, etc); sharp **in·ci·sor** n cutting tooth

in·cite [in-SĪT] vt **-cit·ed, -cit·ing** urge, stir up **in·cite·ment** n

in·clem·ent [in-KLEM-ənt] adj of weather, stormy, severe, cold **in·clem·en·cy** n

in·cline [in-KLĪN] v **-clined, -clin·ing** lean, slope; (cause to) be disposed; bend or lower (the head, etc) ▷ n [IN-klin] slope **in·cli·na·tion** n liking, tendency or preference; sloping surface; degree of deviation

in·clude [in-KLOOD] vt **-clud·ed, -clud·ing** have as (part of) contents; comprise; add in; take in **in·clu·sion** [-zhən] n **in·clu·sive** adj including (everything)

in·cog·ni·to [in-kog-NEE-toh] adv, adj under assumed identity ▷ n, pl **-tos** assumed identity

in·co·her·ent [in-koh-HEER-ənt] adj lacking clarity, disorganized; inarticulate **in·co·her·ence** n

in·come [IN-kum] n amount of money, esp annual, from salary, investments, etc; receipts **income tax** personal, corporate tax levied on annual income

in·com·ing [IN-kum-ing] adj coming in; about to come into office; next

in·com·mode [in-kə-MOHD] vt **-mod·ed, -mod·ing** trouble, inconvenience; disturb **in·com·mo·di·ous** adj cramped;

inconvenient

in·com·mu·ni·ca·do [in-kə-MYOO-ni-kah-doh] *adj, adv* deprived (by force or by choice) of communication with others

in·com·pa·ra·ble [in-] *adj* beyond comparison, unequalled

in·com·pat·i·ble [in-] *adj* inconsistent or conflicting **in·com·pat·i·bil·i·ty** *n*

in·com·pe·tent *adj* not having the necessary ability or skill to do something **in·com·pe·tence** *n*

in·con·gru·ous [in-KONG-groo-əs] *adj* not appropriate; inconsistent; absurd **in·con·gru·i·ty** *n*

in·con·se·quen·tial [in-kon-si-KWEN-shəl] *adj* illogical; irrelevant, trivial

in·con·sid·er·ate *adj* not considering other people

in·con·sist·ent *adj* changeable in behaviour or mood; containing contradictory elements; not in accordance **in·con·sist·en·cy** *n, pl* **-cies**

in·con·tro·vert·i·ble [in-kon-trə-VUR-tə-bəl] *adj* undeniable; indisputable

in·con·ven·ience *n* trouble or difficulty ▷ *v* cause trouble or difficulty to **in·con·ven·ient** *adj*

in·cor·po·rate [in-KOR-pə-rayt] *vt* **-rat·ed, -rat·ing** include; unite into one body; form corporation

in·cor·ri·gi·ble [in-KOR-i-jə-bəl] *adj* beyond correction or reform; firmly rooted

in·crease [in-KREES] *v* **-creased, -creas·ing** make or become greater in size, number, etc ▷ *n* [IN-krees] growth, enlargement, profit **in·creas·ing·ly** *adv* more and more

in·cred·i·ble [in-KRED-ə-bəl] *adj* unbelievable; *inf* marvelous,

amazing

in·cred·u·lous [in-KREJ-ə-ləs] *adj* unbelieving **in·cre·du·li·ty** [-krə-DOO-lə-tee] *n*

in·cre·ment [IN-krə-mənt] *n* increase, esp one of a series **in·cre·men·tal** *adj*

in·crim·i·nate [in-KRIM-ə-nayt] *vt* **-nat·ed, -nat·ing** imply guilt of; accuse of crime **in·crim·i·na·to·ry** *adj*

in·crust [in-KRUST] *v* cover with or form a crust or hard covering

in·cu·bate [IN-kyə-bayt] *vt* **-bat·ed, -bat·ing** provide (eggs, embryos, bacteria, etc) with heat or other favorable condition for development ▷ *vi* develop in this way **in·cu·ba·tion** *n* **in·cu·ba·tor** *n* apparatus for artificially hatching eggs, for rearing premature babies

in·cu·bus [IN-kyə-bəs] *n, pl* **-bi** [-bī] nightmare or obsession; *orig* demon believed to afflict sleeping person

in·cul·cate [in-KUL-kayt] *vt* **-cat·ed, -cat·ing** impress on the mind **in·cul·ca·tion** *n*

in·cum·bent [in-KUM-bənt] *adj* lying, resting (on) ▷ *n* holder of office, esp elective office in government **in·cum·ben·cy** *n* obligation; office or tenure of incumbent **it is incumbent on** it is the duty of

in·cur [in-KUR] *vt* **-curred, -cur·ring** fall into, bring upon oneself **in·cur·sion** [-zhən] *n* invasion, penetration

in·cur·a·ble *adj* not able to be cured; not willing or able to change **in·cur·a·bly** *adv*

in·debt·ed [in-DET-id] *adj* owing gratitude for help, favors, etc; owing money **in·debt·ed·ness** *n*

in·de·cent *adj* morally or sexually

offensive; unsuitable or unseemly **in·de·cen·cy** n

in·de·ci·sive adj unable to make decisions **in·de·ci·sion** n

in·deed' adv in truth; really; in fact; certainly ▷ interj denoting surprise, doubt, etc

in·de·fat·i·ga·ble [in-di-FAT-i-gə-bəl] adj untiring **in·de·fat'i·ga·bly** adv

in·de·fen·si·ble [in-di-FEN-sə-bəl] adj not justifiable or defensible

in·def'i·nite adj without exact limits; vague, unclear **indefinite article** grammar the word a or an

in·del·i·ble [in-DEL-ə-bəl] adj that cannot be blotted out, effaced or erased; producing such a mark **in·del'i·bly** adv

in·del·i·cate [in-DEL-i-kit] adj coarse, embarrassing, tasteless

in·dem·ni·ty [in-DEM-ni-tee] n, pl **-ties** compensation; security against loss **in·dem·ni·fi·ca'tion** n **in·dem'ni·fy** [-fī] vt **-fied, -fy·ing** give indemnity to; compensate

in·dent' v set in (from margin, etc); make notches in ▷ n [IN-dent] indentation; notch **in·den·ta'tion** n **in·den'ture** n contract, esp one binding apprentice to master; indentation ▷ vt **-tured, -tur·ing** bind by indenture

in·de·pend·ent [in-di-PEN-dənt] adj not subject to others; self-reliant; free; valid in itself; politically of no party **in·de·pend'ence** n being independent; self-reliance; self-support

in·de·scrib·a·ble [in-di-SKRĪ-bə-bəl] adj beyond description; too intense, vivid, etc for words **in·de·scrib'a·bly** adv

in·de·ter·mi·nate [in-di-TUR-mə-nit] adj uncertain; inconclusive; incalculable

in·dex [IN-deks] n, pl **-dex·es, -di·ces** [-də-seez] alphabetical list of references, usu at end of book; pointer, indicator; *mathematics* exponent; *economics* quantity indicating relative level of wages, prices, etc compared with date established as standard ▷ vt provide book with index; insert in index; adjust wages, prices, etc to reflect change in some economic indicator

In·di·an [IN-dee-ən] n native of India; *oft offens* person descended from indigenous peoples of N America ▷ adj

in·di·cate [IN-di-kayt] vt **-cat·ed, -cat·ing** point out; state briefly; signify **in·di·ca'tion** n sign; token; explanation **in·dic'a·tive** adj pointing to; grammar stating fact **in'di·ca·tor** n one who, that which, indicates; on vehicle, flashing light showing driver's intention to turn

in·dict [in-DĪT] vt accuse, esp by legal process **in·dict'ment** [-mənt] n

in·dif·fer·ent [in-DIF-ər-ənt] adj uninterested; unimportant; neither good nor bad; inferior; neutral **in·dif'fer·ence** n

in·dig·e·nous [in-DIJ-ə-nəs] adj born in or natural to a country

in·di·gent [IN-di-jənt] adj poor, needy **in'di·gence** n poverty

in·di·ges·tion [in-di-JES-chən] n (discomfort, pain caused by) difficulty in digesting food **in·di·gest'i·ble** adj

in·dig·nant [in-DIG-nənt] adj moved by anger and scorn; angered by sense of injury or injustice **in·dig·na'tion** n **in·dig'ni·ty** n humiliation, insult, slight

in·di·go [IN-də-goh] n, pl **-gos** blue dye obtained from plant; the plant ▷ adj deep blue

in·di·rect' *adj* done or caused by someone or something else; not by a straight route

in·dis·creet' *adj* incautious or tactless in revealing secrets **in·dis·cre'tion** *n*

in·dis·crim·i·nate [in-di-SKRIM-ə-nit] *adj* lacking discrimination; jumbled

in·dis·pen·sa·ble [in-di-SPEN-sə-bəl] *adj* necessary; essential

in·dis·po·si·tion [in-dis-pə-ZISH-ən] *n* sickness; disinclination **in·dis·posed'** [-POHZD] *adj* unwell, not fit; disinclined

in·dis·sol·u·ble [in-di-SOL-yə-bəl] *adj* permanent

in·di·um [IN-dee-əm] *n* soft silver-white metallic element

in·di·vid·u·al [in-də-VIJ-oo-əl] *adj* single; characteristic of single person or thing; distinctive ▷ *n* single person or thing **in·di·vid·u·al·ism** *n* principle of asserting one's independence **in·di·vid·u·al·ist** *n* **in·di·vid·u·al·i·ty** *n* distinctive character; personality **in·di·vid·u·al·ize** *vt* **-ized, -iz·ing** make (or treat as) individual **in·di·vid·u·al·ly** *adv* singly

in·doc·tri·nate [in-DOK-trə-nayt] *vt* **-nat·ed, -nat·ing** implant beliefs in the mind of

in·do·lent [IN-dl-ənt] *adj* lazy **in·do·lence** *n*

in·dom·i·ta·ble [in-DOM-i-tə-bəl] *adj* unyielding

in·door [IN-dor] *adj* within doors; under cover **in·doors** [in-DORZ] *adv*

in·du·bi·ta·ble [in-DOO-bi-tə-bəl] *adj* beyond doubt; certain **in·du·bi·ta·bly** *adv*

in·duce [in-DOOS] *vt* **-duced, -duc·ing** persuade; bring on; cause; produce by induction **in·duce'ment** *n* incentive, attraction

in·duct [in-DUKT] *vt* install in office **in·duc'tion** *n* an inducting; general inference from particular instances; production of electric or magnetic state in body by its being near (not touching) electrified or magnetized body **in·duc'tance** [-təns] *n* **in·duc'tive** *adj*

in·dulge [in-DULJ] *vt* **-dulged, -dulg·ing** gratify; give free course to; pamper; spoil **in·dul'gence** [-jəns] *n* an indulging; extravagance; something granted as a favor or privilege; *R C Church* remission of temporal punishment due after absolution **in·dul'gent** [-jənt] *adj*

in·dus·try [IN-də-stree] *n* manufacture, processing, etc of goods; branch of this; diligence; habitual hard work **in·dus'tri·al** *adj* of industries, trades **in·dus'tri·al·ize** *vt* **-ized, -iz·ing** **in·dus'tri·ous** [-tree-əs] *adj* diligent

in·e·bri·ate [in-EE-bree-ayt] *vt* **-at·ed, -at·ing** make drunk; intoxicate ▷ *adj* [-bree-it] drunken ▷ *n* habitual drunkard **in·e·bri·a'tion** *n* drunkenness

in·ed·i·ble [in-ED-ə-bəl] *adj* not eatable; unfit for food

in·ed·u·ca·ble [in-EJ-uu-kə-bəl] *adj* incapable of being educated, eg through mental retardation

in·ef·fa·ble [in-EF-ə-bəl] *adj* too great or sacred for words; unutterable **in·ef·fa·bil'i·ty** *n*

in·ef·fi·cient *adj* unable to perform a task or function to the best advantage **in·ef·fi'cien·cy** *n*

in·el·i·gi·ble [in-EL-i-jə-bəl] *adj* not fit or qualified (for something) **in·el·i·gi·bil'i·ty** *n*

in·ept' *adj* absurd; out of place;

clumsy **in·ept'i·tude** n

in·ert [in-URT] adj without power of action or resistance; slow, sluggish; chemically unreactive **in·er'tia** [-UR-shà] n inactivity; property by which matter continues in its existing state of rest or motion in straight line, unless that state is changed by external force

in·es·ti·ma·ble [in-ES-tà-mà-bàl] adj too good, too great, to be estimated

in·ev·i·ta·ble [in-EV-i-tà-bàl] adj unavoidable; sure to happen **in·ev·i·ta·bil'i·ty** n

in·ex·o·ra·ble [in-EK-sàr-à-bàl] adj relentless **in·ex'o·ra·bly** adv

in·ex·pe'ri·enced adj having no knowledge or experience of a particular situation, activity, etc **in·ex·pe'ri·ence** n

in·ex·pli·ca·ble [in-EK-spli-kà-bàl] adj impossible to explain

in ex·tre·mis [eks-TREE-mis] Lat at the point of death

in·fal·li·ble [in-FAL-ò-bàl] adj unerring; not liable to fail; certain, sure **in·fal·li·bil'i·ty** n

in·fa·mous [IN-fà-màs] adj notorious; shocking **in'fa·my** [-mee] n, pl **-mies**

in·fant [IN-fànt] n very young child **in'fan·cy** n **in·fan'ti·cide** [-tà-sid] n murder of newborn child; person guilty of this **in'fan·tile** [-fàn-til] adj childish

in·fan·try [IN-fàn-tree] n, pl **-tries** foot soldiers

in·fat·u·ate [in-FACH-oo-ayt] vt **-at·ed, -at·ing** inspire with folly or foolish passion **in·fat'u·at·ed** adj foolishly enamored **in·fat·u·a'tion** n

in·fect [in-FEKT] vt affect (with disease); contaminate **in·fec'tion** [-shàn] n **in·fec'tious** [-shàs] adj

catching, spreading, pestilential

in·fer [in-FUR] vt **-ferred, -fer·ring** deduce, conclude **in'fer·ence** [-fàr-àns] n **in·fer·en'tial** [-fàr-EN-shàl] adj deduced

in·fe·ri·or [in-FEER-ee-àr] adj of poor quality; lower ▷ n one lower (in rank, etc) **in·fe·ri·or'i·ty** n **inferiority complex** psychoanalysis intense sense of inferiority

in·fer'nal [in-FUR-nl] adj devilish; hellish; inf irritating, confounded

in·fer·no [in-FUR-noh] n region of hell; great destructive fire

in·fer'tile adj unable to produce offspring; (of soil) barren, not productive **in·fer·til'i·ty** n

in·fest vt inhabit or overrun in dangerously or unpleasantly large numbers **in·fes·ta'tion** n

in·fi·del·i·ty [in-fi-DEL-i-tee] n unfaithfulness; religious disbelief; disloyalty; treachery **in'fi·del** [-dl] n unbeliever ▷ adj

in·fil'trate [in-FIL-trayt] v **-trat·ed, -trat·ing** trickle through; cause to pass through pores; gain access surreptitiously **in·fil·tra'tion** n

in·fi·nite [IN-fà-nit] adj boundless **in'fi·nite·ly** adv exceedingly **in·fin·i·tes'i·mal** [-TES-à-màl] adj extremely, infinitely small **in·fin'i·ty** n unlimited and endless extent

in·fin·i·tive [in-FIN-i-tiv] adj grammar in form expressing notion of verb without limitation of tense, person, or number ▷ n verb in this form; the form

in·firm [in-FURM] adj physically weak; mentally weak; irresolute **in·fir'ma·ry** [-mà-ree] n hospital; dispensary **in·fir'mi·ty** n, pl **-ties**

in·flame [in-FLAYM] v **-flamed, -flam·ing** rouse

to anger, excitement; cause inflammation in; become inflamed **in·flam·ma·bil·i·ty** n **in·flam·ma·ble** adj easily set on fire; excitable **in·flam·ma·tion** n infection of part of the body, with pain, heat, swelling, and redness **in·flate** [in-FLAYT] v **-flat·ed, -flat·ing** blow up with air, gas; swell; cause economic inflation; raise price, esp artificially **in·fla·tion** n increase in prices and fall in value of money **in·fla·tion·ar·y** adj

in·flect [in-FLEKT] vt modify (words) to show grammatical relationships; bend inward **in·flec·tion** n modification of word; modulation of voice

in·flex·i·ble [in-FLEK-sə-bəl] adj incapable of being bent; stern **in·flex·i·bil·i·ty** n

in·flict [in-FLIKT] vt impose, deliver forcibly **in·flic·tion** n inflicting; punishment

in·flu·ence [IN-floo-əns] n effect of one person or thing on another; power of person or thing having an effect; thing, person exercising this ▷ vt **-enced, -enc·ing** sway; induce; affect **in·flu·en·tial** adj

in·flu·en·za [in-floo-EN-zə] n contagious feverish respiratory virus disease

in·flux [IN-fluks] n a flowing in; inflow

in·form' vt tell; animate ▷ vi give information (about) **in·form·ant** [-ənt] n one who tells **in·for·ma·tion** n what is told, knowledge **in·form·a·tive** adj **in·fo·mer·cial** [in-foh-MUR-shəl] n TV commercial advertising something in an informative way **information superhighway** worldwide network of computers sharing information at high speed

information technology use of computers and electronic technology to store and communicate information

in·for·mal adj relaxed and friendly; appropriate for everyday life or use **in·for·mal·i·ty** n

in·frac·tion n see **INFRINGE**

in·fra·red [in-frə-RED] adj denoting rays below red end of visible spectrum

in·fra·struc·ture [IN-frə-struk-chər] n basic structure or fixed capital items of an organization or economic system

in·fre·quent adj not happening often

in·fringe [in-FRINJ] vt **-fringed, -fring·ing** transgress, break **in·fringe·ment** n **in·frac·tion** n breach; violation

in·fu·ri·ate [in-FYUUR-ee-ayt] vt **-at·ed, -at·ing** enrage

in·fuse [in-FYOOZ] v **-fused, -fus·ing** soak to extract flavor, etc; instill, charge **in·fu·sion** [-FYOO-zhən] n an infusing; liquid extract obtained

in·gen·ious [in-JEEN-yəs] adj clever at contriving; cleverly contrived **in·ge·nu·i·ty** [-jə-NOO-ə-tee] n

in·gé·nue [AN-zhə-noo] n artless girl or young woman; actress playing such a part

in·gen·u·ous [in-JEN-yoo-əs] adj frank; naive, innocent **in·gen·u·ous·ness** n

in·ges·tion [in-JES-chən] n act of introducing food into the body

in·got [ING-gət] n brick of cast metal, esp gold

in·grain [in-GRAYN] vt implant deeply **in·grained'** adj deep-rooted; inveterate

in·gra·ti·ate [in-GRAY-shee-ayt] *v refl* get (oneself) into favor

in·gra·ti·at·ing·ly *adv*

in·grat·i·tude *n* lack of gratitude or thanks

in·gre·di·ent [in-GREE-dee-ảnt] *n* component part of a mixture

in'gress *n* entry, means, right of entrance

in·hab·it *vt* dwell in **in·hab·it·a·ble** *adj* **in·hab·it·ant** [-i-tånt] *n*

in·hale [in-HAYL] *v* **-haled, -hal·ing** breathe in (air, etc) **in·ha·la·tion** *n* esp medical preparation for inhaling **in·hal·er** *n* person who inhales; (also **in'ha·la·tor**) device producing, and assisting inhalation of therapeutic vapors

in·here [in-HEER] *vi* **-hered, -her·ing** of qualities, exist (in); of rights, be vested (in person) **in·her·ent** [-HEER-ảnt] *adj* existing as an inseparable part

in·her·it *vt* receive as heir; derive from parents ▷ *vi* succeed as heir **in·her·it·ance** [-ảns] *n*

in·hib·it *vt* restrain (impulse, desire, etc); hinder (action); forbid **in·hi·bi·tion** *n* repression of emotion, instinct; a stopping or retarding **in·hib·i·to·ry** *adj*

in·hos·pi·ta·ble *adj* not welcoming, unfriendly; difficult to live in, harsh

in·hu·man [in-HYOO-mản] *adj* cruel, brutal; not human **in·hu·man'i·ty** *n*

in·im·i·cal [i-NIM-i-kål] *adj* unfavorable (to); unfriendly; hostile

in·im·i·ta·ble [i-NIM-i-tả-bảl] *adj* defying imitation **in·im'i·ta·bly** *adv*

in·iq·ui·ty [i-NIK-wi-tee] *n, pl* **-ties** gross injustice; wickedness, sin **in·iq'ui·tous** *adj* unfair, sinful, unjust

in·i·tial [i-NISH-ảl] *adj* of, occurring at the beginning ▷ *n* initial letter, esp of person's name ▷ *vt* **-tialed, -tial·ing** mark, sign with one's initials

in·i·ti·ate [i-NISH-ee-ayt] *vt* **-at·ed, -at·ing** originate; begin; admit into closed society; instruct in elements (of) ▷ *n* [-ee-it] initiated person **in·i·ti·a'tion** *n* **in·i·ti·a'tive** *n* first step, lead; ability to act independently ▷ *adj* originating

in·ject [in-JEKT] *vt* introduce (esp fluid, medicine, etc with syringe) **in·jec'tion** *n*

in·junc·tion [in-JUNGK-shản] *n* judicial order to restrain; authoritative order

in·ju·ry [in-jả-ree] *n, pl* **-ries** physical damage or harm; wrong **in·jure** [IN-jảr] *vt* **-jured, -jur·ing** do harm or damage to **in·ju'ri·ous** [-JUU-ree-ảs] *adj*

in·jus·tice [in-JUS-tis] *n* want of justice; wrong; injury; unjust act

ink *n* fluid used for writing or printing ▷ *vt* mark with ink; cover, smear with it

ink·ling [INGK-ling] *n* hint, slight knowledge or suspicion

inlaid SEE INLAY

in·land *n* interior of country ▷ *adj* [IN-lånd] in this; away from the sea; within a country ▷ *adv* [IN-land] in or toward the inland

in'-law *n* relative by marriage esp mother-in-law and father-in-law

in'lay *vt* **-laid, -lay·ing** embed; decorate with inset pattern ▷ *n* inlaid piece or pattern

in'let *n* entrance; small arm of sea, lake, etc; piece inserted

in lo·co pa·ren·tis [LOH-koh pả-REN-tis] *Lat* in place of a parent

in·mate [IN-mayt] *n* occupant, esp

in·most [IN-mohst] *adj* most inward, deepest; most secret

inn *n* restaurant or tavern; country hotel **inn'keep·er** *n*

in·nards [IN-ərdz] *pl n* internal organs or working parts

in·nate [i-NAYT] *adj* inborn; inherent

in·ner [IN-ər] *adj* lying within **in'ner·most** *adj* **inner tube** rubber air tube of pneumatic tire

in'ning *n sport* side's turn at bat; spell, turn

in·no·cent [IN-ə-sənt] *adj* pure; guiltless; harmless ▷ *n* innocent person, esp young child **in·'no·cence** *n*

in·noc·u·ous [i-NOK-yoo-əs] *adj* harmless

in·no·vate [IN-ə-vayt] *vt* **-vat·ed, -vat·ing** introduce changes, new things **in·no·va'tion** *n*

in·nu·en·do [in-yoo-EN-doh] *n, pl* **-dos** allusive remark, hint; indirect accusation

in·nu·mer·a·ble [i-NOO-mər-ə-bəl] *adj* countless; very numerous

in·oc·u·late [i-NOK-yə-layt] *vt* **-lat·ed, -lat·ing** immunize by injecting vaccine **in·oc·u·la'tion** *n*

in·of·fen·sive [in-ə-FEN-siv] *adj* causing no harm

in·op·er·a·ble [in-OP-ər-ə-bəl] *adj* unworkable; *medicine* that cannot be operated on **in·op'er·a·tive** *adj* not operative; ineffective

in·op·por·tune [in-op-ər-TOON] *adj* badly timed

in·or·di·nate [in-OR-dn-it] *adj* excessive

in·or·gan·ic [in-or-GAN-ik] *adj* not having structure or characteristics of living organisms; of substances without carbon

in·pa·tient [IN-pay-shənt] *n* patient who stays in hospital

in·put [IN-puut] *n* act of putting in; that which is put in, as resource needed for industrial production, etc; data, etc fed into a computer

in·quest [IN-kwest] *n* legal or judicial inquiry presided over by a coroner; detailed inquiry or discussion

in·quire [in-KWIR] *vi* **-quired, -quir·ing** seek information **in·quir'er** *n* **in·quir'y** *n, pl* **-quir·ies** question; investigation

in·qui·si·tion [in-kwə-ZISH-ən] *n* searching investigation, official inquiry; **(I-)** *history* organization within the Catholic Church for suppressing heresy **in·quis'i·tor** [-KWIZ-ə-tər] *n*

in·quis·i·tive [in-KWIZ-i-tiv] *adj* curious; prying

in·road [IN-rohd] *n* incursion; encroachment

in·sane [in-SAYN] *adj* mentally deranged; crazy, senseless **in·sane'ly** *adv* like a lunatic, madly; excessively **in·san'i·ty** *n*

in·san·i·tar·y [in-SAN-i-ter-ee] *adj* dirty or unhealthy

in·sa·tia·ble [in-SAY-shə-bəl] *adj* incapable of being satisfied

in·scribe [in-SKRIB] *vt* **-scribed, -scrib·ing** write, engrave (in or on something); mark; dedicate; trace (figure) within another **in·scrip'tion** *n* inscribing; words inscribed on monument, etc

in·scru·ta·ble [in-SKROO-tə-bəl] *adj* mysterious, impenetrable; affording no explanation **in·scru·ta·bil'i·ty** *n*

in·sect [IN-sekt] *n* small invertebrate animal with six legs, usu segmented body and two or four wings **in·sec'ti·cide** [-sīd] *n* preparation for killing insects

in·sec·tiv·o·rous adj insect-eating

in·se·cure [in-si-KYUUR] adj not safe or firm; anxious, not confident

in·sem·i·nate [in-SEM-ə-nayt] vt **-nat·ed, -nat·ing** implant semen into **artificial insemination** impregnation of the female by artificial means

in·sen·sate [in-SEN-sayt] adj without sensation, unconscious; unfeeling

in·sen·si·ble [in-SEN-sə-bəl] adj unconscious; without feeling; not aware; not perceptible **in·sen·si·bly** adv imperceptibly

in·sen·si·tive adj unaware of or ignoring other people's feelings **in·sen·si·tiv·i·ty** n

in·sert [in-SURT] vt introduce; place or put (in, into, between) ▷ n [IN-surt] something inserted **in·ser·tion** [-shən] n

in·set n something extra inserted esp as decoration **in·set'** vt **-set, -set·ting**

in·shore [IN-shor] adj near shore ▷ adv toward shore

in·side [IN-sīd] n inner side, surface, or part; inner circle of influence; pl sl confidential information ▷ adj of, in, or on, inside ▷ adv [in-SĪD] in or into the inside; sl in prison ▷ prep within, on inner side

in·sid·i·ous [in-SID-ee-əs] adj stealthy, treacherous; unseen but deadly

in·sight [IN-sīt] n deep understanding

in·sig·ni·a [in-SIG-nee-ə] n, pl **-ni·as, -ni·a** badge or emblem of honor or office

in·sig·nif·i·cant adj not important **in·sig·nif·i·cance** n

in·sin·cere' adj showing false feelings, not genuine **in·sin·cer·i·ty** n, pl **-ties**

in·sin·u·ate [in-SIN-yoo-ayt] vt **-at·ed, -at·ing** hint; work oneself into favor; introduce gradually or subtly **in·sin·u·a·tion** n

in·sip·id adj dull, tasteless, spiritless

in·sist vi demand persistently; maintain; emphasize **in·sist'ence** n **in·sist'ent** adj

in si·tu [Sī-too] Lat in its original place or position

in·so·lent [IN-sə-lənt] adj arrogantly impudent **in'so·lence** n

in·sol·vent adj unable to pay one's debts **in·sol'ven·cy** n

in·som·ni·a [in-SOM-nee-ə] n sleeplessness **in·som'ni·ac** [-nee-ak] adj, n

in·so·much [in-sə-MUCH] adv to such an extent

in·sou·ci·ant [in-SOO-see-ənt] adj indifferent, careless, unconcerned **in·sou'ci·ance** n

in·spect [in-SPEKT] vt examine closely or officially **in·spec·tion** n **in·spec·tor** n one who inspects; high-ranking police or fire officer

in·spire [in-SPĪR] vt **-spired, -spir·ing** animate, invigorate; arouse, create feeling, thought; give rise to; breathe in, inhale **in·spi·ra·tion** n good idea; creative influence or stimulus

in·stall [in-STAWL] vt have (apparatus) put in; establish; place (person in office, etc) with ceremony **in·stal·la·tion** n act of installing; that which is installed

in·stall·ment [in-STAWL-mənt] n payment of part of debt; any of parts of a whole delivered in succession

in·stance [IN-stəns] n example; particular case; request ▷ vt **-stanced, -stanc·ing** cite

in·stant [IN-stànt] *n* moment, point of time ▷ *adj* immediate; urgent; (of foods) requiring little preparation **in·stan·ta'ne·ous** *adj* happening in an instant **in·stan'ter** *adv* at once **in·stant'ly** *adv* at once **instant messaging** online facility that allows the instant exchange of written messages between people using different computers or cell phones

in·stead [in-STED] *adv* in place (of); as a substitute

in·step *n* top of foot between toes and ankle

in·sti·gate [IN-sti-gayt] *vt* **-gat·ed, -gat·ing** incite, urge; bring about **in·sti·ga'tion** *n*

in·still *vt* implant; inculcate **in·still'ment** *n*

in·stinct [IN-stingkt] *n* inborn impulse or propensity; unconscious skill; intuition **in·stinc'tive** *adj*

in·sti·tute [IN-sti-toot] *vt* **-tut·ed, -tut·ing** establish, found; appoint; set in motion ▷ *n* society for promoting some public good, esp scientific; its building **in·sti·tu'tion** *n* an instituting; establishment for care or education, hospital, college, etc; an established custom or law; *inf* a well-established person **in·sti·tu'tion·al** *adj* of institutions; routine **in·sti·tu'tion·al·ize** *vt* **-ized, -iz·ing** place in an institution esp for care of mentally ill; make or become an institution

in·struct [in-STRUKT] *vt* teach; inform; order; brief (jury, lawyer) **in·struc'tion** *n* teaching; order ▷ *pl* directions **in·struc'tive** *adj* informative; useful

in·stru·ment [IN-strà-mànt] *n* tool, implement, means, person, thing used to make, do, measure, etc; mechanism for producing

musical sound; legal document **in·stru·men'tal** *adj* acting as instrument or means; helpful; belonging to, produced by musical instruments **in·stru·men'tal·ist** *n* player of musical instrument **in·stru·men·tal'i·ty** *n*, *pl* **-ties** agency, means **in·stru·men·ta'tion** *n* arrangement of music for instruments

in·sub·or·di·nate [in-sà-BOR-dn-it] *adj* not submissive; mutinous, rebellious **in·sub·or·di·na'tion** *n*

in·su·lar [IN-sà-làr] *adj* of an island; remote, detached; narrow-minded or prejudiced **in·su·lar'i·ty** *n*

in·su·late [IN-sà-layt] *vt* **-lat·ed, -lat·ing** prevent or reduce transfer of electricity, heat, sound, etc; isolate, detach **in·su·la'tion** *n*

in·su·lin [IN-sà-lin] *n* pancreatic hormone, used in treating diabetes

in·sult' *vt* behave rudely to; offend ▷ *n* [IN-sult] offensive remark; affront **in·sult'ing** *adj*

in·su·per·a·ble [in-SOO-pàr-à-bàl] *adj* that cannot be overcome or surmounted; unconquerable

in·sure [in-SHUUR] *v* **-sured, -sur·ing** contract for payment in event of loss, death, etc, by payment of premiums; make such contract about; make safe (against) **in·sur'a·ble** *adj* **in·sur'ance** *n* **in·sur'er** *n* insurance policy; contract of insurance

in·sur·gent [in-SUR-jànt] *adj* in revolt ▷ *n* rebel **in·sur'gence** *n*, **in·sur·rec'tion** *n* revolt

in·tact [in-TAKT] *adj* untouched; uninjured

in·tag·li·o [in-TAL-yoh] *n*, *pl* **-tagl·ios** engraved design; gem so cut

in·take [IN-tayk] n what is taken in; quantity taken in; opening for taking in; in car, air passage into carburetor

in·tan'gi·ble adj not clear or definite enough to be seen or felt easily

in·te·ger [IN-ti-jər] n whole number; whole of anything

in·te·gral [IN-ti-grəl] adj constituting an essential part of a whole **in'te·grate** vt **-grat·ed, -grat·ing** combine into one whole; unify diverse elements (of community, etc) **in·te·gra'tion** n **integral calculus** branch of mathematics of changing quantities that calculates total effects of the change **integrated circuit** tiny electronic circuit, usu on silicon chip

in·teg·ri·ty [in-TEG-ri-tee] n honesty; original perfect state

in·teg·u·ment [in-TEG-yə-mənt] n natural covering; skin, rind, husk

in·tel·lect [IN-tl-ekt] n power of thinking and reasoning **in·tel·lec'tu·al** adj of, appealing to intellect; having good intellect ▷ n one endowed with intellect and attracted to intellectual things

in·tel·li·gent [in-TEL-i-jənt] adj having, showing good intellect; quick at understanding; informed **intel'li·gence** n quickness of understanding; mental power or ability; intellect; information, news, esp military information **intel·li·gent'si·a** [-JENT-see-ə] n intellectual or cultured classes **intel'li·gi·ble** [-jə-bəl] adj understandable

in·tem·per·ate [in-TEM-pər-it] adj drinking alcohol to excess; immoderate; unrestrained **in·tem'per·ance** [-əns] n

in·tend' vt propose, mean (to do,

say, etc) **in·tend'ed** adj planned, future ▷ n inf proposed spouse

in·tense [in-TENS] adj strong or acute; emotional **in·ten·si·fi·ca'tion** n **in·ten'si·fy** v **-fied, -fy·ing** make or become stronger; increase **in·ten'si·ty** n intense quality; strength **in·ten'sive** adj characterized by intensity or emphasis on specified factor

in·tent' n purpose ▷ adj concentrating (on); resolved, bent; preoccupied, absorbed **in·ten'tion** n purpose, aim **in·ten'tion·al** adj

in·ter [in-TUR] vt **in·terred, -ter·ring** bury **in·ter'ment** n

inter- prefix between, among, mutually: **interglacial; interrelation**

in·ter·act [in-tər-AKT] vi act on each other **in·ter·ac'tion** n

in·ter·cede [in-tər-SEED] vi **-ced·ed, -ced·ing** plead in favor of; mediate **in·ter·ces'sion** n

in·ter·cept [in-tər-SEPT] vt cut off; seize, stop in transit **in·ter·cep'tion** n **in·ter·cept'or, -er** n one who, that which intercepts; fast fighter plane, missile, etc

in·ter·change [in-tər-CHAYNJ] v **-changed, -chang·ing** (cause to) exchange places ▷ n [IN-tər-chaynj] interchanging; highway intersection **in·ter·change'a·ble** adj able to be exchanged in position or use

in·ter·con·ti·nen·tal [in-tər-kon-tn-EN-tl] adj connecting continents; (of missile) able to reach one continent from another

in·ter·course [IN-tər-kors] n mutual dealings; communication; sexual joining of two people; copulation

in·ter·dict [IN-tər-dikt] n in Catholic church, decree restraining faithful from receiving certain

sacraments; formal prohibition
in·ter·dict' vt prohibit, forbid;
restrain **in·ter·dic·tion** n

in·ter·est [IN-tər-ist] n concern,
curiosity; thing exciting this; sum
paid for use of borrowed money; legal
concern; right, advantage, share
▷ vt excite, cause to feel interest
in·ter·est·ing adj

in·ter·face [IN-tər-fays] n area,
surface, boundary linking two
systems

in·ter·fere [in-tər-FEER] vi **-fered,
-fer·ing** meddle, intervene; clash
in·ter·fer·ence n act of interfering;
radio interruption of reception
by atmospherics or by unwanted
signals

in·ter·fer·on [in-tər-FEER-on]
n a cellular protein that stops
development of an invading virus

in·ter·im [IN-tər-əm] n meantime
▷ adj temporary, intervening

in·te·ri·or [in-TEER-ee-ər] adj
inner; inland; indoors ▷ n inside;
inland region

in·ter·ject [in-tər-JEKT]
vt interpose (remark, etc)
in·ter·jec·tion n exclamation;
interjected remark

in·ter·lard [in-tər-LAHRD] v
intersperse

in·ter·loc·u·tor [in-tər-LOK-
yə-tər] n one who takes part
in conversation; middle man
in line of minstrel performers
in·ter·loc·u·to·ry adj of a court
decree, issued before the final
decision in an action

in·ter·lop·er [IN-tər-lohp-ər] n
one intruding upon another's affairs;
intruder

in·ter·lude [IN-tər-lood] n
interval (in play, etc); something
filling an interval

in·ter·mar·ry [in-tər-MAR-
ee] vi **-ried, -ry·ing** (of families,
races, religions) become linked by
marriage; marry within one's family
in·ter·mar·riage n

in·ter·me·di·ate [in-tər-MEE-
dee-it] adj coming between;
interposed **in·ter·me·di·ar·y** n

in·ter·mez·zo [in-tər-MET-soh] n,
pl **-zos** short performance between
acts of play or opera

in·ter·mi·na·ble [in-TUR-mə-nə-
bəl] adj endless **in·ter·mi·na·bly**
adv

in·ter·mis·sion [in-tər-MISH-ən]
n short interval between parts of a
concert, play, etc **in·ter·mit·tent**
adj occurring at intervals

in·tern' [in-TURN] vt confine to
special area or camp **in·tern·ment**
n **in·tern·ee'** n

in·tern², in·terne [IN-turn] n
recent medical school graduate
residing in hospital and working
under supervision as member
of staff; trainee in occupation or
profession **in·tern·ship** n

in·ter·nal [in-TUR-nl] adj
inward; interior; within (a country,
organization) **internal combustion**
process of exploding mixture of air
and fuel within engine cylinder

in·ter·na·tion·al [in-tər-NASH-
ə-nl] adj of relations between
nations ▷ n labor union, etc with
units, members, in more than one
country

in·ter·ne·cine [in-tər-NEE-seen]
adj mutually destructive; deadly

In·ter·net, in·ter·net [IN-tər-
net] n large international public
access computer network

in·ter·po·late [in-TUR-pə-layt]
vt **-lat·ed, -lat·ing** insert new (esp
misleading) matter (in book, etc);
interject (remark); mathematics
estimate a value between known

values **in·ter·po·la·tion** n
in·ter·pose [in-tər-POHZ] v
-posed, -pos·ing ▷ vt insert;
say as interruption; put in the
way ▷ vi intervene; obstruct
in·ter·po·si·tion [-pə-ZISH-ən] n
in·ter·pret [in-TUR-prit]
v explain; translate, esp
orally; art render, represent
in·ter·pre·ta·tion n
in·ter·reg·num [in-tər-REG-nəm]
n, pl **-nums** interval between reigns;
gap in continuity
in·ter·ro·gate [in-TER-ə-
gayt] vt **-gat·ed, -gat·ing**
question, esp closely or
officially **in·ter·ro·ga·tion** n
in·ter·rog·a·tive adj questioning
▷ n word used in asking question
in·ter·rog·a·to·ry adj of inquiry
▷ n question, set of questions
in·ter·rupt [in-tə-RUPT] v break
in (upon); stop the course of; block
in·ter·rup·tion n
in·ter·sect [in-tər-SEKT] vt divide
by passing across or through ▷ vi
meet and cross **in·ter·sec·tion** n
point where lines, roads cross
in·ter·sperse [in-tər-SPURS]
vt **-spersed, -spers·ing** sprinkle
(something with or something
among or in)
in·ter·stel·lar [in-tər-STEL-ər]
(of the space) between stars
in·ter·stice [in-TUR-stis] n, pl
-stic·es [-stə-seez] chink, gap,
crevice **in·ter·sti·tial** [-STISH-
əl] adj
in·ter·val [IN-tər-vəl] n
intervening time or space; pause,
break; short period between parts of
play, concert, etc; difference (of pitch)
in·ter·vene [in-tər-VEEN] vi
-vened, -ven·ing come into a
situation in order to change it;
be, come between or among;

occur in meantime; interpose
in·ter·ven·tion n
in·tes·tate [in-TES-tayt] adj not
having made a will ▷ n person dying
intestate **in·tes·ta·cy** [-tə-see] n
in·tes·tine [in-TES-tin] n (usu
pl) lower part of alimentary canal
between stomach and anus
in·tes·ti·nal adj of bowels
in·ti·mate[1] [IN-tə-mit] adj
closely acquainted, familiar;
private; extensive; having sexual
relations (with) ▷ n intimate friend
in·ti·ma·cy [-mə-see] n
in·ti·mate[2] [IN-tə-mayt] vt
-mat·ed, -mat·ing imply;
announce **in·ti·ma·tion** n notice
in·tim·i·date [in-TIM-i-dayt]
vt **-dat·ed, -dat·ing** frighten
into submission; deter by threats
in·tim·i·da·tion n
in·to [IN-too] prep expresses
motion to a point within; indicates
change of state; indicates coming
up against, encountering; indicates
arithmetical division
in·tol·er·a·ble adj more than can
be endured
in·tone [in-TOHN] vt **-toned,
-ton·ing** chant; recite in monotone
in·to·na·tion n modulation of
voice; intoning; accent
in·tox·i·cate [in-TOK-si-kayt]
vt **-cat·ed, -cat·ing** make drunk;
excite to excess **in·tox·i·cant**
[-kənt] adj, n intoxicating (liquor)
intr. intransitive
intra- prefix within: intravenous
in·trac·ta·ble [in-TRAK-tə-bəl]
adj difficult to influence; hard to
control
in·tra·net [IN-trə-net] n computing
local network that makes use of
Internet technology
in·tran·si·gent [in-TRAN-si-jənt]
adj uncompromising, obstinate

in·tra·u·ter·ine [in-trə-YOO-tər-in] *adj* within the womb

in·tra·ve·nous [in-trə-VEE-nəs] *adj* into a vein

in·trep·id [in-TREP-id] *adj* fearless, undaunted **in·tre·pid·i·ty** *n*

in·tri·cate [in-tri-kit] *adj* involved, puzzlingly entangled **in·tri·ca·cy** *n, pl* **-cies**

in·trigue [in-TREEG] *n* underhanded plot; secret love affair ▷ *v* **-trigued, -tri·guing** ▷ *vi* carry on intrigue ▷ *vt* interest, puzzle

in·trin·sic [in-TRIN-sik] *adj* inherent, essential **in·trin·si·cal·ly** *adv*

intro- *prefix* into, within: introduce; introvert

in·tro·duce [in-trə-DOOS] *vt* **-duced, -duc·ing** make acquainted; present; bring in; bring forward; bring into practice; insert **in·tro·duc·tion** *n* an introducing; presentation of one person to another; preliminary section or treatment **in·tro·duc·to·ry** *adj* preliminary

in·tro·spec·tion *n* [in-trə-SPEK-shən] examination of one's own thoughts **in·tro·spec·tive** *adj*

in·tro·vert [in-trə-vurt] *n* psychoanalysis one who looks inward rather than at the external world **in·tro·ver·sion** [-zhən] *n* **in·tro·vert·ed** *adj*

in·trude [in-TROOD] *v* **-trud·ed, -trud·ing** thrust (oneself) in uninvited **in·tru·sion** [-zhən] *n* **in·tru·sive** *adj*

in·tu·i·tion [in-too-ISH-ən] *n* immediate mental apprehension without reasoning; immediate insight **in·tu·it** *v* **in·tu·i·tive** *adj*

In·u·it [IN-oo-it] *n* one of race of indigenous people of Alaska, N Canada, and Greenland ▷ *adj*

in·un·date [IN-ən-dayt] *vt* **-dat·ed, -dat·ing** flood; overwhelm **in·un·da·tion** *n*

in·ure [in-YUUR] *vt* **-ured, -ur·ing** accustom, esp to hardship, danger, etc

in·vade [in-VAYD] *vt* **-vad·ed, -vad·ing** enter by force with hostile intent; overrun; pervade **in·va·sion** *n*

in·va·lid¹ [IN-və-lid] *n* one suffering from chronic ill health ▷ *adj* ill, suffering from sickness or injury ▷ *v* become an invalid; retire from active service because of illness, etc

in·val·id² [in-VAL-id] *adj* not valid

in·val·u·a·ble [in-VAL-yoo-ə-bəl] *adj* priceless

invasion see INVADE

in·veigh [in-VAY] *v* speak violently (against) **in·vec·tive** *n* abusive speech or writing, vituperation

in·vei·gle [in-VAY-gəl] *vt* **-gled, -gling** entice, seduce, wheedle

in·vent [in-VENT] *vt* devise, originate; fabricate (falsehoods, etc) **in·ven·tion** *n* that which is invented; ability to invent; contrivance; deceit; lie **in·ven·tive** *adj* resourceful; creative **in·ven·tor** *n*

in·ven·to·ry [IN-vən-tor-ee] *n, pl* **-ries** detailed list of goods, etc ▷ *vt* **-ried, -ry·ing** make list of

in·vert [in-VURT] *vt* turn upside down; reverse position, relations of **in·verse** [-verse] *adj* inverted; opposite ▷ *n* **in·verse·ly** *adv* **in·ver·sion** [-zhən] *n*

in·ver·te·brate [in-VUR-tə-brit] *n* animal having no vertebral column ▷ *adj* spineless

in·vest [in-VEST] *vt* lay out (money, time, effort, etc) for profit or advantage; install; endow; poetry cover as with garment **in·ves·ti·ture** [-chər] *n* formal installation of person in office or rank **in·vest·ment** n investing; money invested; stocks, bonds, etc bought

in·ves·ti·gate [in-VES-ti-gayt] v inquire into; examine **in·ves·ti·ga'tion** n

in·vet·er·ate [in-VET-ər-it] adj deep-rooted; long established, confirmed

in·vid·i·ous [in-VID-ee-əs] adj likely to cause ill will or envy

in·vig·or·ate [in-VIG-ə-rayt] vt -at·ed, -at·ing give vigor to, strengthen

in·vin·ci·ble [in-VIN-sə-bəl] adj unconquerable **in·vin·ci·bil'i·ty** n

in·vi·o·la·ble [in-Vī-ə-lə-bəl] adj not to be profaned; sacred; unalterable **in·vi'o·late** [-lit] adj unhurt; unprofaned; unbroken

in·vis·i·ble [in-VIZ] adj not able to be seen **in·vis·i·bil'i·ty** n

in·vite [in-VīT] vt -vit·ed, -vit·ing request the company of; ask courteously; ask for; attract; call forth ▷ n [IN-vīt] inf an invitation **in·vi·ta'tion** n

in·voice [IN-vois] n itemized bill for goods or services sold ▷ vt -voiced, -voic·ing make or present an invoice

in·voke [in-VOHK] vt -voked, -vok·ing call on; appeal to; ask earnestly for; summon **in·vo·ca'tion** n

in·vol·un·tar·y [in-VOL-ən-ter-ee] adj not done willingly; unintentional; instinctive

in·vo·lute [IN-və-loot] adj complex; coiled spirally; (also **in·vo·lut'ed**) rolled inward

in·volve [in-VOLV] vt -volved, -volv·ing include; entail; implicate (person); concern; entangle **involved** adj complicated;

concerned (in)

in·vul·ner·a·ble adj not able to be wounded or harmed

in·ward [IN-wərd] adj internal; situated within; spiritual, mental ▷ adv toward the inside; into the mind **in'ward·ly** adv in the mind; internally

i·o·dine [ī-ə-dīn] n nonmetallic element found in seaweed and used in antiseptic solution, photography, etc **i'o·dize** vt -dized, -diz·ing treat or react with iodine

i·on [ī-ən] n electrically charged atom or group of atoms **i·on'ic** adj **i·on·i·za'tion** n **i'on·ize** vt -ized, -iz·ing change into ions **i·on'o·sphere** n region of atmosphere about 50 to 250 miles (80 to 400 km) above Earth

I·on·ic [ī-ON-ik] adj architecture distinguished by scroll-like decoration on columns

i·o·ta [ī-OH-tə] n the Greek letter i; (usu with not) very small amount

IP ad·dress n Internet protocol address: numeric code that identifies all computers that are connected to the Internet

iPod ® [ī-pod] n small portable digital audio player capable of storing thousands of tracks downloaded from the Internet or transferred from CDs

ip·so fac·to [IP-soh FAK-toh] Lat by that very fact

Ir chemistry iridium

ir- prefix same as **in-1** or **in-2**

ire [īr] n anger, wrath **i·ras·ci·ble** [i-RAS-ə-bəl] adj hot-tempered **i·ras'ci·bly** adv angry **i·rate** [ī-RAYT] adj angry

ir·i·des·cent [ir-i-DES-ənt] adj exhibiting changing colors like those of the rainbow **ir·i·des'cence** n

i·rid·i·um [i-RID-ee-əm] n very

hard, corrosion-resistant metallic element

i·ris [í-iris] *n* circular membrane of eye containing pigment; plant with sword-shaped leaves and showy flowers

irk [urk] *vt* irritate, vex **irk'some** [-sum] *adj* tiresome

i·ron [í-ərn] *n* metallic element, much used for tools, etc, and the raw material of steel; tool, etc, of this metal; appliance used, when heated, to smooth cloth; metal-headed golf club ▷ *pl* fetters ▷ *adj* of, like, iron; inflexible, unyielding; robust ▷ *v* smooth, cover, fetter, etc, with iron or an iron **i·ron·clad** protected with or as with iron **iron curtain** any barrier that separates communities or ideologies **iron lung** apparatus for administering artificial respiration

i·ro·ny [í-rə-nee] *n, pl* **-nies** (usu humorous or mildly sarcastic) use of words to mean the opposite of what is said; event, situation opposite of that expected **i·ron'ic** [-RON-ik] *adj* of, using, irony

ir·ra·di·ate [i-RAY-dee-ayt] *vt* **-at·ed, -at·ing** treat by irradiation; shine upon, throw light upon, light up **ir·ra·di·a'tion** *n* impregnation by X-rays, light rays

ir·ra·tion·al *adj* not based on or not using logical reasoning

ir·re·fran·gi·ble [i-ri-FRAN-jə-bəl] *adj* inviolable; in optics, not susceptible to refraction

ir·ref·u·ta·ble [i-REF-yə-tə-bəl] *adj* that cannot be refuted, disproved

ir·reg·u·lar *adj* not regular or even; not conforming to accepted practice; (of a word) not following the typical pattern of formation in a language **ir·reg·u·lar'i·ty** *n, pl* **-ties**

ir·rel'e·vant *adj* not connected with the matter in hand **ir·rel'e·vance** *n*

ir·rep·a·ra·ble [i-REP-ər-ə-bəl] *adj* not able to be repaired or remedied

ir·re·place'a·ble *adj* impossible to replace

ir·re·sist'i·ble *adj* too attractive or strong to resist

ir·res'o·lute *adj* unable to make decisions

ir·re·spec'tive [ir-i-SPEK-tiv] *adj* without taking account (of)

ir·re·spon'si·ble *adj* not showing or not done with due care for the consequences of one's actions or attitudes

ir·rev·o·ca·ble [i-REV-ə-kə-bəl] *adj* not able to be changed, undone, altered

ir·ri·gate [IR-i-gayt] *vt* **-gat·ed, -gat·ing** water by artificial channels, pipes, etc **ir·ri·ga'tion** *n*

ir·ri·tate [IR-i-tayt] *vt* **-tat·ed, -tat·ing** annoy; inflame; stimulate **ir·ri·ta·ble** *adj* easily annoyed **ir·ri'tant** *adj, n* (person or thing) causing irritation **ir·ri·ta'tion** *n*

Is. Isaiah

is [iz] third person singular, present indicative of **BE**

Is·lam [iz-LAHM] *n* Muslim faith or world **Is·lam'ic** *adj*

is·land [í-lənd] *n* piece of land surrounded by water; raised area for pedestrians in middle of road

isle [Il] *n* island **is·let** [í-lit] *n* little island

i·so·bar [í-sə-bahr] *n* line on map connecting places of equal mean barometric pressure

i·so·late [í-sə-layt] *vt* **-lat·ed, -lat·ing** place apart or alone **i·so·la'tion** *n* **i·so·la'tion·ism** *n* policy of not participating in international affairs

i·so·mer [ī-sə-mər] *n* substance with same molecules as another but different atomic arrangement **i·so·mer·ic** *adj*

i·so·met·ric [ī-sə-ME-trik] *adj* having equal dimensions; relating to muscular contraction without movement **i·so·met·rics** *pl n* system of isometric exercises

i·sos·ce·les [ī-SOS-ə-leez] *adj* of triangle, having two sides equal

i·so·therm [ī-sə-thurm] *n* line on map connecting points of equal mean temperature

i·so·tope [ī-sə-tohp] *n* atom of element having a different nuclear mass and atomic weight from other atoms in same element **i·so·top·ic** *adj*

ISP Internet service provider: business providing its customers with connection to the Internet

is·sue [ISH-oo] *n* sending or giving out officially or publicly; number or amount so given out; discharge; offspring, children; topic of discussion; question, dispute; outcome, result ▷ *v* **-sued, -su·ing** ▷ *vi* go out; result in; arise (from) ▷ *vt* emit, give out, send out; distribute, publish

isth·mus [IS-məs] *n* neck of land between two seas

it *pron* neuter pronoun of the third person **its** *adj* belonging to it **it's** it is; it has **it·self** *pron* emphatic form of **it**

i·tal·ic [i-TAL-ik] *adj* of type, sloping **i·tal·ics** *pl n* this type, now used for emphasis, etc **i·tal·i·cize** [-siz] *vt* put in italics

itch [ich] *vi, n* (feel) irritation in the skin **itch·y** *adj* **itch·i·er, itch·i·est**

i·tem [ī-təm] *n* single thing in list, collection, etc; piece of information; entry in account, etc **i·tem·ize** *vt* **-ized, -iz·ing**

it·er·ate [IT-ə-rayt] *vt* **-at·ed, -at·ing** repeat **it·er·a·tion** *n* **it·er·a·tive** *adj*

i·tin·er·ant [i-TIN-ər-ənt] *adj* traveling from place to place; working for a short time in various places; traveling on circuit **i·tin·er·ar·y** *n, pl* **-ar·ies** record, line of travel; route; guidebook

i·vo·ry [ī-və-ree] *n, pl* **-ries** hard white substance of the tusks of elephants, etc **ivory tower** seclusion, remoteness

i·vy [ī-vee] *n, pl* **-vies** climbing evergreen plant **i·vied** *adj* covered with ivy

j

jab *vt* **jabbed, jab•bing** poke roughly; thrust, stab abruptly ▷ *n* poke; punch

jab•ber [JAB-ər] *v* chatter; utter, talk rapidly, incoherently **Jab′ber•wock•y** *n* nonsense, esp in verse

jack [jak] *n* fellow, man; *inf* sailor; male of some animals; device for lifting heavy weight, esp automobile; playing card with picture of soldier or servant; socket and plug connection for electrical equipment; small flag, esp national, at sea ▷ *vt* (usu with *up*) lift (an object) with a jack **jack-of-all-trades** *pl* **jacks** person adept at many kinds of work

jack•al [JAK-əl] *n* wild, gregarious animal of Asia and Africa closely allied to dog

jack•ass [JAK-as] *n* male donkey; blockhead

jack•et [JAK-it] *n* outer garment, short coat; outer casing, cover

jack•knife [JAK-nīf] *n, pl* **-knives** clasp knife; dive with sharp bend at waist in midair ▷ *v* **-knifed, -knif•ing** bend sharply, eg an articulated truck forming a sharp angle with its trailer

jack•pot [JAK-pot] *n* large prize; accumulated stakes, as in poker

jac•quard [JAK-ahrd] *n* fabric in which design is incorporated into the weave

Ja•cuz•zi ® [jə-KOO-zee] *n* device that swirls water in a bath; bath with this device

jade¹ [jayd] *n* ornamental semiprecious stone, usu dark green; this color

jade² *n* sorry or worn-out horse; disreputable woman **jad′ed** *adj* tired and unenthusiastic

jag *n* sharp or ragged projection; spree **jag′ged** [-id] *adj*

jag•uar [JAG-wahr] *n* large S Amer spotted cat

jail [jayl] *n* building for confinement of criminals or suspects ▷ *vt* send to, confine in prison **jail′bait** [-bayt] *n sl* underage girl with whom sexual intercourse is considered a crime **jail′er** *n* **jail′bird** *n* hardened criminal

ja•lop•y [jə-LOP-ee] *n, pl* **-lop•ies** *inf* old car

jam *vt* **jammed, jam•ming** pack together; (cause to) stick together and become unworkable; apply fiercely; squeeze; *radio* block (another station) with impulses of equal wavelength ▷ *n* fruit preserved by boiling with sugar; crush; delay of traffic; awkward situation **jam-packed** *adj* filled to capacity **jam session** [improvised jazz session]

jamb [jam] *n* side post of arch, door, etc

jam•bo•ree [jam-bə-REE] *n* large gathering or rally of scouts; spree, celebration

jan•gle [JANG-gəl] *v* **-gled, -gling**

(cause to) sound harshly, as bell; (of nerves) irritate ▷ *n* harsh sound

jan·i·tor [JAN-i-tər] *n* custodian, cleaner

jar[1] [jahr] *n* round vessel of glass, earthenware, etc; *inf* drink of beer, whiskey, etc

jar[2] *v* **jarred, jar·ring** (cause to) vibrate suddenly, violently; have disturbing, painful effect on ▷ *n* jarring sound; shock, etc

jar·gon [JAHR-gən] *n* specialized language concerned with particular subject; pretentious or nonsensical language

jas·per [JAS-pər] *n* red, yellow, dark green or brown quartz

jaun·dice [JAWN-dis] *n* disease marked by yellowness of skin; bitterness, ill humor; prejudice ▷ *v* **-diced, -dic·ing** make, become prejudiced, bitter, etc

jaunt [jawnt] *n* short pleasure trip ▷ *vi* make one

jaun·ty [JAWN-tee] *adj* **-ti·er, -ti·est** sprightly; brisk; smart, trim **jaun'ti·ly** *adv*

Java ® [JAH-və] *n* computer programming language that is widely used on the Internet

jave·lin [JAV-lin] *n* spear, esp for throwing in sporting events

jaw *n* one of bones in which teeth are set; ▷ *pl* mouth; *fig* narrow opening of a gorge or valley; gripping part of vise, etc ▷ *vi sl* talk lengthily

jay *n* noisy bird of brilliant plumage

jay'walk·er *n* careless pedestrian **jay'walk** *vi*

jazz *n* syncopated music and dance **jazz'y** *adj* **-jazz·i·er, jazz·i·est** flashy, showy **jazz up** play as jazz; make more lively, appealing

jeal·ous [JEL-əs] *adj* distrustful of the faithfulness (of); envious; suspiciously watchful

jeans [jeenz] *pl n* casual trousers, esp of denim

jeer *v* scoff, deride ▷ *n* scoff, taunt, gibe

Je·ho·vah [ji-HO-və] *n* God

je·june [ji-JOON] *adj* simple, naive; meager

jell *v* congeal; assume definite form

jel·ly [JEL-ee] *n, pl* **-lies** semitransparent food made with gelatin, becoming softly stiff as it cools; anything of the consistency of this **jel'ly·fish** *n* jellyfish small sea animal

jeop·ard·y [JEP-ər-dee] *n* danger **jeop'ard·ize** *vt* **-ized, -iz·ing** endanger

Jer. Jeremiah

jerk [jurk] *n* sharp, abruptly stopped movement; twitch; sharp pull; *sl* stupid person, inconsequential person ▷ *v* move or throw with a jerk **jerk'i·ly** *adv* **jerk'y** *adj* **jerk·i·er, jerk·i·est** uneven, spasmodic

jer·sey [JUR-zee] *n, pl* **-seys** knitted sweater; machine-knitted fabric; (J-) breed of cow

jest *n, vi* joke **jest'er** *n history* professional clown at court

Jes·u·it [JEZH-oo-it] *n* member of Society of Jesus, order founded by Ignatius Loyola in 1534 **Jes·u·it'i·cal** *adj* of Jesuits; (j-) crafty, using overly subtle reasoning

jet[1] *n* stream of liquid, gas, etc, esp shot from small hole; the small hole; spout, nozzle; aircraft driven by jet propulsion ▷ *v* **jet·ted, -jet·ting** throw out; shoot forth **jet-black** *adj* deep black **jet lag** fatigue caused by crossing time zones in jet aircraft **jet propulsion** propulsion by thrust provided by jet of gas or liquid **jet ski** small self-propelled vehicle resembling a scooter, which skims across water on a flat keel

jet² *n* hard black mineral capable of brilliant polish

jet•sam [JET-sàm] *n* goods thrown out to lighten ship and later washed ashore **jet'ti•son** [-tə-sàn] *vt* abandon; throw overboard

jet•ty [JET-ee] *n*, *pl* **-ties** small pier, wharf

Jew [joo] *n* one of Hebrew ancestry; one who practices Judaism **Jew'ish** *adj* **Jew'ry** *n* the Jews **Jew's harp** *n* small musical instrument held between teeth and played by finger

jew•el [JOO-əl] *n* precious stone; ornament containing one; precious thing **jew'el•er** *n* dealer in jewels **jew'el•ry** *n*

jib *n* triangular sail set forward of mast; projecting arm of crane or derrick

jibe see **GIBE**

jif•fy [JIF-ee] *n*, *pl* **-fies** *inf* very short period of time

jig *n* lively dance; music for it; small mechanical device; guide for cutting, etc; *angling* any of various lures ▷ *v* **jigged, jig•ging** dance jig; make jerky up-and-down movements **jig'saw** *n* machine-mounted saw for cutting curves, etc **jigsaw puzzle** picture stuck on board and cut into interlocking pieces with jigsaw

jig•ger [JIG-ər] *n* small glass holding and pouring measure of whiskey, etc

jig•gle [JIG-əl] *v* **-gled, -gling** move (up and down, etc) with short jerky movements

jilt *vt* cast off (lover)

jim•my [JIM-ee] *n*, *pl* **-mies** short steel crowbar ▷ *vt* **-mied, -my•ing** force open with a jimmy

jin•gle [JING-gàl] *n* mixed metallic noise, as of shaken chain; catchy, rhythmic verse, song, etc ▷ *v* **-gled,**

-gling (cause to) make jingling sound

jin•go•ism [JING-goh-iz-àm] *n* chauvinism **jin•go•is'tic** *adj*

jinks [jingks] *pl n* **high jinks** boisterous merrymaking

jinx [jingks] *n* force, person, thing bringing bad luck ▷ *v* be or put a jinx on

jit•ters [JIT-ərz] *pl n* worried nervousness, anxiety **jit'ter•y** *adj* **-ter•i•er, -ter•i•est** nervous

jiujitsu *n* see **JUJITSU**

jive [jīv] *n* (dance performed to) swing music, esp of 1950s ▷ *v* **jived, jiv•ing** play, dance to, swing music; *sl* tease; fool

job *n* piece of work, task; position, office; *inf* difficult task; *sl* a crime, esp robbery **job'ber** *n* wholesale merchant **job'less** [-lis] *adj*, *pl n* unemployed (people)

jock•ey [JOK-ee] *n*, *pl* **-eys** professional rider in horse races ▷ *v* **-eyed, -ey•ing** (used with for) maneuver

jo•cose [joh-KOHS] *adj* waggish, humorous **jo•cos'i•ty** [-KOS-i-tee] *n* **joc'u•lar** [-yə-lər] *adj* joking; given to joking **joc•u•lar'i•ty** *n*

joc•und [JOK-ənd] *adj* merry, cheerful **jo•cun•di•ty** [joh-KUN-di-tee] *n*, *pl* **-ties**

jodh•purs [JOD-pərz] *pl n* tight-legged riding breeches

jog *v* **jogged, jog•ging** ▷ *vi* run slowly or move at trot, esp for physical exercise ▷ *vt* jar, nudge; remind, stimulate ▷ *n* jogging **jog'ger** *n* jogging

jog•gle [JOG-əl] *v* **-gled, -gling** move to and fro in jerks; shake

John [jon] *n* name; (**j-**) *sl* toilet; *sl* prostitute's customer

joie de vi•vre [zhwad VEE-vrà] Fr enjoyment of life, ebullience

join vt put together, fasten, unite; become a member (of) ▷vi become united, connected; (with up) enlist; take part (in) ▷n joining; place of joining, seam **join'er** n maker of finished woodwork; one who joins

joint n arrangement by which two things fit together, rigidly or loosely; place of this; sl house, place, etc; sl disreputable bar or nightclub; sl marijuana cigarette ▷adj common; shared by two or more ▷vt connect by joints; divide at the joints **joint'ly** adv **out of joint** dislocated; disorganized

joist n one of the parallel beams stretched from wall to wall on which to fix floor or ceiling

joke [johk] n thing said or done to cause laughter; something not in earnest, or ridiculous ▷vi **joked**, **jok'ing** make jokes **jok'er** n one who jokes; inf fellow; extra card in pack, counting as highest card in some games

jol·ly [JOL-ee] adj **-li·er**, **-li·est** jovial, festive, merry ▷vt **-lied**, **-ly·ing** (esp with along) (try to) make person, occasion, etc happier

jolt [johlt] n sudden jerk; bump; shock; inf a strong drink ▷v move, shake with jolts

joss [jos] n Chinese idol **joss house** Chinese temple **joss stick** stick of Chinese incense

jos·tle [JOS-əl] v **-tled**, **-tling** knock or push against

jot n small amount, whit ▷vt **jot·ted**, **jot·ting** write briefly; make note of **jot'ting** n quick note; memorandum

joule [jool] n electricity unit of work or energy

jour·nal [JUR-nl] n daily newspaper or other periodical; daily record; logbook; part of axle or shaft resting on the bearings **jour·nal·ese'** [-EEZ] n journalist's jargon; style full of clichés **jour'nal·ism** n editing, writing in periodicals

jour·ney [JUR-nee] n, pl **-neys** going to a place, excursion; distance traveled ▷vi **-neyed**, **-ney·ing** travel

joust [jowst] n history encounter with lances between two mounted knights ▷vi engage in joust

jo·vi·al [JOH-vee-əl] adj convivial, merry, gay **jo·vi·al'i·ty** n

jowl n cheek, jaw; outside of throat when prominent

joy [joi] n gladness, pleasure, delight; cause of this **joy'ful** [-fuul] adj **joy'less** [-lis] adj **joy'ride** n (high-speed) automobile trip **joy'stick** n inf control stick of aircraft or computer device

ju·bi·lant [JOO-bə-lənt] adj exultant **ju·bi·la·tion** n

ju·bi·lee [JOO-bə-lee] n time of rejoicing, esp 25th (silver) or 50th (golden) anniversary

Jud. Judges

Ju·da·ic [joo-DAY-ik] adj Jewish **Ju'da·ism** n

judge [juj] n officer appointed to try cases in law courts; one who decides in a dispute, contest, etc; one able to form a reliable opinion, arbiter; umpire; in Jewish history, ruler ▷v **judged**, **judg·ing** ▷vi act as judge ▷vt act as judge of; try, estimate; decide **judg'ment** n faculty of judging; sentence of court; opinion; misfortune regarded as sign of divine displeasure

ju·di·ca·ture [JOO-di-kə-chər] n administration of justice; body of judges **ju·di'cial** [-DISH-əl] adj of or by a court or judge; proper to a judge; discriminating **ju·di'ci·ar·y**

[-shee-er-ee] *n, pl* **-ar·ies** system of courts and judges **ju·di·cious** [-shəs] *adj* well-judged, sensible, prudent

ju·do [JOO-doh] *n* modern sport derived from jujitsu

jug *n* vessel for liquids, with handle and small spout; its contents; *sl* prison ▷ *vt* **jugged, jug·ging** stew (esp hare) in jug

jug·ger·naut [JUG-ər-nawt] *n* large overpowering, destructive force

jug·gle [JUG-əl] *v* **-gled, -gling** throw and catch (several objects) so most are in the air simultaneously; manage, manipulate (accounts, etc) to deceive ▷ *n* **jug·gler** *n*

jug·u·lar vein [JUG-yə-lər] one of three large veins of the neck returning blood from the head

juice [joos] *n* liquid part of vegetable, fruit, or meat; *sl* electric current; *sl* fuel used to run engine; vigor, vitality **juic·y** *adj* **juic·i·er, juic·i·est** succulent; scandalous, improper

ju·jit·su [joo-JIT-soo] *n* the Japanese art of wrestling and self-defense

ju·jube [JOO-joo-bee] *n* lozenge of gelatin, sugar, etc; a fruit

ju·lep [JOO-lip] *n* sweet drink; medicated drink

Jul·ian calendar [JOOL-yən] *adj* of Julius Caesar **Julian calendar** calendar as adjusted by Julius Caesar in 46 BC, in which the year was made to consist of 365 days, 6 hours, instead of 365 days

ju·li·enne [joo-lee-EN] *n* kind of clear soup ▷ *adj* of food, cut into thin strips or small pieces ▷ *vt*

jum·ble [JUM-bəl] *vt* **-bled, -bling** mingle, mix in confusion ▷ *n* confused heap, muddle

jum·bo [JUM-boh] *n, inf* elephant; anything very large

jump *v* (cause to) spring, leap (over); move hastily; pass or skip (over) ▷ *vi* move hastily; rise steeply; parachute from aircraft; start, jerk (with astonishment, etc); of faulty film, etc, make abrupt movements ▷ *v* come off (tracks, rails, etc); attack without warning ▷ *n* act of jumping; obstacle to be jumped; distance, height jumped; sudden rise in prices **jump'er** *n* one who, that which jumps; sleeveless dress; electric cable to connect discharged car battery to external battery to aid starting of engine **jump'y** *adj* **jump·i·er, jump·i·est** nervous **jump'suit** *n* one-piece garment of trousers and top

junc·tion [JUNGK-shən] *n* railroad station, etc where lines, routes join; place of joining, joining

junc·ture [JUNGK-chər] *n* state of affairs

jun·gle [JUNG-gəl] *n* tangled vegetation of equatorial forest; land covered with it; tangled mass; condition of intense competition, struggle for survival

jun·ior [JOON-yər] *adj* younger; of lower standing ▷ *n* junior person

ju·ni·per [JOO-nə-pər] *n* evergreen shrub with berries yielding oil of juniper, used for medicine and gin making

junk[1] [jungk] *n* discarded, useless objects; *inf* nonsense; *sl* narcotic drug esp heroin **junk·ie**, **junk·y** *n, pl* **-junk·ies** *inf* drug addict **junk food** food, often of low nutritional value, eaten in addition to or instead of regular meals **junk mail** unsolicited mail advertising goods or services

junk[2] *n* Chinese sailing vessel

jun·ket [JUNG-kit] n curdled milk flavored and sweetened; pleasure trip esp one paid for by others ▷ vi go on a junket

jun·ta [HUUN-tə] n group of military officers holding power in a country

Ju·pi·ter [JOO-pi-tər] n Roman chief of gods; largest of the planets

ju·ris·dic·tion [juur-is-DIK-shən] n administration of justice; authority; territory covered by it

ju·ris·pru·dence [-PROO-dəns] n science of, skill in, law

ju·rist n one skilled in law

ju·ry [JUUR-ee] n, pl **-ries** body of persons sworn to render verdict in court of law; body of judges of competition **ju·ror** n member of jury

just adj fair; upright, honest; proper; right; equitable ▷ adv exactly; barely; at this instant; merely; only;

really **jus·tice** n quality of being just; fairness; judicial proceedings; judge; magistrate **jus·ti·fy** vt **-fied**, **-fy·ing** prove right, true or innocent; vindicate; excuse **jus·ti·fi·a·ble** adj **jus·ti·fi·ca·tion** [-kay-shən] n

jut vi **jut·ted**, **jut·ting** project, stick out ▷ n projection

jute [joot] n fiber of certain plants, used for rope, canvas, etc

ju·ve·nile [JOO-və-nl] adj young; of, for young children; immature ▷ n young person, child; male actor **ju·ve·nil·i·a** pl n works produced in author's youth **juvenile court** court dealing with young offenders or children in need of care **juvenile delinquent** young person guilty of some offense, antisocial behavior, etc

jux·ta·pose [JUK-stə-pohz] vt **-posed**, **-pos·ing** put side by side **jux·ta·po·si·tion** n contiguity, being side by side

K Kelvin; *chemistry* potassium

ka·bob [kə-BOB], **ke·bab** [kə-BAB] *n* dish of small pieces of meat, tomatoes, etc grilled on skewers

kale [kayl] *n* type of cabbage

ka·lei·do·scope [kə-LĪ-də-skohp] *n* optical toy for producing changing symmetrical patterns by multiple reflections of colored glass chips, etc, in inclined mirrors enclosed in tube; any complex, frequently changing pattern **ka·lei·do·scop·ic** [-SKOP-ik] *adj* swiftly changing

ka·mi·ka·ze [kah-mi-KAH-zə] *n* suicidal attack, esp as in World War II, by Japanese pilots

kan·ga·roo [kang-gə-ROO] *n, pl* **-roos** Aust marsupial with very strongly developed hind legs for jumping **kangaroo court** irregular, illegal court

ka·pok [KAY-pok] *n* tropical tree; fiber from its seed pods used to stuff cushions, etc

ka·put [kah-PUUT] *adj sl* ruined, out of order, no good

ka·ra·te [kə-RAH-tee] *n* Japanese system of unarmed combat using feet, hands, elbows, etc as weapons in a variety of ways

kar·ma [KAHR-mə] *n Buddhism, Hinduism* one's actions seen as affecting fate for next reincarnation

kart [kahrt] *n* miniature low-powered racing car; (also **go-kart**)

kay·ak [KĪ-ak] *n* Inuit canoe made of sealskins stretched over frame; any canoe of this design

ka·zoo [kə-ZOO] *n, pl* **-zoos** cigar-shaped musical instrument producing nasal sound

kbyte *computing* kilobyte

kebab, kebob see **KABOB**

ked·ger·ee [KEJ-ə-ree] *n* East Indian dish of fish cooked with rice, eggs, etc

keel *n* lowest longitudinal support on which ship is built **keel'haul** *vt* formerly, punish by hauling under keel of ship; rebuke severely **keel over** turn upside down; collapse suddenly

keen¹ *adj* **-er, -est** sharp; acute; eager; shrewd, strong **keen'ly** *adv* **keen'ness** *n*

keen² *n* funeral lament ▷ *vi* wail over the dead

keep *v* **kept, keep·ing** retain possession of, not lose; store; cause to continue; take charge of; maintain, detain; provide upkeep; reserve; remain good; remain; continue ▷ *n* living or support; charge or care; central tower of castle, stronghold **keep'er** *n* **keep'ing** *n* harmony, agreement; care, charge, possession **keep'sake** *n* thing treasured for sake of giver

keg *n* small barrel usu holding 5 to 10 gallons (19 to 38 liters)

kelp *n* large seaweed; its ashes, yielding iodine

Kel'vin *adj* of thermometric scale starting at absolute zero (-273.15° Celsius) ▷ *n* SI unit of temperature

ken *n* range of knowledge ▷ *vt*

kenned or **kent, ken•ning** Scot know

ken•do [KEN-doh] n Japanese sport of fencing, using bamboo staves

ken•nel [KEN-l] n house, shelter for dog; (oft pl) place for breeding, boarding dogs ▷ vt -neled, -nel•ing put into kennel

kept pt/pp of KEEP

ker•chief [KUR-chif] n square scarf used as head covering; handkerchief

ker•nel [KUR-nl] n inner seed of nut or fruit stone; central, essential part

ker•o•sene [KER-à-seen] n fuel distilled from petroleum or coal and shale

ketch [kech] n two-masted sailing vessel

ketch•up [KECH-əp] n condiment of vinegar, tomatoes, etc

ket•tle [KET-l] n metal vessel with spout and handle, esp for boiling water **ket'tle•drum** n musical instrument made of membrane stretched over copper, brass, etc hemisphere **a fine kettle of fish** awkward situation, mess

key [kee] n instrument for operating lock, winding clock, etc; something providing control, explanation, means of achieving an end, etc; music set of related notes; operating lever of typewriter, piano, computer, etc; mode of thought ▷ vt (also **key in**) enter (text) using a keyboard; provide symbols on map, etc to assist identification of positions on it ▷ adj vital; most important **key'board** [-bord] n set of keys on piano, computer, etc **key'hole** n hole for inserting key into lock; any shape resembling this **key'note** [-noht] n dominant idea; basic note of musical key **key'pad** n small keyboard with push buttons **key'stone** n central stone of arch that locks all in position

khak•i [KAK-ee] adj dull yellowish-brown ▷ n, pl **khakis** khaki cloth; (usu pl) military uniform

Khmer [kmair] n member of a people of Cambodia

Ki. Kings

kib•ble [KIB-əl] vt -bled, -bling grind into small pieces ▷ n dry dog food prepared in this way

kib•butz [ki-BUUTS] n in Israel, Jewish communal agricultural settlement **kib•butz'nik** n member of kibbutz

ki•bosh [KI-bosh] n inf nonsense **to put the kibosh on** silence; check; defeat

kick [kik] vi strike out with foot; score with a kick; be recalcitrant; recoil ▷ vt strike or hit with foot; sl free oneself of (drug habit, etc) ▷ n foot blow; recoil; excitement; thrill **kick'back** n strong reaction; money paid illegally for favors done, etc **kick off** v start game of football; begin (discussion, etc) **kick-start** v start motorcycle engine, etc by pedal that is kicked downward

kid n young goat; leather of its skin; inf child ▷ v **kid•ded, kid•ding** (of a goat) give birth; inf tease, deceive; inf behave, speak in fun

kid'nap vt -napped, -nap•ping seize and hold for ransom **kid'nap•per** n

kid•ney [KID-nee] n, pl -neys either of the pair of organs that secrete urine; animal kidney used as food; nature, kind **kidney bean** common bean, kidney-shaped at maturity

kill vt deprive of life; destroy; neutralize; pass (time); weaken or dilute; inf tire, exhaust; inf cause to suffer pain; inf quash, defeat, veto ▷ n act of killing; animals, etc killed in hunt; enemy troops, aircraft, etc killed or destroyed in combat **kill'er** n one who, that which, kills **kill'ing** adj inf very tiring; very funny ▷ n sudden success, esp on stock market

kiln n furnace, oven

kil·o [KEE-loh] n short for KILOGRAM

kilo- comb form one thousand: kiloliter; kilometer

kil·o·byte [KIL-ə-bit] n computing 1,024 bytes; (loosely) one thousand bytes

kil·o·gram [KIL-ə-gram] n weight of one thousand grams

kil·o·hertz [KIL-ə-hurts] n one thousand cycles per second

kil·o·watt [KIL-ə-wot] n electricity one thousand watts

kilt n short, usu tartan, skirt, deeply pleated, worn orig by Scottish Highlanders **kilt'ed** adj

ki·mo·no [kə-MOH-nə] n, pl **-nos** loose, wide-sleeved Japanese robe, fastened with sash; woman's garment like this

kin n family, relatives ▷ adj related by blood **kin'dred** [-drid] n relationship; relatives ▷ adj similar; related **kin'folk** [-fohk] n **kin'ship** n

kind [kind] n genus, sort, class ▷ adj **-er, -est** sympathetic, considerate; good, benevolent; gentle **kind'li·ness** n adj **-li·er, -li·est** kind, genial ▷ adv **kind'ness** n **kind'heart·ed** adj **in kind** (of payment) in goods rather than money; with something similar

kin·der·gar·ten [KIN-dər-gahr-tn] n class, school for children of about four to six years old

kin·dle [KIN-dl] v **-dled, -dling** ▷ vt set on fire; inspire, excite ▷ vi catch fire **kind'ling** n small wood to kindle fires

ki·net·ic [ki-NET-ik] adj of motion in relation to force **ki·net'ics** n the

branch of mechanics concerned with the study of bodies in motion

king n male sovereign ruler of independent country; monarch; piece in game of chess; playing card with picture of a king; checkers two pieces on top of one another, allowed freedom of movement **king'ly** adj **-li·er, -li·est** royal; appropriate to a king **king'dom** [-dəm] n country ruled by king; realm; sphere **king'fish** n any of several types of fish; inf person in position of authority **king'pin** n swivel pin; central or front pin in bowling; inf chief thing or person **king-size, king-sized** adj inf large; larger than standard size

kink [kingk] n tight twist in rope, wire, hair, etc; crick, as of neck; inf eccentricity ▷ v make, become kinked; put, make kink in; twist **kink'y** adj **kink·i·er, kink·i·est** full of kinks; inf eccentric, esp given to deviant (sexual) practices

ki·osk [KEE-osk] n small, sometimes movable booth selling soft drinks, cigarettes, newspapers, etc

kip·per [KIP-ər] vt cure (fish) by splitting open, rubbing with salt, and drying or smoking ▷ n kippered fish

kirsch [keersh] n brandy made from cherries

kis·met [KIZ-mit] n fate, destiny

kiss n touch or caress with lips; light touch ▷ v **kiss'er** n one who kisses; sl mouth or face **kissing kin** relative(s) familiar enough to greet with polite kiss **kiss of death** apparently friendly ruinous act

kit n outfit, equipment; personal effects, esp of traveler; set of pieces of equipment sold ready to be assembled **kit bag** small bag for holding soldier's or traveler's kit

kitch·en [KICH-ən] n room used for cooking **kitch·en·ette** n small compact kitchen **kitchen garden** garden for raising vegetables, herbs, etc **kitchen sink** sink in kitchen; final item imaginable

kite [kit] n light papered frame flown in wind; large hawk; check drawn against nonexistent funds ▷ **kit·ed, kit·ing** use check in this way; cash or pass such a check

kith n **kith and kin** friends and relatives

kitsch [kich] n vulgarized, pretentious art, literature, etc, usu with popular, sentimental appeal

kit·ten [KIT-n] n young cat

kit·ty [KIT-ee] n, pl **-ties** short for **KITTEN** in some card games, pool of money; communal fund

ki·wi [KEE-wee] n, pl **-wis** any N.Z. flightless bird of the genus *Apteryx*; inf New Zealander **kiwi fruit** fuzzy fruit of Asian climbing plant, the Chinese gooseberry

klax·on [KLAK-sən] n powerful electric horn, used as warning signal

klep·to·ma·ni·a [klep-tə-MAY-nee-ə] n compulsive tendency to steal for the sake of theft **klep·to·ma·ni·ac** n

knack [nak] n acquired facility or dexterity; trick; habit

knap·sack [NAP-sak] n soldier's or traveler's bag to strap to the back, rucksack

knave [nayv] n jack at cards; obs rogue **knav·er·y** n villainy **knav·ish** adj

knead [need] vt work (flour) into dough; work; massage

knee [nee] n joint between thigh and lower leg; part of garment covering knee ▷ vt **kneed, knee·ing** strike, push with knee **knee·cap** n bone in front of knee

kneel [neel] vi **knelt** or **kneeled, kneel·ing** fall, rest on knees

knell [nel] n sound of a bell, esp at funeral or death; portent of doom

knew pt of KNOW

knick·ers [NIK-ərz] pl n loose-fitting short trousers gathered in at knee

knick-knack [NIK-nak] n small ornament or toy

knife [nif] n, pl **knives** cutting blade, esp one in handle, used as implement or weapon ▷ vt **knifed, knif·ing** cut or stab with knife **knife edge** critical, possibly dangerous situation

knight [nit] n Brit man of rank below baronet, having right to prefix *Sir* to his name; member of medieval order of chivalry; champion; piece in chess ▷ vt confer knighthood on **knight'hood** [-huud] n

knish [nit] n turnover filled with potato, meat, etc and fried or baked

knit [nit] v **knit'ted** or **knit, knit·ting** form (garment, etc) by putting together series of loops in wool or other yarn; draw together; unite **knit'ting** n knitted work; act of knitting

knob [nob] n rounded lump, esp at end or on surface of anything **knob·bly** adj **-bi·er, -bi·est**

knock [nok] vt strike, hit; inf disparage; rap audibly; (of engine) make metallic noise, ping ▷ n blow, rap **knock'er** n metal appliance for knocking on door; who or what knocks **knock-kneed** adj having incurved legs **knocked out** exhausted, tired, worn out **knock off** inf cease work; inf copy, plagiarize; sl kill; sl steal **knock out** inf render (opponent) unconscious; overwhelm, amaze; make (something) hurriedly **knock'out** n blow, etc that renders unconscious; *inf* person or thing overwhelmingly attractive **knock up** *sl* make pregnant

knoll [nohl] *n* small rounded hill, mound

knot [not] *n* fastening of strands by looping and pulling tight; cluster; small closely knit group; tie, bond; hard lump, esp of wood where branch joins or has joined in; unit of speed used by ships, equal to one nautical mile per hour; difficulty ▷ *vt* **knot•ted, knot•ting** tie with knot, in knots **knot'ty** *adj* **-ti•er, -ti•est** full of knots; puzzling, difficult **knot'hole** [-hohl] *n* hole in wood where knot has been

know [noh] *v* **knew, known, know•ing** ▷ *vt* be aware of, have information about, be acquainted with, recognize, have experience, understand ▷ *vi* have information or understanding **know'ing** *adj* cunning, shrewd **know'ing•ly** *adv* shrewdly; deliberately **knowl•edge** [NOL-ij] *n* knowing; what one knows; learning **knowl•edge•a•ble** *adj* intelligent, well-informed **know-how** *n* practical knowledge, experience, aptitude **in the know** informed

knuck•le [nuk-əl] *n* bone at finger joint; knee joint of calf or pig ▷ *vt* **-led, -ling** strike with knuckles **knuckle ball** *baseball* pitch delivered by holding ball by thumb and first joints or tips of first two or three fingers **knuckle-dust•er** *n* metal appliances worn on knuckles to add force to blow, brass knuckles **knuckle down** get down (to work) **knuckle under** yield, submit

knurled [nurld] *adj* serrated; gnarled

ko•a•la [koh-AH-lə] *n* marsupial Aust animal, native bear

kohl *n* powdered antimony used orig in Eastern countries for darkening the eyelids

kohl•ra•bi [kohl-RAH-bee] *n, pl* **-bies** type of cabbage with edible stem

ko•peck [KOH-pek] *n* monetary unit of Russia and Belarus, one hundredth of ruble

Ko•ran [kə-RAN] *n* sacred book of Muslims

ko•sher [KOH-shər] *adj* permitted, clean, good, as of food, etc, conforming to the Jewish dietary law; *inf* legitimate, authentic ▷ *n inf* kosher food ▷ *vt* make (food, etc) kosher

kow•tow *n* former Chinese custom of touching ground with head in respect; submission ▷ *vi* (esp with to) prostrate oneself; be obsequious, fawn on

Kr *chemistry* krypton

Krem'lin *n* central government of Russia and, formerly, the Soviet Union

krill [kril] *n, pl* **krill** small shrimplike marine animal

kryp•ton [KRIP-ton] *n* rare gaseous element, present in atmosphere

ku•dos [KOO-dohz] *n* honor; acclaim

ku•du [KOO-doo] *n* Afr antelope with spiral horns

ku•lak [kuu-LAHK] *n* independent well-to-do Russian peasant of Czarist times

kum•quat [KUM-kwot] *n* small Chinese tree; its round orange fruit

kung fu [kung foo] Chinese martial art combining techniques of judo and karate

Kwan•zaa [KWAHN-zə, -zah] *n* African-American festival held from December 26 through January 1

la see LAH

La chemistry lanthanum

la·bel [LAY-bəl] n slip of paper, metal, etc, fixed to object to give information about it; brief, descriptive phrase or term ▷ vt **-beled, -bel·ing**

la·bi·al [LAY-bee-əl] adj of the lips; pronounced with the lips ▷ n labial consonant

la·bor [LAY-bər] n exertion of body or mind; task; workers collectively; effort, pain, of childbirth or time taken for this ▷ vi work hard; strive; maintain normal motion with difficulty; (esp of ship) to be tossed heavily ▷ vt elaborate; stress to excess **la'bored** adj uttered, done, with difficulty **la'bor·er** one who labors, esp person doing manual work for wages **la·bo·ri·ous** [lə-BOR-ee-əs] adj tedious

lab·o·ra·to·ry [LAB-rə-tor-ee] n place for scientific investigations or for manufacture of chemicals

lab·ra·dor [LAB-rə-dor] n breed of large, smooth-coated retriever dog

lab·y·rinth [LAB-ə-rinth] n network of tortuous passages, maze; inexplicable difficulty; perplexity

lab·y·rin·thine [-RIN-thin] adj

lace [lays] n fine patterned openwork fabric; cord, usu one of pair, to draw edges together, eg to tighten shoes, etc; ornamental braid ▷ vt **laced, lac·ing** fasten with laces; flavor with whiskey, etc **lac'y** adj **lac·i·er, lac·i·est** fine, like lace

lac·er·ate [LAS-ə-rayt] vt **-at·ed, -at·ing** tear, mangle; distress **lac·er·a'tion** n

lach·ry·mal [LAK-rə-məl] adj of tears **lach'ry·ma·to·ry** [-mə-tor-ee] adj causing tears or inflammation of eyes **lach'ry·mose** [-mohs] adj tearful

lack [lak] n deficiency, need ▷ vt need, be short of **lack'lus·ter** adj lacking brilliance or vitality

lack·a·dai·si·cal [lak-ə-DAY-zi-kəl] adj languid, listless; lazy, careless

lack·ey [LAK-ee] n, pl **-eys** servile follower; footman ▷ v **-eyed, -ey·ing** be, or play, the lackey; wait upon

la·con·ic [lə-KON-ik] adj using, expressed in few words; brief, terse; offhand, not caring **la·con'i·cal·ly** adv

lac·quer [LAK-ər] n hard varnish ▷ vt coat with this

la·crosse [lə-KRAWS] n ball game played with long-handled racket, or crosse

lac·tic [LAK-tik] adj of milk **lac'tate** vi **-tat·ed, -tat·ing** secrete milk **lac·ta'tion** n **lac·tose** [-tohs] n white crystalline substance occurring in milk

la·cu·na [lə-KYOO-nə] n, pl **-nae** [-nee] gap, missing part, esp in document or series

lad n boy, young fellow

lad·der [LAD-ər] n frame of two poles connected by crossbars called rungs, used for climbing; flaw in stockings, caused by running of torn stitch

lade [layd] vt **lad·ed**, **lad·ed** or **lad·en**, **lad·ing** load; burden; weigh down **lad·ing** n cargo, freight

la·dle [LAYD-l] n spoon with long handle for large bowl ▷ vt **-dled**, **-dling** serve out liquid with a ladle

la·dy [LAY-dee] n, pl **-dies** female counterpart of gentleman; polite term for a woman; title of some women of rank **la·dy·like** adj gracious; well-mannered **Our Lady** the Virgin Mary **la·dy·fin·ger** n small sponge cake in shape of finger **lady-of-the-night** n, pl **ladies-** prostitute

lag[1] vi **lagged**, **lag·ging** go too slowly, fall behind ▷ n lagging, interval of time between events **lag·gard** [-ərd] n one who lags **lag·ging** adj loitering, slow

lag[2] vt **lagged**, **lag·ging** wrap boiler, pipes, etc with insulating material **lagging** n this material

la·ger [LAH-gər] n a light-bodied type of beer ▷ vt age (beer) by storing in tanks

la·goon [lə-GOON] n saltwater lake, enclosed by atoll, or separated by sandbank from sea

lah, la n sixth sol-fa note

la·ic [LAY-ik] adj secular, lay **la·i·cize** [-sīz] vt **-cized**, **-ciz·ing** render secular or lay

laid [layd] pt/pp of LAY **laid-back** adj inf relaxed

lain [layn] pp of LIE

lair n resting place, den of animal

lais·sez faire [les-ay FAIR] n principle of nonintervention, esp by government in commercial affairs; indifference

la·i·ty [LAY-i-tee] n lay worshipers, the people as opposed to clergy

lake [layk] n expanse of inland water

lam n sl hasty escape ▷ vi sl **lammed**, **lam·ming** run away fast; escape **on the lam** sl escaping; hiding esp from police

Lam. Lamentations

la·ma [LAH-mə] n Buddhist priest in Tibet or Mongolia **la·ma·ser·y** n monastery of lamas

lamb [lam] n young of the sheep; its meat; innocent or helpless creature ▷ vi (of sheep); give birth to lamb **lamb'like** adj meek, gentle

lam·baste [lam-BAYST] vt **-bast·ed**, **-bast·ing** beat, reprimand

lam·bent [LAM-bənt] adj (of flame) flickering softly; glowing

lame [laym] adj **lam·er**, **lam·est** crippled in a limb, esp leg; limping; (of excuse, etc) unconvincing ▷ vt **lamed**, **lam·ing** cripple **lame duck** official serving out term of office while waiting for elected successor to assume office; disabled, weak person or thing

la·mé [la-MAY] n, adj (fabric) interwoven with gold or silver thread

la·ment [lə-MENT] v feel, express sorrow (for) ▷ n passionate expression of grief; song of grief **lam·en·ta·ble** [LAM-] adj deplorable **lam·en·ta·tion** n

lam·i·na [LAM-ə-nə] n, pl **-nas** thin plate, scale, flake **lam'i·nate** [-nayt] v **-nat·ed**, **-nat·ing** make (sheet of material) by bonding together two or more thin sheets; split, beat, form into thin sheets; cover with thin sheet of material ▷ n [-nit] laminated sheet **lam·i·na'tion** n

lamp n any of various; appliances (esp electrical) that produce light, heat, radiation, etc; formerly, vessel holding oil burned by wick for lighting **lamp'black** n pigment made from soot **lamp'light** n **lamp'post** n post supporting lamp in street

lam·poon [LAM-] n satire ridiculing person, literary work, etc ▷ vt satirize, ridicule **lam·poon'ist** n

lam·prey [LAM-pree] n, pl **-preys** fish like an eel with a round sucking mouth

lance [lans] n horseman's spear ▷ vt **lanced, lanc·ing** pierce with lance or lancet **lan'ce·o·late** [-see-ò-layt] adj lance-shaped, tapering **lanc'er** n formerly, cavalry soldier armed with lance **lan'cet** [-sit] n pointed two-edged surgical lance

land n solid part of Earth's surface; ground, soil; country; property consisting of land ▷ pl estates ▷ vi come to land, disembark; bring an aircraft from air to land or water; alight, step down; arrive on ground ▷ vt bring to land; come or bring to some point or condition; inf obtain; catch **land'ed** adj possessing, consisting of lands **land'ing** n act of landing; platform between flights of stairs **land'fall** n ship's approach to land at end of voyage **land'locked** adj enclosed by land **land'lord, -la·dy** n person who lets land or houses, etc; owner of apartment house, etc **land'lub·ber** n person ignorant of the sea and ships **land'mark** n boundary mark, conspicuous object, as guide for direction, etc; event, decision, etc considered as important stage in development of something **land'scape** n piece of inland scenery; picture of it; prospect ▷ vt **-scaped, -scap·ing** create, arrange, garden, park, etc **landscape gardener** n person who designs gardens or parks so that they

look attractive **land'slide** n falling of soil, rock, etc down mountainside; overwhelming electoral victory

lane [layn] n narrow road or street; specified route followed by shipping or aircraft; area of road for one stream of traffic

lan·guage [LANG-gwij] n system of sounds, symbols, etc for communicating thought; specialized vocabulary used by a particular group; style of speech or expression; system of words and symbols for computer programming

lan·guish [LANG-gwish] vi be or become weak or faint; be in depressing or painful conditions; droop, pine **lan'guid** adj lacking energy, interest; spiritless, dull **lan'guor** [-gòr] n want of energy or interest; faintness; tender mood; softness of atmosphere **lan'guor·ous** adj

lank [langk] adj lean and tall; straight and limp **lank'y** adj **lank·i·er, lank·i·est**

lan·o·lin [LAN-l-in] n grease from wool used in ointments, etc

lan·tern [LAN-tòrn] n transparent case for lamp or candle; erection on dome or roof to let out smoke, admit light

lan·tha·num [LAN-thò-nòm] n silvery-white ductile metallic element

lan·yard [LAN-yòrd] n short cord for securing knife or whistle; short nautical rope; cord for firing cannon

lap¹ n the part between waist and knees of a person when sitting; fig place where anything lies securely; single circuit of racetrack, track; stage or part of journey; single turn of wound thread, etc ▷ vt **lapped, lap·ping** enfold, wrap around; overtake opponent to be one or more circuits ahead **lap dog** n small pet dog **lap'top** adj (of a computer) small and light enough to be held on the user's lap ▷ n such a computer

lap² vt **lapped, lap·ping** drink by scooping up with tongue; (of waves, etc) beat softly

la·pel [lə-PEL] n part of front of a jacket or coat folded back toward shoulders

lap·i·dar·y [LAP-i-der-ee] adj of stones; engraved on stone; exhibiting extreme refinement; concise and dignified ▷ n, pl **-dar·ies** cutter, engraver of stones

lap·is laz·u·li [LAP-is LAZ-uu-lee] bright blue stone or pigment

lapse [laps] n fall (in standard, condition, virtue, etc); slip; mistake; passing (of time, etc) ▷ vi lapsed, **laps·ing** fall away; end, esp through disuse

lar·board [LAHR-bord] n, adj old term for port (side of ship)

lar·ce·ny [LAHR-sə-nee] n, pl **-nies** theft

lard [lahrd] n prepared pig fat ▷ vt insert strips of bacon in (meat); interperse, decorate (speech with strange words, etc)

lar·der [LAHR-dər] n storeroom for food

large [lahrj] adj **larg·er, larg·est** broad in range or area; great in size, number, etc; liberal; generous ▷ n in a big way **large'ly** adv **larg·gess', lar·gesse'** n bounty; gift; donation **at large** free, not confined; in general; fully

lar·go [LAHR-goh] adv music slow and dignified

lar·i·at [LAR-ee-ət] n lasso

lark¹ [lahrk] n small brown songbird, skylark

lark² n frolic, spree ▷ vi indulge in lark

lar·va [LAHR-və] n, pl **-vae** [-vee] insect in immature but active stage **lar'val** adj

lar·ynx [LAR-ingks] n, pl **-es** part of throat containing vocal cords **lar·yn·gi·tis** [-ji-tis] n inflammation of this

la·sa·gne [lə-ZAHN-yə] n pasta formed in wide, flat sheets; baked dish of this with meat, cheese, tomato sauce, etc

las·civ·i·ous [lə-SIV-ee-əs] adj lustful

la·ser [LAY-zər] n device for concentrating electromagnetic radiation or light of mixed frequencies into an intense, narrow, concentrated beam

lash¹ n stroke with whip; flexible part of whip; eyelash ▷ vt strike with whip, thong, etc; dash against (as waves); attack verbally, ridicule; flick, wave sharply to and fro ▷ vi (with out) hit, kick

lash² vt fasten or bind tightly with cord, etc

las·si·tude [LAS-i-tood] n weariness

las·so [LAS-oh] n, pl **-sos** or **-soes** rope with noose for catching cattle, etc ▷ vt **-soed, -so·ing**

last¹ adj, adv after all others, coming at the end; most recent(ly) ▷ adj only remaining; sup of LATE ▷ n last person or thing **last'ly** adv finally

last² vi continue, hold out, remain alive or unexhausted, endure

last³ n model of foot on which shoes are made, repaired

latch [lach] n fastening for door, consisting of bar, catch for it, and lever to lift it; small lock with spring action ▷ vt fasten with latch **latch'key** [-kee] n

late [layt] adj **lat·er** or **lat·ter, lat·est** or **last** coming after the appointed time; delayed; that was recently but now is not; recently dead; recent in date; of late stage of development ▷ *adv* **late·er, lat·est** after proper time; recently; at, till late hour **late'ly** *adv* not long since

la·tent [LAYT-nt] *adj* existing but not developed; hidden

lat·er·al [LAT-ər-əl] *adj* of, at, from the side **lat'er·al·ly** *adv*

la·tex [LAY-leks] *n* sap or fluid of plants, esp of rubber tree

lath *n, pl* **laths** [lathz] thin strip of wood, or wire mesh **lath'ing** *n*

lathe [layth] *n* machine for turning object while it is being shaped

lath·er [LATH-ər] *n* froth of soap and water; frothy sweat ▷ *v* make frothy; *inf* beat

Lat·in [LAT-n] *n* language of ancient Romans ▷ *adj* of ancient Romans, of, in their language; denoting people speaking a language descended from Latin esp Spanish **La·ti·no** [lə-TEE-noh] *n, pl* **-nos** person of Central or S Amer descent

lat·i·tude [LAT-i-tood] *n* angular distance on meridian reckoned N or S from equator; deviation from a standard; freedom from restriction; scope ▷ *pl* regions

la·trine [lə-TREEN] *n* in army, etc, toilet

lat·ter [LAT-ər] *adj* second of two; later; more recent **lat'ter·ly** *adv*

lat·tice [LAT-is] *n* structure of strips of wood, metal, etc crossing with spaces between; window, gate, so made **lat'ticed** *adj*

laud [lawd] *n* hymn, song, of praise ▷ *vt* **laud'a·ble** praiseworthy **laud'a·bly** *adv* **laud'a·to·ry** [-tor-ee] *adj* expressing, containing, praise

lau·da·num [LAWD-n-əm] *n*

tincture of opium

laugh [laf] *vi* make sounds instinctively expressing amusement, merriment, or scorn ▷ *n* **laugh'a·ble** *adj* ludicrous **laugh'a·bly** *adv* **laugh'ter** *n* **laughing gas** nitrous oxide as anesthetic **laughing stock** object of general derision

launch[1] [lawnch] *vt* set afloat; set in motion; start; propel (missile, spacecraft) into space; hurl, send ▷ *vi* enter on course **launch'er** *n* installation, vehicle, device for launching rockets, missiles, etc

launch[2] *n* large engine-driven boat

laun·dry [LAWN-dree] *n, pl* **-dries** place for washing clothes, esp as a business; clothes, etc for washing **laun'der** *vt* wash and iron **laun·der·ette'** *n* self-service laundry with coin-operated washing, drying machines

lau·re·ate [LOR-ee-ət] *adj* crowned with laurels ▷ *n* person honored for achievements **poet laureate** poet honored as most eminent of country or region

lau·rel [LOR-əl] *n* glossy-leaved shrub, bay tree ▷ *pl* its leaves, emblem of victory or merit

la·va [LAH-və] *n* molten matter thrown out by volcanoes, solidifying as it cools

lav·a·to·ry [LAV-ə-tor-ee] *n* **-ries** washroom; toilet

lave [layv] *vt* **laved, lav·ing** wash, bathe

lav·en·der [LAV-ən-dər] *n* shrub with fragrant flowers; color of the flowers, pale lilac

lav·ish *adj* giving or spending profusely; very, too abundant ▷ *vt* spend, bestow, profusely

law *n* rule binding on community; system of such rules; legal science; knowledge, administration of it; *inf* (member of) police force; general principle deduced from facts; invariable sequence of events in nature **law·ful** [-fəl] *adj* allowed by law **law'ful·ly** *adv* **law'less** [-lis] *adj* ignoring laws; violent **law'yer** *n* professional expert in law **law'-a·bid·ing** [-bīd-ing] *adj* obedient to laws; well-behaved **law'giv·er** *n* one who makes laws **law'suit** [-soot] *n* prosecution of claim in court

lawn¹ *n* stretch of carefully tended turf in garden, etc **lawn tennis** tennis played on grass court

lawn² *n* fine linen

lawyer see LAW

lax [laks] *adj* not strict; lacking precision; loose, slack **lax'a·tive** *adj* having loosening effect on bowels ▷ *n* **lax'i·ty, lax'ness** *n* slackness; looseness of (moral) standards

lay¹ *pt* of LIE¹

lay² *vt* **laid, lay·ing** deposit, set, cause to lie **lay'er** *n* single thickness of some substance, as stratum or coating on surface; laying hen; shoot of plant pegged down or partly covered with soil or plastic to encourage root growth ▷ *vt* propagate plants by making layers **lay'down** *n* in bridge, unbeatable hand held by declarer who plays with all cards exposed to view **lay'out** *n* arrangement, esp of matter for printing **lay off** *vt* dismiss employees during slack period **lay'off** *n* **lay on** provide, supply; apply; strike **lay on hands** place hands on person to be cured **lay out** display; expend; prepare for burial; plan copy for printing, etc; *sl* knock out; *sl* criticize severely **lay waste** devastate

lay³ *n* minstrel's song

lay⁴ *adj* not clerical or professional;

of, or done, by persons not clergymen **lay'man, lay'per·son** *n* ordinary person

lay·ette [lay-ET] *n* clothes, etc for newborn child

laz·ar [LAZ-ər] *n* leper

la·zy [LAY-zee] *adj* **-zi·er, -zi·est** averse to work, indolent **laze** *vi* **lazed, laz·ing** indulge in laziness **la'zi·ly** *adv* **la'zi·ness** *n*

lead¹ [leed] *v* **led, lead·ing** ▷ *vt* guide, conduct; persuade; direct; conduct people ▷ *vi* be, go, play first; result; give access to ▷ *n* leading; that which leads or is used to lead; example; front or principal place, role, etc; cable bringing current to electric instrument **lead'er** *n* one who leads; most important or prominent article in newspaper; (also **leading article**) **lead'er·ship** *n* **leading question** question worded to prompt answer desired **lead time** time between design of product and its production

lead² [led] *n* soft heavy gray metal; plummet, used for sounding depths of water; graphite ▷ *vt* **-ed, -ing** cover, weight or space with lead **lead'en** *adj* of, like lead; heavy; dull **go over like a lead balloon** *sl* fail to arouse interest or support

leaf [leef] *n, pl* **leaves** organ of photosynthesis in plants, consisting of a flat, usu green blade on stem; two pages of book, etc; thin sheet; flap, movable part of table, etc ▷ *vt* turn through (pages, etc) cursorily **leaf'less** [-lis] *adj* **leaf'let** [-lit] *n* small leaf; single sheet, often folded, of printed matter for distribution as eg notice or advertisement **leaf'y** *adj* **leaf·i·er, leaf·i·est**

league¹ [leeg] *n* agreement for mutual help; parties to it; federation of teams, etc; *inf* class, level ▷ *vi*

leagued, lea·guing unite in a
league; combine in an association
lea·guer n member of league
league[2] n obs measure of distance,
about three miles

leak [leek] n hole, defect, that
allows escape or entrance of liquid,
gas, radiation, etc; disclosure ▷ vi let
fluid, etc in or out; (of fluid, etc) find
its way through leak ▷ v (allow to)
become known little
by little **leak·age** [-ij] n leaking;
gradual escape or loss **leak'y** adj
leak·i·er, leak·i·est

lean[1] [leen] adj **-er, -est** lacking fat;
thin; meager; (of mixture of fuel and
air) with too little fuel ▷ n lean part
of meat, mainly muscular tissue

lean[2] v leaned, lean·ing rest
against; bend, incline; tend
(toward); depend, rely (on) **leaning**
n tendency **lean-to** n, pl -tos shed
built against tree or post

leap [leep] v leaped or leapt,
leap·ing spring, jump; spring over
▷ n jump **leap'frog** n game in
which players vaults over another
bending down **leap year** year with
February 29th as extra day, occurring
every fourth year

learn [lurn] v learned or learnt,
learn·ing gain skill, knowledge by
study, practice or teaching; gain
knowledge; be taught; find out
learn'ed [LUR-nid] adj erudite,
deeply read; showing much learning
learn'er n **learn'ing** n knowledge
acquired by study

lease [lees] n contract by which
land or property is rented for stated
time by owner to tenant ▷ v
leased, leas·ing let, rent by, take
on lease

leash [leesh] n thong for holding a
dog; curb ▷ vt hold on leash; restrain

least [leest] adj smallest; sup of

LITTLE ▷ n smallest one ▷ adv in
smallest degree

leath·er [LETH-ər] n prepared
skin of animal **leath'er·y** adj like
leather, tough

leave[1] [leev] v left, leav·ing go
away from; deposit; allow to remain;
depart from; entrust; bequeath; go
away, set out

leave[2] n permission; permission to
be absent from work, duty; period of
such absence; formal parting

leav·en [LEV-ən] n yeast; fig
transforming influence ▷ vt raise
with leaven; influence; modify

lech·er [LECH-ər] n man
given to lewdness **lech'er·ous**
adj lewd; provoking lust;
lascivious **lech'er·ous·ly** adv
lech'er·ous·ness n **lech'er·y** n,
pl **-er·ies**

lec·tern [LEK-tərn] n reading desk,
esp in church; stand with slanted top
to hold book, notes, etc

lec·ture [LEK-chər] n instructive
discourse; speech of reproof ▷ v
-tured, -tur·ing ▷ vi deliver
discourse ▷ vt reprove **lec'tur·er** n

ledge [lej] n narrow shelf sticking
out from wall, cliff, etc; ridge, rock
below surface of sea

ledg·er [LEJ-ər] n book of debit and
credit accounts, chief account book
of firm; flat stone **ledger line** music
short line, above or below stave

lee n shelter; side of anything, esp
ship, away from wind **lee'ward**
[-wərd] adj, n (on) lee side ▷ adv
toward this side **lee'way** n leeward
drift of ship; room for free movement
within limits

leech n species of bloodsucking
worm

leek n plant like onion with long
bulb and thick stem

leer vi glance with malign, sly, or

lascivious expression ▷ *n* such glance

lees [leez] *pl n* sediment of wine, etc; dregs

left¹ *adj* denotes the side that faces west when the front faces north; opposite to the right ▷ *n* the left hand or part; *politics* reforming or radical party; (also **left wing**) ▷ *adv* on or toward the left **left'ist** *n, adj* (person) of the political left

left² *pt/pp of* LEAVE

leg *n* one of limbs on which person or animal walks, runs, stands; part of garment covering leg; anything that supports, as leg of table; stage of journey **leg'gings** *pl n* covering of leather or other material for legs **leg'gy** *adj* -**gi•er**, -**gi•est** long-legged; (of plants) straggling **leg'warm•er** *n* one of pair of long knitted footless socks worn over tights when exercising

leg•a•cy [LEG-ə-see] *n, pl* -**cies** anything left by will, bequest; thing handed down to successor

le•gal [LEE-gəl] *adj* of, appointed or permitted by, or based on, law **le•gal'i•ty** *n* **le'gal•ize** *vt* -**ized**, -**iz•ing** make legal

leg•ate [LEG-it] *n* ambassador, esp papal **le•ga'tion** *n* diplomatic minister and staff; headquarters for these

leg•a•tee [leg-ə-TEE] *n* recipient of legacy

le•ga•to [lə-GAH-toh] *adv music* smoothly

leg•end [LEJ-ənd] *n* traditional story or myth; traditional literature; famous, renowned, person or event; inscription **leg'end•ar•y** *adj*

leg•er•de•main [lej-ər-də-MAYN] *n* juggling, conjuring, sleight of hand, trickery

leg•i•ble [LEJ-ə-bəl] *adj* easily read

leg•i•bil•i•ty *n*

le•gion [LEE-jən] *n* body of infantry in Roman army; various modern military bodies; association of veterans; large number **le'gion•ar•y** *adj, n* **le•gion•naires' disease** [-NAIRZ] serious bacterial disease similar to pneumonia

leg•is•la•tor [LEJ-is-lay-tər] *n* maker of laws **leg•is•late** *vi* -**lat•ed**, -**lat•ing** make laws **leg•is•la'tion** *n* act of legislating; law or laws that are made **leg•is•la•tive** *adj* **leg•is•la•ture** [-chər] *n* body that makes laws of a country or state

le•git•i•mate [lə-JIT-ə-mit] *adj* born in wedlock; lawful, regular; fairly deduced **le•git'i•ma•cy** [-mə-see] *n* **le•git'i•mize** *vt* -**mized**, -**miz•ing** make legitimate

le•gu•mi•nous [li-GYOO-mə-nəs] *adj* (of plants) pod-bearing **leg•ume** [LEG-yoom] *n* leguminous plant

lei [lay] *n* garland of flowers

lei•sure [LEE-zhər] *n* freedom from occupation; spare time **lei'sure•ly** *adj* deliberate, unhurried ▷ *adv* slowly **lei'sured** *adj* with plenty of spare time

leit•mo•tif [LĪT-moh-teef] *n music* recurring theme associated with some person, situation, thought

lem•ming [LEM-ing] *n* rodent of northern regions

lem•on [LEM-ən] *n* pale yellow acid fruit; tree bearing it; its color; *inf* useless or defective person or thing **lem•on•ade** [-AYD] *n* drink made from lemon juice

le•mur [LEE-mər] *n* nocturnal animal like monkey

lend *vt* **lent, lend•ing** give temporary use of; let out for hire or interest; give, bestow **lends itself to** is suitable for

length [lengkth] *n* quality of being

long; measurement from end to end;
duration; extent; piece of a certain
length **length·en** v make, become,
longer; draw out **length·i·ly** adv
length·wise adj, adv **length·y** adj
length·i·er, length·i·est (over)long
at length in full detail; at last
le·ni·ent [LEE-nee-ənt] adj mild,
tolerant, not strict **le·ni·en·cy** n
len·i·ty [LEN-i-tee] n, pl **-ties**
mercy; clemency
lens [lenz] n, pl **-es** piece of glass
or similar material with one or
both sides curved, used to converge
or diverge light rays in cameras,
eyeglasses, telescopes, etc
lent pt/pp of **LEND**
Lent n period of fasting from Ash
Wednesday to Easter **Lent**'an adj of,
in, or suitable to Lent
len·til n edible seed of leguminous
plant **len·tic·u·lar** adj like lentil
len·to [LEN-toh] adv music slowly
le·o·nine [LEE-ə-nīn] adj like a lion
leop·ard [LEP-ərd] n large, spotted,
carnivorous animal of cat family,
like panther
le·o·tard [LEE-ə-tahrd] n tight-
fitting garment covering most of
body, worn by acrobats, dancers, etc
lep·er [LEP-ər] n one suffering from
leprosy; person ignored or despised
lep·ro·sy [LEP-rə-see] n disease
attacking nerves and skin resulting
in loss of feeling in affected parts
lep·rous [-rəs] adj
lep·re·chaun [LEP-rə-kawn] n
mischievous elf of Irish folklore
les·bi·an [LEZ-bee-ən] n a
homosexual woman **les·bi·an·ism**
n
lese maj·es·ty [LEEZ] n treason;
taking of liberties
le·sion [LEE-zhən] n injury,
injurious change in texture or action
of an organ of the body

less adj comp of **LITTLE** not so much
▷ n smaller part, quantity; a lesser
amount ▷ adv to a smaller extent
or degree ▷ prep after deducting,
minus **less'en** vt diminish; reduce
less'er adj less; smaller; minor
les·see [le-SEE] n one to whom
lease is granted
les·son [LES-ən] n installment
of instruction; content of this;
experience that teaches; portion of
Scripture read in church
les·sor [LES-or] n grantor of a lease
lest conj in order that not; for
fear that
let[^1] v let, let·ting ▷ vt allow,
enable, cause; allow to escape; grant
use of for rent, lease ▷ vi be leased
▷ v aux used to express a proposal,
command, threat, assumption
let[^2] n in law, obstacle or hindrance;
in tennis, etc, minor infringement,
esp obstruction of ball by net on
service, requiring replaying of point
le·thal [LEE-thəl] adj deadly
leth·ar·gy [LETH-ər-jee] n, pl **-gies**
apathy, want of energy or interest;
unnatural drowsiness **le·thar·gic**
adj **le·thar·gi·cal·ly** adv
let·ter [LET-ər] n alphabetical
symbol; written message; strict
meaning, interpretation ▷ pl
literature, knowledge of books ▷ vt
mark with, in, letters **let'tered** adj
learned **let'ter·press** n process of
printing from raised type; matter
printed in this way
let·tuce [LET-is] n plant grown for
use in salad
leu·co·cyte [LOO-kə-sīt] n one of
white blood corpuscles
leu·ke·mi·a [loo-KEE-mee-ə] n a
progressive blood disease
Lev. Leviticus
lev·ee[^1] n history reception held by
sovereign on rising; reception in

someone's honor

levee² n river embankment, natural or artificial

lev·el [LEV-əl] adj horizontal; even in surface; consistent in style, quality, etc ▷ n horizontal line or surface; instrument for showing, testing horizontal plane; position on scale; standard, grade; horizontal passage in mine ▷ v **-eled, -el·ing** make level; bring to same level; knock down; aim (gun, or, fig accusation, etc); inf (esp with with) be honest, frank **le'vel-head'ed** [-HED-id] adj not apt to be carried away by emotion

lev·er [LEV-ər] n rigid bar pivoted about a fulcrum to transfer a force with mechanical advantage; handle pressed, pulled, etc; to operate something ▷ vt pry, move, with lever **lev'er·age** [-ij] n action, power of lever; influence; power to accomplish something; advantage

le·vi·a·than [lə-VĪ-ə-thən] n sea monster; anything huge or formidable

lev·i·ta·tion [lev-i-TAY-shən] n the power of raising a solid body into the air supernaturally **lev'i·tate** v **-tat·ed, -tat·ing** (cause to) do this

lev·i·ty [LEV-i-tee] n, pl **-ties** inclination to make a joke of serious matters, frivolity; facetiousness

lev·y [LEV-ee] vt **lev·ied, lev·y·ing** impose (tax); raise (troops) ▷ n, pl **lev·ies** imposition or collection of taxes; enrolling of troops; amount, number levied

lewd [lood] adj **-er, -est** lustful; indecent **lewd'ly** adv **lewd'ness** n

lex·i·con [LEK-si-kon] n dictionary **lex·i·cog'ra·pher** [-ə-fər] n writer of dictionaries **lex·i·cog'ra·phy** n

Li chemistry lithium

li·a·ble [Lī-ə-bəl] adj answerable; exposed (to); subject (to); likely (to) **li·a·bil'i·ty** n state of being liable, obligation; hindrance, disadvantage; pl **-ties** debts

li·ai·son [lee-AY-zon] n union; connection; intimacy, esp secret; person who keeps others in touch with one another

li·ar [Lī-ər] n one who tells lies

li·ba·tion [lī-BAY-shən] n drink poured as offering to the gods; facetious drink of whiskey

li·bel [Lī-bəl] n published statement falsely damaging person's reputation ▷ vt **-beled, -bel·ing** defame falsely **li'bel·ous** adj defamatory

lib·er·al [LIB-ər-əl] adj of political party favoring democratic reforms or favoring individual freedom; generous; tolerant; abundant; (of education) designed to develop general cultural interests ▷ n one who has liberal ideas or opinions **lib'er·al·ism** n **lib·er·al'i·ty** n, pl **-ties** munificence **lib'er·al·ize** vt **-ized, -iz·ing**

lib·er·ate [LIB-ə-rayt] vt **-at·ed, -at·ing** set free **lib·er·a'tion** n

lib·er·tar·i·an [lib-ər-TAIR-ee-ən] n believer in freedom of thought, etc, or in free will ▷ adj

lib·er·tine [LIB-ər-teen] n morally dissolute person ▷ adj dissolute

lib·er·ty [LIB-ər-tee] n freedom; pl **-ties** rights, privileges at liberty free; having the right; out of work **take liberties (with)** be presumptuous

li·bi·do [li-BEE-doh] n, pl **-dos** life force; emotional craving, esp of sexual origin **li·bid'i·nous** adj lustful

li·brar·y [Lī-brer-ee] n, pl **-brar·ies** room, building where books are kept; collection of books, phonograph records, etc; reading, writing room in house **li·brar·i·an** n keeper of library

li·bret·to [li-BRET-oh] n, pl **-tos** or **-ti** [-tee] words of an opera **li·bret·tist** n

lice n see **LOUSE**

li·cense [LĪ-sàns] n (document, certificate, giving) leave, permission; excessive liberty; dissoluteness; writer's, artist's intentional transgression of rules of art; (also **poetic license**) **li'cense** vt **-censed, -cens·ing** grant license to **li·cen·see'** n holder of license

li·cen·tious [li-SEN-shàs] adj dissolute; sexually immoral

li·chen [LĪ-kàn] n small flowerless plants forming crust on rocks, trees, etc

lick [lik] vt pass the tongue over; touch lightly; inf defeat; inf flog, beat ▷ n act of licking; small amount (esp of work, etc); block or natural deposit of salt or other chemical licked by cattle, etc **lick'ing** n beating; defeat

lic·o·rice [LIK-àr-ish] n black substance used in medicine and as a candy; plant, its root from which it is obtained

lid n movable cover; cover of the eye; sl hat

lie¹ [lī] vi **lay, lain, ly·ing** be horizontal, at rest; be situated; remain, be in certain state or position; exist, be found; recline ▷ n manner, direction, position in which thing lies; of a golf ball, its position relative to difficulty of hitting it

lie² vi **lied, ly·ing** make false statement knowingly ▷ n deliberate falsehood **li'ar** [-àr] n untruth said without evil intent **give the lie to** disprove

lien [leen] n right to hold another's property until claim is met

lieu [loo] n place **in lieu of** instead of

lieu·ten·ant [loo-TEN-ànt] n deputy; army, marines rank below captain; navy rank below lieutenant commander; police, fire department officer

life [līf] n, pl **lives** active principle of existence of animals and plants, animate existence; time of its lasting; history of such existence; way of living; vigor, vivacity **life'less** [-lis] adj dead; inert; dull **life'long** adj lasting a lifetime **life belt, life jacket** buoyant device to keep afloat person in danger of drowning **life coach** person whose job it is to improve the quality of his or her clients' lives, by offering advice on professional and personal matters **life style** particular attitudes, habits, etc of person or group **life-support** adj of equipment or treatment necessary to keep a person alive **life'time** n length of time person, animal, or object lives or functions

lift vt raise in position, status, mood, volume, etc; take up and remove; exalt spiritually; inf steal ▷ vi rise ▷ n raising apparatus; ride in car, etc, as passenger; force of air acting at right angles on aircraft wing, so lifting it; inf feeling of cheerfulness, uplift

lig·a·ment [LIG-à-mànt] n band of tissue joining bones **lig'a·ture** [-chàr] n anything that binds; thread for tying up blood vessels or for removing tumors

light¹ [līt] adj **-er, -est** of, or bearing, little weight; not severe; gentle; easy, requiring little effort; trivial; (of industry) producing small, usu consumer goods, using light machinery ▷ adv in light manner

▷v **light•ed** or **lit, light•ing** ▷vi
alight (from vehicle, etc); come by
chance (upon) **light'en** vt reduce,
remove (load, etc) **lights** pl n lungs
of animals as food **light'head'ed**
adj dizzy, inclined to faint; delirious
light'heart'ed adj carefree
light'weight n, adj (person) of
little weight or importance; boxer
weighing between 126 and 135
pounds (56.7 to 61 kg)

light² n electromagnetic radiation
by which things are visible; source
of this, lamp; window; light part of
anything; means or act of setting
fire to; understanding ▷pl traffic
lights ▷adj **-er, -est** bright;
pale, not dark ▷v **light•ed** or **lit,
light•ing** set burning; give light to;
take fire; brighten **light'en** vt make
light **light'ing** n apparatus for
supplying artificial light **light'ning**
n visible discharge of electricity
in atmosphere **light'house** n
tower with a light to guide ships
light-year n astronomy distance
light travels in one year, about six
trillion miles

light•er [LĪ-tər] n device for
lighting cigarettes, etc; flat-
bottomed boat for unloading ships

like¹ [lik] adj resembling; similar;
characteristic of ▷adv in the
manner of ▷pron similar thing
like'li•hood [-huud] n probability
like'ly adj **-li•er, -li•est** probable;
hopeful, promising ▷adv probably
lik'en vt compare **like'ness** n
resemblance; portrait **like'wise** adv
in like manner

like² vt find agreeable,
enjoy, love **lik'a•ble** adj **liking** n
fondness; inclination, taste

li•lac [LĪ-lək] n shrub bearing purple
or white flowers; pale reddish purple
▷adj of this color

Lil•li•pu•tian [lil-i-PYOO-shàn] adj
diminutive ▷n very small person

lilt v sing merrily; move lightly ▷n
rhythmical effect in music, swing
lilt'ing adj

lil•y [LIL-ee] n, pl **lil•ies** bulbous
flowering plant **lil-y-white** adj
white; pure, above reproach; of
an organization or community,
forbidding admission to blacks

limb¹ [lim] n arm or leg; wing;
branch of tree

limb² n edge of sun or moon; edge
of sextant

lim•ber¹ [LIM-bàr] n detachable
front of gun carriage

lim•ber² adj pliant, lithe **limber up**
loosen stiff muscles by exercises

lim•bo¹ [LIM-boh] n, pl **-bos**
supposed region intermediate
between heaven and hell for
the unbaptized; intermediate,
indeterminate place or state

lim•bo² n, pl **-bos** West Indian
dance in which dancers pass under
a bar

lime¹ [lim] n any of various calcium
compounds used in making fertilizer,
cement ▷vt treat, limeing
treat (land) with lime **lime'light**
n formerly, intense white light
obtained by heating lime; glare of
publicity **lime'stone** n sedimentary
rock used in building

lime² n small acid fruit like lemon

lim•er•ick [LIM-ər-ik] n self-
contained, nonsensical, humorous
verse of five lines

lim'it n utmost extent or duration;
boundary ▷vt restrict, restrain,
bound **lim•i•ta'tion** n **lim'it•less**
adj

lim•ou•sine [LIM-ə-zeen] n large,
luxurious car

limp¹ adj **-er, -est** without firmness
or stiffness **limp'ly** adv

limp² *vi* walk lamely ▷ *n* limping gait

lim·pid *adj* clear; translucent
lim·pid'i·ty *n*

linch·pin *n* pin to hold wheel on its axle; essential person or thing

line [lin] *n* long narrow mark; stroke made with pen, etc; continuous length without breadth; row; series, course; telephone connection; progeny; province of activity; shipping company; railroad track; any class of goods; cord; string; wire; advice, guidance ▷ *vt* **lined, lin·ing** cover inside; mark with lines; bring into line; be, form border, edge **lin'e·age** [-ee-ij] *n* descent from, descendants of an ancestor **lin'e·al** *adj* of lines; in direct line of descent **lin'e·a·ment** *n* feature of face **lin'e·ar** *adj* of, in lines **lin·er** [LIN-ər] *n* large ship or aircraft of passenger line **line dancing** form of social dancing performed by rows of people to popular music **lines'man** [-mən] *n sport* official who helps referee, umpire **get a line on** obtain all relevant information about

lin·en [LIN-ən] *adj* made of flax ▷ *n* cloth made of flax; linen articles collectively; sheets, tablecloths, etc, or shirts (orig made of linen)

lin·ger [LING-gər] *vi* delay, loiter; remain long

lin·ge·rie [LAHN-zhə-ree] *n* women's underwear or nightwear

lin·go [LING-goh] *n inf* language, speech esp applied to jargon and slang

lin·gua fran·ca [LING-gwə FRANG-kə] *n, pl* **-fran·cas** language used for communication between people of different mother tongues

lin·gual [LING-gwəl] *adj* of the tongue or language ▷ *n* sound made by the tongue, as *d, l, t* **lin'guist** *n*

one skilled in languages or language study **lin·guis'tic** *adj* of languages or their study **lin·guis'tics** *n* study, science of language

lin·i·ment [LIN-ə-mənt] *n* lotion for rubbing on limbs, etc for relieving pain

lin·ing [Lī-ning] *n* covering the inside of garment, etc

link [lingk] *n* ring of a chain; connection; measure, one hundredth part of surveyor's chain ▷ *vt* join with, as with, link; intertwine ▷ *vi* be so joined **link'age** [-ij] *n*

links [lingks] *pl n* golf course, esp one by the sea

li·no·le·um [li-NOH-lee-əm] *n* floor covering of burlap or canvas with smooth, hard, decorative coating of powdered cork, etc

lin'seed *n* seed of flax plant

lint *n* tiny shreds of yarn; bits of thread; soft material for dressing wounds

lin·tel [LIN-tl] *n* top piece of door or window

li·on [Lī-ən] *n* large animal of cat family **li·on·ess** *n fem* **li'on·ize** *vt* **-ized, -iz·ing** treat as celebrity **li'on·heart·ed** *adj* exceptionally brave

lip *n* upper or lower edge of the mouth; edge or margin; *sl* impudence **lip gloss** cosmetic to give lips sheen **lip'read·ing** *n* method of understanding spoken words by interpreting movements of speaker's lips **lip service** insincere tribute or respect **lip'stick** *n* cosmetic preparation, usu in stick form, for coloring lips

lip·o·suc·tion [LIP-oh-suk-shən, LĪP-oh-] *n* cosmetic procedure removing fat from the body by suction

li·queur [li-KUR] *n* alcoholic liquor

flavored and sweetened

liq·uid [LIK-wid] *adj* fluid, not solid or gaseous; flowing smoothly; (of assets) in form of money or easily converted into money ▷ *n* substance in liquid form **liq·ue·fy** [-wə-fī] *v* **-fied, -fy·ing** make or become liquid **li·quid·i·ty** *n* state of being able to meet financial obligations **liquid air, liquefied gas** air, gas reduced to liquid state on application of increased pressure at low temperature

liq·ui·date [LIK-wi-dayt] *vt* **-dat·ed, -dat·ing** pay (debt); arrange affairs of and dissolve (company); wipe out, kill **liq·ui·da'tion** *n* process of clearing up financial affairs; state of being bankrupt **liq'ui·da·tor** *n* official appointed to liquidate business

liq·uor [LIK-ər] *n* liquid, esp an alcoholic one

li·ra [LEER-ə] *n, pl* **-ras** monetary unit of Turkey and (formerly) Italy

lisle [līl] *n* fine hard-twisted cotton thread

lisp *v* speech defect in which *s* and *z* are pronounced *th*; speak falteringly ▷ *n*

lis·some [LIS-əm] *adj* supple, agile

list[1] *n* inventory, register; catalog; edge of cloth, selvage ▷ *n* [l] field for combat ▷ *vt* place on list

list[2] *vi* (of ship) lean to one side ▷ *n* inclination of ship

lis·ten [LIS-ən] *vi* try to hear, attend to **lis'ten·er** *n*

list·less [LIST-lis] *adj* indifferent, languid

lit *pt/pp* of LIGHT

lit·a·ny [LIT-n-ee] *n, pl* **-nies** prayer with responses from congregation; tedious account

li·ter [LEE-tər] *n* measure of volume of fluid, one cubic decimeter, about

---

1.05 quarts

lit·er·al [LIT-ər-əl] *adj* according to sense of actual words, not figurative; exact in wording; of letters

lit·er·ate [LIT-ər-it] *adj* able to read and write; educated ▷ *n* literate person **lit'er·a·cy** *n*

lit·e·ra·ti [-RAH-tee] *pl n* scholarly, literary people

lit·er·a·ture [LIT-ər-ə-chər] *n* books and writings of a country, period or subject **lit'er·ar·y** *adj* of or learned in literature

lithe [līth] *adj* **lith'er, lith·est** supple, pliant **lithe'some** [-səm] *adj* lissome, supple

lith·i·um [LITH-ee-əm] *n* one of the lightest alkaline metallic elements; this substance used in treatment of depression, etc

li·thog·ra·phy [li-THOG-rə-fee] *n* method of printing from metal or stone block using the antipathy of grease and water with **lith'o·graph** *n* print so produced ▷ *vt* print thus **li·thog'ra·pher** *n*

lit·i·gant [LIT-i-gənt] *n, adj* (person) conducting a lawsuit **lit·i·ga'tion** *n* lawsuit

lit·i·gate [LIT-i-gayt] *v* **-gat·ed, -gat·ing** carry on a lawsuit; contest in law ▷ *vi* contest in law ▷ *vt* **li·ti'gious** [-jəs] *adj* given to engaging in lawsuits; disputatious **li·ti'gious·ness** *n*

lit·mus [LIT-məs] *n* blue dye turned red by acids and restored to blue by alkali **litmus paper** paper impregnated with litmus **litmus test** use of litmus paper to test acidity or alkalinity of a solution; any crucial test based on only one factor

lit·ter [LIT-ər] *n* untidy refuse; odds and ends; young of animal produced at one birth; straw, etc as bedding for animals; portable couch; kind of stretcher for wounded ▷ *vt* strew

with litter; bring forth
lit·tle [LIT-l] *adj* small, not much ▷ *n* small quantity ▷ *adv* slightly
lit·to·ral [LIT-ər-əl] *adj* pert to the shore of sea, lake, ocean ▷ *n* littoral region
lit·ur·gy [LIT-ər-jee] *n, pl* **-gies** prescribed form of public worship **li·tur·gi·cal** *adj*
live[1] [liv] *v* have life; pass one's life; continue in life; continue, last; dwell; feed **liv·a·ble** *adj* suitable for living in; tolerable **living** *n* action of being in life; people now alive; way of life; means of living; church benefice
live[2] [liv] *adj* **liv·er, liv·est** living, alive, active, vital; flaming; (of transmission line, etc) carrying electric current; (of broadcast) transmitted during the actual performance **live·ly** *adj* **-li·er, -li·est** brisk, active, vivid **live·li·ness** *n* **liv·en** *vt* (esp with up) make (more) lively **live·stock** *n* domestic animals **live wire** wire carrying electric current; able, very energetic person
live·li·hood [LIV-lee-huud] *n* means of living; subsistence; support
live·long [LIV-lawng] *adj* of a period of time, lasting throughout, esp as though forever
liv·er [LIV-ər] *n* organ secreting bile; animal liver as food **liv·er·ish** *adj* unwell, as from liver upset; cross, touchy, irritable
liv·er·y [LIV-ə-ree] *n, pl* **-er·ies** distinctive dress of person or group, esp servant('s); care, feeding of horses; a livery stable **livery stable** where horses are kept at a charge or hired out
liv·id [LIV-id] *adj* of a bluish pale color; discolored, as by bruising; of reddish color; *inf* angry, furious

liz·ard [LIZ-ərd] *n* four-footed reptile
Lk. Luke
lla·ma [LAH-mə] *n* woolly-haired animal used as beast of burden in S Amer
load [lohd] *n* burden; amount usu carried at once; actual load carried by vehicle; resistance against which engine has to work; amount of electrical energy drawn from a source ▷ *vt* put load on or into; charge (gun); weigh down **load·ed** *adj* carrying a load; (of dice) dishonestly weighted; biased; (of question) containing hidden trap or implication; *sl* wealthy; *sl* drunk
loadstar, -stone *n* see LODE
loaf[1] [lohf] *n, pl* **loaves** mass of bread as baked; shaped mass of food
loaf[2] *vi* idle, loiter **loaf·er** *n* idler
loam [lohm] *n* fertile soil
loan [lohn] *n* act of lending; thing lent; money borrowed at interest; permission to use ▷ *vt* grant loan of
loath, loth [lohth] *adj* unwilling, reluctant (to) **loathe** [lohth] *vt* **loathed, loath·ing** hate, abhor **loathing** [LOHTH-ing] *n* disgust; repulsion **loath·some** [LOHTH-səm] *adj* disgusting
lob [lob] *vt* **lobbed, lob·bing** in tennis, artillery, etc, ball, shell, sent high in air ▷ *v* hit, fire, thus
lob·by [LOB-ee] *n, pl* **-bies** corridor into which rooms open; passage or room adjacent to legislative chamber; group of people who try to influence members of legislature **lob·by·ing** *n* activity of this group **lob·by·ist** *n*
lobe [lohb] *n* any rounded projection; subdivision of body organ; soft, hanging part of ear **lobed** *adj* **lo·bot·o·my** [lə-BOT-ə-mee] *n, pl* **-mies** surgical incision

into lobe of organ, esp brain

lob·ster [LOB-stər] n shellfish with long tail and claws, turning red when boiled

lo·cal [LOH-kəl] adj of, existing in particular place; confined to a definite spot, district or part of the body; of place; (of train) making many stops ▷ n person belonging to a district; local branch of labor union; local train **lo·cale** [loh-KAL] n scene of event **lo·cal·i·ty** n place, situation; district **lo·cal·ize** vt -ized, -iz·ing assign, restrict to definite place **local anesthetic** one that produces insensibility in one part of body

lo·cate [loh-KAYT] vt -cat·ed, -cat·ing attribute to a place; find the place of; situate **lo·ca·tion** n placing; situation; site of film production away from studio

lock¹ [lok] n appliance for fastening door, lid, etc; mechanism for firing gun; enclosure in river or canal for moving boats from one level to another; air lock; appliance to check the motion of a mechanism; interlocking; block, jam ▷ vt fasten, make secure with lock; place in locked container; join firmly; cause to become immovable; embrace closely ▷ vi become fixed or united; become immovable **lock·er** n small closet with lock **lock·down** n security measure in which those inside a building are required to remain confined in it for a time **lock·jaw** n tetanus locked jaw **lock·out** n exclusion of workmen by employers as means of coercion **lock·smith** n one who makes and mends locks **lock·up** n prison

lock² n tress of hair

lock·et [LOK-it] n small hinged pendant for portrait, etc

lo·co·mo·tive [loh-kə-MOH-tiv] n engine for pulling train on railway tracks ▷ adj having power of moving from place to place **lo·co·mo·tion** n action, power of moving

lo·cus [LOH-kəs] n, pl -ci [-sī] exact place or locality; curve made by all points satisfying certain mathematical condition, or by point, line or surface moving under such condition

lo·cust [LOH-kəst] n destructive winged insect; N Amer tree; wood of this tree

lo·cu·tion [loh-KYOO-shən] n a phrase; speech; mode or style of speaking

lode [lohd] n vein of ore **lode·star** n star that shows the way; any guide on which attention is fixed; Polaris **lode·stone** n magnetic iron ore

lodge [loj] n house, cabin used seasonally or occasionally, eg for hunting, skiing; gatekeeper's house; meeting place of branch of certain fraternal organizations; the branch ▷ v lodged, lodg·ing ▷ vt house; deposit; bring (a charge, etc) against someone ▷ vi live in another's house at fixed rent; come to rest (in, on) **lodg·er** n **lodg·ings** pl n rented room(s) in another person's house

loft [lawft] n space between top story and roof; upper story of warehouse, factory, etc typically with large unpartitioned space; gallery in church, etc ▷ vt send (golf ball, etc) high **loft building** building in which all stories have large unobstructed space once used for manufacturing but now usu are converted to residences **loft·i·ly** adv haughtily **loft·i·ness** n **loft·y** adj **loft·i·er, loft·i·est** of great height; elevated; haughty

log¹ [lawg] n portion of felled

tree stripped of branches; detailed record of voyages, time traveled, etc, of ship, aircraft, etc; apparatus used formerly for measuring ship's speed ▷ vt **logged, log·ging** keep a record of time; travel (specified distance, time) **log'ging** n cutting and transporting logs to river **log in, out** v gain entrance to or leave a computer system by keying in a special command

log² n logarithm

log·a·rithm [LAW-gà-rith-àm] n one of series of arithmetical functions tabulated for use in calculation

log·ger·head [LAW-gàr-hed] n **at loggerheads** quarreling, disputing

log·ic [LOJ-ik] n art or philosophy of reasoning; reasoned thought or argument; coherence of various facts, events, etc **log'i·cal** adj of logic; according to reason; reasonable; apt to reason correctly **lo·gi·cian** [loh-JISH-àn] n

lo·gis·tics [loh-JIS-tiks] n the transport, housing and feeding of troops; organization of any project, operation **lo·gis'ti·cal** adj

lo·go [LOH-goh] n, pl -gos company emblem or similar device

loin n part of body between ribs and hip; cut of meat from this ▷ pl hips and lower abdomen **loin'cloth** n garment covering loins only

loi·ter [LOI-tàr] vi dawdle, hang about; idle **loi'ter·er** n

loll [lol] vi sit, lie lazily; hang out ▷ vt allow to hang out

lone [lohn] adj solitary **lone'ly** adj **-li·er, -li·est** sad because alone; unfrequented; solitary, alone **lone'li·ness** n **lon'er** n one who prefers to be alone **lone'some** [-sàm] adj

long¹ [lawng] adj **-er, -est** having

length, esp great length, in space or time; extensive; protracted ▷ adv for a long time **long'hand** n writing in which words are written out in full by hand rather than on typewriter, etc **long'-play'ing** adj (of record) lasting for 10 to 30 minutes because of its fine grooves **long-range** adj of the future; able to travel long distances without refueling; (of weapons) designed to hit distant target **long shot** competitor, undertaking, bet, etc with small chance of success **long ton** 2240 lbs **long'-wind'ed** adj tediously loquacious

long² vi have keen desire, yearn (for) **long'ing** n yearning

lon·gev·i·ty [lon-JEV-i-tee] n long existence or life; length of existence or life; tenure

lon·gi·tude [LON-ji-tood] n distance east or west from prime meridian **lon·gi·tu'di·nal** adj of length or longitude; lengthwise

long·shore·man [LAWNG-SHOR-màn] n dock laborer

look [luuk] vi direct, use eyes; face; seem; search (for); hope (for); (with after) take care of ▷ n looking; view; search ▷ pl appearance **good looks** beauty **look'a·like** n person who is double of another **look'out** n guard; place for watching; watchman; object of worry, concern **look after** tend **look down on** despise

loom¹ n machine for weaving; middle part of oar

loom² vi appear dimly; seem ominously close; assume great importance

loon¹ n Amer fish-eating diving bird

loon² n stupid, foolish person **loon'y** adj **loon·i·er, loon·i·est** ▷ n, pl -nies **loony bin** inf mental hospital or ward

loop n figure made by curved line

crossing itself; similar rounded shape in cord or rope, etc crossed on itself; contraceptive coil; aerial maneuver in which aircraft describes complete circle ▷ v form loop

loop·hole [LOOP-hohl] *n* means of evading rule without infringing it; vertical slit in building wall, esp for defense

loose [loos] *adj* **loos·er, loos·est** not tight, fastened, fixed, or tense; slack; vague; dissolute ▷ v **loosed, loos·ing** ▷ vt free; unfasten; slacken ▷ vi (with *off*) shoot, let fly **loose·ly** *adv* **loos·en** *vt* make loose **loose·ness** *n* **on the loose** free; on a spree

loot *n, vt* plunder

lop¹ *vt* **lopped, lop·ping** cut away twigs and branches; chop off

lop² *vi* **lopped, lop·ping** hang limply **lop'-eared** *adj* having drooping ears **lop'sid·ed** *adj* with one side lower than the other; badly balanced

lope [lohp] *vi* **loped, lop·ing** run with long, easy strides

lo·qua·cious [loh-KWAY-shəs] *adj* talkative **lo·quac·i·ty** [-KWAS-ə-tee] *n*

lord *n* British nobleman, peer of the realm; feudal superior; one ruling others; owner; (**L-**) God ▷ vi domineer **lord'li·ness** *n* **lord'ly** *adj* **-li·er, -li·est** imperious, proud; fit for a lord **lord'ship** *n* rule, ownership; domain; title of some noblemen

lore [lor] *n* learning; body of facts and traditions

lor·gnette [lorn-YET] *n* pair of eyeglasses mounted on long handle

lorn *adj poet* abandoned; desolate

lose [looz] *v* **lost, los·ing** ▷ vt be deprived of, fail to retain or use; let slip; fail to get; (of clock, etc) run slow (by specified amount); be defeated in ▷ vi suffer loss **loss** [laws] *n* a losing; what is lost; harm or damage resulting from losing **lost** *adj* unable to be found; unable to find one's way; bewildered; not won; not utilized

lot *n* great number; collection; large quantity; share; fate; destiny; item at auction; one of a set of objects used to decide something by chance, as in **to cast lots**; area of land ▷ *pl* great numbers or quantity ▷ *adv* a great deal

loth see **LOATH**

lo·tion [LOH-shən] *n* liquid for washing to reduce itching, etc, improving skin, etc

lot·ter·y [LOT-ə-ree] *n, pl* **-ter·ies** method of raising funds by selling tickets and prizes by chance; any gamble

lot·to [LOT-oh] *n* game of chance like bingo

lo·tus [LOH-təs] *n, pl* **-tus·es** legendary plant whose fruits induce forgetfulness when eaten; Egyptian water lily **lotus position** seated cross-legged position used in yoga, etc

loud [lowd] *adj* **-er, -est** strongly audible; noisy; obtrusive **loud'ly** *adv* **loud'speak·er** *n* instrument for converting electrical signals into sound audible at a distance

lounge [lownj] *vi* **lounged, loung·ing** sit, lie, walk, or stand in a relaxed manner ▷ *n* general waiting, relaxing area in airport, hotel, etc; bar **loung·er** *n* loafer

louse [lows] *n, pl* **lice** a parasitic insect **lous'y** *adj inf* **lous·i·er, lous·i·est** nasty, unpleasant; *sl* (too) generously provided, thickly populated (with); bad; poor; having lice

lout [lowt] *n* crude, oafish person **lout'ish** *adj*

lou·ver [LOO-vər] *n* one of a set of boards or slats set parallel and slanted to admit air but not rain or sunlight; ventilating structure of these

love [luv] *n* warm affection; benevolence; charity; sexual passion; sweetheart; tennis, *etc* score of zero ▷ *v* **loved, lov·ing** ▷ *vt* admire passionately; delight in ▷ *vi* be in love **lov'a·ble** *adj* **love'less** [-lis] *adj* **love'lorn** *adj* forsaken by, pining for a lover **love'li·ness** *n* **love'ly** *adj* **-li·er, -li·est** beautiful, delightful **lov·ing** *adj* affectionate; tender **lov'ing·ly** *adv* **loving cup** formerly passed around at banquet; large cup given as prize **make love (to)** have sexual intercourse (with)

low¹ [loh] *adj* **-er, -est** not tall, high or elevated; humble; commonplace; coarse, vulgar; dejected; ill; not loud; moderate; cheap **low'er** *vt* cause, allow to descend; move down; diminish, degrade ▷ *adj* below in position or rank; at an early stage, period of development **low'li·ness** *n* **low'ly** *adj* **-li·er, -li·est** modest, humble **low'brow** *n* person with no intellectual or cultural interests ▷ *adj* **low'down** *n inf* inside information ▷ *adj* mean, shabby, dishonorable **low frequency** in electricity any frequency of alternating current from about 30 to 300 kilohertz; frequency within audible range **low-key** [-kee] *adj* subdued, restrained, not intense **low'land** *n* low-lying land **low-ten·sion** *adj* carrying, operating at low voltage

low² *vi* of cattle, utter their cry, bellow ▷ *n* cry of cattle, bellow

low·er [LOW-ər] *vi* look gloomy or threatening, as sky; scowl ▷ *n* scowl, frown

loy·al [LOI-əl] *adj* faithful, true to allegiance **loy'al·ly** *adv* **loy'al·ty** *n*

loz·enge [LOZ-inj] *n* small candy or tablet of medicine; rhombus, diamond figure

Lr *chemistry* lawrencium

LSD lysergic acid diethylamide (hallucinogenic drug)

Lu *chemistry* lutetium

lub·ber [LUB-ər] *n* clumsy fellow; unskilled seaman

lu·bri·cate [LOO-bri-kayt] *vt* **-cat·ed, -cat·ing** oil, grease; make slippery **lu'bri·cant** [-kənt] *n* substance used for this **lu·bri·ca'tion** [-KAY-shən] *n* **lu·bric'i·ty** [-BRIS-i-tee] *n, pl* **-ties** slipperiness, smoothness; lewdness

lu·cid [LOO-sid] *adj* clear; easily understood; sane **lu·cid'i·ty** *n*

Lu·ci·fer [LOO-sə-fər] *n* Satan

luck [luk] *n* fortune, good or bad; good fortune; chance **luck'i·ly** *adv* fortunately **luck'less** *adj* having bad luck **luck'y** *adj* **luck·i·er, luck·i·est** having good luck

lu·cre [LOO-kər] *n* money, wealth **lu'cra·tive** [-krə-tiv] *adj* very profitable **filthy lucre** *inf* money

lu·di·crous [LOO-di-krəs] *adj* absurd, laughable, ridiculous

lug¹ *v* **lugged, lug·ging** ▷ *vt* drag with effort ▷ *vi* pull hard

lug² *n* projection, tag serving as handle or support; *sl* fellow, blockhead

lug·gage [LUG-ij] *n* traveler's suitcases and other baggage

lu·gu·bri·ous [luu-GOO-bree-əs] *adj* mournful, doleful, gloomy **lu·gu'bri·ous·ly** *adv*

luke·warm [look-worm] *adj* moderately warm, tepid; indifferent

lull *vt* soothe, sing to sleep; make quiet ▷ *vi* become quiet, subside ▷ *n* brief time of quiet in storm, *etc*

lull'a·by [LUL-ə-bie] n, pl -bies lulling song, esp for children

lum·bar [LUM-bahr] adj relating to body between lower ribs and hips **lum·ba'go** [-BAY-goh] n rheumatism in lower part of the back

lum·ber [LUM-bər] n sawn timber; disused articles, useless rubbish ▷vi move heavily ▷vt convert (a number of trees) into lumber; burden with something unpleasant **lum'ber·jack** n logger

lu·men [LOO-mən] n, pl -mi·na [-mə-nə] SI unit of luminous flux

lu·mi·nous [LOO-mə-nəs] adj bright; shedding light; glowing; lucid **lu'mi·nar·y** [-ner-ee] n learned person; prominent person; heavenly body giving light **lu·mi·nes'cence** [-NES-əns] n emission of light at low temperatures by process (eg chemical) not involving burning **lu·mi·nos'i·ty** n

lump n shapeless piece or mass; swelling; large sum ▷vt throw together in one mass or sum ▷vi move heavily **lump'ish** adj clumsy; stupid **lump'y** adj **lump·i·er, lump·i·est** full of lumps; uneven **lump it** inf put up with; accept and endure

lu·nar [LOO-nər] adj relating to the moon

lu·na·tic [LOO-nə-tik] adj insane ▷n insane person **lu'na·cy** n, pl -cies lunatic fringe extreme, radical section of group, etc

lunch n meal taken in the middle of the day ▷v eat, entertain at lunch **lunch'eon** [-ən] n a lunch

lung n one of the two organs of respiration in vertebrates **lung'fish** n type of fish with air-breathing lung

lunge [lunj] vi **lunged, lung·ing** thrust with sword, etc ▷n such thrust; sudden movement of body, plunge

lu·pine¹ [LOO-pin] n leguminous plant with tall spikes of flowers

lu·pine² [LOO-pīn] adj like a wolf

lu·pus [LOO-pəs] n skin disease

lurch n sudden roll to one side ▷vi stagger **leave in the lurch** leave in difficulties

lure [luur] n something that entices; bait; power to attract ▷vt **lured, lur·ing** entice; attract

lu·rid [LUUR-id] adj vivid in shocking detail, sensational; pale, wan; lit with unnatural glare

lurk vi lie hidden **lurk'ing** adj (of suspicion) not definite

lus·cious [LUSH-əs] adj sweet, juicy; extremely pleasurable or attractive

lush¹ -er, -est (of grass, etc) luxuriant and juicy, fresh

lush² n sl heavy drinker; alcoholic

lust n strong desire for sexual gratification; any strong desire ▷vi have passionate desire **lust** [-fəl] **lust'i·ly** adv **lust'y** adj **lust·i·er, lust·i·est** vigorous, healthy

lus·ter [LUST-ər] n gloss, sheen; splendor; renown; glory; glossy material; metallic pottery glaze **lus'trous** [-trəs] adj shining, luminous

lute [loot] n old stringed musical instrument played with the fingers **lute·nist** n

lux [luks] n, pl **lu·ces** [LOO-seez] SI unit of illumination

lux·u·ry [LUK-shə-ree] n, pl -ries possession and use of costly, choice things for enjoyment; enjoyable but not necessary thing; comfortable surroundings **lux·u·ri·ance** [lug-ZHUUR-ee-əns] n abundance, proliferation **lux·u·ri·ant** adj growing thickly;

abundant **lux·u·ri·ate** [-ayt] vi -at·ed, -at·ing indulge in luxury; flourish profusely; take delight (in) **lux·u·ri·ous** adj fond of luxury; self-indulgent; sumptuous

ly·ce·um [lī-SEE-əm] n institution for popular education eg concerts, lectures; public building for this purpose

lye [lī] n water made alkaline with wood ashes, etc for washing

lying pr p of LIE

lymph [limf] n colorless bodily fluid, mainly of white blood cells **lym·phat·ic** adj of lymph; flabby,

sluggish ▷ n vessel in the body conveying lymph

lynch [linch] vt put to death without trial **lynch law** procedure of self-appointed court trying and punishing esp executing accused

lynx [lingks] n animal of cat family

lyre [līr] n instrument like harp

lyr·ic [LIR-ik] **lyr·i·cal** adj of short personal poems expressing emotion; of lyre; meant to be sung **lyric** n lyric poem ▷ pl words of popular song **lyr·i·cist** [-sist] n writer of lyrics; lyric poet **wax lyrical** express great enthusiasm

m

ma·ca·bre [mə-KAH-brə] adj gruesome, ghastly

mac·ad·am [mə-KAD-əm] n road surface made of pressed layers of small broken stones; this stone

mac·a·roon [mak-ə-ROON] n small cookie made of egg whites, almond paste, etc

ma·caw [mə-KAW] n kind of parrot

mace [mays] n spice made of the husk of the nutmeg

Mace ® [mays] n liquid causing tears and nausea, used as spray for riot control

mac·er·ate [MAS-ə-rayt] vt **-at·ed, -at·ing** soften by soaking; cause to waste away

mach (number) [mahk] n the ratio of the air speed of an aircraft to the velocity of sound under given conditions

ma·chet·e [mə-SHET-ee] n broad, heavy knife used for cutting or as a weapon

Mach·i·a·vel·li·an [makee-ə-VEL-ə-ən] adj politically unprincipled, crafty, perfidious, subtle

mach·i·na·tion [mak-ə-NAY-shən] n (usu pl) plotting, intrigue

ma·chine [mə-SHEEN] n apparatus combining action of several parts to apply mechanical force; controlling organization; mechanical appliance; vehicle ▷ vt **-chined, -chin·ing** sew, print, shape, etc with machine **ma·chin·er·y** n, pl **-er·ies** parts of machine collectively; machines **ma·chin·ist** n one who makes or operates machines

ma·chis·mo [mah-CHEEZ-moh] n strong or exaggerated masculine pride or masculinity **ma·cho** [-choh] adj denoting or exhibiting such pride in masculinity ▷ n, pl **-chos** person exhibiting this

mack·er·el [MAK-ər-əl] n edible sea fish with blue and silver stripes

mac·ra·mé [MAK-rə-may] n ornamental webbing of knotted cord

mac·ro·bi·ot·ics [mak-roh-bi-OT-iks] n (with sing v) dietary system advocating grain and vegetables grown without chemical additives **mac·ro·bi·ot·ic** adj, n (relating to the diet of) person practicing macrobiotics

mac·ro·cosm [MAK-rə-koz-əm] n the universe; any large, complete system

mad adj **-der, -dest** suffering from mental disease, insane; wildly foolish; very enthusiastic (about); excited; furious, angry **mad'den** vt make mad **mad'ly** adv **mad'man** n **mad'ness** n insanity; folly

mad·am [MAD-əm] n polite form of address to a woman; woman in charge of house; woman in charge of house of prostitution

made pt/pp of MAKE

Ma·don·na [mə-DON-ə] n the Virgin Mary; picture or statue of her

mad·ri·gal [MAD-ri-gəl] n unaccompanied part song; short love poem or song

mael•strom [MAYL-strəm] n great whirlpool; turmoil

ma•es•to•so [mi-STOH-soh] adv music grandly, in majestic manner

maes•tro [Mī-stroh] n outstanding musician, conductor; man regarded as master of any art

Ma•fi•a [MAH-fee-ə] n international secret organization engaging in crime, orig Italian

mag•a•zine [mag-ə-ZEEN] n periodical publication with stories and articles by different writers; appliance for supplying cartridges automatically to gun; storehouse for explosives or arms

ma•gen•ta [mə-JEN-tə] adj, n (of) purplish-red color

mag•got [MAG-ət] n grub, larva of certain flies **mag′got•y** adj infested with maggots

Ma•gi [MAY-jī] pl n priests of ancient Persia; the wise men from the East at the Nativity

mag•ic [MAJ-ik] n art of supposedly invoking supernatural powers to influence events, etc; any mysterious agency or power; witchcraft; conjuring ▷ adj **mag′i•cal** adj **ma•gi′cian** n one skilled in magic, wizard, conjurer, enchanter

mag•is•trate [MAJ-ə-strayt] n civil officer administering law; justice of the peace **mag•is•te•ri•al** [-STEER-ee-əl] adj of, referring to magistrate; authoritative; weighty **mag′is•tra•cy** [-strə-see] n, pl **-cies** office of magistrate; magistrates collectively

mag•ma [MAG-mə] n paste, suspension; molten rock inside Earth's crust

mag•nan•i•mous [mag-NAN-ə-məs] adj noble, generous, not petty **mag•na•nim′i•ty** n

mag•nate [MAG-nayt] n influential or wealthy person

mag•ne•si•um [mag-NEE-zee-əm] n metallic element **mag•ne′sia** [-zhə] n white powder compound of this used in medicine

mag•net [MAG-nit] n piece of iron, steel having properties of attracting iron, steel and pointing north and south when suspended; lodestone **mag•net′ic** adj with properties of magnet; exerting powerful attraction **mag•net′i•cal•ly** adv **mag′net•ism** [-ni-tiz-əm] n magnetic phenomena; science of this; personal charm or power of attracting others **mag′net•ize** vt **-ized, -iz•ing** make into a magnet; attract as if by magnet; fascinate **mag•ne′to** [-NEE-toh] n, pl **-tos** apparatus for ignition in internal combustion engine

mag•nif•i•cent [mag-NIF-ə-sənt] adj splendid; stately, imposing; excellent **mag•nif′i•cence** n

mag•ni•fy [MAG-nə-fī] v **-fied, -fy•ing** increase apparent size of, as with lens; exaggerate; make greater **mag•ni•fi•ca′tion** [-KAY-shən] n

mag•nil•o•quent [mag-NIL-ə-kwənt] adj speaking pompously; grandiose **mag•nil′o•quence** n

mag•ni•tude [MAG-ni-tood] n importance; greatness; size

mag•num [MAG-nəm] n large wine bottle (approx 1.6 quarts, 1.5 liters)

mag•pie [MAG-pī] n black-and-white bird; incessantly talkative person

ma•ha•ra•jah [mah-hə-RAH-jə] n former title of some Indian princes

ma•ha•ri•shi [mah-hə-REE-shee] n Hindu religious teacher or mystic

ma•hat•ma [mə-HAHT-mə] n Hinduism man of saintly life with supernatural powers; one endowed with great wisdom and power

mahl·stick [MAHL-stik] *n* light stick with ball at one end, held in other hand to support working hand while painting

maid·en [MAYD-n] *n lit* young unmarried woman ▷ *adj* unmarried; of, suited to maiden; first; having blank record **maid**·n woman servant; *lit* young unmarried woman **maid'en·ly** *adj* modest **maid'en·hair** *n* fern with delicate stalks and fronds **maid'en·head** *n* virginity **maiden name** woman's surname before marriage

mail¹ [mayl] *n* letters, etc transported and delivered by the post office; letters, etc conveyed at one time; the postal system; train, ship, etc carrying mail; same as **E-MAIL** ▷ *vt* send by mail **mail'box** *n* (on a computer) the directory in which e-mail messages are stored

mail² *n* armor of interlaced rings or overlapping plates **mailed** *adj* covered with mail

maim [maym] *vt* cripple, mutilate

main [mayn] *adj* chief, principal, leading ▷ *n* principal pipe, line carrying water, gas, etc; chief part; strength, power; *obs* open sea **main'ly** *adv* for the most part, chiefly **main'frame** *computing adj* denoting a high-speed general-purpose computer ▷ *n* such a computer **main'land** *n* stretch of land that forms main part of a country **main'mast** *n* chief mast in ship **main'sail** *n* lowest sail of mainmast **main'spring** *n* chief spring of watch or clock; chief cause or motive **main'stay** *n* rope from mainmast; chief support

main·tain [mayn-TAYN] *vt* carry on; preserve; support; sustain; keep up; keep supplied; affirm; support by argument; defend **main'te·nance** [-tə-nəns] *n* maintaining; means of support; upkeep of buildings, etc; provision of money for separated or divorced spouse

maî·tre d'hô·tel [may-tàr doh-TEL] *n, pl* **maî·tres** [-tàrz] headwaiter, owner, or manager of hotel

maize [mayz] *n* primitive corn with kernels of various colors, Indian corn

maj·es·ty [MAJ-ə-stee] *n* stateliness; sovereignty; grandeur **ma·jes·tic** [mə-] *adj* splendid; regal **ma·jes·ti·cal·ly** *adv*

ma·jor [MAY-jər] *n* military officer ranking next above captain; scale in music; principal field of study at college; person engaged in this ▷ *adj* greater in number, quality, extent; significant, serious **ma·jor'i·ty** *n* greater number; larger party voting together; more than half of votes cast in election; coming of age; rank of major **major-do·mo** [-DOH-moh] *n, pl* **-mos** male servant in charge of large household

make [mayk] *v* **made**, **mak·ing** construct; produce; create; establish; appoint; amount to; cause to do something; accomplish; reach; earn; tend; contribute ▷ *n* brand, type, or style **making** *n* creation ▷ *pl* necessary requirements or qualities **make allowance for** take mitigating circumstance into consideration **make'shift** *n* temporary expedient **make'up** *n* cosmetics; characteristics; layout **make up** compose; compile; complete; compensate; apply cosmetics; invent **on the make** *inf* intent on gain; *sl* seeking sexual relations

mal- *comb form* ill, badly:

malformation; malevolent

ma·lac·ca [mə-LAK-ə] n brown cane used for walking stick

mal·a·droit [mal-ə-DROIT] adj clumsy, awkward

mal·a·dy [MAL-ə-dee] n, pl -dies disease

ma·laise [ma-LAYZ] n vague, unlocated feeling of bodily discomfort

mal·a·prop·ism [MAL-ə-prop-iz-əm] n ludicrous misuse of word

ma·lar·i·a [mə-LAIR-ee-ə] n infectious disease caused by parasite transmitted by bite of some mosquitoes **ma·lar·i·al** adj

mal·con·tent [mal-kən-TENT] adj actively discontented ▷ n malcontent person

male [mayl] adj of sex producing gametes that fertilize female gametes; of men or male animals; of machine part, made to fit inside corresponding recessed female part ▷ n male person or animal

mal·e·dic·tion [mal-i-DIK-shən] n curse

mal·e·fac·tor [MAL-ə-fak-tər] n criminal

ma·lev·o·lent [mə-LEV-ə-lənt] adj full of ill will **ma·lev·o·lence** n

mal·fea·sance [mal-FEE-zəns] n illegal action; official misconduct

mal·ice [MAL-is] n ill will; spite **ma·li·cious** [mə-LISH-əs] adj intending evil or unkindness; spiteful; moved by hatred

ma·lign [mə-LìN] adj evil in influence or effect ▷ vt slander, misrepresent **ma·lig·nan·cy** [-LIG-nən-see] n **ma·lig·nant** adj feeling extreme ill will; (of disease) resistant to therapy; tending to produce death **ma·lig·ni·ty** n malignant disposition

ma·lin·ger [mə-LING-gər] vi feign

illness to escape duty **ma·lin·ger·er** n

mall [mawl] n level, shaded walk; street, shopping area closed to vehicles

mal·le·a·ble [MAL-ee-ə-bəl] adj capable of being hammered into shape; adaptable

mal·let [MAL-it] n (wooden, etc) hammer; croquet or polo stick

mal·nu·tri·tion [mal-noo-TRISH-ən] n inadequate nutrition

mal·o·dor·ous [mal-OH-dər-əs] adj evil-smelling

mal·prac·tice [mal-PRAK-tis] n immoral, careless illegal or unethical conduct

malt [mawlt] n grain used for brewing or distilling ▷ vt make into malt

mal·ware [MAL-wair] n computer program designed to damage or disrupt a system

mam·bo [MAHM-boh] n, pl -bos Latin Amer dance like rumba

mam·mal [MAM-əl] n animal of type that suckles its young **mam·ma·li·an** [-MAY-lee-ən] adj

mam·ma·ry [MAM-ər-ee] adj of, relating to breast or milk-producing gland

mam·mon [MAM-ən] n wealth regarded as source of evil; **(M-)** false god of covetousness

mam·moth [MAM-əth] n extinct animal like an elephant ▷ adj colossal

man n, pl **men** human being; person; human race; adult male; manservant; piece used in chess, etc ▷ vt **manned, man·ning** supply (ship, artillery, etc) with necessary crew; fortify **man'ful** adj brave, vigorous **man'li·ness** n **man'ly** -li·er, -li·est **man'nish** adj like a man **man'han·dle** vt -dled, -dling treat roughly **man·hole** n opening through which person can pass to a drain, sewer, etc **man·hood** [-huud] n **man·kind** [-KĪND] n human beings in general **man·pow·er** n power of human effort; available number of workers **man·slaugh·ter** [-slaw-tər] n culpable homicide without malice aforethought

man·a·cle [MAN-ə-kəl] n fetter, handcuff ▷ vt **-cled, -cling** shackle

man·age [MAN-ij] vt **-aged, -ag·ing** be in charge of, administer; succeed in doing; control; handle, cope with; conduct, carry on; persuade **man·age·a·ble** adj **man·age·ment** n those who manage, as board of directors, etc; administration; skillful use of means; conduct **man·ag·er** n one in charge of business, institution, actor, etc; one who manages efficiently **man·a·ge·ri·al** adj

man·a·tee [MAN-ə-tee] n large, plant-eating aquatic mammal

man·da·rin [MAN-də-rin] n history Chinese high-ranking bureaucrat; fig any high government official; Chinese variety of orange

man·date [MAN-dayt] n command of, or commission to act for, another; commission from United Nations to govern a territory; instruction from electorate to representative or government **man·dat·ed** adj committed to a mandate **man·da·to·ry** [-də-tor-ee] n holder of a mandate **man·da·to·ry** adj compulsory

man·di·ble [MAN-də-bəl] n lower jawbone; either part of bird's beak **man·dib·u·lar** adj, of, like mandible

man·do·lin [MAN-dl-in] n stringed musical instrument

man·drel [MAN-drəl] n axis on which material is supported in a lathe; spindle around which metal is forged

man·drill n large blue-faced baboon

mane [mayn] n long hair on neck of horse, lion, etc

ma·neu·ver [mə-NOO-vər] n contrived, complicated, perhaps deceptive plan or action; skillful management ▷ v employ stratagems, work adroitly; (cause to) perform maneuvers

man·ga·nese [MANG-gə-neez] n metallic element; black oxide of this

mange [maynj] n skin disease of dogs, etc **man·gy** adj **-gi·er, -gi·est** scruffy, shabby

man·ger [MAYN-jər] n eating trough in stable

man·gle[1] [MANG-gəl] n machine for pressing clothes, etc to remove water ▷ vt **-gled, -gling** press in mangle

man·gle[2] vt **-gled, -gling** mutilate, spoil, hack

man·go [MANG-goh] n, pl **-goes** tropical fruit; tree bearing it

man·grove [MANG-grohv] n tropical tree that grows on muddy banks of estuaries

ma·ni·a [MAY-nee-ə] n madness; prevailing craze **ma·ni·ac**, **ma·ni·a·cal, man·ic** adj affected by mania **maniac** n inf mad person; wild enthusiast

man·i·cure [MAN-i-kyuur] n treatment and care of fingernails and hands ▷ vt **-cured, -cur·ing** apply such treatment **man·i·cur·ist** n one who does this professionally

man·i·fest [MAN-ə-fest] adj clearly revealed, visible, undoubted ▷ vt make manifest ▷ n list of cargo for customs **man·i·fes·ta·tion** n **man·i·fest·ly** adv clearly

man·i·fes·to n, pl **-toes** declaration

of policy by political party, government, or movement

man·i·fold [MAN-ə-fohld] *adj* numerous and varied ▷ *n* in internal combustion engine, pipe with several outlets

ma·nip·u·late [mə-NIP-yə-layt] *vt* **-lat·ed, -lat·ing** handle; deal with skillfully; manage; falsify **ma·nip·u·la'tion** *n* act of manipulating, working by hand; skilled use of hands **ma·nip·u·la·tive** *adj*

man·na [MAN-ə] *n* food of Israelites in the wilderness; unexpected benefit

man·ne·quin [MAN-i-kin] *n* person who models clothes, esp at fashion shows; clothing dummy

man·ner [MAN-ər] *n* way thing happens or is done; sort, kind; custom; style ▷ *pl* social behavior **man'ner·ism** *n* person's distinctive habit, trait **man'ner·ly** *adj* polite

man·or [MAN-ər] *n* main house of estate or plantation **ma·no'ri·al** *adj*

man·sard [MAN-sahrd] *n* roof with break in its slope, lower part being steeper than upper

man·sion [MAN-shən] *n* large house

man·tel [MAN-tl] *n* structure around fireplace; mantelpiece **man'tel·piece, -shelf** *n* shelf at top of mantel

man·til·la [man-TIL-ə] *n* in Spain, (lace) scarf worn as headdress

man·tis *n, pl* **-tis·es** genus of insects including the stick insects and leaf insects

man·tle [MAN-tl] *n* loose cloak; covering; incandescent fireproof network hood around gas jet ▷ *vt* **-tled, -tling** cover; conceal **man·tle·piece** *n* mantel

man·tra [MAN-trə] *n* word or phrase repeated as object of concentration in meditation

man·u·al [MAN-yoo-əl] *adj* of, or done with, the hands; by human labor, not automatic ▷ *n* handbook; textbook; organ keyboard

man·u·fac·ture [man-yə-FAK-chər] *vt* **-tured, -tur·ing** process, make (materials) into finished articles; produce (articles); invent, concoct ▷ *n* making of articles, materials, esp in large quantities; anything produced from raw materials **man·u·fac'tur·er** *n*

ma·nure [mə-NUUR] *vt* **-nured, -nur·ing** enrich land ▷ *n* dung, chemical fertilizer (used to enrich land)

man·u·script [MAN-yə-skript] *n* book, document, written by hand; copy for printing ▷ *adj* handwritten or typed

man·y [MEN-ee] *adj* **more, most** numerous ▷ *n, pron* large number

Ma·o·ri [MAH-aw-ree] *n* member of New Zealand aboriginal population; their language

map *n* flat representation of Earth or some part of it, or of the heavens ▷ *vt* **mapped, map·ping** make a map of; (with *out*) plan

ma·ple [MAY-pəl] *n* tree with broad leaves, a variety of which (**sugar maple**) yields sugar

ma·quis [mah-KEE] *n* scrubby undergrowth of Mediterranean countries; name adopted by French resistance movement in WWII

mar [mahr] *vt* **marred, mar·ring** spoil, impair

mar·a·bou [MAR-ə-boo] *n* kind of stork; its soft white lower tail feathers, formerly used to trim hats, etc; kind of silk

ma·rac·a [mə-RAH-kə] *n* percussion instrument of gourd

containing dried seeds, etc

mar·a·schi·no [mar-ə-SKEE-noh] n liqueur made from cherries

mar·a·thon [MAR-ə-thon] n long-distance race; endurance contest

ma·raud [mə-RAWD] v make raid for plunder; pillage **ma·raud'er** n

mar·ble [MAHR-bəl] n kind of limestone capable of taking polish; slab of, sculpture in this; small ball used in children's game **mar'bled** adj having mottled appearance, like marble; (of beef) streaked with fat

march [mahrch] vi walk with military step; go, progress ▷ vt cause to march ▷ n action of marching; distance marched in day; tune to accompany marching

mar·chion·ess [MAHR-shə-nis] n wife, widow of marquis

Mar·di Gras [MAHR-dee grah] n festival of Shrove Tuesday; revelry celebrating this

mare [mair] n female horse **mare's-nest** n supposed discovery that proves worthless

mar·ga·rine [MAHR-jər-in] n butter substitute made from vegetable fats

mar·gin [MAHR-jin] n border, edge; space around printed page; amount allowed beyond what is necessary **mar'gin·al** adj

mar·i·gold [MAR-i-gohld] n plant with yellow flowers

ma·ri·jua·na [mar-ə-WAH-nə] n dried flowers and leaves of hemp plant, used as narcotic

ma·ri·na [mə-REE-nə] n mooring facility for yachts and pleasure boats

mar·i·nade [mar-ə-NAYD] n seasoned, flavored liquid used to soak fish, meat, etc before cooking **mar'i·nate** vt **-nat·ed, -nat·ing**

ma·rine [mə-REEN] adj of the sea or shipping; used at, found in sea ▷ n shipping, fleet; soldier trained for land or sea combat **mar'i·ner** n sailor

mar·i·on·ette [mar-ee-ə-NET] n puppet worked with strings

mar·i·tal [MAR-i-tl] adj relating to marriage

mar·i·time [MAR-i-tīm] adj connected with seafaring; naval; bordering on the sea

mar·jo·ram [MAHR-jər-əm] n aromatic herb

mark¹ [mahrk] n line, dot, scar, etc; sign, token; inscription; letter, number showing evaluation of schoolwork, etc; indication; target ▷ vt make a mark on; be distinguishing mark of; indicate; notice; watch; assess, eg examination paper ▷ vi take notice **mark'er** n one who, that which marks; counter used at card playing, etc; sl an IOU **marks'man** n skilled shot

mark² n former German monetary unit

mar·ket [MAHR-kit] n assembly, place for buying and selling; demand for goods; center for trade ▷ vt offer or produce for sale **mar'ket·a·ble** adj

mar·ma·lade [MAHR-mə-layd] n preserve usually made of oranges, lemons, etc

mar·mo·re·al [mahr-MOR-ee-əl] adj of or like marble

ma·roon¹ [mə-ROON] n brownish-red; firework ▷ adj of the color

ma·roon² vt leave (person) on deserted island or coast; isolate, cut off by any means

mar·quee [mahr-KEE] n rooflike shelter with open sides; rooflike projection above theater, etc displaying name of play, etc being performed

mar·quis [MAHR-kwis] *n* nobleman of rank below duke

mar·row [MAR-oh] *n* fatty substance inside bones; vital part

mar·ry [MAR-ee] *v* **-ried, -ry·ing** join as husband and wife; unite closely **mar·riage** [MAR-ij] *n* state of being married; wedding **mar·riage·a·ble** *adj*

Mars [mahrz] *n* Roman god of war; planet nearest but one to Earth **Mar·tian** [MAHR-shən] *n* supposed inhabitant of Mars ▷ *adj* of Mars

marsh [mahrsh] *n* low-lying wet land **marsh·y** *adj* **marsh·i·er, marsh·i·est**

mar·shal [MAHR-shəl] *n* high officer of state; law enforcement officer ▷ *vt* **-shaled, -shal·ing** arrange in due order; conduct with ceremony **field marshal** in some nations, military officer of the highest rank

marsh·mal·low [MAHRSH-mal-oh] *n* spongy candy orig made from root of **marsh mallow**; shrubby plant growing near marshes

mar·su·pi·al [mahr-SOO-pee-əl] *n* animal that carries its young in pouch, eg kangaroo ▷ *adj*

mar·ten [MAHR-tn] *n* weasel-like animal; its fur

mar·tial [MAHR-shəl] *adj* relating to war; warlike, brave **court martial** see **COURT** **martial law** law enforced by military authorities in times of danger or emergency

mar·tin *n* species of swallow

mar·ti·net [mahr-tn-ET] *n* strict disciplinarian

mar·ti·ni [mahr-TEE-nee] *n, pl* **-nis** cocktail containing gin and vermouth

mar·tyr [MAHR-tər] *n* one put to death for not renouncing beliefs; one who suffers in some cause; one in constant suffering ▷ *vt* make martyr of **mar·tyr·dom** [-dəm] *n*

mar·vel [MAHR-vəl] *vi* **-veled, -vel·ing** wonder ▷ *n* wonderful thing **mar·vel·ous** *adj* amazing; wonderful

mar·zi·pan [MAHR-zə-pan] *n* paste of almonds, sugar, etc used in candies, cakes, etc

mas·car·a [ma-SKAIR-ə] *n* cosmetic for darkening eyelashes and eyebrows

mas·cot [MAS-kot] *n* animal, person or thing supposed to bring luck

mas·cu·line [MAS-kyə-lin] *adj* relating to males; manly; of the grammatical gender to which names of males belong

mash *n* grain, meal mixed with warm water; warm food for horses, etc ▷ *vt* make into a mash; crush into soft mass or pulp

mask *n* covering for face; surgery covering for nose and mouth; disguise, pretense ▷ *vt* cover with mask; hide, disguise

mas·och·ism [MAS-ə-kiz-əm] *n* abnormal condition in which pleasure (esp sexual) is derived from pain, humiliation, etc **mas·och·ist** *n* **mas·och·is·tic** *adj*

ma·son [MAY-sən] *n* worker in stone; (M-) Freemason **Ma·son·ic** *adj* of Freemasonry **ma·son·ry** *n* stonework; (M-) Freemasonry

masque [mask] *n* history form of theatrical performance

mas·quer·ade [mas-kə-RAYD] *n* masked ball ▷ *vi* **-ad·ed, -ad·ing** appear in disguise

Mass *n* service of the Eucharist

mass *n* quantity of matter; dense collection of this; large quantity or number ▷ *v* form into a mass **mas'sive** *adj* large and heavy **mass-**

pro·duce' *vt* **-duced, -duc·ing** produce standardized articles in large quantities **mass production** manufacturing of standardized goods in large quantities **the masses** the common people

mas·sa·cre [MAS-ə-kər] *n* indiscriminate, large-scale killing, esp of unresisting people ▷ *vt* **-cred, -cring** kill indiscriminately

mas·sage [mə-SAHZH] *n* rubbing and kneading of muscles, etc as curative treatment ▷ *vt* **-saged, -sag·ing** apply this treatment to **mas·seur** [-SUR] (*fem*) **-seuse** [-SOOS] *n* one who practices massage

mast *n* pole for supporting ship's sails; tall upright support for aerial, etc

mas·tec·to·my [ma-STEK-tə-mee] *n, pl* **-mies** surgical removal of a breast

mas·ter [MAS-tər] *n* one in control; employer; head of household; owner; document, etc from which copies are made; captain of merchant ship; expert; great artist; teacher ▷ *vt* overcome; acquire knowledge of or skill in **mas·ter·ful** *adj* imperious, domineering **mas·ter·ly** *adj* showing great competence **mas·ter·y** *n* full understanding (of); expertise; authority; victory **master key** one that opens many different locks **mas·ter·mind** *vt* plan, direct ▷ *n* **mas·ter·piece** *n* outstanding work

mas·tic [MAS-tik] *n* gum obtained from certain trees; pasty substance

mas·ti·cate [MAS-ti-kayt] *vt* **-cat·ed, -cat·ing** chew **mas·ti·ca·tion** *n*

mas·tiff *n* large dog

mas·toid *adj* nipple-shaped ▷ *n* prominence on bone behind human ear **mas·toid·i'tis** *n* inflammation of this area

mas·tur·bate [MAS-tər-bayt] *v* **-bat·ed, -bat·ing** stimulate (one's own) genital organs **mas·tur·ba'tion** *n*

mat¹ *n* small rug; piece of fabric to protect another surface or to wipe feet on, etc; thick tangled mass ▷ *v* **mat·ted, mat·ting** form into such mass **go to the mat** struggle unyieldingly

mat² see MATTE

mat·a·dor [MAT-ə-dor] *n* bullfighter who slays bulls in bullfights

match¹ [mach] *n* contest, game; equal; person, thing exactly corresponding to another; marriage; person regarded as eligible for marriage ▷ *vt* get something corresponding to (color, pattern, etc); oppose, put in competition (with); arrange marriage for; join (in marriage) ▷ *vi* correspond **match·less** *adj* unequaled **match·mak·er** *n* one who schemes to bring about a marriage

match² *n* small stick with head that ignites when rubbed; fuse **match·box** *n*

mate¹ [mayt] *n* husband, wife; one of pair; officer in merchant ship ▷ *v* **mat·ed, mat·ing** marry; pair

mate² *n, vt chess* checkmate ▷ *v* **mat·ed, mat·ing** checkmate

ma·te·ri·al [mə-TEER-ee-əl] *n* substance from which thing is made; cloth, fabric ▷ *adj* of matter or body; affecting physical well-being; unspiritual; important, essential **ma·te·ri·al·ism** *n* excessive interest in, desire for money and possessions; doctrine that nothing but matter exists, denying independent existence

of spirit **ma·te·ri·al·is·tic** adj
ma·te·ri·al·ize v -ized, -iz·ing
▷ vi come into existence or view ▷ vt
make material **ma·te·ri·al·ly** adv
appreciably

ma·ter·nal [mə-TUR-nl] adj
motherly; of a mother; related
through mother **ma·ter·ni·ty** n
motherhood

math·e·mat·ics [math-
ə-MAT-iks] n science of
numbers, quantities and
shapes **math·e·mat·i·cal** adj
math·e·ma·ti·cian [-TI-shən] n

mat·i·née [mat-n-AY] n afternoon
performance in theater

ma·tri·arch [MAY-tree-ahrk] n
mother as head and ruler of family
ma·tri·ar·chy n, pl -chies society
with government by women and
descent reckoned in female line

mat·ri·cide [MA-tri-sid] n the
crime of killing one's mother; one
who does this

ma·tric·u·late [mə-TRIK-yə-layt]
v -lat·ed, -lat·ing enroll, be enrolled
as degree candidate in a college or
university **ma·tric·u·la·tion** n

mat·ri·mo·ny [MA-trə-moh-nee]
n marriage **mat·ri·mo·ni·al** adj

ma·trix [MAY-triks] n, pl -tri·ces
[-tri-seez] substance, situation
in which something originates,
takes form, or is enclosed; mold for
casting; mathematics rectangular
array of elements set out in rows
and columns

ma·tron [MAY-trən] n married
woman esp of established social
position; woman who superintends
domestic arrangements of public
institution, boarding school,
etc; woman guard in prison, etc
ma'tron·ly adj sedate

Matt. Matthew

matte [mat] adj of photographic

print, dull, lusterless, not shiny

mat·ter [MAT-ər] n substance of
which thing is made; physical or
bodily substance; affair, business;
cause of trouble; substance of book,
etc ▷ vi be of importance, signify

mat·tock [MA-tək] n tool like pick
with ends of blades flattened for
cutting, hoeing

mat·tress [MA-tris] n stuffed flat
case, often with springs, or foam
rubber pad, used as part of bed **air
mattress** inflatable mattress usu of
rubbery material

ma·ture [mə-CHUUR] adj -tur·er,
-tur·est ripe, completely developed;
grown-up ▷ v -tured, -tur·ing
bring, come to maturity ▷ vi (of
bond, etc) come due **mat·u·ra·tion**
n process of maturing **ma·tu·ri·ty** n
state of being mature

maud·lin [MAWD-lin] adj weakly
or tearfully sentimental

maul [mawl] vt handle roughly;
beat or bruise ▷ n heavy wooden
hammer

maulstick n see MAHLSTICK

mau·so·le·um [maw-sə-LEE-əm]
n stately building as a tomb

mauve [mawv] adj, n (of) pale
purple color

mav·er·ick [MAV-ər-ik] n
unbranded steer, strayed cow;
independent, unorthodox person

maw n stomach, crop

mawk·ish [MAW-kish] adj weakly
sentimental, maudlin; sickening

max·im [MAK-sim] n general
truth, proverb; rule of conduct,
principle

max·i·mum [MAK-sə-məm] n
greatest size or number; highest
point ▷ adj greatest **max'i·mize** vt
-mized, -miz·ing

may v, pt **might** used as an auxiliary
to express possibility, permission,

opportunity, etc **may'be** adv
perhaps; possibly

May'day n international
radiotelephone distress signal

may'fly [MAY-fli] n short-lived
flying insect, found near water

may'hem n in law, depriving
person by violence of limb, member
or organ, or causing mutilation
of body; any violent destruction;
confusion

may·on·naise [may-ə-NAYZ] n
creamy sauce of egg yolks, etc, esp
for salads

may·or [MAY-ər] n head of
municipality **may'or·al** adj
may'or·al·ty [-əl-tee] n (time of)
office of mayor

may·pole [MAY-pohl] n pole set up
for dancing around on **May Day** to
celebrate spring

maze [mayz] n labyrinth; network
of paths, lines; state of confusion

ma·zur·ka [mə-ZUR-kə] n lively
Polish dance like polka; music for it

MC n master of ceremonies

me [mee] pron objective case
singular of first personal pronoun

me'-time n time a person has to
himself or herself, in which to do
something enjoyable

me·a cul·pa [ME-ah KUUL-pah]
Lat my fault

mead·ow [MED-oh] n tract of
grassland

mea·ger [MEE-gər] adj lean, thin,
scanty, insufficient

meal¹ [meel] n occasion when food
is served and eaten; the food

meal² n grain ground to powder
meal'y adj **meal·i·er, meal·i·est**
mealy-mouthed [-mowthd] adj
euphemistic, insincere in what
one says

mean¹ [meen] v **mean** [ment]
mean·ing intend; signify; have

a meaning; have the intention
of behaving ⊳ **mean'ing** n sense,
significance ⊳ adj expressive
mean'ing·ful [-fəl] adj of
great meaning or significance
mean'ing·less adj
mean'ness n

mean² adj **-er, -est** ungenerous,
petty; miserly, niggardly; unpleasant;
callous; shabby; ashamed
mean'ness n

mean³ n thing that is intermediate;
middle point ⊳ pl that by which
thing is done; money; resources ⊳ adj
intermediate in time, quality, etc;
average **means test** inquiry into
person's means to decide eligibility
for pension, grant, etc **mean'time,
-while** adv, n (during) time between
one happening and another **by all
means** certainly **by no means**
not at all

me·an·der [mee-AN-dər] vi flow
windingly; wander aimlessly

mea·sles [MEE-zəlz] n infectious
disease producing rash of red spots
mea'sly -sli·er, -sli·est inf poor,
wretched, stingy; of measles

meas·ure [MEZH-ər] n size,
quantity; vessel, rod, line, etc for
ascertaining size or quantity; unit
of size or quantity; course, plan
of action; law; poetical rhythm;
musical time; poetry tune;
obs dance ⊳ vt **-ured, -ur·ing**
ascertain size, quantity of; be (so
much) in size or quantity; indicate
measurement of; estimate;
bring into competition (against)
meas'ur·a·ble adj **meas'ured** adj
determined by measure; steady;
rhythmical; carefully considered
meas'ure·ment n measuring; size
⊳ pl dimensions

meat [meet] n animal flesh as
food; food **meat'y** adj **meat·i·er,
meat·i·est** (tasting) of, like meat;

brawny; full of import or interest

Mec·ca [MEK-ə] n holy city of Islam; (m-) place that attracts visitors

me·chan·ic [mə-KAN-ik] n one employed or skilled with machinery; skilled worker ▷ pl scientific theory of motion **me·chan'i·cal** adj concerned with machines or operation of them; worked, produced (as though) by machine; acting without thought **me·chan'i·cal·ly** adv

mech·an·ism [MEK-ə-niz-əm] n structure of machine; piece of machinery **mech'a·nize** vt -nized, -niz·ing equip with machinery; make mechanical, automatic; military equip with armored vehicles

med·al [MED-l] n piece of metal with inscription, etc used as reward or memento **me·dal'lion** [mə-DAL-yən] n large medal; various things like this in decorative work **med'al·ist** n winner of a medal; maker of medals

med·dle [MED-l] vi -dled, -dling interfere, busy oneself with unnecessarily **med'dle·some** [-səm] adj

me·di·a [MEE-dee-ə] n pl of MEDIUM used esp of the mass media, radio, TV, etc **media event** event staged for or exploited by mass media

mediaeval see MEDIEVAL

me·di·al [MEE-dee-əl] adj in the middle; pert to a mean or average **me'di·an** adj, n middle (point or line)

me·di·ate [MEE-dee-ayt] v -at·ed, -at·ing ▷ vi intervene to reconcile ▷ vt bring about by mediation ▷ adj depending on mediation **me·di·a'tion** n intervention on behalf of another; act of going between

med·i·cine [MED-i-sin] n drug or remedy for treating disease; science of preventing, diagnosing, alleviating, or curing disease **med'i·cal** [-kəl] adj **me·dic'a·ment** n remedy **med'i·cate** [-kayt] vt -cat·ed, -cat·ing treat, impregnate with medicinal substances **med·i·ca'tion** n **me·dic'i·nal** [-DIS-ə-nəl] adj curative

me·di·e·val [mee-dee-EE-vəl] adj of Middle Ages **me·di·e'val·ist** n student of the Middle Ages

me·di·o·cre [mee-dee-OH-kər] adj neither bad nor good, ordinary, middling; second-rate **me·di·oc'ri·ty** [-OK-rə-tee] n

med·i·tate [MED-i-tayt] v -tat·ed, -tat·ing ▷ vi be occupied in thought; reflect deeply or on spiritual matters; engage in transcendental meditation ▷ vt think about; plan **med·i·ta'tion** [-TAY-shən] n thought; absorption in thought; religious contemplation **med'i·ta·tive** adj thoughtful; reflective

me·di·um [MEE-dee-əm] adj between two qualities, degrees, etc, average ▷ n, pl -di·a or -di·ums middle quality, degree; intermediate substance conveying force; means, agency of communicating news, etc to public, as radio, newspapers, etc; person through whom communication can supposedly be held with spirit world; surroundings; environment

med·ley [MED-lee] n, pl -leys miscellaneous mixture

meds [medz] pl n medicinal substances

Me·du·sa [mə-DOO-sə] n, pl -sas mythology Gorgon whose head turned beholders into stone

meek *adj* **-er, -est** submissive, humble **meek·ly** *adv* **meek·ness** *n*

meer·schaum [MEER-shəm] *n* white substance like clay; tobacco pipe bowl of this

meet *vt* **met, meet·ing** come face to face come face to face with, encounter; satisfy; pay; converge at specified point; assemble; come into contact ▷ *n* meeting, esp for sports **meeting** *n* assembly; encounter

meg·a·bit [MEG-ə-bit] *n* computing 1,048,576 bits; (loosely) one million bits

meg·a·byte [MEG-ə-bit] *n* computing 1,048,576 bytes; (loosely) one million bytes

meg·a·lith [MEG-ə-lith] *n* great stone **meg·a·lith·ic** *adj*

meg·a·lo·ma·ni·a [meg-ə-loh-MAY-nee-ə] *n* desire for, delusions of grandeur, power, etc

meg·a·pix·el [MEG-ə-piks-əl] *n* one million pixels

meg·a·ton [MEG-ə-tun] *n* one million tons; explosive power equal to that of million tons of TNT

meg'ohm *n* electricity one million ohms

mel·an·chol·y [MEL-ən-kol-ee] *n* sadness, dejection, gloom ▷ *adj* gloomy, dejected **mel·an·chol·i·a** [-KOH-lee-ə] *n* former name for DEPRESSION

mé·lange [may-LAHNZH] *n* mixture

mel·a·nin [MEL-ə-nin] *n* dark pigment found in hair, skin, etc of man

me·lee [MAY-lay] *n* confused fight among several people; confusion; turmoil

mel·io·rate [MEEL-yə-rayt] *v* **-rat·ed, -rat·ing** improve **mel·io·ra·tion** *n* **mel·io·rism** *n* doctrine that the world can be improved by human effort

mel·lif·lu·ous [mə-LIF-loo-əs] *adj* (of sound, voice) smooth, sweet

mel·low [MEL-oh] *adj* **-er, -est** ripe; softened by age, experience; soft, not harsh; genial, gay ▷ *v* make, become mellow

mel·o·dra·ma [MEL-ə-dram-ə] *n* play full of sensational and startling situations, often highly emotional; overly dramatic behavior, emotion **mel·o·dra·mat·ic** [-drə-MAT-ik] *adj*

mel·o·dy [MEL-ə-dee] *n, pl* **-dies** series of musical notes that make tune; sweet sound **me·lo·di·ous** [mə-LOH-dee-əs] *adj* pleasing to the ear; tuneful

mel·on [MEL-ən] *n* large, fleshy, juicy fruit

melt *v* **melt·ed, melt·ed** or **mol·ten, melt·ing** (cause to) become liquid by heat; dissolve; soften; waste away; blend (into); disappear **melting** *adj* softening; languishing; tender **melt·down** *n* in nuclear reactor, melting of fuel rods, with possible release of radiation

mem·ber [MEM-bər] *n* any of individuals making up body or society; limb; any part of complex whole

mem·brane [MEM-brayn] *n* thin flexible tissue in plant or animal body

me·men·to [mə-MEN-toh] *n, pl* **-tos** or **-toes** thing serving to remind, souvenir

mem·oir [MEM-wahr] *n* autobiography, personal history, biography; record of events

mem·o·ry [MEM-ə-ree] *n, pl* **-ries** faculty of recollecting, recalling to mind; recollection; thing remembered; length of time one can remember; commemoration; part or faculty of computer that stores information **me·mo·ri·al** *adj* of,

preserving memory ▷ *n* thing, esp a monument, that serves to keep in memory **mem·or·a·ble** *adj* worthy of remembrance, noteworthy
mem·o·ran·dum *n, pl* -**dums** or -**da** note to help the memory, etc; informal letter; note of contract
me·mo·ri·al·ize *vt* -**ized, -iz·ing** commemorate **mem·o·rize** *vt* -**ized, -iz·ing** commit to memory **memory stick** transportable data storage device
men·ace [MEN-is] *n* threat ▷ *vt* -**aced, -ac·ing** threaten, endanger
mé·nage [may-NAHZH] *n* persons of a household **ménage à trois** [ah TWAH] arrangement in which three persons, eg two men and one woman, share sexual relations while occupying same household
me·nag·er·ie [mə-NAJ-ə-ree] *n* exhibition, collection of wild animals
mend *vt* repair, patch; reform, correct, put right ▷ *vi* improve, esp in health ▷ *n* repaired breakage, hole **on the mend** regaining health
men·da·cious [men-DAY-shəs] *adj* untruthful **men·dac·i·ty** [-DAS-i-tee] *n* (tendency to) untruthfulness
men·di·cant *adj* begging ▷ *n* beggar **men·di·can·cy** *n* begging
me·ni·al [MEE-nee-əl] *adj* of work requiring little skill; of household duties or servants; servile ▷ *n* servant; servile person
men·in·gi·tis [men-in-jī-tis] *n* inflammation of the membranes of the brain
me·nis·cus [mə-NIS-kəs] *n* curved surface of liquid; curved lens
men·o·pause [MEN-ə-pawz] *n* final cessation of menstruation
men·stru·a·tion [men-stroo-AY-shən] *n* approximately monthly

discharge of blood and cellular debris from womb of nonpregnant woman **men·stru·al** *adj* **men·stru·ate** *vi* -**at·ed, -at·ing**
men·su·ra·tion [men-shə-RAY-shən] *n* measuring, esp of areas
men·tal [MEN-təl] *adj* of, done by the mind; *inf* slightly mad **men·tal·i·ty** *n* state or quality of mind
men·thol [MEN-thawl] *n* organic compound found in peppermint, used medicinally
men·tion [MEN-shən] *vt* refer to briefly, speak of ▷ *n* acknowledgment; reference to or remark about (person or thing) **men·tion·a·ble** *adj* fit or suitable to be mentioned
men·tor *n* wise, trusted adviser, guide, teacher
men·u [MEN-yoo] *n* list of dishes to be served, or from which to order; *computing* list of options available to user
mer·can·tile [MUR-kən-til] *adj* of, engaged in trade, commerce
mer·ce·nar·y [MUR-sə-ner-ee] *adj* influenced by greed; working merely for reward ▷ *n* -**nar·ies** hired soldier
mer·chant [MUR-chənt] *n* one engaged in trade; storekeeper **mer·chan·dise** *n* merchant's wares **mer·chant·man** [-mən] *n* trading ship **merchant navy** ships engaged in a nation's commerce
mer·cu·ry [MUR-kyə-ree] *n* silvery metal, liquid at ordinary temperature, quicksilver; (**M-**) Roman god of eloquence, messenger of the gods, etc; planet nearest to sun **mer·cu·ri·al** [-KYOO-ree-əl] *adj* relating to, containing mercury; lively, changeable
mer·cy [MUR-see] *n, pl* -**cies**

refraining from infliction of suffering by one who has right, power to inflict it, compassion **mer·ci·ful** [-fəl] *adj* **mer·ci·less** [-lis] *adj*

mere [meer] *adj, sup* **mer·est** only; not more than; nothing but **mere·ly** *adv*

mer·e·tri·cious [mer-i-TRISH-əs] *adj* superficially or garishly attractive; insincere

merge [murj] *v* **merged, merg·ing** (cause to) lose identity or be absorbed **mer·ger** *n* combination of business firms into one; absorption into something greater

me·rid·i·an [mə-RID-ee-ən] *n* circle of Earth passing through poles; imaginary circle in sky passing through celestial poles; highest point reached by star, etc; period of greatest splendor ▷ *adj* of meridian; at peak of something

me·ringue [mə-RANG] *n* baked mixture of white of eggs and sugar; cake of this

mer·it *n* excellence, worth; quality of deserving reward ▷ *pl* excellence ▷ *vt* deserve **mer·i·to·ri·ous** *adj* deserving praise

mer·maid [MUR-mayd] *n* imaginary sea creature with upper part of woman and lower part of fish

mer·ry [MER-ee] *adj* **-ri·er, -ri·est** joyous, cheerful **mer·ri·ly** *adv* **mer·ri·ment** *n*

mesh *n* (one of the open spaces of, or wires, etc forming) network; net ▷ *v* entangle, become entangled; (of gears) engage ▷ *vi* coordinate (with)

mes·mer·ism [MEZ-mə-riz-əm] *n* former term for **HYPNOTISM** **mes·mer·ize** *vt* **-ized, -iz·ing** hypnotize; fascinate; hold spellbound

me·son [MEE-zon] *n* elementary atomic particle

mess *n* untidy confusion; trouble, difficulty; place where military personnel group regularly eat together ▷ *vi* make mess; putter (about); *military* eat in a mess **mess up** make dirty; botch; spoil **mess·y** *adj* **mess·i·er, mess·i·est**

mes·sage [MES-ij] *n* communication sent; meaning, moral **mes·sen·ger** *n* bearer of message

Mes·si·ah [mi-SI-ə] *n* Jews' promised deliverer; Christ **mes·si·an·ic** [mes-ee-AN-ik] *adj*

Messrs [MES-ərz] *pl of* **MR**

met *pt/pp of* **MEET**

meta- *comb form* change: *metamorphose; metathesis*

me·tab·o·lism [mə-TAB-ə-liz-əm] *n* chemical process of living body **met·a·bol·ic** *adj* **met·ab·o·lize** *vt* **-lized, -liz·ing**

met·a·da·ta [MET-ə-day-tə] *n* information that is held as a description of stored data

met·al [MET-l] *n* mineral substance, opaque, fusible and malleable, capable of conducting heat and electricity; object made of metal **me·tal·lic** *adj* **met·al·lur·gist** *n* **met·al·lur·gy** *n* scientific study of extracting, refining metals, and their structure and properties

met·a·mor·pho·sis [met-ə-MOR-fə-sis] *n, pl* **-ses** change of shape, character, etc **met·a·mor·phic** *adj* (esp of rocks) changed in texture, structure by heat, pressure, etc **met·a·mor·phose** [-fohz] *vt* **-phosed, -phos·ing** transform

met·a·phor [MET-ə-for] *n* figure of speech in which term is transferred to something it does not literally apply to; instance of this

met·a·phor·i·cal adj figurative

met·a·phys·ics [met-ə-FIZ-iks] n branch of philosophy concerned with being and knowing

me·tath·e·sis [mə-TATH-ə-sis] n, pl **-ses** [-seez] transposition, esp of letters in word, eg Old English bridd gives modern bird

mete [meet] vt **met·ed, met·ing** measure **mete out** distribute; allot as punishment

me·te·or [MEE-tee-ər] n small, fast-moving celestial body, visible as streak of incandescence if it enters Earth's atmosphere **me·te·or·ic** adj of, like meteor; brilliant but short-lived **me·te·or·ite** n fallen meteor

me·te·or·ol·o·gy [mee-tee-ə-ROL-ə-jee] n study of Earth's atmosphere, esp for weather forecasting

me·ter[1] [MEE-tər] n unit of length in decimal system; SI unit of length; rhythm of poem **met·ric** adj of system of weights and measures in which meter is a unit **met·ri·cal** adj of measurement of poetic meter

meter[2] n that which measures; instrument for recording consumption of gas, electricity, etc

meth·ane [METH-ayn] n inflammable gas, compound of carbon and hydrogen

meth·od [METH-əd] n way, manner; technique; orderliness, system **me·thod·i·cal** adj orderly **meth·od·ol·o·gy** n, pl **-gies** particular method or procedure

Meth·od·ist [METH-ə-dist] n member of any of the churches originated by Wesley and his followers ▷ adj **Meth'od·ism** n

me·tic·u·lous [mə-TIK-yə-ləs] adj (over)particular about details

mé·tier [MAY-tyay] n profession, vocation; one's forte

me·ton·y·my [mi-TON-ə-mee] n figure of speech in which thing is replaced by another associated with it, eg the Oval Office for the president

met·ro·nome [ME-trə-nohm] n instrument that marks musical time by means of ticking pendulum

me·trop·o·lis [mi-TROP-ə-lis] n, pl **-lis·es** chief city of a country, region **me·tro·pol'i·tan** adj of metropolis ▷ n bishop with authority over other bishops of an ecclesiastical province

met·tle [MET-l] n courage, spirit **met'tle·some** [-səm] adj high-spirited

mew [myoo] n cry of cat ▷ vi utter this cry

mez·za·nine [MEZ-ə-neen] n in a theater, lowest balcony or forward part of balcony; in a building, low story between two other stories, esp between first and second stories

mez·zo·so·pran·o [MET-soh-sə-PRAN-oh] n, pl **-pran·os** voice, singer between soprano and contralto

Mg chemistry magnesium

mi [mee] n third sol-fa note

mi·as·ma [mi-AZ-mə] n, pl **-mas** unwholesome or harmful atmosphere

mi·ca [MĪ-kə] n mineral found in glittering scales, plates

mi·crobe [MĪ-krohb] n minute organism; disease germ **mi·cro'bi·al** adj

mi·cro·chip [MĪ-kroh-chip] n small wafer of silicon, etc containing electronic circuits, chip

mi·cro·com·put·er [MĪ-kroh-kəm-pyoo-tər] n computer having a central processing unit contained in one or more silicon chips

mi·cro·cosm [MĪ-krə-koz-əm] n miniature representation, model, etc of some larger system; human beings, society as epitome of universe

mi•cro•fi•ber [Mī-krō-fī-bàr] n very fine synthetic yarn

mi•cro•fiche [Mī-krə-feesh] n microfilm in sheet form

mi•cro•film [Mī-krə-film] n miniaturized recording of manuscript, book on roll of film

mi•crom•e•ter [mi-KROM-i-tàr] n instrument for measuring very small distances or angles

mi•cron [Mī-kron] n unit of length, one millionth of a meter

mi•cro•or•gan•ism [mi-kroh-OR-gà-niz-àm] n organism of microscopic size

mi•cro•pay•ment [mī-kroh-PAY-mànt] n system by which a user pays a small fee to access a specific area of a website

mi•cro•phone [Mī-krà-fohn] n instrument for amplifying, transmitting sounds

mi•cro•proc•es•sor [Mī-kroh-pros-es-àr] n integrated circuit acting as central processing unit in small computer

mi•cro•scope [Mī-krà-skohp] n instrument by which very small body is magnified and made visible **mi•cro•scop•ic** [-SKOP-ik] adj of microscope; very small

mi•cros•co•py [-KROS-kà-pee] n use of microscope

mi•cro•site [Mī-kroh-sīt] n website, often temporary, intended for a specific limited purpose

mi•cro•wave [Mī-kroh-wayv] n electromagnetic wave with wavelength of a few centimeters, used in radar, cooking, etc; microwave oven

mid adj intermediate, in the middle of **mid**day n noon

mid•night n twelve o'clock at night

mid•ship•man [-màn] n student, eg at US Naval Academy, training for commission as naval officer

mid•sum•mer n middle of summer; summer solstice **mid'way** adj, adv halfway **mid'win•ter** n

mid•dle [MID-l] adj equidistant from two extremes; medium; intermediate ▷ n middle point or part **mid'dling** adj mediocre; moderate ▷ adv **Middle Ages** period from about 1000 AD to the 15th century **middle class** social class of business, professional people, etc; middle economic class **mid'dle-class** adj **mid'dle-man** n business person between producer and consumer

midge [mij] n gnat or similar insect

midg•et [MIJ-it] n very small person or thing

mid'riff n middle part of body

midst prep in the middle of ▷ n middle **in the midst of** surrounded by, among

mid•wife [MID-wīf] n trained person who assists at childbirth **mid•wife'ry** [-WiF-à-ree] n art, practice of this

mien [meen] n person's bearing, demeanor or appearance

might¹ [mīt] see **MAY**

might² n power, strength **might'i•ly** adv strongly; powerfully **might'y** adj **might•i•er**, **might•i•est** of great power; strong; valiant; important ▷ adv inf very

mi•graine [Mī-grayn] n severe headache, often with nausea and other symptoms

mi•grate [Mī-grayt] vi **-grat•ed**, **-grat•ing** move from one place to another **mi'grant** [-grànt] n, adj **mi•gra'tion** n act of passing from one place, condition to another;

mild | 348

mi·gra·to·ry [-grə-TOR-ee] *adj* of, capable of migration; (of animals) changing from one place to another according to season

mild [mild] *adj* **-er, -est** not strongly flavored; gentle, merciful; calm or temperate **mild'ly** *adv* **mild'ness** *n*

mil·dew [MIL-doo] *n* destructive fungus on plants or things exposed to damp ▷ *v* become tainted, affect with mildew

mile [mil] *n* measure of length, 1760 yards (1.609 km) **mile'age** *n* distance in miles; traveling expenses per mile; miles traveled (per gallon of gasoline) **mile'stone** *n* stone marker showing distance; significant event, achievement

mi·lieu [mil-YUU] *n* environment, condition in life

mil·i·tar·y [MIL-i-ter-ee] *adj* of, for, soldiers, armies or war ▷ *n* armed services **mil'i·tan·cy** [-tən-see] *n* **mil'i·tant** *adj* aggressive, vigorous in support of cause; prepared, willing to fight **mil'i·ta·rism** [-tə-riz-əm] *n* enthusiasm for military force and methods **mil'i·ta·rize** *vt* **-rized, -riz·ing** convert to military use

mi·li·tia [-LISH-ə] *n* military force of citizens serving full time only in emergencies

mil·i·tate [MIL-i-tayt] *vi* **-tat·ed, -tat·ing** (esp with *against*) have strong influence, effect on

milk *n* white fluid with which mammals feed their young; fluid in some plants ▷ *vt* draw milk from **milk'y** *adj* **milk·i·er, milk·i·est** containing, like milk; (of liquids) opaque, clouded **milk'sop** *n* weak, effeminate fellow; milquetoast **milk teeth** first set of teeth in young mammals **Milky Way** luminous

band of stars, etc stretching across sky, the galaxy

mill *n* factory; machine for grinding, pulverizing grain, paper, etc ▷ *vt* put through mill; cut fine grooves across edges of (eg coins) ▷ *vi* move in confused manner, as cattle or crowds of people **mill'er** *n* **mill'stone** *n* flat circular stone for grinding; heavy emotional or mental burden

mil·len·ni·um [mi-LEN-ee-əm] *n, pl* **-ni·a** [-ni-ə] period of a thousand years during which some claim Christ is to reign on earth; period of a thousand years; period of peace, happiness **millennium bug** *computing* software problem arising from the change in date at the start of the 21st century

mil·let [MIL-it] *n* a cereal grass

milli- *comb form* thousandth: *milligram*; thousandth part of a gram

mil·li·bar [MIL-ə-bahr] *n* unit of atmospheric pressure

mil·li·ner [MIL-ə-nər] *n* maker of, dealer in women's hats, ribbons, etc **mil'li·ner·y** *n* milliner's goods or work

mil·lion [MIL-yən] *n* 1000 thousands **mil·lion·aire'** *n* owner of a million dollars, etc or more; very rich person **mil'lionth** *adj, n*

mil·li·pede [MIL-ə-peed] *n* small arthropod, like centipede, with jointed body and many pairs of legs

milque·toast [MILK-tohst] *n* ineffectual person esp one easily dominated

milt *n* spawn of male fish

mime [mīm] *n* acting without the use of words; actor who does this ▷ *v* **mimed, mim·ing** act in mime

mim·ic [MIM-ik] *vt* **-icked, -ick·ing** imitate (person, manner, etc) esp for satirical effect ▷ *n* one who, or animal that does this, or is

adept at it ▷ *adj* **mim·ic·ry** *n, pl*
-ries mimicking

min·a·ret [min-ə-RET] *n* tall
slender tower of mosque

mince [mins] *v* **minced, minc·ing**
▷ *vt* cut, chop very small; soften or
moderate (words, etc) ▷ *vi* walk,
speak in affected manner ▷ *n*
something minced; mincemeat
minc'ing *adj* affected in manner
mince'meat *n* mixture of minced
apples, currants, spices, sometimes
meat, etc **mince pie** pie containing
mincemeat or mince

mind [mīnd] *n* thinking faculties
as distinguished from the body,
intellectual faculties; memory,
attention; intention; taste; sanity
▷ *vt* take offense at; care for; attend
to; be cautious, careful about
(something); be concerned, troubled
about ▷ *vi* be careful; heed **mind'ful**
[fəl] *adj* heedful; keeping in memory
mind'less [-lis] *adj* stupid, careless
mind candy something that is
entertaining or enjoyable but lacks
depth or significance

mine¹ [mīn] *pron* belonging to me

mine² *n* deep hole for digging out
coal, metals, etc; in war, hidden
deposit of explosive to blow up ship,
etc; land mine; profitable source
▷ *v* **mined, min·ing** ▷ *vt* dig from
mine; make mine in or under; place
explosive mines in, on ▷ *vi* make,
work in mine **mi'ner** *n* one who
works in mine **mine'field** *n* area
of land or sea containing mines
mine'lay·er *n* ship for laying mines
mine'sweep·er *n* ship, helicopter
for clearing away mines

min·er·al [MIN-ər-əl] *n* naturally
occurring inorganic substance,
esp as obtained by mining ▷ *adj*
of, containing, or like minerals
min·er·al·o·gy *n* science of

minerals **mineral water** water
containing some mineral, esp
natural or artificial kinds for drinking

min·e·stro·ne [min-ə-STROH-
nee] *n* type of vegetable soup
containing pasta

min·gle [MING-gəl] *v* **-gled, -gling**
mix, blend, unite, merge

min·i [MIN-ee] *n* something small
or miniature; short skirt; small
computer ▷ *adj*

min·i·a·ture [MIN-ee-ə-chər] *n*
small painted portrait; anything on
small scale ▷ *adj* small-scale, minute

min·i·bus [MIN-ee-bus] *n* small
bus for about fifteen passengers

min·im [MIN-əm] *n* unit of
fluid measure, one-sixtieth of a
dram; *music* note half the length of
semibreve

min·i·mize [MIN-ə-mīz] *vt*
-mized, -miz·ing bring to, estimate
at smallest possible amount
min'i·mal [-məl] *adj* minimum
[-məm] *n, pl* **-mums** lowest size or
quantity ▷ *adj* least possible

min·ion [MIN-yən] *n* favorite;
servile follower

min·is·ter [MIN-ə-stər] *n*
person in charge of government
department; diplomatic
representative; clergyman ▷ *vi*
attend to needs of, take care of
min·is·te'ri·al [-STEER-ee-əl]
adj **min·is·tra'tion** *n* rendering
help, esp to sick **min'is·try** *n, pl*
-tries office of clergyman; body of
ministers forming government; act
of ministering **minister** *n* minister
without **portfolio** minister of state not in
charge of specific department

mink [mingk] *n* variety of weasel;
its (brown) fur

min·now [MIN-oh] *n* small
freshwater fish

mi·nor [MĪ-nər] *adj* lesser;

under age ▷ *n* person below age of legal majority; scale in music

mi·nor·i·ty [mi-NOR-i-tee] *n* lesser number; smaller party voting together; ethical or religious group in a minority in any country; state of being a minor

Min·o·taur [MIN-ə-tor] *n* fabled monster, half bull, half man

min·strel [MIN-strəl] *n* medieval singer, musician, poet ▷ *pl* performers in minstrel show

minstrel show formerly, an entertainment of songs and jokes provided by white performers with blackened faces

mint¹ *n* place where money is coined ▷ *vt* coin, invent

mint² *n* aromatic plant

min·u·et [min-yoo-ET] *n* stately dance; music for it

mi·nus [Mī-nəs] *prep, adj* less, with the deduction of, deprived of; lacking; negative ▷ *n* the sign (-) denoting subtraction

mi·nus·cule [MIN-iss-skyool] *adj* very small

mi·nute¹ [mi-NOOT] *adj* **-nut·er**, **-nut·est** very small; precise **mi·nute·ly** *adv* **mi·nu·ti·ae** [mi-NOO-shee-ie] *pl n* trifles, precise details

min·ute² [MIN-it] *n* 60th part of hour or degree; moment; memorandum ▷ *pl* record of proceedings of meeting, etc

minx [mingks] *n* bold, flirtatious girl

mir·a·cle [MIR-ə-kəl] *n* supernatural event; marvel **mi·rac·u·lous** [mi-RAK-yə-ləs] *adj* **miracle play** drama (esp medieval) based on sacred subject

mi·rage [mi-RAHZH] *n* deceptive image in atmosphere, eg of lake in desert

mire [mir] *n* swampy ground, mud ▷ *vt* **mired, mir·ing** stick in, dirty with mud; entangle, involve

mir·ror [MIR-ər] *n* glass or polished surface reflecting images ▷ *vt* reflect

mirth [murth] *n* merriment, gaiety **mirth'ful** *adj*

MIS management information system(s)

mis- *prefix* wrong(ly), bad(ly)

mis·an·thrope [MIS-ən-throhp] *n* hater of mankind **mis·an·throp·ic** *adj*

mis·ap·pro·pri·ate [mis-ə-PROH-pree-ayt] *vt* **-at·ed, -at·ing** put to dishonest use; embezzle

mis·be·have *v* behave badly **mis·be·hav'iour** *n*

mis·cal·cu·late *vt* calculate or judge wrongly **mis·cal·cu·la'tion** *n*

mis·car·ry [mis-KA-ree] *vi* **-ried, -ry·ing** bring forth young prematurely; go wrong, fail **mis·car'riage** [-KA-rij] *n*

mis·cast [*mus'th*] *v* **-cast, -cast·ing** distribute acting parts wrongly; assign to unsuitable role

mis·cel·la·ne·ous [mis-ə-LAY-nee-əs] *adj* mixed, assorted **mis'cel·la·ny** *n, pl* **-nies** collection of assorted writings in one book; medley

mis·chief [MIS-chif] *n* annoying behavior; inclination to tease, disturb; harm; source of harm or annoyance **mis'chie·vous** [-chi-vəs] *adj* of a child, full of pranks; disposed to mischief; having harmful effect

mis·ci·ble [MIS-ə-bəl] *adj* capable of mixing

mis·con·cep·tion [mis-kən-SEP-shən] *n* wrong idea, belief

mis·con'duct *n* immoral or unethical behaviour

mis·cre·ant [MIS-kree-ənt] n wicked person, evildoer, villain

mis'deed n wrongful act

mis·de·mean·or [mis-di-MEE-nər] n in law, offense less grave than a felony; minor offense

mi'ser [MÎ-zər] n hoarder of money; stingy person **mi'ser·ly** adj avaricious; niggardly

mis·er·a·ble [MIZ-ər-ə-bəl] adj very unhappy, wretched; causing misery; worthless; squalid **mis'er·y** n, pl -**er·ies** great unhappiness; distress; poverty

mis'fit n esp person not suited to surroundings or work

mis·for·tune n (piece of) bad luck

mis·giv·ing n (oft pl) feeling of fear, doubt, etc

mis·guid·ed [mis-GĪ-did] adj foolish, unreasonable

mis'hap n minor accident

mis·in·form vt give incorrect information to **mis·in·for·ma·tion** n

mis·judge v judge wrongly or unfairly **mis·judg'ment** n

mis·lay' vt -**laid**, -**lay·ing** put in place that cannot later be remembered; place wrongly

mis·lead [mis-LEED] vt -**led**, -**lead·ing** give false information to; lead astray **misleading** adj deceptive

mis·man·age vt organize or run (something) badly **mis·man'age·ment** n

mis·no·mer [mis-NOH-mər] n wrong name or term; use of this

mi·sog·y·ny [mi-SOJ-ə-nee] n hatred of women **mi·sog'y·nist** n

mis·place' vt mislay; put in the wrong place; give (trust or affection) inappropriately

mis'print n printing error ▷ vt

mis·pro·nounce' v

pronounce (a word) wrongly **mis·pro·nun·ci·a·tion** n

miss vt fail to hit, reach, find, catch, or notice; be late for; omit; notice or regret absence of; avoid ▷ vi (of engine) misfire ▷ n fact, instance of missing **miss'ing** adj lost; absent

mis'sal [MIS-əl] n book containing prayers, etc of the Mass

mis·shap·en [mis-SHAY-pən] adj badly shaped, deformed

mis·sile [MIS-əl] n that which may be thrown, shot, homed to damage, destroy **guided missile** see also GUIDE

mis·sion [MISH-ən] n specific task or duty; calling in life; delegation; sending or being sent on some service; those sent **mis'sion·ar·y**, pl -**ar·ies** one sent to a place, society to spread religion ▷ adj

mis'sive [MIS-iv] n letter

mis·spell' v spell (a word) wrongly

mis·spent' adj wasted or misused

mist n water vapor in fine drops **mist'y** adj -**i·er**, -**i·est** full of mist; dim; obscure

mis·take [mi-STAYK] n error, blunder ▷ v -**took** [-TUUK], -**tak·en**, -**tak·ing** ▷ vt fail to understand; form wrong opinion about; take (person or thing) for another ▷ vi be in error

mis·ter [MIS-tər] n the full form of MR

mis·tle·toe [MIS-əl-toh] n evergreen parasitic plant with white berries that grows on trees

mis·tress [MIS-tris] n object of man's illicit love; woman with mastery or control; woman owner; woman teacher; obs title given to married woman

mis·un·der·stand v fail to understand properly **mis·un·der·stand'ing** n

mis•use' n incorrect, improper, or careless use ▷ vt use wrongly; treat badly

mite [mīt] n very small insect; anything very small; small contribution but all one can afford

mi•ter [MĪ-tər] n bishop's headdress; joint between two pieces of wood, etc meeting at right angles ▷ vt join with, shape for a miter joint; put miter on

mit•i•gate [MIT-i-gayt] vt -gat•ed, -gat•ing make less severe **mit•i•ga'tion** n

mitt n baseball player's glove esp for catcher, first baseman; sl hand

mit•ten [MIT-n] n glove with two compartments, one for thumb and one for fingers

mix [miks] vt put together, combine, blend, mingle ▷ vi be mixed; associate **mixed** adj composed of different elements, races, sexes, etc **mix'er** n one who, that which mixes; informal party intended to help guests meet one another **mix'ture** [-chər] n **mixed-up** adj confused; emotionally unstable **mix-up** n confused situation; a fight

mks units metric system of units based on the meter, kilogram and second

MMS Multimedia Messaging Service: method of transmitting graphics, video, or sound files and text messages over wireless networks

Mn chemistry manganese

mne•mon•ic [ni-MON-ik] adj helping the memory ▷ n something intended to help the memory

Mo chemistry molybdenum

moan [mohn] n low murmur, usually of pain ▷ v utter with moan, lament

moat [moht] n deep wide ditch esp around castle ▷ vt surround with moat

mob n disorderly crowd of people; mixed assembly ▷ vt **mobbed, mob•bing** attack in mob; crowd around boisterously

mo•bile [MOH-bəl] adj capable of movement; easily moved or changed ▷ n [moh-BEEL] hanging structure of card, plastic, etc designed to move in air currents **mo•bil'i•ty** n **mobile home** large trailer, connected to utilities at a trailer park, etc, used as a residence **mobile phone** another name for **CELL PHONE**

mo•bi•lize [MOH-bə-līz] v -lized, -liz•ing (of armed services) prepare for military service ▷ vt organize for a purpose **mo•bi•li•za'tion** [-ZAY-shən] n in war time, calling up of men and women for active service

moc•ca•sin [MOK-ə-sin] n Amer Indian soft shoe, usu of deerskin

mo•cha [MOH-kə] n type of strong, dark coffee; this flavor

mock [mok] vt make fun of, ridicule; mimic ▷ vi scoff ▷ n act of mocking; laughingstock ▷ adj sham, imitation **mock'er•y** n, pl -er•ies derision; travesty **mocking bird** N Amer bird that imitates songs of others **mock-up** n scale model

mode [mohd] n method, manner; prevailing fashion

mod•el [MOD-l] n miniature representation; pattern; person or thing worthy of imitation; person employed by artist to pose, or by dress designer to display clothing ▷ vt -eled, -el•ing make model of; mold; display (clothing) for dress designer

mo•dem [MOH-dem] n device for connecting two computers via a telephone line

mod•er•ate [MOD-ər-it] adj not

going to extremes, temperate, medium ▷ *n* person of moderate views ▷ *v* [-ayt] make, become less violent or excessive; preside over meeting, etc **mod·er·a·tor** *n* mediator; president of Presbyterian body; arbitrator; person presiding over panel discussion

mod·ern [MOD-ðrn] *adj* of present or recent times; in, of current fashion ▷ *n* person living in modern times **mod·ern·ism** *n* (support of) modern tendencies, thoughts, etc **mod·ern·i·za'tion** [-ZAY-shðn] *n* **mod·ern·ize** [-iz] *vt* **-ized, -iz·ing** bring up to date

mod·est [MOD-ist] *adj* not overrating one's qualities or achievements; shy; moderate, not excessive; decorous, decent **mod·es·ty** *n*

mod·i·cum [MOD-i-kðm] *n* small quantity

mod·i·fy [MOD-ð-fī] *v* (mainly tr) **-fied, -fy·ing** change slightly; tone down **mod·i·fi·ca'tion** *n* **mod·i·fi·er** [-fī-ðr] *n* esp word qualifying another

mod·u·late [MOJ-ð-layt] *v* **-lat·ed, -lat·ing** ▷ *vt* regulate; vary in tone ▷ *vi* change key of music **mod·u·la'tion** *n* modulating; *electronics* superimposing signals onto high-frequency carrier

mod·ule [MOJ-ool] *n* (detachable) unit, section, component with specific function

mo·dus op·e·ran·di [MOH-dðs op-ð-RAN-dee] *Lat* method of operating; tackling task

mo·gul [MOH-gðl] *n* important or powerful person; bump in ski slope

mo·hair [MOH-hair] *n* fine cloth of goat hair; hair of Angora goat

mo·hel [MOH-ðl] *n* in Jewish tradition, person who performs rite of circumcision

moi·e·ty [MOI-i-tee] *n, pl* **-ties** a half

moist *adj* **-er, -est** damp, slightly wet **moist'en** [MOI-sðn] *v*

mois·ture [-chðr] *n* liquid, esp diffused or in drops

mo·lar [MOH-lðr] *adj* (of teeth) for grinding ▷ *n* molar tooth

mo·las·ses [mð-LAS-iz] *n* thick brown syrup, byproduct of process of sugar refining

mold¹ [mohld] *n* hollow object in which metal, etc is cast; pattern for shaping; character; shape, form ▷ *vt* shape or pattern **mold'ing** *n* molded object; ornamental edging; decoration

mold² *n* fungoid growth caused by dampness **mold'y** *adj* **mold·i·er, mold·i·est** stale, musty

mold³ *n* loose soil rich in organic matter **mold'er** *vi* decay or cause to decay into dust

mole¹ [mohl] *n* small dark protuberant spot on the skin

mole² *n* small burrowing animal; spy, informer

mole³ *n* SI unit of amount of substance

mol·e·cule [MOL-ð-kyool] *n* simplest freely existing chemical unit, composed of two or more atoms; very small particle **mo·lec·u·lar** *adj* of, inherent in molecules

mo·lest [mð-LEST] *vt* pester, interfere with so as to annoy or injure; make indecent sexual advances esp to a child

mol·li·fy [MOL-ð-fī] *vt* **-fied, -fy·ing** calm down, placate, soften **mol·li·fi·ca'tion** *n*

mol·lusk [MOL-ðsk] *n* soft-bodied, usu hard-shelled animal, eg snail, oyster

molt [mohlt] v cast or shed fur, feathers, etc ▷ n molting

molten see MELT

mo·lyb·de·num [mə-LIB-də-nəm] n silver-white metallic element

mo·ment [MOH-mənt] n very short space of time; (present) point in time **mo·men·tar·i·ly** adv **mo'men·tar·y** adj lasting only a moment

mo·men·tous [moh-MEN-təs] adj of great importance

mo·men·tum [moh-MEN-təm] n force of a moving body; impetus gained from motion

mon·arch [MON-ərk] n sovereign ruler of a country **mo·nar'chi·cal** adj **mon'ar·chist** n supporter of monarchy **mon'ar·chy** n, pl **-chies** nation ruled by sovereign; monarch's rule

mon·as·ter·y [MON-ə-ster-ee] n, pl **-ter·ies** house occupied by members of religious order **mo·nas·tic** [mə-NAS-tik] adj relating to monks, nuns, or monasteries ▷ n monk, recluse

mon·ey [MUN-ee] n, pl **-eys** or **-ies** banknotes, coin, etc, used as medium of exchange **mon·e·ta·rism** [MON-ə-tə-riz-əm] n theory that inflation is caused by increase in money supply **mon'e·ta·rist** adj, n **mon'e·tar·y** adj **mon·eyed, -ied** [MUN-eed] adj rich

mon·gol·ism [MONG-gə-liz-əm] n a former and non-medical name for DOWN SYNDROME

mon·goose [MON-goos] n, pl **-goos·es** small animal of Asia and Africa noted for killing snakes

mon·grel [MONG-grəl] n animal, esp dog, of mixed breed; hybrid ▷ adj

mon·i·tor [MON-i-tər] n person or device that checks, controls, warns or keeps record of something; pupil assisting teacher with conduct of class; television set used in a studio for checking program being transmitted; computing cathode ray tube with screen for viewing data; type of large lizard ▷ vt watch, check on **mon'i·to·ry** [-tor-ee] adj giving warning

monk [munk] n one of a religious community of men living apart under vows **monk'ish** adj

mon·key [MUN-kee] n, pl **-keys** long-tailed primate; mischievous child ▷ vi meddle, fool (with) **monkey wrench** one with adjustable jaw

mono- comb form single: monosyllabic

mon·o·chrome [MON-ə-krohm] n representation in one color ▷ adj of one color **mon·o·chro·mat·ic** adj

mon·o·cle [MON-ə-kəl] n single eyeglass

mo·noc·u·lar [mə-NOK-yə-lər] adj one-eyed

mo·nog·a·my [mə-NOG-ə-mee] n custom of being married to one person at a time **mo·nog'a·mous** adj

mon·o·gram [MON-ə-gram] n design of one or more letters interwoven

mon·o·graph [MON-ə-graf] n short scholarly book on single subject

mon·o·lith [MON-ə-lith] n monument consisting of single standing stone **mon·o·lith'ic** adj of or like a monolith; massive, inflexible

mon·o·logue [MON-ə-lawg] n dramatic composition with only one speaker; long speech by one person

mon·o·ma·ni·a [mon-ə-MAY-nee-ə] n excessive preoccupation with one thing

mo·nop·o·ly [mə-NOP-ə-lee] n, pl **-lies** exclusive control of commerce, privilege, etc **mo·nop'o·lize** vt **-lized, -liz·ing** claim, take exclusive possession of

mon·o·rail [MON-ə-rayl] n railway with cars running on or suspended from single rail

mon·o·the·ism [MON-ə-thee-iz-əm] n belief in only one God

mon·o·tone [MON-ə-tohn] n continuing on one note

mo·not·o·nous [mə-NOT-n-əs] adj lacking in variety, dull, wearisome **mo·not'o·ny** n

mon·soon n seasonal wind of SE Asia; very heavy rainfall season

mon·ster [MON-stər] n fantastic imaginary beast; misshapen animal or plant; very wicked person; huge person, animal or thing ▷ adj huge **mon·stros·i·ty** n monstrous being; deformity; distortion **mon'strous** [-strəs] adj of, like monster; unnatural; enormous; horrible

mon·tage [mon-TAHZH] n elements of two or more pictures imposed upon a single background to give a unified effect; method of editing a film

month [munth] n one of twelve periods into which the year is divided; period of moon's revolution around Earth **month'ly** adj happening or payable once a month ▷ adv once a month ▷ n magazine published every month

mon·u·ment [MON-yə-mənt] n anything that commemorates, esp a building or statue **mon·u·men·tal** [-MEN-tl] adj vast, lasting; of or serving as monument

mooch vi sl borrow without intending to repay; beg

mood[1] n state of mind and feelings

mood'y adj **mood·i·er, mood·i·est** gloomy, pensive; changeable in mood

mood[2] n grammar form indicating function of verb

moon n satellite that takes lunar month to revolve around Earth; any secondary planet ▷ vi go about dreamily **moon'light** n **moon'shine** n inf whiskey, esp corn liquor, illicitly distilled; nonsense; moonlight **moon'stone** n transparent semiprecious stone

moor[1] n tract of open uncultivated land, often hilly and overgrown with heath

moor[2] v secure (ship) with chains or ropes **moor'ings** pl n ropes, etc for mooring; something providing stability, security

moose [moos] n N Amer deer with large antlers

moot adj that is open to argument, debatable; purely academic

mop n bundle of yarn, cloth, etc on end of stick, used for cleaning; tangle (of hair, etc) ▷ vt **mopped, mop·ping** clean, wipe with mop or other absorbent material

mope [mohp] vi **moped, mop·ing** be gloomy, apathetic

mo·ped [MOH-ped] n light motorized bicycle

mo·raine [mə-RAYN] n accumulated mass of debris, earth, stones, etc, deposited by glacier

mor·al [MOR-əl] adj pert to right and wrong conduct; of good conduct ▷ n practical lesson, e g of fable ▷ pl habits with respect to right and wrong, esp in matters of sex **mor'al·ist** n teacher of morality **mo·ral·i·ty** [mə-RAL-ə-tee] n good moral conduct; moral goodness or badness; kind of medieval drama, containing moral lesson **mor'al·ize**

v **-ized, -iz·ing** ▷ *vi* write, think about moral aspect of things ▷ *vt* interpret morally **moral victory** triumph that is psychological rather than practical

mo·rale [mə-RAL] *n* degree of confidence, hope of person or group

mo·rass [mə-RAS] *n* marsh; mess

mor·a·to·ri·um [mor-ə-TOR-ee-əm] *n, pl* **-ri·ums** *or* **-ri·a** act authorizing postponement of payments, etc; delay

mor'bid *adj* unduly interested in death; gruesome; diseased

mor·dant [MOR-dnt] *adj* biting; corrosive; scathing ▷ *n* substance that fixes dyes

more [mor] *adj* greater in quantity or number; *comp of* **MANY** *or* **MUCH** ▷ *adv* to a greater extent; in addition ▷ *pron* greater or additional amount or number **more·o·ver** *adv* besides, further

mor·ga·nat·ic marriage [mor-gə-NAT-ik] marriage of king or prince in which wife does not share husband's rank or possessions and children do not inherit from father

morgue [morg] *n* mortuary; newspaper reference file or file room

mor·i·bund [MOR-ə-bund] *adj* dying; stagnant

Mor·mon [MOR-mən] *n* member of religious sect founded in US

morn'ing *n* early part of day until noon **morning-after pill** woman's contraceptive pill for use within hours after sexual intercourse **morning glory** plant with trumpet-shaped flowers that close in late afternoon

mo·roc·co [mə-ROK-oh] *n* goatskin leather

mo·ron [MOR-on] *n* (formerly) person with low intelligence quotient; *inf* fool **mo·ron'ic** *adj*

mo·rose [mə-ROHS] *adj* sullen, moody

morph [morf] *v* cause or undergo change of shape or appearance via computer graphic effects

mor·phine [MOR-feen] *n* narcotic extract of opium used to induce sleep and relieve pain

mor·phol·o·gy [mor-FOL-ə-jee] *n* science of structure of organisms; form and structure of words of a language

Morse [mors] *n* system of telegraphic signaling in which letters of alphabet are represented by combinations of dots and dashes, or short and long flashes

mor·sel [MOR-səl] *n* fragment, small piece

mor·tal [MOR-tl] *adj* subject to death; causing death ▷ *n* mortal creature **mor·tal'i·ty** *n* state of being mortal; great loss of life; death rate **mor·tal·ly** *adv* fatally; deeply, intensely

mor·tar [MOR-tər] *n* mixture of lime, sand and water for holding bricks and stones together; small cannon firing over short range; vessel in which substances are pounded **mor·tar·board** [-bord] *n* square academic cap

mort·gage [MOR-gij] *n* conveyance of property as security for debt with provision that property be reconveyed on payment within agreed time ▷ *vt* **-gaged, -gag·ing** convey by mortgage; pledge as security **mort·ga·gee'** *n* person to whom property is mortgaged **mort'ga·gor, -ger** *n* person who mortgages property

mor·ti·fy [MOR-tə-fī] *v* **-fied, -fy·ing** humiliate; subdue by self-denial; (of flesh) be affected with gangrene **mor·ti·fi·ca'tion**

[-fi-KAY-shən] n

mor•tise [MOR-tis] n hole in piece of wood, etc to receive the tongue (tenon) and end of another piece ▷ vt **-tised, -tis•ing** make mortise in; fasten by mortise and tenon

mor•tu•ar•y [MOR-choo-er-ee] n, pl **-ar•ies** funeral parlor ▷ adj of, for burial; pert to death

mo•sa•ic [moh-ZAY-ik] n picture or pattern of small surfaces of colored stone, glass, etc; this process of decoration

Mo•sa•ic [moh-ZAY-ik] adj of Moses

mosh vi dance violently and frantically with others in group at rock concert ▷ n

Moslem n see **MUSLIM**

mosque [mosk] n Muslim temple

mos•qui•to [mə-SKEE-toh] n, pl **-toes** or **-tos** any of various kinds of flying, biting insects

moss [maws] n small plant growing in masses on moist surfaces **moss'y** adj **moss•i•er, moss•i•est** covered with moss

most [mohst] adj greatest in size, number, or degree; sup of **MUCH** or **MANY** ▷ n greatest number, amount, or degree ▷ adv in the greatest degree; abbrev of **ALMOST most'ly** adv for the most part, generally, on the whole

mo•tel [moh-TEL] n roadside hotel with accommodation for motorists and their vehicles

mo•tet [moh-TET] n short sacred vocal composition

moth [mawth] n usu nocturnal insect like butterfly; its grub **moth'ball** n small ball of camphor or naphthalene to repel moths from stored clothing, etc ▷ vt put in mothballs; store, postpone, etc **moth'eat•en** adj eaten, damaged by grub of moth; decayed, scruffy

moth•er [MUTH-ər] n female parent; head of religious community of women ▷ adj natural, native, inborn ▷ vt act as mother to **moth'er•hood** [-huud] n **moth'er•ly** adj **mother-in-law** mother of one's wife or husband **mother of pearl** iridescent lining of certain shells

mo•tif [moh-TEEF] n dominating theme; recurring design

mo•tion [MOH-shən] n process or action or way of moving; proposal in meeting; application to judge ▷ vt direct by sign **mo'tion•less** [-lis] adj still, immobile

mo•tive [MOH-tiv] n that which makes person act in particular way; inner impulse ▷ adj causing motion **mo'ti•vate** vt **-vat•ed, -vat•ing** instigate; incite **mo•ti•va'tion** [-VAY-shən] n

mot•ley [MOT-lee] adj miscellaneous, varied; multicolored

mo•to•cross [MOH-toh-kraws] n motorcycle race over rough course

mo•tor [MOH-tər] n that which imparts movement; machine to supply motive power; automobile ▷ vi travel by automobile **mo'tor•ist** n user of automobile **mo'tor•ize** vt **-ized, -iz•ing** equip with motor **motor home** large motor vehicle with living quarters, used for recreational travel

mot•tle [MOT-l] vt **-tled, -tling** mark with blotches, variegate ▷ n arrangement of blotches; blotch on surface

mot•to [MOT-oh] n, pl **-toes** saying adopted as rule of conduct; short inscribed sentence; word or sentence on badge or banner

mound [mownd] n heap of earth or stones; small hill

mount [mownt] vi rise; increase;

get on horseback ▷ vt get up on; frame (picture); fix, set up; provide with horse ▷ n that on which thing is supported or fitted; horse; hill

moun·tain [MOWN-tn] n hill of great size; surplus **moun·tain·eer** n one who lives among or climbs mountains **moun·tain·ous** adj very high, rugged **mountain bike** bicycle with straight handlebars and broad, thick tires, for cycling over rough terrain

moun·te·bank [MOWN-tà-bangk] n charlatan, fake

Moun·tie [MOWN-tee] n inf member of Royal Canadian Mounted Police

mourn [morn] v feel, show sorrow (for) **mourn'er** n **mourn'ful** [-fəl] adj sad; dismal **mourn'ful·ly** adv **mourn'ing** n grieving; conventional signs of grief for death; clothes of mourner

mouse [mows] n, pl **mice** [mīs] small rodent; computing hand-operated device for moving the cursor, clicking on icons, etc without keying ▷ vi catch, hunt mice; prowl **mous'er** n cat used for catching mice **mous'y** adj **mous·i·er**, **mous·i·est** like mouse, esp in color; meek, shy

mousse [moos] n sweet dessert of flavored cream whipped and frozen

moustache SEE MUSTACHE

mouth [mowth] n opening in head for eating, speaking, etc; opening into anything hollow; outfall of river; entrance to harbor, etc ▷ vt [mowth] declaim, esp in public; form (words) with lips without speaking; take, move in mouth **mouth'piece** n end of anything placed between lips, eg pipe; spokesman

move [moov] v **moved, mov·ing** ▷ vt change position of; stir

emotions in; incite; propose for consideration ▷ vi change places; change one's dwelling, etc; take action ▷ n a moving; motion toward some goal **mov'a·ble** adj, n **move'ment** n process, action of moving; moving parts of machine; division of piece of music

mov·ie [MOO-vee] n inf cinema film

mow [moh] v **mowed, mowed** or **mown, mow·ing** cut (grass, etc) **mow'er** n person or machine that mows

MP3, Mpeg-1 la·yer3 n computing Motion Picture Expert Group-1, Audio Layer-3: digital compression format used to reduce audio files to a fraction of their original size without loss of sound quality

Mr mister

Mrs title of married woman

Ms title used instead of Miss or Mrs

Mt chemistry meitnerium

much adj **more, most** existing in quantity ▷ n large amount; a great deal; important matter ▷ adv in a great degree; nearly

mu·ci·lage [MYOO-sə-lij] n gum, glue

muck [muk] n horse, cattle dung; unclean refuse; insulting remarks ▷ vt make dirty **muck'y** adj **muck·i·er, muck·i·est** dirty; messy; unpleasant **muck out** v remove muck from **muck up** v inf ruin, bungle, confuse

mu·cus [MYOO-kəs] n viscid fluid secreted by mucous membrane **mu'cous** [-kəs] adj resembling mucus; secreting mucus; slimy **mucous membrane** lining of canals and cavities of the body

mud n wet and soft earth; inf slander **mud'dy** adj **-di·er, -di·est**

mud·dle [MUD-əl] vt **-dled, -dling**

(esp with *up*) confuse; bewilder; mismanage ▷ *n* confusion; tangle

mu·ez·zin [myoo-EZ-in] *n* crier who summons Muslims to prayer

muff¹ *n* tube-shaped covering to keep the hands warm

muff² *vt* miss, bungle, fail in

muf·fin *n* cup-shaped quick bread

muf·fle [MUF-əl] *vt* **-fled, -fling** wrap up, esp to deaden sound **muf·fler** [-lər] *n* on motor vehicles, device for accomplishing this; scarf

muf·ti [MUF-tee] *n* plain clothes as distinguished from uniform, eg of soldier

mug¹ *n* drinking cup

mug² *n sl* face; *sl* ruffian, criminal ▷ *vt* **mugged, mug·ging** rob violently **mug·ger** [-ər] *n*

mug·gy [MUG-ee] *adj* **-gi·er, -gi·est** damp and stifling

Mu·ham·mad, Mo·ham·med [muu-HAM-əd] *n* prophet and founder of Islam **Mu·ham·mad·an** *adj, n* Muslim

mu·lat·to [mə-LAT-oh] *adj, n, pl* **-oes** (child) of one white and one black parent

mul·ber·ry [MUL-ber-ee] *n, pl* **-ries** tree whose leaves are used to feed silkworms; its purplish fruit

mulch *n* straw, leaves, etc, spread as protection for roots of plants ▷ *vt* protect thus

mule [myool] *n* animal that is cross between female horse and male donkey; hybrid; spinning machine; small locomotive; slipper **mul·ish** *adj* obstinate

mull *vt* heat (wine) with sugar and spices; think (over), ponder

mul·lah [MUL-ə] *n* Muslim theologian

mul·let¹ [MUL-it] *n* edible sea fish

mul·let² *n* haircut in which the hair is short at the top and sides and long

at the back

mul·lion [MUL-yən] *n* upright dividing bar in window

multi-, mult- *comb form* many: *multiracial; multistory*

mul·ti·far·i·ous [mul-tə-FAIR-ee-əs] *adj* of various kinds or parts

mul·ti·ple [MUL-tə-pəl] *adj* having many parts ▷ *n* quantity that contains another an exact number of times **mul·ti·pli·cand'** *n* mathematics number to be multiplied **mul·ti·pli·ca·tion** *n* **mul·ti·plic'i·ty** [-PLIS-i-tee] *n* variety, greatness in number **mul'ti·ply** [-plī] *v* **-plied, -ply·ing** (cause to) increase in number, quantity, or degree ▷ *vt* combine (two numbers or quantities) by multiplication; increase in number by reproduction

mul·ti·plex [MUL-tə-pleks] *adj* telecommunications capable of transmitting numerous messages over same wire or channel

mul·ti·tude [MUL-ti-tood] *n* great number; great crowd; populace **mul·ti·tu'di·nous** *adj* very numerous

mum *adj* silent **mum's the word** keep silent

mum·ble [MUM-bəl] *v* **-bled, -bling** speak indistinctly, mutter

mum·my [MUM-ee] *n, pl* **-mies** embalmed body **mum'mi·fy** *vt* **-fied, -fy·ing**

mumps *n* infectious disease marked by swelling in the glands of the neck

munch *v* chew noisily and vigorously; crunch

mun·dane [mun-DAYN] *adj* ordinary, everyday; belonging to this world, earthly

mu·nic·i·pal [myuu-NIS-ə-pəl] *adj* belonging to affairs of city or town

mu·nic·i·pal·i·ty n, pl **-ties** city or town with local self-government; its governing body

mu·nif·i·cent [myoo-NIF-ə-sənt] adj very generous **mu·nif·i·cence** n bounty

mu·ni·tions [myoo-NISH-ənz] pl n military stores

mu·ral [MYUUR-əl] n painting on a wall ▷ adj of or on a wall

mur·der [MUR-dər] n unlawful premeditated killing of human being ▷ vt kill thus **mur·der·ous** adj

murk n thick darkness **murk·y** adj **murk·i·er, murk·i·est** gloomy

mur·mur [MUR-mər] n low, indistinct sound ▷ vi make such a sound; complain ▷ vt utter in a low voice

mus·cle [MUS-əl] n part of body that produces movement by contracting; system of muscles **mus·cu·lar** [-kyə-lər] adj with well-developed muscles; strong; of, like muscle **mus·cle-bound** adj with muscles stiff through overdevelopment **muscular dystrophy** disease with wasting of muscles **muscle in** inf force one's way into **muscle shirt** inf shirt that leaves full arm exposed

muse [myooz] vi **mused, mus·ing** ponder; consider meditatively; be lost in thought

Muse [myooz] n one of the nine goddesses inspiring learning and the arts

mu·se·um [myoo-ZEE-əm] n place housing collection of natural, artistic, historical or scientific objects

mush[1] n soft pulpy mass; cloying sentimentality **mush·y** adj **mush·i·er, mush·i·est**

mush[2] vi travel over snow with dog team and sled ▷ vt spur on (sled) dogs ▷ interj go!

mush·room n fungoid growth, typically with stem and cap structure, some species edible ▷ vi shoot up rapidly; expand **mushroom cloud** large cloud resembling mushroom, esp from nuclear explosion

mu·sic [MYOO-zik] n art form using melodious and harmonious combination of notes; laws of this; composition in this art **mu·si·cal** adj of, like music; interested in, or with instinct for, music; pleasant to ear ▷ n play, motion picture in which music plays essential part **mu·si·cian** n **mu·si·col·o·gist** [-jist] n **mu·si·col·o·gy** n scientific study of music

musical comedy light dramatic entertainment of songs, dances, etc

musk n scent obtained from gland of **musk deer**; various plants with similar scent **musk·y** adj **musk·i·er, musk·i·est musk ox** ox of Arctic Amer **musk·rat** n N Amer rodent found near water; its fur

mus·ket [MUS-kit] n history infantryman's gun **mus·ket·eer'** n

Mus·lim [MUZ-lim] n follower of religion of Islam ▷ adj of religion, culture, etc of Islam

mus·lin [MUZ-lin] n fine cotton fabric

mus·sel [MUS-əl] n bivalve shellfish

must[1] v aux be obliged to, or certain to ▷ n something one must do

must[2] n newly-pressed grape juice; unfermented wine

mus·tache, mous·tache [MUS-tash] n hair on the upper lip

mus·tang n wild horse

mus·tard [MUS-tərd] n powder made from the seeds of a plant, used

in paste as a condiment; the plant
mustard gas poisonous gas causing
blistering, lung damage, etc
mus•ter [MUS-tər] v assemble ▷ n
assembly, esp for exercise, inspection
mus•ty [MUS-tee] adj **-ti•er,
-ti•est** moldy, stale **must** n
mus'ti•ness n
mu•tate [MYOO-tayt] v **-tat•ed,
-tat•ing** (cause to) undergo
mutation **mu'ta•ble** [-tə-bəl]
adj liable to change **mu'tant**
[-tənt] n mutated animal, plant,
etc **mu•ta'tion** [-TAY-shən] n
change, esp genetic change causing
divergence from kind or racial type
mu'ta•tive adj
mute [myoot] adj **mut•er, mut•est**
dumb; silent ▷ n person incapable of
speech; music contrivance to soften
tone of instruments **mut'ed** adj (of
sound) muffled; (of light) subdued
mu•ti•late [MYOOT-l-ayt] vt
-lat•ed, -lat•ing deprive of a limb
or other part; damage; deface
mu•ti•la'tion n
mu•ti•ny [MYOOT-n-ee] n, pl
-nies rebellion against authority,
esp against officers of disciplined
body ▷ vi **-nied, -ny•ing** commit
mutiny **mu•ti•neer'** n **mu'ti•nous**
adj rebellious
mutt n inf (mongrel) dog
mut•ter [MUT-ər] vi speak with
mouth nearly closed, indistinctly;
grumble ▷ vt utter in such tones ▷ n
(act of) muttering
mut•ton [MUT-ən] n flesh of sheep
used as food **mut•ton•chops** pl n
side whiskers broad at jaw, narrow at
temples **mut'ton•head** [-hed] n inf
slow-witted person
mu•tu•al [MYOO-choo-əl] adj
done, possessed, etc, by each of
two with respect to the other;

reciprocal; common to both or
all **mu•tu•al'i•ty** n **mutual fund**
investment company selling shares
to public with repurchase on request
muz•zle [MUZ-əl] n mouth and
nose of animal; cover for these to
prevent biting; open end of gun
▷ vt **-zled, -zling** put muzzle on;
silence, gag
my [mī] adj belonging to me
my•self' pron emphatic or reflexive
form of I or ME
my•col•o•gy [mī-KOL-ə-jee] n
science of fungi
my•o•pi•a [mī-OH-pee-ə] n
nearsightedness; obtuseness
my•op'ic adj
myr•i•ad [MIR-ee-əd] adj
innumerable ▷ n large indefinite
number
myrrh [mur] n aromatic gum,
formerly used as incense
mys•ter•y [MIS-tə-ree] n, pl **-teries**
obscure or secret thing; anything
strange or inexplicable; religious
rite; in Middle Ages, biblical play
mys•te'ri•ous [-TEER-ee-əs] adj
mys•tic [MIS-tik] n one who seeks
divine, spiritual knowledge, esp by
prayer, contemplation, etc ▷ adj of
hidden meaning, esp in religious
sense **mys'ti•cal** adj **mys'ti•cism**
[-siz-əm] n
mys•ti•fy [MIS-tə-fī] vt
-fied, -fy•ing bewilder, puzzle
mys•ti•fi•ca'tion [-KAY-shən] n
mys•tique [mi-STEEK] n aura of
mystery, power, etc
myth [mith] n tale with
supernatural characters or
events; invented story; imaginary
person or object **myth'i•cal** adj
myth•o•log'i•cal [-LOJ-ə-kəl] adj
my•thol'o•gy n, pl **-gies** myths
collectively; study of them

n

N *chemistry* nitrogen; *physics* newton

Na *chemistry* sodium

na·bob [NAY-bob] *n* wealthy, powerful person

na·cre [NAY-kər] *n* mother-of-pearl

na·dir [NAY-dər] *n* point opposite the zenith; lowest point

nag¹ *v* **nagged, nag·ging** scold or annoy constantly; cause pain to constantly ▷ *n* nagging; one who nags

nag² *n* old horse; *sl* any horse; small horse for riding

nai·ad [NAY-ad] *n* water nymph

nail [nayl] *n* horny shield at ends of fingers, toes; claw; small metal spike for fastening wood, etc ▷ *vt* fasten with nails; *inf* catch **hit the nail on the head** do or say the right thing

na·ive [nah-EEV] *adj* simple, unaffected, ingenuous **na·ive·té** [-eev-TAY] *n*

nak·ed [NAY-kid] *adj* without clothes; exposed, bare; undisguised **naked eye** the eye unassisted by any optical instrument

name [naym] *n* word by which person, thing, etc is denoted; reputation; title; credit; family; famous person ▷ *vt* **named, nam·ing** give name to; call by name; entitle; appoint; mention; specify **name·less** [-lis] *adj* without a name; indescribable; too dreadful to be mentioned; obscure **name·ly** *adv* that is to say **name·sake** *n* person named after another; person with same name as another **name and shame** make public the name of (a wrongdoer) in order to bring public condemnation on him or her

nap¹ *vi* **napped, nap·ping** take short sleep, esp in daytime ▷ *n* short sleep

nap² *n* downy surface on cloth made by projecting fibers

na·palm [NAY-pahm] *n* jellied gasoline, highly incendiary, used in bombs, etc

nape [nayp] *n* back of neck

naph·tha [NAF-thə] *n* inflammable oil distilled from coal, etc **naph·tha·lene** [-leen] *n* white crystalline product distilled from coal tar, used in disinfectants, mothballs, etc

nap·kin *n* cloth, paper for wiping fingers or lips at table

nar·cis·sus [nahr-SIS-əs] *n*, *pl* **nar·cis·sus** genus of bulbous plants including daffodil, jonquil, esp one with white flowers **nar·cis·sism** *n* abnormal love and admiration of oneself **nar·cis·sist** *n*

nar·cot·ic [nahr-KOT-ik] *n* any of a group of drugs, including morphine and opium, producing numbness and stupor, used medicinally but addictive ▷ *adj*

nar·rate [NAR-ayt] *vt* **-rat·ed, -rat·ing** relate, recount, tell (story) **nar·ra·tion** *n* **nar·ra·tive** [-rə-tiv] *n* account, story ▷ *adj* relating **nar·ra·tor** [-ray-tər] *n*

nar·row [NAR-oh] *adj* **-er, -est**

of little breadth, or width esp in comparison to length; limited; barely adequate or successful ▷ v make, become narrow **nar'rows** pl n narrow part of straits **nar'row·ness** n **narrow-minded** adj illiberal; bigoted **narrow-mindedness** n prejudice, bigotry

na·sal [NAY-zəl] adj of nose ▷ n sound partly produced in nose **na'sal·ly** adv

nas·cent [NAYS-ənt] adj just coming into existence; springing up

nas·tur·tium [na-STUR-shəm] n garden plant with red or orange flowers

nas·ty [NAS-tee] adj **-ti·er, -ti·est** foul, disagreeable, unpleasant **nas'ti·ly** adv **nas'ti·ness** n

na·tal [NAYT-l] adj of birth

na·tion [NAY-shən] n people or race organized as a country **na'tion·al** [NASH-ə-nl] adj belonging or pert to a nation; public, general ▷ n member of a nation **na'tion·al·ism** n loyalty, devotion to one's country; movement for independence of country, area, ruled by another **na·tion·al·i·ty** n, pl **-ties** national quality or feeling; fact of belonging to particular nation; member of this **na'tion·al·ize** vt **-ized, -iz·ing** convert (private industry, resources, etc) to government control

na·tive [NAY-tiv] adj inborn; born in particular place; found in pure state; that was place of one's birth ▷ n one born in a place; member of indigenous people of a country; species of plant, animal, etc originating in a place **Native American** n person descended from the original inhabitants of the American continent ▷ adj of Native Americans

na·tiv·i·ty [nə-TIV-i-tee] n, pl **-ties** birth; time, circumstances of birth; **(N-)** birth of Christ

nat·ter [NAT-ər] vi talk idly

nat·ty [NAT-ee] adj **ti·er, -ti·est** neat and smart; spruce **nat'ti·ly** adv

na·ture [NAY-chər] n innate or essential qualities of person or thing; class, sort; life force; **(N-)** power underlying all phenomena in material world; material world as a whole; unspoiled scenery or countryside, and plants and animals in it; disposition; temperament **nat·u·ral** [NACH-ə-əl] adj of, according to, occurring in, provided by, nature; inborn; normal; unaffected; illegitimate ▷ n something, somebody well suited for something; music symbol used to remove effect of sharp or flat preceding it **nat'u·ral·ist** n student of natural history **nat·u·ral·is·tic** adj of imitating nature in effect or characteristics **nat'u·ral·ize** vt **-ized, -iz·ing** admit to citizenship; accustom to different climate or environment **nat'u·ral·ly** adv of or according to nature; by nature; of course **natural history** study of animals and plants

naught [nawt] n nothing; nought **naugh·ty** [NAW-tee] adj **-ti·er, -ti·est** disobedient, not behaving well; mildly indecent, tasteless **naugh'ti·ly** adv

nau·se·a [NAW-zee-ə] n feeling that precedes vomiting **nau'se·ate** vt **-at·ed, -at·ing** sicken **nau'seous** [NAW-shəs] adj **nau'se·at·ing** adj disgusting; causing nausea

nau·ti·cal [NAW-ti-kəl] adj of seamen or ships; marine **nautical mile** 6080.20 feet (1853.25 meters)

nau·ti·lus [NAWT-l-əs] n, pl **-lus·es** univalvular shellfish

naval see NAVY

nave [nayv] n main part of church

na·vel [NAY-vəl] n umbilicus, small scar, depression in middle of abdomen where umbilical cord was attached

nav·i·gate [NAV-i-gayt] v **-gat·ed, -gat·ing** plan, direct, plot path or position of ship, etc; travel **nav'i·ga·ble** adj **nav·i·ga'tion** n science of directing course of seagoing vessel, or of aircraft in flight; shipping **nav'i·ga·tor** n one who navigates

na·vy [NAY-vee] n, pl **-vies** fleet; warships of country with their crews and organization ▷ adj navy-blue **na'val** adj of the navy **navy-blue** adj very dark blue

Na·zi [NAHT-see] n member of the National Socialist political party in Germany, 1919–45; one who thinks, acts, like a Nazi ▷ adj

Nb chemistry niobium

Nd chemistry neodymium

Ne chemistry neon

Ne·an·der·thal [nee-AN-dər-thawl] adj of a type of primitive man; (n-) primitive

neap [neep] adj low **neap tide** the low tide at the first and third quarters of the moon

near [neer] prep close to ▷ adv **-er, -est** at or to a short distance ▷ adj **-er, -est** close at hand; closely related; narrow, so as barely to escape; stingy; (of vehicles, horses, etc) at driver's left ▷ v approach **near'by** adj adjacent **near'ly** adv closely; almost

neat [neet] adj **-er, -est** tidy, orderly; efficient; precise, deft; cleverly worded; undiluted; simple and elegant **neat'ly** adv

neb·u·la [NEB-yə-lə] n, pl **-lae** [-lee] astronomy diffuse cloud of particles, gases **neb'u·lous** adj cloudy; vague, indistinct

nec·es·sar·y [NES-ə-ser-ee] adj needful, requisite, that must be done; unavoidable, inevitable **nec'es·sar·i·ly** adv **ne·ces'si·tate** vt **-tat·ed, -tat·ing** make necessary **ne·ces'si·tous** adj poor, needy, destitute **ne·ces'si·ty** n, pl **-ties** something needed, requisite; constraining power or state of affairs; compulsion; poverty

neck [nek] n part of body joining head to shoulders; narrower part of a bottle, etc; narrow piece of anything between wider parts ▷ vi embrace, cuddle **neck'lace** [-lis] n ornament around the neck

nec·ro·man·cy [NEK-rə-man-see] n magic, esp by communication with dead **nec'ro·man·cer** n wizard

ne·crop·o·lis [nə-KROP-ə-lis] n, pl **-lis·es** cemetery

nec·tar [NEK-tər] n honey of flowers; drink of the gods

nec·tar·ine [nek-tə-REEN] n variety of peach

nee [nay] adj indicating maiden name of married woman

need vt want, require ▷ n (state, instance of) want; requirement; necessity; poverty **need'ful** adj necessary, requisite **need'less** adj unnecessary **needs** adv (preceded or foll by must) necessarily **need'y** adj **need·i·er, need·i·est** poor, in want

nee·dle [NEE-dl] n **-dled, -dling** pointed pin with an eye and no head, for sewing; long, pointed pin for knitting; pointer of gauge, dial; magnetized bar of compass; stylus for record player; leaf of fir, pine, etc; obelisk; hypodermic syringe ▷ vt inf goad, provoke **nee'dle·craft, -work** n embroidery, sewing

ne·far·i·ous [ni-FAIR-ee-əs] *adj* wicked **ne·far·i·ous·ness** *n*

ne·gate [ni-GAYT] *vt* **-gat·ed, -gat·ing** deny, nullify **ne·ga·tion** *n* contradiction, denial

neg·a·tive [NEG-ə-tiv] *adj* expressing denial or refusal; lacking enthusiasm, energy, interest; not positive; of electrical charge having the same polarity as the charge of an electron ▷ *n* negative word or statement; photography picture made by action of light on chemicals in which lights and shades are reversed

ne·glect [ni-GLEKT] *vt* disregard, take no care of; fail to do; omit through carelessness ▷ *n* fact of neglecting or being neglected **ne·glect'ful** *adj*

neg·li·gee [NEG-li-zhay] *n* woman's light, gauzy nightgown or dressing gown

neg·li·gence [NEG-li-jəns] *n* neglect; carelessness **neg'li·gent** *adj* **neg'li·gi·ble** *adj* able to be disregarded; very small or unimportant

ne·go·ti·ate [ni-GOH-shee-ayt] *v* **-at·ed, -at·ing** ▷ *vi* discuss with view to mutual settlement ▷ *vt* arrange by conference; transfer (bill, check, etc); get over, past, around (obstacle) **ne·go'ti·a·ble** [-shə-bəl] *adj* **ne·go·ti·a'tion** [-shee-AY-shən] *n* dealing with another on business; discussion; transference (of bill, check, etc)

Ne·gro [NEE-groh] *n, pl* **-groes** *oft offens* dark-skinned person of African ancestry ▷ *adj*

neigh [nay] *n* cry of horse ▷ *vi* utter this cry

neigh·bor [NAY-bər] *n* one who lives near another **neigh'bor·hood** *n* district; people of a district; region

around about **neigh'bor·ing** *adj* situated nearby **neigh'bor·ly** *adj* as or befitting a good or friendly neighbor; friendly; helpful

nei·ther [NEE-thər] *adj, pron* not the one or the other ▷ *adv* not on the one hand; not either ▷ *conj* nor yet

nem·e·sis [NEM-ə-sis] *n, pl* **-ses** [-seez] retribution; (**N-**) the goddess of vengeance

neo- *comb form* new, later, revived in modified form, based upon: *neoclassicism*

neo·con·ser·va·tism [nee-oh-kən-SUR-və-tiz-əm] *n* conservative tendency among supporters of the political left that has become characterized by its support of hawkish foreign policies

Ne·o·lith·ic [nee-ə-LITH-ik] *adj* of the later Stone Age

ne·ol·o·gism [nee-OL-ə-jiz-əm] *n* newly coined word or phrase

ne·on [NEE-on] *n* one of the inert constituent gases of the atmosphere, used in illuminated signs and lights

ne·o·phyte [NEE-ə-fīt] *n* new convert; beginner, novice

neph·ew [NEF-yoo] *n* brother's or sister's son

ne·phri·tis [nə-FRĪ-tis] *n* inflammation of kidneys **ne·phro·sis** [-FROH-sis] *n* degenerative disease of kidneys

nep·o·tism [NEP-ə-tiz-əm] *n* undue favoritism toward one's relations

Nep·tune [NEP-toon] *n* god of the sea; planet second farthest from sun

nep·tu·ni·um [nep-TOO-nee-əm] *n* synthetic metallic element

nerd [nurd] *n sl* boring person obsessed with a particular subject

nerve [nurv] *n* sinew, tendon; fiber or bundle of fibers conveying feeling, impulses to motion, etc to

and from brain and other parts of
body; assurance; coolness in danger;
audacity; ▷ *pl* irritability; unusual
sensitiveness to fear, annoyance,
etc **nerve'less** [-lis] *adj* without
nerves; useless; weak; paralyzed
nerv'ous [-əs] *adj* excitable;
timid, apprehensive, worried; of the
nerves **nerv'y** [-ee] *adj* **nerv·i·er,
nerv·i·est** nervous, jumpy, irritable;
on edge **nervous breakdown**
condition of mental, emotional
disturbance, disability

nest *n* place in which bird lays and
hatches its eggs; animal's breeding
place; snug retreat ▷ *vi* make, have
a nest **nest egg** (fund of) money
in reserve

nes·tle [NES-əl] *vi* **-tled, -tling**
settle comfortably, usu pressing in or
close to something

nest'ling *n* bird too young to
leave nest

net' *n* openwork fabric of meshes
of cord, etc; piece of it used to catch
fish, etc; (**N-**) short for **INTERNET** ▷ *vt*
net·ted, net·ting cover with, or
catch in, net; catch, ensnare **netting**
n string or wire net **net'ball** *n* tennis
return shot that hits top of net and
remains in play **net·i·quette** [NET-
i-kit] *n* informal code of behaviour
on the Internet

net² *n* left after all deductions;
free from deduction ▷ *vt* **net·ted,
net·ting** gain, yield as clear profit
neth·er [NETH-ər] *adj* lower
ne·tsu·ke [NET-skee] *n* carved
wooden or ivory toggle or button
worn in Japan
net·tle [NET-l] *n* plant with
stinging hairs on the leaves ▷ *vt*
-tled, -tling irritate, provoke
net·work [NET-wurk] *n* system
of intersecting lines, roads, etc;
interconnecting group of people or

things; in broadcasting, group of
stations connected to transmit same
programs simultaneously; *computing*
system of interconnected computers
neu·ral [NUUR-əl] *adj* of the nerves
neu·ral·gia [nuu-RAL-jə] *n* pain
in, along nerves, esp of face and head
neu·ri·tis [nuu-RĪ-tis] *n*
inflammation of nerves
neu·rol·o·gy [nuu-ROL-ə-
jee] *n* science, study of nerves
neu·rol·o·gist *n*
neu·ro·sis [nuu-ROH-sis] *n, pl*
-ses [-seez] relatively mild mental
disorder **neu·rot·ic** *adj* suffering
from nervous disorder; abnormally
sensitive ▷ *n* neurotic person
neu·ter [NOO-tər] *adj* neither
masculine nor feminine ▷ *n* neuter
word; neuter gender ▷ *vt* castrate,
spay (domestic animals)
neu·tral [NOO-trəl] *adj* taking
neither side in war, dispute, etc;
without marked qualities; belonging
to neither of two classes ▷ *n* neutral
nation or a citizen of one; neutral
gear **neu·tral·i·ty** **neu·tral·ize**
vt **-ized, -iz·ing** make ineffective;
counterbalance **neutral gear** in
vehicle, position of gears that leaves
transmission disengaged
neu·tron [NOO-tron] *n* electrically
neutral particle of the nucleus of an
atom **neutron bomb** nuclear bomb
designed to destroy people but not
buildings
nev·er [NEV-ər] *adv* at no time
nev·er·the·less *adv* for all that,
notwithstanding
ne·vus [NEE-vəs] *n* congenital
mark on skin; birthmark, mole
new [noo] *adj* **-er, -est** not
existing before, fresh; that has
lately come into some state or
existence; unfamiliar, strange ▷ *adv*

newly **new·ly** adv recently, fresh
new·ness n **New Age** cultural movement originating in the 1980s, characterized by such things as alternative medicine, astrology, and meditation **new·com·er** n recent arrival **new·fan·gled** [-FANG-əld] adj of new fashion

new·el [NOO-əl] n central pillar of winding staircase; post at top or bottom of staircase rail

news [nooz] n report of recent happenings, tidings; interesting fact not previously known **news·cast** n news broadcast **news·deal·er** n shopkeeper who sells newspapers and magazines **news·flash** n brief news item, oft interrupting radio, TV program **news·group** n electronic discussion group on the Internet that is devoted to a specific topic **news·pa·per** n periodical publication containing news, advertisements, etc **news·print** n paper of the kind used for newspapers, etc **news·reel** n motion picture giving news **news·room** n room where news is received and prepared for publication or broadcast **news·wor·thy** [-wur-thee] adj **-thi·er**, **-thi·est** sufficiently interesting or important to be reported as news

newt [noot] n small, tailed amphibious creature

new·ton [NOOT-n] n SI unit of force

next [nekst] adj, adv nearest; immediately following **next of kin** nearest relative(s)

nex·us [NEK-səs] n, pl **nexus** tie; connection, link

Ni chemistry nickel

nib·ble [NIB-əl] v **-bled**, **-bling** take little bites of ▷ n little bite

nice [nis] adj **nic·er**, **nic·est** pleasant; friendly; kind; attractive; subtle, fine; careful, exact; difficult to decide **nice·ly** adv **ni·ce·ty** n, pl **-ties** minute distinction or detail; subtlety; precision

niche [nich] n recess in wall; suitable place in life, public estimation, etc

nick [nik] vt make notch in, indent; sl steal ▷ n notch; exact point of time **in the nick of time** at the last possible moment

nick·el [NIK-əl] n silver-white metal much used in alloys and plating; five-cent piece

nick·name [NIK-naym] n familiar name added to or replacing an ordinary name

nic·o·tine [NIK-ə-teen] n poisonous oily liquid in tobacco

niece [nees] n brother's or sister's daughter

nif·ty [NIFT-ee] adj **-tier**, **-tiest** inf neat or smart

nig·gard [NIG-ərd] n mean, stingy person **nig·gard·ly** adj, adv **nig·gard·li·ness** n

nig·gle [NIG-əl] vi **-gled**, **-gling** find fault continually; annoy **niggling** adj petty; irritating and persistent

nigh [ni] adj, adv, prep lit near

night [nit] n time of darkness between sunset and sunrise; end of daylight; dark **night·ie** n inf nightgown **night·ly** adj happening, done every night; of the night ▷ adv every night; by night **night·cap** n cap worn in bed; inf late-night (alcoholic) drink **night·club** n establishment for dancing, music, etc open until early morning **night·gown** n woman's or child's loose gown worn in bed **night·in·gale** n small Old World bird that sings usu at night **night·mare**

[-mair] n very bad dream; terrifying experience **night'time** n

ni·hil·ism [Nĭ-ä-liz-əm] n rejection of all religious and moral principles; opposition to all constituted authority, or government **ni'hil·ist** n **ni·hil·is'tic** adj

nim·ble [NIM-bəl] adj **-bler, -blest** agile, active, quick, dexterous **nim'bly** adv

nim·bus [NIM-bəs] n, pl **-bi** [-bī] or **-bus·es** rain or storm cloud; cloud of glory, halo

nine [nīn] adj, n cardinal number next above eight **ninth** adj, n **ninth'ly** adv **nine·teen'** adj, n nine more than ten **nine·teenth'** adj **nine'ty** adj, n nine tens **nine'ti·eth** adj **nine'pins** n game where wooden pins are set up to be knocked down by rolling ball, skittles

nip v **nipped, nip·ping** pinch sharply; detach by pinching, bite; check growth (of plants) thus; inf steal; inf beat (opponent) by close margin hurry ▷ n pinch; check to growth; sharp coldness of weather; small alcoholic drink **nip'per** n thing (eg crab's claw) that nips; inf small boy ▷ pl pincers **nip'py** adj **-pi·er, -pi·est** inf cold; quick

nip·ple [NIP-əl] n point of a breast, teat; anything like this

nir·va·na [nir-VAH-nə] n Buddhism absolute blessedness; Hinduism merging of individual in supreme spirit

nit n egg of louse or other parasite **nit'pick·ing** adj, inf overconcerned with detail, esp to find fault **nit'pick** v show such overconcern; criticize over petty faults **nit'wit** n inf fool **nit·ty-grit'ty** n sl basic facts, details

ni·tro·gen [Nī-trə-jən] n one of the gases making up the air

ni'trate n compound of nitric acid and an alkali **ni'tric** adj **ni'trous** adj **ni·trog·e·nous** [-TROJ-ə-nəs] adj of, containing nitrogen **ni·tro·glyc'er·in** [-troh-GLIS-ə-rin] n explosive liquid

No chemistry nobelium

no [noh] adj not any, not a; not at all ▷ adv expresses negative reply to question or request ▷ n, pl **noes** refusal; denial; negative vote or voter **no one** nobody **no-go** adj sl not operating; canceled **no man's land** waste or unclaimed land; contested land between two opposing forces **no way** inf absolutely not

no·bel·i·um [noh-BEL-ee-əm] n synthetic element produced from curium

no·ble [NOH-bəl] adj **-bler, -blest** of the nobility; showing, having high moral qualities; impressive, excellent ▷ n member of the nobility **no·bil'i·ty** n in some countries, class holding special rank, usu hereditary; being noble **no'bly** adv

no·bod·y [NOH-bod-ee] pron no person; no one ▷ n, pl **-bod·ies** person of no importance

noc·tur·nal [nok-TUR-nl] adj of, in, by night; active by night **noc·turne** [NOK-turn] n dreamy piece of music

nod v **nod·ded, nod·ding** bow head slightly and quickly in assent, command, etc; let head droop with sleep ▷ n act of nodding **nodding acquaintance** slight knowledge of person or subject **give the nod to** inf express approval of **nod off** fall asleep

node [nohd] n knot or knob; point at which curve crosses itself **no'dal** [-əl] adj

nod·ule [NOJ-ool] n little knot; rounded irregular mineral mass

No·el [noh-EL] n Christmas; **(n-)** Christmas carol

nog n drink made with beaten eggs; eggnog; peg, block

nog·gin [NOG-ən] n small amount of liquor; small mug; inf head

noise [noyz] n any sound, esp disturbing one; clamor, din; loud outcry; talk or interest ▷ vt rumor **noise·less** [-lis] adj without noise, quiet, silent **nois·i·ly** adv **nois·y** adj **nois·i·er, nois·i·est** making much noise; clamorous

noi·some [NOI-səm] adj disgusting; noxious

no·mad [NOH-mad] n member of tribe with no fixed dwelling place; wanderer **no·mad·ic** adj

nom de plume [nom də PLOOM] Fr writer's assumed name; pen name; pseudonym

no·men·cla·ture [NOH-mən-klay-chər] n terminology of particular science, etc

nom·i·nal [NOM-ə-nəl] adj in name only; (of fee, etc) small, insignificant; of a name or names **nom·i·nal·ly** adv in name only; not really

nom·i·nate [NOM-ə-nayt] vt **-nat·ed, -nat·ing** propose as candidate; appoint to office **nom·i·na·tion** n **nom·i·na·tive** [-nə-tiv] adj, n (of) case of nouns, pronouns when subject of verb **nom·i·nee'** n candidate

non- prefix indicating: negation: nonexistent; refusal or failure: noncooperation; exclusion from a specified class: nonfiction; lack or absence: nonevent

non·a·ge·nar·i·an [non-ə-jə-NAIR-ee-ən] adj aged between ninety and ninety-nine ▷ n person of such age

non·ag·gres'sion n policy of not attacking other countries

non·al·co·hol'ic adj containing no alcohol

nonce [nons] n **for the nonce** for the occasion only; for the present

non·cha·lant [non-shə-LAHNT] adj casually unconcerned, indifferent, cool **non'cha·lance** n

non·com·bat·ant [non-kəm-BAT-nt] n civilian during war; member of army who does not fight, eg chaplain

non·com·mit'tal [non-kə-MIT-l] adj avoiding definite preference or pledge

non com·pos men·tis [NON KOM-pohs MEN-tis] Lat of unsound mind

non·con·duc'tor n substance that is a poor conductor of heat, electricity, or sound

non·con·trib'u·to·ry adj denoting a pension scheme for employees, the premiums of which are paid entirely by the employer

non·de·script [non-di-SKRIPT] adj lacking distinctive characteristics; indeterminate

none [nun] pron no one, not any ▷ adj no ▷ adv in no way **none·the·less'** adv despite that, however

non·en·ti·ty [non-EN-ti-tee] n, pl **-ties** insignificant person, thing; nonexistent thing

non·e·vent' n disappointing or insignificant occurrence

non·ex·ist'ent adj not existing, imaginary **nonexistence** n

non·fic'tion n writing that deals with facts or real events

non·in·ter·ven'tion n refusal to intervene in the affairs of others

non·pa·reil [non-pə-REL] adj unequaled, matchless ▷ n person or thing unequaled or unrivaled;

small bead of colored sugar used to decorate cakes, etc; flat round piece of chocolate covered with this sugar

non·pay'ment n failure to pay money owed

non·plus vt -plussed, -plus·sing disconcert, confound, or bewilder completely

non·prof·it adj not run with the intention of making a profit

non·sense [NON-sens] n lack of sense; absurd language; silly conduct **non·sen'si·cal** adj ridiculous; meaningless; without sense

non se·qui·tur [non SEK-wi-tər] Lat statement with little or no relation to what preceded it

non·smok·er n person who does not smoke **non-smok'ing, no-smok'ing** adj denoting an area in which smoking is forbidden

non·stand·ard adj denoting language that is not regarded as correct by educated native speakers

non·start·er n person or idea that has little chance of success

non·stick adj coated with a substance that food will not stick to when cooked

non·stop adj, adv without a stop

non·tox·ic adj not poisonous

non·vi·o·lent adj using peaceful methods to bring about change **non·vi·o·lence** n

noo·dle¹ [NOOD-l] n strip of pasta served in soup, etc

noodle² n simpleton, fool; sl the head

nook [nuuk] n sheltered corner, retreat

noon n midday, twelve o'clock **noon'day** n noon **noon'tide** n the time about noon

noose [noos] n running loop; snare ▷ vt **noosed, noos·ing** catch,

ensnare in noose, lasso

nor conj and not

Nor·dic [NOR-dik] adj pert to peoples of Germanic stock, eg Scandinavians

norm n average level of achievement; rule or authoritative standard; model; standard type or pattern **nor'mal** adj ordinary; usual; conforming to type ▷ n geometry perpendicular **nor'mal·ly** adv

north n direction to the right of person facing the sunset; part of the world, of country, etc toward this point ▷ adv toward or in the north ▷ adj to, from, or in the north **north·er·ly** [NOR-thər-lee] adj (of wind) from the north ▷ n a wind from the north **north'ern** adj north or in the north **north'ern·er** n person from the north **north'ward** [NORTH-wərd] adj **north'ward(s)** adv

nose [nohz] n organ of smell, used also in breathing; any projection resembling a nose, as prow of ship, aircraft, etc ▷ v **nosed, nos·ing** (cause to) move forward slowly and carefully ▷ vt touch with nose; smell, sniff ▷ vi smell; pry **nos·y** adj **nos·i·er, nos·i·est** inquisitive **nose'dive** n downward sweep of aircraft; any sudden sharp fall **nose'gay** n bunch of flowers

nos·tal·gia [no-STAL-jə] n longing for return of past events; homesickness **nos·tal'gic** adj

nos·tril [NOS-tril] n one of the two external openings of the nose

nos·trum [NOS-trəm] n quack medicine; secret remedy

not adv expressing negation, refusal, denial

no·ta be·ne [NOH-tah BE·ne] Lat note well

no·ta·ble [NOH-tə-bəl] adj worthy of note, remarkable ▷ n person of distinction **no·ta·bil·i·ty** *n, pl* **-ties** prominence; an eminent person **no'ta·bly** *adv*

no·ta·tion [noh-TAY-shàn] *n* representation of numbers, quantities, by symbols; set of such symbols

notch [noch] *n* V-shaped cut or indentation; *inf* step, grade ▷ *vt* make notches in

note [noht] *n* brief comment or record; short letter; promissory note; symbol for musical score; single tone; indication, hint; fame; notice; regard ▷ *pl* brief jottings written down for future reference ▷ *vt* **not·ed, not·ing** observe, record; heed **noted** *adj* well-known; celebrated **note'book** *n* small book with blank pages for writing **note'wor·thy** [-wur-thee] *adj* worth noting, remarkable

noth·ing [NUTH-ing] *n* no thing, not anything, nought ▷ *adv* not at all, in no way

no·tice [NOH-tis] *n* observation, attention, consideration; warning, intimation, announcement; advance notification of intention to end a contract, etc, as of employment; review ▷ *vt* **-ticed, -tic·ing** observe, mention; give attention to **no'tice·a·ble** *adj* conspicuous; attracting attention; appreciable

no·ti·fy [NOH-tə-fī] *vt* **-fied, -fy·ing** report; give notice of or to **no·ti·fi·ca'tion** [-KAY-shàn] *n*

no·tion [NOH-shàn] *n* concept; opinion; whim ▷ *pl* small items eg buttons, thread for sale in store **no'tion·al** *adj* speculative, imaginary, abstract

no·to·ri·ous [noh-TOR-ee-əs] *adj* known for something bad; well-known **no·to·ri'e·ty** [-tə-RĪ-i-tee] *n* discreditable publicity

not·with·stand·ing *prep* in spite of ▷ *adv* all the same ▷ *conj* although

nou·gat [NOO-gàt] *n* chewy candy containing nuts, fruit, etc

nought [nawt] *n* nothing; figure o

noun [nown] *n* word used as name of person, idea, or thing, substantive

nour·ish [NUR-ish] *vt* feed; nurture; tend; encourage

nou·velle cui·sine [noo-vel kwee-ZEEN] *Fr* style of preparing and presenting food with light sauces and unusual combinations of flavors

no·va [NOH-və] *n, pl* **-vas** star that suddenly becomes brighter then loses brightness through months or years

nov·el¹ [NOV-əl] *n* fictitious tale in book form **nov'el·ist** *n* writer of novels

novel² *adj* new, recent; strange **nov'el·ty** *n, pl* **-ties** newness; something new or unusual; small ornament, trinket

no·ve·na [noh-VEE-nə] *n* RC Church prayers, services usu extending over nine consecutive days

nov·ice [NOV-is] *n* one new to anything; beginner; candidate for admission to religious order **no·vi·ti·ate** [noh-VISH-ee-it] *n* probationary period; part of religious house for novices; novice

now *adv* at the present time; immediately; (often with *just*) recently ▷ *conj* seeing that, since **now'a·days** *adv* in these times, at present

no·where [NOH-hwair] *adv* not in any place or state

no·wise [NOH-wiz] *adv* not in any manner or degree

nox·ious [NOK-shəs] *adj* poisonous, harmful

noz·zle [NOZ-əl] n pointed spout, esp at end of hose

Np chemistry neptunium

NT New Testament

nu·ance [NOO-ahns] n delicate shade of difference, in color, tone of voice, etc

nub n small lump; main point (of story, etc)

nu·bile [NOO-bil] adj marriageable **nu·bil'i·ty** n

nu·cle·us [NOO-klee-əs] n, pl -cle·i [-klee-i] center, kernel; beginning meant to receive additions; core of the atom **nu'cle·ar** [-klee-ər] adj of, pert to atomic nucleus **nuclear energy** energy released by nuclear fission **nuclear fission** disintegration of the atom **nuclear reaction** change in structure and energy content of atomic nucleus by interaction with another nucleus, particle **nuclear reactor** see REACTOR **nuclear winter** period of extremely low temperatures and little light after nuclear war

nude [nood] n state of being naked; (picture, statue, etc of) naked person ▷ adj naked **nud'ism** n practice of nudity **nud'ist** n **nu'di·ty** n

nudge [nuj] vt **nudged, nudg·ing** touch slightly esp with elbow to gain someone's attention, prod someone into action ▷ n such touch

nu·ga·to·ry [NOO-gə-tor-ee] adj trifling; futile

nug·get [NUG-it] n rough lump of native gold; anything of significance, value

nui·sance [NOO-səns] n something or someone harmful, offensive, annoying or disagreeable

null adj of no effect, void **nul'li·fy** [-fī] vt **-fied, -fy·ing** cancel; make useless or ineffective **nul'li·ty** n state of being null and void

Num. Numbers

numb [num] adj **-er, -est** deprived of feeling, esp by cold ▷ vt make numb; deaden

num·ber [NUM-bər] n sum or aggregate; word or symbol saying how many; single issue of a journal, etc, issued in different series; classification as to singular or plural; song, piece of music; performance; company, collection; identifying number, as of particular house, telephone, etc; inf measure, correct estimation of ▷ vt count; class, reckon; give a number to; amount to **num'ber·less** adj countless **number crunching** inf large-scale processing of numerical data

nu·mer·al [NOO-mər-əl] n sign or word denoting a number **nu'mer·ate** vt **-at·ed, -at·ing** count **nu'mer·a'tion** n **nu'mer·a·tor** n top part of fraction, figure showing how many of the fractional units are taken **nu·mer·i·cal** adj of, in respect of, number or numbers **nu'mer·ous** [-əs] adj many

nu·met·al [noo-MET-l] n type of rock music featuring sounds typical of heavy metal but also influenced by rap and hip-hop

nu·mis·mat·ic [noo-miz-MAT-ik] adj of coins **nu·mis·mat'ics** n the study of coins **nu·mis'ma·tist** [-mə-tist] n

nun n woman living (in convent) under religious vows **nun'ner·y** n, pl **-ies** convent of nuns

nun·cu·pa·tive [NUNG-kyə-pay-tiv] adj of a will, oral; not written

nup·tial [NUP-shəl] adj of, relating to marriage **nup'tials** pl n marriage; wedding ceremony

nurse [nurs] n person trained

for care of sick or injured; woman tending another's child ▷ vt **nursed, nurs·ing** act as nurse to; suckle; pay special attention to; harbor (grudge, etc) **nurs'er·y** n, pl **-er·ies** room for children; rearing place for plants **nurs'er·y·man** [-mən] n one who raises plants for sale **nursing home** institution for housing and caring for the aged or chronically ill

nur·ture [NUR-chər] n bringing up; education; rearing; nourishment ▷ vt **-tured, -tur·ing** bring up; educate

nut n fruit consisting of hard shell and kernel; hollow metal collar into which a screw fits; sl the head; sl eccentric or crazy person ▷ vi **nut·ted, nut·ting** gather nuts **nut'ty** adj **-ti·er, -ti·est** of, like nut; pleasant to taste and bite; sl insane, crazy; eccentric **nuts** adj sl insane **nut'hatch** n small songbird **nut'meg** n aromatic seed

of Indian tree
nu·tri·ent [NOO-tree-ənt] adj nourishing ▷ n something nutritious

nu·tri·ment [NOO-trə-mənt] n nourishing food **nu·tri'tion** [-TRISH-ən] n food; act of nourishing; study of this process **nu·tri'tion·ist** n one trained in nutrition **nu·tri'tious, nu'tri·tive** adj nourishing; promoting growth

nuz·zle [NUZ-əl] vi **-zled, -zling** burrow, press with nose; nestle

ny·lon [NĪ-lon] n synthetic material used for fabrics, bristles, ropes, etc ▷ pl stockings made of this

nymph [nimf] n legendary semidivine maiden of sea, woods, mountains, etc

nym·pho·ma·ni·a [nim-fə-MAY-nee-ə] n abnormally intense sexual desire in women **nym·pho·ma'ni·ac** n

O

O *chemistry* oxygen

oaf [ohf] *n* lout; dolt

oak [ohk] *n* common, deciduous forest tree **oak'en** [-in] *adj* of oak

oa•kum [OH-kəm] *n* loose fiber, used for caulking, got by unraveling old rope

oar [or] *n* wooden lever with broad blade worked by the hands to propel boat; oarsman ▷ *v* row **oars•man** [ORZ-mən] *n, pl* -**men** **oars'manship** *n* skill in rowing

o•a•sis [oh-AY-sis] *n, pl* -**ses** [-seez] fertile spot in desert; place serving as pleasant change from routine

oat [oht] *n* (usu *pl*) grain of cereal grass; the plant **oat'en** [-in] *adj* **oat'meal** [-meel] *n*

oath [ohth] *n, pl* **oaths** [ohthz] confirmation of truth of statement by naming something sacred; curse

ob•bli•ga•to [ob-li-GAH-toh] *adj, n, pl* -**tos** or -**ti** [-tee] (in musical score) essential; essential part of a musical score

ob•du•rate [OB-duu-rit] *adj* stubborn, unyielding **ob'du•ra•cy** [-rə-see]

o•be•di•ence [oh-BEE-dee-əns] *n* submission to authority

o•be•di•ent *adj* willing to obey; compliant; dutiful

o•bei•sance [oh-BAY-səns] *n* deference; a bow or curtsy

ob•e•lisk [OB-ə-lisk] *n* tapering rectangular stone column, with pyramidal apex

o•bese [oh-BEES] *adj* very fat, corpulent **o•be'si•ty** *n*

o•bey [oh-BAY] *vt* do the bidding of; act in accordance with ▷ *vi* do as ordered; submit to authority

ob•fus•cate [OB-fə-skayt] *vt* -**cat•ed, -cat•ing** perplex; darken; make obscure

o•bit•u•ar•y [oh-BICH-oo-er-ee] *n, pl* -**ar•ies** notice, record of death; biographical sketch of deceased person, esp in newspaper; (also **ob'it**)

ob•ject¹ [OB-jikt] *n* material thing; that to which feeling or action is directed; end or aim; *grammar* word dependent on verb or preposition **object lesson** lesson with practical and concrete illustration **no object** not an obstacle or hindrance

ob•ject² [əb-JEKT] *vt* state in opposition ▷ *vi* feel dislike or reluctance to something **ob•jec'tion** *n* **ob•jec'tion•a•ble** *adj* disagreeable; justly liable to objection

ob•jec•tive [əb-JEK-tiv] *adj* external to the mind; impartial ▷ *n* thing or place aimed at **ob•jec•tiv'i•ty** [ob-jek-TIV-]

ob•jur•gate [OB-jər-gayt] *vt* -**gat•ed, -gat•ing** scold, reprove **ob•jur•ga'tion** *n*

ob•late [OB-layt] *adj* of a sphere, flattened at the poles

o•blige [ə-BLIJ] *vt* **o•bliged, o•blig•ing** bind morally or legally to do service to; compel **ob'li•gate** *vt* -**gat•ed, -gat•ing** bind esp by legal contract; put under

obligation **ob·li·ga'tion** n binding duty, promise; debt of gratitude
o·blig'a·to·ry adj required; binding
o·blig'ing adj ready to serve others, civil, helpful, courteous
o·blique [ə-BLEEK] adj slanting; indirect **o·blique'ly** adv
o·bliq'ui·ty [-BLIK-wi-tee] n, pl **-ties** slant; dishonesty **oblique angle** one not a right angle
ob·lit·er·ate [ə-BLIT-ə-rayt] vt **-at·ed, -at·ing** blot out, efface, destroy completely
ob·liv·i·on [ə-BLIV-ee-ən] n forgetting or being forgotten
ob·liv'i·ous adj forgetful; unaware
ob·long [OB-lawng] adj rectangular, with adjacent sides unequal ▷ n oblong figure
ob·lo·quy [OB-lə-kwee] n, pl **-quies** reproach; abuse; disgrace; detraction
ob·nox·ious [əb-NOK-shəs] adj offensive, disliked, odious
o·boe [OH-boh] n woodwind instrument **o'bo·ist** n
ob·scene [əb-SEEN] adj indecent, lewd, repulsive **ob·scen'i·ty** [-SEN-i-tee] n
ob·scure [əb-SKYUUR] adj **-scur·er, -scur·est** unclear, indistinct; unexplained; dark, dim; humble ▷ vt **-scured, -scur·ing** make unintelligible; dim; conceal
ob·scu'rant [-SKYUUR-ənt] n one who opposes enlightenment or reform **ob·scu'rant·ism** n
ob·scu'ri·ty n indistinctness; lack of intelligibility; darkness; obscure, esp unrecognized, place or position
ob·se·quies [OB-si-kweez] pl n funeral rites
ob·se·qui·ous [əb-SEE-kwee-əs] adj servile, fawning
ob·serve [əb-ZURV] v **-served, -serv·ing** ▷ vt notice, remark; watch; note systematically; keep, follow ▷ vi make a remark
ob·serv'ance [-əns] n paying attention; keeping
ob·serv'ant adj quick to notice; careful in observing **ob·serv·a'tion** n action, habit of observing; noticing; remark **ob·serv'a·to·ry** [-və-tor-ee] n, pl **-ries** place for watching stars, etc
ob·sess [əb-SES] vt haunt, fill the mind **ob·ses'sion** [-SESH-ən] n fixed idea; domination of the mind by one idea **ob·ses'sive** adj
ob·sid·i·an [əb-SID-ee-ən] n fused volcanic rock, forming hard, dark, natural glass
ob·so·lete [ob-sə-LEET] adj disused, out of date **ob·so·les'cent** [-LES-ənt] adj going out of use
ob·sta·cle [OB-stə-kəl] n hindrance; impediment, barrier, obstruction
ob·stet·rics [əb-STE-triks] n branch of medicine concerned with childbirth and care of women before and after childbirth **ob·stet'ric** adj **ob·ste·tri'cian** [-shən] n
ob·sti·nate [OB-stə-nit] adj stubborn; self-willed; unyielding; hard to overcome or cure **ob'sti·na·cy** n
ob·strep·er·ous [əb-STREP-ər-əs] adj unruly, noisy, boisterous
ob·struct [əb-STRUKT] vt block up; hinder; impede **ob·struc'tion** n **ob·struc'tion·ist** n one who deliberately opposes transaction of business
ob·tain [əb-TAYN] vt get; acquire; procure by effort ▷ vi be customary **ob·tain'a·ble** adj procurable
ob·trude [əb-TROOD] vt **-trud·ed, -trud·ing** thrust forward unduly **ob·tru'sion** [-TROO-zhən] n **ob·tru'sive** adj forward, pushing

ob·tuse [əb-TOOS] adj dull of perception; stupid; greater than right angle; not pointed

ob·verse [OB-vurs] n a fact, idea, etc that is the complement of another; side of coin, medal, etc that has the principal design ▷ adj [ob-VURS]

ob·vi·ate [OB-vee-ayt] vt -at·ed, -at·ing remove, make unnecessary

ob·vi·ous [OB-vee-əs] adj clear, evident; wanting in subtlety

oc·ca·sion [ə-KAY-zhən] n time when thing happens; reason, need; opportunity; special event ▷ vt cause **oc·ca'sion·al** adj happening, found now and then; produced for some special event: occasional music **oc·ca'sion·al·ly** adv sometimes, now and then

Oc·ci·dent [OK-si-dənt] n the West **oc·ci·den'tal** adj

oc·ci·put [OK-sə-put] n back of head **oc·cip'i·tal** adj

oc·clude [ə-KLOOD] vt -clud·ed, -clud·ing shut in or out **oc·clu'sion** [-zhən] n **oc·clu'sive** adj serving to occlude

oc·cult [ə-KULT] adj secret, mysterious; supernatural ▷ n esoteric knowledge ▷ vt hide from view **oc·cul·ta·tion** [ok-əl-TAY-shən] n eclipse **oc'cult·ism** n study of supernatural

oc·cu·py [OK-yə-pī] vt -pied, -py·ing inhabit, fill; employ; take possession of **oc'cu·pan·cy** n fact of occupying; residing **oc'cu·pant** n tenant **oc·cu·pa'tion** n employment; pursuit; fact of occupying; seizure **oc·cu·pa'tion·al** adj pert to occupation, esp of diseases arising from a particular occupation; pert to use of occupations, eg craft, hobbies, etc as means of rehabilitation

oc·cur [ə-KUR] vi -curred, -cur·ring happen; come to mind **oc·cur'rence** n happening

o·cean [OH-shən] n great body of water; large division of this; the sea **o·ce·an'ic** [-shee-AN-ik] adj **o·cea·nol·o·gy** [oh-shə-NOL-ə-jee] n branch of science that relates to ocean

oc·e·lot [OS-ə-lot] n Amer leopardlike cat

o·cher [OH-kər] n various earths used as yellow or brown pigments; this color, from yellow to brown

o'clock [ə-KLOK] adv by the clock

oct-, octa-, octo- comb form eight: octagon; octopus

oc·ta·gon [OK-tə-gon] n plane figure with eight angles **oc·tag'o·nal** adj

oc·tane [OK-tayn] n ingredient of gasoline **octane number** measure of ability of gasoline to reduce engine knock

oc·tave [OK-tiv] n music eighth note above or below given note; this space

oc·ta·vo [ok-TAY-voh] n, pl -vos book in which each sheet is folded three times forming eight leaves

oc·tet [ok-TET] n group of eight; music for eight instruments or singers

oc·to·ge·nar·i·an [ok-tə-jə-NAIR-ee-ən] n person aged between eighty and ninety ▷ adj

oc·to·pus [OK-tə-pəs] n mollusk with eight arms covered with suckers **oc'to·pod** n, adj (mollusk) with eight feet

oc·tu·ple [ok-TUU-pəl] adj eight times as many or as much; eightfold

oc·u·lar [OK-yə-lər] adj of eye or sight

OD [oh-DEE] n overdose esp of dangerous drug; person who has

taken overdose ▷ v **-ed, -ing** take,
die of, overdose

odd adj **-er, -est** strange, queer;
incidental, random; that is one
in addition when the rest have
been divided into equal groups;
not even; not part of a set **odds** pl
n advantage conceded in betting;
likelihood **odd'i·ty** n, pl **-ties** odd
person or thing; quality of being
odd **odd'ments** [-mənts] pl n
remnants; trifles **odds and ends**
odd fragments or scraps

ode [ohd] n lyric poem on particular
subject

o·di·um [OH-dee-əm] n hatred,
widespread dislike **o'di·ous** adj
hateful, repulsive, obnoxious

o·dor [OH-dər] n smell
o·dor·if·er·ous [oh-də-RIF-ər-əs]
adj spreading an odor **o'dor·ize**
vt **-ized, -iz·ing** fill with scent
o'dor·ous adj fragrant; scented
o'dor·less [-lis] adj

od·ys·sey [OD-ə-see] n, pl **-seys**
any long adventurous journey

of [əv] prep denotes removal,
separation, ownership, attribute,
material, quality

off [awf] adv away ▷ prep away
from ▷ adj not operative; canceled
or postponed; bad, sour, etc; distant;
of horses, vehicles, etc, to driver's
right **off-color** adj slightly ill; risqué
off·hand' adj, adv without previous
thought; curt **off-line** [-] (of a
computer) not directly controlled by
a central processor; not connected
to or done via the Internet ▷ adv
off-mes'sage adj not following
the official line, not saying what is
expected **off-road** adj (of a motor
vehicle) designed for use away from
public roads **off'set** n that which
counterbalances, compensates;
method of printing **off·set'** vt

off'spring n children, issue **in the
offing** likely to happen soon

of·fal [AW-fəl] n edible entrails of
animal; refuse

of·fend [ə-FEND] vt hurt feelings
of, displease ▷ vi do wrong

of·fense' n wrong; crime; insult;
sport, military attacking team,
force **of·fen'sive** adj causing
displeasure; aggressive ▷ n position
or movement of attack

of·fer [AW-fər] vt present for
acceptance or refusal; tender;
propose; attempt ▷ vi present itself
▷ n offering, bid **of'fer·er, -or** n
of'fer·to·ry n, pl **-ies** offering of
the bread and wine at the Eucharist;
collection in church service

of·fice [AW-fis] n room(s), building,
in which business, clerical work, etc
is done; commercial or professional
organization; official position;
service; duty; form of worship ▷ pl
task; service **of'fi·cer** n one in
command in army, navy, etc; official

of·fi·cial [ə-FISH-əl] adj with, by,
authority ▷ n one holding office,
esp in public body **of·fi'cial·dom**
[-dəm] n officials collectively,
or their attitudes, work, usu in
contemptuous sense

of·fi·ci·ate [ə-FISH-ee-ayt] vi
-at·ed, -at·ing perform duties of
office; perform ceremony

of·fi·cious [ə-FISH-əs] adj
objectionably persistent in offering
service; interfering

of·ten [AW-fən] adv many times,
frequently **oft** adv poet often

o·gle [OH-gəl] v **o·gled, o·gling**
stare, look (at) amorously ▷ n this
look **o'gler** n

o·gre [OH-gər] n folklore man-
eating giant; monster

ohm n unit of electrical resistance
ohm'me·ter [-ee-tər] n

oil n any of a number of viscous liquids with smooth, sticky feel and wide variety of uses; petroleum; any of variety of petroleum derivatives, esp as fuel or lubricant ▷ vt lubricate with oil; apply oil to **oil'y** adj **oil•i•er**, **oil•i•est** **oil'skin** n cloth treated with oil to make it waterproof **oiled** sl drunk

oint•ment [OINT-mənt] n greasy preparation for healing or beautifying the skin

OK, o•kay [oh-kay] adj, adv int all right ▷ n, pl **OK's** approval ▷ vt **OK'd, OK'ing** approve

o•ka•pi [oh-KAH-pee] n, pl **-pis** Afr animal like short-necked giraffe

old [ohld] adj **old•er** or **old•est** aged, having lived or existed long; belonging to earlier period **old-fash•ioned** [-FASH-ənd] adj in style of earlier period, out of date; fond of old ways **old maid** offens elderly spinster; fussy person

o•le•ag•i•nous [oh-lee-AJ-ə-nəs] adj oily, producing oil; unctuous, fawning

ol•fac•to•ry [ohl-FAK-tə-ree] adj of smelling

ol•i•gar•chy [OL-i-gahr-kee] n, pl **-chies** government by a few **ol•i•gar'chic** adj

ol•ive [OL-iv] n evergreen tree; its oil-yielding fruit; its wood, color ▷ adj grayish-green

O•lym•pi•ad [ə-LIM-pee-ad] n four-year period between Olympic games; celebration of modern Olympic games

om•buds•man [OM-bədz-mən] n, pl **-men** official who investigates citizens' complaints against government; person appointed to perform analogous function in a business

o•me•ga [oh-MAY-gə] n last letter of Greek alphabet; end

om•e•let [OM-lit] n dish of eggs beaten up and cooked in melted butter with other ingredients and seasoning

o•men [OH-mən] n prophetic object or happening **om•i•nous** [OM-ə-nəs] adj boding evil, threatening

o•mit [oh-MIT] vt **o•mit•ted, o•mit•ting** leave out, neglect; leave undone **o•mis•sion** [-MISH-ən] n

omni- comb form all: omnipresent

om•ni•bus [OM-nə-bəs] n bus; book containing several works ▷ adj serving, containing several objects or subjects

om•ni•di•rec•tion•al [om-nə-di-REK-shə-nl] n in radio, denotes transmission, reception in all directions

om•nip•o•tent [om-NIP-ə-tənt] adj all-powerful **om•nip'o•tence** n

om•ni•pres•ent [om-nə-PREZ-ənt] adj present everywhere **om•ni•pres'ence** n

om•nis•cient [om-NISH-ənt] adj knowing everything **om•nis'cience** n

om•niv•o•rous [om-NIV-ər-əs] adj devouring all foods; not selective eg in reading

on prep above and touching, at, near, toward, etc; attached to; concerning; performed upon; during; taking regularly ▷ adj operating; taking place ▷ adv so as to be on; forward; continuously, etc; in progress **on•line'** adj (of a computer) directly controlled by a central processor; connected to, or done via, the Internet ▷ adv **on-mes'sage** adj following the official line, saying what is expected

o•nan•ism [OH-nə-niz-əm] n masturbation

once [wuns] *adv* one time; formerly; ever **once'-o·ver** *n* inf quick examination **at once** immediately; simultaneously

on·co·gene [ONG-kə-jeen] *n* any of several genes that when abnormally activated can cause cancer **on·co·gen·ic** *adj*

on·col·o·gy [ong-KOL-ə-jee] *n* branch of medicine dealing with tumors; study of cancer

one [wun] *adj* lowest cardinal number; single; united; only, without others; identical ▷ *n* number or figure 1; unity; single specimen ▷ *pron* particular but not stated person; any person **one'ness** *n* unity; uniformity; singleness **one·self'** *pron* **one'-sid'ed** *adj* partial; uneven **one-way** *adj* denotes system of traffic circulation in one direction only

on·er·ous [ON-ər-əs] *adj* burdensome

on·ion [UN-yən] *n* edible bulb of pungent flavor **know one's onions** *sl* know one's field, etc thoroughly

on·ly [OHN-lee] *adj* being the one specimen ▷ *adv* solely, merely, exclusively ▷ *conj* but then, excepting that

on·o·mas·tics [on-ə-MAS-tiks] *n* study of proper names

on·o·mat·o·poe·ia [on-ə-mat-ə-PEE-ə] *n* formation of a word by using sounds that resemble or suggest the object or action to be named **on·o·mat·o·poe·ic**, **on·o·mat·o·po·et·ic** *adj*

on·set *n* violent attack; assault; beginning

on·slaught [ON-slawt] *n* attack

on·to [ON-too] *prep* on top of; aware of

on·tog·e·ny [on-TOJ-ə-nee] *n* development of an individual organism

on·tol·o·gy [on-TOL-ə-jee] *n* science of being or reality

o·nus [OH-nəs] *n*, *pl* **-nus·es** responsibility; burden

on·ward [ON-wərd] *adj* advanced or advancing ▷ *adv* in advance, ahead, forward **on'wards** *adv*

on·yx [ON-iks] *n* variety of chalcedony

ooze [ooz] *vi* **oozed**, **ooz·ing** pass slowly out, exude (moisture) ▷ *n* sluggish flow; wet mud; slime

o·pal [OH-pəl] *n* glassy gemstone displaying variegated colors **o·pal·es'cent** *adj*

o·paque [oh-PAYK] *adj* not allowing the passage of light; not transparent **o·pac·i·ty** [-PAS-i-tee] *n*

op. cit. [op sit] in the work cited

o·pen [OH-pən] *adj* not shut or blocked up; without lid or door; bare; undisguised; not enclosed; covered or exclusive; spread out, accessible; frank, sincere ▷ *vt* set open, uncover, give access to; disclose, lay bare; begin; make a hole in ▷ *vi* become open; begin ▷ *n* clear space, unenclosed country; *sport* competition in which all may enter **o'pen·ing** *n* hole, gap; beginning; opportunity ▷ *adj* first; initial **o'pen·ly** *adv* without concealment **o'pen·hand'ed** *adj* generous **o'pen·heart'ed** *adj* frank, magnanimous **o'pen·mind'ed** *adj* unprejudiced **open source** intellectual property, esp computer source code, that is made freely available to the general public **o'pen·work** *n* pattern with interstices

op·er·a [OP-ər-ə] *n* musical drama **op·er·at'ic** *adj* of opera **op·er·et'ta** *n* light, comic opera **op·er·a·tion** [op-ə-RAY-shən] working, way things work; scope; act of surgery; military action **op'er·ate** v **-at·ed, -at·ing** ▷ vt cause to function; effect ▷ vi work; produce an effect; perform act of surgery; exert power **op·er·a'tion·al** adj of operation(s); working **op'er·a·tive** [-ā-tiv] adj working with a special skill; secret agent

o·phid·i·an [oh-FID-ee-ən] adj, n (reptile) of the order including snakes

oph·thal'mic [of-THAL-mik] adj of eyes **oph·thal·mol'o·gist** [-jist] n **oph·thal·mol'o·gy** n study of eye and its diseases **oph·thal'mo·scope** [-skohp] n instrument for examining interior of eye

opiate see **OPIUM**

o·pin·ion [ə-PIN-yən] n what one thinks about something; belief, judgment **o·pine** [oh-PÏN] vt **o·pined, o·pin·ing** think; utter opinion **o·pin'ion·at·ed** adj stubborn in one's opinions; dogmatic

o·pi·um [OH-pee-əm] n sedative-narcotic drug made from poppy **o'pi·ate** [-it] n drug containing opium; narcotic ▷ adj inducing sleep; soothing

o·pos·sum [ə-POS-əm] n small Amer marsupial animal, possum

op·po·nent [ə-POH-nənt] n adversary, antagonist

op·por·tune [op-ər-TOON] adj seasonable, well-timed **op·por·tun'ism** n policy of doing what is expedient at the time regardless of principle **op·por·tun'ist** n, adj **op·por·tu'ni·ty** n, pl **-ties** favorable time or condition; good chance

op·pose [ə-POHZ] vt **-posed, -pos·ing** resist, withstand; contrast; set against **op·po·site** [OP-ə-zit]

adj contrary; facing; diametrically different; adverse ▷ n the contrary ▷ prep, adv facing; on the other side **op·po·si'tion** [-ZISH-ən] n antithesis; resistance; obstruction; hostility; group opposing another; party opposing that in power

op·press [ə-PRES] vt govern with tyranny; weigh down **op·pres'sion** [-PRESH-ən] n act of oppressing; severity; misery **op·pres'sive** adj tyrannical; hard to bear; heavy; hot and tiring (of weather) **op·pres'sor** [-ər] n

op·pro·bri·um [ə-PROH-bree-əm] n disgrace **op·pro'bri·ous** adj reproachful; shameful; abusive

opt vi make a choice **op'ta·tive** [OP-tə-tiv] adj expressing wish or desire

op·tic [OP-tik] adj of eye or sight ▷ n eye **optics** n science of sight and light **op'ti·cal** adj **optical character reader** device for scanning magnetically coded data on labels, cans, etc **op·ti'cian** [-TISH-ən] n maker of, dealer in eyeglasses, contact lenses

op·ti·mism [OP-tə-miz-əm] n disposition to look on the bright side; doctrine that good must prevail in the end; belief that the world is the best possible world **op'ti·mist** n **op·ti·mis'tic** adj

op·ti·mum [OP-tə-məm] adj, n the best, the most favorable

op·tion [OP-shən] n choice; preference; thing chosen; in business, purchased privilege of either buying or selling things at specified price within specified time **op'tion·al** adj leaving to choice

op·tom·e·trist [op-TOM-i-trist] n person qualified in testing eyesight, prescribing corrective lenses, etc **op·tom'e·try** n

op•u•lent [OP-yə-lənt] *adj* rich; copious **op'u•lence** *n* riches, wealth

o•pus [OH-pəs] *n, pl* **o•pus•es** or **op•er•a** [OHP-ə-rə] work; musical composition: Grieg's *opus 53*

or *conj* introduces alternatives; if not

or•a•cle [OR-ə-kəl] *n* divine utterance, prophecy, oft ambiguous, given at shrine of god; the shrine; wise or mysterious adviser **o•rac•u•lar** [aw-RAK-yə-lər] *adj* of oracle; prophetic; authoritative; ambiguous

o•ral [OR-əl] *adj* spoken; by mouth ▷ *n* spoken examination **o'ral•ly** *adv*

or•ange [OR-inj] *n* bright reddish-yellow round fruit; tree bearing it; fruit's color

o•rang•u•tan [aw-RANG-uu-tan] *n* large E Indian ape

or•a•tor [OR-ə-tər] *n* maker of speech; skillful speaker **or•a'tion** [aw-RAY-shən] *n* formal speech **or•a•tor'i•cal** *adj* of orator or oration **or'a•to•ry** *n* speeches; eloquence; small private chapel

or•a•to•ri•o [or-ə-TOR-ee-oh] *n, pl* **-ri•os** semidramatic composition of sacred music

orb *n* globe, sphere; eye, eyeball

or'bit *n* track of planet, satellite, comet, etc, around another heavenly body; field of influence, sphere; eye socket ▷ *v* move in, or put into, an orbit

or•chard [OR-chərd] *n* area for cultivation of fruit trees; the trees

or•ches•tra [OR-kə-strə] *n* band of musicians; place for such band in theater, etc **or•ches'tral** *adj* **or'ches•trate** *vt* **-trat•ed, -trat•ing** compose or arrange music for orchestra; organize, arrange

or•chid [OR-kid] *n* genus of various flowering plants

or•dain [or-DAYN] *vt* admit to

religious ministry; confer holy orders upon; decree, enact; destine **or•di•na'tion** *n*

or•deal [or-DEEL] *n* severe, trying experience; *history* form of trial by which accused underwent severe physical test

or•der [OR-dər] *n* regular or proper arrangement or condition; sequence; peaceful condition of society; rank, class; group; command; request for something to be supplied; mode of procedure; instruction; monastic society ▷ *vt* command; request (something) to be supplied or made; arrange **or'der•li•ness** *n* **or'der•ly** *adj* tidy; methodical; well-behaved ▷ *n* hospital attendant; soldier performing chores for officer

or•di•nal [OR-dn-əl] *adj* showing position in a series ▷ *n* ordinal number

or•di•nance [OR-dn-əns] *n* decree, rule; rite, ceremony

or•di•nar•y [OR-dn-er-ee] *adj* usual, normal; common; plain; commonplace ▷ *n* average condition **or'di•nar•i•ly** *adv*

ord•nance [ORD-nəns] *n* big guns, artillery; military stores

or•dure [OR-jər] *n* dung; filth

ore [or] *n* naturally occurring mineral that yields metal

o•reg•a•no [ə-REG-ə-noh] *n* herb, variety of marjoram

org Internet domain name for an organization, usually a non-profit-making organization

or•gan [OR-gən] *n* musical wind instrument of pipes and stops, played by keys; member of animal or plant carrying out particular function; means of action; medium of information, esp newspaper **or•gan'ic** *adj* of, derived from, living organisms; of bodily organs;

affecting bodily organs; having vital organs; *chemistry* of compounds formed from carbon; grown with fertilizers derived from animal or vegetable matter; organized, systematic **or·gan·i·cal·ly** *adv* **or·gan·ist** *n* organ player

or·gan·ize [OR-gə-niz] *vt* **-nized, -niz·ing** give definite structure; get up, arrange; put into working order; unite in a society **or·gan·ism** *n* organized body or system; plant, animal **or·gan·i·za·tion** *n* act of organizing; body of people; system

or·gasm [OR-gaz-əm] *n* sexual climax

or·gy [OR-jee] *n, pl* **-gies** drunken or licentious revel, debauch; act of immoderation, overindulgence

o·ri·el [OR-ee-əl] *n* projecting part of an upper room with a window; the window

o·ri·ent [OR-ee-ənt] *n* (**O-**) East; luster of best pearls ▷ *adj* rising; (**O-**) Eastern ▷ *vt* [OR-ee-ent] place so as to face east or other known direction; take bearings; determine one's position **o·ri·en·tal** *adj* of, or from, the East ▷ *n* oft offens person from the East or of Eastern descent **o·ri·en·tal·ist** *n* expert in Eastern languages and history **o·ri·en·ta·tion** *n*

or·i·fice [OR-ə-fis] *n* opening, mouth of a cavity, eg pipe

o·ri·ga·mi [or-i-GAH-mee] *n* Japanese art of paper folding

or·i·gin [OR-i-jin] *n* beginning; source; parentage

o·rig·i·nal [ə-RIJ-ə-nl] *adj* primitive, earliest; new, not copied or derived; thinking or acting for oneself; eccentric ▷ *n* pattern, thing from which another is copied; unconventional or strange person **o·rig·i·nal·i·ty** *n* power of

producing something individual to oneself **o·rig'i·nal·ly** *adv* at first; in the beginning

o·rig·i·nate [ə-RIJ-ə-nayt] *v* **-nat·ed, -nat·ing** come or bring into existence, begin **o·rig·i·na·tor** [-tər] *n*

o·ri·ole [OR-ee-ohl] *n* any of several thrushlike birds

O·ri·on [ə-Rī-ən] *n* bright constellation

or·i·son [OR-ə-zən] *n* prayer

or·mo·lu [OR-mə-loo] *n* gilded bronze; gold-colored alloy; articles of these

or·na·ment [OR-nə-mənt] *n* any object used to adorn or decorate; decoration ▷ *vt* [-ment] adorn **or·na·men'tal** *adj* **or·na·men·ta'tion** *n*

or·nate [or-NAYT] *adj* highly decorated or elaborate

or·ni·thol·o·gy [or-nə-THOL-ə-jee] *n* science of birds **or·ni·thol'o·gist** *n*

o·ro·tund [OR-ə-tund] *adj* full, clear, and musical; pompous

or·phan [OR-fən] *n* child bereaved of one or both parents **or'phan·age** [-fə-nij] *n* institution for care of orphans

ortho- *comb form* right, correct **or·tho·dox** [OR-thə-doks] *adj* holding accepted views; conventional **or·tho·dox'y** *n* **or·thog·ra·phy** [or-THOG-rə-fee] *n* correct spelling

or·tho·pe·dic [or-thə-PEE-dik] *adj* for curing deformity, disorder of bones **or·tho·pe'dics** *n* medical specialty dealing with this **or·tho·pe'dist** *n*

Os *chemistry* osmium

os·cil·late [OS-ə-layt] *vi* **-lat·ed, -lat·ing** swing to and fro; waver; fluctuate (regularly) **os·cil·la'tion** *n* *n* **os·cil·la·tor** *n* **os·cil·la·to·ry** *adj* **os·cil·lo·scope** *n* electronic instrument producing visible representation of rapidly changing quantity

os·mi·um [OZ-mee-əm] *n* heaviest known of metallic elements

os·mo·sis [oz-MOH-sis] *n* percolation of fluids through porous partitions **os·mot·ic** *adj*

os·se·ous [OS-ee-əs] *adj* of, like bone; bony **os·si·fi·ca·tion** *n* **os·si·fy** [-fī] *v* **-fied, -fy·ing** turn into bone; grow rigid

os·ten·si·ble [o-STEN-sə-bəl] *adj* apparent; professed **os·ten·si·bly** *adv*

os·ten·ta·tion [os-ten-TAY-shən] *n* show, pretentious display **os·ten·ta·tious** *adj* given to display; showing off

os·te·op·a·thy [os-tee-OP-ə-thee] *n* art of treating disease by removing structural derangement by manipulation, esp of spine **os·te·o·path** *n* one skilled in this art

os·tra·cize [OS-trə-sīz] *vt* **-cized, -ciz·ing** exclude, banish from society, exile **os·tra·cism** [-siz-əm] *n* social boycotting

os·trich *n* large swift-running flightless Afr bird

oth·er [UTH-ər] *adj* not this; not the same; alternative, different ▷ *pron* other person or thing **oth·er·wise** *adv* differently; in another way ▷ *conj* else, if not

o·ti·ose [OH-shee-ohs, OH-tee-ohs] *adj* superfluous; useless

o·ti·tis [oh-TĪ-tis] *n* inflammation of the ear

ot·ter [OT-ər] *n* furry aquatic fish-eating animal

Ot·to·man [OT-ə-mən] *adj* Turkish ▷ *n* Turk; (o-) cushioned, backless seat; (o-) cushioned

footstool

ought [awt] *v aux* expressing duty or obligation or advisability; be bound

Oui·ja® [WEE-jə] *n* board with letters and symbols used to obtain messages at seances

ounce [owns] *n* a weight, sixteenth of avoirdupois pound (28.349 grams), twelfth of troy pound (31.103 grams)

our [OW-ər] *adj* belonging to us **ours** *pron* thing(s) belonging to us **our·selves'** *pron* emphatic or reflexive form of **WE**

oust [owst] *vt* put out, expel

out [owt] *adv* from within, away; wrong; on strike ▷ *adj* not worth considering; not allowed; unfashionable; unconscious; not in use, operation, etc; at an end; not burning; *baseball* failed to get on base ▷ *vt inf* name (public figure) as being homosexual **out·er** *adj* away from the inside **out·er·most** [-mohst] *adj* on extreme outside **out·ing** *n* pleasure excursion **out·ward** [-wurd] *adj, adv* **out·wards** [-wurdz] *adv*

out- *prefix* beyond, in excess: outclass; outdistance; outsize

out·bal·ance [owt-BAL-əns] *vt* **-anced, -anc·ing** outweigh; exceed in weight

out·board [OWT-bord] *adj* of boat's engine, mounted on, outside stern

out·break [OWT-brayk] *n* sudden occurrence, esp of disease or strife

out·burst [OWT-burst] *n* bursting out, esp of violent emotion

out·cast [OWT-kast] *n* someone rejected ▷ *adj*

out·class [owt-KLAS] *vt* excel, surpass

out·come [OWT-kum] *n* result

out·crop [OWT-krop] *n geology*

rock coming out of stratum to the surface ▷ *vi* [owt-KROP] **-cropped, -crop·ping** come out to the surface

out·doors [owt-DORZ] *adv* in the open air **out'door** *adj*

out·fit [OWT-fit] *n* equipment; clothes and accessories; *inf* group or association regarded as a unit **out'fit·ter** *n* one who supplies clothing and accessories

out·flank [owt-FLANGK] *vt* to get beyond the flank of (enemy army); circumvent; outmaneuver

out·go·ing [OWT-goh-ing] *adj* departing; friendly, sociable

out·grow [owt-GROH] *vt* **-grew, -grown, -grow·ing** become too large or too old for; surpass in growth

out·house [OWT-hows] *n* outdoor toilet; shed, etc near main building

out·land·ish [owt-LAN-dish] *adj* queer, extravagantly strange

out·law [OWT-law] *n* one beyond protection of the law; exile, bandit ▷ *vt* make (someone) an outlaw; ban

out·lay [OWT-lay] *n* expenditure

out·let [OWT-let] *n* opening, vent; means of release or escape; market for product or service

out·line [OWT-lin] *n* rough sketch; general plan; lines enclosing visible figure ▷ *vt* **-lined, lin·ing** sketch; summarize

out·look [OWT-luuk] *n* point of view; probable outcome; view

out·ly·ing [OWT-li-ing] *adj* distant, remote

out·mod·ed [owt-MOH-did] *adj* no longer fashionable or current

out·pa·tient [OWT-pay-shànt] *n* patient treated but not kept at hospital

out·put [OWT-puut] *n* quantity produced; *computing* data produced ▷ *vt* *computing* produce (data) at the end of a process

out·rage [OWT-rayj] *n* violation of others' rights; gross or violent offense or indignity; anger arising from this ▷ *vt* **-raged, rag·ing** offend grossly; insult; injure, violate **out·ra'geous** [-RAY-jàs] *adj*

ou·tré [oo-TRAY] *adj* extravagantly odd; bizarre

out·rig·ger [OWT-rig-àr] *n* frame, esp with float attached, outside boat's gunwale; frame on rowing boat's side with rowlock; boat with one

out·right [OWT-rit] *adj* undisturbed; downright; positive ▷ *adv* [owt-rit] completely; once for all; openly

out·set [OWT-set] *n* beginning

out·side [OWT-sid] *n* exterior ▷ *adv* [owt-SID] not inside; in the open air ▷ *adj* [owt-SID] on exterior; remote, unlikely; greatest possible, probable **out·sid'er** *n* person outside specific group; contestant thought unlikely to win

out·skirts [OWT-skurts] *pl n* outer areas, districts, esp of city

out·spok·en [owt-SPOH-kàn] *adj* frank, candid

out·stand·ing [owt-STAN-ding] *adj* excellent; remarkable; unsettled, unpaid

out·strip [owt-STRIP] *vt* **-stripped, -strip·ping** outrun, surpass

out·wit [owt-WIT] *vt* **-wit·ted, -wit·ting** get the better of by cunning

o·val [OH-vàl] *adj* egg-shaped, elliptical ▷ *n* something of this shape

o·va·ry [OH-à-ree] *n, pl* **-ries** female egg-producing organ **o·var'i·an** [-VAIR-ee-àn] *adj*

o·va·tion [oh-VAY-shàn] *n* enthusiastic burst of applause

ov•en [UV-ən] n heated chamber for baking in

o•ver [OH-vər] adv above, above and beyond, going beyond, in excess, too much, past, finished, in repetition, across, downward, etc ▷ prep above; on, upon; more than, in excess of, along, etc ▷ adj upper, outer

over- prefix too much: overeat; above: overlord; on top: overshoe

o•ver•all [OH-vər-awl] adj, adv in total ▷ n coat-shaped protective garment ▷ pl protective garment consisting of trousers with a part extending up over the chest

o•ver•awe' vt affect (someone) with an overpowering sense of awe

o•ver•bal'ance v lose balance

o•ver•bear•ing [oh-vər-BAIR-ing] adj domineering

o•ver•blown [OH-vər-BLOHN] adj excessive, bombastic

o•ver•board [OH-vər-bord] adv from a vessel into the water

o•ver•cast [OH-vər-KAST] adj covered over, esp by clouds

o'ver•coat n heavy coat

o•ver•come [oh-vər-KUM] vt -came, -come, -com•ing conquer; surmount; make powerless

o•ver•crowd' vt fill with more people or things than is desirable **ov•er•crowd'ing** n

o•ver•do' vt do to excess; exaggerate (something)

o'ver•dose n excessive dose of a drug ▷ v take an overdose

o•ver•draft [OH-vər-draft] n withdrawal of money in excess of credit balance on bank account

o•ver•due' adj still due after the time allowed

o•ver•flow' v flow over; be filled beyond capacity ▷ n something that overflows; outlet for excess liquid;

excess amount

o•ver•haul [oh-vər-HAWL] vt examine and set in order, repair; overtake ▷ n [OH-vər-hawl] thorough examination, esp for repairs

o•ver•head [OH-vər-hed] adj over one's head, above ▷ n expense of running a business, over and above cost of manufacturing and of raw materials ▷ adv [OH-vər-HED] aloft, above

o•ver•kill [OH-vər-kil] n capacity, advantage greater than required

o•ver•lap' v share part of the same space or period of time (as) ▷ n area overlapping

o•ver•look [oh-vər-LUUK] vt fail to notice; disregard; look over

o•ver•pow'er v subdue or overcome (someone); make helpless or ineffective **o•ver•pow'er•ing** adj

o•ver•re•act' vi react more strongly than is necessary

o•ver•ride [oh-vər-RĪD] vt -rode, -rid•den, -rid•ing set aside, disregard; cancel; trample down

o•ver•rule' vt reverse the decision of (a person with less power); reverse (someone else's decision)

o•ver•run' v conquer rapidly; spread over (a place) rapidly; extend beyond a set limit

o•ver•seas [OH-vər-SEEZ] adj foreign ▷ adj, adv [oh-vər-SEEZ] to, from place over the sea

o•ver•se•er [OH-vər-see-ər] n supervisor **o•ver•see'** vt -saw, -seen, -see•ing supervise

o•ver•shoot' v go beyond (a mark or target)

o•ver•sight [OH-vər-sīt] n failure to notice; mistake; supervision

o•vert [oh-VURT] adj open, unconcealed **o•vert'ly** adv

o•ver•take [oh-vər-TAYK] vt

-took, -tak·en, -tak·ing move past (vehicle, person) traveling in same direction; come up with in pursuit; catch up

o·ver·tax [oh-vər-TAKS] vt tax too heavily; impose too great a strain on

o·ver·throw [oh-vər-THROH] vt **-threw, -thrown, -throw·ing** upset, overturn; defeat ▷ n [OH-vər-throh] ruin; defeat; fall

o·ver·tone [OH-vər-tohn] n additional meaning, nuance

o·ver·ture [OH-vər-chər] n music orchestral introduction; opening of negotiations; formal offer

o·ver·ween·ing [OH-vər-WEE-ning] adj thinking too much of oneself

o·ver·whelm [oh-vər-HWELM] vt crush; submerge, engulf

o·ver·whelm'ing adj decisive; irresistible

o·ver·wrought [OH-vər-RAWT] adj overexcited; too elaborate

o·vip·a·rous [oh-VIP-ər-əs] adj laying eggs

ov·ule [OV-yool] n unfertilized seed **ov'u·late** [-yə-layt] vi **-lat·ed, -lat·ing** produce, discharge (egg) from ovary

o·vum [OH-vəm] n, pl **o·va** [OH-və] female egg cell, in which development of fetus takes place

owe [oh] vt **owed, ow·ing** be bound to repay, be indebted for **owing** adj owed, due **owing to** caused by, as result of

owl n night bird of prey **owl'ish** adj resembling an owl

own [ohn] adj emphasizes possession ▷ vt possess; acknowledge ▷ vi to confess **own'er·ship** n possession

ox [oks] n, pl **ox·en** large cloven-footed and usu horned farm animal; bull or cow **ox'bow** [-boh] n U-shaped harness collar of ox; bow-shaped bend in river

ox·ide [OK-sīd] n compound of oxygen and another element **ox'i·dize** [-dīz] v **-dized, -diz·ing** (cause to) combine with oxide, rust

ox·y·gen [OK-si-jən] n gas in atmosphere essential to life, combustion, etc **ox'y·gen·ate** vt **-at·ed, -at·ing** combine or treat with oxygen

ox·y·mo·ron [ok-si-MOR-on] n figure of speech in which two ideas of opposite meaning are combined to form an expressive phrase or epithet, such as cruel kindness

oys·ter [OI-stər] n edible bivalve mollusk or shellfish

o·zone [OH-zohn] n form of oxygen with pungent odor **ozone layer** layer of upper atmosphere with concentration of ozone

P

P *chemistry* phosphorus

Pa *chemistry* protactinium

PAC Political Action Committee: political organization formed to raise money for the campaigns of political candidates likely to advance the organization's interests

pace [pays] *n* step; its length; rate of movement; walk, gait ▷ *v* **paced, pac•ing** ▷ *vi* step ▷ *vt* set speed for; cross, measure with steps **pac•er** *n* one who sets the pace for another; horse used for pacing in harness racing **pace'mak•er** *n* esp electronic device surgically implanted in those with heart disease

pa•chin•ko [pə-CHING-koh] *n* Japanese pinball machine

pach•y•derm [PAK-i-durm] *n* thick-skinned animal, such as an elephant **pach•y•der'ma•tous** [-mə-təs] *adj* thick-skinned, stolid

pac•i•fy [PAS-ə-fī] *vt* **-fied, -fy•ing** calm; establish peace **pa•cif'ic** *adj* peaceable; calm, tranquil **pa'ci•fi•er** *n* ring or nipple for baby to suck or chew **pac'i•fism** *n* **pac'i•fist** *n* advocate of abolition of war; one who refuses to help in war

pack [pak] *n* bundle; band of animals; large set of people or things; set of, container for, retail commodities; set of playing cards; mass of floating ice ▷ *vt* put together in suitcase, etc; make into a bundle; press tightly together, cram; fill with things; fill (meeting, etc) with one's own supporters; order off **pack'age** [-ij] *n* parcel; set of items offered together ▷ *vt* **-aged, -ag•ing pack'et** [-it] *n* small parcel; small container (and contents); *inf* large sum of money; small mail, passenger, freight boat **pack'horse** *n* horse for carrying goods **pack ice** loose floating ice that has been compacted together

pact [pakt] *n* covenant, agreement, compact

pad¹ *n* piece of soft material used as a cushion, protection, etc; block of sheets of paper; foot or sole of various animals; place for launching rockets; *sl* residence ▷ *vt* **pad•ded, pad•ding** make soft, fill in, protect, etc, with pad or padding; add to dishonestly **padding** *n* material used for stuffing; literary matter put in simply to increase quantity

pad² *vi* **pad•ded, pad•ding** walk with soft step; travel slowly ▷ *n* sound of soft footstep

pad•dle¹ [PAD-əl] *n* short oar with broad blade at one or each end ▷ *v* **-dled, -dling** move by, as with, paddles; row gently **paddle wheel** wheel with crosswise blades striking water successively to propel ship

pad•dle² *vt* **-dled, -dling** walk with bare feet in shallow water ▷ *n* such a walk

pad•dock [PAD-ək] *n* small grass field or enclosure

pad•dy [PAD-ee] *n, pl* **-dies** rice growing or in the husk **paddy field**

field where rice is grown

pad·lock [PAD-lok] n detachable lock with hinged hoop to go through staple or ring ▷vt fasten thus

pae·an [PEE-ən] n song of triumph or thanksgiving

pa·gan [PAY-gən] adj, n heathen **pa'gan·ism** n

page¹ [payj] n one side of leaf of book, etc; screenful of information from a website or teletext service

page² n boy servant; attendant ▷vt **paged, pag·ing** summon (a person), by bleeper or loudspeaker, in order to pass on a message

page'boy n hair style with hair rolled under usu at shoulder length

pag·eant [PAJ-ənt] n show of persons in costume in procession, dramatic scenes, etc, usu illustrating history; brilliant show **pag'eant·ry** n, pl -ies

pag·i·nate [PAJ-ə-nate] vt **-nat·ed, -nat·ing** number pages of **pag·i·na'tion** n

pa·go·da [pə-GOH-də] n pyramidal temple or tower of Chinese or Indian type

paid [payd] pt of **PAY** **paid-up** adj paid in full

pail [payl] n bucket **pail'ful** [-fəl] n, pl -fuls

pain [payn] n bodily or mental suffering; penalty or punishment ▷pl trouble, exertion ▷vt inflict pain upon **pain'ful** [-fəl] adj **pain'less** [-lis] adj **pain'kill·er** n drug, as aspirin, that reduces pain **pains'tak·ing** adj diligent, careful

paint [paynt] n coloring matter spread on a surface with brushes, roller, spray gun, etc ▷vt portray, color, coat, or make picture of, with paint; apply makeup; describe **paint'er** n **paint'ing** n picture in paint

paint·er [PAYN-tər] n line at bow of boat for tying it up

pair n set of two, esp existing or generally used together ▷v arrange in twos; group or be grouped in twos

pais·ley [PAYZ-lee] n, pl -leys pattern of small curving shapes

pa·ja·mas [pə-JAH-məz] pl n sleeping suit of loose-fitting trousers and jacket

pal inf friend

pal·ace [PAL-is] n residence of king, bishop, etc; stately mansion **pa·la·tial** [pə-LAY-shəl] adj like a palace; magnificent **pal·a·tine** [PAL-ə-tin] adj with royal privileges

pal·ate [PAL-it] n roof of mouth; sense of taste **pal'at·a·ble** adj agreeable to eat **pal'a·tal** [-təl] adj of the palate; made by placing tongue against palate

palatial, palatine SEE **PALACE**

pa·lav·er [pə-LAV-ər] n fuss; conference, discussion

pale¹ [payl] adj **pal·er, pal·est** wan, dim, whitish ▷vi **paled, pal·ing** whiten; lose superiority or importance

pale² n stake, boundary **pal'ing** n upright stakes making up fence **beyond the pale** beyond limits of propriety, safety, etc

pa·le·o·lith·ic [pay-lee-ə-LITH-ik] adj of the old Stone Age

pa·le·on·tol·o·gy [pay-lee-ən-TOL-ə-jee] n study of past geological periods and fossils

pal·ette [PAL-it] n artist's flat board for mixing colors on

pal·i·mo·ny [PAL-ə-moh-nee] n alimony awarded to partner in broken romantic relationship

pal·in·drome [PAL-in-drohm] n word, verse or sentence that is the same when read backward or forward

pal·i·sade [pal-ə-SAYD] *n* fence of stakes ▷ *pl* line of cliffs ▷ *vt* **-sad·ed, -sad·ing** to enclose or protect with one

pall[1] [pawl] *n* cloth spread over a coffin; depressing, oppressive atmosphere **pall'bear·er** *n* one carrying, attending coffin at funeral

pall[2] *vi* become tasteless or tiresome; cloy

pal·let[1] [PAL-it] *n* straw mattress; small bed

pallet[2] *n* portable platform for storing and moving goods

pal·li·ate [PAL-ee-ayt] *vt* **-at·ed, -at·ing** relieve without curing; excuse **pal'li·a·tive** [-ə-tiv] *adj* giving temporary or partial relief ▷ *n* that which excuses, mitigates or alleviates

pal·lid [PAL-id] *adj* pale, wan, colorless **pal'lor** [-ər] *n* paleness

palm [pahm] *n* inner surface of hand; tropical tree; leaf of the tree as symbol of victory ▷ *vt* conceal in palm of hand; pass off by trickery **palm'is·try** *n* fortune telling from lines on palm of hand **palm'y** *adj* **palm·i·er, palm·i·est** flourishing, successful **Palm Sunday** Sunday before Easter **palm'top** *adj* (of a computer) small enough to be held in the hand ▷ *n* such a computer

pal·o·mi·no [pal-ə-MEE-noh] *n, pl* **-nos** golden horse with mane and tail

pal·pa·ble [PAL-pə-bəl] *adj* obvious; certain; that can be touched or felt **pal'pa·bly** *adv*

pal·pate [PAL-payt] *vt* **-pat·ed, -pat·ing** medicine examine by touch

pal·pi·tate [PAL-pi-tayt] *vi* **-tat·ed, -tat·ing** throb; pulsate violently **pal·pi·ta'tion** *n* throbbing; violent, irregular beating of heart

pal·sy [PAWL-zee] *n, pl* **-sies** paralysis, esp with tremors **pal'sied** *adj* affected with palsy

pal·try [PAWL-tree] *adj* **-tri·er, -tri·est** worthless, contemptible, trifling

pam·pas [PAM-pəz] *pl n* vast grassy treeless plains in S Amer

pam·per [PAM-pər] *vt* overindulge, spoil by coddling

pam·phlet [PAM-flit] *n* thin unbound book usu on some topical subject **pam·phlet·eer** *n* writer of these

pan[1] *n* broad, shallow vessel; depression in ground, esp where salt forms ▷ *vt* **panned, pan·ning** wash gold ore in pan; *inf* criticize harshly **pan out** *vi inf* result, esp successfully

pan[2] *v* **panned, pan·ning** move motion picture or TV camera slowly while shooting to cover scene, follow moving object, etc

pan-, pant-, panto- *comb form* all; **panacea; pan-American**

pan·a·ce·a [pan-ə-SEE-ə] *n* universal remedy, cure for all ills

pa·nache [pə-NASH] *n* dashing style

pan·cake [PAN-kayk] *n* thin cake of batter fried in pan; flat cake or stick of compressed makeup ▷ *v* **-caked, -cak·ing** aviation make flat landing by dropping in a level position

pan·chro·mat·ic [pan-kroh-MAT-ik] *adj* photography sensitive to light of all colors

pan·cre·as [PAN-kree-əs] *n* digestive gland behind stomach **pan·cre·at·ic** *adj*

pan·da [PAN-də] *n* large black and white bearlike mammal of China

pan·dem·ic [pan-DEM-ik] *adj* (of disease) occurring over wide area

pan·de·mo·ni·um [pan-də-

MOH-nee-əm] n scene of din and uproar

pan·der [PAN-dər] v (esp with to) give gratification to (weakness or desires) ▷ n pimp

pane [payn] n single piece of glass in a window or door

pan·e·gyr·ic [pan-ə-JIR-ik] n speech of praise pan·e·gyr·i·cal adj laudatory pan·e·gyr·ist n

pan·el [PAN-l] n compartment of surface, usu raised or sunk, for example in a door; any distinct section of something; strip of material inserted in garment; group of persons as team in quiz game, etc; list of jurors, doctors, etc; thin board with picture on it ▷ vt -eled, -el·ing adorn with panels pan·el·ing n paneled work pan·el·ist n member of panel

pang n sudden pain, sharp twinge; compunction

pan·ic [PAN-ik] n sudden and infectious fear; extreme fright; unreasoning terror ▷ adj of fear, etc ▷ v -icked, -ick·ing feel or cause to feel panic pan·ick·y adj inclined to panic; nervous panic button button or switch that operates safety device, for use in emergency panic room secure room within a house, to which a person can flee if someone breaks in panic-stricken, -struck adj panicky

pan·o·ply [PAN-ə-plee] n, pl -plies complete, magnificent array pan·o·plied adj

pan·o·ram·a [pan-ə-RAM-ə] n wide or complete view; picture arranged around spectators or unrolled before them pan·o·ram·ic adj

pan·sy [PAN-zee] n, pl -sies flower, species of violet; sl offens effeminate man

pant vi gasp for breath; yearn; long; throb ▷ n gasp

pan·ta·loon [PAN-tl-oon] n in pantomime, foolish old man who is the butt of clown ▷ pl obs baggy trousers

pan·the·ism [PAN-thee-iz-əm] n identification of God with the universe pan·the·is·tic adj pan·the·on [-thee-ən] n temple of all gods

pan·ther [PAN-thər] n cougar; puma; variety of leopard

pant·ies [PAN-teez] pl n women's undergarment

pan·to·mime [PAN-tə-mim] n dramatic entertainment without speech

pan·try [PAN-tree] n, pl -tries [-treez] room for storing food or utensils

pants pl n trousers; undergarment for lower trunk

pant·y·hose [PAN-tee-hohz] pl n women's one-piece garment combining stockings and panties

pant·y·waist [PAN-tee-wayst] n inf offens effeminate man

pap n soft food for infants, invalids, etc; pulp, mash; idea, book, etc lacking substance

pa·pa·cy [PAY-pə-see] n, pl -cies office of Pope; papal system pa·pal adj of, relating to, the Pope pa·pist n, adj offens Roman Catholic

pa·pa·raz·zo [pah-pə-RAHT-soh] n, pl -raz·zi [-RAHT-see] freelance photographer specializing in candid shots of celebrities

pa·pa·ya [pə-PAH-yə] n tree bearing melon-shaped fruit; its fruit

pa·per [PAY-pər] n material made by pressing pulp of rags, straw, wood, etc, into thin, flat sheets; printed sheet of paper; newspaper; article, essay ▷ pl documents, etc ▷ vt

cover, decorate with paper paper over (try to) conceal (differences, etc) in order to preserve friendship, etc

pa·pier-mâ·ché [PAY-pàr mà-SHAY] *n* pulp from rags or paper mixed with size, shaped by molding and dried hard

pa·poose [pa-POOS] *n* N Amer Indian child

pap·ri·ka [pa-PREE-kà] *n* (powdered seasoning prepared from) type of red pepper

pa·py·rus [pà-Pī-ràs] *n, pl* **-py·ri** [-Pī-rī] species of reed; (manuscript written on) kind of paper made from this plant

par [pahr] *n* equality of value or standing; face value (of stocks and bonds); golf estimated standard score ▷ *vt* **parred, par·ring** golf make par on hole or round **par·i·ty** *n* equality; analogy

para-, par-, pa- *comb form* beside, beyond; *paradigm; parallel; parody*

par·a·ble [PA-rà-bàl] *n* allegory, story with a moral lesson

pa·rab·o·la [pà-RAB-à-là] *n* section of cone cut by plane parallel to the cone's side

par·a·chute [PA-rà-shoot] *n* apparatus extending like umbrella used to retard the descent of a falling body ▷ *v* **-chut·ed, -chut·ing** land or cause to land by parachute **par·a·chut·ist** *n* **golden parachute** employment contract for key employee of company guaranteeing substantial severance pay, etc if company is sold

pa·rade [pà-RAYD] *n* display; muster of troops; parade ground ▷ *v* **-rad·ed, -rad·ing** march; display

par·a·digm [PA-rà-dim] *n* example; model **par·a·dig·mat·ic** [-dig-MAT-ik] *adj*

par·a·dise [PA-rà-dis] *n* heaven; state of bliss; **(P-)** Garden of Eden

par·a·dox [PA-rà-doks] *n* statement that seems absurd or self-contradictory but may be true **par·a·dox·i·cal** *adj*

par·af·fin [PA-rà-fin] *n* waxlike or liquid hydrocarbon mixture used as fuel, solvent, in candles, etc

par·a·gon [PA-rà-gon] *n* pattern or model of excellence

par·a·graph [PA-rà-graf] *n* section of chapter or book; short notice, as in newspaper ▷ *vt* arrange in paragraphs

par·a·keet [PA-rà-keet] *n* small kind of parrot

par·al·lax [PA-rà-laks] *n* apparent difference in object's position or direction as viewed from different points

par·al·lel [PA-rà-lel] *adj* continuously at equal distances; precisely corresponding ▷ *n* line equidistant from another at all points; thing exactly like another; comparison; line of latitude ▷ *vt* **-leled, -lel·ing** represent as similar, compare **par·al·lel·ism** *n* **par·al·lel·o·gram** [-à-gram] *n* four-sided plane figure with opposite sides parallel

pa·ral·y·sis [pà-RAL-à-sis] *n, pl* **-ses** [-seez] incapacity to move or feel, due to damage to nervous system **par·a·lyze** [PA-rà-liz] *vt* **-lyzed, -lyz·ing** affect with paralysis; cripple; make useless or ineffectual **par·a·lyt·ic** [-LIT-ik] *adj, n* (person) affected with paralysis **infantile paralysis** poliomyelitis

par·a·med·i·cal [pa-rà-MED-i-kàl] *adj* of persons working in various capacities in support of medical profession **par·a·med·ic** *n*

pa·ram·e·ter [pə-RAM-i-tər]
n measurable characteristic; any
constant limiting factor

par·a·mil·i·tary [pa-rə-MIL-
i-ter-ee] *adj* of civilian group
organized on military lines or in
support of the military

par·a·mount [PA-rə-mownt] *adj*
supreme, eminent, preeminent, chief

par·a·mour [PA-rə-moor] *n*
old-fashioned lover, esp of a person
married to someone else

par·a·noi·a [pa-rə-NOI-ə] *n*
mental disease with delusions
of fame, grandeur, persecution
par·a·noi·ac *adj, n* **par·a·noid** *adj*
of paranoia; *inf* exhibiting fear of
persecution, etc ▷ *n*

par·a·pet [PA-rə-pit] *n* low
wall, railing along edge of balcony,
bridge, etc

par·a·pher·na·lia [pa-rə-fər-
NAYL-yə] *pl n* personal belongings;
odds and ends of equipment

par·a·phrase [PA-rə-frayz] *n*
expression of meaning of passage
in other words; free translation ▷ *vt*
-phrased, -phras·ing put into
other words

par·a·ple·gi·a [pa-rə-PLEE-jee-
ə] *n* paralysis of lower half of body
par·a·ple·gic *n, adj*

par·a·psy·chol·o·gy [pa-rə-
si-KOL-ə-jee] *n* study of subjects
pert to extrasensory perception, eg
telepathy

par·a·site [PA-rə-sit] *n* animal or
plant living in or on another; self-
interested hanger-on **par·a·sit·ic**
[-SIT-ik] *adj* of the nature of, living
as, parasite **par·a·sit·ism** [-si-tiz-
əm] *n* **par·a·si·tol·o·gy** *n* study of
animal and vegetable parasites, esp
as causes of disease

par·a·sol [PA-rə-sawl] *n*
lightweight umbrella used as
sunshade

par·a·troop·er [PA-rə-troo-pər]
n soldier trained to descend from
airplane by parachute

par·a·ty·phoid [pa-rə-TĪ-foid] *n*
an infectious disease similar to but
distinct from typhoid fever

par·boil [PAHR-boil] *vt* boil until
partly cooked

par·cel [PAHR-səl] *n* packet of
goods, esp one enclosed in paper;
quantity dealt with at one time; tract
of land ▷ *vt* **-celed, -cel·ing** wrap
up; divide into, distribute in parts

parch [pahrch] *v* dry by heating;
make, become hot and dry; scorch;
roast slightly

parch·ment [PAHRCH-mənt] *n*
sheep, goat, calf skin prepared for
writing; manuscript of this

par·don [PAHR-dn] *vt* forgive,
excuse ▷ *n* forgiveness; release from
punishment **par·don·a·ble** *adj*

pare [pair] *vt* **pared, par·ing** trim,
cut edge or surface of; decrease bit by
bit **par·ing** *n* piece pared off, rind

par·e·gor·ic [pa-ri-GOR-ik] *n*
tincture of opium used to stop
diarrhea

par·ent [PAIR-ənt] *n* father or
mother **par·ent·age** *n* descent,
extraction **pa·ren·tal** [pə-REN-tl]
adj **par·ent·hood** [-huud] *n*

pa·ren·the·sis [pə-REN-thə-sis] *n*
word, phrase, etc inserted in passage
independently of grammatical
sequence and usu marked off
by brackets, dashes, or commas
pa·ren·the·ses [-seez] *pl n* round
brackets, () **par·en·thet·i·cal** *adj*

pa·ri·ah [pə-RĪ-ə] *n* social outcast

par·ish [PA-rish] *n* district under
one clergyman; subdivision of
county **pa·rish·ion·er** *n* member,
inhabitant of parish

parity see PAR

park [pahrk] n large area of land in natural state preserved for recreational use; field or stadium for sporting events; large enclosed piece of ground, usu with grass or woodland, attached to country house or for public use; space in camp for military supplies ▷ vt leave for a short time; maneuver (automobile, etc) into a suitable space; inf engage in caressing and kissing in parked automobile

par·ka [PAHR-kə] n warm waterproof coat with hood

par·lance [PAHR-ləns] n way of speaking, conversation; idiom

par·ley [PAHR-lee] n, pl -leys meeting between leaders or representatives of opposing forces to discuss terms ▷ vi -leyed, -ley·ing hold discussion about terms

par·lia·ment [PAHR-lə-mənt] n legislature of some countries **par·lia·men·tar·i·an** [-TAIR-ee-ən] n expert in rules and procedures of a legislature or other formal organization

par·lor [PAHR-lər] n sitting room, room for receiving company in small house; place for milking cows; room or building as business premises, esp undertaker, hairdresser, etc

Par·me·san [PAHR-mə-zahn] n hard dry Italian cheese for grating

pa·ro·chi·al [pə-ROH-kee-əl] adj narrow, provincial; of a parish **pa·ro·chi·al·ism** n

par·o·dy [PA-rə-dee] n, pl -dies composition in which author's style is made fun of by imitation; travesty ▷ vt -died, -dy·ing write parody of **par·o·dist** n

pa·role [pə-ROHL] n early freeing of prisoner on condition of good behavior; word of honor ▷ vt -roled, rol·ing place on parole

par·ox·ysm [PA-rək-siz-əm] n sudden violent attack of pain, rage, laughter

par·quet [pahr-KAY] n flooring of wooden blocks arranged in pattern ▷ vt -queted [-KAYD] -quet·ing [-KAY-ing] lay a parquet

par·ri·cide [PA-rə-sīd] n murder or murderer of a parent

par·rot [PA-rət] n bird with short hooked beak, some varieties of which can imitate speaking; unintelligent imitator ▷ vt imitate or repeat without understanding

par·ry [PA-ree] vt -ried, -ry·ing ward off, turn aside ▷ n, pl -ries act of parrying, esp in fencing

parse [pahrs] vt parsed, pars·ing describe (word), analyze (sentence) in terms of grammar

par·si·mo·ny [PAHR-sə-moh-nee] n stinginess; undue economy **par·si·mo·ni·ous** adj sparing

pars·ley [PAHR-slee] n herb used for seasoning, garnish, etc

pars·nip [PAHR-snip] n edible whitish root vegetable

par·son [PAHR-sən] n clergyman of parish or church; clergyman **par'son·age** n parson's house

part [pahrt] n portion, section, share; division; actor's role; duty ▷ pl region ▷ v divide; separate **part'ing** n division between sections of hair on head; separation; leave-taking **part'ly** adv in part **part song** song for several voices singing in harmony

par·tial [PAHR-shəl] adj not general or complete; prejudiced; fond of **par'tial·ly** adv partly **par·ti·al·i·ty** [pahr-shee-AL-i-tee] n favoritism; fondness for

par·tic·i·pate [pahr-TIS-ə-payt] v **-pat·ed, -pat·ing** share in; take part in **par·tic·i·pant** n **par·tic·i·pa·to·ry** adj

par·ti·ci·ple [PAHR-tə-sip-əl] n adjective made by inflection from verb and keeping verb's relation to dependent words **par·ti·cip'i·al** adj

par·ti·cle [PAHR-ti-kəl] n minute portion of matter; least possible amount; minor part of speech in grammar, prefix, suffix

par·ti·col·ored [PAHR-tee-kul-ərd] adj differently colored in different parts, variegated

par·tic·u·lar [pahr-TIK-yə-lər] adj relating to one, not general; distinct; minute; very exact; fastidious ▷n detail, item ▷pl detailed account; items of information **par·tic'u·lar·ize** vt **-ized, -iz·ing** mention in detail **par·tic'u·lar·ly** adv

par·ti·san [PAHR-tə-zən] n adherent of a party; guerrilla, member of resistance movement ▷adj adhering to faction; prejudiced

par·ti·tion [pahr-TISH-ən] n division; interior dividing wall ▷vt divide, cut into sections

part·ner [PAHRT-nər] n ally or companion; member of a partnership; one who dances with another; a husband or wife; sport one who plays with another against opponents ▷vt be a partner of **part'ner·ship** n association of persons for business, etc

par·tridge [PAHR-trij] n, pl **-tridg·es** game bird of the grouse family

par·tu·ri·tion [pahr-tyuu-RISH-ən] n act of bringing forth young; childbirth

par·ty [PAHR-tee] n, pl **-ties** social assembly; group of persons traveling or working together; group of persons united in opinion; side; person ▷adj of, belonging to, a party or faction **party line** telephone line serving two or more subscribers; policies of political party **party wall** common wall separating adjoining premises

par·ve·nu [PAHR-və-noo] n one newly risen into position of notice, power, wealth; upstart

Pas·cal [PAS-kal] n high-level computer programming language developed as a teaching language

pas·chal [PAS-kəl] adj of Passover or Easter

pass vt go by, beyond, through, etc; exceed; be accepted by; undergo successfully; spend; transfer; exchange; disregard; bring into force, sanction a legislative bill, etc ▷vi go; be transferred from one state or person to another; elapse; undergo examination successfully; be taken as member of religious or racial group other than one's own ▷n way, esp a narrow and difficult way; permit, license, authorization; successful result from test; condition; sport transfer of ball by kick or throw **pass'a·ble** adj (just) acceptable **pass'ing** adj transitory; cursory, casual **pass off** present (something) under false pretenses **pass up** ignore, neglect, reject

pas·sage [PAS-ij] n channel, opening; way through, corridor; part of book, etc; journey, voyage, fare; enactment of rule, law by legislature, etc; conversation, dispute; incident

pas·sé [pa-SAY] adj out-of-date; past the prime

pas·sen·ger [PAS-ən-jər] n traveler, esp by public conveyance

pas·ser·ine [PAS-ər-in] adj of the order of perching birds

pas'sim Lat everywhere, throughout

pas•sion [PASH-ən] n ardent desire, esp sexual; any strongly felt emotion; suffering (esp that of Christ) **pas'sion•ate** [-it] adj (easily) moved by strong emotions

pas•sive [PAS-iv] adj unresisting; submissive; inactive; denoting grammatical voice of verb in which the subject receives the action

pas•siv'i•ty n passive-aggressive adj relating to a personality that harbors aggressive emotions while behaving in a passive manner

passive smoking involuntary inhalation of smoke from other's cigarettes by nonsmoker

Pass•o•ver [PAS-oh-vər] n Jewish spring festival commemorating exodus of Jews from Egypt

pass'port n official document granting permission to pass, travel abroad, etc

pass'word [PAS-wurd] n word, phrase, to distinguish friend from enemy; countersign

past adj ended; gone by; elapsed ▷ n bygone times ▷ adv by; along ▷ prep beyond; after

pas•ta [PAH-stə] n type of food, such as spaghetti, that is made in different shapes from flour and water

paste [payst] n soft composition, as toothpaste; soft plastic mixture or adhesive; fine glass to imitate gems ▷ vt **past•ed, past•ing** fasten with paste **past'y** adj **past•i•er, past•i•est** like paste; white; sickly

pas•tel [pa-STEL] n colored crayon; art of drawing with crayons; pale, delicate color ▷ adj delicately tinted

pas•teur•ize [PAS-chə-rīz] vt **-ized, -iz•ing** sterilize by heat **pas•teur•i•za'tion** n

pas•tiche [pa-STEESH] n literary, musical, artistic work composed of parts borrowed from other works

and loosely connected together; work imitating another's style

pas•tille [pa-STEEL] n lozenge; aromatic substance burned as deodorant or fumigator

pas•time [PAS-tim] n that which makes time pass agreeably; recreation

pas•tor [PAS-tər] n priest or minister in charge of a church **pas'to•ral** adj of, or like, shepherd's or rural life; of office of pastor ▷ n poem describing pastoral life

pas•try [PAY-stree] n, pl **-tries** article of food made chiefly of flour, shortening and water

pas•ture [PAS-chər] n grass for food of cattle; ground on which cattle graze ▷ v **-tured, -tur•ing** (cause to) graze **pas'tur•age** n (right to) pasture

pat¹ vt **pat•ted, pat•ting** tap ▷ n light, quick blow; small mass, as of butter, beaten into shape

pat² adv exactly; fluently; opportunely; glib; exactly right

patch [pach] n piece of cloth sewn on garment; spot; plot of ground; protecting pad for the eye; small contrasting area; short period ▷ vt mend; repair clumsily **patch'y** adj **patch•i•er, patch•i•est** of uneven quality; full of patches **patch'work** n work composed of pieces sewn together; jumble

patch•ou•li [pə-CHOO-lee] n Indian herb; perfume from it

pate [payt] n head; top of head

pâ•té [pa-TAY] n spread of finely chopped liver, etc **pâté de foie gras** [də-fwah-GRAH] one made of goose liver

pa•tel•la [pə-TEL-ə] n, pl **-las** kneecap **pa•tel'lar** adj

pat•ent [PAT-nt] n document securing to person or organization exclusive right to invention ▷ *adj* open; evident; manifest; open to public perusal: *letters patent* ▷ *vt* secure a patent **pat·ent·ee** *n* one who has a patent **pat·ent·ly** *adv* obviously **patent leather** *n* leather (imitation) processed to give hard, glossy surface

pa·ter·fa·mil·i·as [pah-tàr-fò-MIL-ee-òs] *n, pl* **-ases** father of a family

pa·ter·nal [pò-TUR-nl] *adj* fatherly; of a father; related through a father **pa·ter·nal·ism** *n* authority exercised in a way that limits individual responsibility **pa·ter·nal·is·tic** *adj* **pa·ter·ni·ty** *n* relation of a father to his offspring; fatherhood

pa·ter·nos·ter [PAY-tàr-NOS-tàr] *n* Lord's Prayer; beads of rosary

path *n, pl* **paths** [pathz] way or track; course of action **path'name** *n* name of an electronic file or directory together with its position relative to other directories traced back to its source

pa·thet·ic [pò-THET-ik] *adj* affecting or moving tender emotions; distressingly inadequate **pa·thet'i·cal·ly** *adv*

path·o·gen·ic [path-ò-JEN-ik] *adj* producing disease **patho'o·gen** *n* disease-producing agent, eg virus

pa·thol·o·gy [pò-THOL-ò-jee] *n* science of diseases **path·o·log·i·cal** [-LOJ-i-kòl] *adj* of the science of disease; due to disease; compulsively motivated **pa·thol'o·gist** *n*

pa·thos [PAY-thos] *n* power of exciting tender emotions

pa·tient [PAY-shònt] *adj* bearing trials calmly ▷ *n* person under medical treatment **pa'tience** *n* quality of enduring; card game for one player

pat·i·na [pò-TEE-nò] *n* fine layer on a surface; sheen of age on woodwork

pat·i·o [PAT-ee-oh] *n, pl* **-ios** (usu paved) area adjoining house for lounging, etc

pat·ois [PA-twah] *n* regional dialect

pa·tri·arch [PAY-tree-ahrk] *n* father and founder of family, esp Biblical **pa·tri·ar·chal** *adj* venerable

pa·tri·cian [pò-TRISH-òn] *n* noble of ancient Rome; one of noble birth ▷ *adj* of noble birth

pat·ri·cide [PA-trò-sìd] *n* murder or murderer of father

pat·ri·mo·ny [PA-trò-moh-nee] *n, pl* **-nies** property inherited from ancestors

pa·tri·ot [PAY-tree-òt] *n* one who loves own country and maintains its interests **pa'tri·ot·ism** *n* [-ò-tiz-òm] love of, loyalty to one's country **pa·tri·ot·ic** [-OT-ik] *adj* inspired by love of one's country

pa·trol [pò-TROHL] *n* regular circuit by guard; person, small group patrolling; unit of Boy Scouts or Girl Scouts ▷ *v* **-trolled, -trol·ling** go around on guard, or reconnoitering

pa·tron [PAY-tràn] *n* one who sponsors or aids artists, charities, etc; protector; regular customer; guardian saint; one who has disposition of benefice, etc **pa'tron·age** *n* support given by, or position of, a patron **pa'tron·ize** *vt* **-ized, -iz·ing** assume air of superiority toward; frequent as customer; encourage

pat·ro·nym·ic [pa-trò-NIM-ik] *n* name derived from that of parent or an ancestor

pat·ter [PAT-àr] *vi* make noise, as sound of quick, short steps; tap in quick succession; pray, talk rapidly

▷ n quick succession of taps; *inf* glib, rapid speech

pat·tern [PAT-ərn] n arrangement of repeated parts; design; shape to direct cutting of cloth, etc; model; specimen ▷ vt (with *on, after*) model; decorate with pattern

pat·ty [PAT-ee] n, pl -**ties** a little pie; thin round piece of meat, candy, etc

pau·ci·ty [PAW-si-tee] n scarcity; smallness of quantity; fewness

paunch [pawnch] n belly; potbelly

pau·per [PAW-pər] n poor person, esp formerly, one supported by the public **pau·per·ism** n destitution; extreme poverty **pau·per·ize** vt -**ized, -iz·ing** reduce to pauperism

pause [pawz] vi **paused, paus·ing** cease for a time ▷ n stop or rest

pave [payv] vt **paved, pav·ing** form surface with stone or brick **pave·ment** [-mənt] n paved floor, footpath; material for paving **pave the way for** lead up to; facilitate entrance of

pa·vil·ion [pə-VIL-yən] n clubhouse on playing field, etc; building for housing exhibition, etc; large ornate tent

paw n foot of animal ▷ v scrape with forefoot; handle roughly; stroke with the hands

pawn[1] vt deposit (article) as security for money borrowed ▷ n article deposited **pawn·bro·ker** n lender of money on goods pledged

pawn[2] n piece in chess; *fig* person used as mere tool

pay v **paid, pay·ing** ▷ vt give money, etc, for goods or services rendered; compensate; give or bestow; be profitable to; (with *out*) release bit by bit, as rope ▷ vi be remunerative; be profitable; (with *out*) spend ▷ n wages; paid employment **pay·a·ble** adj justly due; profitable **pay·ee**[1] n person to whom money is paid or due **pay·ment** [-mənt] n discharge of debt **pay·load** n part of cargo earning revenue; explosive power of missile, etc **paying guest** boarder, lodger, esp in private house **pay television** programs provided for viewers who pay monthly or per-program fees

Pb *chemistry* lead

pc politically correct; personal computer

Pd *chemistry* palladium

PDF Portable Document Format: a format in which electronic documents may be viewed

pea [pee] n fruit, growing in pods, of climbing plant; the plant **pea-green** adj of shade of green like color of green peas **pea green** this color **pea soup** thick soup made of green peas; *inf* thick fog

peace [pees] n freedom from war; harmony; quietness of mind; calm; repose **peace·a·ble** adj disposed to peace **peace·a·bly** adv **peace·ful** adj free from war, tumult; mild; undisturbed

peach [peech] n stone fruit of delicate flavor; *inf* person or thing very pleasant; pinkish-yellow color **peach·y** adj **peach·i·er, peach·i·est** like peach; *inf* fine, excellent

pea·cock [PEE-kok] n male of bird with fanlike tail, brilliantly colored **pea·hen** n fem **pea·fowl** n peacock or peahen

peak [peek] n pointed end of anything, esp hill's sharp top; point of greatest development, etc; sharp increase; projecting piece on front of cap ▷ v (cause to) form, reach peaks **peaked** adj like, having a

peak peak·ed [PEE-kid] sickly, wan, drawn

peal [peel] n loud sound or succession of loud sounds; changes rung on set of bells; chime ▷ vi sound loudly

pea·nut [PEE-nut] n pea-shaped nut that ripens underground; the plant ▷ pl inf trifling amount of money

pear [pair] n tree yielding sweet, juicy fruit; the fruit **pear-shaped** adj shaped like a pear, heavier at the bottom than the top

pearl [purl] n hard, lustrous structure found in several mollusks, esp pearl oyster and used as jewel **pearl'y** adj **pearl·i·er, pearl·i·est** like pearls

peas·ant [PEZ-ənt] n in certain countries, member of low social class, esp in rural district; boorish person **peas'ant·ry** n peasants collectively

peat [peet] n decomposed vegetable substance found in bogs; turf of it used for fuel **peat moss** dried peat, used as mulch, etc

peb·ble [PEB-əl] n small roundish stone; pale, transparent rock crystal; grainy, irregular surface ▷ vt **-bled, -bling** pave, cover with pebbles

pe·can [pi-KAHN] n Amer tree, species of hickory, allied to walnut; its edible nut

pec·ca·dil·lo [pek-ə-DIL-oh] n, pl **-loes** slight offense; petty crime

pec·ca·ry [PEK-ə-ree] n, pl **-ries** vicious Amer animal allied to pig

peck¹ [pek] n fourth part of bushel, equal to 8.81 liters; great deal

peck² v pick, strike with or as with beak; nibble ▷ n quick kiss **peck'ish** adj inf irritable

pecs [peks] pl n inf pectoral muscles

pec·tin [PEK-tin] n gelatinizing substance obtained from ripe fruits **pec'tic** adj congealing; denoting pectin

pec·to·ral [PEK-tər-əl] adj of the breast ▷ n pectoral part of organ; breastplate

pec·u·late [PEK-yə-layt] v **-lat·ed, -lat·ing** embezzle; steal **pec·u·la'tion** n

pe·cu·liar [pi-KYOOL-yər] adj strange; particular; belonging to **pe·cu·li·ar'i·ty** n oddity; characteristic; distinguishing feature

pe·cu·ni·ar·y [pi-KYOO-nee-er-ee] adj relating to, or consisting of, money

ped·a·gogue [PED-ə-gog] n schoolmaster; pedant **ped·a·gog'ic** [-GOJ-ik] adj

ped·al [PED-l] n something to transmit motion from foot; foot lever to modify tone or swell of musical instrument; music note, usu bass, held through successive harmonies ▷ adj of a foot ▷ v **-daled, -dal·ing** propel bicycle, etc by using its pedals; use pedal

ped·ant [PED-ənt] n one who overvalues, or insists on, petty details of book learning, grammatical rules, etc **pe·dan'tic** adj **ped'ant·ry** n, pl **-ries**

ped·dle [PED-l] vt **-dled, -dling** go around selling goods **ped'dler, ped'lar** n

ped·er·ast [PED-ə-rast] n man who has homosexual relations with boy **ped'er·as·ty** n

ped·es·tal [PED-ə-stl] n base of column, pillar **put on a pedestal** idealize

pe·des·tri·an [pə-DES-tree-ən] n one who goes on foot; walker ▷ adj going on foot; commonplace; dull, uninspiring

pe·di·at·rics [pee-dee-A-triks] n branch of medicine dealing with diseases and disorders of children **pe·di·a·tri·cian** [-ə-TRISH-ən] n

ped·i·cel [PED-ə-səl] n small, short stalk of leaf, flower or fruit

ped·i·cure [PED-i-kyoor] n medical or cosmetic treatment of feet

ped·i·gree n register of ancestors; genealogy

ped·i·ment [PED-ə-mənt] n triangular part over Greek portico, etc **ped·i·men·tal** [-MEN-tl] adj

pedlar see PEDDLE

pe·dom·e·ter [pə-DOM-i-tər] n instrument that measures the distance walked

pe·dun·cle [pi-DUNG-kəl] n flower stalk; stalklike structure

peek vi, n peep, glance

peel vt strip off skin, rind or any form of covering ▷ vi come off, as skin, rind ▷ n rind, skin **peeled** adj inf of eyes, watchful **peel·ings** pl n parings

peep[1] vi look slyly or quickly ▷ n such a look

peep[2] vi cry, as chick; chirp ▷ n such a cry

peer[1] n nobleman; one of the same rank, ability, etc **peer·age** [-ij] n body of peers; rank of peer **peer·ess** n fem **peer·less** [-lis] adj without match or equal

peer[2] vi look closely and intently

peeved [peevd] adj sulky, irritated **peeve** vt peeved, peev·ing annoy; vex

pee·vish adj fretful; irritable **pee·vish·ly** adv **pee·vish·ness** [-nis] n annoyance

peg n nail or pin for joining, fastening, marking, etc; (mark of) level, standard, etc ▷ v **pegged, peg·ging** fasten with pegs; stabilize

(prices); inf throw; (with away) persevere **take down a peg** humble (someone)

peign·oir [pain-WAHR] n woman's dressing gown, jacket, wrapper

pe·jo·ra·tive [pi-JOR-ə-tiv] adj (of words, etc) with unpleasant, disparaging connotation

Pe·king·ese [pee-kə-NEEZ] n small Chinese dog

pe·lag·ic [pə-LAJ-ik] adj of the deep sea

pel·i·can [PEL-i-kən] n large, fish-eating waterfowl with large pouch beneath its bill

pel·let [PEL-it] n little ball, pill

pell-mell adv in utter confusion, headlong

pel·lu·cid [pə-LOO-sid] adj translucent; clear

pelt[1] vt strike with missiles ▷ vi throw missiles; rush; fall persistently, as rain

pelt[2] n raw hide or skin

pel·vis n, pl **-vis·es** bony cavity at base of human trunk **pel·vic** adj pert to pelvis

pen[1] n instrument for writing ▷ vt penned, pen·ning compose; write **pen name** author's pseudonym **pen pal** person with whom one corresponds, usu someone whom one has never met

pen[2] n small enclosure, as for sheep ▷ vt penned, pen·ning put, keep in enclosure

pen[3] n female swan

pe·nal [PEEN-l] adj of, incurring, inflicting, punishment **pe·nal·ize** vt -ized, -iz·ing impose penalty on; handicap **pen·al·ty** n, pl -ties punishment for crime or offense; forfeit; sport handicap or disadvantage imposed for infringement of rule, etc

pen·ance [PEN-əns] n suffering

submitted to as expression of
penitence; repentance

pen·chant [PEN-chənt] *n*
inclination, decided taste

pen·cil [PEN-səl] *n* instrument as
of graphite, for writing, etc; *optics*
narrow beam of light ▷ *vt* **-ciled,**
-cil·ing paint or draw; mark with
pencil

pend·ant [PEN-dənt] *n* hanging
ornament **pend·ent** *adj* suspended;
hanging; projecting

pend·ing *prep* during, until ▷ *adj*
awaiting settlement; undecided;
imminent

pen·du·lous [PEN-jə-ləs] *adj*
hanging, swinging **pen·du·lum**
[-ləm] *n* suspended weight
swinging to and fro, esp as regulator
for clock

pen·e·trate [PEN-i-trayt] *vt*
-trat·ed, trat·ing enter into;
pierce; arrive at the meaning of
pen·e·tra·bil·i·ty *n* quality of
being penetrable **pen·e·tra·ble**
[-trə-bəl] *adj* capable of being
entered or pierced **penetrating**
adj sharp; easily heard; subtle; quick
to understand **pen·e·tra·tion** *n*
insight, acuteness **pen·e·tra·tive**
[-tray-tiv] *adj* piercing; discerning

pen·guin [PENG-gwin] *n*
flightless, short-legged swimming
bird

pen·i·cil·lin [pen-ə-SIL-in] *n*
antibiotic drug effective against a
wide range of diseases, infections

pen·in·su·la [pə-NINS-yə-lə] *n*
portion of land nearly surrounded by
water **pen·in·su·lar** *adj*

pe·nis [PEE-nis] *n, pl* **-nis·es**
male organ of copulation (and
of urination) in man and many
mammals

pen·i·tent [PEN-i-tənt] *adj*
affected by sense of guilt ▷ *n* one

that repents of sin **pen·i·tence**
n sorrow for sin; repentance

pen·i·ten·tial [-TEN-shəl] *adj*
of, or expressing, penitence

pen·i·ten·tia·ry [-TEN-shə-ree] *adj*
relating to penance, or to the rules of
penance ▷ *n, pl* **-ries** prison

pen·nant [PEN-ənt] *n* long
narrow flag

pen·non [PEN-ən] *n* small pointed
or swallow-tailed flag

pen·ny [PEN-ee] *n, pl* **-nies** coin,
100th part of dollar; similar coin of
other countries **pen·ni·less** [-lis]
adj having no money; poor **a pretty
penny** *inf* considerable amount
of money

pe·nol·o·gy [pee-NOL-ə-jee] *n*
study of punishment and prevention
of crime

pen·sion [PEN-shən] *n* regular
payment to old people, retired public
officials, workers, etc ▷ *vt* grant
pension to **pen·sion·er** *n*

pen·sive [PEN-siv] *adj* thoughtful
with sadness; wistful

pent *adj* shut up, kept in **pent-up**
adj not released, repressed

pen·ta·gon [PEN-tə-gon] *n*
plane figure having five angles
pen·tag·o·nal [-TAG-ə-nl] *adj*

pen·tam·e·ter [pen-TAM-i-tər] *n*
verse of five metrical feet

Pen·ta·teuch [PEN-tə-tyook] *n*
first five books of Old Testament

pen·tath·lon [pen-TATH-lən] *n*
athletic contest of five events

Pen·te·cost [PEN-ti-kawst] *n*
Christian festival of seventh Sunday
after Easter

pent·house [PENT-hows] *n, pl*
-hous·es [-howz-iz] apartment or
other structure on top, or top floor,
of building

pen·tode [PEN-tohd] *n electronics*
five-electrode vacuum tube, having

anode, cathode and three grids

pe·nult [PEE-nult] *n* last syllable but one of word **pen·ul·ti·mate** [pi-NUL-tà-mit] *adj* next before the last

pe·num·bra [pi-NUM-brà] *n* imperfect shadow; in an eclipse, the partially shadowed region that surrounds the full shadow

pen·u·ry [PEN-yà-ree] *n* extreme poverty; extreme scarcity **pe·nu·ri·ous** [pà-NUUR-ee-às] *adj* niggardly, stingy; poor, scanty

peo·ple [PEE-pàl] *pl n* persons generally; community, nation; race; family ▷ *vt* **-pled, -pling** stock with inhabitants; populate

pep *n inf* vigor; energy; enthusiasm ▷ *vt* **pepped, pep·ping** impart energy to; speed up

pep·per [PEP-àr] *n* fruit of climbing plant that yields pungent aromatic spice; various slightly pungent vegetables, eg capsicum ▷ *vt* season with pepper; sprinkle, dot; pelt with missiles **pep'per·y** *adj* having the qualities of pepper; irritable **pep'per·corn** *n* dried pepper berry; something trifling **pep'per·mint** *n* plant noted for aromatic pungent liquor distilled from it; a candy flavored with this

pep·tic [PEP-tik] *adj* relating to digestion or digestive juices

per [pàr] *prep* for each; by; in manner of

per-, par-, pel-, pil- *prefix* through, thoroughly; perfect; pellucid

per·am·bu·late [pàr-AM-byà-layt] *v* **-lat·ed, -lat·ing** ▷ *vt* walk through or over; traverse ▷ *vi* walk about **per·am'bu·la·tor** *n* baby carriage

per an·num [pàr AN-àm] *Lat* by the year

per·cale [pàr-KAYL] *n* woven

cotton used esp for sheets

per cap·i·ta [pàr KAP-i-tà] *Lat* for each person

per·ceive [pàr-SEEV] *vt* **-ceived, -ceiv·ing** obtain knowledge of through senses; observe; understand **per·ceiv'a·ble** *adj* discernible, recognizable **per·cep'tion** *n* faculty of perceiving; intuitive knowledge **per·cep'tive** *adj*

perception *n see* PERCEIVE

perch¹ [purch] *n* freshwater fish

perch² *n* resting place, as for bird ▷ *vt* place, as on perch ▷ *vi* alight, settle on fixed body; roost; balance on

per·cip·i·ent [pàr-SIP-ee-ànt] *adj* having faculty of perception; perceiving ▷ *n* one who perceives

per·co·late [PUR-kà-layt] *v* **-lat·ed, -lat·ing** pass through fine mesh as liquid; permeate; filter **per'co·la·tor** *n* coffeepot with filter

per·cus·sion [pàr-KUSH-àn] *n* collision; impact; vibratory shock **percussion instrument** musical instrument played by being struck, such as drums or cymbals

per di·em [pàr DEE-àm] *Lat* by the day; for each day

per·di·tion [pàr-DISH-àn] *n* spiritual ruin

per·e·gri·nate [PER-i-grà-nayt] *vi* **-nat·ed, -nat·ing** travel about; roam **per·e·grine** [PER-i-grin] *n* type of falcon

per·emp·to·ry [pà-REMP-tà-ree] *adj* authoritative, imperious; forbidding debate; decisive

per·en·ni·al [pà-REN-ee-àl] *adj* lasting through the years; perpetual, unfailing ▷ *n* plant lasting more

perfect | 402

than two years

per·fect [PUR-fikt] *adj* complete; finished; whole; unspoiled; faultless; correct, precise; excellent; of highest quality ▷ *vt* tense denoting a completed act ▷ *vt* [pər-FEKT] improve; finish; make skillful **per·fect'i·ble** *adj* capable of becoming perfect **per·fec'tion** [-FEK-shən] *n* state of being perfect; faultlessness **per'fect·ly** *adv*

per·fi·dy [PUR-fi-dee] *n* treachery, disloyalty **per·fid'i·ous** *adj*

per·fo·rate [PUR-fə-rayt] *vt* **-rat·ed, -rat·ing** make hole(s) in, penetrate **per·fo·ra'tion** *n* hole(s) made through thing

per·force [pər-FORS] *adv* of necessity

per·form [pər-FORM] *vt* bring to completion; accomplish; fulfill; represent on stage ▷ *vi* function; act part; play, as on musical instrument **per·for'mance** [-məns] *n*

per·fume [PUR-fyoom] *n* agreeable scent; fragrance ▷ *vt* **-fumed, -fum·ing** imbue with an agreeable odor; scent **per·fum'er** *n*

per·func·to·ry [pər-FUNGK-tə-ree] *adj* superficial; hasty; done indifferently

per·go·la [PUR-gə-lə] *n* area covered by plants growing on trellis; the trellis

per·haps [pər-HAPS] *adv* possibly

peri- *prefix* round: *perimeter; period; periphrasis*

per·i·car·di·um [per-i-KAHR-dee-əm] *n, pl* **-di·a** [-dee-ə] membrane enclosing the heart **per·i·car·di'tis** *n* inflammation of this

per·i·he·li·on [per-ə-HEE-lee-ən] *n, pl* **-li·a** [-lee-ə] point in orbit of planet or comet nearest to sun

per·il [PER-əl] *n* danger; exposure

to injury **per'il·ous** *adj* full of peril, hazardous

pe·rim·e·ter [pə-RIM-i-tər] *n* outer boundary of an area; length of this

pe·ri·od [PEER-ee-əd] *n* particular portion of time; a series of years; single occurrence of menstruation; cycle; conclusion; full stop (.) at the end of a sentence; complete sentence ▷ *adj* of furniture, dress, play, etc, belonging to particular time in history **pe·ri·od'ic** *adj* recurring at regular intervals **pe·ri·od'i·cal** *adj, n* (of) publication issued at regular intervals ▷ *adj* of a period; periodic **pe·ri·o·dic'i·ty** [-DIS-i-tee] *n*

per·i·pa·tet·ic [per-ə-pə-TET-ik] *adj* itinerant; walking, traveling about

pe·riph·er·y [pə-RIF-ə-ree] *n, pl* **-er·ies** circumference; surface, outside **pe·riph'er·al** [-ə-rəl] *adj* minor, unimportant; of periphery

pe·riph·ra·sis [pə-RIF-rə-sis] *n, pl* **-ses** [-seez] roundabout speech or phrase; circumlocution **per·i·phras'tic** *adj*

per·i·scope [PER-ə-skohp] *n* instrument used esp in submarines, for giving view of objects on different level

per·ish [PER-ish] *vi* die, waste away; decay, rot **per'ish·a·ble** *adj* that will not last long ▷ *pl n* perishable food

per·i·to·ne·um [per-i-tn-EE-əm] *n, pl* **-ne·ums** or **-to·ne·a** [-EE-ə] membrane lining internal surface of abdomen **per·i·to·ni'tis** [-Nī-tis] *n* inflammation of it

per·i·win·kle [PER-i-wing-kəl] *n* myrtle; small edible shellfish

per·jure [PUR-jər] *vt* **-jured, -jur·ing** be guilty of perjury **per'ju·ry** *n, pl* **-ries** crime of false testimony under oath; false swearing

perk·y [PUR-kee] adj **perk·i·er, perk·i·est** lively, cheerful, jaunty, gay **perk up** make, become cheerful

per·ma·frost [PUR-mà-frawst] n permanently frozen ground

per·ma·nent [PUR-mà-nànt] adj continuing in same state; lasting **per'ma·nence, per'ma·nen·cy** n fixedness **permanent wave** n (treatment of hair producing) longlasting style

per·me·ate [PUR-mee-ayt] vt **-at·ed, -at·ing** pervade, saturate; pass through pores of **per'me·a·ble** [-à-bàl] adj admitting of passage of fluids

per·mit [pàr-MIT] vt **-mit·ted, -mit·ting** allow; give leave to ▷ n [PUR-mit] license to do something; written permission **permis'si·ble** adj allowable **per·mis'sion** n authorization; leave, liberty **per·mis'sive** adj (too) tolerant, lenient, esp as parent

per·mute [pàr-MYOOT] vt **-mut·ed, -mut·ing** interchange **per·mu·ta·tion** [pur-myuu-TAY-shàn] n mutual transference; *mathematics* arrangement of a number of quantities in every possible order

per·ni·cious [pàr-NISH-às] adj wicked or mischievous; extremely hurtful; having quality of destroying or injuring

per·o·ra·tion [per-à-RAY-shàn] n concluding part of oration

per·ox·ide [pà-ROK-sid] n oxide of a given base containing greatest quantity of oxygen; short for **HYDROGEN PEROXIDE**

perp [purp] n *inf* person who has committed a crime

per·pen·dic·u·lar [pur-pàn-DIK-yà-làr] adj at right angles to the plane of the horizon; at right angles

to given line or surface; exactly upright ▷ n line falling at right angles on another line or plane

per·pe·trate [PUR-pi-trayt] vt **-trat·ed, -trat·ing** perform or be responsible for (something bad)

per·pet·u·al [pàr-PECH-oo-àl] adj continuous; lasting for ever **per·pet'u·ate** vt **-at·ed, -at·ing** make perpetual; not to allow to be forgotten **per·pet·u·a'tion** n **per·pe·tu'i·ty** [pur-pi-TOO-i-tee] n

per·plex [pàr-PLEKS] vt puzzle; bewilder; make difficult to understand **per·plex'i·ty** n, pl **-ties** puzzled or tangled state

per·qui·site [PUR-kwi-zit] n any incidental benefit from a certain type of employment; casual payment in addition to salary; something due as a privilege

per se [pur SAY] *Lat* by or in itself

per·se·cute [PUR-si-kyoot] vt **-cut·ed, -cut·ing** oppress because of race, religion, etc; subject to persistent ill-treatment **per·se·cu'tion** n

per·se·vere [pur-sà-VEER] vi **-vered, -ver·ing** persist, maintain effort **per·se·ver'ance** [-àns] n persistence

per·si·flage [PUR-sà-flahzh] n idle talk; frivolous style of treating subject

per·sim·mon [pàr-SIM-àn] n Amer tree; its hard wood; its fruit

per·sist [pàr-SIST] vi continue in spite of obstacles or objections **per·sist'ence** [-àns] n **per·sist'en·cy** n **per·sist'ent** adj persisting; steady; persevering; lasting

per·snick·et·y [pàr-SNIK-i-tee] adj *inf* fussy; fastidious about trifles; snobbishly aloof; requiring great care

per·son [PUR-sǝn] n individual (human) being; body of human being; grammar classification, or one of the classes, of pronouns and verb forms according to the person speaking, spoken to, or spoken of **per·so·na** [pǝr-SOH-nǝ] n, pl **-nas** assumed character **per·son·age** [-ij] n notable person **per·son·al** adj individual, private, or one's own; of, relating to grammatical person **per·son·al·i·ty** n, pl **-ties** distinctive character; a celebrity **per·son·al·ly** adv in person **per·son·ate** vt **-at·ed, -at·ing** pass oneself off as **personal computer** small computer used for word processing, e-mail, computer games, etc **personal property** law all property except land and interests in land that pass to their **personal stereo** very small portable cassette player with headphones **per·son·hood** n condition of being a person who is an individual with inalienable rights
per·son·i·fy [pǝr-SON-ǝ-fī] vt **-fied, -fy·ing** represent as person; typify **per·son·i·fi·ca·tion** n
per·son·nel [pur-sǝ-NEL] n staff employed in a service or institution
per·spec·tive [pǝr-SPEK-tiv] n mental view; art of drawing on flat surface to give effect of solidity and relative distances and sizes; drawing in perspective
per·spi·ca·cious [pur-spi-KAY-shǝs] adj having quick mental insight **per·spi·cac·i·ty** [-KAS-i-tee] n
per·spic·u·ous [pǝr-SPIK-yoo-ǝs] adj clearly expressed; lucid; plain; obvious
per·spire [pǝr-SPIR] v **-spired, -spir·ing** sweat **per·spi·ra·tion**

[-spi-RAY-shǝn] n sweating; sweat
per·suade [pǝr-SWAYD] vt **-suad·ed, -suad·ing** bring (one to do something) by argument, charm, etc; convince **per·sua·sion** [-SWAY-zhǝn] n art, act of persuading; way of thinking or belief **per·sua·sive** adj
pert adj **-er, -est** forward, saucy
per·tain [pǝr-TAYN] vi belong, relate, have reference (to); concern
per·ti·na·cious [pur-tn-AY-shǝs] adj obstinate, persistent **per·ti·nac·i·ty** [-AS-i-tee] n doggedness, resolution
per·ti·nent [PUR-tn-ǝnt] adj to the point **per·ti·nence** n relevance
per·turb [pǝr-TURB] vt disturb greatly; alarm **per·tur·ba·tion** n disturbance; agitation of mind
pe·ruse [pǝ-ROOZ] vt **-rused, -rus·ing** examine, read, esp in slow and careful, or leisurely, manner **pe·rus·al** n
per·vade [pǝr-VAYD] vt **-vad·ed, -vad·ing** spread through; be rife among **per·va·sive** adj
per·vert [pǝr-VURT] vt turn to wrong use; lead astray ⊳ n [PUR-vǝrt] one who shows unhealthy abnormality, esp in sexual matters **per·verse** [pǝr-VURS] adj obstinately or unreasonably wrong; self-willed; headstrong; wayward **per·ver·sion** [-VUR-zhǝn] n
pes·sa·ry [PES-ǝ-ree] n, pl **-ries** instrument used to support mouth and neck of uterus; appliance to prevent conception; medicated suppository
pes·si·mism [PES-ǝ-miz-ǝm] n tendency to see the worst side of things; theory that everything turns to evil **pes·si·mist** n **pes·si·mis·tic** adj
pest n troublesome or harmful thing, person or insect; plague

pest·i·cide [-sīd] n chemical for killing pests, esp insects

pes·tif·er·ous [-ər-əs] adj troublesome; bringing plague

pes·ter [PES-tər] vt trouble or vex persistently; harass

pes·ti·lence [PES-tl-əns] n epidemic disease, esp bubonic plague **pes·ti·lent** adj troublesome; deadly **pes·ti·len·tial** [-LEN-shəl] adj

pes·tle [PES-əl] n instrument with which things are pounded in a mortar

Pet. Peter

pet n animal or person kept or regarded with affection ▷ vt **pet·ted, pet·ting** make pet of; inf hug, embrace, fondle

pet·al [PET-l] n white or colored leaflike part of flower **pet'aled** adj

pe·tard [pi-TAHRD] n formerly, an explosive device **hoist by one's own petard** ruined, destroyed by plot one intended for another

pe·ter [PEE-tər] vi **peter out** inf disappear, lose power gradually

pe·tit [PET-ee] adj law small, petty

pe·tite [pə-TEET] adj small, dainty

pe·ti·tion [pə-TISH-ən] n entreaty, request, espone presented to a governing body or person ▷ vt present petition to **pe·ti·tion·er** n

pet·rel [PE-trəl] n sea bird

pet·ri·fy [PE-trə-fī] vt **-fied, -fy·ing** turn to stone; fig make motionless with fear; make dumb with amazement **pet·ri·fac·tion** n

pe·tro·le·um [pə-TROH-lee-əm] n unrefined oil

pet·ti·coat [PET-ee-koht] n women's undergarment worn under skirts, dresses, etc

pet·ti·fog·ger [PET-ee-fog-ər] n quibbler; unethical lawyer; one given to mean dealing in small matters

pet·ty [PET-ee] adj **-ti·er, -ti·est** unimportant, trivial; small-minded, mean; on a small scale **petty cash** cash kept by firm to pay minor incidental expenses **petty officer** noncommissioned officer in Navy

pet·u·lant [PECH-ə-lənt] adj given to small fits of temper; peevish **pet·u·lance** n peevishness

pe·tu·nia [pi-TOON-yə] n plant with funnel-shaped purple or white flowers

pew [pyoo] n fixed seat in church; inf chair, seat

pew·ter [PYOO-tər] n alloy of tin and lead; utensil of this

pha·lanx [FAY-langks] n, pl **-lanx·es** body of soldiers, etc formed in close array

phal·lus [FAL-əs] n, pl **-lus·es** penis; symbol of it used in primitive rites **phal'lic** adj

phan·tas·ma·go·ri·a [fan-taz-mə-GOR-ee-ə] n crowd of dim or unreal figures; exhibition of illusions

phan·tom [FAN-təm] n apparition; specter, ghost; fancied vision

Phar·aoh [FAIR-oh] n title of ancient Egyptian kings

phar·i·see [FA-rə-see] n sanctimonious person; hypocrite **phar·i·sa·ic** [-SAY-ik] adj

phar·ma·ceu·tic [fahr-mə-SOO-tik] adj of pharmacy **phar·ma·ceu·ti·cal** adj

phar·ma·cist n person qualified to dispense drugs **phar·ma·col·o·gy** [-KOL-ə-jee] n study of drugs

phar·ma·co·poe·ia [-kə-PEE-ə] n official book with list and directions for use of drugs **phar'ma·cy** [-mə-see] n preparation and dispensing of drugs; drugstore

pharm·ing [FAHRM-ing] n practice of growing genetically-modified animals or plants in order to develop drugs and medicines

phar·ynx [FA-ringks] *n, pl* **pha·ryn·ges** [fə-RIN-jeez] cavity forming back part of mouth and terminating in gullet **pha·ryn·ge·al** *adj*

phase [fayz] *n* any distinct or characteristic period or stage in a development or chain of events ▷ *vt* **phased, phas·ing** arrange, execute in stages or to coincide with something else

pheas·ant [FEZ-ənt] *n* game bird with bright plumage

phe·no·bar·bi·tal [fee-noh-BAHR-bi-tawl] *n* drug inducing sleep

phe·nom·e·non [fi-NOM-ə-non] *n, pl* **-na** [-nə] anything appearing or observed; remarkable person or thing **phe·nom·e·nal** *adj* relating to phenomena; remarkable; recognizable or evidenced by senses

Phil. Philippians

phil- *comb form* loving: *philanthropy; philosophy*

phi·lan·der [fi-LAN-dər] *vi* (of man) flirt with, make love to, women, esp with no intention of marrying them **phi·lan·der·er** *n*

phi·lan·thro·py [fi-LAN-thrə-pee] *n, pl* **-pies** practice of doing good to people; love of mankind; a philanthropic organization **phi·lan·throp·ic** *adj* loving mankind; benevolent **phi·lan·thro·pist** *n*

phi·lat·e·ly [fi-LAT-l-ee] *n* stamp collecting **phi·lat·e·list** *n*

phil·is·tine [FIL-ə-steen] *n* ignorant, smug person ▷ *adj*

phi·lol·o·gy [fi-LOL-ə-jee] *n* science of structure and development of languages **phi·lol·o·gist** *n*

phi·los·o·phy [fi-LOS-ə-fee] *n* pursuit of wisdom; study of realities and general principles; system of theories on nature of things or on conduct; calmness of mind **phi·los·o·pher** *n* one who studies, possesses, or originates philosophy **phil·o·soph·i·cal** *adj* of, like philosophy; wise, learned; calm, stoical **phi·los·o·phize** [-fīz] *vi* **-phized, -phiz·ing** reason like philosopher; theorize; moralize

phle·bi·tis [flə-Bī-tis] *n* inflammation of a vein

phlegm [flem] *n* viscid substance formed; by mucous membrane and ejected by coughing, etc; apathy, sluggishness **phleg·mat·ic** [fleg-MAT-ik] *adj* not easily agitated; composed

pho·bi·a [FOH-bee-ə] *n* fear or aversion; unreasoning dislike

phoe·nix [FEE-niks] *n* legendary bird; unique thing

phone [fohn] *n, v inf* telephone **phone card** prepaid card used to pay for telephone calls **phone tag** repeated unsuccessful attempts to contact by telephone

pho·net·ic [fə-NET-ik] *adj* of, or relating to, vocal sounds **pho·net·ics** *n* science of vocal sounds **pho·ne·ti·cian** [foh-ni-TISH-ən] *n*

phono- *comb form* sound: *phonology*

pho·no·graph [FOH-nə-graf] *n* instrument recording and reproducing sounds, record player

pho·ny [FOH-nee] *inf adj* **-ni·er, -ni·est** not genuine; insincere ▷ *n, pl* **pho·nies** phony person or thing

phos·pho·rus [FOS-fər-əs] *n* toxic, flammable, nonmetallic element that appears luminous in the dark **phos·phate** [FOS-fayt] *n* compound of phosphorus

phos·pho·res·cence n faint glow in the dark

pho·to [FOH-toh] n inf short for **PHOTOGRAPH** **photo finish** photo taken at end of race to show placing of contestants

photo- comb form light: photometer; photosynthesis

pho·to·cop·y [FOH-toh-kop-ee] n, pl -cop·ies photographic reproduction ▷ vt -cop·ied, -cop·y·ing

pho·to·e·lec·tron [foh-toh-i-LEK-tron] n electron liberated from metallic surface by action of beam of light

pho·to·gen·ic [foh-tə-JEN-ik] adj capable of being photographed attractively

pho·to·graph [FOH-tə-graf] n picture made by chemical action of light on sensitive film ▷ vt take photograph of **pho·tog·ra·pher** [-tə-fər] n

pho·to·syn·the·sis [foh-tə-SIN-thə-sis] n process by which green plant uses sun's energy to build up carbohydrate reserves

phrase [frayz] n group of words; pithy expression; mode of expression ▷ vt phrased, phras·ing express in words **phra·se·ol·o·gy** [fray-zee-OL-ə-jee] n manner of expression, choice of words **phras·al verb** [-əl] phrase consisting of verb and preposition, often with meaning different to the parts, such as take in meaning deceive

phre·nol·o·gy [frə-NOL-ə-jee] n (formerly) study of skull's shape; theory that character and mental powers are indicated by shape of skull **phre·nol·o·gist** n

phy·lac·ter·y [fi-LAK-tə-ree] n, pl -ter·ies leather case containing religious texts worn by Jewish men during weekday morning prayers

phys·ic [FIZ-ik] n medicine, esp cathartic ▷ pl science of properties of matter and energy **phys·i·cal** adj bodily, as opposed to mental or moral; material; of physics of body **phy·si·cian** n medical doctor **phys·i·cist** n one skilled in, or student of, physics

phys·i·og·no·my [fiz-ee-OG-nə-mee] n, pl -mies judging character by face; face; outward appearance of something

phys·i·ol·o·gy [fiz-ee-OL-ə-jee] n science of normal function of living things **phys·i·ol·o·gist** n

phys·i·o·ther·a·py [fiz-ee-oh-THER-ə-pee] n therapeutic use of physical means, as massage, etc **phys·i·o·ther·a·pist** n

phy·sique [fi-ZEEK] n bodily structure, constitution and development

pi [pī] n mathematics ratio of circumference of circle to its diameter, approx 3.141592

pi·an·o [pee-AN-oh] n, pl -an·os musical instrument with strings that are struck by hammers worked by keyboard; (also **pianofor·te**) **pi·an·ist** [pee-AN-ist] n performer on piano

pi·az·za [pee-AZ-ə] n square, marketplace; veranda

pi·ca [Pī-kə] n printing type of 6 lines to the inch; size of type, 12 point; typewriter type size (10 letters to inch)

pi·ca·dor [PIK-ə-dor] n mounted bullfighter with lance

pic·a·resque [pik-ə-RESK] adj of fiction, esp episodic and dealing with the adventures of rogues

pic·co·lo [PIK-ə-loh] n, pl -los small flute

pick[1] [pik] vt choose, select

carefully; pluck, gather; peck at;
pierce with something pointed;
find occasion for ▷ *n* act of picking;
choicest part **pick'ings** *pl n*
gleanings; odds and ends of profit
pick-me-up *n inf* stimulating drink,
tonic **pick'pock·et** *n* one who steals
from another's pocket **pick'up** *n*
device for conversion of mechanical
energy into electric signals, as in
record player, etc **pickup truck**
small truck with open body **pick
on** find fault with **pick up** raise,
lift; collect; improve, get better;
accelerate

pick² *n* tool with curved steel
crossbar and wooden handle, for
breaking up hard ground or masonry
pick'ax *n* pick

pick·er·el [PIK-ər-əl] *n* small pike
pick·et [PIK-it] *n* prong, pointed
stake; person, esp striker, posted
outside building, etc to prevent use
of facility, deter would-be workers
during strike ▷ *vt* beset as picket;
tether to peg **picket fence** fence of
pickets **picket line** line of pickets

pick·le [PIK-əl] *n* food, esp
cucumber, preserved in brine,
vinegar, etc; liquid used for
preserving; *inf* awkward situation
▷ *pl* pickled vegetables ▷ *vt* **-led,
-ling** preserve in pickle **pickled**
adj sl drunk

pic·nic [PIK-nik] *n* pleasure outing
including meal out of doors ▷ *vi*
-nicked, -nick·ing take part in
picnic

Pict [pikt] *n* member of ancient
people of NE Scotland

pic·ture [PIK-chər] *n* drawing or
painting; mental image; beautiful or
picturesque object ▷ *pl inf* movies
▷ *vt* **-tured, -tur·ing** represent in,
or as in, a picture **pic·to'ri·al** *adj* of,

in, with, painting or pictures; graphic
pic·tur·esque [pik-chə-RESK] *adj*
such as would be effective in picture;
striking, vivid **picture messaging**
practice of sending and receiving
photographs by cell phone **picture
phone** cell phone that can take, send,
and receive photographs

pidg·in [PIJ-ən] *n* language, not a
mother tongue, made up of elements
of two or more other languages

pie [pī] *n* baked dish of fruit, meat,
etc, usu with pastry crust

pie·bald [PĪ-bawld] *adj* irregularly
marked with black and white; motley
▷ *n* piebald horse or other animal

piece [pees] *n* bit, part, fragment;
single object; literary or musical
composition, etc; small object
used in checkers, chess, etc;
firearm ▷ *vt* **pieced, piec·ing**
mend, put together **piece'meal**
adv by, in, or into pieces, a bit at a
time **piece'work** *n* work paid for
according to quantity produced

pièce de ré·sis·tance [pyes də
ray-zee-STAHNS] *Fr* most impressive
item

pied [pīd] *adj* piebald; variegated
pie-eyed [PĪ-īd] *adj sl* drunk
pier [peer] *n* structure running into
sea as landing stage; piece of solid
upright masonry as foundation for
building, etc

pierce [peers] *vt* **pierced, pierc·ing**
make hole in; make a way through
piercing *adj* keen; penetrating

pi·e·ty [PĪ-i-tee] *n*, *pl* **-ties**
godliness; devoutness, goodness;
dutifulness

pig *n* wild or domesticated mammal
killed for pork, ham, bacon; *inf*
greedy, dirty person; *offens sl*
policeman; oblong mass of smelted
metal ▷ *vi* **pigged, pig·ging** of sow,
produce litter **pig'gish** *adj* dirty;

greedy; stubborn **pig'head•ed** adj
obstinate **pig'skin** n (leather made
from) the skin of a pig; inf a football
pig'tail n braid of hair hanging from
back of head
pi•geon [PIJ-ən] n bird of many
wild and domesticated varieties,
often trained to carry messages;
sl dupe **pi'geon•hole** [-hohl] n
compartment for papers in desk, etc
▷ vt **-holed, -hol•ing** defer; classify
pi'geon-toed [-tohd] adj with feet,
toes turned inward
pig•ment [PIG-mənt] n coloring
matter, paint or dye
pigmy see PYGMY
pike[1] [pik] n various types of large,
predatory freshwater fish
pike[2] n spear formerly used by
infantry
pi•laf [PEE-lahf] n Middle Eastern
dish of steamed rice with spices,
sometimes with meat or fowl, etc
pi•las•ter [pi-LAS-tər] n square
column, usu set in wall
pile[1] [pil] n heap; great mass of
building ▷ vt **piled, pil•ing** ▷ vt
heap (up), stack load ▷ vi (with in,
out) move in a group **atomic pile**
nuclear reactor
pile[2] n beam driven into the ground,
esp as foundation for building in
water or wet ground **pile driver**
n machine for driving down piles;
person who operates this machine
pile[3] n nap of cloth, esp of velvet,
carpet, etc; down
piles [pilz] pl n tumors of veins of
rectum, hemorrhoids
pil•fer [PIL-fər] v steal in small
quantities **pil'fer•age** [-ij]
pil'fer•er n
pil'grim n one who journeys to
sacred place; wanderer, wayfarer
pil'grim•age [-ij] n
pill n small ball of medicine

swallowed whole; anything
disagreeable that has to be endured
the pill oral contraceptive **pill'box** n
small box for pills; small concrete fort
pil•lage [PIL-ij] v **-laged, -lag•ing**
plunder, ravage, sack ▷ n seizure of
goods, esp in war; plunder
pil•lar [PIL-ər] n slender, upright
structure, column; prominent
supporter
pil•lo•ry [PIL-ə-ree] n, pl **-ries**
frame with holes for head and hands
in which offender was confined and
exposed to public abuse and ridicule
▷ vt **-ried, -ry•ing** expose to ridicule
and abuse; set in pillory
pil•low [PIL-oh] n cushion for the
head, esp in bed ▷ vt lay on, or as
on, pillow
pi•lot [Pī-lət] n person qualified
to fly an aircraft or spacecraft;
one qualified to take charge of
ship entering or leaving harbor, or
where knowledge of local water
is needed; steersman; guide ▷ adj
experimental and preliminary ▷ vt
act as pilot to; steer **pilot light** small
auxiliary flame lighting main one in
gas appliance, etc
pi•mien•to [pi-MYEN-toh] n, pl
-tos (fruit of the) sweet red pepper;
(also **pi•men'to**)
pimp n one who solicits for
prostitute ▷ vi act as pimp
pim•ple [PIM-pəl] n small pus-filled
spot on the skin **pim'ply** adj **-pli•er,
-pli•est**
pin n short thin piece of stiff wire
with point and head, for fastening;
wooden or metal peg or rivet ▷ vt
pinned, pin•ning fasten with
pin; seize and hold fast **pin'ball**
n table game, where small ball is
shot through various hazards **pin
money** trivial sum **pin'point** vt
mark exactly

pin·a·fore [PIN-ə-for] n child's apron; woman's dress with a bib top

pince-nez [PANS-nay] n, pl **pince-nez** eyeglasses kept on nose by spring

pin·cers [PIN-sərz] pl n tool for gripping, composed of two limbs crossed and pivoted; claws of lobster, etc **pincers movement** military maneuver in which both flanks of a force are attacked simultaneously

pinch vt nip, squeeze; stint; sl steal; sl arrest ▷ n nip; as much as can be taken up between finger and thumb; stress; emergency **pinch'bar** n crowbar

pine¹ [pin] n evergreen coniferous tree; its wood

pine² vi **pined, pin·ing** yearn; waste away with grief, etc

pin·e·al [PIN-ee-əl] adj shaped like pine cone **pineal gland** small cone-shaped gland situated at base of brain

pine·ap·ple [PI-nap-əl] n tropical plant with spiny leaves bearing large edible fruit; the fruit; sl a bomb

ping vi produce brief ringing sound, of engine, knock

pin·guid [PING-gwid] adj oily; fat

pin·ion¹ [PIN-yən] n bird's wing ▷ vt disable or confine by binding wings, arms, etc

pinion² n small cogwheel

pink [pingk] n pale red color; garden plant; best condition, fitness ▷ adj of color pink ▷ vt pierce; finish edge (of fabric) with perforations or scallops

pin·na·cle [PIN-ə-kəl] n highest pitch or point; mountain peak; pointed turret on buttress or roof

pint [pint] n liquid measure, one eighth of gallon (.568 liter)

pin·tle [PIN-tl] n pivot pin

pin'up n picture of sexually attractive person, esp (partly) naked

pi·o·neer [pi-ə-NEER] n explorer; early settler; originator; one of advance party preparing road, etc for troops ▷ vi act as pioneer or leader

pi·ous [PI-əs] adj devout; righteous

pip¹ n seed in fruit; inf something or someone outstanding

pip² n spot on playing cards, dice, or dominoes; inf metal insigne on officer's shoulder showing rank

pip³ n disease of poultry

pipe [pip] n tube of metal or other material; tube with small bowl at end for smoking tobacco; musical instrument, whistle ▷ pl bagpipes ▷ v **piped, pip·ing** play on pipe; utter in shrill tone; convey by pipe; ornament with a piping or fancy edging **pip'er** n player on pipe or bagpipes **piping** n system of pipes; fancy edging or trimming on clothes; act or art of playing on pipe, esp bagpipes **pipe down** inf stop making noise; stop talking **pipe dream** fanciful, impossible plan, etc **pipe'line** n long pipe for transporting oil, water, etc; means of communications **pipe up** inf assert oneself by speaking; speak louder **in the pipeline** yet to come; in process of completion, etc

pi·pette [pi-PET] n slender glass tube to transfer fluids from one vessel to another

pip'pin n kind of apple

pi·quant [PEE-kənt] adj pungent; stimulating **pi'quan·cy** n

pique [peek] n feeling of injury, baffled curiosity or resentment ▷ vt **piqued, piqu·ing** hurt pride of; irritate; stimulate

pi·qué [pi-KAY] n stiff ribbed cotton fabric

pi·ra·nha [pi-RAHN-yə] n, pl -nhas small voracious freshwater fish of

pi·rate [PĪ-rət] *n* sea robber; publisher, etc, who infringes copyright ▷*n, adj* (person) broadcasting illegally **pi'ra·cy** ▷*vt* **-rat·ed, -rat·ing** use or reproduce (artistic work, etc) illicitly **pi'ra·cy** [-see] *n, pl* **-cies**

pir·ou·ette [pir-oo-ET] *n* spinning around on the toe ▷*vi* **-et·ted, -et·ting** do this

pissed [pist] *adj sl* angry, annoyed, or disappointed

pis·ta·chi·o [pi-STASH-ee-oh], *n, pl* **-i·os** small hard-shelled, sweet-tasting nut; tree producing it

pis·til [PIS-tl] *n* seed-bearing organ of flower

pis·tol [PIS-tl] *n* small firearm for one hand ▷*vt* **-toled, -tol·ing** shoot with pistol

pis·ton [PIS-tən] *n* in internal combustion engine, steam engine, etc, cylindrical part propelled to and fro in hollow cylinder by pressure of gas, etc to convert reciprocating motion to rotation

pit *n* deep hole in ground; mine or its shaft; depression; enclosure where cocks are set to fight; servicing, refueling area on automobile racetrack ▷*vt* **pit·ted, pit·ting** set to fight, match; mark with small dents or scars **pit'fall** *n* any hidden danger; covered pit for trapping animals or people

pitch¹ [pich] *vt* cast or throw; set up; set the key of (a tune) ▷*vi* fall headlong; of ship, plunge lengthwise ▷*n* act of pitching; degree, height, intensity; slope; distance propeller advances during one revolution; distance between threads of screw, teeth of saw, etc; acuteness of tone; *baseball* ball delivered by pitcher to batter; *inf* persuasive sales talk **pitch'er** *n baseball* player who delivers ball to batter **pitch'fork** *n* fork for lifting hay, etc ▷*vt* throw with, as with, pitchfork **pitch'out** *n baseball* pitch thrown intentionally beyond batter's reach to improve catcher's chance of putting out base runner attempting to steal

pitch² *n* dark sticky substance obtained from tar or turpentine ▷*vt* coat with this **pitch'y** *adj* **pitch·i·er, -i·est** covered with pitch; black as pitch **pitch-black, -dark** *adj* very dark

pitch·blende [PICH-blend] *n* mineral composed largely of uranium oxide, yielding radium

pitch·er [PICH-ər] *n* large jug; see also **PITCH**

pith *n* tissue in stems and branches of certain plants; essential substance, most important part **pith'i·ly** *adv* **pith'y** *adj* **pith·i·er, pith·i·est** terse, cogent, concise; consisting of pith

pi·ton [PEE-ton] *n* metal spike used in mountain climbing

pit·tance [PIT-ns] *n* small allowance; inadequate wages

pi·tu·i·tar·y [pi-TOO-i-ter-ee] *adj* of, pert to, the endocrine gland at base of brain

pit·y [PIT-ee] *n, pl* **pit·ies** sympathy, sorrow for others' suffering; regrettable fact ▷*vt* **pit·ied, pit·y·ing** feel pity for **pit·e·ous** *adj* deserving pity; sad, wretched **pit'i·a·ble** *adj* **pit·i·ful** [-i-fəl] *adj* woeful; contemptible **pit'i·less** [-i-lis] *adj* feeling no pity; hard, merciless

piv·ot [PIV-ət] *n* shaft or pin on which thing turns ▷*vt* furnish with pivot ▷*vi* hinge on one **piv'ot·al** [-ət-əl] *adj* of, acting as, pivot; of crucial importance

pix·el [PIKS-əl] *n* any of a number of very small picture elements that make up a picture, as on a visual display unit

pix·ie [PIK-see] *n* fairy; mischievous person

pi·zazz [pə-ZAZ] *n inf* sparkle, vitality, glamour

piz·za [PEET-sə] *n* dish of baked disk of dough covered with cheese and tomato sauce and wide variety of garnishes **piz·ze·ri·a** [-REE-ə] *n* place selling pizzas

piz·zi·ca·to [pit-si-KAH-toh] *adj music* played by plucking string of violin, etc, with finger

plac·ard [PLAK-ahrd] *n* paper or card with notice on one side for posting up or carrying, poster ▷ *vt* post placards on; advertise, display on placards

pla·cate [PLAY-klayt] *vt* **-cat·ed, -cat·ing** conciliate, pacify, appease **pla·ca·to·ry** [-kə-tor-ee] *adj*

place [plays] *n* locality, spot; position; stead; duty; town, village, residence, buildings; office, employment; seat, space ▷ *vt* **placed, plac·ing** put in particular place; set; identify; make (order, bet, etc)

pla·ce·bo [plə-SEE-boh] *n, pl* **-bos** sugar pill, etc given to unsuspecting patient as active drug

pla·cen·ta [plə-SEN-tə] *n, pl* **-tas** organ formed in uterus during pregnancy, providing nutrients for fetus; afterbirth

plac·id [PLAS-id] *adj* calm; equable **pla·cid·i·ty** [plə-SID-i-tee] *n* mildness, quiet

pla·gia·rism [PLAY-jə-riz-əm] *n* taking ideas, passages, etc from an author and presenting them, unacknowledged, as one's own **pla·gia·rize** [-rīz] *v* **-rized, -riz·ing**

pla·gia·rist *n*

plague [playg] *n* highly contagious disease, esp bubonic plague; nuisance; affliction ▷ *vt* **plagued, pla·guing** trouble, annoy

plaid [plad] *n* checked or tartan pattern; fabric made of this

plain [playn] *adj* **-er, -est** flat, level; unobstructed, not intricate; clear, obvious; easily understood; simple; ordinary; without decoration; not beautiful ▷ *n* tract of level country ▷ *adv* clearly **plain·ly** [-lee] *adv* **plain'ness** [-nis] *n* **plain clothes** civilian dress, as opposed to uniform **plain dealing** directness and honesty in transactions **plain sailing** unobstructed course of action **plain speaking** frankness, candor

plain·tiff [PLAYN-tif] *n law* one who sues in court

plain·tive [PLAYN-tiv] *adj* sad, mournful, melancholy

plait [playt] *n* braid of hair, straw, etc ▷ *vt* form or weave into braids

plan *n* scheme; way of proceeding; project; design; drawing of horizontal section; diagram, map ▷ *vt* **planned, plan·ning** make plan of; arrange beforehand

planch·et [PLAN-chit] *n* flat sheet of metal; disk of metal from which coin is stamped

plan·chette [plan-SHET] *n* small board used in spiritualism

plane¹ [playn] *n* smooth surface; a level; carpenter's tool for smoothing wood ▷ *vt* **planed, plan·ing** make smooth with one ▷ *adj* perfectly flat or level **plan'er** *n* planing machine

plane² *v* (of aircraft) rise and (of airplane, glide; (of boat, rise and partly skim over water ▷ *n* wing of airplane; airplane

plan·et [PLAN-it] *n* heavenly

body revolving around the sun

plan·e·tar·y [-i-ter-ee] adj of, like, planets

plan·e·tar·i·um [plan-i-TAIR-ee-əm] n an apparatus that shows the movement of sun, moon, stars and planets by projecting lights on the inside of a dome; building in which the apparatus is housed

plan·gent [PLAN-jənt] adj resounding

plank [plangk] n long flat piece of sawn timber ▷ vt cover with planks

plank·ton [PLANGK-tən] n minute animal and vegetable organisms floating in ocean

plant n living organism feeding on inorganic substances and without power of locomotion; such an organism that is smaller than tree or shrub; equipment or machinery needed for manufacture; building and equipment for manufacturing purposes; complete equipment used for heating, air conditioning, etc ▷ vt set in ground, to grow; support, establish; stock with plants; sl hide, esp to deceive or observe **plant'er** n one who plants; ornamental pot or stand for house plants

plan·tain¹ [PLAN-tin] n low-growing weed with broad leaves

plantain² n tropical plant like banana; its fruit

plan·ta·tion [plan-TAY-shən] n estate or large farm for cultivation of tobacco, cotton, etc; wood of planted trees; formerly, colony

plaque [plak] n ornamental plate, tablet; plate of clasp or brooch; filmy deposit on surfaces of teeth, conducive to decay

plas·ma [PLAZ-mə] n clear, fluid portion of blood

plas·ter [PLAS-tər] n mixture of lime, sand, etc for coating walls, etc;

piece of fabric spread with medicinal or adhesive substance ▷ vt apply plaster to; apply like plaster; inf defeat soundly **plas'tered** adj sl drunk

plas·tic [PLAS-tik] n any of a group of synthetic products derived from casein, cellulose, etc that can be readily molded into any form and are extremely durable ▷ adj made of plastic; easily molded, pliant; capable of being molded; produced by molding **plas·tic·i·ty** [pla-STIS-i-tee] n ability to be molded **plastic surgery** repair or reconstruction of missing or malformed parts of the body for medical or cosmetic reasons

plate [playt] n shallow round dish; flat thin sheet of metal, glass, etc; household utensils of gold or silver; device for printing; illustration in book; set of false teeth, part of this that adheres to roof of mouth ▷ vt **plat·ed, plat·ing** cover with thin coating of gold, silver, or other metal **plate'ful** [-fəl] n, pl **-fuls plat'er** n person who plates; inferior race horse **plate glass** kind of thick glass used for mirrors, windows, etc **plate tec·ton'ics** geology study of structure of Earth's crust, esp movement of layers of rocks

pla·teau [pla-TOH] n, pl **-teaus** [-TOHZ] tract of level high land, tableland; period of stability

plat·en [PLAT-n] n printing plate by which paper is pressed against type; roller in typewriter

plat·form n raised level surface or floor, stage; raised area in station from which passengers board trains; political program

plat·i·num [PLAT-n-əm] n white heavy malleable metal

plat·i·tude [PLAT-i-tood] n commonplace remark

plat·i·tu'di·nous *adj*

Pla·ton·ic [plà-TON-ik] *adj* of Plato or his philosophy; **(p-)** (of love) purely spiritual, friendly

pla·toon [plà-TOON] *n* two or more squads of soldiers employed as unit

plat·ter [PLAT-àr] *n* flat dish

plat·y·pus [PLAT-i-pàs] *n*, *pl* **-pus·es** small Aust egg-laying amphibious mammal, with dense fur, webbed feet and ducklike bill; (also **duckbilled platypus**)

plau·dit [PLAW-dit] *n* act of applause, handclapping

plau·si·ble [PLAW-zà-bàl] *adj* apparently fair or reasonable; fair-spoken **plau·si·bil'i·ty** *n*

play *vi* amuse oneself; take part in game; behave carelessly; act a part on the stage; perform on musical instrument; move with light or irregular motion, flicker, etc ▷ *vt* contend with in game; take part in (game); trifle; act the part of; perform (music); perform on (instrument); use, work (instrument) ▷ *n* dramatic piece or performance; sport; amusement; manner of action or conduct; activity; brisk or free movement; gambling **play'boy** *n* rich man who lives only for pleasure **play'ful** [-fàl] *adj* lively **play'group** [-groop] *n* group of young children playing regularly under adult supervision **play'house** *n* theater; small house for children to play in **playing card** one of set of usu 52 cards used in card games **playing field** extensive piece of ground for open-air games **play'thing** *n* toy **play'wright** [-rit] *n* author of plays

pla·za [PLAH-zà] *n* open space or square; complex of retail stores, etc

plea [plee] *n* entreaty; statement of prisoner or defendant; excuse **plead**

v **plead·ed** or **pled, plead·ing** make earnest appeal; address court of law; bring forward as excuse or plea **plea bargaining** procedure in which defendant agrees to plead guilty in return for leniency in sentencing, etc

please [pleez] *v* **pleased, pleas·ing** ▷ *vt* be agreeable to; gratify; delight ▷ *vi* like; be willing ▷ *adv* word of request **pleas'ant** [PLEZ-ànt] *adj* pleasing, agreeable **pleas'ant·ry** [-àn-tree] *n*, *pl* **-ries** joke, humor **pleas·ur·a·ble** [PLEZH-àr-à-bàl] *adj* giving pleasure **pleas'ure** *n* enjoyment; satisfaction; will, choice

pleat [pleet] *n* any of various types of fold made by doubling material back on itself ▷ *vi* make, gather into pleats

plebe [pleeb] *n* at US military and naval academies, member of first-year class

ple·be·ian [pli-BEE-àn] *adj* belonging to the common people; low or rough ▷ *n* one of the common people

pleb·i·scite [PLEB-à-sit] *n* decision by direct voting of the electorate

plec·trum [PLEK-tràm] *n*, *pl* **-trums** small implement for plucking strings of guitar, etc

pledge [plej] *n* promise; thing given over as security; toast ▷ *vt* **pledged, pledg·ing** promise formally; bind or secure by pledge; give over as security

Pleis·to·cene [PLI-stà-seen] *adj* geology of the glacial period of formation

ple·na·ry [PLEE-nà-ree] *adj* complete, without limitations, absolute; of meeting, etc, with all members present

plen·i·po·ten·ti·a·ry [plen-à-pà-TEN-shee-er-ee] *adj*, *n* (envoy) having full powers

plen·i·tude [PLEN-i-tood] *n* completeness, abundance, entirety

plen·ty *n, pl* **-ties** abundance; quite enough **plen·te·ous** [-tee-əs] *adj* ample; rich; copious **plen·ti·ful** [-ti-fəl] *adj* abundant

ple·num [PLEE-nəm] *n, pl* **-nums** space as considered to be full of matter (opposed to vacuum); condition of fullness; space above ceiling, etc for receiving, storing heated or cooled air

ple·o·nasm [PLEE-ə-naz-əm] *n* use of more words than necessary **ple·o·nas·tic** [-NAS-tik] *adj* redundant

pleth·o·ra [PLETH-ər-ə] *n* oversupply **ple·thor·ic** [ple-THOR-ik] *adj*

pleu·ri·sy [PLUUR-ə-see] *n* inflammation of the pleura **pleura** *n* membrane lining the chest and covering the lungs

plex·us [PLEK-səs] *n, pl* **-us·es** network of nerves, or fibers

pli·a·ble [PLĪ-ə-bəl] *adj* easily bent or influenced **pli·a·bil·i·ty** *n* **pli·an·cy** [-ən-see] *n* **pli·ant** *adj* pliable

pli·ers [PLĪ-ərz] *pl n* tool with hinged arms and jaws for gripping

plight[1] [plīt] *n* distressing state; predicament

plight[2] *vt* promise, engage oneself to

Plim·soll line [PLIM-səl] mark on ships indicating maximum displacement permitted when loaded

Pli·o·cene [PLĪ-ə-seen] *n* geology the most recent tertiary deposits

plod *vi* **plod·ded, plod·ding** walk or work doggedly

plop *n* sound of object falling into water ▷ *vi* **plopped, plop·ping** fall

with, as though with, such a sound; make the sound

plot[1] *n* secret plan, conspiracy; essence of story, play, etc ▷ *v* **plot·ted, plot·ting** devise secretly; mark position of; make map of; conspire

plot[2] *n* small piece of land

plov·er [PLUV-ər] *n* one of various shore birds, typically with round head, straight bill and long pointed wings

plow *n* implement for turning up soil; similar implement for clearing snow, etc ▷ *vt* turn up with plow, furrow ▷ *vi* work at slowly **plow'share** [-shair] *n* blade of plow **plow under** bury beneath soil by plowing; overwhelm

ploy [ploi] *n* stratagem; occupation; prank

pluck [pluk] *vt* pull, pick off; strip from; sound strings of (guitar, etc) with fingers, plectrum ▷ *n* courage; sudden pull or tug **pluck'y** *adj* **pluck·i·er, pluck·i·est** courageous

plug *n* thing fitting into and filling a hole; *electricity* device connecting appliance to electricity supply; tobacco pressed hard; *inf* recommendation, advertisement; *sl* worn-out horse ▷ *vt* **plugged, plug·ging** stop with plug; *inf* advertise anything by constant repetition; *sl* punch; *sl* shoot **plug away** work hard **plug in** connect (electrical appliance) with power source by means of plug

plum *n* stone fruit; tree bearing it; choicest part, piece, position, etc; dark reddish-purple color ▷ *adj* choice; plum-colored

plumage see PLUME

plumb [plum] *n* ball of lead attached to string used for sounding, finding the perpendicular, etc ▷ *adj* perpendicular ▷ *adv* perpendicularly; exactly; *inf* downright; honestly ▷ *vt* set exactly upright; find depth of; reach, undergo; equip with, connect to plumbing system **plumb'er** [PLUM-ər] *n* worker who attends to water and sewage systems **plumb'ing** *n* trade of plumber; system of water and sewage pipes **plumb'line** *n* cord with plumb attached

plume [ploom] *n* feather; ornament of feathers, etc ▷ *vt* **plumed, plum·ing** furnish with plumes; pride oneself **plum·age** [PLOO-mij] *n* bird's feathers collectively

plum·met [PLUM-it] *vi* plunge headlong ▷ *n* plumbline

plump[1] *adj* **-er, -est** of rounded form, moderately fat, chubby ▷ *v* make, become plump

plump[2] *vi* sit, fall abruptly; (with *for*) support enthusiastically ▷ *vt* drop, throw abruptly ▷ *adv* suddenly; heavily; directly

plun·der [PLUN-dər] *vt* take by force; rob systematically ▷ *vi* rob ▷ *n* pillage; booty, spoils

plunge [plunj] *v* **plunged, plung·ing** ▷ *vt* put forcibly (into) ▷ *vi* throw oneself (into); enter, rush with violence; descend very suddenly ▷ *n* dive **plung'er** *n* rubber suction cap with handle to unblock drains **take the plunge** *inf* embark on risky enterprise; get married

plunk *v* pluck (string of banjo, etc); drop, fall suddenly and heavily ▷ *vi*

plu·ral [PLUUR-əl] *adj* of, denoting more than one person or thing ▷ *n* word in its plural form **plu'ral·ism** *n* holding of more than one office at a time; coexistence of different social groups, etc, in one society **plu·ral'i·ty** *n, pl* **-ties** of three or more candidates, etc; largest share

of votes

plus *prep* with addition of ▷ *adj* to be added; positive ▷ *n* sign (+) denoting addition; advantage

plush *n* fabric with long nap, long-piled velvet ▷ *adj* **-er, -est** luxurious

Plu·to [PLOO-toh] *n* Greek god of the underworld; farthest planet from the sun

plu·toc·ra·cy [ploo-TOK-rə-see] *n, pl* **-cies** government by the rich; state ruled thus; wealthy class **plu'to·crat** [-tə-krat] *n* wealthy person

plu·to·ni·um [ploo-TOH-nee-əm] *n* radioactive metallic element used esp in nuclear reactors and weapons

ply[1] [plī] *v* **plied, ply·ing** wield; work at; supply pressingly; urge; keep busy; go to and fro, run regularly

ply[2] *n* fold or thickness; strand of yarn **ply'wood** [-wuud] *n* board of thin layers of wood glued together with grains at right angles

Pm *chemistry* promethium

pneu·mat·ic [nuu-MAT-ik] *adj* of, worked by, inflated with wind or air

pneu·mo·nia [nuu-MOHN-yə] *n* inflammation of the lungs

Po *chemistry* polonium

poach[1] [pohch] *vt* take (game) illegally; trample, make swampy or soft ▷ *vi* trespass for this purpose; encroach **poach'er** *n*

poach[2] *vt* simmer (eggs, fish, etc) gently in water, etc **poach'er** *n*

pock [pok] *n* pustule, as in smallpox, etc **pock'marked** *adj*

pock·et [POK-it] *n* small bag inserted in garment; cavity filled with ore, etc; socket, cavity, pouch or hollow; mass of water or air differing from that surrounding it; isolated group or area ▷ *vt* put into one's pocket; appropriate, steal ▷ *adj* small **pocket money** small, regular allowance given to children by parents; allowance for small, occasional expenses **pocket veto** indirect veto of bill by president, governor, who retains bill unsigned until legislative adjournment

pod n long seed vessel, as of peas, beans, etc ▷v **pod·ded, pod·ding** ▷vi form pods ▷vt shed

po·di·um [POH-dee-əm] n small raised platform

po·em [POH-əm] n imaginative composition in rhythmic lines **po·et** [-it] n writer of poems **po'et·ry** n art or work of poet, verse **po·et·ic** [-ET-ik] adj **po·et·i·cal·ly** adv **po'et·as·ter** [-as-tər] n would-be or inferior poet

po·e·sy [-ə-see] n poetry

po·grom [pə-GRUM] n organized persecution and massacre, esp of Jews

poign·ant [POIN-yənt] adj moving; biting, stinging; vivid; pungent **poign'an·cy** n, pl -**cies**

poin·set·ti·a [poin-SET-ee-ə] n orig Amer shrub, widely cultivated for its clusters of scarlet leaves, resembling petals

point n dot, mark; punctuation mark; item, detail; unit of value; position, degree, stage; moment; gist of an argument; purpose; striking or effective part or quality; essential object or thing; sharp end; single unit in scoring; headland; one of direction marks of compass; fine kind of lace; act of pointing; printing unit, one-twelfth of a pica ▷pl electrical contacts in distributor of engine ▷vi show direction or position by extending finger; direct attention; (of dog) indicate position of game by standing facing it ▷vt aim, direct; sharpen; fill up joints with mortar; give value to (words, etc) **point'ed** adj sharp; direct, telling **point'er** n index; indicating rod, etc, used for pointing; indication; dog trained to point

point'less [-lis] adj blunt; futile, irrelevant **point-blank** adj aimed horizontally; plain, blunt ▷adv with level aim (there being no necessity to elevate for distance); at short range

poise [poiz] n composure; self-possession; balance, equilibrium, carriage (of body, etc) ▷v **poised, pois·ing** (cause to be) balanced or suspended ▷vt hold in readiness

poi·son [POI-zən] n substance that kills or injures when introduced into living organism ▷vt give poison to; infect; pervert, spoil **poi'son·ous** adj **poison-pen letter** malicious anonymous letter

poke¹ [pohk] v **poked, pok·ing** ▷vt push, thrust with finger, stick, etc; thrust forward ▷vi make thrusts; pry ▷n act of poking **pok'er** n metal rod for poking fire **pok'y** adj **pok·i·er, pok·i·est** small, confined, cramped

poke² n pig in a poke something bought, accepted, etc without previous inspection

pok·er [POHK-ər] n card game **poker face** expressionless face; person with this

polar adj see **POLE²**

Po·lar·oid ® [POH-lə-roid] n type of plastic that polarizes light; camera that develops print very quickly inside itself

pole¹ [pohl] n long rounded piece of wood, etc ▷vt **poled, pol·ing** propel with pole

pole² n each of the ends of axis of Earth or celestial sphere; each of opposite ends of magnet, electric battery, etc **polar** [POH-lər] adj pert to the N and S pole, or to magnetic poles; directly opposite in tendency, character, etc **po·lar·i·ty** n **po·lar·i·za·tion** [-ZAY-shən] n **po·lar·ize** vt **-rized, -riz·ing** give polarity to; affect light in order to restrict vibration of its waves to certain directions **polar bear** white Arctic bear **poles apart** having completely opposite interests, etc

po·lem·ic [pə-LEM-ik] adj controversial ▷ n war of words, argument **po·lem·i·cal** adj **po·lem·i·cize** [-sīz] vt **-cized, -ciz·ing**

po·lice [pə-LEES] n the civil force that maintains public order ▷ vt **-liced, -lic·ing** keep in order **police officer** n member of police force

pol·i·cy¹ [POL-ə-see] n, pl **-cies** course of action adopted, esp in state affairs; prudence

policy² n, pl **-cies** insurance contract

po·li·o [poh-lee-oh] n (also **po·li·o·my·e·li·tis**) disease of spinal cord characterized by fever and possibly paralysis

pol·ish vt make smooth and glossy; refine ▷ n shine; polishing; substance for polishing; refinement

po·lite [pə-līT] adj **-lit·er, -lit·est** showing regard for others in manners, speech, etc; refined, cultured **po·lite'ness** n courtesy

pol·i·tic [POL-i-tik] adj wise, shrewd, expedient, cunning **pol'i·tics** n art of government; political affairs or life **po·lit'i·cal** adj of the state or its affairs **pol·i·ti·cian** [-TISH-ən] n one engaged in politics **pol'i·ty** n, pl **-ties** form of government; organized state; civil government **politically correct** (esp of language) intended to avoid any implied prejudice

pol·ka [POHL-kə] n, pl **-kas** lively 19th-century dance; music for it

polka dot one of pattern of bold spots on fabric, etc

poll [pohl] n voting; counting of votes; number of votes recorded; canvassing of sample of population to determine general opinion; (top of) head ▷ pl place where votes are cast ▷ vt receive (votes); take votes of; lop, shear; cut horns from animals ▷ vi vote **polled** adj hornless **poll'ster** n one who conducts polls **poll tax** (esp formerly) tax on each person

pol·lard [POL-ərd] n hornless animal of normally horned variety; tree on which a close head of young branches has been made by polling ▷ vt make a pollard of

pol·len [POL-ən] n fertilizing dust of flower **pol'li·nate** vt **-nat·ed, -nat·ing**

pol·lute [pə-LOOT] vt **-lut·ed, -lut·ing** make foul; corrupt; desecrate **pol·lu'tant** [-tənt] n **pol·lu'tion** n

po·lo [POH-loh] n game like hockey played by teams of 4 players on horseback **water polo** game played similarly by swimmers sewn to a side

pol·o·naise [pol-ə-NAYZ] n Polish dance; music for it

pol·ter·geist [POHL-tər-gist] n noisy mischievous spirit

poly- comb form many: polysyllabic

pol·y·an·dry [POL-ee-an-dree] n polygamy in which woman has more than one husband **pol·y·an'drous** adj

pol·y·chrome [POL-ee-krohm] adj many colored ▷ n work of art in many colors **pol·y·chro·mat·ic** adj

pol·y·es·ter [POL-ee-es-tər] n any of large class of synthetic materials used as plastics, textile fibers, etc

pol·y·eth·yl·ene [pol-ee-ETHə-leen] n tough thermoplastic material

po·lyg·a·my [pə-LIG-ə-mee] n custom of being married to several persons at a time **po·lyg·a·mist** n

pol·y·glot [POLE-ee-glot] adj speaking, writing in several languages ▷ n person who speaks, reads and writes in many languages

pol·y·gon [POLE-ee-gon] n figure with many angles or sides

po·lyg·y·ny [pə-LIJ-ə-nee] n polygamy in which one man has more than one wife

pol·y·he·dron [pol-ee-HEE-drən] n solid figure contained by many faces

pol·y·math [POL-ee-math] n learned person

pol·y·mer [POL-ə-mər] n compound, as polystyrene, that has large molecules formed from repeated units **po·lym·er·i·za·tion** [pə-lim-ər-ə-ZAY-shən] n **po·lym·er·ize** [-LIM-ər-iz] vt **-ized, -iz·ing**

pol·yp [POL-ip] n sea anemone, or allied animal; tumor with branched roots

pol·y·sty·rene [pol-ee-STI-reen] n synthetic material used esp as white rigid foam for packing, etc

pol·y·tech·nic [pol-ee-TEK-nik] n college dealing mainly with technical subjects ▷ adj

pol·y·the·ism [POL-ee-thee-iz-əm] n belief in many gods **pol·y·the·is·tic** adj

pol·y·un·sat·u·rat·ed [pol-ee-un-SACH-ə-ray-tid] adj of group of fats that do not form cholesterol in blood

pol·y·u·re·thane [pol-ee-YUUR-ə-thayn] n class of synthetic materials, often in foam or flexible form

po·made [po-MAYD] n scented ointment for hair

po·me·gran·ate [POM-ə-gran-it] n tree; its fruit with thick rind containing many seeds in red pulp

pom·mel [PUM-əl] n front of saddle; knob of sword hilt ▷ vt **-meled, -mel·ing** pummel

pomp n splendid display or ceremony

pom'pom n tuft of ribbon, wool, feathers, etc, decorating hat, shoe, etc

pomp·ous [POM-pəs] adj self-important; ostentatious; of language, inflated, stilted **pom·pos·i·ty** n, pl **-ties**

pon·cho [PON-choh] n, pl **-chos** loose circular cloak with hole for head

pond n small body, pool or lake of still water

pon·der [PON-dər] v muse, meditate, think over; consider, deliberate on

pon·der·ous [PON-dər-əs] adj heavy, unwieldy; boring **pon'der·a·ble** adj able to be evaluated or weighed

pon'tiff n Pope; high priest; bishop **pon·tif'i·cal** adj **pon·tif'i·cate** [-kit] n dignity or office of pontiff **pon·tif'i·cate** [-kayt] vi **-cat·ed, -cat·ing** speak bombastically; act as pontiff

pon·toon' n flat-bottomed boat or metal drum for use in supporting temporary bridge

po·ny [POH-nee] n, pl **-nies** horse of small breed; small horse; very small glass **po'ny·tail** n long hair tied in one bunch at back of head

poo·dle [POOD-l] n pet dog with long curly hair often clipped fancifully

pool¹ n small body of still water;

deep place in river or stream; puddle; swimming pool

pool[2] n common fund or resources; group of people, eg typists, any of whom can work for any of several employers; collective stakes in various games; cartel; variety of billiards ▷ vt put in common fund

poop[1] n ship's stern

poop[2] vt sl exhaust (someone) **poop out** sl fail in something; cease functioning

poop[3] n children's sl excrement ▷ vi defecate

poop[4] n sl pertinent information

poor [puur] adj **-er, -est** having little money; unproductive; inadequate, insignificant; needy; miserable, pitiable; feeble; not fertile **poor'ly** adv, adj not in good health

pop[1] v **popped, pop•ping** ▷ vi make small explosive sound; inf go or come unexpectedly or suddenly ▷ vt cause to make small explosive sound; put or place suddenly ▷ n small explosive sound; inf nonalcoholic soda

pop'corn n any kind of corn with kernels that puff up when roasted; the roasted product **pop-up** adj (of an appliance) characterized by or having a mechanism that pops up; (of a book) having pages that rise when opened to simulate a three-dimensional form; (of a menu on a computer screen, etc) suddenly appearing when an option is selected ▷ n something that appears over or above the open window on a computer screen **pop up** to appear suddenly

pop[2] n inf father; old man

pop[3] n music of general appeal, esp to young people ▷ adj short for **POPULAR**

Pope [pohp] n bishop of Rome and head of R C Church

pop•lar [POP-lər] n tree noted for its slender tallness

pop'lin n corded fabric usu of cotton

pop•pa•dom [POP-ə-dəm] n thin, round, crisp Indian bread

pop•py [POP-ee] n, pl **-pies** bright-flowered plant yielding opium

pop•u•lace [POP-yə-ləs] n the common people; the masses

pop•u•lar [POP-yə-lər] adj finding general favor; of, by the people **pop•u•lar'i•ty** n state or quality of being generally liked **pop'u•lar•ize** vt **-ized, -iz•ing** make popular

pop•u•late [POP-yə-layt] vt **-lat•ed, -lat•ing** fill with inhabitants **pop•u•la'tion** [-LAY-shən] n inhabitants; their number

pop'u•lous [-ləs] adj thickly populated or inhabited

pop•u•list [POP-yə-list] adj claiming to represent the whole of the people ▷ n **pop'u•lism** [-liz-əm] n

por•ce•lain [POR-sə-lin] n fine earthenware, china

porch n covered approach to entrance of building; veranda

por•cine [POR-sin] adj of, like a pig

por•cu•pine [POR-kyə-pīn] n rodent covered with long, pointed quills

pore[1] [por] vi **pored, por•ing** fix eye or mind upon; study closely

pore[2] n minute opening, esp in skin **po•ros•i•ty** [pə-ROS-i-tee] n **por•ous** [POR-əs] adj allowing liquid to soak through; full of pores

pork n pig's flesh as food **pork'er** n pig raised for food **pork'y** adj **pork•i•er, pork•i•est** fleshy, fat

porn, por'no n inf short for **PORNOGRAPHY**

por•nog•ra•phy [por-NOG-rə-fee] n indecent literature,

films, etc **por·nog·ra·pher** n
por·no·graph·ic adj

por·phy·ry [POR-fə-ree] n, pl
-ries reddish stone with embedded
crystals

por·poise [POR-pəs] n blunt-
nosed sea mammal like dolphin

por·ridge [POR-ij] n soft food of
oatmeal, etc boiled in water

port[1] n harbor, haven; town with
harbor

port[2] n larboard or left side of ship
▷ vt turn to left side of a ship

port[3] n strong sweet, usu red,
fortified wine from Portugal

port[4] n opening in side of ship
port·hole n small opening or
window in side of ship

port[5] vt military carry rifle, etc
diagonally across body ▷ n this
position

port·a·ble [POR-tə-bəl] n, adj
(something) easily carried

por·tage [POR-tij] n (cost of)
transport

por·tal [POR-tl] n large doorway or
imposing gate; computing Internet
site providing links to other sites

portal-to-portal pay payment to
worker that includes pay for all time
spent on employer's premises

port·cul·lis [port-KUL-is] n
defense grating to raise or lower in
front of castle gateway

por·tend· vt foretell; be an omen of
por·tent n omen, warning; marvel
por·ten·tous [-təs] adj ominous;
threatening; pompous

por·ter [POR-tàr] n person
employed to carry luggage;
doorkeeper

port·fo·li·o [port-FOH-lee-oh] n,
pl -li·os flat portable case for loose
papers; office of minister of state,
member of cabinet

por·ti·co [POR-ti-koh] n, pl -coes

or -cos colonnade; covered walk

por·tiere [por-TYAIR] n heavy
door curtain

por·tion [POR-shàn] n part, share,
helping; destiny, lot ▷ vt divide
into shares

port·ly [PORT-lee] adj -li·er, -li·est
bulky, stout

port·man·teau [port-MAN-toh]
n, pl -teaus leather suitcase, esp one
opening into two compartments
portmanteau word word made
by putting together parts of other
words, such as motel from motor
and hotel

por·tray· vt make pictures of,
describe **por·trait** [-trit] n likeness
of (face of) person **por·trai·ture**
[-tri-chàr] n **por·tray·al** [-tri-əl] n act
of portraying

pose [pohz] v posed, pos·ing
▷ vt place in attitude; put forward
▷ vi assume attitude, affect or
pretend to be a certain character ▷ n
attitude, esp one assumed for effect
po·seur [poh-ZUR] n one who
assumes affected attitude to create
impression

pos·er [POH-zàr] n puzzling
question

posh adj inf smart, elegant, stylish

pos·it [POZ-it] vt lay down as
principle

po·si·tion [pə-ZISH-àn] n place;
situation; location, attitude; status;
state of affairs; employment;
strategic point ▷ vt place in position

pos·i·tive [POZ-i-tiv] adj
certain; sure; definite, absolute,
unquestionable; utter; downright;
confident; not negative; greater than
zero; electricity having deficiency of
electrons ▷ n something positive;
photography print in which lights
and shadows are not reversed
pos·i·tiv·ism n philosophy

recognizing only matters of fact and experience **pos'i·tiv·ist** n believer in this

pos·i·tron [POZ-i-tron] n positive electron

pos·se [POS-ee] n body of armed people, esp for maintaining law and order

pos·sess [pə-ZES] vt own; (of evil spirit, etc) have mastery of thing possessed; ownership **pos·ses·sion** n act of possessing; **pos·ses·sive** adj n, indicating possession; with excessive desire to possess, control ▷ n possessive case in grammar **pos·ses·sor** n owner

pos·si·ble [POS-ə-bəl] adj that can, or may, be, exist, happen or be done; worthy of consideration ▷ n possible candidate **pos·si·bil'i·ty** n, pl **-ties pos'si·bly** adv perhaps

pos·sum [POS-əm] n opossum **play possum** pretend to be dead, asleep, etc to deceive opponent

post¹ [pohst] n upright pole of timber or metal fixed firmly, usu to support or mark something ▷ vt display; stick up (on notice board, etc); computing make (e-mail) publicly available **post'er** n large advertising bill; one who posts bills **poster paints, colors** flat paints suited for posters

post² n mail; collection or delivery of this; office; situation; point, station, place of duty; place where soldier is stationed; held by body of troops; fort ▷ vt put into mailbox; supply with latest information; station (soldiers, etc) in particular spot; transfer (entries) to ledger ▷ adv with haste **post·age** [POH-stij] n charge for carrying letter **post'al** [-əl] adj **postal money order** written order, available at post office, for payment of sum of

money **post'card** n stamped card sent by mail **post'man** [-mən] n, pl **-men** postal employee who collects or delivers mail **post'mark** n official mark with name of office, etc stamped on letters **post'mas·ter** n official in charge of post office **post'mis·tress** [-tris] n fem **post office** place where postal business is conducted

post- prefix after, behind, later than: postwar

post·date [pohst-DAYT] vt **-dat·ed, -dat·ing** give date later than actual date

poste res·tante [pohst re-STAHNT] Fr direction on mail to indicate that post office should keep traveler's letters till called for

pos·te·ri·or [po-STEER-ee-ər] adj later, hinder ▷ n the buttocks

pos·ter·i·ty [po-STER-i-tee] n later generations; descendants

post·grad·u·ate [pohst-GRAJ-oo-it] adj carried on after graduation ▷ n

post·hu·mous [POS-chə-məs] adj occurring after death; born after father's death; published after author's death **post'hu·mous·ly** adv

post·mor·tem [pohst-MOR-təm] n medical examination of body; evaluation after event, etc ends ▷ adj taking place after death

post·par·tum [pohst-PAHR-təm] adj occurring after childbirth

post·pone [pohs-POHN] vt **-poned, -pon·ing** put off to later time, defer

post·pran·di·al [pohst-PRAN-dee-əl] adj after a meal, esp dinner

post-rock [pohst-ROK] n type of music that often varies from traditional rock in terms of form and instrumentation

post·script [POHST-skript] *n*
addition to letter, book, etc

pos·tu·lant [POS-chǝ-lǝnt] *n*
candidate for admission to religious
order

pos·tu·late [POS-chǝ-layt] *vt*
-lat·ed, -lat·ing take for granted;
lay down as self-evident; stipulate
▷ *n* [-lit] proposition assumed
without proof; prerequisite

pos·ture [POS-chǝr] *n* attitude,
position of body ▷ *v* **-tured,**
-tur·ing pose

po·sy [POH-zee] *n, pl* **-sies** flower;
bunch of flowers

pot *n* round vessel; cooking vessel;
trap, esp for crabs, lobsters; *sl*
marijuana; do a lot ▷ *vt* **pot·ted,**
pot·ting put into, preserve in pot
potted *adj* cooked, preserved, in
a pot; *sl* drunk **pot'hole** *n* pitlike
cavity in rocks, usu limestone,
produced by faulting and water
action; hole worn in road **pot'luck**
n whatever is to be had (to eat)
pot'sherd [-shurd] *n* broken
fragment of pottery **pot shot** easy
or random shot

po·ta·ble [POH-tǝ-bǝl] *adj*
drinkable **po·ta'tion** [-TAY-shǝn] *n*
drink; drinking

pot'ash *n* alkali used in soap, etc;
crude potassium carbonate

po·tas·si·um [pǝ-TAS-ee-ǝm] *n*
white metallic element

po·ta·to [pǝ-TAY-toh] *n, pl* **-toes**
plant with tubers grown for food **hot
potato** topic, etc too threatening
to bring up **sweet potato** trailing
plant; its edible sweetish tubers

po·tent [POHT-nt] *adj* powerful,
influential; (of male) capable of
sexual intercourse **po'ten·cy** *n*
physical or moral power; efficacy

po·ten·tate [POHT-n-tayt] *n* ruler

po·ten·tial [pǝ-TEN-shǝl] *adj*

latent, that may or might but does
not now exist or act ▷ *n* possibility;
amount of potential energy;
electricity level of electric pressure
po·ten·ti·al·i·ty [-shee-AL-i-tee] *n*

po·tion [POH-shǝn] *n* dose of
medicine or poison

pot·pour·ri [poh-puu-REE] *n*
mixture of rose petals, spices, etc;
musical, literary medley

pot·tage [POT-ij] *n* soup or stew

pot·ter [POT-ǝr] *n* maker of
earthenware vessels **pot'ter·y** *n,
pl* **-ter·ies** earthenware; where it is
made; art of making it

pouch [powch] *n* small bag; pocket
▷ *vt* put into one

poul·tice [POHL-tis] *n* soft
composition of cloth, bread, etc,
applied hot to sore or inflamed parts
of the body

poul·try [POHL-tree] *n* domestic
fowl collectively

pounce¹ [powns] *vi* **pounced,**
pounc·ing spring upon suddenly,
swoop (upon) ▷ *n* swoop or sudden
descent

pounce² *n* fine powder used to
prevent ink from spreading on
unsized paper or in pattern making

pound¹ [pownd] *vt* beat, thump;
crush to pieces or powder; walk,
run heavily

pound² *n* unit of troy weight; unit of
avoirdupois weight equal to 0.453 kg;
monetary unit in United Kingdom

pound³ *n* enclosure for stray
animals or officially removed
vehicles; confined space

pound·al [POWN-dl] *n* a unit
of force in the foot-pound-second
system

pour [por] *vi* come out in a stream,
crowd, etc; flow freely; rain heavily
▷ *vt* give out thus; cause to run out

pout [powt] *v* thrust out (lips), look

sulky ▷ *n* act of pouting **pout'er** *n* pigeon with power of inflating its crop

pov·er·ty [POV-ər-tee] *n* state of being poor; poorness; lack of means; scarcity

pow·der [POW-dər] *n* solid matter in fine dry particles; medicine in this form; gunpowder; face powder, etc ▷ *vt* apply powder to; reduce to powder **pow'der·y** *adj*

pow·er [POW-ər] *n* ability to do or act; strength; authority; control; person or thing having authority; mechanical energy; electricity supply; rate of doing work; product from continuous multiplication of number by itself **pow'ered** *adj* having or operated by mechanical or electrical power **pow'er·ful** [-fəl] *adj* **pow'er·less** [-lis] *adj* **pow'er·house, power station** *n* installation for generating and distributing electric power

pow'wow *n* conference ▷ *vi* confer

pox [poks] *n* one of several diseases marked by pustular eruptions of skin; *inf* syphilis

Pr *chemistry* praseodymium

prac·ti·cal [PRAK-ti-kəl] *adj* given to action rather than theory; relating to action or real existence; useful; in effect though not in name; virtual **prac'ti·cal·ly** *adv* **prac'ti·ca·ble** [-kə-bəl] *adj* that can be done, used, etc **prac·ti'tion·er** *n* one engaged in a profession

prac·tice [PRAK-tis] *v* **-ticed, -tic·ing** ▷ *vt* do repeatedly, work at to gain skill; do habitually; put into action ▷ *vi* exercise oneself; exercise profession **practice** *n* habit; mastery or skill; exercise of art or profession; action, not theory

prag·mat·ic [prag-MAT-ik] *adj* concerned with practical

consequence; of the affairs of state **prag'ma·tism** [-mə-tiz-əm] *n* **prag'ma·tist** *n*

prai·rie [PRAIR-ee] *n* large mostly treeless tract of grassland **prairie dog** small Amer rodent allied to marmot **prairie oyster** as remedy for hangover, a drink of raw egg usu with seasonings; as food, testis of a calf

praise [prayz] *n* commendation; fact, state of being praised ▷ *vt* **praised, prais'ing** express approval, admiration of; speak well of; glorify **praise'wor·thy** [-wur-thee] *adj*

pra·line [PRAH-leen] *n* candy made of nuts with caramel covering

prance [prans] *vi* **pranced, pranc·ing** swagger; caper; walk with bounds ▷ *n* prancing

pran·di·al [PRAN-dee-əl] *adj* of a meal, esp dinner

prank [prangk] *n* mischievous trick or escapade, frolic

pra·se·o·dym·i·um [pray-zee-oh-DIM-ee-əm] *n* rare-earth chemical element

prate [prayt] *vi* **prat·ed, prat·ing** talk idly, chatter ▷ *n* idle chatter

prat·tle [PRAT-l] *vi* **-tled, -tling** talk like child ▷ *n* trifling, childish talk **prat'tler** *n* babbler

prawn *n* edible sea crustacean like a shrimp

pray *vt* ask earnestly; entreat ▷ *vi* offer prayers, esp to God **prayer** [prair] *n* action, practice of praying to God; earnest entreaty **pray'er** *n* one who prays

pre- *prefix* before, beforehand: *prenatal; prerecord; preshrunk*

preach [preech] *vi* deliver sermon; give moral, religious advice ▷ *vt* set forth in religious discourse; advocate **preach'er** *n*

pre·am·ble [PREE-am-bəl] *n*

introductory part of document, story, etc

pre·car·i·ous [pri-KAIR-ee-əs] *adj* insecure, unstable, perilous

pre·cau·tion [pri-KAW-shən] *n* previous care to prevent evil or secure good; preventive measure **pre·cau·tion·ar·y** *adj*

pre·cede [pri-SEED] *v* **-ced·ed, -ced·ing** go, come before in rank, order, time, etc **prec·e·dence** [PRES-i-dəns] *n* priority in position, rank, time, etc **prec·e·dent** *n* previous case or occurrence taken as rule

pre·cept [PREE-sept] *n* rule for conduct, maxim **pre·cep·tor** *n* instructor

pre·ces·sion [pree-SESH-ən] *n* act of preceding; motion of spinning body, in which the axis of rotation sweeps out a cone

pre·cinct [PREE-singkt] *n* enclosed, limited area; administrative area of city, esp of police, board of elections ▷ *pl* environs **precinct house** police station

pre·cious [PRE-shəs] *adj* beloved, cherished; of great value, highly valued; rare **pre·ci·os·i·ty** [presh-ee-OS-i-tee] *n* overrefinement in art or literature **pre·cious·ly** *adv*

prec·i·pice [PRES-ə-pis] *n* very steep cliff or rockface **pre·cip·i·tous** *adj* sheer

pre·cip·i·tant [prə-SIP-i-tənt] *adj* hasty, rash; abrupt **pre·cip·i·tance, -tan·cy** *n*

pre·cip·i·tate [pri-SIP-i-tayt] *vt* **-tat·ed, -tat·ing** hasten happening of; throw headlong; *chemistry* cause to be deposited in solid form from solution ▷ *adj* [-i-tit] too sudden; rash, impetuous ▷ *n* [-i-tit] substance chemically precipitated

pre·cip·i·tate·ly [-tit-lee] *adv*
pre·cip·i·ta·tion [-TAY-shən] *n* esp rain, snow, etc

pré·cis [PRAY-see] *n, pl* **pré·cis** [PRAY-seez] abstract, summary

pre·cise [pri-SĪS] *adj* definite; particular; exact, strictly worded; careful in observance; punctilious, formal **pre·cise·ly** *adv* **pre·ci·sion** [-SIZH-ən] *n* accuracy

pre·clude [pri-KLOOD] *vt* **-clud·ed, -clud·ing** prevent from happening; shut out

pre·co·cious [pri-KOH-shəs] *adj* developed, matured early or too soon **pre·coc·i·ty** [-KOS-i-tee] **pre·co·cious·ness** [-KOH-shəs-nis] *n*

pre·con·ceive [pree-kən-SEEV] *vt* **-ceived, -ceiv·ing** form an idea beforehand **pre·con·cep·tion** [-SEP-shən] *n*

pre·con·di·tion [pree-kən-DISH-ən] *n* necessary or required condition

pre·cur·sor [pri-KUR-sər] *n* forerunner **pre·cur·sive** *adj* **pre·cur·so·ry** *adj*

pred·a·to·ry [PRED-ə-tor-ee] *adj* hunting, killing other animals, etc for food; plundering **pred·a·tor** *n* predatory animal

pre·de·ces·sor [PRED-ə-ses-ər] *n* one who precedes another in an office or position; ancestor

pre·des·tine [pri-DES-tin] *vt* **-tined, -tin·ing** decree beforehand, foreordain **pre·des·ti·na·tion** *n*

pre·dic·a·ment [pri-DIK-ə-mənt] *n* perplexing, embarrassing or difficult situation

pred·i·cate [PRED-i-kayt] *vt* **-cat·ed, -cat·ing** affirm, assert; base (on or upon) ▷ *n* [-kit] that which is predicated; *grammar* statement made about a subject

pre·dict [pri-DIKT] *vt* foretell, prophesy **pre·dict·a·ble** *adj*

pre·di·lec·tion [pred-l-EK-shən] *n* preference, liking, partiality

pre·dis·pose [pree-dis-POHZ] *vt* -**posed, -pos·ing** incline, influence someone (toward); make susceptible (to)

pre·dom·i·nate [pri-DOM-ə-nayt] *vi* -**nat·ed, -nat·ing** be main or controlling element **pre·dom·i·nance** [-nəns] *n* **pre·dom·i·nant** *adj* chief

pre·em·i·nent [pree-EM-ə-nənt] *adj* excelling all others, outstanding **pre·em·i·nence** *n*

pre·empt [pree-EMPT] *vt* acquire in advance or act in advance of so as to exclusion of others **pre·emp·tive** *adj*

preen *vt* trim (feathers) with beak, plume; smarten oneself

pre·fab·ri·cate [pree-FAB-ri-kayt] *vt* -**cat·ed, -cat·ing** manufacture buildings, etc in shaped sections, for rapid assembly on the site **pre·fab** *n* building so made

pref·ace [PREF-is] *n* introduction to book, etc ▷ *vt* -**faced, -fac·ing** introduce **pref·a·to·ry** *adj*

pre·fect [PREE-fekt] *n* person put in authority **pre·fec·ture** [PREE-fek-chər] *n* office, residence, jurisdiction of a prefect

pre·fer [pri-FUR] *vt* -**ferred, -fer·ring** like better; promote **pref·er·a·ble** [PREF-ər-ə-bəl] *adj* more desirable **pref·er·a·bly** *adv* **pref·er·ence** [-əns] *n* **pref·er·en·tial** [-EN-shəl] *adj* giving, receiving preference

pre·fix [PREE-fiks] *n* preposition or particle put at beginning of word or title ▷ *vt* put as introduction; put before word to make compound

preg·nant [PREG-nənt] *adj* carrying fetus in womb; full of

meaning, significance; inventive **preg·nan·cy** *n*

pre·hen·sile [pri-HEN-sil] *adj* capable of grasping

pre·his·tor·ic [pree-hi-STOR-ik] *adj* before period in which written history begins **pre·his·to·ry** *n*

prej·u·dice [PREJ-ə-dis] *n* preconceived opinion; bias, partiality; damage or injury likely to happen to person or person's rights as a result of others' action or judgment ▷ *vt* -**diced, -dic·ing** influence; bias; injure **prej·u·di·cial** [-DISH-əl] *adj* injurious; disadvantageous

prel·ate [PREL-it] *n* bishop or other church dignitary of equal or higher rank **prel·a·cy** [-ə-see] *n* prelate's office

pre·lim·i·nar·y [pri-LIM-ə-ner-ee] *adj* preparatory, introductory ▷ *n*, *pl* -**ies** introductory, preparatory statement, action

prel·ude [PRAY-lood] *n* music introductory movement; performance, event, etc serving as introduction ▷ *v* -**ud·ed, -ud·ing** serve as prelude, introduce

pre·mar·i·tal [pree-MA-ri-təl] *adj* occurring before marriage

pre·ma·ture [pree-mə-CHUUR] *adj* happening, done before proper time

pre·med·i·tate [pri-MED-i-tayt] *vt* -**tat·ed, -tat·ing** consider, plan beforehand **pre·med·i·ta·tion** *n*

pre·mier [pri-MEER] *n* prime minister ▷ *adj* chief, foremost; first **pre·mier·ship** *n* office of premier

pre·miere [pri-MEER] *n* first performance of a play, film, etc ▷ *vi* -**miered, -mier·ing** have first performance

prem·ise [PREM-is] *n* logic proposition from which inference is drawn ▷ *pl* house, building with its belongings **premise** *vt* **-mised, -mis·ing** state by way of introduction

pre·mi·um [PREE-mee-əm] *n* prize, bonus; sum paid for insurance; excess over nominal value; great value or regard

pre·mo·ni·tion [pree-mə-NISH-ən] *n* presentiment, foreboding **pre·mon·i·to·ry** [pri-MON-i-tor-ee] *adj*

pre·na·tal [pree-NAYT-l] *adj* occurring before birth

pre·oc·cu·py [pree-OK-yə-pī] *vt* **-pied, -py·ing** occupy to the exclusion of other things **pre·oc·cu·pa'tion** *n* mental concentration or absorption

prep [prep] *n* preppy

pre·pare [pri-PAIR] *v* **-pared, -par·ing** ▷ *vt* make ready; make ▷ *vi* get ready **prep·a·ra'tion** *n* making ready beforehand; something that is prepared, as a medicine; at school, (time spent) preparing work for lesson **pre·par'a·to·ry** [-PA-rə-tor-ee] *adj* serving to prepare; introductory **pre·par'ed·ness** [-id-nis] *n* state of being prepared **preparatory school** private school preparing students for college

pre·pay [pri-PAY] *vt* **-paid, -pay·ing** pay or pay for beforehand **pre·paid'** *adj*

pre·pon·der·ate [pri-PON-də-rayt] *vi* **-at·ed, -at·ing** be of greater weight or power **pre·pon'der·ance** [-əns] *n* superiority of power, numbers, etc

prep·o·si·tion [prep-ə-ZISH-ən] *n* word marking relation between noun or pronoun and other words **prep·o·si'tion·al** *adj*

pre·pos·sess [pree-pə-ZES] *vt* impress, esp favorably,

beforehand; possess beforehand **pre·pos·sess'ing** *adj* inviting favorable opinion, attractive, winning

pre·pos·ter·ous [pri-POS-tər-əs] *adj* utterly absurd, foolish

prep·py, prep·pie [PRE-pee] *n* **-ies** *inf* (person who behaves like) student or former student of preparatory school ▷ *adj*

pre·puce [PRE-pyoos] *n* retractable fold of skin covering tip of penis, foreskin

pre·req·ui·site [pri-REK-wə-zit] *n, adj* (something) required as prior condition

pre·rog·a·tive [pri-ROG-ə-tiv] *n* peculiar power or right, esp as vested in ruler ▷ *adj* privileged

pres·age [PRES-ij] *n* omen, indication of something to come ▷ *vt* **-aged, -ag·ing** foretell

pres·by·o·pi·a [prez-bee-OH-pee-ə] *n* progressively diminishing ability of the eye to focus, esp on near objects, farsightedness

pres·by·ter [PREZ-bi-tər] *n* elder in early Christian church; priest; member of a presbytery **Pres·by·te'ri·an** *adj, n* (member) of Protestant church governed by lay elders **pres'by·ter·y** *n* church court composed of all ministers within a certain district and one or two ruling elders from each church; *R C Church* rectory

pre·science [PRESH-əns] *n* foreknowledge **pres'cient** *adj*

pre·scribe [pri-SKRĪB] *v* **-scribed, -scrib·ing** set out rules for; order; ordain; order use of (medicine) **pre·scrip'tion** *n* prescribing; thing prescribed; written statement of it **pre·scrip'tive** *adj*

pres·ent[1] [PREZ-ənt] *adj* that is here; now existing or happening ▷ *n* present time or tense **pres'ence** n being present; appearance; bearing **pres'ent·ly** adv soon; at present

present² [pri-ZENT] vt introduce formally; show; give; offer; point, aim **pres'ent** n gift **pre·sent'a·ble** adj fit to be seen **pres·en·ta'tion** [-TAY-shàn] n **pre·sent'er** n person who presents, esp an award

pre·sen·ti·ment [pri-ZEN-tà-mànt] n sense of something (esp evil) about to happen

pre·serve [pri-ZURV] vt **-served, -serv·ing** keep from harm, injury or decay; maintain; pickle, can ▷ n special area; that which is preserved, as fruit, etc; place where game is kept for private fishing, shooting ▷ pl preserved vegetables, fruit, etc **pres·er·va'tion** n **pre·serv'a·tive** n chemical put into perishable foods, drinks, etc to keep them from going bad ▷ adj tending to preserve; having quality of preserving

pre·side [pri-ZID] vi **-sid·ed, -sid·ing** be chairperson; superintend **pres'i·dent** [-dànt] n head of organization, company, republic, etc **pres'i·den·cy** n, pl **-cies pres·i·den'tial** [-DEN-shàl] adj

press¹ vt subject to push or squeeze; smooth by pressure or heat; urge steadily, earnestly ▷ vi bring weight to bear; throng; hasten ▷ n pressing; machine for pressing, esp printing machine; printing house; its work or art; newspapers collectively; reporters, journalists; crowd; stress **press'ing** adj urgent; persistent **press agent** person employed to advertise and secure publicity for any person, enterprise, etc **press'man** [-màn] n printer who attends to the press

press² vt force to serve esp in navy or army **press gang** formerly, body of men employed to press men into naval service

pres·sure [PRESH-àr] n act of pressing; influence; authority; difficulties; physics thrust per unit area **pres·sur·i·za'tion** [-ZAY-shàn] n in aircraft, maintenance of normal atmospheric pressure at high altitudes **pres'sur·ize** vt **-ized, -iz·ing** pressure cooker reinforced pot that cooks food rapidly by steam under pressure **pressure group** organized group that exerts influence on policies, public opinion, etc

pres·ti·dig·i·ta·tion [pres-ti-dij-i-TAY-shàn] n sleight of hand **pres·ti·dig'i·ta·tor** n

pres·tige [pre-STEEZH] n reputation; influence depending on it **pres·tig'i·ous** [-STIJ-às] adj

pres·to [PRES-toh] adv music quickly

pre·stressed [PREE-strest] adj (of concrete) containing stretched steel cables for strengthening

pre·sume [pri-ZOOM] v **-sumed, -sum·ing** ▷ vt take for granted ▷ vi take liberties **pre·sum'a·bly** adv probably; doubtlessly **pre·sump'tion** [-ZUM-shàn] n forward, arrogant opinion or conduct; strong probability **pre·sump'tive** adj that may be assumed as true or valid until contrary is proved **pre·sump'tu·ous** [-shoo-às] adj forward, impudent, taking liberties

pre·sup·pose [pree-sà-POHZ] vt **-posed, -pos·ing** assume or take for granted beforehand **pre·sup·po·si'tion** [-ZI-shàn] n previous supposition

pre·tend [pri-TEND] vt claim or allege (something untrue); make

believe, as in play ▷ vi lay claim (to)
pre·tense' n simulation; pretext
pre·tend'er n claimant (to throne)
pre·ten·sion n **pre·ten·tious**
[-shǎs] adj making claim to special
merit or importance; given to
outward show
pre·ter·nat·u·ral [pre-tàr-NACH-
ǎr-ǎl] adj out of ordinary way of
nature; abnormal, supernatural
pre·text [PREE-tekst] n excuse;
pretense
pret·ty [PRIT-ee] adj **-ti·er, -ti·est**
having beauty that is attractive
rather than imposing; charming, etc
▷ adv fairly, moderately **pret'ti·ness**
[-nis] n
pret·zel [PRET-sǎl] n crisp, dry
biscuit usu shaped as knot or stick
pre·vail [pri-VAYL] vi gain
mastery; triumph; be in fashion,
generally established **pre·vail'ing**
adj widespread; predominant
prev·a·lence [-lǎns] n **prev·a·lent**
[-lǎnt] adj extensively existing, rife
pre·var·i·cate [pri-VA-ri-kayt]
vi **-cat·ed, -cat·ing** make evasive
or misleading statements; lie
pre·var'i·ca·tor n
pre·vent [pri-VENT] vt stop, hinder
pre·vent'a·ble adj **pre·ven·tion**
[-shǎn] n **pre·ven·tive** adj, n
pre·view [PREE-vyoo] n advance
showing; a showing of scenes from a
forthcoming film, etc
pre·vi·ous [PREE-vee-ǎs] adj
earlier; preceding; happening before
pre'vi·ous·ly adv before
prey [pray] n animal hunted and
killed by carnivorous animals; victim
▷ vi seize for food; treat as prey;
(with upon) afflict, obsess
price [prïs] n amount, etc for
which thing is bought or sold; cost;
value; reward; odds in betting ▷ vt
priced, pric·ing fix, ask price for

price'less [-lis] adj invaluable; very
funny **pric'ey** [-ee] adj **pric·i·er,
pric·i·est** expensive
prick [prik] vt pierce slightly with
sharp point; cause to feel mental
pain; mark by prick; erect (ears)
▷ n slight hole made by pricking;
pricking or being pricked; sting;
remorse; that which pricks; sharp
point **prick'le** n thorn, spike ▷ vi
-kled, -kling feel tingling or pricking
sensation **prick'ly** adj **-li·er, -li·est**
prickly heat inflammation of skin
with stinging pains
pride [prïd] n too high an opinion of
oneself; worthy self-esteem; feeling
of elation or great satisfaction;
something causing this; group (of
lions) ▷ v refl **prid·ed, prid·ing**
take pride
priest [preest] n official minister
of religion, member of clergy
priest'ess n fem **priest'hood**
[-huud] n **priest'ly** adj **-li·er, -li·est**
prig n self-righteous person who
professes superior culture, morality,
etc **prig'gish** adj
prim adj **prim·mer, prim·mest** very
restrained, formally prudish
pri·ma·cy [PRI-me-see] n state of
being first in rank, grade, etc; office
of PRIMATE[1]
pri·ma don·na [pree-mǎ DON-ǎ]
n, pl **donnas** principal female singer
in opera; temperamental person
pri·ma fa·ci·e [PRI-mǎ FAY-shee]
Lat at first sight; obvious
pri·mal [PRI-mǎl] adj of earliest
age; first, original **pri·ma·ri·ly**
adv **pri·ma·ry** adj chief; of the first
stage, decision, etc; elementary
pri·mate [PRI-mit] n archbishop
primate[2] [PRI-mayt] n one of order
of mammals including monkeys
and man
prime[1] [prïm] adj fundamental;

original; chief; best ▷ n first, best part of anything; youth; full health and vigor ▷ vt **primed, prim·ing** prepare (gun, engine, pump, etc) for use; fill up, eg with information **prime minister** leader of parliamentary government

prime² vt **primed, prim·ing** prepare for paint with preliminary coating of oil, etc **prim·er** [PRIM-ər] n paint, etc for priming

prim·er [PRIM-ər] n elementary schoolbook or manual

pri·me·val [prI-MEE-vəl] adj of the earliest age of the world

prim·i·tive [PRIM-i-tiv] adj of an early undeveloped kind; ancient; crude, rough

pri·mo·gen·i·ture [prI-mə-JEN-i-chər] n rule by which real estate passes to the first born son **pri·mo·gen'i·tor** n earliest ancestor; forefather

pri·mor·di·al [prI-MOR-dee-əl] adj existing at or from the beginning

prince [prins] n son or (in some countries) grandson of king or queen; ruler, chief **prin'cess** n fem **prince'ly** adj **-li·er, -li·est** generous, lavish; stately; magnificent

prin·ci·pal [PRIN-sə-pəl] adj chief in importance ▷ n person for whom another is agent; head of institution, esp school; sum of money lent and yielding interest; chief actor **prin·ci·pal'i·ty** n territory, dignity of prince

prin·ci·ple [PRIN-sə-pəl] n moral rule; settled reason of action; uprightness; fundamental truth or element

print vt reproduce (words, pictures, etc, by pressing inked plates, type, blocks, etc to paper, etc); produce thus; write in imitation of this; impress; photography produce pictures from negatives; stamp (fabric) with colored design ▷ n printed matter; printed lettering; written imitation of printed type; photograph; impression, mark left on surface by thing that has pressed against it; printed cotton fabric **print'er** n person or device engaged in printing **printed circuit** electronic circuit with wiring printed on an insulating base **print'out** n printed information from computer, teleprinter, etc

pri·or [PRI-ər] adj earlier ▷ n chief of religious house or order **pri'or·ess** n fem **pri·or'i·ty** n, pl **-ties** precedence; something given special attention **pri'o·ry** n, pl **-ries** monastery, convent under prior, prioress **prior to** before, earlier

prise [prIz] vt **prised, pris·ing** force open by levering; obtain (information, etc) with difficulty

prism [PRIZ-əm] n transparent solid usu with triangular ends and rectangular sides, used to disperse light into spectrum or refract it in optical instruments, etc **pris·mat'ic** adj of prism shape; (of color) such as is produced by refraction through prism, rainbowlike, brilliant

pris·on [PRIZ-ən] n jail **pris'on·er** n one kept in prison; captive

pris·sy [PRIS-ee] adj **-si·er, -si·est** fussy, prim

pris·tine [pris-TEEN] adj original, primitive, unspoiled, good

pri·vate [PRI-vit] adj secret, not public; reserved for, or belonging to, or concerning, an individual only; personal; secluded; denoting soldier or marine of lowest rank; not controlled by government ▷ n private soldier or marine **pri'va·cy** [-vi-see] n **pri'va·tize** vt **-tized, -tiz·ing** transfer from government or public ownership to private enterprise

pri•va•tion [pri-VAY-shən] *n* want of comforts or necessities; hardship; act of depriving **priv•a•tive** [PRIV-ə-tiv] *adj* of privation or negation

priv•et [PRIV-it] *n* bushy shrub used for hedges

priv•i•lege [PRIV-ə-lij] *n* advantage or favor that only a few obtain; right, advantage belonging to person or class **priv•i•leged** *adj* enjoying special right or immunity

priv•y [PRIV-ee] *adj* admitted to knowledge of secret ▷ *n*, *pl* **priv•ies** outhouse; *law* person having interest in an action

prize¹ [priz] *n* reward given for success in competition; thing striven for; thing won ▷ *adj* winning or likely to win a prize ▷ *vt* **prized, priz•ing** value highly **prize'fight** *n* boxing match for money

prize² *n* ship, property captured in (naval) warfare

pro¹ [proh] *adj, adv* in favor of

pro² *n* professional ▷ *adj* professional

pro- prefix for, instead of, before, in front: *proconsul; pronoun; project*

pro•ac•tive [proh-AK-tiv] *adj* taking the initiative and acting in advance, rather than simply reacting to circumstances and events

prob•a•ble [PROB-ə-bəl] *adj* likely **prob•a•bil'i•ty** *n* likelihood; anything that has appearance of truth **prob'a•bly** *adv*

pro•bate [PROH-bayt] *n* proving of authenticity of will; certificate of this **probate court** court with power over administration of estates of dead persons

pro•ba•tion [proh-BAY-shən] *n* system of releasing lawbreakers, but placing them under supervision for

stated period; testing of candidate before admission to full membership

probe [prohb] *vt* **probed, prob•ing** search into, examine, question closely ▷ *n* that which probes, or is used to probe; thorough inquiry

pro•bi•ty [PROH-bi-tee] *n* honesty, uprightness, integrity

prob•lem [PROB-ləm] *n* matter, etc difficult to deal with or solve; question set for solution; puzzle **prob•le•mat'ic** *adj* questionable; uncertain; disputable

pro•bos•cis [proh-BOS-is] *n*, *pl* **-cis•es** trunk or long snout; *inf* nose, esp prominent one

pro•ceed [prə-SEED] *vi* go forward, continue; be carried on; take legal action **pro•ceeds** [PROH-seedz] *pl n* amount of money or profit received **pro•ce'dur•al** [-SEE-jər-əl] *adj* **pro•ce'dure** *n* act, manner of proceeding; conduct **pro•ceed'ing** *n* act or course of action; transaction ▷ *pl* minutes of meeting; methods of prosecuting charge, claim, etc

proc•ess [PROS-es] *n* series of actions or changes; method of operation; state of going on; action of law; outgrowth ▷ *vt* handle, treat, prepare by special method of manufacture, etc **pro•ces•sion** [prə-SESH-ən] *n* regular, orderly progress; line of persons in formal order **pro•ces'sion•al** *adj* **proc'es•sor** *n* person or device that processes; *computing* same as **CENTRAL PROCESSING UNIT**

pro•claim [proh-KLAYM] *vt* announce publicly, declare **proc•la•ma'tion** [prok-lə-MAY-shən] *n*

pro•cliv•i•ty [proh-KLIV-i-tee] *n*, *pl* **-ties** inclination, tendency

pro•cras•ti•nate [proh-KRAS-tə-nayt] *vi* **-nat•ed, -nat•ing** put

off, delay **pro·cras·ti·na'tion** n
pro·cras'ti·na·tor n
pro·cre·ate [PROH-kree-ayt] vt
-**at·ed, -at·ing** produce offspring,
generate **pro·cre·a'tion** n
Pro·crus·te·an [proh-KRUS-tee-
ən] adj compelling uniformity by
violence
proc·tol·o·gy [prok-TOL-ə-jee]
n medical specialty dealing with
diseases of anus and rectum
proc·tor [PROK-tər] n person
appointed to supervise students
during examinations; university
official with administrative, esp
disciplinary, duties
pro·cure [prə-KYUUR] v -**cured,
-cur·ing** ▷ vt obtain, acquire;
provide; bring about ▷ vi act as pimp
pro·cure'ment n **pro·cur'er** n one
who procures; pimp **pro·cur'ess**
n fem
prod vt **prod·ded, prod·ding** poke
with something pointed; stimulate
to action ▷ n prodding; goad;
pointed instrument
prod·i·gal [PROD-i-gəl] adj
wasteful; extravagant ▷ n
spendthrift **prod·i·gal'i·ty** n
reckless extravagance
prod·i·gy [PROD-i-jee] n, pl
-**gies** person esp precocious child
with some marvelous gift; thing
causing wonder **pro·di·gious**
[prə-DIJ-əs] adj very great, immense;
extraordinary **pro·di'gious·ly** adv
pro·duce [prə-DOOS] vt -**duced,
-duc·ing** bring into existence; yield;
make; bring forward; manufacture;
exhibit; present on stage, film,
TV; geometry extend in length ▷ n
[PROD-oos] that which is yielded or
made, esp vegetables **pro·duc'er**
n person who produces, esp play,
film, etc **prod'uct** [-əkt] n result
of process of manufacture; number

resulting from multiplication
pro·duc'tion n producing; things
produced **pro·duc'tive** adj fertile;
creative; efficient **pro·duc·tiv'i·ty**
n
pro·fam·i·ly [proh-FAM-ə-lee] adj
antiabortion; pro-life
pro·fane [prə-FAYN] adj irreverent,
blasphemous; not sacred ▷ vt
-**faned, -fan·ing** pollute, desecrate
prof·a·na·tion [prof-ə-NAY-shən]
n **pro·fan·i·ty** [prə-FAN-i-tee] n
profane talk or behavior, blasphemy
pro·fess [prə-FES] vt affirm
belief in; confess publicly; assert;
claim, pretend **pro·fess'ed·ly** adv
avowedly **pro·fes'sion** n calling or
occupation; esp learned, scientific
or artistic; a professing; vow of
religious faith on entering religious
order **pro·fes'sion·al** adj engaged
in a profession; engaged in a game
or sport for money ▷ n member of
profession; paid player **pro·fes'sor** n
teacher of highest rank in college or
university **pro·fes·so'ri·al** adj
prof·fer vt, n offer
pro·fi·cient [prə-FISH-ənt] adj
skilled; expert **pro·fi'cien·cy** n
pro·file [PROH-fil] n outline,
esp of face, as seen from side; brief
biographical sketch
prof'it n money gained; benefit
obtained ▷ v benefit **prof'it·a·ble**
adj yielding profit **prof·it·eer'** n
one who makes excessive profits at
the expense of the public ▷ vi do this
prof·li·gate [PROF-li-git] adj
dissolute; reckless, wasteful ▷ n
dissolute person **prof'li·ga·cy**
[-li-gi-see] n
pro for·ma [proh FOR-mə] Lat
prescribing a set form; for the sake
of form
pro·found [prə-FOWND] adj
-**er, -est** very learned; deep

pro·fun·di·ty n
pro·fuse [prə-FYOOS] adj abundant, prodigal **pro·fu·sion** [-FYOO-zhən] n

prog·e·ny [PROJ-ə-nee] n children
pro·gen·i·tor [proh-JEN-i-tər] n ancestor

pro·ges·ter·one [proh-JES-tə-rohn] n hormone that prepares uterus for pregnancy and prevents further ovulation

prog·na·thous [prog-NAY-thəs] adj with projecting lower jaw

prog·no·sis [prog-NOH-sis] n, pl **-ses** [-seez] art of foretelling course of disease by symptoms; forecast **prog·nos·tic** adj of, serving as prognosis ▷ n **prog·nos·ti·cate** **-cat·ed, -cat·ing** foretell

pro·gram [PROH-gram] n plan, detailed notes of intended proceedings; broadcast on radio or television; detailed instructions for a computer ▷ vt **-grammed, -gram·ming** feed program into (computer); arrange detailed instructions for computer **pro'gram·mer** n

prog'ress n onward movement; development ▷ vi [prə-GRES] go forward; improve **pro·gres·sion** n moving forward; advance, improvement; increase or decrease of numbers or magnitudes according to fixed law; music regular succession of chords **pro·gres·sive** adj progressing by degrees; favoring political or social reform

pro·hib·it [proh-HIB-it] vt forbid **pro·hi·bi·tion** n act of forbidding; interdict; interdiction of supply and consumption of alcoholic drinks **pro·hib·i·tive** adj tending to forbid or exclude; (of prices) very high

pro·ject [PROJ-ekt] n plan, scheme; design ▷ v [prə-JEKT]

▷ vt plan; throw; cause to appear on distant background ▷ vi stick out, protrude **pro·jec·tile** [-JEK-til] n heavy missile, esp shell or ball ▷ adj for throwing **pro·jec·tion** n **pro·jec·tion·ist** n operator of film projector **pro·jec·tor** n apparatus for projecting photographic images, films, slides on screen; one that forms scheme or design

pro·lapse [proh-LAPS] n falling, slipping down of part of body from normal position ▷ vi fall or slip down in this way

pro·le·tar·i·at [proh-li-TAIR-ee-ət] n lowest class of community, working class **pro·le·tar'i·an** adj, n

pro-life see PROFAMILY

pro·lif·er·ate [prə-LIF-ə-rayt] v **-at·ed, -at·ing** grow or reproduce rapidly **pro·lif·er·a'tion** n

pro·lif·ic [prə-LIF-ik] adj fruitful; producing much

pro·lix [proh-LIKS] adj wordy, long-winded **pro·lix'i·ty** n

pro·logue [PROH-lawg] n preface, esp speech before a play

pro·long [prə-LAWNG] vt lengthen; protract

prom n social or college dance, esp at end of school year

prom·e·nade [prom-ə-NAYD] n leisurely walk; place made or used for this ▷ vi **-nad·ed, -nad·ing** take leisurely walk; go up and down

prom·i·nent [PROM-ə-nənt] adj sticking out; conspicuous; distinguished **prom'i·nence** n

pro·mis·cu·ous [prə-MIS-kyoo-əs] adj indiscriminate, esp in sexual relations; mixed without distinction **prom·is·cu'i·ty** [-KYOO-ə-tee] n

prom·ise [PROM-is] v **-mised, -mis·ing** ▷ vt give assurance ▷ vi be likely to ▷ n undertaking to do or not to do something; potential

prom·is·ing adj showing good signs, hopeful **prom·is·ing·ly** adv

prom·is·so·ry adj containing promise **promissory note** written promise to pay sum to person named, at specified time

prom·on·to·ry [PROM-ən-tor-ee] n, pl **-ries** point of high land jutting out into the sea, headland

pro·mote [prə-MOHT] vt **-mot·ed, -mot·ing** help forward; move up to higher rank or position; work for; encourage sale of **pro·mot·er** n **pro·mo·tion** n advancement; preferment

prompt adj **-er, -est** done at once; acting with alacrity; punctual; ready ▷ v urge, suggest; help out (actor or speaker) by reading or suggesting next words **prompt·er** n **prompt·ness** [-nis] n **prompt·ly** adv

prom·ul·gate [PROM-əl-gayt] vt **-gat·ed, -gat·ing** proclaim, publish **prom·ul·ga·tion** n

prone [prohn] adj lying face or front downward; inclined (to) **prone·ness** [-nis] n

prong n one tine of fork or similar instrument

pro·noun [PROH-nown] n word used to replace noun **pro·nom·i·nal** adj pert to, like pronoun

pro·nounce [prə-NOWNS] v **-nounced, -nounc·ing** ▷ vt utter formally; form with organs of speech; speak distinctly; declare ▷ vi give opinion or decision **pro·nounce·a·ble** adj **pro·nounced** adj strongly marked, decided **pro·nounce·ment** n declaration **pro·nun·ci·a·tion** n way word, etc is pronounced; articulation

pron·to [PRON-toh] adv inf at once, immediately, quickly

proof n evidence; thing that proves; test, demonstration; trial impression from type or engraved plate; photography print from a negative; standard of strength of alcoholic drink ▷ adj giving impenetrable defense against; of proven strength **proof·read** [-reed] v **-read, -read·ing** read and correct proofs **proof·read·er** n

prop[1] vt propped, prop·ping support, sustain, hold up ▷ n pole, beam, etc; used as support

prop[2] n short for PROPELLER

prop[3] n short for (THEATRICAL) PROPERTY

prop·a·gan·da [prop-ə-GAN-də] n organized dissemination of information to assist or damage political cause, etc **prop·a·gan·dist** n **prop·a·gan·dize** [-dīz] vt **-dized, -diz·ing**

prop·a·gate [pro-pə-gayt] v **-gat·ed, -gat·ing** ▷ vt reproduce, breed, spread by sowing, breeding, etc; transmit ▷ vi breed, multiply **prop·a·ga·tion** n

pro·pane [PROH-payn] n colorless, flammable gas from petroleum

pro·pel [prə-PEL] vt **-pelled, -pel·ling** cause to move forward **pro·pel·lant, -lent** n something causing propulsion, such as rocket fuel **pro·pel·ler** n revolving shaft with blades for driving ship or aircraft **pro·pul·sion** n act of, means of, driving forward **pro·pul·sive, pro·pul·so·ry** adj tending, having power to propel; urging on

pro·pen·si·ty [prə-PEN-si-tee] n, pl **-ties** inclination or bent; tendency; disposition

prop·er [PROP-ər] adj appropriate; correct; conforming to etiquette, decorous; strict; (of noun) denoting individual person or place

prop·er·ty [PROP-ər-tee] n, pl **-ties**

that which is owned; estate whether in lands, goods, or money; quality, attribute of something; article used on stage in play, etc

proph·et [PROF-it] n inspired teacher or revealer of divine will; foreteller of future **proph·e·cy** [-ə-see] n, pl -cies prediction, prophetic utterance **proph·e·sy** [-ə-si] v -sied, -sy·ing foretell, predict; make predictions **pro·phet·ic** adj **pro·phet·i·cal·ly** adv

pro·phy·lac·tic [prof-ə-LAK-tik] n, adj (something) done or used to ward off disease; condom **pro·phy·lax·is** n

pro·pin·qui·ty [proh-PING-kwi-tee] n nearness, proximity, close kinship

pro·pi·ti·ate [prə-PISH-ee-ayt] vt -at·ed, -at·ing appease, gain favor of **pro·pi·ti·a·to·ry** adj **pro·pi·tious** adj favorable, auspicious

pro·po·nent [prə-POH-nənt] n one who advocates something

pro·por·tion [prə-POR-shən] n relative size or number; comparison; due relation between connected things or parts; share; relation ▷ pl dimensions ▷ vt arrange proportions of **pro·por·tion·al, pro·por·tion·ate** adj having a due proportion; corresponding in size, number, etc **pro·por·tion·al·ly** adv

pro·pose [prə-POHZ] v -posed, -pos·ing ▷ vt put forward for consideration; nominate; intend ▷ vi offer marriage **pro·pos·al** n

prop·o·si·tion n offer; statement, assertion; theorem; suggestion of terms; thing to be dealt with; proposal of illicit sexual relations

pro·pound [prə-POWND] vt put forward for consideration or solution

pro·pri·e·tor [prə-PRĪ-i-tər] n

owner **pro·pri·e·tar·y** [-ter-ee] adj belonging to owner; made by firm with exclusive rights of manufacture

pro·pri·e·ty [prə-PRĪ-itee] n, pl -ties properness, correct conduct, fitness

propulsion see PROPEL

pro ra·ta [proh RAY-tə] Lat in proportion

pro·sa·ic [proh-ZAY-ik] adj commonplace, unromantic

pro·sce·ni·um [proh-SEE-nee-əm] n, pl -ni·a [-nee-ə] arch or opening framing stage

pro·scribe [proh-SKRĪB] vt -scribed, -scrib·ing outlaw, condemn **pro·scrip·tion** n

prose [prohz] n speech or writing not verse **pros·y** adj **pros·i·er, pros·i·est** tedious, dull

pros·e·cute [PROS-i-kyoot] vt -cut·ed, -cut·ing carry on, bring legal proceedings against **pros·e·cu·tion** n **pros·e·cu·tor** n

pros·e·lyte [PROS-ə-lit] n convert **pros·e·lyt·ize** [-li-tiz] vt -ized, -iz·ing

pros·o·dy [PROS-ə-dee] n system, study of versification **pros·o·dist** n

pros·pect [PROS-pekt] n expectation, chance for success; view, outlook; likely customer or subscriber; mental view ▷ v explore, esp for gold **pro·spec·tive** adj anticipated; future **pros·pec·tor** n **pro·spec·tus** [prə-SPEK-təs] n, pl -tus·es document describing company, school, etc

pros·per [PROS-pər] vi do well **pros·per·i·ty** n, pl -ties good fortune, well-being **pros·per·ous** adj doing well, successful; flourishing, rich, well-off

pros·tate [PROS-tayt] n gland accessory to male generative organs

pros·the·sis [pros-THEE-sis] n, pl

-ses [-seez] (replacement of part of body with) artificial substitute
pros·ti·tute [PROS-ti-toot] n one who offers sexual intercourse in return for payment ▷ vt **-tut·ed, -tut·ing** make a prostitute of; put to unworthy use **pros·ti·tu·tion** n
pros·trate [PROS-trayt] adj lying flat; crushed, submissive, overcome ▷ vt **-trat·ed, -trat·ing** throw flat on ground; reduce to exhaustion **pros·tra·tion** n
pro·tag·o·nist [proh-TAG-ə-nist] n leading character; principal actor; champion of a cause
pro·te·an [PROH-tee-ən] adj variable; versatile
pro·tect [prə-TEKT] vt defend, guard, keep from harm **pro·tec·tion** n **pro·tec·tion·ist** n one who advocates protecting industries by taxing competing imports **pro·tec·tive** adj **pro·tec·tor** n one who protects; regent **pro·tec·tor·ate** [-tər-it] n relation of country to territory it protects and controls; such territory; office, period of protector of a country
pro·té·gé [PROH-tə-zhay] n one under another's care, protection or patronage **pro·té·gée** n fem
pro·tein [PROH-teen] n any of kinds of organic compounds that form most essential part of food of living creatures
pro·test [PROH-test] n declaration or demonstration of objection ▷ vi [prə-TEST] object; make declaration against; assert formally **prot·es·ta·tion** [prot-ə-STAY-shən] n strong declaration
Prot·es·tant [PROT-ə-stənt] adj belonging to any branch of the Western Christian Church outside the Roman Catholic Church ▷ n member of such church

Prot·es·tant·ism n
proto-, prot- comb form first: prototype
pro·to·col [PROH-tə-kawl] n diplomatic etiquette; draft of terms signed by parties as basis of formal treaty; computing standardized format for exchanging data, esp between different computer systems
pro·ton [PROH-ton] n positively charged particle in nucleus of atom
pro·to·plasm [PROH-tə-plaz-əm] n substance that is living matter of all animal and plant cells
pro·to·type [PROH-tə-tīp] n original, or model, after which thing is copied; pattern
pro·to·zo·an [proh-tə-ZOH-ən] n minute animal of lowest and simplest class
pro·tract [proh-TRAKT] vt lengthen; prolong; delay; draw to scale **pro·tract·ed** adj long drawn out; tedious **pro·trac·tor** n instrument for measuring angles on paper
pro·trude [proh-TROOD] v **-trud·ed, -trud·ing** stick out, project **pro·tru·sion** [-zhən] n **pro·tru·sive** [-siv] adj thrusting forward
pro·tu·ber·ant [proh-TOO-bər-ənt] adj bulging out **pro·tu·ber·ance** [-əns] n bulge, swelling
proud [prowd] adj **-er, -est** feeling or displaying pride; arrogant; gratified; noble; self-respecting; stately **proud·ly** adv **proud flesh** flesh growing around healing wound
Prov. Proverbs
prove [proov] v **proved, proved** or **prov·en, prov·ing** ▷ vt establish validity of; demonstrate; test ▷ vi turn out (to be, etc); (of dough) rise in warm place before baking **proven**

adj proved

prov·e·nance [PROV-ə-nəns] *n* place of origin, source

prov·en·der [PROV-ən-dər] *n* fodder

prov·erb [PROV-ərb] *n* short, pithy, traditional saying in common use **pro·ver·bi·al** [prə-VUR-bee-əl] *adj*

pro·vide [prə-VID] *v* **-vid·ed, -vid·ing** ▷ *vi* make preparation ▷ *vt* supply, equip, prepare, furnish, give **pro·vid·er** *n* provided that; on condition that

prov·i·dent [PROV-i-dənt] *adj* thrifty; showing foresight **prov·i·dence** *n* kindly care of God or nature; foresight; economy **prov·i·den·tial** [-DEN-shəl] *adj* strikingly fortunate, lucky

prov·ince [PROV-əns] *n* division of a country, district; sphere of action ▷ *pl* any part of country outside capital or largest cities **pro·vin·cial** [prə-VIN-shəl] *adj* of a province; unsophisticated; narrow in outlook ▷ *n* unsophisticated person; inhabitant of province **pro·vin·cial·ism** *n* narrowness of outlook; lack of refinement; idiom peculiar to district

pro·vi·sion [prə-VIZH-ən] *n* a providing, esp for the future; thing provided; *law* article of instrument or statute ▷ *pl* food ▷ *vt* supply with food **pro·vi·sion·al** *adj* temporary; conditional

pro·vi·so [prə-VI-zoh] *n*, *pl* **-sos** or **-soes** condition

pro·vo·ca·teur [prə-vok-ə-TUR] *n* one who causes dissension, makes trouble; agitator; see **AGENT PROVOCATEUR**

pro·voke [prə-VOHK] *vt* **-voked, -vok·ing** irritate; incense; arouse; excite; cause **prov·o·ca·tion** [-ə-KAY-shən] *n* **pro·voc·a·tive**

[-VOK-ə-tiv] *adj*

pro·vost [PROH-vohst] *n* one who superintends or presides; high administrative officer of university **provost marshal** head of military police

prow [rhymes with **cow**] *n* bow of vessel

prow·ess [PROW-is] *n* skill; bravery, fighting capacity

prowl *vi* roam stealthily, esp in search of prey or booty ▷ *n* **prowl·er** *n* **on the prowl** searching stealthily; seeking sexual partner

prox·i·mate [PROK-sə-mit] *adj* nearest, next, immediate **prox·im·i·ty** *n*

prox·y [PROK-see] *n*, *pl* **prox·ies** authorized agent or substitute; writing authorizing one to act as this

prude [prood] *n* one who affects excessive modesty or propriety **prud·er·y** *n*, *pl* **-er·ies** **prud·ish** *adj*

pru·dent [PROOD-nt] *adj* careful, discreet; sensible **pru·dence** *n* habit of acting with careful deliberation; wisdom applied to practice **pru·den·tial** *adj*

prune¹ [proon] *n* dried plum

prune² *vt* **pruned, prun·ing** cut out dead parts, excessive branches, etc; shorten, reduce

pru·ri·ent [PRUUR-ee-ənt] *adj* given to, springing from lewd thoughts; having unhealthy curiosity or desire **pru·ri·ence** *n*

pry [pri] *vi* **pried, pry·ing** make furtive or impertinent inquiries; look curiously; force open

Ps. Psalm(s)

psalm [sahm] *n* sacred song; (**P-**) any of the sacred songs making up the Book of Psalms in the Bible **psalm·ist** *n* writer of psalms **psal·mo·dy** [SAHM-ə-dee] *n* art, act of singing sacred music **psal·ter**

[SAWL·tər] *n* book of psalms; (**P-**) copy of the Psalms as separate book **psal·ter·y** [-tə-ree] *n, pl* **-ter·ies** obsolete stringed instrument like lyre

pseu·do [SOO-doh] *adj* sham, fake

pseudo- *comb form* false, sham: *pseudo-Gothic; pseudoscience*

pseu·do·nym [SOOD-n-im] *n* false, fictitious name; pen name

psit·ta·co·sis [sit-ə-KOH-sis] *n* dangerous infectious disease, germ of which is carried by parrots

psy·che [SÍ-kee] *n* human mind or soul

psych·e·del·ic [si-ki-DEL-ik] *adj* of or causing hallucinations; like intense colors, etc experienced during hallucinations

psy·chic [SÍ-kik] *adj* sensitive to phenomena lying outside range of normal experience; of soul or mind; that appears to be outside region of physical law **psy·chi·a·try** [si-KÍ-ə-tree] *n* medical treatment of mental diseases **psy·chi·a·trist** *n* **psy·cho·a·nal'y·sis** [si-koh-] *n* method of studying and treating mental disorders **psy·cho·an'a·lyst** *n* **psy·cho·log·i·cal** [si-kə-LOJ-i-kəl] *adj* of psychology; of the mind **psy·chol'o·gist** *n* **psy·chol'o·gy** *n* study of mind; person's mental makeup **psy·chom'e·try** *n* measurement, testing of psychological processes; supposed ability to divine unknown persons' qualities by handling object used or worn by them **psy'cho·path** *n* person afflicted with severe mental disorder causing him or her to commit antisocial, often violent acts **psy·cho·path'ic** *adj* **psy·cho'sis** *n, pl* **-ses** [-seez] severe mental disorder in which

person's contact with reality becomes distorted **psy·cho'tic** *adj, n* **psy·cho·so·mat'ic** [-sə-MAT-ik] *adj* of physical disorders thought to have psychological causes **psy·cho·ther'a·py** *n* treatment of disease by psychological, not physical, means

psych up [sik] *vt* prepare (oneself or another) psychologically for action, performance, etc

Pt *chemistry* platinum

ptar·mi·gan [TAHR-mi-gàn] *n* bird of grouse family that turns white in winter

PT boat small, fast naval vessel used primarily for torpedoing enemy shipping

pter·o·dac·tyl [ter-ə-DAK-til] *n* extinct flying reptile with large batlike wings

pto·maine [TOH-mayn] *n* any of kinds of poisonous alkaloid found in decaying matter

Pu *chemistry* plutonium

pu·ber·ty [PYOO-bər-tee] *n* sexual maturity

pu·bic [PYOO-bik] *adj* of the lower abdomen

pub·lic [PUB-lik] *adj* of or concerning the public as a whole; not private; open to general observation or knowledge; accessible to all; serving the people ▷ *n* the community or its members **pub·lic·ly** *adv* publicly **pub·lic re·la·tions** promotion of good relations of an organization or business with the general public **public school** local elementary school **public service** government employment **public spirit** interest in and devotion to welfare of community

pub·li·cist [PUB-lə-sist] *n* press agent; writer on public concerns

pub·lic'i·ty *n* process of attracting

public attention; attention thus gained **pub'li·cize** vt **-cized, -ciz·ing** give publicity to; bring to public notice

pub'lish vt prepare and issue for sale (books, music, etc); make generally known; proclaim **pub·li·ca'tion** [-KAY-shàn] n **pub'lish·er** n

puce [pyoos] adj, n purplish-brown (color)

puck[1] [puk] n hard rubber disk used instead of ball in ice hockey

puck[2] n mischievous sprite **puck'ish** adj

puck·er [PUK-àr] v gather into wrinkles ▷ n crease, fold

pud'ding [PUUD-ing] n thick, cooked dessert, often made from flour, milk, eggs, flavoring, etc

pud·dle [PUD-l] n small pool of water; rough cement for lining walls of canals, etc ▷ vt **-dled, -dling** line with puddle; make muddy **puddling** n method of converting pig iron to wrought iron by oxidizing the carbon

pu·den·dum [pyoo-DEN-dàm] n, pl **-da** [-dà] external genital organs, esp of a woman; vulva

pu·er·ile [PYOO-àr-il] adj childish; foolish; trivial

puff n short blast of breath, wind, etc; its sound; type of pastry; laudatory review or advertisement ▷ vi blow abruptly; breathe hard ▷ vt send out in a puff; blow out, inflate; advertise; smoke hard **puff'y** adj **puff·i·er, puff·i·est** short-winded; swollen **puff'ball** n ball-shaped fungus

puf'fin n sea bird with large brightly-colored beak

pug n small snub-nosed dog; sl boxer **pug nose** snub nose

pu·gi·list [PYOO-jà-list] n boxer **pu'gi·lism** n **pu·gi·lis'tic** adj

pug·na·cious [pug-NAY-shàs]

adj given to fighting **pug·nac'i·ty** [-NAS-i-tee] n

puke [pyook] sl vi **puked, puk·ing** vomit ▷ n vomit

pul·chri·tude [PUL-kri-tood] n beauty **pul·chri·tu'di·nous** adj

pull [puul] vt exert force on object to move it toward source of force; strain or stretch; tear; propel by rowing ▷ n act of pulling; force exerted by it; drink of liquor; inf power, influence **pull in** (of train) arrive; attract; sl arrest **pull off** inf carry through to successful issue **pull out** withdraw; extract; (of train) depart; (of car, etc) move away from side of road or move out to overtake **pull over** (of car, etc) drive to side of road and stop **pull someone's leg** make fun of **pull up** tear up; recover lost ground; improve; come to a stop; halt; reprimand

pul·let [PUUL-it] n young hen

pul·ley [PUUL-ee] n, pl **-leys** wheel with groove in rim for cord, used to raise weights by downward pull

Pull·man ® [PUUL-màn] n, pl **-mans** railroad sleeping car or parlor car

pull·o·ver [PUUL-oh-vàr] n sweater without fastening, to be pulled over head

pul·mo·nar·y [PUUL-mà-ner-ee] adj of lungs

pulp n soft, moist, vegetable or animal matter; flesh of fruit; any soft soggy mass ▷ vt reduce to pulp

pul·pit [PUUL-pit] n (enclosed) platform for preacher, minister, rabbi, etc

pul·sar [PUL-sahr] n small dense star emitting radio waves

pulse [puls] n movement of blood in arteries corresponding to heartbeat, discernible to touch, for example in the wrist; any regular beat or vibration **pul·sate** [PUL-sayt] vi **-sat·ed, -sat·ing** throb, quiver **pul·sa·tion** [-SAY-shən] n

pul·ver·ize [PUL-və-riz], **-ized, -iz·ing** reduce to powder; smash or demolish

pu·ma [PYOO-mə] n large Amer feline carnivore, cougar

pum·ice [PUM-is] n light porous variety of lava

pum·mel [PUM-əl] vt **-meled, -mel·ing** strike repeatedly with fists

pump[1] n appliance in which piston and handle are used for raising water, or putting in or taking out air or liquid, etc ▷ vt raise, put in, take out, etc with pump; empty by means of a pump; extract information from ▷ vi work pump; work like pump **pump iron** lift weights as exercise

pump[2] n light shoe

pump'kin n any of varieties of gourd, eaten esp as vegetable, in pie

pun n play on words ▷ vi **punned, pun·ning** make one **pun'ster** [-stər] n

punch[1] n tool for perforating or stamping; blow with fist; vigor ▷ vt stamp, perforate with punch; strike with fist **pull punches** punch lightly; inf lessen, withhold, criticism **punch-drunk** adj inf dazed, as by repeated blows

punch[2] n drink of spirits or wine with fruit juice, spice, etc

punc·til·i·ous [pungk-TIL-ee-əs] adj making much of details of etiquette; very exact, particular **punc·til'i·ous·ness** [-nis] n

punc·tu·al [PUNGK-choo-əl] adj in good time, not late, prompt **punc·tu·al'i·ty** n

punc·tu·ate [PUNGK-choo-ayt] vt **-at·ed, -at·ing** put in punctuation marks; interrupt at intervals; emphasize **punc·tu·a'tion** n

marks, such as commas and colons, put in writing to assist in making sense clear

punc·ture [PUNGK-chər] n small hole made by sharp object, esp in tire; act of puncturing ▷ vt **-tured, -tur·ing** prick hole in, perforate

pun'dit n self-appointed expert

pun·gent [PUN-jənt] adj biting; irritant; piercing; tart; caustic **pun'gen·cy** n

pun·ish vt cause to suffer for offense; inflict penalty on; use or treat roughly **pun·ish·a·ble** adj **pun·ish·ment** n **pu'ni·tive** [PYOO-ni-tiv] adj inflicting or intending to inflict punishment

punk adj, n inferior, rotten, worthless (person or thing); petty (hoodlum); (of) style of rock music

punt[1] n flat-bottomed square-ended boat, propelled by pushing with pole ▷ vt propel thus

punt[2] vt football kick ball before it touches ground, when let fall from hands ▷ n such a kick

punt[3] vi gamble, bet **punt'er** n one who punts; gambler

pu·ny [PYOO-nee] adj **-ni·er, -ni·est** small and feeble

pup n young of certain animals, such as dogs and seals

pu·pa [PYOO-pə] n, pl **-pas** stage between larva and adult in metamorphosis of insect, chrysalis **pu'pal** adj

pu·pil[1] [PYOO-pəl] n person being taught; opening in iris of eye

pup·pet [PUP-it] n small doll or figure of person, etc controlled by operator's hand **pup·pet·eer'** n **puppet show** show with puppets worked by hidden performer

pup·py [PUP-ee] n, pl **-pies** young dog

pur·chase [PUR-chəs] vt **-chased,**

-chas·ing buy ▷ n buying; what is bought; leverage; grip

pur·dah [PUR-də] n Muslim, Hindu custom of keeping women in seclusion; screen, veil to achieve this

pure [pyuur] adj pur·er, pur·est unmixed, untainted; simple; spotless; faultless; innocent; concerned with theory only pure·ly adv pu·ri·fi·ca·tion n pu·ri·fy vt -fied, -fy·ing make, become pure, clear or clean pur·ism n excessive insistence on correctness of language pur·ist n pu·ri·ty n state of being pure

pu·rée [pyuu-RAY] n pulp, soup, of cooked fruit or vegetables put through sieve, etc ▷ vt -réed, -rée·ing

pur·ga·to·ry [PUR-gə-tor-ee] n -ries place or state of torment, pain or distress, esp temporary

purge [purj] vt purged, purg·ing make clean, purify; remove, get rid of; clear out ▷ n act, process of purging; removal of undesirable members from political party, army, etc pur·ga·tive [-gə-tiv] adj, n

Pu·ri·tan [PYUUR-i-tn] n history member of extreme Protestant party; (p-) person of extreme strictness in morals or religion pu·ri·tan·i·cal adj strict in the observance of religious and moral duties; overscrupulous pu·ri·tan·ism n

purl n stitch that forms ridge in knitting ▷ vi knit in purl

pur·loin [pər-LOIN] vt steal; pilfer

pur·ple [PUR-pəl] n, adj -pler, -plest (of) color between crimson and violet

pur·port [pər-PORT] vt claim to be (true, etc); signify; imply ▷ n [PUR-port] meaning; apparent meaning; significance

pur·pose [PUR-pəs] n reason, object; design; aim, intention ▷ vt -posed, -pos·ing intend pur·pose·ly adv on purpose intentionally

purr n pleased noise that cat makes ▷ vi utter this

purse [purs] n small bag for money; handbag; resources; money as prize ▷ v pursed, purs·ing ▷ vt pucker in wrinkles ▷ vi become wrinkled and drawn in purs·er n ship's officer who keeps accounts

pur·sue [pər-SOO] v -sued, -su·ing ▷ vt run after; chase; aim at; engage in; continue; follow ▷ vi go in pursuit; continue pur·su·ance [-əns] n carrying out pur·su·ant [-ənt] adv accordingly pur·su·er n pur·suit [-SOOT] n running after, attempt to catch; occupation

pu·ru·lent adj see PUS

pur·vey [pər-VAY] vt supply (provisions) pur·vey·or n

pur·view [PUR-vyoo] n scope, range

pus n yellowish matter produced by suppuration pu·ru·lence [PYUUR-ə-ləns] n pu·ru·lent adj forming, discharging pus; septic

push [puush] vt move, try to move away by pressure; drive or impel; sl sell (esp narcotic drugs) illegally ▷ vi make thrust; advance with steady effort ▷ n thrust; persevering self-assertion; big military advance push·er n push·y adj push·i·er, push·i·est given to pushing oneself

pu·sil·lan·i·mous [pyoo-sə-LAN-ə-məs] adj cowardly pu·sil·la·nim·i·ty [-lə-NIM-ə-tee] n

puss [puus], pus·sy n, pl -ses, -sies inf cat

puss·y·foot [PUUS-ee-fuut] vi move stealthily; act indecisively, procrastinate

pus·tule [PUS-chuul] *n* pimple containing pus

put [puut] *vt* **put, put·ting** place; set; express; throw (esp shot) ▷ *n* throw **put across** express, carry out successfully **put off** postpone; disconcert; repel **put up** erect; accommodate; nominate

pu·ta·tive [PYOO-tə-tiv] *adj* reputed, supposed

pu·trid [PYOO-trid] *adj* decomposed; rotten **pu·tre·fy** [-trə-fī] *v* **-fied, -fy·ing** make or become rotten **pu·tre·fac·tion** *n* **pu·tres·cent** [-ənt] *adj* becoming rotten

putsch [puuch] *n* surprise attempt to overthrow the existing power, political revolt

putt [put] *vt* strike (golf ball) along ground in direction of hole **putt·er** *n* golf club for putting; person who putts

put·ter [PUT-ər] *vi* work, act in feeble, unsystematic way

put·ty [PUT-ee] *n, pl* **-ties** paste of ground chalk and oil as used by glaziers ▷ *vt* **-tied, -ty·ing** fix, fill with putty

puz·zle [PUZ-əl] *v* **-zled, -zling** perplex or be perplexed ▷ *n* bewildering, perplexing question, problem or toy **puz·zle·ment** *n*

pyg·my, pig·my [PIG-mee] *n, pl* **-mies** abnormally undersized person; (**P-**) member of one of dwarf peoples of Equatorial Africa ▷ *adj* undersized

py·lon [PĪ-lon] *n* post, tower, esp for guiding aviators; steel tower for supporting power lines

py·or·rhe·a [pī-ə-REE-ə] *n* inflammation of the gums with discharge of pus and loosening of teeth

pyr·a·mid [PIR-ə-mid] *n* solid figure with sloping sides meeting at apex; structure of this shape, esp ancient Egyptian; group of persons or things arranged, organized, like pyramid **py·ram'i·dal** *adj*

pyre [pīr] *n* pile of wood for burning a dead body

py·ri·tes [pi-RĪ-teez] *n, pl* **py·ri·tes** sulfide of a metal, esp iron pyrites

py·ro·ma·ni·ac [pī-rə-MAY-nee-ak] *n* person with uncontrollable desire to set things on fire

py·rom·e·ter [pī-ROM-i-tər] *n* instrument for measuring very high temperature

py·ro·tech·nics [pī-rə-TEK-niks] *n* manufacture, display of fireworks

Pyr·rhic victory [PIR-ik] one won at too high cost

py·thon [PĪ-thon] *n* large nonpoisonous snake that crushes its prey

pyx [piks] *n* vessel in which consecrated Host is preserved

q

Q.E.D. which was to be shown or proved

qua [kway] *prep* in the capacity of

quack [kwak] *n* harsh cry of duck; pretender to medical or other skill ▷ *vi* (of duck) utter cry

quadr-, quadri- *comb form* four: quadrilateral

quad·ran·gle [KWOD-rang-gəl] *n* four-sided figure; four-sided courtyard in a building **quad·ran·gu·lar** [-gyə-lər] *adj*

quad·rant [KWOD-rənt] *n* quarter of circle; instrument for taking angular measurements **quad·rat·ic** *adj* of equation, involving square of unknown quantity

quad·ra·phon·ic [kwod-rə-FON-ik] *adj* of a sound system using four independent speakers

quad·ri·lat·er·al [kwod-rə-LAT-ər-əl] *adj* four-sided ▷ *n* four-sided figure

quad·rille [kwo-DRIL] *n* square dance; music played for it

quad·ril·lion [kwo-DRIL-yən] *n* cardinal number of 1 followed by 15 zeros

quad·ru·man·ous [kwo-DROO-mə-nəs] *adj* of apes, etc having four feet that can be used as hands

quad·ru·ped [KWOD-ruu-ped] *n* four-footed animal

quad·ru·ple [kwo-DROO-pəl] *adj* fourfold ▷ *v* **-pled, -pling** make, become four times as much **quad·ru·pli·cate** [-kit] *adj* fourfold

quad·ru·plet [kwo-DRUP-lit] *n* one of four offspring born at one birth

quaff [kwof] *v* drink heartily or in one swallow

quag·mire [KWAG-mir] *n* bog, swamp

quail[1] [kwayl] *n* small bird of partridge family

quail[2] *vi* flinch; cower

quaint [kwaynt] *adj* **-er, -est** interestingly old-fashioned or odd; curious; whimsical **quaint'ness** [-nis] *n*

quake [kwayk] *vi* **quaked, quak·ing** shake, tremble

Quak·er [KWAY-kər] *n* member of Christian sect, the **Society of Friends**

qual·i·fy [KWOL-ə-fī] *v* **-fied, -fy·ing** make oneself competent; moderate; limit; make competent; ascribe quality to; describe **qual·i·fi·ca'tion** *n* thing that qualifies; attribute; restriction; qualifying

qual·i·ty [KWOL-i-tee] *n*, *pl* **-ties** attribute, characteristic, property; degree of excellence; rank **qual'i·ta·tive** *adj* depending on quality

qualm [kwahm] *n* misgiving; sudden feeling of sickness, nausea

quan·da·ry [KWAN-dree] *n*, *pl* **-ries** state of perplexity, puzzling situation, dilemma

quan·ti·ty [KWON-ti-tee] *n*, *pl* **-ties** size, number, amount; specified or considerable amount

quan·ti·fy [-fī] vt **-fied, -fy·ing** discover, express quantity of

quan·ti·ta·tive adj **quan'tum** [-təm] n, pl **-ta** [-tə] desired or required amount **quantum leap, jump** inf sudden large change, increase, or advance **quantum theory** theory that in radiation, energy of electrons is discharged not continuously but in discrete units, or quanta

quar·an·tine [KWOR-ən-teen] n isolation to prevent spreading of infection ▷ vt **-tined, -tin·ing** put, keep in quarantine

quark [kwork] n physics any of several hypothetical particles thought to be fundamental units of matter

quar·rel [KWOR-əl] n angry dispute; argument ▷ vi **-reled, -rel·ing** argue; find fault with **quar'rel·some** [-səm] adj

quar·ry¹ [KWOR-ee] n, pl **-ries** object of hunt or pursuit; prey

quarry² n, pl **-ries** excavation where stone, etc is obtained from ground for building, etc ▷ v **-ried, -ry·ing** get from quarry

quart [kwort] n liquid measure, quarter of gallon or 2 pints (0.964 liter)

quar·ter [KWOR-tər] n fourth part; 25 cents; region, district; mercy ▷ pl lodgings ▷ vt divide into quarters; lodge **quar'ter·ly** adj happening, due, etc each quarter of year ▷ n, pl **-lies** quarterly periodical **quar·tet'** n group of four musicians; music for four performers **quar'to** n, pl **-tos** size of book in which sheets are folded into four leaves ▷ adj of this size **quar'ter·deck** n after part of upper deck used esp for official, ceremonial purposes **quarter horse** small, powerful breed of horse bred

for short races **quar'ter·mas·ter** n officer responsible for quarters, clothing, etc

quartz [kworts] n stone of pure crystalline silica **quartz'ite** [-īt] n quartz rock **quartz timepiece** watch or clock operated by a vibrating quartz crystal

qua·sar [KWAY-zahr] n extremely distant starlike object emitting powerful radio waves

quash [kwosh] vt annul; reject; subdue forcibly

quasi- [KWAY-zī] comb form seemingly, resembling but not actually being: quasi-scientific

quat·er·nar·y [KWOT-ər-ner-ee] adj of the number four; having four parts; **(Q-)** geology of most recent period after Tertiary

quat·rain [KWO-trayn] n four-line stanza, esp rhymed alternately

qua·ver [KWAY-vər] n say or sing in quavering tones ▷ vi tremble, shake, vibrate ▷ n musical note half length of crotchet; quavering trill

quay [kee] n solid, fixed landing stage; wharf

quea·sy [KWEE-zee] adj **-si·er, -si·est** inclined to, or causing, sickness

queen [kween] n king's wife; female ruler; piece in chess; fertile female bee, wasp, etc; playing card with picture of a queen, ranking between king and jack; sl offens male homosexual **queen'ly** adj **-li·er, -li·est**

queer [kweer] adj **-er, -est** odd, strange; sl usu offens homosexual ▷ n sl usu offens homosexual ▷ vt spoil; interfere with

quell [kwel] vt crush, put down; allay; pacify

quench [kwench] vt slake; extinguish, put out, suppress

quer·u·lous [KWER-ə-ləs] *adj* fretful, peevish, whining

que·ry [KWEER-ee] *n, pl* **-ries** question; mark of interrogation ▷ *vt* **-ried, -ry·ing** question

quest [kwest] *n, vi* search

ques·tion [KWES-chən] *n* sentence seeking for answer; that which is asked; interrogation; inquiry; problem; point for debate; debate, strife ▷ *vt* ask questions of, interrogate; dispute; doubt **ques·tion·a·ble** *adj* doubtful, esp not clearly true or honest **ques·tion·naire'** *n* list of questions drawn up for formal answer

queue [kyoo] *n* line of waiting persons, vehicles; sequence of computer tasks awaiting action ▷ *vi* **queued, queu·ing** (with *up*) wait in line; arrange computer tasks in queue

quib·ble [KWIB-əl] *n* trivial objection ▷ *v* **-bled, -bling** make this

quiche [keesh] *n* open pielike dish of cheese, etc on light pastry shell

quick [kwik] *adj* **-er, -est** rapid, swift; keen; brisk; hasty ▷ *n* part of body sensitive to pain; sensitive flesh **the quick** *obs* living people **quick·en** *v* make, become faster or more lively **quick'ie** *n inf* a quick drink, etc **quick'ly** *adv* **quick'sand** *n* loose wet sand easily yielding to pressure and engulfing persons, animals, etc **quick'silver** *n* mercury **quick-tempered** *adj* irascible

quid pro quo [KWID proh KWOH] *Lat* something given in exchange

qui·es·cent [kwee-ES-ənt] *adj* at rest, inactive, inert; silent **qui·es·cence** *n*

qui·et [KWI-it] *adj* **-er, -est** with little or no motion or noise; undisturbed; not showy or obtrusive ▷ *n* state of peacefulness, absence of noise or disturbance ▷ *v* make, become quiet **qui'et·ly** *adv* **qui·e·tude** *n*

quill [kwil] *n* large feather; hollow stem of this; pen, plectrum made from feather; spine of porcupine

quilt [kwilt] *n* padded coverlet ▷ *vt* stitch (two pieces of cloth) with pad between

quince [kwins] *n* acid pear-shaped fruit; tree bearing it

qui·nine [KWI-nīn] *n* bitter drug made from bark of tree, used to treat fever, and as mixer

quin·quen·ni·al [kwin-KWEN-ee-əl] *adj* occurring once in, or lasting, five years

quin·sy [KWIN-zee] *n* inflammation of throat or tonsils

quint [kwint] *n* short for **QUINTUPLET**

quin·tes·sence [kwin-TES-əns] *n* purest form, essential feature; embodiment **quin·tes·sen'tial** [-tə-SEN-shəl] *adj*

quin·tet [kwin-TET] *n* set of five singers or players; composition for five voices or instruments

quin·tu·plet [kwin-TUP-lit] *n* one of five offspring born at one birth

quip [kwip] *n, v* **quipped, quip·ping** (utter) witty saying

quire [kwīr] *n* 24 sheets of writing paper

quirk [kwurk] *n* individual peculiarity of character; unexpected twist or turn

quis·ling [KWIZ-ling] *n* traitor who aids occupying enemy force

quit [kwit] *v* **quit** or **quit·ted, quit·ting** stop doing a thing; depart; leave, go away from; cease from ▷ *adj* free, rid **quits** *adj* on equal or even terms by repayment, etc **quit'tance** *n*

[KWIT-ns] *n* discharge; receipt
quit'ter one lacking perseverance
quite [kwīt] *adv* wholly, completely;
very considerably; somewhat, rather
▷ *interj* exactly, just so
quiv•er[1] [KWIV-ər] *vi* shake or
tremble ▷ *n* quivering; vibration
quiver[2] *n* carrying case for arrows
quix•ot•ic [kwik-SOT-ik] *adj*
unrealistically and impractically
optimistic, idealistic, chivalrous
quiz [kwiz] *n, pl* **quiz•zes**
entertainment in which general
or specific knowledge of players is
tested by questions; examination,
interrogation ▷ *vt* **quizzed,**
quiz•zing question, interrogate
quiz'zi•cal *adj* questioning;
mocking
quoit [kwoit] *n* ring for throwing
at peg as a game ▷ *pl* the game in
which quoits are tossed at a stake in

the ground in attempts to encircle it
quo•rum [KWOR-əm] *n* least
number that must be present in
meeting to make its transactions
valid
quo•ta [KWOH-tə] *n* share to be
contributed or received; specified
number, quantity, that may be
imported or admitted
quote [kwoht] *vt* **quot•ed,**
quot•ing copy or repeat passages
from; refer to, esp to confirm view;
state price for **quot'a•ble** *adj*
quo•ta'tion *n*
quoth [kwohth] *v obs* said
quo•tid•i•an [kwoh-TID-ee-ən] *adj*
daily; everyday, commonplace
quo•tient [KWOH-shənt] *n*
number resulting from dividing one
number by another
q.v. which see: used to refer a reader
to another item in the same book

r

Ra *chemistry* radium

rab·bet [RAB-it] *n* recess, groove cut into piece of timber to join with matching piece ▷ *vt* **-bet·ed, -bet·ing** cut rabbet in

rab·bi [RAB-i] *n, pl* **-bis** Jewish learned man, spiritual leader, teacher **rab·bin·i·cal** *adj*

rab·bit *n* small burrowing rodent like hare ▷ *vi* hunt rabbits **rabbit punch** sharp blow to back of neck; *see* **RAREBIT**

rab·ble [RAB-əl] *n* crowd of vulgar, noisy people; mob

rab·id *adj* relating to or having rabies; furious; mad; fanatical

ra·bies [RAY-beez] *n* acute infectious viral disease transmitted by dogs, etc

rac·coon [ra-KOON] *n* small N Amer mammal

race¹ [rays] *n* contest of speed, as in running, swimming, etc; contest, rivalry; strong current of water, esp leading to water wheel ▷ *v* meeting for horse racing ▷ *v* **raced, rac·ing** ▷ *vt* cause to run rapidly ▷ *vi* run swiftly; of engine, pedal, etc, to move rapidly and erratically, esp on removal of resistance **rac·er** *n* person, vehicle, animal that races

race² *n* group of people of common ancestry with distinguishing physical features (skin color, etc); species; type **ra·cial** [RAY-shəl] *adj* **rac·ism** *n* belief in innate superiority of particular race; antagonism toward members of different race based on this belief **rac·ist** *adj, n*

rack¹ [rak] *n* framework for displaying or holding baggage, books, hats, bottles, etc; *mechanics* straight bar with teeth on its edge, to work with pinion; instrument of torture by stretching ▷ *vt* stretch on rack or wheel; torture; stretch, strain **rack·ing** *adj* agonizing (pain)

rack² *n* **rack and ruin** destruction

rack³ *n* neck or rib section of mutton, lamb, pork

rack·et¹ [RAK-it] *n* loud noise, uproar; occupation by which money is made illegally **rack·et·eer** [rak-i-TEER] *n* one making illegal profits **rack·et·y** *adj* noisy

rack·et², rac·quet [RAK-it] *n* bat used in tennis, etc ▷ *pl* ball game played in paved, walled court

rac·on·teur [rak-ən-TUR] *n* skilled storyteller

racquet *see* **RACKET²**

rac·y [RAY-see] *adj* **rac·i·er, rac·i·est** spirited; lively; having strong flavor; spicy; piquant **rac·i·ly** *adv* **rac·i·ness** *n*

ra·dar [RAY-dahr] *n* device for finding range and direction by ultrahigh frequency point-to-point radio waves, which reflect back to their source and reveal position and nature of objects sought

radial *see* **RADIUS**

ra·di·ate [RAY-dee-ayt] *v* **-at·ed, -at·ing** emit, be emitted in rays; spread out from center **ra·di·ance**

[-əns] n brightness; splendor
ra·di·ant [-ənt] adj beaming;
shining; emitting rays **ra·di·a·tion**
n transmission of heat, light, etc
from one body to another; particles,
rays, emitted in nuclear decay; act of
radiating **ra·di·a·tor** n that which
radiates, esp heating apparatus
for rooms; cooling apparatus of
automobile engine
rad·i·cal [RAD-i-kəl] adj
fundamental, thorough; extreme;
of root ▷ n person of extreme
(political) views; number expressed
as root of another; group of atoms
of several elements that remain
unchanged in a series of chemical
compounds
ra·di·o [RAY-dee-oh] n, pl **-di·os**
use of electromagnetic waves for
broadcasting, communication,
etc; device for receiving, amplifying
radio signals; broadcasting, content
of radio program ▷ vt **-di·oed,**
-di·o·ing transmit message, etc
by radio
radio- comb form of rays, of
radiation, of radium: *radiology*
ra·di·o·ac·tive [ray-dee-oh-
AK-tiv] adj emitting invisible
rays that penetrate matter
ra·di·o·ac·tiv·i·ty n
ra·di·og·ra·phy [ray-dee-OG-rə-
fee] n production of image on film or
plate by radiation
ra·di·ol·o·gy [ray-dee-OL-ə-jee]
n science of use of rays in medicine
ra·di·ol·o·gist n
ra·di·o·ther·a·py [ray-dee-
oh-THER-ə-pee] n diagnosis and
treatment of disease by x-rays
rad·ish n pungent root vegetable
ra·di·um [RAY-dee-əm] n
radioactive metallic element
ra·di·us [RAY-dee-əs] n, pl **-di·i**
[-dee-ī] straight line from center to

circumference of circle; outer of two
bones in forearm **ra·di·al** [-əl] adj
arranged like radii of circle; of ray or
rays; of radius
ra·dome [RAY-dohm] n dome-
shaped housing for radar
ra·don [RAY-don] n radioactive
gaseous element
raf·fi·a [RAF-fee-ə] n prepared
palm fiber for making mats, etc
raff·ish adj disreputable
raf·fle [RAF-əl] n lottery in which
an article is assigned by lot to one
of those buying tickets ▷ vt **-fled,**
-fling dispose of by raffle
raft n floating structure of logs,
planks, etc
raf·ter [RAF-tər] n one of the main
beams of a roof
raft·ing [RAF-ting] n sport of
traveling on rivers by raft **raft·er** n
participant in this
rag¹ n fragment of cloth; torn
piece; *inf* newspaper, etc, esp
one considered worthless; piece
of ragtime music ▷ pl tattered
clothing **rag·ged** [RAG-id] adj
shaggy; torn; clothed in torn clothes;
lacking smoothness **rag·bag** n
confused assortment **rag·time** n
style of jazz piano music
rag² vt ragged, rag·ging tease;
torment; play practical jokes on
rag·a·muf·fin [RAG-ə-muf-in] n
ragged, dirty person or child
rage [rayj] n violent anger or
passion; fury; aggressive behavior
associated with a certain activity,
eg, road rage ▷ vi **raged, rag·ing**
speak, act with fury; proceed
violently and without check (as
storm, battle, etc); be widely and
violently prevalent **all the rage**
very popular
rag·lan [RAG-lən] adj of sleeves
that continue to the neck so that

there are no shoulder seams

ra·gout [ra-GOO] n highly seasoned stew of meat and vegetables

raid [rayd] n rush, attack; foray ▷ vt make raid on

rail¹ [rayl] n horizontal bar, esp as part of fence, track, etc; sl line of cocaine for sniffing **rail'ing** n fence, barrier made of rails supported by posts **rail'head** [-hed] n farthest point to which railway line extends **rail'road, rail'way** n track of steel rails on which trains run; company operating railroad

rail² vi utter abuse; scoff; scold; reproach **rail'er·y** [-ə-ree] n, pl **-ler·ies** banter

rail³ n any of kinds of marsh birds

rai·ment [RAY-mənt] n clothing

rain [rayn] n moisture falling in drops from clouds; fall of such drops ▷ vi fall as rain ▷ vt pour down like rain **rain'y** adj **rain·i·er, rain·i·est rain'bow** [-boh] n arch of prismatic colors in sky **rain'coat** n light water-resistant overcoat

raise [rayz] vt **raised, rais·ing** lift up; set up; build; increase; elevate; promote; heighten; as pitch of voice; breed into existence; levy, collect; end (siege) **raise Cain** [KAYN] be riotous, angry, etc

rai·sin [RAY-zin] n dried grape

rai·son d'ê·tre [RAY-zohn DE-trə] Fr reason or justification for existence

raj [rahj] n rule, sway, esp in India **ra'jah** n Indian prince or ruler

rake¹ [rayk] n tool with long handle and crosspiece with teeth for gathering hay, leaves, etc ▷ vt **raked, rak·ing** gather, smooth with rake; sweep, search over; sweep with shot **rake-off** n monetary commission, esp illegal

rake² n dissolute or dissipated man

rake³ n slope, esp backward, of ship's funnel, etc ▷ v **raked, rak·ing** incline from perpendicular **rak'ish** adj appearing dashing or speedy

ral·ly [RAL-ee] v **-lied, -ly·ing** bring together, esp what has been scattered, as routed army or dispersed troops; come together; regain health or strength, revive ▷ n act of rallying; assembly, esp outdoor, of any organization; tennis lively exchange of strokes

ram n male sheep; hydraulic machine; battering engine ▷ vt **rammed, ram·ming** force, drive; strike against with force; stuff; strike with ram

RAM [ram] computing random-access memory (as on a hard disk)

ram·ble [RAM-bəl] vi **-bled, -bling** walk without definite route; wander; talk incoherently; spread in random fashion ▷ n rambling walk **ram'bler** n climbing rose; one who rambles

ram·e·kin [RAM-i-kin] n small fireproof dish; food baked in it

ram·i·fy [RAM-ə-fī] v **-fied, -fy·ing** spread in branches, subdivide; become complex **ram·i·fi·ca'tion** n branch, subdivision; process of branching out; consequence

ra·mose [RAY-mōs] adj branching

ramp n gradual slope joining two level surfaces

ram·page [ram-PAYJ] vi **-paged, -pag·ing** dash about violently ▷ n [RAM-payj] angry or destructive behavior **ram·pa'geous** [-jəs] adj

ramp·ant [RAM-pənt] adj violent; rife; rearing

ram·part [RAM-pahrt] n mound, wall for defense

ram·shack·le [RAM-shak-əl] adj tumble-down, rickety, makeshift

ran pt of RUN

ranch n cattle farm ▷ vi manage one **ranch'er** n

ran·cid [RAN-sid] adj smelling or tasting offensive, like stale fat

ran·cor [RANG-kòr] n bitter, inveterate hate **ran'cor·ous** adj malignant; virulent

ran·dom [RAN-dàm] adj made or done by chance, without plan **at random** haphazardly(ly)

rang pt of RING²

range [raynj] n limits; row; scope; sphere; distance missile can travel; distance of mark shot at; place for shooting practice or rocket testing; rank; kitchen stove ▷ vt **ranged, rang·ing** ▷ vt set in row; classify; roam ▷ vi extend; roam; pass from one point to another; fluctuate (as prices) **rang'er** n official in charge of or patrolling park, etc **rang'y** adj **rang·i·er, rang·i·est** with long, slender limbs; spacious **range'find·er** n instrument for finding distance away of given object

rank¹ [rangk] n row, line; order; social class; status; relative place or position ▷ vt draw up in rank, classify ▷ vi have rank, place; have certain distinctions **the ranks** common soldiers **rank and file** (esp in labor unions) great mass or majority of people

rank² adj **-er, -est** growing too thickly, coarse; offensively strong; rancid; vile; flagrant **rank'ly** adv

ran·kle [RANG-kàl] vi **-kled, -kling** fester, continue to cause anger, resentment or bitterness

ran·sack [RAN-sak] vt search thoroughly; pillage, plunder

ran·som [RAN-sàm] n release from captivity by payment; amount paid ▷ vt pay ransom for

rant vi rave in violent, high-sounding language ▷ n noisy, boisterous speech; wild gaiety

rap¹ n smart slight blow; rhythmic monologue performed to music ▷ v **rapped, rap·ping** give rap to; utter abruptly; perform rhythmic monologue to music **rap'per** n singer of rap; person or thing that raps **take the rap** sl take blame, suffer punishment (for), whether guilty or not

rap² n **not care a rap** not care at all

ra·pa·cious [rà-PAY-shàs] adj greedy; grasping **ra·pac'i·ty** [-PAS-i-tee] n

rape [rayp] vt **raped, rap·ing** force (person) to submit unwillingly to sexual intercourse ▷ n act of raping; any violation or abuse **rap'ist** n

rap·id adj quick, swift **rapids** pl n part of river with fast, turbulent current **ra·pid'i·ty** n

ra·pi·er [RAY-pee-àr] n fine-bladed sword for thrusting only

rap·ine [RAP-in] n plunder

rap·port [ra-POR] n harmony, agreement

rap·proche·ment [rap-rohsh-MAHN] n reestablishment of friendly relations, esp between nations

rapt adj engrossed, spellbound **rap'ture** [-chàr] n ecstasy **rap'tur·ous** adj

rare¹ [rair] adj **rar·er, rar·est** uncommon; infrequent; of uncommon quality; of atmosphere, having low density, thin **rare'ly** adv seldom **rar'i·ty** n, pl **-ties** anything rare; rareness

rare² adj **rar·er, rar·est** (of meat) lightly cooked

rare·bit [RAIR-bit] n see WELSH RABBIT

rar·e·fy [RAIR-à-fī] v **-fied, -fy·ing** make, become thin, rare, or less dense; refine

rar·ing [RAIR-ing] *adj inf* enthusiastically willing, ready

ras·cal [RAS-kàl] *n* rogue; naughty (young) person **ras·cal'i·ty** [-KAL-i-tee] *n* roguery, baseness **ras'cal·ly** [-kàl-ee] *adj*

rash¹ *adj* **-er, -est** hasty, reckless, incautious

rash² *n* skin eruption; outbreak, series of (unpleasant) occurrences

rash·er [RASH-àr] *n* serving of bacon, usu three or four slices; thin slice of bacon or ham

rasp *n* harsh, grating noise; coarse file ▷ *v* scrape with rasp; make scraping noise; speak in grating voice; grate upon; irritate

rasp·ber·ry [RAZ-ber-ee] *n* red, juicy edible berry; plant which bears it; *inf* spluttering noise with tongue and lips to show contempt

Ras·ta·far·i·an [ras-tà-FAR-ee-àn] *n, adj* (member) of Jamaican cult regarding Haile Selassie, late emperor of Ethiopia, as the messiah

rat *n* small rodent; *sl* contemptible person, esp deserter, informer, etc ▷ *vi* **rat·ted, rat·ting** *sl* inform (on), betray, desert, abandon; hunt rats **rat'ty** *adj sl* **-ti·er, -ti·est** mean, ill-tempered, irritable **rat race** continual hectic competitive activity **rat'trap** *n* device for catching rats; dilapidated dwelling

ratch·et [RACH-it] *n* set of teeth on bar or wheel allowing motion in one direction only

rate¹ [rayt] *n* proportion between two things; charge; degree of speed, etc ▷ *vt* **rat·ed, rat·ing** value; estimate value of **rat'a·ble** *adj* that can be rated or appraised

rate² *vt* **rat·ed, rat·ing** scold, chide

rath·er [RATH-àr] *adv* to some extent; preferably; more willingly

rat·i·fy [RAT-à-fī] *vt* **-fied, -fy·ing**
confirm **rat·i·fi·ca'tion** [-fi-KAY-shàn] *n*

rat·ing [RAY-ting] *n* credit standing; fixing a rate; classification, esp of ship, enlisted member of armed forces; angry rebuke

ra·tio [RAY-shoh] *n, pl* **-tios** proportion; quantitative relation

ra·ti·oc·i·nate [rash-ee-OS-à-nayt] *vi* **-nat·ed, -nat·ing** reason **ra·ti·oc·i·na'tion** [-NAY-shàn] *n*

ra·tion [RASH-àn] *n* fixed allowance of food, etc ▷ *vt* supply with, limit to certain amount

ra·tion·al [RASH-à-nl] *adj* reasonable, sensible; capable of thinking, reasoning **ra·tion·ale'** [-NAL] *n* reasons given for actions, etc **ra'tion·al·ism** *n* philosophy that regards reason as only guide or authority **ra·tion·al'i·ty** *n* **ra·tion·al·i·za'tion** *n* **ra'tion·al·ize** *vt* **-ized, -iz·ing** justify by plausible reasoning; reorganize to improve efficiency, etc

rat·tan [ra-TAN] *n* climbing palm with jointed stems; cane of this oft used for furniture

rat·tle [RAT-l] *v* **-tled, -tling** ▷ *vi* give out succession of short sharp sounds; clatter ▷ *vt* shake briskly causing a sharp clatter of sounds; confuse, fluster ▷ *n* such sound; instrument for making it; set of horny rings in rattlesnake's tail **rat'tle·snake** *n* poisonous snake

rau·cous [RAW-kàs] *adj* hoarse; harsh

raun·chy [RAWN-chee] *adj inf* **-chi·er, -chi·est** earthy, vulgar, sexy; slovenly

rav·age [RAV-ij] *vt* **-aged, -ag·ing** lay waste, plunder ▷ *n* destruction

rave [rayv] *vi* **raved, rav·ing** talk wildly in delirium or enthusiastically ▷ *n*

rav·el [RAV-əl] vt **-eled, -el·ing** entangle; fray out; disentangle

ra·ven[1] [RAY-vən] n black bird like crow ▷ adj shiny black

raven[2] v seek prey, plunder

rav·en·ous [RAV-ə-nəs] adj very hungry

ra·vine [rə-VEEN] n narrow steep-sided valley worn by stream, gorge

ra·vi·o·li [rav-ee-OH-lee] pl n small, thin pieces of dough filled with highly seasoned, chopped meat and cooked

rav·ish vt enrapture; commit rape upon **rav·ish·ing** adj lovely, entrancing

raw adj **-er, -est** uncooked; not manufactured or refined; skinned; inexperienced, unpracticed, as recruits; sensitive; chilly **raw deal** unfair or dishonest treatment **raw·hide** n untanned hide; whip of this

ray[1] n single line or narrow beam of light, heat, etc; any of set of radiating lines ▷ vi come out in rays; radiate

ray[2] n marine fish, often very large, with winglike pectoral fins and whiplike tail

ray·on n (fabric of) synthetic fiber

raze [rayz] vt **razed, raz·ing** destroy completely; wipe out, delete; level

ra·zor [RAY-zər] n sharp instrument for shaving or for cutting hair

Rb chemistry rubidium

re[1] [ray] n second sol-fa note

re[2] prep with reference to, concerning

Re chemistry rhenium

re- prefix again: re-enter; retrial

reach [reech] vt arrive at; extend; succeed in touching; attain to ▷ vi stretch out hand; extend ▷ n act of reaching; power of touching; grasp;

scope; range; straight stretch of river between two bends

re·act [ree-AKT] vi act in return, opposition or toward former state

re·ac·tance [-əns] n electricity resistance in coil, apart from ohmic resistance, due to current reacting on itself **re·ac·tion** [-AK-shən] n any action resisting another; counter or backward tendency; response; chemical or nuclear change, combination or decomposition **re·ac·tion·ar·y** n, adj, pl **-ar·ies** (person) opposed to change, esp in politics, etc **re·ac·tive** adj chemically active **re·ac·tor** n apparatus in which nuclear reaction is maintained and controlled to produce nuclear energy

read [reed] v **read** [red] **read·ing** ▷ vt look at and understand written or printed matter; learn by reading; interpret mentally; read and utter; interpret; study; understand any indicating instrument; (of instrument) register ▷ vi be occupied in reading; find mentioned in reading **read·a·ble** adj that can be read, or read with pleasure **read·er** n one who reads; university professor's assistant; school textbook; one who reads manuscripts submitted to publisher

re·ad·just v adapt to a new situation **re·ad·just·ment** n

re·ad·mit vt **-mitting, -mitted** let (person, country, etc) back in to a place or organization

read·y [RED-ee] adj **read·i·er, read·i·est** prepared for use or action; willing; prompt **read·i·ly** adv promptly; willingly **read·i·ness** [-nis] n

re·a·gent [ree-AY-jənt] n chemical substance that reacts with another and is used to detect presence of the other

re·al [REE-əl] *adj* existing in fact; happening; actual; genuine; (of property) consisting of land and houses **re·al·ism** *n* regarding things as they are; artistic treatment with this outlook **re·al·is·tic** *adj* **re·al·i·ty** [ri-AL-i-tee] *n* real existence **re·al·ly** *adv* **re·al·ty** *n* real estate **real estate** landed property

re·al·ize [REE-ə-liz] *vt* -ized, -iz·ing apprehend, grasp significance of; make real; convert into money **re·al·i·za·tion** *n*

realm [relm] *n* kingdom, province, domain, sphere

ream¹ [reem] *n* twenty quires or 500 sheets of paper ▷ *pl* large quantity of written matter

ream² *vt* enlarge, bevel out, as in metal **ream·er** *n* tool for this

reap [reep] *v* cut and gather harvest; receive as fruit of previous activity **reap·er** *n*

re·ap·pear *vi* appear again **re·ap·pear·ance** *n*

rear¹ [reer] *n* back part; part of army, procession, etc behind others **rear admiral** lowest flag rank in certain navies **rear·guard** *n* troops protecting rear of army **rear·most** [-mohst] *adj*

rear² *vt* care for and educate (children); breed; erect ▷ *vi* rise, esp on hind feet

re·arm *v* arm again ▷ *vt* equip (army, nation, etc) with better weapons **re·ar·ma·ment** *n*

re·ar·range *vt* organize differently, alter **rearrangement** *n*

rea·son [REE-zən] *n* ground, motive; faculty of thinking; sanity; sensible or logical thought or view ▷ *vi* think logically in forming conclusions ▷ *vt* (usu with *with*) persuade by logical argument

into doing, etc **rea·son·a·ble** *adj* sensible, not excessive; suitable;

re·as·sure [ree-ə-SHUUR] *vt* -sured, -sur·ing restore confidence to

re·bate [REE-bayt] *n* discount, refund ▷ *vt* -bat·ed, -bat·ing deduct

re·bel [ri-BEL] *vi* -belled, -bel·ling revolt, resist lawful authority, take arms against ruling power ▷ *n* [REB-əl] one who rebels; insurgent ▷ *adj* [REB-əl] in rebellion **re·bel·lion** [ri-BEL-yən] *n* organized open resistance to authority, revolt **re·bel·lious** *adj*

re·birth *n* revival or renaissance **re·born** *adj* active again after a period of inactivity

re·boot *v* to shut down and then restart (a computer system)

re·bound [ri-BOWND] *vi* spring back; misfire, esp so as to hurt perpetrator (of plan, deed, etc) ▷ *n* [REE-bownd] act of springing back or recoiling; return

re·buff [ri-BUF] *n* blunt refusal; check ▷ *vt* repulse, snub

re·build *vt* -build·ing, -built build (building, town) again, after severe damage; develop (business, relationship, etc) again after destruction or damage

re·buke [ri-BYOOK] *vt* -buked, -buk·ing reprove, reprimand, find fault with ▷ *n*

re·bus [REE-bəs] *n, pl* -bus·es riddle in which names of things, etc are represented by pictures standing for syllables, etc

re·but [ri-BUT] *vt* -but·ted, -but·ting refute, disprove **re·but·tal** *n*

re·cal·ci·trant [ri-KAL-si-trənt] *adj, n* willfully disobedient (person)

re·call [ri-KAWL] vt recollect, remember; call, summon, order back; annul, cancel; revive, restore ▷ n [REE-kawl] summons to return; ability to remember

re·cant [ri-KANT] vt withdraw statement, opinion, etc **re·can·ta·tion** n

re·ca·pit·u·late [ree-kà-PICH-à-layt] vt -lat·ed, -lat·ing state again briefly; repeat

re·cap·ture vt experience again; capture again

re·cede [ri-SEED] vi -ced·ed, -ced·ing go back; become distant; slope backward; begin balding

re·ceipt [ri-SEET] n written acknowledgment of money received; receiving or being received ▷ vt acknowledge payment of in writing

re·ceive [ri-SEEV] vt -ceived, -ceiv·ing take, accept, get; experience; greet (guests) **re·ceiv·a·ble** adj **re·ceiv·er** n official appointed to receive money; fence, one who takes stolen goods knowing them to have been stolen; equipment in telephone, radio or TV that converts electrical signals into sound, light

re·cent [REE-sànt] adj that has lately happened; new **re·cent·ly** adv

re·cep·ta·cle [ri-SEP-tà-kàl] n vessel, place or space, to contain anything

re·cep·tion [ri-SEP-shàn] n receiving; manner of receiving; welcome; formal party; in broadcasting, quality of signals received **re·cep·tion·ist** n person who receives guests, clients, etc

re·cep·tive [ri-SEP-tiv] adj able, quick, willing to receive new ideas, suggestions, etc **re·cep·tiv·i·ty** n

re·cess [REE-ses] n niche, alcove; hollow; secret, hidden place; remission or suspension of business; vacation, holiday

re·ces·sion [ri-SESH-àn] n period of reduction in economic activity; act of receding **re·ces·sive** adj receding

re·ces·sion·al [ri-SESH-à-nl] n hymn sung while clergy retire

re·cher·ché [rà-SHAIR-shay] adj of studied elegance; exquisite; choice

re·cid·i·vist [ri-SID-à-vist] n one who relapses into crime

rec·i·pe [RES-à-pee] n directions for cooking a dish; prescription; expedient

re·cip·i·ent [ri-SIP-ee-ànt] adj that can or does receive ▷ n one who, that which receives

re·cip·ro·cal [ri-SIP-rà-kàl] adj complementary; mutual; moving backward and forward; alternating **re·cip·ro·cate** [-rà-kayt] v -cat·ed, -cat·ing ▷ vt give and receive mutually; return ▷ vi move backward and forward **rec·i·proc·i·ty** [res-à-PROS-i-tee] n

re·cite [ri-SĪT] vt -cit·ed, -cit·ing repeat aloud, esp to audience **re·cit·al** [-àl] n musical performance, usu by one person; act of reciting; narration of facts, etc; story; public entertainment of recitations, etc **rec·i·ta·tion** n recital, usu from memory, of poetry or prose; recountal **rec·i·ta·tive** [res-i-tà-TEEV] n musical declamation

reck·less [REK-lis] adj heedless, incautious

reck·on [REK-àn] v count; include; consider; inf think, deem; make calculations

re·claim [ri-KLAYM] vt make fit for cultivation; bring back; reform; demand the return of **rec·la·ma·tion** n

re·cline [ri-KLÌN] *vi* **-clined, -clin·ing** sit or lie back on one's side

rec·luse [REK-loos] *n* hermit ▷ *adj* [ri-KLOOS] living in seclusion, shut off from the world **re·clu·sive** *adj*

rec·og·nize [REK-əg-nìz] *vt* **-nized, -niz·ing** know again; treat as valid; notice, show appreciation of **rec·og·ni·tion** *n* **rec·og·niz·a·ble** *adj* **re·cog·ni·zance** [ri-KOG-nə-zəns] *n* avowal; bond by which person undertakes before court to observe some condition; *obs* recognition

re·coil [ri-KOIL] *vi* draw back in horror, etc; go wrong so as to hurt the perpetrator; rebound (esp of gun when fired) ▷ *n* [REE-koil] backward spring; retreat; recoiling

rec·ol·lect [rek-ə-LEKT] *vt* call back to mind, remember

rec·om·mend [rek-ə-MEND] *vt* advise, counsel; praise, commend; make acceptable **rec·om·men·da·tion** *n*

rec·om·pense [REK-əm-pens] *vt* **-pensed, -pens·ing** reward; compensate, make up for ▷ *n* compensation; reward; requital

rec·on·cile [REK-ən-sìl] *vt* **-ciled, -cil·ing** bring back into friendship; adjust, settle, harmonize **rec·on·cil·a·ble** *adj* **rec·on·cil·i·a·tion** *n*

rec·on·dite [REK-ən-dìt] *adj* obscure, abstruse, little known

re·con·di·tion [ree-kən-DISH-ən] *vt* restore to good condition, working order

re·con·noi·ter [ree-kə-NOI-tər] *vt* make preliminary survey of; survey position of enemy ▷ *vi* make reconnaissance **re·con·nais·sance** [ri-KON-ə-səns] *n* examination or survey for military or engineering purposes; scouting

re·con·sid·er *v* think about again, consider changing

re·con·sti·tute [ree-KON-sti-toot] *vt* **-tut·ed, -tut·ing** restore (food) to former state esp by addition of water to a concentrate

re·con·struct *v* rebuild; use evidence to re-create **re·con·struc·tion** *n*

re·cord [REK-ərd] *n* being recorded; document or other thing that records; disk with indentations that phonograph transforms into sound; best recorded achievement; known facts about person's past ▷ *v* [ri-KORD] preserve (sound, TV programs, etc) on plastic disk, magnetic tape, etc for reproduction on playback device ▷ *vt* put in writing; register **re·cord·er** *n* one who, that which records; type of flute **re·cord·ing** *n* process of making records from sound; something recorded, eg radio or TV program **record player** instrument for reproducing sound on disks **off the record** not for publication

re·count [ri-KOWNT] *vt* tell in detail

re·coup [ri-KOOP] *vt* recompense, compensate; recover what has been expended or lost

re·course [REE-kors] *n* (resorting to) source of help; *law* right of action or appeal

re·cov·er [ri-KUV-ər] *vt* regain, get back ▷ *vi* get back health **re·cov·er·y** *n, pl* **-er·ies**

re·cre·ate *v* make happen or exist again

rec·re·a·tion [rek-ree-AY-shən] *n* agreeable or refreshing occupation, relaxation, amusement **rec·re·a·tion·al** *adj*

recreational vehicle large vanlike vehicle equipped to be lived in

re·crim·i·nate [ri-KRIM-ə-nayt] *vi* **-nat·ed, -nat·ing** make countercharge or mutual accusation **re·crim·i·na'tion** *n* mutual abuse and blame

re·cru·desce [ree-kroo-DES] *vi* **-desced, -desc·ing** break out again **re·cru·des'cent** *adj*

re·cruit [ri-KROOT] *n* newly-enlisted soldier; one newly joining society, etc ▷ *vt* enlist fresh soldiers, etc

rec·tan·gle [REK-tang-gəl] *n* oblong four-sided figure with four right angles **rec·tang'u·lar** *adj* shaped thus

rec·ti·fy *vt* **-fied, -fy·ing** put right, correct, remedy, purify **rec·ti·fi·ca'tion** *n* act of setting right; *electricity* conversion of alternating current into direct current **rec'ti·fi·er** [-fi-ər] *n* person or thing that rectifies

rec·ti·lin·e·ar [rek-tl-IN-ee-ər] *adj* in straight line; characterized by straight lines

rec·ti·tude [REK-ti-tood] *n* moral uprightness; honesty of purpose

rec·to [REK-toh] *n, pl* **-tos** right-hand page of book, front of leaf

rec·tor [REK-tər] *n* member of clergy with care of parish; head of certain institutions, chiefly academic **rec'to·ry** *n* rector's house

rec·tum [REK-təm] *n* final section of large intestine **rec'tal** [-tl] *adj*

re·cum·bent [ri-KUM-bənt] *adj* lying down **re·cum'ben·cy** *n*

re·cu·per·ate [ri-KOO-pər-ayt] *v* **-at·ed, -at·ing** restore, be restored from illness, losses, etc; convalesce **re·cu·per·a'tion** *n*

re·cur [ri-KUR] *vi* **-curred, -cur·ring** happen again, return again and again; go or come back in mind **re·cur'rence** [-əns] *n*

repetition **re·cur'rent** [-ənt] *adj*

re·cy·cle [ree-SĪ-kəl] *vt* **-cled, -cling** reprocess a manufactured substance for use again; reuse

red *adj* of color varying from crimson to orange and seen in blood, rubies, glowing fire, etc ▷ *n* the color; communist **red'den** *v* make red; become red; flush **red'dish** *adj* **red-blood·ed** [-blud-id] *adj* vigorous; virile **red'coat** *n* in American Revolution, a British soldier **red flag** danger signal **red-hand·ed** *adj* (caught) in the act **red herring** topic introduced to divert attention from main issue **red-hot** red with heat; creating excitement **red state** US state with a majority of Republican voters **red tape** excessive adherence to official rules **red'wood** [-wuud] *n* giant coniferous tree of California **in the red** operating at loss; in debt **see red** *inf* be very angry

re·deem [ri-DEEM] *vt* buy back; set free; free from sin; make up for **re·demp·tion** [-DEM-shən] *n* **re·deem'a·ble** *adj* **The Re·deem·er** Jesus Christ

re·de·vel·op *v* rebuild or renovate (an area or building) **re·de·vel'op·ment** *n*

red·o·lent [RED-l-ənt] *adj* smelling strongly, fragrant; reminiscent (of) **red'o·lence** *n*

re·dou·ble [ree-DUB-əl] *v* **-bled, -bling** increase, multiply, intensify; double a second time

re·doubt [ri-DOWT] *n* detached outwork in fortifications

re·doubt·a·ble [ri-DOWT-ə-bəl] *adj* dreaded, formidable

re·dound [ri-DOWND] *vt* contribute (to); recoil

re·dress [ri-DRES] *vt* set right; make amends for ▷ *n* [REE-dres]

re·duce [ri-DOOS] *vt* **-duced,**
-duc·ing bring down, lower;
lessen, weaken; bring by force or
necessity to some state or action;
slim; simplify; dilute; *chemistry*
separate substance from others with
which it is combined **re·duc'i·ble**
adj **re·duc'tion** [-DUK-shən] *n*
reducing agent substance used
to deoxidize or lessen density of
another substance

re·dun·dant [ri-DUN-dənt] *adj*
superfluous **re·dun'dan·cy** *n*

re·ech'o *v* **-ech·o·ing, -ech·oed**
echo over and over again, resound

reed *n* various marsh or water
plants; tall straight stem of one;
music vibrating cane or metal strip
of certain wind instruments **reed'y**
adj **reed·i·er, reed·i·est** full of
reeds; like reed instrument, harsh
and thin in tone

reef *n* ridge of rock or coral near
surface of sea; vein of ore; part of
sail that can be rolled up to reduce
area ▷ *vt* take in a reef of **reef'er**
n sailor's close-fitting jacket; *sl*
marijuana cigarette

reek *n* strong (unpleasant) smell
▷ *vi* emit fumes; smell

reel *n* spool on which film is wound;
motion pictures portion of film;
winding apparatus; bobbin; thread
wound on this; lively dance; music
for it; act of staggering ▷ *vt* wind on
reel; draw (in) by means of reel ▷ *vi*
stagger, sway, rock **reel off** recite,
write fluently, quickly

re·fec·to·ry [ri-FEK-tə-ree] *n,*
pl **-ries** dining room in monastery,
college, etc **re·fec'tion** *n* a meal

re·fer [ri-FUR] *v* **-ferred, -fer·ring**
▷ *vi* relate (to), allude ▷ *vt* send to
for information; trace, ascribe to;
submit for decision **re·fer'ral** *n* act,

instance of referring **ref·er·ee'**
n arbitrator; person willing to
whom scientific paper, etc is sent
for judgment of its quality, etc;
umpire ▷ *v* **-eed, -ee·ing** act as
referee **ref'er·ence** [-ins] *n* act
of referring; citation or direction
in book; appeal to judgment of
another; testimonial; one to whom
inquiries as to character, etc may be
made **ref·er·en'dum** *n, pl* **-da** [-də]
submitting of question to electorate

re·fill' *v* fill again ▷ *n* second or
subsequent filling; replacement
supply of something in a permanent
container

re·fine [ri-FIN] *vt* **-fined, -fin·ing**
purify **re·fine'ment** *n* subtlety;
improvement, elaboration;
fineness of feeling, taste or manners
re·fin'er·y *n, pl* **-er·ies** place for
refining sugar, oil, etc

re·fla·tion [ri-FLAY-shən] *n*
(steps taken to produce) increase in
economic activity of country, etc

re·flect [ri-FLEKT] *vt* throw back,
esp rays of light; cast (discredit, etc)
upon ▷ *vi* meditate **re·flec'tion**
[-FLEK-shən] *n* act of reflecting;
return of rays of heat, light, or
waves of sound from surface;
image of object given back by
mirror, etc; conscious thought;
meditation; expression of thought
re·flec'tive *adj* meditative, quiet,
contemplative; throwing back
images **re·flec'tor** *n* polished
surface for reflecting light, etc

re·flex [REE-fleks] *n* reflex
action; reflected image; reflected
light, color, etc ▷ *adj* (of muscular
action) involuntary; reflected; bent
back **re·flex·ive** [ri-FLEK-siv] *adj*
grammar describes verb denoting
agent's action on self **reflex action**
involuntary response to (nerve)

stimulation

re·form [ri-FORM] v improve; abandon evil practices; reconstruct ▷ n improvement

ref·or·ma·tion [ref-ər-MAY-shàn] n

re·form'a·to·ry [ri-FRAK-tà-ree] n, pl -ries institution for reforming juvenile offenders

re·fract [ri-FRAKT] vi change course of light, etc passing from one medium to another **re·frac'tion** n

re·frac·to·ry [ri-FRAK-tà-ree] adj unmanageable; difficult to treat or work; medicine resistant to treatment; resistant to heat

re·frain¹ [ri-FRAYN] vi abstain (from)

re·frain² n phrase or verse repeated regularly esp in song or poem; chorus

re·fran·gi·ble [ri-FRAN-jà-bàl] adj that can be refracted

re·fresh [ri-FRESH] vt give freshness to; revive; renew; brighten; provide with refreshment **re·fresh'er** n that which refreshes **re·fresh'ment** n that which refreshes, esp food, drink; restorative

re·frig·er·ate [ri-FRIJ-à-rayt] vt -at·ed, -at·ing freeze; cool **re·frig'er·ant** n refrigerating substance ▷ adj **re·frig·er·a·tor** n apparatus in which foods, drinks are kept cool

ref·uge [REF-yooj] n shelter, protection, retreat, sanctuary **ref·u·gee** [ref-yuu-JEE] n one who seeks refuge, esp in foreign country

re·fund [ri-FUND] vt pay back ▷ n [REE-fund] return of money; amount returned

re·fur·bish [ree-FUR-bish] vt furbish, furnish or brighten anew

re·fuse¹ [ri-FYOOZ] v -fused,
-fus·ing decline, deny, reject

re·fus'al n denial of anything demanded or offered; option

ref·use² [REF-yoos] n rubbish, useless matter

re·fute [ri-FYOOT] vt -fut·ed,
-fut·ing disprove **re·fut'a·ble** adj

ref·u·ta·tion [ref-yuu-TAY-shàn] n

re·gal [REE-gàl] adj of, like a king **re·ga·li·a** [ri-GAY-lee-à] pl n insignia of royalty, as used at coronation, an order, etc; emblems of high office, an order, etc **re·gal·i·ty** [ri-GAL-i-tee] n, pl -ties

re·gale [ri-GAYL] vt -galed,
-gal·ing give pleasure to; feast

re·gard [ri-GAHRD] vt look at; consider; relate to; heed ▷ n look; attention; particular respect; esteem ▷ pl expression of good will **re·gard'ful** adj heedful, careful **re·gard'less** adj heedless ▷ adv in spite of everything

re·gat·ta [ri-GAT-à] n meeting for yacht or boat races

re·gen·er·ate [ri-JEN-à-rayt] v -at·ed, -at·ing cause spiritual rebirth; reform morally; reproduce, re-create; reorganize ▷ adj [-à-rit] born anew **re·gen·er·a'tion** n **re·gen'er·a·tive** adj

re·gent [REE-jànt] n ruler of kingdom during absence, minority, etc, of its monarch ▷ adj ruling **re'gen·cy** n status, (period of) office of regent

reg·gae [REG-ay] n style of popular West Indian music with strong beat

reg·i·cide [REJ-à-sīd] n one who kills a king; this crime

re·gime [rà-ZHEEM] n system of government, administration **regime change** transition from one political regime to another, esp through concerted political or military action

reg•i•men [REJ-ə-mən] n prescribed system of diet, etc; rule

reg•i•ment [REJ-ə-mənt] n organized body of troops as unit of army ▷ vt [REJ-ə-ment] discipline, organize rigidly or too strictly **reg•i•men'tal** adj of regiment

re•gion [REE-jən] n area, district; stretch of country; part of the body; sphere, realm; administrative division of a country **re'gion•al** adj

reg•is•ter [REJ-ə-stər] n list; catalogue; roll; device for registering; written record; range of voice or instrument ▷ v show, be shown on meter, face, etc ▷ vt enter in register; record; show; set down in writing; printing, photography cause to correspond precisely **reg'is•trar** [-trahr] n keeper of a register esp in college or university **reg•is•tra'tion** n **reg'is•try** n, pl -tries register; place where registers are kept, esp of births, marriages, deaths

re•gorge [ri-GORJ] v -gorged, -gorg•ing vomit up

re•gress [ri-GRES] vi return, revert to former place, condition, etc ▷ n **re•gres'sion** [-shən] n act of returning; retrogression **re•gres'sive** adj falling back

re•gret [ri-GRET] vt -gret•ted, -gret•ting feel sorry, distressed for loss of or on account of ▷ n sorrow, distress for thing done or left undone or lost **re•gret'ful** adj **re•gret'ta•ble** adj

reg•u•lar [REG-yə-lər] adj normal; habitual; done, occurring, according to rule; periodical; straight; level; living under rule; belonging to standing army ▷ n regular soldier; regular customer **reg•u•lar'i•ty** n **reg'u•lar•ize** vt -ized, -iz•ing **reg•u•late** [REG-yə-layt] vt -lat•ed, -lat•ing adjust; arrange;

direct; govern; put under rule **reg•u•la'tion** n **reg'u•la•tor** n contrivance to produce uniformity of motion, as flywheel, governor, etc

re•gur•gi•tate [ri-GUR-ji-tayt] v vomit; bring back (swallowed food) into mouth

re•ha•bil•i•tate [ree-hə-BIL-i-tayt] vt -tat•ed, -tat•ing help (person) to readjust to society after a period of illness, imprisonment, etc; restore to reputation or former position; make fit again; reinstate

re•hash [ree-HASH] vt rework, reuse ▷ n [REE-hash] old materials presented in new form

re•hearse [ri-HURS] vt -hearsed, -hears•ing practice (play, etc); repeat aloud; say over again; train, drill **re•hears'al** n

reign [rayn] n period of sovereign's rule ▷ vi be ruler; be supreme

re•im•burse [ree-im-BURS] vt -bursed, -burs•ing refund; pay back **re•im•burse'ment** n

rein [rayn] n narrow strap attached to bit to guide horse; instrument for governing ▷ vt check, manage with reins; control **give free rein to** remove restraints

re•in•car•na•tion [ree-in-kahr-NAY-shən] n rebirth of soul in successive bodies; one of series of such transmigrations **re•in•car'nate** [-KAHR-nayt] vt -nat•ed, -nat•ing

rein•deer [RAYN-deer] n deer, with large branched antlers, that lives in the arctic regions

re•in•force [ree-in-FORS] vt -forced, -forc•ing strengthen with new support, material, force; strengthen with additional troops, ships, etc **re•in•force'ment** n **reinforced concrete** concrete strengthened internally by steel bars

re·in·state [ree-in-STAYT] vt -stat·ed, -stat·ing replace, restore, reestablish

re·it·er·ate [ree-IT-ə-rayt] vt -at·ed, -at·ing repeat again and again **re·it·er·a·tion** n repetition **re·it·er·a·tive** [-ət-ə-tiv] adj

re·ject [ri-JEKT] vt refuse to accept; put aside; discard; renounce ▷ n [REE-jekt] person or thing rejected as not up to standard **re·jec·tion** n refusal

re·joice [ri-JOIS] v -joiced, -joic·ing make or be joyful, merry; gladden; exult

re·join [ree-JOIN] vt reply; join again **re·join·der** [ri-JOIN-dər] n answer, retort

re·ju·ve·nate [ri-JOO-və-nayt] vt -nat·ed, -nat·ing restore to youth **re·ju·ve·na·tion** n **re·ju·ve·nes·cence** [ri-joo-və-NES-əns] n process of growing young again

re·lapse [ri-LAPS] vi -lapsed, -laps·ing fall back into evil, illness etc ▷ n [REE-laps] return of bad habits, illness, etc

re·late [ri-LAYT] v -lat·ed, -lat·ing ▷ vt narrate, recount; establish relation between; have reference or relation to ▷ vi (with to) form sympathetic relationship

re·la·tion [ri-LAY-shən] n relative quality or condition; connection by blood or marriage; connection between things; act of relating; narrative **re·la·tion·ship** n **rel·a·tive** [REL-ə-tiv] adj dependent on relation to something else, not absolute; having reference or relation (to) ▷ n one connected by blood or marriage; relative word or thing **rel·a·tiv·i·ty** n state of being related; subject of two theories of Albert Einstein, dealing with relationships of space, time and motion, and acceleration and gravity

re·lax [ri-LAKS] vt make loose or slack ▷ vi become loosened or slack; ease up from effort or attention; become more friendly, less strict **re·lax·a·tion** [ree-] n relaxing recreation; alleviation; abatement

re·lay [REE-lay] n fresh set of people or animals relieving others; electricity device for making or breaking local circuit ▷ vt -layed, -lay·ing pass on, as message **relay race** race between teams of which each runner races part of distance

re·lease [ri-LEES] vt -leased, -leas·ing give up, surrender, set free; permit showing of (movie, etc) ▷ n setting free; releasing; written discharge; permission to show publicly; film, record, etc newly issued

rel·e·gate [REL-i-gayt] vt -gat·ed, -gat·ing banish, consign; demote **rel·e·ga·tion** n

re·lent [ri-LENT] vi give up harsh intention, become less severe **re·lent·less** [-lis] adj pitiless; merciless

rel·e·vant [REL-ə-vənt] adj having to do with the matter in hand, to the point **rel·e·vance** n

reliable, reliance see RELY

rel·ic [REL-ik] n thing remaining, esp as memorial of saint; memento ▷ pl remains, traces

re·lief [ri-LEEF] n alleviation, end of pain, distress, etc; money, food given to victims of disaster, poverty, etc; release from duty; one who relieves another; freeing of besieged city, etc; projection of carved design from surface; distinctness, prominence **re·lieve** [ri-LEEV] vt -lieved, -liev·ing bring or give relief to **relief map** map showing elevations and depressions of country in relief

re·li·gion [ri-LIJ-ən] n system of belief in, worship of a supernatural power or god **re·li'gious** adj pert to religion; pious; conscientious **re·li'gious·ly** adv in religious manner; scrupulously; conscientiously

re·lin·quish [ri-LING-kwish] vt give up, abandon

rel·i·quar·y [REL-i-kwer-ee] n, pl -**quar·ies** case or shrine for holy relics

rel·ish [REL-ish] n enjoy, like ▷ n liking, gusto; appetizing savory food, such as pickle; taste or flavor

re·luc·tant [ri-LUK-tənt] adj unwilling, loath, disinclined **re·luc'tance** n

re·ly [ri-LĪ] vi -**lied, -ly·ing** depend (on); trust **re·li·a·bil'i·ty** n **re·li'a·ble** adj trustworthy, dependable **re·li'ance** [ri-LĪ-əns] n trust; confidence; dependence **re·li'ant** [-ənt] adj confident; trustful

re·main [ri-MAYN] vi stay, be left behind; continue; abide; last **remains** pl n relics, esp of ancient buildings; dead body **re·main'der** n rest, what is left after subtraction ▷ vt offer (end of consignment of goods, material, etc) at reduced prices

re·mand [ri-MAND] vt send back, esp into custody

re·mark [ri-MAHRK] vi make casual comment (on) ▷ vt comment, observe; say; take notice of ▷ n observation, comment **re·mark'a·ble** adj noteworthy, unusual **re·mark'a·bly** adv exceedingly; unusually

re·mar·ry v -**ry·ing, -ried** marry again following a divorce or the death of one's previous husband

or wife

rem·e·dy [REM-i-dee] n, pl -**dies** means of curing, counteracting or relieving disease, trouble, etc ▷ vt -**died, -dy·ing** put right **re·me'di·a·ble** adj **re·me'di·al** adj designed, intended to correct specific disability, handicap, etc **re·me·di·a'tion** n

re·mem·ber [ri-MEM-bər] vt retain in, recall to memory ▷ vi have in mind **re·mem'brance** [-brəns] n memory; token; souvenir; reminiscence

re·mind [ri-MĪND] vt cause to remember; put in mind (of) **re·mind'er** n

rem·i·nisce [rem-ə-NIS] vi -**nisced, -nisc·ing** talk, write of past times, experiences, etc **rem·i·nis'cence** n remembering; thing recollected ▷ pl memoirs **rem·i·nis'cent** adj reminding or suggestive (of)

re·miss [ri-MIS] adj negligent, careless

re·mit [ri-MIT] v -**mit·ted, -mit·ting** send money for goods, services, etc, esp by mail; refrain from exacting; give up; restore; return; slacken; forgive (sin, etc) ▷ n law transfer of court record to another court **re·mis'sion** n abatement; reduction in length of prison term; pardon, forgiveness **re·mit'tance** n sending of money; money sent

rem·nant [REM-nənt] n fragment or small piece remaining; oddment

re·mon·strate [ri-MON-strayt] vi -**strat·ed, -strat·ing** protest, reason with, argue **re·mon'strance** [-strəns] n

re·morse [ri-MORS] n regret and repentance **re·morse'ful** [-fəl] adj **re·morse'less** [-lis] adj pitiless

re·mote [ri-MOHT] adj -**mot·er,**

-mot·est far away, distant; aloof; slight **re·mote·ly** adv remote **control** control of apparatus from a distance by electrical device

re·move [ri-MOOV] v **-moved, -mov·ing** ▷ vt take away or off; transfer; withdraw ▷ vi go away, change residence ▷ n degree of difference **re·mov·a·ble** adj **re·mov·al** n

re·mu·ner·ate [ri-MYOO-nð-rayt] vt reward, pay **re·mu·ner·a·tion** n **re·mu·ner·a·tive** adj

ren·ais·sance [ren-ð-SAHNS] n revival, rebirth, esp revival of learning in 14th to 16th centuries

re·nal [REEN-l] adj of the kidneys

re·nas·cent [ri-NAS-ðnt] adj springing up again into being

rend v rent, **rend·ing** tear, wrench apart; burst, break, split

ren·der [REN-dðr] vt submit, present; give in return, deliver up; cause to become; portray, represent; melt down; cover with plaster

ren·dez·vous [RAHN-de-voo] n, pl **rendezvous** [-vooz] meeting place; appointment; haunt; assignation ▷ vi **-voused** [-vood] **-vous·ing** [-voo-ing] meet, come together

ren·di·tion [ren-DISH-ðn] n performance; translation

ren·e·gade [REN-i-gayd] n deserter; outlaw; rebel ▷ adj

re·nege [ri-NIG] vi **-neged, -neg·ing** (usu with on) go back on (promise, etc); in cards, break rule

re·new [ri-NOO] vt begin again; reaffirm; make valid again; make new; revive; restore to former state; replenish ▷ vi be made new; grow again **re·new·a·bil·i·ty** n quality of being renewable **re·new·a·ble** adj **re·new·al** n revival, restoration; regeneration

ren·net [REN-it] n lining

membrane of calf's fourth stomach; preparation from this membrane for curdling milk

re·nounce [ri-NOWNS] vt **-nounced, -nounc·ing** give up, cast off; disown; abjure; resign, as title or claim **re·nun·ci·a·tion** n

ren·o·vate [REN-ð-vayt] vt restore, repair, renew, do up **ren·o·va·tion** n

re·nown [ri-NOWN] n fame

rent¹ n payment for use of land, buildings, machines, etc ▷ vt hold by lease; let **rent·al** [RENT-ðl] n sum payable as rent

rent² n tear; fissure; pt/pp of **REND**

renunciation SEE **RENOUNCE**

rep¹ n fabric with corded surface for upholstery, etc

rep² adj, n short for **REPERTORY (COMPANY)**

rep³ n short for **REPRESENTATIVE**

re·paid [ri-PAYD] pt/pp of **REPAY**

re·pair¹ [ri-PAIR] vt make whole, sound again; mend; patch; restore ▷ n **re·pair·a·ble** adj **rep·a·ra·tion** [rep-ð-RAY-shðn] n repairing; amends, compensation

repair² vi resort (to), go

re·past [ri-PAST] n a meal

re·pa·tri·ate [ri-PAY-tree-ayt] vt **-at·ed, -at·ing** send (someone) back to own country

re·pay [ri-PAY] vt **-paid, -pay·ing** pay back, refund; make return for **re·pay'ment** n

re·peal [ri-PEEL] vt revoke, annul, cancel ▷ n act of repealing

re·peat [ri-PEET] vt say, do again; reproduce; recur ▷ vi recur; of food, be tasted repeatedly for some time after being eaten ▷ n act, instance of repeating, esp TV show broadcast again **re·peat·ed·ly** adv again and again; frequently **re·peat'er** n firearm that can be discharged many times without reloading; watch that strikes every hour **rep·e·ti·tion** [rep-i-TISH-ən] n act of repeating; thing repeated; piece learned by heart and repeated **rep·e·ti'tious** adj repeated unnecessarily **re·pet'i·tive** adj repeated

re·pel [ri-PEL] vt **-pelled, -pel·ling** drive back, ward off; refuse; be repulsive to **re·pel'lent** [-ənt] adj distasteful; resisting water, etc ▷ n that which repels, esp chemical to repel insects

re·pent [ri-PENT] vi wish one had not done something; feel regret for deed or omission ▷ vt feel regret for **re·pent'ance** [-əns] n contrition **re·pent'ant** [-ənt] adj

re·per·cus·sion [ree-pər-KUSH-ən] n indirect effect, oft unpleasant; recoil; echo

rep·er·to·ry [REP-ər-tor-ee] n, pl **-ries** repertoire, collection; store **rep'er·toire** [-twahr] n stock of plays, songs, etc that performer or company can give **repertory theater** theater with permanent company producing succession of plays

repetition, repetitious, repetitive see REPEAT

re·pine [ri-PĪN] vi **-pined, -pin·ing** fret, complain

re·place [ri-PLAYS] vt **-placed, -plac·ing** substitute for; put back

re·play [REE-play] n (also **instant replay**) immediate reshowing on TV of incident in sport, esp in slow motion; replaying of a match ▷ vt [ree-PLAY]

re·plen·ish [ri-PLEN-ish] vt fill up again **re·plen'ish·ment** n

re·plete [ri-PLEET] adj filled, gorged

rep·li·ca [REP-li-kə] n exact copy; facsimile, duplicate **rep·li·cate** [REP-li-kayt] vt **-cat·ed, -cat·ing** make, be a copy of **rep·li·ca·tion** n **rep'li·ca·ble** adj

re·ply [ri-PLĪ] v **-plied, -ply·ing** answer or respond ▷ n, pl **-lies** answer or response

re·port [ri-PORT] n account, statement; written statement of child's progress at school; rumor; repute; bang ▷ vt announce, relate; make, give account of; take down in writing; complain about ▷ vi make report; act as reporter; present oneself (to) **re·port'er** n one who reports, esp for newspaper

re·pose [ri-POHZ] n rest; composure; sleep ▷ v **-posed, -pos·ing** ▷ vi rest ▷ vt lay to rest; place; rely, lean (on) **re·pos'i·tor·y** [-POZ-i-tor-ee] n, pl **-tor·ies** place where valuables are deposited for safekeeping; store

rep·re·hend [rep-ri-HEND] vt find fault with **rep·re·hen'si·ble** adj deserving censure; unworthy **rep·re·hen'sion** n censure

rep·re·sent [rep-ri-ZENT] vt stand for; deputize for; act, play; symbolize; make out to be; call up by description or portrait **rep·re·sen·ta'tion** n **rep·re·sen'ta·tive** n one chosen to stand for group; (traveling) salesman ▷ adj typical

re·press [ri-PRES] vt keep down or under, quell, check **re·pres'sion** [-PRESH-ən] n restraint **re·pres'sive** adj

re·prieve [ri-PREEV] vt **-prieved, -priev·ing** suspend execution of (condemned person); give temporary relief (to) ▷ n postponement or cancellation of punishment; respite; last-minute intervention

rep·ri·mand [REP-rə-mand] n

sharp rebuke ▷ vt rebuke sharply

re·print' vt print further copies of (a book) ▷ n reprinted copy

re·pris·al [ri-PRĪ-zəl] n retaliation

re·proach [ri-PROHCH] vt blame, rebuke ▷ n scolding, upbraiding; expression of this; thing bringing discredit **re·proach'ful** [-fəl] adj

rep·ro·bate [REP-rà-bayt] adj depraved; rejected by God ▷ n depraved or disreputable person ▷ vt **-bat·ed, -bat·ing** disapprove of, reject

re·pro·duce [ree-prà-DOOS] v **-duced, -duc·ing** ▷ vt produce copy of; bring new individuals into existence; re-create, produce anew ▷ vi propagate; generate **re·pro·duc'i·ble** adj **re·pro·duc'tion** n process of reproducing; that which is reproduced; facsimile, as of painting, etc **re·pro·duc'tive** adj

re·prove [ri-PROOV] vt **-proved, -prov·ing** censure, rebuke **re·proof'** n

rep·tile [REP-til, REP-tīl] n cold-blooded, air breathing vertebrate with horny scales or plates, as snake, tortoise, etc **rep·til'i·an** adj

re·pub·lic [ri-PUB-lik] n country without monarch in which supremacy of people or their elected representatives is formally acknowledged **re·pub'li·can** adj, n

re·pu·di·ate [ri-PYOO-dee-ayt] vt **-at·ed, -at·ing** reject authority or validity of; cast off, disown **re·pu·di·a'tion** n

re·pug·nant [ri-PUG-nənt] adj offensive; distasteful; contrary **re·pug'nance** n dislike, aversion; incompatibility

re·pulse [ri-PULS] vt **-pulsed, -puls·ing** drive back; rebuff; repel ▷ n driving back, rejection, rebuff

re·pul·sion [-shən] n distaste, aversion; physics force separating two objects **re·pul'sive** adj loathsome, disgusting

re·pute [ri-PYOOT] vt **-put·ed, -put·ing** reckon, consider ▷ n reputation, credit **rep'u·ta·ble** adj of good repute; respectable **rep·u·ta'tion** n estimation in which person is held; character; good name

re·quest [ri-KWEST] n asking; thing asked for ▷ vt ask

Req·ui·em [REK-wee-əm] n Mass for the dead; (r-) music for this

re·quire [ri-KWĪR] vt **-quired, -quir·ing** want, need; demand **re·quire'ment** n essential condition; specific need; want

req·ui·site [REK-wà-zit] adj necessary; essential ▷ n

req·ui·si·tion [rek-wà-ZISH-ən] n formal demand, such as for materials or supplies ▷ vt demand (supplies); press into service

re·quite [ri-KWĪT] vt **-quit·ed, -quit·ing** repay

re·scind [ri-SIND] vt cancel, annul **re·scis'sion** [-SIZH-ən] n

res·cue [RES-kyoo] vt **-cued, -cu·ing** save, deliver, extricate ▷ n **res'cu·er** n

re·search [ri-SURCH] n investigation, esp scientific study to discover facts ▷ v carry out investigations (on, into)

re·sem·ble [ri-ZEM-bəl] vt **-bled, -bling** be like; look like **re·sem'blance** n

re·sent [ri-ZENT] vt show, feel indignation at; retain bitterness about **re·sent'ful** [-fəl] adj **re·sent'ment** [-mənt] n

re·serve [ri-ZURV] vt **-served, -serv·ing** hold back, set aside, keep for future use ▷ n (also pl) something, esp money, troops, etc kept for emergencies; (also **reservation**) area of land reserved for particular purpose or for use by particular group of people, etc; reticence, concealment of feelings or friendliness **re·ser·va'tion** n reserving; thing reserved; doubt; exception or limitation **reserved** adj not showing feelings, lacking cordiality **re·serv'ist** n one serving in reserve

res·er·voir [REZ-ər-vwahr] n enclosed area for storage of water, esp for community supplies; receptacle for liquid, gas, etc; place where anything is kept in store

re·shuf'fle n reorganization ▷v reorganize

re·side [ri-ZID] vt **-sid·ed, -sid·ing** dwell permanently **res·i·dence** [REZ-i-dəns] n home; house **res'i·den·cy** n dwelling; position or period of medical resident **res'i·dent** [-dənt] adj, n **res·i·den'tial** adj (of part of town) consisting mainly of residences; of, connected with residence; providing living accommodation **resident** physician in residence at hospital and serving on staff to obtain advanced training

res·i·due [REZ-i-doo] n what is left, remainder **re·sid'u·al** [ri-ZIJ-oo-əl] adj **residuals** pl n additional payments to performers for reruns of film, TV programs, etc in which they appear

re·sign [ri-ZIN] vt give up ▷vi give up office, employment, etc; reconcile (oneself) to **re·sig·na'tion** [-ig-NAY-shən] n resigning; being resigned, submission **re·signed'** [-ZIND] adj content to endure

re·sil·ient [ri-ZIL-yənt] adj capable of returning to normal after

stretching, etc, elastic; (of person) recovering quickly from shock, etc **re·sil'ience, -ien·cy** n

res·in [REZ-in] n sticky substance formed in and oozing from plants, esp firs and pines **res'in·ous** [-nəs] adj of, like resin

re·sist [ri-ZIST] v withstand, oppose **re·sist'ance** [-əns] n act of resisting; opposition; hindrance; *electricity* opposition offered by circuit to passage of current through it **re·sist'ant** [-ənt] adj **re·sist'i·ble** adj **re·sis·tiv'i·ty** n measure of electrical resistance **re·sist'or** n component of electrical circuit producing resistance

res·o·lute [REZ-ə-loot] adj determined **res·o·lu'tion** n resolving; firmness; purpose or thing resolved upon; decision or vote of assembly

re·solve [ri-ZOLV] vt **-solved, -solv·ing** make up one's mind; decide with effort of will; form by resolution of vote; separate component parts of; make clear ▷n resolution; fixed purpose

res·o·nance [REZ-ə-nəns] n echoing, esp in deep tone; sound produced by body vibrating in sympathy with neighboring source of sound **res'o·nant** [-nənt] adj **res'o·nate** vi, vt **-nat·ed, -nat·ing**

re·sort [ri-ZORT] vi have recourse; frequent ▷n place for vacations; recourse; frequented place; haunt

re·sound [ri-ZOWND] vi echo, ring, go on sounding **re·sound'ing** adj echoing; thorough

re·source [ri-ZORS, ri-SORS] n capability, ingenuity; that to which one resorts for support; expedient ▷pl source of economic wealth; supply that can be drawn on; means of support, funds **re·source'ful**

[-fəl] adj

re·spect [ri-SPEKT] n deference; esteem; point or aspect; reference, relation ▷ vt treat with esteem; show consideration for **re·spect·a·bil'i·ty** n **re·spect'a·ble** adj worthy of respect, decent; fairly good **re·spect'ful** adj **re·spect'ing** prep concerning **re·spect'ive** adj relating separately to each of those in question; several, separate

res·pi·ra·tion [res-pə-RAY-shən] n breathing **res·pi·ra·tor** n apparatus worn over mouth and breathed through as protection against dust, poison gas, etc or to provide artificial respiration **res'pi·ra·to·ry** [-rə-tor-ee] adj

res·pite [RES-pit] n pause; interval; suspension of labor; reprieve

re·splend·ent [ri-SPLEN-dənt] adj brilliant, splendid; shining **re·splend'en·cy** [-ən-see] n

re·spond [ri-SPOND] vi answer; act in answer to stimulus; react **re·spond'ent** adj replying ▷ n one who answers; defendant **re·sponse'** n answer **re·spon'sive** adj readily reacting to some influence

re·spon·si·ble [ri-SPON-sə-bəl] adj liable to answer for; accountable; dependable; involving responsibility; of good credit or position **re·spon·si·bil'i·ty** n state of being answerable; duty; charge; obligation

rest' n repose; freedom from exertion, etc; that on which anything rests or leans; pause, esp in music; support ▷ vi take rest; be supported ▷ vt give rest to; place on support **rest'ful** adj **rest'less** [-lis] adj offering no rest; uneasy, impatient **rest home** residential

establishment providing care for aged, convalescent, etc

rest² n remainder; others ▷ vi remain; continue to be

res·tau·rant [RES-tər-ənt] n commercial establishment serving food **res·tau·ra·teur'** [-ə-TUR] n keeper of one

res·ti·tu·tion [res-ti-TOO-shən] n giving back or making up; reparation, compensation

res·tive [RES-tiv] adj restless; resisting control, impatient

re·store [ri-STOR] vt **-stored**, **-stor·ing** build up again, repair, renew; reestablish; give back **res·to·ra·tion** n **re·stor'a·tive** adj restoring ▷ n medicine to strengthen, etc **re·stor'er** n

re·strain [ri-STRAYN] vt check, hold back; prevent; confine **re·straint'** n restraining, control, esp self-control **restraining order** order issued by a civil court to a potential abuser to keep away from another specified person

re·strict [ri-STRIKT] vt limit, restrict **re·stric'tion** n limitation; restraint; rule **re·stric'tive** adj **re·strict'ed** adj denying residence, membership to persons of certain races, ethnic groups, etc

re·sult [ri-ZULT] vi follow as consequence; happen; end ▷ n effect, outcome **re·sult'ant** [-ZUL-tnt] adj arising as result

re·sume [ri-ZOOM] vt **-sumed**, **-sum·ing** begin again **ré·su·mé** [REZ-uu-may] n summary, abstract; brief statement of one's qualifications for employment, public office, etc **re·sump'tion** [-shən] n resuming; fresh start

re·sur·gence [ri-SUR-jəns] n rising again **re·sur'gent** adj

res·ur·rect [rez-ə-REKT] vt

restore to life, resuscitate; use once more (something discarded, etc) **res•ur•rec'tion** *n* rising again (esp from dead); revival

re•sus•ci•tate [ri-SUS-i-tayt] *vt* **-tat•ed, -tat•ing** revive to life, consciousness

re•tail [REE-tayl] *n* sale in small quantities ▷ *adv* at retail ▷ *v* sell, be sold, retail; recount

re•tain [ri-TAYN] *vt* keep; engage services of **re•tain'er** *n* fee to retain professional adviser, esp lawyer **re•ten'tion** [-shən] *n* **re•ten'tive** *adj* capable of retaining, remembering

re•tal•i•ate [ri-TAL-ee-ayt] *v* **-at•ed, at•ing** repay in kind; revenge **re•tal•i•a'tion** *n* **re•tal'i•a•to•ry** *adj*

re•tard [ri-TAHRD] *vt* make slow or late; keep back; impede development of **re•tard'ed** *adj* underdeveloped, esp mentally **re•tar•da'tion** *n*

retch [rech] *vi* try to vomit

ret•i•cent [RET-ə-sənt] *adj* reserved in speech; uncommunicative **ret'i•cence** *n*

ret•i•na [RET-n-ə] *n, pl* **-nas** light-sensitive membrane at back of eye **ret'i•nal** *adj* **ret•i•ni'tis** [-NĪ-tis] *n* inflammation of retina

ret•i•nue [RET-n-yoo] *n* band of followers or attendants

re•tire [ri-TĪR] *v* **-tired, -tir•ing** ▷ *vi* give up office or work; go away; withdraw; go to bed ▷ *vt* cause to retire **retired** *adj* that has retired from office, etc **re•tire'ment** [-mənt] *n* **re•tir'ing** *adj* unobtrusive, shy

re•tort [ri-TORT] *vt* reply; repay in kind, retaliate; hurl back (charge, etc) ▷ *vi* reply with countercharge ▷ *n* vigorous reply or repartee; vessel with bent neck used for distilling

re•touch [ree-TUCH] *vt* touch up, improve by new touches, esp of paint, etc

re•trace [ri-TRAYS] *vt* **-traced, -trac•ing** go back over (a route, etc) again

re•tract [ri-TRAKT] *v* draw back, recant **re•tract'a•ble** *adj* **re•trac'tion** *n* drawing or taking back, esp of statement, etc **re•trac'tor** *n* muscle; surgical instrument

re•tread [ree-TRED] *vt* restore tread to worn rubber tire ▷ *n* [REE-tred] retreaded tire; *sl* person returned to work after dismissal; person training for new type of work; *inf* reworked old idea, etc

re•treat [ri-TREET] *vi* move back from any position; retire ▷ *n* act of, or military signal for, retiring, withdrawal; place to which anyone retires esp for meditation; refuge; sunset call on bugle

re•trench [ri-TRENCH] *vt* reduce expenditure, esp by dismissing staff; cut down

ret•ri•bu•tion [re-trə-BYOO-shən] *n* recompense, esp for evil deeds; vengeance

re•trieve [ri-TREEV] *vt* **-trieved, -triev•ing** fetch back again; restore; rescue from ruin; recover, esp information from computer; regain **re•triev'al** *n* **re•triev'er** *n* dog trained to retrieve game

ret•ro•ac•tive [re-troh-AK-tiv] *adj* applying or referring to the past

ret•ro•grade [RE-trə-grayd] *adj* going backward, reverting; reactionary **ret•ro•gres'sion** [-GRE-shən] *n* **ret•ro•gres'sive** *adj*

ret•ro•spect [RE-trə-spekt] *n* looking back, survey of past **ret•ro•spec'tion** [-SPEK-shən] *n* **ret•ro•spec'tive** *adj*

re·trous·sé [ri-troo-SAY] adj of nose, turned upward

re·turn [ri-TURN] vi go, come back ▷ vt give, send back; report officially; elect ▷ n returning, being returned; profit; official report esp tax return

re·un·ion [ree-YOON-yàn] n gathering of people who have been apart **re·u·nite'** v bring or come together again after a separation

Rev. Revelations

rev n inf revolution (of engine) ▷ v revved, rev·ving (oft with up) increase speed of revolution (of engine)

re·val·ue [ree-VAL-yoo] v -ued, -u·ing adjust exchange value of currency upward

re·vamp [ree-VAMP] vt renovate, restore

re·veal [ri-VEEL] vt make known; show **rev·e·la'tion** n

rev·eil·le [REV-à-lee] n morning bugle call, etc to waken soldiers

rev·el [REV-àl] vi -eled, -el·ing take pleasure (in); make merry ▷ n (usu pl) merrymaking **rev'el·ry** n festivity

re·venge [ri-VENJ] n retaliation for wrong done; act that satisfies this; desire for this ▷ v -venged, -veng·ing ▷ vt avenge; make retaliation for ▷ v refl avenge oneself **re·venge'ful** [-fàl] adj vindictive; resentful

rev·e·nue [REV-àn-yoo] n income, esp of nation, as taxes, etc

re·ver·ber·ate [ri-VUR-bà-rayt] v -at·ed, -at·ing echo, resound, throw back (sound, etc)

re·vere [ri-VEER] vt -vered, -ver·ing hold in great regard or religious respect **rev'er·ence** [-àns] n revering; awe mingled with respect and esteem; veneration **rev'er·end** [-ànd] adj (esp as prefix

to clergyman's name) worthy of reverence **rev'er·ent** [-ànt] adj showing reverence **rev·er·en'tial** adj marked by reverence

rev·er·ie [REV-à-ree] n daydream, absent-minded state

re·verse [ri-VURS] v -versed, -vers·ing (of vehicle) (cause to) move backward ▷ vt turn upside down or other way round; change completely ▷ n opposite, contrary; side opposite, obverse; defeat; reverse gear ▷ adj opposite, contrary **re·ver'sal** [-sàl] n **re·vers'i·ble** adj **reverse gear** mechanism enabling vehicle to move backward

re·vert [ri-VURT] vi return to former state; come back to subject; refer to a second time; turn backward **re·ver'sion** [-VUR-zhàn] n (of property) rightful passing to owner or designated heir, etc

re·vet·ment [ri-VET-mànt] n facing of stone, sandbags, etc for wall

re·view [ri-VYOO] vt examine; look back on; reconsider; hold, make, write review of ▷ n general survey; critical notice of book, etc; periodical with critical articles; inspection of troops; revue **re·view'er** n writer of reviews

re·vile [ri-VÎL] vt -viled, -vil·ing be viciously scornful of, abuse

re·vise [ri-VÎZ] vt -vised, -vis·ing look over and correct; change, alter **re·vi'sion** [-zhàn] n reexamination for purpose of correcting; act of revising; revised copy **re·vi'sion·ism** n departure from generally accepted theory, interpretation **re·vi'sion·ist** adj, n

re·vive [ri-VÎV] v -vived, -viv·ing bring, come back to life, vigor, use, etc **re·viv'al** [-vàl] n esp of religious fervor **re·viv'al·ist** n organizer of religious revival

re·voke [ri-VOHK] vt **-voked, -vok·ing** take back, withdraw; cancel **rev·o·ca·ble** [-ə-kə-bəl] adj **rev·o·ca'tion** n repeal

re·volt [ri-VOHLT] n rebellion ▷ vi rise in rebellion; feel disgust ▷ vt affect with disgust **re·volt'ing** adj disgusting, horrible

re·volve [ri-VOLV] v **-volved, -volv·ing** ▷ vi turn around, rotate; be centered on ▷ vt rotate

rev·o·lu'tion n violent overthrow of government; great change; complete rotation, turning or spinning around **rev·o·lu'tion·ar·y** adj, n **rev·o·lu'tion·ize** vt **-ized, -iz·ing** change considerably; bring about revolution in

re·volv·er [ri-VOL-vər] n repeating pistol with revolving cylinder

re·vue, re·view [ri-VYOO] n theatrical entertainment with topical sketches and songs

re·vul·sion [ri-VUL-shən] n sudden violent change of feeling; marked repugnance or abhorrence

re·ward [ri-WORD] vt pay, make return for service, conduct, etc ▷ n reward; satisfaction; personal satisfaction, worthwhile

re·ward'ing adj giving personal satisfaction, worthwhile

re·wind' v run (tape or film) back to an earlier point in order to replay

Rf chemistry rutherfordium

Rh chemistry rhodium

rhap·so·dy [RAP-sə-dee] n, pl **-dies** enthusiastic or high-flown (musical) composition or utterance **rhap·sod'ic** adj **rhap'so·dize** [-sə-dīz] v **-dized, -diz·ing**

rhe·o·stat [REE-ə-stat] n instrument for regulating the value of the resistance in an electric circuit

rhe·sus [REE-səs] n small, long-tailed monkey of S Asia **rhesus factor, Rh factor** feature distinguishing different types of human blood

rhet·o·ric [RET-ər-ik] n art of effective speaking or writing; artificial or exaggerated language **rhe·tor·i·cal** [ri-TOR-i-kəl] adj (of question) not requiring an answer **rhet·o·ri'cian** [-RISH-ən] n

rheu·ma·tism [ROO-mə-tiz-əm] n painful inflammation of joints or muscles **rheu·mat'ic** [ruu-MAT-ik] adj, n **rheu·ma·toid** [ROO-mə-toid] adj of, like rheumatism

Rh factor SEE RHESUS

rhi·noc·er·os [rī-NOS-ər-əs] n, pl **-os·es** large thick-skinned animal with one or two horns on nose

rho·di·um [ROH-dee-əm] n hard metal like platinum

rhom·bus [ROM-bəs] n, pl **-bus·es** or **-bi** [-bī] equilateral but not right-angled parallelogram, diamond-shaped figure

rhu·barb [ROO-bahrb] n garden plant of which the fleshy stalks are cooked and used as fruit; laxative from root of allied Chinese plant; sl argument, fight

rhyme [rīm] n identity of sounds at ends of lines of verse, or in words; word or syllable identical in sound to another; verse marked by rhyme ▷ vt **rhymed, rhym·ing** make rhymes

rhythm [RITH-əm] n measured beat or flow, esp of words, music, etc **rhyth'mic** adj **rhyth'mi·cal·ly** adv

rib¹ n one of curved bones springing from spine and forming framework of upper part of body; cut of meat including rib(s); curved timber of framework of boat; raised series of rows in knitting, etc ▷ vt **ribbed, rib'bing** furnish, mark with ribs; knit to form a rib pattern **rib'bing** n

rib² vt inf **ribbed, rib·bing** tease, ridicule **rib'bing** n

rib·ald [RIB-əld] adj irreverent,

scurrilous; indecent ▷ *n* ribald
person **rib'ald·ry** *n* vulgar, indecent
talk

rib·bon [RIB-ən] *n* narrow band of
fabric used for trimming, tying, etc;
long strip or line of anything **ribbon
development** building of houses,
etc along main road leading out of
town, etc

ri·bo·fla·vin [Rī-bah-flay-vin] *n*
form of vitamin B

rice [rīs] *n* cereal plant; its seeds
as food **rice paper** fine (edible)
Chinese paper

rich *adj* **-er, -est** wealthy; fertile;
abounding; valuable; (of food)
containing much fat or sugar;
mellow; amusing ▷ *n* the wealthy
classes **rich·es** [RICH-iz] *pl n*
wealth **rich'ly** *adv*

rick·ets [RIK-its] *n* disease of
children marked by softening of
bones, bow legs, etc, caused by
vitamin D deficiency **rick'et·y** *adj*
-et·i·er, -et·i·est shaky, insecure,
unstable; suffering from rickets

rick·shaw [RIK-shaw] *n* light two-
wheeled man-drawn Asian vehicle

ric·o·chet [rik-ə-SHAY] *vi* **-cheted**
[-SHAYD] **-chet·ing** [-SHAY-ing] (of
bullet) rebound or be deflected by
solid surface or water ▷ *n* bullet or
shot to which this happens

rid *vt* **rid** or **rid·ded, rid·ding** clear,
relieve of; free; deliver **rid·dance**
[RID-ns] *n* clearance; act of ridding;
deliverance; relief

rid·den [RID-n] *pp of* **RIDE** *adj*
afflicted or affected by the thing
specified: *disease-ridden*

rid·dle¹ [RID-l] *n* question made
puzzling to test one's ingenuity;
enigma; puzzling thing, person ▷ *vi*
-dled, -dling speak in, make riddles

rid·dle² *vt* **-dled, -dling** pierce
with many holes **riddled with** full

of, esp holes

ride [rīd] *v* **rode, rid·den, rid·ing**
sit on and control or propel (horse,
bicycle, etc); be carried on or across
▷ *vi* go on horseback or in vehicle;
lie at anchor ▷ *vt* travel over ▷ *n*
journey on horse, etc, or in any
vehicle **rid·er** *n* one who rides;
supplementary clause; addition to
a document

ridge [rij] *n* long narrow hill; long,
narrow elevation on surface; line of
meeting of two sloping surfaces ▷ *vt*
ridged, ridg·ing form into ridges

ri·dic·u·lous [ri-DIK-yə-ləs] *adj*
deserving to be laughed at, absurd,
foolish **rid·i·cule** [RID-i-kyool]
n treatment of person or thing as
ridiculous ▷ *vt* **-culed, -cul·ing**
laugh at, deride

rife [rīf] *adj* prevalent, common

rif·fle [RIF-əl] *v* **-fled, -fling** flick
through (pages, etc) quickly

riff'raff *n* rabble, disreputable
people

ri·fle [Rī-fəl] *vt* **-fled, -fling** search
and rob; ransack; make spiral grooves
in (gun barrel, etc) ▷ *n* firearm with
long barrel **rifling** *n* arrangement of
grooves in gun barrel; pillaging

rift *n* crack, split, cleft

rig *vt* **rigged, rig·ging** provide
(ship) with spars, ropes, etc; equip;
set up, esp as makeshift; arrange in
dishonest way ▷ *n* way ship's masts
and sails are arranged; apparatus for
drilling for oil and gas; tractor-trailer
truck; style of dress **rigging** *n* ship's
spars and ropes; lifting tackle

right [rīt] *adj* just; in accordance
with truth and duty; true; correct;
proper; of side that faces east when
front is turned to north; *politics*
(also **right wing**) conservative or
reactionary; straight; upright; of
outer or more finished side of fabric

▷ vt bring back to vertical position; do justice to ▷ vi come back to vertical position ▷ n claim, title, etc allowed or due; what is right, just or due; conservative political party; punch, blow with right hand ▷ adj straight; properly; very; on or to right side **right'ful** [-fəl] adj **right'ly** adv right angle; angle of 90 degrees **right of way** law right to pass over someone's land; path used; right to drive; right to proceed

right·eous [RĪ-chəs] adj just, upright; godly; virtuous; good; honest

rig·id [RIJ-id] adj inflexible; harsh, stiff **ri·gid'i·ty** n

rig·ma·role [RIG-mə-rohl] n meaningless string of words; long, complicated procedure

rig·or[1] [RIG-ər] n sudden coldness attended by shivering **rig·or mor'tis** stiffening of body after death

rigor[2] n harshness, severity, strictness; hardship **rig'or·ous** adj stern, harsh, severe

rile [rīl] vt **riled, ril·ing** inf anger, annoy

rill n small stream

rim n edge, border, margin; outer ring of wheel ▷ vt **rimmed, rim·ming** furnish with rim; coat or encrust; basketball, golf of ball, go around basket, hole, and not drop in **rimmed** adj bordered, edged **rim'less** adj

rime [rīm] n hoarfrost **rim'y** adj **rim·i·er, rim·i·est**

rind [rīnd] n outer coating of fruits, etc

ring[1] n circle of gold, etc, esp for finger; any circular band, coil, rim, etc; circle of persons; enclosed area, esp roped-in square for boxing ▷ vt **ringed, ring·ing** put ring round; mark (bird, etc) with ring **ring'er**

n one who rings bells; sl student, athlete, racehorse, etc participating in examination, sporting event, etc under false pretenses or fraudulently in place of another **dead ringer** sl person, thing apparently identical to another **ring'lead·er** [-leed-ər] n instigator of mutiny, riot, etc

ring'let [-lit] n curly lock of hair

ring'worm [-wurm] n fungal skin disease in circular patches

ring[2] vi **rang, rung, ring·ing** give out clear resonant sound, as bell; resound; cause (bell) to sound; telephone ▷ n a ringing; telephone call **ring'tone** n tune played by a cell phone when it receives a call

rink [ringk] n sheet of ice for skating or hockey; floor for roller skating

rinse [rins] vt **rinsed, rins·ing** remove soap (from washed clothes, hair, etc) by applying clean water; wash lightly ▷ n a rinsing; liquid to tint hair

ri·ot [RĪ-ət] n tumult, disorder; loud revelry; disorderly, unrestrained disturbance; profusion ▷ vi make, engage in riot **ri'ot·ous** adj unruly, rebellious, wanton

R.I.P. rest in peace

rip[1] vt **ripped, rip·ping** cut, tear away, slash, rend ▷ n rent, tear **rip'cord** n cord pulled to open parachute **rip'saw** n saw with coarse teeth (used for cutting wood along grain) **rip off** sl steal, cheat, overcharge **rip'off** n sl act of stealing, overcharging, etc

rip[2] n strong current, esp one moving away from the shore

ri·par·i·an [ri-PAIR-ee-ən] adj of, on banks of river

ripe [rīp] adj **rip·er, rip·est** ready to be reaped, eaten, etc; matured; (of judgment, etc) sound **rip'en** v grow ripe; mature

ri·poste [ri-POHST] *n* verbal retort; counterstroke; *fencing* quick lunge after parry

rip·ple [RIP-əl] *n* slight wave, ruffling of surface; anything like this; sound like ripples of water ▷ v **-pled, -pling** ▷ *vi* flow, form into little waves; (of sounds) rise and fall gently ▷ *vt* form ripples on

rise [rīz] *vi* **rose, ris·en, ris·ing** get up; move upward; appear above horizon; reach higher level; increase in value or price; rebel; adjourn; have its source ▷ *n* rising; upslope; increase, esp of prices **ris·er** *n* one who rises, esp from bed; vertical part of stair step **rising** *n* revolt ▷ *adj* increasing in rank, maturity

ris·i·ble [RIS-ə-bəl] *adj* inclined to laugh; laughable **ris·i·bil·i·ty** *n, pl* **-ties**

risk *n* chance of disaster or loss ▷ *vt* venture; put in jeopardy; take chance of **risk'y** *adj* **risk·i·er, risk·i·est** dangerous; hazardous

ri·sot·to [ri-SAW-toh] *n* dish of rice cooked in stock with various other ingredients

ris·qué [ri-SKAY] *adj* suggestive of indecency

rite [rīt] *n* formal practice or custom, esp religious **rit·u·al** [RICH-oo-əl] *n* prescribed order or book of rites; regular, stereotyped action or behavior ▷ *adj* concerning rites **rit'u·al·ism** *n* practice of ritual

ri·val [RĪ-vəl] *n* one that competes with another for favor, success, etc ▷ *vt* **-valed, -val·ing** vie with ▷ *adj* in position of rival **ri'val·ry** *n* keen competition

riv·er [RIV-ər] *n* large natural stream of water; copious flow

riv·et [RIV-it] *n* bolt for fastening metal plates, the end being put through holes and then beaten flat ▷ *vt* **-et·ed, -et·ing** fasten with rivets; cause to be fixed or held firmly, esp in surprise, horror, etc **riv'et·er** *n*

riv·u·let [RIV-yə-lit] *n* small stream

Rn *chemistry* radon

roach [rohch] *n* cockroach; *sl* butt of marijuana cigarette

road [rohd] *n* track, way prepared for passengers, vehicles, etc; direction, way; street **road'block** *n* barricade across road to stop traffic for inspection, etc **road hog** selfish, aggressive driver **road map** map intended for drivers, showing roads, distances, etc in a country or area; plan or guide for future actions **road'run·ner** *n* large cuckoo of W US, Mexico, C Amer able to run quickly **road'side** *n, adj* **road'ster** *n obs* touring car **road warrior** *inf* frequent business traveler **road'work** [-wurk] *n* repairs to road; running, jogging along country roads as exercise for boxers **road'worth·y** [-wur-thee] *adj* (of vehicle) mechanically sound

roam [rohm] *v* wander about, rove **roam'er** *n*

roan [rohn] *adj* (of horses) having coat in which main color is thinly interspersed with another, esp bay, sorrel or chestnut mixed with white or gray ▷ *n* roan horse

roar [ror] *v* make or utter loud deep hoarse sound as of lion, thunder, voice in anger, etc ▷ *n* such a sound **roar'ing** *adj* brisk and profitable ▷ *adv* noisily

roast [rohst] *v* bake, cook in closed oven; cook by exposure to open fire; make, be very hot ▷ *n* piece of meat for roasting; *inf* roasting ▷ *adj* roasted **roast'ing** *n* severe criticism, scolding; session of good-natured scolding by way of tribute to honored person

rob vt **robbed, rob·bing** plunder, steal from; pillage, defraud **rob'ber** n **rob'ber·y** n, pl-**ber·ies**

robe [rohb] n long outer garment, often denoting rank or office ▷ v **robed, rob·ing** ▷ vt dress ▷ vi put on robes, vestments

rob'in n large thrush with red breast **robin's-egg blue** pale green to light blue

ro·bot [ROH-bət] n automated machine, esp performing functions in human manner; person of machine-like efficiency **ro·bot·ics** [roh-BOT-iks] n science of designing and using robots

ro·bust [roh-BUST] adj sturdy, strong **ro·bust'ness** [-nis] n

roc [rok] n monstrous bird of Arabian mythology

rock¹ [rok] n stone; large rugged mass of stone; sl diamond, gem **rock'er·y** n, pl-**er·ies** mound or grotto of stones or rocks for plants in a garden **rock'y** adj **rock·i·er, rock·i·est** having many rocks; rugged, presenting difficulty **rock bottom** lowest possible level **between a rock and a hard place** between equally unattractive alternatives

rock² v (cause to) sway to and fro ▷ n style of pop music derived from rock-'n'-roll **rock'er** n curved piece of wood, etc on which thing may rock **rocking chair** chair allowing the sitter to rock backwards and forwards **rock-'n'-roll** n popular dance rhythm **rock the boat** inf disrupt smooth routine of company, etc **off one's rocker** sl insane

rock·et [ROK-it] n self-propelling device powered by burning of explosive contents (used as firework, for display, signaling, line carrying, weapon, etc); vehicle propelled by rocket engine, as weapon or carrying spacecraft ▷ vi move fast, esp upward, as rocket **rock'et·ry** n

ro·co·co [rə-KOH-koh] adj of furniture, architecture, etc having much conventional decoration in style of early 18th century work in France; tastelessly florid

rod n slender straight bar, stick; cane; old unit of length equal to 5.5 yards

rode pt of RIDE

ro·dent [ROHD-nt] n animal with teeth specialized for gnawing, such as a rat or squirrel

ro·de·o [ROH-dee-oh] n display of skills, competition, with bareback riding, cattle handling techniques, etc

roe [roh] n mass of eggs in fish

roent·gen [RENT-gən] n measuring unit of radiation dose

rogue [rohg] n rascal, knave, scoundrel; mischief-loving person or child; wild beast of savage temper, living apart from herd **ro'guish** adj **rogue state** sovereign political power that conducts its policy in a dangerously unpredictable way, disregarding international law

rois·ter [ROI-stər] vi be noisy, boisterous, bragging **roist'er·er** n reveler

role, rôle [rohl] n actor's part; specific task or function

roll [rohl] v move by turning over and over ▷ vt wind around; smooth out with roller ▷ vi move, sweep along; undulate; turn from side to side; of aircraft, turn about a line from nose to tail in flight ▷ n act of flying down and turning over and over or from side to side; piece of paper, etc rolled up; any object thus shaped, eg jelly roll; list, catalogue; bread baked into small oval or round; continuous sound, as of drums, thunder, etc **roll·er** n cylinder of wood, stone, metal, etc used for pressing, crushing, smoothing, supporting thing to be moved, winding thing on, etc; long wave of sea **roll call** act of calling over list of names, as in schools or army **roller bearings** bearings of hardened steel rollers **Roll'er·blade ®** n roller skate with the wheels set in a straight line, mounted on a boot **roller coaster** small gravity railroad in amusement park with steep ascents and descents for frightening riders; any experience with similar ups and downs **roller skate** skate with wheels instead of runner **roller towel** loop of towel on roller **rolling pin** cylindrical roller for pastry or dough **rolling stock** locomotives, freight cars, etc of railroad **roll top** n desk, flexible lid sliding in grooves; such a desk **roll up** appear, turn up; increase, accumulate

rol·lick·ing [ROL-i-king] adj boisterously jovial and merry

ro·ly-po·ly [ROH-lee-poh-lee] adj round, plump ▷ n round, plump person or thing

ROM [rom] computing read-only memory (permanently recorded on a computer chip)

Rom. Romans

Ro·man [ROH-mǎn] adj of Rome or Roman Catholic Church **Roman Catholic** member of Roman Catholic Church **Roman Catholic Church** the Christian church that acknowledges supremacy of the Pope **Roman numerals** letters I, V, X, L, C, D, M used to represent numbers in manner of Romans **roman type** plain upright letters,

ordinary style of printing

roman á clef [roh-mah-na-KLAY] n, pl **romans á clef** [roh-mah-na-KLAY] Fr novel that disguises real events and people

ro·mance [roh-MANS] n love affair, esp intense and happy one; mysterious or exciting quality; tale of chivalry; tale with scenes remote from ordinary life; literature like this; picturesque falsehood ▷ v -manced, -manc·ing ▷ vi exaggerate, fantasize ▷ vt inf woo, court **Romance language** any of vernacular languages of certain countries, developed from Latin, as French, Spanish, etc **ro·man·tic** adj characterized by romance; of or dealing with love; of literature, etc, preferring passion and imagination to proportion and finish ▷ n **ro·man·ti·cism** [-ti-sizm] n **ro·man·ti·cize** vi -cized, -ciz·ing **Ro·man·esque** [rohm-ǎn-NESK] adj, n (in) style of round-arched vaulted architecture of period between Classical and Gothic

romp vi run, play wildly, joyfully ▷ n spell of romping; easy victory **romp·ers** [-ǎrz] pl n child's loose one-piece garment **romp home** win easily

ron·deau [ron-DOH] n, pl -deaux [-DOHZ] short poem with opening words used as refrain **ron·del** n extended rondeau **ron·de·let** [ron-dl-ET] n short rondeau

ron·do [RON-doh] n, pl -dos piece of music with leading theme to which return is continually made

roof n, pl **roofs** outside upper covering of building; top, covering part of anything ▷ vt put roof on, over

rook³ [ruuk] n bird of crow family ▷ vt swindle, cheat **rook'er·y** n, pl

-er·ies colony of rooks

rook² n chess piece shaped like a castle

rook·ie [RUUK-ee] n recruit, esp in army; *sport* professional athlete playing in first season

room n space; space enough; division of house; scope, opportunity ▷pl lodgings **room'y** adj

room·i·er, room·i·est spacious

roost n perch for poultry ▷vi perch **roost'er** n male of domestic fowl; cock

root¹ n part of plant that grows down into earth and conveys nourishment to plant; plant with edible root, such as a carrot; vital part; (also **roots**) source, origin, original cause of anything; *anatomy* embedded portion of tooth, nail, hair, etc; primitive word from which other words are derived; factor of a quantity that, when multiplied by itself the number of times indicated, gives the quantity ▷v (cause to) take root; pull by roots; dig, burrow

root² vi cheer; applaud; encourage **root'er** n

rope [rohp] n thick cord ▷vt **roped, rop·ing** secure, mark off with rope **rope in** inf entice, lure by deception

ro·sa·ry [ROH-zə-ree] n, pl **-ries** series of prayers; string of beads for counting these prayers as they are recited; rose garden, bed of roses

rose¹ [rohz] n shrub, climbing plant usu with prickly stems and fragrant flowers; the flower; perforated flat nozzle for hose, watering can, etc; pink color ▷adj of this color

ro·se·ate [ROH-zee-it] adj rose-colored, rosy **ro·sette** [roh-ZET] n rose-shaped bunch of ribbon; rose-shaped architectural ornament

ros'y adj **ros·i·er, ros·i·est**

flushed; hopeful, promising **rose-colored** adj having color of rose; unwarrantably optimistic **rose window** circular window with series of mullions branching from center **rose of Sharon** [SHAR-ən] low, spreading small tree or shrub with white, purplish or red flowers

rose² pt of RISE

ro·sé [roh-ZAY] n pink wine

rose·mar·y [ROHZ-mair-ee] n evergreen fragrant flowering shrub; its leaves and flowers used as seasoning

Ro·si·cru·cian [roh-zi-KROO-shən] n member of secret order devoted to occult law ▷adj

Ro·si·cru·cian·ism n

ros·in [ROZ-in] n resin esp used for rubbing on bows of violins, etc

ros·ter [ROS-tər] n list or plan showing turns of duty

ros·trum [ROS-trəm] n, pl **-tra** [-trə] or **-trums** platform, stage, pulpit; beak or bill of a bird

rot v **rot·ted, rot·ting** decompose naturally; corrupt ▷n decay, putrefaction; any disease producing decomposition of tissue; nonsense **rot'ten** adj decomposed, putrid; corrupt

ro·ta·ry [ROH-tə-ree] adj (of movement) circular; operated by rotary movement **ro·tate** [ROH-tayt] v **-tat·ed, -tat·ing** (cause to) move around center or on pivot **ro·ta'tion** n rotation; regular succession **Rotary Club** one of international association of businessmen's clubs **Ro·tar'i·an** n member of such

rote [roht] n habitual, mechanical repetition **by rote** by memory

ro·tis·ser·ie [roh-TIS-ə-ree] n (electrically driven) rotating spit for cooking meat

ro·tor [ROH-tər] n rotating portion of a dynamo motor or turbine

rotten SEE ROT

ro·tund [roh-TUND] adj round; plump; sonorous **ro·tun·di·ty** n

rouble SEE RUBLE

rou·é [roo-AY] n dissolute or dissipated man; rake

rouge [roozh] n red powder, cream used to color cheeks ▷ v **rouged**, **roug·ing** color with rouge

rough [ruf] adj **-er, -est** not smooth, of irregular surface; violent, stormy, boisterous; rude; uncivil; lacking refinement; approximate; in preliminary form ▷ vt make rough; plan out approximately; (with it) live without usual comforts, rough ▷ n rough condition or area; sketch **diamond in the rough** excellent, valuable but unsophisticated person **rough·en** [-n] vt **rough·age** [RUF-ij] n unassimilated portion of food promoting proper intestinal action **rough·house** [-hows] n, v **-housed, -hous·ing** fight, row

rou·lette [roo-LET] n game of chance played with revolving dishlike wheel and ball

round [rownd] adj **-er, -est** spherical, cylindrical, circular, curved; full, complete; roughly correct; large, considerable; plump; unqualified, positive ▷ adv with circular or circuitous course ▷ n thing round in shape; recurrent duties; stage in competition; customary course, as of postman; game (of golf); one of several periods in boxing match, etc; cartridge for firearm; rung; movement in circle ▷ prep about; on all sides of ▷ v make, become round ▷ vt round **round·ers** n British ball game resembling baseball **round·ly** adv plainly;

thoroughly **round·a·bout'** adj not straightforward **round robin** sports tournament in which all contestants play one another **round up** drive (cattle) together; collect and arrest criminals

roun·de·lay [ROWN-dl-ay] n simple song with refrain

rouse [rowz] v **roused, rous·ing** ▷ vt wake up, stir up, excite to action; cause to rise ▷ vi waken

roust·a·bout [ROWST-ə-bowt] n laborer working in circus, oil rig, etc

rout [rowt] n overwhelming defeat, disorderly retreat; noisy rabble ▷ vt scatter and put to flight

route [root] n road, chosen way **go the route** inf see through to the end; baseball pitch complete game

rou·tine [roo-TEEN] n regularity of procedure, unvarying round; regular course ▷ adj ordinary, regular

roux [roo] n fat and flour cooked together as thickener for sauces

rove [rohv] v **roved, rov·ing** wander, roam **rov·er** n one who roves; pirate

row¹ [roh] n number of things in a straight line; rank; file; line

row² v propel boat by oars ▷ n spell of rowing **row'boat** n

row³ [rhymes with **cow**] n dispute; disturbance ▷ vi quarrel noisily

row·dy [ROW-dee] adj **-di·er, -di·est** disorderly, noisy and rough ▷ n person like this

roy·al [ROI-əl] adj of, worthy of, befitting, patronized by, king or queen; splendid **roy·al·ist** n supporter of monarchy **roy·al·ty** n royal dignity or power; royal persons; payment to owner of land for right to work minerals, or to inventor for use of invention; payment to author depending on sales

Ru chemistry ruthenium

rub v **rubbed, rub·bing** ▷ vt apply pressure to with circular or backward and forward movement; clean, polish, dry, thus; pass hand over; abrade, chafe; remove by friction ▷ vi come into contact accompanied by friction; become frayed or worn by friction ▷ n rubbing; impediment

rub·ber¹ [RUB-ər] n coagulated sap of rough, elastic consistency, of certain tropical trees; piece of rubber, etc used for erasing; thing for rubbing; person who rubs; *sl* condom ▷ adj of rubber **rub·ber·ize** vt **-ized, -iz·ing** coat, impregnate, treat with rubber **rub·ber·y** adj **rub·ber·neck** v gawk at **rubber stamp** device for imprinting dates, etc; automatic authorization

rubber² n series of odd number of games or contests at various games, such as bridge; two out of three games won **rubber match** deciding contest between tied opponents

rub·bish [RUB-ish] n refuse, waste material, garbage; anything worthless; trash, nonsense **rub·bish·y** adj valueless

rub·ble [RUB-əl] n fragments of stone, etc; builders' rubbish

ru·bel·la [roo-BEL-ə] n mild contagious viral disease, German measles

ru·bi·cund [ROO-bi-kund] adj ruddy

ru·ble, rou·ble [ROO-bəl] n unit of currency of Russia and Belarus

ru·bric [ROO-brik] n title, heading; direction in liturgy; instruction

ru·by [ROO-bee] n **-bies** precious red gem; its color ▷ adj of this color

ruck·sack [RUK-sak] n pack carried on back, knapsack

ruck·us [RUK-əs] n uproar, disturbance

rud·der [RUD-ər] n flat piece hinged to boat's stern or rear of aircraft to steer by

rud·dy [RUD-ee] adj **-di·er, -di·est** of fresh or healthy red color; rosy; florid

rude [rood] adj impolite; coarse; vulgar; primitive; roughly made; uneducated; sudden, violent **rude·ly** adv **rude·ness** n

ru·di·ments [ROO-də-mənts] pl n elements; first principles **ru·di·men·ta·ry** adj

rue¹ [roo] v **rued, ru·ing** grieve for; regret; deplore; repent ▷ n sorrow; repentance **rue·ful** [-fəl] adj sorry; regretful; dejected; deplorable

rue² n plant with evergreen bitter leaves

ruff n starched and frilled collar; natural collar of feathers, fur, etc on some birds and animals; type of shore bird **ruf·fle** vt **-fled, -fling** rumple, disorder; annoy, put out; frill, pleat ▷ n frilled trimming

ruff² n cards trump

ruf·fi·an [RUF-ee-ən] n violent, lawless person

rug n small, oft shaggy or thick-piled floor mat; thick woolen wrap, coverlet; *sl* toupee, hairpiece **rug·rat** n inf small child

rug·by [RUG-bee] n form of football with two teams of 15 players

rug·ged [RUG-id] adj rough; broken; unpolished; harsh, austere

ru·in [ROO-in] n decay, destruction; downfall; fallen or broken state; loss of wealth, position, etc ▷ pl ruined buildings, etc ▷ vt reduce to ruins; bring to decay or destruction; spoil; impoverish **ru·in·a·tion** n **ru·in·ous** adj causing or characterized by ruin or destruction

rule [rool] n principle; precept;

authority; government; what is usual; control; measuring stick ▷ vt **ruled, rul·ing** govern; decide; mark with straight lines; draw (line) **rul'er** n one who governs; stick for measuring or ruling lines

rum n liquor distilled from sugar cane

rum·ba [RUM-bə] n, pl **-bas** rhythmic dance, orig Cuban; music for it

rum·ble [RUM-bəl] vi **-bled, -bling** make noise as of distant thunder, heavy vehicle, etc; sl engage in gang street fight ▷ n noise like thunder, etc; gang street fight

ru·mi·nate [ROO-mə-nayt] vi **-nat·ed, -nat·ing** chew cud; ponder over; meditate **ru'mi·nant** [-nənt] adj, n cud-chewing (animal) **ru·mi·na'tion** [-NAY-shən] n quiet meditation and reflection **ru'mi·na·tive** [-mə-nā-tiv] adj

rum·mage [RUM-ij] v **-maged, -mag·ing** search thoroughly ▷ n **rummage sale** sale of miscellaneous, usu secondhand, items

rum·my[1] [RUM-ee] n card game

rum·my[2] [RUM-ee] n, pl **-mies** sl drunkard

ru·mor [ROO-mər] n hearsay, common talk, unproved statement ▷ vt put out as, by way of, rumor

rump n tail end; buttocks

rum·ple [RUM-pəl] v, n **-pled, -pling** crease, wrinkle

rum·pus [RUM-pəs] n, pl **-us·es** disturbance; noise and confusion

run v **ran, run, run·ning** ▷ vi move with more rapid gait than walking; go quickly; flow; flee; compete in race, contest, election; revolve; continue; function; travel according to schedule; fuse; melt; spread over; have certain meaning ▷ vt cross by running; expose oneself (to risk, etc); cause to run; (of newspaper) print, publish; transport and dispose of (smuggled goods); manage; operate ▷ n act, spell of running; rush; tendency, course; period; sequence; heavy demand; enclosure for domestic poultry, animals; ride in car; series of unraveled stitches; ladder; score of one at baseball; steep snow-covered course for skiing **run'ner** n racer; messenger; curved piece of wood on which sleigh slides; any similar appliance; slender stem of plant running along ground forming new roots at intervals; strip of cloth, carpet **running** adj continuous; consecutive; flowing; discharging; effortless; entered for race; used for running ▷ n act of moving or flowing quickly; management **run'ny** adj **-ni·er, -ni·est** tending to flow or exude moisture **run'down** n summary **run-down** adj exhausted **run down** stop working; reduce; exhaust; denigrate **run'way** n level stretch where aircraft take off and land **in the running** having fair chance in competition

rung[1] n crossbar or spoke, esp in ladder

rung[2] pp of RING[2]

runt n small animal, below usual size of species; offens undersized person

ru·pee [roo-PEE] n monetary unit of India and Pakistan

rup·ture [RUP-chər] n breaking, breach; hernia ▷ v **-tured, tur·ing** break; burst, sever

ru·ral [RUUR-əl] adj of the country; rustic

ruse [rooz] n stratagem, trick

rush[1] vt impel, carry along violently and rapidly; take by sudden assault

▷*vi* cause to hurry; move violently or rapidly ▷*n* rushing, charge; hurry; eager demand for; heavy current (of air, water, etc) ▷*adj* done with speed; characterized by speed **rush hour** period at beginning and end of day when many people are traveling to and from work

rush² *n* marsh plant with slender pithy stem; the stems as material for baskets

rusk *n* kind of sweet raised bread esp used for feeding babies

rus·set [RUS-it] *adj* reddish-brown ▷*n* the color; apple with skin of this color

rust *n* reddish-brown coating formed on iron by oxidation; disease of plants ▷*v* contract, affect with rust **rust'y** *adj* **rust·i·er, rust·i·est** coated with rust, of rust color; out of practice **rust'proof** *adj*

rus·tic [RUS-tik] *adj* of, or as of, country people; rural; of rough manufacture; made of untrimmed tree limbs ▷*n* country person, peasant **rus'ti·cate** *v* **-cat·ed, -cat·ing** ▷*vt* send to, house in, country ▷*vi* live a country life

rus·tle¹ [RUS-əl] *vi* **-tled, -tling** make sound as of blown dead leaves, etc ▷*n* this sound

rustle² *vt* **-tled, -tling** steal (cattle) **rus'tler** *n* cattle thief

rut¹ *n* furrow made by wheel; settled habit or way of living; groove **rut'ty** *adj* **-ti·er, -ti·est**

rut² *n* periodic sexual excitement among animals ▷*vi* **rut·ted, rut·ting** be under influence of this

ruth·less [ROOTH-lis] *adj* pitiless, merciless

RV *n* recreational vehicle

rye [rī] *n* grain used for forage and bread; plant bearing it; whisky made from rye

S

S chemistry sulfur

Sab·bath [SAB-əth] n Saturday, devoted to worship and rest from work in Judaism and certain Christian churches; Sunday, observed by Christians as day of worship and rest **sab·bat·i·cal** [sə-BAT-ə-kəl] adj, n (denoting) leave granted to university staff, etc for study

sa·ber [SAY-bər] n curved cavalry sword; fencing sword having two cutting edges and blunt point

sa·ble [SAY-bəl] n small weasellike animal of cold regions; its fur; black ▷ adj black

sab·o·tage [SAB-ə-tahzh] n intentional damage done to roads, machines, etc, esp secretly in war ▷ vt **-taged, -tag·ing sab·o·teur** [sab-ə-TUR] n

sac [sak] n pouchlike structure in an animal or vegetable body

sac·cha·rin [SAK-ər-in] n artificial sweetener **sac·cha·rine** [-in] adj excessively sweet

sac·er·do·tal [sas-ər-DOHT-l] adj of priests

sa·chet [sa-SHAY] n small envelope or bag, esp one holding scented powder

sack [sak] n large bag, orig of coarse material; pillaging; sl dismissal; sl bed ▷ vt pillage (captured town); sl fire (person) from a job **sack·ing** n material for sacks **sack·cloth** [SAK-klawth] n coarse fabric used for sacks and worn as sign of mourning

sac·ra·ment [SAK-rə-mənt] n one of certain ceremonies of Christian church esp Eucharist **sac·ra·men·tal** adj

sa·cred [SAY-krid] adj dedicated, regarded as holy; set apart, reserved; inviolable; connected with, intended for religious use

sac·ri·fice [SAK-rə-fīs] n giving something up for sake of something else; act of giving up; thing so given up; making of offering to a god; thing offered ▷ vt **-ficed, -fic·ing** offer as sacrifice; give up; sell at very cheap price **sac·ri·fi·cial** [-FISH-l] adj

sac·ri·lege [SAK-rə-lijj] n misuse, desecration of something sacred **sac·ri·le·gious** [-LEE]-əs] adj profane; desecrating

sac·ro·sanct [SAK-roh-sangkt] adj preserved by religious fear against desecration or violence; inviolable

sac·rum [SAK-rəm] n, pl **sac·ra** [SAK-rə] five vertebrae forming compound bone at base of spinal column

sad adj **sad·der, sad·dest** sorrowful; unsatisfactory, deplorable **sad·den** [SAD-n] vt make sad

sad·dle [SAD-l] n rider's seat to fasten on horse, bicycle, etc; anything resembling a saddle; cut of mutton, venison, etc for roasting; ridge of hill ▷ vt **-dled, -dling** put saddle on; lay burden, responsibility on

sa·dism [SAY-diz-əm] n form of (sexual) perversion marked by love of inflicting pain **sa·dist** n **sa·dis·tic**

[sə-DIS-tik] adj

sa·fa·ri [sə-FAH-ree] n (party making) overland (hunting) journey, esp in Africa **safari park** park where lions, etc may be viewed by public from automobiles

safe [sayf] adj **saf·er, saf·est** secure, protected; uninjured, out of danger; not involving risk; trustworthy; sure, reliable; cautious ▷ n strong lockable container; structure for storing meat, etc **safe·ly** adv **safe·ty** n **safe-conduct** [KON-dukt] n a permit to pass somewhere **safe·guard** [-GAHRD] n protection ▷ vt protect **safety glass** glass resistant to fragmenting when broken

saf·fron [SAF-rən] n crocus; orange colored flavoring obtained from it; the color ▷ adj orange

sag vi **sagged, sag·ging** sink in middle; hang sideways; curve downward under pressure; give way; tire; (of clothes) hang loosely ▷ n droop

sa·ga [SAH-gə] n legend of Norse heroes; any long (heroic) story

sa·ga·cious [sə-GAY-shəs] adj wise **sa·gac'i·ty** [-GAS-i-tee] n

sage¹ [sayj] n very wise person ▷ adj **sag·er, sag·est** wise

sage² n aromatic herb

said [sed] pt/pp of SAY

sail [sayl] n piece of fabric stretched to catch wind for propelling ship, etc; act of sailing; journey upon the water; ships collectively; arm of windmill ▷ vi travel by water; move smoothly; begin voyage ▷ vt navigate **sail'er** n seaman; one who sails **sail'board** [-bord] n craft used for windsurfing like surfboard with mast and single sail

saint [saynt] n (title of) person formally recognized (esp by R C Church) after death, as having gained by holy deeds a special place in heaven; exceptionally good person **saint'ed** [-id] adj canonized; sacred **saint'li·ness** [-nis] n holiness **saint'ly** adj

sake¹ [sayk] n cause, account; end, purpose **for the sake of** on behalf of; to please or benefit

sa·ke² [SAH-kee] n Japanese alcoholic drink made of fermented rice

sa·laam [sə-LAHM] n bow of salutation, mark of respect in East ▷ vt salute

salable adj see SALE

sa·la·cious [sə-LAY-shəs] adj excessively concerned with sex, lewd

sal·ad [SAL-əd] n mixed vegetables, or fruit, used as food without cooking, oft combined with fish, meat, etc ▷ adj **salad days** period of youthful inexperience **salad dressing** oil, vinegar, herbs, etc mixed together as sauce for salad

sal·a·man·der [SAL-ə-man-dər] n variety of lizard; portable space heater

sa·la·mi [sə-LAH-mee] n variety of highly-spiced sausage

sal·a·ry [SAL-ə-ree] n, pl **-ries** fixed regular payment to persons employed usu in nonmanual work **sal'a·ried** adj

sale [sayl] n selling; selling of goods at unusually low prices; auction **sal'a·ble** adj capable of being sold **sales'per·son** n one who sells goods, etc in store; one traveling to sell goods, esp as representative of firm **sales'man·ship** n art of selling or presenting goods in most effective way

sa·li·ent [SAY-lee-ənt] adj prominent, noticeable; jutting out ▷ n salient angle, esp in fortification or line of battle

sa·line [SAY-leen] *adj* containing, consisting of a chemical salt, esp common salt; salty **sa·lin·i·ty** [sə-LIN-i-tee] *n*

sa·li·va [sə-LI-və] *n* liquid that forms in mouth, spittle **sal·i·var·y** [SAL-ə-ver-ee] *adj* **sal'i·vate** *v* **-vat·ed, -vat·ing**

sal·low [SAL-oh] *adj* of unhealthy pale or yellowish color

sal·ly [SAL-ee] *n, pl* **-lies** rushing out, esp by troops; outburst; witty remark ▷ *vi* **-lied, -ly·ing** rush; set out

salm·on [SAM-ən] *n* large silvery fish with orange-pink flesh valued as food; color of its flesh ▷ *adj* of this color

sal·mo·nel·la [sal-mə-NEL-ə] *n, pl* **-lae** [-nee] bacteria causing disease (esp food poisoning)

sa·lon [sə-LON] *n* (reception room for) guests in fashionable household; commercial premises of hairdressers, beauticians, etc

sa·loon [sə-LOON] *n* principal cabin or sitting room in passenger ship; bar; public room for specified use, eg billiards

salt [sawlt] *n* white powdery or granular crystalline substance consisting mainly of sodium chloride, used to season or preserve food; chemical compound of acid and metal; wit ▷ *vt* season, sprinkle with, spread, preserve with salt **salt'y** *adj* **salt·i·er, salt·i·est** of, like salt **old salt** sailor **salt'cel·lar** [-sel-ər] *n* salt shaker **salt lick** deposit, block of salt licked by game, cattle, etc **salt pan** *n* depression encrusted with salt after partial draining away of water **salt·pe·ter** [sawlt-PEE-tər] *n* potassium nitrate used in gunpowder **with a pinch**

of salt allowing for exaggeration **worth one's salt** efficient

sa·lu·bri·ous [sə-LOO-bree-əs] *adj* favorable to health, beneficial

Sa·lu·ki [sə-LOO-kee] *n* tall hound with silky coat

sal·u·tar·y [SAL-yə-ter-ee] *adj* wholesome, resulting in good

sa·lute [sə-LOOT] *v* **-lut·ed, -lut·ing** greet with words or sign; acknowledge with praise ▷ *vi* perform military salute ▷ *n* word, sign by which one greets another; motion of arm as mark of respect to superior, etc in military usage; firing of guns as military greeting of honor **sal·u·ta·tion** [-yə-TAY-shən] *n*

sal·vage [SAL-vij] *n* act of saving ship or other property from danger of loss; property so saved ▷ *vt* **-vaged, -vag·ing**

sal·va·tion [sal-VAY-shən] *n* fact or state of being saved, esp of soul

salve [sav] *n* healing ointment ▷ *vt* **salved, salv·ing** anoint with such, soothe

sal·ver [SAL-vər] *n* (silver) tray for presentation of food, letters, etc

sal·vo [SAL-voh] *n, pl* **-vos** or **-voes** simultaneous discharge of guns, etc

Sam. Samuel

Sa·mar·i·tan [sə-MAR-i-tn] *n* native of ancient Samaria; **(s-)** benevolent person

sam·ba [SAM-bə] *n* dance of S Amer origin; music for it

same [saym] *adj* identical with, not different, unchanged; uniform; just mentioned previously **same'ness** [-nis] *n* similarity; monotony

sam·o·var [SAM-ə-vahr] *n* Russian tea urn

Sam·o·yed [sam-ə-YED] *n* dog with thick white coat and tightly curled tail

sam·pan *n* small oriental boat

sam•ple [SAM-pəl] *n* specimen ▷ *vt* **-pled, -pling** take, give sample of; try; test; select; use part of (old sound recording) in new recording

sam'pler beginner's exercise in embroidery **sampling** *n* the taking of samples; sample

sam•u•rai [SAM-uu-rī] *n*, *pl* **samurai** member of ancient Japanese warrior caste

san•a•to•ri•um [san-ə-TOR-ee-əm] *n*, *pl* **-ri•ums** or **-ri•a** [-ree-ə] hospital, esp for chronically ill; health resort

sanc•ti•fy [SANGK-tə-fī] *vt* **-fied, -fying** set apart as holy; free from sin **sanc•ti•fi•ca'tion** *n* **sanc'ti•ty** *n*, *pl* **-ti•ties** saintliness; sacredness; inviolability **sanc'tu•ar•y** [-choo-er-ee] *n*, *pl* **-ar•ies** holy place; part of church nearest altar; place of special holiness in synagogue; place where fugitive was safe from arrest or violence; place protected by law where animals, etc can live without interference **sanc'tum** [SANGK-təm] *n* sacred place or shrine; person's private room **sanctum sanc•to•rum** [sangk-TOR-əm] *n* holy of holies in Temple in Jerusalem; sanctum

sanc•ti•mo•ni•ous [sangk-tə-MOH-nee-əs] *adj* making a show of piety, holiness **sanc•ti•mo'ni•ous•ness** *n*

sanc•tion [SANGK-shən] *n* permission, authorization; penalty for breaking law ▷ *pl* boycott or other coercive measure esp by one country against another regarded as having violated a law, right, etc ▷ *vt* allow, authorize, permit

sand *n* substance consisting of small grains of rock or mineral, esp on beach or in desert ▷ *pl* stretches or banks of this, usually forming seashore ▷ *vt* polish, smooth with sandpaper; cover, mix with sand **sand'er** *n* (power) tool for smoothing surfaces **sand'y** *adj* sand-colored; consisting of, covered with sand **sand'bag** *n* bag filled with sand or soil, used as protection against gunfire, floodwater, etc and as weapon ▷ *vt* **-bagged, -bag•ging** beat, hit with sandbag; *inf* in football, tackle passer as if from ambush **sand'blast** *n* jet of sand blown from a nozzle under pressure for cleaning, grinding, etc ▷ *vt* **sand'pa•per** *n* paper with sand stuck on it for scraping or polishing wood, etc **sand'pit, sand'box** *n* quantity of sand for children to play in **sand'stone** *n* rock composed of sand

san•dal [SAN-dl] *n* shoe consisting of sole attached by straps

sand'wich *n* two slices of bread with meat or other food between; anything resembling this ▷ *vt* insert between two other things

sane [sayn] *adj* **san•er, san•est** of sound mind; sensible, rational **san•i•ty** [SAN-i-tee] *n*

sang pt of SING

sang-froid [sahn-FRWAH] *n* Fr composure; indifference; self-possession

san•guine [SANG-gwin] *adj* cheerful, confident; ruddy in complexion **san•gui•nar•y** [SANG-gwə-ner-ee] *adj* accompanied by bloodshed; bloodthirsty

san•i•tar•y [SAN-i-ter-ee] *adj* helping protection of health against dirt, etc **san•i•ta'tion** *n* measures, apparatus for preservation of public health

sank pt of SINK

San'skrit *n* ancient language

of India

sap[1] *n* moisture that circulates in plants; energy ▷*v* **sapped, sap·ping** drain off sap **sap'ling** *n* young tree

sap[2] *v* **sapped, sap·ping** undermine; destroy insidiously; weaken ▷*n* trench dug in order to approach or undermine enemy position **sap'per** [-pər] *n* soldier doing this

sap[3] *n sl* foolish, gullible person

sa·pi·ent [SAY-pee-ənt] *adj usu ironical* wise; discerning; shrewd; knowing **sa'pi·ence** *n*

Sap·phic [SAF-ik] *adj* of Sappho, a Grecian poet; denoting a kind of verse ▷*n* Sapphic verse **sap'phism** [SAF-iz-əm] *n* lesbianism

sap·phire [SAF-ir] *n* (usu blue) precious stone; deep blue

sar·a·band [SAR-ə-band] *n* slow, stately Spanish dance; music for it

sar·casm [SAHR-kaz-əm] *n* bitter or wounding ironic remark; such remarks; taunt; sneer; irony; use of such expressions **sar·cas'tic** [-KAS-tik] *adj* **sar·cas'ti·cal·ly** *adv*

sar·coph·a·gous [sahr-KOF-ə-gəs] *adj* carnivorous

sar·coph·a·gus [sahr-KOF-ə-gəs] *n, pl* **-gi** [-jī] stone coffin

sar·dine [sahr-DEEN] *n* small fish of herring family, usu preserved in oil

sar·don·ic [sahr-DON-ik] *adj* characterized by irony, mockery or derision

sar·don·yx [sahr-DON-iks] *n* gemstone, variety of chalcedony

sar·gas·sum [sahr-CAS-əm], **sar·gas·so** [-GAS-oh] *n* gulfweed, type of floating seaweed

sa·ri [SAHR-ee] *n, pl* **-ris** Hindu woman's robe

sa·rong [sə-RAWNG] *n* skirtlike garment worn in Asian and Pacific countries

sar·sa·pa·ril·la [sas-pə-RIL-ə] *n* (flavor of) drink like root beer orig made from root of plant

sar·to·ri·al [sahr-TOR-ee-əl] *adj* of tailor, tailoring, or men's clothes

sash[1] *n* decorative belt, ribbon, wound around the body

sash[2] *n* window frame opened by moving up and down in grooves

sas·sa·fras [SAS-ə-fras] *n* tree of laurel family with aromatic bark used medicinally

sat pt/pp of **sɪt**

Sa·tan [SAYT-n] *n* the devil **sa·tan·ic** [sə-TAN-ik] **sa·tan'i·cal** *adj* devilish, fiendish

satch·el [SACH-əl] *n* small bag, oft with shoulder strap

sate [sayt] *vt* **sat·ed, sat·ing** satisfy a desire or appetite fully or excessively

sat·el·lite [SAT-l-īt] *n* celestial body or manmade projectile orbiting planet; person, country, etc dependent on another

sa·ti·ate [SAY-shee-ayt] *vt* **-at·ed, at·ing** satisfy to the full; surfeit **sa·ti·a'tion** *n* **sa·ti·e·ty** [sə-TĪ-i-tee] *n* feeling of having had too much

sat·in [SAT-n] *n* fabric (of silk, nylon, etc) with glossy surface on one side **sat'in·y** *adj* of, like satin

sat·ire [SAT-īr] *n* composition in which vice, folly or foolish person is held up to ridicule; use of ridicule or sarcasm to expose vice and folly **sa·tir·i·cal** [sə-TIR-i-kəl] *adj* of nature of satire; sarcastic; bitter **sat'i·rist** *n* **sat'i·rize** *vt* **-rized, -riz·ing** make object of satire; censure thus

sat·is·fy [SAT-is-fī] *vt* **-fied, -fy·ing** content, meet wishes of; pay; fulfill, supply adequately;

convince **sat·is·fac'tion** n **sat·is·fac'to·ry** adj

sa·trap [SAY-trap] n provincial governor in ancient Persia; subordinate ruler, oft despotic

sat·u·rate [SACH-ə-rayt] vt **-rat·ed, -rat·ing** soak thoroughly; cause to absorb moisture; amount; chemistry cause substance to combine to its full capacity with another; shell or bomb heavily **sat·u·ra'tion** n act, result of saturating

Sat·urn [SAT-ərn] n Roman god; one of planets **sat·ur·nine** [SAT-ər-nin] adj gloomy; sluggish in temperament, dull, morose **Sat·ur·na'li·a** [-NAY-lee-ə], n, pl **-li·as** ancient festival of Saturn; **(s-)** noisy revelry, orgy

sa·tyr [SAY-tər] n woodland deity, part man, part goat; lustful man

sauce [saws] n liquid added to food to enhance flavor; inf impudence; sl whiskey ▷ vt **sauced, sauc·ing** add sauce to; inf be cheeky, impudent to **sau'ci·ly** adv **sau'cy** adj **-ci·er, -ci·est** impudent **sauce'pan** n cooking pot with long handle

sau·cer [SAW-sər] n curved plate put under cup; shallow depression

sau·er·kraut [SOW-ər-krowt] n German dish of finely shredded and pickled cabbage

sau·na [SAW-nə] n steam bath, orig Finnish

saun·ter [SAWN-tər] vi walk in leisurely manner, stroll ▷ n leisurely walk or stroll

sau·ri·an [SOR-ee-ən] n one of the order of reptiles including the alligator, lizard, etc

sau·sage [SAW-sij] n chopped seasoned meat enclosed in thin tube of animal intestine or synthetic material **sausage meat** meat prepared for this

sau·té [soh-TAY] adj cooked or browned in pan with little butter, oil, etc ▷ vt **-téed, -té·ing** cook in this way

Sau·ternes [soh-TURN] n sweet white wine from S Bordeaux, France; **(s-)** similar wine made elsewhere

sav·age [SAV-ij] adj wild; ferocious; brutal; uncivilized; primitive ▷ n member of savage tribe, barbarian ▷ vt **-aged, -ag·ing** attack ferociously **sav'age·ry** n

sa·van·na, sa·van·nah [sə-VAN-ə] n extensive open grassy plain

sa·vant [sa-VAHNT] n person of learning

save [sayv] v **saved, sav·ing** ▷ vt rescue, preserve; protect; secure; keep for future, lay by; prevent need of; spare; except; computing keep (data) by moving to location for storage ▷ vi lay by money ▷ prep except ▷ conj but **saving** adj frugal; thrifty; delivering from sin; excepting; compensating ▷ prep except ▷ n economy ▷ pl money, earnings put by for future use

sav·ior [SAYV-yər] n person who rescues another; **(S-)** Christ

sa·voir-faire [sav-wahr-FAIR] n Fr ability to do, say, the right thing in any situation

sa·vor [SAY-vər] n characteristic taste; flavor; odor; distinctive quality ▷ vi have particular smell or taste; have suggestion (of) ▷ vt give flavor to; have flavor of; enjoy, appreciate **sa'vor·y** adj attractive to taste or smell; not sweet

sa·vor·y [SAY-və-ree] n, pl **-vor·ies** aromatic herb used in cooking

sav·vy [SAV-ee] vt inf **-vied, -vy·ing** understand ▷ n wits, intelligence

saw[1] n tool for cutting wood, etc

by tearing it with toothed edge ▷ v
sawed, sawed or **sawn, saw·ing**
cut with saw; make movements
of sawing **saw'dust** n fine wood
fragments made in sawing **saw'mill**
n mill where timber is sawed by
machine into planks, etc
saw² pt of SEE
saw³ n wise saying, proverb
sax·i·frage [SAK-sà-frij] n alpine
or rock plant
Sax·on [SAK-sàn] n member of
West Germanic people who settled
widely in the early Middle
Ages ▷ adj
sax·o·phone [SAK-sà-fohn] n
keyed wind instrument
say vt **said** [sed], **say·ing, says**
[sez] speak; pronounce; state;
express; take as example or as near
enough; form and deliver opinion
▷ n what one has to say; chance of
saying it; share in decision **saying** n
maxim, proverb
Sb chemistry antimony
Sc chemistry scandium
scab [skab] n crust formed over
wound; skin disease; disease of
plants; strikebreaker **scab'by** adj
-bi·er, -bi·est
scab·bard [SKAB-àrd] n sheath for
sword or dagger
scab·rous [SKAYB-ràs] adj having
rough surface; thorny; indecent; risky
scaf·fold [SKAF-àld] n temporary
platform for workmen; gallows
scaf'fold·ing n (material for
building) scaffold
sca·lar [SKAY-làr] n variable
quantity, eg time, having magnitude
but no direction ▷ adj
scald [skawld] vt burn with hot
liquid or steam; clean, sterilize with
boiling water; heat (liquid) almost to
boiling point ▷ n injury by scalding
scale¹ [skayl] n one of the thin,

overlapping plates covering fishes
and reptiles; thin flake; incrustation
that forms in boilers, etc ▷ v **scaled,
scal·ing** ▷ vt remove scales from
▷ vi come off in scales **scal'y** adj
scal·i·er, scal·i·est resembling or
covered in scales **scale insect** plant
pest covered by waxy secretion
scale² n (chiefly in pl) weighing
instrument ▷ v **scaled, scal·ing**
weigh in scales; have weight of
scale³ n graduated table or
sequence of marks at regular
intervals used as reference or for
fixing standards, as in making
measurements, in music, etc; ratio
of size between a thing and a model
or map of it; (relative) degree, extent
▷ vt **scaled, scal·ing** climb ▷ adj
proportionate **scale up, down**
increase or decrease proportionately
in size
sca·lene [SKAY-leen] adj (of
triangle) with three unequal sides
scal·lop [SKOL-àp] n edible
shellfish; edging in small curves like
edge of scallop shell ▷ vt shape like
scallop shell; cook in scallop shell or
dish like one
scalp [skalp] n skin and hair of top
of head ▷ vt cut off scalp of
scal·pel [SKAL-pàl] n small surgical
knife
scam [skam] n inf a dishonest
scheme
scamp [skamp] n mischievous
person or child ▷ v do or make
hastily or carelessly
scam·per [SKAM-pàr] vi run about;
run hastily from place to place ▷ n
scam·pi [SKAM-pee] n, pl **scampi**
large shrimp; dish of these sautéed in
oil or butter and garlic
scan [skan] v **scanned, scan·ning**
look at carefully, scrutinize; measure
or read (verse) by metrical feet;

examine, search by systematically varying the direction of a radar or sonar beam; glance over quickly; (of verse) conform to metrical rules ▷ *n* scanning **scan'ner** *n* device, esp electronic, that scans **scan'sion** [-shən] *n*

scan·dal [SKAN-dl] *n* action, event generally considered disgraceful; malicious gossip **scan'dal·ize** vt **-ized, -iz·ing** shock **scan'dal·ous** [-dl-əs] *adj* outrageous, disgraceful

scant [skant] *adj* **-er, -est** barely sufficient or not sufficient **scant'i·ly** *adv* **scant'y** *adj* **scant·i·er, scant·i·est scant·ies** [SKAN-teez] *n* very brief underpants

scape·goat [SKAYP-goht] *n* person bearing blame for others **scape'grace** [-grays] *n* rascal; unscrupulous person

scap·u·la [SKAP-yà-là] *n, pl* **-las** shoulder blade **scap'u·lar** [-làr] *adj* of scapula ▷ *n* loose sleeveless monastic garment

scar [skar] *n* mark left by healed wound, burn or sore; change resulting from emotional distress ▷ *v* **scarred, scar·ring** mark, heal with scar

scar·ab [SKA-ràb] *n* sacred beetle of ancient Egypt; gem cut in shape of this

scarce [skairs] *adj* hard to find; existing or available in insufficient quantity; uncommon **scarce'ly** *adv* only just; not quite; definitely or probably not **scar'ci·ty** [-si-tee] *n*

scare [skair] *vt* **scared, scar·ing** frighten ▷ *n* fright, sudden panic **scar'y** *adj* **scar·i·er, scar·i·est scare'crow** [-kroh] *n* thing set up to frighten birds from crops; badly dressed or miserable looking person **scare·mon·ger** [-mung-gàr] *n* one who spreads alarming rumors

scarf¹ [skarf] *n, pl* **scarfs** or **scarves** long narrow strip, large piece of material to put around neck, head, etc

scarf² *n, pl* **scarfs** part cut away from each of two pieces of timber to be jointed longitudinally; joint so made ▷ *vt* cut or join in this way

scar·i·fy [SKA-rà-fī] *vt* **-fied, -fy·ing** scratch, cut slightly all over; lacerate; stir surface soil of; criticize mercilessly

scar·let [SKAHR-lit] *n* a brilliant red color; cloth or clothing of this color ▷ *adj* of this color; immoral, esp unchaste **scarlet fever** infectious fever with scarlet rash

scarp [skahrp] *n* steep slope; inside slope of ditch in fortifications

scath·ing [SKAYth-ing] *adj* harshly critical; cutting; damaging

scat·ter [SKAT-àr] *v* throw in various directions; put here and there; sprinkle ▷ *vi* disperse ▷ *n* **scat'ter·brain** [-brayn] *n* silly, careless person

scav·enge [SKAV-inj] *v* **-enged, -eng·ing** search for (anything usable) usu among discarded material **scav'en·ger** *n* person who scavenges; animal, bird that feeds on refuse

scene [seen] *n* place of action of novel, play, etc; place of any action; subdivision of play; view; episode; display of strong emotion **scen'er·y** *n, pl* **-er·ies** natural features of area; constructions of wood, canvas, etc used on stage to represent a place where action is happening **sce'nic** *adj* picturesque; of or on the stage **sce·nar·i·o** [si-NAIR-ee-oh] *n, pl* **-i·os** summary of plot (of play, etc) or plan

scent [sent] *n* distinctive smell, esp pleasant one; trail, clue; perfume

▷ *vt* detect or track (by smell); suspect, sense; fill with fragrance

scep·ter [SEP-tər] *n* ornamental staff as symbol of royal power; royal dignity

sched·ule [SKEJ-uul] *n* plan of procedure for a project; list; timetable ▷ *vt* **-uled, -ul·ing** enter in schedule; plan to occur at certain time **on schedule** on time

sche·ma [SKEE-mə] *n, pl* **-ma·ta** [-mə-tə] *or* **-mas** overall plan or diagram **sche·mat·ic** *adj* presented as plan or diagram **sche·ma·tize** [-tiz] *v* **-tized, -tiz·ing**

scheme [skeem] *n* plan, design; project; outline ▷ *v* **schemed, schem·ing** devise, plan, esp in underhand manner **schem·er** *n*

scher·zo [SKERT-soh] *n* music light playful composition

schism [SIZ-əm] *n* (group resulting from) division in political party, church, etc **schis·mat·ic** *n, adj*

schist [shist] *n* crystalline rock that splits into layers

schiz·o·phre·ni·a [skit-sə-FREE-nee-ə] *n* mental disorder involving deterioration of, confusion about personality **schiz·o·phren·ic** [-FREN-ik] *adj, n* **schiz·oid** [-soid] *adj* relating to schizophrenia

schmaltz [shmahlts] *n* excessive sentimentality **schmaltz·y** *adj* **schmaltz·i·er, schmaltz·i·est**

schnapps [shnops] *n* spirit distilled from potatoes; any strong spirit

schnit·zel [SHNIT-səl] *n* thin slice of meat, esp veal

scholar *n* see **SCHOOL¹**

school¹ [skool] *n* institution for teaching children or for giving instruction in any subject; buildings of such institution; group of thinkers, writers, artists, etc with principles or methods in common ▷ *vt* educate; bring under control, train **school bus** vehicle used to transport children to or from school or on school-related activities **school·man** *n* medieval philosopher **schol·ar** [SKOL-ər] *n* learned person; one taught in school; one quick to learn **schol·ar·ly** *adj* learned, erudite **schol·ar·ship** *n* learning; prize, grant to student for payment of school or college fees **scho·las·tic** [skə-LAS-tik] *adj* of schools or scholars, or education; pedantic

school² *n* large number (of fish, whales, etc)

schoon·er [SKOO-nər] *n* fore-and-aft rigged vessel with two or more masts; tall glass

schot·tische [SHOT-ish] *n* kind of dance; music for this

sci·at·i·ca [sī-AT-i-kə] *n* neuralgia of hip and thigh; pain in sciatic nerve **sci·at·ic** *adj* of the hip; of sciatica

sci·ence [SĪ-əns] *n* systematic study and knowledge of natural or physical phenomena; any branch of study concerned with observed material facts **sci·en·tif·ic** *adj* of the principles of science; systematic **sci·en·tif·i·cal·ly** *adv* **sci·en·tist** *n* one versed in natural science **science fiction** stories set in the future making imaginative use of scientific knowledge

scim·i·tar [SIM-i-tər] *n* oriental curved sword

scin·til·late [SIN-tl-ayt] *vi* **-lat·ed, -lat·ing** sparkle; be animated, witty, clever **scin·til·la·tion** *n*

sci·on [SĪ-ən] *n* descendant, heir; slip for grafting

scis·sors [SIZ-ərs] *pl n* cutting instrument with two crossed pivoted blades

scle·ro·sis [skli-ROH-sis] n, pl **-ses** [-seez] a hardening of bodily organs, tissues, etc **scle·rot·ic** [-ROT-ik] adj

scoff [skof] vt express derision for ▷ n derision; mocking words **scoff·er** n

scold [skohld] vt find fault; reprimand, be angry with ▷ n someone who does this **scold·ing** n

sconce [skons] n bracket candlestick on wall

scone [skohn] n small plain biscuit baked on griddle or in oven

scoop [skoop] n small shovel-like tool for ladling, hollowing out, etc; inf exclusive news item; inf information ▷ vt ladle out; hollow out, rake in with scoop; make sudden profit; beat (rival newspaper, etc)

scoot [skoot] vi inf move off quickly **scoot·er** n child's vehicle propelled by pushing on ground with one foot; light motorcycle; (also **motor scooter**)

scope [skohp] n range of activity or application; room, opportunity

scorch [skorch] v burn, be burned, on surface; parch; shrivel; wither ▷ n slight burn **scorch·er** n inf very hot day

score [skor] n points gained in game, competition; group of 20; musical notation; mark or notch, esp to keep tally; reason, account; grievance ▷ pl lots ▷ v **scored, scor·ing** ▷ vt gain points in game; mark; cross out; arrange music (for) ▷ vi keep tally of points; succeed

scorn [skorn] n contempt, derision ▷ vt despise **scorn·ful** [-fəl] adj derisive **scorn·ful·ly** adv

scor·pi·on [SKOR-pee-ən] n small lobster-shaped animal with sting at end of jointed tail

Scot [skot] n native of Scotland

Scot·tish adj **Scotch** n whisky distilled in Scotland **Scots** adj Scottish ▷ n English dialect spoken in Scotland **Scots·man** [-mən] **Scots·wom·an** n

scotch [skoch] vt put an end to

scot-free [skot-free] adj without harm or loss

scoun·drel [SKOWN-drəl] n villain, blackguard **scoun·drel·ly** adv

scour[1] [skowr] vt clean, polish by rubbing; clear or flush out

scour[2] v move rapidly along or over (territory) in search of something

scourge [skurj] n whip, lash; severe affliction; pest; calamity ▷ vt **scourged, scourg·ing** flog; punish severely

scout [skowt] n one sent out to reconnoiter; (**S-**) member of organization for young people which aims to develop character and responsibility ▷ vi go out, act as scout; reconnoiter **scout·mas·ter** n leader of troop of Boy Scouts

scow [skow] n unpowered barge

scowl [skowl] vi frown gloomily or sullenly ▷ n angry or gloomy expression

scrab·ble [SKRAB-əl] v **-bled, -bling** scrape at with hands, claws in disorderly manner ▷ n (**S-**) ® board game in which words are formed by letter tiles

scrag [skrag] n lean person or animal; lean end of a neck of mutton **scrag·gy** adj **-gi·er, -gi·est** thin, bony

scrag·gly [SKRAG-lee] adj **-gli·er, -gli·est** untidy

scram[1] [skram] v **scrammed, scram·ming** inf go away hastily, get out

scram[2] n emergency shutdown of nuclear reactor ▷ v **scrammed, scram·ming**

scram·ble [SKRAM-bəl] v **-bled, -bling** ▷ vi move along or up by crawling, climbing, etc; struggle with others (for); (of aircraft, aircrew) take off hurriedly ▷ vt mix up; cook (eggs) beaten up with milk; render (speech) unintelligible by electronic device ▷ n scrambling; rough climb; disorderly proceeding; emergency takeoff of military aircraft

scrap [skrap] n small piece or fragment; leftover material; inf fight ▷ v **scrapped, scrap·ping** break up, discard as useless; fight **scrap'py** adj **-pi·er, -pi·est** unequal in quality; badly finished **scrap'book** [-buuk] n book in which newspaper clippings, etc are kept

scrape [skrayp] vt **scraped, scrap·ing** rub with something sharp; clean, smooth thus; grate; scratch; rub with harsh noise ▷ n act, sound of scraping; awkward situation, esp as result of escapade **scrap'er** n instrument for scraping; contrivance on which mud, etc is scraped from shoes

scratch [skrach] vt score, make narrow surface wound with claws, nails, or anything pointed; make marks on with pointed instruments; scrape (skin) with nails to relieve itching; remove, withdraw from list, race, etc ▷ vi use claws or nails, esp to relieve itching ▷ n wound, mark or sound made by scratching; line or starting point ▷ adj got together at short notice; impromptu; golf without any allowance **scratch'y** adj **scratch·i·er, scratch·i·est scratch hit** baseball weak hit barely enabling batter to reach first base

scrawl [skrawl] vt write, draw untidily ▷ n thing scrawled; careless writing

scrawn·y [SKRAW-nee] adj

scrawn·i·er, scrawn·i·est thin, bony

scream [skreem] vi utter piercing cry, esp of fear, pain, etc; be very obvious ▷ vt utter in a scream ▷ n shrill, piercing cry; inf very funny person or thing

scree [skree] n loose shifting stones; slope covered with these

screech [skreech] vi, n scream

screed [skreed] n long (tedious) letter, passage or speech; thin layer of cement; in masonry, board used to make level

screen [skreen] n device to shelter from heat, light, draft, observation, etc; anything used for such purpose; mesh over doors, windows to keep out insects; white or silvered surface on which photographic images are projected; windscreen; wooden or stone partition in church ▷ vt shelter, hide; protect from detection; show (film); scrutinize; examine (group of people) for presence of disease, weapons, etc; examine for political motives; *electricity* protect from stray electric or magnetic fields **screen saver** computing software that produces changing images on a monitor when the computer is operating but idle **the screen** motion pictures generally

screw [skroo] n (nail-like device or cylinder with) spiral thread cut to engage similar thread or to bore into material (wood, etc) to pin or fasten; anything resembling a screw in shape, esp in spiral form; propeller; twist ▷ vt fasten with screw; twist around; extort **screw'y** adj **screw·i·er, screw·i·est** sl crazy, eccentric **screw'driv·er** n tool for turning screws; drink of vodka and orange juice **screw up** sl bungle, distort

scrib·ble [SKRIB-əl] v **-bled, -bling** write, draw carelessly; make meaningless marks with pen or pencil ▷ n something scribbled

scribe [skrīb] n writer; copyist ▷ v scribed, scrib·ing scratch a line with pointed instrument

scrim·mage [SKRIM-ijj] n scuffle; football a play ▷ v **-maged, -mag·ing** engage in scrimmage

scrimp [skrimp] vt make too small or short; treat meanly **scrimp'y** adj **scrimp·i·er, scrimp·i·est**

scrip [skrip] n written certificate esp of holding fractional share of stock; paper certificates issued in place of money

script [skript] n (system or style of) handwriting; written characters; written text of film, play, radio or television program ▷ vt write a script

scrip·ture [SKRIP-chər] n sacred writings; (**S-**) the Bible **scrip'tur·al** adj

scrof·u·la [SKROF-yə-lə] n tuberculosis of lymphatic glands, esp of neck **scrof'u·lous** [-ləs] adj

scroll [skrohl] n roll of parchment or paper; list; ornament shaped thus ▷ v computing move (text) up or down on a VDU screen

scro·tum [SKROH-təm] n, pl **-tums** pouch containing testicles

scrounge [skrownj] v **scrounged, scroung·ing** get without cost, by begging **scroung'er** n

scrub¹ [skrub] vt **scrubbed, scrub·bing** clean with hard brush and water; scour; sl cancel, get rid of ▷ n scrubbing

scrub² n stunted trees; brushwood **scrub'by** adj **-bi·er, -bi·est** covered with scrub; stunted; shabby

scruff [skruf] n nape (of neck)

scrum [skrum] n rugby restarting of play in which opposing packs of forwards push against each other to gain possession of the ball

scrunch [skrunch] v crumple or crunch or be crumpled or crunched ▷ n act or sound of scrunching

scrun'chie [SKRUNCH-ee] n loop of elastic covered loosely with fabric, used to hold the hair in a ponytail

scru·ple [SKROO-pəl] n doubt or hesitation about what is morally right; weight of 20 grains ▷ v **-pled, -pling** hesitate **scru'pu·lous** [-pyə-ləs] adj extremely conscientious; thorough; attentive to small points

scru·ti·ny [SKROOT-n-ee] n, pl **-nies** close examination; critical investigation; searching look **scru·ti·nize** vt **-nized, -niz·ing** examine closely

scu·ba [SKOO-bə] n, adj (relating to) self-contained underwater breathing apparatus

scud [skud] vi **scud·ded, scud·ding** run fast; run before wind

scuff [skuf] vi drag, scrape with feet in walking ▷ vt scrape with feet; scratch (something) by scraping ▷ n act, sound of scuffing ▷ pl thong sandals **scuffed** adj (of shoes) scraped or slightly grazed

scuf·fle [SKUF-əl] vi **-fled, -fling** fight in disorderly manner; shuffle ▷ n

scull [skul] n oar used in stern of boat; short oar used in pairs ▷ v propel, move by means of scull(s)

scul·ler·y [SKUL-ə-ree] n, pl **-ler·ies** place for washing dishes, etc

scul·lion [SKUL-yən] n despicable person; kitchen servant doing menial work

sculp·ture [SKULP-chər] n art of forming figures in relief or solid; product of this art ▷ vt **-tured, -tur·ing** represent by sculpture

sculpt v **sculp'tur·al** adj with qualities proper to sculpture **sculp·tor, sculp'tress** [-tris] n

scum [skum] n froth or other floating matter on liquid; waste part of anything; vile person(s) or thing(s) **scum'my** adj **-mi·er, -mi·est**

scup·per [SKUP-ər] n hole in ship's side level with deck to carry off water

scurf [skurf] n flaky matter on scalp, dandruff **scurf'y** adj **scurf·i·er, scurf·i·est**

scur·ril·ous [SKUR-ə-ləs] adj coarse, indecently abusive **scur·ril·i·ty** [skə-RIL-ə-tee] n, pl **-ties**

scur·ry [SKUR-ee] vi **-ried, -ry·ing** run hastily ▷ n, pl **-ries** bustling haste; flurry

scur·vy [SKUR-vee] n disease caused by lack of vitamin C ▷ adj **-vi·er, -vi·est** afflicted with the disease; mean, contemptible

scut·tle¹ [SKUT-l] n fireside container for coal

scuttle² vi **-tled, -tling** rush away; run hurriedly ▷ n

scuttle³ vt **-tled, -tling** make hole in ship to sink it; abandon, cause to be abandoned

scut·work [SKUT-wurk] n inf menial work

scythe [sith] n manual implement with long curved blade for cutting grass, grain ▷ vt **scythed, scyth·ing** cut with scythe

Se chemistry selenium

sea [see] n mass of salt water covering greater part of Earth; broad tract of this; waves; swell; large quantity; vast expanse **sea'board** [-bord] n coast **sea'far·ing** [-fair-ing] adj occupied in sea voyages **sea horse** fish with pony plated body and horselike head **sea lion** kind of large seal **sea'man** [-mən]

n sailor **sea'sick·ness** n nausea caused by motion of ship **sea'sick** adj **sea urchin** marine animal, echinus **sea'weed** n plant growing in sea **sea'wor·thy** [-wurth-ee] adj **-thi·er, -thi·est** in fit condition to put to sea

seal¹ [seel] n piece of metal or stone engraved with device for impression on wax, etc; impression thus made (on letters, etc); device; material preventing passage of water, air, oil, etc; (also **seal'er**) ▷ vt affix seal to ratify, authorize; mark with stamp as evidence of some quality; keep close or secret; settle; make watertight, airtight, etc

seal² n amphibious furred carnivorous mammal with flippers as limbs ▷ vi hunt seals **seal'er** n person or ship engaged in sealing **seal'skin** n skin, fur of seals

seam [seem] n line of junction of two edges, eg of two pieces of cloth, or two planks; thin layer, stratum ▷ vt mark with furrows or wrinkles **seam'less** [-lis] adj **seam'y** adj **seam·i·er, seam·i·est** sordid; marked with seams **seam'stress** [-stris] n sewing woman

sé·ance [SAY-ahns] n meeting at which spiritualists attempt to communicate with the dead

sear [seer] vt scorch, brand with hot iron; deaden

search [surch] v look over or through to find something; probe into, examine ▷ n act of searching; quest **search'ing** adj keen; thorough; severe **search engine** computing Internet service enabling users to search for items of interest online **search'light** n powerful electric light with concentrated beam

sea·son [SEE-zən] n one of

four divisions of year associated with type of weather and stage of agriculture; period during which thing happens, grows, is active, etc; proper time ▷ vt flavor with salt, herbs, etc; make edible or ready for use; make experienced **sea·son·a·ble** adj appropriate for the season; opportune; fit **sea·son·al** [-əl] adj depending on, varying with seasons **sea·son·ing** n flavoring **in season** (of an animal) in heat **season ticket** one for series of events within a certain time

seat [seet] n thing for sitting on; buttocks; right to seat (eg in legislature, etc); place where something is located, centered; locality of disease, trouble, etc; country house ▷ vt make to sit; provide sitting accommodation for; install firmly

se·ba·ceous [si-BAY-shəs] adj of, pert to fat; secreting fat, oil

se·cant [SEE-kant] n mathematics (secant of an angle) reciprocal of its cosine; line that intersects a curve

se·cede [si-SEED] vi **-ced·ed, -ced·ing** withdraw formally from federation, union, etc **se·ces·sion** [-SESH-ən] n

se·clude [si-KLOOD] vt **-clud·ed, -clud·ing** guard from, remove from sight, view, contact with others **secluded** adj remote; private **se·clu·sion** [-KLOO-zhən] n

sec·ond [SEK-ənd] adj next after first; alternate; additional; of lower quality ▷ n person or thing coming second; attendant; sixtieth part of minute; square radii of time; moment ▷ pl inferior goods ▷ vt support; support (motion in meeting) so that discussion may be in order **sec·ond·hand'** adj bought after use by another; not original **second**

sight faculty of seeing events before they occur

sec·ond·ar·y [SEK-ən-der-ee] adj subsidiary, of less importance; developed from, or dependent on, something else; education after primary stage **sec·ond·ar·i·ly** adv

se·cret [SEE-krit] adj kept, meant to be kept from knowledge of others; hidden; private ▷ n thing kept secret **se·cre·cy** [-krə-see] n, pl **-cies** keeping or being kept secret **se·cre·tive** adj given to having secrets; uncommunicative; reticent **se·cre·tive·ness** [-tiv-nis] n

sec·re·tar·y [SEK-ri-ter-ee] n, pl **-tar·ies** one employed by individual or organization to deal with papers and correspondence, keep records, prepare business, etc; member of presidential cabinet **sec·re·tar·i·al** [-TAIR-ee-əl] adj **sec·re·tar·i·at** [-ət] n body of secretaries; building occupied by secretarial staff

se·crete [si-KREET] vt **-cret·ed, -cret·ing** hide; conceal; (of gland, etc) collect and supply particular substance in body **se·cre·tion** n

sect [sekt] n group of people (within religious body, etc) with common interest; faction **sec·tar·i·an** [-TAIR-ee-ən] adj of a sect; narrow-minded

sec·tion [SEK-shən] n part cut off; division; portion; distinct part of city, country, people, etc; cutting; drawing of anything as if cut through **sec·tion·al** adj

sec·tor [SEK-tər] n part or subdivision; part of circle enclosed by two radii and the arc they cut off

sec·u·lar [SEK-yə-lər] adj worldly; lay, not religious; not monastic; lasting for, or occurring once in, an age; centuries old **sec·u·lar·ism** n **sec·u·lar·ist** n one who believes that religion should have no place in civil affairs **sec·u·lar·i·za·tion** n **sec'u·lar·ize** vt -ized, -iz·ing transfer from religious to lay possession or use

se·cure [si-KYOOR] adj -cur·er, -cur·est safe; free from fear, anxiety; firmly fixed; certain; sure, confident ▷ vt -cured, -cur·ing gain possession of; make safe; free (creditor) from risk of loss; make firm **se·cur'i·ty** n, pl -ties state of safety; protection; that which secures; assurance; anything given as bond, caution or pledge; one who becomes surety for another

se·dan [si-DAN] n enclosed automobile body with two or four doors **sedan chair** history closed chair for one person, carried on poles by bearers

se·date' [si-DAYT] adj calm, collected, serious

sedate² vt -dat·ed, -dat·ing make calm by sedative **se·da'tion** n **sed'a·tive** adj having soothing or calming effect ▷ n sedative drug

sed·en·ta·ry [SED-n-ter-ee] adj done sitting down; sitting much

Se·der [SAY-dər] n ritual for the first or first two nights of Passover

sed·i·ment [SED-ə-mənt] n matter that settles to the bottom of liquid; dregs, lees **sed·i·men·ta·ry** adj

se·di·tion [si-DISH-ən] n speech or action threatening authority of a state **se·di'tious** [-shəs] adj

se·duce [si-DOOS] vt -duced, -duc·ing persuade to commit some (wrong) deed, esp sexual intercourse; tempt; attract **se·duc'er**, **se·duc'tress** n **se·duc'tion** [-DUK-shən] n **se·duc'tive** adj alluring; winning

sed·u·lous [SEJ-ə-ləs] adj diligent; industrious; persevering; persistent **se·du·li·ty** [si-DOO-li-tee] n

see' v saw, seen, see·ing perceive with eyes or mentally; observe; watch; find out; reflect; come to know; interview; make sure; accompany; perceive; consider; understand **seeing** conj since; in view of the fact that

see² n diocese, office, or jurisdiction of bishop

seed n reproductive germs of plants; one grain of this; such grains saved or used for sowing; origin; sperm; offspring ▷ vt sow with seed; arrange draw for tennis or other tournament, so that best players do not meet in early rounds ▷ vi produce seed **seed'ling** n young plant raised from seed **seed'y** adj **seed·i·er, seed·i·est** shabby; gone to seed; unwell, ill

seek v sought [sawt] **seek·ing** make search or inquiry for; search

seem vi appear (to be or to do); look; appear to one's judgment **seem'ing** adj apparent but not real **seem'ing·ly** adv

seem·ly [SEEM-lee] adj -li·er, -li·est becoming and proper **seem'li·ness** [-nis] n

seen pp of SEE

seep vi trickle through slowly, as water, ooze

seer n prophet

seer·suck·er [SEER-suk-ər] n light cotton fabric with slightly crinkled surface

see'saw n game in which children sit at opposite ends of plank supported in middle and swing up and down; plank used for this ▷ vi move up and down

seethe [seeth] vi **seethed**, **seeth·ing** boil, foam; be very agitated; be in constant movement

(as large crowd, etc)

seg·ment [SEG-mənt] *n* piece cut off; section ▷ *v* [SEG-ment] to divide into segments
seg·men·ta·tion *n*

seg·re·gate [SEG-ri-gayt] *vt* **-gat·ed, -gat·ing** set apart from rest; dissociate; separate; isolate
seg·re·ga·tion *n*

se·gue [SAY-gway] *vi* **-gued, -gue·ing** proceed from one section or piece of music to another without break; make a transition smoothly eg from one topic of conversation to another ▷ *n*

seis·mic [SIZ-mik] *adj* pert to earthquakes **seis·mo·graph** [-mə-graf] *n* instrument to record earthquakes **seis·mo·log·ic·al** pert to seismology **seis·mol·o·gist** [-MOL-ə-jist] *n* one versed in seismology **seis·mol·o·gy** *n* science concerned with study of earthquakes

seize [seez] *v* **seized, seiz·ing** ▷ *vt* grasp; lay hold of; capture ▷ *vi* in machine, of bearing or piston, to stick tightly through overheating **seiz·ure** [SEE-zhər] *n* act of taking, esp by legal writ, as goods; sudden onset of disease

sel·dom [SEL-dəm] *adv* not often, rarely

se·lect [si-LEKT] *vt* pick out, choose ▷ *adj* choice, picked; exclusive **se·lec·tion** *n* **se·lec·tive** *adj* **se·lec·tiv·i·ty** *n*

se·le·ni·um [si-LEE-nee-əm] *n* nonmetallic element with photoelectric properties

sel·e·nog·ra·phy [sel-ə-NOG-rə-fee] *n* study of surface of moon

self *pron, pl* **selves** used reflexively or to express emphasis ▷ *adj* (of color, etc) same throughout, uniform ▷ *n* one's own person or individuality

self·ish *adj* concerned unduly over personal profit or pleasure; lacking consideration for others; greedy **self·ish·ly** *adv* **self·less** [-lis] *adj* having no regard for self; unselfish

self- *prefix* used with many main words to mean: of oneself or itself; by, to, in, due to, for, or from the self; automatic(ally) **self-ad·dressed'** *adj* addressed to the sender **self-as·sured'** *adj* confident **self-cen'tered** *adj* totally preoccupied with one's own concerns **self-con'fi·dent** *adj* **self-con·tained'** *adj* containing everything needed, complete; (of an apartment) having its own facilities **self-con·trol'** *n* ability to control one's feelings and reactions **self-de·fense'** *n* defending of oneself or one's property **self-em·ployed'** *adj* earning a living from one's own business **self-ev'i·dent** *adj* obvious without proof **self-help'** *n* use of one's own abilities to solve problems; practice of solving one's problems within a group of people with similar problems **self-in·dul'gent** *adj* tending to indulge one's desires **self-in'ter·est** *adj* one's own advantage **self-rais'ing** *adj* (of flour) containing a raising agent **self-sat'is·fied** *adj* conceited

self-con'scious [-KON-shəs] *adj* unduly aware of oneself; conscious of one's acts or states

self-de·ter·mi·na·tion [-di-turmə-NAY-shən] *n* the right of person or nation to decide for itself

self-made' [-mayd] *adj* having achieved wealth, status, etc by one's own efforts

self-pos·sessed' [-pə-ZEST] *adj* calm, composed **self-pos·ses'sion** [-pə-ZESH-ən] *n*

self-re·spect' [-ri-SPEKT] *n* proper

sense of one's own dignity and integrity

self-right·eous [-Ri-chəs] adj smugly sure of one's own powers

self·same [-saym] adj very same

self-seek·ing [-] n (having) preoccupation with one's own interests

self-ser·vice [-SUR-vis] adj, n (of) the serving of oneself in a store or restaurant

self-suf·fi·cient [-sə-FISH-ənt] adj sufficient in itself; relying on one's own powers

self-will n obstinacy; willfulness **self-willed** [-] adj headstrong

sell v sold, sell·ing hand over for a price; stock, have for sale; make someone accept; find purchasers; inf betray, cheat ▷ n inf hoax **sell'er** n **sell'out** n disposing of completely by selling; betrayal

selt·zer (water) [SELT-sər] n effervescent (mineral) water

sel·vage [SEL-vij] n finished, unfraying edge of cloth

se·man·tic [si-MAN-tik] adj relating to meaning of words or symbols **se·man·tics** n study of linguistic meaning

sem·a·phore [SEM-ə-for] n post with movable arms for signaling; system of signaling by human or mechanical arms

sem·blance [SEM-bləns] n (false) appearance; image, likeness

se·men [SEE-mən] n fluid carrying sperm of male animals; sperm

se·mes·ter [si-MES-tər] n (half-year) session of academic year in many universities, colleges

sem·i [SEM-i] n inf semitrailer

semi- comb form half, partly, not completely: semicircle

sem·i·breve [SEM-ee-breev] n musical note half the length of a breve

sem·i·cir·cle [SEM-i-sur-kəl] n half of circle **sem·i·cir·cu·lar** [-SUR-kyə-lər] adj

sem·i·co·lon [SEM-i-koh-lən] n punctuation mark (;)

sem·i·con·duc·tor [sem-i-kən-DUK-tər] n physics substance with an electrical conductivity that increases with temperature or voltage

sem·i·de·tached [sem-ee-di-TACHT] adj, n (of) house joined to another on one side only

sem·i·fi·nal [sem-ee-FIN-l] n match, round, etc before final

sem·i·nal [SEM-ə-nl] adj capable of developing; influential, important; rudimentary; of semen or seed

sem·i·nar [SEM-ə-nahr] n meeting of group (of students) for discussion

sem·i·nar·y [SEM-ə-ner-ee] n, pl -nar·ies college for priests **sem·i·nar'i·an** n student at seminary

sem·i·pre·cious [sem-ee-PRESH-əs] adj (of gemstones) having less value than precious stones

sem·i·skilled [sem-ee-SKILD] adj partly skilled, trained but not for specialized work

Sem·ite [SEM-It] n member of ancient and modern peoples including Jews and Arabs; Jew **Se·mit·ic** [sə-MIT-ik] adj denoting a Semite; Jewish

sem·i·tone [SEM-ee-tohn] n musical half tone

sem·i·trail·er [SEM-i-tray-lər] n trailer used for hauling freight, having wheels at back but supported by towing vehicle in front

sem·o·li·na [sem-ə-LEE-nə] n milled product of durum wheat, used for pasta, etc

sen·ate [SEN-it] n upper legislative body of country; upper council of university, etc **sen·a·tor** [-ə-tər] n **sen·a·to·ri·al** [-TOR-ee-əl] adj

send vt **sent, send·ing** cause to go or be conveyed; dispatch; transmit (by radio)

se·nile [SEE-nil] adj showing weakness of old age **se·nil·i·ty** [si-NIL-i-tee] n

sen·ior [SEEN-yər] adj superior in rank or standing; older ▷ n superior; elder person **sen·ior·i·ty** [-YOR-i-tee] n

se·ñor [sayn-YOR] n Sp title of respect, like Mr. **se·ñor·a** n Mrs **se·ño·ri·ta** [-REE-tə] n Miss

sen·sa·tion [sen-SAY-shən] n operation of sense, feeling, awareness; excited feeling, state of excitement; exciting event; strong impression; commotion **sen·sa·tion·al** adj producing great excitement; melodramatic; of perception by senses **sen·sa·tion·al·ism** n use of sensational language, etc to arouse intense emotional excitement; doctrine that sensations are basis of all knowledge

sense [sens] n any of bodily faculties of perception or feeling; sensitiveness of any or all of these faculties; ability to perceive, mental alertness; consciousness; meaning; coherence, intelligible meaning; sound practical judgment ▷ vt **sensed, sens·ing** perceive; understand **sense·less** [-lis] adj

sen·si·ble [SEN-sə-bəl] adj reasonable, wise; perceptible by senses; aware, mindful; considerable, appreciable **sen·si·bil·i·ty** n ability to feel esp emotional or moral feelings **sen·si·bly** adv

sen·si·tive [SEN-si-tiv] adj open to, acutely affected by, external impressions; easily affected or altered; easily upset by criticism; responsive to slight changes **sen·si·tiv·i·ty** n **sen·si·tize** [-tiz] vt **-tized, -tiz·ing** make sensitive, esp make photographic film, etc) sensitive to light

sen·sor [SEN-sər] n device that responds to stimulus

sen·so·ry [SEN-sə-ree] adj relating to organs, operation, of senses

sen·su·al [SEN-shoo-əl] adj of senses only and not of mind; given to pursuit of pleasures of sense; self-indulgent; licentious **sen·su·al·ist** n

sen·su·ous [SEN-shoo-əs] adj stimulating, or apprehended by, senses esp in aesthetic manner

sent pt/pp of SEND

sen·tence [SEN-tns] n combination of words that is complete as expressing a thought; judgment passed on criminal by court or judge ▷ vt **-tenced, -tenc·ing** pass sentence on, condemn **sen·ten·tial** [-TEN-shəl] adj of sentence **sen·ten·tious** [-shəs] adj full of axioms and maxims; pithy; pompously moralizing **sen·ten·tious·ness** n

sen·tient [SEN-shənt] adj capable of feeling; feeling; thinking **sen·tience** n

sen·ti·ment [SEN-tə-mənt] n tendency to be moved by feeling rather than reason; verbal expression of feeling; mental feeling, emotion; opinion **sen·ti·men·tal** adj given to indulgence in sentiment and in its expression; weak; sloppy **sen·ti·men·tal·i·ty** n

sen·ti·nel [SEN-tn-l] n sentry

sen·try [SEN-tree] n, pl **-tries** soldier on watch

se·pal [SEE-pəl] n leaf or division of

the calyx of a flower

sep·a·rate [SEP-ə-rayt] v **-rat·ed, -rat·ing** ▷vt part; divide; sever; put apart; occupy place between ▷vi withdraw, become parted from ▷adj [SEP-ər-it] disconnected, apart, distinct, individual **sep·a·ra·ble** adj **sep·a·ra·tion** [-RAY-shən] n disconnection; law living apart of married people without divorce **sep·a·ra·tor** n that which separates; apparatus for separating cream from milk

se·pi·a [SEE-pee-ə] n reddish-brown pigment made from a fluid secreted by the cuttlefish ▷adj of this color

sep·sis n presence of pus-forming bacteria in body

sep·ten·ni·al [sep-TEN-ee-əl] adj lasting, occurring every seven years

sep·tet' n music for seven instruments or voices; group of seven performers

sep·tic [SEP-tik] adj of, caused by, sepsis; (of wound) infected **sep·ti·ce·mi·a** [-SEE-mee-ə] n blood poisoning

sep·tu·a·ge·nar·i·an [sep-choo-ə-jə-NAIR-ee-ən] adj aged between seventy and eighty ▷n

se·pul·cher [SEP-əl-kər] n tomb; burial vault **se·pul·chral** [sə-PUL-krəl] adj of burial, or the grave; mournful; gloomy **sep·ul·ture** [-əl-chər] n burial

se·quel [SEE-kwəl] n consequence; continuation, eg of story

se·quence [SEE-kwəns] n arrangement of things in successive order; section, episode of motion picture **se·quen·tial** [si-KWEN-shəl] adj

se·ques·ter [si-KWES-tər] vt separate; seclude; put aside **se·ques·trate** [-KWES-trayt] vt

-trat·ed, -trat·ing confiscate; divert or appropriate income of property to satisfy claims against its owner **se·ques·tra·tion** [-TRAY-shən] n

se·quin [SEE-kwin] n small ornamental metal disk or spangle on dresses, etc; orig Venetian gold coin

se·quoi·a [si-KWOI-ə] n giant Californian coniferous tree

se·ragl·io [si-RAL-yoh] n, pl **-ragl·ios** harem, palace, of Turkish sultan

ser·aph [SER-əf] n, pl **-a·phim** [-ə-fim] member of highest order of angels

ser·e·nade [ser-ə-NAYD] n sentimental piece of music or song of type addressed to woman by lover esp at evening ▷v **-nad·ed, -nad·ing** sing serenade (to someone)

ser·en·dip·i·ty [ser-ən-DIP-i-tee] n faculty of making fortunate discoveries by accident

se·rene [sə-REEN] adj calm, tranquil; unclouded; quiet, placid **se·ren·i·ty** [-REN-i-tee] n

serf [surf] n one of class of medieval laborers bound to, and transferred with, land **serf'dom** [-dəm] n

serge [surj] n strong hard-wearing twilled worsted fabric

ser·geant [SAHR-jənt] n noncommissioned officer in Army, Marine Corps, police department **sergeant major** noncommissioned Army officer serving as chief administrative assistant; noncommissioned officer ranking above first sergeant in Marine Corps **sergeant at arms** legislative, organizational officer assigned to keep order, etc

se·ries [SEER-eez] n, pl **series** sequence; succession; set (eg of radio, TV programs with same characters, setting, but different stories) **se·ri·al** [SEER-ee-əl] n story or play produced in successive episodes or installments; periodical publication ▷ adj **se'ri·al·ize** v **-ized, -iz·ing** publish, present as serial **serial killer** murderer who commits series of murders in same pattern oft in same locality

ser·if [SUR-if] n small line finishing off stroke of letter

se·ri·ous [SEER-ee-əs] adj thoughtful, solemn; earnest, sincere; of importance; giving cause for concern

ser·mon [SUR-mən] n discourse of religious instruction or exhortation spoken or read from pulpit; any similar discourse **ser'mon·ize** vi **-ized, -iz·ing** talk like preacher; compose sermons

ser·pent [SUR-pənt] n snake **serp'en·tine** [-teen] adj like, shaped like, serpent

ser·rate [SER-ayt], **ser·rat·ed** [SER-ay-tid] adj having notched, sawlike edge **ser·ra'tion** n

se·rum [SEER-əm] n, pl **-rums** watery animal fluid, esp thin part of blood as used for inoculation or vaccination

serve [surv] v **served, serv·ing** (mainly tr) work for, under, another; attend (to customers) in store, etc; provide; help to (food, etc); present (food, etc) in particular way; provide with regular supply of; be member of military unit; pay homage to; spend time doing; be useful, suitable enough; tennis, etc put (ball) into play ▷ n tennis, etc act of serving ball **ser'vant** [-vənt] n personal or domestic attendant **serv'er** [-vər] n person who serves; computing computer or program that supplies

data to other machines on a network **serv'ice** [-vis] n the act of serving, helping, assisting; system organized to provide for needs of public; maintenance of vehicle; use; readiness, availability for use; set of dishes, etc; form, session, of public worship ▷ pl armed forces ▷ vt **-iced, -ic·ing** overhaul **serv'ice·a·ble** adj in working order, usable; durable **service road** narrow road giving access to houses, stores, etc **service station** place supplying fuel, oil, maintenance for motor vehicles

ser·vile [SUR-vil] adj slavish, without independence; cringing; fawning; menial **serv·il'i·ty** n

ser·vi·tude [SUR-vi-tood] n bondage, slavery

ser·vo·mech·an·ism [SUR-voh-mek-ə-niz-əm] n electronic device for converting small mechanical, hydraulic or other type of force into larger, esp in steering mechanisms

ses·a·me [SES-ə-mee] n plant with seeds used as herbs and for making oil

ses·sion [SESH-ən] n meeting of court, etc; assembly; continuous series of such meetings; any period devoted to an activity; school or university term: summer session

set vt **set, set·ting** (mainly tr) put or place in specified position or condition; cause to sit; fix, point, put up; make ready; become firm or fixed; establish; prescribe, allot; put to music; (of hair, arrange while wet, so that it dries in position; of sun, go down; have direction ▷ adj fixed, established; deliberate; formal, arranged beforehand; unvarying ▷ n act or state of being set; bearing, posture; radio, TV complete apparatus for reception or transmission; *theater, films* organized settings and equipment to form ensemble of scene; number of things, persons associated as being similar, complementary or used together; *mathematics* group of numbers, objects, etc with at least one common property **set'back** *n* anything that hinders or impedes **set'up** *n* position; organization **set up** establish; *inf* treat, as to drinks; *inf* framing, entrap; *inf* lure into embarrassing, dangerous, situation **set shot** *basketball* shot at basket taken from standing position and relatively distant from basket

set·tee' *n* couch

set·ter [SET-ər] *n* various breeds of gun dog

set·ting [SET-ing] *n* background; surroundings; scenery and other stage accessories; act of fixing; decorative metalwork holding precious stone, etc in position; tableware and cutlery for (single place at) table; descending below horizon of sun; music for song

set·tle [SET-l] *v* **-tled, -tling** ▷ *vt* arrange, put in order; establish; make firm or secure or quiet; decide upon; end (dispute, etc); pay; bestow (property) by legal deed ▷ *vi* come to rest; subside; become clear; take up residence; subside, sink to bottom; come to agreement **set'tle·ment** [-mənt] *n* act of settling; place newly inhabited; money bestowed legally; subsidence (of building) **set·tler** [SET-lər] *n* colonist

sev·en [SEV-ən] *adj, n* cardinal number, next after six **sev'enth** *adj* the ordinal number **sev'en·teen'** *adj, n* ten and seven **sev'en·ty** *adj, n, pl* **-ties** ten times seven

sev·er [SEV-ər] *v* separate, divide; cut off **sev·er·ance** [-əns] *n*

severance pay compensation paid by a firm to an employee for loss of employment

sev·er·al [SEV-ər-əl] *adj* some, a few; separate; individual; various; different ▷ *pron* indefinite small number **sev'er·al·ly** *adv* apart from others; singly

se·vere [sə-VEER] *adj* **-ver·er, -ver·est** strict; rigorous; hard to do; harsh; austere; extreme **se·ver·i·ty** [-VER-i-tee]

sew [soh] *v* **sewed, sewn** or **sewed, sew·ing** join with needle and thread; make by sewing

sew·age [SOO-ij] *n* refuse, waste matter, excrement conveyed in sewer **sew'er** *n* underground drain to remove waste water and refuse **sew'er·age** *n* arrangement of sewers; sewage

sex [seks] *n* state of being male or female; males or females collectively; sexual intercourse ▷ *adj* concerning sex ▷ *vt* ascertain sex of **sex'ism** *n* discrimination on basis of sex **sex'ist** *n, adj* **sex·u·al** [SEK-shoo-əl] *adj* **sex'y** *adj* **sex·i·er, sex·i·est** sexual intercourse act of procreation in which male's penis is inserted into female's vagina

sex·a·ge·nar·i·an [sek-sə-jə-NAIR-ee-ən] *adj, n* (person) sixty to seventy years old

sex·tant [SEK-stənt] *n* navigator's instrument for measuring elevations of heavenly body, etc

sex·tet [seks-TET] *n* (composition for) six singers or players; group of six

sex·ton [SEK-stən] *n* official who takes care of church building and its contents and sometimes assists in burial of dead; official who takes care of synagogue and sometimes assists cantor in conducting services

Sg *chemistry* seaborgium

shab·by [SHAB-ee] adj **-bi·er, -bi·est** faded, worn, ragged; poorly dressed; mean, dishonorable; stingy **shab'bi·ly** adv **shab'bi·ness** [-nis] n

shack [shak] n rough hut **shack up (with)** sl live (with) esp as husband and wife without being legally married

shack·le [SHAK-əl] n metal ring or fastening for prisoner's wrist or ankle; anything that confines ▷ vt **-led, -ling** fasten with shackles; hamper

shade [shayd] n partial darkness; shelter, place sheltered from light, heat, etc; darker part of anything; depth of color; tinge; ghost; screen; anything used to screen; window blind ▷ pl sl sunglasses ▷ vt **shad·ed, shad·ing** screen from light, darken; represent shades in drawing **shad'y** adj **shad·i·er, shad·i·est** shielded from sun; dim; dubious; dishonest; dishonorable

shad·ow [SHAD-oh] n dark figure projected by anything that intercepts rays of light; patch of shade; slight trace; indistinct image; gloom; inseparable companion ▷ vt cast shadow over; follow and watch closely **shad'ow·y** adj

shaft n straight rod, stem, handle; arrow; ray, beam (of light); revolving rod for transmitting power; one of the bars between which horse is harnessed; entrance boring of mine

shag¹ n matted wool or hair; long-napped cloth; coarse shredded tobacco **shag'gy** adj **-gi·er, -gi·est** covered with rough hair or wool; tousled; unkempt

shag² vt **shagged, shag·ging** chase after; baseball in practice, chase and catch fly balls

shah n formerly, ruler of Iran

shake [shayk] v **shook** [shuuk]

shak·en (cause to) move with quick vibrations; tremble; grasp the hand (of another) in greeting; upset; wave, brandish ▷ n act of shaking; vibration; jolt; inf short period of time, jiffy **shak'i·ly** adv **shak'y** adj **shak·i·er, shak·i·est** unsteady, insecure

shale [shayl] n flaky, sedimentary rock

shall [shal] v, pt **should** used as an auxiliary to make the future tense or to indicate intention, obligation, or inevitability

shal·lot [SHAL-ət] n kind of small onion

shal·low [SHAL-oh] adj **-er, -est** not deep; having little depth of water; superficial; not sincere ▷ n shallow place

sham adj, n imitation, counterfeit ▷ vt **shammed, sham·ming** pretend, feign

sham·ble [SHAM-bəl] vi **-bled, -bling** walk in shuffling, awkward way

sham·bles [SHAM-bəlz] n messy, disorderly thing or place

shame [shaym] n emotion caused by consciousness of guilt or dishonor in one's conduct or state; cause of disgrace; ignominy; pity, hard luck ▷ vt **shamed, sham·ing** cause to feel shame; disgrace; force by shame (into) **shame'ful** [-fəl] adj disgraceful **shame·less** [-lis] adj with no sense of shame; indecent **shame'faced** [-faysd] adj ashamed

sham·poo [sham-POO] n various preparations of liquid soap for washing hair, carpets, etc; this process ▷ vt **-pooed, -poo·ing** use shampoo to wash

sham·rock [SHAM-rok] n cloverlike plant with three leaves on each stem, esp as Irish emblem

shang·hai [SHANG-hī] vt **-haied, -hai·ing** force, trick someone to do something

shank n lower leg; shinbone; stem of thing **shank of the evening** best or main part of the evening

shan·tung n soft, natural Chinese silk

shan·ty¹ [SHAN-tee] n, pl **-ties** temporary wooden building; crude dwelling

shanty² see CHANTEY

shape [shayp] n external form or appearance, esp of a woman; mold, pattern; condition, esp of physical fitness ▷ v **shaped, shap·ing** ▷ vt form, mold, fashion, make ▷ vi develop **shape'less** [-lis] adj **shape'ly** adj **-li·er, -li·est** well-proportioned

shard [shahrd] n broken fragment, esp of earthenware

share¹ [shair] n portion; quota; lot; unit of ownership in corporation ▷ v **shared, shar·ing** give, take a share; join with others in doing, using, something **share'hold·er** n

share² n blade of plow

shark [shahrk] n large sometimes predatory sea fish; person who cheats others; person of great ability in cards, etc

sharp [shahrp] adj **-er, -est** having keen cutting edge or fine point; keen; not gradual or gentle; brisk; clever; harsh; dealing cleverly but unfairly; shrill; strongly marked, esp in outline ▷ adv promptly ▷ n music note half a tone above natural pitch; cheat, swindler; (also **sharp'er**) **sharp'en** vt make sharp **sharp'shoot·er** n marksman

shat·ter [SHAT-ər] v break in pieces; ruin (plans, etc); disturb (person) greatly

shave [shayv] v **shaved, shaved** or **shav·en, shav·ing** cut close, esp hair of face or head; pare away; graze; reduce ▷ n shaving **shav'ings** pl n parings **close shave** narrow escape

shawl n piece of fabric to cover woman's shoulders or head

she [shee] pron 3rd person singular feminine pronoun

sheaf [sheef] n, pl **sheaves** bundle, esp corn; loose leaves of paper

shear [sheer] vt **sheared, sheared** or **shorn, shear·ing** clip hair, wool from; cut through; trim (eg hedge); fracture **shears** pl n large pair of scissors; mechanical shearing, cutting instrument

sheath [sheeth] n, pl **sheaths** [sheethz] close-fitting cover, esp for knife or sword; scabbard; condom **sheathe** [sheeth] vt **sheathed, sheath·ing** put into sheath

she·bang [shə-BANG] n inf situation, matter, esp whole shebang

shed¹ n roofed shelter used for storage or as workshop

shed² vt **shed, shed·ding** (cause to) pour forth (eg tears, blood); cast off

sheen n gloss

sheep n ruminant animal bred for wool and meat **sheep'ish** adj embarrassed, shy **sheep-dip** n solution in which sheep are immersed to kill vermin and germs in fleece **sheep'dog** n dog of various breeds orig for herding sheep **sheep'skin** n skin of sheep (with fleece) used for clothing, rug or without fleece for parchment; inf diploma

sheer¹ adj **-er, -est** perpendicular; of material, very fine, transparent; absolute, unmitigated

sheer² vi deviate from course; swerve; turn aside

sheet¹ n large piece of cotton, etc

to cover bed; broad piece of any thin material; large expanse ▷ vt cover with sheet

sheet² n rope fastened in corner of sail **sheet anchor** large anchor for emergency

sheik [shayk, sheek] n Arab chief

shek·el [SHEK-əl] n monetary unit of Israel ▷ pl inf money

shelf n, pl **shelves** board fixed horizontally (on wall, etc) for holding things; ledge

shell n outer case (esp of egg, nut, etc); husk; explosive projectile; outer part of structure left when interior is removed; racing shell ▷ vt take shell from; take out of shell; fire at with shells **racing shell** long light racing boat for rowing by crew of one or more **shell'fish** n mollusk; crustacean **shell shock** battle fatigue, nervous disorder caused by bursting of shells or bombs **shell out** inf pay up

shel·lac [shə-LAK] n varnish ▷ vt **-lacked, -lack·ing** coat with shellac

shel·ter [SHEL-tər] n place, structure giving protection; protection; refuge; haven ▷ vt give protection to; screen ▷ vi take shelter

shelve [shelv] vt **shelved, shelv·ing** ▷ vt put on a shelf; put off; cease to employ; defer indefinitely ▷ vi slope gradually

she·nan·i·gans [shə-NAN-i-gənz] pl n inf frolicking; playing tricks, etc

shep·herd [SHEP-ərd] n person who tends sheep ▷ vt guide, watch over **shep'herd·ess** [-is] n fem

sher·bet [SHUR-bit] n frozen fruit-flavored dessert like ices but with gelatin, etc added

sher·iff n law enforcement officer

Sher·pa [SHUR-pà] n, pl **-pas** or **-pa** member of a Tibetan people

sher·ry [SHER-ee] n, pl **-ries** fortified wine from S Spain

shib·bo·leth [SHIB-ə-lith] n custom, word, etc distinguishing people of particular class or group; test word, pet phrase of sect or party

shield [sheeld] n piece of armor carried on arm; any protection used to stop blows, missiles, etc; any protective device; sports trophy ▷ vt cover, protect

shift v (cause to) move, change position ▷ n relay of workers; time of their working; evasion; expedient; removal; woman's underskirt or dress **shift'i·ness** [-nis] n **shift'less** [-lis] adj lacking in resource or character **shift'y** adj **shift·i·er, shift·i·est** evasive, of dubious character

shil·le·lagh [shə-LAY-lə] n (in Ireland) cudgel

shil'ling n former Brit coin, now 5 pence; monetary unit in various countries

shil·ly·shal·ly [SHIL-ee-shal-ee] vi **-lied, -ly·ing** waver ▷ n wavering, indecision

shim·mer [SHIM-ər] vi shine with quivering light ▷ n such light; glimmer

shin n front of lower leg ▷ v **shinned, shin·ning** climb with arms and legs **shin'bone** [-bohn] n tibia

shin'dig n inf elaborate party, dance, etc

shine [shin] v **shone, shin·ing** give out, reflect light; perform very well, excel; cause to shine by polishing ▷ n brightness, luster; polishing **shin'y** adj **shin·i·er, shin·i·est**

shin·gle¹ [SHIN-gəl] n wooden roof and wall tile ▷ vt **-gled, -gling** cover with shingles

shingle² n mass of pebbles

shin·gles [SHIN-gəlz] n disease causing inflammation along a nerve

Shin·to [SHIN-toh] n native Japanese religion **Shin'to·ism** n

ship n large seagoing vessel ▷ v **shipped, ship·ping** put on or send (esp by ship); embark; take employment on ship **ship'ment** [-mənt] n act of shipping; goods shipped **shipping** n freight transport business; ships collectively **ship'shape** [-shayp] adj orderly, trim **ship'wreck** [-rek] n destruction of a ship through storm, collision, etc ▷ vt cause to undergo shipwreck **ship'yard** n place for building and repair of ships **ship out** leave by ship; inf quit, resign, be fired

shirk [shurk] vt evade, try to avoid (duty, etc)

shirr [shur] vt gather (fabric) into parallel rows ▷ n series of gathered rows decorating a dress, blouse, etc; (also **shir'ring**)

shirt [shurt] n garment for upper part of body

shiv n sl knife

shiv·er [SHIV-ər] vi tremble, usu with cold or fear; shudder; vibrate ▷ n act, state, of shivering

shiver[2] v splinter, break in pieces ▷ n splinter

shoal [shohl] n stretch of shallow water; sandbank or bar ▷ v make, become, shallow

shock[1] [shok] vt horrify, scandalize ▷ n violent or damaging blow; emotional disturbance; state of weakness, illness, caused by physical or mental shock; paralytic stroke; collision; effect on sensory nerves of electric discharge **shock'er** n person or thing that shocks or distresses **shock absorber** device (esp in automobiles) to absorb shocks

shock[2] n group of corn sheaves placed together

shock[3] n mass of hair ▷ adj shaggy **shock'head·ed** [-hed-id] adj

shod·dy [SHOD-ee] adj -di·er, -di·est worthless, trashy, second-rate, of poor material

shoe [shoo] n, pl **shoes** covering for foot, not enclosing ankle; metal rim or curved bar put on horse's hoof; various protective plates or undercoverings ▷ vt **shod** or **shoed, shod** or **shoed, shoe·ing** protect, furnish with shoe or shoes **shoe'string** adj, n very small (amount of money, etc)

shone pt/pp of SHINE

shoo interj go away! ▷ vt **shooed, shoo·ing** drive away **shoo-in** n inf person or thing certain to win or succeed; match or contest that is easy to win

shook [shuuk] pt of SHAKE

shoot v shot, shoot·ing hit, wound, kill with missile fired from weapon; discharge weapon; send, slide, push rapidly; photograph, film; hunt; sprout ▷ n young branch, sprout; shooting competition; hunting expedition

shop n store, place for retail sale of goods and services; workshop, factory ▷ vi **shopped, shop·ping** visit stores to buy or examine **shop'lift·er** n one who steals from store **shop stew·ard** [STOO-ərd] labor union representative of workers in factory, etc **talk shop** talk of one's business, etc at unsuitable moments

shore[1] [shor] n edge of sea or land

shore[2] vt **shored, shor·ing** prop (up)

shorn pp of SHEAR

short ▷ adj -er, -est not long; not tall; brief, hasty; not reaching quantity or standard required; wanting, lacking; abrupt, rude; **stock exchange** not in possession of stock shares when selling them ▷ *adv* suddenly, abruptly; without reaching end ▷ *n* short film ▷ *pl* short trousers **short'age** [-ij] *n* deficiency **short'en** *v* **short'ly** *adv* soon; briefly **short'bread** [-bred] *n* butter cookie **short'cake** [-kayk] cake made of butter, flour and sugar; dessert of biscuit dough with fruit topping **short circuit** electricity connection, often accidental, of low resistance between two parts of circuit **short'com'ing** [-kum-ing] *n* failing; defect **short'hand** *n* method of rapid writing by signs or contractions **short'-hand'ed** *adj* lacking the usual or necessary number of workers, helpers **short list** selected list of candidates (esp for job) from which final selection will be made **short shrift** summary treatment **short ton** ton (2000 lbs) **short wave** radio wave of frequency greater than 1600 kHz

short·en·ing [SHORT-ning] *n* fat used to make cake, etc rich and crumbly; pr p of **SHORTEN**

shot *n* act of shooting; missile; lead in small pellets; marksman, shooter; try, attempt; photograph; short film sequence; dose; hypodermic injection ▷ *adj* woven so that color is different, according to angle of light; pt/pp of **SHOOT**

should [shuud] *v* past tense of **shall** used as an auxiliary to make the subjunctive mood or to indicate obligation or possibility

shoul·der [SHOHL-dər] *n* part of body to which arm or foreleg is attached; anything resembling shoulder; side of road ▷ *vt* undertake; bear (burden); accept

505 | shrapnel

(responsibility); put on one's shoulder ▷ *vi* make way by pushing **shoulder blade** [blayd] shoulder bone

shout [showt] *n* loud cry ▷ *v* utter (cry, etc) with loud voice

shove [shuv] *vt* **shoved, shov·ing** push ▷ *n* push **shove off** *inf* go away

shovel [SHUV-əl] *n* instrument for scooping, lifting earth, etc ▷ *vt* **-eled, -el·ing** lift, move (as) with shovel

show [shoh] *v* **showed, shown, show·ing** expose to view; point out; display; exhibit; explain; prove; guide; accord (favor, etc); appear; be noticeable ▷ *n* display, exhibition; spectacle; theatrical or other entertainment; indication; competitive event; ostentation; semblance; pretense **show'i·ly** *adv* **show'y** *adj* **show·i·er, show·i·est** gaudy; ostentatious **show'down** *n* confrontation; final test **show jump·ing** horse-riding competition to demonstrate skill in jumping obstacles **show'man** [-mən] *n*, *pl* **-men** organizer of theatrical events, circuses, etc; one skilled at presenting anything in effective way **show off** exhibit to invite admiration; behave in this way **show-off** *n* **show up** reveal; expose; embarrass; arrive

show·er [SHOW-ər] *n* short fall of rain; anything coming down like rain; kind of bath in which person stands while being sprayed with water; party to present gifts to a person, as a prospective bride ▷ *vt* bestow liberally ▷ *vi* take bath in shower **show'er·y** *adj*

shrank pt of **SHRINK**

shrap·nel [SHRAP-nəl] *n* shell filled with pellets that scatter on bursting; shell splinters

shred n fragment, torn strip; small amount ▷ vt or **shred·ded**, **shred·ding** cut, tear to shreds

shrew [shroo] n animal like mouse; bad-tempered woman; scold **shrew'ish** adj nagging

shrewd [shrood] adj **-er**, **-est** astute, intelligent; crafty **shrewd'ness** [-nis] n

shriek [shreek] n shrill cry; piercing scream ▷ v screech

shrike [shrik] n bird of prey with heavy hooked bill

shrill adj piercing, sharp in tone ▷ v utter in such tone **shril'ly** adv

shrimp n, pl shrimp or **shrimps** small edible crustacean; pl inf undersized person ▷ vi go catching shrimps

shrine [shrin] n place (building, tomb, alcove) of worship, usu associated with saint

shrink [shreenk] v shrank or **shrunk, shrunk** or **shrunk·en**, **shrink·ing** become smaller; retire, flinch, recoil; make smaller ▷ n sl psychiatrist, psychotherapist **shrink'age** [-ij] n

shrive [shriv] v shrove or shrived, **shriv·en** or **shrived, shriv·ing** give absolution to **shrift** n obs confession; absolution

shriv·el [SHRIV-əl] vi **-eled, -el·ing** shrink and wither

shroud [shrowd] n sheet, wrapping, for corpse; anything that covers, envelops like shroud ▷ pl set of ropes to masthead ▷ vt put shroud on; screen, veil; wrap up

Shrove Tuesday [shrohv] day before Ash Wednesday

shrub n bushy plant; drink of fruit juices, etc oft with alcohol **shrub'ber·y** [-ər-ee] n, pl-**ber·ies** planting of shrubs; shrubs

collectively

shrug v shrugged, shrug·ging raise shoulders, as sign of indifference, ignorance, etc; move (shoulders) thus; (with off) dismiss as unimportant ▷ n shrugging

shrunk, shrunken pp of SHRINK

shuck [shuk] n shell, husk, pod ▷ vt remove husks, etc from **shucks** interj inf used as mild expression of regret

shud·der [SHUD-ər] vi shake, tremble violently, esp with horror ▷ n shuddering, tremor

shuf·fle [SHUF-əl] vi **-fled, -fling** move feet without lifting them; dance like this; act evasively ▷ vt mix (cards); (with off) evade, pass to another ▷ n shuffling; rearrangement

shun vt shunned, shun·ning avoid; keep away from

shunt vt push aside; divert; move (train) from one line to another

shut v shut, shut·ting close; bar; forbid entrance to **shut'ter** [-ər] n movable window screen, usu hinged to frame; device in camera admitting light as required to film or plate **shut down** close or stop factory, machine, etc

shut·tle [SHUT-l] n instrument that threads weft between threads of warp in weaving; similar appliance in sewing machine; plane, bus, etc traveling to and fro over short distance ▷ v **-tled, -tling** (cause to) move back and forth **shut'tle·cock** n small, light cone with cork stub and fan of feathers used as a ball in badminton

shy[1] [shi] adj shy·er or shi·er, shy·est or shi·est awkward in company; timid, bashful; reluctant; scarce, lacking in card games, not having enough money for bet, etc) ▷ v **shied, shy·ing** start back

in fear; show sudden reluctance ▷ *n*,
pl **shies** start of fear by horse **shy·ly**
adv **shy·ness** [-nis] *n*

shy² *vt, n* **shied**, **shy·ing** throw

shy·ster [SHY-stər] *n inf* dishonest,
deceitful person, esp unprofessional
lawyer

SI Fr Système International (d'Unités),
international system of units of
measurement based on units of ten

Si *chemistry* silicon

Si·a·mese cat [SI-ə-MEEZ] breed
of cat with blue eyes

Siamese twins nontechnical name
for CONJOINED TWINS

sib·i·lant [SIB-ə-lənt] *adj* hissing
▷ *n* speech sound with hissing effect

sib·ling *n* person's brother or
sister ▷ *adj*

sib·yl [SIB-əl] *n* woman endowed
with spirit of prophecy **sib·yl·line**
[-een] *adj* occult

sic [sik] *Lat* thus: oft used to call
attention to a quoted mistake

sick [sik] *adj* **-er, -est** inclined to
vomit, vomiting; not well or healthy,
physically or mentally; macabre,
sadistic, morbid; bored, tired;
disgusted **sick·en** [-ən] *v* make,
become, feel sick; disgust; nauseate
sick·ly *adj* unhealthy, weakly;
inducing nausea **sick·ness** [-nis] *n*
sick bay place set aside for treating
sick people, esp aboard ships
sick·le [SIK-əl] *n* reaping hook

side [sid] *n* one of the surfaces of
object, esp upright inner or outer
surface; either surface of thing
having only two; part of body that
is to right or left; region nearer
or farther than, or right or left of,
dividing line, etc; region; aspect
or part; one of two parties or sets
of opponents; sect, faction; line of
descent traced through one parent
▷ *adj* at, in, the side; subordinate,

incidental ▷ *vi* **sid·ed, sid·ing** (usu
with *with*) take up cause of **siding**
n short line of rails on which trains
or wagons are shunted from main
line **side·board** [-bord] *n* piece of
furniture for holding dishes, etc in
dining room **side·burns** [-burnz]
pl n man's side whiskers **side·car**
n small car attached to side of
motorcycle; cocktail made with
brandy, orange liqueur and lemon
juice **side·kick** *n* pal; assistant
side·light [-līt] *n* esp either of two
lights on vessel for use at night; item
of incidental information **side·line**
n sport boundary of playing area;
subsidiary interest or activity
side·long [-lawng] *adj* lateral, not
directly forward ▷ *adv* obliquely
side·man [-man] *n*, *pl* **-men** instrumentalist
in band **side·track** *v* deviate
from main topic ▷ *n* **side·walk** *n*
footpath beside road **side·ways**
[-wayz] *adv* to or from the side;
laterally

si·de·re·al [si-DEER-ee-əl] *adj*
relating to, fixed by, stars

si·dle [SID-l] *vi* **-dled, -dling** move
in furtive or stealthy manner; move
sideways

SIDS Sudden Infant Death Syndrome,
unexplained death of baby while
asleep

siege [seej] *n* besieging of town or
fortified place

si·en·na [see-EN-ə] *n* (pigment of)
brownish-yellow color

si·er·ra [see-ER-ə] *n* range of
mountains with jagged peaks

si·es·ta [see-ES-tə] *n* rest, sleep
in afternoon

sieve [siv] *n* device with network
or perforated bottom for sifting ▷ *v*
sieved, siev·ing sift; strain

sift *vt* separate (eg with sieve)
coarser portion from finer; examine

closely **sift·er** n

sigh [si] v, n (utter) long audible breath **sigh for** yearn for, grieve for

sight [sit] n faculty of seeing; seeing; thing seen; view; glimpse; device for guiding eye; spectacle; inf pitiful or ridiculous or unusual object; inf large number, great deal ▷ vt catch sight of; adjust sights of gun, etc **for sore eyes** inf person or thing one is glad to see **sight·less** [-lis] adj **sight-read** [-reed] v **-read** [-red] **-read·ing** [-reed-ing] play, sing music without previous preparation **sight·see** v visit (place) to look at interesting sights

sign [sin] n mark, gesture, etc to convey some meaning; (board, placard, bearing) notice, warning, etc; symbol; omen; evidence ▷ vt put one's signature to; ratify ▷ vi make sign or gesture; affix signature; use symbols of sign language **sign language** gestures used for communicating with deaf people

sig·nal [SIG-nəl] n sign to convey order or information, esp on railroads; that which in first place impels any action; sequence of electrical impulses or radio waves transmitted or received ▷ adj remarkable, striking ▷ v **-naled, -nal·ing** make signals to; give orders, etc by signals **sig'nal·ize** vt **-ized, -iz·ing** make notable

sig·na·to·ry [SIG-nə-tor-ee] n, pl **-ries** one of those who sign agreements, treaties

sig·na·ture [SIG-nə-chər] n person's name written by self; act of writing it **signature tune** theme song

sig·net [SIG-nit] n small seal

sig·nif·i·cant [sig-NIF-i-kənt] adj revealing; designed to make something known; important

sig·nif·i·cance [-kəns] n import, weight; meaning **sig·ni·fi·ca'tion** n meaning

sig·ni·fy [SIG-nə-fī] v **-fied, -fy·ing** mean; indicate; denote; imply; be of importance

si·gnor [SEEN-yor] n Italian title of respect, like Mr. **si·gno·ra** [sin-YOR-ə] n Mrs **si·gno·ri'na** [seen-yə-REEN-ə] n Miss

Sikh [seek] n member of Hindu religious sect

si·lage [SĪ-lij] n fodder crop harvested while green and stored in state of partial fermentation

si·lence [SĪ-ləns] n absence of noise; refraining from speech ▷ vt **-lenced, -lenc·ing** make silent; put a stop to **si'lenc·er** n device to reduce noise of firearm **si'lent** adj

sil·hou·ette [sil-oo-ET] n outline of object seen against light background; profile portrait in black ▷ vt **-et·ted, -et·ting** show in or as if in silhouette

sil·i·ca [SIL-i-kə] n naturally occurring dioxide of silicon **si·li·ceous** [sə-LEE-shəs] adj **si·li·co·sis** [si-li-KOH-sis] n lung disease caused by inhaling silica dust over a long period

sil·i·con [SIL-i-kən] n brittle metalloid element found in sand, clay, stone, widely used in chemistry, industry **sil'i·cone** [-kohn] n large class of synthetic substances, related to silicon and used in chemistry, industry, medicine

silk n fiber made by larvae (**silkworms**) of a certain moth; thread, fabric made from this **silk'en** adj made of, like silk; soft; smooth; dressed in silk **silk'i·ness** [-nis] n

sill n ledge beneath window; bottom part of door or window frame

sil·ly [SIL-ee] *adj* **-li·er, -li·est**
foolish; trivial; feebleminded
sil'li·ness [-nis] *n*

si·lo [SY-loh] *n, pl* **-los** pit, tower for
storing fodder or grain; underground
missile launching site

silt *n* mud deposited by water ▷ *v*
fill, be choked with silt **sil·ta'tion** *n*

sil·ver [SIL-vər] *n* white precious
metal; things made of it; silver
coins; cutlery ▷ *adj* made of silver;
resembling silver or its color; having
pale luster, as moon; soft, melodious,
as sound; bright ▷ *vt* coat with silver
sil'ver·y *adj* **silver birch** tree having
silvery white peeling bark **silver
wedding** 25th wedding anniversary

sim·i·an [SIM-ee-ən] *adj* of,
like apes

sim·i·lar [SIM-ə-lər] *adj*
resembling, like **sim·i·lar'i·ty** *n*
likeness; close resemblance

sim·i·le [SIM-ə-lee] *n* comparison
of one thing with another, using *as* or
like, esp in poetry

si·mil·i·tude [si-MIL-i-tood] *n*
outward appearance, likeness; guise

sim·mer [SIM-ər] *v* keep or be just
bubbling or just below boiling point;
to be in state of suppressed anger
or laughter

sim·per [SIM-pər] *vi* smile, utter in
silly or affected way ▷ *n*

sim·ple [SIM-pəl] *adj* **-pler,
-plest** not complicated; plain;
not combined or complex;
ordinary, mere; guileless; stupid
sim'ple·ton [-tən] *n* foolish person
sim·plic'i·ty [-PLIS-ə-tee] *n, pl* **-ties**
simpleness, clearness, artlessness
sim·pli·fi·ca'tion *n* **sim·pli·fy** [-fī]
vt **-fied, -fy·ing** make simple, plain
or easy **sim·plis'tic** *adj* extremely
simple, naive **sim'ply** *adv* **simple
fraction** one in which both the
numerator and the denominator are

whole numbers

sim·u·late [SIM-yə-layt] *vt*
-lat·ed, -lat·ing make pretense of;
reproduce, copy, esp conditions of
particular situation **sim·u·la'tion** *n*
sim'u·la·tor *n*

si·mul·ta·ne·ous [sī-məl-TAY-
nee-əs] *adj* occurring at the same
time **si·mul·ta·ne'i·ty** [-tə-NEE-i-
tee] *n* **simulta'ne·ous·ly** *adv*

sin *n* transgression of divine or moral
law, esp committed consciously;
offense against principle or standard
▷ *vi* **sinned, sin·ning** commit sin
sin'ful [-fəl] *adj* of nature of sin;
guilty of sin **sin'ful·ly** *adv*

since [sins] *prep* during or
throughout period of time after
▷ *conj* from time when; because
▷ *adv* from that time

sin·cere [sin-SEER] *adj* not
hypocritical, actually moved by or
feeling apparent emotions; true,
genuine; unaffected **sin·cere'ly** *adv*
sin·cer'i·ty [-SER-i-tee] *n*

sine [sīn] *n* mathematical function,
esp ratio of length of hypotenuse to
opposite side in right triangle

si·ne·cure [SĪ-ni-kyuur] *n* office
with pay but minimal duties

si·ne di·e [SĪ-nee DĪ-ee] *Lat* with no
date, indefinitely postponed

si·ne qua non [SĪ-nee kway
non] *Lat* essential condition or
requirement

sin·ew [SIN-yoo] *n* tough, fibrous
cord joining muscle to bone ▷ *pl*
muscles, strength **sin'ew·y** *adj*
stringy; muscular

sing *v* **sang, sung, sing·ing** utter
musical sounds; hum, whistle,
ring; utter (words) with musical
modulation; celebrate in song or
poetry **sing'song** [-sawng] *adj*
monotonously regular in tone,
rhythm

singe [sinj] *vt* **singed, singe·ing**
burn surface of ▷ *n* act or effect of
singeing

sin·gle [SING-gəl] *adj* one only;
alone, separate; unmarried; for one;
formed of only one part, fold, etc;
wholehearted, straightforward ▷ *n*
single thing; photography record
with one short item on each side;
baseball one-base hit ▷ *vt* **-gled,
-gling** pick (out); make single
sin'gly *adv* **single file** persons,
things arranged in one line **single-
hand·ed** [adj] without assistance
singles bar bar or club that is social
meeting place esp for single people
sin·gu·lar [SING-gyə-lər] *adj*
remarkable; unusual; unique;
denoting one person or thing
sin·gu·lar·i·ty [-ties] something
unusual **sin'gu·lar·ly** [-lər-lee] *adv*
particularly; peculiarly
sin·is·ter [SIN-ə-stər] *adj*
threatening; evil-looking; wicked;
unlucky; heraldry on bearer's left-
hand side **sin'is·trous** [-trəs] *adj*
ill-omened
sink [singk] *v* **sank** or **sunk, sunk**
or **sunk·en, sink·ing** become
submerged (in water); drop, give
way; decline in value, health, etc;
penetrate (into); cause to sink; make
by digging out; invest ▷ *n* receptacle
with pipe for carrying away waste
water; cesspool; place of corruption,
vice **sink'er** *n* weight for fishing line
sink'hole [-hohl] *n* low land where
drainage collects; cavity formed in
rock by water **sinking fund** money
set aside at intervals for payment of
particular liability at fixed date
Sino- *comb form* Chinese, of China:
Sino-American relations
sin·u·ous [SIN-yoo-əs] *adj*
curving, devious, lithe **sin·u·os'i·ty**
[-OS-i-tee] *n, pl* **-ties**

si·nus [SI-nəs] *n, pl* **-nus·es** cavity,
esp air passages in bones of skull
si·nus·i'tis [-SI-tis] *n* inflammation
of sinus
sip *v* **sipped, sip·ping** drink in very
small portions ▷ *n*
si·phon [SI-fən] *n* device, esp
bent tube, that uses atmospheric or
gaseous pressure to draw liquid from
container ▷ *v* draw off thus; draw off
in small amounts
sir [sur] *n* polite term of address for a
man; (**S-**) title of knight or baronet
sire [sir] *n* male parent, esp of horse
or domestic animal; term of address
to king ▷ *v* **sired, sir·ing** beget
si·ren [SI-rən] *n* device making loud
wailing noise, esp giving warning of
danger; legendary sea nymph who
lured sailors to destruction; alluring
woman
sir·loin [SUR-loin] *n* prime cut of
loin of beef
si·sal [SI-səl] *n* (fiber of) plant used
in making ropes
sis·sy [SIS-ee] *adj, n, pl* **-sies** weak,
cowardly (person); effeminate boy
or man
sis·ter [SIS-tər] *n* daughter of same
parents; woman fellow member
esp of religious body ▷ *adj* closely
related, similar **sis'ter·hood**
[-huud] *n* relation of sister; order,
band of women **sis'ter·ly** *adj* **sister-
in-law** *n* sister of husband or wife;
brother's wife
sit [sit] *v* **sat, sit·ting** (mainly intr)
adopt posture or rest on buttocks;
thighs; perch; incubate; pose for
portrait; occupy official position;
hold session; remain; take
examination; keep watch over
baby, etc **sit in** protest by refusing
to move from place **sit-in** *n* such
protest
si·tar [si-TAHR] *n* stringed musical

instrument, esp of India **si•tar'ist** n

site [sīt] n place, location; space for, with, a building; same as **WEBSITE** **site map** plan of a website showing its contents and where it can be viewed

sit•u•ate [SICH-oo-ayt] v **-at•ed, -at•ing** place, locate **sit•u•a'tion** n place, position; state of affairs; employment, post

six [siks] adj, n cardinal number one more than five **sixth** adj ordinal number ▷ n sixth part **six'teen'** n, adj six and ten **six'ty** n, adj, pl **-ties** six times ten

size¹ [sīz] n bigness, dimensions; one of series of standard measurements of clothes, etc; inf state of affairs ▷ vt **sized, siz'ing** arrange according to size **siz'a•ble, size'a•ble** adj quite large **size up** inf assess (person, situation, etc)

size² n gluelike sealer, filler ▷ vt **sized, siz'ing** coat, treat with size

siz•zle [SIZ-l] v, n **-zled, -zling** (make) hissing, spluttering sound as of frying **siz'zler** [-lər] n inf hot day

skate¹ [skayt] n steel blade attached to boot, for gliding over ice ▷ vi **skat•ed, skat•ing** glide as on skates **skat'er** n **skate'board** n small board mounted on roller-skate wheels

skate² n large marine ray

ske•dad•dle [ski-DAD-l] vi inf **-dled, -dling** flee; run away hurriedly

skeet n shooting sport with clay target propelled from trap to simulate flying bird

skein [skayn] n quantity of yarn, wool, etc in loose knot; flight of wildfowl

skel•e•ton [SKEL-i-tn] n bones of animal; bones separated from flesh and preserved in their natural position; very thin person; outline,

draft, framework; nucleus ▷ adj reduced to a minimum; drawn in outline; not in detail **skel•e•tal** [-tl] adj **skeleton key** key filed down so as to open many different locks

skep•tic [SKEP-tik] n one who maintains doubt or disbelief; agnostic; unbeliever **skep'ti•cal** [-kəl] adj **skep'ti•cism** [-siz-əm] n

sketch [skech] n rough drawing; brief account; essay; short humorous play ▷ v make sketch (of) **sketch'y** adj **sketch•i•er, sketch•i•est** omitting detail; incomplete; inadequate

skew [skyoo] vi move obliquely ▷ adj slanting; crooked

skew•er [SKYOO-ər] n pin to fasten (meat) together ▷ v pierce or fasten (as though) with skewer

ski [skee] n, pl **skis** long runner fastened to boot for sliding over snow or water ▷ v **skied, ski•ing** slide on skis; go skiing

skid v **skid•ded, skid•ding** slide (sideways), esp vehicle out of control with wheels not rotating ▷ n instance of this; device to facilitate sliding, eg in moving heavy objects **skid'dy** adj **-di•er, -di•est**

skiff n small boat

skill n practical ability, cleverness, dexterity **skilled** adj having, requiring knowledge, united with readiness and dexterity **skill'ful** [-fəl] adj expert, masterly; adroit

skil•let [SKIL-it] n small frying pan

skim v **skimmed, skim•ming** remove floating matter from surface of liquid; glide over lightly and rapidly; read thus; move thus **skim milk, skimmed milk** milk from which cream has been removed

skimp vt give short measure; do thing imperfectly **skimp'y** adj

skimp·i·er, skimp·i·est meager; scanty

skin n outer covering of vertebrate body, lower animal or fruit; animal skin used as material or container; film on surface of cooling liquid, etc; complexion ▷vt **skinned, skin·ning** remove skin of **skin'ny** adj **-ni·er, -ni·est** thin **skin-deep** adj superficial; slight **skin diving** underwater swimming using breathing apparatus **skin'flint** n miser, niggard **skin graft** transplant of piece of healthy skin to wound to form new skin **skin-tight** [-tīt] adj fitting close to skin

skip¹ v **skipped, skip·ping** leap lightly; jump a rope as it is swung under one; pass over, omit ▷n act of skipping

skip² n large bucket, container for transporting people, materials in mines, etc

skip·per [SKIP-ər] n captain of ship, plane or team ▷vt captain

skirl [skurl] n sound of bagpipes

skir·mish [SKUR-mish] n fight between small parties, small battle ▷vi fight briefly or irregularly

skirt [skurt] n woman's garment hanging from waist; lower part of woman's dress, coat, etc; outlying part; sl offens woman ▷vi border; go around **skirt'ing** n material for women's skirts

skit n short satirical piece, esp theatrical sketch

skit'tish adj frisky, frivolous

skit·tle [SKIT-l] n bottle-shaped object used as a target in some games ▷pl game in which players try to knock over skittles by rolling a ball at them

skoal [skohl] interj (as a toast) to your health

skul·dug·ger·y [skul-DUG-ə-ree]

n, pl **-ger·ies** trickery

skulk vi sneak out of the way; lurk **skulk'er** n

skull n bony case that encloses brain **skull'cap** n close-fitting cap

skunk n small N Amer animal that emits evil-smelling fluid; inf mean person

sky [skī] n, pl **skies** apparently dome-shaped expanse extending upward from the horizon; outer space; heavenly regions ▷vt **skied, sky·ing** inf hit, throw (ball) high **sky'div·ing** n parachute jumping with delayed opening of parachute **sky'light** [-līt] n window in roof or ceiling **sky'scrap·er** [-skrayp-ər] n very tall building

slab n thick, broad piece

slack [slak] adj loose; sluggish; careless, negligent; not busy ▷n loose part, as of rope ▷vi be idle or lazy **slack'en** v become looser; become slower, abate

slacks [slaks] pl n informal trousers worn by men or women

slag n refuse of smelted metal

slain pp of SLAY

slake [slayk] vt **slaked, slak·ing** satisfy (thirst, desire, etc); combine (lime) with water to produce calcium hydroxide

sla·lom [SLAH-ləm] n, v race over winding course in skiing, automobile racing, etc

slam v **slammed, slam·ming** shut noisily; bang; hit; dash down; inf criticize harshly ▷n (noise of) this action **slam dunk** n basketball forceful downward basket; inf clearcut success ▷vt **slam-dunked', slam-dunk'ing** basketball shoot (ball) in a slam dunk **grand slam** cards winning of all tricks; sport winning of selected group of major tournaments in one year

slan·der [SLAN-dər] n false or malicious statement about person ▷v utter such statement **slan·der·ous** adj

slang n words, etc or meanings of these used very informally for novelty or vividness or for the sake of unconventionality

slant v slope; put at angle; write, present (news, etc) with bias ▷n slope; point of view; idea ▷adj sloping, oblique **slant'wise** [-wiz] adv

slap n blow with open hand or flat instrument ▷vt **slapped, slap·ping** strike thus; put on, down carelessly or messily **slap'dash** adj careless and abrupt **slap'stick** n broad boisterous comedy

slash vt gash; lash; cut, slit; criticize unmercifully ▷n gash; cutting stroke; slashing punctuation mark, either / or \

slat n narrow strip of wood or metal as in window blinds, etc

slate [slayt] n kind of stone that splits easily in flat sheets; piece of this for covering roof or, formerly, for writing on ▷vt **slat·ed, slat·ing** cover with slates

slath·er [SLATH-ər] n inf generous amount ▷vt **-ered, -er·ing** spread, apply thickly

slat·tern [SLAT-ərn] n slut **slatt'ern·ly** adj slovenly, untidy

slaugh·ter [SLAW-tər] n killing ▷vt kill **slaugh'ter·ous** adj **slaugh'ter·house** [-hows] n place for butchering animals for food

slave [slayv] n captive, person without freedom or personal rights; one dominated by another or by a habit, etc ▷vi **slaved, slav·ing** work like slave **slav'er** n person, ship engaged in slave traffic **slav'er·y** n **slav'ish** adj servile

slav·er [SLAV-ər] vi dribble saliva from mouth; fawn ▷n saliva running from mouth

slay vt slew, slain, slay·ing kill; inf impress, esp by being very funny **slay'er** n killer

slea·zy [SLEE-zee] adj -zi·er, -zi·est sordid **sleaze** [sleez] n sl sordidness; contemptible person

sled n carriage on runners for sliding on snow; toboggan ▷v **sled·ded, sled·ding**

sledge [slej] n sledgehammer; sled **sledge·ham·mer** [SLEJ-ham-ər] n heavy hammer with long handle

sleek adj -er, -est glossy, smooth, shiny

sleep n unconscious state regularly occurring in humans and animals; slumber, repose; inf dried particles oft found in corners of eyes after sleeping ▷v **slept, sleep·ing** take rest in sleep, slumber; accommodate for sleeping **sleep'er** n one who sleeps; railroad sleeping car; inf person, firm, etc that succeeds unexpectedly **sleep'i·ly** adv **sleep'i·ness** [-nis] n **sleep'less** [-lis] adj **sleep'y** adj **sleep·i·er, sleep·i·est sleeping sickness** Afr disease spread by tsetse fly **sleep'o·ver** n instance of spending the night at another person's home

sleet n rain and snow or hail falling together

sleeve [sleev] n part of garment that covers arm; case surrounding shaft; phonograph record cover ▷vt **sleeved, sleev·ing** furnish with sleeves **sleeved** adj **sleeve'less** [-lis] adj **have up one's sleeve** have something prepared secretly for emergency or as trick

sleigh [slay] n sled

sleight [slit] n dexterity; trickery; deviousness **sleight of hand**

(manual dexterity in) conjuring; juggling; legerdemain

slen·der [SLEN-dər] *adj* slim, slight; feeble

slept *pt/pp of* **SLEEP**

sleuth [slooth] *n* detective; bloodhound ▷ *vt* track

slew[1] [sloo] *pt of* **SLAY**

slew[2] *v* swing around

slew[3] *n inf* large number or quantity

slice [slis] *n* thin flat piece cut off; share; spatula; slice of pizza ▷ *vt* **sliced, slic·ing** cut into slices; cut cleanly; hit with bat, club, etc at angle

slick [slik] *adj* smooth; smooth-tongued; flattering; superficially attractive; sly ▷ *vt* make glossy, smooth ▷ *n* slippery area; patch of oil on water

slide [slid] *v* **slid, slid** *or* **slid·den, slid·ing** slip smoothly along; glide, as over ice; pass imperceptibly; deteriorate morally ▷ *n* sliding; surface, track for sliding; sliding part of mechanism; piece of glass holding object to be viewed under microscope; photographic transparency **slide rule** mathematical instrument of two parts, one of which slides upon the other, for rapid calculations **sliding scale** schedule for automatically varying one thing (eg wages) according to fluctuations of another (eg cost of living)

slight [slit] *adj* small, trifling; not substantial, fragile; slim, slender ▷ *vt* disregard; neglect ▷ *n* indifference; act of discourtesy

slim [slim] *adj* **slim·mer, slim·mest** thin; slight ▷ *v* **slimmed, slim·ming** reduce person's weight by diet and exercise **slim'ness** *n* **slim'line** *adj* appearing slim; pert to slimness

slime [slim] *n* greasy, thick, liquid

mud or similar substance **slim'y** *adj* **slim·i·er, slim·i·est** like slime; fawning

sling *n* strap, loop with string attached at each end for hurling stone; bandage for supporting wounded limb; rope, belt, etc for hoisting, carrying weights ▷ *vt* **slung, sling·ing** throw; hoist, swing by rope

slink *vi* **slunk, slink·ing** move stealthily, sneak **slink'y** *adj* **slink·i·er, slink·i·est** sinuously graceful; (of clothes, etc) figure-hugging

slip[1] *v* **slipped, slip·ping** (cause to) move smoothly, easily, quietly; pass out of (mind, etc); (of motor vehicle clutch) engage partially, fail ▷ *vi* lose balance by sliding; fall from person's grasp; (usu *with up*) make mistake; decline in health, morals ▷ *vt* put on or take off easily, quickly; let go (anchor, etc); dislocate (bone) ▷ *n* act or occasion of slipping; mistake; petticoat; small piece of paper; plant cutting; launching slope on which ships are built; covering for pillow; small child **slip'shod** *adj* slovenly, careless **slip'stream** *n* aviation stream of air driven astern by engine

slip[2] *n* clay mixed with water to creamy consistency, used for decorating ceramic ware

slip·per [SLIP-ər] *n* light shoe for indoor use **slip'pered** *adj*

slip·per·y [SLIP-ə-ree] *adj* so smooth as to cause slipping or to be difficult to hold or catch; changeable; unreliable; crafty; wily

slit *v* **slit, slit·ting** make long straight cut in; cut in strips ▷ *n*

slith·er [SLITH-ər] *vi* slide unsteadily (down slope, etc)

sliv·er [SLIV-ər] *n* thin small piece torn off something; splinter

slob n slovenly, coarse person
slob·ber [SLOB-ər] v slaver; be weakly and excessively demonstrative ▷ n running saliva; maudlin speech
sloe [sloh] n blue-black, sour fruit of blackthorn **sloe-eyed** adj dark-eyed; slanty-eyed **sloe gin** [jin] n liqueur of sloes steeped in gin
slog v slogged, slog·ging hit vigorously, esp in boxing; work or study with dogged determination; move, work with difficulty ▷ n
slo·gan [SLOH-gən] n distinctive phrase (in advertising, etc)
sloop n small one-masted vessel; history small warship
slop v slopped, slop·ping spill; splash in spilled liquid; watery food; dirty liquid ▷ pl liquid refuse **slop'py** adj -pi·er, -pi·est careless, untidy; sentimental; wet, muddy
slope [slohp] v sloped, slop·ing ▷ vt place slanting ▷ vi lie in, follow an inclined course; go furtively ▷ n slant; upward, downward inclination
slosh n watery mud, etc ▷ v splash **sloshed** adj sl drunk
slot n narrow hole or depression; slit for coins ▷ vt slot·ted, slot·ting put in slot; sort; place in series, organization **slot machine** automatic machine worked by insertion of coin
sloth [slawth] n sluggish S Amer animal; sluggishness **sloth'ful** [-fəl] adj lazy, idle
slouch [slowch] vi walk, sit, etc in lazy or ungainly, drooping manner ▷ n, adj (of hat) with wide, flexible brim
slough[1] [rhymes with cow] n bog
slough[2] [sluf] n skin shed by snake ▷ v shed (skin); drop off
slov·en [SLUV-ən] n dirty, untidy person **slov'en·ly** adj -li·er, -li·est

untidy; careless; disorderly ▷ adv
slow [sloh] adj -er, -est lasting a long time; moving at low speed; behind the true time; dull ▷ v slacken speed (of) **slow motion** motion picture showing movement greatly slowed down **slow'poke** [-pohk] n person slow in moving, acting, deciding, etc
sludge [sluj] n slush, ooze; sewage
slug[1] n land snail with no shell; bullet **slug'gard** [-ərd] n lazy, idle person **slug'gish** adj slow; lazy, inert; not functioning well **slug'gish·ness** n
slug[2] v slugged, slug·ging hit, slog ▷ n inf heavy blow; shot of whiskey **slug'ger** n hard-hitting boxer, baseball batter
sluice [sloos] n gate, door to control flow of water ▷ vt sluiced, sluic·ing pour water over, through
slum n squalid street or neighborhood ▷ vi slummed, slum·ming visit slums **slum'lord** n landlord who owns buildings in slums and neglects them
slum·ber [SLUM-bər] vi, n sleep **slum'ber·er** n
slump v fall heavily; relax ungracefully; decline suddenly in value, volume or esteem ▷ n sudden decline; (of prices, etc) sharp fall; depression
slung pt/pp of SLING
slunk pt/pp of SLINK
slur vt slurred, slur·ring pass over lightly; run together (words, musical notes); disparage ▷ n slight, stigma; music curved line above or below notes to be slurred
slurp v eat, drink noisily
slur·ry [SLUR-ee] n, pl -ries muddy liquid mixture as cement, mud, etc
slush n watery, muddy substance; excessive sentimentality **slush'y** adj

slush·i·er, slush·i·est slush fund fund for financing bribery, corruption

slut n offens promiscuous woman **slut'tish** adj

sly [slī] adj **sly·er** or **sli·er**, **sly·est** or **sli·est** cunning, wily, knowing; secret, deceitful **sly'ly, sli'ly** adv **sly'ness** [-nis] n

Sm chemistry samarium

smack [smak] n taste, flavor; sl heroin ▷ vi taste (of); suggest

smack² vt slap; open and close (lips) with loud sound ▷ n smacking slap; crack; such sound; loud kiss ▷ adv inf squarely; directly **smack'dab'** adv inf smack

smack³ n small sailing vessel, usu for fishing

small [smawl] adj **-er, -est** little, unimportant; petty; short; weak; mean ▷ n small slender part esp of the back **small hours** hours just after midnight **small-mind·ed** [-mīnd-id] adj having narrow views; petty **small'pox** n contagious disease **small talk** light, polite conversation

smarm·y [SMAHR-mee] adj **smarm·i·er, smarm·i·est** unpleasantly suave; fawning

smart [smahrt] adj **-er, -est** astute; brisk; clever, witty; impertinent; trim, well dressed; fashionable; causing stinging pain ▷ v feel, cause pain ▷ n sharp pain **smart'en** vt **smart'ly** adv **smart'ness** [-nis] n **smart al'eck** conceited person, know-it-all **smart ass** sl offens smart aleck **smart card** plastic card with integrated circuit capable of storing and processing data, used for identification, bank and store transactions, etc **smart'phone** n combination of cell phone and handheld computer

smash vt break violently; strike

hard; ruin; destroy ▷ vi break; dash violently against ▷ n heavy blow; collision (of vehicles, etc); total financial failure; inf popular success **smashed** adj sl very drunk or affected by drugs **smash'er** n attractive person, thing

smat·ter·ing [SMAT-ər-ing] n slight superficial knowledge

smear [smeer] vt rub with grease, etc; smudge, spread with dirt, grease, etc ▷ n mark made thus; sample of secretion for medical examination; slander

smell v **smelled** or **smelt, smell'ing** perceive by nose; suspect; give out odor; use nose ▷ n faculty of perceiving odors by nose; anything detected by sense of smell **smell'y** adj **smell·i·er, smell·i·est** with strong (unpleasant) smell

smelt² vt extract metal from ore **smelt'er** n

smelt² n fish of salmon family

smid·gen [SMIJ-ən] n very small amount

smile [smīl] n curving or parting of lips in pleased or amused expression ▷ v **smiled, smil·ing** wear, assume a smile; approve, favor

smirch [smurch] vt dirty, sully; disgrace, discredit ▷ n stain; disgrace

smirk [smurk] n smile expressing scorn, smugness ▷ v

smite [smīt] vt **smote, smit'ten** or **smit, smit'ing** strike; attack; afflict; affect, esp with love or fear

smith n worker in iron, gold, etc **smith'y** n, pl **smith·ies** blacksmith's workshop; blacksmith

smith·er·eens [SMITH-ər-eenz] pl n small bits

smock [smok] n loose outer garment ▷ vt gather by sewing in honeycomb pattern **smock'ing** n

smog n mixture of smoke and fog

smoke [smohk] n cloudy mass of suspended particles that rises from fire or anything burning; spell of tobacco smoking ▷ vb **smoked, smok·ing** ▷ vi give off smoke; inhale and expel tobacco smoke ▷ vt use (tobacco) by smoking; expose to smoke (esp in curing fish, etc) **smok·er** n one who smokes; informal party

smol·der [SMOHL-dər] vi burn slowly without flame; (of feelings) exist in suppressed state

smooch v, n inf kiss, cuddle

smooth [smooth] adj not rough, even of surface or texture; sinuous; flowing; calm, soft, soothing; suave, plausible; free from jolts ▷ vt make smooth; quiet **smooth·ly** adv

smor·gas·bord [SMOR-gəs-bord] n buffet meal of assorted dishes

smote pt of SMITE

smoth·er [SMUTH-ər] v suffocate; envelop; suppress ▷ vi be suffocated

SMS Short Message Server, system for sending messages of no more than 160 characters to a cell phone

smudge [smuj] v **smudged, smudg·ing** make smear, stain, dirty mark (on) ▷ n

smug adj **smug·ger, smug·gest** self-satisfied, complacent **smug·ly** adv

smug·gle [SMUG-əl] vt **-gled, -gling** import, export without paying customs duties; conceal, take secretly **smug·gler** n

smut n piece of soot, particle of dirt; lewd or obscene talk, etc; disease of grain ▷ vt **smut·ted, smut·ting** blacken, smudge **smut·ty** adj **-ti·er, -ti·est** soiled with smut, soot; obscene, lewd

Sn chemistry tin

snack [snak] n light portion of food eaten hastily between meals ▷ vi eat

thus **snack bar** lunchroom at which light meals are served

snag n difficulty; sharp protuberance; hole, loop in fabric caused by sharp object; obstacle (eg tree branch, etc in river bed) ▷ vt **snagged, snag·ging** catch, damage on snag

snail [snayl] n slow-moving mollusk with shell; slow, sluggish person **snail·like** adj **snail mail** n inf conventional mail, as opposed to e-mail; the conventional postal system **snail-mail** vt send by the conventional postal system, rather than by e-mail

snake [snayk] n long scaly limbless reptile, serpent ▷ v **snaked, snak·ing** move like snake **snak·y** adj **snak·i·er, snak·i·est** twisted or winding **snake in the grass** hidden enemy

snap v **snapped, snap·ping** break suddenly; make cracking sound; bite (at) suddenly; speak suddenly, angrily ▷ n act of snapping; fastener; snapshot; inf easy task; brief period, esp of cold weather ▷ adj sudden, unplanned, arranged quickly **snap·py** adj **-pi·er, -pi·est** irritable; inf quick; inf smart, fashionable **snap·drag·on** n plant with flowers that can be opened like a mouth **snap·shot** n informal photograph

snare [snair] n (noose used as) trap ▷ vt **snared, snar·ing** catch with one

snarl [snahrl] n growl of angry dog; tangle, knot ▷ vi utter snarl; grumble

snatch [snach] v make quick grab or bite (at); seize, catch ▷ n grab; fragment; short part

sneak [sneek] vi **sneaked, sneak·ing** slink; move about furtively; act in mean, underhand manner ▷ n mean, treacherous person **sneak'ing** adj secret but persistent **sneak pre'view** unannounced showing of movie before general release

sneak·ers [SNEEK-ərz] pl n flexible, informal sports shoes

sneer n scornful, contemptuous expression or remark ▷ v

sneeze [sneez] vi sneezed, **sneez·ing** emit breath through nose with sudden involuntary spasm and noise ▷ n

snick·er [SNIK-ər] n sly, disrespectful laugh, esp partly stifled ▷ v

snide [snīd] adj snid·er, snid·est malicious, supercilious

sniff vi inhale through nose with sharp hiss; (with at) express disapproval, etc by sniffing ▷ vt take up through nose, smell ▷ n **sniff'le** vi -fled, -fling sniff noisily through nose, esp when suffering from a cold in the head; snuffle

snig·ger [SNIG-ər] n snicker

snip vt snipped, snip·ping cut, cut bits off ▷ n act, sound of snipping; bit cut off; inf small, insignificant, impertinent person **snip·pet** [SNIP-it] n shred, fragment, clipping **snips** pl n tool for cutting

snipe [snīp] n wading bird ▷ v sniped, snip·ing shoot at enemy from cover; (with at) criticize, attack (person) slyly **snip'er** n

snit n irritated state of mind

snitch [snich] vt inf steal ▷ vi inform ▷ n informer

sniv·el [SNIV-əl] vi -eled, -el·ing sniffle to show distress; whine

snob n one who pretentiously judges others by social rank, etc **snob'ber·y** n **snob'bish** adj of or like a snob

snook·er [SNUUK-ər] n game like pool played with balls ▷ vt leave (opponent) in unfavorable position; place (someone) in difficult situation; sl cheat

snoop v pry, meddle; peer into ▷ n one who acts thus; snooping

snoot·y [SNOOT-ee] adj **snoot·i·er, snoot·i·est** inf haughty

snooze [snooz] vi snoozed, **snooz·ing** take short sleep ▷ n nap

snore [snor] vi snored, snor·ing breathe noisily when asleep ▷ n

snor·kel [SNOR-kəl] n tube for breathing underwater ▷ vi swim, fish using this

snort vi make (contemptuous) noise by driving breath through nostrils; sl inhale drug ▷ n noise of snorting; sl shot of liquor; sl amount of drug inhaled

snot n vulg mucus from nose **snot·ty** [-tee] adj -ti·er, -ti·est inf arrogant

snout [snowt] n animal's nose

snow [snoh] n frozen vapor that falls in flakes; sl cocaine ▷ v fall, sprinkle as snow; let fall, throw down like snow; cover with snow; sl overwhelm; sl deceive **snow'y** adj snow·i·er, snow·i·est of, like snow; covered with snow; very white **snow'ball** n snow pressed into hard ball for throwing ▷ v increase rapidly; play, fight with snowballs **snow blind·ness** temporary blindness due to brightness of snow **snow'board** n board like surfboard for descending ski slopes **snow'drift** n bank of deep snow **snow fence** fence for erecting in winter beside exposed road **snow job** sl attempt to deceive by flattery or exaggeration **snow line** elevation above which snow does not melt **snow'shoes**

[-shooz] pl n shoes like rackets for traveling on snow **snow under** cover and block with snow; fig overwhelm

snub vt snubbed, snub·bing insult (esp by ignoring) intentionally ▷ n, adj short and blunt **snub-nosed** adj

snuff[1] n powdered tobacco for inhaling through nose **up to snuff** inf up to a standard

snuff[2] n extinguish (esp candle, etc)

snuf·fle [SNUF-əl] vi -fled, -fling breathe noisily, with difficulty

snug adj -ger, -gest warm, comfortable **snug·gle** v -gled, -gling lie close to for warmth or affection **snug'ly** adv

so[1] [soh] adv to such an extent; in such a manner; very; the case being such; accordingly ▷ conj therefore; in order that; with the result that ▷ interj well! **so-called** adj called by but doubtfully deserving that name **so long** inf goodbye

so[2] see SOL

soak [sohk] v steep; absorb; drench; lie in liquid; sl overcharge (customer) ▷ n soaking; sl habitual drunkard

soap [sohp] n compound of alkali and oil used in washing ▷ vt apply soap to **soap'y** adj **soap·i·er, soap·i·est** soap opera radio or TV serial of domestic life

soar [sor] vi fly high; increase, rise (in price, etc)

sob vi sobbed, sob·bing catch breath, esp in weeping ▷ n sobbing **sob story** tale of personal distress told to arouse sympathy

so·ber [SOH-bər] adj -ber·er, -ber·est not drunk; temperate; subdued; dull, plain; solemn ▷ v make, become sober **so·bri·e·ty** [sə-BRI-i-tee] n state of being sober

so·bri·quet [SOH-brə-kay] n

nickname; assumed name

soc·cer [SOK-ər] n ball game played with feet and spherical ball

so·cia·ble [SOH-shə-bəl] adj friendly; convivial **so·cia·bil'i·ty** n

so·cial [SOH-shəl] adj living in communities; relating to society; sociable ▷ n informal gathering **so'cial·ite** n member of fashionable society **so'cial·ize** v -ized, -iz·ing **so'cial·ly** adv **social security** government-sponsored provision for the disabled, unemployed, aged, etc **social work** work to improve welfare of others

so·cial·ism [SOH-shə-liz-əm] n political system that advocates public ownership of means of production, distribution and exchange **so'cial·ist** n, adj

so·ci·e·ty [sə-SI-i-tee] n, pl -ties living associated with others; those so living; companionship; company; association; club; fashionable people collectively

so·ci·ol·o·gy [soh-see-OL-ə-jee] n study of societies

sock[1] [sok] n cloth covering for foot

sock[2] vt hit ▷ n blow

sock·et [SOK-it] n hole or recess for something to fit into

So·crat·ic [sə-KRAT-ik] adj of, like Greek philosopher Socrates

sod n lump of earth with grass

so·da [SOH-də] n compound of sodium; soda water **soda water** water charged with carbon dioxide

sod·den [SOD-n] adj soaked; drunk; heavy and lumpy

so·di·um [SOH-dee-əm] n metallic alkaline element **sodium bicarbonate** white crystalline soluble compound; (also **bicarbonate of soda**)

sod·om·y [SOD-ə-mee] n anal intercourse **sod'om·ite** n

so·fa [SOH-fə] n upholstered couch with back and arms, for two or more people

soft [sawft] adj **-er, -est** yielding easily to pressure, not hard; mild; easy; subdued; quiet, gentle; (too) lenient; oversentimental; foolish, stupid; (of water) containing few mineral salts; (of drugs) not liable to cause addiction **soft'en** [SAWF-ən] v make, become soft or softer; mollify; lighten; mitigate; make less loud **soft'ly** adv gently, quietly **soft'ball** n (ball used in) variation of baseball using larger, softer ball **soft drink** one that is nonalcoholic **soft goods** nondurable goods, eg curtains, rugs **soft soap** inf flattery **soft'ware** n programs used with a computer **soft'wood** [-wuud] n wood of coniferous tree

sog·gy [SOG-ee] adj **-gi·er, -gi·est** soaked with liquid; damp and heavy

soil¹ n earth, ground; country, territory

soil² v make, become dirty; tarnish; defile ▷ n dirt; sewage; stain

soi·ree [swah-RAY] n private evening party esp with music

so·journ [SOH-jurn] vi stay for a time ▷ n short stay **so'journ·er** n

sol, so n fifth sol-fa note

sol·ace [SOL-is] n, vt **-aced, -ac·ing** comfort in distress

so·lar [SOH-lər] adj of the sun **solar plex'us** network of nerves at pit of stomach

sold pt/pp of SELL

sol·der [SOD-ər] n easily-melted alloy used for joining metal ▷ vt join with it **soldering iron** tool for melting and applying solder

sol·dier [SOHL-jər] n one serving in army ▷ vi serve in army; inf loaf; (with on) persist doggedly **sol'dier·ly** adj

sole¹ [sohl] adj one and only, unique; solitary **sole'ly** adv alone; only; entirely

sole² n underside of foot; underpart of shoe, etc ▷ vt sole, sol·ing fit with sole

sole³ n small edible flatfish

sol·e·cism [SOL-ə-siz-əm] n breach of grammar or etiquette

sol·emn [SOL-əm] adj serious; formal; impressive **sol'emn·ly** adv **so·lem·ni·ty** [sə-LEM-ni-tee] n **sol·em·nize** [SOL-əm-nīz] vt **-nized, -niz·ing** celebrate, perform; make solemn

so·le·noid [SOH-lə-noid] n coil of wire as part of electrical apparatus

sol-fa [sohl-FAH] n music system of syllables sol, fa, etc sung in scale

so·lic·it [sə-LIS-it] vt request; accost; urge; entice **so·lic·i·ta·tion** n **so·lic·i·tor** n one who solicits **so·lic·i·tous** adj anxious; eager; earnest **so·lic·i·tude** n

sol·id adj not hollow; compact; composed of one substance; firm; massive; reliable, sound ▷ n body of three dimensions; substance not liquid or gas **sol·i·dar·i·ty** n unity of interests; united condition **so·lid·i·fy** v **-fied, -fy·ing** make, become solid or firm; harden **so·lid·i·ty** n

so·lil·o·quy [sə-LIL-ə-kwee] n, pl **-quies** (esp in drama) thoughts spoken by person while alone **so·lil'o·quize** vi **-quized, -quiz·ing**

sol·ip·sism [SOL-ip-siz-əm] n doctrine that self is the only thing known to exist **sol'ip·sist** n

sol·i·tar·y [SOL-i-ter-ee] adj alone, single ▷ n hermit **sol'i·taire** n game for one person played with cards or with pegs set in board; single precious stone set by itself **sol·i·tude** [SOH-li-tyood] *n* state of being alone; loneliness

so·lo [SOH-loh] *n, pl* **-los** music for one performer ▷ *adj* not concerted; unaccompanied, alone; piloting airplane alone **so·lo·ist** *n*

sol·stice [SOL-stis] *n* either shortest (winter) or longest (summer) day of year

solve [solv] *vt* **solved, solv·ing** work out, explain; find answer to **sol·u·bil·i·ty** [sol-yə-BIL-i-tee] *n* **sol·u·ble** *adj* capable of being dissolved in liquid; able to be solved or explained **so·lu·tion** [sə-LOO-shən] *n* answer to problem; dissolving; liquid with something dissolved in it **solv·a·ble** *adj* **sol·ven·cy** [-vən-see] *n* **sol·vent** *adj* able to meet financial obligations ▷ *n* liquid with power of dissolving

som·ber [SOM-bər] *adj* dark, gloomy

som·bre·ro [som-BRAIR-oh] *n, pl* **-bre·ros** wide-brimmed hat worn in Mexico, Spain, etc

some [sum] *adj* denoting an indefinite number, amount or extent; one or other; amount of; certain; approximately ▷ *pron* portion, quantity **some·bod·y** *n* some person; important person **some·how** *adv* by some means unknown **some·thing** *n* thing not clearly defined; indefinite amount, quantity or degree **-something** *comb form* (person) of an age above a given figure: thirtysomething **some·time** *adv* formerly; at some (past or future) time ▷ *adj* former **some·times** *adv* occasionally; now and then **some·what** [-hwot] *adv* to some extent, rather **some·where** [-hwair] *adv*

som·er·sault [SUM-ər-sawlt] *n* tumbling head over heels

som·nam·bu·list [som-NAM-byə-list] *n* sleepwalker **som·nam·bu·lism** *n*

som·no·lent [SOM-nə-lənt] *adj* drowsy; causing sleep **som·no·lence** *n*

son [sun] *n* male child **son-in-law** *n* daughter's husband

so·nar [SOH-nahr] *n* device like echo sounder

so·na·ta [sə-NAH-tə] *n* piece of music in several movements **son·a·ti·na** [son-ə-TEE-nə] *n* short sonata

son et lumière [saw-nay-luu-MYAIR] *Fr* entertainment staged at night at famous place, building, giving dramatic history of it with lighting and sound effects

song [sawng] *n* singing; poem, etc for singing **song'ster** *n* singer; songbird **song'stress** [-stris] *n fem*

son·ic [SON-ik] *adj* pert to sound waves **sonic boom** explosive sound caused by aircraft traveling at supersonic speed

son·net [SON-it] *n* fourteen-line poem with definite rhyme scheme **son·net·eer** [son-i-TEER] *n* writer of this

so·no·rous [sə-NOR-ees, SAHN-ər-us] *adj* giving out (deep) sound, resonant **so·nor'i·ty** *n*

soon *adv* in a short time; before long; early, quickly

soot [suut] *n* black powdery substance formed by burning of coal, etc **soot'y** *adj* **soot·i·er, soot·i·est** of, like soot

sooth [sooth] *n* truth **sooth'say·er** *n* one who foretells future; diviner

soothe [sooth] *vt* **soothed, sooth·ing** make calm, tranquil;

relieve (pain, etc)

sop *n* piece of bread, etc soaked in liquid; concession, bribe ▷ *vt* **sopped, sop·ping** steep in water, etc; soak (up) **sopping** *adj* completely soaked

soph·ist [SOF-ist] *n* fallacious reasoner, quibbler **soph'ism** [-izm] *n* specious argument **soph'ist·ry** *n*

so·phis·ti·cate [sə-FIS-ti-kayt] *vt* **-cat·ed, -cat·ing** make artificial, spoil, falsify, corrupt ▷ *n* [-kit] sophisticated person **sophisticated** *adj* having refined or cultured tastes, habits; worldly wise; superficially clever; complex **so·phis·ti·ca'tion** *n*

soph·o·more [SOF-ə-mor] *n* student in second year at high school or college **soph·o·mor'ic** *adj* intellectually pretentious

sop·o·rif·ic [sop-ə-RIF-ik] *adj* causing sleep (esp by drugs)

so·pra·no [sə-PRAN-oh] *n, pl* **-pra·nos** highest voice in women and boys; singer with this voice; musical part for it

sor·bet [sor-BAY] *n* sherbet

sor·cer·er [SOR-sər-ər] *n* magician **sor'cer·ess** [-ris] *n fem* **sor'cer·y** *n, pl* **-ies** witchcraft, magic

sor·did *adj* mean, squalid; ignoble, base **sor'did·ly** *adv* **sor'did·ness** [-nis] *n*

sore [sor] *adj* **sor·er, sor·est** painful; causing annoyance; severe; distressed; annoyed ▷ *adv obs* grievously, intensely ▷ *n* sore place, ulcer, boil, etc **sore'ly** *adv* grievously; greatly

sor·ghum [SOR-gəm] *n* kind of grass cultivated for grain

sor·rel [SOR-əl] *n* plant; reddish-brown color; horse of this color ▷ *adj* of this color

sor·row [SOR-oh] *n* pain of

mind, grief, sadness ▷ *vi* grieve

sor'row·ful [-fəl] *adj*

sor·ry [SOR-ee] *adj* **-ri·er, -ri·est** feeling pity or regret; distressed; miserable, wretched; mean, poor **sor'ri·ly** *adv*

sort *n* kind or class ▷ *vt* classify **sort'er** *n*

sor·tie [SOR-tee] *n* sally by besieged forces

SOS *n* international code signal of distress; call for help

so-so [SOH-soh] *adj* mediocre ▷ *adv* tolerably

sot *n* habitual drunkard

sot·to vo·ce [SOT-oh VOH-chee] It in an undertone

souf·flé [soo-FLAY] *n* dish of eggs beaten to froth, flavored and baked; dessert like this of various ingredients

sough [rhymes with **cow**] *n* low murmuring sound as of wind in trees

sought [sawt] pt/pp of **SEEK**

soul [sohl] *n* spiritual and immortal part of human being; example, pattern; person; (also **soul music**) type of Black music combining urban blues with jazz, pop, etc **soul'ful** [-fəl] *adj* full of emotion or sentiment **soul'less** [-lis] *adj* mechanical; lacking sensitivity or nobility; heartless, cruel

sound¹ [sownd] *n* what is heard; noise ▷ *vi* make a sound; seem; give impression of ▷ *vt* cause to sound; utter **sound barrier** hypothetical barrier to flight at speed of sound waves **sound bite** short pithy statement extracted from a longer speech for use esp in television or radio news reports **sound track** recorded sound accompaniment of motion picture, etc

sound² *adj* **-er, -est** in good condition; solid; of good judgment;

legal; solvent; thorough; effective; watertight; deep **sound'ly** adv thoroughly

sound³ vt find depth of, as water; ascertain views of; probe **sound'ings** pl n measurements taken by sounding

sound⁴ n channel; strait

soup [soop] n liquid food made by boiling or simmering meat, vegetables, etc **soup'y** adj

soup•i•er, soup•i•est like soup; murky; sentimental

sour [sowr] adj acid; gone bad; rancid; peevish; disagreeable ▷ v make, become sour **sour'ness** [-nis] n **sour'puss** [-puus] n inf sullen, sour-faced person

source [sors] n origin, starting point; spring

souse [rhymes with **LOUSE**] v soused, sous•ing plunge, drench; pickle ▷ n sousing; brine for pickling; sl drunkard **soused** adj sl drunk

south [sowth] n cardinal point opposite north; region, part of country, etc lying to that side ▷ adj, adv (that is) toward south **south'ward** [-wĕrd] adj, adv **south'wards** [-wĕrdz] adv **south•er•ly** [SUTH-ĕr-lee] adj toward south ▷ n, pl -lies wind from the south **south•ern** [SUTH-ĕrn] adj in south **south•west•er** [sowth-WES-tĕr] n wind, storm from the southwest

sou•ve•nir [soo-vŏ-NEER] n keepsake, memento

sov•er•eign [SOV-rin] n king, queen; former British gold coin worth 20 shillings ▷ adj supreme; efficacious **sov'er•eign•ty** n, pl -ties supreme power and right to exercise it; dominion; independent state

so•vi•et [SOH-vee-et] n formerly, elected council at various levels of government in USSR; (**S-**) official or citizen of the former USSR ▷ adj of the former USSR

sow¹ [soh] v sowed, sown or sowed, sow•ing ▷ vi scatter, plant seed ▷ vt scatter, deposit (seed); spread abroad

sow² [rhymes with **cow**] n female adult pig

soy•bean [SOI-been] n edible bean used as livestock feed, meat substitute, etc

soy sauce [SOI saws] sauce made by fermenting soybeans in brine

spa [spah] n medicinal spring; place, resort with one

space [spays] n extent; room; period; empty place; area; expanse; region beyond Earth's atmosphere ▷ vt spaced, spac•ing place at intervals **spa'cious** [-shŏs] adj roomy, extensive **space'craft**, **space'ship** n vehicle for travel beyond Earth's atmosphere **space shuttle** vehicle for repeated space flights **space'suit** n sealed, pressurized suit worn by astronaut

spade¹ [spayd] n tool for digging **spade'work** [SPAYD-wurk] n arduous preparatory work

spade² n leaf-shaped black symbol on playing card

spa•ghet•ti [spŏ-GET-ee] n pasta in form of long strings

spake [spayk] obs pt of **SPEAK**

spam computing sl v spams, spamming, spammed send unsolicited text messages simultaneously to many cell phones ▷ n unsolicited e-mail or text messages sent in this way

span n space from thumb to little finger as measure; extent; space; stretch of arch, etc ▷ vt spanned, span•ning stretch over; measure

span•gle [SPANG-gəl] *n* small shiny metallic ornament ▷*vt* **-gled, -gling** decorate with spangles

span•iel [SPAN-yəl] *n* breed of dog with long ears and silky hair

spank [spangk] *vt* slap with flat of hand, etc esp on buttocks ▷*n* **spank'ing** *n* series of spanks ▷*adj* quick, lively; large, fine

spar[1] [spahr] *n* pole, beam, esp as part of ship's rigging

spar[2] *vi* **sparred, spar•ring** box; dispute, esp in fun ▷*n* sparring

spar[3] *n* any of kinds of crystalline mineral

spare [spair] *vt* **spared, spar•ing** leave unhurt; show mercy; abstain from using; do without; give away ▷*adj* additional; in reserve; thin; lean; scanty ▷*n* spare part (for machine) **sparing** *adj* economical, careful

spark [spahrk] *n* small glowing or burning particle; flash of light produced by electrical discharge; vivacity, humor; trace; in internal-combustion engines, electric spark (in spark plug) that ignites explosive mixture in cylinder ▷*v* emit sparks; kindle, excite; *obs* woo

spar•kle [SPAHR-kəl] *vi* **-kled, -kling** glitter; effervesce; scintillate ▷*n* small spark; glitter; flash; lustre **sparkling** *adj* flashing; glittering; brilliant; lively; (of wines) effervescent

spar•row [SPA-roh] *n* small finch

sparse [spahrs] *adj* **spars•er, spars•est** thinly scattered

Spar•tan [SPAHR-tn] *adj* hardy; austere; frugal; undaunted

spasm [SPAZ-əm] *n* sudden convulsive (muscular) contraction; sudden burst of activity, etc

spas•mod•ic [spaz-MOD-ik] *adj* occurring in spasms

spas•tic [SPAS-tik] *n* *oft considered offens* person who has cerebral palsy ▷*adj* affected by involuntary muscle contractions: *spastic colon*; *oft considered offens* suffering from cerebral palsy

spat[1] *pt* of **SPIT**[1]

spat[2] *n* short gaiter

spat[3] *n* slight quarrel ▷*vi* **spat•ted, spat•ting** quarrel

spate [spayt] *n* rush, outpouring; flood

spa•tial [SPAY-shəl] *adj* of, in space

spat•ter [SPAT-ər] *vt* splash, cast drops over ▷*vi* be scattered in drops ▷*n* slight splash; sprinkling

spat•u•la [SPACH-ə-lə] *n* utensil with broad, flat blade for various purposes

spav•in *n* injury to, growth on horse's leg **spav'ined** *adj* lame, decrepit

spawn *n* eggs of fish, frog, etc ▷*vi* (of fish or frog) cast eggs; produce in great numbers

spay *vt* remove ovaries from (animal)

speak [speek] *v* **spoke, spo•ken, speak•ing** utter words; converse; deliver discourse; utter; pronounce; express; communicate in **speak'er** *n* one who speaks; one who specializes in speechmaking; (**S-**) official chairman of US House of Representatives, other legislative bodies; loudspeaker **speak'er•phone** *n* telephone including an external microphone and loudspeaker, allowing several people to participate in a call

spear [speer] *n* long pointed weapon; slender shoot, as of asparagus ▷*vt* transfix, pierce, wound with spear **spear'head** [-hed] *n* leading force in attack, campaign ▷ vt

spear·mint [SPEER-mint] n type of mint

spec [spek] n **on spec** inf as a risk or gamble

spe·cial [SPESH-əl] adj beyond the usual; particular, individual; distinct; limited **spe'cial·ist** n one who devotes self to special subject or branch of subject **etc spe'cial·ty** n, pl **-ties** special product, skill, characteristic, etc **spe'cial·ize** v **-ized, -iz·ing** ▷ vi be specialist; be adapted to special function or environment ▷ vt make special

spe·cie [SPEE-shee] n coined, as distinct from paper, money

spe·cies [SPEE-sheez] n, pl **species** sort, kind, esp animals, etc; class; subdivision

spe·cif·ic [spə-SIF-ik] adj definite; exact in detail; characteristic of a thing or kind **spe·cif'i·cal·ly** adv **spec'i·fy** vt **-fied, -fy·ing** state definitely or in detail **spec·i·fi·ca'tion** [-KAY-shən] n detailed description of something to be made, done **specific gravity** ratio of density of substance to that of water

spec·i·men [SPES-ə-mən] n part typifying whole; individual example

spe·cious [SPEE-shəs] adj deceptively plausible, but false **spe'cious·ly** adv **spe'cious·ness** [-nis] n

speck [spek] n small spot, particle ▷ vt spot **speck·le** [SPEK-l] n, vt **-led, -ling** speck

spec·ta·cle [SPEK-tə-kəl] n show; thing exhibited; ridiculous sight **spectacles** pl n eyeglasses **spec·tac'u·lar** adj impressive; showy; grand; magnificent ▷ n lavishly produced performance **spec·ta·tor** [SPEK-tay-tər] n one

who looks on

spec·ter [SPEK-tər] n ghost; image of something unpleasant **spec'tral** [-trəl] adj ghostly

spec·trum [SPEK-trəm] n, pl **-tra** [-trə] band of colors into which beam of light can be decomposed eg by prism; range (of eg opinions, occupations) **spec'tro·scope** [-trə-skohp] n instrument for producing, examining physical spectra

spec·u·late [SPEK-yə-layt] vi **-lat·ed, -lat·ing** guess, conjecture; engage in (risky) commercial transactions **spec·u·la'tion** n **spec'u·la·tive** [-lə-tiv] adj given to, characterized by speculation **spec'u·la·tor** n

spec·u·lum [SPEK-yə-ləm] n, pl **-lums** mirror; reflector of polished metal, esp in reflecting telescopes

speech n act, faculty of speaking; words, language; conversation; discourse; (formal) talk given before audience **speech'i·fy** vi **-fied, -fy·ing** make speech, esp long and tedious one **speech'less** [-lis] adj mute; at a loss for words

speed n swiftness; rate of progress; degree of sensitivity of photographic film; sl amphetamine ▷ v **sped** or **speed·ed, speed·ing** move quickly; drive vehicle at high speed; further; expedite **speed'ing** n driving (vehicle) at high speed, esp over legal limit **speed'i·ly** adv **speed'y** adj **speed·i·er, speed·i·est** quick; rapid; nimble; prompt **speed'boat** n light fast motorboat **speed·om·e·ter** [-OM-ə-tər] n instrument to show speed of vehicle **speed'way** n track for automobile or motorcycle racing

spe·le·ol·o·gy [spee-lee-OL-ə-jee] n study, exploring of caves **spe·le·ol'o·gist** n

spell[1] vt **spelled** or **spelt, spell·ing** give letters of in order; read letter by letter; indicate; result in **spelling** n **spell'check·er** n computing program that finds words in a document that are not recognized as being correctly spelled **spell out** make explicit

spell[2] n magic formula; enchantment **spell'bound** [-bownd] adj enchanted; entranced

spell[3] n (short) period of time, work

spend vt **spent, spend·ing** pay out; pass (time) on activity, etc; use up completely **spend'thrift** n wasteful person

sperm [spurm] n male reproductive cell; semen **sper·mat·ic** adj of sperm **sperm'i·cide** [-sīd] n drug, etc that kills sperm

sper·ma·cet·i [spur-mə-SET-ee] n white, waxy substance obtained from oil from head of sperm whale **sperm whale** large, toothed whale

spew [spyoo] v vomit; gush

sphag·num [SFAG-nàm] n moss that grows in bogs

sphere [sfeer] n ball, globe; range; field of action; status; position; province **spher·i·cal** [SFER-i-kàl] adj

sphinc·ter [SFINGK-tàr] n ring of muscle surrounding opening of hollow bodily organ

sphinx [sfingks] n, pl **-es** figure in Egypt with lion's body and human head; (**S-**) the great statue of this near the pyramids of Giza; monster, half woman, half lion; enigmatic person

spice [spis] n aromatic or pungent vegetable substance; spices collectively; anything that adds flavor, relish, piquancy, interest, etc ▷ vt **spiced, spic·ing** season with spices, flavor **spic'y** adj **spic·i·er,**

spic·i·est flavored with spices; slightly indecent, risqué

spick-and-span [SPIK-ən-SPAN] adj spotlessly clean; neat, smart, new-looking

spi·der [SPI-dàr] n small eight-legged creature that spins web to catch prey **spi'der·y** adj

spiel [speel] n inf glib (sales) talk ▷ vi deliver spiel, recite **spiel'er** n

spig·ot [SPIG-àt] n peg or plug; faucet

spike [spīk] n sharp point; sharp pointed object; long flower cluster with flowers attached directly to the stalk ▷ vt **spiked, spik·ing** pierce, fasten with spike; render ineffective; add alcohol to (drink)

spill v **spilled** or **spilt, spill·ing** (cause to) pour from, flow over, fall out, esp unintentionally; upset; be lost or wasted ▷ n spillway; spillage **spill'age** [-ij] n amount spilled **spill'way** n passageway through which excess water spills

spin v **spun, spin·ning** (cause to) revolve rapidly; whirl; twist into thread; prolong; tell (a story); fish with lure ▷ n spinning; (of aircraft) descent in dive with continued rotation; rapid run or ride; politics interpretation (of event, speech, etc) to gain partisan advantage **spinning** n act, process of drawing out and twisting into threads, as wool, cotton, flax, etc **spinning wheel** household machine with large wheel turned by treadle for spinning wool, etc into thread **spin doctor** inf person who provides a favourable slant to a news item or policy on behalf of a political personality or party **spin-dry** vt **-dried, -dry·ing** spin clothes in (washing) machine to remove excess water **spin machine** group of people acting together to present news or information in a way that creates a particular impression

spin·ach [SPIN-ich] n dark green leafy vegetable

spin·dle [SPIN-dl] n rod, axis for spinning **spin'dly** adj **-dli·er, -dli·est** long and slender; attenuated

spin'drift n spray blown along surface of sea

spine [spīn] n backbone; thin spike, esp on fish, etc; ridge; back of book **spi'nal** [-əl] adj **spine'less** [-lis] adj lacking spine; cowardly

spin·et [SPIN-it] n small piano; small harpsichord

spin·na·ker [SPIN-ə-kər] n large yacht sail

spin·ster [SPIN-stər] n unmarried woman

spi·ral [SPI-rəl] n continuous curve drawn at ever increasing distance from fixed point; anything resembling this; football kick or pass turning on longer axis ▷ v **-raled, -ral·ing** of eg football or inflation, (cause to) take spiral course ▷ adj

spire [spīr] n pointed part of steeple; pointed stem of plant

spir'it n life principle animating body; disposition; liveliness; courage; frame of mind; essential character or meaning; soul; ghost; liquid got by distillation, alcohol ▷ pl emotional state; strong alcoholic drink eg whiskey ▷ vt carry away mysteriously **spir'it·ed** [-id] adj lively **spir'it·less** [-lis] adj listless, apathetic **spir·it·u·al** [-choo-əl] adj given to, interested in things of the spirit ▷ n religious song, hymn **spir'it·u·al·ism** n belief that spirits of the dead communicate with the living **spir'it·u·al·ist** n **spir'it·u·ous** adj alcoholic **spirit**

level glass tube containing bubble in liquid, used to check horizontal, vertical surfaces

spirt n see SPURT

spit¹ v spit or spat, spit·ting eject saliva; eject from mouth ▷ n spitting, saliva **spit·tle** [SPIT-l] n saliva **spit'ball** n illegal pitch of baseball moistened with saliva by pitcher; ball of chewed paper used as missile **spit·toon'** n vessel to spit into **spit'fire** n person, esp woman or girl, with fiery temper

spit² n sharp rod to put through meat for roasting; sandy point projecting into the sea ▷ vt **spit·ted, spit·ting** thrust through

spite [spīt] n malice ▷ vt **spit·ed, spit·ing** thwart spitefully **spite'ful** [-fəl] adj **in spite of** prep regardless of; notwithstanding

splash v scatter liquid about or on, over something; print, display prominently ▷ n sound of this; patch, esp of color; (effect of) extravagant display; small amount

splat n wet, slapping sound

splat·ter [SPLAT-ər] v, n spatter

splay adj spread out; slanting; turned outward ▷ vt spread out; twist outward ▷ n slanted surface **splay'foot·ed** [-fuut-id] adj flat and broad (of foot)

spleen n organ in the abdomen; anger; irritable or morose temper **sple·net·ic** [splə-NET-ik] adj

splen'did adj magnificent, brilliant, excellent **splen'did·ly** adv **splen'dor** [-dər] n

splice [splīs] vt spliced, splic·ing join by interweaving strands; join (wood) by overlapping; inf join in marriage ▷ n spliced joint

spline [splīn] n narrow groove, ridge, strip, esp joining wood, etc

splint n rigid support for broken

limb, etc

splin·ter [SPLIN-tàr] *n* thin fragment ▷ *vi* break into fragments, shiver **splinter group** group that separates from main party, organization, oft after disagreement

split *v* split, split'ting break asunder; separate; divide; sl depart ▷ *n* crack, fissure; dessert of fruit, usu banana, and ice cream

splotch [sploch] *n, v,* splash, daub **splotch'y** *adj* splotch·i·er, splotch·i·est

splurge [splurj] *v* splurged, splurg·ing spend money extravagantly ▷ *n*

splut·ter [SPLUT-àr] *v* make hissing, spitting sounds; utter incoherently with spitting sounds ▷ *n*

spoil *v* spoiled or spoilt, spoil·ing damage, injure; damage manners or behavior of (esp child) by indulgence; pillage; go bad ▷ *n* booty; waste material, esp in mining; (also **spoil'age**) **spoil'er** *n* slowing device on aircraft wing, etc **spoiling for** eager for

spoke[1] *pt of* SPEAK **spokes'per·son, -wo·man, -man** *n* one deputed to speak for others

spoke[2] *n* radial bar of a wheel

spoken *pp of* SPEAK

spo·li·a·tion [spoh-lee-AY-shàn] *n* act of spoiling; robbery; destruction **spo'li·ate** [-ayt] *v* -at·ed, -at·ing despoil, plunder, pillage

spon·dee *n* metrical foot consisting of two long syllables

sponge [spunj] *n* marine animal; its skeleton, or a synthetic substance like it, used to absorb liquids; type of light cake ▷ *v* **sponged, spong·ing** ▷ *vt* wipe with sponge ▷ *vi* live meanly at expense of others; cadge **spong'er** *n* sl one who cadges, or

lives at expense of others **spon'gy** *adj* -gi·er, -gi·est spongelike; wet and soft

spon·sor [SPON-sàr] *n* one promoting, advertising something; one who agrees to give money to a charity on completion of specified activity by another; one taking responsibility (esp for welfare of child at baptism, ie godparent); guarantor ▷ *vt* act as sponsor **spon'sor·ship** *n*

spon·ta·ne·ous [spon-TAY-nee-às] *adj* voluntary; natural; not forced; produced without external force **spon·ta·ne'i·ty** [-tà-NEE-i-tee] *n*

spoof *n* mild satirical mockery; trick, hoax ▷ *v*

spook *n* ghost ▷ *vt* haunt **spook'y** *adj* spook·i·er, spook·i·est

spool *n* reel, bobbin

spoon *n* implement with shallow bowl at end of handle for carrying food to mouth, etc ▷ *vt* lift with spoon **spoon'ful** [-fàl] *n, pl* **-fuls** [-fàlz] **spoon'fed** *adj* fed (as if) with spoon; pampered

spoon·er·ism [SPOO-nà-riz-àm] *n* amusing transposition of initial consonants, such as *half-warmed fish* for *half-formed wish*

spoor [spuur] *n* trail of wild animals ▷ *v* follow spoor

spo·rad·ic [spà-RAD-ik] *adj* intermittent; scattered, single **spo·rad'i·cal·ly** *adv*

spore [spor] *n* minute reproductive organism of some plants and protozoans

sport *n* game, activity for pleasure, competition, exercise; enjoyment; mockery; cheerful person, good loser ▷ *vt* wear (esp ostentatiously) ▷ *vi* frolic; play (sport) **sport'ing** *adj* of sport; behaving with fairness, generosity **sport'ive** *adj*

playful **sports car** fast (open) car
sports jacket man's casual jacket
sports·man [-mǎn] n, pl -men one
who engages in sport; good loser
sports'man·ship n good sport
sport utility vehicle powerful four-wheel drive
vehicle for rough terrain

spot n small mark, stain; blemish;
pimple; place; (difficult) situation
▷ vt **spot·ted, spot·ting** mark
with spots; detect; observe; blemish
spot'less [-lis] adj unblemished;
pure **spot'less·ly** adv **spot'ty**
-ti·er, -ti·est with spots; uneven
spot check random examination
spot'light n powerful light
illuminating small area; center of
attention

spouse [spows] n husband or wife
spous·al [SPOWZ-əl] n, adj (of)
marriage

spout [spowt] v pour out; inf
speechify ▷ n projecting tube or
lip for pouring liquids; copious
discharge

sprain n, vt wrench or twist (of
muscle, etc)

sprang pt of **SPRING**

sprat n small sea fish

sprawl vi lie or sit about awkwardly;
spread in rambling, unplanned way
▷ n sprawling

spray[1] n (device for producing) fine
drops of liquid ▷ vt sprinkle with
shower of fine drops

spray[2] n branch, twig with buds,
flowers, etc; floral ornament, brooch,
etc like this

spread [spred] v **spread,
spread'ing** extend; stretch out; open
out; scatter; distribute; unfold; cover
▷ n extent; increase; ample meal;
food that can be spread on bread, etc
spread-ea·gle adj with arms and
legs outstretched **spread'sheet** n
computer program for manipulating

figures

spree n session of overindulgence;
romp

sprig n small twig; ornamental
design like this; small headless nail

spright·ly [SPRIT-lee] adj **-li·er,
-li·est** lively, brisk **spright'li·ness**
[-nis] n

spring v **sprang, sprung,
spring·ing** leap; shoot up or forth;
come into being; appear; grow;
become bent or tight; produce
unexpectedly; set off (trap) ▷ n
leap; recoil; piece of coiled or bent
metal with much resilience; flow
of water from earth; first season
of year **spring'y** adj **spring·i·er,
spring·i·est** elastic **spring'board**
[-bord] n flexible board for diving;
anything that supplies impetus
for action

sprin·kle [SPRING-kəl] vt **-kled,
-kling** scatter small drops on, strew
sprin'kler n sprinkling n small
amount or number

sprint vt run short distance at great
speed ▷ n such run, race **sprint'er** n
one who sprints

sprit n small spar set diagonally
across a fore-and-aft sail in order to
extend it

sprite [sprit] n fairy, elf

sprock·et [SPROK-it] n projection
on wheel or capstan for engaging
chain; wheel with these

sprout [sprowt] vi put forth shoots,
spring up ▷ n shoot **Brus'sels
sprout** [-sǎlz] kind of miniature
cabbage

spruce[1] [sproos] n variety of fir

spruce[2] adj **spruc·er, spruc·est**
neat in dress ▷ v spruced,
spruc·ing (with up) make (oneself)
spruce

sprung pp of **SPRING**

spry [spri] adj **spry·er** or **spri·er,**

spry·est or **spri·est** nimble, vigorous

spud n inf potato

spume [spyoom] n, vi **spumed, spum·ing** foam, froth

spun pt/pp of **SPIN**

spunk n courage, spirit

spur n pricking instrument attached to horseman's heel; incitement; stimulus; projection on rooster's leg; projecting mountain range; branch (road, etc) ▷ vt **spurred, spur·ring** equip with spurs; urge on

spu·ri·ous [SPYUUR-ee-əs] adj not genuine

spurn vt reject with scorn, thrust aside

spurt v send, come out in jet; rush suddenly ▷ n jet; short sudden effort, esp in race

sput·nik [SPUUT-nik] n one of series of Russian satellites

sput·ter [SPUT-ər] v splutter

spu·tum [SPYOO-təm] n, pl -**ta** [-tə] spittle

spy [spī] n, pl **spies** one who watches (esp in rival countries, companies, etc) and reports secretly ▷ v **spied, spy·ing** act as spy; catch sight of **spy'glass** n small telescope **spy'ware** n software secretly installed in a computer via the Internet to gather and transmit information about the user

squab·ble [SKWOB-əl] vi -**bled, -bling** engage in petty, noisy quarrel, bicker ▷ n

squad [skwod] n small party, esp of soldiers or police **squad car** police patrol automobile; (also **patrol car**) **squad·ron** [-rən] n division of an air force, fleet, or cavalry regiment

squal·id [SKWOL-id] adj mean and dirty **squal'or** [-ər] n

squall [skwawl] n harsh cry; sudden gust of wind; short storm ▷ vi yell

squan·der [SKWON-dər] vt spend wastefully, dissipate

square [skwair] n equilateral rectangle; area of this shape; in town, open space (of this shape); product of a number multiplied by itself; instrument for drawing right angles; sl person behind the times ▷ adj square in form; honest; straight; even; level; equal; denoting a measure of area; inf straightforward, honest; sl ignorant of current trends in dress, music, etc, conservative ▷ v **squared, squar·ing** ▷ vt make square; find square of; pay ▷ vi fit, suit **square'ly** adv **square off** get ready to dispute or fight **square root** number that, multiplied by itself, gives number of which it is factor

squash [skwosh] vt crush flat; pulp; suppress; humiliate (person) ▷ n act of squashing; (also **squash racquets**) game played with rackets and soft balls in walled court; plant bearing gourds used as a vegetable

squat [skwot] vi **squat·ted** or **squat, squat·ting** sit on heels; act as squatter ▷ adj **squat·ter, squat·test** short and thick **squatter** n one who settles on land or occupies house without permission

squaw [skwaw] n offens Amer Indian woman; sl wife

squawk [skwawk] n short harsh cry, esp of bird ▷ v utter this

squeak [skweek] v, n (make) short shrill sound

squeal [skweel] n long piercing squeak ▷ v make one; sl turn informer, supply information (about another) **squeal'er** n

squeam·ish [SKWEEM-ish] adj easily nauseated; easily shocked; overscrupulous

squee·gee [SKWEE-jee] *n* tool with rubber blade for clearing water (from glass, etc, spreading wet paper, etc) ▷ *vt* **-geed, -gee·ing** press, smooth with a squeegee

squeeze [skweez] *vt* **squeezed, squeez·ing** press; wring; force; hug; subject to extortion ▷ *n* act of squeezing; period of hardship, difficulty caused by weakness

squelch [skwelch] *vt* squash; silence with crushing rebuke, etc ▷ *vi* make, walk with wet sucking sound, as in walking through mud ▷ *n*

squib [skwib] *n* small (faulty) firework; short piece of writing; short news story

squid [skwid] *n* type of cuttlefish

squig·gle [SKWIG-əl] *n* wavy, wriggling mark ▷ *vi* **-gled, -gling** wriggle; draw squiggle

squint [skwint] *vi* look with eyes partially closed; have the eyes turned in different directions; glance sideways; look askance ▷ *n* partially closed eyes; crossed eyes; *inf* a glance

squire [skwir] *n* country gentleman

squirm [skwurm] *vi* wriggle; be embarrassed ▷ *n*

squir·rel [SKWUR-əl] *n* small graceful bushy-tailed tree animal ▷ *vt* **-reled, -rel·ing** store or hide (possession) for future use

squirt [skwurt] *v* (of liquid) force, be forced through narrow opening ▷ *n* jet; *inf* short or insignificant person; *inf* (impudent) youngster

squish [skwish] *v, n* (make) soft splashing sound

Sr *chemistry* strontium

stab *v* **stabbed, stab·bing** pierce, strike (at) with pointed weapon ▷ *n* blow, wound so inflicted; sudden unpleasant sensation; attempt

sta·bi·lize [STAY-bə-liz] *vt* **-ized, -iz·ing** make steady, restore to equilibrium, esp of money values, prices and wages **sta·bi·li·za'tion** *n* **sta'bi·liz·er** *n* device to maintain equilibrium of ship, aircraft, etc

sta·ble¹ [STAY-bəl] *n* building for horses; racehorses of particular owner, establishment; such establishment ▷ *vt* **-bled, -bling** put into, lodge in, a stable

stable² [-blər, -blest] firmly fixed; steadfast, resolute **sta·bil·i·ty** [stə-BIL-ə-tee] *n* steadiness; ability to resist change of any kind **sta'bly** *adv*

stac·ca·to [stə-KAH-toh] *adj, adv music* with notes sharply separated; abrupt

stack [stak] *n* ordered pile, heap; chimney ▷ *vt* pile in stack; control aircraft waiting to land so that they fly safely at different altitudes

sta·di·um [STAY-dee-əm] *n, pl* **-di·ums** open-air or covered arena for athletics, etc

staff¹ *n, pl* **staffs** body of officers or workers; personnel; pole ▷ *vt* employ personnel; supply with personnel

staff² *n, pl* **staffs** or **staves** five lines on which music is written

stag *n* adult male deer ▷ *adj* for men only: *stag party*

stage [stayj] *n* period, division of development; raised floor or platform; (platform of) theater; scene of action; stopping place of stagecoach, etc on road, distance between two of them; separate unit of space rocket, which can usu be jettisoned ▷ *vt* **staged, stag·ing** put (play) on stage; arrange, bring about **stag'y** *adj* **stag·i·er, stag·i·est** theatrical **by easy stages** unhurriedly; gradually **stage**

whisper loud whisper intended to be heard by audience

stag•ger [STAG-ər] vi walk unsteadily ▷ vt astound; arrange in overlapping or alternating positions, times; distribute over a period ▷ n act of staggering **stag'gers** n form of vertigo; disease of horses **stag•ger•ing** adj astounding

stag•nate [STAG-nayt] vi **-nat•ed, -nat•ing** cease to flow or develop **stag•na'tion** n **stag'nant** [-nənt] adj sluggish; not flowing; foul, impure

staid [stayd] adj of sober and quiet character, sedate **staid'ly** adv **staid'ness** [-nis] n

stain [stayn] v spot, mark; apply liquid coloring to (wood, etc); bring disgrace upon ▷ n **stain'less** adj **stainless steel** rustless steel alloy

stairs [stairz] pl n set of steps, esp as part of house **stair'case, -way** n structure enclosing stairs; stairs **stair'well** n vertical opening enclosing staircase

stake [stayk] n sharpened stick or post; money wagered or contended for ▷ vt **staked, stak•ing** secure, mark out with stakes; wager, risk

sta•lac•tite [stə-LAK-tīt] n lime deposit like icicle on roof of cave

sta•lag•mite [stə-LAG-mīt] n lime deposit like pillar on floor of cave

stale [stayl] adj **stal•er, stal•est** old, lacking freshness; hackneyed; lacking energy, interest through monotony **stale'mate** n chess draw through one player being unable to move; deadlock, impasse

stalk[1] [stawk] n plant's stem; anything like this

stalk[2] v follow, approach stealthily; walk in stiff and stately manner; pursue persistently and, sometimes, attack (a person with whom one is

obsessed) ▷ n stalking **stalk'er** n **stalk'ing-horse** n pretext

stall [stawl] n compartment in stable, etc; booth for display and sale of goods; seat in choir or chancel of church; slowdown ▷ v put in stall; stick fast; (motor engine) unintentionally stop; (aircraft) lose flying speed; delay; hinder

stal•lion [STAL-yən] n uncastrated male horse, esp for breeding

stal•wart [STAWL-wərt] adj strong, brave; staunch ▷ n stalwart person

sta•men [STAY-mən] n male organ of a flowering plant

stam•i•na [STAM-ə-nə] n power of endurance, vitality

stam•mer [STAM-ər] v speak, say with repetition of syllables, stutter ▷ n habit of so speaking **stam'mer•er** n

stamp vi put down foot with force ▷ vt impress mark on; affix postage stamp; fix in memory; reveal, characterize ▷ n stamping with foot; imprinted mark; appliance for marking; piece of gummed paper printed with device as evidence of postage, etc; character

stam•pede [stam-PEED] n sudden frightened rush, esp of herd of cattle, crowd ▷ v **-ped•ed, -ped•ing** cause, take part in stampede

stance [stans] n manner, position of standing; attitude; point of view

stanch [stawnch] vt stop flow (of blood) from

stan•chion [STAN-shən] n upright bar, support ▷ vt make secure with stanchion

stand v **stood** [stuud] **stand•ing** have, take, set in upright position; remain; be situated; remain firm or stationary; cease to move; endure; adhere to principles; offer oneself as a candidate; be symbol, etc of; provide free treat to ▷ *n* holding firm; position; halt; something on which thing can be placed; structure from which spectators watch sport, etc; stop made by traveling entertainer, etc: *one-night stand* **standing** *n* reputation, status; duration ▷ *adj* erect; permanent, lasting; stagnant; performed from stationary position: *standing jump* **stand·by** [-bi] *n, pl* **-bys** [-biz] someone, something that can be relied on **stand·in** *n* substitute **stand over** watch closely; postpone

stand·ard [STAN-dàrd] *n* accepted example of something against which others are judged; degree, quality; flag; weight or measure to which others must conform; post ▷ *adj* usual, regular; average; of recognized authority, competence; accepted as correct **stand·ard·ize** *vt* **-ized, -iz·ing** regulate by a standard

stand·off [STAND-awf] *n* (objectionable) aloofness; *sport* a tie ▷ *adj* (objectionably) aloof; reserved

stand·point *n* point of view, opinion; mental attitude

stank pt of **STINK**

stan·nous [STAN-às] *adj* of, containing tin

stan·za [STAN-zà] *n, pl* **-zas** group of lines of verse

sta·ple [STAY-pàl] *n* U-shaped piece of metal with pointed ends to drive into wood for use as ring; paper fastener; main product; fiber; pile of wool, etc ▷ *adj* principal; regularly produced or made for market ▷ *vt* **-pled, -pling** fasten with staple; sort, classify (wool, etc) according to length of fibre **sta·pler** *n* small device for fastening papers together

star [stahr] *n* celestial body, seen

as twinkling point of light; asterisk; celebrated player, actor; medal, jewel, etc of apparent shape of star ▷ *v* **starred, star·ring** adorn with stars; mark (with asterisk); feature as star performer; play leading role in film, etc ▷ *adj* leading, most important, famous **star'ry** *adj* **-ri·er, -ri·est** covered with stars **star'dom** [-dàm] *n* **star'fish** *n* small star-shaped sea creature

star·board [STAHR-bàrd] *n* right-hand side of ship, looking forward ▷ *adj* of, on this side

starch *n* substance forming the main food element in bread, potatoes, etc, and used mixed with water, for stiffening laundered fabrics; *inf* boldness; vigor; energy ▷ *vt* stiffen thus **starch'y** *adj* **starch·i·er, starch·i·est** containing starch; stiff; formal; prim

stare [stair] *vi* **stared, star·ing** look fixedly at; gaze with eyes wide open; be obvious or visible to ▷ *n* staring, fixed gaze **stare down** abash by staring at; defeat by staring

stark [stahrk] *adj* **-er, -est** blunt, bare; desolate; absolute ▷ *adv* completely

start [stahrt] *vt* begin; set going ▷ *vi* begin, esp journey; make sudden movement ▷ *n* beginning; abrupt movement; advantage of a lead in a race **start'er** *n* electric motor starting car engine; competitor in, supervisor of, start of race

star·tle [STAHR-tl] *vt* **-tled, -tling** give a fright to

starve [stahrv] *v* **starved, starv·ing** (cause to) suffer or die from hunger **star·va'tion** [-VAY-shàn] *n*

stash *vt* put away, store, hide ▷ *n* anything stashed; place for this; *sl* supply of illicit drugs

state [stayt] n condition; place, situation; politically organized people eg any of the fifty states of the USA; government; rank; pomp ▷ vt **stat•ed, stat•ing** express in words **stated** adj fixed; regular; settled **state'ly** adj -li•er, -li•est dignified, lofty **state'ment** [-mənt] n expression in words; account **state'room** [-ruum] n private cabin on ship **states'man** [-mən] n, pl -men respected political leader **states'man•ship** n statesman's art

stat•ic [STAT-ik] adj motionless, inactive; pert to bodies at rest, or in equilibrium ▷ n electrical interference in radio reception **stat'i•cal•ly** adv

sta•tion [STAY-shən] n place where traffic stops or is placed; stopping place for railroad trains, buses; local office for police force, fire department, etc; place equipped for radio or television transmission; post; status; position in life ▷ vt put in position **sta'tion•ar•y** [-er-ee] adj not moving, fixed; not changing **sta•tion•er** [STAY-shən-ər] n dealer in writing materials, etc **sta'tion•er•y** n

sta•tis•tic [stə-TIS-tik] n numerical fact collected and classified systematically **sta•tis•tics** n science of classifying and interpreting numerical information **sta•tis'ti•cal** [-kəl] adj **stat•is•ti•cian** [stat-i-STISH-ən] n one who compiles and studies statistics

stat•ue [STACH-oo] n solid carved or cast image of person, animal, etc **stat'u•ar•y** n statues collectively **stat•u•esque** [-esk] adj like statue; dignified

stat•ure [STACH-ər] n bodily height; greatness

sta•tus [STAY-təs] n position, rank; prestige; relation to others **status quo** [kwoh] existing state of affairs

stat•ute [STACH-oot] n written law **stat'u•to•ry** [-ə-tor-ee] adj enacted, defined or authorized by statute

staunch [stawnch] adj -er, -est trustworthy, loyal

stave [stayv] n one of the pieces forming barrel; verse, stanza; music staff ▷ vt **staved** or **stove, stav•ing** break hole in; ward (off)

stay[1] v **stayed, stay•ing** remain; sojourn; pause; wait; endure; stop; hinder; postpone ▷ n remaining, sojourning; check; restraint; deterrent; postponement

stay[2] n support, prop, rope supporting mast, etc ▷ pl formerly, laced corsets

stead [sted] n place **in stead** in place (of) **in good stead** of service

stead•y [STED-ee] adj **stead•i•er, stead•i•est** firm; regular; temperate; industrious; reliable ▷ vt **stead•ied, stead•y•ing** make steady **stead'i•ly** adv **stead'i•ness** [-nis] n **stead'fast** [-fəst] adj firm, fixed, unyielding **stead'fast•ly** adv

steak [stayk] n slice of meat, esp beef; slice of fish

steal [steel] v **stole, sto•len, steal•ing** rob; move silently; take without right or leave

stealth [stelth] n secret or underhanded procedure, behavior **stealth'i•ly** adv **stealth'y** adj **stealth•i•er, stealth•i•est**

steam [steem] n vapor of boiling water; inf power, energy ▷ vi give off steam; rise in vapor; move by steam power ▷ vt cook or treat with steam **steam'er** n steam-propelled ship; vessel for cooking or treating with steam **steam engine** engine

worked or propelled by steam
steam'roll·er n large roller, orig moved by steam, for leveling road surfaces, etc; any great power used to crush opposition ▷ vt crush

steed n poetry horse

steel n hard and malleable metal made by mixing carbon in iron; tool, weapon of steel ▷ vt harden **steel'y** adj **steel·i·er, steel·i·est**

steep[1] adj -er, -est rising, sloping abruptly; precipitous; (of prices) very high or exorbitant; unreasonable **steep'en** v **steep'ly** adv **steep'ness** n

steep[2] v soak, saturate ▷ n act or process of steeping; the liquid used

stee·ple [STEE-pəl] n church tower with spire **stee'ple·chase** [-] n horse race with ditches and fences to jump; foot race with hurdles, etc to jump **stee'ple·jack** n one who builds, repairs chimneys, steeples, etc

steer[1] vt guide, direct course of vessel, motor vehicle, etc ▷ vi direct one's course **steer'age** [-ij] n formerly, cheapest accommodation on ship **steer'ing wheel** n wheel turned by the driver of a vehicle in order to steer it

steer[2] n castrated bull

stein [stīn] n earthenware beer mug

ste·le [STEE-lee] n ancient carved stone pillar or slab

stel·lar [STEL-ər] adj of stars

stem[1] n stalk, trunk; long slender part, as in tobacco pipe; part of word to which inflections are added; foremost part of ship **stem cell** histology undifferentiated embryonic cell that gives rise to specialized cells, such as blood, bone, etc

stem[2] vt **stemmed, stem·ming** check, stop, dam up

stench n evil smell

sten·cil [STEN-səl] n thin sheet pierced with pattern which is brushed over with paint or ink, leaving pattern on surface under it; the pattern; the plate; pattern made ▷ vt **-ciled, -cil·ing**

ste·nog·ra·phy [stə-NOG-rə-fee] n shorthand writing **sten·og'ra·pher** n **sten·o·graph'ic** adj

stent n surgical implant to keep an artery open

sten·to·ri·an [sten-TOR-ee-ən] adj (of voice) very loud

step v **stepped, step·ping** move and set down foot; proceed (in this way); measure in paces ▷ n act of stepping; sound made by stepping; mark made by foot; manner of walking; series of foot movements forming part of dance; gait; pace; measure, act, stage in proceeding; board, rung, etc to put foot on; degree in scale; mast socket; promotion ▷ pl portable stepladder with hinged prop attached, stepladder **step'lad·der** n four-legged stepladder having broad flat steps

step-child [STEP-child] n, pl **-chil·dren** [-CHIL-drən] child of husband or wife by former marriage; person, organization, idea, etc treated improperly **step'broth·er** n **step'fa·ther** n **step'moth·er** n **step'sis·ter** n

steppe [step] n extensive treeless plain in European and Asiatic Russia

stere [steer] n cubic meter

ster·e·o·phon·ic [ster-ee-ə-FON-ik] adj (of sound) giving effect of coming from many directions **ster'e·o** adj, n (of, for) stereophonic record player, etc

ster·e·o·scop·ic [ster-ee-ə-SKOP-ik] adj having three-dimensional effect

ster·e·o·type [STER-ee-ə-tīp] n

metal plate for printing cast from type; something (monotonously) familiar, conventional, predictable ▷vt **-typed, -typ·ing** make stereotype of

ster·ile [STER-əl] adj unable to produce fruit, crops, young, etc; free from (harmful) germs **ster·il·i·ty** [stə-RIL-ə-tee] n **ster·i·li·za·tion** n process or act of making sterile **ster·i·lize** vt **-lized, -liz·ing** render sterile

ster·ling [STUR-ling] adj genuine, true; of solid worth, dependable; in British money ▷n British money

stern[1] [sturn] adj severe, strict **stern·ly** adv **stern·ness** [-nis] n

stern[2] n rear part of ship

ster·num [STUR-nəm] n the breast bone

ster·to·rous [STUR-tər-əs] adj with sound of heavy breathing, hoarse snoring

stet Lat let it stand (proofreader's direction to cancel alteration previously made)

steth·o·scope [STETH-ə-skohp] n instrument for listening to action of heart, lungs, etc

Stet·son ® [STET-sàn] n type of broad-brimmed hat esp cowboy hat

ste·ve·dore [STEE-vi-dor] n one who loads or unloads ships

stew [stoo] n food cooked slowly in closed vessel; state of excitement, agitation or worry ▷v cook by stewing; worry **stew in one's own juice** suffer consequences of one's own actions

stew·ard [STOO-àrd] n one who manages another's property; official managing race meeting, assembly, etc; attendant on ship's or aircraft's passengers **stew·ard·ess** [-is] n fem

stick [stik] n long, thin piece of

wood; anything shaped like a stick; inf uninteresting person ▷v **stuck, stick·ing** v pierce, stab; place, fasten, as by pins, glue; protrude; bewilder; inf impose disagreeable responsibility on (someone) ▷vi adhere; come to stop, jam; remain; be fastened; protrude **stick·er** n adhesive label: bumper sticker **stick·y** adj **stick·i·er, stick·i·est** covered with, like adhesive substance; (of weather) warm, humid; inf difficult, unpleasant **stick shift** automobile transmission with manually operated shift lever

stick·ler [STIK-lər] n person who insists on something

stiff adj **-er, -est** not easily bent or moved; rigid; awkward; difficult; thick, not fluid; formal; stubborn; unnatural; strong or fresh, as breeze; inf excessive ▷n sl corpse; sl a drunk ▷vt sl fail to tip (waiter, etc) **stiff·en** [-in] v **stiff·ly** adv **stiff-necked** [-nekt] adj obstinate, stubborn; haughty

sti·fle [STIF-əl] vt **-fled, -fling** smother, suppress

stig·ma [STIG-mə] n, pl **-mas** or **-ma·ta** [-MAH-tə] distinguishing mark esp of disgrace **stig·ma·tize** vt **-tized, -tiz·ing** mark with stigma

sti·let·to [sti-LET-oh] n, pl **-tos** or **-toes** small dagger; small boring tool ▷adj thin, pointed like a stiletto

still[1] adj **-er, -est** motionless, noiseless, at rest ▷vt quiet ▷adv to this time; yet; even ▷n photograph esp of motion picture scene **still·born** adj born dead **still life** a painting of inanimate objects

still[2] n apparatus for distilling

stilt n pole with footrests for walking raised from ground; long post supporting building, etc **stilt·ed** [-id] adj stiff in manner, pompous

stim•u•lus [STIM-yə-ləs] *n*, *pl* **-li** [-lī] something that rouses to activity; incentive **stim'u•lant** [-lənt] *n* drug, etc acting as a stimulus **stim'u•late** *vt* **-lat•ed, -lat•ing** rouse up, spur **stim'u•lat•ing** *adj* acting as stimulus **stim•u•la'tion** *n* **stim'u•la•tive** [-lə-tiv] *adj*

sting *v* **stung, sting•ing** thrust sting into; cause sharp pain to; *sl* cheat, take advantage of, esp by overcharging; feel sharp pain ▷ *n* (wound, pain, caused by) sharp pointed organ, often poisonous, of certain insects and animals; *sl* illegal operation conducted by police, etc to collect evidence against criminals

stin•gy [STIN-jee] *adj* **-gi•er, -gi•est** mean; avaricious; niggardly **stin'gi•ness** [-nis] *n*

stink *vi* **stank** or **stunk, stunk stink•ing** give out strongly offensive smell; *inf* be markedly inferior ▷ *n* such smell, stench; *inf* fuss, bother; scandal

stint *vt* be frugal, miserly to (someone) or with (something) ▷ *n* allotted amount of work or time; limitation, restriction

sti•pend [STI-pend] *n* payment, esp scholarship or fellowship allowance given to student **sti•pen'di•ar•y** [-dee-er-ee] *adj* receiving stipend

stip•ple [STIP-əl] *vt* **-pled, -pling** engrave, paint in dots ▷ *n* this process

stip•u•late [STIP-yə-layt] *vi* **-lat•ed, -lat•ing** specify in making a bargain **stip•u•la'tion** *n* proviso; condition

stir [stur] *v* **stirred, stir•ring** (begin to) move; rouse; cause trouble; set, keep in motion; excite

▷ *n* commotion, disturbance

stir•rup [STUR-əp] *n* metal loop hung from strap for supporting foot of rider on horse

stitch [stich] *n* movement of needle in sewing, etc; its result in the work; sharp pain in side; least fragment (of clothing) ▷ *v* sew

stock [stok] *n* goods, material stored, esp for sale or later use; reserve, fund; shares in, or capital of, company, etc; standing, reputation; farm animals (livestock); plant, stem from which cuttings are taken; handle of gun, tool, etc; liquid broth produced by boiling meat, etc; flowering plant; lineage ▷ *pl* *history* frame to secure feet, hands (of offender); frame to support ship during construction ▷ *adj* kept in stock; standard, hackneyed ▷ *vt* keep, store; supply with livestock, fish, etc **stock'y** *adj* **stock•i•er, stock•i•est** thickset **stock'brok•er** [-brohk-ər] *n* agent for buying, selling stocks and bonds **stock car** ordinary automobile strengthened and modified for a form of racing in which automobiles often collide **stock ex•change** institution for buying and selling shares **stock'pile** *v* acquire and store large quantity of (something) **stock-still** *adj* motionless **stock'tak•ing** *n* examination, counting and valuing of goods in a store, etc **put stock in** believe, trust

stock•ade [sto-KAYD] *n* enclosure of stakes, barrier

stock•ing [STOK-ing] *n* close-fitting covering for leg and foot

stodg•y [STOJ-ee] *adj* **stodg•i•er, stodg•i•est** heavy, dull

sto•gy [STOH-gee] *n, pl* **-gies** cheap cigar

sto•ic [STOH-ik] *adj* capable of

much self-control, great endurance without complaint ▷ *n* stoical person **sto'i•cal** [-kəl] *adj*

stoke [stohk] *v* **stoked, stok•ing** feed, tend fire or furnace **stok'er** *n*

stole¹ [stohl] *pt of* STEAL

stole² *n* long scarf or shawl

sto•len [stohl-ən] *pp of* STEAL

stol'id *adj* hard to excite; heavy, slow, apathetic

stom•ach [STUM-ək] *n* sac forming chief digestive organ in any animal; appetite; desire, inclination ▷ *vt* put up with

stomp *vi* put down foot with force

stone [stohn] *n* (piece of) rock; gem; hard seed of fruit; hard deposit formed in kidneys, bladder; British unit of weight, 14 lbs ▷ *vt* **stoned, ston•ing** throw stones at; free (fruit) from stones **stoned** *adj sl* stupefied by alcohol or drugs **ston'y** *adj* **ston•i•er, ston•i•est** of, like stone; hard; cold **stone-broke** [-brohk] *adj* with no money left

stone-dead *adj* completely dead

stone-deaf *adj* completely deaf

stone'wall *v* stall; evade; filibuster

stone'ware [-wair] *n* heavy common pottery

stood [stuud] *pt/pp of* STAND

stooge [stooj] *n* performer always the butt of another's jokes; anyone taken advantage of by another

stool *n* backless chair; excrement

stoop¹ *vi* lean forward or down, bend; swoop; abase, degrade oneself ▷ *n* stooping carriage of the body

stoop² *n* steps or small porch in front of house

stop *v* **stopped, stop•ping** check, bring to halt; prevent; interrupt; suspend; desist from; fill up an opening; cease, come to a halt; stay ▷ *n* stopping or becoming stopped; any device for altering or regulating pitch; set of pipes in organ having tones of a distinct quality **stop'page** [-ij] *n* **stop'per** [-ər] *n* plug for closing bottle, etc **stop'gap** *n* temporary substitute **stop'off, stop'o•ver** *n* short break in journey **stop'watch** *n* one that can be stopped for exact timing eg of race **pull out all the stops** use all available means

store [stor] *v* **stored, stor•ing** stock, furnish, keep; *computing* enter or retain (data) ▷ *n* retail store; abundance; stock; place for keeping goods; warehouse ▷ *pl* stocks of goods, provisions **stor'age** *n* in **store** in readiness; imminent

stork *n* large wading bird

storm *n* violent weather with wind, rain, hail, sand, snow, etc; assault on fortress; violent outbreak, discharge ▷ *vt* assault; take by storm ▷ *vi* rage **storm'y** *adj* **storm•i•er, storm•i•est** like storm; (emotionally) violent

sto•ry¹ [STOR-ee] *n, pl* **-ries** (book, piece of prose, etc) telling about events, happenings; lie

sto•ry² *n, pl* **-ries** horizontal division of a building

stoup [stoop] *n* small basin for holy water

stout [stowt] *adj* **-er, -est** fat; sturdy, resolute ▷ *n* kind of beer **stout'ly** *adv* **stout'ness** [-nis] *n*

stove¹ [stohv] *n* apparatus for cooking, heating, etc

stove² *pt/pp of* STAVE

stow [stoh] *vt* pack away **stow'age** [-ij] *n* **stow'a•way** *n* one who hides in ship to obtain free passage

strad•dle [STRAD-l] *v* **-dled, -dling** ▷ *vt* bestride ▷ *vi* spread legs wide ▷ *n*

strafe [strayf] *vt* **strafed, straf•ing** attack (esp with bullets, rockets) from air

strag·gle [STRAG-əl] vi **-gled, -gling** stray, get dispersed, linger **strag'gler** n

straight [strayt] adj **-er, -est** without bend; honest; level; in order; (of whiskey) undiluted, neat; expressionless; (of drama, actor, etc) serious; sl heterosexual ▷ n straight condition or part ▷ adv direct **straight'en** [-in] v **straight'a·way** adv immediately **straight·for·ward** [-wərd] adj open, frank; simple; honest

strain¹ [strayn] vt stretch tightly; stretch to full or to excess; filter ▷ vi make great effort ▷ n stretching force; violent effort; injury from being strained; burst of music or poetry; great demand; (condition caused by) overwork, worry, etc; tone of speaking or writing **strain'er** [-ər] n filter, sieve

strain² n breed or race; type (esp in biology); trace, streak

strait [strayt] n channel of water connecting two larger areas of water ▷ pl position of difficulty or distress ▷ adj narrow; strict **strait'en** [-in] vt make strait, narrow; press with poverty **strait'jack·et** n jacket to confine arms of violent person **strait-laced** [-layst] adj austere, strict; puritanical

strand¹ v run aground; leave, be left in difficulties or helpless

strand² n one single string or wire of rope, etc

strange [straynj] adj **strang·er, strang·est** odd; queer; unaccustomed; foreign; uncommon; wonderful; singular **stran'ger** n unknown person; foreigner; one unaccustomed (to) **strange'ness** [-nis] n

stran·gle [STRANG-gəl] vt **-gled,**

-gling kill by squeezing windpipe; suppress **stran·gu·la·tion** [-gyə-LAY-shən] n strangling

strap n strip, esp of leather ▷ vt **strapped, strap'ping** fasten, beat with strap **strap'ping** adj tall and powerful **strap'hang·er** n in bus, subway car, one who has to stand, steadying self with strap provided for this purpose

strat·a·gem [STRAT-ə-jəm] n plan, trick **strat'e·gy** [-ə-jee] n, pl **-gies** art of war; overall plan **strat'e·gist** n **stra·te·gic** [strə-TEE-jik] adj

strat·o·sphere [STRAT-ə-sfeer] n upper part of the atmosphere from approx 11 km to 50 km above Earth's surface

stra·tum [STRAY-təm] n, pl **stra·ta** [-tə] layer, esp of rock; class in society **strat'i·fy** v **-fied, -fy·ing** form, deposit in layers **strat·i·fi·ca'tion** n

straw n stalks of grain; single stalk; long, narrow tube used to suck up liquid **straw'ber·ry** n creeping plant producing a red, juicy fruit; the fruit

stray vi wander; digress; get lost ▷ adj strayed; occasional, scattered ▷ n stray animal

streak [streek] n long line or band; element, trace ▷ vt mark with streaks ▷ vi move fast; run naked in public **streak'y** adj **streak·i·er, streak·i·est** having streaks; striped

stream [streem] n flowing body of water or other liquid; steady flow ▷ vi flow; run with liquid; float, wave in the air ▷ vt discharge, send in stream **stream'er** [-ər] n (paper) ribbon, narrow flag

stream·lined [STREEM-lind] adj (of train, motor, etc) built so as to offer least resistance to air

street n road in town, etc usu lined

with houses **street'car** n vehicle (esp electrically driven and for public transport) running usu on rails laid on roadway **street'walk·er** n prostitute **street'wise, -smart** adj inf adept at surviving in urban, oft criminal, environment

strength [strengkth] n quality of being strong; power; capacity for exertion or endurance; vehemence; force; full or necessary number of people **strength'en** v make stronger, reinforce **on the strength of** relying on; because of

stren·u·ous [STREN-yoo-əs] adj energetic; earnest

strep·to·coc·cus [strep-tə-KOK-əs] n, pl **-coc·ci** [-KOK-sī] genus of bacteria

strep·to·my·cin [strep-tə-Mī-sin] n antibiotic drug

stress n emphasis; strain; impelling force; effort; tension ▷ vt emphasize; accent; put mechanical stress on

stretch [strech] vt extend; exert to utmost; tighten, pull out; reach out ▷ vi reach; have elasticity ▷ n stretching, being stretched, expanse; spell **stretch'er** n person, thing that stretches; appliance on which disabled person is carried; bar linking legs of chair

strew [stroo] vt **strewed, strewn** or **strewed, strew·ing** scatter over surface, spread

stri·ate [STRĪ-ayt] vt **-at·ed, -at·ing** mark with streaks; score **stri·a'tion** n **striated** adj streaked, furrowed, grooved

strick·en [STRIK-ən] adj seriously affected by disease, grief, famine; afflicted; pp of **STRIKE**

strict [strikt] adj **-er, -est** stern, not lax or indulgent; defined; without exception

stric·ture [STRIK-chər] n critical remark; constriction

stride [strīd] vi **strode, strid·den, strid·ing** walk with long steps ▷ n single step; its length; regular pace **hit one's stride** reach the level at which one consistently functions best

stri·dent [STRĪD-nt] adj harsh in tone; loud; urgent

strife [strīf] n conflict; quarreling

strike [strīk] v **struck, struck** or **strick·en, strik·ing** hit (against); ignite; (of snake) bite; arrive at, come upon; of plants (cause to) take root; attack; hook (fish); sound (time) as bell in clock, etc; baseball swing and miss a pitch, etc ▷ vt affect; enter mind of; discover (gold, oil, etc); dismantle, remove; make (coin) ▷ vi cease work as protest or to make demands ▷ n act of striking **strik'er** n **striking** adj noteworthy, impressive **strike it rich** meet unexpected financial success **strike off** remove **strike out** fail in a venture; baseball make three strikes

string n (length of) thin cord or other material; strand, row; series; fiber in plants ▷ pl conditions ▷ vt **strung, string·ing** provide with, thread on string; form in line, series **stringed** adj (of musical instruments) furnished with strings **string'y** adj **string·i·er, string·i·est** like string; fibrous

strin·gent [STRIN-jənt] adj strict, rigid, binding **strin'gen·cy** n severity

strip v **stripped, strip·ping** lay bare, take covering off; dismantle; deprive (of); undress ▷ n long, narrow piece of land **strip'per** n person who performs a striptease **strip'tease** [-teez] n nightclub or theater act in which stripper undresses in time to music

stripe [strip] *n* narrow mark, band; chevron as symbol of military rank; style, kind

strip'ling *n* a youth

strive [striv] *vi* **strove** or **strived, striv•en** or **strived, striv•ing** try hard, struggle, contend

strobe [strohb] *n* apparatus that produces high-intensity flashing light

strode [strohd] *pt of* **STRIDE**

stroke [strohk] *n* blow; sudden action, occurrence; apoplexy; mark of pen, pencil, brush, etc; chime of clock; completed movement in series; act, manner of striking (ball, etc); style, method of swimming; rower sitting nearest stern setting the rate; act of stroking ▷ *vt* **stroked, strok•ing** set time in rowing; pass hand lightly over

stroll [strohl] *vi* walk in leisurely or idle manner ▷ *n*

strong [strawng] *adj* **-er, -est** powerful, robust, healthy; difficult to break; noticeable; intense; emphatic; not diluted; having a certain number **strong'hold** [-hohld] *n* fortress

stron•ti•um [STRON-shee-əm] *n* silvery-white chemical element **strontium go** radioactive isotope of strontium present in fallout of nuclear explosions

strop *n* leather for sharpening razors ▷ *vt* **stropped, strop•ping** sharpen on one

strove [strohv] *pt of* **STRIVE**

struck *pt/pp of* **STRIKE**

struc•ture [STRUK-chər] *n* (arrangement of parts in) construction, building, etc; form; organization ▷ *vt* **-tured, -tur•ing** give structure to **struc'tur•al** [-chər-əl] *adj*

strug•gle [STRUG-əl] *vi* **-gled,**

-gling contend; fight; proceed, work, move with difficulty and effort ▷ *n*

strum *vt* **strummed, strum•ming** strike notes of guitar, etc

strum•pet [STRUM-pit] *n* promiscuous woman; prostitute

strung *pt/pp of* **STRING**

strut *vi* **strut•ted, strut•ting** walk affectedly or pompously ▷ *n* brace; rigid support, usu set obliquely; strutting gait

strych•nine [STRIK-nin] *n* poison obtained from nux vomica seeds

stub *n* remnant of anything, eg pencil, cigarette, etc; retained portion of check, etc ▷ *vt* **stubbed, stub•bing** strike (eg toes) against fixed object; extinguish by pressing against surface **stub'by** *adj* **-bi•er, -bi•est** short, broad

stub•ble [STUB-əl] *n* stumps of cut grain, etc after cutting; short growth of beard

stub•born [STUB-ərn] *adj* unyielding, obstinate **stub'born•ness** [-nis] *n*

stuc•co [STUK-oh] *n, pl* **-coes** or **-cos** plaster ▷ *vt* **-coed, -co•ing** apply stucco to (wall)

stuck *pt/pp of* **STICK**

stud¹ *n* nail with large head; type of button; vertical wall support ▷ *vt* **stud'ded, stud'ding** set with studs **stud'ding**

stud² *n* stallion; set of horses, kept for breeding; *sl* man known for sexual prowess **stud'book** [-buuk] *n* book giving pedigree of noted or thoroughbred animals, esp horses **stud farm** establishment where horses are kept for breeding

stu•di•o [STOO-dee-oh] *n, pl* **-di•os** workroom of artist, photographer, etc; building, room where motion pictures, TV or radio shows are made, broadcast; apartment of one main room

stud·y [STUD-ee] v **stud·ied, stud·y·ing** be engaged in learning; make study of; try constantly to do; consider; scrutinize ▷ n, pl **stud·ies** effort to acquire knowledge; report, etc produced as result of study; sketch **stu·dent** [STOOD-nt] n one who studies, esp at college, etc **studied** adj carefully designed, premeditated **stu·di·ous** [STOO-dee-əs] adj fond of study; thoughtful; painstaking; deliberate **stu'di·ous·ly** adv

stuff v pack, cram, fill (completely); eat large amount; fill with seasoned mixture; fill (animal's skin) with material to preserve lifelike form ▷ n material, fabric; any substance **stuff'ing** n material for stuffing, esp seasoned mixture for inserting in poultry, etc before cooking **stuff'y** adj **stuff·i·er, stuff·i·est** lacking fresh air; dull, conventional **stuffed shirt** pompous person

stul·ti·fy [STUL-tə-fī] vt **-fied, -fy·ing** make ineffectual **stul·ti·fi·ca'tion** n

stum·ble [STUM-bəl] vi **-bled, -bling** trip and nearly fall; falter ▷ n **stumbling block** obstacle

stump n remnant of tree, tooth, etc, when main part has been cut away; part of leg or arm remaining after amputation ▷ vt confuse, puzzle ▷ vi walk heavily, noisily **stump'y** adj **stump·i·er, stump·i·est** short and thickset

stun vt **stunned, stun·ning** knock senseless; amaze

stung pt/pp of STING

stunk pp of STINK

stunt¹ vt check growth of, dwarf **stunt'ed** adj underdeveloped; undersized

stunt² n feat of dexterity or daring; anything spectacular, usually done to gain publicity

stu·pe·fy [STOO-pə-fī] vt **-fied, -fy·ing** make insensitive, lethargic; astound **stu·pe·fac'tion** n

stu·pen·dous [stoo-PEN-dəs] adj astonishing; amazing; huge

stu·pid [STOO-pid] adj **-er, -est** slow-witted; silly; in a stupor **stu·pid'i·ty** n, pl **-ties**

stu·por [STOO-pər] n dazed state; insensibility **stu'por·ous** adj

stur·dy [STUR-dee] adj **-di·er, -di·est** robust, strongly built; vigorous **stur'di·ly** adv

stur·geon [STUR-jən] n fish yielding caviar

stut·ter [STUT-ər] v speak with difficulty; stammer ▷ n

sty¹ [stī] n, pl **sties** place to keep pigs in; hovel, dirty place

sty² n, pl **sties** inflammation on edge of eyelid

Styg·i·an [STIJ-ee-ən] adj of river Styx in Hades; gloomy; infernal

style [stīl] n manner of writing, doing, etc; designation; sort; elegance, refinement; superior manner, quality; design ▷ vt **styled, styl·ing** shape, design; adapt; designate **styl'ish** adj fashionable **styl'ist** n one cultivating style in literary or other execution; designer; hairdresser **styl·is'tic** adj **styl'ize** vt **-ized, -iz·ing** give conventional stylistic form to

sty·lus [STĪ-ləs] n, pl **-lus·es** writing instrument; (in record player) tiny point running in groove of record

sty·mie [STĪ-mee] vt **-mied, -my·ing** hinder, thwart

styp·tic [STIP-tik] adj, n (designating) a substance that stops bleeding

suave [swahv] *adj* **suav·er,**
suav·est smoothly polite, affable,
bland **suav'i·ty** *n*

sub submarine; submarine sandwich;
substitute *vi* *inf* **subbed, sub·bing**
serve as substitute

sub- *prefix* under, less than, in lower
position, subordinate, forming
subdivision, etc: *subaquatic;*
subheading; subnormal; subsoil

sub·com·mit·tee [SUB-kə-
mit-ee] *n* section of committee
functioning separately from main
body

sub·con·scious [sub-KON-shəs]
adj acting, existing without one's
awareness ▷ *n* psychology that part
of the human mind unknown, or only
partly known to possessor

sub·cu·ta·ne·ous [sub-kyoo-
TAY-nee-əs] *adj* under the skin

sub·di·vide [sub-di-VID] *vt*
-vid·ed, -vid·ing divide again
sub'di·vi·sion [-vizh-ən] *n*

sub·due [səb-DOO] *v* **-dued,**
-du·ing overcome **subdued'** *adj*
cowed, quiet; (of light) not bright
or intense

subject [SUB-jikt] *n* theme, topic;
that about which something is
predicated; conscious self; one
under power of another ▷ *adj* owing
allegiance; subordinate; dependent;
liable (to) ▷ *vt* [səb-JEKT] cause
to undergo; make liable; subdue
sub·jec'tion [-JEK-shən] *n* act of
bringing, or state of being, under
control **sub·ject'ive** *adj* based on
personal feelings, not impartial;
of the self; existing in the mind;
displaying artist's individuality
sub·jec·tiv'i·ty *n*

sub·ju·dice [sub JOO-di-see] *Lat*
under judicial consideration

sub·ju·gate [SUB-jə-gayt] *vt*
-gat·ed, -gat·ing force to submit;

conquer **sub·ju·ga'tion** *n*

sub·junc·tive [səb-JUNGK-tiv] *n*
mood used mainly in subordinate
clauses expressing wish, possibility
▷ *adj* in, of, that mood

sub·let' *vt* **-let, -let·ting** (of tenant)
let to another all or part of what
tenant has rented

sub·li·mate [SUB-lə-mayt] *vt*
-mat·ed, -mat·ing psychology
direct energy (esp sexual) into
activities considered more socially
acceptable; refine ▷ *n* [-mit]
chemistry material obtained
when substance is sublimed
sub·li·ma'tion *n* psychology
unconscious diversion of sexual
impulses towards new aim and
activities; chemistry process in
which a solid changes directly into
a vapor

sub·lime [sə-BLIM] *adj* elevated;
eminent; majestic; inspiring awe;
exalted ▷ *v* **-limed, -lim·ing**
chemistry change or cause to change
from solid to vapor **sub·lime'ly** *adv*

sub·lim·i·nal [sub-LIM-ə-nl] *adj*
resulting from processes of which
the individual is not aware

sub·ma·rine [sub-mə-REEN] *n*
ship that can travel below surface of
sea and remain submerged for long
periods ▷ *adj* below surface of sea
submarine sandwich overstuffed
sandwich of meats, cheese, etc in
long loaf of Italian bread

sub·merge [səb-MURJ] *v*
-merged, -merg·ing place, go
under water **sub·mer'sion** [-MUR-
zhən] *n*

sub·mit [səb-MIT] *v* **-mit·ted,**
-mit·ting surrender; put forward
for consideration; surrender;
defer **sub·mis'sion** [-MISH-ən] *n*
sub·mis'sive *adj* meek, obedient

sub·or·di·nate [sə-BOR-dn-it]

adj of lower rank or less importance ▷ n inferior; one under order of another ▷ vt [-dn-ayt] **-nat·ed, -nat·ing** make, treat as subordinate **sub·or·di·na'tion** [-NAY-shàn] n

sub·orn [sà-BORN] vt bribe to do evil **sub·or·na·tion** [sub-or-NAY-shàn] n

sub·poe·na [sà-PEE-nà] n writ requiring attendance at court of law ▷ vt **-naed, -na·ing** summon by such order

sub·scribe [sàb-SKRIB] v **-scribed, -scrib·ing** pay, promise to pay (contribution); write one's name at end of document **sub·scrip'tion** n subscribing; money paid

sub·se·quent [SUB-si-kwànt] adj later, following or coming after in time

sub·ser·vi·ent [sàb-SUR-vee-ànt] adj submissive, servile **sub·ser'vi·ence** n

sub·side [sàb-SID] vi **-sid·ed, -sid·ing** abate, come to an end; sink; settle; collapse **sub·sid'ence** n

sub·sid·i·ar·y [sàb-SID-ee-er-ee] adj supplementing; secondary; auxiliary ▷ n, pl **-ar·ies**

sub·si·dize [SUB-si-diz] vt **-dized, -diz·ing** help financially; pay grant to **sub'si·dy** [-dee] n, pl **-dies** money granted

sub·sist [sàb-SIST] vi exist, sustain life **sub·sist'ence** [-àns] n the means by which one supports life; livelihood

sub·son·ic [sub-SON-ik] adj concerning speeds less than that of sound

sub·stance [SUB-stàns] n matter; particular kind of matter; chief part, essence; wealth **sub·stan'tial** [sàb-STAN-shàl] adj considerable; of real value; solid, big, important; really existing **sub·stan'ti·ate**

[-shee-ayt] vt **-at·ed, -at·ing** bring evidence for, confirm, prove **sub·stan·ti·a'tion** n **sub·stan'tive** [-stàn-tiv] adj having independent existence; real, fixed ▷ n noun

sub·sti·tute [SUB-sti-toot] v **-tut·ed, -tut·ing** put, serve in exchange (for) ▷ n thing, person put in place of another; deputy **sub·sti·tu'tion** n

sub·sume [sàb-SOOM] vt **-sumed, -sum·ing** incorporate (idea, case, etc) under comprehensive heading, classification

sub·tend [sàb-TEND] vt be opposite to and delimit

sub·ter·fuge [SUB-tàr-fyooj] n trick, lying excuse used to evade something

sub·ter·ra·ne·an [sub-tà-RAY-nee-àn] adj underground; in concealment

sub·ti·tle [SUB-tit-l] n secondary title of book; written translation of film dialogue, superimposed on film

sub·tle [SUT-l] adj **-tler, -tlest** not immediately obvious; ingenious; acute; crafty; intricate; delicate; making fine distinctions **sub'tle·ty** [-tee] n, pl **-ties**

sub·tract [sàb-TRAKT] vt take away, deduct **sub·trac'tion** [-TRAK-shàn] n

sub·trop·i·cal [sub-TROP-i-kàl] adj of regions bordering on the tropics

sub'urb n residential area on outskirts of city **sub·ur'ban** [sà-BUR-bàn] adj **sub·ur'bi·a** [-bee-à] n suburbs of a city

sub·ven·tion [sàb-VEN-shàn] n subsidy

sub·vert [sàb-VURT] vt overthrow; corrupt **sub·ver'sion** [-zhàn] n **sub·ver'sive** [-siv] adj

sub'way n underground passage;

underground railroad

suc·ceed [sək-SEED] *vi* accomplish purpose; turn out satisfactorily; follow ▷ *vt* follow, take place of **suc·cess'** *n* favorable accomplishment, attainment, issue or outcome; successful person or thing **suc·cess'ful** [-fəl] *adj* **suc·ces'sion** [-SESH-ən] *n* following; series; succeeding **suc·ces'sive** *adj* following in order; consecutive **suc·ces'sor** [-ər] *n*

suc·cinct [sək-SINGKT] *adj* terse, concise **suc·cinct'ly** *adv* **suc·cinct'ness** [-nis] *n*

suc·cor [SUK-ər] *vt, n* help in distress

suc·cu·bus [SUK-yə-bəs] *n, pl* **-bi** [-bī] female demon fabled to have sexual intercourse with sleeping men

suc·cu·lent [SUK-yə-lənt] *adj* juicy, full of juice; (of plant) having thick, fleshy leaves ▷ *n* such plant **suc·cu·lence** [-ləns] *n*

suc·cumb [sə-KUM] *vi* yield, give way; die

such *adj* of the kind or degree mentioned; so great, so much; so made, etc; of the same kind **such'like** *adj* such ▷ *pron* other such things

suck [suk] *vt* draw into mouth; hold (dissolve) in mouth; draw in ▷ *n* sucking **suck'er** *n* person, thing that sucks; organ, appliance that adheres by suction; shoot coming from root or base of stem of plant; *inf* person easily deceived or taken in **suck·le** [SUK-əl] *v* **-led, -ling** feed from the breast **suck'ling** *n* unweaned infant

suc·tion [SUK-shən] *n* drawing or sucking of air or fluid; force produced by difference in pressure

sud·den [SUD-n] *adj* done,

occurring unexpectedly; abrupt, hurried **sud'den·ness** [-dən-is] *n*

su·dor·if·ic [soo-də-RIF-ik] *adj* causing perspiration ▷ *n* medicine that produces sweat

suds [sudz] *pl n* froth of soap and water, lather; *sl* beer

sue [soo] *v* **sued, su·ing** ▷ *vt* prosecute; seek justice from ▷ *vi* make application or entreaty; beseech

suede [swayd] *n* leather with soft, velvety finish

su·et [SOO-it] *n* hard animal fat from sheep, cow, etc

suf·fer [SUF-ər] *v* undergo, endure, experience (pain, etc); allow **suf·fer·a·ble** *adj* **suf·fer·ance** [-əns] *n* toleration

suf·fice [sə-FĪS] *v* **-ficed, -fic·ing** be adequate, satisfactory (for) **suf·fi·cien·cy** [sə-FISH-ən-see] *n* adequate amount **suf·fi'cient** [-ənt] *adj* enough, adequate

suf·fix [SUF-iks] *n* letter or word added to end of word ▷ *vt* add, annex to the end

suf·fo·cate [SUF-ə-kayt] *v* **-cat·ed, -cat·ing** kill, be killed by deprivation of oxygen; smother

suf·frage [SUF-rij] *n* vote or right of voting **suf'fra·gist** *n* one claiming a right of voting **suf·fra·gette'** *n fem*

suf·fuse [sə-FYOOZ] *vt* **-fused, -fus·ing** well up and spread over **suf·fu'sion** [-FYOO-zhən] *n*

sug·ar [SHUUG-ər] *n* sweet crystalline vegetable substance ▷ *vt* sweeten, make pleasant (with sugar) **sug'ar·y** *adj* **sugar cane** plant from whose juice sugar is obtained **sugar daddy** *inf* wealthy (elderly) man who pays for (esp sexual) favors of younger woman

sug·gest [səg-JEST] *vt* propose:

call up the idea of **sug·gest'i·ble** *adj* easily influenced **sug·gest'ion** [-chǝn] *n* hint; proposal; insinuation of impression, belief, etc. into mind **sug·gest'ive** *adj* containing, open to suggestion, esp of something indecent

su·i·cide [SOO-ǝ-sīd] *n* (act of) one who takes own life **su·i·cid'al** [-ǝl] *adj*

suit [soot] *n* set of clothing; garment worn for particular event, purpose; one of four sets in pack of cards; action at law ▷*v* make, be fit or appropriate for; be acceptable to (someone) **suit'a·ble** *adj* fitting, proper, convenient; becoming **suit'a·bly** *adv* **suit'case** [-kays] *n* flat rectangular traveling case

suite [sweet] *n* matched set esp furniture; set of rooms

suit·or [SOOT-ǝr] *n* wooer; one who sues; petitioner

sul·fate [SUL-fayt] *n* salt formed by sulfuric acid in combination with any base

sul·fon·a·mides [sul-FON-ǝ-mīdz] *n* group of drugs used as internal germicides in treatment of many bacterial diseases

sul·fur [SUL-fǝr] *n* pale yellow nonmetallic element **sul·fur·ic** [sul-FYUUR-ik] *adj*

sulk *vi* be silent, resentful, esp to draw attention to oneself ▷*n* this mood **sulk'y** *adj* **sulk·i·er, sulk·i·est**

sul·len [SUL-ǝn] *adj* unwilling to talk or be sociable, morose; dismal; dull

sul·ly [SUL-ee] *vt* **-lied, -ly·ing** stain, tarnish, disgrace

sul·tan [SUL-tn] *n* ruler of Muslim country **sul·tan'a** *n* sultan's wife or concubine; kind of raisin **sul·try** [SUL-tree] *adj* **-tri·er,**

-tri·est (of weather) hot, humid; (of person) looking sensual

sum *n* amount, total; problem in arithmetic ▷*v* **summed, sum·ming** add up; make summary of main parts

sum·ma·ry [SUM-ǝ-ree] *n, pl* **-ries** abridgment or statement of chief points of longer document, speech, etc; abstract ▷*adj* done quickly **sum·mar·i·ly** [sǝ-MAIR-ǝ-lee] *adv* speedily; abruptly **sum'ma·rize** [-ǝ-rīz] *vt* **-rized, -riz·ing** make summary of; present briefly and concisely

sum·mer [SUM-ǝr] *n* second, warmest season ▷*vi* pass the summer **sum'mer·y** *adj*

sum·mit *n* top, peak **summit conference** meeting of heads of governments **sum'mit·ry** [-mi-tree] *n* practice, art of holding summit conferences

sum·mon [SUM-ǝn] *vt* demand attendance of; call on; bid witness appear in court; gather up (energies, etc) **sum'mons** *n* call; authoritative demand

sump *n* place or receptacle (esp as oil reservoir in engine) where fluid collects

sump·tu·ous [SUMP-choo-ǝs] *adj* lavish, magnificent; costly **sump'tu·ous·ness** [-nis] *n* **sump'tu·ar·y** [-er-ee] *adj* pert to or regulating expenditure

sun *n* luminous body around which Earth and other planets revolve; its rays ▷*v* **sunned, sun·ning** expose (self) to sun's rays **sun'ny** *adj* **-ni·er, -ni·est** like the sun; warm; cheerful **sun'bath·ing** [-bayth-ing] *n* exposure of whole or part of body to sun's rays **sun'beam** [-beem] *n* ray of sun **sun'burn** *n* inflammation of skin due to excessive exposure to

sun **sun•down** n sunset **sun•spot** n dark patch appearing temporarily on sun's surface **sun•stroke** [-strohk] n illness caused by prolonged exposure to intensely hot sun **sun•tan** n coloring of skin by exposure to sun

sun•dae [SUN-day] n ice cream topped with fruit, etc

sun•der [SUN-dər] vt separate, sever

sun•dry [SUN-dree] adj several, various **sun'dries** pl n odd items not mentioned in detail

sung pp of **SING**

sunk, sunk•en [-in] pp of **SINK**

sup v **supped, sup•ping** take by sips; take supper ▷ n mouthful of liquid

su•per [SOO-pər] adj very good ▷ n short for **SUPERINTENDENT**

super- prefix above, greater, exceeding(ly): superhuman; superman; supertanker

su•per•a•ble [SOO-pər-ə-bəl] adj capable of being overcome; surmountable

su•per•an•nu•ate [soo-pər-AN-yoo-ayt] vt **-at•ed, -at•ing** pension off; discharge or dismiss as too old

su•perb [suu-PURB] adj splendid, grand, impressive

su•per•charge [SOO-pər-chahrj] vt **-charged, -charg•ing** charge, fill to excess **su'per•charg'er** n (internal-combustion engine) device to ensure complete filling of cylinder with explosive mixture when running at high speed

su•per•cil•i•ous [soo-pər-SIL-ee-əs] adj displaying arrogant pride, scorn, indifference

su•per•cil'i•ous•ness [-nis] n

su•per•fi•cial [soo-pər-FISH-əl] adj of or on surface; not careful or thorough; without depth, shallow

su•per•flu•ous [suu-PUR-floo-əs]

adj extra, unnecessary; excessive; left over **su•per•flu'i•ty** [-FLOO-i-tee], n pl **-ties** superabundance; unnecessary amount

su•per•high•way [soo-pər-HI-way] n broad multilane highway for travel at high speeds

su•per•in•tend [soo-pər-in-TEND] v have charge of; overlook; supervise

su•per•in•tend'ent n esp person in charge of building maintenance

su•pe•ri•or [sə-PEER-ee-ər] adj greater in quality or quantity; upper, higher in position, rank or quality; showing consciousness of being so

su•pe•ri•or'i•ty n quality of being higher, greater, or more excellent

su•per•la•tive [sə-PUR-lə-tiv] adj of, in highest degree or quality; surpassing; grammar denoting form of adjective, adverb meaning most ▷ n grammar superlative degree of adjective or adverb

su•per•mar•ket [SOO-pər-mahr-kit] n large self-service store selling chiefly food and household goods

su•per•mod•el [SOO-pər-mod-l] n famous and highly-paid fashion model

su•per•nal [suu-PUR-nl] adj celestial

su•per•nat•u•ral [soo-pər-NACH-ər-əl] adj being beyond the powers or laws of nature; miraculous ▷ n being, place, etc of miraculous powers

su•per•nu•mer•ar•y [soo-pər-NOO-mə-rer-ee] adj in excess of normal number, extra ▷ n, pl **-ar•ies** extra person or thing

su•per•script [SOO-pər-skript] n, adj (character) printed, written above the line

su•per•sede [soo-pər-SEED] vt **-sed•ed, -sed•ing** take the place of; set aside, discard, supplant

su·per·size [SOO-pər-sïz] *adj* larger than standard size ▷ *vt* increase the size of

su·per·son·ic [soo-pər-SON-ik] *adj* denoting speed greater than that of sound

su·per·sti·tion [soo-pər-STISH-ən] *n* religion, opinion or practice based on belief in luck or magic **su·per·sti·tious** *adj*

su·per·vene [soo-pər-VEEN] *vi* **-vened, -ven·ing** happen, as an interruption or change **su·per·ven·tion** [-shən] *n*

su·per·vise [SOO-pər-viz] *vt* **-vised, -vis·ing** oversee; direct; inspect and control; superintend **su·per·vi·sion** [-VIZH-ən] *n* **su·per·vis·or** *n*

su·pine [soo-PIN] *adj* lying on back with face upward; indolent ▷ *n* [SOO-pïn] Latin verbal noun

sup·per [SUP-ər] *n* (light) evening meal

sup·plant [sə-PLANT] *vt* take the place of, esp unfairly; oust

sup·ple [SUP-əl] *adj* **-pler, -plest** pliable; flexible; compliant **sup·ply** [SUP-lee] *adv*

sup·ple·ment [SUP-lə-mənt] *n* thing added to fill up, supply deficiency, esp extra part added to book, etc; additional number of periodical, usu on special subject; separate, often illustrated section published periodically with newspaper ▷ *vt* add to; supply deficiency **sup·ple·men·ta·ry** [-tə-ree] *adj* additional

sup·pli·ant [SUP-lee-ənt] *adj* petitioning ▷ *n* petitioner

sup·pli·cate [SUP-li-kayt] *v* **-cat·ed, -cat·ing** beg humbly, entreat **sup·pli·cant** [-li-kənt] *n* **sup·pli·ca·tion** [-KAY-shən] *n* **sup·pli·ca·to·ry** [-kə-tor-ee]

sup·ply [sə-PLI] *vt* **-plied, -ply·ing** furnish; make available; provide ▷ *n, pl* **-plies** supplying, substitute; stock, store

sup·port [sə-PORT] *vt* hold up; sustain; assist ▷ *n* supporting, being supported; means of support **sup·port·a·ble** *adj* **sup·port·er** *n* adherent **sup·port·ing** *adj* (of motion picture, etc role) less important **sup·port·ive** *adj*

sup·pose [sə-POHZ] *vt* **-posed, -pos·ing** assume as theory; take for granted; accept as likely; (in passive) be expected, obliged; ought **sup·posed'** *adj* **sup·pos·ed·ly** [sə-POH-zid-lee] *adv* **sup·po·si·tion** [-ZISH-ən] *n* assumption; belief without proof; conjecture **sup·po·si·tious** *adj* **sup·pos·i·ti·tious** [sə-poz-i-TISH-əs] *adj* sham; spurious; counterfeit **sup·pos·i·to·ry** [sə-POZ-i-tor-ee] *n, pl* **-ries** medication (in capsule) for insertion in orifice of body

sup·press [sə-PRES] *vt* put down, restrain; crush, stifle; keep or withdraw from publication **sup·pres·sion** [-PRESH-ən] *n*

sup·pu·rate [SUP-yə-rayt] *vi* **-rat·ed, -rat·ing** fester, form pus **sup·pu·ra·tion** [-shən] *n*

supra- *prefix* above, over: supranational

su·preme [sə-PREEM] *adj* highest in authority or rank; utmost **su·prem·a·cy** [-PREM-ə-see] *n* position of being supreme

sur·cease [sur-SEES] *vi* **-ceased, -ceas·ing** cease, desist ▷ *n* cessation

sur·charge [SUR-chahrj] *n* additional charge ▷ *vt* [sur-CHAHRJ] **-charged, -charg·ing** make additional charge

sure [shuur] *adj* certain;

trustworthy; without doubt ▷ *adv inf* certainly **sure·ly** *adv* **sur·e·ty** [SHUUR-i-tee] *n*, *pl* **-ties** one who takes responsibility for another's obligations; security against damage, etc; certainty

surf *n* waves breaking on shore ▷ *v* swim in, ride surf; move quickly through a medium such as the World Wide Web **surf·ing** *n* this sport **surf·er** *n* one who (often) goes surfing **surf·board** *n* board used in surfing

sur·face [SUR-fis] *n* outside face of body; exterior; plane; top, visible side; superficial appearance; outward impression ▷ *adj* involving the surface only; going no deeper than surface ▷ *v* **-faced**, **-fac·ing** (cause to) come to surface; put a surface on

sur·feit [SUR-fit] *n* excess; disgust caused by excess ▷ *v* feed to excess; provide anything in excess

surge [surj] *n* wave; sudden increase; *electricity* sudden rush of current in circuit ▷ *v* **surged**, **surg·ing** move in large waves; swell, billow; rise precipitately

sur·geon [SUR-jǝn] *n* physician who performs operations **sur·ger·y** *n* medical treatment by operation **sur·gi·cal** [-kǝl] *adj*

sur·ly [SUR-lee] *adj* **-li·er**, **-li·est** gloomily morose; ill-natured; cross and rude **sur·li·ness** [-nis] *n*

sur·mise [sǝr-MIZ] *v*, *n*, **-mised**, **-mis·ing** guess; conjecture

sur·mount [sǝr-MOWNT] *vt* get over, overcome **sur·mount·a·ble** *adj*

sur·name [SUR-naym] *n* family name

sur·pass [sǝr-PAS] *vt* go beyond; excel; outstrip **sur·pass·a·ble** *adj* **sur·pass·ing** *adj* excellent; exceeding others

sur·plice [SUR-plis] *n* loose white vestment worn by clergy and choir members

sur·plus *n* what remains over in excess

sur·prise [sǝr-PRIZ] *vt* **-prised**, **-pris·ing** cause surprise to; astonish; take, come upon unexpectedly; startle (someone) into action thus ▷ *n* what takes unawares; something unexpected; emotion aroused by being taken unawares

sur·re·al·ism [sǝ-REE-ǝ-liz-ǝm] *n* movement in art and literature emphasizing expression of the unconscious **sur·re·al** *adj* **sur·re·al·ist** *n*, *adj*

sur·ren·der [sǝ-REN-dǝr] *vt* hand over, give up ▷ *vi* yield; cease resistance; capitulate ▷ *n* act of surrendering

sur·rep·ti·tious [sur-ǝp-TISH-ǝs] *adj* done secretly or stealthily; furtive

sur·ro·gate [SUR-ǝ-gayt, SUR-ǝ-git] *n* deputy, esp of bishop; substitute; judicial officer supervising probate of wills **surrogate mother** woman who bears child on behalf of childless woman

sur·round [sǝ-ROWND] *vt* be, come all around, encompass; encircle; hem in ▷ *n* border, edging **sur·round·ings** *pl n* conditions, scenery, etc around a person, place, environment

sur·tax [SUR-taks] *n* additional tax

sur·veil·lance [sǝr-VAY-lǝns] *n* close watch, supervision **sur·veil·lant** *adj*, *n*

sur·vey [sǝr-VAY] *vt* view, scrutinize; inspect, examine; measure, map (land) ▷ *n* [SUR-vay], *pl* **-veys** a surveying; inspection;

report incorporating results of survey **sur•vey•or** n

sur•vive [sər-VIV] v **-vived, -viv•ing** vt outlive; come through alive ▷ vi continue to live or exist

sur•viv•al [-əl] n continuation of existence of persons, things, etc **sur•vi•vor** [-ər] n one left alive when others have died; one who continues to function despite setbacks

sus•cep•ti•ble [sə-SEP-tə-bəl] adj yielding readily (to); capable (of); impressionable **sus•cep•ti•bil'i•ty** n

sus•pect [sə-SPEKT] vt doubt innocence of; have impression of existence or presence of; be inclined to believe that; mistrust ▷ adj [SUS-pekt] of suspected character ▷ n [SUS-pekt] suspected person

sus•pend [sə-SPEND] vt hang up; cause to cease for a time; debar from an office or privilege; keep inoperative; sustain in fluid **sus•pend'ers** pl n straps for supporting trousers, etc

sus•pense [sə-SPENS] n state of uncertainty, esp while awaiting news, an event, etc; anxiety, worry **sus•pen•sion** [-shən] n state of being suspended; springs on axle of body of vehicle **sus•pen•so•ry** [-sə-ree] adj

sus•pi•cion [sə-SPISH-ən] n suspecting, being suspected; slight trace **sus•pi'cious** adj

sus•tain [sə-STAYN] vt keep, hold up; endure; keep alive; confirm **sus•tain'a•ble** adj **sus'te•nance** [-nəns] n food

su•ture [SOO-chər] n act of sewing; sewing up of a wound; material used for this; a joining of the bones of the skull ▷ vt **-tured, -tur•ing** join by suture

SUV sport utility vehicle

su•ze•rain [SOO-zə-rin] n sovereign with rights over autonomous state; feudal lord **su'ze•rain•ty** [-tee] n

svelte [svelt] adj **svelt•er, svelt•est** lightly built, slender; sophisticated

swab [swob] n mop; pad of surgical cotton, etc for cleaning, taking specimen, etc; sl sailor, low or unmannerly fellow ▷ vt **swabbed, swab'bing** clean with swab

swad•dle [SWOD-l] vt **-dled, -dling** swathe **swaddling clothes** history long strips of cloth for wrapping infant

swag n sl stolen property

swag•ger [SWAG-ər] vi strut; boast ▷ n strutting gait; boastful, overconfident manner

swain [swayn] n rustic lover

swal•low¹ [SWOL-oh] vt cause, allow to pass down gullet; engulf; suppress, keep back; believe gullibly ▷ n act of swallowing

swallow² n migratory bird with forked tail and skimming manner of flight

swam pt of **swim**

swamp [swomp] n bog ▷ vt entangle in swamp; overwhelm; flood **swamp'y** adj **swamp•i•er, swamp•i•est**

swan [swon] n large, web-footed water bird with graceful curved neck **swan song** fabled song of a swan before death; last act, etc before death

swank [swangk] vi swagger; show off ▷ n smartness; style **swank'y** adj **swank•i•er, swank•i•est** smart; showy

swap [swop] n, v **swapped, swap'ping** exchange; barter

swarm [sworm] n large cluster of

insects; vast crowd ▷ vi (of bees) be on the move in swarm; gather in large numbers

swarth•y [SWOR-thee] adj **swarth•i•er, swarth•i•est** of dark complexion

swash•buck•ler [SWOSH-buk-lər] n swaggering daredevil person **swash'buck'ling** adj

swas•ti•ka [SWOS-ti-kə] n form of cross with arms bent at right angles, used as emblem by Nazis

swat [swot] vt **swat•ted, swat•ting** hit smartly; kill, esp insects

swath [swoth] n line of grass or grain cut and thrown together by scythe or mower; whole sweep of scythe or mower

swathe [swoth] vt **swathed, swath•ing** cover with wraps or bandages

sway v swing unsteadily; (cause to) vacillate in opinion, etc; influence opinion, etc ▷ n control; power; swaying motion

swear [swair] v **swore, sworn, swear•ing** ▷ vt promise on oath; cause to take an oath ▷ vi declare; use profanity

sweat [swet] n moisture oozing from, forming on skin, esp in humans ▷ v **sweat** or **sweat•ed, sweat•ing** (cause to) exude sweat; toil; employ at wrongfully low wages; worry; want anxiously **sweat'y** adj **sweat•i•er, sweat•i•est sweat'shirt** [-shurt] n long-sleeved cotton pullover

sweat•er [SWET-ər] n knitted pullover or cardigan with or without sleeves

sweep v **swept, sweep•ing** ▷ vi effect cleaning with broom; pass quickly or magnificently; extend in continuous curve ▷ vt clean with broom; carry impetuously ▷ n act

of cleaning with broom; sweeping motion; wide curve; range; long oar; one who cleans chimneys **sweeping** adj wide-ranging; without limitations, reservations **sweep'stakes** n gamble in which winner takes stakes contributed by all; type of lottery; risky venture promising great return

sweet adj **-er, -est** tasting like sugar; agreeable; kind, charming; fresh, fragrant; in good condition; tuneful; gentle, dear, beloved ▷ n small piece of sweet food; something pleasant ▷ pl cake, etc containing much sugar **sweet'en** [-in] v sweeten **sweet'en•er** [-ən-ər] n **sweet'bread** [-bred] n animal's pancreas used as food **sweet'heart** n lover **sweetheart contract** collusive contract between labor union and company benefiting latter **sweet'meat** n sweetened delicacy eg small cake, candy **sweet potato** trailing plant; its edible, sweetish, starchy tubers **sweet talk** inf flattery **sweet-talk** v inf coax, flatter

swell v **swelled, swol•len** [SWOHL-ən] or **swelled, swell•ing** expand ▷ vi be greatly filled with pride, emotion ▷ n act of swelling or being swollen; wave of sea; mechanism in organ to vary volume of sound; inf person of high social standing ▷ adj inf stylish, socially prominent; fine

swel•ter [SWEL-tər] vi be oppressed with heat

swept pt/pp of **sweep**

swerve [swurv] vi **swerved, swerv•ing** swing around, change direction during motion; turn aside (from duty, etc) ▷ n swerving

swift adj **-er, -est** rapid, quick, ready ▷ n bird like a swallow

swig n inf large swallow of drink ▷ v

inf **swigged, swig·ging** drink thus
swill *v* drink greedily; feed (pigs)
with swill ▷ *n* liquid or wet pig
food; greedy drinking; kitchen
refuse; drivel
swim *v* **swam, swum, swim·ming**
▷ *vi* support and move oneself in
water; float; be flooded; have feeling
of dizziness ▷ *vt* cross by swimming;
compete in by swimming ▷ *n* spell
of swimming **swim'ming·ly** *adv*
successfully, effortlessly
swin·dle [SWIN-dl] *n*, *v* **-dled,
-dling** cheat **swind'ler** [-lər] *n*
swind'ling *n*
swine [swin] *n*, *pl* **swine** pig;
contemptible person **swin'ish** *adj*
swing *v* **swung, swing·ing** (cause
to) move to and fro; (cause to) pivot,
turn; hang; arrange, play music with
(jazz) rhythm ▷ *vi* be hanged; hit out
(at) ▷ *n* act, instance of swinging;
seat hung to swing on; fluctuation
(esp eg in voting pattern) **swing'er**
n sl person regarded as modern and
lively or sexually promiscuous
swipe [swip] *v* **swiped, swip·ing**
strike with wide, sweeping or
glancing blow; *inf* steal; pass
(a plastic card, such as a credit
card) through a machine which
electronically reads information
on the card
swirl [swurl] *v* (cause to) move with
eddying motion ▷ *n* such motion
swish *v* (cause to) move with
audible hissing sound ▷ *n* the
sound; *sl* effeminate homosexual
male ▷ *adj sl* effeminate
switch [swich] *n* mechanism to
complete or interrupt electric circuit,
etc; abrupt change; flexible stick or
twig; tufted end of animal's tail; type
of women's hairpiece ▷ *vi* shift,
change; swing ▷ *vt* affect (current,
etc) with switch; change abruptly;

strike with switch **switch'back**
road, railway with steep rises and
descents **switch'board** [-bord]
n installation for establishing or
varying connections in telephone
and electric circuits
swiv·el [SWIV-əl] *n* mechanism of
two parts that can revolve the one
on the other ▷ *v* **-eled, -el·ing** turn
(on swivel)
swollen [SWOH-lən] *pp* of SWELL
swoon *vi*, *n* faint
swoop *vi* dive, as hawk ▷ *n* act of
swooping; sudden attack
sword [sord] *n* weapon with long
blade for cutting or thrusting
swore *v* *pt* of SWEAR
sworn *v* *pp* of SWEAR ▷ *adj* bound
by or as if by an oath: *sworn enemies*
swum *pp* of SWIM
swung *pt/pp* of SWING
syb·a·rite [SIB-ə-rīt] *n* lover of
luxury **syb·a·rit'ic** [-RIT-ik] *adj*
syc·o·phant [SIK-ə-fənt] *n*
one using flattery to gain favors
syc·o·phan'tic [-FAN-tik] *adj*
syc·o·phan·cy [-fən-see] *n*
syl·la·ble [SIL-ə-bəl] *n* division
of word as unit for pronunciation
syl·lab'ic *adj* **syl·lab'i·fy** *vt* **-fied,
-fy·ing**
syl·la·bus [SIL-ə-bəs] *n*, *pl* **-bus·es,
-bi** [-bī] outline of a course of study;
list of subjects studied in course
syl·lo·gism [SIL-ə-jiz-əm] *n* form
of logical reasoning consisting
of two premises and conclusion
syl·lo·gis'tic *adj*
sylph [silf] *n* slender, graceful
woman; sprite
syl·van [SIL-vən] *adj* of forests,
trees
sym- see SYN-
sym·bi·o·sis [sim-bee-OH-sis] *n*,
pl **-ses** [-seez] living together of
two organisms of different kinds,

esp to their mutual benefit; similar relationship involving people, etc **sym·bi·ot·ic** [-OT-ik] adj

sym·bol [SIM-bəl] n sign; thing representing or typifying something **sym·bol'ic** adj **sym·bol'i·cal·ly** adv **sym'bol·ism** n use of, representation by symbols; movement in art holding that work of art should express idea in symbolic form **sym'bol·ist** n, adj **sym'bol·ize** vt **-ized, -iz·ing**

sym·me·try [SIM-ə-tree] n, pl **-tries** proportion between parts; balance of arrangement between two sides; order **sym·met'ri·cal** adj having due proportion in its parts; harmonious; **sym·met'ri·cal·ly** adv

sym·pa·thy [SIM-pə-thee] n, pl **-thies** feeling for another in pain, etc; compassion, pity; sharing of emotion, interest, desire, etc; fellow feeling **sym·pa·thet'ic** adj **sym'pa·thize** [-thiz] vi **-thized, -thiz·ing**

sym·pho·ny [SIM-fə-nee] n, pl **-nies** composition for full orchestra; harmony of sounds **sym·phon'ic** [-FON-ik] adj **sym·pho'ni·ous** [-FOH-nee-əs] adj harmonious

sym·po·si·um [sim-POH-zee-əm] n, pl **-si·a** [-zee-ə] conference, meeting; discussion, writings on a given topic

symp·tom [SIMP-təm] n change in body indicating its state of health or disease; sign, token **symp·to·mat'ic** adj

syn- prefix with, together, alike: *synchronize; syncopate*

syn·a·gogue [SIN-ə-gog] n (place of worship of) Jewish congregation

syn·chro·nize [SING-krə-nīz] v **-nized, -niz·ing** ▷ vt make agree in time ▷ vi happen at same time **syn·chro·ni·za'tion**

n **syn'chro·nous** [-nis] adj simultaneous

syn·co·pate [SING-kə-payt] vt **-pat·ed, -pat·ing** accentuate weak beat in bar of music **syn·co·pa'tion** n

syn·di·cate [SIN-di-kit] n body of people, delegates associated for some enterprise ▷ v [-kayt] **-cat·ed, -cat·ing** form syndicate ▷ vt publish in many newspapers at the same time

syn·drome [SIN-drohm] n combination of several symptoms in disease; symptom, set of symptoms or characteristics

syn·ec·do·che [si-NEK-də-kee] n figure of speech by which whole of thing is put for part or part for whole, such as *sail* for *ship*

syn·er·gy [SIN-ər-jee] n potential ability for people or groups to be more successful working together than on their own

syn·od [SIN-əd] n church council; convention

syn·o·nym [SIN-ə-nim] n word with (nearly) same meaning as another **syn·on·y·mous** [si-NON-ə-məs] adj

syn·op·sis [si-NOP-sis] n, pl **-ses** [-seez] summary, outline **syn·op'tic** adj of, like synopsis; having same viewpoint

syn·tax [SIN-taks] n part of grammar treating of arrangement of words in sentence **syn·tac'tic** adj

syn·the·sis [SIN-thə-sis] n, pl **-ses** [-seez] putting together, combination **syn'the·size** v **-sized, -siz·ing** make artificially **syn'the·siz·er** [-siz-ər] n electronic keyboard instrument capable of reproducing a wide range of musical sounds **syn·thet'ic** adj artificial; of synthesis

syph·i·lis [SIF-ə-lis] *n* contagious venereal disease **syph·i·lit'ic** *adj*

sy·ringe [sə-RINJ] *n* instrument for drawing in liquid by piston and forcing it out in fine stream or spray; squirt ▷ *vt* **-ringed, -ring·ing** spray, cleanse with syringe

syr·up [SIR-əp] *n* thick solution obtained in process of refining sugar, molasses, etc; any liquid like this, esp in consistency **syr'up·y** *adj*

sys·tem [SIS-təm] *n* complex whole, organization; method; classification **sys·tem·at'ic** *adj* methodical **sys·tem·a·tize** [-tiz] *vt* **-tized, -tiz·ing** reduce to system; arrange methodically **sys·tem'ic** *adj* affecting entire body or organism

sys·to·le [SIS-tə-lee] *n* contraction of heart and arteries for expelling blood and carrying on circulation **sys·tol·ic** [sis-TOL-ik] *adj* contracting; of systole

T *chemistry* tritium **to a T** precisely, to a nicety

Ta *chemistry* tantalum

tab *n* tag, label, short strap **keep tabs on** *inf* keep watchful eye on

tab·er·na·cle [TAB-ər-nak-əl] *n* portable shrine of Israelites; receptacle containing reserved Eucharist; place of worship

ta·ble [TAY-bəl] *n* piece of furniture consisting of flat board supported by legs; food; set of facts, figures arranged in lines or columns ▷ *vt* **-bled, -bling** lay on table; lay aside (motion, etc) for possible but unlikely consideration in future **ta'ble·land** *n* plateau, high flat area **ta'ble·spoon** *n* spoon used for serving food, or table secretly; as bribe; drunk

tab·leau [ta-BLOH] *n, pl* **-leaux** or **-leaus** [-BLOHZ] group of persons, silent and motionless, arranged to represent some scene; dramatic scene

ta·ble d'hôte [TAH-bəl DOHT] *n, pl* **ta·bles d'hôte** [TAH-bəl DOHT] *Fr* meal, with limited choice of dishes, at a fixed price

tab·let [TAB-lit] *n* pill of compressed powdered medicinal substance; writing pad; slab of stone, wood, etc, esp used formerly for writing on

tab'loid *n* (illustrated) popular small-sized newspaper usu with terse, sensational headlines

ta·boo [tə-BOO] *adj* forbidden or disapproved of ▷ *n, pl* **-boos** prohibition resulting from social conventions, etc; thing prohibited ▷ *vt* **-booed, -boo·ing** place under taboo

tab·u·lar [TAB-yə-lər] *adj* shaped, arranged like a table **tab·u·late** [-layt] *vt* **-lat·ed, -lat·ing** arrange (figures, facts, etc) in tables

tacho- *comb form* speed: tachometer

ta·chom·e·ter [ta-KOM-i-tər] *n* device for measuring speed, esp of revolving shaft (eg in automobile) and hence revolutions per minute

tac·it [TAS-it] *adj* implied but not spoken; silent **tac'it·ly** *adv* **tac'i·turn** *adj* talking little; habitually silent

tack[1] [tak] *n* small nail; long loose stitch; *nautical* course of ship obliquely to windward; course, direction ▷ *vt* nail with tacks; stitch lightly; append, attach; sail to windward

tack[2] *n* riding harness for horses

tack·le [TAK-əl] *n* equipment, apparatus, esp for fishing; lifting appliances with ropes; *football* lineman between guard and end ▷ *vt* **-led, -ling** take in hand; grip, grapple with; undertake to cope with, master, etc; *football* seize, bring down (ball-carrier)

tack·y [TAK-ee] *adj* **tack·i·er, tack·i·est** sticky; not quite dry; dowdy, shabby **tack'i·ness** [-nis] *n*

ta·co [TAK-oh] *n* **-cos** usu fried tortilla folded or wrapped round filling

tact [takt] n skill in dealing with people or situations; delicate perception of the feelings of others **tact'ful** [-fəl] adj **tact'less** [-lis] adj

tac•tics [TAK-tiks] n art of handling troops, ships in battle; adroit management of a situation; plans for this **tac•ti•cal** [TAK-ti-kəl] adj **tac•ti'cian** [-TISH-ən] n

tac•tile [TAK-til] adj of, relating to the sense of touch

tad•pole [TAD-pohl] n immature frog, in its first state before gills and tail are absorbed

taf•fe•ta [TAF-i-tə] n smooth, stiff fabric of silk, nylon, etc

taf•fy [TAF-ee] n, pl **-fies** candy of molasses and sugar

tag¹ n label identifying or showing price of (something); ragged, hanging end; pointed end of shoelace, etc; trite saying or quotation; any appendage ▷ vt **tagged, tag•ging** append, add (on); trail (along) behind

tag² n children's game where one being chased becomes the chaser upon being touched ▷ vt **tagged, tag•ging** touch **tag wrestling** wrestling match for teams of two, where one partner may replace the other upon being touched on hand

tail [tayl] n flexible prolongation of animal's spine; lower or inferior part of anything; appendage; rear part of aircraft; inf person employed to follow another ▷ pl reverse side of coin; tail coat ▷ vt remove tail of; inf follow closely, trail **tail'ings** pl n waste left over from some (eg industrial) process **tail'less** [-lis] adj **tail'board** [-bord] n removable or hinged rear board on truck, etc **tail end** last part **tail'light** n light carried at rear of vehicle **tail'spin**

n spinning dive of aircraft; sudden (eg emotional, financial) collapse **tail'wind** n wind coming from behind **tail off** diminish gradually, dwindle **turn tail** run away

tai•lor [TAY-lər] n maker of outer clothing, esp for men **tailor-made** adj made by tailor; well-fitting; appropriate

taint [taynt] v affect or be affected by pollution, corruption, etc ▷ n defect, flaw; infection, contamination

take [tayk] v took [tuuk], tak•en, tak•ing ▷ vt grasp, get hold of; get; receive, assume; adopt; accept; understand; consider; carry, conduct; use; capture; consume; subtract; require ▷ vi be effective; please; go ▷ n motion pictures (recording of) scene, sequence photographed without interruption; inf earnings, receipts **tak'ing** adj charming **take'off** n instant at which aircraft becomes airborne; commencement of flight **take after** resemble in face or character **take down** write down; dismantle; humiliate **take in** understand; make (garment, etc) smaller; deceive **take in vain** blaspheme; be facetious **take off** (of aircraft) leave ground; inf go away; inf mimic **take to** become fond of

tal•cum pow'der [TAL-kəm] powder, usu scented, to absorb body moisture, deodorize, etc

tale [tayl] n story, narrative; report; fictitious story

tal•ent [TAL-ənt] n natural ability or power; ancient weight or money **tal'ent•ed** [-id] adj gifted

tal•is•man [TAL-is-mən] n, pl **-mans** object supposed to have magic power; amulet **tal•is•man'ic** [-MAN-ik] adj

talk [tawk] vi express, exchange

ideas, etc in words ▷ *vt* express in speech, utter; discuss ▷ *n* speech, lecture; conversation; rumor

talk·a·tive *adj* fond of talking

talking-to *n*, *pl* **-tos** reproof **talk show** TV or radio program in which guests are interviewed without pay

tall [tawl] *adj* high; of great stature **tall story** unlikely and probably untrue tale

tal·low [TAL-oh] *n* melted and clarified animal fat ▷ *vt* smear with this

tal·ly [TAL-ee] *vi* **-lied, -ly·ing** correspond one with the other; keep record ▷ *n*, *pl* **-lies** record, account, total number

Tal·mud [TAHL-muud] *n* body of Jewish law **Tal·mud·ic** [-MUUD-ik] *adj*

tal·on [TAL-ən] *n* claw

tam·bou·rine [tam-bə-REEN] *n* flat half-drum with jingling disks of metal attached

tame [taym] *adj* **tam·er, tam·est** not wild, domesticated; subdued; uninteresting ▷ *vt* make tame **tame'ly** *adv* in a tame manner; without resisting

tamp *vt* pack, force down by repeated blows

tam·per [TAM-pər] *vi* interfere (with) improperly; meddle

tam'pon *n* plug of lint, cotton, etc inserted in wound, body cavity, to stop flow of blood, absorb secretions, etc

tan *n*, *adj* **tan·ner, tan·nest** (of) brown color of skin after long exposure to rays of sun, etc ▷ *v* **tanned, tan·ning** (cause to) go brown; (of animal hide) convert to leather by chemical treatment **tan'ner** *n* **tan'ner·y** *n* place where hides are tanned **tan'nic** *adj* **tan'nin** *n* vegetable substance used as

tanning agent **tan'bark** *n* bark of certain trees, yielding tannin

tang *n* strong pungent taste or smell; trace, hint; spike, barb **tang'y** *adj* **tang·i·er, tang·i·est**

tan·gent [TAN-jənt] *n* line that touches a curve without cutting; divergent course ▷ *adj* touching, meeting without cutting **tan·gen'tial** [-JEN-shəl] *adj* **tan·gen'tial·ly** *adv*

tan·ge·rine [tan-jə-REEN] *n* citrus tree; its fruit, a variety of orange

tan·gi·ble [TAN-jə-bəl] *adj* that can be touched; definite; palpable; concrete

tan·gle [TANG-gəl] *n* confused mass or situation ▷ *vt* **-gled, -gling** twist together in muddle; contend (with)

tan·go [TANG-goh] *n*, *pl* **-gos** dance of S Amer origin

tank *n* storage vessel for liquids or gas; armored motor vehicle moving on tracks; cistern; reservoir **tank'er** *n* ship, truck, etc for carrying liquid in bulk

tan·kard [TANG-kərd] *n* large drinking cup of metal or glass; its contents, esp beer

tannin see TAN

tan·ta·lize [TAN-tə-liz] *vt* **-lized, -liz·ing** torment by appearing to offer something desired; tease

tan·ta·mount [TAN-tə-mownt] *adj* equivalent in value or signification; equal, amounting (to)

tan·trum [TAN-trəm] *n* childish outburst of temper

tap¹ *v* **tapped, tap·ping** strike lightly but with some noise ▷ *n* slight blow, rap

tap² *n* valve with handle to regulate or stop flow of fluid in pipe, etc; stopper, plug permitting liquid to be drawn from cask, etc; steel tool for forming internal screw threads ▷ *vt* **tapped, tap·ping** put tap in; draw off with or as with tap; make secret connection to telephone wire to overhear conversation on it; make connection for supply of electricity at intermediate point in supply line; form internal threads in

tape [tayp] *n* narrow long strip of fabric, paper, etc; magnetic recording of music, data, etc ▷ *vt* **taped, tap·ing** record (speech, music, etc) **tape deck** device for playing magnetic tape recordings **tape measure** tape of fabric, metal marked off in centimeters, inches, etc **tape recorder** apparatus for recording sound on magnetized tape and playing it back **tape'worm** [-wurm] *n* long flat worm parasitic in animals and people

ta·per [TAY-pər] *vi* become gradually thinner toward one end ▷ *n* thin candle; long wick covered with wax; a narrowing

tap·es·try [TAP-ə-stree] *n*, *pl*-**tries** fabric decorated with designs in colors sewn by needles **tap'es·tried** *adj*

tap·i·o·ca [tap-ee-OH-kə] *n* beadlike starch made from cassava root, used esp in puddings, as thickener, etc

ta·pir [TAY-pər] *n* Amer animal with elongated snout, allied to pig

tap'root *n* large single root growing straight down

tar¹ [tahr] *n* thick black liquid distilled from coal, etc ▷ *vt* **tarred, tar·ring** coat, treat (as though) with tar **tarred with same brush** (made to appear) guilty of same misdeeds

tar² *n inf* sailor

tar·an·tel·la [ta-rən-TEL-ə] *n* lively Italian dance; music for it

ta·ran·tu·la [tə-RAN-chuu-lə] *n*, *pl* -**las** any of various large (poisonous) hairy spiders

tar·dy [TAHR-dee] *adj* -**di·er**, -**di·est** slow, late **tar'di·ly** *adv*

tare [tair] *n* weight of wrapping, container for goods; unladen weight of vehicle

tar·get [TAHR-git] *n* mark to aim at in shooting; thing aimed at; object of criticism; butt

tar·iff [TA-rif] *n* tax levied on imports, etc; list of charges; bill

tarn [tahrn] *n* small mountain lake

tar·nish [TAHR-nish] *v* (cause to) become stained, lose shine or become dimmed or sullied ▷ *n* discoloration, blemish

ta·ro [TAHR-oh] *n*, *pl* -**ros** plant of Pacific islands now cultivated widely; its edible tuber

ta·rot [TA-roh] *n* one of special pack of cards now used mainly in fortunetelling

tar·pau·lin [tahr-PAW-lin] *n* (sheet of) heavy hard-wearing waterproof fabric

tar·ry *vi* -**ried, -ry·ing** linger, delay; stay behind

tart¹ [tahrt] *n* small pie filled with fruit, jam, etc; *sl* promiscuous woman; prostitute

tart² *adj* -**er, -est** sour; sharp; bitter

tar·tan [TAHR-tn] *n* woolen cloth woven in pattern of colored checks, esp in colors, patterns associated with Scottish clans; such pattern

tar·tar¹ [TAHR-tər] *n* crust deposited on teeth; deposit formed during fermentation of wine

tartar² *n* ill-tempered person, difficult to deal with; (**T-**) member of group of peoples including Mongols and Turks

task *n* piece of work (esp unpleasant or difficult) set or undertaken ▷ *vt* assign task to; exact **task force** naval or military unit dispatched to carry out specific undertaking; any similar group in government, industry **task·mas·ter** n (stern) overseer **take to task** reprove

tas·sel [TAS-əl] n ornament of fringed knot of threads, etc; tuft **tas'seled** adj

taste [tayst] n sense by which flavor, quality of substance is detected by the tongue; this act or sensation; (brief) experience of something; small amount; preference, liking; power of discerning, judging; discretion, delicacy ▷v **tast·ed, tast·ing** observe or distinguish the taste of a substance; take small amount into mouth; experience ▷vi have specific flavor **taste'ful** [-fəl] adj in good style; with, showing good taste **taste'less** [-lis] adj **tast'y** adj **tast·i·er, tast·i·est** pleasantly or highly flavored **taste bud** small organ of taste on tongue

tat v **tat·ted, tat·ting** make by tatting **tatting** n type of handmade lace

tat·ter [TAT-ər] n make or become ragged, worn to shreds ▷n ragged piece

tat·tle vi, n, v **-tled, -tling** gossip, chatter

tat·too¹ [ta-TOO] n, pl **-toos** beat of drum and bugle call; military spectacle or pageant

tattoo² vt **-tooed, -too·ing** mark skin in patterns, etc by pricking and filling punctures with indelible colored inks ▷n, pl **-toos** mark so made

tat·ty [TAT-ee] adj **-ti·er, -ti·est** shabby, worn out

taught [tawt] pt/pp of TEACH

taunt [tawnt] vt provoke, deride with insulting words, etc ▷n instance of this; words used for this

taut [tawt] adj **-er, -est** drawn tight; under strain

tau·tol·o·gy [taw-TOL-ə-gee] n, pl **-gies** needless repetition of same thing in other words in same sentence **tau·to·log·i·cal** [-tə-LOJ-ə-kəl] adj

tav·ern [TAV-ərn] n bar; inn

taw·dry [TAW-dree] adj **-dri·er, -dri·est** showy, but cheap and without taste, flashy **taw'dri·ness** [-nis] n

taw·ny [TAW-nee] adj, n **-ni·er, -ni·est** (of) light (yellowish) brown

tax [taks] n compulsory payments by wage earners, companies, etc imposed by government to raise revenue; heavy demand on something ▷vt impose tax on; strain; accuse, blame **tax'a·ble** adj **tax·a'tion** n levying of taxes **tax'pay·er** n **tax return** statement supplied to authorities of personal income and tax due

tax·i [TAK-see] n, pl **tax·is** (also **tax'i·cab**) motor vehicle for hire with driver ▷vi **tax·ied tax·i·ing** or **tax·y·ing** (of aircraft) run along ground under its own power; ride in taxi

tax·i·der·my [TAK-si-dur-mee] n art of stuffing, mounting animal skins to give them lifelike appearance **tax'i·der·mist** n

tax·on·o·my [tak-SON-ə-mee] n science, practice of classification, esp of biological organisms

Tb chemistry terbium

T-bone steak loin steak with T-shaped bone

Tc chemistry technetium

Te see TI

Te chemistry tellurium

tea [tee] n dried leaves of plant

cultivated esp in (sub)tropical Asia; infusion of it as beverage; various herbal beverages; tea, cakes, etc as light afternoon meal; *sl* marijuana **tea bag** small porous bag of paper containing tea leaves **tea'spoon** *n* small spoon for stirring tea, etc

teach [teech] *v* **taught** [tawt] **teach'ing** instruct; educate; train; impart knowledge of; act as teacher **teach'er** *n*

teak [teek] *n* East Indian tree; very hard wood obtained from it

teal [teel] *n* type of small duck; greenish-blue color

team [teem] *n* set of animals, players of game, etc associated in activity ▷ *vi* (usu *with up*) (cause to) make a team **team'ster** *n* driver of truck or team of draft animals **team spirit** subordination of individual desire for good of team **team'work** *n* cooperative work by team acting as unit

tear¹ [teer] *n* drop of fluid appearing in and falling from eye **tear'ful** [-fəl] *adj* inclined to weep; involving tears **tear gas** irritant gas causing abnormal watering of eyes, and temporary blindness **tear-jerk-er** [TEER-jur-kər] *n inf* excessively sentimental story, moving picture, etc

tear² [tair] *v* **tore, torn, tear-ing** pull apart, rend; become torn; rush ▷ *n* hole, cut or split

tease [teez] *vt* **teased, teas-ing** tantalize, torment, irritate, bait; pull apart fibers of ▷ *n* one who teases

teat [teet] *n* nipple of female breast; rubber nipple of baby's feeding bottle

tech-ni-cal [TEK-ni-kəl] *adj* of, specializing in industrial, practical or mechanical arts and applied sciences; skilled in practical and mechanical arts; belonging to

particular art or science; according to letter of the law **tech-ni-cal'i-ty** *n* point of procedure; state of being technical **tech-ni'cian** [-NISH-ən] *n* one skilled in technique of an art **tech-nique** [tek-NEEK] *n* method of performance in an art; skill required for mastery of subject **technical college** higher educational institution specializing in mechanical and industrial arts and applied science, etc **technical knockout** *boxing* termination of bout by referee who judges that one boxer is not fit to continue

tech-noc-ra-cy [tek-NOK-rə-see] *n* government by technical experts; example of this **tech'no-crat** [-nə-krat] *n*

tech-nol-o-gy [tek-NOL-ə-gee] *n, pl* **-gies** application of practical, mechanical sciences to industry, commerce; technical methods, skills, knowledge **tech-no-log'i-cal** *adj*

tec-ton-ic [tek-TON-ik] *adj* of construction or building; *geology* pert to (forces or condition of) structure of Earth's crust **tec-ton'ics** *n* art, science of building

te-di-ous [TEE-dee-əs] *adj* causing fatigue or boredom, monotonous **te'di-um** [-əm] *n* monotony

tee *n* *golf* slightly raised ground from which first stroke of hole is made; small peg supporting ball for this stroke **tee off** make first stroke of hole in golf; *sl* scold; *sl* irritate

teem *vi* abound with; swarm; be prolific; pour, rain heavily

teens [teenz] *pl n* years of life from 13 to 19 **teen'age** *adj* **teen'ag-er** *n* person in teens

teepee *n* see **TEPEE**

tee-ter [TEE-tər] *vi* seesaw or make similar movements; vacillate

teeth *pl* of **TOOTH**

teethe [teeth] vi **teethed,**
teeth·ing (of baby) grow first teeth
teething ring ring on which baby
can bite

tee·to·tal [tee-TOHT-l] adj
pledged to abstain from alcohol
tee·to'tal·er n

tele- comb form at a distance, and
from far off: telecommunications; by
telephone: telebanking; or of involving
television: telecast

tel·e·cast [TELI-kast] v, n -cast
or -cast·ed, -cast·ing (broadcast)
TV program

tel·e·com·mu·ni·ca·tions [tel-
i-kà-myoo-ni-KAY-shànz] n science
and technology of communications
by telephony, radio, TV, etc

tel·e·gram [TEL-i-gram] n
message sent by telegraph

tel·e·graph [TEL-i-graf] n
electrical apparatus for transmitting
messages at a distance; any
signaling device for transmitting
messages ▷ v communicate by
telegraph **tel·e·graph'ic** adj
te·leg'ra·pher n one who works
telegraph **te·leg'ra·phy** n science
of telegraph; use of telegraph

tel·e·mar·ket·ing [tel-à-MAHR-
ki-ting] n selling or advertising by
telephone, television

tel·e·ol·o·gy [tel-ee-OL-à-jee]
n doctrine of final causes; belief
that things happen because of
the purpose or design that will be
fulfilled by them

tel·e·pa·thy [tà-LEP-à-thee] n
action of one mind on another at a
distance **tel·e·path'ic** [-à-PATH-
ik] adj

tel·e·phone [tel-à-FOHN] n
apparatus for communicating sound
to hearer at a distance ▷ v -phoned,
-phon·ing communicate, speak by
telephone **tel·e·phon'ic** [-FON-ik]

adj **te·leph·o·ny** [tà-LEF-à-nee] n

tel·e·pho·to [TEL-à-foh-toh] adj
(of lens) producing magnified image
of distant object

Tel·e·Promp·Ter ® [TEL-à-
promp-tàr] n off-camera device
to enable TV performer to refer to
magnified script out of sight of the
cameras

tel·e·scope [TEL-à-skohp] n
optical instrument for magnifying
images of distant objects ▷ v
-scoped, -scop·ing slide or drive
together, esp parts designed to fit
one inside the other; make smaller,
shorter **tel·e·scop'ic** [-SKOP-ik]

tel·e·text [TEL-i-tekst] n
electronic system that shows
information, news, graphics on
subscribers' TV screens

tel·e·vi·sion [TEL-à-vizh-àn]
n system of producing on screen
images of distant objects, events, etc
by electromagnetic radiation; device
for receiving this transmission and
converting it to optical images;
programs, etc viewed on TV set
tel'e·vise [-viz] vt -vised, -vis·ing
transmit by TV; make, produce as
TV program

tel·e·work·ing [TELi-wurk-ing] n
use of home computers, telephones,
etc, to enable a person to work from
home while maintaining contact
with colleagues or customers
tel'e·work·er n

tell v told, tell·ing ▷ vt let
know; order, direct; narrate, make
known; discern; distinguish; count
▷ vi give account; be of weight,
importance; reveal secrets **tel'ler**
n narrator; bank cashier **telling** adj
effective, striking **tell'tale** n sneak;
automatic indicator ▷ adj revealing

tel·lu·ri·um [te-LUUR-ee-àm] n
nonmetallic bluish-white element

tel·lu'ric adj

tem·blor [TEM-blòr] n earthquake

te·mer·i·ty [tə-MER-i-tee] n boldness, audacity

temp n inf one employed on temporary basis

tem·per [TEM-pər] n frame of mind; anger, oft noisy; mental constitution; degree of hardness of steel, etc ▷ vt restrain, qualify, moderate; harden; bring to proper condition

tem·pe·ra [TEM-pər-ə] n emulsion used as painting medium ▷ n painting made with this

tem·per·a·ment [TEM-pər-ə-mənt] n natural disposition; emotional mood; mental constitution **tem·per·a·men·tal** adj given to extremes of temperament, moody; of, occasioned by temperament

tem·per·ate [TEM-pər-it] adj not extreme; showing, practicing moderation **tem'per·ance** [-əns] n moderation; abstinence, esp from alcohol

tem·per·a·ture [TEM-pər-ə-chər] n degree of heat or coldness; inf (abnormally) high body temperature

tem·pest [TEM-pist] n violent storm **tem·pes·tu·ous** [tem-PES-choo-əs] adj turbulent; violent, stormy

tem·plate [TEM-plit] n mold, pattern to help shape something accurately

tem·ple¹ [TEM-pəl] n building for worship; shrine

tem·ple² n flat part on either side of forehead

tem·po [TEM-poh] n, pl -pos rate, rhythm, esp in music

tem·po·ral [TEM-pə-rəl] adj of time; of this life or world, secular

tem·po·rar·y [TEM-pə-rer-ee] adj lasting, used only for a time ▷ n, pl -ies person employed on temporary basis **tem·po·rar·i·ly** adv

tem·po·rize [TEM-pə-rīz] vi -ized, -iz·ing use evasive action; hedge; gain time by negotiation, etc; conform to circumstances **tem'po·riz·er** n

tempt vt try to persuade, entice, esp to something wrong or unwise; dispose, cause to be inclined to **temp·ta·tion** [-TAY-shən] n act of tempting; thing that tempts **tempt'er, tempt'ress** n **tempt'ing** adj attractive, inviting

ten n, adj cardinal number next after nine **tenth** adj, n ordinal number

ten·a·ble [TEN-ə-bəl] adj able to be held, defended, maintained

te·na·cious [tə-NAY-shəs] adj holding fast; retentive; stubborn **te·nac'i·ty** [-NAS-i-tee] n

ten·ant [TEN-ənt] n one who holds lands, house, etc on rent or lease **ten'an·cy** n, pl -cies

tend¹ vi be inclined; be conducive; make in direction of **ten'den·cy** [-dən-see] n, pl -cies inclination, bent **ten·den·tious** [-DEN-shəs] adj having, showing tendency or bias; controversial

tend² vt take care of, watch over **tend'er** n small boat carried by yacht or ship; carriage for fuel and water attached to steam locomotive; one who tends: *bartender*

ten·der¹ [TEN-dər] adj not tough or hard; easily injured; gentle, loving, affectionate; delicate, soft **ten'der·ness** [-nis] n **ten'der·ize** vt -ized, -iz·ing soften (meat) by pounding or by treating (it) with substance made for this purpose **ten'der·foot** [-fuut] n, pl -feet or -foots newcomer, esp to ranch, etc

tender² vt offer ▷ vi make offer or

estimate ▷ *n* offer; offer or estimate for contract to undertake specific work; what may legally be offered in payment

ten·don [TEN-dən] *n* sinew attaching muscle to bone, etc **ten·di·ni'tis** [-Nī-tis] *n* inflammation of tendon

ten'dril *n* slender curling stem by which climbing plant clings to anything; curl, as of hair

ten·e·ment [TEN-ə-mənt] *n* run-down apartment house, esp in slum

ten·et [TEN-it] *n* doctrine, belief

ten·nis *n* game in which ball is struck with racket by players on opposite sides of net, lawn tennis **tennis elbow** strained muscle as a result of playing tennis

ten·on [TEN-ən] *n* tongue put on end of piece of wood, etc, to fit into a mortise

ten·or [TEN-ər] *n* male voice between alto and bass; music for singer with this; general course, meaning

tense¹ [tens] *n* modification of verb to show time of action

tense² *adj* **tens·er, tens·est** stretched tight; strained; taut; emotionally strained ▷ *v* **tensed, tens·ing** make, become tense

ten'sile [-səl] *adj* of, relating to tension; capable of being stretched

ten'sion [-shən] *n* stretching; strain when stretched; emotional strain or excitement; hostility; suspense; *electricity* voltage

tent *n* portable shelter of canvas, etc

ten·ta·cle [TEN-tə-kəl] *n* elongated, flexible organ of some animals (eg octopus) used for grasping, feeding, etc

ten·ta·tive [TEN-tə-tiv] *adj* done as a trial; experimental; cautious

ten·ter·hooks [TEN-tər-huuks]

pl n **on tenterhooks** in anxious suspense

ten·u·ous [TEN-yoo-əs] *adj* flimsy, uncertain; thin, fine, slender

ten·ure [TEN-yər] *n* (length of time of) possession, holding of office, position, etc

te·pee, tee·pee [TEE-pee] *n* N Amer Indian cone-shaped tent of animal skins

tep'id *adj* moderately warm, lukewarm; half-hearted

te·qui·la [tə-KEE-lə] *n* Mexican alcoholic liquor

tera- *comb form* denoting one million million (10^{12}): *terameter*

ter·bi·um [TUR-bee-əm] *n* rare metallic element

ter·cen·ten·a·ry [tur-sen-TEN-ə-ree] *adj, n, pl* **-nar·ies** (of) three-hundredth anniversary

term [turm] *n* word, expression; limited period of time; period during which courts sit, schools are open, etc; limit, end ▷ *pl* conditions; mutual relationship ▷ *vt* name, designate

ter·mi·nal [TUR-mə-nl] *adj* at, forming an end; pert to, forming a terminus; (of disease) ending in death ▷ *n* terminal part or structure; extremity; point where current enters, leaves electrical device (eg battery); device permitting operation of computer at some distance from it

ter·mi·nate [TUR-mə-nayt] *v* **-nat·ed, -nat·ing** bring, come to an end **ter·mi·na'tion** [-shən] *n*

ter·mi·nol·o·gy [tur-mə-NOL-ə-jee] *n, pl* **-gies** set of technical terms or vocabulary; study of terms

ter·mi·nus [TUR-mə-nəs] *n, pl* **-ni** [-nī] finishing point; farthest limit; railroad station, bus station, etc at end of long-distance line

ter•mite [TUR-mīt] n insect, some species of which feed on and damage wood; (also **white ant**)

ter•race [TER-ǝs] n raised level place; level cut out of hill; row, street of houses built as one block ▷ vt **-raced, -rac•ing** form into, furnish with terrace

ter•ra cot•ta [TER-ǝ KOT-ǝ] hard unglazed pottery; its color, a brownish-red

ter•ra fir•ma [FUR-mǝ] Lat firm ground; dry land

ter•rain [tǝ-RAYN] n area of ground, esp with reference to its physical character

ter•ra•pin [TER-ǝ-pin] n type of aquatic tortoise

ter•rar•i•um [tǝ-RAIR-ee-ǝm] n, pl **-i•ums** enclosed container in which small plants, animals are kept

ter•raz•zo [tǝ-RAZ-oh] n floor, wall finish of chips of stone set in mortar and polished

ter•res•tri•al [tǝ-RES-tree-ǝl] adj of the earth; of, living on land

ter•ri•ble [TER-ǝ-bǝl] adj serious; dreadful, frightful; excessive; causing fear **ter'ri•bly** adv

ter•ri•er [TER-ee-ǝr] n small dog of various breeds, orig for following quarry into burrow

ter•rif•ic [tǝ-RIF-ik] adj very great; inf good, excellent; terrible, awe-inspiring

ter•ri•fy [TER-ǝ-fī] vt **-fied, -fy•ing** fill with fear, dread

ter•ri•to•ry [TER-i-tor-ee] n, pl **-ries** region; geographical area under control of a political unit, esp a sovereign state; area of knowledge **ter•ri•to'ri•al** adj

ter•ror [TER-ǝr] n great fear; inf troublesome person or thing **ter'ror•ism** n use of violence, intimidation to achieve ends;

state of terror **ter'ror•ist** n, adj **ter'ror•ize** vt **-ized, -iz•ing** force, oppress by fear, violence

terse [turs] adj **ters•er, ters•est** expressed in few words, concise; abrupt

ter•ti•ar•y [TUR-shee-er-ee] adj third in degree, order, etc ▷ n (T-) geological period before Quaternary

tes•sel•late [TES-ǝ-layt] vt **-lat•ed, -lat•ing** make, pave, inlay with mosaic of small tiles; (of identical shapes) fit together exactly **tes'ser•a** [-ǝr-ǝ] n, pl **-ae** [-ee] stone used in mosaic

test vt try, put to the proof; carry out test(s) on ▷ n (critical) examination; means of trial **test'ing** adj difficult **test case** lawsuit viewed as means of establishing precedent **test tube** narrow cylindrical glass vessel used in scientific experiments **test-tube baby** baby conceived in artificial womb

tes•ta•ment [TES-tǝ-mǝnt] n law will; declaration; (T-) one of the two main divisions of the Bible **tes•ta•men'ta•ry** adj

tes•tate [TES-tayt] adj having left a valid will **tes'ta•cy** n [-tǝ-see] state of being testate **tes'ta•tor** [-tay-tǝr] (fem) **tes•ta•trix** [te-STAY-triks] n maker of will

tes•ti•cle [TES-ti-kǝl] n either of two male reproductive glands

tes•ti•fy [TES-tǝ-fī] v **-fied, -fy•ing** declare; bear witness (to)

tes•ti•mo•ny [TES-tǝ-moh-nee] n, pl **-nies** affirmation; evidence **tes•ti•mo'ni•al** [-ǝl] n certificate of character, ability, etc; gift, reception, etc by organization or person expressing regard for recipient ▷ adj

tes•tis n, pl **-tes** [-teez] testicle

tes'ty adj **-ti•er, -ti•est** irritable,

short-tempered **tes'ti·ly** *adv*

tet·a·nus [TET-n-əs] *n* acute infectious disease producing muscular spasms, contractions; (also **lockjaw**)

tête-à-tête [TAYT-ə-TAYT] *n, pl* **tête-à-têtes** [-tayts] *Fr* private conversation

teth·er [TETH-ər] *n* rope or chain for fastening (grazing) animal ▷ *vt* tie up with rope **be at the end of one's tether** have reached limit of one's endurance

Teu·ton·ic [too-TON-ik] *adj* German; of ancient Teutons

text [tekst] *n* (actual words of) book, passage, etc; passage of Scriptures, etc, esp as subject of discourse ▷ *v* send text message (to)

tex'tu·al [-choo-əl] *adj*, of, in a text **text'book** *n* book of instruction on particular subject **text message** message, usu in form of coded abbreviations, sent from cell phone to cell phone

tex·tile [TEKS-til] *n* any fabric or cloth, esp woven ▷ *adj* of (the making of) fabrics

tex·ture [TEKS-chər] *n* character, structure; consistency

Th *chemistry* thorium

tha·lid·o·mide [thə-LID-ə-mid] *n* drug formerly used as sedative, but found to cause abnormalities in developing fetus

thal·li·um [THAL-ee-əm] *n* highly toxic metallic element **thal'lic** *adj*

than [than] *conj* introduces second part of comparison

thank [thangk] *vt* express gratitude to; say thanks; hold responsible **thanks** *pl n* words of gratitude **thank'ful** [-fəl] *adj* grateful, appreciative **thank'less** [-lis] *adj* having, bringing no thanks; unprofitable **Thanks·giv'ing Day** public holiday in US, Canada

that [that] *adj, pron* used to refer to something already mentioned or familiar, or further away ▷ *conj* used to introduce a clause ▷ *pron* used to introduce a relative clause

thatch [thach] *n* reeds, straw, etc used as roofing material ▷ *vt* to roof (a house) with reeds, straw, etc **thatch'er** *n*

thaw *v* melt; (cause to) unfreeze; defrost; become warmer, or more genial ▷ *n* a melting (of frost, etc)

the [thə, thee] *adj* the definite article

the·a·ter [THEE-ə-tər] *n* place where plays, etc are performed; drama, dramatic works generally; large room with (tiered) seats, used for lectures, etc; surgical operating room **the·at'ri·cal** *adj*, of, for the theater; exaggerated, affected

thee [thee] *pron obs* objective and dative of **THOU**

theft *n* stealing

their [thair] *adj* of or associated with them **theirs** *pron* (thing or person) belonging to them

the·ism [THEE-iz-əm] *n* belief in creation of universe by one god **the'ist** *n*

them [them] *pron* refers to people or things other than the speaker or those addressed **themselves** *pron* emphatic and reflexive form of **THEY** or **THEM**

theme [theem] *n* main idea or topic of conversation, book, etc; subject of composition; recurring melody in music **the·mat'ic** [thə-MAT-ik] *adj* **theme park** leisure area designed around one subject **theme song** one associated with particular program, person, etc

then [then] *adv* at that time; next; that being so

thence [thens] *adv obs* from that

place, point of reasoning, etc

the·oc·ra·cy [thee-OK-rà-see] n, pl **-cies** government by a deity or a priesthood **the·o·crat·ic** [-à-KRAT-ik] adj

the·od·o·lite [thee-OD-l-it] n surveying instrument for measuring angles

the·ol·o·gy [thee-OL-à-jee] n, pl **-gies** systematic study of religion(s) and religious belief(s) **the·o·lo·gian** [thee-à-LOH-jàn] n

the·o·rem [THEE-àr-àm, THEER-àm] n proposition that can be demonstrated by argument

the·o·ry [THEE-à-ree] n, pl **-ries** supposition to account for something; system of rules and principles; rules and reasoning, etc as distinguished from practice **the·o·ret·i·cal** adj based on theory; speculative, as opposed to practical **the·o·rize** vi **-rized, -riz·ing** form theories, speculate

the·os·o·phy [thee-OS-à-fee] n any of various religious, philosophical systems claiming possibility of intuitive insight into divine nature

ther·a·py [THER-à-pee] n, pl **-pies** healing treatment **ther·a·peu·tic** [-PYOO-tik] adj of healing; serving to improve or maintain health **ther·a·peu·tics** n art of healing **ther·a·pist** n psychotherapist

there [thair] adv in that place; to that point **there·by** adv by that means **there·fore** adv in consequence, that being so **there·up·on** conj at that point, immediately afterward

therm [thurm] n unit of measurement of heat **ther·mal** [-àl] adj of, pert to heat; hot, warm (esp of a spring, etc)

therm·i·on [THURM-i-àn] n ion

emitted by incandescent body

therm·i·on·ic [thur-mee-ON-ik] adj pert to thermion

thermo- comb form related to, caused by or producing heat

ther·mo·dy·nam·ics [thur-moh-di-NAM-iks] n the science that deals with the interrelationship and interconversion of different forms of energy

ther·mom·e·ter [thà-MOM-à-tàr] n instrument to measure temperature **ther·mo·met·ric** [thur-mà-MET-rik] adj

ther·mo·nu·cle·ar [thur-moh-NOO-klee-àr] adj involving nuclear fusion

ther·mo·plas·tic [thur-mà-PLAS-tik] n plastic that retains its properties after being melted and solidified ▷ adj

ther·mos [THUR-màs] n double-walled flask with vacuum between flask, for keeping contents of inner flask at temperature at which they were inserted

ther·mo·stat [THUR-mà-stat] n apparatus for automatically regulating temperature **ther·mo·stat·ic** adj

the·sau·rus [thi-SOR-às] n book containing lists of synonyms and antonyms; dictionary of selected words, topics

these [theez] pl of THIS

the·sis [THEE-sis] n, pl **-ses** [-seez] written work submitted for degree, diploma; theory maintained in argument

thes·pi·an [THES-pee-àn] adj theatrical ▷ n actor, actress

they [thay] pron the third person plural pronoun

thick [thik] adj **-er, -est** having great thickness, not thin; dense, crowded; viscous; (of voice)

throaty; *inf* stupid, insensitive; *inf* friendly ▷ *n* busiest, most intense part **thick·en** [THIK-ən] *v* make, become thick; become more involved, complicated **thick'ly** *adv* **thick'ness** [-nis] *n* dimensions of anything measured through it, at right angles to length and breadth; state of being thick; layer **thick·et** [THIK-it] *n* thick growth of small trees **thick'set** *adj* sturdy and solid of body; set closely together

thief [theef] *n, pl* **thieves** one who steals **thieve** [theev] *v* **thieved, thiev·ing** steal **thiev'ish** *adj*

thigh [thi] *n* upper part of leg

thim·ble [THIM-bəl] *n* cap protecting end of finger when sewing

thin *adj* **thin·ner, thin·nest** of little thickness; slim; lean; of little density; sparse; fine; loose, not close-packed; *inf* unlikely ▷ *v* **thinned, thin·ning** make, become thin **thin'ness** [-nis] *n*

thine [thin] *pron, adj obs* belonging to thee

thing *n* material object; any possible object of thought

think [thingk] *v* **thought** [thawt] **think·ing** ▷ *vi* have one's mind at work; reflect, meditate; reason; deliberate; imagine; hold opinion ▷ *vt* conceive, consider as in the mind; believe; esteem **think'a·ble** *adj* able to be conceived, considered, possible, feasible **thinking** *adj* reflecting **think tank** group of experts studying specific problems

third [thurd] *adj* ordinal number corresponding to three ▷ *n* third part **third degree** violent interrogation **third party** *law* person involved by chance or only incidentally in legal proceedings, etc **third rail** rail through which electrical current is supplied to an electric vehicle; issue that is avoided by politicians because of its controversial nature **Third World** developing countries of Africa, Asia, Latin Amer

thirst [thurst] *n* desire to drink; feeling caused by lack of drink; craving; yearning ▷ *v* feel lack of drink **thirst'y** *adj* **thirst·i·er, thirst·i·est**

thir·teen [thur-TEEN] *adj, n* three plus ten **thir'ty** *n, adj, pl* **-ties** three times ten

this [this] *adj, pron* used to refer to a thing or person nearby, just mentioned, or about to be mentioned ▷ *adj* used to refer to the present time: *this morning*

this·tle [THIS-əl] *n* prickly plant with dense flower heads

thong [thawng] *n* narrow strip of leather, strap; type of light sandal

tho·rax [THOR-aks] *n* part of body between neck and belly **tho·rac·ic** [thaw-RAS-ik] *adj*

tho·ri·um [THOR-ee-əm] *n* radioactive metallic element

thorn *n* prickle on plant; spine; bush noted for its thorns; anything that causes trouble or annoyance **thorn'y** *adj* **thorn·i·er, thorn·i·est**

thor·ough [THUR-oh] *adj* careful, methodical; complete, entire **thor'ough·ly** *adv* **thor'ough·bred** *adj* of pure breed ▷ *n* purebred animal, esp horse **thor'ough·fare** [-fair] *n* road or passage open at both ends; right of way

those [thohz] *adj, pron* pl of **THAT**

thou [thow] *pron, pl* **ye** or **you** *obs* the second person singular pronoun

though [thoh] *conj* in spite of the fact that, even if ▷ *adv* nevertheless

thought [thawt] *n* process of thinking; what one thinks; product of thinking; meditation; pt/pp of **THINK**

thought'ful [-fəl] adj considerate; showing careful thought; engaged in meditation; attentive **thought'less** [-lis] adj inconsiderate, careless, heedless

thou·sand [THOW-zənd] n, adj cardinal number, ten hundred

thrall [thrawl] n slavery; slave, bondsman **thrall'dom** [-dəm] n bondage

thrash vt beat, whip soundly; defeat soundly; thresh ▷ vi move, plunge (esp arms, legs) in wild manner **thrash out** argue about from every angle; solve by exhaustive discussion

thread [thred] n fine cord; yarn; ridge cut spirally on screw; theme, meaning ▷ vt put thread into; fit film, magnetic tape, etc into machine; put on thread; pick (one's way, etc) **thread'bare** [-bair] adj worn, with nap rubbed off; meager; shabby

threat [thret] n declaration of intention to harm, injure, etc; person or thing regarded as dangerous **threat·en** [THRET-n] vt utter threats against; menace

three n, adj cardinal number, one more than two **three-ply** [-plī] adj having three layers (as wood) or strands (as wool) **three'some** [-səm] n group of three **three-di·men·sion·al, 3-D** adj having three dimensions; simulating the effect of depth

thresh v beat, rub (wheat, etc) to separate grain from husks and straw; thrash

thresh·old [THRESH-ohld] n bar of stone or wood forming bottom of doorway; entrance; starting point; point at which a stimulus is perceived, or produces a response

threw [throo] pt of **THROW**

thrice [thrīs] adv three times

thrift n saving, economy; savings organization; genus of plant, sea pink **thrift'y** adj **thrift·i·er, thrift·i·est** economical, frugal, sparing

thrill n sudden sensation of excitement and pleasure ▷ v (cause to) feel a thrill; vibrate, tremble **thrill'er** n book, motion picture, etc with story of mystery, suspense **thrill'ing** adj exciting

thrive [thrīv] vi **thrived** or **throve** [throhv], **thrived** or **thriv·en, thriv·ing** grow well; flourish, prosper

throat [throht] n front of neck; either or both of passages through it **throat'y** adj **throat·i·er, throat·i·est** (of voice) hoarse

throb vi **throbbed, throb·bing** beat, quiver strongly, pulsate ▷ n pulsation, beat; vibration

throes [throhz] pl n condition of violent pangs, pain, etc **in the throes of** in the process of

throm·bo·sis [throm-BOH-sis] n formation of clot of coagulated blood in blood vessel or heart

throne [throhn] n ceremonial seat, powers and duties of king or queen ▷ vt **throned, thron·ing** place on throne, declare king, etc

throng [thrawng] n, v crowd

throt·tle [THROT-l] n device controlling amount of fuel entering engine and thereby its speed ▷ vt **-tled, -tling** strangle; suppress; restrict (flow of liquid, etc)

through [throo] prep from end to end, from side to side of; between the sides of; in consequence of; by means or fault of ▷ adv from end to end; to the end ▷ adj completed; finished; continuous; (of transport, traffic) not stopping **through·out'**

[-OWT] adv, prep in every part (of)
through'put [-puut] n quantity of material processed, esp by computer
through train train that travels whole (unbroken) length of trip journey **carry through** accomplish
throve [throhv] pt of **THRIVE**
throw [throh] vt threw [throo], thrown, throw•ing fling, cast; move, put abruptly, carelessly; give, hold (party, etc); cause to fall; shape on potter's wheel; move (switch, lever, etc); inf baffle, disconcert ▷ n act or distance of throwing
throw'back n one who, that which reverts to character of an ancestor; this process
thrush¹ n songbird
thrush² n fungal disease of mouth, esp in infants; foot disease of horses
thrust v thrust, thrust•ing push, drive; stab; push one's way ▷ n lunge, stab with pointed weapon, etc; cutting remark; propulsive force or power
thud n dull heavy sound ▷ vi
thud•ded, thud•ding make thud
thug n brutal, violent person
thumb [thum] n first, shortest, thickest finger of hand ▷ vt make dirty with thumb; make hitchhiker's signal to get ride; flick through (pages of book, etc)
thump n dull heavy blow; sound of one ▷ vt strike heavily
thun•der [THUN-dər] n loud noise accompanying lightning ▷ vi rumble with thunder; make noise like thunder ▷ vt utter loudly **thun'der•ous** [-əs] adj **thun'der•bolt** [-bohlt] n **thun'der•clap** n lightning flash followed by peal of thunder; anything totally unexpected and unpleasant **thun'der•struck** adj amazed
thus [thus] adv in this way;

therefore
thwack [thwak] vt, n whack
thwart [thwort] vt foil, frustrate, baffle ▷ adv obs across ▷ n seat across a boat
thy [thi] adj obs belonging to thee **thy•self'** pron emphasized form of **THOU**
thyme [tim] n aromatic herb
thy•mus [THI-məs] n small ductless gland in upper part of chest
thy•roid gland [THI-roid] endocrine gland controlling body growth, situated (in people) at base of neck
ti, te [tee] n seventh sol-fa note
Ti chemistry titanium
ti•ar•a [tee-AR-ə] n a woman's jeweled head ornament, coronet
tib•i•a [TIB-ee-ə] n, pl -i•as thicker inner bone of lower leg
tic [tik] n spasmodic twitch in muscles, esp of face
tick¹ [tik] n slight tapping sound, as of watch movement; small mark (✓) ▷ vt mark with tick ▷ vi make the sound **tick•er tape** continuous paper ribbon **tick off** mark off; reprimand; make angry **tick over** (of engine) idle; continue to function smoothly
tick² n small insect-like parasite living on and sucking blood of warm-blooded animals
tick³ n mattress case **tick'ing** n strong material for mattress covers
tick•et [TIK-it] n card, paper entitling holder to admission, travel, etc; list of candidates of one party for election ▷ vt attach label to; issue tickets to
tick•le [TIK-əl] v -led, -ling ▷ vt touch, stroke, poke (person, part of body, etc) to produce laughter, etc; please, amuse ▷ vi be irritated, itch ▷ n act, instance of this **tick'lish**

adj sensitive to tickling; requiring care or tact

tid'bit *n* tasty morsel of food; pleasing scrap (of scandal, etc)

tide [tīd] *n* rise and fall of sea happening twice each lunar day; stream; season, time **tid'al** [-al] *adj* of; like tide **tidal wave** great wave, esp produced by earthquake **tide over** help someone for a while, esp by loan, etc

ti•dings [TĪ-dingz] *pl n* news

ti•dy [TĪ-dee] *adj* **-di•er, -di•est** orderly, neat; of fair size ▷ *vt* **-died, -dy•ing** put in order

tie [tī] *v* **tied, ty•ing** equal (score of) ▷ *vt* fasten, bind, secure; restrict ▷ *n* that with which anything is bound; restriction, restraint; long, narrow piece of material worn knotted around neck; bond; connecting link; drawn game, contest; match, game in eliminating competition **tie'-dye•ing** *n* way of dyeing cloth in patterns by tying sections tightly so they will not absorb dye

tier [teer] *n* row, rank, layer

tiff *n* petty quarrel

ti•ger [TĪ-gər] *n* large carnivorous feline animal

tight [tīt] *adj* **-er, -est** taut, tense; closely fitting; secure, firm; not allowing passage of water, etc; cramped; *inf* mean, stingy; *sl* drunk **tights** *pl n* one-piece clinging garment covering body from waist to feet **tight'en** [-ən] *v* **tight'rope** *n* rope stretched taut above the ground, on which acrobats perform

tile [tīl] *n* flat piece of ceramic, plastic, etc; material used for roofs, walls, floors, drainpipes, etc ▷ *vt* **tiled, til•ing** cover with tiles

till[1] *prep* up to the time of ▷ *conj* to the time that

till[2] *vt* cultivate **till'er** *n*

till[3] *n* drawer for money in store; cash register

til•ler [TIL-ər] *n* lever to move rudder of boat

tilt *v* incline, slope, slant; tip up ▷ *vi* take part in medieval combat with lances; thrust, aim (at) ▷ *n* slope, incline; *history* combat for mounted men with lances, joust

tim•ber [TIM-bər] *n* wood for building, etc; trees suitable for the sawmill **tim'bered** *adj* made of wood; covered with trees **timber line** geographical limit beyond which trees will not grow

tim•bre [TAM-bər] *n* quality of musical sound, or sound of human voice

time [tīm] *n* existence as a succession of states; hour; duration; period; point in duration; opportunity; occasion; leisure; tempo ▷ *vt* **timed, tim•ing** choose time for; note time taken by **time'ly** *adj* at opportune or appropriate time **time** [-ər] *n* person, device for recording or indicating time **time bomb** bomb containing a timing mechanism that determines when it will explode; situation which, if allowed to continue, will develop into a serious problem **time frame** period of time within which certain events are scheduled to occur **time-honored** [-on-ərd] *adj* respectable because old **time-lag** *n* period of time between cause and effect **time'piece** [-pees] *n* watch, clock **time share** *n* system of part ownership of vacation property for specified period each year **time'ta•ble** *n* plan showing hours of work, times of arrival and departure, etc **Greenwich Mean Time** [GREN-ich] world standard time, time as settled by passage of sun over the meridian at Greenwich, England

tim'id *adj* easily frightened; lacking self-confidence **ti·mid'i·ty** *n* **tim'or·ous** [-ər-əs] *adj* timid; indicating fear

tim·pa·ni [TIM-pə-nee] *pl n* set of kettledrums **tim'pa·nist** *n*

tin *n* malleable metal ▷ *vt* **tinned, tin·ning** coat with tin **tin'ny** *adj* **-ni·er, -ni·est** (of sound) thin, metallic; cheap, shoddy

tinc·ture [TINGK-chər] *n* solution of medicinal substance in alcohol; color, stain ▷ *vt* **-tured, -tur·ing** color, tint

tin·der [TIN-dər] *n* dry easily-burning material used to start fire

tine [tīn] *n* tooth, spike of fork, antler, etc

tinge [tinj] *n* slight trace, flavor ▷ *vt* **tinged, tinge·ing** color, flavor slightly

tin·gle [TING-gəl] *vi* **-gled, -gling** feel thrill or prickling sensation ▷ *n*

tink·er [TING-kər] *n* formerly, traveling mender of pots and pans ▷ *vi* fiddle, meddle (eg with machinery) often inexpertly

tin·kle [TING-kəl] *v* **-kled, -kling** (cause to) give out series of light sounds like small bell ▷ *n* this sound or action

tin·sel [TIN-səl] *n* glittering metallic substance for decoration; anything sham and showy

tint *n* color; shade of color; tinge ▷ *vt* dye, give tint to

ti·ny [TĪ-nee] *adj* **-ni·er, -ni·est** very small, minute

tip¹ *n* slender or pointed end of anything; piece of metal, leather, etc protecting an extremity ▷ *vt* **tipped, tip·ping** put a tip on

tip² *n* small present of money given for service rendered; helpful piece of information; warning, hint ▷ *vt* **tipped, tip·ping** give tip to **tip'ster** [-stər] *n* one who sells tips about races, etc

tip³ *v* **tipped, tip·ping** ▷ *vt* tilt, upset; touch lightly ▷ *vi* topple over

tip·ple [TIP-əl] *v* **-pled, -pling** drink (liquor) habitually, esp in small quantities ▷ *n* drink of liquor **tip'pler** [-lər] *n*

tip·sy *adj* **-si·er, -si·est** drunk, partly drunk

tip·toe *vi* **-toed, -to·ing** walk on ball of foot and toes; walk softly

ti·rade [TĪ-rayd] *n* long speech, generally vigorous and hostile, denunciation

tire¹ [tīr] *v* **tired, tir·ing** ▷ *vt* reduce energy of, esp by exertion; bore; irritate ▷ *vi* become tired, wearied, bored **tire'some** [-səm] *adj* wearisome, irritating, tedious

tire² *n* (inflated) rubber or synthetic rubber ring over rim of road vehicle

tis·sue [TISH-oo] *n* substance of animal body, plant, etc; fine, soft paper, esp used as handkerchief, etc; fine woven fabric; interconnection eg of lies

tit¹ *n* any of various small songbirds

tit² *n sl* female breast

ti·tan·ic [tī-TAN-ik] *adj* huge, epic

ti·ta·ni·um [tī-TAY-nee-əm] *n* rare metal of great strength and rust-resisting qualities

tit for tat blow for blow, retaliation

tithe [tīth] *n* esp formerly, one tenth part of agricultural produce paid for the upkeep of the clergy or as tax ▷ *v* **tithed, tith·ing** *vt* exact tithes from ▷ *vi* give, pay tithe

ti·tian [TISH-ən] *adj* (of hair) reddish-gold, auburn

tit·il·late [TIT-l-ayt] *vt* **-lat·ed, -lat·ing** tickle, stimulate agreeably

ti·tle [TĪT-l] *n* name of book;

heading; name; appellation denoting rank; legal right or document proving it; *sport* championship **title deed** legal document as proof of ownership

tit•ter [TIT-ər] *vi* laugh in suppressed way ▷ *n* such laugh

tit•tle [TIT-l] *n* whit, detail

tit•tle-tat•tle [TIT-l-tat-l] *n, vi* -**tled, -tling** gossip

tit•u•lar [TICH-ə-lər] *adj* pert to title; nominal; held by virtue of a title

tiz•zy [TIZ-ee] *n sl, pl* -**zies** state of confusion, anxiety

Tl *chemistry* thallium

Tm *chemistry* thulium

to *prep* toward, in the direction of; as far as; used to introduce a comparison, ratio, indirect object, infinitive, etc ▷ *adv* to the required or normal state or position

toad [tohd] *n* animal like frog **toad'y** *n, pl* **toad•ies** obsequious flatterer, sycophant ▷ *vi* **toad•ied, toad•y•ing** do this **toad'stool** *n* fungus like mushroom, but usu poisonous

toast [tohst] *n* slice of bread crisped and browned on both sides by heat; tribute, proposal of health, success, etc made by company of people and marked by drinking together; one toasted ▷ *vt* crisp and brown (as bread); drink toast to; dry or warm at fire **toast'er** *n* electrical device for toasting bread

to•bac•co [tə-BAK-oh] *n, pl* -**cos** or -**coes** plant with leaves used for smoking; the prepared leaves

to•bog•gan [tə-BOG-ən] *n* sled for sliding down slope of snow ▷ *vi* slide on one

toc•ca•ta [tə-KAH-tə] *n* rapid piece of music for keyboard instrument

toc•sin [TOK-sin] *n* alarm signal, bell

to•day [tə-DAY] *n* this day ▷ *adv* on this day; nowadays

tod•dle [TOD-l] *vi* -**dled, -dling** walk with unsteady short steps ▷ *n* toddling **tod'dler** [-lər] *n* child beginning to walk

tod•dy [TOD-ee] *n, pl* -**dies** sweetened mixture of alcoholic liquor, hot water, etc

to-do [tə-DOO] *n inf, pl* -**dos** fuss, commotion

toe [toh] *n* digit of foot; anything resembling toe in shape or position ▷ *vt* **toed, toe•ing** reach, touch with toe **toe the line** conform

tof•fee [TAW-fee] *n* brittle candy made of sugar and butter, etc

to•ga [TOH-gə] *n, pl* -**gas** loose outer garment worn by ancient Romans

to•geth•er [tə-GETH-ər] *adv* in company, simultaneously ▷ *adj sl* (well) organized

tog•gle [TOG-əl] *n* small wooden, metal peg fixed crosswise on cord, wire, etc and used for fastening as button; any similar device

togs [togz] *pl n* clothes

toil *n* heavy work or task ▷ *vi* labor **toil'worn** *adj* weary with toil; hard and lined

toi•let [TOI-lit] *n* lavatory; ceramic toilet bowl; process of washing, dressing; articles used for this

to•ken [TOH-kən] *n* sign or object used as evidence; symbol; disk used as money ▷ *adj* nominal, slight

told [tohld] *pt/pp of* TELL

tol•er•ate [TOL-ə-ayt] *vt* -**at•ed, -at•ing** put up with; permit **tol'er•a•ble** *adj* bearable; fair, moderate **tol'er•ance** [-əns] *n* (degree of) ability to endure stress, pain, radiation, etc **tol'er•ant** [-ənt] *adj* disinclined to interfere with others' ways or opinions; forbearing; broad-minded

toll¹ [tohl] vt make (bell) ring slowly at regular intervals; announce death thus ▷ vi ring thus ▷ n tolling sound

toll² n tax, esp for the use of bridge or road; loss, damage incurred through accident, disaster, etc

tom n male of some animals, esp cat

tom·a·hawk [TOM-ə-hawk] n formerly, fighting ax of N Amer Indians ▷ vt strike, kill with one

to·ma·to [tə-MAY-toh] n, pl **-toes** plant with red fruit; the fruit, used in salads, etc

tomb [toom] n grave; monument over one **tomb'stone** n gravestone

tom·boy [TOM-boi] n girl who acts, dresses in boyish way

tome [tohm] n large book or volume

tom·fool·er·y [tom-FOO-lə-ree] n, pl **-er·ies** nonsense, silly behavior

to·mog·ra·phy [tə-MOG-rə-fee] n technique used to obtain an X-ray photograph of a plane section of the human body or some other object

to·mor·row [tə-MOR-oh] adv, n (on) the day after today

tom-tom n drum associated with N Amer Indians or with Asia

ton [tun] n measure of weight equal to 2000 pounds or 907 kilograms (short ton); measure of weight equal to 2240 pounds or 1016 kilograms (long ton) **ton·nage** [TUN-ij] n carrying capacity; charge per ton; ships collectively

tone [tohn] n quality of musical sound; quality of voice, color, etc; general character, style; healthy condition ▷ vt **toned, ton·ing** give tone to; blend, harmonize (with) **ton'er** [-ər] n substance that modifies color or composition

ton·al [-əl] adj **to·nal·i·ty** n, pl **-ties tone poem** orchestral work based on story, legend, etc

tongs [tongz] pl n large pincers, esp for handling coal, sugar

tongue [tung] n muscular organ inside mouth, used for speech, taste, etc; various things shaped like this; language, speech, voice

ton·ic [TON-ik] n medicine to improve bodily tone or condition; music keynote; music first note of scale ▷ adj invigorating, restorative; of tone **tonic (water)** mineral water oft containing quinine

to·night [tə-NIT] n this night; the coming night ▷ adv on this night

ton·sil [TON-səl] n gland in throat **ton·sil·li·tis** [-Lī-tis] n inflammation of tonsils **ton·sil·lec·to·my** [-sə-LEK-tə-mee] n, pl **-mies** surgical removal of tonsil(s)

ton·sure [TON-shər] n shaving of part of head as religious or monastic practice; part shaved ▷ vt **-sured, -sur·ing** shave thus

too adv also, in addition; in excess, overmuch

took [tuuk] pt of TAKE

tool n implement or appliance for mechanical operations; servile helper; means to an end ▷ vt work on with tool, esp chisel stone; indent design on leather book cover, etc **tool'ing** n decorative work; setting up, etc of tools, esp for machine operation **tool'bar** n row of buttons displayed on a computer screen, allowing the user to select various functions

tooth n, pl **teeth** bonelike projection in gums of upper and lower jaws of vertebrates; various pointed things like this; prong, cog

top¹ n highest part, summit; highest

rank; first in merit; garment for upper part of body; lid, stopper of bottle, etc ▷ vt **topped, top'ping** cut off, pass, reach, surpass top; provide top for **top'less** [-lis] adj (of costume, woman) with no covering for breasts **top'most** [-mohst] adj supreme; highest **top dressing** layer of fertilizer spread on the surface of land **top hat** man's hat with tall cylindrical crown **top-heavy** adj unbalanced; with top too heavy for base **top'notch** adj excellent, first-class **top-secret** adj needing highest level of secrecy, security **top'soil** n surface layer of soil; more fertile soil spread on lawns, etc

top² n toy that spins on tapering point or ball bearing

to·paz [TOH-paz] n precious stone of various colors

to·pee [toh-PEE] n lightweight hat made of pith

to·pi·ar·y [TOH-pee-er-ee] adj (of shrubs) shaped by cutting or pruning, made ornamental by trimming or training ▷ n

top·ic [TOP-ik] n subject of discourse, conversation, etc **top'i·cal** [-ik-əl] adj up-to-date, having news value; of topic

to·pog·ra·phy [tə-POG-rə-fee] n, pl **-phies** (description of) surface features of a place **to·pog'ra·pher** n

top·ple [TOP-əl] v **-pled, -ling** (cause to) fall over, collapse

top·sy-tur·vy [TOP-see-TUR-vee] adj, adv upside down, in confusion

tor n high, rocky hill

To·rah [TOH-rə] n parchment on which is written the Pentateuch

torch n portable hand light containing electric battery and bulb; burning brand, etc; any apparatus burning with hot flame, eg for welding **torch'bear·er** [-bair-ər] n

tore pt of TEAR²

tor·e·a·dor [TOR-ee-ə-dor] n bullfighter

tor·ment v torture in body or mind; afflict; tease ▷ n [TOR-ment] suffering, torture, agony of body or mind

torn pp of TEAR²

tor·na·do [tor-NAY-doh] n, pl **-does** whirlwind; violent storm

tor·pe·do [tor-PEE-doh] n, pl **-does** cylindrical self-propelled underwater missile with explosive warhead, fired esp from submarine ▷ vt **-doed, -do·ing** strike, sink with, as with, torpedo

tor·pid adj sluggish, apathetic **tor·por** [TOR-pər] n torpid state

torque [tork] n collar, similar ornament of twisted gold or other metal; mechanics rotating or twisting force

tor·rent [TOR-ənt] n a rushing stream; downpour **tor·ren·tial** [tə-REN-shəl] adj resembling a torrent; overwhelming

tor·rid [TOR-id] adj parched, dried with heat; highly emotional **Torrid Zone** land between tropics

tor·sion [TOR-shən] n twist, twisting

tor·so [TOR-soh] n, pl **-sos** (statue of) body without head or limbs; trunk

tort n law private or civil wrong

tor·til·la [tor-TEE-yə] n, pl **-til·las** thin Mexican pancake

tor·toise [TOR-təs] n four-footed reptile covered with shell of horny plates **tor·toise·shell** n mottled brown shell of hawksbill turtle used commercially as adj

tor·tu·ous [TOR-choo-əs] adj winding, twisting; involved; not straightforward

tor·ture [TOR-chər] n infliction

of severe pain ▷ *vt* **-tured, -tur·ing** subject to torture **tor·tur·er** *n*

toss [taws] *vt* throw up, about ▷ *vi* be thrown; fling oneself about ▷ *n* act of tossing

tot[1] *n* very small child

tot[2] *v* **tot·ted, tot·ting** (with *up*) add up; amount to

to·tal [TOHT-l] *n* whole amount; sum, aggregate ▷ *adj* complete, entire, full, absolute ▷ *v* **-taled, -tal·ing** to; add up **to·tal·i·ty** *n*, *pl* **-ties**

to·tal·i·za·tor [TOHT-l-ə-zay-tər] *n* machine to operate system of betting at racetrack in which money is paid out to winners in proportion to their bets

to·tal·i·tar·i·an [toh-tal-i-TAIR-ee-ən] *adj* of dictatorial, one-party government

tote[1] [toht] *n* short for **TOTALIZATOR**

tote[2] *vt* **tot·ed, tot·ing** haul, carry

to·tem [TOH-təm] *n* tribal badge or emblem **totem pole** post carved, painted with totems, esp by Amer Indians

tot·ter [TOT-ər] *vi* walk unsteadily; begin to fall

touch [tuch] *n* sense by which qualities of object, etc are perceived by touching; characteristic manner or ability; touching; slight blow, stroke, contact, amount, etc ▷ *vt* come into contact with; put hand on; reach; affect emotions of; deal with, handle; eat, drink; *sl* (try to) borrow from ▷ *vi* be in contact; (with *on*) refer to **touch'ing** *adj* emotionally moving ▷ *prep* concerning **touch'y** *adj* **touch·i·er, touch·i·est** easily offended, sensitive **touch'down** *n* football crossing of goal line with football; act of, moment of, landing of aircraft **touch'stone** *n* criterion **touch and go** precarious (situation)

touch base make contact, renew communication

tou·ché [too-SHAY] *interj* acknowledgment that blow (orig in fencing), remark, etc has been successful

tough [tuf] *adj* **-er, -est** strong, resilient, not brittle; sturdy; able to bear hardship, strain; difficult; needing effort to chew; rough; uncivilized; violent; unlucky, unfair ▷ *n* rough, violent person **tough'en** [-ən] *v* **tough'ness** [-nis] *n*

tou·pee [too-PAY] *n* man's hairpiece, wig

tour [toor] *n* traveling around; journey to one place after another; excursion ▷ *v* make tour (of) **tour'ism** *n* tourist travel; this as an industry **tour'ist** *n* one who travels for pleasure

tour de force [toor də FORS] *Fr* brilliant stroke, achievement

tour·ma·line [TUUR-mə-lin] *n* crystalline mineral used for optical instruments and as gem

tour·na·ment [TUUR-nə-mənt] *n* competition, contest usu with several stages to decide overall winner **tour'ney** [TUUR-nee] *n*, *pl* **-neys** tournament

tour·ni·quet [TUR-ni-kit] *n* bandage, surgical instrument to constrict artery and stop bleeding

tou·sle [TOW-zəl] *vt* **-sled, -sling** tangle, ruffle; treat roughly

tout [towt] *vi* solicit trade (usu in undesirable fashion); obtain and sell information about racehorses, etc ▷ *n* one who touts

tow[1] [toh] *vt* drag along behind, esp at end of rope ▷ *n* towing or being towed; vessel, vehicle in tow **tow'path** *n* path beside canal, river, orig for towing

tow[2] *n* fiber of hemp, flax **tow-**

head·ed [-hed-id] *adj* with pale-colored, or rumpled hair

to·ward [tord], **to·wards** [tords] *prep* in direction of; with regard to; as contribution to

tow·el [TOW-əl] *n* cloth for wiping off moisture after washing **tow'el·ing** *n* material used for making towels

tow·er [TOW-ər] *n* tall strong structure often forming part of church or other large building; fortress ▷ *vi* stand very high; loom (over)

town *n* collection of dwellings, etc larger than village and smaller than city **town'ship** *n* small town **towns'peo·ple** *n*

tox·ic [TOK-sik] *adj* poisonous; due to poison **tox·e·mi·a** [tok-SEEM-ee-ə] *n* blood poisoning **tox·ic'i·ty** [-IS-i-tee] *n* strength of a poison **tox·i·col·o·gy** [tok-si-KOL-ə-jee] *n* study of poisons **tox'in** *n* poison of bacterial origin

toy [toi] *n* something designed to be played with; (miniature) replica ▷ *adj* very small ▷ *vi* act idly, trifle

trace[1] [trays] *n* track left by anything; indication; minute quantity ▷ *vt* **traced, trac·ing** follow course, track of; find out; make plan of; draw or copy exactly, esp using tracing paper **trace element** chemical element occurring in very small quantity in soil, etc **tracer** bullet or shell that leaves visible trail so that aim can be checked **tracing paper** transparent paper placed over drawing, map, etc to enable exact copy to be taken

trace[2] *n* chain, strap by which horse pulls vehicle **kick over the traces** become defiant, independent

tra·che·a [TRAY-kee-ə] *n, pl -che·as** windpipe **tra'che·al** [-əl]

adj **tra·che·ot'o·my** [-OT-ə-mee] *n, pl -mies** surgical incision into trachea

tra·cho·ma [trə-KOH-mə] *n* contagious viral disease of eye

track [trak] *n* mark, line of marks, left by passage of anything; path; rough road; course; railroad line; distance between two road wheels on one axle; circular jointed metal band driven by wheels as on tank, bulldozer, etc; course for running or racing; separate section on phonograph record; class, division of schoolchildren grouped together because of similar ability ▷ *vt* follow trail or path of; find thus **track record** past accomplishments of person, company, etc

tract[1] [trakt] *n* wide expanse, area; *anatomy* system of organs, etc with particular function

tract[2] *n* treatise or pamphlet, esp religious one **trac'tate** [-tayt] *n* short tract

trac·ta·ble [TRAK-tə-bəl] *adj* easy to manage, docile, amenable

trac·tion [TRAK-shən] *n* action of drawing, pulling **traction engine** locomotive running on surfaces other than tracks

trac·tor [TRAK-tər] *n* motor vehicle for hauling, pulling, etc

trade [trayd] *n* commerce, business; buying and selling; any profitable pursuit; those engaged in trade ▷ *v* **trad·ed, trad·ing** engage in trade; buy and sell; barter **trade-in** *n* used article given in part payment for new **trade'mark, -name** *n* distinctive mark (secured by legal registration) on maker's goods **trades'man** [-mən] *n, pl -men** person engaged in trade; skilled worker **trade union** society of workers for protection of their interests **trade wind** wind blowing constantly toward equator in certain parts of globe

tra·di·tion [trà-DISH-ən] n unwritten body of beliefs, facts, etc handed down from generation to generation; custom, practice of long standing; process of handing down

tra·duce [trà-DOOS] vt **-duced, -duc·ing** slander

traf·fic [TRAF-ik] n vehicles passing to and fro in street, town, etc; (illicit) trade ▷ vi **-ficked, -fick·ing** trade, esp in illicit goods, eg drugs **traf'fick·er** n trader **traffic lights** set of colored lights at road junctions, etc to control flow of traffic

trag·e·dy [TRAJ-i-dee] n, pl **-dies** sad or calamitous event; dramatic, literary work dealing with serious, sad topic and with ending marked by (inevitable) disaster **tra·ge·di·an** [trə-JEE-dee-ən] n actor in, writer of tragedies **trag'ic** adj of, in manner of tragedy; disastrous; appalling **trag'i·cal·ly** adv

trail [trayl] vt drag behind one ▷ vi be drawn behind; hang, grow loosely ▷ n track or trace; thing that trails; rough ill-defined track in wild country **trail'er** n vehicle towed by another vehicle; trailing plant; *motion pictures* advertisement of forthcoming film **trailer park** site for parking mobile homes, usu providing facilities for trailer residents **trailer trash** offens poor person or people living in trailer parks

train [trayn] vt educate, instruct, exercise; cause to grow in particular way; aim (gun, etc) ▷ vi follow course of training, esp to achieve physical fitness for athletics ▷ n line of railroad vehicles joined to locomotive; succession, esp of thoughts, events, etc; procession of animals, vehicles, etc traveling together; trailing part of dress; body of attendants **train·ee'** n one training to be skilled worker, esp in industry

traipse [trayps] vi inf **traipsed, traips·ing** walk wearily

trait [trayt] n characteristic feature

trai·tor [TRAY-tər] n one who betrays or is guilty of treason **trai'tor·ous** [-əs] adj disloyal; guilty of treachery

tra·jec·to·ry [trə-JEK-tə-ree] n, pl **-ries** line of flight, (curved) path of projectile

tram·mel [TRAM-əl] n anything that restrains or holds captive; type of compass or is guilty of treason ▷ vt **-meled, -mel·ing** restrain; hinder

tramp vi travel on foot, esp as vagabond or for pleasure; walk heavily ▷ n homeless person who travels about on foot; walk; tramping; vessel that takes cargo wherever shippers desire

tram·ple [TRAM-pəl] vt **-pled, -pling** tread on and crush under foot

tram·po·line [tram-pə-LEEN] n tough canvas sheet stretched horizontally with elastic cords, etc to frame, for gymnastic, acrobatic use

trance [trans] n unconscious or dazed state; state of ecstasy or total absorption

tran·quil [TRANG-kwil] adj calm, quiet; serene **tran·quil'li·ty** n **tran'quil·ize** vt **-ized, -iz·ing** make calm **tran'quil·iz·er** n drug that induces calm, tranquil state

trans- prefix across, through, beyond: *transnational*; changing thoroughly: *transliterate*

trans·act [tran-SAKT] vt carry through; negotiate; conduct (affair, etc) **trans·ac·tion** n performing of any business; that which is performed; single sale or purchase ▷ pl proceedings; reports of a society

trans·ceiv·er [tran-SEE-vàr] n combined radio transmitter and receiver

tran·scend [tran-SEND] vt rise above; exceed; surpass **tran·scend'ent** adj **tran·scen·den'tal** adj surpassing experience; supernatural; abstruse **transcendental meditation** process seeking to induce detachment from problems, etc by system of meditation

tran·scribe [tran-SKRĪB] vt -**scribed, -scrib·ing** copy out; record for later broadcast; arrange (music) for different instrument **tran·script** n copy

tran·sept n transverse part of cruciform church; either of its arms

trans·fer [trans-FUR] vt -**ferred, -fer·ring** move, send from one person, place, etc to another ▷ n [TRANS-fur] removal of person or thing from one place to another; design that can be transferred from one surface to another by pressure, heat, etc **trans·fer'a·ble** adj **trans·fer'ence** n transfer

trans·fig·ure [trans-FIG-yàr] vt -**ured, -ur·ing** alter appearance of

trans·fix [trans-FIKS] vt astound, stun; pierce

trans·form' vt change shape, character of **trans·for·ma·tion** n **trans·form'er** n electricity apparatus for changing voltage of alternating current

trans·fuse [trans-FYOOZ] vt -**fused, -fus·ing** convey from one vessel to another, esp blood from healthy person to one injured or ill **trans·fu·sion** [-FYOO-zhàn] n

trans·gress [trans-GRES] vt break (law); sin **trans·gres·sion** [-GRESH-àn] n **trans·gres·sor** n

tran·sient [TRAN-shànt] adj fleeting, not permanent **tran·sience** n

tran·sis·tor [tran-ZIS-tàr] n electronics small semiconducting device used to amplify electric currents; inf portable radio using transistors

tran·sit n, v -**sit·ed, -sit·ing** (make) passage, crossing **tran·si·tion** [-ZISH-àn] n change from one state to another **tran·si·tion·al** adj **tran·si·tive** adj (of verb) requiring direct object **tran·si·to·ry** adj not lasting long, transient

trans·late [trans-LAYT] vt -**lat·ed, -lat·ing** turn from one language into another; interpret **trans·la·tion** n **trans·la·tor** n

trans·lit·er·ate [trans-LIT-àr-ayt] vt -**at·ed, -at·ing** write in the letters of another alphabet **trans·lit·er·a'tion** n

trans·lu·cent [trans-LOO-sànt] adj letting light pass through, semitransparent **trans·lu'cence** n

trans·mi·grate [trans-MĪ-grayt] vi -**grat·ed, -grat·ing** (of soul) pass into another body **trans·mi·gra·tion** n

trans·mit [trans-MIT] vt -**mit·ted, -mit·ting** send, cause to pass to another place, person, etc; communicate; send out (signals) by means of radio waves; broadcast (radio, television program) **trans·mis·sion** n transference; gear by which power is communicated from engine to road wheels **trans·mit'tal** n transmission

trans·mog·ri·fy [trans-MOG-rà-fī] vt inf -**fied, -fy·ing** change completely esp into bizarre form

trans·mute [trans-MYOOT] vt **-mut·ed, -mut·ing** change in form, properties, or nature **trans·mu·ta·tion** n

tran·som [TRAN-sǝm] n window above door; crosspiece separating the door and window

trans·par·ent [trans-PA-rǝnt] adj letting light pass without distortion; that can be seen through distinctly; obvious **trans·par·en·cy** n, pl **-cies** quality of being transparent; photographic slide; picture made visible by light behind it

tran·spire [tran-SPIR] vi **-spired, -spir·ing** become known; inf happen; (of plants) give off water vapor through leaves **tran·spi·ra·tion** n

trans·plant [trans-PLANT] vt move and plant again in another place; transfer organ surgically from one body to another ▷ n [TRANS-plant] surgical transplanting of organ; anything transplanted **trans·plan·ta·tion** n

trans·port [trans-PORT] vt convey from one place to another; enrapture ▷ n [TRANS-port] means of conveyance; ships, aircraft, etc used in transporting supplies, troops, etc; a ship, etc so used

trans·pose [trans-POHZ] vt **-posed, -pos·ing** change order of; interchange; put music into different key **trans·po·si·tion** [-pǝ-ZISH-ǝn] n

trans·sub·stan·ti·a·tion n [tran-sǎb-stan-shee-AY-shǎn] doctrine that substance of bread and wine changes into substance of Christ's body when consecrated in Eucharist

trans·verse [trans-VURS] adj lying across; at right angles

trans·ves·tite [trans-VES-tit] n person seeking sexual pleasure by wearing clothes normally worn by opposite sex

trap n snare, device for catching game, etc; anything planned to deceive, betray, etc; arrangement of pipes to prevent escape of gas; movable opening, etc; sl mouth ▷ vt **trapped, trap·ping** catch, ensnare **trap·per** n one who traps animals for their fur **trap·door** n door in floor or roof

tra·peze [tra-PEEZ] n horizontal bar suspended from two ropes for use in gymnastics, acrobatic exhibitions, etc **trapeze artist** one who performs on trapeze

trap·e·zoid [TRAP-ǝ-zoid] n quadrilateral with two parallel sides

trap·pings [TRAP-ingz] pl n equipment, ornaments

trash n rubbish; nonsense **trash·y** adj **trash·i·er, trash·i·est** worthless, cheap

trau·ma [TROW-mǝ, TRAW-mǝ] n nervous shock; injury **trau·mat·ic** adj of, causing, caused by trauma

tra·vail [trǝ-VAYL] vi, n labor, toil

trav·el [TRAV-ǝl] v **-eled, -el·ing** go, move from one place to another ▷ n act of traveling, esp as tourist; machinery distance component is allowed to move ▷ pl (account of) traveling **trav·el·er** n **trav·e·logue** [TRAV-ǝ-log] n film, etc about travels

trav·erse [trǝ-VURS] vt **-ersed, -ers·ing** cross, go through or over; (of gun) move laterally ▷ n [TRA-vurs] anything set across; partition; mountaineering face, steep slope to be crossed from side to side ▷ adj being, lying across

trav·es·ty [TRAV-ǝ-stee] n, pl **-ties** farcical, grotesque imitation; mockery ▷ vt **-tied, -ty·ing** make, be a travesty of

trawl n net dragged at deep levels behind special boat, to catch fish, shrimp, etc ▷ vi fish with one **trawl'er** n trawling vessel

tray n flat board, usu with rim, for carrying things; any similar utensil

treach·er·y [TRECH-ã-ree] n, pl **-er·ies** deceit, betrayal **treach'er·ous** [-rãs] adj disloyal; unreliable, dangerous

trea·cle [TREE-kãl] n cloying sentimentally; Brit molasses

tread [tred] v trod, trod·den or trod, tread·ing set foot on; trample; oppress; walk ▷ n treading; fashion of walking; upper surface of step; part of motor vehicle tire in contact with ground **tread'mill** n dreary routine, etc

trea·dle [TRED-l] n lever worked by foot to turn wheel

trea·son [TREE-zãn] n violation by citizen of allegiance to country or ruler; treachery; disloyalty **trea'son·a·ble** adj constituting treason **trea'son·ous** adj

treas·ure [TREZH-ãr] n riches; stored wealth or valuables ▷ vt **-ured, -ur·ing** prize, cherish; store up **treas'ur·er** n official in charge of funds **treas'ur·y** n, pl **-ur·ies** place for treasure; government department in charge of finance **treasure-trove** [-trohv] n treasure found hidden (with no evidence of ownership)

treat n (treet) pleasure, entertainment given ▷ vt deal with, act toward; give medical treatment to; (with of) discourse on; entertain, esp with food or drink ▷ v negotiate **treat'ment** n method of counteracting a disease; care or mode of treating; manner of handling an artistic medium

trea·tise [TREE-tis] n book discussing a subject, formal essay

trea·ty [TREE-tee] n, pl **-ties** signed contract between nations, etc

tre·ble [TREB-l] adj threefold, triple; music high-pitched ▷ n soprano voice; part of music for it; singer with such voice ▷ v **-bled, -bling** increase threefold **tre'bly** [-blee] adv

tree n large perennial plant with woody trunk; beam; anything (eg genealogical chart) resembling tree, or tree's structure ▷ vt **treed, tree·ing** force, drive up tree; plant with trees

tre·foil [TREE-foil] n plant with three-lobed leaf, clover; carved ornament like this

trek vi, n trekked, trek·king (make) long difficult journey

trel·lis [TREL-is] n lattice or grating of light bars fixed crosswise ▷ vt screen, supply with one

trem·ble [TREM-bãl] vi **-bled, -bling** quiver, shake; feel fear, anxiety ▷ n involuntary shaking; quiver; tremor

tre·men·dous [tri-MEN-dãs] adj vast, immense; exciting, unusual; excellent

trem·o·lo [TREM-ã-loh] n, pl **-los** quivering or vibrating effect in singing or playing

trem·or [TREM-ãr] n quiver; shaking; minor earthquake

trem·u·lous [TREM-yã-lãs] adj quivering slightly; fearful, agitated

trench n long narrow ditch, esp as shelter in war ▷ vt cut grooves or ditches in **trench coat** double-breasted waterproof overcoat

trench·ant [TRENCH-ãnt] adj cutting, incisive, biting

trend n direction, tendency, inclination, drift **trend'y** adj,

trend·i·er, trend·i·est consciously fashionable (person) **trend'i·ness** [-nis] *n*

tre·pan [tri-PAN] *n* instrument for cutting circular pieces, esp for skull ▷ *vt* **-panned, -pan·ning**

trep·i·da·tion [trep-i-DAY-shàn] *n* fear, anxiety

tres·pass [TRES-pàs] *vi* intrude (on) property, etc of another; transgress, sin ▷ *n* wrongful entering on another's land; wrongdoing

tress *n* long lock of hair

tres·tle [TRES-l] *n* board fixed on pairs of spreading legs and used as support; structural member of bridge

tri- *comb form* three or thrice; **trilingual;** occurring every three: **triweekly**

tri·ad [TRI-ad] *n* group of three; *chemistry* element, radical with valence of three

tri·al [TRI-àl] *n* act of trying, testing; experimental examination; *law* conduct of case before judge, jury; thing, person that strains endurance or patience

tri·an·gle [TRI-ang-gàl] *n* figure with three angles; percussion musical instrument **tri·an'gu·lar** [-làr] *adj*

tribe [trib] *n* subdivision of race of people **trib'al** [-àl] *adj*

trib·u·la·tion [trib-yà-LAY-shàn] *n* misery, trouble, affliction, distress; cause of this

tri·bu·nal [trà-BYOON-l] *n* law court; body appointed to inquire into and decide specific matter; place, seat of judgment

trib·u·tar·y [TRIB-yà-ter-ee] *n, pl* **-tar·ies** stream flowing into another ▷ *adj* auxiliary; contributory; paying tribute

trib·ute [TRIB-yoot] *n* sign of honor or recognition; tax paid by one country to another as sign of subjugation

trice [tris] *n* moment **in a trice** instantly

tri·chi·na [tri-KĪ-nà] *n, pl* **-nae** [-nee] minute parasitic worm **trich·i·no·sis** [trik-à-NOH-sis] disease caused by this

trick [trik] *n* deception; prank; mannerism; illusion; feat of skill or cunning; knack; cards played in one round; spell of duty; *sl* prostitute's customer, sexual act ▷ *vt* cheat; hoax; deceive **trick'ster** *n* **trick'y** *adj* **trick·i·er, trick·i·est** difficult, needing careful handling; crafty

trick·le [TRIK-l] *v* **-led, -ling** (cause to) run, flow, move in thin stream or drops

tri·col·or [TRI-kul-àr] *adj* three colored ▷ *n* tricolor flag

tri·cy·cle [TRI-sì-kàl] *n* child's three-wheeled bike

tri·dent [TRID-nt] *n* three-pronged fork or spear

tri·en·ni·al [tri-EN-ee-àl] *adj* happening every, or lasting, three years

tri·fle [TRI-fàl] *n* insignificant thing or matter; small amount ▷ *vi* **-fled, -fling** toy (with); act, speak idly **tri'fler** [-flàr] *n*

trig·ger [TRIG-àr] *n* catch that releases spring esp to fire gun ▷ *vt* (oft with *off*) start, set in action, etc **trigger-happy** *adj* tending to irresponsible, ill-considered behavior, esp in use of firearms

trig·o·nom·e·try [trig-à-NOM-i-tree] *n* branch of mathematics dealing with relations of sides and angles of triangles **trig·o·no·met'ric** [-nà-MET-rik] *adj*

tri·lat·er·al [tri-LAT-àr-àl] *adj* having three sides

trill vi sing with quavering voice; sing lightly; warble ▷ n such singing or sound

tril·lion [TRIL-yàn] n number 1 followed by 12 zeroes

tril·o·gy [TRIL-ā-jee] n, pl -gies series of three related (literary) works

trim adj **trim·mer, trim·mest** neat, smart; slender; in good order ▷ vt **trimmed, trim·ming** shorten slightly by cutting; prune; decorate; adjust; put in good order; adjust balance of (ship, aircraft) ▷ n decoration; order, state of being trim; haircut that neatens existing style; upholstery, accessories in automobile; edging material, as inside woodwork around doors, windows, etc **trimming** n (oft pl) decoration, addition; inf a defeat ▷ pl garnish to main dish

tri·ma·ran [TRĪ-mà-ran] n three-hulled vessel

trin·i·ty [TRIN-i-tee] n the state of being threefold; (**T-**) the three persons of the Godhead

trin·i·tar·i·an [-TAIR-ee-àn] n, adj

trin·ket [TRING-kit] n small ornament, trifle

tri·o [TREE-oh] n, pl **tri·os** group of three; music for three players

tri·ode [TRĪ-ohd] n electronics three-electrode vacuum tube

trip n (short) journey for pleasure; stumble; switch; sl hallucinatory experience caused by drug ▷ v **tripped, trip·ping** (cause to) stumble; (cause to) make false step, mistake ▷ vi run lightly; skip; dance; sl take hallucinatory drugs ▷ vt operate (switch)

tri·par·tite [trī-PAHR-tīt] adj having, divided into three parts

tripe [trīp] n stomach of cow, etc prepared for food; sl nonsense

tri·ple [TRIP-àl] adj threefold ▷ v

-pled, -pling treble; hit triple ▷ n baseball three-base hit **trip·let** [TRIP-lit] n three of a kind; one of three offspring born at one birth **trip·lex** adj threefold; (of apartment) having three floors **trip'ly** [-lee] adv

trip·li·cate [TRIP-li-kit] adj threefold ▷ n state of being triplicate; one of set of three copies ▷ vt [-kayt] **-cat·ed, -cat·ing** make threefold

tri·pod [TRĪ-pod] n stool, stand, etc with three feet

trip·tych [TRIP-tik] n carving, set of pictures (esp altarpiece) on three panels hinged side by side

trite [trīt] adj hackneyed, banal

trit·i·um [TRIT-ee-àm] n radioactive isotope of hydrogen

tri·umph [TRĪ-àmf] n great success; victory; exultation ▷ vi achieve great success or victory; prevail; exult **tri·um'phal** [-UMF-àl] adj **tri·um'phant** [-fànt] adj victorious

tri·um·vi·rate [trī-UM-vàr-it] n joint rule by three persons

triv·et [TRIV-it] n metal bracket or stand for pot or kettle

triv·i·a [TRIV-ee-à] pl n petty, unimportant things, details **triv'i·al** adj of little consequence; commonplace **triv·i·al'i·ty** n, pl -ties

tro·chee [TROH-kee] n in verse, foot of two syllables, first long and second short **tro·cha'ic** [-KAY-ik] adj

trod pt/pp of TREAD **trod'den** [TROD-àn] pp of TREAD

trog·lo·dyte [TROG-là-dīt] n cave dweller

Tro·jan [TROH-jàn] adj, n (inhabitant) of ancient Troy; steadfast or persevering (person)

troll¹ [trohl] vt fish for by dragging

baited hook or lure through water

troll² n supernatural being in Scandinavian mythology and folklore

trol·ley [TROL-ee] n, pl **-leys** small wheeled table for food and drink; wheeled cart for moving goods, etc; streetcar

trol·lop [TROL-əp] n promiscuous or slovenly woman

trom·bone [trom-BOHN] n deep-toned brass wind instrument with sliding tube **trom·bon·ist** n

troop n group or crowd of persons or animals; unit of cavalry ▷ pl soldiers ▷ vi move in a troop, flock **troop'er** n cavalry soldier; state police officer

trope [trohp] n figure of speech

tro·phy [TROH-fee] n, pl **-phies** prize, award, as shield, cup; memorial of victory, hunt, etc ▷ adj inf regraded as highly desirable symbol of wealth or success: a *trophy wife*

trop·ic [TROP-ik] n either of two lines of latitude at 23½°N (**tropic of Cancer**) or 23½°S (**tropic of Capricorn**) ▷ pl area of Earth's surface between these lines **trop'i·cal** [-kəl] adj pert to, within tropics; (of climate) very hot

trot vi **trot·ted**, **trot·ting** (of horse) move at medium pace, lifting feet in diagonal pairs; (of person) run easily with short strides ▷ n trotting, jog **trot'ter** n horse trained to trot in race; foot of certain animals, esp pig

troth [trawth] n fidelity, truth

trou·ba·dour [TROO-bà-dor] n one of school of early poets and singers

trou·ble [TRUB-əl] n state or cause of mental distress, pain, inconvenience; care, effort ▷ v **-bled, -bling** ▷ vt be trouble to ▷ vi be inconvenienced, concerned

(about); be agitated; take pains, exert oneself **trou'ble·some** [-səm] adj

trough [trawf] n long open vessel, esp for animals' food or water; hollow between two waves; *meteorology* area of low pressure

trounce [trowns] vt **trounced, trounc·ing** beat thoroughly, thrash

troupe [troop] n company of performers **troup'er** n

trou·sers [TROW-zərz] pl n two-legged outer garment with legs reaching to the ankles

trous·seau [TROO-soh] n, pl **-seaux** [-sohz] bride's outfit of clothing

trout [trowt] n freshwater sport and food fish

trow·el [TROW-əl] n small tool like spade for spreading mortar, lifting plants, etc ▷ vt **-eled, -el·ing** work with or as if with trowel

troy weight [troi] system of weights used for gold, silver and gems

tru·ant [TROO-ənt] n one absent without leave, esp child so absenting self from school ▷ adj **tru'an·cy** [-ən-see] n, pl **-cies**

truce [troos] n temporary cessation of fighting; respite, lull

truck¹ [truk] n wheeled (motor) vehicle for moving goods

truck² n **have no truck with** refuse to be involved with

truck·le [TRUK-əl] vi **-led, -ling** yield weakly (to)

truc·u·lent [TRUK-yə-lənt] adj aggressive, defiant **truc·u·lence** [-ləns] n

trudge [truj] vi **trudged, trudg·ing** walk laboriously ▷ n laborious or wearisome walk

true [troo] adj **tru·er, tru·est** in accordance with facts; faithful;

exact, correct; genuine **tru·ism**
[TROO-iz-əm] n self-evident truth
tru·ly adv exactly; really; sincerely
truth [trooth] n state of being true;
something that is true **truth'ful**
[-fəl] adj accustomed to speak the
truth; accurate, exact
truf·fle [TRUF-əl] n edible fungus
growing underground; candy
resembling this
truism [TROO-iz-əm] n see TRUE
trump n card of suit temporarily
ranking above others ▷ vt take trick
with a trump **trump up** concoct,
fabricate
trump·er·y [TRUM-pə-ree] adj
showy but worthless ▷ n, pl **-er·ies**
worthless finery; trash; worthless
stuff
trum·pet [TRUM-pit] n metal
wind instrument like horn ▷ vi
blow trumpet; make sound like one,
as elephant ▷ vt proclaim, make
widely known
trun·cate [TRUNG-kayt] vt
-cat·ed, -cat·ing cut short
trun·cheon [TRUN-chən] n
police officer's club; staff of office or
authority; baton
trun·dle [TRUN-dəl] vt **-dled,
-dling** roll, as a thing on little wheels
trunk n main stem of tree; person's
body without or excluding head and
limbs; box for clothes, etc; elephant's
proboscis ▷ pl man's bathing suit
trunk line main line of railroad,
telephone, etc
truss vt fasten up, tie up ▷ n
support; medical device of belt,
etc to hold hernia in place; pack,
bundle; cluster of flowers at end of
single stalk
trust n confidence; firm belief;
reliance; combination of producers
to reduce competition and keep up
prices; care, responsibility; property

held for another ▷ vt rely on; believe
in; expect, hope; consign for care
trust·ee' n one legally holding
property on another's behalf; trusty
trust·ee'ship n **trust'ful** [-fəl]
adj inclined to trust; credulous
trust'wor·thy [-wur-thee] adj
reliable; dependable; honest; safe
trust'y adj **trust·i·er, trust·i·est**
faithful; reliable ▷ n, pl **trust·ies**
trustworthy convict with special
privileges
truth [trooth] see TRUE
try [trī] v **tried, try·ing** ▷ vi
attempt, endeavor ▷ vt attempt;
test; make demands upon;
investigate (case); examine (person)
in court of law; purify or refine (as
metals) ▷ n, pl **tries** attempt, effort
tried adj proved; afflicted **trying** adj
upsetting, annoying; difficult
tryst [trist] n appointment to meet;
place appointed
tsar [zahr] see CZAR
tset·se [TSET-see] n Afr
bloodsucking fly whose bite
transmits various diseases to man
and animals
T-shirt [TEE-shurt] n informal
(short-sleeved) undershirt, sweater
usu of cotton
T square n T-shaped ruler for
drawing parallel lines, right angles,
etc
tsu·na·mi [tsuu-NAH-mee] n tidal
wave, usu caused by an earthquake
under the sea
tub n open wooden vessel like
bottom half of barrel; small round
container; bath; inf short, fat
person; old, slow ship, etc
tu·ba [TOO-bə] n, pl **-bas** valved
brass wind instrument of low pitch
tube [toob] n long, narrow, hollow
cylinder; flexible cylinder with cap to
hold liquids, pastes **tu'bu·lar** [-byə-

lər] *adj* like tube

tu·ber [TOO-bər] *n* fleshy underground stem of some plants, eg potato **tu'ber·ous** [-əs] *adj*

tu·ber·cle [TOO-bər-kəl] *n* any small rounded nodule on skin, etc; small lesion of tissue, esp produced by tuberculosis **tu·ber·cu·lar** (tuu-BUR-kyə-lər) **tu·ber'cu·lin** *n* extraction from bacillus used to test for and treat tuberculosis

tu·ber·cu·lo'sis *n* communicable disease, esp of lungs

tuck [tuk] *vt* push, fold into small space; gather, stitch in folds; draw, roll together ▷ *n* stitched fold **tuck'er** *n* strip of linen or lace formerly worn across bosom by women ▷ *vt inf* weary; tire

tu·fa [TOO-fə] *n* porous rock formed as deposit from springs, etc

tuf·fet [TUF-it] *n obs* small mound or seat

tuft *n* bunch of feathers, threads, etc

tug *vt* **tugged, tug·ging** pull hard or violently; haul; jerk forward ▷ *n* violent pull; ship used to tow other vessels **tug of war** contest in which two teams pull against one another on a rope; hard-fought contest for supremacy

tu·i·tion [too-ISH-ən] *n* teaching, instruction; fee for instruction

tu·lip [TOO-lip] *n* plant with bright cup-shaped flowers

tulle [tool] *n* kind of fine thin silk or lace

tum·ble [TUM-bəl] *v* **-bled, -bling** (cause to) fall or roll, twist, etc (esp in play); rumple, disturb ▷ *n* fall; somersault **tum'bler** *n* stemless drinking glass; acrobat; spring catch in lock **tum'ble-down** *adj* dilapidated **tumble to** *inf* realize, understand

tu·me·fy [TOO-mə-fī] *v*

-fied, -fy·ing (cause to) swell

tu·mes·cence [too-MES-əns] *n*
tu·mes'cent [-ənt] *adj* (becoming) swollen

tu·mor [TOO-mər] *n* abnormal growth in or on body

tu·mult [TOO-məlt] *n* violent uproar, commotion **tu·mult'u·ous** [-MUL-choo-əs] *adj*

tu·na [TOO-nə] *n* large marine food and game fish

tun·dra [TUN-drə] *n* vast treeless zone between ice cap and timber line of N America and Eurasia

tune [toon] *n* melody; quality of being in pitch; adjustment of musical instrument; concord; frame of mind ▷ *vt* **tuned, tun·ing** put in tune; adjust machine to obtain most efficient running; adjust radio circuit **tune'ful** [-fəl] *adj* **tun'er** [-ər] *n*

tune in adjust (radio, TV) to receive (a station, program)

tung·sten [TUNG-stən] *n* grayish-white metal, used in lamp filaments, some steels, etc

tu·nic [TOO-nik] *n* close-fitting jacket forming part of uniform; loose hip-length or knee-length garment

tun·nel [TUN-l] *n* underground passage, esp as track for railroad line; burrow of a mole, etc ▷ *v* **-neled, -nel·ing** make tunnel (through)

tur·ban [TUR-bən] *n* in certain countries, man's headdress, made by coiling length of cloth around head or a cap; woman's hat like this

tur·bid *adj* muddy, not clear; disturbed **tur·bid'i·ty** *n*

tur·bine [TUR-bin] *n* rotary engine driven by steam, gas, water or air playing on blades

turbo- *comb form* of, relating to, or driven by a turbine

tur·bu·lent [TUR-byə-lənt] *adj* in commotion; swirling; riotous

tur•bu•lence [-ləns] n esp instability of atmosphere causing gusty air currents, etc

tu•reen [tuu-REEN] n serving dish for soup

turf n, pl **turfs** short grass with earth bound to it by matted roots; grass, esp as lawn; sl claimed territory of gang ▷ vt lay with turf

tur•gid [TUR-jid] adj swollen, inflated; bombastic **tur•gid′i•ty** n

tur•key [TUR-kee] n large bird reared for food; sl loser, naive person; sl a flop

Turk•ish [TUR-kish] adj of, pert to Turkey, the Turks **Turkish bath** steam bath **Turkish delight** gelatin candy flavored and coated with powdered sugar

tur′moil n confusion and bustle, commotion

turn v move around, rotate; change, reverse, alter position or direction (of); (oft with into) change in nature, character, etc ▷ vt make, shape on lathe ▷ n act of turning; inclination, etc; period, spell; turning; short walk; (part of) rotation; performance **turn′ing** n road, path leading off main route **turn′coat** [-koht] n one who forsakes own party or principles **turn′out** n number of people appearing for some purpose, occasion; way in which person is dressed, equipped **turn′o•ver** n total sales made by business over certain period; rate at which employees leave and are replaced; small pastry; football, basketball loss of ball to opponents through mistake **turn′pike** n history (gate across) road where toll was paid; highway **turn′stile** n revolving gate for controlling admission of people **turn′ta•ble** n revolving platform **turn down** refuse **turn up** appear;

be found; increase (flow, volume)

tur′nip n plant with globular root used as food

tur•pen•tine [TUR-pən-tin] n resin obtained from certain trees; oil made from this **turps** n short for turpentine

tur•pi•tude [TUR-pi-tood] n depravity

tur•quoise [TUR-kwoiz] n bluish-green precious stone; this color

tur•ret [TUR-it] n small tower; revolving armored tower for guns on warship, tank, etc

tur•tle [TUR-tl] n (esp sea) tortoise

tusk n long pointed side tooth of an elephant, walrus, etc

tus•sle [TUS-əl] n, v **-sled, -sling** fight, wrestle, struggle

tu•te•lage [TOOT-l-ij] n act, office of tutor or guardian **tu′te•lar•y** [-ler-ee] adj

tu•tor [TOO-tər] n one teaching individuals or small groups ▷ v teach thus **tu•to′ri•al** [-TOR-ee-əl] n period of instruction with tutor

tu•tu [TOO-too] n, pl **-tus** short, stiff skirt worn by ballerinas

tux•e•do [tuk-SEE-doh] n, pl **-dos** dinner jacket

TV television **TV dinner** frozen meal in tray for heating before serving **TV game** game played on TV screen using special attachment

twad•dle [TWOD-l] n silly talk

twain [twayn] n two in twain asunder

twang n vibrating metallic sound; nasal speech ▷ v (cause to) make such sounds

tweak [tweek] vt pinch and twist or pull ▷ n

tweed n rough-surfaced cloth used for clothing ▷ pl suit of tweed

tween n child of about 8 to 12 years of age

tweet *n, vi* chirp **tweet'er** *n* small loudspeaker reproducing high-frequency sounds

tweez•ers [TWEE-zərz] *pl n* small forceps or tongs

twelve [twelv] *n, adj* cardinal number two more than ten **twelfth** *adj* the ordinal number 12

twen•ty [TWEN-tee] *n, adj, pl* **-ties** cardinal number, four times ten **twen'ti•eth** [-tee-ith] *adj* the ordinal number 20 ▷ *n* **twenty-four-seven, 24/7** *adj, adv* inf all the time

twerp [twurp] *n sl* silly person

twice [twis] *adv* two times

twid•dle [TWID-l] *v* **-dled, -dling** fiddle; twist

twig *n* small branch, shoot

twi•light [TWÍ-lit] *n* soft light after sunset

twill *n* fabric woven so as to have surface of parallel ridges

twin *n* one of pair, esp two children born together ▷ *adj* being a twin ▷ *v* **twinned, twin•ning** pair, be paired

twine [twin] *v* **twined, twin•ing** twist, coil around ▷ *n* string, cord

twinge [twinj] *n* momentary sharp, shooting pain; qualm

twin•kle [TWING-kəl] *vi* **-kled, -kling** shine with dancing or quivering light, sparkle ▷ *n* twinkling; flash; gleam of amusement in eyes **twinkling** *n* very brief time

twirl [twurl] *vt* turn or twist round quickly; whirl; twiddle

twist *v* make, become spiral, by turning with one end fast; distort; change; wind ▷ *n* thing twisted **twist'er** *n* person or thing that twists; inf tornado, whirlwind **twist'y** *adj* **twist•i•er, twist•i•est**

twit *n* foolish person ▷ *vt* **twit•ted, twit•ting** taunt

twitch [twich] *v* give momentary sharp pull or jerk (to) ▷ *n* such pull or jerk; spasmodic jerk, spasm

twit•ter [TWIT-ər] *vi* giggle; talk idly; (of birds) utter succession of tremulous sounds ▷ *n* such succession of notes

two [too] *n, adj* cardinal number, one more than one **two'fold** *adj, adv* **two-faced** *adj* double-dealing, deceitful; with two faces **two-stroke** [-strohk] *adj* (of internal-combustion engine) making one explosion to every two strokes of piston

ty•coon [ti-KOON] *n* powerful, influential businessperson

tyke [tik] *n* small, cheeky child; small (mongrel) dog

tympani see TIMPANI

type [tip] *n* class; sort; model; pattern; characteristic build; specimen; block bearing letter used for printing; such pieces collectively ▷ *vt* **typed, typ•ing** print with typewriter; typify; classify **type'script** *n* typewritten document or copy **type'writ•er** *n* keyed writing machine **typ'ist** *n* one who operates typewriter **ty'po** *n, pl* **ty•pos** inf error in typing, printing

ty•phoid [Tí-foid] *n* acute infectious disease, affecting esp intestines ▷ *adj* **ty•phus** [Tí-fəs] *n* infectious disease

ty•phoon [ti-FOON] *n* violent tropical storm or cyclone

typ•i•cal [TIP-i-kəl] *adj* true to type; characteristic **typ'i•cal•ly** *adv* **typ•i•fy** [TIP-i-fī] *vt* **-fied, -fy•ing** serve as type or model of

ty•pog•ra•phy [ti-POG-rə-fee] *n* art of printing; style of printing **ty•po•graph'i•cal** *adj* **ty•pog'ra•pher** [-POG-rə-fər] *n*

ty•rant [TÍ-rənt] *n* oppressive or

cruel ruler; one who forces own will on others cruelly and arbitrarily **ty·ran·ni·cal** [ti-RAN-i-kəl] *adj* despotic; ruthless **tyr·an·nize** [TIR-ə-niz] *v* **-nized, -niz·ing** exert ruthless or tyrannical authority (over) **tyr'an·nous** [-ə-nəs] *adj* **tyr'an·ny** *n* despotism **ty·ro** [ti-roh] *n, pl* **-ros** novice, beginner

U

U *chemistry* uranium

u·biq·ui·tous [yoo-BIK-wi-tàs] *adj* everywhere at once; omnipresent **u·biq·ui·ty** *n*

ud·der [UD-ər] *n* milk-secreting organ of cow, etc

ug·ly [UG-lee] *adj* **-li·er, -li·est** unpleasing, repulsive to the sight, hideous; ill-omened; threatening **ug'li·ness** [-nis] *n*

u·kase [yoo-KAYS] *n* an arbitrary command

u·ku·le·le [yoo-kà-LAY-lee] *n* small four-stringed guitar, esp of Hawaii

ul·cer [UL-sàr] *n* open sore on skin, mucous membrane that is slow to heal **ul'cer·ate** *v* **-at·ed, -at·ed** make, form ulcer(s) **ul·cer·a'tion** *n*

ul·lage [UL-ij] *n* quantity by which a container falls short of being full

ul·na [UL-nà] *n, pl* **-nae** [-nee] longer of two bones of forearm

ul·te·ri·or [ul-TEER-ee-àr] *adj* lying beneath, beyond what is revealed or evident (eg motives); situated beyond

ul·ti·mate [UL-tà-mit] *adj* last; highest; most significant; fundamental **ul·ti·ma'tum** [-MAY-tàm] *n, pl* **-tums** or **-ta** [-tà] final proposition; final terms offered

ul·tra- *prefix* beyond, excessively: *ultramodern*

ul'tra·high frequency [UL-trà-hi] (band of) radio waves of very short wavelength

ul·tra·ma·rine [ul-trà-mà-REEN] *n* blue pigment

ul·tra·son·ic [ul-trà-SON-ik] *adj* of sound waves beyond the range of human ear

ul·tra·vi·o·let [ul-trà-VĪ-à-lit] *adj* of electromagnetic radiation (eg of sun, etc) beyond limit of visibility at violet end of spectrum

um·bel [UM-bàl] *n* umbrella-like flower cluster with stalks springing from central point **um·bel·lif'er·ous** [-LIF-àr-às] *adj* bearing umbel(s)

um·ber [UM-bàr] *n* dark brown pigment

um·bil·i·cal [um-BIL-i-kàl] *adj* of (region of) navel **umbilical cord** cordlike structure connecting fetus with placenta of mother; cord joining astronaut to spacecraft, etc

um·brage [UM-brij] *n* offense, resentment

um·brel·la [um-BREL-à] *n* folding circular cover of nylon, etc on stick, carried in hand to protect against rain, heat of sun; anything shaped or functioning like an umbrella

um·pire [UM-pir] *n* person chosen to decide question, or to decide disputes and enforce rules in a game ▷ *v* **-pired, -pir·ing** act as umpire (in)

un- *prefix* not: *unidentified*; denoting reversal of an action: *untie*; denoting removal from: *unthrone*

un·ac·count·a·ble [un-à-KOWNT-à-bàl] *adj* that cannot be explained

u·nan·i·mous [yoo-NAN-ə-məs] *adj* in complete agreement; agreed by all **u·na·nim·i·ty** [yoo-nə-NIM-ə-tee] *n*

un·as·sum·ing [un-ə-SOO-ming] *adj* not pretentious; modest

un·a·vail·ing [un-ə-VAY-ling] *adj* useless; futile

un·a·ware [un-ə-WAIR] *adj* not aware, uninformed **un·a·wares** [-WAIRZ] *adv* without previous warning; unexpectedly

un·bear·a·ble *adj* not able to be endured

un·bos·om [un-BUUZ-əm] *vt* tell or reveal (one's secrets, etc)

un·can·ny [un-KAN-ee] *adj* weird, mysterious; extraordinary

un·cer·tain *adj* not able to be accurately known or predicted; not able to be depended upon; changeable

un·cle [UNG-kəl] *n* brother of father or mother; husband of aunt

un·com·fort·a·ble *adj* not physically relaxed; anxious or uneasy

un·com·mon *adj* not happening or encountered often; in excess of what is normal

un·com·pli·men·ta·ry [un-kom-plə-MEN-tə-ree] *adj* not complimentary; insulting, derogatory

un·con·di·tion·al *adj* without conditions or limitations

un·con·scion·a·ble [un-KON-shə-nə-bəl] *adj* unscrupulous, unprincipled; excessive

un·con·scious [un-KON-shəs] *adj* insensible; not aware; not knowing, of thoughts, memories, etc of which one is not normally aware ▷ *n* these thoughts **un·con·scious·ness** [-nis] *n*

un·couth [un-KOOTH] *adj* clumsy, boorish; without ease or polish

unc·tion [UNGK-shən] *n* anointing; excessive politeness; soothing words or thoughts

unc·tu·ous [-choo-əs] *adj* slippery, greasy; oily in manner, gushing

un·de·cid·ed *adj* not having made up one's mind; (of an issue or problem) not agreed or decided upon

un·der [UN-dər] *prep* below, beneath; bound by, included in; less than; subjected to; known by; in the time of ▷ *adv* in lower place or condition ▷ *adj* lower

under- *prefix* beneath, below, lower: *underground*

un·der·car·riage [UN-dər-ka-rij] *n* landing gear of vehicle esp aircraft

un·der·charge [UN-dər-CHAHRJ] *vt* -charged, -charg·ing charge less than proper amount ▷ *n* [UN-dər-chahrj] too low a charge

un·der·class [UN-dər-klas] *n* the most economically disadvantaged people, such as the long-term unemployed

un·der·coat [UN-dər-koht] *n* coat of paint applied before top coat

un·der·dog [UN-dər-dawg] *n* person or team in a weak or underprivileged position

un·der·go [UN-dər-GOH] *vt* -went, -gone, -go·ing experience, endure, sustain

un·der·grad·u·ate [UN-dər-GRAJ-oo-it] *n* student at college who has not received degree

un·der·ground [UN-dər-ground] *adj* under the ground; secret ▷ *adv* secretly ▷ *n* secret but organized resistance to government in power; subway

un·der·hand [UN-dər-hand] *adj* secret, sly; *sport* (of softball pitch, etc) with hand swung below shoulder level

un·der·lie [un-dər-LĪ] *vt* -lay,

-lain, -ly·ing be situated under, lie beneath

un·der·line [UN-dər-lin] vt **-lined, -lin·ing** put line under; emphasize

un·der·ling [UN-dər-ling] n subordinate

un·der·mine [un-dər-MIN] vt **-mined, -min·ing** wear away base, support of; weaken insidiously

un·der·neath [un-dər-NEETH] adv, prep under or beneath ▷ adj, n lower (part or surface)

un·der·pass [UN-dər-pas] n section of road passing under another road, railroad line, etc

un·der·stand [un-dər-STAND] v **-stood** [-stuud] **-stand·ing** know and comprehend; realize ▷ vt infer; take for granted **un·der·stand'a·ble** adj **un·der·stand·ing** n intelligence; opinion; agreement ▷ adj sympathetic

un·der·stud·y [UN-dər-stud-ee] n, pl **-stud·ies** one prepared to take over theatrical part from performer if necessary ▷ vt **-stud·ied, -stud·y·ing** work as understudy to (performer)

un·der·take [un-dər-TAYK] vt **-took** [-tuuk], **-tak·en, -tak·ing** make oneself responsible for; enter upon; promise **un'der·tak·er** n one who arranges funerals **un'der·tak·ing** n that which is undertaken; project; guarantee

un·der·tone [UN-dər-tohn] n quiet, dropped tone of voice; underlying tone or suggestion

un·der·tow [UN-dər-toh] n backwash of wave; current beneath surface moving in different direction from surface current

un·der·wear [UN-dər-wair] n (also **un'der·clothes**) garments worn next to skin

un·der·world [UN-dər-wurld] n criminals and their associates; mythology abode of the dead

un·der·write [un-dər-RIT] vt **-wrote, -writ·ten, -writ·ing** agree to pay; accept liability in insurance policy **un'der·writ·er** n agent for insurance or stock issue

un·do [un-DOO] vt **-did, -done, -do·ing** untie, unfasten; reverse; cause downfall of **un·do'ing** n **un·done** adj [un-DUN] ruined; not performed

un·du·late [UN-jə-layt] v **-lat·ed, -lat·ing** move up and down like waves **un·du·la'tion** n

un·earth [un-URTH] vt dig up; discover

un·eas·y [un-EE-zee] adj **-eas·i·er, -eas·i·est** anxious; uncomfortable **un·eas'i·ness** [-nis] n

un·em·ployed [un-im-PLOID] adj having no paid employment, out of work **un·em·ploy'ment** [-mənt] n

un·e·quiv'o·cal adj completely clear in meaning

un·err·ing [un-ER-ing] adj not missing the mark; consistently accurate

un·fail'ing adj continuous or reliable

un·fair' adj not right, fair, or just

un·fit' adj unqualified or unsuitable; in poor physical condition

un·fold' v open or spread out from a folded state; reveal or be revealed

un·for·get'ta·ble adj impossible to forget, memorable

un·for'tu·nate adj unlucky, unsuccessful, or unhappy; regrettable or unsuitable ▷ n unlucky person

un·gain·ly [un-GAYN-lee] adj **-li·er, -li·est** awkward, clumsy

un·gain·li·ness [-nis] n

un·guent [UNG-gwànt] n
ointment

un·hap·py adj sad or depressed;
unfortunate or unlucky

un·health·y adj likely to cause
poor health; not fit or well; morbid,
unnatural

uni- comb form one: unicorn; uniform

u·ni·corn [YOO-ni-korn] n
mythical horselike animal with
single long horn

u·ni·form [YOO-ni-form] n
identifying clothes worn by
members of same group eg soldiers,
nurses, etc ▷ adj not changing,
unvarying; regular, consistent;
conforming to same standard or
rule **u·ni·form·i·ty** n sameness
u'ni·form·ly adv

u·ni·fy [YOO-nə-fī] v -fied, -fy·ing
make or become one **u·ni·fi·ca·tion**
[-KAY-shən] n

u·ni·lat·er·al [yoo-nə-LAT-ər-əl]
adj one-sided; (of contract) binding
one party only

un·ion [YOON-yən] n joining
into one; state of being joined;
result of being joined; federation,
combination of states, etc; labor
union, trade union **un'ion·ize**
-ized, -iz·ing organize (workers)
into labor union

u·nique [yoo-NEEK] adj being only
one of its kind; unparalleled

u·ni·son [YOO-nə-sən] n music
singing, etc of same note as others;
agreement, harmony, concord

u·nit [YOO-nit] n single thing or
person; standard quantity; group of
people or things with one purpose

u·nite [yoo-NĪT] v u·nit·ed,
u·nit·ing ▷ vt join into one,
connect; associate; cause to adhere
▷ vi become one; combine **u·ni·ty**
[-nə-tee] n state of being one;

harmony; agreement, uniformity;
combination of separate parts into
connected whole; mathematics the
number one

u·ni·verse [YOO-nə-vurs] n all
existing things considered as
constituting systematic whole;
the world **u·ni·ver·sal** [-səl]
adj relating to all things or all
people; applying to all members of
a community **u·ni·ver·sal'i·ty**
[-SAL-ə-tee] n

u·ni·ver·si·ty [yoo-nə-VUR-
si-tee] n, pl -ties educational
institution for research, study,
examination and award of degrees in
various branches of learning

un·kempt adj of rough or uncared-
for appearance

un·less conj if not, except

un·men·tion·a·ble adj
unsuitable as a topic of conversation

un·moved adj not affected by
emotion, indifferent

un·or·tho·dox adj (of ideas,
methods, etc) unconventional and
not generally accepted; (of a person)
having unusual opinions or methods

un·pleas·ant adj not pleasant or
agreeable

un·rav·el [un-RAV-əl] vt -eled,
-el·ing undo, untangle

un·re·mit·ting [un-ri-MIT-ing]
adj never slackening or stopping

un·re·quit·ed adj not returned:
unrequited love

un·roll v open out or unwind
(something rolled or coiled) or (of
something rolled or coiled) become
opened out or unwound

un·ru·ly [un-ROO-lee] adj -li·er,
-li·est badly behaved, ungovernable,
disorderly

un·sa·vor·y [un-SAY-və-ree] adj
distasteful, disagreeable

un·sight·ly [un-SĪT-lee] adj ugly

un·suit·a·ble *adj* not right or appropriate for a particular purpose

un·ten·a·ble [un-TEN-ə-bəl] *adj* (of theories, etc) incapable of being maintained; defended

un·think·a·ble [un-THING-kə-bəl] *adj* out of the question; inconceivable; unreasonable

un·til *conj* up to the time that ▷ *prep* in or throughout the period before

un·to [UN-too] *prep* to

un·touched [un-TUCHT] *adj* not touched; not harmed

un·touch'a·ble *adj* not able to be touched ▷ *n* esp formerly, non-caste Hindu, forbidden to be touched by one of caste

un·to·ward [un-TORD] *adj* awkward, inconvenient

un·tram·meled [un-TRAM-əld] *adj* not confined, not constrained

un·u·su·al *adj* uncommon or extraordinary

un·wield·y [un-WEEL-dee] *adj* **-wield·i·er, -wield·i·est** awkward, big, heavy to handle; clumsy

un·wit·ting *adj* not knowing; not intentional

un·wrap' *v* remove the wrapping from (something)

up *prep* from lower to higher position; along ▷ *adv* in to higher position, source, activity, etc; indicating completion **up'ward** *adj, adv* **up'wards** *adv* up against; confronted with

up- *comb form* up, upper, upwards: *uproot; upgrade*

up·braid [up-BRAYD] *vt* scold, reproach

up'bring·ing *n* rearing and education of children

up·date [up-DAYT] *vt* **-dat·ed, -dat·ing** bring up to date ▷ *n*

up·front [up-frunt] *adj inf* open,

frank ▷ *adj, adv inf* (of money) paid out at beginning of business arrangement

up·grade [up-GRAYD] *vt* **-grad·ed, -grad·ing** promote to higher position; improve

up·heav·al [up-HEE-vəl] *n* sudden or violent disturbance

up·hold [up-HOHLD] *vt* **-held, -hold·ing** maintain, support, etc

up·hol·ster [up-HOHL-stər] *vt* fit springs, padding and coverings on chairs, etc **up·hol'ster·er** *n* one who does this work **up·hol'ster·y** *n*

up'keep *n* act, process or cost of keeping something in good repair

up·lift *vt* raise aloft ▷ *n* [UP-lift] a lifting up; mental, social or emotional improvement

up·load *vt computing* transfer data from a single computer to a server or host

up·on [ə-PON] *prep* on

up·per [UP-ər] *adj* higher, situated above; comp of **up** ▷ *n* upper part of boot or shoe **up'per·cut** *n* short-arm upward blow **up'per·most** [-mohst] *adj* sup of **up**

up·right [UP-rīt] *adj* erect; honest, just ▷ *adv* vertically ▷ *n* thing standing upright, eg post in framework

up·ris·ing [UP-rī-zing] *n* rebellion, revolt

up·roar [UP-ror] *n* tumult, disturbance **up·roar'i·ous** [-ee-əs] *adj* rowdy

up·set *vt* **-set, -set·ting** overturn; distress; disrupt; make ill ▷ *n* [UP-set] unexpected defeat; confusion; trouble; overturning

up'shot *n* outcome, end

up·stage [up-stayj] *adj* of back of stage ▷ *vt* **-staged, -stag·ing** draw attention away from another to oneself

up·start [UP-stahrt] n one suddenly raised to wealth, power, etc

up·tight [up-tīt] adj sl displaying tense nervousness, irritability; repressed

u·ra·ni·um [yuu-RAY-nee-əm] n white radioactive metallic element, used as chief source of nuclear energy

U·ra·nus [YUUR-ə-nəs] n Greek god, personification of sky; seventh planet from the sun

ur·ban [UR-bàn] adj relating to town or city; describing modern pop music of African-American origin, such as hip-hop **ur·ban·ize** vt **-ized, -iz·ing** change countryside to residential or industrial area

ur·bane [ur-BAIN] adj elegant, sophisticated **ur·ban·i·ty** [-BAN-i-tee] n

ur·chin n mischievous, unkempt child

u·re·a [yuu-REE-ə] n substance occurring in urine

u·re·thra [yuu-REE-thrə] n canal conveying urine from bladder out of body

urge [urj] vt **urged, urg·ing** exhort earnestly; entreat; drive on ▷ n strong desire **ur·gen·cy** [-jən-see] n, pl **-cies ur·gent** [-jənt] adj pressing; needing attention at once **ur·gent·ly** adv

u·rine [YUUR-in] n fluid excreted by kidneys to bladder and passed as waste from body **u·ric** adj **u·ri·nal** [YUUR-ə-nl] n (place with) sanitary fitting used by men for urination **ur·i·nar·y** adj **u·ri·nate** vi **-nat·ed, -nat·ing** discharge urine

URL computing uniform resource locator: standardized address of a location on the Internet

urn n vessel like vase, esp for ashes of the dead; large container with tap for making and dispensing tea,

coffee, etc

ur·sine [UR-sin] adj of, like a bear

us pron pl the objective case of the pronoun **WE**

USB port n computing type of serial port for connecting peripheral devices in a computing system

use [yooz] vt **used, us·ing** employ, avail oneself of; exercise; exploit; consume ▷ n [yoos] employment, application to a purpose; need to employ; serviceableness; profit; habit **us·a·ble** [YOO-zə-bàl] adj fit for use **us·age** [YOOS-ij] n act of using; custom; customary way of using **used** [yoozd] adj secondhand, not new **use·ful** [YOOS-fàl] adj of use; helpful; serviceable **use·ful·ness** [-nis] n **use·less·ness** [-lis-nis] n **used to** [yoost] adj accustomed to ▷ vt did so formerly **us·er** n **us·er friendly** [YOO-zər] (of computer, etc) easily understood and operated **us·er·name** n computing account name that, with a password, allows access to a computing system; part of an e-mail address before the @ symbol

ush·er [USH-ər] n doorkeeper, one showing people to seats, etc ▷ vt introduce, announce; inaugurate

u·su·al [YOO-zhoo-àl] adj habitual, ordinary **u·su·al·ly** adv as a rule; generally, commonly

u·surp [yoo-SURP] vt seize wrongfully **u·sur·pa·tion** [yoo-sər-PAY-shàn] n violent or unlawful seizing of power **u·surp·er** n

u·su·ry [YOO-zhə-ree] n lending of money at excessive interest; such interest **u·su·rer** n money lender **u·su·ri·ous** [-ZHUUR-ee-əs] adj

u·ten·sil [yoo-TEN-sàl] n vessel, implement, esp in domestic use

u·ter·us [YOO-tər-əs] n, pl **-us·es** womb **u·ter·ine** [-tər-in] adj

u•til•i•ty [yoo-TIL-i-tee] *n*, *pl* **-ties** usefulness; benefit; useful thing; a public service, such as electricity
▷ *adj* made for practical purposes

u•til•i•tar•i•an [-TAIR-ee-ən] *adj* useful rather than beautiful

u•til•i•tar•i•an•ism *n* doctrine that morality of actions is to be tested by their utility, esp that the greatest good of the greatest number should be the sole end of public action **u•ti•li•za•tion** [-ZAY-shən] *n* **u'ti•lize** *vt* **-lized, -liz•ing** make use of

ut•most [UT-mohst] *adj* to the highest degree; extreme, furthest
▷ *n* greatest possible amount

u•to•pi•a [yoo-TOH-pee-ə] *n* imaginary state with perfect political and social conditions, or constitution **u•to'pi•an** [-pee-ən] *adj* ideally perfect but impracticable

ut•ter¹ [UT-ər] *vt* express, emit audibly, say; put in circulation (forged bills, counterfeit coin)

ut'ter•ance [-əns] *n* act of speaking; expression in words; spoken words

utter² *adj* complete, total, absolute **ut'ter•ly** *adv*

ut•ter•most [UT-ər-mohst] *adj* farthest out; utmost ▷ *n* highest degree

u•vu•la [YOO-vyə-lə] *n*, *pl* **-las** or **-lae** [-lee] pendent fleshy part of soft palate **u'vu•lar** [-lər] *adj*

ux•o•ri•ous [uk-SOR-ee-əs] *adj* excessively fond of one's wife

V *chemistry* vanadium

va·cant [VAY-kànt] *adj* without thought, empty; unoccupied **va'can·cy** [-kàn-see] *n, pl* **-cies** state of being unoccupied; unfilled position, accommodation, etc

va·cate [VAY-kayt] *vt* **-cat·ed, -cat·ing** make empty **va·ca'tion** [-KAY-shàn] *n* act of vacating; holidays; time when schools and courts, etc are closed

vac·ci·nate [VAK-sà-nayt] *vt* **-nat·ed, -nat·ing** inoculate with vaccine as protection against a specific disease **vac·ci·na'tion** *n* **vac·cine** [vak-SEEN] *n* any substance used for inoculation against disease

vac·il·late [VAS-à-layt] *vi* **-lat·ed, -lat·ing** fluctuate in opinion; waver; move to and fro **vac·il·la'tion** *n* indecision; wavering; unsteadiness

vac·u·um [VAK-yoom] *n, pl* **-u·ums** place, region containing no matter and from which all or most air, gas has been removed ▷ *v* clean with vacuum cleaner **va·cu'i·ty** [va-KYOO-i-tee] *n* **vac'u·ous** [VAK-yoo-às] *adj* vacant; expressionless; unintelligent **vacuum cleaner**

apparatus for removing dust by suction **vac'uum-packed** *adj* contained in packaging from which air has been removed

vag·a·bond [VAG-à-bond] *n* person with no fixed home; wandering beggar or thief ▷ *adj* like a vagabond

va·gar·y [VAY-gà-ree] *n, pl* **-gar·ies** something unusual, erratic; whim

va·gi·na [và-JI-nà] *n, pl* **-nas** passage from womb to exterior **vag·i·nal** [VAJ-à-nl] *adj*

va·grant [VAY-grànt] *n* vagabond, tramp ▷ *adj* wandering, esp without purpose **va'gran·cy** *n, pl* **-cies**

vague [vayg] *adj* **va·guer** [-gèr] **va·guest** [-gàst] indefinite or uncertain; indistinct; not clearly expressed; absent-minded

vain [vayn] *adj* **-er, -est** conceited; worthless, useless; unavailing; foolish **vain'ly** *adv*

vain·glo·ry [VAYN-glor-ee] *n* boastfulness, vanity **vain·glo'ri·ous** *adj*

val·ance [VAL-àns] *n* short curtain around base of bed, etc

vale [vayl] *n poetry* valley

val·e·dic·tion [val-i-DIK-shàn] *n* farewell **val·e·dic·to'ri·an** [-TOR-ee-àn] *n* **val·e·dic'to·ry** [-DIK-tà-ree] *n* farewell address ▷ *adj*

va·lence [VAY-làns], **va·len·cy** [-làn-see] *n chemistry* combining power of element or atom

val·en·tine [VAL-àn-tīn] *n* (one receiving) card, gift, expressing affection, on Saint Valentine's Day, Feb. 14th

val·et [va-LAY] *n* gentleman's personal servant

val·e·tu·di·nar·y [val-i-TOOD-n-er-ee] *adj* sickly; infirm **val·e·tu·di·nar'i·an** [-NAIR-ee-àn] *n* person obliged or disposed to live the life of an invalid

Val·hal·la [val-HAL-ə] n Norse mythology place of immortality for heroes slain in battle

val·iant [VAL-yənt] adj brave, courageous

val·id adj sound; capable of being justified; of binding force in law **va·lid·i·ty** [və-LID-i-tee] n soundness; power to convince; legal force **val'i·date** vt **-dat·ed, -dat·ing** make valid

va·lise [və-LEES] n traveling bag

Val·kyr·ie [val-KEER-ee, VAL-ker-ee] n one of the Norse war goddesses who chose the slain and guided them to Valhalla

val·ley [VAL-ee] n, pl **-leys** low area between hills; river basin

val·or [VAL-ər] n bravery **val'or·ous** [-əs] adj

val·ue [VAL-yoo] n worth; utility; equivalent; importance ▷ pl principles, standards ▷ vt **-ued, -u·ing** estimate value of; hold in respect; prize **val'u·a·ble** [-ə-bəl] adj precious; worthy; capable of being valued ▷ n (usu pl) valuable thing **val·u·a'tion** [-AY-shən] n estimated worth **value·less** [-lis] adj worthless **value added tax** n tax on difference between cost of basic materials and cost of article made from them

valve [valv] n device to control passage of fluid, etc through pipe; anatomy part of body allowing one-way passage of fluids; any of separable parts of shell of mollusk; music device on brass instrument for lengthening tube

va·moose [va-MOOS] v **-moosed, -moos·ing** sl depart quickly

vamp¹ n woman who deliberately allures men ▷ v exploit (man) as vamp

vamp² n something patched up; front part of shoe upper ▷ vt patch up, rework; jazz improvise

vam·pire [VAM-pīr] n (in folklore) corpse that rises from dead to drink blood of the living **vampire bat** one that sucks blood of animals

van¹ n large covered truck, esp for furniture; smaller such vehicle for camping, etc

van² n short for **VANGUARD**

va·na·di·um [və-NAY-dee-əm] n metallic element used in manufacture of hard steel

van·dal [VAN-dl] n one who wantonly and deliberately damages or destroys **van'dal·ism** n **van'dal·ize** vt **-ized, -iz·ing**

vane [vayn] n weather vane; blade of propeller; fin on bomb, etc; sight on quadrant

van·guard [VAN-gahrd] n leading, foremost group, position, etc

va·nil·la [və-NIL-ə] n tropical climbing orchid; its seed(pod); essence of this used for flavoring

van·ish vi disappear; fade away

van·i·ty [VAN-i-tee] n, pl **-ties** excessive pride or conceit; ostentation

van·quish [VANG-kwish] vt subdue in battle; conquer, overcome

vap·id adj flat, dull, insipid **va·pid·i·ty** [və-PID-i-tee] n

va·por [VAY-pər] n gaseous form of a substance more familiar as liquid or solid; steam; mist; invisible moisture in air **va'por·ize** [-pə-rīz] v **-ized, -iz·ing** convert into, pass off in, vapor

var·i·a·ble see **VARY**

var·i·cose [VAR-i-kohs] adj of vein, swollen, twisted

var·i·e·gate [VAR-ee-i-gayt] vt **-gat·ed, -gat·ing** diversify by patches of different colors

var·i·e·gat·ed [va-ree-OR-əm] *adj* streaked, spotted, dappled

va·ri·e·ty [və-RI-i-tee] *n, pl* **-ties** state of being varied or various; diversity; varied assortment; sort or kind

var·i·o·rum [va-ree-OR-əm] *adj, n* (edition) with notes by various commentators

var·i·ous [VAIR-ee-əs] *adj* manifold, diverse, of several kinds

var·nish [VAHR-nish] *n* resinous solution put on a surface to make it hard and shiny ▷ *vt* apply varnish to

var·y [VAIR-ee] *v* **var·ied, var·y·ing** (cause to) change, diversify, differ, deviate **var·i·a·bil·i·ty** **var·i·a·ble** *adj* changeable; unsteady or fickle ▷ *n* something subject to variation **var·i·ance** [-əns] *n* state of discord, discrepancy **var·i·ant** [-ənt] *adj* different ▷ *n* difference in form; alternative form or reading **var·i·a·tion** [-AY-shən] *n* alteration; extent to which thing varies; modification **var·ied** *adj* diverse; modified; variegated

vas *n, pl* **va·sa** [VA-sə] vessel, tube carrying bodily fluid

vas·cu·lar [VAS-kyə-lər] *adj* of, with vessels for conveying sap, blood, etc

vase [vayz] *n* vessel, jar as ornament or for holding flowers

vas·ec·to·my [va-SEK-tə-mee] *n, pl* **-mies** contraceptive measure of surgical removal of part of vas bearing sperm from testicle

vas·sal [VAS-əl] *n* holder of land by feudal tenure; dependent

vast *adj* **-er, -est** very large **vast·ly** [-lee] *adv* **vast·ness** [-nis] *n*

vat *n* large tub, tank

Vat·i·can [VAT-i-kən] *n* Pope's palace; papal authority

vaude·ville [VAWD-vil] *n*

theatrical entertainment with songs, juggling acts, dance, etc

vault¹ [vawlt] *n* arched roof; arched apartment; cellar; burial chamber; place for storing valuables ▷ *vt* build with arched roof

vault² *v* spring, jump over with the hands resting on something ▷ *n* such jump **vaulting horse** padded apparatus for support of hands in gymnastics

vaunt [vawnt] *v, n* boast **vaunt·ed** [-id] excessively praised

VDU visual display unit, monitor

veal [veel] *n* calf flesh as food

vec·tor [VEK-tər] *n* quantity (eg force) having both magnitude and direction; disease-carrying organism, esp insect; compass direction, course

veer *vi* change direction; change one's mind

veg·e·ta·ble [VEJ-tə-bəl] *n* plant, esp edible one; *inf* person who has lost use of mental and physical faculties; dull person ▷ *adj* of, from, concerned with plants

veg·e·tar·i·an [vej-i-TAIR-ee-ən] *n* one who does not eat meat ▷ *adj* **veg·e·tar·i·an·ism**

veg·e·tate [VEJ-i-tayt] *vi* **-tat·ed, -tat·ing** (of plants) grow, develop; (of person) live dull, unproductive life **veg·e·ta·tion** *n* plants collectively; plants growing in a place; process of plant growth **veg·e·ta·tive** [-tay-tiv] *adj*

ve·he·ment [VEE-ə-mənt] *adj* marked by intensity of feeling; vigorous; forcible **ve·he·mence** [-məns] *n*

ve·hi·cle [VEE-i-kəl] *n* means of conveying; means of expression; medium **ve·hic·u·lar** [-HIK-yə-lər] *adj*

veil [vayl] *n* light material to cover

face or head; mask, cover ▷ *vt* cover with, as with, veil **veiled** *adj* disguised **take the veil** become a nun

vein [vayn] *n* tube in body taking blood to heart; rib of leaf or insect's wing; fissure in rock filled with ore; streak; distinctive trait, strain, etc; mood ▷ *vt* mark with streaks

ve•nous [VEE-nəs] *adj* of veins

veld, veldt [velt] *n* elevated grassland in S Afr

vel•lum [VEL-əm] *n* parchment of calf skin used for manuscripts or bindings; paper resembling this

ve•loc•i•ty [və-LOS-i-tee] *n*, *pl* **-ties** rate of motion in given direction, esp of inanimate things; speed

ve•lour [və-LUUR] *n* fabric with velvety finish

ve•lum [VEE-ləm] *n*, *pl* **-la** [-lə] zoology membranous covering or organ; soft palate

vel•vet [VEL-vit] *n* silk or cotton fabric with thick, short pile **vel•vet•een** [-ə-TEEN] *n* cotton fabric resembling velvet **vel'vet•y** *adj* of, like velvet; soft and smooth

ve•nal [VEEN-l] *adj* guilty of taking, prepared to take, bribes; corrupt **ve•nal'i•ty** *n*

vend *vt* sell **ven•dor** [VEN-dər] *n* **vending machine** one that automatically dispenses goods when money is inserted

ven•det•ta [ven-DET-ə] *n* bitter, prolonged feud

ve•neer [və-NEER] *n* thin layer of fine wood; superficial appearance ▷ *vt* cover with veneer

ven•er•a•ble [VEN-ər-ə-bəl] *adj* worthy of reverence **ven•er•ate** [VEN-ə-rayt] *vt* **-at•ed, -at•ing** look up to, respect, revere **ven•er•a'tion** *n*

ve•ne•re•al [və-NEER-ee-əl] *adj*

(of disease) transmitted by sexual intercourse; infected with venereal disease; of, relating to genitals or sexual intercourse

ven•er•y [VEN-ə-ree] *n obs* pursuit of sexual gratification

Ve•ne•tian [və-NEE-shən] *adj* of Venice, port in NE Italy ▷ *n* native or inhabitant of Venice **Venetian blind** window blind made of thin horizontal slats that turn to let in more or less light

ven•geance [VEN-jəns] *n* revenge; retribution for wrong done **venge'ful** [-fəl] *adj*

ve•ni•al [VEE-nee-əl] *adj* pardonable

ven•i•son [VEN-ə-sən] *n* flesh of deer as food

ven•om [VEN-əm] *n* poison; spite **ven'om•ous** [-əs] *adj* poisonous

venous [VEE-nəs] see **VEIN**

vent¹ *n* small hole or outlet ▷ *vt* give outlet to; utter; pour forth

vent² *n* vertical slit in garment esp at back of jacket

ven•ti•late [VEN-tl-ayt] *vt* **-lat•ed, -lat•ing** supply with fresh air; bring into discussion **ven'ti•la•tor** *n*

ven•tral [VEN-trəl] *adj* abdominal

ven•tri•cle [VEN-tri-kəl] *n* cavity, hollow in body, esp in heart or brain **ven•tric'u•lar** [-TRIK-yə-lər] *adj*

ven•tril•o•quist [ven-TRIL-ə-kwist] *n* one who can so speak that the sounds seem to come from some other person or place **ven•tril'o•quism** *n*

ven•ture [VEN-chər] *v* **-tured, -tur•ing** *vt* expose to hazard; risk ▷ *vi* dare; have courage to do something or go somewhere ▷ *n* risky undertaking; speculative commercial undertaking **ven'ture•some** [-səm] *adj*

ven·ue [VEN-yoo] *n* law district in which case is tried; meeting place; location

Ve·nus [VEE-nəs] *n* Roman goddess of love; planet between Earth and Mercury **Venus's flytrap** insect-eating plant

ve·ra·cious [və-RAY-shəs] *adj* truthful; true **ve·rac·i·ty** [-RAS-i-tee] *n*

ve·ran·da, ve·ran·dah [və-RAN-də] *n* open or partly enclosed porch on outside of house

verb [vurb] *n* part of speech used to express action or being **ver·bal** [VUR-bəl] *adj* of, by, or relating to words spoken rather than written; of, like a verb **ver·bal·ize** *v* **-ized, -iz·ing** put into words, speak **ver·bal·ly** *adv* **ver·ba·tim** [vər-BAY-tim] *adv, adj* word for word, literal

ver·bi·age [VUR-bee-ij] *n* excess of words **ver·bose** [vər-BOHS] *adj* wordy, long-winded **ver·bos·i·ty** [-BOS-i-tee] *n*

ver·dant [VUR-dnt] *adj* green and fresh **ver·dure** [-jər] *n* greenery; freshness

ver·dict [VUR-dikt] *n* decision of a jury; opinion reached after examination of facts

ver·di·gris [VUR-di-grees] *n* green film on copper

verdure [VUR-jər] *see* **VERDANT**

verge [vurj] *n* edge; brink *9 v* **verged, verg·ing** come close to; be on the border of

ver·i·fy [VER-ə-fī] *vt* **-fied, -fy·ing** prove, confirm truth of; test accuracy of **ver·i·fi·a·ble** *adj*

ver·i·si·mil·i·tude [ver-ə-si-MIL-i-tood] *n* appearance of truth; likelihood

ver·i·ta·ble [VER-i-tə-bəl] *adj* actual, true, genuine **ver·i·ta·bly**

adv

ver·i·ty [VER-i-tee] *n, pl* **-ties** truth; reality; true assertion

ver·mi·cide [VUR-mə-sīd] *n* substance to destroy worms **ver·mi·form** *adj* shaped like a worm: *vermiform appendix*

ver·mil·ion [vər-MIL-yən] *adj, n* (of) bright red color or pigment

ver·min [VUR-min] *n* injurious animals, parasites, etc

ver·mouth [vər-MOOTH] *n* wine flavored with aromatic herbs, etc

ver·nac·u·lar [vər-NAK-yə-lər] *n* commonly spoken language or dialect of particular country or place *9 adj* of vernacular; native

ver·nal [VUR-nl] *adj* of spring

ver·ni·er [VUR-nee-ər] *n* sliding scale for obtaining fractional parts of subdivision of graduated scale

ver·sa·tile [VUR-sə-tl] *adj* capable of or adapted to many different uses, skills, etc; liable to change **ver·sa·til·i·ty** *n*

verse [vurs] *n* stanza or short subdivision of poem or the Bible; poetry; line of poetry **ver·si·fy** [VUR-sə-fī] *v* **-fied, -fy·ing** turn into verse **ver·si·fi·ca·tion** *n* **versed in** skilled

ver·sion [VUR-zhən] *n* description from certain point of view; translation; adaptation

ver·so [VUR-soh] *n* back of sheet of printed paper, left-hand page

ver·sus [VUR-səs] *prep* against

ver·te·bra [VUR-tə-brə] *n, pl* **-brae** [-bree] single section of backbone **ver·te·bral** [-brəl] *adj* of the spine **ver·te·brate** [-brit] *n* animal with backbone *9 adj*

ver·tex [VUR-teks] *n, pl* **-ti·ces** [-tə-seez] summit

ver·ti·cal [VUR-ti-kəl] *adj* at right angles to the horizon; upright;

overhead

ver·ti·go [VUR-ti-goh] *n, pl* **-goes** giddiness **ver·tig·i·nous** [vər-TIJ-ə-nəs] *adj* dizzy

verve [vurv] *n* enthusiasm; spirit; energy, vigor

ver·y [VER-ee] *adj* exact, ideal; same; complete; actual ▷ *adv* extremely, to great extent

ves·i·cle [VES-i-kəl] *n* small blister, bubble, or cavity **ve·sic·u·lar** [və-SIK-yə-lər] *adj*

ves·pers [VES-pərz] *pl n* evening church service; evensong

ves·sel [VES-əl] *n* any object used as a container, esp for liquids; ship, large boat; tubular structure conveying liquids (eg blood) in body

vest *n* sleeveless garment worn under jacket or coat ▷ *vt* place; bestow; confer; clothe **vest'ment** [-mənt] *n* robe or official garment **vested interest** strong personal interest in particular state of affairs

ves·tal [VES-tl] *adj* pure, chaste

ves·ti·bule [VES-tə-byool] *n* entrance hall, lobby

ves·tige [VES-tij] *n* small trace, amount **ves·tig'i·al** [-TIJ-ee-əl] *adj*

ves·try [VES-tree] *n, pl* **-tries** room in church for keeping vestments, holding meetings, etc

vet *n* short for VETERINARIAN ▷ *vt* **vet·ted, vet·ting** examine; check

vet·er·an [VET-ər-ən] *n* one who has served a long time, esp in fighting services ▷ *adj* long-serving

vet·er·i·nar·i·an [vet-ər-ə-NAIR-ee-ən] *n* one qualified to treat animal ailments **vet'er·i·nar·y** [-nər-ee] *adj* of, concerning the health of animals ▷ *n* veterinarian

ve·to [VEE-toh] *n, pl* **-toes** power of rejecting piece of legislation, or preventing it from coming into effect; any prohibition ▷ *vt* **-toed, -to·ing** enforce veto against; forbid with authority

vex [veks] *vt* annoy; distress **vex·a·tion** *n* cause of irritation; state of distress **vex·a'tious** *adj* **vexed** *adj* cross; annoyed; much discussed

vi·a [VI-ə] *adv* by way of

vi·a·ble [VI-ə-bəl] *adj* practicable; able to live and grow independently **vi·a·bil'i·ty** *n*

vi·a·duct [VI-ə-dukt] *n* bridge over valley for a road or railroad

Vi·a·gra ® [vi-AG-rə] *n* drug used to treat impotence in men

vi·al [VI-əl] *n* small bottle for medicine, perfume

vi·ands [VI-əndz] *pl n* food esp delicacies

vi·bra·harp [VI-brə-hahrp] *n* musical instrument like xylophone, but with electronic resonators, that produces a gentle vibrato; (also **vi'bra·phone**)

vi·brate [VI-brayt] *v* **-brat·ed, -brat·ing** (cause to) move to and fro rapidly and continuously; give off (light or sound) by vibration ▷ *vi* oscillate; quiver **vibes** *pl n inf* emotional reactions between people; atmosphere of a place **vi'brant** [-brənt] *adj* throbbing; vibrating; appearing vigorous, lively **vi·bra'tion** *n* a vibrating **vi·bra·to** [vi-BRAH-toh] *n, pl* **-os** vibrating effect in music

vic·ar [VIK-ər] *n* member of clergy in charge of parish **vic'ar·age** [-ij] *n* vicar's house **vi·car·i·al** [vī-KAIR-ee-əl] *adj* of vicar

vi·car·i·ous [vī-KAIR-ee-əs] *adj* obtained, enjoyed or undergone through sympathetic experience of another's experiences; suffered, done, etc as substitute for another

vice [vis] n evil or immoral habit or practice; criminal immorality esp prostitution; fault, imperfection

vice- comb form in place of, second to: *vice-chairman; viceroy*

vice·roy [VIS-roi] n ruler acting for king in province or dependency **vice·re·gal** adj

vi·ce ver·sa [VI-sə·VUR-sə] Lat conversely, the other way round

vi·cin·i·ty [vi-SIN-i-tee] n, pl -ties neighborhood

vi·cious [VISH-əs] adj wicked, cruel; ferocious, dangerous; leading to vice

vi·cis·si·tude [vi-SIS-i-tood] n change of fortune; ▷ pl ups and downs of fortune

vic·tim [VIK-tim] n person or thing killed, injured, etc as result of another's deed, or accident, circumstances, etc; person cheated; sacrifice **vic·tim·i·za·tion** [-ZAY-shən] n **vic·tim·ize** vt -mized, -miz·ing punish unfairly; make victim of

vic·tor [VIK-tər] n conqueror; winner **vic·to·ri·ous** [vik-TOR-ee-əs] adj winning; triumphant **vic·to·ry** [-tə-ree] n, pl -ries winning of battle, etc

vict·ual [VIT-l] n (usu in pl) food ▷ vt -ualed, -ual·ing supply with or obtain food

vi·cu·na [vi-KOO-nə] n S Amer animal like llama; fine, light cloth made from its wool

vi·de [VI-dee] Lat see **vide in·fra** [IN-frə] see below **vide su·pra** [SOO-prə] see above

vi·de·li·cet [vi-DEL-ə-sit] Lat namely

vid·e·o [VID-ee-oh] adj relating to or used in transmission or production of TV image ▷ n apparatus for recording TV programs; film, etc on videocassette for viewing on this apparatus **video call** call made via a camera phone, allowing the participants to see each other as they talk **videocassette** cassette containing video tape **videocassette recorder** tape recorder for vision and sound signals, used for recording and playing back TV programs and films on cassette **video game** any of various games played on video screen using electronic control **videotape** magnetic tape on which to record TV program **videotape recorder** tape recorder for signals for TV broadcast **vid·e·o·tex** n means of providing written or graphical representation of computerized information on TV screen for information retrieval, shopping at home, etc

vie [vy] vi **vied, vy·ing** (foll by **with, for**) contend, compete against or for someone, something

view [vyoo] n survey by eyes or mind; range of vision; picture; scene; opinion; purpose ▷ vt look at; survey; consider **view·er** n one who views; one who watches TV; optical device to assist viewing of photographic slides **viewfinder** n device on camera enabling user to see what will be included in photograph **viewpoint** n way of regarding a subject; position commanding view of landscape

vig·il [VIJ-əl] n a keeping awake, watch; eve of church festival **vig·i·lance** [-ləns] n **vig·i·lant** [-lənt] adj watchful, alert

vig·i·lan·te [vij-ə-LAN-tee] n one (esp as member of group) who unofficially takes on duty of enforcing law

vi·gnette [vin-YET] n short literary essay, sketch; photograph or portrait with the background shaded off

vig·or [VIG-ər] n force, strength; energy, activity **vig'or·ous** [-əs] adj strong; energetic; flourishing

Vi·king [Vī-king] n medieval Scandinavian seafarer, raider, settler

vile [vīl] adj **vil·er, vil·est** very wicked, shameful; disgusting; despicable **vil·i·fy** [VIL-ə-fī] vt **-fied, -fy·ing** speak ill of; slander **vil·i·fi·ca'tion** [-fi-KAY-shən] n

vil·la [VIL-ə] n large, luxurious, country house

vil·lage [VIL-ij] n small group of houses in country area

vil·lain [VIL-ən] n wicked person; inf mischievous person **vil'lain·ous** [-əs] adj wicked; vile **vil'lain·y** n, pl **-lain·ies**

vim n force, energy

vin·ai·grette [vin-ə-GRET] n small bottle of smelling salts; type of salad dressing ⊳ adj (of food) served with vinaigrette

vin·di·cate [VIN-di-kayt] vt **-cat·ed, -cat·ing** clear of charges; justify; establish the truth or merit of **vin·di·ca'tion** n

vin·dic·tive [vin-DIK-tiv] adj revengeful; inspired by resentment

vine [vīn] n climbing plant bearing grapes **vine·yard** [VIN-yərd] n plantation of vines **vin·tage** [-tij] n gathering of the grapes; the yield; wine of particular year; time of origin ⊳ adj best and most typical **vint'ner** [-nər] n dealer in wine

vin·e·gar [VIN-i-gər] n acid liquid obtained from wine and other alcoholic liquors **vin'e·gar·y** adj like vinegar; sour; bad-tempered

vi·nyl [Vīn-l] n plastic material with variety of domestic and industrial uses

vi·ol [Vī-əl] n early stringed instrument preceding violin

vi·o·la¹ [vee-OH-lə] n large violin with lower range

vi·o·la² [Vī-OH-lə] n single-colored variety of pansy

vi·o·late [Vī-ə-layt] vt **-lat·ed, -lat·ing** break (law, agreement, etc), infringe; rape; outrage, desecrate **vi'o·la·ble** [-lə-bəl] adj **vi·o·la'tion** [-LAY-shən] n

vi·o·lent [Vī-ə-lənt] adj marked by, due to, extreme force, passion or fierceness; of great force; intense **vi'o·lence** [-lins] n

vi·o·let [Vī-ə-lit] n plant with small bluish-purple or white flowers; the flower; bluish-purple color ⊳ adj of this color

vi·o·lin [Vī-ə-LIN] n small four-stringed musical instrument **vi·o·lin'ist** n **vi·o·lon·cel·lo** [vee-ə-lən-CHEL-oh] n see CELLO

VIP very important person

vi·per [Vī-pər] n venomous snake

vi·ra·go [vi-RAH-goh] n, pl **-goes** or **-gos** abusive woman

vir·gin [VUR-jin] n one who has not had sexual intercourse ⊳ adj without experience of sexual intercourse; unsullied, fresh; (of land) untilled **vir·gin·al** [VUR-jə-nl] adj; of, like virgin ⊳ n type of spinet **vir·gin'i·ty** n

vir·ile [VIR-əl] adj (of male) capable of copulation or procreation; strong, forceful **vi·ril'i·ty** [-RIL-i-tee] n

virology [vi-ROL-ə-jee] see VIRUS

vir·tu·al [VUR-choo-əl] adj so in effect, though not in appearance or name **vir'tu·al·ly** adv practically, almost **virtual reality** computer-generated environment that seems real to the user

vir·tue [VUR-choo] n moral goodness; good quality; merit; inherent power **vir'tu·ous** [-əs] adj morally good; chaste

vir·tu·o·so [vur-choo-OH-soh] n, pl -sos or -si [-see] one with special skill, esp in a fine art **vir·tu·os'i·ty** n great technical skill, esp in a fine art as music

vir·u·lent [VIR-yə-lənt] adj very infectious, poisonous, etc; malicious

vi·rus [VI-rəs] n any of various submicroscopic organisms, some causing disease; computing program that propagates itself, via disks and electronic networks, to cause disruption **vi·rol'o·gy** n study of viruses

vi·sa [VEEZ-ə] n, pl -sas endorsement on passport permitting the bearer to travel to country of issuing government **visa** vt -saed, -sa·ing approve visa for (someone)

vis·age [VIZ-ij] n face

vis·à·vis [vee-zà-VEE] Fr in relation to, regarding; opposite to

vis·cer·a [VIS-ər-ə] pl n large internal organs of body, esp of abdomen **visc'er·al** [-əl] adj

vis·cid [VIS-id] adj sticky, of a consistency like molasses **vis·cid'i·ty** n

vis·cous [VIS-kəs] adj thick and sticky **vis·cos'i·ty** n, pl -ties

vise [vis] n appliance with screw jaw for holding things while working on them

vis·i·ble [VIZ-ə-bəl] adj that can be seen **vis·i·bil'i·ty** n degree of clarity of atmosphere, esp for navigation **vis'i·bly** adv

vi·sion [VIZH-ən] n sight; insight; dream; phantom; imagination **vi'sion·ar·y** [-er-ee] adj marked by vision; impractical ▷ n, pl -ar·ies mystic; impractical person

vis·it [VIZ-it] v go, come and see, stay temporarily with (someone) ▷ n stay; call at person's home, etc; official call **vis·it·a'tion** [-ə-TAY-

shən] n formal visit or inspection; affliction or plague **vis'i·tor** n

vi·sor [VI-zər] n front part of helmet made to move up and down before the face; eyeshade, esp on car; peak on cap

vis·ta [VIS-tə] n view, esp distant view

vis·u·al [VIZH-oo-əl] adj of sight; visible **vis·u·al·ize** vt -ized, -iz·ing form mental image of **vis·u·al·i·za'tion** n

vi·tal [VIT-l] adj necessary to, affecting life; living, animated; essential; highly important **vi'tals** pl n vital organs of body **vi·tal'i·ty** n life, vigor **vi'tal·ize** [-tə-līz] vt -ized, -iz·ing give life to; lend vigor to **vi'tal·ly** adv

vi·ta·min [VI-tə-min] n any of group of substances occurring in foodstuffs and essential to health

vi·ti·ate [VISH-ee-ayt] vt -at·ed, -at·ing spoil; deprive of efficacy; invalidate **vi·ti·a'tion** n

vit·re·ous [VI-tree-əs] adj of glass; glassy **vit·ri·fy** [VI-trə-fī] v -fied, -fy·ing convert into glass, or glassy substance **vit·ri·fi·ca'tion** n

vit·ri·ol [VI-tree-əl] n sulfuric acid; caustic speech **vit·ri·ol'ic** adj

vi·tu·per·ate [vi-TOO-pə-rayt] vt -at·ed, -at·ing abuse in words, revile **vi·tu'per·a·tive** adj

vi·va·cious [vi-VAY-shəs] adj lively, gay, sprightly **vi·vac'i·ty** [-VAS-i-tee] n

vi·va vo·ce [VI-və VOH-see] Lat adj, adv by word of mouth ▷ n in European universities, oral examination

viv·id [VIV-id] adj bright, intense; clear; lively, animated; graphic **viv'id·ly** adv

viv·i·fy [VIV-ə-fī] vt -fied, -fy·ing animate, inspire

vi·vip·a·rous [vi-VIP-ər-əs] *adj* bringing forth young alive

viv·i·sec·tion [viv-ə-SEK-shən] *n* dissection of, or operating on, living animals **viv·i·section·ist** *n*

vix·en [VIK-sən] *n* female fox; spiteful woman **vix·en·ish** *adj*

viz. short for VIDELICET

vi·zier [vi-ZEER] *n* (formerly) high official in some Muslim countries

vo·cab·u·lary [voh-KAB-yə-ler-ee] *n, pl* **-lar·ies** list of words, usu in alphabetical order; stock of words used in particular language, etc

vo·cal [VOH-kəl] *adj* of, with, or giving out voice; outspoken, articulate ▷ *n* piece of popular music that is sung **vo·cal·ist** *n* singer **vo·cal·ize** *vt* **-ized, -iz·ing** utter with voice

vo·ca·tion [voh-KAY-shən] *n* (urge, inclination, predisposition to) particular career, profession, etc **vo·ca·tion·al** [-əl] *adj*

voc·a·tive [VOK-ə-tiv] *n* in some languages, case of nouns used in addressing a person

vo·cif·er·ate [voh-SIF-ə-rayt] *v* **-at·ed, -at·ing** exclaim, cry out **vo·cif·er·ous** [-əs] *adj* shouting, noisy

vod·ka [VOD-kə] *n* Russian spirit distilled from grain, potatoes, etc

vogue [vohg] *n* fashion, style; popularity

voice [vois] *n* sound given out by person in speaking, singing, etc; quality of the sound; expressed opinion; (right to) share in discussion; verbal forms proper to relation of subject and action ▷ *vt* **voiced, voic·ing** give utterance to, express **voice·less** [-lis] *adj* **voice mail** electronic system for recording and storage of telephone messages, which can then be checked later or accessed remotely

void *adj* empty; destitute; not legally binding ▷ *n* empty space ▷ *vt* make ineffectual or invalid; empty out

vol·a·tile [VOL-ə-tl] *adj* evaporating quickly; lively; fickle, changeable **vol·a·til·i·ty** *n* **vol·a·ti·lize** *v* **-lized, -liz·ing** (cause to) evaporate

vol·ca·no [vol-KAY-noh] *n, pl* **-noes, -nos** hole in Earth's crust through which lava, ashes, smoke, etc are discharged; mountain so formed **vol·can·ic** *adj* **vol·can·ol·o·gy** [-kə-NOL-ə-jee] *n* study of volcanoes and volcanic phenomena, vulcanology

vole [vohl] *n* small rodent

vo·li·tion [voh-LISH-ən] *n* act, power of willing; exercise of the will

vol·ley [VOL-ee] *n, pl* **-leys** simultaneous discharge of weapons or missiles; rush of oaths, questions, etc; *tennis* flight, return of moving ball before it touches ground ▷ *v* **-leyed, -ley·ing** discharge; utter; fly, strike etc in volley **vol·ley·ball** *n* team game where large ball is hit by hand over high net

volt [vohlt] *n* unit of electric potential **volt·age** [-ij] *n* electric potential difference expressed in volts **volt·me·ter** *n*

volte-face [vohlt-FAHS] *n, pl* **volte-face** Fr complete reversal of opinion or direction

vol·u·ble [VOL-yə-bəl] *adj* talking easily, readily and at length **vol·u·bly** *adv* **vol·u·bil·i·ty** *n*

vol·ume [VOL-yəm] *n* space occupied; bulk, mass; amount; power, fullness of voice or sound; control on radio, etc for adjusting this; book; part of book bound in one cover **vol·u·met·ric** *adj* pert to measurement by volume

vo·lu·mi·nous [və-LOO-mə-nəs] adj bulky, copious

vol·un·tar·y [VOL-ən-ter-ee] adj having, done by free will; done without payment; supported by freewill contributions; spontaneous ▷ n, pl -**tar·ies** organ solo in church service **vol·un·tar·i·ly** adv **vol·un·teer** n one who offers service, joins force, etc of own free will ▷ v offer oneself or one's services

vo·lup·tu·ous [və-LUP-choo-əs] adj of, contributing to pleasures of the senses **vo·lup·tu·ar·y** [-er-ee] n, pl -**ar·ies** one given to luxury and sensual pleasures

vo·lute [və-LOOT] n spiral or twisting turn, form or object

vom·it v eject (contents of stomach) through mouth ▷ n matter vomited

voo·doo n, pl -**doos** practice of black magic, esp in W Indies, witchcraft ▷ vt -**dooed, -doo·ing** affect by voodoo

vo·ra·cious [vaw-RAY-shəs] adj greedy, ravenous **vo·rac·i·ty** [-RAS-i-tee] n

vor·tex [VOR-teks] n, pl -**ti·ces** [-tə-seez] whirlpool; whirling mass or motion

vo·ta·ry [VOH-tə-ree] n, pl -**ries** one vowed to service or pursuit **vo·tive** [-tiv] adj given, consecrated by vow

vote [voht] n formal expression of choice; individual pronouncement; right to give it, in question or election; result of voting; that which is given or allowed by vote ▷ v **vot·ed, vot·ing** express, declare opinion, choice, preference, etc by vote; authorize, enact, etc by vote

vouch [vowch] vi (with for) guarantee, make oneself responsible for **vouch·er** n document proving

correctness of item in accounts, or to establish facts; ticket as substitute for cash **vouch·safe** [-SAYF] vt -**safed, -saf·ing** agree, condescend to grant or do something

vow n solemn promise, esp religious one ▷ vt promise, threaten by vow

vow·el [VOW-əl] n any speech sound pronounced without stoppage or friction of the breath; letter standing for such sound: a, e, i, o, u

voy·age [VOI-ij] n journey, esp long one, by sea or air ▷ vi -**aged, -ag·ing** make voyage **voy·ag·er** n

vo·yeur [vwah-YUR] n one obtaining sexual pleasure by watching sexual activities of others

vul·can·ize [VUL-kə-nīz] vt -**ized, -iz·ing** treat (rubber) with sulfur at high temperature to increase its durability **vul'can·ite** n rubber so hardened **vul·can·i·za'tion** n **vul·can·ol'o·gy** see **VOLCANOLOGY**

vul·gar [VUL-gər] adj offending against good taste; coarse; common **vul·gar'i·an** [-GAIR-ee-ən] n vulgar (rich) person **vul'gar·ism** n coarse, obscene word, phrase **vul·gar'i·ty** n, pl -**ties** **vul·gar·i·za'tion** [-gə-ri-ZAY-shən] n **vul'gar·ize** vt -**ized, -iz·ing** make vulgar or too common

Vul·gate [VUL-gayt] n fourth-century Latin version of the Bible

vul·ner·a·ble [VUL-nər-ə-bəl] adj capable of being physically or emotionally wounded or hurt; exposed, open to attack, persuasion, etc

vul·pine [VUL-pin] adj of foxes; foxy

vul·ture [VUL-chər] n large bird that feeds on carrion **vul'tur·ous** [-əs] adj of vulture; rapacious

vul·va [VUL-və] n, pl -**vas** external genitals of human female

vy·ing [VĪ-ing] pr p of VIE

through air or water ▷ *n* breath of
wind; odor, whiff

wag *v* **wagged, wag·ging** (cause
to) move rapidly from side to side
▷ *n* instance of wagging; humorous,
witty person **wag'gish** *adj*

wage [wayj] *n* (oftn in pl) payment
for work done ▷ *vt* **waged, wag·ing**
carry on

wa·ger [WAY-jər] *n, vt* bet

wag·on [WAG-ən] *n* four-wheeled
vehicle for heavy loads **off the
wagon** *sl* drinking alcoholic
beverages again **on the wagon** *sl*
abstaining from alcoholic beverages

waif [wayf] *n* homeless person,
esp child

wail [wayl] *v* cry out, lament ▷ *n*
mournful cry

wain·scot [WAYN-skət] *n*
wooden lining of walls of room ▷ *vt*
-scot·ed, -scot·ting line thus

waist [wayst] *n* part of body
between hips and ribs; various
narrow central parts **waist·coat**
[WES-kət] *n brit* vest **waist'line**
n line, size of waist (of person,
garment)

wait [wayt] *v* stay in one place,
remain inactive in expectation
(of something); be prepared for
(something); delay ▷ *vi* serve in
restaurant, etc ▷ *n* act or period
of waiting **wait'er** *n* attendant
serving diners at hotel, restaurant,
etc; one who waits **wait·ress** [WAY-
tris] *n fem*

waive [wayv] *vt* **waived, waiv·ing**
forgo; not to insist on **waiv'er** *n*
(written statement of) this act

wake¹ [wayk] *v* **waked** *or* **woke,
waked** *or* **wok·en, wak·ing** rouse
from sleep; stir up ▷ *n* vigil; watch
beside dead person **wak·en** [WAY-kən] *v*
wake **wake'ful** [-fəl] *adj*

wake² *n* track or path left by

W *chemistry* tungsten

wack·y [WAK-ee] *adj* **wack·i·er,
wack·i·est** *inf* eccentric or funny
wack'i·ness [-nis] *n*

wad [wod] *n* small pad of fibrous
material; thick roll of paper money;
sum of money ▷ *vt* **wad·ded,
wad·ding** line, pad, stuff, etc with
wad **wad'ding** *n* stuffing

wad·dle [WOD-l] *vi* **-dled, -dling**
walk like duck ▷ *n* this gait

wade [wayd] *vi* **wad·ed, wad·ing**
walk through something that
hampers movement, esp water;
proceed with difficulty **wad'er**
n person or bird that wades ▷ *pl*
angler's high waterproof boots

wa·di [WO-dee] *n, pl* **-dis** in the
East, watercourse that is dry except
in wet season

wa·fer [WAY-fər] *n* thin, crisp
biscuit; thin slice of anything; thin
disk of unleavened bread used in the
Eucharist

waf·fle¹ [WOF-əl] *n* kind of batter
cake with gridlike design

waf·fle² *inf vi* **-fled, -fling** speak,
write in vague wordy manner ▷ *n*
vague speech, etc; nonsense

waft [wahft] *vt* convey smoothly

anything that has passed, as track of
turbulent water behind ship

walk [wawk] v (cause, assist to)
move, travel on foot at ordinary pace
▷ vt cross, pass through by walking;
escort, conduct by walking ▷ n act,
instance of walking; path or other
place or route for walking; manner of
walking; occupation, career **walk'er**
n one who walks; framework of
metal for support while walking
walk·ie·talk·ie [WAW-kee-TAWK-
kee] n portable radio set containing
both transmission and receiver
units **walking stick** stick, cane
carried while walking **Walk·man ®**
[WAWK-man] n small portable
cassette player, radio, etc equipped
with headphones **walk'out** n
strike; act of leaving as a protest
walk'o·ver n unopposed or easy
victory

wall [wawl] n structure of brick,
stone, etc serving as fence, side
of building, etc; surface of one;
anything resembling this ▷ vt
enclose with wall; block up with
wall **wall'flow·er** n garden flower,
often growing on walls; at dance,
person who remains seated for lack
of partner **wall'pa·per** n paper, usu
patterned, to cover interior walls

wal·la·by [WOL-ə-bee] n, pl-bies
Aust marsupial similar to and smaller
than kangaroo

wal·let [WOL-it] n small
folding case, esp for paper money,
documents, etc

wall·eyed [WAWL-īd] adj having
eyes turned outward in squint;
having eyes with pale irises

wal·lop [WOL-əp] inf vt beat
soundly; strike hard ▷ n stroke
or blow **wal'lop·er** n inf one
who wallops **wal'lop·ing** inf n
thrashing ▷ adj, adv very, great(ly)

wal·low [WOL-oh] vi roll (in liquid
or mud); revel (in) ▷ n

wal·nut [WAWL-nut] n large nut
with crinkled shell splitting easily
into two halves; the tree; its wood

wal·rus [WAWL-rəs] n large sea
mammal with long tusks

waltz [wawlts] n ballroom dance;
music for it ▷ v

wam·pum [WOM-pəm] n beads
made of shells, formerly used by
N Amer Indians as money and for
ornament

wan [won] adj **wan·ner, wan·nest**
pale, sickly complexioned; pallid

wand [wond] n stick, usu straight
and slender, esp as carried by
magician, etc

wan·der [WON-dər] v roam,
ramble ▷ vi go astray, deviate ▷ n
wan'der·er n **wan'der·lust** n
irrepressible urge to wander or travel

wane [wayn] vi, n **waned, wan·ing**
decline; (of moon) decrease in size

wan·gle [WANG-gəl] vt -gled,
-gling inf manipulate, manage in
skillful way

want [wont] v desire; lack ▷ n
desire; need; deficiency **want'ed**
[-id] adj being sought, esp by the
police **want'ing** adj lacking; below
standard

wan·ton [WON-tən] adj dissolute;
without motive, thoughtless;
unrestrained ▷ n wanton person

war [wor] n fighting between
nations; state of hostility; conflict,
contest ▷ vi **warred, war·ring**
make war **war'like** adj of, for war;
fond of war **war·ri·or** [WOR-ee-
ər] n fighter **war cry** cry used by
attacking troops in war; distinctive
word, phrase used by political party,
etc **war'fare** [-fair] n hostilities
war'head [-hed] n part of
missile, etc containing explosives

war•mon•ger [WOR-mung-gàr] n one fostering, encouraging war

war'ship n vessel armed, armored for naval warfare

war•ble [WOR-bàl] vi -bled, -bling sing with trills **war•bler** [-blàr] n person or bird that warbles; any of various kinds of small songbirds

ward [word] n division of city, hospital, etc; minor under care of guardian; guardianship; curved bar in lock, groove in key that prevents incorrectly cut key opening lock **ward'room** n officers' mess on warship **ward off** avert, repel

war•den [WOR-dn] n person, officer in charge of prison

ward•robe [WOR-drohb] n piece of furniture for hanging clothes in; person's supply of clothes; costumes of theatrical company

ware [wair] n goods; articles collectively ▷ pl goods for sale; commodities; merchandise **ware'house** n storehouse for goods prior to distribution and sale ▷ vt store for future shipment or use

war•lock [WOR-lok] n wizard, sorcerer

warm [worm] adj moderately hot; serving to maintain heat; affectionate; ardent; earnest; hearty; (of color) having yellow or red for a basis ▷ v make, become warm **warm'ly** adv **warmth** n mild heat; cordiality; vehemence, anger

warn [worn] vt put on guard; caution, admonish; give advance information to; notify authoritatively **warn'ing** n hint of harm, etc; admonition; advance notice of

warp [worp] v (cause to) twist (out of shape); pervert or be perverted ▷ n state, condition of being warped; lengthwise threads on loom

war•rant [WOR-ànt] n authority; document giving authority ▷ vt guarantee; authorize, justify **war•ran•tee'** n person given warranty **war'ran•tor** [-tàr] n person, company giving warranty **war'ran•ty** [-tee] n, pl -ties guarantee of quality of goods; security **warrant officer** officer in certain armed services holding rank between commissioned and noncommissioned officer

war•ren [WOR-àn] n (burrows inhabited by) colony of rabbits

warrior [WOR-ee-àr] n see WAR

wart [wort] n small hard growth on skin **wart hog** kind of Afr wild pig

war•y [WAIR-ee] adj **war•i•er, war•i•est** watchful, cautious, alert **war'i•ly** adv

was [wuz, woz] v first and third person sing pt of BE

wash [wosh] v clean (oneself, clothes, etc) esp with water, soap, etc ▷ vi be washable; inf able to be proved true ▷ vt move, be moved by water; flow, sweep over, against ▷ n act of washing; clothes washed at one time; sweep of water, esp set up by moving ship; thin coat of color **wash'a•ble** adj capable of being washed without damage, etc **wash'er** n one who, that which, washes; ring put under a nut **wash'ing** n clothes to be washed **wash'y** adj **wash•i•er, wash•i•est** dilute; watery; insipid **wash'out** n rainout; inf complete failure

wasp [wosp] n striped stinging insect resembling bee **wasp'ish** adj irritable, snappish **wasp waist** very small waist

waste [wayst] v **wast•ed, wast•ing** ▷ vt expend uselessly, use extravagantly; fail to take advantage of; lay desolate ▷ vi dwindle; pine

away ▷ *n* act of wasting; what is
wasted; desert ▷ *adj* worthless,
useless; desert; wasted **wast·age**
[WAY-stij] *n* loss by use or decay;
losses as result of wastefulness
waste'ful [-fəl] *adj* extravagant
waste'ful·ness [-nis] *n* waste
product discarded material in
manufacturing process; excreted
urine, feces **wast·rel** [WAY-strəl] *n*
wasteful person, spendthrift
watch [woch] *vt* observe closely;
guard ▷ *vi* wait expectantly (for); be
on watch ▷ *n* portable timepiece
for wrist, pocket, etc; state of being
on the lookout; guard; spell of duty
watch'ful [-fəl] *adj* **watch'mak·er**
n one skilled in making and repairing
watches **watch'man** [-mən] *n, pl*
-men person guarding building, etc,
esp at night **watch'word** [-wurd] *n*
password; rallying cry
wa·ter [WAW-tər] *n* transparent,
colorless, odorless, tasteless liquid,
substance of rain, river, etc; body
of water; river; lake; sea; tear; urine
▷ *vt* put water on or into; irrigate or
provide with water ▷ *vi* salivate; (of
eyes) fill with tears; take in or obtain
water **wa'ter·y** *adj* **water buffalo**
oxlike Asian animal **water closet**
[KLOZ-it] toilet **wa'ter·col·or** *n*
pigment mixed with water; painting
in this **wa'ter·course** *n* stream
wa'ter·cress *n* plant growing in
clear ponds and streams **wa'ter·fall**
n perpendicular descent of waters
of river, stream **wa'ter·logged**
adj saturated, filled with water
wa'ter·mark *n* faint translucent
design stamped on substance of
sheet of paper **wa'ter·proof** *adj* not
letting water through ▷ *vt* make
waterproof **wa'ter·shed** *n* area
drained by a river; important division
between conditions, phases **water-**

ski·ing *n* sport of riding over water
on ski towed by speedboat **water
sports** various sports, as swimming,
windsurfing, that take place in or
on water **water·tight** [-tīt] *adj* so
fitted as to prevent water entering
or escaping; with no loopholes or
weak points
watt [wot] *n* unit of electric power
watt'age [-ij] *n* electric power
expressed in watts
wat·tle [WOT-l] *n* fleshy pendent
lobe on head or neck of certain birds,
eg turkey
wave [wayv] *v* **waved, wav·ing**
move to and fro, as hand in greeting
or farewell; signal by waving; give,
take shape of waves (as hair, etc) ▷ *n*
ridge and trough on water, etc; act,
gesture of waving; vibration, as in
radio waves, of electric and magnetic
forces alternating in direction;
prolonged spell of something;
upsurge; wavelike shapes in the
hair, etc **wav'y** [-ee] *adj* **wav·i·er,
wav·i·est wave'length** *n* distance
between same points of two
successive sound waves
wav·er [WAY-vər] *vi* hesitate, be
irresolute; be, become unsteady
wax¹ [waks] *n* yellow, soft, pliable
material made by bees; this or
similar substance used for sealing,
making candles, etc; waxy secretion
of ear ▷ *vt* **waxed, wax·ing** put
wax on **wax'y** [-ee] *adj* **wax·i·er,
wax·i·est** like wax **wax'wing** *n*
small songbird **wax'work** [-wurk] *n*
lifelike figure, esp of famous person,
reproduced in wax
wax² *vi* **waxed, wax·ing** grow,
increase
way *n* manner; method; means;
track; direction; path; passage;
course; route; progress; state or
condition **way'far·er** [-fair-ər]

n traveler, esp on foot **way·lay** *vt* **-laid, -lay·ing** lie in wait for and accost, attack **way'side** *n* side or edge of a road ▷ *adj* **way'ward** [-wàrd] *adj* capricious, perverse, willful **way'ward·ness** [-nis] *n*

we [wee] *pron* first person plural pronoun

weak [week] *adj* **-er, -est** lacking strength; feeble; fragile; delicate; easily influenced; faint **weak·en** [WEE-kàn] *v* **weak'ling** *n* feeble creature **weak'ly** *adj* weak; sickly ▷ *adv*

wealth [welth] *n* riches; abundance **wealth'y** *adj* **wealth·i·er, wealth·i·est**

wean [ween] *vt* accustom to food other than mother's milk; win over, coax away from

weap·on [WEP-àn] *n* implement to fight with; anything used to get the better of an opponent **weap'on·ry** [-ree] *n*

wear [wair] *v* **wore, worn, wear·ing** ▷ *vt* have on the body; show; produce (hole, etc) by rubbing, etc; harass or weaken ▷ *vi* last; become impaired by use; (of time) pass slowly ▷ *n* act of wearing; things to wear; damage caused by use; ability to resist effects of constant use

wea·ry [WEER-ee] *adj* **-ri·er, -ri·est** tired, exhausted, jaded; tiring; tedious ▷ *v* **-ried, -ry·ing** make, become weary **wea'ri·ness** [-ree-nis] *n* **wea'ri·some** [-ree-sàm] *adj* causing weariness

wea·sel [WEE-zàl] *n* small carnivorous mammal with long body and short legs

weath·er [WETH-àr] *n* day-to-day meteorological conditions, esp temperature, cloudiness, etc of a place ▷ *adj* toward the wind ▷ *vt* affect by weather; endure; resist; come safely through; sail to windward of **weath'er·vane** [-vain] *n* rotating vane to show which way wind blows

weave [weev] *v* **wove** or **weaved, wo·ven** or **wove, weav·ing** ▷ *vt* form into texture or fabric by interlacing, esp on loom; fashion, construct ▷ *vi* become woven; make one's way, esp with side to side motion **weav'er** [-àr] *n*

web *n* woven fabric; net spun by spider; membrane between toes of waterfowl, frogs, etc **the Web** short for **WORLD WIDE WEB web address** another name for **URL web'bing** *n* strong fabric woven in strips **web'cam** *n* camera that transmits images over the Internet **web'cast** *n* broadcast of an event over the Internet **web'log** *n* person's online journal **web'mail** *n* system of electronic mail that allows account holders to access their mail via an Internet site **web'site** *n* group of pages on the World Wide Web with a single address

web·er [WEB-àr] *n* SI unit of magnetic flux

wed *vt* **wed·ded, wed·ding** marry; unite closely **wedding** *n* act of marrying, nuptial ceremony **wed'lock** *n* marriage

wedge [wej] *n* piece of wood, metal, etc, thick at one end, tapering to a thin edge ▷ *vt* **wedged, wedg·ing** fasten, split with wedge; stick by compression or crowding

weed *n* plant growing where undesired; *inf* tobacco; *sl* marijuana; thin, sickly person, animal ▷ *vt* clear of weeds **weed'y** *adj* **weed·i·er, weed·i·est** full of weeds; thin, weakly **weed out** remove, eliminate what is unwanted

weeds [weedz] *pl n obs* (widow's) mourning clothes

week *n* period of seven days, esp one beginning on Sunday and ending on Saturday; hours, days of work in seven-day period **week'ly** *adj, adv* happening, done, published, etc once a week ▷ *n* newspaper or magazine published once a week **week'day** *n* any day of week except Sunday and usu Saturday **week'end** *n* (at least) Saturday and Sunday, esp considered as rest period

weep *v* **wept, weeping** shed tears (for); grieve **weep'y** *adj* **weep·i·er, weep·i·est weeping willow** willow with drooping branches

wee·vil [WEE-vəl] *n* small beetle harmful to cotton, etc

weft *n* cross threads in weaving, woof

weigh [way] *vt* find weight of; consider; raise (anchor) ▷ *vi* have weight; be burdensome **weight** *n* measure of the heaviness of an object; quality of heaviness; heavy mass; object of known mass for weighing; unit of measurement of weight; importance, influence ▷ *vt* add weight to **weight'y** *adj* **weight·i·er, weight·i·est** heavy; onerous; important; momentous

weir [weer] *n* small dam in river or stream; fence or net in stream, etc for catching fish

weird [weerd] *adj* **-er, -est** unearthly, uncanny; strange, bizarre

wel·come [WEL-kəm] *adj* received gladly; freely permitted ▷ *n, interj* kindly greeting ▷ *vt* **-comed, -com·ing** greet with pleasure; receive gladly

weld *vt* unite metal by softening with heat; unite closely ▷ *n* welded joint **weld'er** *n* person who welds; machine used in welding

weld'ment [-mənt] *n* welded assembly

wel·fare [WEL-fair] *n* well-being **welfare state** system in which the government takes responsibility for the social, economic, etc security of its citizens

well[1] *adv* in good manner or degree; suitably; intimately; fully; favorably, kindly; to a considerable degree ▷ *adj* **bet·ter, best** in good health; suitable ▷ *interj* exclamation of surprise, interrogation, etc **well-being** *n* state of being well, happy, or prosperous **well-disposed** *adj* inclined to be friendly, kindly (toward) **well-mannered** *adj* having good manners **well-off** *adj* fairly rich **well-read** [-red] *adj* having read much **well-spoken** *adj* speaking fluently, graciously, aptly **well-to-do** *adj* moderately wealthy

well[2] *n* hole sunk into the earth to reach water, gas, oil, etc; spring; any shaft like a well ▷ *vi* spring, gush

Welsh *adj* of Wales ▷ *n* language, people of Wales **Welsh rabbit, rarebit** dish of melted cheese, beer, spices on toast

welsh *vi* inf fail to pay debt or fulfill obligation; (also **welch**) **welsh'er** [-ər] **welch·er** [WELCH-ər] *n*

welt *n* raised, strengthened seam; weal ▷ *vt* provide with welt; thrash

wel·ter [WEL-tər] *vi* roll or tumble ▷ *n* turmoil, disorder

wel·ter·weight [WEL-tər-wayt] *n* boxing weight between light and middle; boxer of this weight

wen *n* cyst, esp on scalp

wench *n obs, now facetious* young woman

wend *v* go, travel

went *pt* of **go**

wept *pt/pp* of **weep**

were [wur] past indicative, plural

and subjunctive sing and pl of **BE**

were·wolf [WAIR-wuulf] n, pl **-wolves** (in folklore) human being turned into wolf

west n part of sky where sun sets; part of country, region etc to this side; occident ▷ adj that is toward or in this region ▷ adv to the west **west·er·ly** [-ǝr-lee] adj **west·ward** [-wǝrd] adj, adv **west·ward(s)** adv toward the west **west·ern** [-ǝrn] adj of, in the west ▷ n (in film, story, etc about cowboys or frontiersmen in western US **go west** inf die

wet adj **wet·ter, wet·test** having water or other liquid on a surface or being soaked in it; rainy; not yet dry (paint, ink, etc) ▷ v **wet** or **wet·ted, wet·ting** make wet ▷ n moisture, rain **wet blanket** one depressing spirits of others **wet·land** [-lǝnd] n area of swamp or marsh **wet nurse** woman suckling another's child **wet suit** close-fitting rubber suit worn by divers, etc

whack [hwak] vt strike with sharp resounding blow ▷ n such blow; sl share; inf attempt **whack·ing** adj inf big, enormous

whale [hwayl] n large fish-shaped sea mammal **whal·er** n person, ship employed in hunting whales **whale·bone** n horny elastic substance from projections of upper jaw of certain whales **whal·ing** n a **whale of a time** inf very enjoyable time

wharf [hworf] n platform at harbor, on river, etc for loading and unloading ships

what [hwut, hwot] pron which thing; that which; request for statement to be repeated ▷ adj which; as much as; how great, surprising, etc ▷ interj exclamation

---

of surprise, anger, etc **what·ev·er** pron anything which; of what kind it may be **what·not** n small stand with shelves; something, anything of same kind

wheat [hweet] n cereal plant with thick four-sided seed spikes of which bread is chiefly made **wheat·en** [-ǝn] adj **wheat germ** [-jurm] embryo of wheat kernel

whee·dle [HWEED-l] v **-dled, -dling** coax, cajole

wheel [hweel] n circular frame or disk (with spokes) revolving on axle; anything like a wheel in shape or function; act of turning; steering wheel ▷ v (cause to) turn as if on axis; (cause to) move on or as if on wheels; (cause to) change course, esp in opposite direction **wheel·bar·row** [-ba-roh] n barrow with one wheel **wheel·base** [-bays] n distance between front and rear hubs of vehicle **wheel·chair** n chair mounted on large wheels, used by people who cannot walk

wheeze [hweez] vi **wheezed, wheez·ing** breathe with difficulty and whistling noise ▷ n this sound; story, etc told too often **wheez·y** [-ee] adj **wheez·i·er, wheez·i·est**

whelp [hwelp] n pup, cub ▷ v produce whelps

when [hwen] adv at what time ▷ conj at the time that; although; since ▷ pron at which (time) **when·ev·er** adv, conj at whatever time

whence [hwens] adv, conj obs from what place or source; how

where [hwair] adv, conj at what place; at or to the place in which **where'a·bouts** adv, conj in what, which place ▷ n present position **where·as'** conj considering that; while, on the contrary **where·by'**

[-Bi] *conj* by which **where·fore**
adv obs why ▷ *conj* consequently
where·up·on' *conj* at which point
wher·ev'er *adv* at whatever place
where·with·al [-with-awl] *n*
necessary funds, resources, etc
whet [hwet] *vt* **whet·ted,**
whetting sharpen; stimulate
whet'stone *n* stone for sharpening
tools

wheth·er [HWETH-ər] *conj*
introduces the first of two
alternatives, of which the second
may be expressed or implied

whey [hway] *n* watery part of milk
left after separation of curd in cheese
making

which [hwich] *adj* used in requests
for a selection from alternatives
▷ *pron* which person or thing; the
thing *who* **which·ev'er** *pron*

whiff [hwif] *n* brief smell or
suggestion of; puff of air ▷ *v* smell

while [hwil] *conj* in the time that;
in spite of the fact that, although;
whereas ▷ *vt* **whiled, whil·ing** pass
(time, usu idly) ▷ *n* period of time

whim [hwim] *n* sudden,
passing fancy **whim'si·cal** [-zi-
kəl] *adj* fanciful; full of whims
whim·si·cal'i·ty [-zi-KAL-i-tee] *n*,
pl **-ties whim'sy** [-zee] *n*, *pl* **-sies**
whim; caprice

whim·per [HWIM-pər] *vi* cry or
whine softly; complain in this way
▷ *n* such cry or complaint

whine [hwin] *n* high-pitched
plaintive cry; peevish complaint ▷ *vi*
whined, whin·ing utter this

whin·ny [HWIN-ee] *vi* **-nied,**
-ny·ing neigh softly ▷ *n*

whip [hwip] *v* **whipped, whip·ping**
▷ *vt* strike with whip; thrash; beat
(cream, eggs) to a froth; lash; pull,
remove, quickly ▷ *vi* dart ▷ *n*
lash attached to handle for urging

or punishing; one who enforces
attendance, voting, etc of political
party; elastic quality permitting
bending in mast, fishing rod, etc;
whipped dessert **whip'lash** *n* injury
to neck as result of sudden jerking of
unsupported head **whipping boy**
scapegoat

whip·pet [HWIP-it] *n* racing dog
like small greyhound

whir [hwur] *v* **whirred, whir·ring**
(cause to) fly, spin, etc with buzzing
or whizzing sound; bustle ▷ *n* this
sound

whirl [hwurl] *v* swing rapidly
around; move rapidly in a circular
course; drive at high speed ▷ *n*
whirling movement; confusion,
bustle, giddiness **whirl'pool** *n*
circular current, eddy **whirl'wind** *n*
wind whirling around while moving
forward ▷ *adj*

whisk [hwisk] *v* brush, sweep,
beat lightly; move, remove, quickly;
beat to a froth ▷ *n* light brush;
eggbeating implement

whisk·er [HWIS-kər] *n* any of the
long stiff hairs at side of mouth of
cat or other animal; any of hairs on a
man's face **by a whisker** only just

whis·key [HWIS-kee] *n*, *pl* **-keys**
alcoholic liquor distilled from
fermented cereals **whis'ky** *n*, *pl* **-kies**
Scotch or Canadian whiskey

whis·per [HWIS-pər] *v* speak
in soft, hushed tones, without
vibration of vocal cords; rustle ▷ *n*
such speech; trace or suspicion;
rustle

whist [hwist] *n* card game

whis·tle [HWIS-əl] *v* **-tled, -tling**
▷ *vi* produce shrill sound by forcing
breath through rounded, nearly
closed lips; make such a sound ▷ *vt*
utter, summon, etc by whistle ▷ *n*
such sound; any similar sound;

instrument to make it **whis•tler** [HWIS-lər] n **whistle-blower** n person who informs on or puts stop to something

whit [hwit] n **not a whit** not the slightest amount

white [hwit] adj **whit•er, whit•est** of the color of snow; pale; light in color; having a light-colored skin ▷ n color of snow; white pigment; white part; clear fluid round yolk of egg; Caucasian person **whit'en** [-ən] v **white ant** termite **white-collar** adj denoting nonmanual salaried workers **white elephant** useless, unwanted, gift or possession **white flag** white banner or cloth used as signal of surrender or truce **white hope** one (formerly, a white person) expected to bring honor or glory to his group, team, etc **white lie** minor, unimportant lie **white paper** government report on matter recently investigated **white slave** woman, child forced or enticed away for purposes of prostitution **white'wash** [-wosh] n substance for whitening walls, etc ▷ vt apply this; cover up, gloss over, suppress

whith•er [HWITH-ər] adv to what place; to which

whit•tle [HWIT-l] vt **-tled, -tling** cut, carve with knife; pare away **whittle down** reduce gradually, wear (away)

whiz [hwiz] n loud hissing sound; inf person skillful at something ▷ v **whizzed, whiz•zing** move with such sound, or make it; inf move quickly **take a whizz** inf urinate

who [hoo] pron relative and interrogative pronoun, always referring to persons **who•dun'it** n inf detective story **who•ev'er** pron who, any one or every one that

whole [hohl] adj complete;

containing all elements or parts; entire; not defective or imperfect; healthy ▷ n complete thing or system **whol'ly** adv sincere; enthusiastic **whole'sale** [-sayl] n sale of goods in large quantities to retailers ▷ adj dealing by wholesale; extensive ▷ vt **-saled, -sal•ing wholesal•er** n **whole'some** [-səm] adj producing good effect, physically or morally **whole-wheat** adj of, pert to flour that contains the complete wheat kernel **on the whole** taking everything into consideration; in general

whom [hoom] pron objective case of WHO

whoop [hwuup] n shout or cry expressing excitement, etc **whoop•ee** [HWUUP-ee] n inf gay, riotous time **make whoopee** participate in wild noisy party; go on spree

whoop•ing cough [HUUP-ing] n infectious disease of mucous membrane lining air passages, marked by convulsive coughing with loud whoop or indrawing of breath

whop•per [HWOP-ər] n inf anything unusually large; monstrous lie **whop'ping** adj

whore [hor] n prostitute

whorl [hwurl] n ring of leaves or petals; turn of spiral; anything forming part of circular pattern, eg lines of human fingerprint

whose [hooz] pron of whom or of which

why [hwi] adv for what cause or reason

wick [wik] n strip of thread feeding flame of lamp or candle with oil, grease, etc

wick•ed [WIK-id] adj evil, sinful;

very bad; mischievous **wick·ed·ness** [-nis] n

wick·er [WIK-ər] n woven cane, etc basketwork; (also **wick·er·work**)

wick·et [WIK-it] n small window, gate; croquet wire arch

wide [wīd] adj **wid·er, wid·est** having a great extent from side to side, broad; having considerable distance between; spacious; liberal; vast; far from the mark; opened fully ▷ adv to the full extent; far from the intended target **wi·den** [WĪD-n] v **width** n breadth **wide'spread** [-spred] adj extending over a wide area

wid·ow [WID-oh] n woman whose husband is dead and who has not married again ▷ vt make a widow of **wid'ow·er** n man whose wife is dead and who has not married again **wid'ow·hood** [-huud] n

wield [weeld] vt hold and use; brandish; manage

wife [wīf] n, pl **wives** a man's partner in marriage, married woman **wife'ly** adj

Wi-Fi [Wī-fī] n system of wireless access to the Internet

wig n artificial hair for the head **wigged** adj

wig·gle [WIG-əl] v **-gled, -gling** (cause to) move jerkily from side to side ▷ n **wiggle room** scope for freedom of action or thought

wig·wam [WIG-wom] n Native American's tent

wild [wīld] adj **-er, -est** not tamed or domesticated; not cultivated; savage; stormy; uncontrolled; random; excited; rash; frantic; (of party, etc) rowdy, unrestrained **wild'ly** adv **wild'ness** [-nis] n **wild'cat** n any of various undomesticated feline animals; wild, savage person ▷ adj unsound,

irresponsible; sudden, unofficial, unauthorized **wildcat strike** strike called without sanction of labor union **wild-goose chase** futile pursuit **wild'life** n wild animals and plants collectively

wil·der·ness [WIL-dər-nis] n desert, waste place; state of desolation or confusion

wild·fire [WĪLD-fīr] n raging, uncontrollable fire; anything spreading, moving fast

wile [wīl] n trick **wil'y** adj **wil·i·er, wil·i·est** crafty, sly

will v aux, pt **would** [wuud] forms moods and tenses indicating intention or conditional result ▷ vi have a wish ▷ vt wish; intend; leave as legacy ▷ n faculty of deciding what one will do; purpose; volition; determination; wish; directions written for disposal of property after death **will'ing** adj ready; given cheerfully **will'ing·ly** adv **will'ing·ness** [-nis] n **will'pow·er** n ability to control oneself, one's actions, impulses

will·ful [WIL-fəl] adj obstinate, self-willed; intentional **will'ful·ness** [-nis] n

will-o'-the-wisp [WIL-ə-thə-WISP] n brief pale flame or phosphorescence sometimes seen over marshes; elusive person or hope

wil·low [WIL-oh] n tree, such as **weeping willow**, with long thin flexible branches; its wood **wil'low·y** adj lithe, slender, supple

wil·ly-nil·ly [WIL-ee-NIL-ee] adv, adj (occurring) whether desired or not

wilt v (cause to) become limp, drooping or lose strength, etc

wimp n inf feeble, ineffective person

wim·ple [WIM-pəl] n garment worn by nun, around face

win *v* **won, win·ning** ⊳ *vi* be successful, victorious ⊳ *vt* get by labor or effort; reach; lure; be successful in; gain the support, consent, etc of ⊳ *n* victory, esp in games **winning** *adj* charming **winnings** *pl n* sum won in game, betting, etc **win-win** *adj* guaranteeing a favourable outcome for everyone involved

wince [wins] *vi* **winced, winc·ing** flinch, draw back, as from pain, etc ⊳ *n* this act

winch *n* machine for hoisting or hauling using cable wound around drum ⊳ *vt* move (something) by using a winch

wind¹ *n* air in motion; breath; flatulence; idle talk; hint or suggestion; scent borne by air ⊳ *vt* **wind·ed, wind·ing** render short of breath, esp by blow, etc; get the scent of **wind·ward** [-wərd] *n* side against which wind is blowing **wind'y** *adj* **wind·i·er, wind·i·est** exposed to wind; talking too much **wind'fall** *n* unexpected good luck; fallen fruit **wind instrument** musical instrument played by blowing or air pressure **wind'mill** *n* wind-driven apparatus with fanlike sails for raising water, crushing grain, etc **wind'pipe** *n* passage from throat to lungs **wind'shield** [-sheeld] *n* protective sheet of glass, etc in front of driver or pilot **wind'sock** *n* cone of material flown on mast at airfield to indicate wind direction **wind'surf·ing** *n* sport of sailing standing up on sailboard holding special boom to control sail

wind² [wīnd] *v* **wound** [wownd] **wind·ing** ⊳ *vi* twine; meander ⊳ *vt* twist around, coil; wrap; make ready for working by tightening spring ⊳ *n* act of winding; single turn of something wound; a turn, curve

wind·lass [WIND-ləs] *n* winch, esp simple one worked by a crank

win·dow [WIN-doh] *n* hole in wall (with glass) to admit light, air, etc; anything similar in appearance or function; area for display of goods behind glass of store front **window dressing** arrangement of goods in a shop window; deceptive display

wine [wīn] *n* fermented juice of grape, etc **wine'press** *n* apparatus for extracting juice from grape

wing *n* feathered limb a bird uses in flying; one of organs of flight of insect or some animals; main lifting surface of aircraft; lateral extension; side portion of building projecting from main central portion; one of sides of stage; flank corps of army on either side; part of car body that surrounds wheels; administrative, tactical unit of air force; faction esp of political party ⊳ *pl* insignia worn by qualified aircraft pilot; sides of stage ⊳ *vi* fly; move, go very fast ⊳ *vt* disable, wound slightly **wing'span** *n* distance between the wing tips of an aircraft, bird, or insect

wink [wingk] *v* close and open (an eye) rapidly, esp to indicate friendliness or as signal; twinkle ⊳ *n* act of winking

win·now [WIN-oh] *vt* blow free of chaff; sift, examine

win·some [WIN-səm] *adj* charming, winning **win'some·ly** *adv*

win·ter [WIN-tər] *n* the coldest season ⊳ *vi* pass, spend the winter **win'try** *adj* **-tri·er, -tri·est** of, like winter; cold

wipe [wīp] *vt* **wiped, wip·ing** rub so as to clean ⊳ *n* wiping **wi'per** *n* one that wipes; automatic wiping apparatus (esp windshield wiper) **wipe out** erase; annihilate; *inf* kill; *sl* beat decisively **wiped-out** *adj* exhausted; intoxicated **wipe'out** *n inf* murder; complete defeat

wire [wīr] *n* metal drawn into thin, flexible strand; something made of wire, eg fence; telegram ▷ *vt* **wired, wir•ing** provide, fasten with wire; send by telegraph **wired** *adj sl* excited or nervous; using computers and the Internet to send and receive information **wiring** *n* system of wires **wir'y** *adj* **wir•i•er, wir•i•est** like wire; lean and tough **wire-haired** *adj* (of various breeds of dog) with short stiff hair

wire-less [wīR-lis] *n obs* term for RADIO *or* RADIO SET ▷ *adj* not requiring wires

wise[1] [wīz] *adj* having intelligence and knowledge; sensible **wis•dom** [WIZ-dàm] *n* (accumulated) knowledge, learning; erudition **wise'ly** *adv* **wise'a•cre** *n* one who wishes to seem wise **wisdom tooth** third molar usually cut about 20th year

wise[2] *n obs* manner

wise-crack [WĪZ-krak] *n inf* flippant (would-be) clever remark

wish *vi* have a desire ▷ *vt* desire ▷ *n* desire; thing desired **wish'ful** [-fàl] *adj* desirous; too optimistic **wish'bone** *n* V-shaped bone above breastbone of fowl

wisp *n* light, delicate streak, as of smoke; twisted handful, usu of straw, etc; stray lock of hair **wisp'y** *adj* **wisp•i•er, wisp•i•est**

wist-ful [WIST-fàl] *adj* longing, yearning; sadly pensive **wist'ful•ly** *adv*

wit *n* ingenuity in connecting amusingly incongruous ideas; person gifted with this power;

sense; intellect; understanding; ingenuity; humor **wit'ti•cism** [-ti-sizm] *n* witty remark **wit'ti•ly** *adv* **wit'ting•ly** *adv* on purpose; knowingly **wit'less** [-lis] *adj* foolish **wit'ty** *adj* **-ti•er, -ti•est**

witch [wich] *n* person, usu female, believed to practice, practicing, or professing to practice (black) magic, sorcery; ugly, wicked woman; fascinating woman **witch'craft** *n* **witch doctor** in certain societies, person appearing to cure or cause injury, disease by magic

with [with] *prep* in company or possession of; against; in relation to; through; by means of **with•al** [with-AWL] *adv* also, likewise **with•in'** *prep, adv*, inside **with•out'** *prep* lacking; *obs* outside

with•draw [with-DRAW] *v* **-drew, -drawn, -draw•ing** draw back or out **with•draw'al** *n* **with•drawn'** *adj* reserved, unsociable

with•er [WITH-àr] *v* (cause to) wilt, dry up, decline **with'er•ing** *adj* (of glance, etc) scornful

with•ers [WITH-àrz] *pl n* ridge between a horse's shoulder blades

with•hold [with-HOHLD] *vt* **-held, -hold•ing** restrain; keep back; refrain from giving

with•stand' *v* **-stood** [-stuud] **-stand•ing** oppose, resist, esp successfully

wit•ness [WIT-nis] *n* one who sees something; testimony; one who gives testimony ▷ *vi* give testimony ▷ *vt* see; attest; see and sign as having seen

wiz•ard [WIZ-àrd] *n* sorcerer, magician; conjurer **wiz'ard•ry** *n*

wiz•ened [WIZ-ànd] *adj* shriveled, wrinkled

WMD weapon(s) of mass destruction: nuclear, chemical, or biological weapons that can cause death or injury on a large scale

wob·ble [WOB-əl] *vi* **-bled, -bling** move unsteadily; sway ▷ *n* an unsteady movement **wob'bly** *adj* **-bli·er, -bli·est**

woe [woh] *n* grief **woe·be·gone** [WOH-bi-gawn] *adj* looking sorrowful **woe'ful** [-fəl] *adj* sorrowful; pitiful; wretched **woe'ful·ly** *adv*

wolf [wuulf] *n, pl* **wolves** wild predatory doglike animal of northern countries; *inf* man who habitually tries to seduce women ▷ *vt* eat ravenously **wolf whistle** whistle by man expressing admiration for a woman **cry wolf** raise false alarm

wolf·ram [WUUL-frəm] *n* tungsten

wol·ver·ine [wuul-və-REEN] *n* carnivorous mammal inhabiting northern regions

wom·an [WUUM-ən] *n, pl* **wom·en** [WIM-in] adult human female; women collectively **wom'an·hood** [-huud] *n* **wom'an·ish** *adj* effeminate **wom'an·ize** *vi* **-ized, -iz·ing** (of man) indulge in many casual affairs with women **wom'an·kind** [-kīnd] *n* **wom'an·ly** *adj* of, proper to woman **women's liberation** movement for removal of attitudes, practices that preserve social, economic, etc inequalities between women and men; (also **women's lib**)

womb [woom] *n* female organ of conception and gestation, uterus

won [wun] *pt/pp of* WIN

won·der [WUN-dər] *n* emotion excited by amazing or unusual thing; marvel, miracle ▷ *vi* be curious about; feel amazement **won'der·ful** [-fəl] *adj* remarkable; very fine **won'der·ment** [-mənt] *n* surprise

won'drous [-drəs] *adj* inspiring wonder; strange

wont [wawnt] *n* custom ▷ *adj* accustomed **wont'ed** [-id] *adj* habitual, established

woo *vt* court, seek to marry **woo'er** [-ər] *n* suitor

wood [wuud] *n* substance of trees, timber; firewood; tract of land with growing trees **wood'ed** [-id] *adj* having (many) trees **wood'en** [-n] *adj* made of wood; obstinate; without expression **wood'y** *adj* **wood'chuck** *n* Amer burrowing rodent **wood'cut** *n* engraving on wood; impression from this **wood'land** [-lənd] *n* woods, forest **wood'peck·er** *n* bird that searches tree trunks for insects **wood'wind** *adj, n* (of) wind instruments of orchestra, orig made of wood

woof [wuuf] *n* the threads that cross the warp in weaving

woof·er [WUUF-ər] *n* loudspeaker for reproducing low-frequency sounds

wool [wuul] *n* soft hair of sheep, goat, etc; yarn spun from this **wool'en** [-in] *adj* **wool'ly** *adj* **-li·er, -li·est** of wool; vague, muddled ▷ *n* [-eez] (oft pl) knitted woolen garment, esp warm undergarment **wool'gath·er·ing** *n* daydreaming

word [wurd] *n* unit of speech or writing regarded by users of a language as the smallest separate meaningful unit; term; message; brief remark; information; promise; command ▷ *vt* express in words, esp in particular way **word'ing** *n* choice and arrangement of words **word'y** *adj* **word·i·er, word·i·est** using more words than necessary, verbose **word processor** keyboard, microprocessor and monitor for electronic organization and storage of written text

wore pt of WEAR

work [wurk] *n* labor; employment; occupation; task; toil; something made or accomplished; production of art or science; book; needlework ▷ *pl* factory; total of person's deeds, writings, etc; *inf* everything, full or extreme treatment; mechanism of clock, etc ▷ *vt* cause to operate; make, shape ▷ *vi* apply effort; labor; operate; be engaged in trade, profession, etc; turn out successfully; ferment **work'a•ble** *adj* **work•a•hol•ic** [wur-kə-HAW-lik] *n* person addicted to work **work'ing class** social class consisting of wage earners, esp manual **working-class** *adj* **work•man** [WURK-mən] *n*, *pl* **-men** manual worker; male worker **work'man•ship** *n* skill of workman; way thing is finished; style **work'shop** *n* place where things are made; discussion group, seminar

world [wurld] *n* the universe; Earth; sphere of existence; mankind, people generally; society **world'ly** *adj* earthly; mundane; absorbed in the pursuit of material gain, advantage; carnal **World Wide Web** global computer network sharing graphics, etc, via the Internet

worm [wurm] *n* small limbless creeping snakelike creature; anything resembling worm in shape or movement; gear wheel with teeth forming part of screw threads; *inf* weak, despised person; *computing* type of virus ▷ *pl* (disorder caused by) infestation of worms, esp in intestines ▷ *vi* crawl ▷ *vt* work (oneself) in insidiously; extract (secret) craftily; rid of worms **worm'-eaten** *adj* full of holes gnawed by worms; old, antiquated **worm'y** *adj* **worm•i•er, worm•i•est**

worm•wood [WURM-wuud] *n* bitter herb; bitterness

worn pp of WEAR

wor•ry [WUR-ee] *v* **-ried, -ry•ing** ▷ *vi* be (unduly) concerned ▷ *vt* trouble, pester, harass; (of dog) seize, shake with teeth ▷ *n, pl* **-ries** (cause of) anxiety, concern **wor'ri•er** *n*

worse [wurs] *adj, adv* comp of BAD, BADLY ▷ *n* **worst** *adj, adv* sup of BAD, BADLY ▷ *n* **wors'en** [-in] *v* make, grow worse; impair; deteriorate

wor•ship [WUR-ship] *vt* **-shiped, -ship•ing** show religious devotion to; adore; love and admire ▷ *n* act of worshiping **wor'ship•er** *n*

wor•sted [WUUS-tid] *n* woolen yarn ▷ *adj* made of woolen yarn; spun from wool

worth [wurth] *adj* having or deserving to have value specified; meriting ▷ *n* excellence; merit, value; virtue; usefulness; price; quantity to be had for a given sum **wor•thy** [WUR-thee] *adj* **-thi•er, -thi•est** virtuous; meriting ▷ *n* one of eminent worth; celebrity **wor'thi•ness** [-thee-nis] *n* **worth•less** [WURTH-lis] *adj* useless **worth•while** [wurth-hwil] *adj* worth the time, effort, etc involved

would [wuud] *v aux* expressing wish, intention, probability; pt of WILL **would-be** [WUUD-bee] *adj* wishing, pretending to be

wound[1] [woond] *n* injury, hurt from cut, stab, etc ▷ *vt* inflict wound on, injure; pain

wound[2] [wohnd] (rhymes with SOUND) pt/pp of WIND[2]

wove [wohv] pt of WEAVE **wo'ven** pp of WEAVE

wow *interj* of astonishment ▷ *n inf* object of astonishment, admiration, etc; variation, distortion in pitch in record player, etc

wraith [rayth] n apparition of a person seen shortly before or after death; specter

wran·gle [RANG-gəl] vi **-gled, -gling** quarrel (noisily); dispute; herd cattle ▷ n noisy quarrel; dispute **wran'gler** [-glər] n cowboy; disputant

wrap [rap] v **wrapped, wrap·ping** cover, esp by putting something around; put around ▷ n sandwich made by wrapping filling in a tortilla, etc **wrap'per** n loose garment; covering **wrapping** n material used to wrap

wrath [rath] n anger **wrath'ful** [-fəl] adj **wrath'ful·ly** adv

wreak [reek] vt inflict (vengeance); cause

wreath [reeth] n something twisted into ring form, esp band of flowers, etc as memorial or tribute on grave, etc **wreathe** [reeth] vt **wreathed, wreath·ing** form into wreath; surround; wind around

wreck [rek] n destruction of ship; wrecked ship; ruin; something ruined ▷ vt cause the wreck of **wreck'age** [-ij] n **wreck'er** n person or thing that destroys; ruins; vehicle for towing disabled, wrecked, etc automobiles, a tow truck

wren [ren] n kind of small songbird

wrench [rench] vt twist; distort; seize forcibly; sprain ▷ n violent twist; tool for twisting or turning; tool for gripping nut or bolt head; sudden pain caused esp by parting

wrest [rest] vt take by force; twist violently

wres·tle [RES-əl] vi **-tled, -tling** fight (esp as sport) by grappling and trying to throw down; strive (with); struggle ▷ n **wrest'ler** [-lər] n

wretch [rech] n despicable person; miserable creature **wretch'ed** [-id] adj **-ed·er, -ed·est** miserable, unhappy; worthless **wretch'ed·ly** adv **wretch'ed·ness** [-nis] n

wrig·gle [RIG-əl] v **-gled, -gling** move with twisting action, as worm; squirm ▷ n this action

wring [ring] vt **wrung, wring·ing** twist; extort; pain; squeeze out

wrin·kle [RING-kəl] n slight ridge or furrow on surface; crease in the skin; fold; pucker; inf [useful trick, hint] ▷ v **-kled, -kling** make, become wrinkled, pucker

wrist [rist] n joint between hand and arm **wrist'let** [-lit] n band worn on wrist

writ [rit] n written command from law court or other authority

write [rīt] v **wrote, writ·ten, writ·ing** ▷ vi mark paper, etc with the symbols that are used to represent words or sounds; compose; send a letter ▷ vt set down in words; compose; communicate in writing **writ'er** n one who writes; author **write-off** n cancellation from accounts as loss; inf person or thing considered hopeless **write-up** n written (published) account of something

writhe [rīth] v **writhed, writh·ing** twist, squirm in or as in pain, etc ▷ vi be acutely embarrassed, etc

wrong [rawng] adj not right or good; not suitable; wicked; incorrect; mistaken; not functioning properly ▷ n that which is wrong; harm; evil ▷ vt do wrong to; think badly of without justification **wrong'do·er** [-doo-ər] n one who acts immorally or illegally **wrong'ful** [-fəl] adj **wrong'ful·ly** adv

wrote [roht] pt of **WRITE**

wrought [rawt] adj (of metals)

shaped by hammering or beating
wrought iron pure form of iron used esp in decorative railings, etc
wrung pt/pp of **WRING**
wry [rī] *adj* **wri·er, wri·est** turned to one side, contorted, askew; sardonic, dryly humorous
wuss [woos] *n, pl* **-us·ses** *sl* feeble person
WWW World Wide Web

X Christ; Christian; cross; Roman numeral, 10; mark indicating something wrong, a choice, a kiss, signature, etc *n* unknown, mysterious person, factor

Xe *chemistry* xenon

xe·non [ZEE-non] *n* colorless, odorless gas occurring in very small quantities in air

xen·o·pho·bi·a [zen-ə-FOH-bee-ə] *n* dislike, hatred, fear, of strangers or aliens **xen·o·pho'bic** *adj*

xe·rog·ra·phy [zi-ROG-rə-fee] *n* photocopying process

Xmas [EKS-məs] *n inf* Christmas

x-rays [EKS-rayz] *pl n* radiation of very short wavelengths, capable of penetrating solid bodies, and printing on photographic plate shadow picture of objects not permeable by rays **x-ray** *v* photograph by x-rays

xy·li·tol [ZĪ-lə-tol] *n* artificial sweetener produced from xylose and used esp in chewing gum

xy·lo·carp [ZĪ-lə-kahrp] *n* hard, woody fruit **xy·lo·carp'ous** *adj* having fruit that becomes hard or woody

xy·lo·graph [ZĪ-lə-graf] *n* wood engraving; impression from wood block

xy·loid [ZĪ-loid] *adj* pert to wood; woody, ligneous

xy·lo·phone [ZĪ-lə-fohn] *n* musical instrument of wooden bars that sound when struck

Y *chemistry* yttrium

Y2K [n] *inf* name for AD 2000 (esp referring to the millennium bug)

yacht [yot] *n* vessel propelled by sail or power, used for racing, pleasure, etc **yachts·man** [YOTS-mən] *n*, *pl*-**men**

ya·hoo [YAH-hoo] *n*, *pl*-**hoos** crude, coarse person

Yah·weh [YAH-we] *n* Jehovah, God

yak [yangk] *n* shaggy-haired, long-horned ox of Central Asia

yam [yangk] *n* large edible tuber, sweet potato

yank [yangk] *v* jerk, tug; pull quickly ▷ *n* quick tug

Yank [yangk], **Yank'ee** *adj, n inf* American

yap [yangk] *vi* yapped, yap·ping bark (as small dog); *sl* talk shrilly, idly ▷ *n* a bark; *sl* the mouth

yard¹ [yahrd] *n* unit of length, 3 feet (36 inches, 0.9144 meter); spar slung across ship's mast to extend sails **yard'stick** *n* 36-inch ruler; formula or standard of measurement or comparison **yard'age** [-ij] *n* measurement of distance in yards; length in yards

yard² *n* piece of enclosed ground

adjoining building and used for some specific purpose, as garden, storage, holding livestock, etc **yard'age** *n* use of yard; charge made for this

yar·mul·ke [YAHR-məl-kə] *n* skullcap worn by Jewish men and boys, esp in synagogue

yarn [yahrn] *n* spun thread; *inf* long involved story

yash·mak [yahsh-MAHK] *n* face veil worn by Muslim women

yaw [n] *vi* of aircraft, etc, turn about vertical axis; deviate temporarily from course

yawl [n] two-masted sailing vessel

yawn [n] *vi* open mouth wide, esp in sleepiness; gape ▷ *n* a yawning

yaws [yawz] *n* contagious tropical skin disease

Yb *chemistry* ytterbium

ye [yee] *pron obs* you

yea [yay] *interj* yes ▷ *n* affirmative vote

year [yeer] *n* time taken by one revolution of Earth around sun, about 365 days; twelve months **year'ling** *n* animal one year old **year'ly** *adv* every year, once a year ▷ *adj* happening, etc once a year

yearn [yurn] *vi* feel longing, desire; be filled with pity, tenderness **yearn'ing** *n*

yeast [yeest] *n* substance used as fermenting, leavening agent, esp in brewing and in baking bread **yeast'y** *adj* yeast·i·er, yeast·i·est of, like yeast; frothy, fermenting; (of time) characterized by excitement, change, etc

yell [n] *v* cry out in loud shrill tone; speak in this way ▷ *n* loud shrill cry; a cheer, shout

yel·low [YEL-oh] *adj* -**er**, -**est** of the color of lemons, gold, etc; *inf* cowardly ▷ *n* this color

yel·low·bel·ly *n, pl*-**lies** *sl* coward

yellow fever acute infectious disease of (sub)tropical climates
yellow jacket type of wasp; *sl* yellow capsule of phenobarbital

yelp *vi, n* (produce) quick, shrill cry

yen[1] *n* Japanese monetary unit

yen[2] *n inf* longing, craving

yeo·man [YOH-màn] *n, pl* **-men** petty officer in U.S. Navy having mainly clerical duties; *brit history* farmer cultivating own land ▷ *adj* performed in valiant, thorough manner

yes *interj* affirms or consents, gives an affirmative answer ▷ *n, pl* **yes·es** affirmative reply **yes-man** *n, pl* **-men** weak person willing to agree to anything

yes·ter·day [YES-tàr-day] *n* day before today; recent time ▷ *adv, adj*

yet *adv* now, still, besides, hitherto; nevertheless ▷ *conj* but, at the same time, nevertheless

yet·i [YET-ee] *n* see **ABOMINABLE SNOWMAN**

yew [yoo] *n* evergreen tree with dark leaves; its wood

Yid·dish [YID-ish] *adj, n* (of, in) language used by many Jews in or from Europe, orig a form of German written in Hebrew letters, with words from Hebrew and many other languages

yield [yeeld] *vt* give or return as food; produce; provide; concede; give up, surrender ▷ *vi* produce; submit; comply; surrender, give way ▷ *n* amount produced, return, profit, result

yo·del [YOHD-l] *vi* **-deled, -del·ing** warble in falsetto tone ▷ *n* falsetto warbling as practiced by Swiss mountaineers

yo·ga [YOH-gà] *n* Hindu philosophical system aiming at spiritual, mental and physical well-being by means of certain physical and mental exercises **yo'gi** [-[gee] *n, pl* **-gis** one who practices yoga

yo·gurt [YOH-gàrt] *n* thick, custard-like preparation of curdled milk

yoke [yohk] *n* wooden bar put across the necks of two animals to hold them together and to which plow, etc can be attached; various objects like a yoke in shape or use; fitted part of garment, esp around neck, shoulders; bond or tie; domination ▷ *vt* **yoked, yok·ing** put a yoke on, couple, unite

yo·kel [YOH-kàl] *n offens* person who lives in the country and is usu simple and old-fashioned

yolk [yohk] *n* yellow central part of egg; oily secretion of skin of sheep

yon *adj obs* or *dial* that or those over there **yon·der** [YON-dàr] *adj* yon ▷ *adv* over there, in that direction

yore [yor] *n poetry* the distant past

York·shire pudding [YORK-shàr] baked batter eaten with roast beef

you [yoo] *pron* referring to person(s) addressed, or to unspecified person(s)

young [yung] *adj* **-er, -est** not far advanced in growth, life or existence; not yet old; immature; junior; recently formed; vigorous ▷ *n* offspring **young·ster** [-stàr] *n* child

your [yuur] *adj* of, belonging to, or associated with you; of, belonging to, or associated with an unspecified person or people in general **yours** *pron* something belonging to you **your·self** *pron, pl* **-selves**

youth [yooth] *n* state or time of being young; state before adult age; young man; young people **youth'ful** [-fàl] *adj*

yowl *v, n* (produce) mournful cry

yo·yo [YOH-yoh] *n, pl* **-yos** toy

consisting of a spool attached to a string, by which it can be spun out and reeled in while attached to the finger

yuc•ca [YUK-ə] *n* tropical plant with stiff lancelike leaves

Yule [yool] *n* the Christmas festival or season

yup•pie [YUP-ee] *n* young urban professional ▷ *adj*

Z

za·ba·glio·ne [zah-bəl-YOH-nee] *n* Italian custardlike dessert of whipped and heated egg yolks, sugar and Marsala wine

za·ny [ZAY-nee] *adj* **-ni·er, -ni·est** comical, funny in unusual way ▷ *n*, *pl* **-nies** eccentric person; silly person

zap *inf vt* **zapped, zap·ping** attack, kill or destroy; *computing* clear from screen, erase; change (TV channels) rapidly by remote control; skip over or delete sound of (commercials)

zeal [zeel] *n* fervor; keenness; enthusiasm **zeal·ot** [ZEL-ət] *n* fanatic; enthusiast **zeal·ous** [-əs] *adj* ardent; enthusiastic; earnest **zeal·ous·ly** *adv*

ze·bra [ZEE-brə] *n*, *pl* **-bras** striped Afr animal like a horse

ze·bu [ZEE-byoo] *n* humped Indian ox or cow

Zen *n* Japanese school teaching contemplation, meditation

ze·nith [ZEE-nith] *n* point of the heavens directly above an observer; point opposite nadir; summit, peak; climax

zeph·yr [ZEF-ər] *n* soft, gentle breeze

zep·pe·lin [ZEP-ə-lin] *n* large, cylindrical, rigid airship

ze·ro [ZEER-oh] *n*, *pl* **-ros, -roes** nothing; figure 0; point on graduated instrument from which positive and negative quantities are reckoned; the lowest point ▷ *vt* **-roed, -ro·ing** reduce to zero; adjust (instrument, etc) to zero

zest *n* enjoyment; excitement, interest, flavor; peel of orange or lemon **zest·ful** [-fəl] *adj*

zig·zag *n* line or course characterized by sharp turns in alternating directions ▷ *vi* **-zagged, -zag·ging** move along in zigzag course

zinc [zingk] *n* bluish-white metallic element with wide variety of uses, esp in alloys as brass, etc

zin·ni·a [ZIN-ee-ə] *n* plant with daisylike, brightly colored flowers

Zi·on [Zī-ən] *n* hill on which Jerusalem stands; modern Jewish nation; Israel; *christian church* heaven **Zi·on·ism** *n* movement to found, support Jewish homeland in what now is state of Israel **Zi·on·ist** *n*, *adj*

zip *n* short whizzing sound; energy, vigor ▷ *v* **zipped, zip·ping** move with zip

zip code [kohd] system of numbers used to aid sorting of mail; (also ZIP code)

zip·per [ZIP-ər] *n* device for fastening with two rows of flexible metal or plastic teeth, interlocked and opened by a sliding clip ▷ *vt* fasten with zipper

zir·con [ZUR-kon] *n* mineral used as gemstone and in industry

zith·er [ZITH-ər] *n* flat stringed instrument

Zn *chemistry* zinc

zo·di·ac [ZOH-dee-ak] *n* imaginary belt of the heavens along which the sun, moon, and chief planets appear to move, divided crosswise into twelve equal areas, called **signs of the zodiac**, each named after a constellation **zo·di·a·cal** [zoh-DĪ-ə-kəl] adj

zom·bie [ZOM-bee] n person appearing lifeless, apathetic, etc; corpse supposedly brought to life by supernatural spirit

zone [zohn] n region with particular characteristics or use; any of the five belts into which tropics and arctic and antarctic circles divide Earth

zoo n place where wild animals are kept, studied, bred and exhibited

zo·og·ra·phy [zoh-OG-rə-fee] n descriptive zoology **zo·og'ra·pher, zo·og'ra·phist** n **zo·o·graph'i·cal** adj

zo·ol·o·gy [zoh-OL-ə-jee] n scientific study of animals; characteristics of particular animals or of fauna of particular area **zo·o·log'i·cal** adj **zo·ol'o·gist** n

zoom v (cause to) make loud buzzing, humming sound; (cause to) go fast or rise, increase sharply ▷ vi (of camera) use lens of adjustable focal length to make subject appear to move closer or farther away **zoom lens** lens used in this way

zo·o·phyte [ZOH-ə-fīt] n animal resembling a plant, such as a sea anemone **zo·o·phyt'ic** [-FIT-ik] adj

Zr chemistry zirconium

zuc·chi·ni [zoo-KEEN-ee] n, pl **-ni** or **-nis** green-skinned summer squash

Zu·lu [ZOO-loo] n member, language of S Afr Bantu tribes

zy·gote [ZĪ-goht] n fertilized egg cell

zy·mot·ic [zī-MOT-ik] adj of, or caused by fermentation; of, caused by infection

PRESIDENTS OF THE USA

George Washington (F)	1789-97
John Adams (F)	1797-1801
Thomas Jefferson (DR)	1801-09
James Madison (DR)	1809-17
James Monroe (DR)	1817-25
John Quincy Adams (DR)	1825-29
Andrew Jackson (D)	1829-37
Martin Van Buren (D)	1837-41
William H Harrison (W)	1841
John Tyler (W)	1841-45
James K Polk (D)	1845-49
Zachary Taylor (W)	1849-50
Millard Fillmore (W)	1850-53
Franklin Pierce (D)	1853-57
James Buchanan (D)	1857-61
Abraham Lincoln (R)	1861-65
Andrew Johnson (R)	1865-69
Ulysses S Grant (R)	1869-77
Rutherford B Hayes (R)	1877-81
James A Garfield (R)	1881
Chester A Arthur (R)	1881-85
Grover Cleveland (D)	1885-89
Benjamin Harrison (R)	1889-93

Grover Cleveland (D)	1893-97
William McKinley (R)	1897-1901
Theodore Roosevelt (R)	1901-09
William H Taft (R)	1909-13
Woodrow Wilson (D)	1913-21
Warren G Harding (R)	1921-23
Calvin Coolidge (R)	1923-29
Herbert C Hoover (R)	1929-33
Franklin D Roosevelt (D)	1933-45
Harry S Truman (D)	1945-53
Dwight D Eisenhower (R)	1953-61
John F Kennedy (D)	1961-63
Lyndon B Johnson (D)	1963-69
Richard M Nixon (R)	1969-74
Gerald R Ford (R)	1974-77
James E Carter Jr (D)	1977-81
Ronald W Reagan (R)	1981-89
George H W Bush (R)	1989-93
William J Clinton (D)	1993-2001
George W Bush (R)	2001-

(D) Democratic; (DR) Democratic Republican;
(F) Federalist; (R) Republican; (W) Whig

STATES OF THE USA

State	Zip	Capital Code	Area (Sq Mi)	Est Pop (2000)
Alabama	AL	Montgomery	53,423	4,447,100
Alaska	AK	Juneau	656,424	626,932
Arizona	AZ	Phoenix	114,006	5,130,632
Arkansas	AK	Little Rock	53,182	2,673,400
California	CA	Sacramento	163,707	33,871,648
Colorado	CO	Denver	104,100	4,301,261
Connecticut	CT	Hartford	5,544	3,405,565
Deleware	DE	Dover	2,489	783,600
Florida	FL	Tallahassee	65,758	15,982,378
Georgia	GA	Atlanta	59,441	8,186,453
Hawaii	HI	Honolulu	10,932	1,211,537
Idaho	ID	Boise	83,574	1,293,953
Illinois	IL	Springfield	57,918	12,419,293
Indiana	IN	Indianapolis	36,420	6,080,485
Iowa	IA	Des Moines	56,276	2,926,324
Kansas	KS	Topeka	82,282	2,688,418
Kentucky	KY	Frankfort	40,411	4,041,769
Louisiana	LA	Baton Rouge	51,843	4,468,976
Maine	ME	Augusta	35,387	1,274,923
Maryland	MD	Annapolis	12,407	5,296,486
Massa-chusetts	MA	Boston	10,555	6,349,097
Michigan	MI	Lansing	96,810	9,938,444
Minnesota	MN	St Paul	86,943	4,919,479
Mississippi	MS	Jackson	48,434	2,844,658
Missouri	MO	Jefferson City	69,709	5,595,211
Montana	MT	Helena	143,046	902,195
Nebraska	NE	Lincoln	77,358	1,711,263
Nevada	NV	Carson City	110,567	1,998,257

State	Zip	Capital	Code	Area (Sq Mi)	Est Pop (2000)
New Hampshire	NH	Concord		9,351	1,235,786
New Jersey	NJ	Trenton		8,722	8,414,350
New Mexico	NM	Santa Fe		123,598	1,819,046
New York	NY	Albany		54,475	18,976,457
North Carolina	NC	Raleigh		53,821	8,049,313
North Dakota	ND	Bismarck		70,704	642,200
Ohio	OH	Columbus		44,828	11,353,140
Oklahoma	OK	Oklahoma City		69,903	3,450,654
Oregon	OR	Salem		98,386	3,421,399
Pennsylvania	PA	Harrisburg		46,058	12,281,054
Rhode Island	RI	Providence		1,545	1,048,319
South Carolina	SC	Columbia		32,007	4,012,012
South Dakota	SD	Pierre		72,121	754,844
Tennessee	TN	Nashville		42,146	5,689,283
Texas	TX	Austin		268,601	20,851,820
Utah	UT	Salt Lake City		84,904	2,233,169
Vermont	VT	Montpelier		9,615	608,827
Virginia	VA	Richmond		42,769	7,078,515
Washington	WA	Olympia		71,303	5,894,121
West Virginia	WV	Charleston		24,231	1,808,344
Wisconsin	WI	Madison		65,503	5,363,675
Wyoming	WY	Cheyenne		97,818	493,782
District of Columbia	DC	-		68	572,059